Sporting News BOOKS

PRO FOOTBALL REGISTER

2005 EDITION

Withdrawn

CONTENTS

EXPLANATION OF ABBREVIATIONS AND TERMS

LEAGUES: AFL: American Football League. **Ar.FL., Arena Football:** Arena Football League. **CFL:** Canadian Football League. **CoFL:** Continental Football League. **NFL:** National Football League. **NFLE:** NFL Europe League. **USFL:** United States Football League. **WFL:** World Football League. **W.L.:** World League. **WLAF:** World League of American Football.

TEAMS: Birm.: Birmingham. **Jack., Jax.:** Jacksonville. **L.A. Raiders:** Los Angeles Raiders. **L.A. Rams:** Los Angeles Rams. **New Eng.:** New England. **N.Y. Giants:** New York Giants. **N.Y. Jets:** New York Jets. **N.Y./N.J.:** New York/New Jersey. **San Ant.:** San Antonio. **San Fran.:** San Francisco. **Sask.:** Saskatchewan. **StL.:** St. Louis.

STATISTICS: Ast.: Assists. **Att.:** Attempts. **Avg.:** Average. **Blk.:** Blocked punts. **Cmp.:** Completions. **FGA:** Field goals attempted. **FGM:** Field goals made. **50+:** Field goals of 50 yards or longer. **F., Fum.:** Fumbles. **G:** Games. **In. 20:** Punts inside 20-yard line. **Int.:** Interceptions. **Lg.:** Longest made field goal. **L:** Lost. **Net avg.:** Net punting average. **No.:** Number. **Rat.:** Passer rating. **Pct.:** Percentage. **Pts.:** Points scored. **Skd.:** Times sacked. **Sks.:** Sacks. **T:** Tied. **TD:** Touchdowns. **Tk.:** Tackles. **2-pt.:** Two-point conversions. **W:** Won. **XPA:** Extra points attempted. **XPM:** Extra points made. **Yds.:** Yards.

POSITIONS: C: Center. **CB:** Cornerback. **DB:** Defensive back. **DE:** Defensive end. **DL:** Defensive lineman. **DT:** Defensive tackle. **FB:** Fullback. **G:** Guard. **K:** Kicker. **LB:** Linebacker. **OL:** Offensive lineman. **OT:** Offensive tackle. **P:** Punter. **QB:** Quarterback. **RB:** Running back. **S:** Safety. **TE:** Tight end. **WR:** Wide receiver.

SINGLE GAME HIGHS (regular season): If a player reached a single game high on numerous occasions—had one rushing touchdown in a game, for example—the most recent occurrence is listed.

EXPLANATION OF AWARDS

AWARDS: Butkus Award: Nation's top college linebacker. **Chuck Bednarik Award:** Nation's top college defensive player. **Dave Rimington Trophy:** Nation's top college center. **Davey O'Brien Award:** Nation's top college quarterback. **Doak Walker Award:** Nation's top college junior or senior running back. **Fred Biletnikoff Award:** Nation's top college wide receiver. **Harlon Hill Trophy:** Nation's top college Division II player. **Heisman Trophy:** Nation's top college player. **Jim Thorpe Award:** Nation's top college defensive back. **Johnny Unitas Award:** Nation's top college senior quarterback. **Lombardi Award:** Nation's top college lineman. **Lou Groza Award:** Nation's top college kicker. **Maxwell Award:** Nation's top college player. **Outland Trophy:** Nation's top college interior lineman. **Ted Hendricks Award:** Nation's top college defensive end. **Walter Payton Award:** Nation's top college Division I-AA player.

A Note on Tackles:

Nearly all of the numbers in the career section are official NFL statistics. However, tackle data is not official. For the sake of consistency, we use NFL game summaries to collect this information, assuming that the standards used in crediting tackles and assists are relatively uniform among the various stat crews at NFL game sites. However, for seasons before 1994 we list the team-supplied totals because no other data is available. For this reason, you may notice that many regular defenders' assist totals have dropped off substantially since 1994. One final note: a few teams never listed assists; instead, they threw them in with overall tackle numbers. This results in zeroes in the assists column for some players prior to 1995, which suggested that those players never assisted on tackles. In all likelihood they probably did pick up some assists, but it's impossible to find out how many.

Sporting News Contributors:

Editors: Dave Sloan; Zach Bodendieck; **Cover Design by:** Chad Painter; **Page layout by:** Chad Painter

ON THE COVER: Peyton Manning and Curtis Martin by Robert Seale/TSN; Shaun Alexander by Albert Dickson/TSN; Torry Holt by Bob Leverone/TSN. ON THE BACK COVER: Michael Vick by Robert Seale/TSN.

NFL statistics compiled by STATS, Inc., a News Corporation company; 8130 Lehigh Avenue, Morton Grove, IL 60053. STATS is a trademark of Sports Team Analysis and Tracking Systems, Inc.

ISBN: 0-89204-774-7

10 9 8 7 6 5 4 3 2 1

VETERAN PLAYERS

Please note for statistical comparisons: In 1982, only nine of 16 games were played due to the cancellation of games because of a player's strike. In 1987, only 15 of 16 games were played due to the cancellation of games in the third week because of a player's strike. Most NFL players also missed games scheduled in the fourth, fifth and sixth weeks.

Sacks became an official NFL statistic in 1982.

Two-point conversions became an official NFL statistic in 1994.

* Indicates league leader.	† Indicates tied for league lead.	... Statistics unavailable, unofficial, or mathematically
‡ Indicates NFC leader.	§ Indicates AFC leader.	impossible to calculate.
∞ Indicates tied for NFC lead.	▲ Indicates tied for AFC lead.	

ABDULLAH, RABIH   RB

PERSONAL: Born April 27, 1975, in Martinsville, Va. ... 6-0/220. ... Full name: Rabih Fard Abdullah. ... Name pronounced: RAH-bee ab-DUE-lah.
HIGH SCHOOL: Barham Clark (Roselle, N.J.).
COLLEGE: Lehigh.
TRANSACTIONS/CAREER NOTES: Signed as non-drafted free agent by Tampa Bay Buccaneers (April 20, 1998). ... Inactive for all 16 games (1998). ... On injured reserve with thumb injury (December 28, 1999-remainder of season). ... Granted free agency (March 2, 2001). ... Re-signed by Buccaneers (March 2, 2001). ... Granted unconditional free agency (March 1, 2002). ... Signed by Chicago Bears (March 6, 2002). ... Released by Bears (September 4, 2004). ... Signed by New England Patriots (September 11, 2004). ... Released by Patriots (November 22, 2004). ... Re-signed by Patriots (December 22, 2004). ... Granted unconditional free agency (March 2, 2005).
CHAMPIONSHIP GAME EXPERIENCE: Played in AFC championship game (2004 season). ... Member of Super Bowl championship team (2004 season).
SINGLE GAME HIGHS (regular season): Attempts—10 (December 3, 2000, vs. Dallas); yards—38 (December 3, 2000, vs. Dallas); and rushing touchdowns—1 (October 10, 2004, vs. Miami).

| | | | RUSHING | | | | RECEIVING | | | | KICKOFF RETURNS | | | | TOTALS | | | |
Year Team	G	GS	Att.	Yds.	Avg.	TD	No.	Yds.	Avg.	TD	No.	Yds.	Avg.	TD	TD	2pt.	Pts.	Fum.
1999—Tampa Bay NFL	15	1	5	12	2.4	0	2	11	5.5	0	0	0	0.0	0	0	0	0	0
2000—Tampa Bay NFL	12	0	16	70	4.4	0	2	14	7.0	0	1	16	16.0	0	0	0	0	0
2001—Tampa Bay NFL	16	0	11	40	3.6	0	2	26	13.0	0	5	92	18.4	0	0	0	0	1
2002—Chicago NFL	16	0	0	0	0.0	0	0	0	0.0	0	9	182	20.2	0	0	0	0	0
2003—Chicago NFL	15	0	18	37	2.1	0	8	55	6.9	0	5	62	12.4	0	0	0	0	0
2004—New England NFL	9	0	13	13	1.0	1	1	9	9.0	0	0	0	0.0	0	1	0	6	0
Pro totals (6 years)	83	1	63	172	2.7	1	15	115	7.7	0	20	352	17.6	0	1	0	6	1

ABRAHAM, DONNIE   CB   JETS

PERSONAL: Born October 8, 1973, in Orangeburg, S.C. ... 5-10/192. ... Full name: Nathaniel Donnell Abraham.
HIGH SCHOOL: Orangeburg-Wilkinson (Orangeburg, S.C.).
COLLEGE: East Tennessee State.
TRANSACTIONS/CAREER NOTES: Selected by Tampa Bay Buccaneers in third round (71st pick overall) of 1996 NFL draft. ... Signed by Buccaneers (July 13, 1996). ... Released by Buccaneers (March 14, 2002). ... Signed by New York Jets (April 24, 2002).
CHAMPIONSHIP GAME EXPERIENCE: Played in NFC championship game (1999 season).
HONORS: Played in Pro Bowl (2000 season).
MISCELLANEOUS: Holds Tampa Bay Buccaneers all-time record for most interceptions (31).

| | | | TOTALS | | | INTERCEPTIONS | | | |
Year Team	G	GS	Tk.	Ast.	Sks.	No.	Yds.	Avg.	TD
1996—Tampa Bay NFL	16	12	50	8	0.0	5	27	5.4	0
1997—Tampa Bay NFL	16	16	44	10	0.0	5	16	3.2	0
1998—Tampa Bay NFL	13	13	32	6	0.0	1	3	3.0	0
1999—Tampa Bay NFL	16	16	65	14	2.0	†7	115	16.4	†2
2000—Tampa Bay NFL	16	16	46	11	0.0	7	82	11.7	0
2001—Tampa Bay NFL	15	5	29	10	0.0	6	98	16.3	0
2002—New York Jets NFL	16	16	47	6	0.0	4	49	12.3	0
2003—New York Jets NFL	8	2	11	0	0.0	1	12	12.0	0
2004—New York Jets NFL	16	16	38	15	0.0	2	66	33.0	1
Pro totals (9 years)	132	112	362	80	2.0	38	468	12.3	3

ABRAHAM, JOHN   DE   JETS

PERSONAL: Born May 6, 1978, in Timmonsville, S.C. ... 6-4/256.
HIGH SCHOOL: Lamar (Timmonsville, S.C.).
COLLEGE: South Carolina.
TRANSACTIONS/CAREER NOTES: Selected by New York Jets in first round (13th pick overall) of 2000 NFL draft. ... Signed by Jets (July 10, 2000). ... On injured reserve with hernia (November 17, 2000-remainder of season). ... On injured reserve with groin injury (December 15, 2003-remainder of season). ... Designated by Jets as franchise player (February 18, 2005).
HONORS: Named defensive end on THE SPORTING NEWS NFL All-Pro team (2001). ... Played in Pro Bowl (2001 and 2002 seasons). ... Named to play in Pro Bowl (2004 season); replaced by Aaron Smith due to injury.

| | | | TOTALS | | | INTERCEPTIONS | | | |
Year Team	G	GS	Tk.	Ast.	Sks.	No.	Yds.	Avg.	TD
2000—New York Jets NFL	6	0	8	4	4.5	0	0	0.0	0
2001—New York Jets NFL	16	15	57	10	13.0	0	0	0.0	0
2002—New York Jets NFL	16	16	48	13	10.0	0	0	0.0	0
2003—New York Jets NFL	7	6	24	8	6.0	0	0	0.0	0
2004—New York Jets NFL	12	12	35	14	9.5	0	0	0.0	0
Pro totals (5 years)	57	49	172	49	43.0	0	0	0.0	0

ADAMS, ANTHONY — DT — 49ERS

PERSONAL: Born June 18, 1980, in Detroit, Mich. ... 6-0/300. ... Full name: Anthony Adams Jr.
HIGH SCHOOL: Martin Luther King (Detroit).
COLLEGE: Penn State.
TRANSACTIONS/CAREER NOTES: Selected by San Francisco 49ers in second round (57th pick overall) of 2003 NFL draft. ... Signed by 49ers (July 25, 2003).

| | | | TOTALS | | |
Year Team	G	GS	Tk.	Ast.	Sks.
2003—San Francisco NFL	14	1	20	6	1.5
2004—San Francisco NFL	14	12	41	7	0.0
Pro totals (2 years)	28	13	61	13	1.5

ADAMS, CHARLIE — WR — BRONCOS

PERSONAL: Born October 23, 1979, in Camp Hill, Pa. ... 6-2/190.
HIGH SCHOOL: Cumberland Valley (Mechanicsburg, Pa.).
COLLEGE: Hofstra.
TRANSACTIONS/CAREER NOTES: Signed as non-drafted free agent by Denver Broncos (April 29, 2002). ... Waived by Broncos (August 31, 2002). ... Re-signed by Broncos (December 31, 2002). ... Assigned by Broncos to Rhein Fire in 2003 NFL Europe enhancement allocation program (February 22, 2003). ... Released by Broncos (August 31, 2003). ... Re-signed by Broncos to practice squad (September 1, 2003). ... Activated (December 5, 2003). ... Re-signed by Broncos to practice squad (December 29, 2003). ... Waived by Broncos (October 2, 2004). ... Re-signed by Broncos (December 8, 2004).

| | | | RECEIVING | | | | TOTALS | | | |
Year Team	G	GS	No.	Yds.	Avg.	TD	TD	2pt.	Pts.	Fum.
2003—Denver NFL	4	0	0	0	0.0	0	0	0	0	0
2004—Denver NFL	4	0	0	0	0.0	0	0	0	0	0
Pro totals (2 years)	8	0	0	0	0.0	0	0	0	0	0

ADAMS, FLOZELL — T — COWBOYS

PERSONAL: Born May 18, 1975, in Chicago, Ill. ... 6-7/343. ... Full name: Flozell Jootin Adams.
HIGH SCHOOL: Proviso West (Hillside, Ill.).
COLLEGE: Michigan State.
TRANSACTIONS/CAREER NOTES: Selected by Dallas Cowboys in second round (38th pick overall) of 1998 NFL draft. ... Signed by Cowboys (July 17, 1998). ... Designated by Cowboys as franchise player (February 21, 2002). ... Granted unconditional free agency (February 28, 2003). ... Re-signed by Cowboys (February 28, 2003).
PLAYING EXPERIENCE: Dallas NFL, 1998-2004. ... Games/Games started: 1998 (16/12), 1999 (16/16), 2000 (16/16), 2001 (16/16), 2002 (16/16), 2003 (16/16), 2004 (16/16). Total: 112/108.
HONORS: Played in Pro Bowl (2003 season). ... Named offensive tackle on THE SPORTING NEWS college All-America third team (1997).

ADAMS, KEITH — LB — EAGLES

PERSONAL: Born November 22, 1979, in Atlanta, Ga. ... 5-11/223. ... Son of Julius Adams, defensive end with New England Patriots (1971-85, '87).
HIGH SCHOOL: Westlake (Atlanta).
COLLEGE: Clemson.
TRANSACTIONS/CAREER NOTES: Selected after junior season by Tennessee Titans in seventh round (232nd pick overall) of 2001 NFL draft. ... Signed by Titans (July 13, 2001). ... Released by Titans (August 31, 2001). ... Signed by Dallas Cowboys to practice squad (November 8, 2001). ... Activated (November 21, 2001). ... Claimed on waivers by Philadelphia Eagles (October 21, 2002). ... Re-signed by Eagles (March 3, 2003). ... Granted free agency (March 3, 2004). ... Re-signed by Eagles (April 30, 2004). ... Granted unconditional free agency (March 2, 2005). ... Re-signed by Eagles (March 18, 2005).
CHAMPIONSHIP GAME EXPERIENCE: Played in NFC championship game (2002, 2003 and 2004 seasons). ... Played in Super Bowl 39 (2004 season).
HONORS: Named linebacker on THE SPORTING NEWS college All-America third team (1999). ... Named linebacker on THE SPORTING NEWS college All-America first team (2000).

| | | | TOTALS | | | INTERCEPTIONS | | | |
Year Team	G	GS	Tk.	Ast.	Sks.	No.	Yds.	Avg.	TD
2001—Dallas NFL	4	0	0	0	0.0	0	0	0.0	0
2002—Dallas NFL	6	5	15	3	0.0	0	0	0.0	0
—Philadelphia NFL	10	0	0	0	0.0	0	0	0.0	0
2003—Philadelphia NFL	15	0	3	1	0.0	0	0	0.0	0
2004—Philadelphia NFL	16	2	30	4	0.0	0	0	0.0	0
Pro totals (4 years)	51	7	48	8	0.0	0	0	0.0	0

ADAMS, MIKE — CB — 49ERS

PERSONAL: Born March 24, 1981, in Paterson, N.J. ... 5-11/193. ... Full name: Michael Carl Adams.
HIGH SCHOOL: Passiac Tech (Paterson, N.J.).
COLLEGE: Delaware.
TRANSACTIONS/CAREER NOTES: Signed as non-drafted free agent by San Francisco 49ers (April 28, 2004). ... Released by 49ers (September 4, 2004). ... Re-signed by 49ers to practice squad (September 6, 2004). ... Activated (November 13, 2004).

| | | | TOTALS | | | INTERCEPTIONS | | | |
Year Team	G	GS	Tk.	Ast.	Sks.	No.	Yds.	Avg.	TD
2004—San Francisco NFL	8	0	4	1	0.0	1	0	0.0	0

PERSONAL: Born June 13, 1973, in Houston, Texas. ... 6-4/335. ... Full name: Sam Aaron Adams. ... Son of Sam Adams Sr., guard with New England Patriots (1972-80) and New Orleans Saints (1981).

HIGH SCHOOL: Cypress Creek (Houston).

COLLEGE: Texas A&M.

TRANSACTIONS/CAREER NOTES: Selected after junior season by Seattle Seahawks in first round (eighth pick overall) of 1994 NFL draft. ... Signed by Seahawks (July 30, 1994). ... Granted unconditional free agency (February 11, 2000). ... Signed by Baltimore Ravens (April 17, 2000). ... Released by Ravens (March 1, 2002). ... Signed by Oakland Raiders (August 19, 2002). ... Released by Raiders (February 27, 2003). ... Signed by Buffalo Bills (March 23, 2003).

CHAMPIONSHIP GAME EXPERIENCE: Played in AFC championship game (2000 and 2002 seasons). ... Member of Super Bowl championship team (2000 season). ... Played in Super Bowl 37 (2002 season).

HONORS: Named defensive lineman on THE SPORTING NEWS college All-America first team (1993). ... Played in Pro Bowl (2000, 2001 and 2004 seasons).

			TOTALS			INTERCEPTIONS			
Year Team	G	GS	Tk.	Ast.	Sks.	No.	Yds.	Avg.	TD
1994—Seattle NFL	12	7	20	7	4.0	0	0	0.0	0
1995—Seattle NFL	16	5	16	10	3.5	0	0	0.0	0
1996—Seattle NFL	16	15	35	5	5.5	0	0	0.0	0
1997—Seattle NFL	16	15	37	15	7.0	0	0	0.0	0
1998—Seattle NFL	16	11	28	3	2.0	1	25	25.0	1
1999—Seattle NFL	13	13	31	7	1.0	0	0	0.0	0
2000—Baltimore NFL	16	16	23	4	2.0	0	0	0.0	0
2001—Baltimore NFL	14	14	18	5	2.0	0	0	0.0	0
2002—Oakland NFL	15	14	18	4	2.0	0	0	0.0	0
2003—Buffalo NFL	15	15	24	9	5.0	1	37	37.0	1
2004—Buffalo NFL	16	16	26	14	5.0	1	0	0.0	0
Pro totals (11 years)	165	141	276	83	39.0	3	62	20.7	2

AHANOTU, CHIDI   DE

PERSONAL: Born October 11, 1970, in Modesto, Calif. ... 6-2/285. ... Full name: Chidi Obioma Ahanotu. ... Name pronounced: CHEE-dee a-HA-noe-too.

HIGH SCHOOL: Berkeley (Calif.).

COLLEGE: California.

TRANSACTIONS/CAREER NOTES: Selected by Tampa Bay Buccaneers in sixth round (145th pick overall) of 1993 NFL draft. ... Signed by Buccaneers (July 9, 1993). ... Granted free agency (February 16, 1996). ... Re-signed by Buccaneers (February 20, 1996). ... On injured reserve with shoulder injury (October 27, 1998-remainder of season). ... Designated by Buccaneers as franchise player (February 12, 1999). ... Re-signed by Buccaneers (July 30, 1999). ... Released by Buccaneers (April 20, 2001). ... Signed by St. Louis Rams (August 20, 2001). ... Granted unconditional free agency (March 1, 2002). ... Signed by Buffalo Bills (August 19, 2002). ... Granted unconditional free agency (February 28, 2003). ... Signed by San Francisco 49ers (August 21, 2003). ... Granted unconditional free agency (March 3, 2004). ... Signed by Miami Dolphins (September 1, 2004). ... Released by Dolphins (October 20, 2004). ... Signed by Tampa Bay Buccaneers (November 10, 2004). ... Granted unconditional free agency (March 2, 2005).

CHAMPIONSHIP GAME EXPERIENCE: Played in NFC championship game (1999 and 2001 seasons). ... Played in Super Bowl 36 (2001 season).

			TOTALS		
Year Team	G	GS	Tk.	Ast.	Sks.
1993—Tampa Bay NFL	16	10	15	16	1.5
1994—Tampa Bay NFL	16	16	31	15	1.0
1995—Tampa Bay NFL	16	15	36	12	3.0
1996—Tampa Bay NFL	13	13	37	10	5.5
1997—Tampa Bay NFL	16	15	38	10	10.0
1998—Tampa Bay NFL	4	4	9	8	0.0
1999—Tampa Bay NFL	16	15	24	9	6.5
2000—Tampa Bay NFL	16	16	28	19	3.5
2001—St. Louis NFL	16	16	21	8	2.0
2002—Buffalo NFL	16	14	30	14	5.0
2003—San Francisco NFL	16	1	21	6	4.0
2004—Miami NFL	5	0	2	1	1.0
—Tampa Bay NFL	8	5	12	4	3.5
Pro totals (12 years)	174	140	304	132	46.5

AIKEN, SAM   WR   BILLS

PERSONAL: Born December 14, 1980, in Clinton, N.C. ... 6-2/204. ... Full name: Samuel Aiken.

HIGH SCHOOL: James Kenan (Warsaw, N.C.).

COLLEGE: North Carolina.

TRANSACTIONS/CAREER NOTES: Selected by Buffalo Bills in fourth round (127th pick overall) of 2003 NFL draft. ... Signed by Bills (July 10, 2003). ... On injured reserve with knee injury (November 26, 2003-remainder of season).

SINGLE GAME HIGHS (regular season): Receptions—4 (January 2, 2005, vs. Pittsburgh); yards—61 (November 21, 2004, vs. St. Louis); and touchdown receptions—0.

			RECEIVING				TOTALS			
Year Team	G	GS	No.	Yds.	Avg.	TD	TD	2pt.	Pts.	Fum.
2003—Buffalo NFL	5	0	3	35	11.7	0	0	0	0	0
2004—Buffalo NFL	16	0	11	148	13.5	0	0	0	0	0
Pro totals (2 years)	21	0	14	183	13.1	0	0	0	0	0

AKERS, DAVID — K — EAGLES

PERSONAL: Born December 9, 1974, in Lexington, Ky. ... 5-10/200. ... Full name: David Roy Akers. ... Name pronounced: A-kers.
HIGH SCHOOL: Tates Creek (Lexington, Ky.).
COLLEGE: Louisville.
TRANSACTIONS/CAREER NOTES: Signed as non-drafted free agent by Carolina Panthers (April 19, 1997). ... Released by Panthers (August 17, 1997). ... Signed by Atlanta Falcons (April 28, 1998). ... Released by Falcons (July 7, 1998). ... Re-signed by Falcons (July 21, 1998). ... Released by Falcons (August 24, 1998). ... Signed by Washington Redskins to practice squad (September 1, 1998). ... Activated (September 15, 1998). ... Released by Redskins (September 22, 1998). ... Signed by Philadelphia Eagles (January 11, 1999). ... Assigned by Eagles to Berlin Thunder in 1999 NFL Europe enhancement allocation program (February 22, 1999).
CHAMPIONSHIP GAME EXPERIENCE: Played in NFC championship game (2001, 2003 and 2004 seasons). ... Played in Super Bowl 39 (2004 season).
HONORS: Named kicker on THE SPORTING NEWS NFL All-Pro team (2001 and 2002). ... Played in Pro Bowl (2001, 2002 and 2004 seasons).

			FIELD GOALS							TOTALS		
Year Team	G	1-29	30-39	40-49	50+	Tot.	Pct.	Lg.		XPM	XPA	Pts.
1998—Washington NFL	1	0-0	0-0	0-2	0-0	0-2	0.0	0		2	2	2
1999—Philadelphia NFL	16	0-0	0-0	2-3	1-3	3-6	50.0	∞53		2	2	11
2000—Philadelphia NFL	16	7-7	14-15	7-10	1-1	29-33	87.9	51		34	36	121
2001—Philadelphia NFL	16	10-10	7-8	7-10	2-3	26-31	83.9	50		37	38	115
2002—Philadelphia NFL	16	9-9	14-16	6-7	1-2	30-34	88.2	51		43	43	133
2003—Philadelphia NFL	16	9-9	7-7	6-10	2-3	24-29	82.8	57		42	42	114
2004—Philadelphia NFL	16	4-4	6-7	15-18	2-3	‡27-‡32	84.4	51		41	42	‡122
Pro totals (7 years)	97	39-39	48-53	43-60	9-15	139-167	83.2	57		201	205	618

ALBRIGHT, ETHAN — C/LS — REDSKINS

PERSONAL: Born May 1, 1971, in Greensboro, N.C. ... 6-5/265. ... Full name: Lawrence Ethan Albright.
HIGH SCHOOL: Grimsley (Greensboro, N.C.).
COLLEGE: North Carolina.
TRANSACTIONS/CAREER NOTES: Signed as non-drafted free agent by Miami Dolphins (April 28, 1994). ... Released by Dolphins (August 22, 1994). ... Re-signed by Dolphins to practice squad (August 29, 1994). ... Released by Dolphins (September 14, 1994). ... Re-signed by Dolphins to practice squad (September 28, 1994). ... Released by Dolphins (November 2, 1994). ... Re-signed by Dolphins (February 16, 1995). ... On injured reserve with knee injury (November 15, 1995-remainder of season). ... Released by Dolphins (August 20, 1996). ... Signed by Buffalo Bills (August 26, 1996). ... Granted free agency (February 13, 1998). ... Re-signed by Bills (April 15, 1998). ... Granted unconditional free agency (February 12, 1999). ... Re-signed by Bills (April 1, 1999). ... Released by Bills (March 1, 2001). ... Signed by Washington Redskins (March 9, 2001). ... Released by Redskins (March 6, 2003). ... Re-signed by Redskins (March 7, 2003) ... Granted unconditional free agency (March 3, 2004). ... Re-signed by Redskins (March 4, 2004). ... Granted unconditional free agency (March 2, 2005). ... Re-signed by Redskins (March 3, 2005).
PLAYING EXPERIENCE: Miami NFL, 1995; Buffalo NFL, 1996-2000; Washington NFL, 2001-2004. ... Games/Games started: 1995 (10/0), 1996 (16/0), 1997 (16/0), 1998 (16/0), 1999 (16/0), 2000 (16/0), 2001 (16/0), 2002 (16/0), 2003 (16/0), 2004 (16/0). Total: 154/0.

ALEXANDER, BRENT — S — GIANTS

PERSONAL: Born July 10, 1971, in Gallatin, Tenn. ... 5-11/200. ... Full name: Ronald Brent Alexander.
HIGH SCHOOL: Gallatin (Tenn.).
COLLEGE: Tennessee State.
TRANSACTIONS/CAREER NOTES: Signed as non-drafted free agent by Arizona Cardinals (April 28, 1994). ... Granted unconditional free agency (February 13, 1998). ... Signed by Carolina Panthers (March 20, 1998). ... Released by Panthers (April 18, 2000). ... Signed by Pittsburgh Steelers (May 30, 2000). ... Released by Steelers (March 23, 2004). ... Signed by New York Giants (May 27, 2004).
CHAMPIONSHIP GAME EXPERIENCE: Played in AFC championship game (2001 season).

			TOTALS			INTERCEPTIONS			
Year Team	G	GS	Tk.	Ast.	Sks.	No.	Yds.	Avg.	TD
1994—Arizona NFL	16	7	26	10	0.0	0	0	0.0	0
1995—Arizona NFL	16	13	51	17	0.5	2	14	7.0	0
1996—Arizona NFL	16	15	52	29	0.0	2	3	1.5	0
1997—Arizona NFL	16	15	54	22	0.0	0	0	0.0	0
1998—Carolina NFL	16	16	68	29	0.0	0	0	0.0	0
1999—Carolina NFL	16	16	65	12	0.0	2	18	9.0	0
2000—Pittsburgh NFL	16	16	61	12	1.5	3	31	10.3	0
2001—Pittsburgh NFL	16	16	52	17	2.0	4	39	9.8	0
2002—Pittsburgh NFL	16	16	50	25	1.0	4	37	9.3	0
2003—Pittsburgh NFL	16	16	60	21	1.0	4	63	15.8	0
2004—New York Giants NFL	16	16	56	24	2.0	3	3	1.0	0
Pro totals (11 years)	176	162	595	221	8.0	24	208	8.7	0

ALEXANDER, ERIC — LB — PATRIOTS

PERSONAL: Born February 8, 1982, in Tyler, Texas. ... 6-2/240.
HIGH SCHOOL: Stephen F. Austin (Port Arthur, Texas).
COLLEGE: Louisiana State.
TRANSACTIONS/CAREER NOTES: Signed as non-drafted free agent by New England Patriots (April 29, 2004). ... Released by Patriots (September 4, 2004). ... Re-signed by Patriots to practice squad (September 6, 2004). ... Activated (December 20, 2004). ... On injured reserve with ankle injury (January 3, 2005-remainder of season).

			TOTALS			INTERCEPTIONS			
Year Team	G	GS	Tk.	Ast.	Sks.	No.	Yds.	Avg.	TD
2004—New England NFL	3	0	0	0	0.0	0	0	0.0	0

ALEXANDER, P.J.　　　　　T　　　　　BRONCOS

PERSONAL: Born December 23, 1978, in Springfield, Mass. ... 6-4/297. ... Full name: Patrick James Alexander.
HIGH SCHOOL: Lincoln (Tallahassee, Fla.).
COLLEGE: Syracuse.
TRANSACTIONS/CAREER NOTES: Signed as non-drafted free agent by New Orleans Saints (April 23, 2002). ... Released by Saints (August 31, 2002). ... Re-signed by Saints to practice squad (September 2, 2002). ... Signed by Denver Broncos off Saints practice squad (October 22, 2003). ... Inactive for nine games (2003).
PLAYING EXPERIENCE: Denver NFL, 2004. ... Games/Games Started: 2004 (5/0). Total: 5/0.

ALEXANDER, ROC　　　　　CB　　　　　BRONCOS

PERSONAL: Born September 23, 1981, in Colorado Springs, Colo. ... 5-10/186. ... Full name: Narond Alexander.
HIGH SCHOOL: Wasson (Colorado Springs, Colo.).
COLLEGE: Washington.
TRANSACTIONS/CAREER NOTES: Signed as non-drafted free agent by Denver Broncos (May 3, 2004).

		TOTALS			INTERCEPTIONS				KICKOFF RETURNS				TOTALS			
Year　Team	G	GS	Tk.	Ast.	Sks.	No.	Yds.	Avg.	TD	No.	Yds.	Avg.	TD	TD	2pt	Pts.	Fum.
2004—Denver NFL	16	1	5	1	0.0	0	0	0.0	0	19	386	20.3	0	0	0	0	0

ALEXANDER, SHAUN　　　　　RB　　　　　SEAHAWKS

PERSONAL: Born August 30, 1977, in Florence, Ky. ... 5-11/225.
HIGH SCHOOL: Boone County (Ky.).
COLLEGE: Alabama.
TRANSACTIONS/CAREER NOTES: Selected by Seattle Seahawks in first round (19th pick overall) of 2000 NFL draft. ... Signed by Seahawks (July 20, 2000). ... Designated by Seahawks as franchise player (February 22, 2005).
HONORS: Named running back on THE SPORTING NEWS college All-America second team (1999). ... Played in Pro Bowl (2003 season). ... Named to play in Pro Bowl (2004 season); replaced by Brian Westbrook due to injury.
SINGLE GAME HIGHS (regular season): Attempts—35 (November 11, 2001, vs. Oakland); yards—266 (November 11, 2001, vs. Oakland); and rushing touchdowns—4 (September 29, 2002, vs. Minnesota).
STATISTICAL PLATEAUS: 100-yard rushing games: 2001 (4), 2002 (4), 2003 (7), 2004 (7). Total: 22.
MISCELLANEOUS: Holds Seattle Seahawks all-time record for most rushing touchdowns (62).

			RUSHING				RECEIVING				TOTALS			
Year　Team	G	GS	Att.	Yds.	Avg.	TD	No.	Yds.	Avg.	TD	TD	2pt.	Pts.	Fum.
2000—Seattle NFL	16	1	64	313	4.9	2	5	41	8.2	0	2	0	12	2
2001—Seattle NFL	16	12	309	1318	4.3	*14	44	343	7.8	2	§16	0	96	4
2002—Seattle NFL	16	16	295	1175	4.0	‡16	59	460	7.8	2	‡18	0	108	3
2003—Seattle NFL	16	15	326	1435	4.4	14	42	295	7.0	2	16	0	96	4
2004—Seattle NFL	16	16	‡353	‡1696	4.8	‡16	23	170	7.4	4	*20	0	120	5
Pro totals (5 years)	80	60	1347	5937	4.4	62	173	1309	7.6	10	72	0	432	18

ALEXANDER, STEPHEN　　　　　TE　　　　　BRONCOS

PERSONAL: Born November 7, 1975, in Chickasha, Okla. ... 6-4/250.
HIGH SCHOOL: Chickasha (Okla.).
COLLEGE: Oklahoma.
TRANSACTIONS/CAREER NOTES: Selected by Washington Redskins in second round (48th pick overall) of 1998 NFL draft. ... Signed by Redskins (July 13, 1998). ... On injured reserve with ankle injury (December 26, 2001-remainder of season). ... Granted unconditional free agency (March 1, 2002). ... Signed by San Diego Chargers (March 21, 2002). ... On injured reserve with groin injury (December 20, 2003-remainder of season). ... Released by Chargers (March 2, 2004). ... Signed by Detroit Lions (June 4, 2004) ... Granted unconditional free agency (March 2, 2005). ... Signed by Denver Broncos (March 25, 2005).
HONORS: Played in Pro Bowl (2000 season).
SINGLE GAME HIGHS (regular season): Receptions—8 (December 29, 2002, vs. Seattle); yards—129 (December 29, 2002, vs. Seattle); and touchdown receptions—2 (September 19, 1999, vs. New York Giants).
STATISTICAL PLATEAUS: 100-yard receiving games: 2002 (1). Total: 1.

			RECEIVING				TOTALS			
Year　Team	G	GS	No.	Yds.	Avg.	TD	TD	2pt.	Pts.	Fum.
1998—Washington NFL	15	5	37	383	10.4	4	4	0	24	2
1999—Washington NFL	15	15	29	324	11.2	3	3	0	18	0
2000—Washington NFL	16	16	47	510	10.9	2	2	0	12	2
2001—Washington NFL	7	5	9	85	9.4	0	0	0	0	0
2002—San Diego NFL	14	14	45	510	11.3	1	1	0	6	1
2003—San Diego NFL	3	0	0	0	0.0	0	0	1	2	0
2004—Detroit NFL	16	15	41	377	9.2	1	1	0	6	0
Pro totals (7 years)	86	70	208	2189	10.5	11	11	1	68	5

ALLEN, BRIAN　　　　　LB　　　　　REDSKINS

PERSONAL: Born April 1, 1978, in Lake City, Fla. ... 6-0/232.
HIGH SCHOOL: Columbia (Lake City, Fla.).
COLLEGE: Florida State.

TRANSACTIONS/CAREER NOTES: Selected by St. Louis Rams in third round (83rd pick overall) of 2001 NFL draft. ... Signed by Rams (June 5, 2001). ... Selected by Houston Texans from Rams in NFL expansion draft (February 18, 2002). ... Claimed on waivers by Carolina Panthers (May 30, 2002). ... Granted free agency (March 3, 2004). ... Re-signed by Panthers (April 23, 2004). ... Granted free agency (March 2, 2005). ... Signed by Washington Redskins (April 6, 2005).

CHAMPIONSHIP GAME EXPERIENCE: Member of Rams for NFC championship game (2001 season); inactive. ... Member of Rams for Super Bowl 36 (2001 season); inactive. ... Played in NFC championship game (2003 season). ... Played in Super Bowl 38 (2003 season).

Year Team	G	GS	TOTALS			INTERCEPTIONS			
			Tk.	Ast.	Sks.	No.	Yds.	Avg.	TD
2001—St. Louis NFL	3	0	0	0	0.0	0	0	0.0	0
2002—Carolina NFL	16	5	27	6	0.0	0	0	0.0	0
2003—Carolina NFL	14	4	22	10	1.0	0	0	0.0	0
2004—Carolina NFL	14	0	11	4	0.0	1	21	21.0	0
Pro totals (4 years)	47	9	60	20	1.0	1	21	21.0	0

ALLEN, DAVID   RB   JAGUARS

PERSONAL: Born February 5, 1978, in Euless, Texas. ... 5-9/195.
HIGH SCHOOL: Liberty (Mo.).
COLLEGE: Kansas State.
TRANSACTIONS/CAREER NOTES: Signed as non-drafted free agent by San Francisco 49ers (April 27, 2001). ... Waived by 49ers (August 30, 2001). ... Signed by Minnesota Vikings (March 27, 2002). ... Waived by Vikings (September 1, 2002). ... Signed by Jacksonville Jaguars to practice squad (November 5, 2002). ... Released by Jaguars (November 12, 2002). ... Re-signed by Jaguars to practice squad (December 17, 2002). ... Activated (January 7, 2003). ... Assigned by Jaguars to Berlin Thunder in 2003 NFL Europe enhancement allocation program (February 22, 2003). ... Released by Jaguars (August 31, 2003). ... Re-signed by Jaguars to practice squad (September 1, 2003). ... Released by Jaguars (September 10, 2003). ... Re-signed by Jaguars (September 16, 2003). ... Released by Jaguars (September 4, 2004). ... Re-signed by Jaguars (December 1, 2004).
SINGLE GAME HIGHS (regular season): Attempts—3 (December 7, 2003, vs. Houston); yards—5 (December 14, 2003, vs. New England); and rushing touchdowns—0.

Year Team	G	GS	RUSHING				RECEIVING				PUNT RETURNS				KICKOFF RETURNS				TOTALS		
			Att.	Yds.	Avg.	TD	No.	Yds.	Avg.	TD	No.	Yds.	Avg.	TD	No.	Yds.	Avg.	TD	TD	2pt.	Pts.
2003—Jac. NFL	14	0	4	8	2.0	0	6	60	10.0	1	27	324	12.0	0	41	831	20.3	0	1	0	6
2004—Jac. NFL	5	0	0	0	0.0	0	2	8	4.0	0	15	144	9.6	0	11	210	19.1	0	0	0	0
Pro totals (2 years)	19	0	4	8	2.0	0	8	68	8.5	1	42	468	11.1	0	52	1041	20.0	0	1	0	6

ALLEN, IAN   T   CARDINALS

PERSONAL: Born July 22, 1978, in Newark, N.J. ... 6-4/310. ... Full name: Ian Ramon Allen.
HIGH SCHOOL: Westlake (Atlanta).
COLLEGE: Purdue.
TRANSACTIONS/CAREER NOTES: Signed as non-drafted free agent by Kansas City Chiefs (April 30, 2001). ... Released by Chiefs (August 28, 2001). ... Signed by Atlanta Falcons to practice squad (January 2, 2002). ... Granted free agency following 2001 season. ... Assigned by Chiefs to Scottish Claymores in 2002 NFL Europe enhancement allocation program (February 12, 2002). ... Signed by Kansas City Chiefs (January 14, 2002). ... Released by Chiefs (September 1, 2002). ... Signed by New York Giants to practice squad (September 10, 2002). ... Activated (October 3, 2002). ... Released by Giants (September 6, 2004). ... Signed by Philadelphia Eagles (September 14, 2004) ... Did not receive qualifying offer from Eagles (March 2, 2005). ... Signed by Arizona Cardinals (April 25, 2005).
PLAYING EXPERIENCE: New York Giants NFL, 2002-2003; Philadelphia NFL, 2004. ... Games/Games started: 2002 (3/0), 2003 (16/11), 2004 (4/0). Total: 23/11.
CHAMPIONSHIP GAME EXPERIENCE: Member of Eagles for NFC championship game (2004 season); inactive. ... Member of Eagles for Super Bowl 39 (2004 season); inactive.

ALLEN, JAMES   LB   SAINTS

PERSONAL: Born November 11, 1979, in Portland, Ore. ... 6-2/245.
HIGH SCHOOL: Thomas Jefferson (Portland, Ore.).
COLLEGE: Oregon State.
TRANSACTIONS/CAREER NOTES: Selected by New Orleans Saints in third round (82nd pick overall) of 2002 NFL draft. ... Signed by Saints (July 22, 2002).

Year Team	G	GS	TOTALS			INTERCEPTIONS			
			Tk.	Ast.	Sks.	No.	Yds.	Avg.	TD
2002—New Orleans NFL	14	1	6	2	0.0	1	0	0.0	1
2003—New Orleans NFL	15	1	10	1	0.0	0	0	0.0	0
2004—New Orleans NFL	16	10	30	16	0.0	0	0	0.0	0
Pro totals (3 years)	45	12	46	19	0.0	1	0	0.0	1

ALLEN, JARED   DE   CHIEFS

PERSONAL: Born April 3, 1982, in Los Gatos, Calif. ... 6-6/265. ... Full name: Jared Scot Allen.
HIGH SCHOOL: Los Gatos (Calif.).
COLLEGE: Idaho State.
TRANSACTIONS/CAREER NOTES: Selected by Kansas City Chiefs in fourth round (126th pick overall) of 2004 NFL draft. ... Signed by Chiefs (July 23, 2004).

Year Team	G	GS	TOTALS			INTERCEPTIONS			
			Tk.	Ast.	Sks.	No.	Yds.	Avg.	TD
2004—Kansas City NFL	15	10	29	2	9.0	0	0	0.0	0

ALLEN, KENDERICK — DT — GIANTS

PERSONAL: Born September 14, 1978, in Bogalusa, La. ... 6-6/315.
HIGH SCHOOL: Bogalusa (La.).
COLLEGE: Louisiana State.
TRANSACTIONS/CAREER NOTES: Signed as non-drafted free agent by New Orleans Saints (May 2, 2003). ... Claimed on waivers by New York Giants (September 6, 2004).

			TOTALS		
Year Team	G	GS	Tk.	Ast.	Sks.
2003—New Orleans NFL	10	1	9	2	0.0
2004—New York Giants NFL	5	2	17	3	1.0
Pro totals (2 years)	15	3	26	5	1.0

ALLEN, LARRY — G — COWBOYS

PERSONAL: Born November 27, 1971, in Los Angeles, Calif. ... 6-3/325. ... Full name: Larry Christopher Allen.
HIGH SCHOOL: Centennial (Compton, Calif.), then Vintage (Napa, Calif.).
JUNIOR COLLEGE: Butte (Calif.) C.c.
COLLEGE: Sonoma State.
TRANSACTIONS/CAREER NOTES: Selected by Dallas Cowboys in second round (46th pick overall) of 1994 NFL draft. ... Signed by Cowboys (July 16, 1994). ... On injured reserve with ankle injury (November 21, 2002-remainder of season).
PLAYING EXPERIENCE: Dallas NFL, 1994-2004. ... Games/Games started: 1994 (16/10), 1995 (16/16), 1996 (16/16), 1997 (16/16), 1998 (16/16), 1999 (11/11), 2000 (16/16), 2001 (16/16), 2002 (5/5), 2003 (16/16), 2004 (16/16). Total: 160/154.
CHAMPIONSHIP GAME EXPERIENCE: Played in NFC championship game (1994 and 1995 seasons). ... Member of Super Bowl championship team (1995 season).
HONORS: Named guard on THE SPORTING NEWS NFL All-Pro team (1995-97 and 1999). ... Played in Pro Bowl (1995-1998, 2000, 2003 and 2004 seasons). ... Named to play in Pro Bowl (1999 season); replaced by Adam Timmerman due to injury. ... Named offensive tackle on THE SPORTING NEWS NFL All-Pro team (1998). ... Named guard on THE SPORTING NEWS NFL All-Pro team (2000 and 2001). ... Named to play in Pro Bowl (2001 season); replaced by Adam Timmerman due to injury.

ALLEN, WILL — CB — GIANTS

PERSONAL: Born August 5, 1978, in Syracuse, N.Y. ... 5-10/196. ... Full name: Will D. Allen.
HIGH SCHOOL: Corcoran (Syracuse, N.Y.).
COLLEGE: Syracuse.
TRANSACTIONS/CAREER NOTES: Selected by New York Giants in first round (22nd pick overall) of 2001 NFL draft. ... Signed by Giants (July 26, 2001). ... On injured reserve with foot injury (December 2, 2003-remainder of season).
HONORS: Named cornerback to THE SPORTING NEWS college All-America third team (2000).

			TOTALS			INTERCEPTIONS			
Year Team	G	GS	Tk.	Ast.	Sks.	No.	Yds.	Avg.	TD
2001—New York Giants NFL	13	12	38	4	0.0	4	27	6.8	0
2002—New York Giants NFL	15	15	50	5	0.0	1	0	0.0	0
2003—New York Giants NFL	12	12	33	7	0.0	2	23	11.5	0
2004—New York Giants NFL	16	16	75	6	1.0	1	11	11.0	0
Pro totals (4 years)	56	55	196	22	1.0	8	61	7.6	0

ALLEN, WILL — DB — BUCCANEERS

PERSONAL: Born June 17, 1982, in Dayton, Ohio. ... 6-1/193.
HIGH SCHOOL: Wayne (Dayton, Ohio).
COLLEGE: Ohio State.
TRANSACTIONS/CAREER NOTES: Selected by Tampa Bay Buccaneers in fourth round (111th pick overall) of 2004 NFL draft. ... Signed by Buccaneers (July 29, 2004).

			TOTALS			INTERCEPTIONS			
Year Team	G	GS	Tk.	Ast.	Sks.	No.	Yds.	Avg.	TD
2004—Tampa Bay NFL	16	0	3	1	0.0	1	0	0.0	0

ALSTON, RICHARD — WR — BROWNS

PERSONAL: Born November 20, 1980, in Warrenton, N.C. ... 5-11/215.
HIGH SCHOOL: Warren County (N.C.).
COLLEGE: East Carolina.
TRANSACTIONS/CAREER NOTES: Signed as non-drafted free agent by Cleveland Browns (February 2, 2004). ... Released by Browns (October 12, 2004). ... Re-signed by Browns to practice squad (October 14, 2004). ... Activated (November 4, 2004).

			RECEIVING				KICKOFF RETURNS				TOTALS			
Year Team	G	GS	No.	Yds.	Avg.	TD	No.	Yds.	Avg.	TD	TD	2pt.	Pts.	Fum.
2004—Cleveland NFL	9	0	0	0	0.0	0	46	1016	22.1	1	1	0	6	2

ALSTOTT, MIKE — FB — BUCCANEERS

PERSONAL: Born December 21, 1973, in Joliet, Ill. ... 6-1/248. ... Full name: Michael Joseph Alstott.
HIGH SCHOOL: Joliet (Ill.) Catholic.
COLLEGE: Purdue.

TRANSACTIONS/CAREER NOTES: Selected by Tampa Bay Buccaneers in second round (35th pick overall) of 1996 NFL draft. ... Signed by Buccaneers (July 21, 1996). ... On injured reserve with neck injury (October 7, 2003-remainder of season).

CHAMPIONSHIP GAME EXPERIENCE: Played in NFC championship game (1999 and 2002 seasons). ... Member of Super Bowl championship team (2002 season).

HONORS: Played in Pro Bowl (1997-2002 seasons).

SINGLE GAME HIGHS (regular season): Attempts—28 (October 28, 2001, vs. Minnesota); yards—131 (September 26, 1999, vs. Denver); and rushing touchdowns—3 (October 28, 2001, vs. Minnesota).

STATISTICAL PLATEAUS: 100-yard rushing games: 1998 (2), 1999 (2), 2001 (2), 2002 (1). Total: 7.

MISCELLANEOUS: Holds Tampa Bay Buccaneers all-time records for most rushing touchdowns (49) and most touchdowns (61).

Year Team	G	GS	RUSHING Att.	Yds.	Avg.	TD	RECEIVING No.	Yds.	Avg.	TD	TOTALS TD	2pt.	Pts.	Fum.
1996—Tampa Bay NFL	16	16	96	377	3.9	3	65	557	8.6	3	6	0	36	4
1997—Tampa Bay NFL	15	15	176	665	3.8	7	23	178	7.7	3	10	0	60	5
1998—Tampa Bay NFL	16	16	215	846	3.9	8	22	152	6.9	1	9	0	54	5
1999—Tampa Bay NFL	16	16	242	949	3.9	7	27	239	8.9	2	9	0	54	6
2000—Tampa Bay NFL	13	13	131	465	3.5	5	13	93	7.2	0	5	0	30	3
2001—Tampa Bay NFL	16	16	165	680	4.1	10	35	231	6.6	1	11	2	70	2
2002—Tampa Bay NFL	16	9	146	548	3.8	5	35	242	6.9	2	7	0	42	4
2003—Tampa Bay NFL	4	3	27	77	2.9	2	10	83	8.3	0	2	0	12	0
2004—Tampa Bay NFL	14	11	67	230	3.4	2	29	202	7.0	0	2	0	12	2
Pro totals (9 years)	126	115	1265	4837	3.8	49	259	1977	7.6	12	61	2	370	31

AMANO, EUGENE — G — TITANS

PERSONAL: Born August 1, 1982, in San Pedro, Calif. ... 6-3/295. ... Full name: Eugene Robert Amano.

HIGH SCHOOL: Rancho Bernardo (Calif.).

COLLEGE: Southeast Missouri State.

TRANSACTIONS/CAREER NOTES: Selected by Tennessee Titans in seventh round (239th pick overall) of 2004 NFL draft. ... Signed by Titans (July 27, 2004).

PLAYING EXPERIENCE: Tennessee NFL, 2004. ... Games/Games started: 2004 (15/2). Total: 15/2.

AMATO, KEN — C/LS — TITANS

PERSONAL: Born May 18, 1977, in Puerto Rico. ... 6-2/245. ... Full name: Kenneth Carlos Amato.

HIGH SCHOOL: Braddock (Miami).

JUNIOR COLLEGE: Moorpark (Calif.).

COLLEGE: Montana State.

TRANSACTIONS/CAREER NOTES: Signed as non-drafted free agent by Carolina Panthers (February 11, 2003). ... Released by Panthers (June 11, 2003). ... Re-signed by Panthers (May 28, 2003). ... Released by Panthers (August 2, 2003). ... Signed by Tennessee Titans (August 12, 2003). ... Released by Titans (October 14, 2003). ... Re-signed by Titans (October 17, 2003).

PLAYING EXPERIENCE: Tennessee NFL, 2003-2004. ... Games/Games started: 2003 (16/0), 2004 (16/0). Total: 32/0.

AMBROSE, ASHLEY — CB

PERSONAL: Born September 17, 1970, in New Orleans, La. ... 5-11/195. ... Full name: Ashley Avery Ambrose.

HIGH SCHOOL: Alcee Fortier (New Orleans).

COLLEGE: Mississippi Valley State.

TRANSACTIONS/CAREER NOTES: Selected by Indianapolis Colts in second round (29th pick overall) of 1992 NFL draft. ... Signed by Colts (August 11, 1992). ... On injured reserve with leg injury (September 14-October 29, 1992); on practice squad (October 21-29, 1992). ... Granted free agency (February 17, 1995). ... Re-signed by Colts (April 29, 1995). ... Granted unconditional free agency (February 16, 1996). ... Signed by Cincinnati Bengals (February 25, 1996). ... Granted unconditional free agency (February 12, 1999). ... Signed by New Orleans Saints (July 13, 1999). ... Granted unconditional free agency (February 11, 2000). ... Signed by Atlanta Falcons (February 12, 2000). ... Released by Falcons (February 21, 2003). ... Signed by Saints (March 3, 2003). ... On injured reserve with knee injury (December 10, 2004-remainder of season). ... Released by Saints (April 1, 2005).

CHAMPIONSHIP GAME EXPERIENCE: Played in AFC championship game (1995 season).

HONORS: Played in Pro Bowl (1996 season).

Year Team	G	GS	TOTALS Tk.	Ast.	Sks.	INTERCEPTIONS No.	Yds.	Avg.	TD
1992—Indianapolis NFL	10	2	6	2	0.0	0	0	0.0	0
1993—Indianapolis NFL	14	6	36	8	0.0	0	0	0.0	0
1994—Indianapolis NFL	16	4	31	4	0.0	2	50	25.0	0
1995—Indianapolis NFL	16	0	11	3	0.0	3	12	4.0	0
1996—Cincinnati NFL	16	16	44	6	0.0	8	63	7.9	1
1997—Cincinnati NFL	16	16	57	2	1.0	3	56	18.7	0
1998—Cincinnati NFL	15	15	36	4	0.0	2	0	0.0	0
1999—New Orleans NFL	16	16	51	6	0.0	6	27	4.5	0
2000—Atlanta NFL	16	16	37	1	0.0	4	‡139	34.7	1
2001—Atlanta NFL	16	16	49	3	0.0	5	43	8.6	0
2002—Atlanta NFL	16	16	42	2	0.0	3	25	8.3	0
2003—New Orleans NFL	16	12	41	6	0.0	3	78	26.0	1
2004—New Orleans NFL	9	6	23	3	0.0	3	19	6.3	0
Pro totals (13 years)	192	141	464	50	1.0	42	512	12.2	3

ANDERSEN, MORTEN   K

PERSONAL: Born August 19, 1960, in Copenhagen, Denmark. ... 6-2/217.
HIGH SCHOOL: Ben Davis (Indianapolis).
COLLEGE: Michigan State.
TRANSACTIONS/CAREER NOTES: Selected by New Orleans Saints in fourth round (86th pick overall) of 1982 NFL draft. ... On injured reserve with sprained ankle (September 15-November 20, 1982). ... Designated by Saints as transition player (February 25, 1993). ... Released by Saints (July 19, 1995). ... Signed by Atlanta Falcons (July 21, 1995). ... Granted unconditional free agency (March 2, 2001). ... Signed by New York Giants (August 29, 2001). ... Granted unconditional free agency (March 1, 2002). ... Signed by Kansas City Chiefs (March 25, 2002). ... On injured reserve with knee injury (December 17, 2002-remainder of season). ... Granted unconditional free agency (February 28, 2003). ... Re-signed by Chiefs (March 18, 2003). ... Released by Chiefs (September 5, 2004). ... Signed by Minnesota Vikings (September 7, 2004). ... Granted unconditional free agency (March 2, 2005).
CHAMPIONSHIP GAME EXPERIENCE: Played in NFC championship game (1998 season). ... Played in Super Bowl 33 (1998 season).
HONORS: Named kicker on THE SPORTING NEWS college All-America first team (1981). ... Named kicker on THE SPORTING NEWS NFL All-Pro team (1985-1987 and 1995). ... Played in Pro Bowl (1985-1988, 1990, 1992 and 1995 seasons).
RECORDS: Holds NFL career records for most games played—354 (December 11, 1983-present); and for most made field goals of 50 or more yards—40. ... Holds NFL single-season record for most made field goals of 50 or more yards—8 (1995). ... Holds NFL single-game record for most made field goals of 50 or more yards—3 (December 10, 1995, vs. New Orleans). ... Shares NFL record for most seasons with 100 or more points—14 (1985-89, 1991-95, 1997-98 and 2002-03). ... New Orleans Saints all-time scoring leader (1,318 points). ... Atlanta Falcons all-time scoring leader (620 points).

| | | FIELD GOALS | | | | | | | TOTALS | | |
Year Team	G	1-29	30-39	40-49	50+	Tot.	Pct.	Lg.	XPM	XPA	Pts.
1982—New Orleans NFL	8	0-0	1-1	1-3	0-1	2-5	40.0	45	6	6	12
1983—New Orleans NFL	16	10-10	3-4	2-6	3-4	18-24	75.0	52	37	38	91
1984—New Orleans NFL	16	9-9	4-5	5-10	2-3	20-27	74.1	53	34	34	94
1985—New Orleans NFL	16	4-5	13-14	11-12	3-4	31-35	‡88.6	§55	27	29	120
1986—New Orleans NFL	16	12-12	6-7	6-6	2-5	26-30	*86.7	53	30	30	108
1987—New Orleans NFL	12	9-9	9-9	8-12	2-6	*28-*36	77.8	52	32	33	110
1988—New Orleans NFL	16	12-13	8-11	5-8	1-4	26-36	72.2	51	44	45	104
1989—New Orleans NFL	16	7-8	10-11	3-6	0-4	20-29	69.0	49	29	29	92
1990—New Orleans NFL	16	5-5	5-6	8-12	3-4	21-27	77.8	52	38	38	113
1991—New Orleans NFL	16	6-6	11-13	6-9	2-4	25-32	78.1	*60	33	34	∞120
1992—New Orleans NFL	16	10-10	8-10	8-11	3-3	29-34	‡85.3	52	33	33	117
1993—New Orleans NFL	16	9-9	7-7	11-14	1-5	28-35	80.0	56	32	32	116
1994—New Orleans NFL	16	9-9	11-14	8-10	0-6	28-†39	71.8	48	29	30	122
1995—Atlanta NFL	16	9-9	11-11	3-8	8-9	‡31-37	83.8	*59	29	30	122
1006 Atlanta NFL	16	5-5	9-11	7-8	1-5	22-29	75.9	∞54	31	31	97
1997—Atlanta NFL	16	11-11	7-7	3-6	2-3	23-27	85.2	∞55	35	35	104
1998—Atlanta NFL	16	8-10	7-7	6-9	2-2	23-28	82.1	53	51	52	120
1999—Atlanta NFL	16	6-6	5-8	4-6	0-1	15-21	71.4	49	34	34	79
2000—Atlanta NFL	16	6-6	6-7	11-15	2-3	25-31	80.6	51	23	23	98
2001—New York Giants NFL	16	8-8	7-8	6-7	2-5	23-28	82.1	51	29	30	98
2002—Kansas City NFL	14	6-6	10-10	5-9	1-1	22-26	84.6	50	*51	*51	117
2003—Kansas City NFL	16	3-3	8-8	5-8	0-1	16-20	80.0	49	*58	*59	106
2004—Minnesota NFL	16	9-9	5-7	4-6	0-0	18-22	81.8	48	45	45	99
Pro totals (23 years)	354	173-178	171-196	136-201	40-83	520-658	79.0	60	798	808	2358

ANDERSON, BENNIE   G   BILLS

PERSONAL: Born February 17, 1977, in St. Louis, Mo. ... 6-5/345. ... Full name: Tyrone Lamar Anderson.
HIGH SCHOOL: Cleveland Junior Naval Academy (St. Louis).
COLLEGE: Tennessee State.
TRANSACTIONS/CAREER NOTES: Signed as non-drafted free agent by St. Louis Rams (May 3, 2000). ... Released by Rams (July 19, 2000). ... Signed by Baltimore Ravens (June 14, 2001). ... Granted unconditional free agency (March 2, 2005). ... Signed by Buffalo Bills (March 31, 2005).
PLAYING EXPERIENCE: Baltimore NFL, 2001-2004. ... Games/Games started: 2001 (16/13), 2002 (16/16), 2003 (16/15), 2004 (16/12). Total: 64/56.

ANDERSON, BRYAN   G   BEARS

PERSONAL: Born March 30, 1980, in Philadelphia. ... 6-4/325. ... Full name: Bryan Michael Anderson.
HIGH SCHOOL: John Bartram (Philadelphia).
COLLEGE: Pittsburgh.
TRANSACTIONS/CAREER NOTES: Selected by Chicago Bears in seventh round (261st pick overall) of 2003 NFL draft. ... Released by Bears (September 4, 2004). ... Re-signed by Bears to practice squad (September 6, 2004). ... Released by Bears (September 17, 2004). ... Re-signed by Bears to practice squad (September 21, 2004). ... Activated (December 11, 2004). ... Assigned by Bears to Rhein Fire in 2005 NFL Europe enhancement allocation program (February 14, 2005).
PLAYING EXPERIENCE: Chicago NFL, 2004. ... Games/Games started: 2004 (4/0). Total: 4/0.

ANDERSON, CHARLIE   DE/LB   TEXANS

PERSONAL: Born December 8, 1981, in Jackson, Miss. ... 6-4/243. ... Full name: Charlie Alexander Anderson.
HIGH SCHOOL: Provine (Jackson, Miss.).
COLLEGE: Mississippi.
TRANSACTIONS/CAREER NOTES: Selected by Houston Texans in sixth round (200th pick overall) of 2004 NFL draft. ... Signed by Texans (July 30, 2004).

| | | | TOTALS | | |
Year Team	G	GS	Tk.	Ast.	Sks.
2004—Houston NFL	15	0	1	1	0.0

ANDERSON, COURTNEY   TE   RAIDERS

PERSONAL: Born November 19, 1980, in Greenville, Texas. ... 6-7/270.
HIGH SCHOOL: Richmond (Calif.).
COLLEGE: San Jose State.
TRANSACTIONS/CAREER NOTES: Selected by Oakland Raiders in seventh round (245th pick overall) of 2004 NFL draft. ... Signed by Raiders (July 9, 2004).
SINGLE GAME HIGHS (regular season): Receptions—3 (October 10, 2004, vs. Indianapolis); yards—38 (October 10, 2004, vs. Indianapolis); and touchdown receptions—1 (October 10, 2004, vs. Indianapolis).

Year Team	G	GS	RECEIVING No.	Yds.	Avg.	TD	TOTALS TD	2pt.	Pts.	Fum.
2004—Oakland NFL	9	4	13	175	13.5	1	1	0	6	0

ANDERSON, DAMIEN   RB   CARDINALS

PERSONAL: Born July 17, 1979, in Wilmington, Ill. ... 5-11/212. ... Full name: Damien Ramone Anderson.
HIGH SCHOOL: Wilmington (Ill.).
COLLEGE: Northwestern.
TRANSACTIONS/CAREER NOTES: Signed as non-drafted free agent by Arizona Cardinals (April 23, 2002). ... Released by Cardinals (September 1, 2002). ... Re-signed by Cardinals to practice squad (September 2, 2002). ... Activated (October 5, 2002). ... Released by Cardinals (September 5, 2004). ... Re-signed by Cardinals (December 24, 2004).
SINGLE GAME HIGHS (regular season): Attempts—23 (October 6, 2002, vs. Carolina); yards—61 (October 6, 2002, vs. Carolina); and rushing touchdowns—0.

Year Team	G	GS	RUSHING Att.	Yds.	Avg.	TD	RECEIVING No.	Yds.	Avg.	TD	KICKOFF RETURNS No.	Yds.	Avg.	TD	TOTALS TD	2pt.	Pts.	Fum.
2002—Arizona NFL	10	1	24	65	2.7	0	3	36	12.0	0	12	227	18.9	0	0	0	0	0
2003—Arizona NFL	16	0	18	68	3.8	0	6	36	6.0	0	2	31	15.5	0	0	0	0	0
2004—Arizona NFL	4	0	1	2	2.0	0	0	0	0.0	0	0	0	0.0	0	0	0	0	0
Pro totals (3 years)	30	1	43	135	3.1	0	9	72	8.0	0	14	258	18.4	0	0	0	0	0

ANDERSON, DWIGHT   CB   RAMS

PERSONAL: Born July 5, 1981, in Spanish Town, Jamaica. ... 5-10/172. ... Full name: Dwight Orlando Anderson.
HIGH SCHOOL: Bloomfield High (Conn.).
JUNIOR COLLEGE: Arizona Western (Yuma, Ariz.).
COLLEGE: South Dakota.
TRANSACTIONS/CAREER NOTES: Signed as non-drafted free agent by St. Louis Rams (April 30, 2004). ... Released by Rams (September 5, 2004). ... Re-signed by Rams to practice squad (September 6, 2004). ... Activated (September 10, 2004).

Year Team	G	GS	TOTALS Tk.	Ast.	Sks.	INTERCEPTIONS No.	Yds.	Avg.	TD	KICKOFF RETURNS No.	Yds.	Avg.	TD	TOTALS TD	2pt.	Pts.	Fum.
2004—St. Louis NFL	12	0	4	1	0.0	0	0	0.0	0	4	71	17.8	0	0	0	0	0

ANDERSON, GARY   K

PERSONAL: Born July 16, 1959, in Parys, South Africa. ... 5-11/193. ... Full name: Gary Allan Anderson.
HIGH SCHOOL: Brettonwood (Durban, South Africa).
COLLEGE: Syracuse.
TRANSACTIONS/CAREER NOTES: Selected by Buffalo Bills in seventh round (171st pick overall) of 1982 NFL draft. ... Signed by Bills for 1982 season. ... Claimed on waivers by Pittsburgh Steelers (September 7, 1982). ... Designated by Steelers as transition player (February 15, 1994). ... On reserve/did not report list (August 23-25, 1994). ... Free agency status changed by Steelers from transition to unconditional (February 17, 1995). ... Signed by Philadelphia Eagles (July 23, 1995). ... Released by Eagles (April 22, 1997). ... Signed by San Francisco 49ers (June 11, 1997). ... Granted unconditional free agency (February 13, 1998). ... Signed by Minnesota Vikings (February 20, 1998). ... Granted unconditional free agency (March 1, 2002). ... Re-signed by Vikings (September 17, 2002). ... Granted unconditional free agency (February 28, 2003). ... Signed by Tennessee Titans (September 11, 2003). ... Granted unconditional free agency (March 3, 2004). ... Re-signed by Titans (September 14, 2004). ... Granted unconditional free agency (March 2, 2005).
CHAMPIONSHIP GAME EXPERIENCE: Played in AFC championship game (1984 and 1994 seasons). ... Played in NFC championship game (1997 and 1998 seasons). ... Member of Vikings for NFC Championship game (2000 season).
HONORS: Played in Pro Bowl (1983, 1985, 1993 and 1998 seasons). ... Named kicker on THE SPORTING NEWS NFL All-Pro team (1998).
RECORDS: Holds NFL career records for most points—2,434; most field goals attempted—672, and most field goals made—538. ... Holds NFL single-season records for most PATs made without a miss—59 (1983); and most points scored without a touchdown—164 (1998). ... Shares NFL record for most seasons with 100 or more points—14 (1983-85, 1988, 1991-94, 1996-2000, 2003). ... Shares NFL single-season record for highest field-goal percentage—100.0 (1998).
POST SEASON RECORDS: Holds NFL postseason career record for most made field goals—32. ... Holds NFL postseason record for most consecutive made field goals—16 (1989-95).
MISCELLANEOUS: Pittsburgh Steelers all-time scoring leader (1,343 points).

Year Team	G	FIELD GOALS 1-29	30-39	40-49	50+	Tot.	Pct.	Lg.	TOTALS XPM	XPA	Pts.
1982—Pittsburgh NFL	9	4-4	1-2	5-5	0-1	10-12	83.3	48	22	22	52
1983—Pittsburgh NFL	16	10-10	9-10	8-10	0-0	27-31	87.1	49	38	39	§119
1984—Pittsburgh NFL	16	8-9	6-9	8-11	2-3	▲24-32	75.0	55	45	45	§117
1985—Pittsburgh NFL	16	13-14	14-15	5-9	1-4	*33-*42	78.6	52	40	40	§139
1986—Pittsburgh NFL	16	6-8	6-7	9-14	0-3	21-32	65.6	45	32	32	95
1987—Pittsburgh NFL	12	8-9	5-5	7-11	2-2	22-27	81.5	52	21	21	87
1988—Pittsburgh NFL	16	12-12	9-10	6-12	1-2	28-36	77.8	52	34	35	118

Year Team	G	FIELD GOALS							TOTALS		
		1-29	30-39	40-49	50+	Tot.	Pct.	Lg.	XPM	XPA	Pts.
1989—Pittsburgh NFL	16	7-7	5-8	9-15	0-0	21-30	70.0	49	28	28	91
1990—Pittsburgh NFL	16	4-4	8-8	8-11	0-2	20-25	80.0	48	32	32	92
1991—Pittsburgh NFL	16	8-10	9-11	5-6	1-6	23-33	69.7	54	31	31	100
1992—Pittsburgh NFL	16	12-13	12-15	4-6	0-2	28-36	77.8	49	29	31	113
1993—Pittsburgh NFL	16	9-10	14-14	5-6	0-0	28-30	§93.3	46	32	32	*116
1994—Pittsburgh NFL	16	8-9	8-9	7-9	1-2	24-29	82.8	50	32	32	104
1995—Philadelphia NFL	16	5-5	9-10	8-12	0-3	22-30	73.3	43	32	33	98
1996—Philadelphia NFL	16	10-11	8-9	7-9	0-0	25-29	86.2	46	40	40	115
1997—San Francisco NFL	16	11-11	9-12	8-10	1-3	29-36	80.6	51	38	38	125
1998—Minnesota NFL	16	12-12	9-9	12-12	2-2	‡35-∞35	*100.0	53	*59	*59	*164
1999—Minnesota NFL	16	6-8	9-11	4-9	0-2	19-30	63.3	44	46	46	103
2000—Minnesota NFL	16	6-6	9-9	7-7	0-1	22-23	95.7	49	‡45	∞45	111
2001—Minnesota NFL	16	7-7	2-4	6-7	0-0	15-18	83.3	44	29	30	74
2002—Minnesota NFL	14	9-9	5-5	3-8	1-1	18-23	78.3	∞53	36	37	90
2003—Tennessee NFL	15	5-5	12-12	10-14	0-0	27-31	87.1	43	42	42	123
2004—Tennessee NFL	15	4-5	4-4	9-12	0-1	17-22	77.3	45	37	37	88
Pro totals (23 years)	353	184-199	182-208	160-225	12-40	538-672	80.1	55	820	827	2434

A

ANDERSON, MARQUES   S

PERSONAL: Born May 26, 1979, in Harbor City, Calif. ... 5-11/210. ... Full name: Marques Deon Anderson.
HIGH SCHOOL: Polytechnic (Long Beach, Calif.).
COLLEGE: UCLA.
TRANSACTIONS/CAREER NOTES: Selected by Green Bay Packers in third round (92nd pick overall) of 2002 NFL draft. ... Signed by Packers (July 9, 2002). ... Traded by Packers to Oakland Raiders for fifth- (C Junius Coston) and sixth- (DE Mike Montgomery) round picks in 2005 draft (September 3, 2004). ... Granted free agency (March 2, 2005).

Year Team	G	GS	TOTALS			INTERCEPTIONS			
			Tk.	Ast.	Sks.	No.	Yds.	Avg.	TD
2002—Green Bay NFL	14	11	41	20	0.0	4	114	28.5	2
2003—Green Bay NFL	16	7	51	20	0.0	1	3	3.0	0
2004—Oakland NFL	14	10	54	18	0.0	1	23	23.0	0
Pro totals (3 years)	44	28	146	58	0.0	6	140	23.3	2

ANDERSON, MIKE   RB   BRONCOS

PERSONAL: Born September 21, 1973, in Winnsboro, S.C. ... 6-0/230. ... Full name: Michael Moschello Anderson.
HIGH SCHOOL: Fairfield (S.C.).
JUNIOR COLLEGE: Mount San Jacinto Community College (Calif.).
COLLEGE: Utah.
TRANSACTIONS/CAREER NOTES: Selected by Denver Broncos in sixth round (189th pick overall) of 2000 NFL draft. ... Signed by Broncos (July 14, 2000). ... On suspended list for violating league substance abuse policy (November 11-December 14, 2003). ... On injured reserve with groin injury (August 31, 2004-entire season).
SINGLE GAME HIGHS (regular season): Attempts—37 (December 3, 2000, vs. New Orleans); yards—251 (December 3, 2000, vs. New Orleans); and rushing touchdowns—4 (December 3, 2000, vs. New Orleans). Total: 8.
STATISTICAL PLATEAUS: 100-yard rushing games: 2000 (6), 2001 (2). Total: 8.

Year Team	G	GS	RUSHING				RECEIVING				TOTALS			
			Att.	Yds.	Avg.	TD	No.	Yds.	Avg.	TD	TD	2pt.	Pts.	Fum.
2000—Denver NFL	16	12	297	1487	§5.0	§15	23	169	7.3	0	15	1	92	4
2001—Denver NFL	16	7	175	678	3.9	4	8	46	5.8	0	4	1	26	1
2002—Denver NFL	15	12	84	386	4.6	2	18	167	9.3	2	4	0	24	2
2003—Denver NFL	12	5	70	257	3.7	3	12	53	4.4	2	5	0	30	2
2004—Denver NFL			Did not play.											
Pro totals (4 years)	59	36	626	2808	4.5	24	61	435	7.1	4	28	2	172	9

ANDERSON, RICHIE   FB

PERSONAL: Born September 13, 1971, in Sandy Spring, Md. ... 6-2/215. ... Full name: Richard Darnoll Anderson II.
HIGH SCHOOL: Sherwood (Sandy Spring, Md.).
COLLEGE: Penn State.
TRANSACTIONS/CAREER NOTES: Selected after junior season by New York Jets in sixth round (144th pick overall) of 1993 NFL draft. ... Signed by Jets (June 10, 1993). ... On injured reserve with ankle injury (December 31, 1993-remainder of season). ... On injured reserve with ankle injury (November 30, 1995-remainder of season). ... Granted unconditional free agency (February 28, 2003). ... Signed by Dallas Cowboys (March 4, 2003). ... On injured reserve with neck injury (December 28, 2004-remainder of season). ... Released by Cowboys (April 28, 2005).
CHAMPIONSHIP GAME EXPERIENCE: Member of Jets for AFC championship game (1998 season); did not play.
HONORS: Played in Pro Bowl (2000 season).
SINGLE GAME HIGHS (regular season): Attempts—10 (November 7, 2004, vs. Cincinnati); yards—74 (November 13, 1994, vs. Green Bay); and rushing touchdowns—1 (October 17, 2004, vs. Pittsburgh).
STATISTICAL PLATEAUS: 100-yard receiving games: 2000 (3). Total: 3.

Year Team	G	GS	RUSHING				RECEIVING				KICKOFF RETURNS				TOTALS		
			Att.	Yds.	Avg.	TD	No.	Yds.	Avg.	TD	No.	Yds.	Avg.	TD	TD	2pt.	Pts.	Fum.
1993—New York Jets NFL	7	0	0	0	0.0	0	0	0	0.0	0	4	66	16.5	0	0	0	0	1
1994—New York Jets NFL	13	5	43	207	4.8	1	25	212	8.5	1	3	43	14.3	0	2	0	12	1
1995—New York Jets NFL	10	0	5	17	3.4	0	5	26	5.2	0	0	0	0.0	0	0	0	0	2

Year Team	G	GS	RUSHING				RECEIVING				KICKOFF RETURNS				TOTALS			
			Att.	Yds.	Avg.	TD	No.	Yds.	Avg.	TD	No.	Yds.	Avg.	TD	TD	2pt.	Pts.	Fum.
1996—New York Jets NFL......	16	13	47	150	3.2	1	44	385	8.8	0	0	0	0.0	0	1	0	6	0
1997—New York Jets NFL......	16	3	21	70	3.3	0	26	150	5.8	1	0	0	0.0	0	1	0	6	2
1998—New York Jets NFL......	8	1	1	2	2.0	0	3	12	4.0	0	0	0	0.0	0	0	0	0	0
1999—New York Jets NFL......	16	9	16	84	5.3	0	29	302	10.4	3	0	0	0.0	0	3	0	18	0
2000—New York Jets NFL......	16	15	27	63	2.3	0	88	853	9.7	2	0	0	0.0	0	2	0	12	2
2001—New York Jets NFL......	16	16	26	102	3.9	0	40	252	6.3	2	0	0	0.0	0	2	0	12	1
2002—New York Jets NFL......	16	16	5	27	5.4	0	45	257	5.7	1	0	0	0.0	0	1	0	6	1
2003—Dallas NFL.................	15	8	70	306	4.4	1	69	493	7.1	4	0	0	0.0	0	5	0	30	1
2004—Dallas NFL.................	12	4	57	246	4.3	1	26	207	8.0	0	0	0	0.0	0	1	0	6	1
Pro totals (12 years)	161	90	318	1274	4.0	4	400	3149	7.9	14	7	109	15.6	0	18	0	108	11

ANDERSON, TIM   DT   BILLS

PERSONAL: Born November 22, 1980, in Fremont, Ohio. ... 6-3/304.
HIGH SCHOOL: Clyde (Ohio).
COLLEGE: Ohio State.
TRANSACTIONS/CAREER NOTES: Selected by Buffalo Bills in third round (74th pick overall) of 2004 NFL draft. ... Signed by Bills (July 26, 2004).

Year Team	G	GS	TOTALS			INTERCEPTIONS			
			Tk.	Ast.	Sks.	No.	Yds.	Avg.	TD
2004—Buffalo NFL	3	0	0	0	0.0	0	0	0.0	0

ANDERSON, WILLIE   T   BENGALS

PERSONAL: Born July 11, 1975, in Whistler, Ala. ... 6-5/340. ... Full name: Willie Aaron Anderson.
HIGH SCHOOL: Vigor (Prichard, Ala.).
COLLEGE: Auburn.
TRANSACTIONS/CAREER NOTES: Selected after junior season by Cincinnati Bengals in first round (10th pick overall) of 1996 NFL draft. ... Signed by Bengals (August 5, 1996).
PLAYING EXPERIENCE: Cincinnati NFL, 1996-2004. ... Games/Games started: 1996 (16/10), 1997 (16/16), 1998 (16/16), 1999 (14/14), 2000 (16/16), 2001 (16/16), 2002 (16/16), 2003 (16/16), 2004 (16/16). Total: 142/136.
HONORS: Played in Pro Bowl (2003 season). ... Named to play in Pro Bowl (2004 season); replaced by Tarik Glenn due to injury.

ANDREWS, SHAWN   T   EAGLES

PERSONAL: Born December 25, 1982, in Camden, Ark. ... 6-4/340. ... Brother of Stacy Andrews, offensive tackle, Cincinnati Bengals.
HIGH SCHOOL: Fairview (Camden, Ark.).
COLLEGE: Arkansas.
TRANSACTIONS/CAREER NOTES: Selected after junior season by Philadelphia Eagles in first round (16th pick overall) of 2004 NFL draft. ... Signed by Eagles (July 27, 2004). ... On injured reserve with leg injury (September 14, 2004-remainder of season).
PLAYING EXPERIENCE: Philadelphia NFL, 2004. ... Games/Games started: 2004 (1/1). Total: 1/1.
HONORS: Named offensive tackle on THE SPORTING NEWS Freshman All-America first team (2001). ... Named offensive tackle on THE SPORTING NEWS college All-America first team (2002 and 2003).

ANDREWS, STACY   T   BENGALS

PERSONAL: Born June 2, 1981, in Camden, Ark. ... 6-5/346. ... Full name: Stacy Dewayne Andrews. ... Brother of Shawn Andrews, offensive tackle, Philadelphia Eagles.
HIGH SCHOOL: Fairview (Camden, Ark.).
COLLEGE: Mississippi.
TRANSACTIONS/CAREER NOTES: Selected by Cincinnati Bengals in fourth round (123rd pick overall) of 2004 NFL draft. ... Signed by Bengals (July 30, 2004).
PLAYING EXPERIENCE: Cincinnati NFL, 2004. ... Games/Games started: 2004 (1/0). Total: 1/0.

ANDRUZZI, JOE   G   BROWNS

PERSONAL: Born August 23, 1975, in Brooklyn, N.Y. ... 6-3/312. ... Full name: Joseph Dominick Andruzzi. ... Name pronounced: ann-DROOZ-ee.
HIGH SCHOOL: Tottenville (Staten Island, N.Y.).
COLLEGE: Southern Connecticut State.
TRANSACTIONS/CAREER NOTES: Signed as non-drafted free agent by Green Bay Packers (April 25, 1997). ... Inactive for all 16 games (1997). ... Assigned by Packers to Scottish Claymores in 1998 NFL Europe enhancement allocations program (February 18, 1998). ... On injured reserve with knee injury (November 23, 1999-remainder of season). ... Released by Packers (August 27, 2000). ... Signed by New England Patriots (September 9, 2000). ... On injured reserve with knee injury (December 7, 2000-remainder of season). ... Granted unconditional free agency (March 2, 2005). ... Signed by Cleveland Browns (March 2, 2005).
PLAYING EXPERIENCE: Green Bay NFL, 1998-1999; New England NFL, 2000-2004. ... Games/Games started: 1998 (15/1), 1999 (8/3), 2000 (11/11), 2001 (16/16), 2002 (13/13), 2003 (16/16), 2004 (16/16). Total: 95/76.
CHAMPIONSHIP GAME EXPERIENCE: Member of Packers for NFC championship game (1997 season); inactive. ... Member of Packers for Super Bowl 32 (1997 season); inactive. ... Played in AFC championship game (2001, 2003 and 2004 seasons). ... Member of Super Bowl championship team (2001, 2003 and 2004 seasons).

ARCHULETA, ADAM — S — RAMS

PERSONAL: Born November 27, 1977, in Chandler, Ariz. ... 6-0/223. ... Full name: Adam J. Archuleta.
HIGH SCHOOL: Chandler (Ariz.).
COLLEGE: Arizona State.
TRANSACTIONS/CAREER NOTES: Selected by St. Louis Rams in first round (20th pick overall) of 2001 NFL draft. ... Signed by Rams (July 29, 2001).
CHAMPIONSHIP GAME EXPERIENCE: Played in NFC championship game (2001 season). ... Played in Super Bowl 36 (2001 season).

				TOTALS			INTERCEPTIONS			
Year Team	G	GS	Tk.	Ast.	Sks.	No.	Yds.	Avg.	TD
2001—St. Louis NFL	13	12	47	9	2.0	0	0	0.0	0
2002—St. Louis NFL	16	16	94	14	2.5	1	2	2.0	0
2003—St. Louis NFL	13	13	71	7	5.0	1	22	22.0	0
2004—St. Louis NFL	16	14	69	14	2.0	0	0	0.0	0
Pro totals (4 years)	58	55	281	44	11.5	2	24	12.0	0

ARMSTEAD, JESSIE — LB — PANTHERS

PERSONAL: Born October 26, 1970, in Dallas, Texas. ... 6-1/237. ... Full name: Jessie W. Armstead.
HIGH SCHOOL: David W. Carter (Dallas).
COLLEGE: Miami (Fla.).
TRANSACTIONS/CAREER NOTES: Selected by New York Giants in eighth round (207th pick overall) of 1993 NFL draft. ... Signed by Giants (July 19, 1993). ... Released by Giants (February 28, 2002). ... Signed by Washington Redskins (March 1, 2002). ... Released by Redskins (February 24, 2004). ... Signed by Carolina Panthers (March 5, 2004). ... On injured reserve with shoulder injury (September 5, 2004-entire season).
CHAMPIONSHIP GAME EXPERIENCE: Played in NFC championship game (2000 season). ... Played in Super Bowl 35 (2000 season).
HONORS: Named outside linebacker on THE SPORTING NEWS NFL All-Pro team (1997). ... Played in Pro Bowl (1997-2001 seasons).

				TOTALS			INTERCEPTIONS			
Year Team	G	GS	Tk.	Ast.	Sks.	No.	Yds.	Avg.	TD
1993—New York Giants NFL	16	0	28	3	0.0	1	0	0.0	0
1994—New York Giants NFL	16	0	33	8	3.0	1	0	0.0	0
1995—New York Giants NFL	16	2	36	10	0.5	1	58	58.0	1
1996—New York Giants NFL	16	16	83	31	3.0	2	23	11.5	0
1997—New York Giants NFL	16	16	101	31	3.5	2	57	28.5	1
1998—New York Giants NFL	16	16	75	26	5.0	2	4	2.0	0
1999—New York Giants NFL	16	16	97	27	9.0	2	35	17.5	0
2000—New York Giants NFL	16	16	76	26	5.0	1	-2	-2.0	0
2001—New York Giants NFL	16	16	64	24	1.5	0	0	0.0	0
2002—Washington NFL	16	16	79	21	3.0	0	0	0.0	0
2003—Washington NFL	16	15	76	17	6.5	0	0	0.0	0
2004—Carolina NFL				Did not play.					
Pro totals (11 years)	176	129	748	224	40.0	12	175	14.6	2

ARMSTRONG, DERICK — WR — TEXANS

PERSONAL: Born April 2, 1979, in Jasper, Texas. ... 6-2/206.
JUNIOR COLLEGE: Tyler (Texas).
COLLEGE: Arkansas-Monticello.
TRANSACTIONS/CAREER NOTES: Signed by Saskatchewan Roughriders of CFL (2002). ... Signed by Houston Texans (January 7, 2003).
SINGLE GAME HIGHS (regular season): Receptions—6 (November 7, 2004, vs. Denver); yards—101 (October 10, 2004, vs. Minnesota); and touchdown receptions—1 (October 10, 2004, vs. Minnesota).
STATISTICAL PLATEAUS: 100-yard receiving games: 2004 (1). Total: 1.

			RECEIVING				TOTALS			
Year Team	G	GS	No.	Yds.	Avg.	TD	TD	2pt.	Pts.	Fum.
2003—Houston NFL	8	1	7	75	10.7	1	1	0	6	0
2004—Houston NFL	14	1	29	415	14.3	1	1	0	6	0
Pro totals (2 years)	22	2	36	490	13.6	2	2	0	12	0

ARRINGTON, LAVAR — LB — REDSKINS

PERSONAL: Born June 20, 1978, in Pittsburgh, Pa. ... 6-3/253. ... Full name: LaVar RaShad Arrington.
HIGH SCHOOL: North Hills (Pittsburgh).
COLLEGE: Penn State.
TRANSACTIONS/CAREER NOTES: Selected after junior season by Washington Redskins in first round (second pick overall) of 2000 NFL draft. ... Signed by Redskins (July 22, 2000). ... On injured reserve with knee injury (December 29, 2004-remainder of season).
HONORS: Named linebacker on THE SPORTING NEWS college All-America first team (1998 and 1999). ... Butkus Award winner (1999). ... Played in Pro Bowl (2001-2003 seasons).

				TOTALS			INTERCEPTIONS			
Year Team	G	GS	Tk.	Ast.	Sks.	No.	Yds.	Avg.	TD
2000—Washington NFL	16	11	43	9	4.0	0	0	0.0	0
2001—Washington NFL	14	14	82	17	0.5	3	120	40.0	1
2002—Washington NFL	16	16	70	25	11.0	0	0	0.0	0
2003—Washington NFL	16	16	77	13	6.0	0	0	0.0	0
2004—Washington NFL	4	2	11	4	1.0	0	0	0.0	0
Pro totals (5 years)	66	59	283	68	22.5	3	120	40.0	1

ASHWORTH, TOM   T   PATRIOTS

PERSONAL: Born October 10, 1977, in Denver, Colo. ... 6-6/305. ... Full name: Thomas F. Ashworth.
HIGH SCHOOL: Cherry Creek (Englewood, Colo.).
COLLEGE: Colorado.
TRANSACTIONS/CAREER NOTES: Signed as non-drafted free agent by San Francisco 49ers (April 27, 2001). ... Released by 49ers (August 27, 2001). ... Signed by New England Patriots to practice squad (September 4, 2001). ... Released by Patriots (October 9, 2001). ... Re-signed by Patriots to practice squad (October 31, 2001). ... Activated (February 11, 2002). ... On injured reserve with back injury (November 6, 2004-remainder of season). ... Granted free agency (March 2, 2005). ... Re-signed by Patriots (March 15, 2005).
PLAYING EXPERIENCE: New England NFL, 2002-2004. ... Games/Games started: 2002 (1/0), 2003 (16/13), 2004 (6/6). Total: 23/19.
CHAMPIONSHIP GAME EXPERIENCE: Played in AFC championship game (2003 season). ... Member of Super Bowl championship team (2003 season).

ASKEW, B.J.   FB   JETS

PERSONAL: Born August 19, 1980, in Cincinnati, Ohio. ... 6-3/233. ... Full name: Bobby DeAngelo Askew Jr.
HIGH SCHOOL: Colerain (Cincinnati).
COLLEGE: Michigan.
TRANSACTIONS/CAREER NOTES: Selected by New York Jets in third round (85th pick overall) of 2003 NFL draft. ... Signed by Jets (July 20, 2003).
SINGLE GAME HIGHS (regular season): Attempts—6 (November 1, 2004, vs. Miami); yards—23 (November 1, 2004, vs. Miami); rushing touchdowns—0.

Year Team	G	GS	RUSHING Att.	Yds.	Avg.	TD	TOTALS TD	2pt.	Pts.	Fum.
2003—New York Jets NFL	16	0	2	9	4.5	0	0	0	0	0
2004—New York Jets NFL	16	0	6	23	3.8	0	0	0	0	0
Pro totals (2 years)	32	0	8	32	4.0	0	0	0	0	0

ASKEW, MATTHIAS   DT   BENGALS

PERSONAL: Born July 1, 1982, in Fort Lauderdale, Fla. ... 6-5/308.
HIGH SCHOOL: Dillard (Fort Lauderdale, Fla.).
COLLEGE: Michigan State.
TRANSACTIONS/CAREER NOTES: Selected after junior season by Cincinnati Bengals in fourth round (114th pick overall) of 2004 NFL draft. ... Signed by Bengals (July 30, 2004). ... On injured reserve with knee injury (December 1, 2004-remainder of season).

Year Team	G	GS	TOTALS Tk.	Ast.	Sks.	INTERCEPTIONS No.	Yds.	Avg.	TD
2004—Cincinnati NFL	5	0	0	2	0.0	0	0	0.0	0

ASOMUGHA, NNAMDI   CB   RAIDERS

PERSONAL: Born July 6, 1981, in Lafayette, La. ... 6-2/210.
HIGH SCHOOL: Narbonne (Los Angeles).
COLLEGE: California.
TRANSACTIONS/CAREER NOTES: Selected by Oakland Raiders in first round (31st pick overall) of 2003 NFL draft. ... Signed by Raiders (July 24, 2003).

Year Team	G	GS	TOTALS Tk.	Ast.	Sks.	INTERCEPTIONS No.	Yds.	Avg.	TD
2003—Oakland NFL	15	1	17	8	0.0	0	0	0.0	0
2004—Oakland NFL	16	7	33	6	1.0	0	0	0.0	0
Pro totals (2 years)	31	8	50	14	1.0	0	0	0.0	0

ATKINS, JAMES   DT   49ERS

PERSONAL: Born June 23, 1978, in Brooklyn, N.Y. ... 6-5/325. ... Full name: James Hodges Atkins.
HIGH SCHOOL: Roosevelt (Yonkers, N.Y.).
JUNIOR COLLEGE: Holmes (Goodman, Miss.), then Nassau (N.Y.).
COLLEGE: Virginia Union.
TRANSACTIONS/CAREER NOTES: Signed as non-drafted free agent by Miami Dolphins (April 25, 2002). ... Claimed on waivers by Tennessee Titans (August 27, 2002). ... Released by Titans (September 10, 2002). ... Re-signed by Titans to practice squad (September 12, 2002). ... Activated (January 31, 2003). ... Released by Titans (September 5, 2004). ... Signed by San Francisco 49ers (September 28, 2004).

Year Team	G	GS	TOTALS Tk.	Ast.	Sks.
2003—Tennessee NFL	13	4	7	5	0.0
2004—San Francisco NFL	3	0	1	0	0.0
Pro totals (2 years)	16	4	8	5	0.0

AYANBADEJO, BRENDON   LB   DOLPHINS

PERSONAL: Born September 6, 1976, in Chicago, Ill. ... 6-1/230. ... Full name: Oladele Brendon Ayanbadejo. ... Brother of Obafemi Ayanbadejo, running back, Arizona Cardinals.
HIGH SCHOOL: Santa Cruz (Calif.).
COLLEGE: UCLA.

TRANSACTIONS/CAREER NOTES: Signed as non-drafted free agent by Atlanta Falcons (April 19, 1999). ... Waived by Falcons (August 23, 1999). ... Signed by Winnipeg Blue Bombers of CFL (2000). ... Signed by British Columbia of CFL (2002). ... Signed by Miami Dolphins (February 4, 2003).

			RUSHING				TOTALS			
Year Team	G	GS	Att.	Yds.	Avg.	TD	TD	2pt.	Pts.	Fum.
2003—Miami NFL	16	0	0	0	0.0	0	0	0	0	0
2004—Miami NFL	16	2	0	0	0.0	0	0	0	0	0
Pro totals (2 years)	32	2	0	0	0.0	0	0	0	0	0

AYANBADEJO, OBAFEMI   FB   CARDINALS

PERSONAL: Born March 5, 1975, in Chicago, Ill. ... 6-2/231. ... Name pronounced: oh-BUH-fem-me eye-an-buh-DAY-ho. ... Brother of Brendon Ayanbadejo, linebacker, Miami Dolphins.
HIGH SCHOOL: Santa Cruz (Calif.).
JUNIOR COLLEGE: Cabrillo College (Calif.).
COLLEGE: San Diego State.
TRANSACTIONS/CAREER NOTES: Signed as non-drafted free agent by Minnesota Vikings (April 25, 1997). ... Released by Vikings (August 18, 1997). ... Re-signed by Vikings (February 6, 1998). ... Assigned by Vikings to England Monarchs in 1998 NFL Europe enhancement allocation program (February 17, 1998). ... Released by Vikings (August 24, 1998). ... Re-signed by Vikings to practice squad (December 24, 1998). ... Activated (December 1, 1998). ... Released by Vikings (December 23, 1998). ... Re-signed by Vikings to practice squad (December 24, 1998). ... Released by Vikings (September 21, 1999). ... Signed by Baltimore Ravens (September 27, 1999). ... On injured reserve with toe injury (November 28, 2000-remainder of season). ... Granted free agency (March 1, 2002). ... Signed by Miami Dolphins (July 25, 2002). ... Released by Dolphins (September 1, 2002). ... Re-signed by Dolphins (January 15, 2003). ... Granted unconditional free agency (March 3, 2004). ... Signed by Arizona Cardinals (March 6, 2004).
SINGLE GAME HIGHS (regular season): Attempts—9 (October 21, 2001, vs. Cleveland); yards—48 (October 21, 2001, vs. Cleveland); and rushing touchdowns—2 (December 12, 2004, vs. San Francisco).

			RUSHING				RECEIVING				TOTALS			
Year Team	G	GS	Att.	Yds.	Avg.	TD	No.	Yds.	Avg.	TD	TD	2pt.	Pts.	Fum.
1998—Minnesota NFL	1	0	0	0	0.0	0	0	0	0.0	0	0	0	0	0
1999—Minnesota NFL	2	0	0	0	0.0	0	0	0	0.0	0	0	0	0	0
—Baltimore NFL	12	0	0	0	0.0	0	1	2	2.0	0	0	0	0	0
2000—Baltimore NFL	8	4	15	37	2.5	1	23	168	7.3	1	2	0	12	0
2001—Baltimore NFL	16	5	46	173	3.8	1	24	121	5.0	1	2	0	12	1
2003—Miami NFL	16	2	1	-2	-2.0	0	12	53	4.4	0	0	0	0	1
2004—Arizona NFL	16	5	30	122	4.1	3	19	171	9.0	1	4	0	24	1
Pro totals (6 years)	71	16	92	330	3.6	5	79	515	6.5	3	8	0	48	3

AYODELE, AKIN   LB   JAGUARS

PERSONAL: Born September 17, 1979, in Dallas, Texas. ... 6-2/251. ... Full name: Akinola James Ayodele.
HIGH SCHOOL: MacArthur (Irving, Texas).
COLLEGE: Purdue.
TRANSACTIONS/CAREER NOTES: Selected by Jacksonville Jaguars in third round (89th pick overall) of 2002 NFL draft. ... Signed by Jaguars (July 11, 2002). ... Granted free agency (March 2, 2005). ... Re-signed by Jaguars (April 21, 2005).

			TOTALS			INTERCEPTIONS			
Year Team	G	GS	Tk.	Ast.	Sks.	No.	Yds.	Avg.	TD
2002—Jacksonville NFL	16	3	49	7	3.0	1	22	22.0	0
2003—Jacksonville NFL	16	16	85	28	1.0	2	15	7.5	0
2004—Jacksonville NFL	16	16	76	17	2.0	0	0	0.0	0
Pro totals (3 years)	48	35	210	52	6.0	3	37	12.3	0

AZUMAH, JERRY   CB   BEARS

PERSONAL: Born September 1, 1977, in Oklahoma City, Okla. ... 5-10/192. ... Name pronounced: ah-ZOO-muh.
HIGH SCHOOL: St. Peter-Marian (Worcester, Mass.).
COLLEGE: New Hampshire.
TRANSACTIONS/CAREER NOTES: Selected by Chicago Bears in fifth round (147th pick overall) of 1999 NFL draft. ... Signed by Bears (June 8, 1999).
HONORS: Named kick returner on The Sporting News NFL All-Pro team (2003 season). ... Played in Pro Bowl (2003 season). ... Walter Payton Award winner (1998).

			TOTALS			INTERCEPTIONS				KICKOFF RETURNS				TOTALS			
Year Team	G	GS	Tk.	Ast.	Sks.	No.	Yds.	Avg.	TD	No.	Yds.	Avg.	TD	TD	2pt.	Pts.	Fum.
1999—Chicago NFL	16	2	17	2	0.0	0	0	0.0	0	0	0	0.0	0	0	0	0	0
2000—Chicago NFL	14	4	21	5	0.0	1	2	2.0	0	4	65	16.3	0	0	0	0	0
2001—Chicago NFL	16	5	42	7	2.0	1	14	14.0	0	0	0	0.0	0	0	0	0	0
2002—Chicago NFL	16	16	69	13	1.0	0	18	0.0	0	41	1191	*29.0	†2	2	0	12	1
2003—Chicago NFL	16	13	68	11	1.0	4	44	11.0	0	42	924	22.0	0	1	0	6	1
2004—Chicago NFL	12	8	39	11	1.5	4	128	32.0	1	0	0	0.0	0	1	0	6	0
Pro totals (6 years)	90	48	256	49	5.5	10	206	20.6	1	87	2180	25.1	2	3	0	18	2

BABER, BILLY   TE   REDSKINS

PERSONAL: Born January 17, 1979, in Charlottesville, Va. ... 6-3/255. ... Full name: William Franklin Baber.
HIGH SCHOOL: Western Albermarle (Va.).
COLLEGE: Virginia.

TRANSACTIONS/CAREER NOTES: Selected by Kansas City Chiefs in fifth round (141st pick overall) of 2001 NFL draft. ... Signed by Chiefs (May 24, 2001). ... Released by Chiefs (September 2, 2001). ... Re-signed by Chiefs to practice squad (September 3, 2001). ... Activated (December 3, 2001). ... Released by Chiefs (August 30, 2004). ... Signed by San Diego Chargers (November 10, 2004). ... Released by Chargers (November 30, 2004). ... Signed by Tampa Bay Buccaneers (December 15, 2004). ... Released by Buccaneers (April 29, 2004). ... Signed by Washington Redskins (May 5, 2005).

SINGLE GAME HIGHS (regular season): Receptions—1 (January 2, 2005, vs. Arizona); yards—20 (December 28, 2003, vs. Chicago); and touchdown receptions—1 (September 29, 2002, vs. Miami).

Year Team	G	GS	RECEIVING No.	Yds.	Avg.	TD	TOTALS TD	2pt.	Pts.	Fum.
2001—Kansas City NFL	1	0	0	0	0.0	0	0	0	0	0
2002—Kansas City NFL	12	2	2	10	5.0	1	1	0	6	0
2003—Kansas City NFL	16	0	1	20	20.0	0	0	0	0	0
2004—Tampa Bay NFL	1	0	1	7	7.0	0	0	0	0	0
Pro totals (4 years)	30	2	4	37	9.3	1	1	0	6	0

B

BABERS, RODERICK   CB

PERSONAL: Born October 6, 1980, in Houston, Texas. ... 5-9/190. ... Full name: Roderick Henri Babers.
HIGH SCHOOL: Lamar (Houston).
COLLEGE: Texas.
TRANSACTIONS/CAREER NOTES: Selected by New York Giants in fourth round (123rd pick overall) of 2003 NFL draft. ... Signed by Giants (July 24, 2003). ... Claimed on waivers by Detroit Lions (September 8, 2003). ... On injured reserve with shoulder injury (November 11, 2003-remainder of season). ... Released by Lions (September 4, 2004). ... Re-signed by Lions to practice squad (September 6, 2004). ... Activated (September 18, 2004). ... On injured reserve with shoulder injury (September 28, 2004-remainder of season). ... Did not receive qualifying offer from Lions (March 2, 2005). ... Signed by Tampa Bay Buccaneers (April 4, 2005). ... Released by Buccaneers (April 26, 2005).

Year Team	G	GS	TOTALS Tk.	Ast.	Sks.	INTERCEPTIONS No.	Yds.	Avg.	TD
2003—Detroit NFL	5	0	3	1	0.0	0	0	0.0	0
2004—Detroit NFL	2	0	0	1	0.0	0	0	0.0	0
Pro totals (2 years)	7	0	3	2	0.0	0	0	0.0	0

BABIN, JASON   LB/DE   TEXANS

PERSONAL: Born May 24, 1980, in Kalamazoo, Mich. ... 6-2/259.
HIGH SCHOOL: Paw Paw (Mich.).
COLLEGE: Western Michigan.
TRANSACTIONS/CAREER NOTES: Selected by Houston Texans in first round (27th pick overall) of 2004 NFL draft. ... Signed by Texans (June 26, 2004).
HONORS: Named defensive end on THE SPORTING NEWS college All-America second team (2003).

Year Team	G	GS	TOTALS Tk.	Ast.	Sks.
2004—Houston NFL	16	16	51	12	4.0

BABINEAUX, JORDAN   SS   SEAHAWKS

PERSONAL: Born August 31, 1982, in Port Arthur, Texas. ... 6-0/200.
HIGH SCHOOL: Lincoln (Texas).
COLLEGE: Southern Arkansas.
TRANSACTIONS/CAREER NOTES: Signed as non-drafted free agent by Seattle Seahawks (April 29, 2004). ... Released by Seahawks (September 5, 2004). ... Re-signed by Seahawks to practice squad (September 6, 2004).

Year Team	G	GS	TOTALS Tk.	Ast.	Sks.
2004—Seattle NFL	6	0	2	1	0.0

BACKUS, JEFF   T   LIONS

PERSONAL: Born September 21, 1977, in Midland, Mich. ... 6-5/305. ... Full name: Jeffrey Carl Backus.
HIGH SCHOOL: Norcross (Ga.).
COLLEGE: Michigan.
TRANSACTIONS/CAREER NOTES: Selected by Detroit Lions in first round (18th pick overall) of 2001 NFL draft. ... Signed by Lions (July 23, 2001).
PLAYING EXPERIENCE: Detroit NFL, 2001-2004. ... Games/Games started: 2001 (16/16), 2002 (16/16), 2003 (16/16), 2004 (16/16). Total: 64/64.

BACON, WAINE   SS   COLTS

PERSONAL: Born April 11, 1979, in Fort Washington, Md. ... 5-10/191.
HIGH SCHOOL: Bishop McNamara (Fort Washington, Md.).
COLLEGE: Alabama.
TRANSACTIONS/CAREER NOTES: Selected by Atlanta Falcons in sixth round (202nd pick overall) of 2003 NFL draft. ... Signed by Falcons (2003). ... Waived by Falcons (August 30, 2003). ... Signed by Tampa Bay Buccaneers to practice squad (September 4, 2003). ... Released by Buccaneers from practice squad (September 9, 2003). ... Signed by Indianapolis Colts to practice squad (December 10, 2003). ... Activated

(January 9, 2004). ... Released by Colts (September 5, 2004). ... Re-signed by Colts to practice squad (September 7, 2004). ... Released by Colts from practice squad (October 1, 2004). ... Re-signed by Colts to practice squad (October 6, 2004). ... Activated (October 9, 2004).

			INTERCEPTIONS		
Year Team	G	No.	Yds.	Avg.	TD
2004—Indianapolis NFL	11	1	0	0.0	0

BADGER, BRAD   T   RAIDERS

PERSONAL: Born January 11, 1975, in Corvallis, Ore. ... 6-4/320.
HIGH SCHOOL: Corvallis (Ore.).
COLLEGE: Stanford.
TRANSACTIONS/CAREER NOTES: Selected by Washington Redskins in fifth round (162nd pick overall) of 1997 NFL draft. ... Signed by Redskins (May 5, 1997). ... Granted free agency (February 11, 2000). ... Tendered offer sheet by Minnesota Vikings (April 10, 2000). ... Redskins declined to match offer (April 11, 2000). ... Released by Vikings (March 12, 2002). ... Signed by Oakland Raiders (April 12, 2002). ... Granted unconditional free agency (February 28, 2003). ... Re-signed by Raiders (March 4, 2003).
PLAYING EXPERIENCE: Washington NFL, 1997-1999; Minnesota NFL, 2000-2001; Oakland NFL, 2002-2004. ... Games/Games started: 1997 (12/1), 1998 (16/16), 1999 (14/4), 2000 (16/0), 2001 (13/12), 2002 (7/0), 2003 (16/11), 2004 (16/12). Total: 110/56.
CHAMPIONSHIP GAME EXPERIENCE: Member of Vikings for NFC Championship game (2000 season); did not play. ... Member of Raiders for AFC championship game (2002 season); inactive. ... Played in Super Bowl 37 (2002 season).

BAILEY, BOSS   LB   LIONS

PERSONAL: Born October 14, 1979, in Folkston, Ga. ... 6-3/233. ... Brother of Champ Bailey, cornerback, Denver Broncos.
HIGH SCHOOL: Charlton County (Ga.).
COLLEGE: Georgia.
TRANSACTIONS/CAREER NOTES: Selected by Detroit Lions in second round (34th pick overall) of 2003 NFL draft. ... Signed by Lions (July 23, 2003). ... On injured reserve with knee injury (December 16, 2004-remainder of season).

			TOTALS			INTERCEPTIONS			
Year Team	G	GS	Tk.	Ast.	Sks.	No.	Yds.	Avg.	TD
2003—Detroit NFL	16	16	68	20	1.5	1	-2	-2.0	0
2004—Detroit NFL	Did not play.								
Pro totals (1 year)	16	16	68	20	1.5	1	-2	-2.0	0

BAILEY, CHAMP   CB   BRONCOS

PERSONAL: Born June 22, 1978, in Folkston, Ga. ... 6-0/192. ... Full name: Roland Champ Bailey. ... Brother of Boss Bailey, linebacker, Detroit Lions.
HIGH SCHOOL: Charlton County (Folkson, Ga.).
COLLEGE: Georgia.
TRANSACTIONS/CAREER NOTES: Selected after junior season by Washington Redskins in first round (seventh pick overall) of 1999 NFL draft. ... Signed by Redskins (July 24, 1999). ... Designated by Redskins as franchise player (February 24, 2004). ... Traded by Redskins with a second-round pick (RB Tatum Bell) in 2004 draft to Denver for RB Clinton Portis (March 4, 2004).
HONORS: Named cornerback on THE SPORTING NEWS college All-America second team (1998). ... Named cornerback on THE SPORTING NEWS NFL All-Pro team (2003 and 2004). ... Bronko Nagurski Award winner (1998). ... Played in Pro Bowl (2000-2004 seasons).

			TOTALS			INTERCEPTIONS				PUNT RETURNS				KICKOFF RETURNS				TOTALS			
Year Team	G	GS	Tk.	Ast.	Sks.	No.	Yds.	Avg.	TD	No.	Yds.	Avg.	TD	No.	Yds.	Avg.	TD	TD	2pt.	Pts.	Fum.
1999—Was. NFL	16	16	61	5	1.0	5	55	11.0	1	0	0	0.0	0	0	0	0.0	0	1	0	6	0
2000—Was. NFL	16	16	52	5	0.0	5	48	9.6	0	1	65	65.0	0	0	0	0.0	0	1	0	6	0
2001—Was. NFL	16	16	49	2	0.0	3	17	5.7	0	0	0	0.0	0	0	0	0.0	0	0	0	0	0
2002—Was. NFL	16	16	62	6	0.0	3	2	0.7	0	24	238	9.9	0	1	17	17.0	0	0	0	0	4
2003—Was. NFL	16	16	67	4	0.0	2	2	1.0	0	0	0	0.0	0	0	0	0.0	0	0	0	0	0
2004—Den. NFL	16	16	68	13	0.0	3	0	0.0	0	0	0	0.0	0	0	0	0.0	0	0	0	0	0
Pro totals (6 years)	96	96	359	35	1.0	21	124	5.9	1	25	303	12.1	0	1	17	17.0	0	2	0	12	4

BAILEY, RODNEY   DE   PATRIOTS

PERSONAL: Born October 7, 1979, in Cleveland, Ohio. ... 6-3/306. ... Full name: Rodney Dwayne Bailey.
HIGH SCHOOL: St. Edwards (Cleveland).
COLLEGE: Ohio State.
TRANSACTIONS/CAREER NOTES: Selected by Pittsburgh Steelers in sixth round (181st pick overall) of 2001 NFL draft. ... Signed by Steelers (June 6, 2001). ... Granted free agency (March 3, 2004). ... Tendered offer sheet by New England Patriots (March 4, 2004). ... Steelers declined to match offer (March 11, 2004). ... On injured reserve with Achilles injury (August 2, 2004-entire season).
CHAMPIONSHIP GAME EXPERIENCE: Played in AFC championship game (2001 season).

			TOTALS		
Year Team	G	GS	Tk.	Ast.	Sks.
2001—Pittsburgh NFL	16	1	8	4	2.0
2002—Pittsburgh NFL	16	0	17	7	5.5
2003—Pittsburgh NFL	16	0	7	2	2.0
2004—New England NFL	Did not play.				
Pro totals (3 years)	48	1	32	13	9.5

BAKER, CHRIS — TE — JETS

PERSONAL: Born November 18, 1979, in Queens, N.Y. ... 6-3/258.
HIGH SCHOOL: Saline (Mich.).
COLLEGE: Michigan State.
TRANSACTIONS/CAREER NOTES: Selected by New York Jets in third round (88th pick overall) of 2002 NFL draft. ... Signed by Jets (July 16, 2002). ... Granted free agency (March 2, 2005). ... Re-signed by Jets (April 5, 2005).
SINGLE GAME HIGHS (regular season): Receptions—3 (October 24, 2004, vs. New England); yards—33 (October 10, 2004, vs. Buffalo); and touchdown receptions—1 (January 2, 2005, vs. St. Louis).

Year Team	G	GS	RECEIVING				KICKOFF RETURNS				TOTALS			
			No.	Yds.	Avg.	TD	No.	Yds.	Avg.	TD	TD	2pt.	Pts.	Fum.
2002—New York Jets NFL	12	0	2	14	7.0	0	3	23	7.7	0	0	0	0	0
2003—New York Jets NFL	16	0	14	137	9.8	0	2	6	3.0	0	0	0	0	0
2004—New York Jets NFL	16	0	18	182	10.1	4	0	0	0.0	0	4	0	24	1
Pro totals (3 years)	44	0	34	333	9.8	4	5	29	5.8	0	4	0	24	1

BAKER, EUGENE — WR

PERSONAL: Born March 18, 1976, in Monroeville, Pa. ... 6-2/183.
HIGH SCHOOL: Shady Side Academy (Monroeville, Pa.).
COLLEGE: Kent State.
TRANSACTIONS/CAREER NOTES: Selected by Atlanta Falcons in fifth round (164th pick overall) of 1999 NFL draft. ... Signed by Falcons (July 7, 1999). ... Released by Falcons (September 5, 1999). ... Re-signed by Falcons to practice squad (September 7, 1999). ... Activated (December 13, 1999). ... Released by Falcons (September 2, 2001). ... Re-signed by Falcons to practice squad (September 4, 2001). ... Released by Falcons (October 2, 2001). ... Signed by Buffalo Bills to practice squad (October 3, 2001). ... Granted free agency following 2001 season. ... Signed by St. Louis Rams (February 19, 2002). ... Released by Rams (August 23, 2002). ... Signed by Carolina Panthers (January 8, 2003). ... Released by Panthers (October 14, 2004).
CHAMPIONSHIP GAME EXPERIENCE: Member of Panthers for NFC championship game (2003 season); inactive. ... Member of Panthers for Super Bowl 38 (2003 season); inactive.
SINGLE GAME HIGHS (regular season): Receptions—5 (December 19, 1999, vs. Tennessee); yards—66 (December 19, 1999, vs. Tennessee); and touchdown receptions—0.

Year Team	G	GS	RECEIVING				PUNT RETURNS				TOTALS			
			No.	Yds.	Avg.	TD	No.	Yds.	Avg.	TD	TD	2pt.	Pts.	Fum.
1999—Atlanta NFL	3	1	7	118	16.9	0	0	0	0.0	0	0	0	0	0
2003—Carolina NFL	1	0	0	0	0.0	0	0	0	0.0	0	0	0	0	0
2004—Carolina NFL	3	0	0	0	0.0	0	8	49	6.1	0	0	0	0	0
Pro totals (3 years)	7	1	7	118	16.9	0	8	49	6.1	0	0	0	0	0

BAKER, JASON — P — PANTHERS

PERSONAL: Born May 17, 1978, in Fort Wayne, Ind. ... 6-1/201.
HIGH SCHOOL: Wayne (Fort Wayne, Ind.).
COLLEGE: Iowa.
TRANSACTIONS/CAREER NOTES: Signed as non-drafted free agent by Philadelphia Eagles (April 23, 2001). ... Released by Eagles (August 28, 2001). ... Signed by San Francisco 49ers (August 29, 2001). ... Released by 49ers (November 26, 2002). ... Signed by Philadelphia Eagles (December 3, 2002). ... Released by Eagles (December 16, 2002). ... Signed by Kansas City Chiefs (May 14, 2003). ... Granted free agency (March 3, 2004). ... Re-signed by Chiefs (April 12, 2004). ... Released by Chiefs (September 4, 2004). ... Re-signed by Chiefs (September 25, 2004). ... Released by Chiefs (October 5, 2004). ... Signed by Indianapolis Colts (November 11, 2004). ... Claimed on waivers by Denver Broncos (December 9, 2004). ... Granted unconditional free agency (March 2, 2005). ... Re-signed by Broncos (March 18, 2005). ... Traded by Broncos with seventh-round pick in 2006 draft to Carolina Panthers for P Todd Sauerbrun (May 19, 2005).

Year Team	G	PUNTING					
		No.	Yds.	Avg.	Net avg.	In. 20	Blk.
2001—San Francisco NFL	16	69	2813	40.8	35.4	21	0
2002—Philadelphia NFL	2	13	445	34.2	29.8	2	0
—San Francisco NFL	11	42	1688	40.2	32.0	12	0
2003—Kansas City NFL	16	80	3156	39.5	33.2	21	1
2004—Kansas City NFL	2	9	340	37.8	26.9	3	0
—Indianapolis NFL	4	0	0	0.0	0.0	0	0
—Denver NFL	4	15	591	39.4	34.4	7	0
Pro totals (4 years)	55	228	9033	39.6	33.3	66	1

BAKER, RASHAD — DB — BILLS

PERSONAL: Born February 22, 1982, in Camden, N.J. ... 5-10/198. ... Full name: Rashad Steward Baker.
HIGH SCHOOL: Woodrow Wilson (Camden, N.J.).
COLLEGE: Tennessee.
TRANSACTIONS/CAREER NOTES: Signed as non-drafted free agent by Buffalo Bills (April 26, 2004).
HONORS: Named defensive back on THE SPORTING NEWS Freshman All-America third team (2000).

Year Team	G	GS	TOTALS			INTERCEPTIONS			
			Tk.	Ast.	Sks.	No.	Yds.	Avg.	TD
2004—Buffalo NFL	14	3	13	6	0.0	1	26	26.0	0

BALL, DAVE   DE   CHARGERS

PERSONAL: Born January 4, 1981, in Fairfield, Calif. ... 6-5/277. ... Full name: David Stewart Ball.
HIGH SCHOOL: Dixon (Calif.).
COLLEGE: UCLA.
TRANSACTIONS/CAREER NOTES: Selected by San Diego Chargers in fifth round (133rd pick overall) of 2004 NFL draft. ... Signed by Chargers (July 29, 2004). ... On injured reserve with toe injury (October 19, 2004-remainder of season).
HONORS: Named defensive end on THE SPORTING NEWS college All-America first team (2003).

			TOTALS		
Year Team	G	GS	Tk.	Ast.	Sks.
2004—San Diego NFL	6	0	2	1	0.0

BALL, JASON   C

PERSONAL: Born March 21, 1979, in Fayetteville, N.C. ... 6-2/301.
HIGH SCHOOL: Londerry (N.H.).
COLLEGE: New Hampshire.
TRANSACTIONS/CAREER NOTES: Signed as non-drafted free agent by San Diego Chargers (April 26, 2002). ... Claimed on waivers by Tampa Bay Buccaneers (October 27, 2004). ... Released by Buccaneers (November 1, 2004).
PLAYING EXPERIENCE: San Diego NFL, 2002-2004. ... Games/Games started: 2002 (16/13), 2003 (8/8), 2004 (3/2). Total: 27/23.

BANKS, TONY   QB   TEXANS

PERSONAL: Born April 5, 1973, in San Diego, Calif. ... 6-4/229. ... Full name: Anthony Lamar Banks.
HIGH SCHOOL: Herbert Hoover (San Diego).
JUNIOR COLLEGE: San Diego Mesa College.
COLLEGE: Michigan State.
TRANSACTIONS/CAREER NOTES: Selected by St. Louis Rams in second round (42nd pick overall) of 1996 NFL draft. ... Signed by Rams (July 15, 1996). ... On injured reserve list with knee injury (December 14, 1998-remainder of season). ... Granted free agency (February 12, 1999). ... Re-signed by Rams (April 17, 1999). ... Traded by Rams to Baltimore Ravens for fifth-round pick (G Cameron Spikes) in 1999 draft and seventh-round pick (traded to Chicago) in 2000 draft (April 17, 1999). ... Granted unconditional free agency (February 11, 2000). ... Re-signed by Ravens (February 17, 2000). ... Released by Ravens (March 1, 2001). ... Signed by Dallas Cowboys (March 28, 2001). ... Released by Cowboys (August 14, 2001). ... Signed by Washington Redskins (August 16, 2001). ... Granted unconditional free agency (March 1, 2002). ... Signed by Houston Texans (August 19, 2002). ... Granted unconditional free agency (February 28, 2003). ... Re-signed by Texans (April 3, 2003). ... On injured reserve with hand injury (December 1, 2003-remainder of season). ... Granted unconditional free agency (March 2, 2005). ... Re-signed by Texans (March 17, 2005).
CHAMPIONSHIP GAME EXPERIENCE: Member of Ravens for AFC championship game (2000 season); did not play. ... Member of Super Bowl championship team (2000 season).
SINGLE GAME HIGHS (regular season): Attempts—49 (September 28, 1997, vs. Oakland); completions—29 (September 6, 1998, vs. New Orleans); yards—401 (November 2, 1997, vs. Atlanta); and touchdown passes—5 (September 10, 2000, vs. Jacksonville).
STATISTICAL PLATEAUS: 300-yard passing games: 1996 (2), 1997 (1), 1999 (1), 2001 (1). Total: 5.
MISCELLANEOUS: Regular-season record as starting NFL quarterback: 35-43 (.449).

			PASSING									RUSHING				TOTALS		
Year Team	G	GS	Att.	Cmp.	Pct.	Yds.	TD	Int.	Avg.	Skd.	Rat.	Att.	Yds.	Avg.	TD	TD	2pt.	Pts.
1996—St. Louis NFL	14	13	368	192	52.2	2544	15	15	6.91	48	71.0	61	212	3.5	0	0	1	2
1997—St. Louis NFL	16	16	487	252	51.7	3254	14	13	6.68	43	71.5	47	186	4.0	1	1	0	6
1998—St. Louis NFL	14	14	408	241	59.1	2535	7	14	6.21	41	68.6	40	156	3.9	3	3	1	20
1999—Baltimore NFL	12	10	320	169	52.8	2136	17	8	6.68	33	81.2	24	93	3.9	0	0	0	0
2000—Baltimore NFL	11	8	274	150	54.7	1578	8	8	5.76	20	69.3	19	57	3.0	0	0	0	0
2001—Washington NFL	15	14	370	198	53.5	2386	10	10	6.45	29	71.3	47	152	3.2	2	2	0	12
2002—Houston NFL		Did not play.																
2003—Houston NFL	7	3	102	61	59.8	693	5	3	6.79	13	84.3	6	27	4.5	0	0	0	0
2004—Houston NFL	5	0	2	1	50.0	16	0	0	8.00	0	77.1	0	0	0.0	0	0	0	0
Pro totals (8 years)	94	78	2331	1264	54.2	15142	76	71	6.50	227	72.5	244	883	3.6	6	6	2	40

BANNAN, JUSTIN   DT   BILLS

PERSONAL: Born April 18, 1979, in Sacramento, Calif. ... 6-3/305.
HIGH SCHOOL: Bella Vista (Fair Oaks, Calif.).
COLLEGE: Colorado.
TRANSACTIONS/CAREER NOTES: Selected by Buffalo Bills in fifth round (139th pick overall) of 2002 NFL draft. ... Signed by Bills (June 21, 2002).

			TOTALS		
Year Team	G	GS	Tk.	Ast.	Sks.
2002—Buffalo NFL	15	0	15	6	1.0
2003—Buffalo NFL	14	1	9	6	0.0
2004—Buffalo NFL	10	0	1	1	0.0
Pro totals (3 years)	39	1	25	13	1.0

BANNISTER, ALEX   WR   SEAHAWKS

PERSONAL: Born April 23, 1979, in Cincinnati, Ohio. ... 6-5/207.
HIGH SCHOOL: Hughes Center (Cincinnati).
COLLEGE: Eastern Kentucky.

TRANSACTIONS/CAREER NOTES: Selected by Seattle Seahawks in fifth round (140th pick overall) of 2001 NFL draft. ... Signed by Seahawks (July 9, 2001). ... Granted free agency (March 3, 2004). ... Re-signed by Seahawks (May 3, 2004). ... On injured reserve with clavicle injury (November 5, 2004-remainder of season). ... Granted unconditional free agency (March 2, 2005). ... Re-signed by Seahawks (March 31, 2005).

HONORS: Played in Pro Bowl (2003 season).

SINGLE GAME HIGHS (regular season): Receptions—2 (October 17, 2004, vs. New England); yards—53 (December 27, 2003, vs. San Francisco); and touchdown receptions—1 (December 27, 2003, vs. San Francisco).

Year Team	G	GS	RECEIVING No.	Yds.	Avg.	TD	TOTALS TD	2pt.	Pts.	Fum.
2001—Seattle NFL	16	0	4	50	12.5	0	1	0	6	0
2002—Seattle NFL	16	1	0	0	0.0	0	0	0	0	0
2003—Seattle NFL	16	2	3	61	20.3	1	1	0	6	0
2004—Seattle NFL	7	1	2	10	5.0	0	0	0	0	0
Pro totals (4 years)	55	4	9	121	13.4	1	2	0	12	0

BANTA, BRADFORD   TE/LS

PERSONAL: Born December 14, 1970, in Baton Rouge, La. ... 6-6/253. ... Full name: Dennis Bradford Banta.
HIGH SCHOOL: University (Baton Rouge, La.).
COLLEGE: Southern California.
TRANSACTIONS/CAREER NOTES: Selected by Indianapolis Colts in fourth round (106th pick overall) of 1994 NFL draft. ... Signed by Colts (July 22, 1994). ... Granted free agency (February 14, 1997). ... Re-signed by Colts (May 14, 1997). ... Granted unconditional free agency (February 11, 2000). ... Re-signed by Colts (March 9, 2000). ... Released by Colts (August 27, 2000). ... Signed by New York Jets (August 29, 2000). ... Granted unconditional free agency (March 2, 2001). ... Signed by Detroit Lions (April 19, 2001). ... On injured reserve with broken clavicle (December 8, 2003-remainder of season). ... Released by Lions (September 4, 2004). ... Signed by Buffalo Bills (December 14, 2004). ... Granted unconditional free agency (March 2, 2005).
PLAYING EXPERIENCE: Indianapolis NFL, 1994-1999; New York Jets NFL, 2000; Detroit NFL, 2001-2003; Buffalo NFL, 2004. ... Games/Games started: 1994 (16/0), 1995 (16/2), 1996 (13/0), 1997 (15/0), 1998 (16/0), 1999 (16/0), 2000 (16/0), 2001 (16/0), 2002 (16/0), 2003 (13/0), 2004 (3/0). Total: 156/2.
CHAMPIONSHIP GAME EXPERIENCE: Played in AFC championship game (1995 season).
SINGLE GAME HIGHS (regular season): Receptions—1 (November 1, 1998, vs. New England); yards—7 (November 1, 1998, vs. New England); and touchdown receptions—0.

BANTA-CAIN, TULLY   LB   PATRIOTS

PERSONAL: Born August 28, 1980, in Mountain View, Calif. ... 6-2/250.
HIGH SCHOOL: Fremont (Mountain View, Calif.).
COLLEGE: California.
TRANSACTIONS/CAREER NOTES: Selected by New England Patriots in seventh round (239th pick overall) of 2003 NFL draft. ... Signed by Patriots (July 21, 2003). ... On physically unable to perform list with groin injury (August 26-October 18, 2003).
CHAMPIONSHIP GAME EXPERIENCE: Played in AFC championship game (2003 and 2004 seasons). ... Member of Super Bowl championship team (2003 and 2004 season).

Year Team	G	GS	TOTALS Tk.	Ast.	Sks.	INTERCEPTIONS No.	Yds.	Avg.	TD
2003—New England NFL	9	0	1	1	1.0	0	0	0.0	0
2004—New England NFL	16	0	6	4	1.5	1	4	4.0	0
Pro totals (2 years)	25	0	7	5	2.5	1	4	4.0	0

BARBER, RONDE   CB   BUCCANEERS

PERSONAL: Born April 7, 1975, in Roanoke, Va. ... 5-10/184. ... Full name: Jamael Oronde Barber. ... Name pronounced: RON-day. ... Twin brother of Tiki Barber, running back, New York Giants.
HIGH SCHOOL: Cave Spring (Roanoke, Va.).
COLLEGE: Virginia.
TRANSACTIONS/CAREER NOTES: Selected after junior season by Tampa Bay Buccaneers in third round (66th pick overall) of 1997 NFL draft. ... Signed by Buccaneers (July 18, 1997). ... Granted free agency (February 11, 2000). ... Re-signed by Buccaneers (June 13, 2000). ... Granted unconditional free agency (March 2, 2001). ... Re-signed by Buccaneers (April 10, 2001).
CHAMPIONSHIP GAME EXPERIENCE: Played in NFC championship game (1999 and 2002 seasons). ... Member of Super Bowl championship team (2002 season).
HONORS: Played in Pro Bowl (2001 and 2004 seasons).

Year Team	G	GS	TOTALS Tk.	Ast.	Sks.	INTERCEPTIONS No.	Yds.	Avg.	TD
1997—Tampa Bay NFL	1	0	4	0	0.0	0	0	0.0	0
1998—Tampa Bay NFL	16	9	59	11	3.0	2	67	33.5	0
1999—Tampa Bay NFL	16	15	54	16	1.0	2	60	30.0	1
2000—Tampa Bay NFL	16	16	67	15	5.5	2	46	23.0	1
2001—Tampa Bay NFL	16	16	56	13	1.0	†10	86	8.6	1
2002—Tampa Bay NFL	16	16	63	12	3.0	2	9	4.5	0
2003—Tampa Bay NFL	16	16	80	19	1.5	2	53	26.5	0
2004—Tampa Bay NFL	16	16	77	15	3.0	3	23	7.7	0
Pro totals (8 years)	113	104	460	101	18.0	23	344	15.0	3

BARBER, SHAWN   LB   CHIEFS

PERSONAL: Born January 14, 1975, in Richmond, Va. ... 6-2/240.
HIGH SCHOOL: Hermitage (Richmond, Va.).
COLLEGE: Richmond.

TRANSACTIONS/CAREER NOTES: Selected by Washington Redskins in fourth round (113th pick overall) of 1998 NFL draft. ... Signed by Redskins (May 13, 1998). ... Granted free agency (March 2, 2001). ... Re-signed by Redskins (June 1, 2001). ... On injured reserve with knee injury (October 2, 2001-remainder of season). ... Granted unconditional free agency (March 1, 2002). ... Signed by Philadelphia Eagles (March 15, 2002). ... Granted unconditional free agency (February 28, 2003). ... Signed by Kansas City Chiefs (March 3, 2003). ... On injured reserve with knee injury (November 10, 2004-remainder of season).
CHAMPIONSHIP GAME EXPERIENCE: Played in NFC championship game (2002 season).

				TOTALS			INTERCEPTIONS			
Year	Team	G	GS	Tk.	Ast.	Sks.	No.	Yds.	Avg.	TD
1998—Washington NFL		16	1	21	6	0.0	1	0	0.0	0
1999—Washington NFL		16	16	82	19	1.0	2	70	35.0	1
2000—Washington NFL		14	14	56	7	2.0	0	0	0.0	0
2001—Washington NFL		3	3	14	3	0.0	0	0	0.0	0
2002—Philadelphia NFL		16	16	69	22	1.0	2	81	40.5	1
2003—Kansas City NFL		16	16	93	20	5.0	1	28	28.0	0
2004—Kansas City NFL		8	8	29	5	1.0	1	10	10.0	0
Pro totals (7 years)		89	74	364	82	10.0	7	189	27.0	2

BARBER, TIKI   RB   GIANTS

PERSONAL: Born April 7, 1975, in Roanoke, Va. ... 5-10/200. ... Full name: Atiim Kiambu Barber. ... Name pronounced: TEE-kee. ... Twin brother of Ronde Barber, cornerback, Tampa Bay Buccaneers.
HIGH SCHOOL: Cave Spring (Roanoke, Va.).
COLLEGE: Virginia.
TRANSACTIONS/CAREER NOTES: Selected by New York Giants in second round (36th pick overall) of 1997 NFL draft. ... Signed by Giants for 1997 season. ... Granted free agency (February 11, 2000). ... Re-signed by Giants (June 8, 2000). ... Granted unconditional free agency (March 2, 2001). ... Re-signed by Giants (March 8, 2001).
CHAMPIONSHIP GAME EXPERIENCE: Played in NFC championship game (2000 season). ... Played in Super Bowl 35 (2000 season).
HONORS: Played in Pro Bowl (2004 season).
SINGLE GAME HIGHS (regular season): Attempts—32 (December 28, 2002, vs. Philadelphia); yards—203 (December 28, 2002, vs. Philadelphia); and rushing touchdowns—2 (November 7, 2004, vs. Chicago).
STATISTICAL PLATEAUS: 100-yard rushing games: 1997 (1), 2000 (1), 2001 (3), 2002 (4), 2003 (4), 2004 (9). Total: 22. 100-yard receiving games: 1999 (1), 2004 (1). Total: 2.
MISCELLANEOUS: Holds New York Giants all-time records for most yards rushing (6,927) and most receptions (474).

				RUSHING				RECEIVING				PUNT RETURNS				KICKOFF RETURNS				TOTALS		
Year	Team	G	GS	All.	Yds.	Avg.	TD	No.	Yds.	Avg	TD	No.	Yds.	Avg.	TD	No.	Yds.	Avg.	TD	TD	2pt.	Pts.
1997—NYG NFL		12	6	136	511	3.8	3	34	299	8.8	1	0	0	0.0	0	0	0	0.0	0	4	1	26
1998—NYG NFL		16	4	52	166	3.2	0	42	348	8.3	3	0	0	0.0	0	14	250	17.9	0	3	0	18
1999—NYG NFL		16	1	62	258	4.2	0	66	609	9.2	2	∞44	‡506	11.5	∞1	12	266	22.2	0	3	0	18
2000—NYG NFL		16	12	213	1006	4.7	8	70	719	10.3	1	‡39	332	8.5	0	1	28	28.0	0	9	0	54
2001—NYG NFL		14	9	166	865	5.2	4	72	577	8.0	0	38	338	8.9	0	0	0	0.0	0	4	1	26
2002—NYG NFL		16	15	304	1387	4.6	11	69	597	8.7	0	1	5	5.0	0	0	0	0.0	0	11	0	66
2003—NYG NFL		16	16	278	1216	4.4	2	69	461	6.7	1	0	0	0.0	0	0	0	0.0	0	3	1	20
2004—NYG NFL		16	14	322	1518	4.7	13	52	578	11.1	2	0	0	0.0	0	0	0	0.0	0	15	0	90
Pro totals (8 years)		122	77	1533	6927	4.5	41	474	4188	8.8	10	122	1181	9.7	1	27	544	20.1	0	52	3	318

BARKER, BRYAN   P

PERSONAL: Born June 28, 1964, in Jacksonville Beach, Fla. ... 6-1/205. ... Full name: Bryan Christopher Barker.
HIGH SCHOOL: Miramonte (Orinda, Calif.).
COLLEGE: Santa Clara.
TRANSACTIONS/CAREER NOTES: Signed as non-drafted free agent by Denver Broncos (May 1988). ... Released by Broncos (July 19, 1988). ... Signed by Seattle Seahawks (1989). ... Released by Seahawks (August 30, 1989). ... Signed by Kansas City Chiefs (May 1, 1990). ... Released by Chiefs (August 28, 1990). ... Re-signed by Chiefs (September 26, 1990). ... Granted unconditional free agency (February 1-April 1, 1991). ... Re-signed by Chiefs for 1991 season. ... Granted unconditional free agency (February 1-April 1, 1992). ... Re-signed by Chiefs for 1992 season. ... Released by Chiefs (1994). ... Signed by Minnesota Vikings (May 18, 1994). ... Released by Vikings (August 30, 1994). ... Signed by Philadelphia Eagles (October 11, 1994). ... Granted unconditional free agency (February 17, 1995). ... Signed by Jacksonville Jaguars (March 7, 1995). ... Granted unconditional free agency (March 2, 2001). ... Signed by Washington Redskins (April 12, 2001). ... On injured reserve with head injury (December 4, 2002-remainder of season). ... Released by Redskins (February 24, 2004). ... Signed by Green Bay Packers (August 23, 2004). ... Granted unconditional free agency (March 2, 2005).
CHAMPIONSHIP GAME EXPERIENCE: Played in AFC championship game (1993, 1996 and 1999 seasons).
HONORS: Played in Pro Bowl (1997 season).

				PUNTING				
Year	Team	G	No.	Yds.	Avg.	Net avg.	In. 20	Blk.
1990—Kansas City NFL		13	64	2479	38.7	33.3	16	0
1991—Kansas City NFL		16	57	2303	40.4	35.0	11	0
1992—Kansas City NFL		15	75	3245	43.3	35.2	16	1
1993—Kansas City NFL		16	76	3240	42.6	35.3	19	1
1994—Philadelphia NFL		11	66	2696	40.8	‡36.2	20	0
1995—Jacksonville NFL		16	82	3591	43.8	*38.6	19	0
1996—Jacksonville NFL		16	69	3016	43.7	35.6	16	0
1997—Jacksonville NFL		16	66	2964	44.9	38.8	27	0
1998—Jacksonville NFL		16	85	3824	45.0	38.5	28	0
1999—Jacksonville NFL		16	78	3260	41.8	36.9	32	0
2000—Jacksonville NFL		16	76	3194	42.0	34.4	29	0
2001—Washington NFL		16	90	3747	41.6	34.8	27	0
2002—Washington NFL		12	48	1924	40.1	30.0	13	0
2003—Washington NFL		16	84	3377	40.2	34.3	24	0
2004—Green Bay NFL		16	66	2644	40.1	33.4	16	0
Pro totals (15 years)		227	1082	45504	42.1	35.6	313	2

BARLOW, KEVAN — RB — 49ERS

PERSONAL: Born January 7, 1979, in Pittsburgh, Pa. ... 6-1/238. ... Full name: Kevan C. Barlow.
HIGH SCHOOL: Peabody (Pittsburgh).
COLLEGE: Pittsburgh.
TRANSACTIONS/CAREER NOTES: Selected by San Francisco 49ers in third round (80th pick overall) of 2001 NFL draft. ... Signed by 49ers (July 25, 2001).
SINGLE GAME HIGHS (regular season): Attempts—30 (December 21, 2003, vs. Philadelphia); yards—154 (December 21, 2003, vs. Philadelphia); and rushing touchdowns—2 (November 14, 2004, vs. Carolina).
STATISTICAL PLATEAUS: 100-yard rushing games: 2003 (2), 2004 (2). Total: 4.

				RUSHING				RECEIVING				TOTALS		
Year Team	G	GS	Att.	Yds.	Avg.	TD	No.	Yds.	Avg.	TD	TD	2pt.	Pts.	Fum.
2001—San Francisco NFL	15	0	125	512	4.1	4	22	247	11.2	1	5	0	30	1
2002—San Francisco NFL	14	0	145	675	4.7	4	14	136	9.7	1	5	0	30	2
2003—San Francisco NFL	16	4	201	1024	5.1	6	35	307	8.8	1	7	0	42	5
2004—San Francisco NFL	15	14	244	822	3.4	7	35	212	6.1	0	7	0	42	2
Pro totals (4 years)	60	18	715	3033	4.2	21	106	902	8.5	3	24	0	144	10

BARNES, BRANDON — LB — REDSKINS

PERSONAL: Born June 12, 1981, in Sikeston, Mo. ... 6-2/247. ... Full name: Brandon Edward Barnes.
HIGH SCHOOL: Sikeston (Mo.).
COLLEGE: Missouri.
TRANSACTIONS/CAREER NOTES: Signed as non-drafted free agent by Baltimore Ravens (April 30, 2004). ... Released by Ravens (September 7, 2004). ... Re-signed by Ravens to practice squad (September 15, 2004). ... Released from Ravens practice squad (September 21, 2004). ... Signed by Washington Redskins (October 6, 2004). ... Released by Redskins (October 19, 2004). ... Re-signed by Redskins to practice squad (October 21, 2004). ... Activated (October 29, 2004).

			TOTALS		
Year Team	G	GS	Tk.	Ast.	Sks.
2004—Washington NFL	12	0	1	0	0.0

BARNES, DARIAN — FB — COWBOYS

PERSONAL: Born February 28, 1980, in Toms River, N.J. ... 6-2/241. ... Full name: Darian Durrell Barnes.
HIGH SCHOOL: North (Toms River, N.J.).
COLLEGE: Hampton.
TRANSACTIONS/CAREER NOTES: Signed as non-drafted free agent by New York Giants (July 24, 2002). ... Claimed on waivers by Tampa Bay Buccaneers (September 2, 2002). ... On injured reserve with shoulder injury (December 16, 2003-remainder of season). ... Traded by Buccaneers to Dallas Cowboys for seventh-round (WR Mark Jones) pick in 2004 draft (April 25, 2004). ... Granted free agency (March 2, 2005). ... Re-signed by Cowboys (April 20, 2005).
CHAMPIONSHIP GAME EXPERIENCE: Played in NFC championship game (2002 season). ... Member of Super Bowl championship team (2002 season).
SINGLE GAME HIGHS (regular season): Attempts—2 (October 10, 2004, vs. New York Giants); yards—7 (October 10, 2004, vs. New York Giants); and rushing touchdowns—0.

				RUSHING				RECEIVING				TOTALS		
Year Team	G	GS	Att.	Yds.	Avg.	TD	No.	Yds.	Avg.	TD	TD	2pt.	Pts.	Fum.
2002—Tampa Bay NFL	6	0	0	0	0.0	0	0	0	0.0	0	0	0	0	0
2003—Tampa Bay NFL	14	0	0	0	0.0	0	1	6	6.0	0	0	0	0	0
2004—Dallas NFL	16	10	5	10	2.0	0	10	59	5.9	1	1	0	6	1
Pro totals (3 years)	36	10	5	10	2.0	0	11	65	5.9	1	1	0	6	1

BARNES, LIONEL — DE

PERSONAL: Born April 19, 1976, in New Orleans, La. ... 6-5/260. ... Full name: Lionel Barnes Jr.
HIGH SCHOOL: Lakenheath American (Suffolk, England).
JUNIOR COLLEGE: Barton County Community College, Kan. (did not play football).
COLLEGE: Louisiana-Monroe.
TRANSACTIONS/CAREER NOTES: Selected by St. Louis Rams in sixth round (176th pick overall) of 1999 NFL draft. ... Signed by Rams (July 19, 1999). ... Claimed on waivers by Indianapolis Colts (October 12, 2000). ... Released by Colts (November 17, 2001). ... Re-signed by Colts (November 21, 2001). ... Granted free agency (March 1, 2002). ... Signed by Jacksonville Jaguars (January 9, 2003). ... On injured reserve with shoulder injury (October 15, 2004-remainder of season). ... Released by Jaguars (April 4, 2005).
CHAMPIONSHIP GAME EXPERIENCE: Member of Rams for NFC championship game (1999 season); inactive. ... Member of Super Bowl championship team (1999 season); inactive.

			TOTALS		
Year Team	G	GS	Tk.	Ast.	Sks.
1999—St. Louis NFL	3	0	0	0	0.0
2000—St. Louis NFL	1	0	0	0	0.0
—Indianapolis NFL	1	0	0	0	0.0
2001—Indianapolis NFL	6	0	0	0	0.0
2003—Jacksonville NFL	13	0	11	2	1.0
2004—Jacksonville NFL	3	3	5	1	1.0
Pro totals (5 years)	27	3	16	3	2.0

BARNETT, NICK LB PACKERS

PERSONAL: Born May 27, 1981, in Fontana, Calif. ... 6-2/233. ... Full name: Nicholas Alexander Barnett.
HIGH SCHOOL: A.B. Miller (Fontana, Calif.).
COLLEGE: Oregon State.
TRANSACTIONS/CAREER NOTES: Selected by Green Bay Packers in first round (29th pick overall) of 2003 NFL draft. ... Signed by Packers (July 21, 2003).

				TOTALS			INTERCEPTIONS			
Year Team	G	GS	Tk.	Ast.	Sks.	No.	Yds.	Avg.	TD	
2003—Green Bay NFL	15	15	84	25	2.0	3	21	7.0	0	
2004—Green Bay NFL	16	16	91	30	3.0	1	16	16.0	0	
Pro totals (2 years)	31	31	175	55	5.0	4	37	9.3	0	

BARRETT, DAVID CB JETS

PERSONAL: Born December 22, 1977, in Waterloo, Iowa. ... 5-10/195.
HIGH SCHOOL: Osceola (Ark.).
COLLEGE: Arkansas.
TRANSACTIONS/CAREER NOTES: Selected by Arizona Cardinals in fourth round (102nd pick overall) of 2000 NFL draft. ... Signed by Cardinals (June 15, 2000). ... Granted free agency (February 28, 2003). ... Re-signed by Cardinals (May 8, 2003). ... Granted unconditional free agency (March 3, 2004). ... Signed by New York Jets (March 6, 2004).

				TOTALS			INTERCEPTIONS			
Year Team	G	GS	Tk.	Ast.	Sks.	No.	Yds.	Avg.	TD	
2000—Arizona NFL	16	0	6	2	0.0	0	0	0.0	0	
2001—Arizona NFL	16	9	49	9	0.0	2	30	15.0	0	
2002—Arizona NFL	14	14	57	17	0.0	3	40	13.3	0	
2003—Arizona NFL	16	16	68	11	0.0	1	25	25.0	0	
2004—New York Jets NFL	16	16	64	14	0.0	2	14	7.0	0	
Pro totals (5 years)	78	55	244	53	0.0	8	109	13.6	0	

BARROW, MIKE LB REDSKINS

PERSONAL: Born April 19, 1970, in Homestead, Fla. ... 6-2/245. ... Full name: Micheal Colvin Barrow.
HIGH SCHOOL: Homestead (Fla.) Senior.
COLLEGE: Miami (Fla.).
TRANSACTIONS/CAREER NOTES: Selected by Houston Oilers in second round (47th pick overall) of 1993 NFL draft. ... Signed by Oilers (July 30, 1993). ... Granted free agency (February 16, 1996). ... Re-signed by Oilers (August 9, 1996). ... Granted unconditional free agency (February 14, 1997). ... Signed by Carolina Panthers (February 20, 1997). ... Released by Panthers (February 22, 2000). ... Signed by New York Giants (March 2, 2000). ... Released by Giants (March 10, 2004). ... Signed by Washington Redskins (April 22, 2004). ... Inactive for 10 games (2004). ... On injured reserve with knee injury (November 24, 2004-remainder of season).
CHAMPIONSHIP GAME EXPERIENCE: Played in NFC championship game (2000 season). ... Played in Super Bowl 35 (2000 season).
HONORS: Named linebacker on THE SPORTING NEWS college All-America first team (1992).

				TOTALS			INTERCEPTIONS			
Year Team	G	GS	Tk.	Ast.	Sks.	No.	Yds.	Avg.	TD	
1993—Houston NFL	16	0	21	5	1.0	0	0	0.0	0	
1994—Houston NFL	16	16	57	37	2.5	0	0	0.0	0	
1995—Houston NFL	13	12	54	32	3.0	0	0	0.0	0	
1996—Houston NFL	16	16	67	39	6.0	0	0	0.0	0	
1997—Carolina NFL	16	16	68	21	8.5	0	0	0.0	0	
1998—Carolina NFL	16	16	97	32	4.0	1	10	10.0	0	
1999—Carolina NFL	16	16	81	25	4.0	0	0	0.0	0	
2000—New York Giants NFL	15	15	72	22	3.5	1	7	7.0	0	
2001—New York Giants NFL	16	16	91	44	6.0	0	0	0.0	0	
2002—New York Giants NFL	15	14	73	37	2.5	0	0	0.0	0	
2003—New York Giants NFL	16	16	111	39	2.0	0	0	0.0	0	
2004—Washington NFL	Did not play.									
Pro totals (11 years)	171	153	792	333	43.0	2	17	8.5	0	

BARRY, KEVIN T PACKERS

PERSONAL: Born July 20, 1979, in Racine, Wis. ... 6-4/335.
HIGH SCHOOL: Washington Park (Racine, Wis.).
COLLEGE: Arizona.
TRANSACTIONS/CAREER NOTES: Signed as non-drafted free agent by Green Bay Packers (April 21, 2002). ... Granted free agency (March 2, 2005). ... Re-signed by Packers (April 22, 2005).
PLAYING EXPERIENCE: Green Bay NFL, 2002-2004. ... Games/Games started: 2002 (14/3), 2003 (16/1), 2004 (13/3). Total: 43/7.

BARTEE, WILLIAM CB CHIEFS

PERSONAL: Born June 25, 1977, in Daytona Beach, Fla. ... 6-1/200.
HIGH SCHOOL: Atlantic (Daytona Beach, Fla.).
JUNIOR COLLEGE: Butler County Community College (Kan.).
COLLEGE: Oklahoma.

TRANSACTIONS/CAREER NOTES: Selected by Kansas City Chiefs in second round (54th pick overall) of 2000 NFL draft. ... Signed by Chiefs (July 21, 2000). ... Granted unconditional free agency (March 3, 2004). ... Re-signed by Chiefs (March 19, 2004).

Year Team	G	GS	TOTALS			INTERCEPTIONS			
			Tk.	Ast.	Sks.	No.	Yds.	Avg.	TD
2000—Kansas City NFL	16	3	23	4	1.0	0	0	0.0	0
2001—Kansas City NFL	16	5	30	2	1.0	0	0	0.0	0
2002—Kansas City NFL	14	13	71	6	0.0	0	0	0.0	0
2003—Kansas City NFL	11	1	18	4	0.0	0	0	0.0	0
2004—Kansas City NFL	14	9	33	5	1.5	0	0	0.0	0
Pro totals (5 years)	71	31	175	21	3.5	0	0	0.0	0

B

BARTON, ERIC LB JETS

PERSONAL: Born September 29, 1977, in Fayetteville, N.C. ... 6-2/245.
HIGH SCHOOL: Thomas A. Edison (Alexandria, Va.).
COLLEGE: Maryland.
TRANSACTIONS/CAREER NOTES: Selected by Oakland Raiders in fifth round (146th pick overall) of 1999 NFL draft. ... Signed by Raiders for 1999 season. ... Granted unconditional free agency (March 3, 2004). ... Signed by New York Jets (March 6, 2004).
CHAMPIONSHIP GAME EXPERIENCE: Member of Raiders for AFC Championship game (2000 season); inactive. ... Played in AFC championship game (2002 season). ... Played in Super Bowl 37 (2002 season).

Year Team	G	GS	TOTALS			INTERCEPTIONS			
			Tk.	Ast.	Sks.	No.	Yds.	Avg.	TD
1999—Oakland NFL	16	3	20	2	3.0	0	0	0.0	0
2000—Oakland NFL	4	0	4	2	0.0	0	0	0.0	0
2001—Oakland NFL	16	1	19	5	0.0	0	0	0.0	0
2002—Oakland NFL	16	16	95	29	6.0	2	5	2.5	0
2003—Oakland NFL	16	16	99	34	0.5	0	0	0.0	0
2004—New York Jets NFL	16	15	77	30	2.5	1	7	7.0	0
Pro totals (6 years)	84	51	314	102	12.0	3	12	4.0	0

BARTRUM, MIKE TE/LS EAGLES

PERSONAL: Born June 23, 1970, in Gallipolis, Ohio. ... 6-4/245. ... Full name: Michael Weldon Bartrum.
HIGH SCHOOL: Meigs (Pomeroy, Ohio).
COLLEGE: Marshall.
TRANSACTIONS/CAREER NOTES: Signed as non-drafted free agent by Kansas City Chiefs (May 5, 1993). ... Released by Chiefs (August 30, 1993). ... Re-signed by Chiefs to practice squad (August 31, 1993). ... Activated (October 27, 1993). ... Released by Chiefs (August 23, 1994). ... Signed by Green Bay Packers (January 20, 1995). ... On injured reserve with broken arm (October 11, 1995-remainder of season). ... Traded by Packers with DE Walter Scott to New England Patriots for past considerations (August 25, 1996). ... On injured reserve with forearm injury (November 12, 1997-remainder of season). ... Granted unconditional free agency (February 13, 1998). ... Re-signed by Patriots (April 7, 1998). ... Released by Patriots (April 10, 2000). ... Signed by Philadelphia Eagles (April 17, 2000). ... Granted unconditional free agency (March 1, 2002). ... Re-signed by Eagles (March 6, 2002).
PLAYING EXPERIENCE: Kansas City NFL, 1993; Green Bay NFL, 1995; New England NFL, 1996-1999; Philadelphia NFL, 2000-2004. ... Games/Games started: 1993 (3/0), 1995 (4/0), 1996 (16/0), 1997 (9/0), 1998 (16/0), 1999 (16/0), 2000 (16/0), 2001 (16/0), 2002 (16/0), 2003 (16/0), 2004 (16/0). Total: 144/0.
CHAMPIONSHIP GAME EXPERIENCE: Member of Chiefs for AFC championship game (1993 season); inactive. ... Played in AFC championship game (1996 season). ... Played in Super Bowl 31 (1996 season) and Super Bowl 39 (2004 season). ... Played in NFC championship game (2001-2004 seasons).
SINGLE GAME HIGHS (regular season): Receptions—3 (January 2, 2005, vs. Cincinnati); yards—27 (January 2, 2005, vs. Cincinnati); and touchdown receptions—1 (September 26, 2004, vs. Detroit).

BASHIR, IDREES S PANTHERS

PERSONAL: Born December 7, 1978, in Decatur, Ga. ... 6-2/198.
HIGH SCHOOL: Dunwoody (Decatur, Ga.).
COLLEGE: Memphis.
TRANSACTIONS/CAREER NOTES: Selected by Indianapolis Colts in second round (37th pick overall) of 2001 NFL draft. ... Signed by Colts (July 25, 2001). ... Granted unconditional free agency (March 2, 2005). ... Signed by Carolina Panthers (March 31, 2005).
CHAMPIONSHIP GAME EXPERIENCE: Member of Colts for AFC championship game (2003 season); inactive.

Year Team	G	GS	TOTALS			INTERCEPTIONS			
			Tk.	Ast.	Sks.	No.	Yds.	Avg.	TD
2001—Indianapolis NFL	15	15	53	24	0.0	1	0	0.0	0
2002—Indianapolis NFL	14	14	36	14	0.0	2	4	2.0	0
2003—Indianapolis NFL	9	9	29	14	0.0	2	9	4.5	0
2004—Indianapolis NFL	13	13	41	17	0.0	0	0	0.0	0
Pro totals (4 years)	51	51	159	69	0.0	5	13	2.6	0

BATES, SOLOMON LB SEAHAWKS

PERSONAL: Born April 18, 1982, in Carver City, Calif. ... 6-1/243. ... Full name: Solomon Augustus Bates.
HIGH SCHOOL: Canyon Springs (Moreno Valley, Calif.).
COLLEGE: Arizona State.
TRANSACTIONS/CAREER NOTES: Selected by Seattle Seahawks in fourth round (135th pick overall) of 2003 NFL draft. ... Signed by Seahawks (July 24, 2003).

Year Team	G	GS	TOTALS Tk.	Ast.	Sks.	INTERCEPTIONS No.	Yds.	Avg.	TD
2003—Seattle NFL	7	0	0	0	0.0	0	0	0.0	0
2004—Seattle NFL	10	3	16	10	0.0	0	0	0.0	0
Pro totals (2 years)	17	3	16	10	0.0	0	0	0.0	0

BATTLE, ARNAZ — WR — 49ERS

PERSONAL: Born February 22, 1980, in Dallas, Texas. ... 6-1/217. ... Full name: Arnaz Jerome Battle.
HIGH SCHOOL: C.E. Byrd (Shreveport, La.).
COLLEGE: Notre Dame.
TRANSACTIONS/CAREER NOTES: Selected by San Francisco 49ers in sixth round (197th pick overall) of 2003 NFL draft. ... Signed by 49ers (July 24, 2003). ... On injured reserve with toe injury (December 10, 2003-remainder of season).
SINGLE GAME HIGHS (regular season): Receptions—2 (October 17, 2004, vs. New York Jets); yards—87 (October 17, 2004, vs. New York Jets); and touchdown receptions—0.

Year Team	G	GS	RUSHING Att.	Yds.	Avg.	TD	RECEIVING No.	Yds.	Avg.	TD	PUNT RETURNS No.	Yds.	Avg.	TD	KICKOFF RETURNS No.	Yds.	Avg.	TD	TOTALS TD	2pt.	Pts.
2003—S.F. NFL	8	0	2	14	7.0	0	0	0	0.0	0	0	0	0.0	0	5	88	17.6	0	0	0	0
2004—S.F. NFL	14	0	2	5	2.5	0	8	143	17.9	0	31	266	8.6	1	13	257	19.8	0	1	0	6
Pro totals (2 years)	22	0	4	19	4.8	0	8	143	17.9	0	31	266	8.6	1	18	345	19.2	0	1	0	6

BATTLE, JULIAN — CB — CHIEFS

PERSONAL: Born July 11, 1981, in Royal Palm Beach, Fla. ... 6-2/205.
HIGH SCHOOL: Wellington (West Palm Beach, Fla.).
JUNIOR COLLEGE: Los Angeles Valley College.
COLLEGE: Tennessee.
TRANSACTIONS/CAREER NOTES: Selected by Kansas City Chiefs in third round (92nd pick overall) of 2003 NFL draft. ... Signed by Chiefs (May 12, 2003).

Year Team	G	GS	TOTALS Tk.	Ast.	Sks.	INTERCEPTIONS No.	Yds.	Avg.	TD
2003—Kansas City NFL	14	0	4	0	0.0	0	0	0.0	0
2004—Kansas City NFL	12	1	10	0	0.0	0	0	0.0	0
Pro totals (2 years)	26	1	14	0	0.0	0	0	0.0	0

BATTLES, AINSLEY — SS

PERSONAL: Born November 6, 1978, in Lilburn, Ga. ... 5-11/204.
HIGH SCHOOL: Parkview (Lilburn, Ga.).
COLLEGE: Vanderbilt.
TRANSACTIONS/CAREER NOTES: Signed as non-drafted free agent by Pittsburgh Steelers (April 21, 2000). ... Claimed on waivers by Jacksonville Jaguars (September 3, 2001). ... Granted free agency (February 28, 2003). ... Re-signed by Jaguars (April 23, 2003). ... Released by Jaguars (June 19, 2003). ... Signed by Steelers (June 7, 2004). ... On injured reserve with hamstring injury (September 13, 2004-remainder of season). ... Granted unconditional free agency (March 2, 2005).

Year Team	G	GS	TOTALS Tk.	Ast.	Sks.	INTERCEPTIONS No.	Yds.	Avg.	TD
2000—Pittsburgh NFL	16	2	0	0	1.0	0	0	0.0	0
2001—Jacksonville NFL	13	11	0	0	1.0	2	26	13.0	0
2002—Jacksonville NFL	16	4	0	0	0.0	1	6	6.0	0
2004—Pittsburgh NFL	1	0	1	0	0.0	0	0	0.0	0
Pro totals (4 years)	46	17	1	0	2.0	3	32	10.7	0

BAUMAN, RASHAD — CB — BENGALS

PERSONAL: Born May 7, 1979, in Tempe, Ariz. ... 5-8/184. ... Full name: Leddure Rashad Bauman.
HIGH SCHOOL: South Mountain (Phoenix).
COLLEGE: Oregon.
TRANSACTIONS/CAREER NOTES: Selected by Washington Redskins in third round (79th pick overall) of 2002 NFL draft. ... Signed by Redskins (July 22, 2002). ... Claimed on waivers by Cincinnati Bengals (September 5, 2004). ... On injured reserve with Achilles injury (November 29, 2004-remainder of season). ... Granted free agency (March 2, 2005). ... Re-signed by Bengals (April 27, 2005).

Year Team	G	GS	TOTALS Tk.	Ast.	Sks.	INTERCEPTIONS No.	Yds.	Avg.	TD
2002—Washington NFL	16	1	9	0	0.0	0	0	0.0	0
2003—Washington NFL	12	2	17	4	0.0	2	1	0.5	0
2004—Cincinnati NFL	4	0	2	1	0.0	0	0	0.0	0
Pro totals (3 years)	32	3	28	5	0.0	2	1	0.5	0

BAXTER, GARY — CB — BROWNS

PERSONAL: Born November 24, 1978, in Tyler, Texas. ... 6-2/215. ... Full name: Gary Wayne Baxter.
HIGH SCHOOL: John Tyler (Tyler, Texas).
COLLEGE: Baylor.

B

TRANSACTIONS/CAREER NOTES: Selected by Baltimore Ravens in second round (62nd pick overall) of 2001 NFL draft. ... Signed by Ravens (July 20, 2001). ... Granted unconditional free agency (March 2, 2005). ... Signed by Cleveland Browns (March 4, 2005).

Year Team	G	GS	TOTALS Tk.	Ast.	Sks.	INTERCEPTIONS No.	Yds.	Avg.	TD
2001—Baltimore NFL	6	0	0	0	0.0	0	0	0.0	0
2002—Baltimore NFL	16	14	69	9	0.0	1	0	0.0	0
2003—Baltimore NFL	16	16	71	12	1.0	3	41	13.7	0
2004—Baltimore NFL	16	16	72	16	2.0	1	33	33.0	0
Pro totals (4 years)	54	46	212	37	3.0	5	74	14.8	0

BAXTER, JARROD FB TEXANS

PERSONAL: Born March 9, 1979, in Dayton, Ohio. ... 6-1/243. ... Full name: Jarrod Anthony Baxter.
HIGH SCHOOL: Highland (Albuquerque, N.M.).
COLLEGE: New Mexico.
TRANSACTIONS/CAREER NOTES: Selected by Houston Texans in fifth round (136th pick overall) of 2002 NFL draft. ... Signed by Texans (July 19, 2002). ... On injured reserve with foot injury (August 18, 2004-entire season). ... Granted free agency (March 2, 2005). ... Re-signed by Texans (March 8, 2005).
SINGLE GAME HIGHS (regular season): Attempts—2 (September 12, 2004, vs. San Diego); yards—7 (September 15, 2002, vs. San Diego); and rushing touchdowns—0.

Year Team	G	GS	RUSHING Att.	Yds.	Avg.	TD	RECEIVING No.	Yds.	Avg.	TD	TOTALS TD	2pt.	Pts.	Fum.
2002—Houston NFL	16	10	7	14	2.0	0	5	33	6.6	1	1	0	6	0
2004—Houston NFL	8	1	2	1	0.5	0	1	3	3.0	0	0	0	0	0
Pro totals (2 years)	24	11	9	15	1.7	0	6	36	6.0	1	1	0	6	0

BEASLEY, AARON CB

PERSONAL: Born July 7, 1973, in Pottstown, Pa. ... 6-0/205. ... Full name: Aaron Bruce Beasley.
HIGH SCHOOL: Pottstown (Pa.), then Valley Forge Military Academy (Wayne, Pa.).
COLLEGE: West Virginia.
TRANSACTIONS/CAREER NOTES: Selected by Jacksonville Jaguars in third round (63rd pick overall) of 1996 NFL draft. ... Signed by Jaguars (May 24, 1996). ... Granted free agency (February 12, 1999). ... Re-signed by Jaguars (March 3, 1999). ... Granted unconditional free agency (February 11, 2000). ... Re-signed by Jaguars (February 11, 2000). ... On injured reserve with shoulder injury (December 21, 2001-remainder of season). ... Released by Jaguars (February 28, 2002). ... Signed by New York Jets (March 8, 2002). ... Released by Jets (February 27, 2004). ... Signed by Atlanta Falcons (March 31, 2004). ... Granted unconditional free agency (March 2, 2005).
CHAMPIONSHIP GAME EXPERIENCE: Played in AFC championship game (1996 and 1999 seasons). ... Played in NFC championship game (2004 season).
MISCELLANEOUS: Holds Jacksonville Jaguars all-time record for most interceptions (15).

Year Team	G	GS	TOTALS Tk.	Ast.	Sks.	INTERCEPTIONS No.	Yds.	Avg.	TD
1996—Jacksonville NFL	9	7	20	9	1.0	1	0	0.0	0
1997—Jacksonville NFL	9	7	25	0	0.0	1	5	5.0	0
1998—Jacksonville NFL	16	15	58	9	0.0	3	35	11.7	0
1999—Jacksonville NFL	16	16	57	9	1.5	6	*200	§33.3	†2
2000—Jacksonville NFL	14	14	45	7	5.0	1	39	39.0	0
2001—Jacksonville NFL	12	12	36	3	0.0	3	0	0.0	0
2002—New York Jets NFL	15	15	59	7	0.0	2	29	14.5	0
2003—New York Jets NFL	16	16	46	15	0.0	3	64	21.3	0
2004—Atlanta NFL	14	3	16	2	1.0	4	115	28.8	0
Pro totals (9 years)	121	105	362	61	8.5	24	487	20.3	2

BEASLEY, FRED FB 49ERS

PERSONAL: Born September 18, 1974, in Montgomery, Ala. ... 6-0/246. ... Full name: Frederick Jerome Beasley.
HIGH SCHOOL: Robert E. Lee (Montgomery, Ala.).
COLLEGE: Auburn.
TRANSACTIONS/CAREER NOTES: Selected by San Francisco 49ers in sixth round (180th pick overall) of 1998 NFL draft. ... Signed by 49ers (July 18, 1998). ... Granted free agency (March 2, 2001). ... Re-signed by 49ers (March 2, 2001). ... Granted unconditional free agency (March 1, 2002). ... Re-signed by 49ers (March 12, 2002).
HONORS: Played in Pro Bowl (2003 season).
SINGLE GAME HIGHS (regular season): Attempts—12 (December 26, 1999, vs. Washington); yards—65 (December 26, 1999, vs. Washington); and rushing touchdowns—2 (December 12, 1999, vs. Atlanta).

Year Team	G	GS	RUSHING Att.	Yds.	Avg.	TD	RECEIVING No.	Yds.	Avg.	TD	TOTALS TD	2pt.	Pts.	Fum.
1998—San Francisco NFL	16	0	0	0	0.0	0	1	11	11.0	0	0	0	0	0
1999—San Francisco NFL	13	11	58	276	4.8	4	32	282	8.8	0	4	0	24	2
2000—San Francisco NFL	15	15	50	147	2.9	3	31	233	7.5	3	6	0	36	0
2001—San Francisco NFL	15	12	23	73	3.2	1	16	99	6.2	0	1	0	6	1
2002—San Francisco NFL	16	14	26	75	2.9	0	22	152	6.9	1	1	0	6	0
2003—San Francisco NFL	16	11	17	24	1.4	0	19	184	9.7	1	1	0	6	0
2004—San Francisco NFL	14	10	9	15	1.7	0	10	44	4.4	0	0	0	0	0
Pro totals (7 years)	105	73	183	610	3.3	8	131	1005	7.7	5	13	0	78	3

BECHT, ANTHONY   TE   BUCCANEERS

PERSONAL: Born August 8, 1977, in Media, Pa. ... 6-5/272.
HIGH SCHOOL: Monsignor Bonner (Drexel Hill, Pa.).
COLLEGE: West Virginia.
TRANSACTIONS/CAREER NOTES: Selected by New York Jets in first round (27th pick overall) of 2000 NFL draft. ... Signed by Jets (May 26, 2000). ... Granted unconditional free agency (March 2, 2005). ... Signed by Tampa Bay Buccaneers (March 15, 2005).
SINGLE GAME HIGHS (regular season): Receptions—6 (December 28, 2003, vs. Miami); yards—63 (November 23, 2003, vs. Jacksonville); and touchdown receptions—2 (October 12, 2003, vs. Buffalo).

			RECEIVING					TOTALS		
Year Team	G	GS	No.	Yds.	Avg.	TD	TD	2pt.	Pts.	Fum.
2000—New York Jets NFL	14	10	16	144	9.0	2	2	0	12	1
2001—New York Jets NFL	16	16	36	321	8.9	5	5	0	30	0
2002—New York Jets NFL	16	16	28	243	8.7	5	5	1	32	0
2003—New York Jets NFL	16	16	40	356	8.9	4	4	1	26	1
2004—New York Jets NFL	16	16	13	100	7.7	1	1	0	6	0
Pro totals (5 years)	78	74	133	1164	8.8	17	17	2	106	2

BECKETT, ROGERS   S

PERSONAL: Born January 31, 1977, in Apopka, Fla. ... 6-2/207.
HIGH SCHOOL: Apopka (Fla.).
COLLEGE: Marshall.
TRANSACTIONS/CAREER NOTES: Selected by San Diego Chargers in second round (43rd pick overall) of 2000 NFL draft. ... Signed by Chargers (July 24, 2000). ... Claimed on waivers by Cincinnati Bengals (June 10, 2003). ... Granted unconditional free agency (March 3, 2004). ... Re-signed by Bengals (March 25, 2004). ... Released by Bengals (March 10, 2005).
HONORS: Named free safety on THE SPORTING NEWS college All-America third team (1999).

			TOTALS			INTERCEPTIONS			
Year Team	G	GS	Tk.	Ast.	Sks.	No.	Yds.	Avg.	TD
2000—San Diego NFL	16	3	28	11	1.0	1	7	7.0	0
2001—San Diego NFL	16	16	73	21	0.0	1	8	8.0	0
2002—San Diego NFL	16	10	32	2	0.0	0	0	0.0	0
2003—Cincinnati NFL	16	9	51	16	3.0	2	11	5.5	0
2004—Cincinnati NFL	7	5	14	5	0.0	0	0	0.0	0
Pro totals (5 years)	71	43	198	55	4.0	4	26	6.5	0

BECKHAM, TONY   CB   TITANS

PERSONAL: Born October 1, 1978, in Gainesville, Fla. ... 6-1/187.
HIGH SCHOOL: Forest (Ocala, Fla.).
COLLEGE: Wisconsin-Stout.
TRANSACTIONS/CAREER NOTES: Selected by Tennesse Titans in fourth round (115th pick overall) of 2002 NFL draft. ... Signed by Titans (July 18, 2002). ... On physically unable to perform list with knee injury (July 31-November 29, 2004). ... Activated (November 29, 2004).
CHAMPIONSHIP GAME EXPERIENCE: Played in AFC championship game (2002 season).

			TOTALS			INTERCEPTIONS			
Year Team	G	GS	Tk.	Ast.	Sks.	No.	Yds.	Avg.	TD
2002—Tennessee NFL	14	0	1	1	0.0	0	0	0.0	0
2003—Tennessee NFL	16	3	14	2	0.0	1	0	0.0	0
2004—Tennessee NFL	5	1	5	0	0.0	0	0	0.0	0
Pro totals (3 years)	35	4	20	3	0.0	1	0	0.0	0

BEDELL, BRAD   OL   PACKERS

PERSONAL: Born February 12, 1977, in Arcadia, Calif. ... 6-4/306.
HIGH SCHOOL: Arcadia (Calif.).
JUNIOR COLLEGE: Mount San Antonio College (Calif.).
COLLEGE: Colorado.
TRANSACTIONS/CAREER NOTES: Selected by Cleveland Browns in sixth round (206th pick overall) of 2000 NFL draft. ... Signed by Browns (July 10, 2000). ... Released by Browns (August 27, 2002). ... Signed by Washington Redskins (2003). ... Claimed on waivers by Miami Dolphins (November 10, 2003). ... Traded by Dolphins to Green Bay Packers for conditional pick in 2006 draft (September 5, 2004). ... Granted unconditional free agency (March 2, 2005). ... Re-signed by Packers (March 9, 2005).

BEISEL, MONTY   LB   PATRIOTS

PERSONAL: Born August 20, 1978, in Douglass, Kan. ... 6-3/238.
HIGH SCHOOL: Douglass (Kan.).
COLLEGE: Kansas State.
TRANSACTIONS/CAREER NOTES: Selected by Kansas City Chiefs in fourth round (107th pick overall) of 2001 NFL draft. ... Signed by Chiefs (July 23, 2001). ... Granted free agency (March 3, 2004). ... Re-signed by Chiefs (March 24, 2004). ... Granted unconditional free agency (March 2, 2005). ... Signed by New England Patriots (April 14, 2005).

Year Team	G	GS	Tk.	Ast.	Sks.	No.	Yds.	Avg.	TD
			TOTALS			INTERCEPTIONS			
2001—Kansas City NFL	16	0	3	3	0.0	0	0	0.0	0
2002—Kansas City NFL	16	0	0	0	0.0	0	0	0.0	0
2003—Kansas City NFL	12	0	8	0	1.0	0	0	0.0	0
2004—Kansas City NFL	11	9	42	9	2.5	1	-1	-1.0	0
Pro totals (4 years)	55	9	53	12	3.5	1	-1	-1.0	0

BELL, JACOB — G — TITANS

PERSONAL: Born March 2, 1981, in Cleveland, Ohio. ... 6-4/306.
HIGH SCHOOL: St. Ignatius (Euclid, Ohio).
COLLEGE: Miami (Ohio).
TRANSACTIONS/CAREER NOTES: Selected by Tennessee Titans in fifth round (138th pick overall) of 2004 NFL draft. ... Signed by Titans (July 30, 2004).
PLAYING EXPERIENCE: Tennessee NFL, 2004. ... Games/Games started: 2004 (15/14). Total: 15/14.

BELL, JASON — CB — TEXANS

PERSONAL: Born April 1, 1978, in Long Beach, Calif. ... 6-0/186. ... Full name: Jason Dewande Bell.
HIGH SCHOOL: Millikan (Long Beach, Calif.).
COLLEGE: UCLA.
TRANSACTIONS/CAREER NOTES: Signed as non-drafted free agent by Dallas Cowboys (April 27, 2001). ... Claimed on waivers by Houston Texans (September 2, 2002). ... Re-signed by Texans (March 18, 2003). ... Granted free agency (March 3, 2004). ... Re-signed by Texans (April 22, 2004). ... On injured reserve with wrist injury (November 17, 2004-remainder of season). ... Granted unconditional free agency (March 2, 2005). ... Re-signed by Texans (March 4, 2005).

Year Team	G	GS	Tk.	Ast.	Sks.	No.	Yds.	Avg.	TD
			TOTALS			INTERCEPTIONS			
2001—Dallas NFL	16	0	0	0	0.0	0	0	0.0	0
2002—Houston NFL	13	0	2	0	0.0	0	0	0.0	0
2003—Houston NFL	13	0	2	0	0.0	0	0	0.0	0
2004—Houston NFL	9	0	0	0	0.0	0	0	0.0	0
Pro totals (4 years)	51	0	4	0	0.0	0	0	0.0	0

BELL, KENDRELL — LB — CHIEFS

PERSONAL: Born July 2, 1978, in Augusta, Ga. ... 6-1/257.
HIGH SCHOOL: Laney (August, Ga.).
JUNIOR COLLEGE: Middle Georgia College.
COLLEGE: Georgia.
TRANSACTIONS/CAREER NOTES: Selected by Pittsburgh Steelers in second round (39th pick overall) of 2001 NFL draft. ... Signed by Steelers (June 11, 2001). ... Granted unconditional free agency (March 2, 2005). ... Signed by Kansas City Chiefs (March 8, 2005).
CHAMPIONSHIP GAME EXPERIENCE: Played in AFC championship game (2001 season). ... Member of Steelers for AFC championship game (2004 season); inactive.
HONORS: Named NFL Rookie of the Year by THE SPORTING NEWS (2001). ... Played in Pro Bowl (2001 season). ... Named to play in Pro Bowl (2002 season); replaced by Donnie Edwards due to injury.

Year Team	G	GS	Tk.	Ast.	Sks.	No.	Yds.	Avg.	TD
			TOTALS			INTERCEPTIONS			
2001—Pittsburgh NFL	16	16	69	13	9.0	0	0	0.0	0
2002—Pittsburgh NFL	12	12	37	13	4.0	0	0	0.0	0
2003—Pittsburgh NFL	16	16	81	19	5.0	1	61	61.0	0
2004—Pittsburgh NFL	3	0	6	2	0.0	0	0	0.0	0
Pro totals (4 years)	47	44	193	47	18.0	1	61	61.0	0

BELL, MARCUS — DT — LIONS

PERSONAL: Born June 1, 1979, in Memphis, Tenn. ... 6-2/339.
HIGH SCHOOL: Kingsbury (Memphis, Tenn.).
COLLEGE: Memphis.
TRANSACTIONS/CAREER NOTES: Selected by Arizona Cardinals in fourth round (123rd pick overall) of 2001 NFL draft. ... Signed by Cardinals (June 4, 2001). ... Granted free agency (March 3, 2004). ... Re-signed by Cardinals (May 7, 2004). ... Released by Cardinals (June 1, 2004). ... Signed by Detroit Lions (June 11, 2004). ... Granted unconditional free agency (March 2, 2005). ... Re-signed by Lions (March 28, 2005).

Year Team	G	GS	Tk.	Ast.	Sks.
			TOTALS		
2001—Arizona NFL	13	0	16	7	0.5
2002—Arizona NFL	16	4	25	9	2.0
2003—Arizona NFL	13	10	21	2	1.0
2004—Detroit NFL	16	0	19	8	2.0
Pro totals (4 years)	58	14	81	26	5.5

BELL, TATUM — RB — BRONCOS

PERSONAL: Born March 2, 1981, in Dallas, Texas. ... 5-11/213.
HIGH SCHOOL: DeSoto (Texas).
COLLEGE: Oklahoma State.

TRANSACTIONS/CAREER NOTES: Selected by Denver Broncos in second round (41st pick overall) of 2004 NFL draft. ... Signed by Broncos (July 30, 2004).

SINGLE GAME HIGHS (regular season): Attempts—17 (December 12, 2004, vs. Miami); yards—123 (December 12, 2004, vs. Miami); and rushing touchdowns—2 (December 12, 2004, vs. Miami).

STATISTICAL PLATEAUS: 100-yard rushing games: 2004 (1). Total: 1.

			RUSHING				RECEIVING				TOTALS			
Year Team	G	GS	Att.	Yds.	Avg.	TD	No.	Yds.	Avg.	TD	TD	2pt.	Pts.	Fum.
2004—Denver NFL	14	0	75	396	5.3	3	5	80	16.0	0	3	0	18	1

BELL, YEREMIAH   CB   DOLPHINS

PERSONAL: Born March 3, 1978, in Winchester, Ky. ... 6-1/200.
HIGH SCHOOL: George Rogers Clark (Winchester, Ky.).
COLLEGE: Eastern Kentucky.
TRANSACTIONS/CAREER NOTES: Selected by Miami Dolphins in sixth round (213th pick overall) of 2003 NFL draft. ... Signed by Dolphins (July 24, 2003). ... On injured reserve with leg injury (December 13, 2004-remainder of season).

			TOTALS			INTERCEPTIONS			
Year Team	G	GS	Tk.	Ast.	Sks.	No.	Yds.	Avg.	TD
2004—Miami NFL	13	0	3	0	0.0	0	0	0.0	0

BELLAMY, JAY   S   SAINTS

PERSONAL: Born July 8, 1972, in Perth Amboy, N.J. ... 5-11/200. ... Full name: John Jay Bellamy. ... Name pronounced: BELL-a-me.
HIGH SCHOOL: Matawan Regional (Aberdeen, N.J.).
COLLEGE: Rutgers.
TRANSACTIONS/CAREER NOTES: Signed as non-drafted free agent by Seattle Seahawks (April 27, 1994). ... On injured reserve with shoulder injury (November 11, 1994-remainder of season). ... Granted unconditional free agency (March 2, 2001). ... Signed by New Orleans Saints (April 4, 2001).

			TOTALS			INTERCEPTIONS			
Year Team	G	GS	Tk.	Ast.	Sks.	No.	Yds.	Avg.	TD
1994—Seattle NFL	3	0	0	0	0.0	0	0	0.0	0
1995—Seattle NFL	15	0	2	1	0.0	0	0	0.0	0
1996—Seattle NFL	16	0	16	2	0.0	3	18	6.0	0
1997—Seattle NFL	16	7	42	10	2.0	1	13	13.0	0
1998—Seattle NFL	16	16	80	18	1.0	3	40	13.3	0
1999—Seattle NFL	16	16	85	11	0.0	4	4	1.0	0
2000—Seattle NFL	16	16	69	18	2.0	4	132	33.0	1
2001—New Orleans NFL	16	16	69	22	2.0	3	21	7.0	0
2002—New Orleans NFL	16	16	67	19	1.5	3	39	13.0	0
2003—New Orleans NFL	16	16	77	17	1.0	3	19	6.3	0
2004—New Orleans NFL	16	16	74	18	0.0	0	0	0.0	0
Pro totals (11 years)	162	119	581	136	9.5	24	286	11.9	1

BELLAMY, RONALD   WR   DOLPHINS

PERSONAL: Born December 28, 1981, in New Orleans, La. ... 6-0/203.
HIGH SCHOOL: Archbishop Shaw (Marrero, La.).
COLLEGE: Michigan.
TRANSACTIONS/CAREER NOTES: Signed as non-drafted free agent by Miami Dolphins (April 28, 2003). ... Waived by Dolphins (August 31, 2003). ... Re-signed by Dolphins to practice squad (October 7, 2003). ... Assigned by Dolphins to Scottish Claymores in 2004 NFL Europe enhancement allocation program (January 31, 2004). ... Released by Dolphins (September 5, 2004). ... Re-signed by Dolphins to practice squad (September 6, 2004). ... Activated (October 2, 2004). ... Released by Dolphins (October 12, 2004). ... Re-signed by Dolphins to practice squad (October 13, 2004). ... Activated (December 28, 2004).
SINGLE GAME HIGHS: (regular season): Receptions—1 (January 2, 2005, vs. Baltimore); yards—8 (January 2, 2005,vs. Baltimore); touchdown receptions—0.

			RECEIVING				TOTALS			
Year Team	G	GS	No.	Yds.	Avg.	TD	TD	2pt.	Pts.	Fum.
2004—Miami NFL	2	0	1	8	8.0	0	0	0	0	0

BENNETT, BRANDON   RB/KR   PANTHERS

PERSONAL: Born February 3, 1973, in Greenville, S.C. ... 5-11/220.
HIGH SCHOOL: Riverside (Greer, S.C.).
COLLEGE: South Carolina.
TRANSACTIONS/CAREER NOTES: Signed as non-drafted free agent by Cleveland Browns (July 25, 1995). ... Released by Browns (August 18, 1995). ... Signed by Chicago Bears to practice squad (December 6, 1995). ... Released by Bears (August 19, 1996). ... Re-signed by Bears to practice squad (September 24, 1996). ... Released by Bears (November 1, 1996). ... Signed by Miami Dolphins to practice squad (November 5, 1996). ... Activated (December 17, 1996); did not play. ... Released by Dolphins (August 12, 1997). ... Signed by Cincinnati Bengals (April 20, 1998). ... Released by Bengals (August 30, 1998). ... Re-signed by Bengals (September 7, 1998). ... Released by Bengals (June 3, 1999). ... Re-signed by Bengals (March 2, 2001). ... Granted unconditional free agency (March 3, 2004). ... Signed by Tampa Bay Buccaneers (March 18, 2004). ... Released by Buccaneers (September 5, 2004). ... Signed by Carolina Panthers (October 26, 2004).
SINGLE GAME HIGHS (regular season): Attempts—25 (December 20, 1998, vs. Pittsburgh); yards—87 (December 13, 1998, vs. Indianapolis); and rushing touchdowns—1 (November 14, 2004, vs. San Francisco).
STATISTICAL PLATEAUS: 100-yard receiving games: 1998 (1). Total: 1.

Year Team	G	GS	Att.	Yds.	Avg.	TD	No.	Yds.	Avg.	TD	No.	Yds.	Avg.	TD	TD	2pt.	Pts.	Fum.
				RUSHING				RECEIVING				KICKOFF RETURNS				TOTALS		
1995—Chicago NFL	Did not play.																	
1996—Miami NFL	Did not play.																	
1997—	Did not play.																	
1998—Cincinnati NFL	14	1	77	243	3.2	2	8	153	19.1	0	3	61	20.3	0	2	0	12	1
1999—	Did not play.																	
2000—Cincinnati NFL	16	0	90	324	3.6	3	19	168	8.8	0	0	0	0.0	0	3	0	18	2
2001—Cincinnati NFL	16	1	50	232	4.6	0	20	150	7.5	0	4	60	15.0	0	0	0	0	1
2002—Cincinnati NFL	12	0	33	155	4.7	0	18	109	6.1	0	49	1231	25.1	1	1	0	6	2
2003—Cincinnati NFL	16	0	56	173	3.1	0	25	176	7.0	1	53	1146	21.6	0	1	0	6	2
2004—Carolina NFL	8	0	6	17	2.8	1	0	0	0.0	0	8	177	22.1	0	1	0	6	0
Pro totals (6 years)	82	2	312	1144	3.7	6	90	756	8.4	1	117	2675	22.9	1	8	0	48	8

B

BENNETT, DARREN   P   VIKINGS

PERSONAL: Born January 9, 1965, in Sydney, Australia. ... 6-5/235. ... Full name: Darren Leslie Bennett.
HIGH SCHOOL: Applecross (Perth, Western Australia).
COLLEGE: None.
TRANSACTIONS/CAREER NOTES: Played Australian Rules Football (1987-1993). ... Signed as non-drafted free agent by San Diego Chargers (April 14, 1994). ... Released by Chargers (August 28, 1994). ... Re-signed by Chargers to practice squad (August 29, 1994). ... Assigned by Chargers to Amsterdam Admirals in 1995 World League enhancement allocation program (February 20, 1995). ... Granted unconditional free agency (February 11, 2000). ... Re-signed by Chargers (March 7, 2000). ... Granted unconditional free agency (March 3, 2004). ... Signed by Minnesota Vikings (March 20, 2004).
HONORS: Named punter on THE SPORTING NEWS NFL All-Pro team (1995). ... Played in Pro Bowl (1995 and 2000 seasons).

				PUNTING			
Year Team	G	No.	Yds.	Avg.	Net avg.	In. 20	Blk.
1994—San Diego NFL	Did not play.						
1995—San Diego NFL	16	72	3221	44.7	36.6	28	0
1996—San Diego NFL	16	87	3967	45.6	37.2	23	0
1997—San Diego NFL	16	89	3972	44.6	37.7	26	1
1998—San Diego NFL	16	95	4174	43.9	36.8	27	0
1999—San Diego NFL	16	89	3910	43.9	*38.7	32	0
2000—San Diego NFL	16	92	4248	*46.2	36.2	23	0
2001—San Diego NFL	16	78	3308	42.4	36.9	25	0
2002—San Diego NFL	16	87	3540	40.7	34.3	31	2
2003—San Diego NFL	16	82	3436	41.9	36.2	28	0
2004—Minnesota NFL	15	57	2240	39.3	35.3	18	0
Pro totals (10 years)	159	828	36016	43.5	36.6	261	3

BENNETT, DREW   WR   TITANS

PERSONAL: Born August 26, 1978, in Berkeley, Calif. ... 6-5/206. ... Full name: Andrew Russell Bennett.
HIGH SCHOOL: Miramonte (Calif.).
COLLEGE: UCLA.
TRANSACTIONS/CAREER NOTES: Signed as non-drafted free agent by Tennessee Titans (April 22, 2001). ... Granted free agency (March 3, 2004). ... Re-signed by Titans (March 3, 2004).
CHAMPIONSHIP GAME EXPERIENCE: Played in AFC championship game (2002 season).
SINGLE GAME HIGHS (regular season): Receptions—13 (December 19, 2004, vs. Oakland); yards—233 (December 13, 2004, vs. Kansas City); and touchdown receptions—3 (December 13, 2004, vs. Kansas City).
STATISTICAL PLATEAUS: 100-yard receiving games: 2003 (1), 2004 (5). Total: 6.

Year Team	G	GS	No.	Yds.	Avg.	TD	TD	2pt.	Pts.	Fum.
			RECEIVING				TOTALS			
2001—Tennessee NFL	14	1	24	329	13.7	1	1	1	8	0
2002—Tennessee NFL	16	7	33	478	14.5	2	2	0	12	0
2003—Tennessee NFL	12	8	32	504	15.8	4	4	0	24	0
2004—Tennessee NFL	16	16	80	1247	15.6	11	11	0	66	3
Pro totals (4 years)	58	32	169	2558	15.1	18	18	1	110	3

BENNETT, MICHAEL   RB   VIKINGS

PERSONAL: Born August 13, 1978, in Milwaukee, Wis. ... 5-9/209.
HIGH SCHOOL: Milwaukee Tech.
COLLEGE: Wisconsin.
TRANSACTIONS/CAREER NOTES: Selected after junior season by Minnesota Vikings in first round (27th pick overall) of 2001 NFL draft. ... Signed by Vikings (July 30, 2001). ... On physically unable to perform list with foot injury (August 25, 2003). ... Activated (October 31, 2003).
HONORS: Played in Pro Bowl (2002 season).
SINGLE GAME HIGHS (regular season): Attempts—29 (October 27, 2002, vs. Chicago); yards—167 (November 10, 2002, vs. New York Giants); and rushing touchdowns—2 (December 9, 2001, vs. Tennessee).
STATISTICAL PLATEAUS: 100-yard rushing games: 2001 (2), 2002 (5), 2003 (1). Total: 8.

Year Team	G	GS	Att.	Yds.	Avg.	TD	No.	Yds.	Avg.	TD	TD	2pt.	Pts.	Fum.
			RUSHING				RECEIVING				TOTALS			
2001—Minnesota NFL	13	13	172	682	4.0	2	29	226	7.8	1	3	0	18	0
2002—Minnesota NFL	16	16	255	1296	5.1	5	37	351	9.5	1	6	0	36	4
2003—Minnesota NFL	8	7	90	447	5.0	1	12	132	11.0	0	1	0	6	2
2004—Minnesota NFL	11	7	70	276	3.9	1	21	207	9.9	1	2	0	12	1
Pro totals (4 years)	48	43	587	2701	4.6	9	99	916	9.3	3	12	0	72	7

BENTLEY, KEVIN   LB   SEAHAWKS

PERSONAL: Born December 29, 1979, in North Hills, Calif. ... 6-1/240. ... Full name: Kevin Kinte Bentley.
HIGH SCHOOL: Montclair (Calif.).
COLLEGE: Northwestern.
TRANSACTIONS/CAREER NOTES: Selected by Cleveland Browns in fourth round (101st pick overall) of 2002 NFL draft. ... Signed by Browns (July 16, 2002). ... Did not receive qualifying offer from Browns (March 2, 2005). ... Signed by Seattle Seahawks (March 12, 2005).

Year Team	G	GS	TOTALS Tk.	Ast.	Sks.	INTERCEPTIONS No.	Yds.	Avg.	TD
2002—Cleveland NFL	12	0	20	14	0.0	0	0	0.0	0
2003—Cleveland NFL	16	14	55	36	0.0	1	25	25.0	0
2004—Cleveland NFL	16	3	35	16	0.0	0	0	0.0	0
Pro totals (3 years)	44	17	110	66	0.0	1	25	25.0	0

BENTLEY, LECHARLES   G/C   SAINTS

PERSONAL: Born November 7, 1979, in Cleveland, Ohio. ... 6-2/313.
HIGH SCHOOL: St. Ignatius (Cleveland).
COLLEGE: Ohio State.
TRANSACTIONS/CAREER NOTES: Selected by New Orleans Saints in second round (44th pick overall) of 2002 NFL draft. ... Signed by Saints (July 28, 2002). ... On injured reserve with knee injury (December 26, 2003-remainder of season).
PLAYING EXPERIENCE: New Orleans NFL, 2002-2004. ... Games/Games started: 2002 (14/14), 2003 (13/13), 2004 (16/16). Total: 43/43.
HONORS: Named center on THE SPORTING NEWS college All-America first team (2001). ... Named to play in Pro Bowl (2003 season); replaced by Steve Hutchinson due to injury.

BERGER, MITCH   P   SAINTS

PERSONAL: Born June 24, 1972, in Kamloops, B.C. ... 6-4/228.
HIGH SCHOOL: North Delta (Vancouver).
JUNIOR COLLEGE: Tyler (Texas) Junior College.
COLLEGE: Colorado.
TRANSACTIONS/CAREER NOTES: Selected by Philadelphia Eagles in sixth round (193rd pick overall) of 1994 NFL draft. ... Signed by Eagles (July 11, 1994). ... Released by Eagles (October 10, 1994). ... Signed by Cincinnati Bengals to practice squad (October 13, 1994). ... Released by Bengals (November 30, 1994). ... Signed by Chicago Bears (March 7, 1995). ... Released by Bears (May 4, 1995). ... Signed by Indianapolis Colts (May 16, 1995). ... Claimed on waivers by Green Bay Packers (August 24, 1995). ... Released by Packers (August 27, 1995). ... Signed by Bears (November 7, 1995). ... Released by Bears (November 13, 1995). ... Signed by Minnesota Vikings (April 19, 1996). ... Granted unconditional free agency (February 11, 2000). ... Re-signed by Vikings (February 21, 2000). ... On injured reserve with knee injury (December 18, 2001-remainder of season). ... Released by Vikings (February 22, 2002). ... Signed by St. Louis Rams (April 22, 2002). ... Granted unconditional free agency (February 28, 2003). ... Signed by New Orleans Saints (March 7, 2003).
CHAMPIONSHIP GAME EXPERIENCE: Played in NFC championship game (1998 and 2000 seasons).
HONORS: Named punter on THE SPORTING NEWS NFL All-Pro team (1999). ... Played in Pro Bowl (1999 and 2004 seasons).

Year Team	G	No.	Yds.	PUNTING Avg.	Net avg.	In. 20	Blk.
1994—Philadelphia NFL	5	25	951	38.0	31.3	8	0
1995—	Did not play.						
1996—Minnesota NFL	16	88	3616	41.1	32.3	26	2
1997—Minnesota NFL	14	73	3133	42.9	34.1	22	0
1998—Minnesota NFL	16	55	2458	44.7	37.0	17	0
1999—Minnesota NFL	16	61	2769	‡45.4	‡38.4	18	0
2000—Minnesota NFL	16	62	2773	‡44.7	36.2	16	0
2001—Minnesota NFL	12	47	2046	43.5	32.9	10	0
2002—St. Louis NFL	16	72	3020	41.9	32.7	26	0
2003—New Orleans NFL	16	71	3144	44.3	*38.2	28	1
2004—New Orleans NFL	16	85	3704	43.6	*39.0	28	0
Pro totals (10 years)	143	639	27614	43.2	35.5	199	3

BERLIN, EDDIE   WR   BEARS

PERSONAL: Born January 14, 1978, in Urbandale, Iowa. ... 5-11/195.
HIGH SCHOOL: Urbandale (Iowa).
COLLEGE: Northern Iowa.
TRANSACTIONS/CAREER NOTES: Selected by Tennessee Titans in fifth round (159th pick overall) of 2001 NFL draft. ... Signed by Titans (July 9, 2001). ... Granted free agency (March 3, 2004). ... Re-signed by Titans (June 4, 2004). ... Granted unconditional free agency (March 2, 2005). ... Signed by Chicago Bears (March 23, 2005).
CHAMPIONSHIP GAME EXPERIENCE: Played in AFC championship game (2002 season).
SINGLE GAME HIGHS (regular season): Receptions—4 (October 17, 2004, vs. Houston); yards—69 (December 19, 2004, vs. Oakland); and touchdown receptions—1 (October 11, 2004, vs. Green Bay).

Year Team	G	GS	RECEIVING No.	Yds.	Avg.	TD	PUNT RETURNS No.	Yds.	Avg.	TD	KICKOFF RETURNS No.	Yds.	Avg.	TD	TOTALS TD	2pt.	Pts.	Fum.
2001—Tennessee NFL	11	0	2	28	14.0	0	0	0	0.0	0	13	253	19.5	0	0	0	0	0
2002—Tennessee NFL	16	0	1	14	14.0	0	0	0	0.0	0	13	260	20.0	0	0	0	0	0
2003—Tennessee NFL	14	0	1	50	50.0	1	0	0	0.0	0	4	73	18.3	0	1	0	6	2
2004—Tennessee NFL	16	1	20	278	13.9	1	7	26	3.7	0	0	0	0.0	0	1	0	6	0
Pro totals (4 years)	57	1	24	370	15.4	2	7	26	3.7	0	30	586	19.5	0	2	0	12	2

BERNARD, ROCKY   DT   SEAHAWKS

PERSONAL: Born April 19, 1979, in Baytown, Texas. ... 6-3/293. ... Full name: Robert Bernard.
HIGH SCHOOL: Sterling (Baytown, Texas).
COLLEGE: Texas A&M.
TRANSACTIONS/CAREER NOTES: Selected by Seattle Seahawks in fifth round (146th pick overall) of 2002 NFL draft. ... Signed by Seahawks (July 11, 2002). ... Granted free agency (March 2, 2005). ... Re-signed by Seahawks (May 19, 2005).

| | | | | TOTALS | |
Year Team	G	GS	Tk.	Ast.	Sks.
2002—Seattle NFL	16	2	34	15	4.0
2003—Seattle NFL	12	0	11	5	2.0
2004—Seattle NFL	14	1	26	13	3.5
Pro totals (3 years)	42	3	71	33	9.5

BERRIAN, BERNARD   WR   BEARS

PERSONAL: Born December 27, 1980, in Winton, Calif. ... 6-1/185.
HIGH SCHOOL: Atwater (Winton, Calif.).
COLLEGE: Fresno State.
TRANSACTIONS/CAREER NOTES: Selected by Chicago Bears in third round (78th pick overall) of 2004 NFL draft. ... Signed by Bears (July 28, 2004).
HONORS: Named kick returner on THE SPORTING NEWS college All-America fourth team (2001).
SINGLE GAME HIGHS (regular season): Receptions—2 (January 2, 2005, vs. Green Bay); yards—49 (October 31, 2004, vs. San Francisco); and touchdown receptions—1 (November 7, 2004, vs. New York Giants).

| | | | RUSHING | | | | RECEIVING | | | | PUNT RETURNS | | | | KICKOFF RETURNS | | | | TOTALS | | |
Year Team	G	GS	Att.	Yds.	Avg.	TD	No.	Yds.	Avg.	TD	No.	Yds.	Avg.	TD	No.	Yds.	Avg.	TD	TD	2pt.	Pts.
2004—Chi. NFL	16	1	8	28	3.5	0	15	225	15.0	2	2	10	5.0	0	17	385	22.6	0	2	0	12

BERRY, BERTRAND   DE   CARDINALS

PERSONAL: Born August 15, 1975, in Houston, Texas. ... 6-3/275. ... Full name: Bertrand Demond Berry.
HIGH SCHOOL: Humble (Texas).
COLLEGE: Notre Dame.
TRANSACTIONS/CAREER NOTES: Selected by Indianapolis Colts in third round (86th pick overall) of 1997 NFL draft. ... Signed by Colts (July 9, 1997). ... Granted free agency (February 11, 2000). ... Signed by St. Louis Rams (July 20, 2000). ... Released by Rams (August 20, 2000). ... Signed by Denver Broncos (January 3, 2001). ... Granted unconditional free agency (March 3, 2004). ... Signed by Arizona Cardinals (March 6, 2004).
HONORS: Played in Pro Bowl (2004 season).

| | | | | TOTALS | |
Year Team	G	GS	Tk.	Ast.	Sks.
1997—Indianapolis NFL	10	1	4	7	0.0
1998—Indianapolis NFL	16	12	38	11	4.0
1999—Indianapolis NFL	16	0	5	2	1.0
2000—			Did not play.		
2001—Denver NFL	14	0	14	2	2.0
2002—Denver NFL	16	1	10	2	6.5
2003—Denver NFL	16	16	23	14	11.5
2004—Arizona NFL	16	16	40	8	‡14.5
Pro totals (7 years)	104	46	134	46	39.5

BERTON, SEAN   TE   VIKINGS

PERSONAL: Born October 31, 1979, in Columbia, S.C. ... 6-4/272.
HIGH SCHOOL: Hempfield (Greensburg, Pa.).
COLLEGE: North Carolina State.
TRANSACTIONS/CAREER NOTES: Signed as non-drafted free agent by Minnesota Vikings (May 1, 2003). ... Released by Vikings (August 31, 2004). ... Re-signed by Vikings (September 22, 2004).
SINGLE GAME HIGHS (regular season): Receptions—3 (December 24, 2004, vs. Green Bay); yards—24 (December 24, 2004, vs. Green Bay); and touchdown receptions—0.

| | | | RECEIVING | | | | TOTALS | | | |
Year Team	G	GS	No.	Yds.	Avg.	TD	TD	2pt.	Pts.	Fum.
2003—Minnesota NFL	16	0	0	0	0.0	0	0	0	0	0
2004—Minnesota NFL	14	7	9	78	8.7	0	0	0	0	0
Pro totals (2 years)	30	7	9	78	8.7	0	0	0	0	0

BETTIS, JEROME   RB   STEELERS

PERSONAL: Born February 16, 1972, in Detroit, Mich. ... 5-11/255. ... Full name: Jerome Abram Bettis.
HIGH SCHOOL: Mackenzie (Detroit).
COLLEGE: Notre Dame.
TRANSACTIONS/CAREER NOTES: Selected after junior season by Los Angeles Rams in first round (10th pick overall) of 1993 NFL draft. ... Signed by Rams (July 22, 1993). ... Rams franchise moved to St. Louis (April 12, 1995). ... Traded by Rams with third-round pick (LB Steven Conley) in 1996 draft to Pittsburgh Steelers for second-round pick (TE Ernie Conwell) in 1996 draft and fourth-round pick (traded to Miami)

in 1997 draft (April 20, 1996). ... Granted unconditional free agency (February 14, 1997). ... Re-signed by Steelers (February 17, 1997). ... Granted unconditional free agency (March 2, 2001). ... Re-signed by Steelers (March 2, 2001).
CHAMPIONSHIP GAME EXPERIENCE: Played in AFC championship game (1997, 2001 and 2004 seasons).
HONORS: Named NFL Rookie of the Year by THE SPORTING NEWS (1993). ... Played in Pro Bowl (1993, 1994, 1996, 1997 and 2004 seasons). ... Named to play in Pro Bowl (2001 season); replaced by Corey Dillon due to injury.
SINGLE GAME HIGHS (regular season): Attempts—39 (January 2, 1994, vs. Chicago); yards—212 (December 12, 1993, vs. New Orleans); and rushing touchdowns—3 (September 12, 2004, vs. Oakland).
STATISTICAL PLATEAUS: 100-yard rushing games: 1993 (7), 1994 (4), 1996 (10), 1997 (10), 1998 (6), 1999 (2), 2000 (7), 2001 (5), 2002 (1), 2003 (2), 2004 (6). Total: 60.

Year Team	G	GS	RUSHING				RECEIVING				TOTALS			
			Att.	Yds.	Avg.	TD	No.	Yds.	Avg.	TD	TD	2pt.	Pts.	Fum.
1993—Los Angeles Rams NFL	16	12	‡294	1429	4.9	7	26	244	9.4	0	7	0	42	4
1994—Los Angeles Rams NFL	16	16	319	1025	3.2	3	31	293	9.5	1	4	∞2	28	5
1995—St. Louis NFL	15	13	183	637	3.5	3	18	106	5.9	0	3	0	18	4
1996—Pittsburgh NFL	16	12	320	1431	4.5	11	22	122	5.5	0	11	0	66	7
1997—Pittsburgh NFL	15	15	*375	1665	4.4	7	15	110	7.3	2	9	0	54	6
1998—Pittsburgh NFL	15	15	316	1185	3.8	3	16	90	5.6	0	3	0	18	2
1999—Pittsburgh NFL	16	16	299	1091	3.6	7	21	110	5.2	0	7	0	42	2
2000—Pittsburgh NFL	16	16	355	1341	3.8	8	13	97	7.5	0	8	0	48	1
2001—Pittsburgh NFL	11	11	225	1072	§4.8	4	8	48	6.0	0	4	0	24	3
2002—Pittsburgh NFL	13	11	187	666	3.6	9	7	57	8.1	0	9	0	54	1
2003—Pittsburgh NFL	16	10	246	811	3.3	7	13	86	6.6	0	7	1	44	5
2004—Pittsburgh NFL	15	6	250	941	3.8	13	6	46	7.7	0	13	0	78	1
Pro totals (12 years)	180	153	3369	13294	3.9	82	196	1409	7.2	3	85	3	516	41

BETTS, LADELL   RB   REDSKINS

PERSONAL: Born August 27, 1979, in Blue Springs, Mo. ... 5-10/222. ... Full name: Matthew Betts.
HIGH SCHOOL: Blue Springs (Mo.).
COLLEGE: Iowa.
TRANSACTIONS/CAREER NOTES: Selected by Washington Redskins in second round (56th pick overall) of 2002 NFL draft. ... Signed by Redskins (July 23, 2002).
SINGLE GAME HIGHS (regular season): Attempts—26 (January 2, 2005, vs. Minnesota); yards—118 (January 2, 2005, vs. Minnesota); and rushing touchdowns—1 (January 2, 2005, vs. Minnesota).
STATISTICAL PLATEAUS: 100-yard rushing games: 2002 (1), 2004 (1). Total: 2.

Year Team	G	GS	RUSHING				RECEIVING				KICKOFF RETURNS				TOTALS		
			Att.	Yds.	Avg.	TD	No.	Yds.	Avg.	TD	No.	Yds.	Avg.	TD	TD	2pt.	Pts. Fum.
2002—Washington NFL	11	0	65	307	4.7	1	12	154	12.8	0	28	690	24.6	0	1	0	6 2
2003—Washington NFL	9	1	77	255	3.3	2	15	167	11.1	0	3	59	19.7	0	2	0	12 0
2004—Washington NFL	16	1	90	371	4.1	1	15	108	7.2	0	23	528	23.0	0	1	0	6 0
Pro totals (3 years)	36	2	232	933	4.0	4	42	429	10.2	0	54	1277	23.6	0	4	0	24 2

BEVERLY, ERIC   G   FALCONS

PERSONAL: Born March 28, 1974, in Cleveland, Ohio. ... 6-3/300. ... Full name: Eric Raymonde Beverly.
HIGH SCHOOL: Bedford Heights (Ohio).
COLLEGE: Miami (Ohio).
TRANSACTIONS/CAREER NOTES: Signed as non-drafted free agent by Detroit Lions (April 24, 1997). ... Released by Lions (August 24, 1997). ... Re-signed by Lions to practice squad (August 26, 1997). ... Activated (December 20, 1997). ... Active for one game (1997); did not play. ... Granted free agency (March 2, 2001). ... Tendered offer sheet by Miami Dolphins (March 8, 2001). ... Offer matched by Lions (March 15, 2001). ... On injured reserve with ankle injury (December 13, 2003-remainder of season). ... Granted unconditional free agency (March 3, 2004). ... Signed by Atlanta Falcons (March 10, 2004).
PLAYING EXPERIENCE: Detroit NFL, 1998-2003; Atlanta NFL, 2004. ... Games/Games started: 1998 (16/0), 1999 (16/2), 2000 (16/7), 2001 (16/16), 2002 (15/3), 2003 (13/13), 2004 (13/3). Total: 105/44.
CHAMPIONSHIP GAME EXPERIENCE: Played in NFC championship game (2004 season).

BIBLA, MARTIN   G   FALCONS

PERSONAL: Born October 4, 1979, in Mountaintop, Pa. ... 6-3/306. ... Full name: Martin John Bibla.
HIGH SCHOOL: Crestwood (Mountaintop, Pa.).
COLLEGE: Miami (Fla.).
TRANSACTIONS/CAREER NOTES: Selected by Atlanta Falcons in fourth round (116th pick overall) of 2002 NFL draft. ... Signed by Falcons (June 19, 2002).
PLAYING EXPERIENCE: Atlanta NFL, 2002-2004. ... Games/Games started: 2002 (10/0), 2003 (10/2), 2004 (11/0). Total: 31/2.

BIDWELL, JOSH   P   BUCCANEERS

PERSONAL: Born March 13, 1976, in Roseburg, Ore. ... 6-3/220. ... Full name: Joshua John Bidwell.
HIGH SCHOOL: Douglas (Winston, Ore.).
COLLEGE: Oregon.
TRANSACTIONS/CAREER NOTES: Selected by Green Bay Packers in fourth round (133rd pick overall) of 1999 NFL draft. ... Signed by Packers (July 24, 1999). ... On non-football illness list with cancer (September 5, 1999-entire season). ... Granted free agency (February 28, 2003). ... Re-signed by Packers (April 30, 2003). ... Granted unconditional free agency (March 3, 2004). ... Signed by Tampa Bay Buccaneers (March 13, 2004).
HONORS: Named punter on THE SPORTING NEWS college All-America second team (1998).

Year—Team			PUNTING					
	G	No.	Yds.	Avg.	Net avg.	In. 20	Blk.
1999—Green Bay NFL	Did not play.						
2000—Green Bay NFL	16	78	3003	38.5	34.6	22	0
2001—Green Bay NFL	16	82	3485	42.5	36.5	21	0
2002—Green Bay NFL	16	79	3296	41.7	35.7	26	0
2003—Green Bay NFL	16	69	2875	41.7	35.1	16	0
2004—Tampa Bay NFL	16	82	3472	42.3	36.8	23	1
Pro totals (5 years)	80	390	16131	41.4	35.8	108	1

BIERRIA, TERREAL — SS

PERSONAL: Born October 10, 1980, in Slidell, La. ... 6-3/211.
HIGH SCHOOL: Salmen (Slidell, La.).
COLLEGE: Georgia.
TRANSACTIONS/CAREER NOTES: Selected after junior season by Seattle Seahawks in fourth round (120th pick overall) of 2002 NFL draft. ... Signed by Seahawks (July 25, 2002). ... Granted free agency (March 2, 2005).

Year—Team			TOTALS			INTERCEPTIONS			
	G	GS	Tk.	Ast.	Sks.	No.	Yds.	Avg.	TD
2002—Seattle NFL	14	0	0	0	0.0	0	0	0.0	0
2004—Seattle NFL	15	12	47	22	0.0	1	10	10.0	0
Pro totals (2 years)	29	12	47	22	0.0	1	10	10.0	0

BINN, DAVID — C/LS — CHARGERS

PERSONAL: Born February 6, 1972, in San Mateo, Calif. ... 6-3/223. ... Full name: David Aaron Binn.
HIGH SCHOOL: San Mateo (Calif.).
COLLEGE: California.
TRANSACTIONS/CAREER NOTES: Signed as non-drafted free agent by San Diego Chargers (April 28, 1994). ... Granted unconditional free agency (February 13, 1998). ... Re-signed by Chargers (February 25, 1998). ... Granted unconditional free agency (February 11, 2000). ... Re-signed by Chargers (February 11, 2000). ... Granted unconditional free agency (March 1, 2002). ... Re-signed by Chargers (March 5, 2002). ... Granted unconditional free agency (February 28, 2003). ... Re-signed by Chargers (March 3, 2003). ... Granted unconditional free agency (March 3, 2004). ... Re-signed by Chargers (March 4, 2004).
PLAYING EXPERIENCE: San Diego NFL, 1994-2004. ... Games/Games started: 1994 (16/0), 1995 (16/0), 1996 (16/0), 1997 (16/0), 1998 (15/0), 1999 (16/0), 2000 (16/0), 2001 (16/0), 2002 (16/0), 2003 (16/0), 2004 (16/0). Total: 175/0.
CHAMPIONSHIP GAME EXPERIENCE: Played in AFC championship game (1994 season). ... Played in Super Bowl 29 (1994 season).

BIRD, CORY — S

PERSONAL: Born August 10, 1978, in Atlantic City, N.J. ... 5-10/213. ... Full name: Cory James Bird.
HIGH SCHOOL: Oakcrest (Mays Landing, N.J.).
COLLEGE: Virginia Tech.
TRANSACTIONS/CAREER NOTES: Selected by Indianapolis Colts in third round (91st pick overall) of 2001 NFL draft. ... Signed by Colts (July 25, 2001). ... On injured reserve with hip injury (November 20, 2002-remainder of season). ... Granted free agency (March 3, 2004). ... Re-signed by Colts (March 26, 2004). ... Granted unconditional free agency (March 2, 2005).
CHAMPIONSHIP GAME EXPERIENCE: Played in AFC championship game (2003 season).

Year—Team			TOTALS			INTERCEPTIONS			
	G	GS	Tk.	Ast.	Sks.	No.	Yds.	Avg.	TD
2001—Indianapolis NFL	14	0	20	5	0.5	0	0	0.0	0
2002—Indianapolis NFL	6	4	10	5	0.0	0	0	0.0	0
2003—Indianapolis NFL	12	0	2	0	0.0	0	0	0.0	0
2004—Indianapolis NFL	13	4	21	8	0.0	0	0	0.0	0
Pro totals (4 years)	45	8	53	18	0.5	0	0	0.0	0

BIRK, MATT — C — VIKINGS

PERSONAL: Born July 23, 1976, in St. Paul, Minn. ... 6-4/309. ... Full name: Matthew Robert Birk.
HIGH SCHOOL: Cretin-Derham Hall (St. Paul, Minn.).
COLLEGE: Harvard.
TRANSACTIONS/CAREER NOTES: Selected by Minnesota Vikings in sixth round (173rd pick overall) of 1998 NFL draft. ... Signed by Vikings (June 24, 1998). ... Granted free agency (March 2, 2001). ... Re-signed by Vikings (March 6, 2001).
PLAYING EXPERIENCE: Minnesota NFL, 1998-2004. ... Games/Games started: 1998 (7/0), 1999 (15/0), 2000 (16/16), 2001 (16/16), 2002 (16/16), 2003 (16/16), 2004 (12/11). Total: 98/75.
CHAMPIONSHIP GAME EXPERIENCE: Member of Vikings for NFC championship game (1998 season); did not play. ... Played in NFC championship game (2000 season).
HONORS: Named center on THE SPORTING NEWS NFL All-Pro team (2003). ... Played in Pro Bowl (2000, 2003 and 2004 seasons). ... Named to play in Pro Bowl (2001 season); replaced by Jeremy Newberry due to injury.

BLACK, JORDAN — T/G — CHIEFS

PERSONAL: Born January 28, 1980, in Garland, Texas. ... 6-5/304. ... Full name: Brian Jordan Black.
HIGH SCHOOL: Dallas Christian (Mesquite, Texas).
COLLEGE: Notre Dame.

B

TRANSACTIONS/CAREER NOTES: Selected by Kansas City Chiefs in fifth round (153rd pick overall) of 2003 NFL draft.
PLAYING EXPERIENCE: Kansas City NFL, 2004. ... Games/Games started: 2004 (16/4). Total: 16/4.

BLADE, WILLIE   DT   COWBOYS

PERSONAL: Born February 7, 1979, in Warner Robins, Ga. ... 6-3/315.
HIGH SCHOOL: Warner Robins (Ga.).
JUNIOR COLLEGE: Butler County Community College (Kan.).
COLLEGE: Mississippi State.
TRANSACTIONS/CAREER NOTES: Selected by Dallas Cowboys in third round (93rd pick overall) of 2001 NFL draft. ... Signed by Cowboys (July 23, 2001). ... On injured reserve with wrist injury (August 28, 2001-entire season). ... Claimed on waivers by Houston Texans (September 2, 2002). ... Released by Texans (December 24, 2002). ... Signed by Cowboys (January 7, 2003). ... Granted free agency (March 3, 2004). ... Re-signed by Cowboys (April 13, 2004). ... Claimed on waivers by New York Giants (July 28, 2004). ... Claimed on waivers by Jacksonville Jaguars (July 30, 2004). ... Released by Jaguars (November 9, 2004). ... Signed by Cowboys (January 21, 2005). ... Assigned by Cowboys to Berlin Thunder in 2005 NFL Europe enhancement allocation program (January 31, 2005).

					TOTALS		
Year	Team	G	GS	Tk.	Ast.	Sks.
2003—Dallas NFL		15	14	11	5	1.0
2004—Jacksonville NFL		5	1	1	1	0.0
Pro totals (2 years)		20	15	12	6	1.0

BLAKE, JEFF   QB

PERSONAL: Born December 4, 1970, in Daytona Beach, Fla. ... 6-1/223. ... Son of Emory Blake, running back with Toronto Argonauts of CFL (1974).
HIGH SCHOOL: Seminole (Sanford, Fla.).
COLLEGE: East Carolina.
TRANSACTIONS/CAREER NOTES: Selected by New York Jets in sixth round (166th pick overall) of 1992 NFL draft. ... Signed by Jets (July 14, 1992). ... Inactive for all 16 games (1993). ... Claimed on waivers by Cincinnati Bengals (August 29, 1994). ... Granted free agency (February 17, 1995). ... Re-signed by Bengals (May 8, 1995). ... On injured reserve with wrist injury (December 24, 1998-remainder of season). ... Granted unconditional free agency (February 11, 2000). ... Signed by New Orleans Saints (February 11, 2000). ... On injured reserve with broken foot (November 20, 2000-remainder of season). ... Released by Saints (March 1, 2002). ... Signed by Baltimore Ravens (April 24, 2002). ... Granted unconditional free agency (February 28, 2003). ... Signed by Arizona Cardinals (March 12, 2003). ... Released by Cardinals (February 4, 2004). ... Signed by Philadelphia Eagles (May 28, 2004). ... Granted unconditional free agency (March 2, 2005).
CHAMPIONSHIP GAME EXPERIENCE: Member of Eagles for NFC championship game (2004 season); inactive. ... Member of Eagles for Super Bowl 39 (2004 season); inactive.
HONORS: Played in Pro Bowl (1995 season).
SINGLE GAME HIGHS (regular season): Attempts—50 (October 27, 2002, vs. Pittsburgh); completions—33 (September 10, 2000, vs. San Diego); yards—387 (November 6, 1994, vs. Seattle); and touchdown passes—4 (December 6, 1999, vs. San Francisco).
STATISTICAL PLATEAUS: 300-yard passing games: 1994 (2), 1995 (1), 1996 (2), 1997 (1), 1998 (1), 1999 (1), 2002 (2), 2003 (2). Total: 12.
MISCELLANEOUS: Regular-season record as starting NFL quarterback: 39-61 (.390).

				PASSING								RUSHING				TOTALS		
Year	Team	G	GS	Att.	Cmp.	Pct.	Yds.	TD	Int.	Avg.	Skd.	Rat.	Att.	Yds.	Avg.	TD	TD	2pt.	Pts.
1992—New York Jets NFL		3	0	9	4	44.4	40	0	1	4.44	2	18.1	2	-2	-1.0	0	0	0	0
1993—New York Jets NFL		Did not play.																	
1994—Cincinnati NFL		10	9	306	156	51.0	2154	14	9	7.04	19	76.9	37	204	5.5	1	1	1	8
1995—Cincinnati NFL		16	16	567	§326	57.5	3822	§28	17	6.74	24	82.1	53	309	5.8	2	2	1	14
1996—Cincinnati NFL		16	16	549	308	56.1	3624	24	14	6.60	44	80.3	72	317	4.4	2	2	0	12
1997—Cincinnati NFL		11	11	317	184	58.0	2125	8	7	6.70	39	77.6	45	234	5.2	3	3	0	18
1998—Cincinnati NFL		8	2	93	51	54.8	739	3	3	7.95	15	78.2	15	103	6.9	0	0	0	0
1999—Cincinnati NFL		14	12	389	215	55.3	2670	16	12	6.86	30	77.6	63	332	5.3	2	2	0	12
2000—New Orleans NFL		11	11	302	184	60.9	2025	13	9	6.71	24	82.7	57	243	4.3	1	1	0	6
2001—New Orleans NFL		1	0	1	0	0.0	0	0	0	0.00	0	39.6	1	-1	-1.0	0	0	0	0
2002—Baltimore NFL		11	10	295	165	55.9	2084	13	11	7.06	30	77.3	39	106	2.7	1	1	0	6
2003—Arizona NFL		13	13	367	208	56.7	2247	13	15	6.12	19	69.6	30	177	5.9	2	2	1	14
2004—Philadelphia NFL		3	0	37	18	48.6	126	1	1	3.41	2	54.6	3	6	2.0	0	0	0	0
Pro totals (12 years)		117	100	3232	1819	56.3	21656	133	99	6.70	248	77.9	417	2028	4.9	14	14	3	90

BLAKLEY, DWAYNE   TE   FALCONS

PERSONAL: Born August 10, 1979, in St. Joseph, Mo. ... 6-4/257. ... Full name: Dwayne David Blakley.
HIGH SCHOOL: Central (St. Joseph, Mo.).
COLLEGE: Missouri.
TRANSACTIONS/CAREER NOTES: Signed as non-drafted free agent by Kansas City Chiefs (2002). ... Released by Chiefs (August 31, 2002). ... Re-signed by Chiefs to practice squad (September 1, 2002). ... Activated (January 2, 2003). ... Assigned by Chiefs to Rhein Fire in 2003 NFL Europe enhancement allocation program (January 31, 2003). ... Released by Chiefs (August 31, 2003). ... Signed by San Diego Chargers to practice squad (September 17, 2003). ... Released by Chargers from practice squad (October 7, 2003). ... Signed by Tennessee Titans (January 26, 2004). ... Assigned by Titans to Rhein Fire in 2004 NFL Europe enhancement allocation program (February 14, 2004). ... Claimed on waivers by Atlanta Falcons (September 6, 2004).
SINGLE GAME HIGHS (regular season): Receptions—1 (December 26, 2004, vs. New Orleans); yards—13 (October 10, 2004, vs. Detroit); and touchdown receptions—0.

				RECEIVING				TOTALS			
Year	Team	G	GS	No.	Yds.	Avg.	TD	TD	2pt.	Pts.	Fum.
2004—Atlanta NFL		15	1	4	35	8.8	0	0	0	0	0

BLAYLOCK, DERRICK — RB — JETS

PERSONAL: Born August 23, 1979, in Atlanta, Texas. ... 5-9/210.
HIGH SCHOOL: Atlanta (Texas).
COLLEGE: Stephen F. Austin.
TRANSACTIONS/CAREER NOTES: Selected by Kansas City Chiefs in fifth round (150th pick overall) of 2001 NFL draft. ... Signed by Chiefs (June 8, 2001). ... Granted free agency (March 3, 2004). ... Re-signed by Chiefs (March 24, 2004). ... Granted unconditional free agency (March 2, 2005). ... Signed by New York Jets (March 4, 2005).
SINGLE GAME HIGHS (regular season): Attempts—33 (November 14, 2004, vs. New Orleans); yards—186 (November 14, 2004, vs. New Orleans); and rushing touchdowns—4 (October 24, 2004, vs. Atlanta).
STATISTICAL PLATEAUS: 100-yard rushing games: 2004 (1). Total: 1. 100-yard receiving games: 2003 (1). Total: 1.

Year Team	G	GS	RUSHING				RECEIVING				KICKOFF RETURNS				TOTALS			
			Att.	Yds.	Avg.	TD	No.	Yds.	Avg.	TD	No.	Yds.	Avg.	TD	TD	2pt.	Pts.	Fum.
2002—Kansas City NFL	12	0	16	72	4.5	0	5	47	9.4	0	3	49	16.3	0	0	0	0	0
2003—Kansas City NFL	16	0	22	112	5.1	2	15	181	12.1	1	1	32	32.0	0	3	0	18	1
2004—Kansas City NFL	12	5	118	539	4.6	8	25	246	9.8	1	1	22	22.0	0	9	0	54	0
Pro totals (3 years)	40	5	156	723	4.6	10	45	474	10.5	2	5	103	20.6	0	12	0	72	1

BLEDSOE, DREW — QB — COWBOYS

PERSONAL: Born February 14, 1972, in Ellensburg, Wash. ... 6-5/238.
HIGH SCHOOL: Walla Walla (Wash.).
COLLEGE: Washington State.
TRANSACTIONS/CAREER NOTES: Selected after junior season by New England Patriots in first round (first pick overall) of 1993 NFL draft. ... Signed by Patriots (July 6, 1993). ... Traded by Patriots to Buffalo Bills for first-round pick (traded to Chicago) in 2003 draft (April 21, 2002). ... Released by Bills (February 22, 2005). ... Signed by Dallas Cowboys (February 23, 2005).
CHAMPIONSHIP GAME EXPERIENCE: Played in AFC championship game (1996 and 2001 seasons). ... Played in Super Bowl 31 (1996 season). ... Member of Super Bowl championship team (2001 season); did not play.
HONORS: Played in Pro Bowl (1994, 1996, 1997 and 2002 seasons).
RECORDS: Holds NFL single-season record for most passes attempted—691 (1994). ... Holds NFL single-game records for most passes completed—45; most passes attempted—70; and most passes attempted without an interception—70 (November 13, 1994, vs. Minnesota). ... Tied for most consecutive years leading league in passing attempts—3 (1994-1996).
SINGLE GAME HIGHS (regular season): Attempts—70 (November 13, 1994, vs. Minnesota); completions—45 (November 13, 1994, vs. Minnesota); yards—463 (September 15, 2002, vs. Minnesota); and touchdown passes—4 (December 5, 2004, vs. Miami).
STATISTICAL PLATEAUS: 300-yard passing games: 1993 (1), 1994 (6), 1995 (2), 1996 (4), 1997 (3), 1998 (4), 1999 (5), 2000 (1), 2002 (7), 2003 (1). Total: 34.
MISCELLANEOUS: Regular-season record as starting NFL quarterback: 86-85 (.503). ... Postseason record as starting NFL quarterback: 3-3 (.500). ... Holds New England Patriots all-time record for most yards passing (29,657).

Year Team	G	GS	PASSING									RUSHING				TOTALS		
			Att.	Cmp.	Pct.	Yds.	TD	Int.	Avg.	Skd.	Rat.	Att.	Yds.	Avg.	TD	TD	2pt.	Pts.
1993—New England NFL	13	12	429	214	49.9	2494	15	15	5.81	16	65.0	32	82	2.6	0	0	0	0
1994—New England NFL	16	16	*691	*400	57.9	*4555	25	*27	6.59	22	73.6	44	40	0.9	0	0	0	0
1995—New England NFL	15	15	*636	323	50.8	3507	13	16	5.51	23	63.7	20	28	1.4	0	0	0	0
1996—New England NFL	16	16	*623	*373	59.9	4086	27	15	6.56	30	83.7	24	27	1.1	0	0	0	0
1997—New England NFL	16	16	522	314	60.2	3706	28	15	7.10	30	87.7	28	55	2.0	0	0	0	0
1998—New England NFL	14	14	481	263	54.7	3633	20	14	7.55	36	80.9	28	44	1.6	0	0	0	0
1999—New England NFL	16	16	§539	305	56.6	3985	19	§21	7.39	55	75.6	42	101	2.4	0	0	0	0
2000—New England NFL	16	16	531	312	58.8	3291	17	13	6.20	45	77.3	47	158	3.4	2	2	0	12
2001—New England NFL	2	2	66	40	60.6	400	2	2	6.06	5	75.3	5	18	3.6	0	0	0	0
2002—Buffalo NFL	16	16	610	375	61.5	4359	24	15	7.15	54	86.0	27	67	2.5	2	2	0	12
2003—Buffalo NFL	16	16	471	274	58.2	2860	11	12	6.07	*49	73.0	24	29	1.2	2	2	0	12
2004—Buffalo NFL	16	16	450	256	56.9	2932	20	16	6.52	37	76.6	22	37	1.7	0	0	0	0
Pro totals (12 years)	172	171	6049	3449	57.0	39808	221	181	6.58	402	76.7	343	686	2.0	6	6	0	36

BLY, DRE' — CB — LIONS

PERSONAL: Born May 22, 1977, in Chesapeake, Va. ... 5-9/185. ... Full name: Donald Andre Bly.
HIGH SCHOOL: Western Branch (Chesapeake, Va.).
COLLEGE: North Carolina.
TRANSACTIONS/CAREER NOTES: Selected after junior season by St. Louis Rams in second round (41st pick overall) of 1999 NFL draft. ... Signed by Rams (July 16, 1999). ... Granted unconditional free agency (February 28, 2003). ... Signed by Detroit Lions (March 1, 2003).
CHAMPIONSHIP GAME EXPERIENCE: Played in NFC championship game (1999 and 2001 seasons). ... Member of Super Bowl championship team (1999 season). ... Played in Super Bowl 36 (2001 season).
HONORS: Named cornerback on THE SPORTING NEWS college All-America first team (1996). ... Named cornerback on THE SPORTING NEWS college All-America third team (1997). ... Played in Pro Bowl (2003 and 2004 seasons).

Year Team	G	GS	TOTALS			INTERCEPTIONS				PUNT RETURNS				KICKOFF RETURNS				TOTALS			
			Tk.	Ast.	Sks.	No.	Yds.	Avg.	TD	No.	Yds.	Avg.	TD	No.	Yds.	Avg.	TD	TD	2pt.	Pts.	Fum.
1999—StL. NFL	16	2	16	1	0.0	3	53	17.7	1	0	0	0.0	0	1	1	1.0	0	1	0	6	0
2000—StL. NFL	16	3	39	4	1.0	3	44	14.7	0	0	0	0.0	0	9	163	18.1	0	0	0	0	0
2001—StL. NFL	16	4	28	2	0.0	6	150	25.0	†2	7	71	10.1	0	6	128	21.3	0	2	0	12	1
2002—StL. NFL	16	16	58	6	1.0	2	0	0.0	0	8	138	17.3	1	1	5	5.0	0	2	0	12	0
2003—Det. NFL	14	14	52	8	1.0	6	89	14.8	1	3	22	7.3	0	0	0	0.0	0	2	0	12	0
2004—Det. NFL	13	13	32	6	0.0	4	107	26.8	1	0	0	0.0	0	0	0	0.0	0	1	0	6	0
Pro totals (6 years)	91	52	225	27	3.0	24	443	18.5	5	18	231	12.8	1	17	297	17.5	0	8	0	48	2

BOBER, CHRIS   C   CHIEFS

PERSONAL: Born December 24, 1976, in Omaha, Neb. ... 6-5/310.
HIGH SCHOOL: South (Omaha, Neb.).
COLLEGE: Nebraska-Omaha.
TRANSACTIONS/CAREER NOTES: Signed as non-drafted free agent by New York Giants (April 20, 2000). ... Released by Giants (August 27, 2000). ... Re-signed by Giants to practice squad (August 29, 2000). ... Activated (November 6, 2000); did not play. ... Granted free agency (February 28, 2003). ... Re-signed by Giants (April 21, 2003). ... Granted unconditional free agency (March 3, 2004). ... Signed by Kansas City Chiefs (March 12, 2004).
PLAYING EXPERIENCE: New York Giants NFL, 2001-2003; Kansas City NFL, 2004. ... Games/Games started: 2001 (16/0), 2002 (15/15), 2003 (16/16), 2004 (12/2). Total: 59/33.

BOCKWOLDT, COLBY   LB   SAINTS

PERSONAL: Born April 14, 1981, in Odgen, Utah. ... 6-1/237.
HIGH SCHOOL: Northridge (Sunset, Utah).
COLLEGE: Brigham Young.
TRANSACTIONS/CAREER NOTES: Selected by New Orleans Saints in seventh round (240th pick overall) of 2004 NFL draft. ... Signed by Saints (July 27, 2004).

			TOTALS			INTERCEPTIONS			
Year Team	G	GS	Tk.	Ast.	Sks.	No.	Yds.	Avg.	TD
2004—New Orleans NFL	16	7	31	6	1.0	0	0	0.0	0

BODDEN, LEIGH   CB   BROWNS

PERSONAL: Born September 24, 1981, in Hyattsville, Md. ... 6-1/200. ... Full name: Leigh Edmond Bodden.
HIGH SCHOOL: Northwestern (Hyattsville, Md).
COLLEGE: Duquesne.
TRANSACTIONS/CAREER NOTES: Signed as non-drafted free agent by Cleveland Browns (May 2, 2003). ... On injured reserve with pectoral injury (November 9, 2004-remainder of season).

			TOTALS			INTERCEPTIONS			
Year Team	G	GS	Tk.	Ast.	Sks.	No.	Yds.	Avg.	TD
2003—Cleveland NFL	13	1	9	0	0.0	1	1	1.0	0
2004—Cleveland NFL	8	1	11	0	0.0	0	0	0.0	0
Pro totals (2 years)	21	2	20	0	0.0	1	1	1.0	0

BOERIGTER, MARC   WR   CHIEFS

PERSONAL: Born May 4, 1978, in Hastings, Neb. ... 6-3/220. ... Full name: Marc Robert Boerigter.
HIGH SCHOOL: Hastings (Neb.).
COLLEGE: Hastings (Neb.).
TRANSACTIONS/CAREER NOTES: Signed by Calgary Stampeders of CFL (May 12, 2000). ... Signed as non-drafted free agent by Kansas City Chiefs (February 7, 2002). ... On injured reserve with knee injury (September 1, 2004-entire season). ... Granted free agency (March 2, 2005). ... Re-signed by Chiefs (April 19, 2005).
CHAMPIONSHIP GAME EXPERIENCE: Member of CFL championship team (2001).
RECORDS: Shares NFL record for longest pass reception (from Trent Green)—99 yards, touchdown (December 22, 2002, vs. San Diego).
SINGLE GAME HIGHS (regular season): Receptions—5 (December 22, 2002, vs. San Diego); yards—144 (December 22, 2002, vs. San Diego); and touchdown receptions—2 (December 22, 2002, vs. San Diego).
STATISTICAL PLATEAUS: 100-yard receiving games: 2002 (1). Total: 1.

			RECEIVING				TOTALS			
Year Team	G	GS	No.	Yds.	Avg.	TD	TD	2pt.	Pts.	Fum.
2000—Calgary CFL	18	0	63	1092	17.3	8	8	0	48	0
2001—Calgary CFL	18	0	48	931	19.4	11	11	0	66	0
2002—Kansas City NFL	16	2	20	420	21.0	8	8	0	48	0
2003—Kansas City NFL	15	0	11	158	14.4	0	0	0	0	0
2004—Kansas City NFL			Did not play.							
CFL totals (2 years)	36	0	111	2023	18.2	19	19	0	114	0
NFL totals (2 years)	31	2	31	578	18.6	8	8	0	48	0
Pro totals (4 years)	67	2	142	2601	18.3	27	27	0	162	0

BOIMAN, ROCKY   LB   TITANS

PERSONAL: Born January 24, 1980, in Cincinnati, Ohio. ... 6-4/236. ... Full name: Rocky Michael Boiman.
HIGH SCHOOL: St. Xavier (Cincinnati).
COLLEGE: Notre Dame.
TRANSACTIONS/CAREER NOTES: Selected by Tennessee Titans in fourth round (133rd pick overall) of 2002 NFL draft. ... Signed by Titans (July 24, 2002).
CHAMPIONSHIP GAME EXPERIENCE: Played in AFC championship game (2002 season).

			TOTALS			INTERCEPTIONS			
Year Team	G	GS	Tk.	Ast.	Sks.	No.	Yds.	Avg.	TD
2002—Tennessee NFL	16	0	1	0	0.0	0	0	0.0	0
2003—Tennessee NFL	16	2	23	13	1.5	2	70	35.0	1
2004—Tennessee NFL	7	6	8	11	0.0	0	0	0.0	0
Pro totals (3 years)	39	8	32	24	1.5	2	70	35.0	1

BOLDEN, JURAN — CB — BUCCANEERS

PERSONAL: Born June 27, 1974, in Washington, DC. ... 6-2/207.
HIGH SCHOOL: Hillsborough (Tampa).
JUNIOR COLLEGE: Mississippi Delta J.C.
TRANSACTIONS/CAREER NOTES: Signed by Winnipeg Blue Bombers of CFL (April 1995). ... Selected by Atlanta Falcons in fourth round (127th pick overall) of 1996 NFL draft. ... Signed by Falcons (July 20, 1996). ... On injured reserve with knee injury (December 9, 1996-remainder of season). ... Claimed on waivers by Green Bay Packers (September 30, 1998). ... Claimed on waivers by Carolina Panthers (October 27, 1998). ... Released by Panthers (February 12, 1999). ... Signed by Kansas City Chiefs (April 19, 1999). ... Released by Chiefs (September 5, 1999). ... Re-signed by Chiefs (September 21, 1999). ... Released by Chiefs (December 21, 1999). ... Signed by Blue Bombers of CFL (June 8, 2000). ... Signed by Atlanta Falcons (January 10, 2002). ... Granted unconditional free agency (February 28, 2003). ... Re-signed by Falcons (April 28, 2003), ... On active/physically unable to perform list with knee injury (July 25, 2003). ... Activated (October 31, 2003). ... Granted unconditional free agency (March 3, 2004). ... Signed by Jacksonville Jaguars (March 23, 2004). ... Released by Jaguars (March 3, 2005). ... Signed by Tampa Bay Buccaneers (March 29, 2005).

				TOTALS			INTERCEPTIONS			
Year Team	G	GS	Tk.	Ast.	Sks.	No.	Yds.	Avg.	TD
1995—Winnipeg CFL	9	9	17	...	0.0	6	28	4.7	0
1996—Atlanta NFL	9	0	0	0	0.0	0	0	0.0	0
1997—Atlanta NFL	14	1	7	0	0.0	0	0	0.0	0
1998—Atlanta NFL	3	0	3	0	0.0	0	0	0.0	0
—Green Bay NFL	3	0	0	0	0.0	0	0	0.0	0
—Carolina NFL	6	0	0	0	0.0	0	0	0.0	0
1999—Kansas City NFL	7	0	0	0	0.0	0	0	0.0	0
2002—Atlanta NFL	14	6	23	6	0.0	4	25	6.3	0
2003—Atlanta NFL	8	8	22	3	0.0	3	61	20.3	1
2004—Jacksonville NFL	13	0	17	4	0.0	0	0	0.0	0
CFL totals (1 year)	9	9	17	...	0.0	6	28	4.7	0
NFL totals (7 years)	77	15	72	13	0.0	7	86	12.3	1
Pro totals (8 years)	86	24	89		0.0	13	114	8.8	1

BOLDIN, ANQUAN — WR — CARDINALS

PERSONAL: Born October 3, 1980, in Pahokee, Fla. ... 6-1/218.
HIGH SCHOOL: Pahokee (Fla.).
COLLEGE: Florida State.
TRANSACTIONS/CAREER NOTES: Selected after junior season by Arizona Cardinals in second round (54th pick overall) of 2003 NFL draft. ... Signed by Cardinals (July 24, 2003).
HONORS: Played in Pro Bowl (2003 season). ... Named NFL Rookie of the Year by THE SPORTING NEWS (2003).
RECORDS: Holds NFL single-season record for most receptions by a rookie—101 (2003).
SINGLE GAME HIGHS (regular season): Receptions—10 (December 21, 2003, vs. Seattle); yards—217 (September 7, 2003, vs. Detroit); and touchdown receptions—2 (November 23, 2003, vs. St. Louis).
STATISTICAL PLATEAUS: 100-yard receiving games: 2003 (5), 2004 (2). Total: 7.

			RUSHING				RECEIVING				PUNT RETURNS				TOTALS			
Year Team	G	GS	Att.	Yds.	Avg.	TD	No.	Yds.	Avg.	TD	No.	Yds.	Avg.	TD	TD	2pt.	Pts.	Fum.
2003—Arizona NFL	16	16	5	40	8.0	0	101	1377	13.6	8	20	130	6.5	0	8	0	48	3
2004—Arizona NFL	10	9	1	3	3.0	0	56	623	11.1	1	0	0	0.0	0	1	0	6	1
Pro totals (2 years)	26	25	6	43	7.2	0	157	2000	12.7	9	20	130	6.5	0	9	0	54	4

BOLLER, KYLE — QB — RAVENS

PERSONAL: Born June 17, 1981, in Burbank, Calif. ... 6-3/220.
HIGH SCHOOL: Hart (Newhall, Calif.).
COLLEGE: California.
TRANSACTIONS/CAREER NOTES: Selected by Baltimore Ravens in first round (19th pick overall) of 2003 NFL draft. ... Signed by Ravens (July 31, 2003).
SINGLE GAME HIGHS (regular season): Attempts—43 (September 7, 2003, vs. Pittsburgh); completions—24 (October 31, 2004, vs. Philadelphia); yards—302 (October 19, 2003, vs. Cincinnati); and touchdown passes—4 (December 12, 2004, vs. New York Giants).
STATISTICAL PLATEAUS: 300-yard passing games: 2003 (1). Total: 1.
MISCELLANEOUS: Regular-season record as starting NFL quarterback: 14-11 (.560).

			PASSING								RUSHING				TOTALS		
Year Team	G	GS	Att.	Cmp.	Pct.	Yds.	TD	Int.	Avg.	Skd.	Rat.	Att.	Yds.	Avg.	TD	TD	2pt.	Pts.
2003—Baltimore NFL	11	9	224	116	51.8	1260	7	9	5.63	17	62.4	30	62	2.1	0	0	0	0
2004—Baltimore NFL	16	16	464	258	55.6	2559	13	11	5.52	35	70.9	53	189	3.6	1	1	0	6
Pro totals (2 years)	27	25	688	374	54.4	3819	20	20	5.55	52	68.1	83	251	3.0	1	1	0	6

BOLLINGER, BROOKS — QB — JETS

PERSONAL: Born November 15, 1979, in Grand Forks, N.D. ... 6-1/205.
HIGH SCHOOL: Central (Grand Forks, N.D.).
COLLEGE: Wisconsin.
TRANSACTIONS/CAREER NOTES: Selected by New York Jets in sixth round (200th pick overall) of 2003 NFL draft.
SINGLE GAME HIGHS (regular season): Attempts—9 (November 28, 2004, vs. Arizona); completions—5 (November 28, 2004, vs. Arizona); yards—60 (November 28, 2004, vs. Arizona); and touchdown passes—0.

			PASSING								RUSHING				TOTALS		
Year Team	G	GS	Att.	Cmp.	Pct.	Yds.	TD	Int.	Avg.	Skd.	Rat.	Att.	Yds.	Avg.	TD	TD	2pt.	Pts.
2004—New York Jets NFL	1	0	9	5	55.6	60	0	0	6.67	1	76.2	1	2	2.0	0	0	0	0

BOOKER, MARTY — WR — DOLPHINS

PERSONAL: Born July 31, 1976, in Marrero, La. ... 6-0/212. ... Full name: Marty Montez Booker.
HIGH SCHOOL: Jonesboro-Hodge (Jonesboro, La.).
COLLEGE: Louisiana-Monroe.
TRANSACTIONS/CAREER NOTES: Selected by Chicago Bears in third round (78th pick overall) of 1999 NFL draft. ... Signed by Bears (July 22, 1999). ... Granted free agency (March 1, 2002). ... Re-signed by Bears (June 21, 2002). ... Traded by Bears to Miami Dolphins with a third-round pick (LB Channing Crowder) in 2005 draft for DE Adewale Ogunleye (August 23, 2004).
HONORS: Played in Pro Bowl (2002 season).
SINGLE GAME HIGHS (regular season): Receptions—12 (October 7, 2002, vs. Green Bay); yards—198 (September 8, 2002, vs. Minnesota); and touchdown receptions—3 (November 18, 2001, vs. Tampa Bay).
STATISTICAL PLATEAUS: 100-yard receiving games: 1999 (1), 2001 (2), 2002 (3), 2003 (1), 2004 (1). Total: 8.

| | | | RECEIVING | | | | TOTALS | | | |
Year Team	G	GS	No.	Yds.	Avg.	TD	TD	2pt.	Pts.	Fum.
1999—Chicago NFL	9	4	19	219	11.5	3	3	0	18	0
2000—Chicago NFL	15	7	47	490	10.4	2	2	0	12	2
2001—Chicago NFL	16	16	100	1071	10.7	8	8	0	48	2
2002—Chicago NFL	16	16	97	1189	12.3	6	6	0	36	0
2003—Chicago NFL	13	13	52	715	13.8	4	4	0	24	1
2004—Miami NFL	15	15	50	638	12.8	1	1	0	6	0
Pro totals (6 years)	84	71	365	4322	11.8	24	24	0	144	5

B

BOONE, ALFONSO — DT — BEARS

PERSONAL: Born January 11, 1976, in Saginaw, Mich. ... 6-4/318.
HIGH SCHOOL: Arthur Hill (Saginaw, Mich.).
JUNIOR COLLEGE: Mount San Antonio J.C.
COLLEGE: Central State (did not play football).
TRANSACTIONS/CAREER NOTES: Selected after sophomore season by Detroit Lions in seventh round (253rd pick overall) of 2000 NFL draft. ... Signed by Lions (July 16, 2000). ... Released by Lions (August 27, 2000). ... Re-signed by Lions to practice squad (August 29, 2000). ... Signed by Chicago Bears off Lions practice squad (November 21, 2000). ... Inactive for five games (2000).

| | | | TOTALS | | |
Year Team	G	GS	Tk.	Ast.	Sks.
2001—Chicago NFL	11	0	7	2	2.0
2002—Chicago NFL	16	5	19	2	1.5
2003—Chicago NFL	16	6	24	1	1.0
2004—Chicago NFL	12	2	8	3	2.5
Pro totals (4 years)	55	13	58	11	7.0

BOSCHETTI, RYAN — DT — REDSKINS

PERSONAL: Born October 7, 1981, in Belmont, Calif. ... 6-4/300. ... Full name: Ryan S. Boschetti.
HIGH SCHOOL: Carlmont (Belmont, Calif).
JUNIOR COLLEGE: College of San Mateo (Calif.).
COLLEGE: UCLA.
TRANSACTIONS/CAREER NOTES: Signed as non-drafted free agent by Washington Redskins (April 29, 2004). ... Released by Redskins (September 5, 2004). ... Re-signed by Redskins to practice squad (September 6, 2004). ... Activated (November 26, 2004).

| | | | TOTALS | | |
Year Team	G	GS	Tk.	Ast.	Sks.
2004—Washington NFL	3	1	3	3	0.0

BOSTON, DAVID — WR — DOLPHINS

PERSONAL: Born August 19, 1978, in Houston, Texas. ... 6-2/240.
HIGH SCHOOL: Humble (Texas).
COLLEGE: Ohio State.
TRANSACTIONS/CAREER NOTES: Selected after junior season by Arizona Cardinals in first round (eighth pick overall) of 1999 NFL draft. ... Signed by Cardinals (August 2, 1999). ... Granted unconditional free agency (February 28, 2003). ... Signed by San Diego Chargers (March 5, 2003). ... Suspended by Chargers for conduct detrimental to team (September 25, 2003). ... Reinstated (September 29, 2003). ... Traded by Chargers to Miami Dolphins for a sixth-round pick (G Wes Sims) in 2005 draft and a player to be named (March 15, 2004). San Diego acquired CB Jamar Fletcher (March 16, 2004). ... On injured reserve with knee injury (August 31, 2004-entire season). ... Released by Dolphins (March 7, 2005). ... Re-signed by Dolphins (May 18, 2005).
HONORS: Named wide receiver on THE SPORTING NEWS college All-America second team (1998). ... Named wide receiver on THE SPORTING NEWS NFL All-Pro team (2001). ... Played in Pro Bowl (2001 season).
SINGLE GAME HIGHS (regular season): Receptions—14 (October 5, 2003, vs. Jacksonville); yards—184 (December 3, 2003, vs. Cincinnati); and touchdown receptions—2 (November 23, 2003, vs. Cincinnati).
STATISTICAL PLATEAUS: 100-yard receiving games: 1999 (1), 2000 (4), 2001 (9), 2002 (2), 2003 (2). Total: 18.

| | | | RUSHING | | | | RECEIVING | | | | PUNT RETURNS | | | | TOTALS | | | |
Year Team	G	GS	Att.	Yds.	Avg.	TD	No.	Yds.	Avg.	TD	No.	Yds.	Avg.	TD	TD	2pt.	Pts.	Fum.
1999—Arizona NFL	16	8	5	0	0.0	0	40	473	11.8	2	7	62	8.9	0	2	0	12	2
2000—Arizona NFL	16	16	3	9	3.0	0	71	1156	16.3	7	0	0	0.0	0	7	0	42	2
2001—Arizona NFL	16	16	5	35	7.0	0	98	*1598	16.3	8	0	0	0.0	0	8	0	48	1
2002—Arizona NFL	8	8	2	29	14.5	0	32	512	16.0	1	0	0	0.0	0	1	0	6	0
2003—San Diego NFL	14	14	3	18	6.0	0	70	880	12.6	7	0	0	0.0	0	7	1	44	2
2004—Miami NFL						Did not play.												
Pro totals (5 years)	70	62	18	91	5.1	0	311	4619	14.9	25	7	62	8.9	0	25	1	152	7

BOULWARE, MICHAEL — SS/LB — SEAHAWKS

PERSONAL: Born September 17, 1981, in Columbia, S.C. ... 6-3/223. ... Brother of Peter Boulware, linebacker, Baltimore Ravens (1997-2004).
HIGH SCHOOL: Spring Valley (Columbia, S.C.).
COLLEGE: Florida State.
TRANSACTIONS/CAREER NOTES: Selected by Seattle Seahawks in second round (53rd pick overall) of 2004 NFL draft. ... Signed by Seahawks (July 28, 2004).

Year Team	G	GS	TOTALS Tk.	Ast.	Sks.	INTERCEPTIONS No.	Yds.	Avg.	TD
2004—Seattle NFL	16	4	40	13	1.0	5	69	13.8	1

BOULWARE, PETER — LB

PERSONAL: Born December 18, 1974, in Columbia, S.C. ... 6-4/255. ... Full name: Peter Nicholas Boulware. ... Name pronounced: BOWL-ware. ... Brother of Michael Boulware, linebacker, Seattle Seahawks.
HIGH SCHOOL: Spring Valley (Columbia, S.C.).
COLLEGE: Florida State.
TRANSACTIONS/CAREER NOTES: Selected after junior season by Baltimore Ravens in first round (fourth pick overall) of 1997 NFL draft. ... Signed by Ravens (August 16, 1997). ... On physically unable to perform list with ankle injury (July 26-August 16, 2002). ... On physically unable to perform list with knee and toe injuries (September 4, 2004-entire season). ... Released by Ravens (May 11, 2005).
CHAMPIONSHIP GAME EXPERIENCE: Played in AFC championship game (2000 season). ... Member of Super Bowl championship team (2000 season).
HONORS: Named defensive end on THE SPORTING NEWS college All-America first team (1996). ... Played in Pro Bowl (1998, 1999 and 2002 seasons). ... Named to play in Pro Bowl (2003 season); replaced by Willie McGinest due to injury.
MISCELLANEOUS: Holds Baltimore Ravens all-time record for most sacks (67.5).

Year Team	G	GS	TOTALS Tk.	Ast.	Sks.	INTERCEPTIONS No.	Yds.	Avg.	TD
1997—Baltimore NFL	16	16	43	15	11.5	0	0	0.0	0
1998—Baltimore NFL	16	16	38	23	8.5	0	0	0.0	0
1999—Baltimore NFL	16	11	31	8	10.0	0	0	0.0	0
2000—Baltimore NFL	16	15	33	6	7.0	0	0	0.0	0
2001—Baltimore NFL	16	14	45	22	§15.0	0	0	0.0	0
2002—Baltimore NFL	16	16	57	16	7.0	1	6	6.0	0
2003—Baltimore NFL	15	14	42	16	8.5	0	0	0.0	0
2004—Baltimore NFL	Did not play.								
Pro totals (7 years)	111	102	289	106	67.5	1	6	6.0	0

BOUMAN, TODD — QB — SAINTS

PERSONAL: Born August 1, 1972, in Ruthton, Minn. ... 6-2/226. ... Name pronounced: Bow-man.
HIGH SCHOOL: Ruthton (Minn.).
COLLEGE: St. Cloud State.
TRANSACTIONS/CAREER NOTES: Signed as non-drafted free agent by Minnesota Vikings (April 25, 1997). ... Released by Vikings (August 23, 1997). ... Re-signed by Vikings to practice squad (August 25, 1997). ... Activated (December 5, 1997). ... Inactive for all 16 games (1999). ... Assigned by Vikings to Barcelona Dragons in 1999 NFL Europe enhancement allocation program (February 22, 1999). ... Inactive for all 16 games (2000). ... Traded by Vikings to New Orleans Saints for sixth-round pick (LB Mike Nattiel) in 2003 draft (March 13, 2003).
CHAMPIONSHIP GAME EXPERIENCE: Member of Vikings for NFC championship game (1998 and 2000 seasons); inactive.
SINGLE GAME HIGHS (regular season): Attempts—38 (December 16, 2001, vs. Detroit); completions—21 (December 9, 2001, vs. Tennessee); yards—348 (December 9, 2001, vs. Tennessee); and touchdown passes—4 (December 9, 2001, vs. Tennessee).
STATISTICAL PLATEAUS: 300-yard passing games: 2001 (1). Total: 1.
MISCELLANEOUS: Regular-season record as starting NFL quarterback: 1-2 (.333).

Year Team	G	GS	PASSING Att.	Cmp.	Pct.	Yds.	TD	Int.	Avg.	Skd.	Rat.	RUSHING Att.	Yds.	Avg.	TD	TOTALS TD	2pt.	Pts.
2000—Minnesota NFL	Did not play.																	
2001—Minnesota NFL	5	3	89	51	57.3	795	8	4	8.93	4	98.3	9	61	6.8	0	0	0	0
2002—Minnesota NFL	1	0	6	3	50.0	85	0	0	14.17	2	95.8	1	9	9.0	0	0	0	0
2003—New Orleans NFL	4	0	13	7	53.8	81	1	0	6.23	2	98.6	3	1	0.3	0	0	0	0
2004—New Orleans NFL	16	0	0	0	0.0	0	0	0	0.00	0	0.0	0	0	0.0	0	0	0	0
Pro totals (4 years)	26	3	108	61	56.5	961	9	4	8.90	8	98.6	13	71	5.5	0	0	0	0

BOWEN, MATT — S — REDSKINS

PERSONAL: Born November 12, 1976, in Glen Ellyn, Ill. ... 6-1/207.
HIGH SCHOOL: Glenbard West (Glen Ellyn, Ill.).
COLLEGE: Iowa.
TRANSACTIONS/CAREER NOTES: Selected by St. Louis Rams in sixth round (198th pick overall) of 2000 NFL draft. ... Signed by Rams (July 7, 2000). ... On injured reserve with broken foot (October 3-November 6, 2001). ... Released by Rams (November 6, 2001). ... Signed by Green Bay Packers (November 30, 2001). ... Granted free agency (February 28, 2003). ... Tendered offer sheet by Washington Redskins (March 8, 2003). ... Packers declined to match offer (March 11, 2003). ... On injured reserve with knee injury (October 13, 2004-remainder of season).

Year Team	G	GS	TOTALS Tk.	Ast.	Sks.	INTERCEPTIONS No.	Yds.	Avg.	TD
2000—St. Louis NFL	16	2	14	2	0.0	0	0	0.0	0
2001—St. Louis NFL	1	0	0	0	0.0	0	0	0.0	0
—Green Bay NFL	5	0	0	0	0.0	0	0	0.0	0

Year—Team	G	GS	TOTALS Tk.	Ast.	Sks.	INTERCEPTIONS No.	Yds.	Avg.	TD
2002—Green Bay NFL	16	6	29	16	0.0	1	0	0.0	0
2003—Washington NFL	16	16	76	9	0.0	3	44	14.7	0
2004—Washington NFL	5	5	17	4	2.0	0	0	0.0	0
Pro totals (5 years)	59	29	136	31	2.0	4	44	11.0	0

BOWENS, DAVID — DE — DOLPHINS

PERSONAL: Born July 3, 1977, in Denver, Colo. ... 6-3/260. ... Full name: David Walter Bowens.
HIGH SCHOOL: St. Mary's (Orchard Lake, Mich.).
COLLEGE: Western Illinois.
TRANSACTIONS/CAREER NOTES: Selected after junior season by Denver Broncos in fifth round (158th pick overall) of 1999 NFL draft. ... Signed by Broncos (July 22, 1999). ... Traded by Broncos to Green Bay Packers for fourth-round pick (C Ben Hamilton) in 2001 draft (February 24, 2000). ... Traded by Packers to Buffalo Bills for TE Bobby Collins (August 7, 2001). ... Claimed on waivers by Washington Redskins (September 3, 2001). ... Released by Redskins (September 26, 2001). ... Signed by Miami Dolphins (October 22, 2001). ... Granted unconditional free agency (February 28, 2003). ... Re-signed by Dolphins (March 6, 2003). ... On active/non-football injury list with knee injury (July 24-November 25, 2003).

Year—Team	G	GS	TOTALS Tk.	Ast.	Sks.
1999—Denver NFL	16	0	7	0	1.0
2000—Green Bay NFL	14	0	19	7	3.5
2001—Miami NFL	8	0	5	1	1.0
2002—Miami NFL	14	0	9	7	1.5
2003—Miami NFL	4	0	2	0	1.0
2004—Miami NFL	16	15	26	14	7.0
Pro totals (6 years)	72	15	68	29	15.0

BOWENS, TIM — DT — DOLPHINS

PERSONAL: Born February 7, 1973, in Okolona, Miss. ... 6-4/325. ... Full name: Timothy L. Bowens.
HIGH SCHOOL: Okolona (Miss.).
JUNIOR COLLEGE: Itawamba Community College (Miss.).
COLLEGE: Mississippi.
TRANSACTIONS/CAREER NOTES: Selected after junior season by Miami Dolphins in first round (20th pick overall) of 1994 NFL draft. ... Signed by Dolphins (June 2, 1994). ... Designated by Dolphins as franchise player (February 13, 1998). ... Re-signed by Dolphins (August 21, 1998). ... On injured reserve with torn biceps muscle (January 3, 1999-remainder of playoffs). ... Released by Dolphins (February 28, 2002). ... Re-signed by Dolphins (February 28, 2002). ... On injured reserve with back injury (October 27, 2004-remainder of season).
HONORS: Named to play in Pro Bowl (1998 season); replaced by Cortez Kennedy due to injury. ... Played in Pro Bowl (2002 season).

Year—Team	G	GS	TOTALS Tk.	Ast.	Sks.	INTERCEPTIONS No.	Yds.	Avg.	TD
1994—Miami NFL	16	15	44	8	3.0	0	0	0.0	0
1995—Miami NFL	16	16	34	7	2.0	0	0	0.0	0
1996—Miami NFL	16	16	41	7	3.0	0	0	0.0	0
1997—Miami NFL	16	16	34	14	5.0	0	0	0.0	0
1998—Miami NFL	16	16	21	9	0.0	0	0	0.0	0
1999—Miami NFL	16	15	18	16	1.5	0	0	0.0	0
2000—Miami NFL	15	15	29	11	2.5	1	0	0.0	0
2001—Miami NFL	15	15	30	18	3.0	0	0	0.0	0
2002—Miami NFL	16	16	24	12	0.0	0	0	0.0	0
2003—Miami NFL	13	13	20	7	2.0	0	0	0.0	0
2004—Miami NFL	2	2	2	1	0.0	0	0	0.0	0
Pro totals (11 years)	157	155	297	110	22.0	1	0	0.0	0

BOYER, BRANT — LB — BROWNS

PERSONAL: Born June 27, 1971, in Ogden, Utah. ... 6-1/240. ... Full name: Brant T. Boyer.
HIGH SCHOOL: North Summit (Coalville, Utah).
JUNIOR COLLEGE: Snow College (Utah).
COLLEGE: Arizona.
TRANSACTIONS/CAREER NOTES: Selected by Miami Dolphins in sixth round (177th pick overall) of 1994 NFL draft. ... Signed by Dolphins (July 11, 1994). ... Released by Dolphins (September 21, 1994). ... Re-signed by Dolphins to practice squad (September 22, 1994). ... Activated (October 5, 1994). ... Selected by Jacksonville Jaguars from Dolphins in NFL expansion draft (February 15, 1995). ... Released by Jaguars (August 27, 1995). ... Re-signed by Jaguars (December 13, 1995). ... Released by Jaguars (August 25, 1996). ... Re-signed by Jaguars (September 24, 1996). ... Released by Jaguars (September 25, 1996). ... Re-signed by Jaguars (September 27, 1996). ... Granted free agency (February 13, 1998). ... Re-signed by Jaguars (March 18, 1998). ... On injured reserve with neck injury (December 2, 1998-remainder of season). ... Granted unconditional free agency (February 12, 1999). ... Re-signed by Jaguars (March 15, 1999). ... Released by Jaguars (March 1, 2001). ... Signed by Cleveland Browns (March 12, 2001). ... On injured reserve with foot injury (August 30, 2004-entire season).
CHAMPIONSHIP GAME EXPERIENCE: Played in AFC championship game (1996 and 1999 seasons).

Year—Team	G	GS	TOTALS Tk.	Ast.	Sks.	INTERCEPTIONS No.	Yds.	Avg.	TD
1994—Miami NFL	14	0	1	1	0.0	0	0	0.0	0
1995—Jacksonville NFL	2	0	0	0	0.0	0	0	0.0	0
1996—Jacksonville NFL	12	0	4	1	0.0	0	0	0.0	0
1997—Jacksonville NFL	16	2	18	6	1.5	0	0	0.0	0
1998—Jacksonville NFL	11	0	10	2	1.0	0	0	0.0	0

Year Team	G	GS	TOTALS			INTERCEPTIONS			
			Tk.	Ast.	Sks.	No.	Yds.	Avg.	TD
1999—Jacksonville NFL	15	0	18	5	4.0	1	5	5.0	0
2000—Jacksonville NFL	12	5	19	4	3.5	1	12	12.0	0
2001—Cleveland NFL	16	1	50	15	0.0	2	12	6.0	0
2002—Cleveland NFL	16	1	34	7	3.0	1	1	1.0	0
2003—Cleveland NFL	15	7	39	16	0.0	1	4	4.0	0
2004—Cleveland NFL	Did not play.								
Pro totals (10 years)	129	16	193	57	13.0	6	34	5.7	0

BRACKETT, GARY — LB — COLTS

PERSONAL: Born May 23, 1980, in Glassboro, N.J. ... 5-11/235.
COLLEGE: Rutgers.
TRANSACTIONS/CAREER NOTES: Signed as non-drafted free agent by Indianapolis Colts (May 2, 2003).
CHAMPIONSHIP GAME EXPERIENCE: Played in AFC championship game (2003 season).

Year Team	G	GS	TOTALS			INTERCEPTIONS			
			Tk.	Ast.	Sks.	No.	Yds.	Avg.	TD
2003—Indianapolis NFL	16	0	12	2	1.0	1	31	31.0	1
2004—Indianapolis NFL	15	1	12	9	0.0	2	2	1.0	0
Pro totals (2 years)	31	1	24	11	1.0	3	33	11.0	1

BRADFORD, COREY — WR

PERSONAL: Born December 8, 1975, in Baton Rouge, La. ... 6-1/201. ... Full name: Corey Lamon Bradford.
HIGH SCHOOL: Clinton (La.).
JUNIOR COLLEGE: Hinds Community College (Miss.).
COLLEGE: Jackson State.
TRANSACTIONS/CAREER NOTES: Selected by Green Bay Packers in fifth round (150th pick overall) of 1998 NFL draft. ... Signed by Packers (July 17, 1998). ... Re-signed by Packers (March 20, 2001). ... Granted free agency (March 2, 2001). ... Granted unconditional free agency (March 1, 2002). ... Signed by Houston Texans (March 11, 2002). ... Granted unconditional free agency (March 2, 2005).
SINGLE GAME HIGHS (regular season): Receptions—7 (September 29, 2002, vs. Philadelphia); yards—217 (October 12, 2003, vs. Tennessee); and touchdown receptions—2 (October 20, 2002, vs. Cleveland).
STATISTICAL PLATEAUS: 100-yard receiving games: 1999 (1), 2001 (2), 2002 (1), 2003 (1). Total: 5.
MISCELLANEOUS: Holds Houston Texans all-time record for most touchdown receptions (13).

Year Team	G	GS	RECEIVING				TOTALS			
			No.	Yds.	Avg.	TD	TD	2pt.	Pts.	Fum.
1998—Green Bay NFL	8	0	3	27	9.0	0	0	0	0	1
1999—Green Bay NFL	16	2	37	637	17.2	5	5	1	32	1
2000—Green Bay NFL	2	2	0	0	0.0	0	0	0	0	0
2001—Green Bay NFL	16	6	31	526	17.0	2	2	0	12	1
2002—Houston NFL	16	16	45	697	15.5	6	6	0	36	0
2003—Houston NFL	16	6	24	460	19.2	4	4	0	24	0
2004—Houston NFL	15	10	27	399	14.8	3	3	0	18	0
Pro totals (7 years)	89	42	167	2746	16.4	20	20	1	122	3

BRADLEY, JON

PERSONAL: Born January 13, 1981, in West Helena, Ark. ... 6-0/301.
HIGH SCHOOL: Barton (Ark.).
COLLEGE: Arkansas State.
TRANSACTIONS/CAREER NOTES: Signed as non-drafted free agent by Philadelphia Eagles (April 27, 2004). ... Released by Eagles (September 5, 2004). ... Signed by Tampa Bay Buccaneers to practice squad (October 20, 2004). ... Activated (November 6, 2004). ... Released by Buccaneers (December 17, 2004). ... Re-signed by Buccaneers to practice squad (December 18, 2004). ... Activated (January 10, 2005).

Year Team	G	GS	TOTALS		
			Tk.	Ast.	Sks.
2004—Tampa Bay NFL	6	0	5	0	1.0

BRADY, KYLE — TE — JAGUARS

PERSONAL: Born January 14, 1972, in New Cumberland, Pa. ... 6-6/278. ... Full name: Kyle James Brady.
HIGH SCHOOL: Cedar Cliff (Camp Hill, Pa.).
COLLEGE: Penn State.
TRANSACTIONS/CAREER NOTES: Selected by New York Jets in first round (ninth pick overall) of 1995 NFL draft. ... Signed by Jets (July 17, 1995). ... Designated by Jets as transition player (February 12, 1999). ... Tendered offer sheet by Jacksonville Jaguars (February 16, 1999). ... Jets declined to match offer (February 18, 1999).
CHAMPIONSHIP GAME EXPERIENCE: Played in AFC championship game (1998 and 1999 seasons).
HONORS: Named tight end on THE SPORTING NEWS college All-America second team (1994).
SINGLE GAME HIGHS (regular season): Receptions—10 (October 29, 2000, vs. Dallas); yards—138 (October 29, 2000, vs. Dallas); and touchdown receptions—2 (October 19, 1998, vs. New England).
STATISTICAL PLATEAUS: 100-yard receiving games: 2000 (2). Total: 2.

Year Team	G	GS	RECEIVING				TOTALS			
			No.	Yds.	Avg.	TD	TD	2pt.	Pts.	Fum.
1995—New York Jets NFL	15	11	26	252	9.7	2	2	0	12	0
1996—New York Jets NFL	16	16	15	144	9.6	1	1	1	8	1
1997—New York Jets NFL	16	14	22	238	10.8	2	2	0	12	1
1998—New York Jets NFL	16	16	30	315	10.5	5	5	0	30	1
1999—Jacksonville NFL	13	12	32	346	10.8	1	1	1	8	0
2000—Jacksonville NFL	16	15	64	729	11.4	3	3	1	20	0
2001—Jacksonville NFL	16	16	36	386	10.7	2	2	0	12	0
2002—Jacksonville NFL	16	16	43	461	10.7	4	4	0	24	0
2003—Jacksonville NFL	16	14	29	281	9.7	1	1	0	6	3
2004—Jacksonville NFL	11	8	14	103	7.4	1	1	0	6	0
Pro totals (10 years)	151	138	311	3255	10.5	22	22	3	138	6

BRADY, TOM — QB — PATRIOTS

PERSONAL: Born August 3, 1977, in San Mateo, Calif. ... 6-4/225. ... Full name: Thomas Brady.
HIGH SCHOOL: Serra (San Mateo, Calif.).
COLLEGE: Michigan.
TRANSACTIONS/CAREER NOTES: Selected by New England Patriots in sixth round (199th pick overall) of 2000 NFL draft. ... Signed by Patriots (July 14, 2000).
CHAMPIONSHIP GAME EXPERIENCE: Played in AFC championship game (2001, 2003 and 2004 seasons). ... Member of Super Bowl championship team (2001, 2003 and 2004 seasons).
HONORS: Named Most Valuable Player of Super Bowl 36 (2001 season) and Super Bowl 38 (2003 season). ... Played in Pro Bowl (2001, 2003 and 2004 seasons).
SINGLE GAME HIGHS (regular season): Attempts—55 (November 10, 2002, vs. Chicago); completions—39 (September 22, 2002, vs. Kansas City); yards—410 (September 22, 2002, vs. Kansas City); and touchdown passes—4 (September 22, 2002, vs. Kansas City).
STATISTICAL PLATEAUS: 300-yard passing games: 2001 (1), 2002 (3), 2003 (2), 2004 (2). Total: 8.
MISCELLANEOUS: Selected by Montreal Expos organization in 18th round of free-agent draft (June 1, 1995); did not sign. ... Regular-season record as starting NFL quarterback: 48-14 (.774). ... Postseason record as starting NFL quarterback: 9-0 (1.000).

Year Team	G	GS	PASSING								RUSHING				TOTALS		
			Att.	Cmp.	Pct.	Yds.	TD	Int.	Avg.	Skd.	Rat.	Att.	Yds.	Avg.	TD	TD	2pt.	Pts.
2000—New England NFL	1	0	3	1	33.3	6	0	0	2.00	0	42.4	0	0	0.0	0	0	0	0
2001—New England NFL	15	14	413	264	63.9	2843	18	12	6.88	41	86.5	36	43	1.2	0	0	0	0
2002—New England NFL	16	16	601	373	62.1	3764	*28	14	6.26	31	85.7	42	110	2.6	1	1	0	6
2003—New England NFL	16	16	527	317	60.2	3620	23	12	6.87	32	85.9	42	63	1.5	1	1	0	6
2004—New England NFL	16	16	474	288	60.8	3692	28	14	7.79	26	92.6	43	28	0.7	0	0	0	0
Pro totals (5 years)	64	62	2018	1243	61.6	13925	97	52	6.90	130	87.5	163	244	1.5	2	2	0	12

BRAHAM, RICH — C/G — BENGALS

PERSONAL: Born November 6, 1970, in Morgantown, W.Va. ... 6-4/305. ... Name pronounced: BRAY-um.
HIGH SCHOOL: University (Morgantown, W.Va.).
COLLEGE: West Virginia.
TRANSACTIONS/CAREER NOTES: Selected by Arizona Cardinals in third round (76th pick overall) of 1994 NFL draft. ... Signed by Cardinals (July 30, 1994). ... Claimed on waivers by Cincinnati Bengals (November 18, 1994). ... On injured reserve with ankle injury (August 29, 1995-entire season). ... Granted free agency (February 14, 1997). ... Tendered offer sheet by New England Patriots (April 8, 1997). ... Offer matched by Bengals (April 15, 1997). ... On injured reserve with knee injury (December 3, 1998-remainder of season). ... Granted unconditional free agency (March 2, 2001). ... Re-signed by Bengals (March 12, 2001). ... Granted free agency (February 28, 2003). ... Re-signed by Bengals (April 30, 2003). ... Granted unconditional free agency (March 3, 2004). ... Re-signed by Bengals (March 8, 2004). ... On injured reserve with knee injury (December 18, 2004-remainder of season). ... Granted unconditional free agency (March 2, 2005). ... Re-signed by Bengals (May 13, 2005).
PLAYING EXPERIENCE: Cincinnati NFL, 1994-2004. ... Games/Games started: 1994 (3/0), 1996 (16/16), 1997 (16/16), 1998 (12/12), 1999 (16/16), 2000 (9/9), 2001 (16/16), 2002 (15/15), 2003 (16/15), 2004 (10/10). Total: 129/125.
HONORS: Named offensive lineman on THE SPORTING NEWS college All-America second team (1993).

BRANCH, COLIN — S — PANTHERS

PERSONAL: Born March 2, 1980, in Cincinnati, Ohio. ... 5-11/205. ... Brother of Calvin Branch, safety with Oakland Raiders (1997-2000).
HIGH SCHOOL: Carlsbad (Calif.).
COLLEGE: Stanford.
TRANSACTIONS/CAREER NOTES: Selected by Carolina Panthers in fourth round (119th pick overall) of 2003 NFL draft. ... Signed by Panthers (July 26, 2003).
CHAMPIONSHIP GAME EXPERIENCE: Played in NFC championship game (2003 season). ... Played in Super Bowl 38 (2003 season).

Year Team	G	GS	TOTALS			INTERCEPTIONS			
			Tk.	Ast.	Sks.	No.	Yds.	Avg.	TD
2003—Carolina NFL	16	0	2	0	0.0	0	0	0.0	0
2004—Carolina NFL	16	15	40	14	0.0	3	79	26.3	0
Pro totals (2 years)	32	15	42	14	0.0	3	79	26.3	0

BRANCH, DEION — WR — PATRIOTS

PERSONAL: Born July 18, 1979, in Albany, Ga. ... 5-9/193. ... Full name: Anthony Branch.
HIGH SCHOOL: Monroe (Ga.).
JUNIOR COLLEGE: Jones County (Miss.).

COLLEGE: Louisville.
TRANSACTIONS/CAREER NOTES: Selected by New England Patriots in second round (65th pick overall) of 2002 NFL draft.
CHAMPIONSHIP GAME EXPERIENCE: Played in AFC championship game (2003 and 2004 seasons). ... Member of Super Bowl championship team (2003 and 2004 seasons).
HONORS: Named wide receiver on THE SPORTING NEWS college All-America third team (2001). ... Named Most Valuable Player of Super Bowl 39 (2004 season).
POST SEASON RECORDS: Shares Super Bowl single-game record for most receptions—11 (February 6, 2005, vs. Philadelphia).
SINGLE GAME HIGHS (regular season): Receptions—13 (September 29, 2002, vs. San Diego); yards—128 (September 29, 2002, vs. San Diego); and touchdown receptions—1 (January 2, 2005, vs. San Francisco).
STATISTICAL PLATEAUS: 100-yard receiving games: 2002 (2), 2003 (1), 2004 (1). Total: 3.

			RECEIVING				PUNT RETURNS				KICKOFF RETURNS				TOTALS			
Year Team	G	GS	No.	Yds.	Avg.	TD	No.	Yds.	Avg.	TD	No.	Yds.	Avg.	TD	TD	2pt.	Pts.	Fum.
2002—New England NFL.......	13	7	43	489	11.4	2	2	58	29.0	0	36	863	24.0	0	2	0	12	1
2003—New England NFL.......	15	12	57	803	14.1	3	4	26	6.5	0	0	0	0.0	0	3	0	18	0
2004—New England NFL.......	9	9	35	454	13.0	4	1	0	0.0	0	0	0	0.0	0	4	0	24	1
Pro totals (3 years)	37	28	135	1746	12.9	9	7	84	12.0	0	36	863	24.0	0	9	0	54	2

BRANDON, SAM — S — BRONCOS

PERSONAL: Born July 5, 1979, in Toledo, Ohio. ... 6-2/200.
HIGH SCHOOL: Riverside (Calif.).
COLLEGE: Nevada-Las Vegas.
TRANSACTIONS/CAREER NOTES: Selected by Denver Broncos in fourth round (131st pick overall) of 2002 NFL draft. ... Signed by Broncos (July 19, 2002). ... Granted free agency (March 2, 2005). ... Re-signed by Broncos (May 3, 2005).

			TOTALS			INTERCEPTIONS			
Year Team	G	GS	Tk.	Ast.	Sks.	No.	Yds.	Avg.	TD
2002—Denver NFL	16	2	14	3	0.0	0	0	0.0	0
2003—Denver NFL	16	10	33	14	0.0	1	0	0.0	0
2004—Denver NFL	9	0	0	0	0.0	0	0	0.0	0
Pro totals (3 years)	41	12	47	17	0.0	1	0	0.0	0

BRANDT, DAVID — C — CHARGERS

PERSONAL: Born September 25, 1977, in Grand Rapids, Mich. ... 6-4/311.
HIGH SCHOOL: Jenison (Mich.).
COLLEGE: Michigan.
TRANSACTIONS/CAREER NOTES: Signed as non-drafted free agent by Washington Redskins (April 25, 2002). ... Announced retirement (July 24, 2002). ... Traded by Redskins to Green Bay Packers for conditional seventh-round pick in 2004 draft (March 31, 2003). ... Released by Packers (September 1, 2003). ... Signed by San Diego Chargers (October 8, 2003). ... Released by Chargers (March 2, 2004). ... Re-signed by Chargers (March 11, 2004). ... Released by Chargers (December 11, 2004). ... Re-signed by Chargers (March 4, 2005).
PLAYING EXPERIENCE: Washington NFL, 2001; San Diego NFL, 2004. ... Games/Games started: 2001 (13/1), 2004 (3/0). Total: 16/1.

BRAYTON, TYLER — DE — RAIDERS

PERSONAL: Born November 20, 1979, in Richland, Wash. ... 6-6/280.
HIGH SCHOOL: Pasco (Wash.).
COLLEGE: Colorado.
TRANSACTIONS/CAREER NOTES: Selected by Oakland Raiders in first round (32nd pick overall) of 2003 NFL draft. ... Signed by Raiders (July 24, 2003).

			TOTALS			INTERCEPTIONS			
Year Team	G	GS	Tk.	Ast.	Sks.	No.	Yds.	Avg.	TD
2003—Oakland NFL	16	16	48	13	2.5	0	0	0.0	0
2004—Oakland NFL	15	15	37	8	2.5	1	24	24.0	0
Pro totals (2 years)	31	31	85	21	5.0	1	24	24.0	0

BREES, DREW — QB — CHARGERS

PERSONAL: Born January 15, 1979, in Austin, Texas. ... 6-0/209. ... Full name: Drew Christopher Brees.
HIGH SCHOOL: Westlake (Austin, Texas).
COLLEGE: Purdue.
TRANSACTIONS/CAREER NOTES: Selected by San Diego Chargers in second round (32nd pick overall) of 2001 NFL draft. ... Signed by Chargers (August 7, 2001). ... Designated by Chargers as franchise player (February 22, 2005). ... Re-signed by Chargers (March 4, 2005).
HONORS: Named quarterback to THE SPORTING NEWS college All-America third team (2000). ... Maxwell Award winner (2000). ... Played in Pro Bowl (2004 season).
SINGLE GAME HIGHS (regular season): Attempts—50 (November 17, 2002, vs. San Francisco); completions—29 (November 17, 2002, vs. San Francisco); yards—378 (November 28, 2004, vs. Kansas City); and touchdown passes—5 (October 31, 2004, vs. Oakland).
STATISTICAL PLATEAUS: 300-yard passing games: 2002 (3), 2003 (1), 2004 (1). Total: 5.
MISCELLANEOUS: Regular-season record as starting NFL quarterback: 21-21 (.500). ... Postseason record as starting NFL quarterback: 0-1 (.000).

			PASSING										RUSHING				TOTALS		
Year Team	G	GS	Att.	Cmp.	Pct.	Yds.	TD	Int.	Avg.	Skd.	Rat.	Att.	Yds.	Avg.	TD	TD	2pt.	Pts.	
2001—San Diego NFL	1	0	27	15	55.6	221	1	0	8.19	2	94.8	2	18	9.0	0	0	0	0	
2002—San Diego NFL	16	16	526	320	60.8	3284	17	16	6.24	24	76.9	38	130	3.4	1	1	0	6	

Year Team	G	GS	PASSING								RUSHING				TOTALS		
			Att.	Cmp.	Pct.	Yds.	TD	Int.	Avg.	Skd.	Rat.	Att.	Yds.	Avg.	TD	TD	2pt.	Pts.
2003—San Diego NFL	11	11	356	205	57.6	2108	11	15	5.92	21	67.5	21	84	4.0	0	1	0	6
2004—San Diego NFL	15	15	400	262	65.5	3159	27	7	7.90	18	104.8	53	85	1.6	2	2	0	12
Pro totals (4 years)	43	42	1309	802	61.3	8772	56	38	6.70	65	83.2	114	317	2.8	3	4	0	24

BREWER, JACK   S

PERSONAL: Born January 8, 1979, in Fort Worth, Texas. ... 6-0/194.
HIGH SCHOOL: Grapevine (Texas).
COLLEGE: Minnesota.
TRANSACTIONS/CAREER NOTES: Signed as non-drafted free agent by Minnesota Vikings (April 24, 2002). ... On injured reserve with pectoral injury (November 12, 2003-remainder of season). ... Claimed on waivers by New York Giants (March 18, 2004). ... Granted free agency (March 2, 2005).

Year Team	G	GS	TOTALS			INTERCEPTIONS			
			Tk.	Ast.	Sks.	No.	Yds.	Avg.	TD
2002—Minnesota NFL	15	1	8	2	0.0	2	24	12.0	0
2003—Minnesota NFL	6	0	0	0	0.0	0	0	0.0	0
2004—New York Giants NFL	13	0	0	0	0.0	0	0	0.0	0
Pro totals (3 years)	34	1	8	2	0.0	2	24	12.0	0

BRIDGES, JEREMY   G/T   CARDINALS

PERSONAL: Born April 19, 1980, in Fort Wayne, Ind. ... 6-4/301.
HIGH SCHOOL: South Pike (McComb, Miss.).
COLLEGE: Southern Miss.
TRANSACTIONS/CAREER NOTES: Selected by Philadelphia Eagles in sixth round (185th pick overall) of 2003 NFL draft. ... Signed by Eagles (July 16, 2003). ... Inactive for all 16 games (2003). ... Claimed on waivers by Arizona Cardinals (September 6, 2004).
PLAYING EXPERIENCE: Arizona NFL, 2004. ... Games/Games started: 2004 (14/8). Total: 14/8.
CHAMPIONSHIP GAME EXPERIENCE: Member of Eagles for NFC championship game (2003 season); inactive.

BRIEN, DOUG   K   BEARS

PERSONAL: Born November 24, 1970, in Bloomfield, N.J. ... 6-0/185. ... Full name: Douglas Robert Zachariah Brien.
HIGH SCHOOL: De La Salle Catholic (Concord, Calif.).
COLLEGE: California.
TRANSACTIONS/CAREER NOTES: Selected by San Francisco 49ers in third round (85th pick overall) of 1994 NFL draft. ... Signed by 49ers (July 27, 1994). ... Released by 49ers (October 16, 1995). ... Signed by New Orleans Saints (October 31, 1995). ... Granted free agency (February 14, 1997). ... Re-signed by Saints (July 17, 1997). ... Released by Saints (March 1, 2001). ... Signed by Indianapolis Colts (December 5, 2001). ... Released by Colts (December 15, 2001). ... Signed by Tampa Bay Buccaneers (December 27, 2001). ... Granted unconditional free agency (March 1, 2002). ... Signed by Minnesota Vikings (April 29, 2002). ... On physically unable to perform list with knee injury (July 27-August 2, 2002). ... Released by Vikings (October 23, 2002). ... Signed by New York Jets (March 21, 2003). ... Granted unconditional free agency (March 3, 2004). ... Re-signed by Jets (March 6, 2004). ... Released by Jets (April 28, 2005). ... Signed by Chicago Bears (May 12, 2005).
CHAMPIONSHIP GAME EXPERIENCE: Played in NFC championship game (1994 season). ... Member of Super Bowl championship team (1994 season).
POST SEASON RECORDS: Shares Super Bowl single-game record for most extra points—7 (January 29, 1995, vs. San Diego).

Year Team	G	FIELD GOALS							TOTALS		
		1-29	30-39	40-49	50+	Tot.	Pct.	Lg.	XPM	XPA	Pts.
1994—San Francisco NFL	16	5-5	5-6	5-8	0-1	15-20	75.0	48	*60	*62	105
1995—San Francisco NFL	6	4-4	0-1	2-6	1-1	7-12	58.3	51	19	19	40
—New Orleans NFL	8	4-4	4-6	4-6	0-1	12-17	70.6	47	16	16	52
1996—New Orleans NFL	16	4-4	9-10	5-7	3-4	21-25	84.0	‡54	18	18	81
1997—New Orleans NFL	16	3-3	10-10	6-9	4-5	23-27	85.2	53	22	22	91
1998—New Orleans NFL	16	7-7	3-3	6-6	4-6	20-22	90.9	56	31	31	91
1999—New Orleans NFL	16	9-11	6-7	7-9	2-2	24-29	82.8	52	20	21	92
2000—New Orleans NFL	16	7-7	4-5	12-15	0-2	23-29	79.3	48	37	37	106
2001—Indianapolis NFL	1	0-0	0-0	0-0	0-0	0-0	0	0	0	0	0
—Tampa Bay NFL	2	2-2	1-1	2-3	0-0	5-6	83.3	42	2	2	17
2002—Minnesota NFL	6	3-3	1-1	1-2	0-0	5-6	83.3	42	5	7	20
2003—New York Jets NFL	16	5-5	15-15	7-8	0-4	27-32	84.4	48	24	24	105
2004—New York Jets NFL	16	9-10	4-6	10-11	1-2	24-29	82.8	53	33	34	105
Pro totals (11 years)	151	62-65	62-71	67-90	15-28	206-254	81.1	56	287	293	905

BRIGGS, LANCE   LB   BEARS

PERSONAL: Born November 12, 1980, in Sacramento, Calif. ... 6-1/238. ... Full name: Lance Marell Briggs.
HIGH SCHOOL: Elk Grove (Sacramento).
COLLEGE: Arizona.
TRANSACTIONS/CAREER NOTES: Selected by Chicago Bears in third round (68th pick overall) of 2003 NFL draft. ... Signed by Bears (July 25, 2003).

Year Team	G	GS	TOTALS			INTERCEPTIONS			
			Tk.	Ast.	Sks.	No.	Yds.	Avg.	TD
2003—Chicago NFL	16	13	62	13	0.0	1	45	45.0	1
2004—Chicago NFL	16	16	102	24	0.5	1	38	38.0	1
Pro totals (2 years)	32	29	164	37	0.5	2	83	41.5	2

B

BRIGHTFUL, LAMONT   CB/KR

PERSONAL: Born January 29, 1979, in Oak Harbor, Wash. ... 5-10/160. ... Full name: Lamont Eugene Brightful.
HIGH SCHOOL: Mariner (Everett, Wash.).
COLLEGE: Eastern Washington.
TRANSACTIONS/CAREER NOTES: Selected by Baltimore Ravens in sixth round (195th pick overall) of 2002 NFL draft. ... Signed by Ravens (July 25, 2002). ... Claimed on waivers by Miami Dolphins (September 6, 2004). ... Released by Dolphins (September 21, 2004).

			TOTALS			INTERCEPTIONS				PUNT RETURNS				KICKOFF RETURNS				TOTALS			
Year Team	G	GS	Tk.	Ast.	Sks.	No.	Yds.	Avg.	TD	No.	Yds.	Avg.	TD	No.	Yds.	Avg.	TD	TD	2pt.	Pts.	Fum.
2002—Bal. NFL	12	0	0	0	0.0	0	0	0.0	0	15	241	16.1	1	34	701	20.6	0	1	0	6	3
2003—Bal. NFL	16	0	2	0	0.0	0	0	0.0	0	†45	351	7.8	0	29	716	24.7	0	0	0	0	2
2004—Mia. NFL	2	0	0	0	0.0	0	0	0.0	0	9	89	9.9	0	5	126	25.2	0	0	0	0	3
Pro totals (3 years)	30	0	2	0	0.0	0	0	0.0	0	69	681	9.9	1	68	1543	22.7	0	1	0	6	8

BROCK, RAHEEM   DE

PERSONAL: Born June 10, 1978, in Newark, N.J. ... 6-4/274.
HIGH SCHOOL: Dobbins (Germantown, Md.).
COLLEGE: Temple.
TRANSACTIONS/CAREER NOTES: Selected by Philadelphia Eagles in seventh round (238th pick overall) of 2002 NFL draft. ... Signed by Eagles (July 25, 2002). ... Released by Eagles (July 25, 2002). ... Signed by Indianapolis Colts (July 28, 2002). ... Granted free agency (March 2, 2005).
CHAMPIONSHIP GAME EXPERIENCE: Played in AFC championship game (2003 season).

			TOTALS			INTERCEPTIONS			
Year Team	G	GS	Tk.	Ast.	Sks.	No.	Yds.	Avg.	TD
2002—Indianapolis NFL	13	6	12	7	1.0	0	0	0.0	0
2003—Indianapolis NFL	16	16	23	14	2.0	0	0	0.0	0
2004—Indianapolis NFL	16	16	36	11	6.5	0	0	0.0	0
Pro totals (3 years)	45	38	71	32	9.5	0	0	0.0	0

BROMELL, LORENZO   DE

PERSONAL: Born September 23, 1975, in Georgetown, S.C. ... 6-6/260. ... Full name: Lorenzo Alexis Bromell.
HIGH SCHOOL: Choppee (Georgetown, S.C.).
JUNIOR COLLEGE: Georgia Military College.
COLLEGE: Clemson.
TRANSACTIONS/CAREER NOTES: Selected by Miami Dolphins in fourth round (102nd pick overall) of 1998 draft. ... Signed by Dolphins (July 10, 1998). ... Granted free agency (March 2, 2001). ... Re-signed by Dolphins (April 19, 2001). ... Granted unconditional free agency (March 1, 2002). ... Signed by Minnesota Vikings (April 12, 2002). ... Released by Vikings (August 31, 2003). ... Signed by Oakland Raiders (November 19, 2003). ... Granted unconditional free agency (March 3, 2004). ... Signed by New York Giants (April 5, 2004). ... On physically unable to perform list with knee injury (July 30-November 9, 2004). ... On injured reserve with knee injury (December 2, 2004-remainder of season). ... Released by Giants (February 22, 2005).

			TOTALS		
Year Team	G	GS	Tk.	Ast.	Sks.
1998—Miami NFL	14	0	16	7	8.0
1999—Miami NFL	15	1	10	7	5.0
2000—Miami NFL	8	0	11	1	2.0
2001—Miami NFL	16	1	20	12	6.5
2002—Minnesota NFL	16	1	22	7	4.0
2003—Oakland NFL	6	4	8	6	2.0
2004—New York Giants NFL	2	0	3	0	0.0
Pro totals (7 years)	77	7	90	40	27.5

BRONSON, ZACK   S

PERSONAL: Born January 28, 1974, in Jasper, Texas. ... 6-1/204. ... Full name: Robert Zack Bronson.
HIGH SCHOOL: Jasper (Texas).
COLLEGE: McNeese State.
TRANSACTIONS/CAREER NOTES: Signed as non-drafted free agent by San Francisco 49ers (May 2, 1997). ... On injured reserve with foot injury (December 29, 1999-remainder of season). ... Granted free agency (February 11, 2000). ... Re-signed by 49ers (June 15, 2000). ... Granted unconditional free agency (March 2, 2001). ... Re-signed by 49ers (May 15, 2001). ... Released by 49ers (June 2, 2004). ... Signed by St. Louis Rams (September 4, 2004). ... On injured reserve with ankle injury (September 9, 2004-entire season). ... Granted unconditional free agency (March 2, 2005).
CHAMPIONSHIP GAME EXPERIENCE: Played in NFC championship game (1997 season).

			TOTALS			INTERCEPTIONS			
Year Team	G	GS	Tk.	Ast.	Sks.	No.	Yds.	Avg.	TD
1997—San Francisco NFL	16	0	18	6	0.0	1	22	22.0	0
1998—San Francisco NFL	11	1	17	0	0.0	4	34	8.5	0
1999—San Francisco NFL	15	2	17	6	0.0	0	0	0.0	0
2000—San Francisco NFL	9	7	31	7	0.0	3	75	25.0	0
2001—San Francisco NFL	16	16	57	6	0.0	7	‡165	23.6	†2
2002—San Francisco NFL	5	5	16	5	0.0	3	28	9.3	0
2003—San Francisco NFL	12	12	37	5	0.0	1	22	22.0	0
2004—St. Louis NFL			Did not play.						
Pro totals (7 years)	84	43	193	35	0.0	19	346	18.2	2

BROOKING, KEITH — LB — FALCONS

PERSONAL: Born October 30, 1975, in Senoia, Ga. ... 6-2/245. ... Full name: Keith Howard Brooking.
HIGH SCHOOL: East Coweta (Sharpsburg, Ga.).
COLLEGE: Georgia Tech.
TRANSACTIONS/CAREER NOTES: Selected by Atlanta Falcons in first round (12th pick overall) of 1998 NFL draft. ... Signed by Falcons (June 29, 1998). ... On injured reserve with foot injury (November 1, 2000-remainder of season).
CHAMPIONSHIP GAME EXPERIENCE: Played in NFC championship game (1998 and 2004 seasons). ... Played in Super Bowl 33 (1998 season).
HONORS: Played in Pro Bowl (2001, 2003 and 2004 seasons). ... Named to play in Pro Bowl (2002 season); replaced by Shelton Quarles due to injury.

				TOTALS			INTERCEPTIONS			
Year Team	G	GS	Tk.	Ast.	Sks.	No.	Yds.	Avg.	TD
1998—Atlanta NFL	15	0	21	5	0.0	1	12	12.0	0
1999—Atlanta NFL	13	13	73	21	2.0	0	0	0.0	0
2000—Atlanta NFL	5	5	28	8	1.0	0	0	0.0	0
2001—Atlanta NFL	16	16	102	25	3.5	2	17	8.5	0
2002—Atlanta NFL	16	16	111	29	0.0	2	24	12.0	0
2003—Atlanta NFL	16	16	126	18	0.0	0	0	0.0	0
2004—Atlanta NFL	16	16	86	16	2.5	3	41	13.7	0
Pro totals (7 years)	97	82	547	122	9.0	8	94	11.8	0

BROOKS, AARON — QB — SAINTS

PERSONAL: Born March 24, 1976, in Newport News, Va. ... 6-4/220. ... Full name: Aaron Lafette Brooks.
HIGH SCHOOL: Homer L. Ferguson (Newport News, Va.).
COLLEGE: Virginia.
TRANSACTIONS/CAREER NOTES: Selected by Green Bay Packers in fourth round (131st pick overall) of 1999 NFL draft. ... Signed by Packers (July 27, 1999). ... Traded by Packers with TE Lamont Hall to New Orleans Saints for LB K.D. Williams and third-round pick (traded to San Francisco) in 2001 draft (July 31, 2000).
SINGLE GAME HIGHS (regular season): Attempts—60 (November 21, 2004, vs. Denver); completions—34 (November 21, 2004, vs. Denver); yards—441 (December 3, 2000, vs. Denver); and touchdown passes—5 (December 14, 2003, vs. New York Giants).
STATISTICAL PLATEAUS: 100-yard rushing games: 2000 (1). Total: 1. 300-yard passing games: 2000 (1), 2001 (3), 2002 (1), 2003 (1), 2004 (2). Total: 8.
MISCELLANEOUS: Regular-season record as starting NFL quarterback: 35-34 (.507). ... Postseason record as starting NFL quarterback: 1-1 (.500).

			PASSING								RUSHING				TOTALS		
Year Team	G	GS	Att.	Cmp.	Pct.	Yds.	TD	Int.	Avg.	Skd.	Rat.	Att.	Yds.	Avg.	TD	TD	2pt.	Pts.
1999—Green Bay NFL	Did not play.																	
2000—New Orleans NFL	8	5	194	113	58.2	1514	9	6	7.80	15	85.7	41	170	4.1	2	2	0	12
2001—New Orleans NFL	16	16	558	312	55.9	3832	26	∞22	6.87	50	76.4	80	358	4.5	1	1	0	6
2002—New Orleans NFL	16	16	528	283	53.6	3572	∞27	15	6.77	36	80.1	62	253	4.1	2	2	∞2	16
2003—New Orleans NFL	16	16	518	306	59.1	3546	24	8	6.85	34	88.8	54	175	3.2	2	2	0	12
2004—New Orleans NFL	16	16	542	309	57.0	3810	21	16	7.03	41	79.5	58	173	3.0	4	4	0	24
Pro totals (5 years)	72	69	2340	1323	56.5	16274	107	67	6.95	176	81.5	295	1129	3.8	11	11	2	70

BROOKS, BARRETT — T — STEELERS

PERSONAL: Born May 5, 1972, in St. Louis, Mo. ... 6-4/325.
HIGH SCHOOL: McCluer North (Florissant, Mo.).
COLLEGE: Kansas State.
TRANSACTIONS/CAREER NOTES: Selected by Philadelphia Eagles in second round (58th pick overall) of 1995 NFL draft. ... Signed by Eagles (July 19, 1995). ... Granted free agency (February 13, 1998). ... Re-signed by Eagles (April 21, 1998). ... Granted unconditional free agency (February 12, 1999). ... Signed by Detroit Lions (April 12, 1999). ... Granted unconditional free agency (March 2, 2001). ... Signed by Cleveland Browns (July 29, 2001). ... Released by Browns (September 1, 2001). ... Signed by Denver Broncos (March 15, 2002). ... Released by Broncos (September 1, 2002). ... Signed by Green Bay Packers (September 26, 2002). ... Released by Packers (October 12, 2002). ... Re-signed by Packers (October 15, 2002). ... Released by Packers (December 9, 2002). ... Signed by Giants (December 17, 2002). ... Granted uncondition-al free agency (February 28, 2003). ... Re-signed by Giants (March 4, 2003). ... Released by Giants (August 31, 2003). ... Signed by Pittsburgh Steelers (October 22, 2003). ... Active for one game (2003); did not play. ... Re-signed by Steelers (April 15, 2004). ... Granted unconditional free agency (March 2, 2005). ... Re-signed by Steelers (March 28, 2005).
PLAYING EXPERIENCE: Philadelphia NFL, 1995-1998; Detroit NFL, 1999-2000; Green Bay NFL, 2002; Pittsburgh NFL, 2004. ... Games/Games started: 1995 (16/16), 1996 (16/15), 1997 (16/14), 1998 (16/1), 1999 (16/12), 2000 (15/4), 2002 (2/0), 2004 (5/0). Total: 102/62.
CHAMPIONSHIP GAME EXPERIENCE: Member of Steelers for AFC championship game (2004 season); inactive.

BROOKS, DERRICK — LB — BUCCANEERS

PERSONAL: Born April 18, 1973, in Pensacola, Fla. ... 6-0/235. ... Full name: Derrick Dewan Brooks.
HIGH SCHOOL: Booker T. Washington (Pensacola, Fla.).
COLLEGE: Florida State.
TRANSACTIONS/CAREER NOTES: Selected by Tampa Bay Buccaneers in first round (28th pick overall) of 1995 NFL draft. ... Signed by Buccaneers (May 3, 1995).
CHAMPIONSHIP GAME EXPERIENCE: Played in NFC championship game (1999 and 2002 seasons). ... Member of Super Bowl championship team (2002 season).
HONORS: Named linebacker on THE SPORTING NEWS college All-America first team (1993 and 1994). ... Played in Pro Bowl (1997-2000 and 2002 seasons). ... Named linebacker on THE SPORTING NEWS NFL All-Pro team (1999, 2000, 2002 and 2003). ... Named to play in Pro Bowl (2001 season); replaced by Dexter Coakley due to injury. ... Named to play in Pro Bowl (2003 season); replaced by Dexter Coakley due to injury. ... Named to play in Pro Bowl (2004 season); replaced by Mark Fields due to injury.

B

Year Team	G	GS	TOTALS Tk.	Ast.	Sks.	INTERCEPTIONS No.	Yds.	Avg.	TD
1995—Tampa Bay NFL	16	13	60	19	1.0	0	0	0.0	0
1996—Tampa Bay NFL	16	16	92	41	0.0	1	6	6.0	0
1997—Tampa Bay NFL	16	16	102	43	1.5	2	13	6.5	0
1998—Tampa Bay NFL	16	16	*123	35	0.0	1	25	25.0	0
1999—Tampa Bay NFL	16	16	‡118	36	2.0	4	61	15.3	0
2000—Tampa Bay NFL	16	16	*123	23	1.0	1	34	34.0	1
2001—Tampa Bay NFL	16	16	80	33	0.0	3	65	21.7	0
2002—Tampa Bay NFL	16	16	88	30	1.0	5	218	43.6	*3
2003—Tampa Bay NFL	16	16	73	30	1.0	2	56	28.0	1
2004—Tampa Bay NFL	16	16	109	28	3.0	1	3	3.0	0
Pro totals (10 years)	160	157	968	318	10.5	20	481	24.1	5

B

BROOKS, ETHAN   T

PERSONAL: Born April 27, 1972, in Hartford, Conn. ... 6-6/330.
HIGH SCHOOL: Westminster (Simsbury, Conn.).
COLLEGE: Williams.
TRANSACTIONS/CAREER NOTES: Selected by Atlanta Falcons in seventh round (229th pick overall) of 1996 NFL draft. ... Signed by Falcons (June 7, 1996). ... Assigned by Falcons to Frankfurt Galaxy in 1997 World League enhancement allocation program (February 19, 1997). ... Released by Falcons (August 27, 1997). ... Signed by St. Louis Rams (November 20, 1997). ... Inactive for five games (1997). ... Released by Rams (July 19, 1999). ... Signed by Arizona Cardinals (February 3, 2000). ... Granted unconditional free agency (March 2, 2001). ... Signed by Denver Broncos (March 15, 2001). ... Released by Broncos (August 28, 2001). ... Signed by Baltimore Ravens (August 2, 2002). ... Granted unconditional free agency (February 28, 2003). ... Re-signed by Ravens (March 13, 2003). ... Granted unconditional free agency (March 2, 2005).
PLAYING EXPERIENCE: Atlanta NFL, 1996; St. Louis NFL, 1998; Arizona NFL, 2000; Baltimore NFL, 2002-2004. ... Games/Games started: 1996 (2/0), 1998 (15/0), 2000 (14/3), 2002 (15/13), 2003 (15/3), 2004 (14/7). Total: 75/26.

BROUSSARD, JAMALL   WR   BENGALS

PERSONAL: Born August 19, 1981, in Nederland, Texas. ... 5-9/172.
HIGH SCHOOL: Kingwood (Texas), then Naval Academy Prep (Newport, R.I.).
JUNIOR COLLEGE: College of the Canyons (Santa Clarita, Calif.).
COLLEGE: San Jose State.
TRANSACTIONS/CAREER NOTES: Signed as non-drafted free agent by Cincinnati Bengals (April 27, 2004). ... Released by Bengals (September 5, 2004). ... Re-signed by Bengals to practice squad (September 6, 2004). ... Signed by Carolina Panthers off Bengals practice squad (October 14, 2004). ... Released by Panthers (January 1, 2005). ... Signed by Cincinnati Bengals (January 4, 2005).

Year Team	G	GS	RECEIVING No.	Yds.	Avg.	TD	PUNT RETURNS No.	Yds.	Avg.	TD	KICKOFF RETURNS No.	Yds.	Avg.	TD	TOTALS TD	2pt.	Pts.	Fum.
2004—Carolina NFL	8	0	0	0	0.0	0	10	43	4.3	0	24	555	23.1	0	0	0	0	2

BROWN, ALEX   DE   BEARS

PERSONAL: Born June 4, 1979, in Jasper, Fla. ... 6-3/262. ... Full name: Alex James Brown.
HIGH SCHOOL: Hamilton County (White Springs, Fla.).
COLLEGE: Florida.
TRANSACTIONS/CAREER NOTES: Selected by Chicago Bears in fourth round (104th pick overall) of 2002 NFL draft. ... Signed by Bears (July 24, 2002).
HONORS: Named defensive end on THE SPORTING NEWS college All-America first team (1999). ... Named defensive end on THE SPORTING NEWS college All-America second team (2001).

Year Team	G	GS	TOTALS Tk.	Ast.	Sks.	INTERCEPTIONS No.	Yds.	Avg.	TD
2002—Chicago NFL	15	9	31	9	2.5	0	0	0.0	0
2003—Chicago NFL	16	16	48	10	5.5	1	0	0.0	0
2004—Chicago NFL	16	16	41	10	6.0	0	0	0.0	0
Pro totals (3 years)	47	41	120	29	14.0	1	0	0.0	0

BROWN, ANTONIO   KR   REDSKINS

PERSONAL: Born March 3, 1978, in Miami, Fla. ... 5-10/175. ... Full name: Antonio Duval Brown.
HIGH SCHOOL: Central (Miami, Fla.).
COLLEGE: West Virginia.
TRANSACTIONS/CAREER NOTES: Signed as non-drafted free agent by Buffalo Bills (March 25, 2003). ... Released by Bills (August 31, 2004). ... Signed by Washington Redskins (November 3, 2004).

Year Team	G	GS	RECEIVING No.	Yds.	Avg.	TD	PUNT RETURNS No.	Yds.	Avg.	TD	KICKOFF RETURNS No.	Yds.	Avg.	TD	TOTALS TD	2pt.	Pts.	Fum.
2003—Buffalo NFL	16	0	0	0	0.0	0	25	111	4.4	0	48	1046	21.8	0	0	0	0	1
2004—Washington NFL	3	0	0	0	0.0	0	10	89	8.9	0	1	66	66.0	0	0	0	0	1
Pro totals (2 years)	19	0	0	0	0.0	0	35	200	5.7	0	49	1112	22.7	0	0	0	0	2

BROWN, CHAD   LB   PATRIOTS

PERSONAL: Born July 12, 1970, in Altadena, Calif. ... 6-2/245. ... Full name: Chadwick Everett Brown.
HIGH SCHOOL: John Muir (Pasadena, Calif.).
COLLEGE: Colorado.

TRANSACTIONS/CAREER NOTES: Selected by Pittsburgh Steelers in second round (44th pick overall) of 1993 NFL draft. ... Signed by Steelers (July 26, 1993). ... Granted unconditional free agency (February 14, 1997). ... Signed by Seattle Seahawks (February 15, 1997). ... On injured reserve with broken foot (November 12, 2002-remainder of season). ... Released by Seahawks (April 21, 2005). ... Signed by New England Patriots (May 11, 2005).

CHAMPIONSHIP GAME EXPERIENCE: Played in AFC championship game (1994 and 1995 seasons). ... Played in Super Bowl 30 (1995 season).

HONORS: Named linebacker on THE SPORTING NEWS NFL All-Pro team (1996 and 1998). ... Played in Pro Bowl (1996, 1998 and 1999 seasons).

			TOTALS			INTERCEPTIONS			
Year Team	G	GS	Tk.	Ast.	Sks.	No.	Yds.	Avg.	TD
1993—Pittsburgh NFL	16	9	43	26	3.0	0	0	0.0	0
1994—Pittsburgh NFL	16	16	90	29	8.5	1	9	9.0	0
1995—Pittsburgh NFL	10	10	20	10	5.5	0	0	0.0	0
1996—Pittsburgh NFL	14	14	50	31	13.0	2	20	10.0	0
1997—Seattle NFL	15	15	75	29	6.5	0	0	0.0	0
1998—Seattle NFL	16	16	117	32	7.5	1	11	11.0	0
1999—Seattle NFL	15	15	87	30	5.5	0	0	0.0	0
2000—Seattle NFL	16	16	71	23	6.0	1	0	0.0	0
2001—Seattle NFL	16	16	80	26	8.5	0	0	0.0	0
2002—Seattle NFL	8	8	42	8	6.0	0	0	0.0	0
2003—Seattle NFL	14	13	74	12	7.0	1	-1	-1.0	0
2004—Seattle NFL	7	7	26	11	1.0	0	0	0.0	0
Pro totals (12 years)	163	155	775	267	78.0	6	39	6.5	0

BROWN, CHRIS   RB   TITANS

PERSONAL: Born April 17, 1981, in Winfield, Ill. ... 6-3/219. ... Full name: Christopher Rajean Brown.

HIGH SCHOOL: Naperville North (Ill.).

COLLEGE: Colorado.

TRANSACTIONS/CAREER NOTES: Selected after junior season by Tennessee Titans in third round (93rd pick overall) of 2003 NFL draft. ... Signed by Titans (July 21, 2003).

SINGLE GAME HIGHS (regular season): Attempts—32 (October 31, 2004, vs. Cincinnati); yards—152 (September 19, 2004, vs. Indianapolis); and rushing touchdowns—2 (October 11, 2004, vs. Green Bay).

STATISTICAL PLATEAUS: 100-yard rushing games: 2004 (6). Total: 6.

			RUSHING				RECEIVING				TOTALS			
Year Team	G	GS	Att.	Yds.	Avg.	TD	No.	Yds.	Avg.	TD	TD	2pt.	Pts.	Fum.
2003—Tennessee NFL	11	0	56	221	3.9	0	8	61	7.6	0	0	0	0	1
2004—Tennessee NFL	11	11	220	1067	§4.9	6	20	147	7.4	0	6	0	36	6
Pro totals (2 years)	22	11	276	1288	4.7	6	28	208	7.4	0	6	0	36	7

BROWN, CORNELL   LB   RAVENS

PERSONAL: Born March 15, 1975, in Englewood, N.J. ... 6-0/240. ... Full name: Cornell Desmond Brown. ... Brother of Ruben Brown, guard, Chicago Bears.

HIGH SCHOOL: E.C. Glass (Lynchburg, Va.).

COLLEGE: Virginia Tech.

TRANSACTIONS/CAREER NOTES: Selected by Baltimore Ravens in sixth round (194th pick overall) of 1997 NFL draft. ... Signed by Ravens (July 10, 1997). ... Granted free agency (February 11, 2000). ... Re-signed by Ravens (April 25, 2000) ... Granted unconditional free agency (March 2, 2001). ... Re-signed by Ravens (May 23, 2001). ... Released by Ravens (September 5, 2001). ... Signed by Oakland Raiders (February 21, 2002). ... Released by Raiders (June 10, 2002). ... Signed by Ravens (August 20, 2002). ... Granted unconditional free agency (February 28, 2003). ... Re-signed by Ravens (March 18, 2003).

CHAMPIONSHIP GAME EXPERIENCE: Member of Ravens for AFC Championship game (2000 season); inactive. ... Member of Super Bowl championship team (2000 season).

HONORS: Named defensive lineman on THE SPORTING NEWS college All-America first team (1995).

			TOTALS			INTERCEPTIONS			
Year Team	G	GS	Tk.	Ast.	Sks.	No.	Yds.	Avg.	TD
1997—Baltimore NFL	16	1	11	0	0.5	1	21	21.0	0
1998—Baltimore NFL	16	1	3	2	0.0	0	0	0.0	0
1999—Baltimore NFL	16	5	21	7	1.0	0	0	0.0	0
2000—Baltimore NFL	16	1	13	6	3.0	0	0	0.0	0
2002—Baltimore NFL	16	14	36	23	1.5	0	0	0.0	0
2003—Baltimore NFL	16	3	16	2	1.0	0	0	0.0	0
2004—Baltimore NFL	13	0	4	3	0.0	0	0	0.0	0
Pro totals (7 years)	109	25	104	43	7.0	1	21	21.0	0

BROWN, COURTNEY   DE   BRONCOS

PERSONAL: Born February 14, 1978, in Charleston, S.C. ... 6-4/290. ... Full name: Courtney Lanair Brown.

HIGH SCHOOL: Macedonia (Alvin, S.C.).

COLLEGE: Penn State.

TRANSACTIONS/CAREER NOTES: Selected by Cleveland Browns in first round (first pick overall) of 2000 NFL draft. ... Signed by Browns (May 10, 2000). ... On injured reserve with ankle injury (January 2, 2002-remainder of season). ... On injured reserve with knee injury (December 18, 2002-remainder of season). ... On injured reserve with biceps injury (December 9, 2003-remainder of season). ... On injured reserve with foot injury (September 21, 2004-remainder of season). ... Released by Browns (March 14, 2005). ... Signed by Denver Broncos (March 30, 2005).

HONORS: Named defensive end on THE SPORTING NEWS college All-America first team (1999).

Year Team	G	GS	TOTALS		
			Tk.	Ast.	Sks.
2000—Cleveland NFL	16	16	61	8	4.5
2001—Cleveland NFL	5	5	14	7	4.5
2002—Cleveland NFL	11	11	30	12	2.0
2003—Cleveland NFL	13	13	29	9	6.0
2004—Cleveland NFL	2	2	2	0	0.0
Pro totals (5 years)	47	47	136	36	17.0

BROWN, DANTE   RB

PERSONAL: Born July 28, 1980, in Cincinnati, Ohio. ... 6-1/215.
HIGH SCHOOL: Swainsboro, Ga.
JUNIOR COLLEGE: Middle Georgia (Cochran, Ga.).
COLLEGE: Memphis.
TRANSACTIONS/CAREER NOTES: Signed as non-drafted free agent by Pittsburgh Steelers (May 2, 2003). ... Released by Steelers (August 31, 2003). ... Re-signed by Steelers to practice squad (September 1, 2003). ... Activated (September 16, 2003). ... Released by Steelers (September 5, 2004). ... Re-signed by Steelers to practice squad (September 6, 2004). ... Activated (November 11, 2004). ... Released by Steelers (November 23, 2004). ... Signed by Cleveland Browns to practice squad (November 27, 2004). ... Signed by Buffalo Bills off Browns practice squad (December 22, 2004). ... Activated (December 23, 2004). ... Released by Bills (May 17, 2005).
SINGLE GAME HIGHS (regular season): Attempts—1 (November 14, 2004, vs. Cleveland); yards—2 (November 14, 2004, vs. Cleveland); and rushing touchdowns—0.

Year Team	G	GS	RUSHING				TOTALS			
			Att.	Yds.	Avg.	TD	TD	2pt.	Pts.	Fum.
2004—Pittsburgh NFL	1	0	1	2	2.0	0	0	0	0	0

BROWN, DEE   RB   CHIEFS

PERSONAL: Born May 12, 1978, in Clearwater, Fla. ... 5-10/215. ... Full name: Dadrian L. Brown.
HIGH SCHOOL: Lake Brantley (Fla.).
COLLEGE: Syracuse.
TRANSACTIONS/CAREER NOTES: Selected by Carolina Panthers in sixth round (175th pick overall) of 2001 NFL draft. ... Signed by Panthers (July 18, 2001). ... On injured reserve with ankle injury (September 1, 2001-entire season). ... Released by Panthers (August 31, 2003). ... Signed by Pittsburgh Steelers (December 10, 2003). ... Released by Steelers (March 11, 2004). ... Signed by Atlanta Falcons (April 30, 2004). ... Waived by Falcons (May 18, 2004). ... Signed by Cleveland Browns (July 31, 2004). ... Released by Browns (September 21, 2004). ... Re-signed by Browns (September 28, 2004). ... Released by Browns (October 20, 2004). ... Signed by Kansas City Chiefs (April 21, 2005).
SINGLE GAME HIGHS (regular season): Attempts—27 (December 1, 2002, vs. Cleveland); yards—122 (December 1, 2002, vs. Cleveland); and rushing touchdowns—2 (December 22, 2002, vs. Chicago).
STATISTICAL PLATEAUS: 100-yard rushing games: 2002 (1). Total: 1.

Year Team	G	GS	RUSHING				KICKOFF RETURNS				TOTALS			
			Att.	Yds.	Avg.	TD	No.	Yds.	Avg.	TD	TD	2pt.	Pts.	Fum.
2002—Carolina NFL	14	3	102	360	3.5	4	13	253	19.5	0	5	0	30	4
2003—Pittsburgh NFL	1	0	0	0	0.0	0	0	0	0.0	0	0	0	0	0
2004—Cleveland NFL	5	0	0	0	0.0	0	13	243	18.7	0	0	0	0	0
Pro totals (3 years)	20	3	102	360	3.5	4	26	496	19.1	0	5	0	30	4

BROWN, ERIC   S

PERSONAL: Born March 20, 1975, in San Antonio, Texas. ... 6-1/213. ... Full name: Eric Jon Brown.
HIGH SCHOOL: Judson (Converse, Texas).
JUNIOR COLLEGE: Blinn College (Texas).
COLLEGE: Mississippi State.
TRANSACTIONS/CAREER NOTES: Selected by Denver Broncos in second round (61st pick overall) of 1998 NFL draft. ... Signed by Broncos (July 16, 1998). ... On injured reserve with knee injury (November 18, 1999-remainder of season). ... Granted unconditional free agency (March 1, 2002). ... Signed by Houston Texans (August 5, 2002). ... Granted unconditional free agency (February 28, 2003). ... Re-signed by Texans (March 17, 2003). ... Released by Texans (March 14, 2005).
CHAMPIONSHIP GAME EXPERIENCE: Member of Broncos for AFC championship game (1998 season); inactive. ... Member of Super Bowl championship team (1998 season); inactive.

Year Team	G	GS	TOTALS			INTERCEPTIONS			
			Tk.	Ast.	Sks.	No.	Yds.	Avg.	TD
1998—Denver NFL	11	10	24	7	0.0	0	0	0.0	0
1999—Denver NFL	10	10	59	15	1.5	1	13	13.0	0
2000—Denver NFL	16	16	77	14	1.0	3	9	3.0	0
2001—Denver NFL	16	16	64	13	3.0	2	0	0.0	0
2002—Houston NFL	15	15	58	9	0.5	2	7	3.5	0
2003—Houston NFL	16	16	69	23	0.5	1	5	5.0	0
2004—Houston NFL	13	4	3	3	0.0	0	0	0.0	0
Pro totals (7 years)	97	87	354	84	6.5	9	34	3.8	0

BROWN, FAKHIR   CB   SAINTS

PERSONAL: Born September 21, 1977, in Detroit, Mich. ... 5-11/192. ... Full name: Fakhir Hamin Brown. ... Name pronounced: fah-KEAR.
HIGH SCHOOL: Mansfield (La.).
COLLEGE: Grambling State.

TRANSACTIONS/CAREER NOTES: Signed by Toronto Argonauts of CFL (April 6, 1998). ... Signed as non-drafted free agent by San Diego Chargers (April 20, 1999). ... Released by Chargers (September 4, 1999). ... Re-signed by Chargers to practice squad (September 7, 1999). ... Activated (October 9, 1999). ... Released by Chargers (October 15, 1999). ... Re-signed by Chargers to practice squad (October 16, 1999). ... Activated (October 22, 1999). ... Released by Chargers (September 3, 2001). ... Signed by Oakland Raiders (January 24, 2002). ... Released by Raiders (April 26, 2002). ... Signed by New Orleans Saints (July 17, 2002).

Year Team	G	GS	TOTALS Tk.	Ast.	Sks.	INTERCEPTIONS No.	Yds.	Avg.	TD
1998—Toronto CFL	6	...	...	...	0.0	1	0	0.0	0
1999—San Diego NFL	9	3	29	2	0.0	0	0	0.0	0
2000—San Diego NFL	9	8	28	7	0.0	1	0	0.0	0
2002—New Orleans NFL	12	0	15	0	0.0	0	0	0.0	0
2003—New Orleans NFL	16	0	18	4	0.0	0	0	0.0	0
2004—New Orleans NFL	16	10	53	1	0.0	2	0	0.0	0
CFL totals (1 year)	6	...	...	...	0.0	1	0	0.0	0
NFL totals (5 years)	62	21	143	14	0.0	3	0	0.0	0
Pro totals (6 years)	68	...	...	...	0.0	4	0	0.0	0

BROWN, JOSH — K — SEAHAWKS

PERSONAL: Born April 29, 1979, in Tulsa, Okla. ... 6-0/202. ... Full name: Joshua Brown.
HIGH SCHOOL: Foyil (Okla.).
COLLEGE: Nebraska.
TRANSACTIONS/CAREER NOTES: Selected by Seattle Seahawks in seventh round (222nd pick overall) of 2003 NFL draft. ... Signed by Seahawks (June 20, 2003).

Year Team	G	FIELD GOALS 1-29	30-39	40-49	50+	Tot.	Pct.	Lg.	TOTALS XPM	XPA	Pts.
2003—Seattle NFL	16	5-5	10-11	6-11	1-3	22-30	73.3	*58	48	48	114
2004—Seattle NFL	16	8-8	8-9	6-7	1-1	23-25	‡92.0	54	40	40	109
Pro totals (2 years)	32	13-13	18-20	12-18	2-4	45-55	81.8	58	88	88	223

BROWN, KRIS — K — TEXANS

PERSONAL: Born December 23, 1976, in Southlake, Texas. ... 5-11/205.
HIGH SCHOOL: Carroll (Southlake, Texas).
COLLEGE: Nebraska.
TRANSACTIONS/CAREER NOTES: Selected by Pittsburgh Steelers in seventh round (228th pick overall) of 1999 NFL draft. ... Signed by Steelers (June 29, 1999). ... Granted free agency (March 1, 2002). ... Signed by Houston Texans (March 25, 2002).
CHAMPIONSHIP GAME EXPERIENCE: Played in AFC championship game (2001 season).
MISCELLANEOUS: Houston Texans all-time scoring leader (237 points).

Year Team	G	FIELD GOALS 1-29	30-39	40-49	50+	Tot.	Pct.	Lg.	TOTALS XPM	XPA	Pts.
1999—Pittsburgh NFL	16	7-7	9-10	8-11	1-1	25-29	86.2	51	30	31	105
2000—Pittsburgh NFL	16	9-9	9-10	6-9	1-2	25-30	83.3	52	32	33	107
2001—Pittsburgh NFL	16	7-7	15-20	6-15	2-2	30-*44	68.2	†55	34	37	124
2002—Houston NFL	16	3-4	1-1	11-14	2-5	17-24	70.8	51	20	20	71
2003—Houston NFL	16	4-4	8-8	5-6	1-4	18-22	81.8	50	27	27	81
2004—Houston NFL	16	7-7	3-5	6-9	1-3	17-24	70.8	50	34	34	85
Pro totals (6 years)	96	37-38	45-54	42-64	8-17	132-173	76.3	55	177	182	573

BROWN, MARK — LB — JETS

PERSONAL: Born May 19, 1980, in Patterson, N.J. ... 6-0/238.
HIGH SCHOOL: Germantown (Tenn.).
COLLEGE: Auburn.
TRANSACTIONS/CAREER NOTES: Signed as non-drafted free agent by New York Jets (May 2, 2003). ... Released by Jets (August 31, 2003). ... Re-signed by Jets to practice squad (September 1, 2003). ... Released by Jets (October 16, 2003). ... Re-signed by Jets (November 11, 2003).

Year Team	G	GS	TOTALS Tk.	Ast.	Sks.	INTERCEPTIONS No.	Yds.	Avg.	TD
2003—New York Jets NFL	1	0	0	0	0.0	0	0	0.0	0
2004—New York Jets NFL	12	6	8	5	0.0	0	0	0.0	0
Pro totals (2 years)	13	6	8	5	0.0	0	0	0.0	0

BROWN, MICHAEL — LB — FALCONS

PERSONAL: Born January 16, 1980, in Louisville, Ky. ... 5-10/220.
HIGH SCHOOL: Butler (Louisville, Ky.).
COLLEGE: Louisville.
TRANSACTIONS/CAREER NOTES: Signed as non-drafted free agent by Tampa Bay Buccaneers (April 28, 2003). ... Released by Buccaneers (August 29, 2003). ... Re-signed by Buccaneers to practice squad (December 16, 2003). ... Released by Buccaneers (September 5, 2004). ... Signed by Washington Redskins (September 21, 2004). ... Released by Redskins (October 5, 2004). ... Signed by Atlanta Falcons (2005).

B

BROWN, MIKE   S   BEARS

PERSONAL: Born February 13, 1978, in Scottsdale, Ariz. ... 5-10/212.
HIGH SCHOOL: Saguaro (Scottsdale, Ariz.).
COLLEGE: Nebraska.
TRANSACTIONS/CAREER NOTES: Selected by Chicago Bears in second round (39th pick overall) of 2000 NFL draft. ... Signed by Bears (July 23, 2000). ... On injured reserve with Achilles injury (September 21, 2004-remainder of season).

			TOTALS			INTERCEPTIONS			
Year Team	G	GS	Tk.	Ast.	Sks.	No.	Yds.	Avg.	TD
2000—Chicago NFL	16	16	79	17	0.0	1	35	35.0	1
2001—Chicago NFL	16	16	51	11	3.0	5	81	16.2	†2
2002—Chicago NFL	16	15	72	12	0.0	3	16	5.3	0
2003—Chicago NFL	16	16	61	14	0.0	2	0	0.0	0
2004—Chicago NFL	2	2	9	1	0.0	0	0	0.0	0
Pro totals (5 years)	66	65	272	55	3.0	11	132	12.0	3

BROWN, MILFORD   G   TEXANS

PERSONAL: Born August 15, 1980, in Montgomery, Ala. ... 6-4/331.
HIGH SCHOOL: Carver (Montgomery, Ala.).
JUNIOR COLLEGE: East Mississippi (Scooba, Miss.).
COLLEGE: Florida State.
TRANSACTIONS/CAREER NOTES: Selected by Houston Texans in sixth round of NFL supplemental draft (September 27, 2002). ... On injured reserve with knee injury (December 26, 2003-remainder of season). ... Granted free agency (March 2, 2005). ... Re-signed by Texans (April 15, 2005).
PLAYING EXPERIENCE: Houston NFL, 2003-2004. ... Games/Games started: 2003 (3/2), 2004 (2/2). Total: 5/4.

BROWN, ORLANDO   T   RAVENS

PERSONAL: Born December 12, 1970, in Washington, DC. ... 6-7/360. ... Full name: Orlando Claude Brown.
HIGH SCHOOL: Howard D. Woodson (Washington, D.C.).
COLLEGE: South Carolina State.
TRANSACTIONS/CAREER NOTES: Signed as non-drafted free agent by Cleveland Browns (May 13, 1993). ... On injured reserve with shoulder injury (August 30, 1993-entire season). ... Browns franchise moved to Baltimore and renamed Ravens for 1996 season (March 11, 1996). ... Granted unconditional free agency (February 12, 1999). ... Signed by Browns (February 17, 1999). ... On suspended list for abusing an official (December 22, 1999-remainder of season). ... On physically unable to perform list with eye injury (August 27-September 19, 2000). ... Released by Browns (September 19, 2000). ... Signed by Baltimore Ravens (March 18, 2003). ... Granted unconditional free agency (March 3, 2004). ... Re-signed by Ravens (March 12, 2004).
PLAYING EXPERIENCE: Cleveland NFL, 1993-1995; Baltimore NFL, 1996-1998; Cleveland NFL, 1999; Baltimore NFL, 2003-2004. ... Games/Games started: 1994 (14/8), 1995 (16/16), 1996 (16/16), 1997 (16/16), 1998 (13/13), 1999 (15/15), 2003 (16/13), 2004 (14/13), Total: 120/110.

BROWN, RALPH   CB   VIKINGS

PERSONAL: Born September 16, 1978, in Hacienda Heights, Calif. ... 5-10/185. ... Full name: Ralph Brown II.
HIGH SCHOOL: Bishop Amat (La Puente, Calif.).
COLLEGE: Nebraska.
TRANSACTIONS/CAREER NOTES: Selected by New York Giants in fifth round (140th pick overall) of 2000 NFL draft. ... Signed by Giants (July 18, 2000). ... On injured reserve with kidney injury (October 3, 2000-remainder of season). ... Granted free agency (February 28, 2003). ... Re-signed by Giants (April 19, 2003). ... On injured reserve with shoulder injury (December 16, 2003-remainder of season). ... Granted unconditional free agency (March 3, 2004). ... Signed by Washington Redskins (March 18, 2004). ... Released by Redskins (August 31, 2004). ... Signed by Minnesota Vikings (September 14, 2004).
HONORS: Named cornerback on THE SPORTING NEWS college All-America first team (1999).

			TOTALS			INTERCEPTIONS			
Year Team	G	GS	Tk.	Ast.	Sks.	No.	Yds.	Avg.	TD
2000—New York Giants NFL	2	0	0	0	0.0	0	0	0.0	0
2001—New York Giants NFL	8	0	0	2	0.0	0	0	0.0	0
2002—New York Giants NFL	16	2	18	4	0.0	1	19	19.0	0
2003—New York Giants NFL	11	7	29	5	1.0	2	51	25.5	1
2004—Minnesota NFL	12	0	6	1	0.0	0	0	0.0	0
Pro totals (5 years)	49	9	53	12	1.0	3	70	23.3	1

BROWN, RAY   G   REDSKINS

PERSONAL: Born December 12, 1962, in Marion, Ark. ... 6-5/318. ... Full name: Leonard Ray Brown Jr.
HIGH SCHOOL: Marion (Ark.).
COLLEGE: Arkansas State.
TRANSACTIONS/CAREER NOTES: Selected by St. Louis Cardinals in eighth round (201st pick overall) of 1986 NFL draft. ... Signed by Cardinals (July 14, 1986). ... On injured reserve with knee injury (October 17-November 21, 1986). ... Released by Cardinals (September 7, 1987). ... Re-signed by Cardinals as replacement player (September 25, 1987). ... On injured reserve with finger injury (November 12-December 17, 1987). ... Cardinals franchise moved to Phoenix (March 15, 1988). ... Granted unconditional free agency (February 1, 1989). ... Signed by Washington Redskins (March 10, 1989). ... On injured reserve with knee injury (September 5-November 4, 1989). ... On injured reserve with knee injury (September 4, 1990-January 4, 1991). ... Granted unconditional free agency (February 1-April 1, 1991). ... Re-signed by Redskins for 1991 season. ... On injured reserve with elbow injury (August 27, 1991-entire season). ... Granted unconditional free agency

(February 16, 1996). ... Signed by San Francisco 49ers (March 1, 1996). ... Released by 49ers (June 3, 2002). ... Signed by Detroit Lions (August 20, 2002). ... Granted unconditional free agency (February 28, 2003). ... Re-signed by Lions (March 13, 2003). ... Granted unconditional free agency (March 3, 2004). ... Signed by Washington Redskins (August 11, 2004). ... Granted unconditional free agency (March 2, 2005). ... Re-signed by Redskins (March 30, 2005).

PLAYING EXPERIENCE: St. Louis NFL, 1986-1987; Phoenix NFL, 1988; Washington NFL, 1989-1995; San Francisco NFL, 1996-2001; Detroit NFL, 2002-2003; Washington NFL, 2004. ... Games/Games started: 1986 (11/4), 1987 (7/3), 1988 (15/1), 1989 (7/0), 1992 (16/8), 1993 (16/14), 1994 (16/16), 1995 (16/16), 1996 (16/16), 1997 (15/15), 1998 (16/16), 1999 (16/16), 2000 (16/16), 2001 (16/16), 2002 (16/16), 2003 (16/16), 2004 (16/14), Total: 247/203.

CHAMPIONSHIP GAME EXPERIENCE: Played in NFC championship game (1997 season).

HONORS: Played in Pro Bowl (2001 season).

BROWN, RUBEN — G — BEARS

PERSONAL: Born February 13, 1972, in Englewood, N.J. ... 6-3/300. ... Full name: Ruben Pernell Brown. ... Brother of Cornell Brown, linebacker, Baltimore Ravens.
HIGH SCHOOL: E.C. Glass (Lynchburg, Va.).
COLLEGE: Pittsburgh.
TRANSACTIONS/CAREER NOTES: Selected by Buffalo Bills in first round (14th pick overall) of 1995 NFL draft. ... Signed by Bills (June 20, 1995). ... Granted unconditional free agency (February 11, 2000). ... Re-signed by Bills (March 31, 2000). ... Released by Bills (March 1, 2004). ... Signed by Chicago Bears (April 2, 2004). ... On injured reserve with neck injury (November 27, 2004-remainder of season).
PLAYING EXPERIENCE: Buffalo NFL, 1995-2003; Chicago NFL, 2004. ... Games/Games started: 1995 (16/16), 1996 (14/14), 1997 (16/16), 1998 (13/13), 1999 (14/14), 2000 (16/16), 2001 (16/16), 2002 (16/16), 2003 (15/15), 2004 (9/9). Total: 145/145.
HONORS: Named offensive lineman on THE SPORTING NEWS college All-America second team (1994). ... Played in Pro Bowl (1996-2003 seasons).

BROWN, RUFUS — CB — REDSKINS

PERSONAL: Born July 18, 1980, in San Antonio, Texas. ... 5-9/188.
HIGH SCHOOL: Austin (El Paso, Texas).
COLLEGE: Florida State.
TRANSACTIONS/CAREER NOTES: Signed as non-drafted free agent by Washington Redskins (April 27, 2004). ... Released by Redskins (September 6, 2004). ... Re-signed by Redskins to practice squad (September 6, 2004). ... Activated (December 29, 2004). ... Assigned by Redskins to Hamburg Sea Devils in 2005 NFL Europe enhancement allocation program (February 14, 2005).

				TOTALS			INTERCEPTIONS			
Year	Team	G	GS	Tk.	Ast.	Sks.	No.	Yds.	Avg.	TD
2004—Washington NFL		1	0	0	0	0.0	0	0	0.0	0

BROWN, SHELDON — CB — EAGLES

PERSONAL: Born March 19, 1979, in Lancaster, S.C. ... 5-10/200.
HIGH SCHOOL: Lewisville (Richburg, S.C.).
COLLEGE: South Carolina.
TRANSACTIONS/CAREER NOTES: Selected by Philadelphia Eagles in second round (59th pick overall) of 2002 NFL draft. ... Signed by Eagles (July 25, 2002).
CHAMPIONSHIP GAME EXPERIENCE: Played in NFC championship game (2002-2004 seasons). ... Played in Super Bowl 39 (2004 season).

			TOTALS			INTERCEPTIONS			
Year Team	G	GS	Tk.	Ast.	Sks.	No.	Yds.	Avg.	TD
2002—Philadelphia NFL	16	0	8	4	1.0	2	41	20.5	0
2003—Philadelphia NFL	16	3	37	6	1.0	1	10	10.0	0
2004—Philadelphia NFL	16	16	66	23	3.0	2	33	16.5	0
Pro totals (3 years)	48	19	111	33	5.0	5	84	16.8	0

BROWN, TIM — WR

PERSONAL: Born July 22, 1966, in Dallas, Texas. ... 6-0/195. ... Full name: Timothy Donell Brown.
HIGH SCHOOL: Woodrow Wilson (Dallas).
COLLEGE: Notre Dame.
TRANSACTIONS/CAREER NOTES: Selected by Los Angeles Raiders in first round (sixth pick overall) of 1988 NFL draft. ... Signed by Raiders (July 14, 1988). ... On injured reserve with knee injury (September 12, 1989-remainder of season). ... Granted free agency (February 1, 1992). ... Re-signed by Raiders (August 13, 1992). ... Designated by Raiders as transition player (February 25, 1993). ... Tendered offer sheet by Denver Broncos (March 11, 1994). ... Offer matched by Raiders (March 16, 1994). ... Raiders franchise moved to Oakland (July 21, 1995). ... Released by Raiders (August 5, 2004). ... Signed by Tampa Bay Buccaneers (August 10, 2004). ... Granted unconditional free agency (March 2, 2005).
CHAMPIONSHIP GAME EXPERIENCE: Played in AFC championship game (1990, 2000 and 2002 seasons). ... Played in Super Bowl 37 (2002 season).
HONORS: Named wide receiver on THE SPORTING NEWS college All-America first team (1986 and 1987). ... Heisman Trophy winner (1987). ... Named College Football Player of the Year by THE SPORTING NEWS (1987). ... Named kick returner on THE SPORTING NEWS NFL All-Pro team (1988). ... Played in Pro Bowl (1988, 1991, 1993-1997 and 2001 seasons). ... Named wide receiver on THE SPORTING NEWS NFL All-Pro team (1997). ... Named to play in Pro Bowl (1999 season); replaced by Terry Glenn due to injury.
RECORDS: Holds NFL rookie-season record for most combined yards gained—2,317 (1988).
SINGLE GAME HIGHS (regular season): Receptions—14 (December 21, 1997, vs. Jacksonville); yards—190 (October 24, 1999, vs. New York Jets); and touchdown receptions—3 (August 31, 1997, vs. Tennessee).
STATISTICAL PLATEAUS: 100-yard receiving games: 1988 (1), 1991 (1), 1992 (1), 1993 (4), 1994 (4), 1995 (6), 1996 (2), 1997 (7), 1998 (3), 1999 (6), 2000 (2), 2001 (4), 2002 (1), 2003 (1). Total: 43.

MISCELLANEOUS: Holds Raiders franchise all-time record for most receptions (1,070), most yards receiving (14,734), most touchdowns (104) and most receiving touchdowns (99).

			RUSHING				RECEIVING				PUNT RETURNS				KICKOFF RETURNS				TOTALS		
Year Team	G	GS	Att.	Yds.	Avg.	TD	No.	Yds.	Avg.	TD	No.	Yds.	Avg.	TD	No.	Yds.	Avg.	TD	TD	2pt.	Pts.
1988—L.A. Raiders	16	9	14	50	3.6	1	43	725	16.9	5	§49	§444	9.1	0	†41	*1098	*26.8	†1	7	0	42
1989—L.A. Raiders	1	1	0	0	0.0	0	1	8	8.0	0	4	43	10.8	0	3	63	21.0	0	0	0	0
1990—L.A. Raiders	16	0	0	0	0.0	0	18	265	14.7	3	34	295	8.7	0	0	0	0.0	0	3	0	18
1991—L.A. Raiders	16	1	5	16	3.2	0	36	554	15.4	5	29	§330	11.4 ▲1	1	1	29	29.0	0	6	0	36
1992—L.A. Raiders	15	12	3	-4	-1.3	0	49	693	14.1	7	37	383	10.4	0	2	14	7.0	0	7	0	42
1993—L.A. Raiders	16	16	2	7	3.5	0	80	§1180	14.8	7	40	§465	11.6	1	0	0	0.0	0	8	0	48
1994—L.A. Raiders	16	16	0	0	0.0	0	89	§1309	14.7	9	40	*487	12.2	0	0	0	0.0	0	9	0	54
1995—Oak. NFL	16	16	0	0	0.0	0	89	§1342	15.1	10	36	364	10.1	0	0	0	0.0	0	10	0	60
1996—Oak. NFL	16	16	6	35	5.8	0	90	1104	12.3	9	32	272	8.5	0	1	24	24.0	0	9	0	54
1997—Oak. NFL	16	16	5	19	3.8	0	†104	§1408	13.5	5	0	0	0.0	0	1	7	7.0	0	5	1	32
1998—Oak. NFL	16	16	1	-7	-7.0	0	81	1012	12.5	9	3	23	7.7	0	0	0	0.0	0	9	0	54
1999—Oak. NFL	16	16	1	4	4.0	0	90	1344	14.9	6	0	0	0.0	0	0	0	0.0	0	6	0	36
2000—Oak. NFL	16	16	3	12	4.0	0	76	1128	14.8	11	0	0	0.0	0	0	0	0.0	0	11	0	66
2001—Oak. NFL	16	16	4	39	9.8	0	91	1165	12.8	9	6	111	18.5	1	0	0	0.0	0	10	0	60
2002—Oak. NFL	16	16	6	19	3.2	0	81	930	11.5	2	10	55	5.5	0	0	0	0.0	0	2	0	12
2003—Oak. NFL	16	15	0	0	0.0	0	52	567	10.9	2	0	0	0.0	0	0	0	0.0	0	2	0	12
2004—T.B. NFL	15	4	0	0	0.0	0	24	200	8.3	1	6	48	8.0	0	0	0	0.0	0	1	0	6
Pro totals (17 years)	255	202	50	190	3.8	1	1094	14934	13.7	100	326	3320	10.2	3	49	1235	25.2	1	105	1	632

BROWN, TONY — DE — 49ERS

PERSONAL: Born September 29, 1980, in Chattanooga, Tenn. ... 6-1/280. ... Full name: Tony Anthony Brown.
HIGH SCHOOL: City (Chattanooga, Tenn.).
COLLEGE: Memphis.
TRANSACTIONS/CAREER NOTES: Signed as non-drafted free agent by Carolina Panthers (May 2, 2003). ... Released by Panthers (August 31, 2003). ... Signed by Miami Dolphins (December 13, 2003). ... Released by Dolphins (September 6, 2004). ... Signed by San Francisco 49ers (September 7, 2004).

			TOTALS		
Year Team	G	GS	Tk.	Ast.	Sks.
2004—San Francisco NFL	16	4	19	3	1.0

BROWN, TROY — WR — PATRIOTS

PERSONAL: Born July 2, 1971, in Barnwell, S.C. ... 5-10/196. ... Full name: Troy Fitzgerald Brown.
HIGH SCHOOL: Blackville-Hilda (Blackville, S.C.).
JUNIOR COLLEGE: Lees-McRae College (N.C.).
COLLEGE: Marshall.
TRANSACTIONS/CAREER NOTES: Selected by New England Patriots in eighth round (198th pick overall) of 1993 NFL draft. ... Signed by Patriots (July 16, 1993). ... On injured reserve with quadriceps injury (December 31, 1993-remainder of season). ... Released by Patriots (August 28, 1994). ... Re-signed by Patriots (October 19, 1994). ... Granted unconditional free agency (February 14, 1997). ... Re-signed by Patriots (March 10, 1997). ... Granted unconditional free agency (February 11, 2000). ... Re-signed by Patriots (February 26, 2000). ... Granted unconditional free agency (March 2, 2005). ... Re-signed by Patriots (May 23, 2005).
CHAMPIONSHIP GAME EXPERIENCE: Played in AFC championship game (1996, 2001, 2003 and 2004 seasons). ... Member of Patriots for Super Bowl 31 (1996 season); inactive. ... Member of Super Bowl championship team (2001, 2003 and 2004 seasons).
HONORS: Played in Pro Bowl (2001 season).
SINGLE GAME HIGHS (regular season): Receptions—16 (September 22, 2002, vs. Kansas City); yards—176 (September 22, 2002, vs. Kansas City); and touchdown receptions—2 (October 1, 2000, vs. Denver).
STATISTICAL PLATEAUS: 100-yard receiving games: 1997 (2), 1999 (1), 2000 (4), 2001 (3), 2002 (2), 2003 (1). Total: 13.

			RUSHING				RECEIVING				PUNT RETURNS				KICKOFF RETURNS				TOTALS		
Year Team	G	GS	Att.	Yds.	Avg.	TD	No.	Yds.	Avg.	TD	No.	Yds.	Avg.	TD	No.	Yds.	Avg.	TD	TD	2pt.	Pts.
1993—N.E. NFL	12	0	0	0	0.0	0	2	22	11.0	0	25	224	9.0	0	15	243	16.2	0	0	0	0
1994—N.E. NFL	9	0	0	0	0.0	0	0	0	0.0	0	24	202	8.4	0	1	14	14.0	0	0	0	0
1995—N.E. NFL	16	0	0	0	0.0	0	14	159	11.4	0	0	0	0.0	0	31	672	21.7	0	1	0	6
1996—N.E. NFL	16	0	0	0	0.0	0	21	222	10.6	0	0	0	0.0	0	29	634	21.9	0	0	0	0
1997—N.E. NFL	16	6	1	-18	-18.0	0	41	607	14.8	6	0	0	0.0	0	0	0	0.0	0	6	0	36
1998—N.E. NFL	10	0	0	0	0.0	0	23	346	15.0	1	17	225	13.2	0	0	0	0.0	0	1	0	6
1999—N.E. NFL	13	1	0	0	0.0	0	36	471	13.1	1	38	405	10.7	0	8	271	33.9	0	1	0	6
2000—N.E. NFL	16	15	6	46	7.7	0	83	944	11.4	4	39	504	12.9	1	2	15	7.5	0	5	0	30
2001—N.E. NFL	16	13	11	91	8.3	0	101	1199	11.9	5	29	413	*14.2	*2	1	13	13.0	0	7	0	42
2002—N.E. NFL	14	13	3	14	4.7	0	97	890	9.2	3	24	175	7.3	0	0	0	0.0	0	3	1	20
2003—N.E. NFL	12	10	6	27	4.5	0	40	472	11.8	4	29	293	10.1	0	0	0	0.0	0	4	0	24
2004—N.E. NFL	12	0	0	0	0.0	0	17	184	10.8	1	12	83	6.9	0	0	0	0.0	0	1	0	6
Pro totals (12 years)	162	58	27	160	5.9	0	475	5516	11.6	25	237	2524	10.6	3	87	1862	21.4	0	29	1	176

BROWNING, JOHN — DT — CHIEFS

PERSONAL: Born September 30, 1973, in Miami, Fla. ... 6-5/297.
HIGH SCHOOL: North Miami (Fla.).
COLLEGE: West Virginia.
TRANSACTIONS/CAREER NOTES: Selected by Kansas City Chiefs in third round (68th pick overall) of 1996 NFL draft. ... Signed by Chiefs (July 24, 1996). ... On injured reserve with Achilles' tendon injury (September 1, 1999-entire season). ... Granted unconditional free agency (February 11, 2000). ... Re-signed by Chiefs (February 11, 2000). ... On injured reserve with shoulder injury (October 25, 2001-remainder of season).

B

Year Team	G	GS	TOTALS Tk.	Ast.	Sks.	INTERCEPTIONS No.	Yds.	Avg.	TD
1996—Kansas City NFL	13	2	17	4	2.0	0	0	0.0	0
1997—Kansas City NFL	14	13	29	4	4.0	0	0	0.0	0
1998—Kansas City NFL	8	8	20	10	0.0	0	0	0.0	0
1999—Kansas City NFL	Did not play.								
2000—Kansas City NFL	16	16	38	10	6.0	1	0	0.0	0
2001—Kansas City NFL	6	6	15	5	1.5	0	0	0.0	0
2002—Kansas City NFL	16	16	33	6	7.0	0	0	0.0	0
2003—Kansas City NFL	16	16	37	5	0.5	0	0	0.0	0
2004—Kansas City NFL	16	7	32	7	4.5	0	0	0.0	0
Pro totals (8 years)	105	84	221	51	25.5	1	0	0.0	0

BRUCE, ISAAC   WR   RAMS

B

PERSONAL: Born November 10, 1972, in Fort Lauderdale, Fla. ... 6-0/188. ... Full name: Isaac Isidore Bruce.
HIGH SCHOOL: Dillard (Fort Lauderdale, Fla.).
JUNIOR COLLEGE: West Los Angeles Junior College, then Santa Monica (Calif.) Junior College.
COLLEGE: Memphis.
TRANSACTIONS/CAREER NOTES: Selected by Los Angeles Rams in second round (33rd pick overall) of 1994 NFL draft. ... Signed by Rams (July 13, 1994). ... On injured reserve with sprained right knee (December 9, 1994-remainder of season). ... Rams franchise moved to St. Louis (April 12, 1995). ... On injured reserve with hamstring injury (December 9, 1998-remainder of season).
CHAMPIONSHIP GAME EXPERIENCE: Played in NFC championship game (1999 and 2001 seasons). ... Member of Super Bowl championship team (1999 season). ... Played in Super Bowl 36 (2001 season).
HONORS: Named wide receiver on THE SPORTING NEWS NFL All-Pro team (1999). ... Played in Pro Bowl (1996 and 1999 season). ... Named to play in Pro Bowl (2000 season); replaced by Torry Holt due to injury. ... Named to play in Pro Bowl (2001 season); replaced by Joe Horn due to injury.
SINGLE GAME HIGHS (regular season): Receptions—15 (December 24, 1995, vs. Miami); yards—233 (November 2, 1997, vs. Atlanta); and touchdown receptions—4 (October 10, 1999, vs. San Francisco).
STATISTICAL PLATEAUS: 100-yard receiving games: 1995 (9), 1996 (5), 1997 (2), 1998 (2), 1999 (4), 2000 (4), 2001 (3), 2002 (2), 2003 (2), 2004 (6). Total: 39.
MISCELLANEOUS: Holds Rams franchise all-time records for most receptions (777), most yards receiving (11,753) and most receiving touchdowns (74).

Year Team	G	GS	RUSHING Att.	Yds.	Avg.	TD	RECEIVING No.	Yds.	Avg.	TD	TOTALS TD	2pt.	Pts.	Fum.
1994—Los Angeles Rams NFL	12	0	1	2	2.0	0	21	272	13.0	3	3	0	18	0
1995—St. Louis NFL	16	16	3	17	5.7	0	119	1781	15.0	13	13	1	80	2
1996—St. Louis NFL	16	16	1	4	4.0	0	84	*1338	15.9	7	7	0	42	1
1997—St. Louis NFL	12	12	0	0	0.0	0	56	815	14.6	5	5	0	30	1
1998—St. Louis NFL	5	5	1	30	30.0	0	32	457	14.3	1	1	0	6	0
1999—St. Louis NFL	16	16	5	32	6.4	0	77	1165	15.1	12	12	1	74	0
2000—St. Louis NFL	16	16	1	11	11.0	0	87	1471	16.9	9	9	0	54	1
2001—St. Louis NFL	16	16	4	23	5.8	0	64	1106	17.3	6	6	0	36	4
2002—St. Louis NFL	16	16	3	18	6.0	0	79	1075	13.6	7	7	0	42	2
2003—St. Louis NFL	15	15	2	17	8.5	0	69	981	14.2	5	5	0	30	0
2004—St. Louis NFL	16	16	0	0	0.0	0	89	1292	14.5	6	6	0	36	5
Pro totals (11 years)	156	144	21	154	7.3	0	777	11753	15.1	74	74	2	448	16

BRUENER, MARK   TE   TEXANS

PERSONAL: Born September 16, 1972, in Olympia, Wash. ... 6-4/258. ... Full name: Mark Frederick Bruener. ... Name pronounced: BREW-ner.
HIGH SCHOOL: Aberdeen (Wash.).
COLLEGE: Washington.
TRANSACTIONS/CAREER NOTES: Selected by Pittsburgh Steelers in first round (27th pick overall) of 1995 NFL draft. ... Signed by Steelers (July 25, 1995). ... On injured reserve with knee injury (November 29, 1996-remainder of season). ... On injured reserve with shoulder injury (November 21, 2001-remainder of season). ... On physically unable to perform list with foot injury (July 25-30, 2002). ... On injured reserve with knee injury (December 3, 2002-remainder of season). ... Released by Steelers (February 27, 2004). ... Signed by Houston Texans (March 22, 2004).
CHAMPIONSHIP GAME EXPERIENCE: Played in AFC championship game (1995 and 1997 seasons). ... Played in Super Bowl 30 (1995 season).
SINGLE GAME HIGHS (regular season): Receptions—5 (December 13, 1997, vs. New England); yards—51 (November 28, 1999, vs. Cincinnati); and touchdown receptions—1 (November 23, 2003, vs. Cleveland).

Year Team	G	GS	RECEIVING No.	Yds.	Avg.	TD	TOTALS TD	2pt.	Pts.	Fum.
1995—Pittsburgh NFL	16	13	26	238	9.2	3	3	0	18	0
1996—Pittsburgh NFL	12	12	12	141	11.8	0	0	1	2	0
1997—Pittsburgh NFL	16	16	18	117	6.5	6	6	0	36	1
1998—Pittsburgh NFL	16	16	19	157	8.3	2	2	0	12	0
1999—Pittsburgh NFL	14	14	18	176	9.8	0	0	0	0	0
2000—Pittsburgh NFL	16	16	17	192	11.3	3	3	0	18	0
2001—Pittsburgh NFL	9	9	12	98	8.2	0	0	0	0	0
2002—Pittsburgh NFL	12	12	13	66	5.1	1	1	0	6	0
2003—Pittsburgh NFL	14	0	2	12	6.0	1	1	0	6	0
2004—Houston NFL	16	11	4	52	13.0	0	0	0	0	0
Pro totals (10 years)	141	119	141	1249	8.9	16	16	1	98	1

BRUNELL, MARK   QB   REDSKINS

PERSONAL: Born September 17, 1970, in Los Angeles, Calif. ... 6-1/217. ... Full name: Mark Allen Brunell.
HIGH SCHOOL: St. Joseph (Santa Maria, Calif.).
COLLEGE: Washington.
TRANSACTIONS/CAREER NOTES: Selected by Green Bay Packers in fifth round (118th pick overall) of 1993 NFL draft. ... Signed by Packers (July 1, 1993). ... Traded by Packers to Jacksonville Jaguars for third- (FB William Henderson) and fifth-round (RB Travis Jervey) picks in 1995 draft (April 21, 1995). ... Traded by Jaguars to Washington Redskins for third-round pick (traded to Green Bay) in 2004 draft (March 3, 2004).
CHAMPIONSHIP GAME EXPERIENCE: Played in AFC championship game (1996 and 1999 seasons).
HONORS: Played in Pro Bowl (1996, 1997 and 1999 seasons). ... Named Outstanding Player of Pro Bowl (1996 season).
SINGLE GAME HIGHS (regular season): Attempts—52 (October 20, 1996, vs. St. Louis); completions—37 (October 20, 1996, vs. St. Louis); yards—432 (September 22, 1996, vs. New England); and touchdown passes—4 (November 29, 1998, vs. Cincinnati).
STATISTICAL PLATEAUS: 300-yard passing games: 1995 (2), 1996 (6), 1997 (3), 1998 (2), 1999 (3), 2000 (3), 2001 (2), 2002 (1), 2004 (1). Total: 23.
MISCELLANEOUS: Regular-season record as starting NFL quarterback: 66-60 (.524). ... Postseason record as starting NFL quarterback: 4-4 (.500). ... Holds Jacksonville Jaguars all-time record for most yards passing (25,698) and most touchdown passes (144).

				PASSING							RUSHING				TOTALS		
Year Team	G	GS	Att.	Cmp.	Pct.	Yds.	TD	Int.	Avg.	Skd.	Rat.	Att.	Yds.	Avg.	TD	TD	2pt.	Pts.
1993—Green Bay NFL	Did not play.																	
1994—Green Bay NFL	2	0	27	12	44.4	95	0	0	3.52	2	53.8	6	7	1.2	1	1	0	6
1995—Jacksonville NFL	13	10	346	201	58.1	2168	15	7	6.27	39	82.6	67	480	7.2	4	4	0	24
1996—Jacksonville NFL	16	16	557	353	§63.4	*4367	19	§20	*7.84	*50	84.0	80	396	5.0	3	3	2	22
1997—Jacksonville NFL	14	14	435	264	60.7	3281	18	7	§7.54	33	§91.2	48	257	5.4	2	2	0	12
1998—Jacksonville NFL	13	13	354	208	58.8	2601	20	9	7.35	28	89.9	49	192	3.9	0	0	0	0
1999—Jacksonville NFL	15	15	441	259	58.7	3060	14	9	6.94	29	82.0	47	208	4.4	1	1	1	8
2000—Jacksonville NFL	16	16	512	311	60.7	3640	20	14	7.11	*54	84.0	48	236	4.9	2	2	0	12
2001—Jacksonville NFL	15	15	473	289	61.1	3309	19	13	7.00	*57	84.1	39	224	5.7	1	1	0	6
2002—Jacksonville NFL	15	15	416	245	58.9	2788	17	7	6.70	34	85.7	43	207	4.8	0	0	0	0
2003—Jacksonville NFL	3	3	82	54	65.9	484	2	0	5.90	9	89.7	8	19	2.4	1	1	0	6
2004—Washington NFL	9	9	237	118	49.8	1194	7	6	5.04	15	63.9	19	62	3.3	0	0	0	0
Pro totals (11 years)	131	126	3880	2314	59.6	26987	151	92	6.96	350	83.9	454	2288	5.0	15	15	3	96

BRUSCHI, TEDY   LB   PATRIOTS

PERSONAL: Born June 9, 1973, in San Francisco, Calif. ... 6-1/247. ... Full name: Tedy Lacap Bruschi. ... Name pronounced: BREW-ski.
HIGH SCHOOL: Roseville (Calif.).
COLLEGE: Arizona.
TRANSACTIONS/CAREER NOTES: Selected by New England Patriots in third round (86th pick overall) of 1996 NFL draft. ... Signed by Patriots (July 17, 1996). ... Granted free agency (February 12, 1999). ... Re-signed by Patriots (June 1, 1999). ... Granted unconditional free agency (February 11, 2000). ... Re-signed by Patriots (March 22, 2000).
CHAMPIONSHIP GAME EXPERIENCE: Played in AFC championship game (1996, 2001, 2003 and 2004 seasons). ... Played in Super Bowl 31 (1996 season). ... Member of Super Bowl championship team (2001, 2003 and 2004 seasons).
HONORS: Named defensive lineman on THE SPORTING NEWS college All-America first team (1994 and 1995). ... Played in Pro Bowl (2004 season).

			TOTALS			INTERCEPTIONS			
Year Team	G	GS	Tk.	Ast.	Sks.	No.	Yds.	Avg.	TD
1996—New England NFL	16	0	10	1	4.0	0	0	0.0	0
1997—New England NFL	16	1	25	5	4.0	0	0	0.0	0
1998—New England NFL	16	7	48	26	2.0	0	0	0.0	0
1999—New England NFL	14	14	71	36	2.0	1	1	1.0	0
2000—New England NFL	16	16	68	38	1.0	0	0	0.0	0
2001—New England NFL	15	9	54	19	2.0	2	7	3.5	0
2002—New England NFL	11	9	45	20	4.5	2	75	37.5	▲2
2003—New England NFL	16	16	79	49	2.0	3	26	8.7	†2
2004—New England NFL	16	16	75	45	3.5	3	70	23.3	0
Pro totals (9 years)	136	88	475	239	25.0	11	179	16.3	4

BRYANT, ANTONIO   WR   BROWNS

PERSONAL: Born March 9, 1981, in Miami, Fla. ... 6-1/196.
HIGH SCHOOL: Miami Northwestern.
COLLEGE: Pittsburgh.
TRANSACTIONS/CAREER NOTES: Selected after junior season by Dallas Cowboys in second round (63rd pick overall) of 2002 NFL draft. ... Signed by Cowboys (July 26, 2002). ... Traded by Cowboys to Cleveland Browns for WR Quincy Morgan (October 19, 2004).
HONORS: Named wide receiver on THE SPORTING NEWS college All-America second team (2000).
SINGLE GAME HIGHS (regular season): Receptions—8 (November 28, 2004, vs. Cincinnati); yards—170 (December 29, 2002, vs. Washington); and touchdown receptions—2 (December 5, 2004, vs. New England).
STATISTICAL PLATEAUS: 100-yard receiving games: 2002 (1), 2004 (6). Total: 7.

			RUSHING				RECEIVING				TOTALS			
Year Team	G	GS	Att.	Yds.	Avg.	TD	No.	Yds.	Avg.	TD	TD	2pt.	Pts.	Fum.
2002—Dallas NFL	16	15	6	40	6.7	0	44	733	‡16.7	6	6	0	36	3
2003—Dallas NFL	16	5	2	0	0.0	0	39	550	14.1	2	2	0	12	0
2004—Dallas NFL	5	1	0	0	0.0	0	16	266	16.6	0	0	0	0	1
—Cleveland NFL	10	7	0	0	0.0	0	42	546	13.0	4	4	0	24	0
Pro totals (3 years)	47	28	8	40	5.0	0	141	2095	14.9	12	12	0	72	4

BRYANT, FERNANDO — CB — LIONS

PERSONAL: Born March 26, 1977, in Albany, Ga. ... 5-10/175. ... Full name: Fernando Antoneiyo Bryant.
HIGH SCHOOL: Riverdale (Murfreesboro, Tenn.).
COLLEGE: Alabama.
TRANSACTIONS/CAREER NOTES: Selected by Jacksonville Jaguars in first round (26th pick overall) of 1999 NFL draft. ... Signed by Jaguars (August 9, 1999). ... On injured reserve with foot injury (January 1, 2002-remainder of season). ... Granted unconditional free agency (March 3, 2004). ... Signed by Detroit Lions (March 5, 2004).
CHAMPIONSHIP GAME EXPERIENCE: Played in AFC championship game (1999 season).

				TOTALS			INTERCEPTIONS			
Year Team	G	GS	Tk.	Ast.	Sks.	No.	Yds.	Avg.	TD
1999—Jacksonville NFL	16	16	61	9	0.0	2	0	0.0	0
2000—Jacksonville NFL	14	14	37	6	0.0	1	0	0.0	0
2001—Jacksonville NFL	10	9	49	5	0.0	0	0	0.0	0
2002—Jacksonville NFL	16	16	57	2	0.0	1	26	26.0	0
2003—Jacksonville NFL	16	16	61	9	0.0	1	0	0.0	0
2004—Detroit NFL	10	10	42	8	0.0	0	0	0.0	0
Pro totals (6 years)	82	81	307	39	0.0	5	26	5.2	0

BRYANT, MATT — K — BUCCANEERS

PERSONAL: Born May 29, 1975, in Orange, Texas. ... 5-9/200.
HIGH SCHOOL: Bridge City (Orange, Texas).
JUNIOR COLLEGE: Panola Junior College, then Trinity Valley Community College (Texas).
COLLEGE: Baylor.
TRANSACTIONS/CAREER NOTES: Signed as non-drafted free agent by New York Giants (January 9, 2002). ... Assigned by Giants to Frankfurt Galaxy in 2002 NFL Europe enhancement allocation program (February 12, 2002). ... Released by Giants (August 30, 2002). ... Re-signed by Giants to practice squad (September 2, 2002). ... Activated (September 3, 2002). ... Released by Giants (July 30, 2004). ... Signed by Dallas Cowboys (August 11, 2004). ... Released by Cowboys (September 5, 2004). ... Signed by Indianapolis Colts (October 8, 2004). ... Released by Colts (October 11, 2004). ... Signed by Miami Dolphins (October 13, 2004). ... Released by Dolphins (November 10, 2004). ... Signed by Tampa Bay Buccaneers (March 2, 2005).

		FIELD GOALS							TOTALS		
Year Team	G	1-29	30-39	40-49	50+	Tot.	Pct.	Lg.	XPM	XPA	Pts.
2002—New York Giants NFL	16	9-9	14-19	3-4	0-0	26-32	81.3	47	30	32	108
2003—New York Giants NFL	11	3-4	4-5	4-5	0-0	11-14	78.6	47	17	17	50
2004—Indianapolis NFL	1	0-0	0-0	0-1	0-0	0-1	0.0	0	5	5	5
—Miami NFL	3	1-1	0-0	2-2	0-0	3-3	100.0	47	7	7	16
Pro totals (3 years)	31	13-14	18-24	9-12	0-0	40-50	80.0	47	59	61	179

BRYANT, RODERICK — CB

PERSONAL: Born February 17, 1981, in Washington, DC. ... 6-1/190.
HIGH SCHOOL: Friendly (Maryland).
JUNIOR COLLEGE: West Hills (Coalinga, Calif.).
COLLEGE: Idaho.
TRANSACTIONS/CAREER NOTES: Signed as non-drafted free agent by New York Jets (April 30, 2004). ... Released by Jets (March 2, 2005).

				TOTALS			INTERCEPTIONS			
Year Team	G	GS	Tk.	Ast.	Sks.	No.	Yds.	Avg.	TD
2004—New York Jets NFL	13	0	2	0	0.0	0	0	0.0	0

BRYANT, TONY — DE — SAINTS

PERSONAL: Born September 3, 1976, in Marathon, Fla. ... 6-6/282.
HIGH SCHOOL: Marathon (Fla.).
JUNIOR COLLEGE: Copiah-Lincoln (Miss.).
COLLEGE: Florida State.
TRANSACTIONS/CAREER NOTES: Selected by Oakland Raiders in second round (40th pick overall) of 1999 NFL draft. ... Signed by Raiders (July 22, 1999). ... On injured reserve (December 7, 2002-remainder of season). ... Released by Raiders (July 24, 2003). ... Signed by New Orleans Saints (December 26, 2003). ... Granted unconditional free agency (March 2, 2005). ... Re-signed by Saints (March 22, 2005).
CHAMPIONSHIP GAME EXPERIENCE: Played in AFC championship game (2000 season).

			TOTALS		
Year Team	G	GS	Tk.	Ast.	Sks.
1999—Oakland NFL	10	0	0	0	4.5
2000—Oakland NFL	16	16	0	0	5.5
2001—Oakland NFL	16	16	0	0	5.0
2002—Oakland NFL	8	8	0	0	2.5
2004—New Orleans NFL	16	0	7	4	2.0
Pro totals (5 years)	66	40	7	4	19.5

BRYANT, WENDELL — DT — CARDINALS

PERSONAL: Born September 12, 1980, in St. Louis, Mo. ... 6-5/303.
HIGH SCHOOL: Ritenour (St. Louis).
COLLEGE: Wisconsin.

B

TRANSACTIONS/CAREER NOTES: Selected by Arizona Cardinals in first round (12th pick overall) of 2002 NFL draft. ... Signed by Cardinals (September 12, 2002). ... On suspended list for violating league substance abuse policy (September 6-October 6, 2004).
HONORS: Named defensive tackle on THE SPORTING NEWS college All-America second team (2001).

Year Team		G	GS	TOTALS Tk.	Ast.	Sks.
2002—Arizona NFL		14	4	12	8	1.5
2003—Arizona NFL		12	5	16	3	0.0
2004—Arizona NFL		3	0	1	0	0.0
Pro totals (3 years)		29	9	29	11	1.5

B

BRYSON, SHAWN — RB — LIONS

PERSONAL: Born November 20, 1976, in Franklin, N.C. ... 6-1/230. ... Full name: Adrian Shawn Bryson.
HIGH SCHOOL: Franklin (N.C.).
COLLEGE: Tennessee.
TRANSACTIONS/CAREER NOTES: Selected by Buffalo Bills in third round (86th pick overall) of 1999 NFL draft. ... Signed by Bills (July 27, 1999). ... On injured reserve with knee injury (August 30, 1999-entire season). ... Granted free agency (March 1, 2002). ... Re-signed by Bills (May 6, 2002). ... On injured reserve with knee injury (October 18, 2002-remainder of season). ... Granted unconditional free agency (February 28, 2003). ... Signed by Detroit Lions (March 24, 2003). ... Granted unconditional free agency (March 3, 2004). ... Re-signed by Lions (March 23, 2004).
SINGLE GAME HIGHS (regular season): Attempts—28 (December 30, 2001, vs. New York Jets); yards—130 (December 23, 2001, vs. Atlanta); and rushing touchdowns—2 (December 23, 2001, vs. Atlanta).
STATISTICAL PLATEAUS: 100-yard rushing games: 2001 (2), 2003 (1). Total: 3.

Year Team	G	GS	RUSHING Att.	Yds.	Avg.	TD	RECEIVING No.	Yds.	Avg.	TD	KICKOFF RETURNS No.	Yds.	Avg.	TD	TOTALS TD	2pt.	Pts.	Fum.
1999—Buffalo NFL	Did not play.																	
2000—Buffalo NFL	16	7	161	591	3.7	0	32	271	8.5	2	8	122	15.3	0	2	1	14	1
2001—Buffalo NFL	15	3	80	341	4.3	0	9	59	6.6	0	16	299	18.7	0	2	0	12	0
2002—Buffalo NFL	6	0	13	35	2.7	0	1	9	9.0	0	1	18	18.0	0	0	0	0	1
2003—Detroit NFL	16	13	158	606	3.8	3	54	340	6.3	0	0	0	0.0	0	3	0	18	2
2004—Detroit NFL	16	1	50	264	5.3	0	44	322	7.3	0	2	27	13.5	0	0	0	0	1
Pro totals (5 years)	69	24	462	1837	4.0	5	140	1001	7.2	2	27	466	17.3	0	7	1	44	5

BRZEZINSKI, DOUG — G

PERSONAL: Born March 11, 1976, in Livonia, Mich. ... 6-4/305. ... Full name: Douglas Gregory Brzezinski. ... Name pronounced: bruh-ZHIN-skee.
HIGH SCHOOL: Detroit Catholic Central.
COLLEGE: Boston College.
TRANSACTIONS/CAREER NOTES: Selected by Philadelphia Eagles in third round (64th pick overall) of 1999 NFL draft. ... Signed by Eagles (July 28, 1999). ... Granted free agency (March 1, 2002). ... Re-signed by Eagles (March 28, 2002). ... Granted unconditional free agency (February 28, 2003). ... Signed by Carolina Panthers (March 12, 2003). ... On injured reserve with hip injury (November 9, 2004-remainder of season). ... Released by Panthers (February 28, 2005).
PLAYING EXPERIENCE: Philadelphia NFL, 1999-2002; Carolina NFL, 2003-2004. ... Games/Games started: 1999 (16/16), 2000 (16/0), 2001 (16/1), 2002 (16/5), 2003 (1/0), 2004 (8/8). Total: 73/30.
CHAMPIONSHIP GAME EXPERIENCE: Played in NFC championship game (2001 and 2002 seasons). ... Member of Panthers for NFC championship game (2003 season); inactive. ... Member of Panthers for Super Bowl 38 (2003 season); inactive.
HONORS: Named offensive guard on THE SPORTING NEWS college All-America first team (1998).

BUA, TONY — LB — DOLPHINS

PERSONAL: Born February 11, 1980, in River Ridge, La. ... 5-11/212. ... Full name: Anthony Bua.
HIGH SCHOOL: John Curtis (River Ridge, La.).
COLLEGE: Arkansas.
TRANSACTIONS/CAREER NOTES: Selected by Miami Dolphins in fifth round (160th pick overall) of 2004 NFL draft. ... Signed by Dolphins (July 30, 2004). ... On injured reserve with quadriceps injury (December 17, 2004-remainder of season).

Year Team	G	GS	TOTALS Tk.	Ast.	Sks.	INTERCEPTIONS No.	Yds.	Avg.	TD
2004—Miami NFL	7	0	0	0	0.0	0	0	0.0	0

BUCHANAN, RAY — CB

PERSONAL: Born September 29, 1971, in Chicago, Ill. ... 5-9/185. ... Full name: Raymond Louis Buchanan.
HIGH SCHOOL: Proviso East (Maywood, Ill.).
COLLEGE: Louisville.
TRANSACTIONS/CAREER NOTES: Selected by Indianapolis Colts in third round (65th pick overall) of 1993 NFL draft. ... Signed by Colts (July 26, 1993). ... Designated by Colts as transition player (February 13, 1997). ... Tendered offer sheet by Atlanta Falcons (February 25, 1997). ... Colts declined to match offer (March 3, 1997). ... Granted unconditional free agency (February 21, 2001). ... Re-signed by Falcons (February 21, 2001). ... On suspended list for violating league substance abuse policy (September 11-October 14, 2002). ... Released by Falcons (March 1, 2004). ... Signed by Oakland Raiders (April 5, 2004). ... Released by Raiders (March 1, 2005).
CHAMPIONSHIP GAME EXPERIENCE: Played in AFC championship game (1995 season). ... Played in NFC championship game (1998 season). ... Played in Super Bowl 33 (1998 season).
HONORS: Played in Pro Bowl (1998 season).

Year Team	TOTALS					INTERCEPTIONS				PUNT RETURNS				TOTALS			
	G	GS	Tk.	Ast.	Sks.	No.	Yds.	Avg.	TD	No.	Yds.	Avg.	TD	TD	2pt.	Pts.	Fum.
1993—Indianapolis NFL	16	5	44	21	0.0	4	45	11.3	0	0	0	0.0	0	0	0	0	0
1994—Indianapolis NFL	16	16	76	24	1.0	8	221	27.6	†3	0	0	0.0	0	3	0	18	0
1995—Indianapolis NFL	16	16	68	15	1.0	2	60	30.0	0	16	113	7.1	0	0	0	0	1
1996—Indianapolis NFL	13	13	53	9	0.5	2	32	16.0	0	12	201	16.8	0	0	0	0	0
1997—Atlanta NFL	16	16	48	4	0.0	5	49	9.8	0	0	37	0.0	0	0	0	0	0
1998—Atlanta NFL	16	16	54	7	0.0	7	102	14.6	0	1	4	4.0	0	0	0	0	0
1999—Atlanta NFL	16	16	59	5	1.0	4	81	20.2	1	0	0	0.0	0	1	0	6	0
2000—Atlanta NFL	16	16	69	11	0.0	6	114	19.0	0	0	0	0.0	0	0	0	0	0
2001—Atlanta NFL	16	16	63	8	0.0	5	85	17.0	0	0	0	0.0	0	0	0	0	0
2002—Atlanta NFL	12	11	42	5	0.0	2	9	4.5	0	0	0	0.0	0	0	0	0	0
2003—Atlanta NFL	15	8	37	1	0.0	1	2	2.0	0	0	0	0.0	0	0	0	0	0
2004—Oakland NFL	16	16	63	24	0.0	1	27	27.0	0	0	0	0.0	0	0	0	0	0
Pro totals (12 years)	184	165	676	134	3.5	47	827	17.6	4	29	355	12.2	0	4	0	24	1

B

BUCHANON, PHILLIP   CB   TEXANS

PERSONAL: Born September 19, 1980, in Fort Myers, Fla. ... 5-10/185. ... Full name: Phillip Darren Buchanon.
HIGH SCHOOL: Lehigh (Fla.).
COLLEGE: Miami (Fla.).
TRANSACTIONS/CAREER NOTES: Selected after junior season by Oakland Raiders in first round (17th pick overall) of 2002 NFL draft. ... Signed by Raiders (July 25, 2002). ... On injured reserve with wrist injury (October 25, 2002-remainder of season). ... Traded by Raiders to Houston Texans for second- (traded to N.Y. Jets) and third-round (LB Kirk Morrison) picks in 2005 draft (April 20, 2005).

Year Team	TOTALS					INTERCEPTIONS				PUNT RETURNS				KICKOFF RETURNS				TOTALS			
	G	GS	Tk.	Ast.	Sks.	No.	Yds.	Avg.	TD	No.	Yds.	Avg.	TD	No.	Yds.	Avg.	TD	TD	2pt.	Pts.	Fum.
2002—Oak. NFL	6	2	21	0	0.0	2	81	40.5	1	15	178	11.9	1	0	0	0.0	0	2	0	12	2
2003—Oak. NFL	16	10	42	2	0.0	6	§176	29.3	†2	36	491	13.6	†2	2	25	12.5	0	4	0	24	3
2004—Oak. NFL	14	14	50	9	0.0	3	69	23.0	1	21	121	5.8	0	0	0	0.0	0	1	0	6	2
Pro totals (3 years)	36	26	113	11	0.0	11	326	29.6	4	72	790	11.0	3	2	25	12.5	0	7	0	42	7

BUCKHALTER, CORRELL   RB   EAGLES

PERSONAL: Born October 6, 1978, in Collins, Miss. ... 6-0/222.
HIGH SCHOOL: Collins (Miss.).
COLLEGE: Nebraska.
TRANSACTIONS/CAREER NOTES: Selected by Philadelphia Eagles in fourth round (121st pick overall) of 2001 NFL draft. ... Signed by Eagles (May 24, 2001). ... On physically unable to perform list with knee injury (July 27, 2002-entire season). ... Granted free agency (March 3, 2004). ... Re-signed by Eagles (April 30, 2004). ... On injured reserve with knee injury (August 23, 2004-entire season). ... Granted unconditional free agency (March 2, 2005). ... Re-signed by Eagles (March 3, 2005).
CHAMPIONSHIP GAME EXPERIENCE: Played in NFC championship game (2001 and 2003 seasons).
SINGLE GAME HIGHS (regular season): Attempts—23 (November 2, 2003, vs. Atlanta); yards—134 (October 7, 2001, vs. Arizona); and rushing touchdowns—2 (October 26, 2003, vs. New York Jets).
STATISTICAL PLATEAUS: 100-yard rushing games: 2001 (1), 2003 (2). Total: 3.

Year Team		RUSHING				RECEIVING				TOTALS			
	G	GS	Att.	Yds.	Avg.	TD	No.	Yds.	Avg.	TD	TD	2pt.	Pts.	Fum.
2001—Philadelphia NFL	15	6	129	586	4.5	2	13	130	10.0	0	2	0	12	2
2002—Philadelphia NFL			Did not play.											
2003—Philadelphia NFL	15	5	126	542	4.3	8	10	133	13.3	1	9	0	54	3
2004—Philadelphia NFL			Did not play.											
Pro totals (2 years)	30	11	255	1128	4.4	10	23	263	11.4	1	11	0	66	5

BUCKLEY, TERRELL   CB

PERSONAL: Born June 7, 1971, in Pascagoula, Miss. ... 5-10/180. ... Full name: Douglas Terrell Buckley.
HIGH SCHOOL: Pascagoula (Miss.).
COLLEGE: Florida State.
TRANSACTIONS/CAREER NOTES: Selected after junior season by Green Bay Packers in first round (fifth pick overall) of 1992 NFL draft. ... Signed by Packers (September 11, 1992). ... Granted roster exemption for one game (September 1992). ... Traded by Packers to Miami Dolphins for past considerations (April 3, 1995). ... Granted unconditional free agency (February 11, 2000). ... Signed by Denver Broncos (July 20, 2000). ... Granted unconditional free agency (March 2, 2001). ... Signed by New England Patriots (July 13, 2001). ... Granted unconditional free agency (March 1, 2002). ... Signed by Tampa Bay Buccaneers (July 8, 2002). ... Released by Buccaneers (September 1, 2002). ... Signed by New England Patriots (September 5, 2002). ... Granted unconditional free agency (February 28, 2003). ... Signed by Dolphins (March 13, 2003). ... Granted unconditional free agency (March 3, 2004). ... Signed by Patriots (June 8, 2004). ... Released by Patriots (September 5, 2004). ... Signed by New York Jets (September 8, 2004). ... Granted unconditional free agency (March 2, 2005).
CHAMPIONSHIP GAME EXPERIENCE: Played in AFC championship game (2001 season). ... Member of Super Bowl championship team (2001 season).
HONORS: Named defensive back on THE SPORTING NEWS college All-America second team (1990). ... Jim Thorpe Award winner (1991). ... Named defensive back on THE SPORTING NEWS college All-America first team (1991).

Year Team	TOTALS					INTERCEPTIONS				PUNT RETURNS				TOTALS			
	G	GS	Tk.	Ast.	Sks.	No.	Yds.	Avg.	TD	No.	Yds.	Avg.	TD	TD	2pt.	Pts.	Fum.
1992—Green Bay NFL	14	12	30	2	0.0	3	33	11.0	1	21	211	10.0	1	2	0	12	7
1993—Green Bay NFL	16	16	47	1	0.0	2	31	15.5	0	11	76	6.9	0	0	0	0	1
1994—Green Bay NFL	16	16	48	11	0.0	5	38	7.6	0	0	0	0.0	0	0	0	0	0
1995—Miami NFL	16	4	23	3	0.0	1	0	0.0	0	0	0	0.0	0	0	0	0	0
1996—Miami NFL	16	16	46	7	0.0	6	*164	27.3	1	3	24	8.0	0	1	0	6	1

Year Team	G	GS	TOTALS			INTERCEPTIONS				PUNT RETURNS				TOTALS			
			Tk.	Ast.	Sks.	No.	Yds.	Avg.	TD	No.	Yds.	Avg.	TD	TD	2pt.	Pts.	Fum.
1997—Miami NFL	16	16	67	18	0.0	4	26	6.5	0	4	58	14.5	0	1	0	6	0
1998—Miami NFL	16	16	44	7	0.0	8	157	19.6	1	29	354	12.2	0	1	0	6	1
1999—Miami NFL	16	11	30	5	1.0	3	3	1.0	0	8	13	1.6	0	0	0	0	0
2000—Denver NFL	16	16	35	3	0.0	6	110	18.3	1	2	10	5.0	0	1	0	6	0
2001—New England NFL	15	1	24	2	1.0	3	76	25.3	1	0	0	0.0	0	1	0	6	0
2002—New England NFL	16	2	21	0	0.0	4	50	12.5	0	0	0	0.0	0	0	0	0	1
2003—Miami NFL	16	5	39	11	0.0	2	75	37.5	1	1	2	2.0	0	1	0	6	1
2004—New York Jets NFL	16	0	8	2	0.0	3	30	10.0	0	0	0	0.0	0	0	0	0	0
Pro totals (13 years)	205	131	462	72	2.0	50	793	15.9	6	79	748	9.5	1	8	0	48	13

B

BUCKNER, BRENTSON   DT   PANTHERS

PERSONAL: Born September 30, 1971, in Columbus, Ga. ... 6-2/310. ... Full name: Brentson Andre Buckner. ... Name pronounced: BRENT-son.

HIGH SCHOOL: Carver (Columbus, Ga.).

COLLEGE: Clemson.

TRANSACTIONS/CAREER NOTES: Selected by Pittsburgh Steelers in second round (50th pick overall) of 1994 NFL Draft. ... Signed by Steelers (July 23, 1994). ... Traded by Steelers to Kansas City Chiefs for seventh-round pick (traded to San Diego) in 1997 draft (April 4, 1997). ... Claimed on waivers by Cincinnati Bengals (August 25, 1997). ... Granted unconditional free agency (February 13, 1998). ... Signed by San Francisco 49ers (May 26, 1998). ... On physically unable to perform list with pulled quadricep muscle (July 17-August 15, 1998). ... Granted unconditional free agency (February 12, 1999). ... Re-signed by 49ers (April 7, 1999). ... Granted unconditional free agency (February 11, 2000). ... Re-signed by 49ers (August 8, 2000). ... Granted unconditional free agency (March 2, 2001). ... Signed by Carolina Panthers (April 21, 2001). ... On suspended list for violating league substance abuse policy (November 4-December 2, 2002). ... Activated (December 2, 2002).

CHAMPIONSHIP GAME EXPERIENCE: Played in AFC championship game (1994 and 1995 seasons). ... Played in NFC championship game (2003 season). ... Played in Super Bowl 30 (1995 season) and Super Bowl 38 (2003 season).

Year Team	G	GS	TOTALS			INTERCEPTIONS			
			Tk.	Ast.	Sks.	No.	Yds.	Avg.	TD
1994—Pittsburgh NFL	13	5	13	5	2.0	0	0	0.0	0
1995—Pittsburgh NFL	16	16	29	19	3.0	0	0	0.0	0
1996—Pittsburgh NFL	15	14	24	12	3.0	0	0	0.0	0
1997—Cincinnati NFL	14	5	32	7	0.0	0	0	0.0	0
1998—San Francisco NFL	13	0	10	6	0.5	0	0	0.0	0
1999—San Francisco NFL	16	6	29	15	1.0	0	0	0.0	0
2000—San Francisco NFL	16	16	41	14	7.0	0	0	0.0	0
2001—Carolina NFL	16	10	28	10	4.5	1	29	29.0	0
2002—Carolina NFL	12	12	24	8	5.0	0	0	0.0	0
2003—Carolina NFL	12	12	20	3	0.5	0	0	0.0	0
2004—Carolina NFL	15	15	28	13	3.5	1	8	8.0	0
Pro totals (11 years)	158	111	278	112	30.0	2	37	18.5	0

BULGER, MARC   QB   RAMS

PERSONAL: Born April 5, 1977, in Pittsburgh, Pa. ... 6-3/215. ... Full name: Marc Robert Bulger.

HIGH SCHOOL: Central Catholic (Pittsburgh).

COLLEGE: West Virginia.

TRANSACTIONS/CAREER NOTES: Selected by New Orleans Saints in sixth round (168th pick overall) of 2000 NFL draft. ... Signed by Saints (July 13, 2000). ... Released by Saints (August 22, 2000). ... Signed by St. Louis Rams to practice squad (October 24, 2000). ... Released by Rams (October 31, 2000). ... Signed by Atlanta Falcons to practice squad (December 1, 2000). ... Released by Falcons (December 13, 2000). ... Re-signed by Rams (January 12, 2001). ... Granted free agency (March 3, 2004). ... Re-signed by Rams (May 4, 2004).

CHAMPIONSHIP GAME EXPERIENCE: Member of Rams for NFC championship game (2001 season); inactive. ... Member of Rams for Super Bowl 36 (2001 season); inactive.

HONORS: Played in Pro Bowl (2003 season). ... Named Outstanding Player of Pro Bowl (2003 season).

SINGLE GAME HIGHS (regular season): Attempts—53 (November 29, 2004, vs. Green Bay); completions—36 (November 10, 2002, vs. San Diego); yards—453 (November 10, 2002, vs. San Diego); and touchdown passes—4 (November 10, 2002, vs. San Diego).

STATISTICAL PLATEAUS: 300-yard passing games: 2002 (3), 2003 (4), 2004 (4). Total: 11.

MISCELLANEOUS: Regular-season record as starting NFL quarterback: 26-10 (.722). ... Post-season record as starting NFL quarterback: 1-2 (.333).

Year Team	G	GS	PASSING									RUSHING				TOTALS		
			Att.	Cmp.	Pct.	Yds.	TD	Int.	Avg.	Skd.	Rat.	Att.	Yds.	Avg.	TD	TD	2pt.	Pts.
2002—St. Louis NFL	7	7	214	138	64.5	1826	14	6	8.53	12	101.5	12	-13	-1.1	1	1	0	6
2003—St. Louis NFL	15	15	532	336	63.2	‡3845	22	†22	7.23	37	81.4	29	75	2.6	4	4	0	24
2004—St. Louis NFL	14	14	485	321	66.2	3964	21	14	8.17	41	93.7	19	89	4.7	3	3	0	18
Pro totals (3 years)	36	36	1231	795	64.6	9635	57	42	7.83	90	89.7	60	151	2.5	8	8	0	48

BULLUCK, KEITH   LB   TITANS

PERSONAL: Born April 4, 1977, in Suffern, N.Y. ... 6-3/235. ... Full name: Keith J. Bulluck.

HIGH SCHOOL: Clarkstown (New City, N.Y.).

COLLEGE: Syracuse.

TRANSACTIONS/CAREER NOTES: Selected by Tennessee Titans in first round (30th pick overall) of 2000 NFL draft. ... Signed by Titans (July 19, 2000).

CHAMPIONSHIP GAME EXPERIENCE: Played in AFC championship game (2002 season).

HONORS: Played in Pro Bowl (2003 season).

Year—Team	G	GS	Tk.	Ast.	Sks.	No.	Yds.	Avg.	TD
			TOTALS			INTERCEPTIONS			
2000—Tennessee NFL	16	1	10	7	0.0	1	8	8.0	1
2001—Tennessee NFL	15	3	26	19	1.0	2	21	10.5	0
2002—Tennessee NFL	16	16	101	26	1.0	1	5	5.0	0
2003—Tennessee NFL	16	16	106	31	3.0	2	9	4.5	0
2004—Tennessee NFL	16	16	99	53	5.0	2	25	12.5	0
Pro totals (5 years)	79	52	342	136	10.0	8	68	8.5	1

BURGESS, DERRICK — LB/DE — RAIDERS

PERSONAL: Born August 12, 1978, in Lake City, S.C. ... 6-2/266.
HIGH SCHOOL: Eleanor Roosevelt (Greenbelt, Md.).
COLLEGE: Mississippi.
TRANSACTIONS/CAREER NOTES: Selected by Philadelphia Eagles in third round (63rd pick overall) of 2001 NFL draft. ... Signed by Eagles (July 26, 2001). ... On injured reserve with Achilles injury (September 6, 2003-entire season). ... Granted unconditional free agency (March 2, 2005). ... Signed by Oakland Raiders (March 12, 2005).
CHAMPIONSHIP GAME EXPERIENCE: Played in NFC championship game (2001 and 2004 seasons). ... Member of Eagles for NFC championship game (2002 season); inactive. ... Played in Super Bowl 39 (2004 season).

Year—Team	G	GS	Tk.	Ast.	Sks.	No.	Yds.	Avg.	TD
			TOTALS			INTERCEPTIONS			
2001—Philadelphia NFL	16	4	24	6	6.0	0	0	0.0	0
2002—Philadelphia NFL	1	0	1	0	0.0	0	0	0.0	0
2003—Philadelphia NFL			Did not play.						
2004—Philadelphia NFL	12	11	20	4	2.5	0	0	0.0	0
Pro totals (3 years)	29	15	45	10	8.5	0	0	0.0	0

BURLESON, NATE — WR — VIKINGS

PERSONAL: Born August 19, 1981, in Seattle, Wash. ... 6-0/192.
HIGH SCHOOL: O'Dea (Seattle).
COLLEGE: Nevada.
TRANSACTIONS/CAREER NOTES: Selected by Minnesota Vikings in third round (71st pick overall) of 2003 NFL draft. ... Signed by Vikings (July 23, 2003).
SINGLE GAME HIGHS (regular season): Receptions—11 (November 14, 2004, vs. Green Bay); yards—141 (November 14, 2004, vs. Green Bay); and touchdown receptions—2 (December 19, 2004, vs. Detroit).
STATISTICAL PLATEAUS: 100-yard receiving games: 2004 (4). Total: 4.

Year—Team	G	GS	Att.	Yds.	Avg.	TD	No.	Yds.	Avg.	TD	No.	Yds.	Avg.	TD	No.	Yds.	Avg.	TD	TD	2pt.	Pts.
			RUSHING				RECEIVING				PUNT RETURNS				KICKOFF RETURNS				TOTALS		
2003—Min. NFL	16	9	0	0	0.0	0	29	455	15.7	2	1	0	0.0	0	0	0	0.0	0	2	0	12
2004—Min. NFL	16	15	6	49	8.2	0	68	1006	14.8	9	25	214	8.6	1	2	51	25.5	0	10	1	62
Pro totals (2 years)	32	24	6	49	8.2	0	97	1461	15.1	11	26	214	8.2	1	2	51	25.5	0	12	1	74

BURNS, CURRY — S — GIANTS

PERSONAL: Born February 12, 1981, in Miami, Fla. ... 6-0/216.
HIGH SCHOOL: Jackson (Miami).
COLLEGE: Louisville.
TRANSACTIONS/CAREER NOTES: Selected by Houston Texans in seventh round (217th pick overall) of 2003 NFL draft. ... Signed by Texans (June 4, 2003). ... Waived by Texans (August 25, 2003). ... Re-signed by Texans (December 2, 2003). ... Released by Texans (August 31, 2004). ... Signed by New England Patriots to practice squad (September 15, 2004). ... Signed by New York Giants off Patriots practice squad (October 6, 2004).

Year—Team	G	GS	Tk.	Ast.	Sks.	No.	Yds.	Avg.	TD
			TOTALS			INTERCEPTIONS			
2003—Houston NFL	1	0	0	0	0.0	0	0	0.0	0
2004—New York Giants NFL	8	2	17	3	0.0	1	12	12.0	0
Pro totals (2 years)	9	2	17	3	0.0	1	12	12.0	0

BURNS, JOE — RB — BILLS

PERSONAL: Born September 15, 1979, in Thomasville, Ga. ... 5-9/215. ... Full name: Joe Frank Burns.
HIGH SCHOOL: Thomas County (Ga.).
COLLEGE: Georgia Tech.
TRANSACTIONS/CAREER NOTES: Signed as non-drafted free agent by Buffalo Bills (April 26, 2002).
SINGLE GAME HIGHS (regular season): Attempts—8 (September 28, 2003, vs. Philadelphia); yards—29 (December 7, 2003, vs. New York Jets); and rushing touchdowns—0.

Year—Team	G	GS	Att.	Yds.	Avg.	TD	No.	Yds.	Avg.	TD	No.	Yds.	Avg.	TD	TD	2pt.	Pts.	Fum.
			RUSHING				RECEIVING				KICKOFF RETURNS				TOTALS			
2002—Buffalo NFL	10	0	5	7	1.4	0	0	0	0.0	0	1	35	35.0	0	0	0	0	0
2003—Buffalo NFL	16	1	39	113	2.9	0	7	62	8.9	0	1	17	17.0	0	0	0	0	1
2004—Buffalo NFL	16	0	20	73	3.7	0	1	7	7.0	0	0	0	0.0	0	0	0	0	0
Pro totals (3 years)	42	1	64	193	3.0	0	8	69	8.6	0	2	52	26.0	0	0	0	0	1

BURNS, KEITH   LB   BRONCOS

PERSONAL: Born May 16, 1972, in Greeleyville, S.C. ... 6-2/235. ... Full name: Keith Bernard Burns.
HIGH SCHOOL: T. C. Williams (Alexandria, Va.).
JUNIOR COLLEGE: Navarro College (Texas).
COLLEGE: Oklahoma State.
TRANSACTIONS/CAREER NOTES: Selected by Denver Broncos in seventh round (210th pick overall) of 1994 NFL draft. ... Signed by Broncos (July 12, 1994). ... Granted free agency (February 14, 1997). ... Re-signed by Broncos (June 30, 1997). ... Granted unconditional free agency (February 12, 1999). ... Signed by Chicago Bears (April 6, 1999). ... Released by Bears (August 27, 2000). ... Signed by Broncos (September 19, 2000). ... Granted unconditional free agency (March 2, 2001). ... Re-signed by Broncos (April 6, 2001). ... Released by Broncos (February 26, 2003). ... Re-signed by Broncos (February 27, 2003). ... Granted unconditional free agency (March 3, 2004). ... Signed by Tampa Bay Buccaneers (March 9, 2004). ... Granted unconditional free agency (March 2, 2005). ... Signed by Denver Broncos (March 25, 2005).
CHAMPIONSHIP GAME EXPERIENCE: Played in AFC championship game (1997 and 1998 seasons). ... Member of Super Bowl championship team (1997 and 1998 seasons).

			TOTALS			INTERCEPTIONS			
Year Team	G	GS	Tk.	Ast.	Sks.	No.	Yds.	Avg.	TD
1994—Denver NFL	11	1	15	3	0.0	0	0	0.0	0
1995—Denver NFL	16	0	10	3	1.5	0	0	0.0	0
1996—Denver NFL	16	0	1	0	0.0	0	0	0.0	0
1997—Denver NFL	16	0	1	0	0.0	0	0	0.0	0
1998—Denver NFL	16	0	7	2	0.0	0	0	0.0	0
1999—Chicago NFL	15	0	5	0	0.0	1	15	15.0	0
2000—Denver NFL	13	0	0	0	0.0	0	0	0.0	0
2001—Denver NFL	16	0	0	0	0.0	0	0	0.0	0
2002—Denver NFL	16	1	0	0	0.0	0	0	0.0	0
2003—Denver NFL	16	0	2	1	0.0	0	0	0.0	0
2004—Tampa Bay NFL	16	0	0	0	0.0	0	0	0.0	0
Pro totals (11 years)	167	2	41	9	1.5	1	15	15.0	0

BURRESS, PLAXICO   WR   GIANTS

PERSONAL: Born August 12, 1977, in Norfolk, Va. ... 6-5/226.
HIGH SCHOOL: Green Run (Virginia Beach, Va.).
COLLEGE: Michigan State.
TRANSACTIONS/CAREER NOTES: Selected after junior season by Pittsburgh Steelers in first round (eighth pick overall) of 2000 NFL draft. ... Signed by Steelers (July 20, 2000). ... On injured reserve with wrist injury (December 1, 2000-remainder of season). ... Granted unconditional free agency (March 2, 2005). ... Signed by New York Giants (March 18, 2005).
CHAMPIONSHIP GAME EXPERIENCE: Played in AFC championship game (2001 and 2004 seasons).
SINGLE GAME HIGHS (regular season): Receptions—9 (November 10, 2002, vs. Atlanta); yards—253 (November 10, 2002, vs. Atlanta); and touchdown receptions—2 (October 31, 2004, vs. New England).
STATISTICAL PLATEAUS: 100-yard receiving games: 2001 (4), 2002 (4), 2003 (3), 2004 (1). Total: 12.

			RECEIVING				TOTALS			
Year Team	G	GS	No.	Yds.	Avg.	TD	TD	2pt.	Pts.	Fum.
2000—Pittsburgh NFL	12	8	22	273	12.4	0	0	0	0	1
2001—Pittsburgh NFL	16	16	66	1008	15.3	6	6	0	36	1
2002—Pittsburgh NFL	16	15	78	1325	17.0	7	7	1	44	2
2003—Pittsburgh NFL	16	16	60	860	14.3	4	4	0	24	1
2004—Pittsburgh NFL	11	11	35	698	19.9	5	5	0	30	1
Pro totals (5 years)	71	66	261	4164	16.0	22	22	1	134	6

BUSH, STEVE   TE   49ERS

PERSONAL: Born July 4, 1974, in Paradise Valley, Ariz. ... 6-3/267. ... Full name: Steven Jack Bush.
HIGH SCHOOL: Paradise Valley (Phoenix).
COLLEGE: Arizona State.
TRANSACTIONS/CAREER NOTES: Signed as non-drafted free agent by Cincinnati Bengals (April 25, 1997). ... Granted free agency (February 11, 2000). ... Re-signed by Bengals (April 25, 2000). ... Granted unconditional free agency (March 2, 2001). ... Signed by St. Louis Rams (July 20, 2001). ... Released by Rams (August 27, 2001). ... Signed by Arizona Cardinals (November 6, 2001). ... Released by Cardinals (June 1, 2004). ... Signed by Green Bay Packers (June 9, 2004). ... Released by Packers (September 24, 2004). ... Signed by San Francisco 49ers (December 1, 2004). ... Granted unconditional free agency (March 2, 2005). ... Re-signed by 49ers (May 5, 2005).
SINGLE GAME HIGHS (regular season): Receptions—4 (December 21, 2002, vs. San Francisco); yards—31 (December 24, 2000, vs. Philadelphia); and touchdown receptions—1 (January 2, 2005, vs. New England).

			RECEIVING				TOTALS			
Year Team	G	GS	No.	Yds.	Avg.	TD	TD	2pt.	Pts.	Fum.
1997—Cincinnati NFL	16	0	0	0	0.0	0	0	0	0	0
1998—Cincinnati NFL	12	2	4	39	9.8	0	0	0	0	0
1999—Cincinnati NFL	13	0	1	4	4.0	0	0	0	0	0
2000—Cincinnati NFL	16	0	3	39	13.0	0	0	0	0	0
2001—Arizona NFL	9	7	8	80	10.0	0	0	0	0	0
2002—Arizona NFL	16	12	19	121	6.4	1	1	0	6	0
2003—Arizona NFL	16	4	11	71	6.5	1	1	0	6	0
2004—San Francisco NFL	5	2	2	10	5.0	1	1	0	6	0
Pro totals (8 years)	103	27	48	364	7.6	3	3	0	18	0

BUTLER, JERAMETRIUS   CB   RAMS

PERSONAL: Born November 28, 1978, in Dallas, Texas. ... 5-10/181.
HIGH SCHOOL: Carter (Dallas).
COLLEGE: Kansas State.
TRANSACTIONS/CAREER NOTES: Selected after junior season by St. Louis Rams in fifth round (145th pick overall) of 2001 NFL draft. ... Signed by Rams (June 27, 2001). ... Granted free agency (March 3, 2004). ... Tendered offer sheet by Washington Redskins (March 5, 2004). ... Offer matched by Rams (March 11, 2004).
CHAMPIONSHIP GAME EXPERIENCE: Played in NFC championship game (2001 season). ... Played in Super Bowl 36 (2001 season).

				TOTALS			INTERCEPTIONS			
Year Team	G	GS	Tk.	Ast.	Sks.	No.	Yds.	Avg.	TD
2001—St. Louis NFL	16	0	8	2	0.0	0	0	0.0	0
2002—St. Louis NFL	9	0	2	0	0.0	0	0	0.0	0
2003—St. Louis NFL	16	15	64	7	0.0	4	72	18.0	0
2004—St. Louis NFL	16	16	73	5	0.0	5	15	3.0	0
Pro totals (4 years)	57	31	147	14	0.0	9	87	9.7	0

BUTLER, ROBB   S   CHARGERS

PERSONAL: Born September 14, 1981, in Pittsburgh, Pa. ... 6-0/217.
HIGH SCHOOL: Perry (Pittsburgh, Pa.).
COLLEGE: Robert Morris.
TRANSACTIONS/CAREER NOTES: Signed as non-drafted free agent by San Diego Chargers (May 4, 2004). ... Released by Chargers (September 5, 2004). ... Re-signed by Chargers to practice squad (September 6, 2004). ... Activated (November 30, 2004).

			TOTALS			INTERCEPTIONS				KICKOFF RETURNS				TOTALS			
Year Team	G	GS	Tk.	Ast.	Sks.	No.	Yds.	Avg.	TD	No.	Yds.	Avg.	TD	TD	2pt.	Pts.	Fum.
2004—San Diego NFL	5	0	3	1	0.0	0	0	0.0	0	2	35	17.5	0	0	0	0	0

CAIN, JEREMY   LB   BEARS

PERSONAL: Born December 8, 1981, in Boynton Beach, Fla. ... 6-1/235. ... Full name: Jeremy Robert Cain.
HIGH SCHOOL: Taravella (Coral Springs, Fla.), then St. Thomas Aquinas (Fort Lauderdale, Fla.).
COLLEGE: Massachusetts.
TRANSACTIONS/CAREER NOTES: Signed as non-drafted free agent by Chicago Bears (April 26, 2004). ... Released by Bears (September 5, 2004). ... Re-signed by Bears to practice squad (September 6, 2004). ... Activated (November 15, 2004).

			TOTALS			INTERCEPTIONS			
Year Team	G	GS	Tk.	Ast.	Sks.	No.	Yds.	Avg.	TD
2004—Chicago NFL	5	0	0	2	0.0	0	0	0.0	0

CALDWELL, RECHE   WR   CHARGERS

PERSONAL: Born March 28, 1979, in Tampa, Fla. ... 6-0/215. ... Full name: Donald Reche Caldwell Jr.
HIGH SCHOOL: Jefferson (Tampa, Fla.).
COLLEGE: Florida.
TRANSACTIONS/CAREER NOTES: Selected after junior season by San Diego Chargers in second round (48th pick overall) of 2002 NFL draft. ... Signed by Chargers (July 22, 2002). ... On injured reserve with knee injury (October 20, 2004-remainder of season).
SINGLE GAME HIGHS (regular season): Receptions—4 (September 19, 2004, vs. New York Jets); yards—110 (October 3, 2004, vs. Tennessee); and touchdown receptions—1 (October 3, 2004, vs. Tennessee).
STATISTICAL PLATEAUS: 100-yard receiving games: 2004 (1). Total: 1.

			RUSHING				RECEIVING				PUNT RETURNS				KICKOFF RETURNS				TOTALS		
Year Team	G	GS	Att.	Yds.	Avg.	TD	No.	Yds.	Avg.	TD	No.	Yds.	Avg.	TD	No.	Yds.	Avg.	TD	TD	2pt.	Pts.
2002—S.D. NFL	16	2	2	9	4.5	0	22	208	9.5	0	2	-2	-1.0	0	9	220	24.4	0	3	1	20
2003—S.D. NFL	9	4	5	39	7.8	0	8	80	10.0	0	0	0	0.0	0	0	0	0.0	0	0	0	0
2004—S.D. NFL	6	6	4	45	11.3	0	18	310	17.2	3	0	0	0.0	0	0	0	0.0	0	3	0	18
Pro totals (3 years)	31	12	11	93	8.5	0	48	598	12.5	6	2	-2	-1.0	0	9	220	24.4	0	6	1	38

CALICO, TYRONE   WR   TITANS

PERSONAL: Born November 9, 1980, in Millington, Tenn. ... 6-4/222.
HIGH SCHOOL: Millington (Tenn.).
COLLEGE: Middle Tennessee State.
TRANSACTIONS/CAREER NOTES: Selected by Tennessee Titans in second round (60th pick overall) of 2003 NFL draft. ... Signed by Titans (July 21, 2003). ... On injured reserve with knee injury (November 19, 2004-remainder of season).
SINGLE GAME HIGHS (regular season): Receptions—4 (October 12, 2003, vs. Houston); yards—92 (October 12, 2003, vs. Houston); and touchdown receptions—1 (November 9, 2003, vs. Miami).

			RUSHING				RECEIVING				TOTALS			
Year Team	G	GS	Att.	Yds.	Avg.	TD	No.	Yds.	Avg.	TD	TD	2pt.	Pts.	Fum.
2003—Tennessee NFL	14	2	1	5	5.0	0	18	297	16.5	4	4	1	26	0
2004—Tennessee NFL	1	0	0	0	0.0	0	2	13	6.5	0	0	0	0	0
Pro totals (2 years)	15	2	1	5	5.0	0	20	310	15.5	4	4	1	26	0

CALMUS, ROCKY   LB   TITANS

PERSONAL: Born August 1, 1979, in Tulsa, Okla. ... 6-3/238.
HIGH SCHOOL: Jenks (Okla.).
COLLEGE: Oklahoma.
TRANSACTIONS/CAREER NOTES: Selected by Tennessee Titans in third round (77th pick overall) of 2002 NFL draft. ... Signed by Titans (July 24, 2002). ... On injured reserve with hamstring injury (December 11, 2004-remainder of season).
CHAMPIONSHIP GAME EXPERIENCE: Member of Titans for AFC championship game (2002 season); inactive.
HONORS: Named linebacker on THE SPORTING NEWS college All-America first team (2001). ... Butkus Award winner (2001).

			TOTALS			INTERCEPTIONS			
Year Team	G	GS	Tk.	Ast.	Sks.	No.	Yds.	Avg.	TD
2002—Tennessee NFL	13	1	7	4	0.0	0	0	0.0	0
2003—Tennessee NFL	10	9	35	9	1.0	2	26	13.0	0
2004—Tennessee NFL	4	3	12	3	0.0	0	0	0.0	0
Pro totals (3 years)	27	13	54	16	1.0	2	26	13.0	0

CAMPBELL, DAN   TE   COWBOYS

PERSONAL: Born April 13, 1976, in Clifton, Texas. ... 6-5/262. ... Full name: Daniel Allen Campbell.
HIGH SCHOOL: Glen Rose (Texas).
COLLEGE: Texas A&M.
TRANSACTIONS/CAREER NOTES: Selected by New York Giants in third round (79th pick overall) of 1999 NFL draft. ... Signed by Giants (July 29, 1999). ... Granted free agency (March 1, 2002). ... Re-signed by Giants (March 27, 2002). ... Granted unconditional free agency (February 28, 2003). ... Signed by Dallas Cowboys (March 11, 2003). ... On injured reserve with foot injury (September 30, 2004-remainder of season).
CHAMPIONSHIP GAME EXPERIENCE: Played in NFC championship game (2000 season). ... Played in Super Bowl 35 (2000 season).
SINGLE GAME HIGHS (regular season): Receptions—4 (November 10, 2002, vs. Minnesota); yards—35 (November 10, 2002, vs. Minnesota); and touchdown receptions—1 (November 9, 2003, vs. Buffalo).

			RECEIVING				TOTALS			
Year Team	G	GS	No.	Yds.	Avg.	TD	TD	2pt.	Pts.	Fum.
1999—New York Giants NFL	12	1	0	0	0.0	0	0	0	0	0
2000—New York Giants NFL	16	5	8	46	5.8	3	3	0	18	1
2001—New York Giants NFL	16	13	13	148	11.4	1	1	0	6	0
2002—New York Giants NFL	16	16	22	175	8.0	1	1	0	6	0
2003—Dallas NFL	16	16	20	195	9.8	1	1	0	6	0
2004—Dallas NFL	3	2	2	16	8.0	0	0	0	0	0
Pro totals (6 years)	79	53	65	580	8.9	6	6	0	36	1

CAMPBELL, KELLY   WR   VIKINGS

PERSONAL: Born July 23, 1980, in Atlanta, Ga. ... 5-10/173.
HIGH SCHOOL: Mays (Atlanta).
COLLEGE: Georgia Tech.
TRANSACTIONS/CAREER NOTES: Signed non-drafted free agent by Minnesota Vikings (April 26, 2002). ... Released by Vikings (September 24, 2002). ... Re-signed by Vikings to practice squad (September 26, 2002). ... Activated (November 6, 2002). ... Granted free agency (March 2, 2005). ... Re-signed by Vikings (March 15, 2005).
SINGLE GAME HIGHS (regular season): Receptions—6 (November 24, 2002, vs. New England); yards—115 (November 16, 2003, vs. Oakland); and touchdown receptions—2 (December 29, 2002, vs. Detroit).
STATISTICAL PLATEAUS: 100-yard receiving games: 2003 (1). Total: 1.

			RECEIVING				KICKOFF RETURNS				TOTALS			
Year Team	G	GS	No.	Yds.	Avg.	TD	No.	Yds.	Avg.	TD	TD	2pt.	Pts.	Fum.
2002—Minnesota NFL	6	2	13	176	13.5	3	0	0	0.0	0	3	0	18	1
2003—Minnesota NFL	15	6	25	522	20.9	4	5	101	20.2	0	4	0	24	2
2004—Minnesota NFL	16	3	19	364	19.2	1	35	760	21.7	0	1	0	6	1
Pro totals (3 years)	37	11	57	1062	18.6	8	40	861	21.5	0	8	0	48	4

CAMPBELL, KHARY   LB   REDSKINS

PERSONAL: Born April 4, 1979, in Brooklyn, N.Y. ... 6-3/250.
HIGH SCHOOL: Sylvania Southview (Toledo, Ohio).
COLLEGE: Bowling Green.
TRANSACTIONS/CAREER NOTES: Signed as non-drafted free agent by Dallas Cowboys (April 26, 2002). ... Released by Cowboys (August 27, 2002). ... Re-signed by Cowboys to practice squad (September 3, 2002). ... Signed by New York Jets off Cowboys practice squad (September 25, 2002). ... Re-signed by Jets (April 2, 2003). ... Waived by Jets (September 30, 2003). ... Signed by Washington Redskins (April 5, 2004). ... On injured reserve with knee injury (November 16, 2004-remainder of season).

			TOTALS			INTERCEPTIONS			
Year Team	G	GS	Tk.	Ast.	Sks.	No.	Yds.	Avg.	TD
2002—New York Jets NFL	9	0	0	0	0.0	0	0	0.0	0
2003—New York Jets NFL	4	0	3	0	0.0	0	0	0.0	0
2004—Washington NFL	9	0	2	0	0.0	0	0	0.0	0
Pro totals (3 years)	22	0	5	0	0.0	0	0	0.0	0

C

CAMPBELL, MARK   TE   BILLS

PERSONAL: Born December 6, 1975, in Clawson, Mich. ... 6-6/255.
HIGH SCHOOL: Bishop Foley (Madison Heights, Mich.).
COLLEGE: Michigan.
TRANSACTIONS/CAREER NOTES: Signed as non-drafted free agent by Cleveland Browns (April 23, 1999). ... On injured reserve with ankle injury (December 14, 1999-remainder of season). ... On injured reserve with leg injury (September 1, 2001-entire season). ... Traded by Browns to Buffalo Bills for undisclosed pick in 2004 draft (February 28, 2003). ... On injured reserve with knee injury (December 8, 2004-remainder of season).
SINGLE GAME HIGHS (regular season): Receptions—7 (October 27, 2002, vs. New York Jets); yards—55 (December 21, 2003, vs. Miami); and touchdown receptions—3 (November 21, 2004, vs. St. Louis).

			RECEIVING				KICKOFF RETURNS				TOTALS		
Year Team	G	GS	No.	Yds.	Avg.	TD	No.	Yds.	Avg.	TD	TD	2pt.	Pts.	Fum.
1999—Cleveland NFL	14	4	9	131	14.6	0	3	28	9.3	0	0	0	0	0
2000—Cleveland NFL	16	10	12	80	6.7	1	3	30	10.0	0	1	0	6	0
2002—Cleveland NFL	16	16	25	179	7.2	3	2	21	10.5	0	3	0	18	0
2003—Buffalo NFL	16	11	34	339	10.0	1	0	0	0.0	0	1	0	6	0
2004—Buffalo NFL	12	12	17	203	11.9	5	0	0	0.0	0	5	0	30	1
Pro totals (5 years)	74	53	97	932	9.6	10	8	79	9.9	0	10	0	60	1

CAREY, VERNON   G   DOLPHINS

PERSONAL: Born July 31, 1981, in Miami, Fla. ... 6-5/325. ... Full name: Vernon A. Carey.
HIGH SCHOOL: Northwestern (Miami, Fla.).
COLLEGE: Miami (Fla.).
TRANSACTIONS/CAREER NOTES: Selected by Miami Dolphins in first round (19th pick overall) of 2004 NFL draft. ... Signed by Dolphins (July 30, 2004).
PLAYING EXPERIENCE: Miami NFL, 2004. ... Games/Games started: 2004 (14/2). Total: 14/2.

CARLISLE, COOPER   G/T   BRONCOS

PERSONAL: Born August 11, 1977, in Greenville, Miss. ... 6-5/295. ... Full name: Cooper Morrison Carlisle.
HIGH SCHOOL: McComb (Miss.).
COLLEGE: Florida.
TRANSACTIONS/CAREER NOTES: Selected by Denver Broncos in fourth round (112th pick overall) of 2000 NFL draft. ... Signed by Broncos (July 19, 2000). ... Granted unconditional free agency (March 2, 2005). ... Re-signed by Broncos (March 18, 2005).
PLAYING EXPERIENCE: Denver NFL, 2000-2004. ... Games/Games started: 2000 (13/0), 2001 (16/0), 2002 (1/0), 2003 (16/2), 2004 (16/4). Total: 62/6.

CARNEY, JOHN   K   SAINTS

PERSONAL: Born April 20, 1964, in Hartford, Conn. ... 5-11/185. ... Full name: John Michael Carney.
HIGH SCHOOL: Cardinal Newman (West Palm Beach, Fla.).
COLLEGE: Notre Dame.
TRANSACTIONS/CAREER NOTES: Signed as non-drafted free agent by Cincinnati Bengals (May 1, 1987). ... Released by Bengals (August 10, 1987). ... Signed as replacement player by Tampa Bay Buccaneers (September 24, 1987). ... Released by Buccaneers (October 14, 1987). ... Re-signed by Buccaneers (April 5, 1988). ... Released by Buccaneers (August 23, 1988). ... Re-signed by Buccaneers (November 22, 1988). ... Granted unconditional free agency (February 1-April 1, 1989). ... Re-signed by Buccaneers (April 13, 1989). ... Released by Buccaneers (September 5, 1989). ... Re-signed by Buccaneers (December 13, 1989). ... Granted unconditional free agency (February 1, 1990). ... Signed by San Diego Chargers (April 1, 1990). ... Released by Chargers (August 28, 1990). ... Signed by Los Angeles Rams (September 21, 1990). ... Released by Rams (September 26, 1990). ... Signed by Chargers (October 3, 1990). ... Granted free agency (February 1, 1992). ... Re-signed by Chargers (July 27, 1992). ... Granted free agency (March 1, 1993). ... Re-signed by Chargers (June 9, 1993). ... Granted unconditional free agency (February 17, 1994). ... Re-signed by Chargers (April 6, 1994). ... On injured reserve with knee injury (November 15, 1997-remainder of season). ... Granted unconditional free agency (March 2, 2001). ... Signed by New Orleans Saints (August 5, 2001). ... Granted unconditional free agency (March 1, 2002). ... Re-signed by Saints (March 12, 2002). ... Granted unconditional free agency (February 28, 2003). ... Re-signed by Saints (March 7, 2003).
CHAMPIONSHIP GAME EXPERIENCE: Played in AFC championship game (1994 season). ... Played in Super Bowl 29 (1994 season).
HONORS: Named kicker on THE SPORTING NEWS NFL All-Pro team (1994). ... Played in Pro Bowl (1994 season).
MISCELLANEOUS: San Diego Chargers all-time scoring leader (1,076 points).

		FIELD GOALS							TOTALS		
Year Team	G	1-29	30-39	40-49	50+	Tot.	Pct.	Lg.	XPM	XPA	Pts.
1988—Tampa Bay NFL	4	2-3	0-1	0-1	0-0	2-5	40.0	29	6	6	12
1989—Tampa Bay NFL	1	0-0	0-0	0-0	0-0	0-0	0.0	0	0	0	0
1990—Los Angeles Rams NFL	1	0-0	0-0	0-0	0-0	0-0	0.0	0	0	0	0
—San Diego NFL	12	10-10	6-7	3-3	0-1	19-21	90.5	43	27	28	84
1991—San Diego NFL	16	7-7	6-8	4-10	2-4	19-29	65.5	54	31	31	88
1992—San Diego NFL	16	13-14	5-7	7-8	1-3	26-32	81.3	50	35	35	113
1993—San Diego NFL	16	8-8	14-17	7-12	2-3	31-40	77.5	51	31	33	124
1994—San Diego NFL	16	12-12	15-15	5-9	2-2	†34-§38	89.5	50	33	33	*135
1995—San Diego NFL	16	8-8	10-11	3-5	0-2	21-26	80.8	45	32	33	95
1996—San Diego NFL	16	11-13	8-8	7-12	3-3	29-36	80.6	53	31	31	118
1997—San Diego NFL	4	3-3	2-2	2-2	0-0	7-7	100.0	41	5	5	26
1998—San Diego NFL	16	11-12	5-5	8-10	2-3	26-30	86.7	54	19	19	97
1999—San Diego NFL	16	15-15	6-8	9-12	1-1	31-36	86.1	50	22	23	115
2000—San Diego NFL	16	4-4	5-7	7-10	2-4	18-25	72.0	▲54	27	27	81

Year Team	G	FIELD GOALS							TOTALS		
		1-29	30-39	40-49	50+	Tot.	Pct.	Lg.	XPM	XPA	Pts.
2001—New Orleans NFL	15	7-7	11-11	8-12	1-1	27-31	87.1	50	32	32	113
2002—New Orleans NFL	16	9-9	11-13	11-12	0-1	31-35	‡88.6	48	37	37	130
2003—New Orleans NFL	16	6-6	10-12	5-9	1-3	22-30	73.3	50	36	37	102
2004—New Orleans NFL	16	3-3	12-15	5-6	2-3	22-27	81.5	53	38	38	104
Pro totals (17 years)	229	129-134	126-147	91-133	19-34	365-448	81.5	54	442	448	1537

CARPENTER, DWAINE   S   49ERS

PERSONAL: Born November 4, 1976, in Pinehurst, N.C. ... 6-1/203. ... Full name: Dwaine L. Carpenter.
HIGH SCHOOL: West Montgomery (Wadeville, N.C.).
COLLEGE: North Carolina A&T.
TRANSACTIONS/CAREER NOTES: Signed as non-drafted free agent by San Francisco 49ers (May 27, 2003).

Year Team	G	GS	TOTALS			INTERCEPTIONS			
			Tk.	Ast.	Sks.	No.	Yds.	Avg.	TD
2003—San Francisco NFL	15	2	18	1	0.0	0	0	0.0	0
2004—San Francisco NFL	15	6	43	5	2.0	1	31	31.0	0
Pro totals (2 years)	30	8	61	6	2.0	1	31	31.0	0

C

CARPENTER, KEION   S   FALCONS

PERSONAL: Born October 31, 1977, in Baltimore, Md. ... 5-11/205. ... Full name: Keion Eric Carpenter.
HIGH SCHOOL: Woodlawn (Baltimore).
COLLEGE: Virginia Tech.
TRANSACTIONS/CAREER NOTES: Signed as non-drafted free agent by Buffalo Bills (April 19, 1999). ... Granted free agency (March 1, 2002). ... Signed by Atlanta Falcons (March 6, 2002). ... Granted unconditional free agency (February 28, 2003). ... Re-signed by Falcons (April 10, 2003). ... Granted unconditional free agency (March 3, 2004). ... Re-signed by Falcons (March 30, 2004). ... On injured reserve with knee injury (June 10, 2004-entire season). ... Granted unconditional free agency (March 2, 2005). ... Re-signed by Falcons (March 26, 2005).

Year Team	G	GS	TOTALS			INTERCEPTIONS			
			Tk.	Ast.	Sks.	No.	Yds.	Avg.	TD
1999—Buffalo NFL	10	0	0	0	0.0	0	0	0.0	0
2000—Buffalo NFL	12	12	30	3	0.0	5	63	12.6	0
2001—Buffalo NFL	15	10	24	10	0.0	0	0	0.0	0
2002—Atlanta NFL	16	16	43	6	0.0	4	82	20.5	1
2003—Atlanta NFL	15	8	29	2	0.0	3	22	7.3	0
2004—Atlanta NFL			Did not play.						
Pro totals (5 years)	68	46	126	21	0.0	12	167	13.9	1

CARR, DAVID   QB   TEXANS

PERSONAL: Born July 21, 1979, in Bakersfield, Calif. ... 6-3/220.
HIGH SCHOOL: Stockdale (Bakersfield, Calif.).
COLLEGE: Fresno State.
TRANSACTIONS/CAREER NOTES: Selected by Houston Texans in first round (first pick overall) of 2002 NFL draft. ... Signed by Texans (April 20, 2002).
RECORDS: Holds NFL single-season record for most times sacked—76 (2002).
SINGLE GAME HIGHS (regular season): Attempts—42 (October 10, 2004, vs. Minnesota); completions—27 (October 10, 2004, vs. Minnesota); yards—372 (October 10, 2004, vs. Minnesota) and touchdown passes—3 (October 10, 2004, vs. Minnesota).
STATISTICAL PLATEAUS: 300-yard passing games: 2003 (1), 2004 (2). Total: 3.
MISCELLANEOUS: Regular-season record as starting NFL quarterback: 14-29 (.326). ... Holds Houston Texans all-time records for most yards passing (8,136) and passing touchdowns (34).

Year Team	G	GS	PASSING									RUSHING				TOTALS		
			Att.	Cmp.	Pct.	Yds.	TD	Int.	Avg.	Skd.	Rat.	Att.	Yds.	Avg.	TD	TD	2pt.	Pts.
2002—Houston NFL	16	16	444	233	52.5	2592	9	15	5.84	*76	62.8	59	282	4.8	3	3	0	18
2003—Houston NFL	12	11	295	167	56.6	2013	9	13	6.82	15	69.5	27	151	5.6	2	2	0	12
2004—Houston NFL	16	16	466	285	61.2	3531	16	14	7.58	*49	83.5	73	299	4.1	0	0	0	0
Pro totals (3 years)	44	43	1205	685	56.8	8136	34	42	6.75	140	72.5	159	732	4.6	5	5	0	30

CARROLL, AHMAD   CB   PACKERS

PERSONAL: Born August 4, 1983, in Atlanta, Ga. ... 5-10/185.
HIGH SCHOOL: Douglass (Atlanta, Ga.).
COLLEGE: Arkansas.
TRANSACTIONS/CAREER NOTES: Selected after junior season by Green Bay Packers in first round (25th pick overall) of 2004 NFL draft. ... Signed by Packers (August 2, 2004).
HONORS: Named cornerback on THE SPORTING NEWS Freshman All-America third team (2001).

Year Team	G	GS	TOTALS			INTERCEPTIONS			
			Tk.	Ast.	Sks.	No.	Yds.	Avg.	TD
2004—Green Bay NFL	14	11	43	3	2.0	1	0	0.0	0

CARSON, LEONARDO   DT   COWBOYS

PERSONAL: Born February 11, 1977, in Mobile, Ala. ... 6-2/292. ... Full name: Leonardo Tremayne Carson.
HIGH SCHOOL: Shaw (Mobile, Ala.).
COLLEGE: Auburn.
TRANSACTIONS/CAREER NOTES: Selected by San Diego Chargers in fourth round (113th pick overall) of 2000 NFL draft. ... Signed by Chargers (July 20, 2000). ... On injured reserve with shoulder injury (November 17, 2000-remainder of season). ... Granted free agency (February 28, 2003). ... Re-signed by Chargers (April 15, 2003). ... Released by Chargers (October 14, 2003). ... Signed by Dallas Cowboys (October 18, 2003). ... On injured reserve with triceps injury (December 16, 2003-remainder of season). ... On reserve/suspended list for violating league personal conduct policy (September 5-14, 2004). ... Granted unconditional free agency (March 2, 2005). ... Re-signed by Cowboys (March 4, 2005).

			TOTALS		
Year Team	G	GS	Tk.	Ast.	Sks.
2000—San Diego NFL	4	0	2	0	0.0
2001—San Diego NFL	16	13	24	9	3.0
2002—San Diego NFL	16	6	22	9	3.5
2003—San Diego NFL	5	0	2	0	0.0
—Dallas NFL	8	0	13	5	1.5
2004—Dallas NFL	15	15	29	14	0.5
Pro totals (5 years)	**64**	**34**	**92**	**37**	**8.5**

CARSTENS, JORDAN   DT   PANTHERS

C

PERSONAL: Born January 22, 1981, in Carroll, Iowa. ... 6-5/300.
HIGH SCHOOL: Panorama (Bagely, Iowa).
COLLEGE: Iowa State.
TRANSACTIONS/CAREER NOTES: Signed as non-drafted free agent by Carolina Panthers (April 26, 2004). ... Released by Panthers (September 4, 2004). ... Re-signed by Panthers to practice squad (September 7, 2004). ... Activated (October 13, 2004).

			TOTALS		
Year Team	G	GS	Tk.	Ast.	Sks.
2004—Carolina NFL	12	1	10	3	0.0

CARSWELL, DWAYNE   TE   BRONCOS

PERSONAL: Born January 18, 1972, in Jacksonville, Fla. ... 6-3/290.
HIGH SCHOOL: University Christian (Jacksonville).
COLLEGE: Liberty.
TRANSACTIONS/CAREER NOTES: Signed as non-drafted free agent by Denver Broncos (May 2, 1994). ... Released by Broncos (August 26, 1994). ... Re-signed by Broncos to practice squad (August 30, 1994). ... Activated (November 25, 1994). ... On reserve/suspended list (October 18-26, 2004).
CHAMPIONSHIP GAME EXPERIENCE: Played in AFC championship game (1997 and 1998 seasons). ... Member of Super Bowl championship team (1997 and 1998 seasons).
HONORS: Played in Pro Bowl (2001 season).
SINGLE GAME HIGHS (regular season): Receptions—6 (December 16, 2001, vs. Kansas City); yards—68 (October 22, 2000, vs. Cincinnati); and touchdown receptions—1 (October 17, 2004, vs. Oakland).

			RECEIVING				TOTALS			
Year Team	G	GS	No.	Yds.	Avg.	TD	TD	2pt.	Pts.	Fum.
1994—Denver NFL	4	0	0	0	0.0	0	0	0	0	0
1995—Denver NFL	9	2	3	37	12.3	0	0	0	0	0
1996—Denver NFL	16	2	15	85	5.7	0	0	0	0	0
1997—Denver NFL	16	3	12	96	8.0	1	1	0	6	0
1998—Denver NFL	16	1	4	51	12.8	0	0	0	0	0
1999—Denver NFL	16	11	24	201	8.4	2	2	0	12	0
2000—Denver NFL	16	16	49	495	10.1	3	3	0	18	0
2001—Denver NFL	16	16	34	299	8.8	4	4	1	26	0
2002—Denver NFL	16	7	21	189	9.0	1	1	0	6	0
2003—Denver NFL	16	10	6	53	8.8	1	1	0	6	0
2004—Denver NFL	15	14	22	198	9.0	1	1	0	6	0
Pro totals (11 years)	**156**	**82**	**190**	**1704**	**9.0**	**13**	**13**	**1**	**80**	**0**

CARTER, ANDRE   DE   49ERS

PERSONAL: Born May 12, 1979, in Denver, Colo. ... 6-4/265.
HIGH SCHOOL: Oak Grove (San Jose, Calif.).
COLLEGE: California.
TRANSACTIONS/CAREER NOTES: Selected by San Francisco 49ers in first round (seventh pick overall) of 2001 NFL draft. ... Signed by 49ers (July 26, 2001). ... On injured reserve with back injury (December 22, 2004-remainder of season).
HONORS: Named defensive end on THE SPORTING NEWS college All-America first team (2000).

			TOTALS		
Year Team	G	GS	Tk.	Ast.	Sks.
2001—San Francisco NFL	15	15	40	7	6.5
2002—San Francisco NFL	16	16	44	10	12.5
2003—San Francisco NFL	15	15	27	7	6.5
2004—San Francisco NFL	7	6	7	3	2.0
Pro totals (4 years)	**53**	**52**	**118**	**27**	**27.5**

CARTER, DYSHOD — DB — BROWNS

PERSONAL: Born June 18, 1978, in Denver, Colo. ... 5-10/195. ... Full name: Dyshod Vontae Carter.
HIGH SCHOOL: Thomas Jefferson (Denver).
COLLEGE: Kansas State.
TRANSACTIONS/CAREER NOTES: Signed as non-drafted free agent by Kansas City Chiefs (April 26, 2001). ... Released by Chiefs (August 28, 2001). ... Signed by Cleveland Browns to practice squad (October 9, 2001). ... Activated (October 24, 2001). ... Released by Browns (November 7, 2001). ... Re-signed by Browns to practice squad (November 9, 2001). ... Activated (November 29, 2001). ... Released by Browns (August 27, 2002). ... Signed by New England Patriots to practice squad (December 12, 2002). ... Assigned by Patriots to Scottish Claymores in 2003 NFL Europe enhancement allocation program (February 4, 2003). ... Released by Patriots (August 28, 2003). ... Signed by Arizona Cardinals (February 27, 2004). ... Released by Cardinals (August 31, 2004). ... Re-signed by Cardinals (September 14, 2004). ... Claimed on waivers by Browns (December 2, 2004).

				TOTALS			INTERCEPTIONS			
Year Team	G	GS	Tk.	Ast.	Sks.	No.	Yds.	Avg.	TD
2001—Cleveland NFL	5	0	0	0	0.0	0	0	0.0	0
2004—Arizona NFL	6	0	3	0	0.0	0	0	0.0	0
—Cleveland NFL	5	0	2	0	0.0	0	0	0.0	0
Pro totals (2 years)	16	0	5	0	0.0	0	0	0.0	0

CARTER, JONATHAN — WR — JETS

C

PERSONAL: Born March 20, 1979, in Anniston, Ala. ... 6-0/180.
HIGH SCHOOL: Lineville (Ala.).
COLLEGE: Troy.
TRANSACTIONS/CAREER NOTES: Selected by New York Giants in fifth round (162nd pick overall) of 2001 NFL draft. ... Signed by Giants (July 26, 2001). ... Released by Giants (September 2, 2001). ... Re-signed by Giants to practice squad (September 3, 2001). ... Activated (December 29, 2001). ... Claimed on waivers by New York Jets (October 8, 2002). ... Re-signed by Jets (April 2, 2003) ... On injured reserve with knee injury (December 9, 2003-remainder of season). ... Granted free agency (March 2, 2005). ... Re-signed by Jets (April 5, 2005).
SINGLE GAME HIGHS (regular season): Receptions—2 (December 12, 2004, vs. Pittsburgh); yards—62 (November 16, 2003, vs. Indianapolis); and touchdown receptions—1 (September 12, 2004, vs. Cincinnati).

			RECEIVING				KICKOFF RETURNS				TOTALS			
Year Team	G	GS	No.	Yds.	Avg.	TD	No.	Yds.	Avg.	TD	TD	2pt.	Pts.	Fum.
2001—New York Giants NFL	2	0	0	0	0.0	0	8	155	19.4	0	0	0	0	0
2002—New York Giants NFL	1	0	0	0	0.0	0	1	14	14.0	0	0	0	0	0
2003—New York Jets NFL	9	0	4	93	23.3	1	18	517	28.7	1	2	0	12	0
2004—New York Jets NFL	13	1	10	173	17.3	1	17	374	22.0	0	1	0	6	2
Pro totals (4 years)	25	1	14	266	19.0	2	44	1060	24.1	1	3	0	18	2

CARTER, KERRY — RB — SEAHAWKS

PERSONAL: Born December 19, 1980, in Port of Spain, Trinidad. ... 6-1/238.
HIGH SCHOOL: Henry Car (Ontario).
COLLEGE: Stanford.
TRANSACTIONS/CAREER NOTES: Signed as non-drafted free agent by Seattle Seahawks (May 1, 2003).
SINGLE GAME HIGHS (regular season): Attempts—4 (November 7, 2004, vs. San Francisco); yards—15 (November 7, 2004, vs. San Francisco); and rushing touchdowns—0.

			RUSHING				KICKOFF RETURNS				TOTALS			
Year Team	G	GS	Att.	Yds.	Avg.	TD	No.	Yds.	Avg.	TD	TD	2pt.	Pts.	Fum.
2003—Seattle NFL	16	0	3	-2	-0.7	0	8	185	23.1	0	0	0	0	0
2004—Seattle NFL	16	0	4	15	3.8	0	21	448	21.3	0	0	0	0	0
Pro totals (2 years)	32	0	7	13	1.9	0	29	633	21.8	0	0	0	0	0

CARTER, KEVIN — DE — DOLPHINS

PERSONAL: Born September 21, 1973, in Miami, Fla. ... 6-5/290. ... Full name: Kevin Louis Carter. ... Brother of Bernard Carter, linebacker with Jacksonville Jaguars (1995).
HIGH SCHOOL: Lincoln (Tallahassee, Fla.).
COLLEGE: Florida.
TRANSACTIONS/CAREER NOTES: Selected by St. Louis Rams in first round (sixth pick overall) of 1995 NFL draft. ... Signed by Rams (July 17, 1995). ... Designated by Rams as franchise player (February 22, 2001). ... Traded by Rams to Tennessee Titans for first-round pick (DT Ryan Pickett) in 2001 draft (March 28, 2001). ... Released by Titans (February 21, 2005). ... Signed by Miami Dolphins (March 7, 2005).
CHAMPIONSHIP GAME EXPERIENCE: Played in NFC championship game (1999 season). ... Member of Super Bowl championship team (1999 season). ... Played in AFC championship game (2002 season).
HONORS: Named defensive lineman on THE SPORTING NEWS college All-America first team (1994). ... Named defensive end on THE SPORTING NEWS NFL All-Pro team (1999). ... Played in Pro Bowl (1999 and 2002 seasons).

			TOTALS		
Year Team	G	GS	Tk.	Ast.	Sks.
1995—St. Louis NFL	16	16	33	4	6.0
1996—St. Louis NFL	16	16	39	16	9.5
1997—St. Louis NFL	16	16	32	10	7.5
1998—St. Louis NFL	16	16	49	11	12.0
1999—St. Louis NFL	16	16	30	4	*17.0
2000—St. Louis NFL	16	13	31	4	10.5
2001—Tennessee NFL	16	16	28	8	2.0

Year Team	G	GS	TOTALS Tk.	Ast.	Sks.
2002—Tennessee NFL	16	16	27	15	10.0
2003—Tennessee NFL	16	16	29	19	5.5
2004—Tennessee NFL	16	16	26	23	6.0
Pro totals (10 years)	160	157	324	114	86.0

CARTER, KI-JANA — RB

PERSONAL: Born September 12, 1973, in Westerville, Ohio. ... 5-10/226. ... Full name: Kenneth Leonard Carter. ... Name pronounced: KEE-john-uh.

HIGH SCHOOL: Westerville (Ohio) South.

COLLEGE: Penn State.

TRANSACTIONS/CAREER NOTES: Selected after junior season by Cincinnati Bengals in first round (first pick overall) of 1995 NFL draft. ... Signed by Bengals (July 19, 1995). ... On injured reserve with knee injury (August 22, 1995-entire season). ... On injured reserve with wrist injury (September 7, 1998-remainder of season). ... On injured reserve with knee injury (September 29, 1999-remainder of season). ... Released by Bengals (June 1, 2000). ... Signed by Washington Redskins (July 31, 2001). ... Granted unconditional free agency (March 1, 2002). ... Signed by Green Bay Packers (June 14, 2002). ... Released by Packers (August 27, 2002). ... Signed by New Orleans Saints (August 18, 2003). ... Released by Saints (August 31, 2003). ... Re-signed by Saints (September 23, 2003). ... On injured reserve with toe injury (November 26, 2003-remainder of season). ... Granted unconditional free agency (March 3, 2004). ... Re-signed by Saints (May 20, 2004). ... Released by Saints (September 11, 2004). ... Re-signed by Saints (September 14, 2004). ... Released by Saints (September 18, 2004). ... Re-signed by Saints (September 21, 2004). ... Released by Saints (December 4, 2004).

HONORS: Named running back on THE SPORTING NEWS college All-America first team (1994).

SINGLE GAME HIGHS (regular season): Attempts—19 (August 31, 1997, vs. Arizona); yards—104 (September 21, 1997, vs. Denver); and rushing touchdowns—2 (December 30, 2001, vs. New Orleans).

STATISTICAL PLATEAUS: 100-yard rushing games: 1997 (1). Total: 1.

			RUSHING				RECEIVING				TOTALS			
Year Team	G	GS	Att.	Yds.	Avg.	TD	No.	Yds.	Avg.	TD	TD	2pt.	Pts.	Fum.
1995—Cincinnati NFL	Did not play.													
1996—Cincinnati NFL	16	4	91	264	2.9	8	22	169	7.7	1	9	0	54	2
1997—Cincinnati NFL	15	10	128	464	3.6	7	21	157	7.5	0	7	0	42	3
1998—Cincinnati NFL	1	0	2	4	2.0	0	6	25	4.2	0	0	0	0	0
1999—Cincinnati NFL	3	0	6	15	2.5	1	3	24	8.0	0	1	0	6	0
2000—	Did not play.													
2001—Washington NFL	14	0	63	308	4.9	3	13	83	6.4	0	3	0	18	1
2003—New Orleans NFL	8	0	19	72	3.8	1	1	11	11.0	0	1	0	6	0
2004—New Orleans NFL	2	0	10	17	1.7	0	0	0	0.0	0	0	0	0	0
Pro totals (7 years)	59	14	319	1144	3.6	20	66	469	7.1	1	21	0	126	6

CARTER, QUINCY — QB

PERSONAL: Born October 13, 1977, in Decatur, Ga. ... 6-2/213.

HIGH SCHOOL: Southwest DeKalb (Decatur, Ga.).

COLLEGE: Georgia.

TRANSACTIONS/CAREER NOTES: Selected after junior season by Dallas Cowboys in second round (53rd pick overall) of 2001 NFL draft. ... Signed by Cowboys (July 19, 2001). ... Released by Cowboys (August 4, 2004). ... Signed by New York Jets (August 24, 2004). ... Granted unconditional free agency (March 2, 2005).

HONORS: Named College Football Freshman of the Year by THE SPORTING NEWS (1998).

SINGLE GAME HIGHS (regular season): Attempts—47 (December 28, 2003, vs. New Orleans); completions—29 (November 23, 2003, vs. Carolina); yards—321 (September 15, 2003, vs. New York Giants); and touchdown passes—3 (October 3, 2003, vs. Detroit).

STATISTICAL PLATEAUS: 300-yard passing games: 2003 (1). Total: 1.

MISCELLANEOUS: Regular-season record as starting NFL quarterback: 18-16 (.529). ... Post-season record as NFL starting quarterback: 0-1 (.000).

			PASSING									RUSHING				TOTALS		
Year Team	G	GS	Att.	Cmp.	Pct.	Yds.	TD	Int.	Avg.	Skd.	Rat.	Att.	Yds.	Avg.	TD	TD	2pt.	Pts.
2001—Dallas NFL	8	8	176	90	51.1	1072	5	7	6.09	12	63.0	45	150	3.3	1	1	0	6
2002—Dallas NFL	7	7	221	125	56.6	1465	7	8	6.63	19	72.3	27	91	3.4	0	0	0	0
2003—Dallas NFL	16	16	505	292	57.8	3302	17	21	6.54	37	71.4	68	257	3.8	2	2	0	12
2004—New York Jets NFL	7	3	58	35	60.3	498	3	1	8.59	12	98.2	12	20	1.7	0	0	0	0
Pro totals (4 years)	38	34	960	542	56.5	6337	32	37	6.60	80	71.7	152	518	3.4	3	3	0	18

CARTER, TIM — WR — GIANTS

PERSONAL: Born September 21, 1979, in Atlanta, Ga. ... 6-0/200. ... Full name: Timothy M. Carter.

HIGH SCHOOL: Lakewood (St. Petersburg, Fla.).

COLLEGE: Auburn.

TRANSACTIONS/CAREER NOTES: Selected by New York Giants in second round (46th pick overall) of 2002 NFL draft. ... Signed by Giants (July 25, 2002). ... On injured reserve with Achilles' tendon injury (November 12, 2002-remainder of season). ... On injured reserve with concussion (December 12, 2003-remainder of season). ... On injured reserve with hip injury (October 13, 2004-remainder of season).

SINGLE GAME HIGHS (regular season): Receptions—4 (September 12, 2004, vs. Philadelphia); yards—63 (September 19, 2004, vs. Washington); and touchdown receptions—1 (September 19, 2004, vs. Washington).

			RUSHING				RECEIVING				PUNT RETURNS				KICKOFF RETURNS				TOTALS		
Year Team	G	GS	Att.	Yds.	Avg.	TD	No.	Yds.	Avg.	TD	No.	Yds.	Avg.	TD	No.	Yds.	Avg.	TD	TD	2pt.	Pts.
2002—NYG NFL	5	0	3	28	9.3	0	2	37	18.5	0	0	0	0.0	0	5	78	15.6	0	0	0	0
2003—NYG NFL	12	2	0	0	0.0	0	26	309	11.9	0	0	0	0.0	0	1	9	9.0	0	0	0	0
2004—NYG NFL	5	0	2	23	11.5	0	12	182	15.2	1	0	0	0.0	0	0	0	0.0	0	1	0	6
Pro totals (3 years)	22	2	5	51	10.2	0	40	528	13.2	1	0	0	0.0	0	6	87	14.5	0	1	0	6

CARTER, TYRONE   S   STEELERS

PERSONAL: Born March 31, 1976, in Fort Lauderdale, Fla. ... 5-8/190.
HIGH SCHOOL: Ely (Pompano Beach, Fla.).
COLLEGE: Minnesota.
TRANSACTIONS/CAREER NOTES: Selected by Minnesota Vikings in fourth round (118th pick overall) of 2000 NFL draft. ... Signed by Vikings (July 5, 2000). ... Granted free agency (February 28, 2003). ... Signed by New York Jets (April 14, 2003). ... Released by Jets (March 1, 2004). ... Signed by Minnesota Vikings (March 11, 2004). ... Released by Vikings (September 10, 2004). ... Signed by Pittsburgh Steelers (October 20, 2004). ... Granted unconditional free agency (March 2, 2005). ... Re-signed by Steelers (April 5, 2005).
CHAMPIONSHIP GAME EXPERIENCE: Played in NFC championship game (2000 season). ... Played in AFC championship game (2004 season).
HONORS: Jim Thorpe Award winner (1999). ... Named strong safety on THE SPORTING NEWS college All-America first team (1999).

			TOTALS			INTERCEPTIONS				KICKOFF RETURNS				TOTALS			
Year Team	G	GS	Tk.	Ast.	Sks.	No.	Yds.	Avg.	TD	No.	Yds.	Avg.	TD	TD	2pt.	Pts.	Fum.
2000—Minnesota NFL	15	7	29	9	0.0	0	0	0.0	0	17	389	22.9	0	0	0	0	0
2001—Minnesota NFL	15	7	45	5	1.0	0	0	0.0	0	0	0	0.0	0	1	0	6	0
2002—Minnesota NFL	16	7	42	6	0.0	1	13	13.0	0	17	350	20.6	0	0	0	0	0
2003—New York Jets NFL	16	10	59	23	0.0	2	37	18.5	0	0	0	0.0	0	0	0	0	0
2004—Pittsburgh NFL	9	0	4	0	0.0	0	0	0.0	0	0	0	0.0	0	0	0	0	0
Pro totals (5 years)	71	31	179	43	1.0	3	50	16.7	0	34	739	21.7	0	1	0	6	0

CARTWRIGHT, ROCK   FB   REDSKINS

PERSONAL: Born December 3, 1979, in Conroe, Texas. ... 5-7/223.
HIGH SCHOOL: Conroe (Texas).
JUNIOR COLLEGE: Trinity Valley Community College (Texas).
COLLEGE: Kansas State.
TRANSACTIONS/CAREER NOTES: Selected by Washington Redskins in seventh round (257th pick overall) of 2002 NFL draft.. ... Signed by Redskins (July 19, 2002). ... Granted free agency (March 2, 2005). ... Re-signed by Redskins (April 13, 2005).
SINGLE GAME HIGHS (regular season): Attempts—21 (December 14, 2003, vs. Dallas); yards—94 (December 14, 2003, vs. Dallas); and rushing touchdowns—1 (December 27, 2003, vs. Philadelphia).

			RUSHING				RECEIVING				KICKOFF RETURNS				TOTALS			
Year Team	G	GS	Att.	Yds.	Avg.	TD	No.	Yds.	Avg.	TD	No.	Yds.	Avg.	TD	TD	2pt.	Pts.	Fum.
2002—Washington NFL	16	0	3	22	7.3	0	11	121	11.0	1	10	169	16.9	0	1	0	6	1
2003—Washington NFL	15	3	107	411	3.8	4	18	176	9.8	0	2	26	13.0	0	4	0	24	2
2004—Washington NFL	13	0	2	0	0.0	0	0	0	0.0	0	0	0	0.0	0	0	0	0	0
Pro totals (3 years)	44	3	112	433	3.9	4	29	297	10.2	1	12	195	16.3	0	5	0	30	3

CASH, CHRIS   CB   LIONS

PERSONAL: Born July 13, 1980, in Stockton, Calif. ... 5-10/185.
HIGH SCHOOL: Franklin (Stockton, Calif.).
JUNIOR COLLEGE: Palomar College (Calif.).
COLLEGE: Southern California.
TRANSACTIONS/CAREER NOTES: Selected by Detroit Lions in sixth round (175th pick overall) of 2002 NFL draft. ... Signed by Lions (July 23, 2002). ... On injured reserve with knee injury (August 25, 2003-entire season). ... Granted free agency (March 2, 2005). ... Re-signed by Lions (April 6, 2005).

			TOTALS			INTERCEPTIONS			
Year Team	G	GS	Tk.	Ast.	Sks.	No.	Yds.	Avg.	TD
2002—Detroit NFL	16	12	79	12	0.0	1	11	11.0	0
2003—Detroit NFL	Did not play.								
2004—Detroit NFL	11	5	25	4	0.0	1	0	0.0	0
Pro totals (2 years)	27	17	104	16	0.0	2	11	5.5	0

CASON, AVEION   RB   RAMS

PERSONAL: Born July 12, 1979, in St. Petersburg, Fla. ... 5-10/204. ... Full name: Aveion Marquel Cason.
HIGH SCHOOL: Lakewood (St. Petersburg, Fla.).
COLLEGE: Illinois State.
TRANSACTIONS/CAREER NOTES: Signed as non-drafted free agent by St. Louis Rams (April 23, 2001). ... Released by Rams (September 25, 2001). ... Re-signed by Rams to practice squad (September 26, 2001). ... Released by Rams (September 28, 2001). ... Signed by Detroit Lions (November 19, 2001). ... Traded by Lions to Dallas Cowboys for seventh-round pick (RB Brandon Drumm) in 2003 draft (April 27, 2003). ... On injured reserve with knee injury (December 10, 2003-remainder of season). ... Granted free agency (March 3, 2004). ... Re-signed by Cowboys (April 14, 2004). ... Claimed on waivers by Arizona Cardinals (September 1, 2004). ... Released by Cardinals (September 5, 2004). ... Signed by Rams (December 7, 2004).
SINGLE GAME HIGHS (regular season): Attempts—10 (December 15, 2002, vs. Tampa Bay); yards—77 (September 7, 2003, vs. Atlanta); and rushing touchdowns—1 (November 23, 2003, vs. Carolina).

			RUSHING				RECEIVING				KICKOFF RETURNS				TOTALS			
Year Team	G	GS	Att.	Yds.	Avg.	TD	No.	Yds.	Avg.	TD	No.	Yds.	Avg.	TD	TD	2pt.	Pts.	Fum.
2001—St. Louis NFL	1	0	0	0	0.0	0	0	0	0.0	0	4	73	18.3	0	0	0	0	1
—Detroit NFL	5	0	11	31	2.8	0	4	32	8.0	0	0	0	0.0	0	0	0	0	1
2002—Detroit NFL	10	3	26	107	4.1	0	19	288	15.2	2	2	48	24.0	0	2	0	12	0
2003—Dallas NFL	10	0	40	220	5.5	2	17	142	8.4	0	5	81	16.2	0	2	0	12	2
2004—St. Louis NFL	3	0	0	0	0.0	0	0	0	0.0	0	14	310	22.1	0	0	0	0	0
Pro totals (4 years)	29	3	77	358	4.6	2	40	462	11.6	2	25	512	20.5	0	4	0	24	4

CAVER, QUINTON LB CHIEFS

PERSONAL: Born August 22, 1978, in Anniston, Ala. ... 6-4/241.
HIGH SCHOOL: Anniston (Ala.).
COLLEGE: Arkansas.
TRANSACTIONS/CAREER NOTES: Selected by Philadelphia Eagles in second round (55th pick overall) of 2001 NFL draft. ... Signed by Eagles (July 27, 2001). ... Released by Eagles (October 21, 2002). ... Signed by Kansas City Chiefs (October 28, 2002). ... On injured reserve with shoulder injury (December 14, 2002-remainder of season). ... Released by Chiefs (August 31, 2003). ... Re-signed by Chiefs (September 16, 2003). ... Granted free agency (March 3, 2004). ... Re-signed by Chiefs (March 3, 2004). ... Granted unconditional free agency (March 2, 2005). ... Re-signed by Chiefs (April 14, 2005).
CHAMPIONSHIP GAME EXPERIENCE: Played in NFC championship game (2001 season).

| | | | | TOTALS | | | INTERCEPTIONS | | | |
Year Team	G	GS	Tk.	Ast.	Sks.	No.	Yds.	Avg.	TD
2001—Philadelphia NFL	11	0	7	2	0.0	0	0	0.0	0
2002—Philadelphia NFL	5	0	0	0	0.0	0	0	0.0	0
—Kansas City NFL	1	0	0	0	0.0	0	0	0.0	0
2003—Kansas City NFL	12	0	1	0	0.0	0	0	0.0	0
2004—Kansas City NFL	16	4	24	4	0.0	0	0	0.0	0
Pro totals (4 years)	45	4	32	6	0.0	0	0	0.0	0

CELESTIN, OLIVER CB JETS

C

PERSONAL: Born February 25, 1981, in New Orleans, La. ... 6-0/207.
HIGH SCHOOL: St. Augustine (New Orleans, La.).
COLLEGE: Texas Southern.
TRANSACTIONS/CAREER NOTES: Signed as non-drafted free agent by Cleveland Browns (May 2, 2003). ... Released by Browns (August 25, 2003). ... Signed by Minnesota Vikings (June 17, 2004). ... Released by Vikings (September 4, 2004). ... Re-signed by Vikings to practice squad (September 6, 2004). ... Released by Vikings from practice squad (September 14, 2004). ... Re-signed by Vikings to practice squad (September 22, 2004). ... Signed by New York Jets off Vikings practice squad (November 9, 2004).

| | | | | TOTALS | | | INTERCEPTIONS | | | |
Year Team	G	GS	Tk.	Ast.	Sks.	No.	Yds.	Avg.	TD
2004—New York Jets NFL	8	0	5	0	0.0	0	0	0.0	0

CESAIRE, JACQUES DT CHARGERS

PERSONAL: Born August 30, 1980, in Worcester, Mass. ... 6-2/295.
HIGH SCHOOL: Gardner (Mass.).
COLLEGE: Southern Connecticut State.
TRANSACTIONS/CAREER NOTES: Signed as non-drafted free agent by San Diego Chargers (May 2, 2003).

| | | | TOTALS | | |
Year Team	G	GS	Tk.	Ast.	Sks.
2003—San Diego NFL	4	0	1	2	0.0
2004—San Diego NFL	16	12	18	6	0.5
Pro totals (2 years)	20	12	19	8	0.5

CHAMBERLIN, FRANK LB TEXANS

PERSONAL: Born January 2, 1978, in Mahwah, N.J. ... 6-1/235. ... Full name: Frank Jacob Chamberlin.
HIGH SCHOOL: Mahwah (N.J.).
COLLEGE: Boston College.
TRANSACTIONS/CAREER NOTES: Selected by Tennessee Titans in fifth round (160th pick overall) of 2000 NFL draft. ... Signed by Titans (July 7, 2000). ... Granted free agency (February 28, 2003). ... Re-signed by Titans (March 9, 2003). ... Released by Titans (September 2, 2003). ... Signed by Cincinnati Bengals (November 25, 2003). ... On injured reserve with biceps injury (August 30, 2004-entire season). ... Granted unconditional free agency (March 2, 2005). ... Signed by Houston Texans (March 17, 2005).
CHAMPIONSHIP GAME EXPERIENCE: Played in AFC championship game (2002 season).

| | | | | TOTALS | | | INTERCEPTIONS | | | |
Year Team	G	GS	Tk.	Ast.	Sks.	No.	Yds.	Avg.	TD
2000—Tennessee NFL	12	0	0	1	0.0	0	0	0.0	0
2001—Tennessee NFL	16	0	8	3	1.0	0	0	0.0	0
2002—Tennessee NFL	15	3	11	5	0.0	0	0	0.0	0
2003—Cincinnati NFL	5	0	0	0	0.0	0	0	0.0	0
2004—Cincinnati NFL	Did not play.								
Pro totals (4 years)	48	3	19	9	1.0	0	0	0.0	0

CHAMBERS, CHRIS WR DOLPHINS

PERSONAL: Born August 12, 1978, in Cleveland, Ohio. ... 5-11/210.
HIGH SCHOOL: Bedford (Ohio).
COLLEGE: Wisconsin.
TRANSACTIONS/CAREER NOTES: Selected by Miami Dolphins in second round (52nd pick overall) of 2001 NFL draft. ... Signed by Dolphins (July 23, 2001).
SINGLE GAME HIGHS (regular season): Receptions—9 (November 21, 2004, vs. Seattle); yards—153 (December 28, 2003, vs. New York Jets); and touchdown receptions—3 (November 27, 2003, vs. Dallas).
STATISTICAL PLATEAUS: 100-yard receiving games: 2001 (3), 2002 (2), 2003 (2), 2004 (4). Total: 11.

Year Team	G	GS	RUSHING Att.	Yds.	Avg.	TD	RECEIVING No.	Yds.	Avg.	TD	TOTALS TD	2pt.	Pts.	Fum.
2001—Miami NFL	16	7	1	-11	-11.0	0	48	883	*18.4	7	7	0	42	2
2002—Miami NFL	15	15	6	78	13.0	0	52	734	14.1	3	3	0	18	1
2003—Miami NFL	16	16	4	30	7.5	0	64	963	15.0	§11	11	0	66	1
2004—Miami NFL	15	15	9	76	8.4	0	69	898	13.0	7	7	1	44	1
Pro totals (4 years)	62	53	20	173	8.7	0	233	3478	14.9	28	28	1	170	5

CHAMBERS, KIRK — T — BROWNS

PERSONAL: Born March 19, 1979, in Provo, Utah. ... 6-7/313.
HIGH SCHOOL: Provo (Utah).
COLLEGE: Stanford.
TRANSACTIONS/CAREER NOTES: Selected by Cleveland Browns in sixth round (176th pick overall) of 2004 NFL draft. ... Signed by Browns (July 23, 2004).
PLAYING EXPERIENCE: Cleveland NFL, 2004. ... Games/Games started: 2004 (6/0). Total: 6/0.

CHANDLER, CHRIS — QB

PERSONAL: Born October 12, 1965, in Everett, Wash. ... 6-4/224. ... Full name: Christopher Mark Chandler. ... Brother of Greg Chandler, catcher with San Francisco Giants organization (1978); and son-in-law of John Brodie, quarterback with San Francisco 49ers (1957-73).
HIGH SCHOOL: Everett (Wash.).
COLLEGE: Washington.
TRANSACTIONS/CAREER NOTES: Selected by Indianapolis Colts in third round (76th pick overall) of 1988 NFL draft. ... Signed by Colts (July 23, 1988). ... On injured reserve with knee injury (October 3, 1989-remainder of season). ... Traded by Colts to Tampa Bay Buccaneers for first round pick (LB Quentin Coryatt) in 1992 draft (August 7, 1990). ... Claimed on waivers by Phoenix Cardinals (November 6, 1991). ... Granted unconditional free agency (February 17, 1994). ... Signed by Los Angeles Rams (May 6, 1994). ... Granted unconditional free agency (February 17, 1995). ... Signed by Houston Oilers (March 10, 1995). ... Traded by Oilers to Atlanta Falcons for fourth- (WR Derrick Mason) and sixth-round (traded to New Orleans) picks in 1997 draft (February 24, 1997). ... Released by Falcons (February 25, 2002). ... Signed by Chicago Bears (April 12, 2002). ... Released by Bears (March 19, 2004). ... Signed by St. Louis Rams (March 23, 2004). ... Released by Rams (February 22, 2005).
CHAMPIONSHIP GAME EXPERIENCE: Played in NFC championship game (1998 season). ... Played in Super Bowl 33 (1998 season).
HONORS: Played in Pro Bowl (1997 and 1998 seasons).
SINGLE GAME HIGHS (regular season): Attempts—50 (November 18, 2001, vs. Green Bay); completions—29 (November 18, 2001, vs. Green Bay); yards—431 (December 23, 2001, vs. Buffalo); and touchdown passes—4 (November 28, 1999, vs. Carolina).
STATISTICAL PLATEAUS: 300-yard passing games: 1992 (1), 1995 (1), 1998 (1), 1999 (2), 2001 (2). Total: 7.
MISCELLANEOUS: Regular-season record as starting NFL quarterback: 67-85 (.441). ... Postseason record as starting NFL quarterback: 2-1 (.667).

Year Team	G	GS	PASSING Att.	Cmp.	Pct.	Yds.	TD	Int.	Avg.	Skd.	Rat.	RUSHING Att.	Yds.	Avg.	TD	TOTALS TD	2pt.	Pts.
1988—Indianapolis NFL	15	13	233	129	55.4	1619	8	12	6.95	18	67.2	46	139	3.0	3	3	0	18
1989—Indianapolis NFL	3	3	80	39	48.8	537	2	3	6.71	3	63.4	7	57	8.1	1	1	0	6
1990—Tampa Bay NFL	7	3	83	42	50.6	464	1	6	5.59	15	41.4	13	71	5.5	1	1	0	6
1991—Tampa Bay NFL	6	3	104	53	51.0	557	4	8	5.36	10	47.6	18	79	4.4	0	0	0	0
—Phoenix NFL	3	2	50	25	50.0	289	1	2	5.78	7	57.8	8	32	4.0	0	0	0	0
1992—Phoenix NFL	15	13	413	245	59.3	2832	15	15	6.86	29	77.1	36	149	4.1	1	1	0	6
1993—Phoenix NFL	4	2	103	52	50.5	471	3	2	4.57	4	64.8	3	2	0.7	0	0	0	0
1994—L.A. Rams NFL	12	6	176	108	61.4	1352	7	2	7.68	7	93.8	18	61	3.4	1	1	0	6
1995—Houston NFL	13	13	356	225	63.2	2460	17	10	6.91	21	87.8	28	58	2.1	2	2	1	14
1996—Houston NFL	12	12	320	184	57.5	2099	16	11	6.56	25	79.7	28	113	4.0	0	0	0	0
1997—Atlanta NFL	14	14	342	202	59.1	2692	20	7	7.87	39	95.1	43	158	3.7	0	0	0	0
1998—Atlanta NFL	14	14	327	190	58.1	3154	25	12	*9.65	45	100.9	36	121	3.4	2	2	0	12
1999—Atlanta NFL	12	12	307	174	56.7	2339	16	11	7.62	32	83.5	16	57	3.6	1	1	0	6
2000—Atlanta NFL	14	13	331	192	58.0	2236	10	12	6.76	40	73.5	21	60	2.9	0	0	0	0
2001—Atlanta NFL	14	14	365	223	61.1	2847	16	14	7.80	41	84.1	25	84	3.4	0	0	0	0
2002—Chicago NFL	9	7	161	103	64.0	1023	4	4	6.35	23	79.8	10	32	3.2	0	0	0	0
2003—Chicago NFL	8	6	192	107	55.7	1050	3	7	5.47	14	61.3	14	35	2.5	0	0	1	2
2004—St. Louis NFL	5	2	62	35	56.5	463	2	8	7.47	7	51.4	1	2	2.0	0	0	0	0
Pro totals (17 years)	180	152	4005	2328	58.1	28484	170	146	7.11	380	79.1	371	1310	3.5	12	12	2	76

CHANDLER, JEFF — K — REDSKINS

PERSONAL: Born June 18, 1979, in Jacksonville, Fla. ... 6-2/218. ... Full name: Jeffrey Robin Chandler.
HIGH SCHOOL: Mandarin (Jacksonville, Fla.).
COLLEGE: Florida.
TRANSACTIONS/CAREER NOTES: Selected by San Francisco 49ers in fourth round (102nd pick overall) of 2002 NFL draft. ... Signed by 49ers (July 21, 2002). ... Waived by 49ers (September 16, 2003). ... Signed by Jacksonville Jaguars (March 16, 2004). ... Released by Jaguars (August (21, 2004). ... Signed by St. Louis Rams (October 20, 2004). ... Released by Rams (October 25, 2004). ... Signed by Carolina Panthers to practice squad (November 16, 2004). ... Activated (November 19, 2004). ... Released by Panthers (November 30, 2004). ... Signed by Washington Redskins (December 16, 2004).

Year Team	G	FIELD GOALS 1-29	30-39	40-49	50+	Tot.	Pct.	Lg.	TOTALS XPM	XPA	Pts.
2002—San Francisco NFL	6	3-3	1-1	4-7	0-1	8-12	66.7	47	14	14	38
2003—San Francisco NFL	2	5-5	1-1	0-1	0-0	6-7	85.7	35	7	8	25
2004—Carolina NFL	2	0-0	0-2	0-0	0-0	0-2	0.0	0	8	8	8
—Washington NFL	3	4-4	0-0	1-1	0-1	5-6	83.3	49	6	6	21
Pro totals (3 years)	13	12-12	2-4	5-9	0-2	19-27	70.4	49	35	36	92

CHATHAM, MATT   LB   PATRIOTS

PERSONAL: Born June 28, 1977, in Newton, Iowa. ... 6-4/250.
HIGH SCHOOL: Sioux City (Iowa).
COLLEGE: South Dakota.
TRANSACTIONS/CAREER NOTES: Signed as non-drafted free agent by St. Louis Rams (April 26, 1999). ... Released by Rams (June 26, 1999). ... Signed by Rams (February 11, 2000). ... Claimed on waivers by New England Patriots (August 28, 2000). ... Released by Patriots (September 2, 2001). ... Re-signed by Patriots to practice squad (September 4, 2001). ... Activated (September 22, 2001). ... Released by Patriots (September 25, 2001). ... Re-signed by Patriots to practice squad (September 26, 2001). ... Activated (October 3, 2001). ... On injured reserve with hand injury (December 11, 2002-remainder of season). ... Granted free agency (February 28, 2003). ... Re-signed by Patriots (April 11, 2003). ... On physically unable to perform list with leg injury (September 4-October 24, 2004).
CHAMPIONSHIP GAME EXPERIENCE: Played in AFC championship game (2001, 2003 and 2004 seasons). ... Member of Super Bowl championship team (2001, 2003 and 2004 seasons).

				TOTALS			INTERCEPTIONS			
Year	Team	G	GS	Tk.	Ast.	Sks.	No.	Yds.	Avg.	TD
2000—New England NFL		6	0	0	0	0.0	0	0	0.0	0
2001—New England NFL		11	0	2	0	0.0	0	0	0.0	0
2002—New England NFL		13	0	2	0	0.0	0	0	0.0	0
2003—New England NFL		16	4	14	7	1.5	0	0	0.0	0
2004—New England NFL		5	0	0	0	0.0	0	0	0.0	0
Pro totals (5 years)		51	4	18	7	1.5	0	0	0.0	0

CHATMAN, ANTONIO   WR/KR   PACKERS

PERSONAL: Born February 12, 1979, in Jackson, Ala. ... 5-9/184. ... Full name: Antonio Tavaras Chatman.
HIGH SCHOOL: Dorsey (Los Angeles, Calif.).
JUNIOR COLLEGE: El Camino (Torrence, Calif.).
COLLEGE: Cincinnati.
TRANSACTIONS/CAREER NOTES: Signed as non-drafted free agent by San Francisco 49ers (April 26, 2001). ... Released by 49ers (August 24, 2001). ... Signed by Green Bay Packers (June 2, 2003).
SINGLE GAME HIGHS (regular season): Receptions—5 (October 17, 2004, vs. Detroit); yards—50 (October 17, 2004, vs. Detroit); and touchdown receptions—1 (December 19, 2004, vs. Jacksonville).

				RUSHING				RECEIVING				PUNT RETURNS				KICKOFF RETURNS				TOTALS		
Year	Team	G	GS	Att.	Yds.	Avg.	TD	No.	Yds.	Avg.	TD	No.	Yds.	Avg.	TD	No.	Yds.	Avg.	TD	TD	2pt.	Pts.
2003—G.B. NFL		16	0	0	0	0.0	0	0	0	0.0	0	33	277	8.4	0	36	804	22.3	0	0	0	0
2004—G.B. NFL		16	2	4	36	9.0	0	22	246	11.2	1	32	245	7.7	0	25	565	22.6	0	1	0	6
Pro totals (2 years)		32	2	4	36	9.0	0	22	246	11.2	1	65	522	8.0	0	61	1369	22.4	0	1	0	6

CHATMAN, JESSE   RB   CHARGERS

PERSONAL: Born September 22, 1979, in Houston, Texas. ... 5-8/247.
HIGH SCHOOL: Franklin (Seattle).
COLLEGE: Eastern Washington.
TRANSACTIONS/CAREER NOTES: Signed as non-drafted free agent by San Diego Chargers (April 26, 2002). ... Granted free agency (March 2, 2005). ... Re-signed by Chargers (March 30, 2005).
SINGLE GAME HIGHS (regular season): Attempts—14 (December 19, 2004, vs. Cleveland); yards—103 (October 10, 2004, vs. Jacksonville); and rushing touchdowns—1 (October 24, 2004, vs. Carolina).
STATISTICAL PLATEAUS: 100-yard rushing games: 2004 (1). Total: 1.

				RUSHING				RECEIVING				KICKOFF RETURNS				TOTALS			
Year	Team	G	GS	Att.	Yds.	Avg.	TD	No.	Yds.	Avg.	TD	No.	Yds.	Avg.	TD	TD	2pt.	Pts.	Fum.
2002—San Diego NFL		10	0	6	19	3.2	0	3	44	14.7	0	0	0	0.0	0	0	0	0	0
2003—San Diego NFL		16	0	8	17	2.1	0	5	54	10.8	0	2	31	15.5	0	0	0	0	0
2004—San Diego NFL		15	0	65	392	6.0	3	2	17	8.5	0	4	89	22.3	0	3	0	18	1
Pro totals (3 years)		41	0	79	428	5.4	3	10	115	11.5	0	6	120	20.0	0	3	0	18	1

CHAVOUS, COREY   S   VIKINGS

PERSONAL: Born January 15, 1976, in Aiken, S.C. ... 6-1/205. ... Name pronounced: CHAY-vus.
HIGH SCHOOL: Silver Bluff (Aiken, S.C.).
COLLEGE: Vanderbilt.
TRANSACTIONS/CAREER NOTES: Selected by Arizona Cardinals in second round (33rd pick overall) of 1998 NFL draft. ... Signed by Cardinals (July 23, 1998). ... Granted free agency (March 2, 2001). ... Re-signed by Cardinals (July 13, 2001). ... Granted unconditional free agency (March 1, 2002). ... Signed by Minnesota Vikings (March 25, 2002).
HONORS: Played in Pro Bowl (2003 season).

				TOTALS			INTERCEPTIONS			
Year	Team	G	GS	Tk.	Ast.	Sks.	No.	Yds.	Avg.	TD
1998—Arizona NFL		16	5	20	5	0.0	2	0	0.0	0
1999—Arizona NFL		15	4	28	8	0.0	1	1	1.0	0
2000—Arizona NFL		16	1	39	3	0.0	1	0	0.0	0
2001—Arizona NFL		14	14	59	12	0.0	1	0	0.0	0
2002—Minnesota NFL		16	16	66	17	1.0	3	76	25.3	0
2003—Minnesota NFL		16	16	74	11	0.0	8	143	17.9	1
2004—Minnesota NFL		16	16	59	20	0.0	1	0	0.0	0
Pro totals (7 years)		109	72	345	76	1.0	17	220	12.9	2

CHEEK, STEVE   P

PERSONAL: Born April 18, 1977, in Westfield, N.J. ... 6-4/205. ... Full name: Stephen Andrew Cheek.
HIGH SCHOOL: Westfield (N.J.).
COLLEGE: Humboldt State.
TRANSACTIONS/CAREER NOTES: Signed as non-drafted free agent by San Francisco 49ers (April 25, 2001). ... Released by 49ers (August 28, 2001). ... Re-signed by 49ers (February 6, 2002). ... Released by 49ers (March 19, 2002). ... Signed by Philadelphia Eagles (April 22, 2002). ... Released by Eagles (August 26, 2002). ... Signed by New York Giants (January 7, 2003). ... Assigned by Giants to Berlin Thunder in 2003 NFL Europe enhancement allocation program (January 31, 2003). ... Released by Giants (September 1, 2003). ... Signed by Houston Texans (February 10, 2004). ... Traded by Texans to Kansas City Chiefs for future considerations (September 1, 2004). ... Released by Chiefs (September 25, 2004). ... Re-signed by Chiefs to practice squad (September 28, 2004). ... Activated (October 13, 2004). ... Released by Chiefs (December 22, 2004).

			PUNTING				
Year Team	G	No.	Yds.	Avg.	Net avg.	In. 20	Blk.
2004—Kansas City NFL	12	42	1643	39.1	31.6	8	0

CHERRY, JE'ROD   S

PERSONAL: Born May 30, 1973, in Charlotte, N.C. ... 6-1/210. ... Full name: Je'Rod L. Cherry. ... Name pronounced: juh-ROD.
HIGH SCHOOL: Berkeley (Calif.).
COLLEGE: California.
TRANSACTIONS/CAREER NOTES: Selected by New Orleans Saints in second round (40th pick overall) of 1996 NFL draft. ... Signed by Saints (July 3, 1996). ... Granted free agency (February 12, 1999). ... Re-signed by Saints (July 21, 1999). ... Granted unconditional free agency (February 11, 2000). ... Signed by Oakland Raiders (February 19, 2000). ... Released by Raiders (August 27, 2000). ... Signed by Philadelphia Eagles (September 20, 2000). ... Granted unconditional free agency (March 2, 2001). ... Signed by New England Patriots (July 25, 2001). ... Granted unconditional free agency (February 28, 2003). ... Re-signed by Patriots (March 5, 2003). ... Granted unconditional free agency (March 3, 2004). ... Re-signed by Patriots (March 16, 2004). ... Released by Patriots (September 5, 2004). ... Re-signed by Patriots (October 6, 2004). ... Released by Patriots (December 24, 2004). ... Re-signed by Patriots (December 29, 2004). ... Granted unconditional free agency (March 2, 2005).
CHAMPIONSHIP GAME EXPERIENCE: Played in AFC championship game (2001, 2003 and 2004 seasons). ... Member of Super Bowl championship team (2001, 2003 and 2004 seasons).

			TOTALS			INTERCEPTIONS			
Year Team	G	GS	Tk.	Ast.	Sks.	No.	Yds.	Avg.	TD
1996—New Orleans NFL	13	0	6	2	0.0	0	0	0.0	0
1997—New Orleans NFL	16	0	6	0	0.0	0	0	0.0	0
1998—New Orleans NFL	14	0	23	4	2.0	0	0	0.0	0
1999—New Orleans NFL	16	0	13	1	0.0	0	0	0.0	0
2000—Philadelphia NFL	13	0	0	0	0.0	0	0	0.0	0
2001—New England NFL	16	0	2	1	0.0	0	0	0.0	0
2002—New England NFL	16	0	1	0	0.0	0	0	0.0	0
2003—New England NFL	11	0	4	0	1.0	0	0	0.0	0
2004—New England NFL	12	0	1	1	0.0	0	0	0.0	0
Pro totals (9 years)	127	0	56	9	3.0	0	0	0.0	0

CHESTER, LARRY   DT   DOLPHINS

PERSONAL: Born October 17, 1975, in Hammond, La. ... 6-2/325.
HIGH SCHOOL: Hammond (La.).
JUNIOR COLLEGE: Southwest Mississippi Junior College.
COLLEGE: Temple.
TRANSACTIONS/CAREER NOTES: Signed as non-drafted free agent by Indianapolis Colts (April 24, 1998). ... Released by Colts (August 31, 1998). ... Re-signed by Colts to practice squad (September 2, 1998). ... Activated (September 11, 1998). ... Granted free agency (March 2, 2001). ... Signed by Carolina Panthers (May 15, 2001). ... Granted unconditional free agency (March 1, 2002). ... Signed by Miami Dolphins (March 5, 2002). ... On injured reserve with knee injury (September 21, 2004-remainder of season).

			TOTALS		
Year Team	G	GS	Tk.	Ast.	Sks.
1998—Indianapolis NFL	14	2	20	3	3.0
1999—Indianapolis NFL	16	8	31	10	1.0
2000—Indianapolis NFL	15	0	10	6	2.5
2001—Carolina NFL	11	5	26	10	0.5
2002—Miami NFL	16	16	26	11	1.5
2003—Miami NFL	15	15	20	18	0.0
2004—Miami NFL	2	2	7	0	0.0
Pro totals (7 years)	89	48	140	58	8.5

CHILLAR, BRANDON   LB   RAMS

PERSONAL: Born October 21, 1982, in Los Angeles, Calif. ... 6-2/253. ... Full name: Brandon O'Neil Chillar.
HIGH SCHOOL: Carlsbad (Calif.).
COLLEGE: UCLA.
TRANSACTIONS/CAREER NOTES: Selected by St. Louis Rams in fourth round (130th pick overall) of 2004 NFL draft. ... Signed by Rams (July 15, 2004).

			TOTALS			INTERCEPTIONS			
Year Team	G	GS	Tk.	Ast.	Sks.	No.	Yds.	Avg.	TD
2004—St. Louis NFL	16	5	14	5	0.0	0	0	0.0	0

CHREBET, WAYNE   WR   JETS

PERSONAL: Born August 14, 1973, in Garfield, N.J. ... 5-10/188. ... Name pronounced: kra-BET.
HIGH SCHOOL: Garfield (N.J.).
COLLEGE: Hofstra.
TRANSACTIONS/CAREER NOTES: Signed as non-drafted free agent by New York Jets (April 25, 1995). ... On injured reserve with post-concussion syndrome (November 12, 2003-remainder of season).
CHAMPIONSHIP GAME EXPERIENCE: Played in AFC championship game (1998 season).
SINGLE GAME HIGHS (regular season): Receptions—12 (October 13, 1996, vs. Jacksonville); yards—162 (October 13, 1996, vs. Jacksonville); and touchdown receptions—2 (December 29, 2002, vs. Green Bay).
STATISTICAL PLATEAUS: 100-yard receiving games: 1996 (1), 1997 (1), 1998 (5), 1999 (1), 2000 (2), 2001 (1). Total: 11.

			RECEIVING				PUNT RETURNS				TOTALS			
Year Team	G	GS	No.	Yds.	Avg.	TD	No.	Yds.	Avg.	TD	TD	2pt.	Pts.	Fum.
1995—New York Jets NFL	16	16	66	726	11.0	4	0	0	0.0	0	4	0	24	1
1996—New York Jets NFL	16	9	84	909	10.8	3	28	139	5.0	0	3	0	18	5
1997—New York Jets NFL	16	1	58	799	13.8	3	0	0	0.0	0	3	0	18	0
1998—New York Jets NFL	16	15	75	1083	14.4	8	0	0	0.0	0	8	0	48	0
1999—New York Jets NFL	11	11	48	631	13.1	3	0	0	0.0	0	3	0	18	0
2000—New York Jets NFL	16	16	69	937	13.6	8	0	0	0.0	0	8	0	48	0
2001—New York Jets NFL	15	15	56	750	13.4	1	0	0	0.0	0	1	0	6	0
2002—New York Jets NFL	15	15	51	691	13.5	9	0	0	0.0	0	9	0	54	2
2003—New York Jets NFL	7	5	27	289	10.7	1	0	0	0.0	0	1	0	6	0
2004—New York Jets NFL	16	1	31	397	12.8	1	0	0	0.0	0	1	0	6	0
Pro totals (10 years)	144	104	565	7212	12.8	41	28	139	5.0	0	41	0	246	8

CHRISTIE, STEVE   K

PERSONAL: Born November 13, 1967, in Hamilton, ON. ... 6-0/195. ... Full name: Geoffrey Stephen Christie.
HIGH SCHOOL: Trafalgar (Oakville, Ont.).
COLLEGE: William & Mary.
TRANSACTIONS/CAREER NOTES: Signed as non-drafted free agent by Tampa Bay Buccaneers (May 8, 1990). ... Granted unconditional free agency (February 1, 1992). ... Signed by Buffalo Bills (February 5, 1992). ... Granted unconditional free agency (March 2, 2001). ... Re-signed by Bills (April 22, 2001). ... On injured reserve with groin injury (September 8-October 3, 2001). ... Released by Bills (October 3, 2001). ... Signed by San Diego Chargers (November 29, 2001). ... Granted unconditional free agency (March 1, 2002). ... Re-signed by Chargers (March 29, 2002). ... Granted unconditional free agency (February 28, 2003). ... Re-signed by Chargers (April 7, 2003). ... Granted unconditional free agency (March 3, 2004). ... Signed by Jacksonville Jaguars (August 26, 2004). ... Released by Jaguars (September 3, 2004). ... Signed by New York Giants (September 7, 2004). ... Granted unconditional free agency (March 2, 2005).
CHAMPIONSHIP GAME EXPERIENCE: Played in AFC championship game (1992 and 1993 seasons). ... Played in Super Bowl 27 (1992 season) and Super Bowl 28 (1993 season).
POST SEASON RECORDS: Holds Super Bowl single-game record for longest field goal—54 yards (January 30, 1994, vs. Dallas). ... Shares NFL postseason single-game record for most field goals made—5; and most field goals attempted—6 (January 17, 1993, at Miami).
MISCELLANEOUS: Buffalo Bills all-time scoring leader (1,011 points).

		FIELD GOALS							TOTALS		
Year Team	G	1-29	30-39	40-49	50+	Tot.	Pct.	Lg.	XPM	XPA	Pts.
1990—Tampa Bay NFL	16	7-7	10-13	4-5	2-2	23-27	85.2	54	27	27	96
1991—Tampa Bay NFL	16	5-5	7-11	3-4	0-0	15-20	75.0	49	22	22	67
1992—Buffalo NFL	16	11-11	3-6	7-8	3-5	24-30	80.0	†54	§43	§44	115
1993—Buffalo NFL	16	4-5	12-12	6-9	1-6	23-32	71.9	*59	36	37	105
1994—Buffalo NFL	16	11-12	6-7	5-7	2-2	24-28	85.7	52	§38	§38	110
1995—Buffalo NFL	16	13-14	13-15	3-6	2-5	31-40	77.5	51	33	35	126
1996—Buffalo NFL	16	5-6	12-14	7-8	0-1	24-29	82.8	48	33	33	105
1997—Buffalo NFL	16	6-6	9-12	8-10	1-2	24-30	80.0	†55	21	21	93
1998—Buffalo NFL	16	11-13	12-14	9-11	1-3	33-*41	80.5	52	41	41	§140
1999—Buffalo NFL	16	12-12	7-10	3-9	3-3	25-34	73.5	52	33	33	108
2000—Buffalo NFL	16	13-15	4-6	9-13	0-1	26-35	74.3	48	31	31	109
2001—San Diego NFL	5	4-4	3-5	2-2	0-0	9-11	81.8	41	6	6	33
2002—San Diego NFL	16	8-8	5-6	4-9	1-3	18-26	69.2	53	35	35	89
2003—San Diego NFL	16	7-7	3-3	3-7	2-3	15-20	75.0	51	36	36	81
2004—New York Giants NFL	16	9-9	6-8	4-7	3-4	22-28	78.6	53	33	33	99
Pro totals (15 years)	229	126-134	112-142	77-115	21-40	336-431	78.0	59	468	473	1476

CHUKWURAH, PATRICK   LB   BRONCOS

PERSONAL: Born March 1, 1979, in Nigeria. ... 6-1/250.
HIGH SCHOOL: MacArthur (Texas).
COLLEGE: Wyoming.
TRANSACTIONS/CAREER NOTES: Selected by Minnesota Vikings in fifth round (157th pick overall) of 2001 NFL draft. ... Signed by Vikings (July 24, 2001). ... Claimed on waivers by Houston Texans (March 2, 2003). ... Released by Texans (August 31, 2003). ... Signed by Denver Broncos (December 24, 2003). ... Released by Broncos (December 26, 2004). ... Re-signed by Broncos (January 13, 2005).

			TOTALS			INTERCEPTIONS			
Year Team	G	GS	Tk.	Ast.	Sks.	No.	Yds.	Avg.	TD
2001—Minnesota NFL	16	3	0	0	2.5	0	0	0.0	0
2002—Minnesota NFL	11	2	0	0	0.0	0	0	0.0	0
2004—Denver NFL	14	0	2	2	1.0	0	0	0.0	0
Pro totals (3 years)	41	5	2	2	3.5	0	0	0.0	0

C

CIURCIU, VINNY   LB   PANTHERS

PERSONAL: Born May 2, 1980, in Hackensack, N.J. ... 6-0/235. ... Full name: Vincenzo Ciurciu.
HIGH SCHOOL: St. Joseph (Paramus, N.J.).
COLLEGE: Boston College.
TRANSACTIONS/CAREER NOTES: Signed as non-drafted free agent by Carolina Panthers (May 2, 2003). ... Released by Panthers (August 31, 2003). ... Signed by Tampa Bay Buccaneers (October 7, 2003). ... Released by Buccaneers (December 2, 2003). ... Signed by Carolina Panthers to practice squad (December 5, 2003). ... Activated (December 20, 2003).

Year Team	G	GS	TOTALS Tk.	Ast.	Sks.	INTERCEPTIONS No.	Yds.	Avg.	TD
2003—Tampa Bay NFL	8	0	0	0	0.0	0	0	0.0	0
—Carolina NFL	2	0	0	0	0.0	0	0	0.0	0
2004—Carolina NFL	16	4	23	8	0.0	0	0	0.0	0
Pro totals (2 years)	26	4	23	8	0.0	0	0	0.0	0

CLAIBORNE, CHRIS   LB   RAMS

C

PERSONAL: Born July 26, 1978, in San Diego, Calif. ... 6-3/259.
HIGH SCHOOL: John W. North (Riverside, Calif.).
COLLEGE: Southern California.
TRANSACTIONS/CAREER NOTES: Selected after junior season by Detroit Lions in first round (ninth pick overall) of 1999 NFL draft. ... Signed by Lions (July 24, 1999). ... Granted unconditional free agency (February 28, 2003). ... Signed by Minnesota Vikings (March 24, 2003). ... Granted unconditional free agency (March 2, 2005). ... Signed by St. Louis Rams (March 3, 2005).
HONORS: Butkus Award winner (1998). ... Named inside linebacker on THE SPORTING NEWS college All-America first team (1998).

Year Team	G	GS	TOTALS Tk.	Ast.	Sks.	INTERCEPTIONS No.	Yds.	Avg.	TD
1999—Detroit NFL	15	13	50	16	1.5	0	0	0.0	0
2000—Detroit NFL	16	14	65	39	0.5	1	1	1.0	0
2001—Detroit NFL	16	16	77	43	4.0	2	11	5.5	0
2002—Detroit NFL	16	15	72	29	4.5	3	63	21.0	1
2003—Minnesota NFL	12	12	61	19	3.0	1	3	3.0	0
2004—Minnesota NFL	12	12	39	18	1.0	1	15	15.0	1
Pro totals (6 years)	87	82	364	164	14.5	8	93	11.6	2

CLANCY, KENDRICK   DT   GIANTS

PERSONAL: Born September 17, 1978, in Tuscaloosa, Ala. ... 6-1/305.
HIGH SCHOOL: Holt (Tuscaloosa, Ala.).
JUNIOR COLLEGE: East Central Community College (Miss.).
COLLEGE: Mississippi.
TRANSACTIONS/CAREER NOTES: Selected by Pittsburgh Steelers in third round (72nd pick overall) of 2000 NFL draft. ... Signed by Steelers (July 16, 2000). ... Granted free agency (February 28, 2003). ... Re-signed by Steelers (April 16, 2003). ... Granted unconditional free agency (March 3, 2004). ... Re-signed by Steelers (April 28, 2004). ... Released by Steelers (September 5, 2004). ... Re-signed by Steelers (October 20, 2004). ... Granted unconditional free agency (March 2, 2005). ... Signed by New York Giants (March 11, 2005).
CHAMPIONSHIP GAME EXPERIENCE: Played in AFC championship game (2001 and 2004 seasons).
HONORS: Named defensive tackle on THE SPORTING NEWS college All-America third team (1999).

Year Team	G	GS	TOTALS Tk.	Ast.	Sks.	INTERCEPTIONS No.	Yds.	Avg.	TD
2000—Pittsburgh NFL	9	0	5	3	0.0	0	0	0.0	0
2001—Pittsburgh NFL	16	4	6	4	0.0	1	3	3.0	0
2002—Pittsburgh NFL	7	0	1	0	0.0	0	0	0.0	0
2003—Pittsburgh NFL	10	0	3	0	0.0	0	0	0.0	0
2004—Pittsburgh NFL	8	0	7	1	0.0	0	0	0.0	0
Pro totals (5 years)	50	4	22	8	0.0	1	3	3.0	0

CLARK, DALLAS   TE   COLTS

PERSONAL: Born June 12, 1979, in Livermore, Iowa. ... 6-3/252.
HIGH SCHOOL: Twin River Valley (Livermore, Iowa).
COLLEGE: Iowa.
TRANSACTIONS/CAREER NOTES: Selected after junior season by Indianapolis Colts in first round (24th pick overall) of 2003 NFL draft. ... Signed by Colts (August 9, 2003).
CHAMPIONSHIP GAME EXPERIENCE: Played in AFC championship game (2003 season).
SINGLE GAME HIGHS (regular season): Receptions—5 (November 16, 2003, vs. New York Jets); yards—102 (November 14, 2004, vs. Houston); and touchdown receptions—2 (November 14, 2004, vs. Houston).
STATISTICAL PLATEAUS: 100-yard receiving games: 2003 (1), 2004 (1). Total: 2.

Year Team	G	GS	RECEIVING No.	Yds.	Avg.	TD	TOTALS TD	2pt.	Pts.	Fum.
2003—Indianapolis NFL	10	10	29	340	11.7	1	1	0	6	0
2004—Indianapolis NFL	15	13	25	423	16.9	5	5	0	30	2
Pro totals (2 years)	25	23	54	763	14.1	6	6	0	36	2

CLARK, DANNY   LB   RAIDERS

PERSONAL: Born May 9, 1977, in Blue Island, Ill. ... 6-2/245. ... Full name: Daniel Clark IV.
HIGH SCHOOL: Hillcrest (Ill.).
COLLEGE: Illinois.
TRANSACTIONS/CAREER NOTES: Selected by Jacksonville Jaguars in seventh round (245th pick overall) of 2000 NFL draft. ... Signed by Jaguars (June 6, 2000). ... Granted free agency (February 28, 2003). ... Re-signed by Jaguars (May 5, 2003). ... Granted unconditional free agency (March 3, 2004). ... Signed by Oakland Raiders (March 12, 2004).

				TOTALS			INTERCEPTIONS		
Year Team	G	GS	Tk.	Ast.	Sks.	No.	Yds.	Avg.	TD
2000—Jacksonville NFL	16	0	4	0	0.0	0	0	0.0	0
2001—Jacksonville NFL	13	3	18	3	0.0	0	0	0.0	0
2002—Jacksonville NFL	16	16	69	22	2.0	1	7	7.0	0
2003—Jacksonville NFL	16	9	26	11	0.0	0	0	0.0	0
2004—Oakland NFL	16	16	99	31	2.0	0	0	0.0	0
Pro totals (5 years)	77	44	216	67	4.0	1	7	7.0	0

CLARK, DESMOND   TE   BEARS

C

PERSONAL: Born April 20, 1977, in Bartow, Fla. ... 6-3/255. ... Full name: Desmond Darice Clark.
HIGH SCHOOL: Kathleen (Lakeland, Fla.).
COLLEGE: Wake Forest.
TRANSACTIONS/CAREER NOTES: Selected by Denver Broncos in sixth round (179th pick overall) of 1999 NFL draft. ... Signed by Broncos (June 14, 1999). ... Granted free agency (March 1, 2002). ... Re-signed by Broncos (April 16, 2002). ... Claimed on waivers by Miami Dolphins (September 2, 2002). ... Granted unconditional free agency (February 28, 2003). ... Signed by Chicago Bears (March 1, 2003).
SINGLE GAME HIGHS (regular season): Receptions—7 (November 5, 2001, vs. Oakland); yards—94 (October 28, 2001, vs. New England); and touchdown receptions—1 (December 5, 2004, vs. Minnesota).

			RECEIVING				TOTALS			
Year Team	G	GS	No.	Yds.	Avg.	TD	TD	2pt.	Pts.	Fum.
1999—Denver NFL	9	0	1	5	5.0	0	0	0	0	0
2000—Denver NFL	16	2	27	339	12.6	3	3	0	18	0
2001—Denver NFL	16	4	51	566	11.1	6	6	0	36	3
2002—Miami NFL	11	0	2	42	21.0	0	0	0	0	0
2003—Chicago NFL	15	15	44	433	9.8	2	2	0	12	2
2004—Chicago NFL	15	13	24	282	11.8	1	1	0	6	1
Pro totals (6 years)	82	34	149	1667	11.2	12	12	0	72	6

CLARK, RYAN   S   REDSKINS

PERSONAL: Born October 12, 1979, in Marrero, La. ... 5-11/200. ... Full name: Ryan Terry Clark.
HIGH SCHOOL: Shaw (New Orleans).
COLLEGE: Louisiana State.
TRANSACTIONS/CAREER NOTES: Signed as non-drafted free agent by New York Giants (April 26, 2002). ... Released by Giants (October 21, 2002). ... Re-signed by Giants to practice squad (October 23, 2002). ... Activated (January 8, 2003). ... Released by Giants (May 27, 2004). ... Signed by Washington Redskins (July 31, 2004).

				TOTALS			INTERCEPTIONS		
Year Team	G	GS	Tk.	Ast.	Sks.	No.	Yds.	Avg.	TD
2002—New York Giants NFL	6	0	0	1	0.0	0	0	0.0	0
2003—New York Giants NFL	16	4	17	0	1.0	0	0	0.0	0
2004—Washington NFL	15	11	61	14	0.0	0	0	0.0	0
Pro totals (3 years)	37	15	78	15	1.0	0	0	0.0	0

CLAUSS, JARED   DT   TITANS

PERSONAL: Born April 7, 1981, in West Des Moines, Iowa. ... 6-4/294.
HIGH SCHOOL: Valley (West Des Moines, Iowa).
COLLEGE: Iowa.
TRANSACTIONS/CAREER NOTES: Selected by Tennessee Titans in seventh round (230th pick overall) of 2004 NFL draft. ... Signed by Titans (July 23, 2004).

			TOTALS		
Year Team	G	GS	Tk.	Ast.	Sks.
2004—Tennessee NFL	14	1	4	3	0.0

CLAYBROOKS, DEVONE   DT

PERSONAL: Born September 15, 1977, in Martinsville, Va. ... 6-3/292. ... Full name: Natravis DeVone Claybrooks.
HIGH SCHOOL: Bassett (Va.).
COLLEGE: East Carolina.
TRANSACTIONS/CAREER NOTES: Signed as non-drafted free agent by Green Bay Packers (May 18, 2001). ... Released by Packers (September 2, 2001). ... Signed by Tampa Bay Buccaneers to practice squad (September 4, 2001). ... Released by Buccaneers (October 16, 2001). ... Signed by Cleveland Browns to practice squad (October 30, 2001). ... Activated (November 7, 2001); did not play. ... Assigned by Browns to Rhein Fire in 2002 NFL Europe enhancement allocation program (February 12, 2002). ... Released by Browns (July 26, 2002). ... Signed by Buccaneers to practice squad (November 6, 2002). ... Activated (November 15, 2002). ... Released by Buccaneers (November 18,

2002). ... Re-signed by Buccaneers to practice squad (November 20, 2002). ... Activated (November 23, 2002). ... Released by Buccaneers (August 31, 2003). ... Signed by San Francisco 49ers (September 30, 2003). ... Waived by 49ers (December 23, 2003). ... Signed by Atlanta Falcons (December 29, 2003). ... Waived by Falcons (March 9, 2004). ... Signed by Buccaneers (May 5, 2004). ... Released by Buccaneers (August 31, 2004). ... Signed by Dallas Cowboys to practice squad (October 5, 2004). ... Activated (November 2, 2004). ... Granted unconditional free agency (March 2, 2005).

CHAMPIONSHIP GAME EXPERIENCE: Played in NFC championship game (2002 season). ... Member of Super Bowl championship team (2002 season).

				TOTALS			INTERCEPTIONS			
Year Team	G	GS	Tk.	Ast.	Sks.	No.	Yds.	Avg.	TD	
2002—Tampa Bay NFL	2	0	2	3	0.0	0	0	0.0	0	
2003—San Francisco NFL	3	0	0	1	0.0	0	0	0.0	0	
2004—Dallas NFL	8	0	0	2	0.0	0	0	0.0	0	
Pro totals (3 years)	13	0	2	6	0.0	0	0	0.0	0	

CLAYTON, MICHAEL — WR — BUCCANEERS

PERSONAL: Born October 13, 1982, in Baton Rouge, La. ... 6-4/197. ... Full name: Michael Rashard Clayton.
HIGH SCHOOL: Christian Life Academy (Baton Rouge, La.).
COLLEGE: Louisiana State.
TRANSACTIONS/CAREER NOTES: Selected after junior season by Tampa Bay Buccaneers in first round (15th pick overall) of 2004 NFL draft. ... Signed by Buccaneers (July 23, 2004).
SINGLE GAME HIGHS (regular season): Receptions—9 (December 12, 2004, vs. San Diego); yards—145 (December 12, 2004, vs. San Diego); and touchdown receptions—2 (December 26, 2004, vs. Carolina).
STATISTICAL PLATEAUS: 100-yard receiving games: 2004 (2). Total: 2.

			RUSHING				RECEIVING				TOTALS			
Year Team	G	GS	Att.	Yds.	Avg.	TD	No.	Yds.	Avg.	TD	TD	2pt.	Pts.	Fum.
2004—Tampa Bay NFL	16	13	5	30	6.0	0	80	1193	14.9	7	7	0	42	1

CLEELAND, CAM — TE

PERSONAL: Born August 15, 1975, in Sedro-Woolley, Wash. ... 6-5/270. ... Full name: Cameron Ross Cleeland.
HIGH SCHOOL: Sedro Woolley (Wash.).
COLLEGE: Washington.
TRANSACTIONS/CAREER NOTES: Selected by New Orleans Saints in second round (40th pick overall) of 1998 NFL draft. ... Signed by Saints (June 9, 1998). ... On injured reserve with Achilles injury (August 22, 2000-entire season). ... Granted free agency (March 2, 2001). ... Re-signed by Saints (March 19, 2001). ... On injured reserve with Achilles injury (December 26, 2001-remainder of season). ... Granted unconditional free agency (March 1, 2002). ... Signed by New England Patriots (March 28, 2002). ... Granted unconditional free agency (February 28, 2003). ... Signed by St. Louis Rams (April 4, 2003). ... Granted unconditional free agency (March 3, 2004). ... Re-signed by Rams (June 8, 2004). ... Granted unconditional free agency (March 2, 2005).
SINGLE GAME HIGHS (regular season): Receptions—10 (December 27, 1998, vs. Buffalo); yards—112 (December 27, 1998, vs. Buffalo); and touchdown receptions—2 (October 14, 2001, vs. Carolina).
STATISTICAL PLATEAUS: 100-yard receiving games: 1998 (1). Total: 1.

			RECEIVING				TOTALS			
Year Team	G	GS	No.	Yds.	Avg.	TD	TD	2pt.	Pts.	Fum.
1998—New Orleans NFL	16	16	54	684	12.7	6	6	0	36	1
1999—New Orleans NFL	11	8	26	325	12.5	1	1	1	8	1
2000—New Orleans NFL			Did not play.							
2001—New Orleans NFL	9	7	13	138	10.6	4	4	0	24	1
2002—New England NFL	12	1	16	112	7.0	1	1	0	6	0
2003—St. Louis NFL	16	10	10	145	14.5	0	0	0	0	1
2004—St. Louis NFL	16	9	7	57	8.1	0	0	0	0	0
Pro totals (6 years)	80	51	126	1461	11.6	12	12	1	74	4

CLEMENT, ANTHONY — T — BRONCOS

PERSONAL: Born April 10, 1976, in Lafayette, La. ... 6-8/337.
HIGH SCHOOL: Cecilia (La.).
COLLEGE: Louisiana-Lafayette.
TRANSACTIONS/CAREER NOTES: Selected by Arizona Cardinals in second round (36th pick overall) of 1998 NFL draft. ... Signed by Cardinals (June 16, 1998). ... On injured reserve with back injury (November 17, 1998-remainder of season). ... Granted free agency (March 2, 2001). ... Re-signed by Cardinals (May 7, 2001). ... Granted unconditional free agency (March 1, 2002). ... Re-signed by Cardinals (March 3, 2002). ... On injured reserve with triceps injury (November 23, 2002-remainder of season). ... Released by Cardinals (April 25, 2005). ... Signed by Denver Broncos (April 26, 2005).
PLAYING EXPERIENCE: Arizona NFL, 1998-2004. ... Games/Games started: 1998 (1/0), 1999 (16/14), 2000 (16/16), 2001 (16/16), 2002 (1/0), 2003 (16/16), 2004 (16/7). Total: 82/69.

CLEMENTS, NATE — CB — BILLS

PERSONAL: Born December 12, 1979, in Shaker Heights, Ohio. ... 6-0/209.
HIGH SCHOOL: Shaker Heights (Ohio).
COLLEGE: Ohio State.
TRANSACTIONS/CAREER NOTES: Selected after junior season by Buffalo Bills in first round (21st pick overall) of 2001 NFL draft. ... Signed by Bills (July 28, 2001).
HONORS: Played in Pro Bowl (2004 season).

Year Team	G	GS	TOTALS			INTERCEPTIONS				PUNT RETURNS				KICKOFF RETURNS				TOTALS			
			Tk.	Ast.	Sks.	No.	Yds.	Avg.	TD	No.	Yds.	Avg.	TD	No.	Yds.	Avg.	TD	TD	2pt.	Pts.	Fum.
2001—Buf. NFL	16	11	55	10	1.0	3	48	16.0	1	4	81	20.2	1	30	628	20.9	0	2	0	12	1
2002—Buf. NFL	16	16	51	13	0.0	6	82	13.7	1	4	20	5.0	0	0	0	0.0	0	1	0	6	1
2003—Buf. NFL	16	16	51	11	0.0	3	54	18.0	1	14	137	9.8	0	0	0	0.0	0	1	0	6	3
2004—Buf. NFL	16	16	58	20	0.5	6	77	12.8	1	35	327	9.3	1	1	14	14.0	0	2	0	12	3
Pro totals (4 years)	64	59	215	54	1.5	18	261	14.5	4	57	565	9.9	2	31	642	20.7	0	6	0	36	8

CLEMONS, CHRIS   LB   REDSKINS

PERSONAL: Born October 30, 1981, in Griffin, Ga. ... 6-3/234.
HIGH SCHOOL: Griffin (Ga.).
COLLEGE: Georgia.
TRANSACTIONS/CAREER NOTES: Signed as non-drafted free agent by Washington Redskins (April 28, 2003). ... On injured reserve with knee injury (August 31, 2003-entire season). ... Released by Redskins (September 5, 2004). ... Signed by Cleveland Browns to practice squad (September 29, 2004). ... Signed by Redskins off Browns practice squad (November 24, 2004). ... Activated (November 24, 2004).

Year Team	G	GS	TOTALS			INTERCEPTIONS			
			Tk.	Ast.	Sks.	No.	Yds.	Avg.	TD
2004—Washington NFL	6	0	6	0	3.0	0	0	0.0	0

CLEMONS, DUANE   DE   BENGALS

C

PERSONAL: Born May 23, 1974, in Riverside, Calif. ... 6-5/275.
HIGH SCHOOL: John W. North (Riverside, Calif.).
COLLEGE: California.
TRANSACTIONS/CAREER NOTES: Selected after junior season by Minnesota Vikings in first round (16th pick overall) of 1996 NFL draft. ... Signed by Vikings (July 25, 1996). ... Granted unconditional free agency (February 11, 2000). ... Signed by Kansas City Chiefs (March 24, 2000). ... Released by Chiefs (February 26, 2003). ... Signed by Cincinnati Bengals (May 13, 2003).
CHAMPIONSHIP GAME EXPERIENCE: Played in NFC championship game (1998 season).

Year Team	G	GS	TOTALS		
			Tk.	Ast.	Sks.
1996—Minnesota NFL	13	0	2	5	0.0
1997—Minnesota NFL	13	3	23	1	7.0
1998—Minnesota NFL	16	3	17	8	2.5
1999—Minnesota NFL	16	9	29	7	9.0
2000—Kansas City NFL	12	12	47	9	7.5
2001—Kansas City NFL	16	15	37	12	7.0
2002—Kansas City NFL	16	16	28	8	2.0
2003—Cincinnati NFL	16	13	35	7	6.0
2004—Cincinnati NFL	14	14	32	18	6.5
Pro totals (9 years)	132	85	250	75	47.5

CLIFTON, CHAD   T   PACKERS

PERSONAL: Born June 26, 1976, in Martin, Tenn. ... 6-5/330. ... Full name: Jeffrey Chad Clifton.
HIGH SCHOOL: Westview (Martin, Tenn.).
COLLEGE: Tennessee.
TRANSACTIONS/CAREER NOTES: Selected by Green Bay Packers in second round (44th pick overall) of 2000 NFL draft. ... Signed by Packers (July 24, 2000). ... On injured reserve with hip injury (December 4, 2002-remainder of season). ... Designated by Packers as franchise player (February 24, 2004). ... Re-signed by Packers (March 3, 2004).
PLAYING EXPERIENCE: Green Bay NFL, 2000-2004. ... Games/Games started: 2000 (13/10), 2001 (14/13), 2002 (10/9), 2003 (16/16), 2004 (16/16). Total: 69/64.
HONORS: Named offensive tackle on THE SPORTING NEWS college All-America second team (1999).

CLOUD, MICHAEL   RB   GIANTS

PERSONAL: Born July 1, 1975, in Charleston, S.C. ... 5-10/205. ... Full name: Michael Alexander Cloud.
HIGH SCHOOL: Portsmouth (R.I.).
COLLEGE: Boston College.
TRANSACTIONS/CAREER NOTES: Selected by Kansas City Chiefs in second round (54th pick overall) of 1999 NFL draft. ... Signed by Chiefs (July 30, 1999). ... Granted unconditional free agency (February 28, 2003). ... Signed by New England Patriots (June 23, 2003). ... On suspended list for violating league substance abuse policy (August 31-October 5, 2003). ... Released by Patriots (September 3, 2004). ... Signed by New York Giants (September 6, 2004). ... Granted unconditional free agency (March 2, 2005). ... Re-signed by Giants (March 18, 2005).
CHAMPIONSHIP GAME EXPERIENCE: Member of Patriots for AFC championship game (2003 season); inactive. ... Member of Patriots for Super Bowl 38 (2003 season); inactive.
SINGLE GAME HIGHS (regular season): Attempts—16 (December 22, 2002, vs. San Diego); yards—73 (October 5, 2003, vs. Tennessee); and rushing touchdowns—2 (October 31, 2004, vs. Minnesota).

Year Team	G	GS	RUSHING				RECEIVING				KICKOFF RETURNS				TOTALS			
			Att.	Yds.	Avg.	TD	No.	Yds.	Avg.	TD	No.	Yds.	Avg.	TD	TD	2pt.	Pts.	Fum.
1999—Kansas City NFL	11	0	35	128	3.7	0	3	25	8.3	0	2	28	14.0	0	0	0	0	0
2000—Kansas City NFL	16	0	30	84	2.8	1	2	16	8.0	0	36	779	21.6	0	2	0	12	0
2001—Kansas City NFL	15	0	7	54	7.7	1	0	0	0.0	0	8	174	21.8	0	1	0	6	0
2002—Kansas City NFL	14	2	49	115	2.3	2	6	48	8.0	0	0	0	0.0	0	2	0	12	0
2003—New England NFL	5	1	27	118	4.4	5	1	8	8.0	0	2	38	19.0	0	5	0	30	0
2004—New York Giants NFL	10	0	21	90	4.3	3	1	3	3.0	0	8	175	21.9	0	3	0	18	0
Pro totals (6 years)	71	7	169	589	3.5	12	13	100	7.7	0	56	1194	21.3	0	13	0	78	0

COADY, RICH — S — FALCONS

PERSONAL: Born January 26, 1976, in Dallas, Texas. ... 6-1/210. ... Full name: Richard Joseph Coady IV. ... Son of Rich Coady, tight end/center with Chicago Bears (1970-74).
HIGH SCHOOL: J.J. Pearce (Richardson, Texas).
COLLEGE: Texas A&M.
TRANSACTIONS/CAREER NOTES: Selected by St. Louis Rams in third round (68th pick overall) of 1999 NFL draft. ... Signed by Rams (July 16, 1999). ... On injured reserve with neck injury (December 13, 2000-remainder of season). ... Claimed on waivers by Tennessee Titans (August 29, 2002). ... Granted unconditional free agency (February 28, 2003). ... Signed by Indianapolis Colts (March 6, 2003). ... Traded by Colts to St. Louis Rams for seventh-round pick (K David Kimball) in 2004 draft (August 31, 2003). ... Granted unconditional free agency (March 3, 2004). ... Re-signed by Rams (March 23, 2004). ... Granted unconditional free agency (March 2, 2005). ... Signed by Atlanta Falcons (March 7, 2005).
CHAMPIONSHIP GAME EXPERIENCE: Played in NFC championship game (1999 season). ... Member of Super Bowl championship team (1999 season). ... Member of Rams for NFC championship game (2001 season); inactive. ... Member of Rams for Super Bowl 36 (2001 season); inactive. ... Played in AFC championship game (2002 season).

				TOTALS			INTERCEPTIONS			
Year Team	G	GS	Tk.	Ast.	Sks.	No.	Yds.	Avg.	TD
1999—St. Louis NFL	16	0	3	0	0.0	1	11	11.0	0
2000—St. Louis NFL	12	2	17	1	0.0	0	0	0.0	0
2001—St. Louis NFL	12	2	18	3	1.0	0	0	0.0	0
2002—Tennessee NFL	14	2	10	3	0.0	1	24	24.0	1
2003—St. Louis NFL	13	5	26	3	0.0	0	0	0.0	0
2004—St. Louis NFL	16	5	34	6	0.0	0	0	0.0	0
Pro totals (6 years)	83	16	108	16	1.0	2	35	17.5	1

COAKLEY, DEXTER — LB — RAMS

PERSONAL: Born October 20, 1972, in Charleston, S.C. ... 5-10/231. ... Full name: William Dexter Coakley.
HIGH SCHOOL: Wando (Mt. Pleasant, S.C.), then Fork Union (Va.) Military Academy.
COLLEGE: Appalachian State.
TRANSACTIONS/CAREER NOTES: Selected by Dallas Cowboys in third round (65th pick overall) of 1997 NFL draft. ... Signed by Cowboys (July 14, 1997). ... Granted free agency (February 11, 2000). ... Re-signed by Cowboys (April 28, 2000). ... Granted unconditional free agency (March 2, 2001). ... Re-signed by Cowboys (March 8, 2001). ... Released by Cowboys (March 1, 2005). ... Signed by St. Louis Rams (March 2, 2005).
HONORS: Played in Pro Bowl (1999, 2001 and 2003 seasons).

				TOTALS			INTERCEPTIONS			
Year Team	G	GS	Tk.	Ast.	Sks.	No.	Yds.	Avg.	TD
1997—Dallas NFL	16	16	69	20	2.5	1	6	6.0	0
1998—Dallas NFL	16	16	55	17	2.0	1	18	18.0	0
1999—Dallas NFL	16	16	62	14	1.0	4	119	29.7	1
2000—Dallas NFL	16	16	75	12	0.0	0	0	0.0	0
2001—Dallas NFL	15	15	72	23	0.0	2	39	19.5	†2
2002—Dallas NFL	16	16	81	23	1.0	1	52	52.0	1
2003—Dallas NFL	16	16	71	25	1.0	1	24	24.0	0
2004—Dallas NFL	16	16	51	17	0.0	0	0	0.0	0
Pro totals (8 years)	127	127	536	151	7.5	10	258	25.8	4

COATES, SHERROD — LB — BROWNS

PERSONAL: Born December 22, 1978, in Boynton Beach, Fla. ... 6-2/242.
HIGH SCHOOL: Santa Luces County (Boynton Beach, Fla.).
COLLEGE: Western Kentucky.
TRANSACTIONS/CAREER NOTES: Signed as non-drafted free agent by Cleveland Browns (May 2, 2003). ... Released by Browns (September 5, 2004). ... Re-signed by Browns (November 30, 2004).

				TOTALS			INTERCEPTIONS			
Year Team	G	GS	Tk.	Ast.	Sks.	No.	Yds.	Avg.	TD
2003—Cleveland NFL	16	0	0	0	0.0	0	0	0.0	0
2004—Cleveland NFL	5	0	0	0	0.0	0	0	0.0	0
Pro totals (2 years)	21	0	0	0	0.0	0	0	0.0	0

COBBS, CEDRIC — RB — PATRIOTS

PERSONAL: Born January 9, 1981, in Little Rock, Ark. ... 6-0/225.
HIGH SCHOOL: Fair (Little Rock, Ark.).
COLLEGE: Arkansas.
TRANSACTIONS/CAREER NOTES: Selected by New England Patriots in fourth round (128th pick overall) of 2004 NFL draft. ... Signed by Patriots (July 30, 2004). ... On physically unable to perform list with leg injury (September 5-October 30, 2004).
CHAMPIONSHIP GAME EXPERIENCE: Member of Patriots for AFC championship game (2004 season); inactive. ... Member of Patriots for Super Bowl 39 (2004 season); inactive.
SINGLE GAME HIGHS (regular season): Attempts—16 (December 5, 2004, vs. Cleveland); yards—29 (December 5, 2004, vs. Cleveland); and rushing touchdowns—0.

			RUSHING				RECEIVING				KICKOFF RETURNS				TOTALS			
Year Team	G	GS	Att.	Yds.	Avg.	TD	No.	Yds.	Avg.	TD	No.	Yds.	Avg.	TD	TD	2pt.	Pts.	Fum.
2004—New England NFL	3	0	22	50	2.3	0	0	0	0.0	0	0	0	0.0	0	0	0	0	1

COCHRAN, ANTONIO DE SEAHAWKS

PERSONAL: Born June 21, 1976, in Montezuma, Ga. ... 6-4/299. ... Full name: Antonio Desez Cochran.
HIGH SCHOOL: Macon County (Montezuma, Ga.).
JUNIOR COLLEGE: Middle Georgia College.
COLLEGE: Georgia.
TRANSACTIONS/CAREER NOTES: Selected by Seattle Seahawks in fourth round (115th pick overall) of 1999 NFL draft. ... Signed by Seahawks (July 27, 1999). ... Granted free agency (March 1, 2002). ... Re-signed by Seahawks (May 2, 2002). ... Granted unconditional free agency (February 28, 2003). ... Re-signed by Seahawks (March 4, 2003).

			TOTALS			INTERCEPTIONS			
Year Team	G	GS	Tk.	Ast.	Sks.	No.	Yds.	Avg.	TD
1999—Seattle NFL	4	0	2	0	0.0	0	0	0.0	0
2000—Seattle NFL	15	0	19	3	0.5	0	0	0.0	0
2001—Seattle NFL	16	2	26	5	4.5	0	0	0.0	0
2002—Seattle NFL	16	16	37	15	3.0	1	9	9.0	0
2003—Seattle NFL	15	7	23	6	1.0	0	0	0.0	0
2004—Seattle NFL	16	7	27	9	6.5	1	0	0.0	0
Pro totals (6 years)	82	32	134	38	15.5	2	9	4.5	0

COLBERT, KEARY WR PANTHERS

PERSONAL: Born May 21, 1982, in Oxnard, Calif. ... 5-10/193.
HIGH SCHOOL: Hueneme (Oxnard, Calif.).
COLLEGE: Southern California.
TRANSACTIONS/CAREER NOTES: Selected by Carolina Panthers in second round (62nd pick overall) of 2004 NFL draft. ... Signed by Panthers (July 23, 2004).
SINGLE GAME HIGHS (regular season): Receptions—7 (October 24, 2004, vs. San Diego); yards—115 (October 10, 2004, vs. Denver); and touchdown receptions—2 (November 28, 2004, vs. Tampa Bay).
STATISTICAL PLATEAUS: 100-yard receiving games: 2004 (2). Total: 2.

			RECEIVING				TOTALS			
Year Team	G	GS	No.	Yds.	Avg.	TD	TD	2pt.	Pts.	Fum.
2004—Carolina NFL	15	15	47	754	16.0	5	5	1	32	1

COLCLOUGH, RICARDO CB STEELERS

PERSONAL: Born April 18, 1982, in Sumter, S.C. ... 5-11/186. ... Full name: Ricardo Sanchez Colclough Coot.
HIGH SCHOOL: Sumter (S.C.).
COLLEGE: Tusculum.
TRANSACTIONS/CAREER NOTES: Selected by Pittsburgh Steelers in second round (38th pick overall) of 2004 NFL draft. ... Signed by Steelers (July 18, 2004).
CHAMPIONSHIP GAME EXPERIENCE: Played in AFC championship game (2004 season).

			TOTALS			INTERCEPTIONS				PUNT RETURNS				KICKOFF RETURNS				TOTALS			
Year Team	G	GS	Tk.	Ast.	Sks.	No.	Yds.	Avg.	TD	No.	Yds.	Avg.	TD	No.	Yds.	Avg.	TD	TD	2pt.	Pts.	Fum.
2004—Pit. NFL	16	0	13	4	1.5	0	0	0.0	0	1	13	13.0	0	26	566	21.8	0	0	0	0	3

COLE, COLIN DT PACKERS

PERSONAL: Born June 24, 1980, in Toronto, Ont. ... 6-2/299.
HIGH SCHOOL: South Plantation (Fla.).
COLLEGE: Iowa.
TRANSACTIONS/CAREER NOTES: Signed as non-drafted free agent by Minnesota Vikings (May 2, 2003). ... Released by Vikings (September 9, 2003). ... Re-signed by Vikings to practice squad (September 25, 2003). ... Activated (September 30, 2003). ... Released by Vikings (October 8, 2003). ... Signed by Detroit Lions (December 23, 2003). ... Released by Lions (September 4, 2004). ... Re-signed by Lions to practice squad (September 6, 2004). ... Released by Lions (September 8, 2004). ... Signed by Green Bay Packers to practice squad (September 16, 2004). ... Activated (November 30, 2004).

			TOTALS		
Year Team	G	GS	Tk.	Ast.	Sks.
2004—Green Bay NFL	3	1	6	1	0.0

COLEMAN, COSEY G BROWNS

PERSONAL: Born October 27, 1978, in Clarkston, Ga. ... 6-4/322. ... Full name: Cosey Clinton Coleman.
HIGH SCHOOL: DeKalb (Clarkston, Ga.).
COLLEGE: Tennessee.
TRANSACTIONS/CAREER NOTES: Selected after junior season by Tampa Bay Buccaneers in second round (51st pick overall) of 2000 NFL draft. ... Signed by Buccaneers (July 23, 2000). ... Granted unconditional free agency (March 3, 2004). ... Re-signed by Buccaneers (March 23, 2004). ... Granted unconditional free agency (March 2, 2005). ... Signed by Cleveland Browns (March 8, 2005).
PLAYING EXPERIENCE: Tampa Bay NFL, 2000-2004. ... Games/Games started: 2000 (8/0), 2001 (16/16), 2002 (15/15), 2003 (16/16), 2004 (16/16). Total: 71/63.
CHAMPIONSHIP GAME EXPERIENCE: Played in NFC championship game (2002 season). ... Member of Super Bowl championship team (2002 season).

C

COLEMAN, ERIK — DB — JETS

PERSONAL: Born May 6, 1982, in Sacramento, Calif. ... 5-10/200. ... Full name: Erik James Coleman.
HIGH SCHOOL: Lewis and Clark (Spokane, Wash.).
COLLEGE: Washington State.
TRANSACTIONS/CAREER NOTES: Selected by New York Jets in fifth round (143rd pick overall) of 2004 NFL draft. ... Signed by Jets (May 26, 2004).

Year Team	G	GS	TOTALS Tk.	Ast.	Sks.	INTERCEPTIONS No.	Yds.	Avg.	TD	PUNT RETURNS No.	Yds.	Avg.	TD	KICKOFF RETURNS No.	Yds.	Avg.	TD	TOTALS TD	2pt.	Pts.	Fum.
2004—NYJ NFL	16	16	67	21	2.0	4	43	10.8	0	0	0	0.0	0	0	0	0.0	0	0	0	0	0

COLEMAN, KENYON — DE — COWBOYS

PERSONAL: Born April 10, 1979, in Fontana, Calif. ... 6-5/284. ... Full name: Kenyon Octavia Coleman.
HIGH SCHOOL: Alta Loma (Calif.).
COLLEGE: UCLA.
TRANSACTIONS/CAREER NOTES: Selected by Oakland Raiders in fifth round (147th pick overall) of 2002 NFL draft. ... Signed by Raiders (July 24, 2002). ... Traded by Raiders to Dallas Cowboys for a seventh-round pick (later returned to Dallas) in 2004 draft (August 31, 2003).
CHAMPIONSHIP GAME EXPERIENCE: Member of Raiders for AFC championship game (2002 season); inactive. ... Member of Raiders for Super Bowl 37 (2002 season); inactive.
HONORS: Named defensive end on THE SPORTING NEWS college All-America third team (2001).

Year Team	G	GS	TOTALS Tk.	Ast.	Sks.
2002—Oakland NFL	1	0	1	0	0.0
2003—Dallas NFL	16	0	10	4	1.0
2004—Dallas NFL	12	0	9	0	1.0
Pro totals (3 years)	29	0	20	4	2.0

COLEMAN, MARCO — DE — BRONCOS

PERSONAL: Born December 18, 1969, in Dayton, Ohio. ... 6-3/270. ... Full name: Marco Darnell Coleman.
HIGH SCHOOL: Patterson Co-op (Dayton, Ohio).
COLLEGE: Georgia Tech.
TRANSACTIONS/CAREER NOTES: Selected after junior season by Miami Dolphins in first round (12th pick overall) of 1992 NFL draft. ... Signed by Dolphins (August 1, 1992). ... Designated by Dolphins as transition player (February 25, 1993). ... Tendered offer sheet by San Diego Chargers (February 28, 1996). ... Dolphins declined to match offer (March 7, 1996). ... Granted unconditional free agency (February 12, 1999). ... Signed by Washington Redskins (June 3, 1999). ... Granted unconditional free agency (February 11, 2000). ... Re-signed by Redskins (February 29, 2000). ... Released by Redskins (June 3, 2002). ... Signed by Jacksonville Jaguars (June 20, 2002). ... Released by Jaguars (August 30, 2003). ... Signed by Philadelphia Eagles (September 5, 2003). ... Granted unconditional free agency (March 3, 2004). ... Signed by Denver Broncos (March 11, 2004). ... Granted unconditional free agency (March 2, 2005). ... Re-signed by Broncos (April 19, 2005).
CHAMPIONSHIP GAME EXPERIENCE: Played in AFC championship game (1992 season). ... Played in NFC championship game (2003 season).
HONORS: Named linebacker on THE SPORTING NEWS college All-America second team (1991). ... Played in Pro Bowl (2000 season).

Year Team	G	GS	TOTALS Tk.	Ast.	Sks.	INTERCEPTIONS No.	Yds.	Avg.	TD
1992—Miami NFL	16	15	61	23	6.0	0	0	0.0	0
1993—Miami NFL	15	15	35	19	5.5	0	0	0.0	0
1994—Miami NFL	16	16	34	9	6.0	0	0	0.0	0
1995—Miami NFL	16	16	33	12	6.5	0	0	0.0	0
1996—San Diego NFL	16	15	34	8	4.0	0	0	0.0	0
1997—San Diego NFL	16	16	39	9	2.0	1	2	2.0	0
1998—San Diego NFL	16	16	46	5	3.5	0	0	0.0	0
1999—Washington NFL	16	16	54	13	6.5	0	0	0.0	0
2000—Washington NFL	16	16	41	11	12.0	0	0	0.0	0
2001—Washington NFL	12	12	33	6	4.5	0	0	0.0	0
2002—Jacksonville NFL	16	16	29	7	5.0	0	0	0.0	0
2003—Philadelphia NFL	13	0	11	2	0.5	0	0	0.0	0
2004—Denver NFL	16	16	21	7	2.5	0	0	0.0	0
Pro totals (13 years)	200	185	471	131	64.5	1	2	2.0	0

COLEMAN, MARCUS — CB — TEXANS

PERSONAL: Born May 24, 1974, in Dallas, Texas. ... 6-2/206.
HIGH SCHOOL: Lake Highlands (Dallas).
COLLEGE: Texas Tech.
TRANSACTIONS/CAREER NOTES: Selected by New York Jets in fifth round (133rd pick overall) of 1996 NFL draft. ... Signed by Jets (July 11, 1996). ... Granted unconditional free agency (February 11, 2000). ... Re-signed by Jets (February 14, 2000). ... Selected by Houston Texans from Jets in NFL expansion draft (February 18, 2002). ... On injured reserve with shoulder injury (December 7, 2004-remainder of season).
CHAMPIONSHIP GAME EXPERIENCE: Played in AFC championship game (1998 season).

Year Team	G	GS	TOTALS Tk.	Ast.	Sks.	INTERCEPTIONS No.	Yds.	Avg.	TD
1996—New York Jets NFL	13	4	25	6	0.0	1	23	23.0	0
1997—New York Jets NFL	16	2	8	2	0.0	1	24	24.0	0
1998—New York Jets NFL	14	0	5	1	0.0	0	0	0.0	0

Year Team	G	GS	TOTALS			INTERCEPTIONS			
			Tk.	Ast.	Sks.	No.	Yds.	Avg.	TD
1999—New York Jets NFL	16	10	51	11	0.0	6	165	27.5	1
2000—New York Jets NFL	16	16	50	6	0.0	4	6	1.5	0
2001—New York Jets NFL	16	16	58	11	0.0	2	41	20.5	0
2002—Houston NFL	16	16	60	12	0.0	1	0	0.0	0
2003—Houston NFL	15	15	57	12	0.0	▲7	95	13.6	0
2004—Houston NFL	12	12	45	11	0.0	2	116	58.0	1
Pro totals (9 years)	134	91	359	72	0.0	24	470	19.6	2

COLEMAN, ROD   DT   FALCONS

PERSONAL: Born August 16, 1976, in Vicksburg, Miss. ... 6-2/285. ... Full name: Roderick Coleman.
HIGH SCHOOL: Simon Gratz (Philadelphia).
COLLEGE: East Carolina.
TRANSACTIONS/CAREER NOTES: Selected by Oakland Raiders in fifth round (153rd pick overall) of 1999 NFL draft. ... Signed by Raiders (July 24, 1999). ... Granted unconditional free agency (March 3, 2004). ... Signed by Atlanta Falcons (March 8, 2004).
CHAMPIONSHIP GAME EXPERIENCE: Played in AFC championship game (2000 and 2002 seasons). ... Played in NFC championship game (2004 season). ... Played in Super Bowl 37 (2002 season).

Year Team	G	GS	TOTALS			INTERCEPTIONS			
			Tk.	Ast.	Sks.	No.	Yds.	Avg.	TD
1999—Oakland NFL	3	0	1	0	0.0	0	0	0.0	0
2000—Oakland NFL	13	1	16	4	6.0	0	0	0.0	0
2001—Oakland NFL	14	6	35	11	6.0	0	0	0.0	0
2002—Oakland NFL	14	2	33	5	11.0	0	0	0.0	0
2003—Oakland NFL	16	12	44	8	5.5	0	0	0.0	0
2004—Atlanta NFL	13	13	32	9	11.5	1	39	39.0	1
Pro totals (6 years)	73	34	161	37	40.0	1	39	39.0	1

COLES, LAVERANUES   WR   JETS

PERSONAL: Born December 29, 1977, in Jacksonville, Fla. ... 5-11/193.
HIGH SCHOOL: Jean Ribault (Jacksonville).
COLLEGE: Florida State.
TRANSACTIONS/CAREER NOTES: Selected by New York Jets in third round (78th pick overall) of 2000 NFL draft. ... Signed by Jets (May 1, 2000). ... Granted free agency (February 28, 2003). ... Tendered offer sheet by Washington Redskins (March 13, 2003). ... Jets declined to match offer (March 19, 2003). ... Traded by Redskins to New York Jets for WR Santana Moss (March 9, 2005).
HONORS: Played in Pro Bowl (2003 season).
SINGLE GAME HIGHS (regular season): Receptions—12 (December 12, 2004, vs. Philadelphia); yards—180 (September 14, 2003, vs. Atlanta); and touchdown receptions—2 (December 21, 2003, vs. Chicago).
STATISTICAL PLATEAUS: 100-yard receiving games: 2000 (1), 2001 (1), 2002 (4), 2003 (4), 2004 (3). Total: 13.

Year Team	G	GS	RUSHING				RECEIVING				KICKOFF RETURNS				TOTALS			
			Att.	Yds.	Avg.	TD	No.	Yds.	Avg.	TD	No.	Yds.	Avg.	TD	TD	2pt.	Pts.	Fum.
2000—New York Jets NFL	13	3	2	15	7.5	0	22	370	16.8	1	11	207	18.8	0	1	1	8	0
2001—New York Jets NFL	16	16	10	108	10.8	0	59	868	14.7	7	9	211	23.4	0	7	0	42	1
2002—New York Jets NFL	16	16	6	39	6.5	0	89	1264	14.2	5	0	0	0.0	0	5	1	32	1
2003—Washington NFL	16	16	10	39	3.9	0	82	1204	14.7	6	0	0	0.0	0	6	0	36	0
2004—Washington NFL	16	16	3	-3	-1.0	0	90	950	10.6	1	0	0	0.0	0	1	0	6	1
Pro totals (5 years)	77	67	31	198	6.4	0	342	4656	13.6	20	20	418	20.9	0	20	2	124	3

COLLINS, KERRY   QB   RAIDERS

PERSONAL: Born December 30, 1972, in Lebanon, Pa. ... 6-5/245. ... Full name: Kerry Michael Collins.
HIGH SCHOOL: Wilson (West Lawn, Pa.).
COLLEGE: Penn State.
TRANSACTIONS/CAREER NOTES: Selected by Carolina Panthers in first round (fifth pick overall) of 1995 NFL draft. ... Signed by Panthers (July 17, 1995). ... Granted free agency (February 13, 1998). ... Re-signed by Panthers (July 24, 1998). ... Claimed on waivers by New Orleans Saints (October 14, 1998). ... Granted unconditional free agency (February 12, 1999). ... Signed by New York Giants (February 19, 1999). ... Released by Giants (April 28, 2004). ... Signed by Oakland Raiders (May 24, 2004).
CHAMPIONSHIP GAME EXPERIENCE: Played in NFC championship game (1996 and 2000 season). ... Played in Super Bowl 35 (2000 season).
HONORS: Maxwell Award winner (1994). ... Davey O'Brien Award winner (1994). ... Named quarterback on THE SPORTING NEWS college All-America first team (1994). ... Played in Pro Bowl (1996 season).
RECORDS: Shares NFL single-season record for most fumbles—23 (2001).
SINGLE GAME HIGHS (regular season): Attempts—59 (October 12, 2003, vs. New England); completions—36 (January 6, 2002, vs. Green Bay); passing yards—386 (January 6, 2002, vs. Green Bay); and touchdown passes—5 (December 19, 2004, vs. Tennessee).
STATISTICAL PLATEAUS: 300-yard passing games: 1995 (2), 1996 (1), 1997 (1), 1998 (2), 1999 (2), 2000 (3), 2001 (5), 2002 (4), 2003 (3), 2004 (4). Total: 27.
MISCELLANEOUS: Selected by Detroit Tigers organization in 26th round of free-agent draft (June 4, 1990); did not sign. ... Selected by Toronto Blue Jays organization in 58th round of free-agent draft (June 4, 1994); did not sign. ... Regular-season record as starting NFL quarterback: 62-68 (.477). ... Postseason record as starting NFL quarterback: 3-3 (.500).

Year Team	G	GS	PASSING								RUSHING				TOTALS		
			Att.	Cmp.	Pct.	Yds.	TD	Int.	Avg.	Skd.	Rat.	Att.	Yds.	Avg.	TD	TD	2pt.	Pts.
1995—Carolina NFL	15	13	433	214	49.4	2717	14	19	6.27	24	61.9	42	74	1.8	3	3	0	18
1996—Carolina NFL	13	12	364	204	56.0	2454	14	9	6.74	18	79.4	32	38	1.2	0	0	1	2
1997—Carolina NFL	13	13	381	200	52.5	2124	11	*21	5.57	27	55.7	26	65	2.5	1	1	0	6

Year Team	G	GS	PASSING									RUSHING				TOTALS		
			Att.	Cmp.	Pct.	Yds.	TD	Int.	Avg.	Skd.	Rat.	Att.	Yds.	Avg.	TD	TD	2pt.	Pts.
1998—Carolina NFL..................	4	4	162	76	46.9	1011	8	5	6.24	10	70.8	7	40	5.7	0	0	1	2
—New Orleans NFL	7	7	191	94	49.2	1202	4	10	6.29	21	54.5	23	113	4.9	1	1	0	6
1999—New York Giants NFL	10	7	331	190	57.4	2318	8	11	7.00	16	73.3	19	36	1.9	2	2	1	14
2000—New York Giants NFL....	16	16	529	311	58.8	3610	22	13	6.82	28	83.1	41	65	1.6	1	1	0	6
2001—New York Giants NFL....	16	16	‡568	327	57.6	3764	19	16	6.63	36	77.1	39	73	1.9	0	0	0	0
2002—New York Giants NFL....	16	16	545	335	61.5	‡4073	19	14	‡7.47	24	85.4	44	-3	-0.1	0	0	0	0
2003—New York Giants NFL....	13	13	500	284	56.8	3110	13	16	6.22	28	70.7	17	49	2.9	0	0	1	2
2004—Oakland NFL..............	14	13	513	289	56.3	3495	21	†20	6.81	25	74.8	16	36	2.3	0	0	0	0
Pro totals (10 years)	137	130	4517	2524	55.9	29878	153	154	6.61	257	73.3	306	586	1.9	8	8	4	56

COLLINS, TODD   QB   CHIEFS

PERSONAL: Born November 5, 1971, in Walpole, Mass. ... 6-4/228.
HIGH SCHOOL: Walpole (Mass.).
COLLEGE: Michigan.
TRANSACTIONS/CAREER NOTES: Selected by Buffalo Bills in second round (45th pick overall) of 1995 NFL draft. ... Signed by Bills (July 10, 1995). ... Claimed on waivers by Kansas City Chiefs (August 25, 1998). ... Active for three games (1998); did not play. ... Active for all 16 games (1999); did not play. ... Active for all 16 games (2000); did not play. ... Granted unconditional free agency (February 28, 2003). ... Re-signed by Chiefs (March 24, 2003).
SINGLE GAME HIGHS (regular season): Attempts—44 (October 6, 1996, vs. Indianapolis); completions—25 (November 23, 1997, vs. Tennessee); yards—309 (October 6, 1996, vs. Indianapolis); and touchdown passes—3 (September 7, 1997, vs. New York Jets).
STATISTICAL PLATEAUS: 300-yard passing games: 1996 (1). Total: 1.
MISCELLANEOUS: Regular-season record as starting NFL quarterback: 7-10 (.412).

Year Team	G	GS	PASSING									RUSHING				TOTALS		
			Att.	Cmp.	Pct.	Yds.	TD	Int.	Avg.	Skd.	Rat.	Att.	Yds.	Avg.	TD	TD	2pt.	Pts.
1995—Buffalo NFL	7	1	29	14	48.3	112	0	1	3.86	6	44.0	9	23	2.6	0	0	0	0
1996—Buffalo NFL	7	3	99	55	55.6	739	4	5	7.46	11	71.9	21	43	2.0	0	0	0	0
1997—Buffalo NFL	14	13	391	215	55.0	2367	12	13	6.05	39	69.5	30	77	2.6	0	0	0	0
1998—Kansas City NFL			Did not play.															
1999—Kansas City NFL			Did not play.															
2000—Kansas City NFL			Did not play.															
2001—Kansas City NFL	1	0	4	3	75.0	40	0	0	10.00	0	106.2	2	6	3.0	0	0	0	0
2002—Kansas City NFL	3	0	6	5	83.3	73	1	0	12.17	0	156.9	1	7	7.0	0	0	0	0
2003—Kansas City NFL	5	0	12	9	75.0	74	0	0	6.17	0	90.3	8	-7	-0.9	0	0	0	0
2004—Kansas City NFL	2	0	5	1	20.0	42	0	0	8.40	0	62.1	1	4	4.0	0	0	0	0
Pro totals (7 years)	39	17	546	302	55.3	3447	17	19	6.31	56	70.4	72	153	2.1	0	0	0	0

COLOMBO, MARC   T   BEARS

PERSONAL: Born October 8, 1978, in Bridgewater, Mass. ... 6-8/325. ... Full name: Marc Edward Colombo.
HIGH SCHOOL: Bridgewater-Raynham (Bridgewater, Mass.).
COLLEGE: Boston College.
TRANSACTIONS/CAREER NOTES: Selected by Chicago Bears in first round (29th pick overall) of 2002 NFL draft. ... Signed by Bears (July 25, 2002). ... On injured reserve with knee injury (November 26, 2002-remainder of season). ... On physically unable to perform list with knee injury (August 27-November 4, 2003). ... On injured reserve with knee injury (November 4, 2003-remainder of season). ... On physically unable to perform list with knee injury (September 4-November 8, 2004).
PLAYING EXPERIENCE: Chicago NFL, 2002-2004. ... Games/Games started: 2002 (10/5), 2004 (8/2), Total: 18/7.

COLVIN, ROSEVELT   LB   PATRIOTS

PERSONAL: Born September 5, 1977, in Indianapolis, Ind. ... 6-3/250.
HIGH SCHOOL: Broad Ripple (Indianapolis).
COLLEGE: Purdue.
TRANSACTIONS/CAREER NOTES: Selected by Chicago Bears in fourth round (111th pick overall) of 1999 NFL draft. ... Signed by Bears (July 21, 1999). ... Granted free agency (March 1, 2002). ... Re-signed by Bears (April 19, 2002). ... Granted unconditional free agency (February 28, 2003). ... Signed by New England Patriots (March 11, 2003). ... On injured reserve with hip injury (September 22, 2003-remainder of season).
CHAMPIONSHIP GAME EXPERIENCE: Played in AFC championship game (2004 season). ... Member of Super Bowl championship team (2004 season).

Year Team	G	GS	TOTALS			INTERCEPTIONS			
			Tk.	Ast.	Sks.	No.	Yds.	Avg.	TD
1999—Chicago NFL..........................	11	0	10	2	2.0	0	0	0.0	0
2000—Chicago NFL..........................	13	8	25	9	3.0	0	0	0.0	0
2001—Chicago NFL..........................	16	13	60	10	10.5	2	22	11.0	0
2002—Chicago NFL..........................	16	15	55	9	10.5	0	0	0.0	0
2003—New England NFL....................	2	2	3	2	2.0	0	0	0.0	0
2004—New England NFL....................	16	1	18	14	5.0	0	0	0.0	0
Pro totals (6 years)	74	39	171	46	33.0	2	22	11.0	0

COMELLA, GREG   FB

PERSONAL: Born July 29, 1975, in Wellesley, Mass. ... 6-1/240. ... Name pronounced: Ka-MELL-uh.
HIGH SCHOOL: Xaverian Brothers (Westwood, Mass.).
COLLEGE: Stanford.

C

TRANSACTIONS/CAREER NOTES: Signed as non-drafted free agent by New York Giants (April 24, 1998). ... Granted free agency (March 2, 2001). ... Re-signed by Giants (April 18, 2001). ... Granted unconditional free agency (March 1, 2002). ... Signed by Tennessee Titans (April 19, 2002). ... Released by Titans (August 31, 2003). ... Signed by Houston Texans (September 1, 2003). ... Granted unconditional free agency (March 3, 2004). ... Signed by Tampa Bay Buccaneers (March 3, 2004). ... Granted unconditional free agency (March 2, 2005).
CHAMPIONSHIP GAME EXPERIENCE: Played in NFC championship game (2000 season). ... Played in Super Bowl 35 (2000 season). ... Member of Titans for AFC championship game (2002 season); inactive.
SINGLE GAME HIGHS (regular season): Attempts—3 (November 5, 2000, vs. Cleveland); yards—19 (September 10, 2000, vs. Philadelphia); and rushing touchdowns—0.

			RUSHING				RECEIVING				TOTALS			
Year Team	G	GS	Att.	Yds.	Avg.	TD	No.	Yds.	Avg.	TD	TD	2pt.	Pts.	Fum.
1998—New York Giants NFL	16	0	1	6	6.0	0	1	3	3.0	0	0	0	0	0
1999—New York Giants NFL	16	3	1	0	0.0	0	8	39	4.9	0	0	0	0	0
2000—New York Giants NFL	16	12	10	45	4.5	0	36	274	7.6	0	0	0	0	2
2001—New York Giants NFL	16	13	4	15	3.8	0	39	253	6.5	1	1	0	6	2
2002—Tennessee NFL	12	7	1	0	0.0	0	10	70	7.0	0	0	0	0	1
2003—Houston NFL	5	0	0	0	0.0	0	0	0	0.0	0	0	0	0	0
2004—Tampa Bay NFL	7	0	0	0	0.0	0	1	12	12.0	0	0	0	0	0
Pro totals (7 years)	88	35	17	66	3.9	0	95	651	6.9	1	1	0	6	5

COMPTON, MIKE — G/C — JAGUARS

PERSONAL: Born September 18, 1970, in Richlands, Va. ... 6-6/310. ... Full name: Michael Eugene Compton.
HIGH SCHOOL: Richlands (Va.).
COLLEGE: West Virginia.
TRANSACTIONS/CAREER NOTES: Selected by Detroit Lions in third round (68th pick overall) of 1993 NFL draft. ... Signed by Lions (June 4, 1993). ... Granted unconditional free agency (March 2, 2001). ... Signed by New England Patriots (April 2, 2001). ... On injured reserve with foot injury (September 22, 2003-remainder of season). ... Granted unconditional free agency (March 3, 2004). ... Signed by Jacksonville Jaguars (March 9, 2004). ... Released by Jaguars (September 5, 2004). ... Re-signed by Jaguars (September 23, 2004).
PLAYING EXPERIENCE: Detroit NFL, 1993-2000; New England NFL, 2001-2003; Jacksonville NFL, 2004. ... Games/Games started: 1993 (8/0), 1994 (3/0), 1995 (16/7), 1996 (15/15), 1997 (16/16), 1998 (16/16), 1999 (15/15), 2000 (16/16), 2001 (16/16), 2002 (16/16), 2003 (2/2), 2004 (13/0). Total: 152/119.
CHAMPIONSHIP GAME EXPERIENCE: Played in AFC championship game (2001 season). ... Member of Super Bowl championship team (2001 season).
HONORS: Named center on THE SPORTING NEWS college All-America first team (1992).

CONATY, BILL — C

PERSONAL: Born March 8, 1973, in Baltimore, Md. ... 6-2/300. ... Full name: William B. Conaty. ... Name pronounced: CON-uh-tee.
HIGH SCHOOL: Milford (Conn.) Academy, then Camden Catholic (Cherry Hill, N.J.).
COLLEGE: Virginia Tech.
TRANSACTIONS/CAREER NOTES: Signed as non-drafted free agent by Buffalo Bills (April 25, 1997). ... Released by Bills (August 24, 1997). ... Re-signed by Bills to practice squad (August 26, 1997). ... Activated (September 6, 1997). ... Released by Bills (September 22, 1997). ... Re-signed by Bills to practice squad (September 24, 1997). ... Granted free agency (March 2, 2001). ... Re-signed by Bills (June 12, 2001). ... Granted unconditional free agency (March 1, 2002). ... Re-signed by Bills (March 8, 2002). ... Granted unconditional free agency (February 28, 2003). ... Signed by New England Patriots (2003). ... On injured reserve with leg injury (August 27, 2003-August 31, 2003). ... Waived by Patriots (August 31, 2003). ... Signed by Dallas Cowboys (November 5, 2003). ... Released by Cowboys (December 26, 2003). ... Signed by Minnesota Vikings (August 5, 2004). ... Released by Vikings (September 5, 2004). ... Re-signed by Vikings (October 13, 2004). ... Released by Vikings (November 9, 2004). ... Re-signed by Vikings (November 25, 2004). ... Granted unconditional free agency (March 2, 2005).
PLAYING EXPERIENCE: Buffalo NFL, 1997-2002; Minnesota NFL, 2004. ... Games/Games started: 1997 (1/0), 1998 (15/1), 1999 (7/1), 2000 (16/0), 2001 (16/16), 2002 (11/0), 2004 (8/0). Total: 74/18.
HONORS: Named center on THE SPORTING NEWS college All-America first team (1996).

CONNOT, SCOTT — S — CHIEFS

PERSONAL: Born June 24, 1981, in Spencer, Neb. ... 6-3/216. ... Full name: Scott Paul Connot.
HIGH SCHOOL: Naper (Spencer, Neb.).
COLLEGE: South Dakota State.
TRANSACTIONS/CAREER NOTES: Signed as non-drafted free agent by Kansas City Chiefs (April 27, 2004). ... Released by Chiefs (September 5, 2004). ... Re-signed by Chiefs to practice squad (September 16, 2004). ... Activated (December 9, 2004). ... Assigned by Chiefs to Amsterdam Admirals in 2005 NFL Europe enhancement allocation program (February 14, 2005).

			TOTALS			INTERCEPTIONS			
Year Team	G	GS	Tk.	Ast.	Sks.	No.	Yds.	Avg.	TD
2004—Kansas City NFL	2	0	0	0	0.0	0	0	0.0	0

CONWAY, CURTIS — WR

PERSONAL: Born January 13, 1971, in Los Angeles, Calif. ... 6-1/200. ... Full name: Curtis LaMont Conway.
HIGH SCHOOL: Hawthorne (Calif.).
JUNIOR COLLEGE: El Camino College (Calif.).
COLLEGE: Southern California.
TRANSACTIONS/CAREER NOTES: Selected after junior season by Chicago Bears in first round (seventh pick overall) of 1993 NFL draft. ... Signed by Bears (May 24, 1993). ... Granted free agency (February 16, 1996). ... Re-signed by Bears (March 4, 1996). ... On injured reserve with shoulder injury (December 22, 1999-remainder of season). ... Granted unconditional free agency (February 11, 2000). ... Signed by San Diego Chargers (February 22, 2000). ... Released by Chargers (February 27, 2003). ... Signed by New York Jets (March 20, 2003). ... Released by Jets (March 8, 2004). ... Signed by San Francisco 49ers (June 2, 2004). ... Granted unconditional free agency (March 2, 2005).

HONORS: Named kick returner on THE SPORTING NEWS college All-America second team (1992).
SINGLE GAME HIGHS (regular season): Receptions—11 (December 30, 2001, vs. Seattle); yards—156 (December 30, 2001, vs. Seattle); and touchdown receptions—3 (October 15, 1995, vs. Jacksonville).
STATISTICAL PLATEAUS: 100-yard receiving games: 1994 (1), 1995 (3), 1996 (4), 1997 (3), 1999 (1), 2000 (2), 2001 (4), 2002 (3), 2004 (1). Total: 22.

Year Team	G	GS	RUSHING				RECEIVING				KICKOFF RETURNS				TOTALS			
			Att.	Yds.	Avg.	TD	No.	Yds.	Avg.	TD	No.	Yds.	Avg.	TD	TD	2pt.	Pts.	Fum.
1993—Chicago NFL	16	7	5	44	8.8	0	19	231	12.2	2	21	450	21.4	0	2	0	12	1
1994—Chicago NFL	13	12	6	31	5.2	0	39	546	14.0	2	10	228	22.8	0	2	1	14	2
1995—Chicago NFL	16	16	5	77	15.4	0	62	1037	16.7	12	0	0	0.0	0	12	0	72	0
1996—Chicago NFL	16	16	8	50	6.3	0	81	1049	13.0	7	0	0	0.0	0	7	0	42	1
1997—Chicago NFL	7	7	3	17	5.7	0	30	476	15.9	1	0	0	0.0	0	1	0	6	0
1998—Chicago NFL	15	15	5	48	9.6	0	54	733	13.6	3	0	0	0.0	0	3	0	18	1
1999—Chicago NFL	9	8	1	-2	-2.0	0	44	426	9.7	4	0	0	0.0	0	4	0	24	2
2000—San Diego NFL	14	14	3	31	10.3	0	53	712	13.4	5	0	0	0.0	0	5	0	30	0
2001—San Diego NFL	16	16	7	116	16.6	1	71	1125	15.8	6	0	0	0.0	0	7	0	42	1
2002—San Diego NFL	13	13	7	53	7.6	2	57	852	14.9	5	0	0	0.0	0	7	0	42	2
2003—New York Jets NFL	16	15	0	0	0.0	0	46	640	13.9	2	0	0	0.0	0	2	0	12	0
2004—San Francisco NFL	16	5	0	0	0.0	0	38	403	10.6	3	0	0	0.0	0	3	1	20	0
Pro totals (12 years)	167	144	50	465	9.3	3	594	8230	13.9	52	31	678	21.9	0	55	2	334	10

CONWELL, ERNIE   TE   SAINTS

PERSONAL: Born August 17, 1972, in Renton, Wash. ... 6-2/255. ... Full name: Ernest Harold Conwell.
HIGH SCHOOL: Kentwood (Kent, Wash.).
COLLEGE: Washington.
TRANSACTIONS/CAREER NOTES: Selected by St. Louis Rams in second round (59th pick overall) of 1996 NFL draft. ... Signed by Rams (June 25, 1996). ... On injured reserve with knee injury (October 28, 1998-remainder of season). ... On physically unable to perform list with knee injury (August 30-November 9, 1999). ... Granted unconditional free agency (February 11, 2000). ... Re-signed by Rams (February 11, 2000). ... Granted unconditional free agency (February 28, 2003). ... Signed by New Orleans Saints (April 14, 2003). ... On injured reserve with ankle injury (November 20, 2003-remainder of season).
CHAMPIONSHIP GAME EXPERIENCE: Played in NFC championship game (1999 and 2001 seasons). ... Member of Super Bowl championship team (1999 season). ... Played in Super Bowl 36 (2001 season).
SINGLE GAME HIGHS (regular season): Receptions—6 (September 28, 2003, vs. Indianapolis); yards—88 (September 28, 2003, vs. Indianapolis); and touchdown receptions—1 (September 12, 2004, vs. Seattle).

Year Team	G	GS	RUSHING				RECEIVING				TOTALS			
			Att.	Yds.	Avg.	TD	No.	Yds.	Avg.	TD	TD	2pt.	Pts.	Fum.
1996—St. Louis NFL	10	8	0	0	0.0	0	15	164	10.9	0	0	0	0	0
1997—St. Louis NFL	16	16	0	0	0.0	0	38	404	10.6	4	4	0	24	0
1998—St. Louis NFL	7	7	0	0	0.0	0	15	105	7.0	0	0	0	0	0
1999—St. Louis NFL	3	0	0	0	0.0	0	1	11	11.0	0	0	0	0	0
2000—St. Louis NFL	16	1	2	23	11.5	0	5	40	8.0	0	0	0	0	0
2001—St. Louis NFL	16	13	7	28	4.0	1	38	431	11.3	4	5	0	30	2
2002—St. Louis NFL	16	10	6	30	5.0	1	34	419	12.3	2	3	0	18	0
2003—New Orleans NFL	10	10	0	0	0.0	0	26	290	11.2	2	2	0	12	1
2004—New Orleans NFL	16	10	0	0	0.0	0	10	102	10.2	1	1	0	6	0
Pro totals (9 years)	110	75	15	81	5.4	2	182	1966	10.8	13	15	0	90	3

COOK, DAMION   T   DOLPHINS

PERSONAL: Born April 16, 1979, in Nashville, Tenn. ... 6-5/330. ... Full name: Damion Lamar Cook.
HIGH SCHOOL: American Heritage (Fort Lauderdale, Fla.).
COLLEGE: Bethune-Cookman.
TRANSACTIONS/CAREER NOTES: Signed as non-drafted free agent by Baltimore Ravens (April 27, 2001). ... Released by Ravens (September 1, 2001). ... Signed by Chicago Bears (September 28, 2001). ... Inactive for 15 games (2001). ... Assigned by Bears to Barcelona Dragons in 2002 NFL Europe enhancement allocation program (February 12, 2002). ... Released by Bears (September 1, 2002). ... Signed by Miami Dolphins to practice squad (September 10, 2002). ... Signed by Ravens off Dolphins practice squad (September 23, 2002). ... Granted free agency (March 3, 2004). ... Re-signed by Ravens (May 17, 2004). ... Claimed on waivers by Cleveland Browns (November 18, 2004). ... Granted unconditional free agency (March 2, 2005). ... Signed by Miami Dolphins (March 21, 2005).
PLAYING EXPERIENCE: Baltimore NFL, 2002-2004; Cleveland NFL, 2004. ... Games/Games started: 2002 (3/0), 2003 (1/0), 2004 (6/6). Total: 10/6.

COOK, JAMEEL   FB   BUCCANEERS

PERSONAL: Born February 8, 1979, in Miami, Fla. ... 5-10/237. ... Full name: Jameel A. Cook.
HIGH SCHOOL: Southridge (Miami).
COLLEGE: Illinois.
TRANSACTIONS/CAREER NOTES: Selected after junior season by Tampa Bay Buccaneers in sixth round (174th pick overall) of 2001 NFL draft. ... Signed by Buccaneers (July 16, 2001). ... Granted free agency (March 3, 2004). ... Re-signed by Buccaneers (April 19, 2004). ... Granted unconditional free agency (March 2, 2005). ... Re-signed by Buccaneers (March 16, 2005).
CHAMPIONSHIP GAME EXPERIENCE: Played in NFC championship game (2002 season). ... Member of Super Bowl championship team (2002 season).
SINGLE GAME HIGHS (regular season): Attempts—2 (October 28, 2001, vs. Minnesota); yards—2 (October 28, 2001, vs. Minnesota); and rushing touchdowns—0.

Year Team	G	GS	RUSHING				RECEIVING				TOTALS			
			Att.	Yds.	Avg.	TD	No.	Yds.	Avg.	TD	TD	2pt.	Pts.	Fum.
2001—Tampa Bay NFL	16	3	2	2	1.0	0	17	89	5.2	0	0	0	0	0
2002—Tampa Bay NFL	14	1	0	0	0.0	0	4	43	10.8	0	0	0	0	0
2003—Tampa Bay NFL	14	8	1	-1	-1.0	0	20	120	6.0	1	1	0	6	0
2004—Tampa Bay NFL	12	5	0	0	0.0	0	7	44	6.3	1	1	0	6	0
Pro totals (4 years)	56	17	3	1	0.3	0	48	296	6.2	2	2	0	12	0

COOLEY, CHRIS — TE — REDSKINS

PERSONAL: Born July 11, 1982, in Powell, Wyo. ... 6-3/265.
HIGH SCHOOL: Logan (Utah).
COLLEGE: Utah State.
TRANSACTIONS/CAREER NOTES: Selected by Washington Redskins in third round (81st pick overall) of 2004 NFL draft. ... Signed by Redskins (July 26, 2004).

Year Team	G	GS	RECEIVING				TOTALS			
			No.	Yds.	Avg.	TD	TD	2pt.	Pts.	Fum.
2004—Washington NFL	16	9	37	314	8.5	6	6	0	36	0

COOPER, CHRIS — DE — 49ERS

PERSONAL: Born December 27, 1977, in Lincoln, Neb. ... 6-5/285.
HIGH SCHOOL: Lincoln Southeast (Neb.).
COLLEGE: Nebraska-Omaha.
TRANSACTIONS/CAREER NOTES: Selected by Oakland Raiders in sixth round (184th pick overall) of 2001 NFL draft. ... Signed by Raiders (July 21, 2001). ... Traded by Raiders to Dallas Cowboys for future considerations (September 11, 2004). ... Released by Cowboys (November 2, 2004). ... Signed by San Francisco 49ers (November 10, 2004). ... Granted unconditional free agency (March 2, 2005). ... Re-signed by 49ers (March 5, 2005).
CHAMPIONSHIP GAME EXPERIENCE: Played in AFC championship game (2002 season). ... Played in Super Bowl 37 (2002 season).

Year Team	G	GS	TOTALS			INTERCEPTIONS			
			Tk.	Ast.	Sks.	No.	Yds.	Avg.	TD
2001—Oakland NFL	11	1	14	8	2.0	1	0	0.0	0
2002—Oakland NFL	16	1	14	5	1.0	0	0	0.0	0
2003—Oakland NFL	16	9	40	9	2.5	0	0	0.0	0
2004—Dallas NFL	2	0	0	0	0.0	0	0	0.0	0
—San Francisco NFL	8	2	11	4	1.0	0	0	0.0	0
Pro totals (4 years)	53	13	79	26	6.5	1	0	0.0	0

COOPER, DEKE — S — JAGUARS

PERSONAL: Born October 18, 1977, in Swainsboro, Ga. ... 6-2/210.
HIGH SCHOOL: Evansville (Ind.).
COLLEGE: Notre Dame.
TRANSACTIONS/CAREER NOTES: Signed as non-drafted free agent by Arizona Cardinals (April 18, 2000). ... Released by Cardinals (August 22, 2000). ... Re-signed by Cardinals (February 15, 2001). ... Assigned by Cardinals to Rhein Fire in 2001 NFL Europe enhancement allocation program (February 18, 2001). ... Released by Cardinals (September 1, 2001). ... Signed by Cleveland Browns to practice squad (September 20, 2001). ... Released by Browns (October 9, 2001). ... Signed by Carolina Panthers (January 16, 2002). ... Assigned by Panthers to Rhein Fire in 2002 NFL Europe enhancement allocation program (February 12, 2002). ... Released by Panthers (September 1, 2002). ... Re-signed by Panthers to practice squad (September 3, 2002). ... Activated (October 10, 2002). ... Waived by Panthers (August 31, 2003). ... Re-signed by Panthers to practice squad (September 3, 2003). ... Signed by Jacksonville Jaguars off Panthers practice squad (September 17, 2003). ... Granted free agency (March 2, 2005). ... Re-signed by Jaguars (March 22, 2005).

Year Team	G	GS	TOTALS			INTERCEPTIONS			
			Tk.	Ast.	Sks.	No.	Yds.	Avg.	TD
2002—Carolina NFL	10	0	0	0	0.0	0	0	0.0	0
2003—Jacksonville NFL	14	10	35	16	0.0	1	12	12.0	0
2004—Jacksonville NFL	16	0	21	3	1.0	1	0	0.0	0
Pro totals (3 years)	40	10	56	19	1.0	2	12	6.0	0

COOPER, JARROD — S — RAIDERS

PERSONAL: Born March 31, 1978, in Akron, Ohio. ... 6-0/215.
HIGH SCHOOL: Pearland (Texas).
COLLEGE: Kansas State.
TRANSACTIONS/CAREER NOTES: Selected by Carolina Panthers in fifth round (143rd pick overall) of 2001 NFL draft. ... Signed by Panthers (July 19, 2001). ... On injured reserve with knee injury (October 16, 2002-remainder of season). ... On suspended list for violating league substance abuse policy (November 19-December 15, 2003). ... Granted free agency (March 3, 2004). ... Re-signed by Panthers (May 15, 2004). ... Claimed on waivers by Oakland Raiders (October 29, 2004). ... Granted unconditional free agency (March 2, 2005). ... Re-signed by Raiders (April 5, 2005).
CHAMPIONSHIP GAME EXPERIENCE: Played in NFC championship game (2003 season). ... Played in Super Bowl 38 (2003 season).

Year Team	G	GS	TOTALS			INTERCEPTIONS			
			Tk.	Ast.	Sks.	No.	Yds.	Avg.	TD
2001—Carolina NFL	16	0	9	1	0.0	0	0	0.0	0
2002—Carolina NFL	6	0	2	0	0.0	0	0	0.0	0
2003—Carolina NFL	12	0	1	0	0.0	0	0	0.0	0
2004—Carolina NFL	6	0	0	0	0.0	0	0	0.0	0
—Oakland NFL	9	0	13	0	1.0	0	0	0.0	0
Pro totals (4 years)	49	0	25	1	1.0	0	0	0.0	0

C

COOPER, JOSH DE 49ERS

PERSONAL: Born December 5, 1980, in Marietta, Ga. ... 6-3/261. ... Full name: Josh Martez Cooper.
HIGH SCHOOL: Marietta (Ga.).
COLLEGE: Mississippi.
TRANSACTIONS/CAREER NOTES: Signed as non-drafted free agent by San Francisco 49ers (May 3, 2004). ... Released by 49ers (September 5, 2004). ... Re-signed by 49ers to practice squad (September 6, 2004). ... Activated (September 25, 2004). ... Waived by 49ers (September 27, 2004). ... Re-signed by 49ers to practice squad (September 28, 2004). ... Activated (December 30, 2004).

Year Team	G	GS	TOTALS Tk.	Ast.	Sks.
2004—San Francisco NFL	1	0	0	0	0.0

COOPER, MARQUIS LB BUCCANEERS

PERSONAL: Born March 11, 1982, in Mesa, Ariz. ... 6-3/213.
HIGH SCHOOL: Highland (Gilbert, Ariz.).
COLLEGE: Washington.
TRANSACTIONS/CAREER NOTES: Selected by Tampa Bay Buccaneers in third round (79th pick overall) of 2004 NFL draft. ... Signed by Buccaneers (July 29, 2004).

Year Team	G	GS	TOTALS Tk.	Ast.	Sks.	INTERCEPTIONS No.	Yds.	Avg.	TD
2004—Tampa Bay NFL	14	0	1	0	0.0	0	0	0.0	0

COOPER, STEPHEN LB CHARGERS

PERSONAL: Born June 19, 1979, in Wareham, Mass. ... 6-1/235.
HIGH SCHOOL: Wareham (Mass.).
COLLEGE: Maine.
TRANSACTIONS/CAREER NOTES: Signed as non-drafted free agent by San Diego Chargers (May 2, 2003).

Year Team	G	GS	TOTALS Tk.	Ast.	Sks.	INTERCEPTIONS No.	Yds.	Avg.	TD
2003—San Diego NFL	16	0	5	3	1.0	1	25	25.0	0
2004—San Diego NFL	16	2	25	8	0.0	0	0	0.0	0
Pro totals (2 years)	32	2	30	11	1.0	1	25	25.0	0

COPPER, TERRANCE WR COWBOYS

PERSONAL: Born March 12, 1982, in Washington, N.C. ... 6-0/201.
HIGH SCHOOL: Washington (N.C.).
COLLEGE: East Carolina.
TRANSACTIONS/CAREER NOTES: Signed as non-drafted free agent by Dallas Cowboys (April 30, 2004). ... Released by Cowboys (September 5, 2004). ... Re-signed by Cowboys to practice squad (September 7, 2004). ... Activated (October 30, 2004).
SINGLE GAME HIGHS (regular season): Receptions—3 (November 21, 2004, vs. Baltimore); yards—44 (November 21, 2004, vs. Baltimore); and touchdown receptions—1 (December 6, 2004, vs. Seattle).

Year Team	G	GS	RECEIVING No.	Yds.	Avg.	TD	KICKOFF RETURNS No.	Yds.	Avg.	TD	TOTALS TD	2pt.	Pts.	Fum.
2004—Dallas NFL	10	0	7	84	12.0	1	16	307	19.2	0	1	0	6	0

CORTEZ, JOSE K

PERSONAL: Born May 27, 1975, in San Vicente, El Salvador. ... 5-11/200. ... Full name: Jose Antonio Cortez.
HIGH SCHOOL: Van Nuys (Calif.).
JUNIOR COLLEGE: Los Angeles Valley College.
COLLEGE: Oregon State.
TRANSACTIONS/CAREER NOTES: Signed as non-drafted free agent by Cleveland Browns (April 23, 1999). ... Released by Browns (June 3, 1999). ... Signed by San Diego Chargers (June 14, 1999). ... Released by Chargers (August 30, 1999). ... Signed by New York Giants to practice squad (December 14, 1999). ... Activated (December 17, 1999). ... Released by Giants (December 21, 1999). ... Signed by San Diego Chargers (January 18, 2000). ... Released by Chargers (August 27, 2000). ... Signed by San Francisco 49ers (May 9, 2001). ... Released by 49ers (November 26, 2002). ... Signed by Washington Redskins (December 2, 2002). ... Claimed on waivers by Kansas City Chiefs (March 14, 2003). ... Released by Chiefs (August 25, 2003). ... Signed by Minnesota Vikings (October 17, 2003). ... Released by Vikings (October 28, 2003). ... Re-signed by Vikings (November 10, 2004). ... Released by Vikings (May 26, 2005).

Year Team	G	FIELD GOALS 1-29	30-39	40-49	50+	Tot.	Pct.	Lg.	TOTALS XPM	XPA	Pts.
1999—New York Giants NFL	1	0-0	0-0	0-0	0-0	0-0	0.0	0	0	0	0
2001—San Francisco NFL	16	7-9	6-7	4-8	1-1	18-25	72.0	52	47	47	101
2002—San Francisco NFL	10	8-10	7-8	3-6	0-0	18-24	75.0	45	25	25	79
—Washington NFL	4	3-3	1-1	1-4	0-0	5-8	62.5	44	9	9	24
2003—Minnesota NFL	2	0-0	0-0	0-0	0-0	0-0	0.0	0	0	0	0
2004—Minnesota NFL	8	0-0	0-0	0-0	0-0	0-0	0.0	0	0	0	0
Pro totals (5 years)	41	18-22	14-16	8-18	1-1	41-57	71.9	52	81	81	204

COTCHERY, JERRICHO   WR   JETS

PERSONAL: Born June 16, 1982, in Birmingham, Ala. ... 6-0/207.
HIGH SCHOOL: Phillips (Birmingham, Ala.).
COLLEGE: North Carolina State.
TRANSACTIONS/CAREER NOTES: Selected by New York Jets in fourth round (108th pick overall) of 2004 NFL draft. ... Signed by Jets (July 29, 2004).
SINGLE GAME HIGHS (regular season): Receptions—2 (January 2, 2005, vs. St. Louis); yards—18 (December 26, 2004, vs. New England); and touchdown receptions—0.

			RUSHING				RECEIVING				PUNT RETURNS				KICKOFF RETURNS				TOTALS		
Year Team	G	GS	Att.	Yds.	Avg.	TD	No.	Yds.	Avg.	TD	No.	Yds.	Avg.	TD	No.	Yds.	Avg.	TD	TD	2pt.	Pts.
2004—NYJ NFL	12	0	0	0	0.0	0	6	60	10.0	0	0	0	0.0	0	13	362	27.8	1	1	0	6

COUSIN, TERRY   CB   JAGUARS

PERSONAL: Born April 11, 1975, in Miami, Fla. ... 5-9/185.
HIGH SCHOOL: Miami Beach Senior.
COLLEGE: South Carolina.
TRANSACTIONS/CAREER NOTES: Signed as non-drafted free agent by Chicago Bears (April 25, 1997). ... Released by Bears (August 24, 1997). ... Re-signed by Bears to practice squad (August 26, 1997). ... Activated (October 25, 1997). ... Released by Bears (October 28, 1997). ... Re-signed by Bears to practice squad (October 30, 1997). ... Activated (November 15, 1997). ... Granted free agency (February 11, 2000). ... Re-signed by Bears (April 18, 2000). ... Claimed on waivers by Atlanta Falcons (August 28, 2000). ... Granted unconditional free agency (March 2, 2001). ... Signed by Miami Dolphins (March 15, 2001). ... Granted unconditional free agency (March 1, 2002). ... Signed by Carolina Panthers (March 19, 2002). ... Released by Panthers (March 5, 2004). ... Signed by New York Giants (March 24, 2004). ... Released by Giants (February 22, 2005). ... Signed by Jacksonville Jaguars (March 8, 2005).
CHAMPIONSHIP GAME EXPERIENCE: Played in NFC championship game (2003 season). ... Played in Super Bowl 38 (2003 season).

			TOTALS			INTERCEPTIONS			
Year Team	G	GS	Tk.	Ast.	Sks.	No.	Yds.	Avg.	TD
1997—Chicago NFL	6	0	2	2	0.0	0	0	0.0	0
1998—Chicago NFL	16	12	50	12	0.0	1	0	0.0	0
1999—Chicago NFL	16	9	43	12	0.0	2	1	0.5	0
2000—Atlanta NFL	15	0	4	0	0.0	0	0	0.0	0
2001—Miami NFL	16	3	37	13	2.0	0	0	0.0	0
2002—Carolina NFL	16	16	44	15	1.0	2	4	2.0	0
2003—Carolina NFL	13	13	45	4	2.0	0	0	0.0	0
2004—New York Giants NFL	16	5	32	7	0.0	1	6	6.0	0
Pro totals (8 years)	114	58	257	65	5.0	6	11	1.8	0

COWART, SAM   LB   VIKINGS

PERSONAL: Born February 26, 1975, in Jacksonville, Fla. ... 6-2/245.
HIGH SCHOOL: Mandarin (Jacksonville, Fla.).
COLLEGE: Florida State.
TRANSACTIONS/CAREER NOTES: Selected by Buffalo Bills in second round (39th pick overall) of 1998 NFL draft. ... Signed by Bills (July 20, 1998). ... On injured reserve with Achilles' tendon injury (September 26, 2001-remainder of season). ... Granted unconditional free agency (March 1, 2002). ... Signed by New York Jets (March 6, 2002). ... Traded by Jets to Minnesota Vikings for seventh-round pick (traded to New England) in 2005 draft (March 18, 2005).
HONORS: Named outside linebacker on THE SPORTING NEWS college All-America first team (1997). ... Played in Pro Bowl (2000 season).

			TOTALS			INTERCEPTIONS			
Year Team	G	GS	Tk.	Ast.	Sks.	No.	Yds.	Avg.	TD
1998—Buffalo NFL	16	11	54	18	0.0	2	23	11.5	0
1999—Buffalo NFL	16	16	79	46	1.0	0	0	0.0	0
2000—Buffalo NFL	12	12	88	41	5.5	2	4	2.0	0
2001—Buffalo NFL	1	1	0	2	0.0	0	0	0.0	0
2002—New York Jets NFL	16	16	91	36	2.0	0	0	0.0	0
2003—New York Jets NFL	15	15	96	44	2.0	0	0	0.0	0
2004—New York Jets NFL	9	2	21	5	0.0	0	0	0.0	0
Pro totals (7 years)	85	73	429	192	10.5	4	27	6.8	0

COX, TORRIE   CB   BUCCANEERS

PERSONAL: Born October 29, 1980, in Miami, Fla. ... 5-10/181. ... Full name: Torrie Tywan Cox.
HIGH SCHOOL: Northwestern (Miami).
COLLEGE: Pittsburgh.
TRANSACTIONS/CAREER NOTES: Selected by Tampa Bay Buccaneers in sixth round (205th pick overall) of 2003 NFL draft. ... On injured reserve with knee injury (August 22, 2003-entire season).

			INTERCEPTIONS				PUNT RETURNS				KICKOFF RETURNS				TOTALS			
Year Team	G	GS	No.	Yds.	Avg.	TD	No.	Yds.	Avg.	TD	No.	Yds.	Avg.	TD	TD	2pt.	Pts.	Fum.
2003—Tampa Bay NFL			Did not play.															
2004—Tampa Bay NFL	10	0	1	55	55.0	1	0	0	0.0	0	33	866	26.2	0	1	0	6	0
Pro totals (1 year)	10	0	1	55	55.0	1	0	0	0.0	0	33	866	26.2	0	1	0	6	0

CRAFT, JASON   CB   SAINTS

PERSONAL: Born February 13, 1976, in Denver, Colo. ... 5-10/187. ... Full name: Jason Donell Andre Craft.
HIGH SCHOOL: Denver East.
JUNIOR COLLEGE: Denver Community College.
COLLEGE: Colorado State.
TRANSACTIONS/CAREER NOTES: Selected by Jacksonville Jaguars in fifth round (160th pick overall) of 1999 NFL draft. ... Signed by Jaguars (May 18, 1999). ... Granted free agency (March 1, 2002). ... Tendered offer sheet by New Orleans Saints (March 5, 2002). ... Offer sheet matched by Jaguars (March 12, 2002). ... On injured reserve with knee injury (December 19, 2003-remainder of season). ... Traded by Jaguars to New Orleans Saints for fifth-round pick (CB Chris Thompson) in 2004 draft (April 8, 2004). ... Granted unconditional free agency (March 2, 2005). ... Re-signed by Saints (March 11, 2005).
CHAMPIONSHIP GAME EXPERIENCE: Played in AFC championship game (1999 season).

				TOTALS			INTERCEPTIONS			
Year Team	G	GS	Tk.	Ast.	Sks.	No.	Yds.	Avg.	TD
1999—Jacksonville NFL	16	0	2	0	0.0	0	0	0.0	0
2000—Jacksonville NFL	16	3	22	5	0.0	0	0	0.0	0
2001—Jacksonville NFL	16	8	45	6	0.0	2	4	2.0	0
2002—Jacksonville NFL	16	16	49	9	0.0	3	0	0.0	0
2003—Jacksonville NFL	6	6	17	9	0.0	2	29	14.5	0
2004—New Orleans NFL	14	0	14	2	0.0	0	0	0.0	0
Pro totals (6 years)	84	33	149	31	0.0	7	33	4.7	0

CRAMER, CASEY   TE   PANTHERS

PERSONAL: Born January 5, 1982, in Middleton, Wis. ... 6-2/235. ... Full name: Casey R. Cramer.
COLLEGE: Dartmouth.
TRANSACTIONS/CAREER NOTES: Selected by Tampa Bay Buccaneers in seventh round (228th pick overall) of 2004 NFL draft. ... Signed by Buccaneers (July 29, 2004). ... Claimed on waivers by New York Jets (September 2, 2004). ... Released by Jets (September 4, 2004). ... Signed by Tennessee Titans to practice squad (September 7, 2004). ... Signed by Carolina Panthers off Titans practice squad (November 10, 2004).

			RUSHING				RECEIVING				TOTALS			
Year Team	G	GS	Att.	Yds.	Avg.	TD	No.	Yds.	Avg.	TD	TD	2pt.	Pts.	Fum.
2004—Carolina NFL	6	1	0	0	0.0	0	0	0	0.0	0	0	0	0	0

CRAVER, KEYUO   CB   SAINTS

PERSONAL: Born August 22, 1980, in Dallas, Texas. ... 5-10/195.
HIGH SCHOOL: Harleton (Texas).
COLLEGE: Nebraska.
TRANSACTIONS/CAREER NOTES: Selected by New Orleans Saints in fourth round (125th pick overall) of 2002 NFL draft. ... Signed by Saints (July 24, 2002). ... On suspended list for violating league substance abuse policy (October 7-November 11, 2003). ... On suspended list for violating league substance abuse policy (August 25, 2004-entire season).
HONORS: Named cornerback on THE SPORTING NEWS college All-America first team (2001).

			TOTALS			INTERCEPTIONS				PUNT RETURNS				TOTALS			
Year Team	G	GS	Tk.	Ast.	Sks.	No.	Yds.	Avg.	TD	No.	Yds.	Avg.	TD	TD	2pt.	Pts.	Fum.
2002—New Orleans NFL	10	1	9	3	0.0	0	0	0.0	0	1	0	0.0	0	1	0	6	1
2003—New Orleans NFL	12	0	2	0	0.0	0	0	0.0	0	2	22	11.0	0	0	0	0	0
2004—New Orleans NFL	Did not play.																
Pro totals (2 years)	22	1	11	3	0.0	0	0	0.0	0	3	22	7.3	0	1	0	6	1

CRAYTON, PATRICK   WR   COWBOYS

PERSONAL: Born April 7, 1979, in DeSoto, Texas. ... 6-0/200.
COLLEGE: Northwestern Oklahoma State.
TRANSACTIONS/CAREER NOTES: Selected by Dallas Cowboys in seventh round (216th pick overall) of 2004 NFL draft. ... Signed by Cowboys (July 27, 2004). ... Released by Cowboys (October 2, 2004). ... Re-signed by Cowboys to practice squad (October 5, 2004). ... Activated (October 30, 2004).
SINGLE GAME HIGHS (regular season): Receptions—5 (January 2, 2005, vs. New York Giants); yards—58 (January 2, 2005, vs. New York Giants); and touchdown receptions—1 (December 26, 2004, vs. Washington).

			RUSHING				RECEIVING				PUNT RETURNS				KICKOFF RETURNS				TOTALS		
Year Team	G	GS	Att.	Yds.	Avg.	TD	No.	Yds.	Avg.	TD	No.	Yds.	Avg.	TD	No.	Yds.	Avg.	TD	TD	2pt.	Pts.
2004—Dal. NFL	8	0	0	0	0.0	0	12	162	13.5	1	4	34	8.5	0	0	0	0.0	0	1	0	6

CRECION, GABRIEL   TE

PERSONAL: Born July 9, 1977, in West Hills, Calif. ... 6-5/255. ... Full name: Gabriel John Crecion.
HIGH SCHOOL: Chaminade (West Hills, Calif.).
COLLEGE: UCLA.
TRANSACTIONS/CAREER NOTES: Signed as non-drafted free agent by San Francisco 49ers (February 18, 2003). ... Assigned by 49ers to Barcelona Dragons in 2003 NFL Europe enhancement allocation program (March 25, 2003). ... Released by 49ers (August 31, 2003). ... Re-signed by 49ers (December 31, 2003). ... Released by 49ers (September 5, 2004). ... Re-signed by 49ers to practice squad (October 13, 2004). ... Activated (October 16, 2004). ... Released by 49ers (October 19, 2004).
MISCELLANEOUS: Selected by Baltimore Orioles organization in 19th round of free-agent draft (June 1, 1996); did not sign. ... Selected by New York Yankees organization in 16th round of free-agent draft (June 1, 1998); did not sign.

			RECEIVING				TOTALS			
Year Team	G	GS	No.	Yds.	Avg.	TD	TD	2pt.	Pts.	Fum.
2004—San Francisco NFL	1	0	0	0	0.0	0	0	0	0	0

C

CROCKER, CHRIS   S   BROWNS

PERSONAL: Born March 9, 1980, in Chesapeake, Va. ... 5-11/194. ... Full name: Christopher Alan Crocker.
HIGH SCHOOL: Deep Creek (Chesapeake, Va.).
COLLEGE: Marshall.
TRANSACTIONS/CAREER NOTES: Selected by Cleveland Browns in third round (84th pick overall) of 2003 NFL draft. ... Signed by Browns (July 31, 2003).

				TOTALS			INTERCEPTIONS			
Year Team	G	GS	Tk.	Ast.	Sks.	No.	Yds.	Avg.	TD
2003—Cleveland NFL	16	1	21	4	0.0	0	0	0.0	0
2004—Cleveland NFL	12	5	37	10	2.0	1	20	20.0	1
Pro totals (2 years)	28	6	58	14	2.0	1	20	20.0	1

CROCKETT, ZACK   FB   RAIDERS

PERSONAL: Born December 2, 1972, in Pompano Beach, Fla. ... 6-2/240. ... Brother of Henri Crockett, linebacker with Atlanta Falcons (1997-2001) and Minnesota Vikings (2002).
HIGH SCHOOL: Ely (Pompano Beach, Fla.).
JUNIOR COLLEGE: Hinds Community College (Miss.).
COLLEGE: Florida State.
TRANSACTIONS/CAREER NOTES: Selected by Indianapolis Colts in third round (79th pick overall) of 1995 NFL draft. ... Signed by Colts (July 21, 1995). ... On injured reserve with knee injury (October 22, 1996-remainder of season). ... Granted free agency (February 13, 1998). ... Re-signed by Colts (July 23, 1998). ... Claimed on waivers by Jacksonville Jaguars (October 21, 1998). ... Granted unconditional free agency (February 12, 1999). ... Signed by Oakland Raiders (March 16, 1999). ... Granted unconditional free agency (February 28, 2003). ... Re-signed by Raiders (March 4, 2003).
CHAMPIONSHIP GAME EXPERIENCE: Played in AFC championship game (1995, 2000 and 2002 seasons). ... Played in Super Bowl 37 (2002 season).
SINGLE GAME HIGHS (regular season): Attempts—21 (January 2, 2005, vs. Jacksonville); yards—134 (January 2, 2005, vs. Jacksonville); and rushing touchdowns—2 (November 16, 2003, vs. Minnesota).
STATISTICAL PLATEAUS: 100-yard rushing games: 2004 (1). Total: 1.

			RUSHING				RECEIVING				TOTALS			
Year Team	G	GS	Att.	Yds.	Avg.	TD	No.	Yds.	Avg.	TD	TD	2pt.	Pts.	Fum.
1995—Indianapolis NFL	16	0	1	0	0.0	0	2	35	17.5	0	0	0	0	0
1996—Indianapolis NFL	5	5	31	164	5.3	0	11	96	8.7	1	1	0	6	2
1997—Indianapolis NFL	16	11	95	300	3.2	1	15	112	7.5	0	1	0	6	3
1998—Indianapolis NFL	2	1	2	5	2.5	0	1	1	1.0	0	0	0	0	1
—Jacksonville NFL	10	1	0	0	0.0	0	1	4	4.0	0	0	0	0	0
1999—Oakland NFL	13	1	45	91	2.0	4	8	56	7.0	1	5	0	30	0
2000—Oakland NFL	16	3	43	130	3.0	7	10	62	6.2	0	7	0	42	0
2001—Oakland NFL	16	1	57	145	2.5	6	2	10	5.0	0	6	0	36	1
2002—Oakland NFL	16	0	40	118	3.0	8	0	0	0.0	0	8	0	48	0
2003—Oakland NFL	16	6	48	145	3.0	7	7	53	7.6	0	7	0	42	1
2004—Oakland NFL	16	9	48	232	4.8	2	16	87	5.4	0	2	0	12	0
Pro totals (10 years)	142	38	410	1330	3.2	35	73	516	7.1	2	37	0	222	8

CROOM, LARRY   RB   CARDINALS

PERSONAL: Born October 29, 1981, in Long Beach, Calif. ... 5-10/205.
HIGH SCHOOL: Polytechnic (Long Beach, Calif.).
COLLEGE: Nevada-Las Vegas.
TRANSACTIONS/CAREER NOTES: Signed as non-drafted free agent by Arizona Cardinals (April 27, 2004). ... Assigned by Cardinals to Hamburg Sea Devils in 2005 NFL Europe enhancement allocation program (February 14, 2005).
SINGLE GAME HIGHS (regular season): Attempts—18 (December 5, 2004, vs. Detroit); yards—49 (December 5, 2004, vs. Detroit); and rushing touchdowns—0.

			RUSHING				RECEIVING				KICKOFF RETURNS				TOTALS			
Year Team	G	GS	Att.	Yds.	Avg.	TD	No.	Yds.	Avg.	TD	No.	Yds.	Avg.	TD	TD	2pt.	Pts.	Fum.
2004—Arizona NFL	6	1	29	76	2.6	0	2	16	8.0	0	16	314	19.6	0	0	0	0	2

CROWELL, ANGELO   LB   BILLS

PERSONAL: Born August 16, 1981, in Forsyth County, N.C. ... 6-1/235. ... Full name: Angelo Delvonne Crowell. ... Brother of Germane Crowell, wide receiver with Detroit Lions (1998-2002).
HIGH SCHOOL: North Forsyth (N.C.).
COLLEGE: Virginia.
TRANSACTIONS/CAREER NOTES: Selected by Buffalo Bills in third round (94th pick overall) of 2003 NFL draft. ... Signed by Bills (July 23, 2003).

				TOTALS			INTERCEPTIONS			
Year Team	G	GS	Tk.	Ast.	Sks.	No.	Yds.	Avg.	TD
2003—Buffalo NFL	6	0	0	0	0.0	0	0	0.0	0
2004—Buffalo NFL	16	0	0	1	0.0	0	0	0.0	0
Pro totals (2 years)	22	0	0	1	0.0	0	0	0.0	0

C

CRUMPLER, ALGE   TE   FALCONS

PERSONAL: Born December 23, 1977, in Greenville, N.C. ... 6-2/262. ... Full name: Algernon Darius Crumpler.
HIGH SCHOOL: New Hanover (Wilmington, N.C.).
COLLEGE: North Carolina.
TRANSACTIONS/CAREER NOTES: Selected by Atlanta Falcons in second round (35th pick overall) of 2001 NFL draft. ... Signed by Falcons (May 29, 2001).
CHAMPIONSHIP GAME EXPERIENCE: Played in NFC championship game (2004 season).
HONORS: Played in Pro Bowl (2003 and 2004 seasons).
SINGLE GAME HIGHS (regular season): Receptions—7 (October 31, 2004, vs. Denver); yards—118 (November 14, 2004, vs. Tampa Bay); and touchdown receptions—2 (November 21, 2004, vs. New York Giants).
STATISTICAL PLATEAUS: 100-yard receiving games: 2004 (2). Total: 2.

			RECEIVING				TOTALS			
Year Team	G	GS	No.	Yds.	Avg.	TD	TD	2pt.	Pts.	Fum.
2001—Atlanta NFL	16	12	25	330	13.2	3	3	0	18	1
2002—Atlanta NFL	16	9	36	455	12.6	5	5	0	30	0
2003—Atlanta NFL	16	16	44	552	12.5	3	3	0	18	1
2004—Atlanta NFL	14	14	48	774	16.1	6	6	0	36	1
Pro totals (4 years)	62	51	153	2111	13.8	17	17	0	102	3

CULPEPPER, DAUNTE   QB   VIKINGS

PERSONAL: Born January 28, 1977, in Ocala, Fla. ... 6-4/264.
HIGH SCHOOL: Vanguard (Ocala, Fla.).
COLLEGE: Central Florida.
TRANSACTIONS/CAREER NOTES: Selected by Minnesota Vikings in first round (11th pick overall) of 1999 NFL draft. ... Signed by Vikings (July 30, 1999).
CHAMPIONSHIP GAME EXPERIENCE: Played in NFC championship game (2000 season).
HONORS: Played in Pro Bowl (2000, 2003 and 2004 seasons).
RECORDS: Shares NFL single-season record for most fumbles—23 (2002).
SINGLE GAME HIGHS (regular season): Attempts—53 (September 29, 2002, vs. Seattle); completions—37 (September 20, 2004, vs. Philadelphia); yards—425 (October 17, 2004, vs. New Orleans); and touchdown passes—5 (October 17, 2004, vs. New Orleans).
STATISTICAL PLATEAUS: 300-yard passing games: 2000 (5), 2001 (2), 2002 (2), 2003 (3), 2004 (6). Total: 18.
MISCELLANEOUS: Selected by New York Yankees organization in 26th round of free-agent baseball draft (June 1, 1995); did not sign. ... Regular-season record as starting NFL quarterback: 36-37 (.493). ... Postseason record as starting NFL quarterback: 2-2 (.500).

			PASSING								RUSHING				TOTALS		
Year Team	G	GS	Att.	Cmp.	Pct.	Yds.	TD	Int.	Avg.	Skd.	Rat.	Att.	Yds.	Avg.	TD	TD	2pt.	Pts.
1999—Minnesota NFL	1	0	0	0	0.0	0	0	0	0.00	0	0.0	3	6	2.0	0	0	0	0
2000—Minnesota NFL	16	16	474	297	62.7	3937	†33	16	8.31	34	98.0	89	470	5.3	7	7	0	42
2001—Minnesota NFL	11	11	366	235	64.2	2612	14	13	7.14	33	83.3	71	416	5.9	5	5	2	34
2002—Minnesota NFL	16	16	549	333	60.7	3853	18	*23	7.02	47	75.3	106	609	5.7	10	10	1	62
2003—Minnesota NFL	14	14	454	295	65.0	3479	25	11	‡7.66	37	‡96.4	73	422	5.8	4	4	0	24
2004—Minnesota NFL	16	16	‡548	*379	69.2	*4717	‡39	11	‡8.61	∞46	‡110.9	88	406	4.6	2	2	1	14
Pro totals (6 years)	74	73	2391	1539	64.4	18598	129	74	7.78	197	93.2	430	2329	5.4	28	28	4	176

CUNDIFF, BILLY   K   COWBOYS

PERSONAL: Born March 30, 1980, in Valley Center, Calif. ... 6-1/201. ... Full name: Bill Cundiff.
HIGH SCHOOL: Harlan (Iowa).
COLLEGE: Drake.
TRANSACTIONS/CAREER NOTES: Signed as non-drafted free agent by Dallas Cowboys (April 26, 2002). ... Granted free agency (March 2, 2005). ... Re-signed by Cowboys (April 20, 2005).
RECORDS: Shares NFL single-game record for most field goals—7 (September 15, 2003, vs. New York Giants (OT)).

		FIELD GOALS							TOTALS		
Year Team	G	1-29	30-39	40-49	50+	Tot.	Pct.	Lg.	XPM	XPA	Pts.
2002—Dallas NFL	16	3-3	5-7	4-8	0-1	12-19	63.2	48	25	25	61
2003—Dallas NFL	15	11-11	5-6	4-7	3-5	23-29	79.3	52	30	31	99
2004—Dallas NFL	16	7-7	4-4	9-13	0-2	20-26	76.9	49	31	31	91
Pro totals (3 years)	47	21-21	14-17	17-28	3-8	55-74	74.3	52	86	87	251

CURRY, CLARENCE   CB   CARDINALS

PERSONAL: Born December 7, 1981, in Rochester, Mich. ... 6-1/190.
HIGH SCHOOL: Parsippany (N.J.).
COLLEGE: Villanova.
TRANSACTIONS/CAREER NOTES: Signed as non-drafted free agent by Arizona Cardinals (June 7, 2004). ... Released by Cardinals (August 21, 2004). ... Re-signed by Cardinals to practice squad (November 30, 2004). ... Activated (December 31, 2004).

			TOTALS			INTERCEPTIONS			
Year Team	G	GS	Tk.	Ast.	Sks.	No.	Yds.	Avg.	TD
2004—Arizona NFL	1	0	0	0	0.0	0	0	0.0	0

CURRY, DONTE'   LB   LIONS

PERSONAL: Born July 22, 1978, in Savannah, Ga. ... 6-1/233. ... Full name: Donte Curry.
HIGH SCHOOL: Savannah (Ga.).
JUNIOR COLLEGE: Middle Georgia Junior College.
COLLEGE: Morris Brown.
TRANSACTIONS/CAREER NOTES: Signed as non-drafted free agent by Green Bay Packers (April 24, 2001). ... Released by Packers (September 1, 2001). ... Re-signed by Packers to practice squad (September 3, 2001). ... Signed by Washington Redskins off Packers practice squad (October 3, 2001). ... Claimed on waivers by Detroit Lions (August 28, 2002). ... Re-signed by Lions (March 25, 2003). ... Granted free agency (March 3, 2004). ... Re-signed by Lions (April 21, 2004).

| | | | TOTALS | | | INTERCEPTIONS | | | |
Year Team	G	GS	Tk.	Ast.	Sks.	No.	Yds.	Avg.	TD
2001—Washington NFL	8	0	0	0	0.0	0	0	0.0	0
2002—Detroit NFL	16	10	39	16	3.0	0	0	0.0	0
2003—Detroit NFL	11	0	1	0	0.0	0	0	0.0	0
2004—Detroit NFL	12	0	5	2	0.0	0	0	0.0	0
Pro totals (4 years)	47	10	45	18	3.0	0	0	0.0	0

CURRY, RONALD   WR   RAIDERS

PERSONAL: Born May 28, 1979, in Hampton, Va. ... 6-2/220. ... Full name: Ronald Antonio Curry.
HIGH SCHOOL: Hampton (Va.).
COLLEGE: North Carolina.
TRANSACTIONS/CAREER NOTES: Selected by Oakland Raiders in seventh round (235th pick overall) of 2002 NFL draft. ... Signed by Raiders (July 26, 2002). ... Released by Raiders (September 1, 2002). ... Re-signed by Raiders to practice squad (September 3, 2002). ... Released by Raiders (November 2, 2002). ... Re-signed by Raiders to practice squad (January 22, 2003). ... On injured reserve with Achilles injury (December 8, 2004-remainder of season).
CHAMPIONSHIP GAME EXPERIENCE: Member of Raiders for Super Bowl 37 (2002 season); inactive.
SINGLE GAME HIGHS (regular season): Receptions—10 (October 10, 2004, vs. Indianapolis); yards—141 (December 5, 2004, vs. Kansas City); and touchdown receptions—2 (December 5, 2004, vs. Kansas City).
STATISTICAL PLATEAUS: 100-yard receiving games: 2004 (2). Total: 2.

| | | | RUSHING | | | | RECEIVING | | | | KICKOFF RETURNS | | | | TOTALS | | | |
Year Team	G	GS	Att.	Yds.	Avg.	TD	No.	Yds.	Avg.	TD	No.	Yds.	Avg.	TD	TD	2pt.	Pts.	Fum.
2002—Oakland NFL	1	0	0	0	0.0	0	0	0	0.0	0	3	68	22.7	0	0	0	0	1
2003—Oakland NFL	16	2	1	0	0.0	0	5	31	6.2	0	0	0	0.0	0	0	0	0	1
2004—Oakland NFL	12	3	1	-3	-3.0	0	50	679	13.6	6	4	63	15.8	0	6	0	36	1
Pro totals (3 years)	29	5	2	-3	-1.5	0	55	710	12.9	6	7	131	18.7	0	6	0	36	3

CURTIS, KEVIN   WR   RAMS

PERSONAL: Born July 17, 1978, in Murray, Utah. ... 5-11/186.
HIGH SCHOOL: Bingham (South Jordan, Utah).
JUNIOR COLLEGE: Snow College (Utah).
COLLEGE: Utah State.
TRANSACTIONS/CAREER NOTES: Selected by St. Louis Rams in third round (74th pick overall) of 2003 NFL draft. ... Signed by Rams (July 23, 2003).
SINGLE GAME HIGHS (regular season): Receptions—6 (January 2, 2005, vs. New York Jets); yards—99 (January 2, 2005, vs. New York Jets); and touchdown receptions—1 (November 14, 2004, vs. Seattle).

| | | | RUSHING | | | | RECEIVING | | | | PUNT RETURNS | | | | TOTALS | | | |
Year Team	G	GS	Att.	Yds.	Avg.	TD	No.	Yds.	Avg.	TD	No.	Yds.	Avg.	TD	TD	2pt.	Pts.	Fum.
2003—St. Louis NFL	4	1	0	0	0.0	0	4	13	3.3	0	0	0	0.0	0	0	0	0	0
2004—St. Louis NFL	15	0	3	24	8.0	0	32	421	13.2	2	0	0	0.0	0	2	1	14	1
Pro totals (2 years)	19	1	3	24	8.0	0	36	434	12.1	2	0	0	0.0	0	2	1	14	1

CUSHING, MATT   TE   STEELERS

PERSONAL: Born July 2, 1975, in Chicago, Ill. ... 6-4/251. ... Full name: Matt Jay Cushing.
HIGH SCHOOL: Mount Carmel (Chicago).
COLLEGE: Illinois.
TRANSACTIONS/CAREER NOTES: Signed as non-drafted free agent by Pittsburgh Steelers (April 24, 1998). ... Released by Steelers (August 24, 1998). ... Re-signed by Steelers (February 22, 1999). ... Assigned by Steelers to Amsterdam Admirals in 1999 NFL Europe enhancement allocation program (February 22, 1999). ... Released by Steelers (September 5, 1999). ... Re-signed by Steelers (October 28, 1999). ... Released by Steelers (August 27, 2000). ... Re-signed by Steelers (November 7, 2000). ... Granted free agency (March 1, 2002). ... Re-signed by Steelers (April 12, 2002). ... Released by Steelers (September 24, 2002). ... Re-signed by Steelers (October 22, 2002). ... Released by Steelers (November 5, 2002). ... Re-signed by Steelers (December 3, 2002). ... Granted unconditional free agency (February 28, 2003). ... Re-signed by Steelers (March 17, 2003). ... Granted unconditional free agency (March 3, 2004). ... Re-signed by Steelers (March 4, 2004). ... Granted unconditional free agency (March 2, 2005). ... Re-signed by Steelers (April 8, 2005).
CHAMPIONSHIP GAME EXPERIENCE: Played in AFC championship game (2001 and 2004 seasons).
SINGLE GAME HIGHS (regular season): Receptions—2 (December 23, 2001, vs. Detroit); yards—29 (January 2, 2000, vs. Tennessee); and touchdown receptions—1 (December 23, 2001, vs. Detroit).

| | | | RECEIVING | | | | TOTALS | | | |
Year Team	G	GS	No.	Yds.	Avg.	TD	TD	2pt.	Pts.	Fum.
1999—Pittsburgh NFL	7	1	2	29	14.5	0	0	0	0	0
2000—Pittsburgh NFL	6	1	4	17	4.3	0	0	0	0	0

C

Year Team				RECEIVING				TOTALS			
	G	GS	No.	Yds.	Avg.	TD	TD	2pt.	Pts.	Fum.
2001—Pittsburgh NFL	13	3	5	24	4.8	1	1	0	6	0
2002—Pittsburgh NFL	6	0	1	4	4.0	0	0	0	0	0
2003—Pittsburgh NFL	4	0	0	0	0.0	0	0	0	0	0
2004—Pittsburgh NFL	16	0	1	17	17.0	0	0	0	0	0
Pro totals (6 years)	52	5	13	91	7.0	1	1	0	6	0

DALTON, LIONAL DT CHIEFS

PERSONAL: Born February 21, 1975, in Detroit, Mich. ... 6-1/315.
HIGH SCHOOL: Cooley (Detroit).
COLLEGE: Eastern Michigan.
TRANSACTIONS/CAREER NOTES: Signed as non-drafted free agent by Baltimore Ravens (April 23, 1998). ... Granted free agency (March 2, 2001). ... Re-signed by Ravens (March 29, 2001). ... Granted unconditional free agency (March 1, 2002). ... Signed by Denver Broncos (March 20, 2002). ... Traded by Broncos to Washington Redskins for sixth-round pick (WR Triandos Luke) in 2004 draft (August 26, 2003). ... Released by Redskins (February 24, 2004). ... Signed by Kansas City Chiefs (March 30, 2004).
CHAMPIONSHIP GAME EXPERIENCE: Played in AFC championship game (2000 season). ... Member of Super Bowl championship team (2000 season).

Year Team			TOTALS		
	G	GS	Tk.	Ast.	Sks.
1998—Baltimore NFL	2	0	3	1	0.0
1999—Baltimore NFL	16	2	12	5	1.0
2000—Baltimore NFL	16	1	9	1	0.0
2001—Baltimore NFL	16	3	12	4	0.0
2002—Denver NFL	16	13	24	5	1.0
2003—Washington NFL	12	9	11	3	1.0
2004—Kansas City NFL	16	13	19	2	4.0
Pro totals (7 years)	94	41	90	21	7.0

D

DANIELS, PHILLIP DE REDSKINS

PERSONAL: Born March 4, 1973, in Donaldsonville, Ga. ... 6-3/288. ... Full name: Phillip Bernard Daniels.
HIGH SCHOOL: Seminole County (Donaldsonville, Ga.).
COLLEGE: Georgia.
TRANSACTIONS/CAREER NOTES: Selected by Seattle Seahawks in fourth round (99th pick overall) of 1996 NFL draft. ... Signed by Seahawks (July 17, 1996). ... Granted free agency (February 12, 1999). ... Re-signed by Seahawks (April 6, 1999). ... Granted unconditional free agency (February 11, 2000). ... Signed by Chicago Bears (February 12, 2000). ... On injured reserve with ankle injury (December 13, 2000-remainder of season). ... Released by Bears (March 1, 2004). ... Signed by Washington Redskins (March 2, 2004). ... On injured reserve with wrist and groin injuries (December 8, 2004-remainder of season).

Year Team			TOTALS		
	G	GS	Tk.	Ast.	Sks.
1996—Seattle NFL	15	0	9	2	2.0
1997—Seattle NFL	13	10	24	10	4.0
1998—Seattle NFL	16	15	34	14	6.5
1999—Seattle NFL	16	16	40	8	9.0
2000—Chicago NFL	14	14	37	5	6.0
2001—Chicago NFL	16	16	43	7	9.0
2002—Chicago NFL	13	13	34	9	5.5
2003—Chicago NFL	16	16	41	12	2.5
2004—Washington NFL	5	5	4	0	1.0
Pro totals (9 years)	124	105	266	67	45.5

DANSBY, KARLOS LB CARDINALS

PERSONAL: Born November 3, 1981, in Birmingham, Ala. ... 6-4/243.
HIGH SCHOOL: Woodlawn (Birmingham, Ala.).
COLLEGE: Auburn.
TRANSACTIONS/CAREER NOTES: Selected by Arizona Cardinals in second round (33rd pick overall) of 2004 NFL draft. ... Signed by Cardinals (August 4, 2004).

Year Team			TOTALS			INTERCEPTIONS			
	G	GS	Tk.	Ast.	Sks.	No.	Yds.	Avg.	TD
2004—Arizona NFL	15	11	38	16	5.0	1	2	2.0	0

DARBY, CHARTRIC DT SEAHAWKS

PERSONAL: Born October 22, 1975, in North, S.C. ... 6-0/298. ... Full name: Chartric Terrell Darby.
HIGH SCHOOL: North (S.C.).
COLLEGE: South Carolina State.
TRANSACTIONS/CAREER NOTES: Signed as non-drafted free agent by Baltimore Ravens (April 23, 1998). ... Released by Ravens (August 30, 1998). ... Re-signed by Ravens to practice squad (September 1, 1998). ... Granted free agency after 1998 season. ... Signed by Indianapolis Colts (January 19, 1999). ... Claimed on waivers by Carolina Panthers (April 28, 1999). ... Released by Panthers (August 30, 1999). ... Selected by Rhein Fire in 2000 NFL Europe draft (February 22, 2000). ... Signed by Buccaneers (July 10, 2000). ... Released by Buccaneers (August 27, 2000). ... Re-signed by Buccaneers to practice squad (August 28, 2000). ... Granted free agency (March 3, 2004). ... Re-signed by Buccaneers (April 19, 2004). ... Granted unconditional free agency (March 2, 2005). ... Signed by Seattle Seahawks (March 21, 2005).
CHAMPIONSHIP GAME EXPERIENCE: Played in NFC championship game (2002 season). ... Member of Super Bowl championship team (2002 season).

Year Team	G	GS	TOTALS Tk.	Ast.	Sks.
2001—Tampa Bay NFL	13	0	6	0	2.0
2002—Tampa Bay NFL	16	6	22	6	1.5
2003—Tampa Bay NFL	16	1	8	5	2.0
2004—Tampa Bay NFL	16	16	40	10	0.0
Pro totals (4 years)	61	23	76	21	5.5

DARCHE, JEAN-PHILIPPE　　C/LS　　SEAHAWKS

PERSONAL: Born February 28, 1975, in Montreal, Quebec, Can. ... 6-0/246. ... Full name: Jean-Philipe Darche. ... Brother of Mathieu Darche, left winger, Columbus Blue Jackets.
HIGH SCHOOL: Andre Grassett Junior College (Montreal).
COLLEGE: McGill.
TRANSACTIONS/CAREER NOTES: Signed as non-drafted free agent by Seattle Seahawks (May 11, 2000). ... Granted free agency (February 28, 2003). ... Re-signed by Seahawks (March 26, 2003).
PLAYING EXPERIENCE: Seattle NFL, 2000-2004. ... Games/Games started: 2000 (16/0), 2001 (16/0), 2002 (16/0), 2003 (16/0), 2004 (16/0). Total: 80/0.

DARILEK, TREY　　G　　EAGLES

PERSONAL: Born April 23, 1981, in San Antonio, Texas. ... 6-5/310.
HIGH SCHOOL: Robert E. Lee (San Antonio, Texas).
COLLEGE: Texas-El Paso.
TRANSACTIONS/CAREER NOTES: Selected by Philadelphia Eagles in fourth round (131st pick overall) of 2004 NFL draft. ... Signed by Eagles (July 27, 2004).
PLAYING EXPERIENCE: Philadelphia NFL, 2004. ... Games/Games started: 2004 (3/0). Total: 3/0.
CHAMPIONSHIP GAME EXPERIENCE: Member of Eagles for NFC championship game (2004 season); inactive. ... Member of Eagles for Super Bowl 39 (2004 season); inactive.

DARIUS, DONOVIN　　S　　JAGUARS

PERSONAL: Born August 12, 1975, in Camden, N.J. ... 6-1/225. ... Full name: Donovin Lee Darius.
HIGH SCHOOL: Woodrow Wilson (Camden, N.J.).
COLLEGE: Syracuse.
TRANSACTIONS/CAREER NOTES: Selected by Jacksonville Jaguars in first round (25th pick overall) of 1998 NFL draft. ... Signed by Jaguars (July 23, 1998). ... Designated by Jaguars as franchise player (February 20, 2003). ... Re-signed by Jaguars (March 25, 2003). ... Designated by Jaguars as franchise player (February 24, 2004). ... Re-signed by Jaguars (March 11, 2004). ... Designated by Jaguars as franchise player (February 22, 2005). ... Re-signed by Jaguars (March 1, 2005).
CHAMPIONSHIP GAME EXPERIENCE: Played in AFC championship game (1999 season).
HONORS: Named free safety on THE SPORTING NEWS college All-America first team (1997).

Year Team	G	GS	TOTALS Tk.	Ast.	Sks.	INTERCEPTIONS No.	Yds.	Avg.	TD
1998—Jacksonville NFL	14	14	58	16	0.0	0	0	0.0	0
1999—Jacksonville NFL	16	16	56	19	0.0	4	37	9.3	0
2000—Jacksonville NFL	16	16	65	20	1.0	2	26	13.0	0
2001—Jacksonville NFL	11	11	64	12	0.0	1	39	39.0	0
2002—Jacksonville NFL	14	14	70	8	1.0	1	3	3.0	0
2003—Jacksonville NFL	16	16	55	27	0.0	1	4	4.0	0
2004—Jacksonville NFL	16	16	61	28	0.0	5	80	16.0	0
Pro totals (7 years)	103	103	429	130	2.0	14	189	13.5	0

DARLING, DEVARD　　WR　　RAVENS

PERSONAL: Born April 16, 1982, in Bahamas. ... 6-1/215. ... Full name: Devard Loran Darling.
HIGH SCHOOL: Austin (Houston, Texas).
COLLEGE: Washington State.
TRANSACTIONS/CAREER NOTES: Selected after junior season by Baltimore Ravens in third round (82nd pick overall) of 2004 NFL draft. ... Signed by Ravens (July 26, 2004). ... On injured reserve with heel injury (October 29, 2004-remainder of season).
SINGLE GAME HIGHS (regular season): Receptions—2 (September 26, 2004, vs. Cincinnati); yards—5 (September 26, 2004, vs. Cincinnati); and touchdown receptions—0.

Year Team	G	GS	RECEIVING No.	Yds.	Avg.	TD	KICKOFF RETURNS No.	Yds.	Avg.	TD	TOTALS TD	2pt.	Pts.	Fum.
2004—Baltimore NFL	3	0	2	5	2.5	0	0	0	0.0	0	0	0	0	1

DARLING, JAMES　　LB　　CARDINALS

PERSONAL: Born December 29, 1974, in Denver, Colo. ... 6-1/247. ... Full name: James Jackson Darling.
HIGH SCHOOL: Kettle Falls (Wash.).
COLLEGE: Washington State.
TRANSACTIONS/CAREER NOTES: Selected by Philadelphia Eagles in second round (57th pick overall) of 1997 NFL draft. ... Signed by Eagles (July 16, 1997). ... Granted free agency (February 11, 2000). ... Re-signed by Eagles (April 10, 2000). ... Granted unconditional free agency

(March 2, 2001). ... Signed by New York Jets (March 21, 2001). ... Granted unconditional free agency (February 28, 2003). ... Signed by Arizona Cardinals (March 12, 2003).
HONORS: Named inside linebacker on THE SPORTING NEWS college All-America second team (1996).

Year Team	G	GS	TOTALS Tk.	Ast.	Sks.	INTERCEPTIONS No.	Yds.	Avg.	TD
1997—Philadelphia NFL	16	6	20	8	0.0	0	0	0.0	0
1998—Philadelphia NFL	12	8	20	6	2.0	0	0	0.0	0
1999—Philadelphia NFL	15	10	40	18	0.0	1	33	33.0	0
2000—Philadelphia NFL	16	0	1	3	0.5	0	0	0.0	0
2001—New York Jets NFL	16	0	7	4	0.0	0	0	0.0	0
2002—New York Jets NFL	16	0	28	9	1.0	2	38	19.0	0
2003—Arizona NFL	16	0	21	0	2.0	0	0	0.0	0
2004—Arizona NFL	15	15	73	15	1.0	1	65	65.0	0
Pro totals (8 years)	122	39	210	63	6.5	4	136	34.0	0

DAVENPORT, NAJEH — RB — PACKERS

PERSONAL: Born February 8, 1979, in Raleigh, N.C. ... 6-1/250. ... Full name: Najeh Trenadious Monte Davenport.
HIGH SCHOOL: Miami Central (Fla.).
COLLEGE: Miami (Fla.).
TRANSACTIONS/CAREER NOTES: Selected by Green Bay Packers in fourth round (135th pick overall) of 2002 NFL draft. ... Signed by Packers (July 26, 2002). ... On injured reserve with eye injury (November 20, 2002-remainder of season). ... Granted free agency (March 2, 2005). ... Re-signed by Packers (April 1, 2005).
SINGLE GAME HIGHS (regular season): Attempts—22 (September 22, 2002, vs. Detroit); yards— 178 (November 29, 2004, vs. St. Louis); and rushing touchdowns—1 (November 29, 2004, vs. St. Louis).
STATISTICAL PLATEAUS: 100-yard rushing games: 2004 (1). Total: 1.

Year Team	G	GS	RUSHING Att.	Yds.	Avg.	TD	RECEIVING No.	Yds.	Avg.	TD	KICKOFF RETURNS No.	Yds.	Avg.	TD	TOTALS TD	2pt.	Pts.	Fum.
2002—Green Bay NFL	8	0	39	184	4.7	1	5	33	6.6	0	6	130	21.7	0	1	0	6	1
2003—Green Bay NFL	15	0	77	420	5.5	2	6	38	6.3	0	16	505	31.6	0	2	0	12	4
2004—Green Bay NFL	11	1	71	359	5.1	2	4	33	8.3	0	14	286	20.4	0	2	0	12	1
Pro totals (3 years)	34	1	187	963	5.1	5	15	104	6.9	0	36	921	25.6	0	5	0	30	6

D

DAVEY, ROHAN — QB — PATRIOTS

PERSONAL: Born April 14, 1978, in Clarendon, Jamaica. ... 6-2/245. ... Full name: Rohan St. Patrick Davey.
HIGH SCHOOL: Miami Lakes (Fla.).
COLLEGE: Louisiana State.
TRANSACTIONS/CAREER NOTES: Selected by New England Patriots in fourth round (117th pick overall) of 2002 NFL draft. ... Signed by Patriots (July 21, 2002). ... Assigned by Patriots to Berlin Thunder in 2004 NFL Europe enhancement allocation program (February 9, 2004).
CHAMPIONSHIP GAME EXPERIENCE: Member of Patriots for AFC championship game (2003 season); inactive. ... Member of Patriots for AFC championship game (2004 season); did not play. ... Member of Patriots for Super Bowl 38 (2003 season); inactive. ... Member of Patriots for Super Bowl 39 (2004 season); did not play.
SINGLE GAME HIGHS (regular season): Attempts—7 (September 7, 2003, vs. Buffalo); completions—3 (December 5, 2004, vs. Cleveland); yards—44 (December 5, 2004, vs. Cleveland); and touchdown passes—0.

Year Team	G	GS	PASSING Att.	Cmp.	Pct.	Yds.	TD	Int.	Avg.	Skd.	Rat.	RUSHING Att.	Yds.	Avg.	TD	TOTALS TD	2pt.	Pts.
2002—New England NFL	2	0	2	1	50.0	3	0	0	1.50	0	56.2	2	-4	-2.0	0	0	0	0
2003—New England NFL	1	0	7	3	42.9	31	0	0	4.43	0	56.3	0	0	0.0	0	0	0	0
2004—New England NFL	4	0	10	4	40.0	54	0	0	5.40	0	57.9	4	-1	-0.2	0	0	0	0
Pro totals (3 years)	7	0	19	8	42.1	88	0	0	4.63	0	56.5	6	-5	-0.8	0	0	0	0

DAVID, JASON — CB — COLTS

PERSONAL: Born June 12, 1982, in Covina, Calif. ... 5-8/172. ... Full name: Jason Aeron Walter David.
HIGH SCHOOL: Charter Oak (Covina, Calif.).
COLLEGE: Washington State.
TRANSACTIONS/CAREER NOTES: Selected by Indianapolis Colts in fourth round (125th pick overall) of 2004 NFL draft. ... Signed by Colts (July 28, 2004).

Year Team	G	GS	INTERCEPTIONS No.	Yds.	Avg.	TD	PUNT RETURNS No.	Yds.	Avg.	TD	KICKOFF RETURNS No.	Yds.	Avg.	TD	TOTALS TD	2pt.	Pts.	Fum.
2004—Indianapolis NFL	16	11	4	36	9.0	1	8	50	6.3	0	0	0	0.0	0	1	0	6	0

DAVIS, ANDRA — LB — BROWNS

PERSONAL: Born December 23, 1978, in Live Oak, Fla. ... 6-1/255. ... Full name: Andra Raynard Davis.
HIGH SCHOOL: Suwanee (Live Oak, Fla.).
COLLEGE: Florida.
TRANSACTIONS/CAREER NOTES: Selected by Cleveland Browns in fifth round (141st pick overall) of 2002 NFL draft. ... Signed by Browns (July 18, 2002). ... On injured reserve with knee injury (November 29, 2004-remainder of season). ... Granted free agency (March 2, 2005). ... Re-signed by Browns (March 8, 2005).
HONORS: Named linebacker on THE SPORTING NEWS college All-America second team (2001).

Year—Team	G	GS	TOTALS Tk.	Ast.	Sks.	INTERCEPTIONS No.	Yds.	Avg.	TD
2002—Cleveland NFL	16	0	1	4	0.0	1	0	0.0	0
2003—Cleveland NFL	16	16	96	40	5.0	0	0	0.0	0
2004—Cleveland NFL	11	11	54	16	0.5	3	35	11.7	0
Pro totals (3 years)	43	27	151	60	5.5	4	35	8.8	0

DAVIS, ANDRE'　　　　WR　　　　BROWNS

PERSONAL: Born June 12, 1979, in Niskayuna, N.Y. ... 6-1/195. ... Full name: Andre' N. Davis.
HIGH SCHOOL: Niskayuna (N.Y.).
COLLEGE: Virginia Tech.
TRANSACTIONS/CAREER NOTES: Selected by Cleveland Browns in second round (47th pick overall) of 2002 NFL draft. ... Signed by Browns (July 22, 2002). ... On injured reserve with toe injury (December 2, 2004-remainder of season).
SINGLE GAME HIGHS (regular season): Receptions—7 (November 16, 2003, vs. Arizona); yards—117 (November 16, 2003, vs. Arizona); and touchdown receptions—2 (September 21, 2003, vs. San Francisco).
STATISTICAL PLATEAUS: 100-yard receiving games: 2003 (1), 2004 (1). Total: 2.

Year—Team	G	GS	RUSHING Att.	Yds.	Avg.	TD	RECEIVING No.	Yds.	Avg.	TD	PUNT RETURNS No.	Yds.	Avg.	TD	KICKOFF RETURNS No.	Yds.	Avg.	TD	TOTALS TD	2pt.	Pts.
2002—Cle. NFL	16	4	3	7	2.3	0	37	420	11.4	6	7	33	4.7	0	50	1068	21.4	1	7	0	42
2003—Cle. NFL	16	8	5	28	5.6	0	40	576	14.4	5	1	7	7.0	0	38	803	21.1	0	5	0	30
2004—Cle. NFL	7	7	1	-3	-3.0	0	16	416	26.0	2	0	0	0.0	0	0	0	0.0	0	2	0	12
Pro totals (3 years)	39	19	9	32	3.6	0	93	1412	15.2	13	8	40	5.0	0	88	1871	21.3	1	14	0	84

DAVIS, ANTHONY　　　　T　　　　BUCCANEERS

PERSONAL: Born March 27, 1980, in Paterson, N.J. ... 6-4/322. ... Full name: Anthony Sherrod Davis.
HIGH SCHOOL: Central Lunenburg (Victoria, Va.).
COLLEGE: Virginia Tech.
TRANSACTIONS/CAREER NOTES: Signed as non-drafted free agent by Tampa Bay Buccaneers (April 28, 2003). ... Released by Buccaneers (August 26, 2003). ... Re-signed by Buccaneers to practice squad (September 4, 2003). ... Activated (December 26, 2003).
PLAYING EXPERIENCE: Tampa Bay NFL, 2004. ... Games/Games started: 2004 (2/0). Total: 2/0.

DAVIS, CAREY　　　　RB　　　　FALCONS

PERSONAL: Born March 27, 1981, in St. Louis, Mo. ... 5-10/225. ... Full name: Carey Alexander Davis.
HIGH SCHOOL: Hazelwood Central (St. Louis, Mo.).
COLLEGE: Illinois.
TRANSACTIONS/CAREER NOTES: Signed as non-drafted free agent by Indianapolis Colts (April 30, 2004). ... Released by Colts (September 5, 2004). ... Re-signed by Colts (September 9, 2004). ... Released by Colts (September 10, 2004). ... Signed by Atlanta Falcons (December 15, 2004).

Year—Team	G	GS	RUSHING Att.	Yds.	Avg.	TD	TOTALS TD	2pt.	Pts.	Fum.
2004—Indianapolis NFL	1	0	0	0	0.0	0	0	0	0	0

DAVIS, DOMANICK　　　　RB　　　　TEXANS

PERSONAL: Born October 1, 1980, in Lafayette, La. ... 5-9/221.
HIGH SCHOOL: Breaux Bridge (La.).
COLLEGE: Louisiana State.
TRANSACTIONS/CAREER NOTES: Selected by Houston Texans in fourth round (101st pick overall) of 2003 NFL draft. ... Signed by Texans (July 17, 2003).
SINGLE GAME HIGHS (regular season): Attempts—31 (December 26, 2004, vs. Jacksonville); yards—158 (December 26, 2004, vs. Jacksonville); and rushing touchdowns—2 (November 14, 2004, vs. Indianapolis).
STATISTICAL PLATEAUS: 100-yard rushing games: 2003 (4), 2004 (4). Total: 8.
MISCELLANEOUS: Holds Houston Texans all-time records for most yards rushing (2,219), most rushing touchdowns (21) and most touchdowns (22).

Year—Team	G	GS	RUSHING Att.	Yds.	Avg.	TD	RECEIVING No.	Yds.	Avg.	TD	KICKOFF RETURNS No.	Yds.	Avg.	TD	TOTALS TD	2pt.	Pts.	Fum.
2003—Houston NFL	14	10	238	1031	4.3	8	47	351	7.5	0	3	61	20.3	0	8	0	48	4
2004—Houston NFL	15	15	302	1188	3.9	13	68	588	8.6	1	0	0	0.0	0	14	0	84	4
Pro totals (2 years)	29	25	540	2219	4.1	21	115	939	8.2	1	3	61	20.3	0	22	0	132	8

DAVIS, DON　　　　LB　　　　PATRIOTS

PERSONAL: Born December 17, 1972, in Olathe, Kan. ... 6-1/235.
HIGH SCHOOL: Olathe (Kan.) South.
COLLEGE: Kansas.
TRANSACTIONS/CAREER NOTES: Signed as non-drafted free agent by New York Jets (April 28, 1995). ... Released by Jets (August 27, 1995). ... Signed by Kansas City Chiefs (January 9, 1996). ... Released by Chiefs (August 20, 1996). ... Signed by New Orleans Saints to practice squad (August 27, 1996). ... Activated (October 4, 1996). ... On injured reserve with wrist injury (November 19, 1997-remainder of season). ... Claimed on waivers by Tampa Bay Buccaneers (November 25, 1998). ... Granted free agency (February 12, 1999). ... Re-signed by Buccaneers (May 21, 1999). ... Released by Buccaneers (October 9, 1999). ... Re-signed by Buccaneers (October 19, 1999). ... Granted uncon-

D

ditional free agency (February 11, 2000). ... Re-signed by Buccaneers (July 1, 2000). ... Granted unconditional free agency (March 2, 2001). ... Signed by St. Louis Rams (March 3, 2001). ... Granted unconditional free agency (February 28, 2003). ... Signed by New England Patriots (May 16, 2003). ... Granted unconditional free agency (March 3, 2004). ... Re-signed by Patriots (March 5, 2004). ... Granted unconditional free agency (March 2, 2005). ... Re-signed by Patriots (March 22, 2005).

CHAMPIONSHIP GAME EXPERIENCE: Played in NFC championship game (1999 and 2001 seasons). ... Played in AFC championship game (2003 and 2004 seasons). ... Played in Super Bowl 36 (2001 season). ... Member of Super Bowl championship team (2003 and 2004 seasons).

Year Team	G	GS	TOTALS Tk.	Ast.	Sks.	INTERCEPTIONS No.	Yds.	Avg.	TD
1996—New Orleans NFL	11	0	0	0	0.0	0	0	0.0	0
1997—New Orleans NFL	11	0	0	0	0.0	0	0	0.0	0
1998—New Orleans NFL	4	0	2	2	0.0	0	0	0.0	0
—Tampa Bay NFL	5	0	0	0	0.0	0	0	0.0	0
1999—Tampa Bay NFL	14	0	0	1	0.0	0	0	0.0	0
2000—Tampa Bay NFL	16	0	2	5	0.0	0	0	0.0	0
2001—St. Louis NFL	12	8	16	9	0.0	0	0	0.0	0
2002—St. Louis NFL	16	7	33	6	0.0	1	29	29.0	0
2003—New England NFL	15	0	1	0	0.0	0	0	0.0	0
2004—New England NFL	16	2	10	6	0.0	0	0	0.0	0
Pro totals (9 years)	120	17	64	29	0.0	1	29	29.0	0

DAVIS, DORSETT DE/DT BRONCOS

PERSONAL: Born January 24, 1979, in Shelby, Miss. ... 6-5/305. ... Full name: Dorsett Terrell Davis.
HIGH SCHOOL: East Side (Cleveland, Miss.).
JUNIOR COLLEGE: Mississippi Delta Community College.
COLLEGE: Mississippi State.
TRANSACTIONS/CAREER NOTES: Selected by Denver Broncos in third round (96th pick overall) of 2002 NFL draft. ... Signed by Broncos (July 19, 2002). ... On injured reserve with finger injury (July 31, 2004-entire season). ... Granted free agency (March 2, 2005). ... Re-signed by Broncos (April 6, 2005).

Year Team	G	GS	TOTALS Tk.	Ast.	Sks.
2003—Denver NFL	14	0	8	3	0.0
2004—Denver NFL	Did not play.				
Pro totals (1 year)	14	0	8	3	0.0

DAVIS, JAMES LB LIONS

PERSONAL: Born April 26, 1979, in Stuart, Fla. ... 6-2/240.
HIGH SCHOOL: Martin County (Stuart, Fla.).
COLLEGE: West Virginia.
TRANSACTIONS/CAREER NOTES: Selected by Detroit Lions in fifth round (144th pick overall) of 2003 NFL draft. ... Signed by Lions (July 15, 2003).

Year Team	G	GS	TOTALS Tk.	Ast.	Sks.	INTERCEPTIONS No.	Yds.	Avg.	TD
2003—Detroit NFL	8	1	6	0	0.0	0	0	0.0	0
2004—Detroit NFL	16	15	54	25	3.5	0	0	0.0	0
Pro totals (2 years)	24	16	60	25	3.5	0	0	0.0	0

DAVIS, JEROME T 49ERS

PERSONAL: Born February 4, 1974, in Detroit, Mich. ... 6-5/300.
HIGH SCHOOL: Chadsey (Detroit).
COLLEGE: Minnesota.
TRANSACTIONS/CAREER NOTES: Signed as non-drafted free agent by Detroit Lions (April 24, 1997). ... Released by Lions (August 19, 1997). ... Re-signed by Lions to practice squad (December 23, 1997). ... Assigned by Lions to Frankfurt Galaxy in 1998 NFL Europe enhancement allocation program (February 18, 1998). ... On injured reserve list with leg injury (August 17, 1998-entire season). ... Released by Lions (February 12, 1999). ... Signed by Carolina Panthers (August 2, 1999). ... Released by Panthers (August 30, 1999). ... Signed by Denver Broncos (February 16, 2000). ... Released by Broncos (August 21, 2000). ... Signed by Calgary Stampeders of CFL (October 2000). ... Released by Stampeders (June 27, 2001). ... Signed by San Francisco 49ers (August 7, 2001). ... Released by 49ers (September 3, 2001). ... Re-signed by 49ers (January 23, 2002). ... Assigned by 49ers to Frankfurt Galaxy in 2002 NFL Europe enhancement allocation program (February 12, 2002). ... Released by 49ers (September 7, 2002). ... Re-signed by 49ers to practice squad (September 9, 2002). ... Activated (December 30, 2002). ... Waived by 49ers (August 31, 2003). ... Re-signed by 49ers to practice squad (September 1, 2003). ... Activated (September 17, 2003). ... On reserve/suspended list (September 5-October 11, 2004).
PLAYING EXPERIENCE: Detroit NFL, 1998; Calgary CFL, 2000; San Francisco NFL, 2002-2004. ... Games/Games started: 2000 (2/0), 2002 (2/0), 2003 (2/0), 2004 (2/0), Total: 8/0.

DAVIS, KEITH SS COWBOYS

PERSONAL: Born December 30, 1978, in Dallas, Texas. ... 5-10/193.
HIGH SCHOOL: Italy (Texas).
COLLEGE: Sam Houston State.
TRANSACTIONS/CAREER NOTES: Signed as non-drafted free agent by Dallas Cowboys (April 26, 2002). ... Released by Cowboys (August 31, 2002). ... Re-signed by Cowboys to practice squad (September 3, 2002). ... Released by Cowboys (September 10, 2002). ... Re-signed by Cowboys to practice squad (September 16, 2002). ... Activated (October 12, 2002). ... Released by Cowboys (October 21, 2002). ... Re-signed by Cowboys to practice squad (October 23, 2002). ... Activated (November 21, 2002). ... Re-signed by Cowboys (March 7, 2003). ... Assigned by Cowboys to Berlin Thunder in 2004 NFL Europe enhancement allocation program (February 9, 2004).

Year Team	G	GS	TOTALS			INTERCEPTIONS			
			Tk.	Ast.	Sks.	No.	Yds.	Avg.	TD
2002—Dallas NFL	8	0	0	0	0.0	0	0	0.0	0
2004—Dallas NFL	15	0	0	0	0.0	0	0	0.0	0
Pro totals (2 years)	23	0	0	0	0.0	0	0	0.0	0

DAVIS, LEONARD   G   CARDINALS

PERSONAL: Born September 5, 1978, in Wortham, Texas. ... 6-6/381. ... Full name: Leonard Barnett Davis.
HIGH SCHOOL: Wortham (Texas).
COLLEGE: Texas.
TRANSACTIONS/CAREER NOTES: Selected by Arizona Cardinals in first round (second pick overall) of 2001 NFL draft. ... Signed by Cardinals (August 8, 2001). ... On injured reserve with knee injury (December 24, 2002-remainder of season). ... On injured reserve with knee injury (December 31, 2004-remainder of season).
PLAYING EXPERIENCE: Arizona NFL, 2001-2004. ... Games/Games started: 2001 (16/16), 2002 (15/15), 2003 (14/14), 2004 (15/15). Total: 60/60.
HONORS: Named offensive tackle on THE SPORTING NEWS college All-America first team (2000).

DAVIS, ROB   C/LS   PACKERS

PERSONAL: Born December 10, 1968, in Washington, DC. ... 6-3/283. ... Full name: Robert Emmett Davis.
HIGH SCHOOL: Eleanor Roosevelt (Greenbelt, Md.).
COLLEGE: Shippensburg.
TRANSACTIONS/CAREER NOTES: Signed as non-drafted free agent by New York Jets (April 27, 1993). ... Released by Jets (August 24, 1993). ... Re-signed by Jets (April 29, 1994). ... Released by Jets (August 22, 1994). ... Signed by Baltimore Stallions of CFL (April 1995). ... Signed by Kansas City Chiefs (April 22, 1996). ... Released by Chiefs (August 20, 1996). ... Signed by Chicago Bears (August 28, 1996). ... Released by Bears (August 27, 1997). ... Signed by Green Bay Packers (November 4, 1997). ... On physically unable to perform list with back injury (July 18-August 10, 1998). ... Granted unconditional free agency (March 2, 2001). ... Re-signed by Packers (March 20, 2001).
PLAYING EXPERIENCE: Chicago NFL, 1996; Green Bay NFL, 1997-2004. ... Games/Games started: 1996 (16/0), 1997 (7/0), 1998 (16/0), 1999 (16/0), 2000 (16/0), 2001 (16/0), 2002 (16/0), 2003 (16/0), 2004 (16/0). Total: 135/0.
CHAMPIONSHIP GAME EXPERIENCE: Played in NFC championship game (1997 season). ... Played in Super Bowl 32 (1997 season).

DAVIS, ROD   LB   VIKINGS

PERSONAL: Born April 2, 1981, in Gulfport, Miss. ... 6-2/239.
HIGH SCHOOL: Gulfport (Miss.).
COLLEGE: Southern Miss.
TRANSACTIONS/CAREER NOTES: Selected by Minnesota Vikings in fifth round (155th pick overall) of 2004 NFL draft. ... Signed by Vikings (July 28, 2004).
HONORS: Named linebacker on THE SPORTING NEWS Freshman All-America second team (2000). ... Named linebacker on THE SPORTING NEWS college All-America fourth team (2001) and second team (2003).

Year Team	G	GS	TOTALS			INTERCEPTIONS			
			Tk.	Ast.	Sks.	No.	Yds.	Avg.	TD
2004—Minnesota NFL	14	0	1	0	0.0	0	0	0.0	0

DAVIS, RUSSELL   DT   CARDINALS

PERSONAL: Born March 28, 1975, in Hampton, Va. ... 6-4/310. ... Full name: Russell Morgan Davis.
HIGH SCHOOL: E.E. Smith (Fayetteville, N.C.).
COLLEGE: North Carolina.
TRANSACTIONS/CAREER NOTES: Selected by Chicago Bears in second round (48th pick overall) of 1999 NFL draft. ... Signed by Bears (July 22, 1999). ... Claimed on waivers by Arizona Cardinals (August 28, 2000). ... Granted unconditional free agency (February 28, 2003). ... Re-signed by Cardinals (March 16, 2003).

Year Team	G	GS	TOTALS		
			Tk.	Ast.	Sks.
1999—Chicago NFL	11	8	13	4	2.0
2000—Arizona NFL	13	9	29	9	0.5
2001—Arizona NFL	16	16	37	17	2.0
2002—Arizona NFL	16	16	35	9	2.0
2003—Arizona NFL	15	15	29	9	1.0
2004—Arizona NFL	16	16	39	11	1.0
Pro totals (6 years)	87	80	182	59	8.5

DAVIS, SAMMY   CB   CHARGERS

PERSONAL: Born April 8, 1980, in Humble, Texas. ... 6-0/195. ... Full name: Samuel J. Davis Jr.
HIGH SCHOOL: Humble (Texas).
COLLEGE: Texas A&M.
TRANSACTIONS/CAREER NOTES: Selected by San Diego Chargers in first round (30th pick overall) of 2003 NFL draft. ... Signed by Chargers (July 23, 2003). ... On injured reserve with leg injury (November 30, 2004-remainder of season).

D

Year Team	G	GS	TOTALS Tk.	Ast.	Sks.	INTERCEPTIONS No.	Yds.	Avg.	TD
2003—San Diego NFL	16	16	45	13	0.0	2	48	24.0	0
2004—San Diego NFL	12	10	32	6	0.0	1	4	4.0	0
Pro totals (2 years)	28	26	77	19	0.0	3	52	17.3	0

DAVIS, STEPHEN   RB   PANTHERS

PERSONAL: Born March 1, 1974, in Spartanburg, S.C. ... 6-0/230.
HIGH SCHOOL: Spartanburg (S.C.).
COLLEGE: Auburn.
TRANSACTIONS/CAREER NOTES: Selected by Washington Redskins in fourth round (102nd pick overall) of 1996 NFL draft. ... Signed by Redskins (July 16, 1996). ... Granted free agency (February 12, 1999). ... Re-signed by Redskins (May 12, 1999). ... Designated by Redskins as franchise player (February 11, 2000). ... Released by Redskins (February 26, 2003). ... Signed by Carolina Panthers (March 14, 2003). ... On injured reserve with knee injury (November 13, 2004-remainder of season).
CHAMPIONSHIP GAME EXPERIENCE: Played in NFC championship game (2003 season). ... Played in Super Bowl 38 (2003 season).
HONORS: Played in Pro Bowl (1999, 2000 and 2003 seasons).
SINGLE GAME HIGHS (regular season): Attempts—38 (January 6, 2002, vs. Arizona); yards—189 (December 12, 1999, vs. Arizona); and rushing touchdowns—3 (November 24, 2002, vs. St. Louis).
STATISTICAL PLATEAUS: 100-yard rushing games: 1999 (6), 2000 (5), 2001 (6), 2002 (1), 2003 (7). Total: 25. 100-yard receiving games: 1998 (1). Total: 1.

Year Team	G	GS	RUSHING Att.	Yds.	Avg.	TD	RECEIVING No.	Yds.	Avg.	TD	TOTALS TD	2pt.	Pts.	Fum.
1996—Washington NFL	12	0	23	139	6.0	2	0	0	0.0	0	2	0	12	0
1997—Washington NFL	14	6	141	567	4.0	3	18	134	7.4	0	3	0	18	1
1998—Washington NFL	16	12	34	109	3.2	0	21	263	12.5	2	2	0	12	0
1999—Washington NFL	14	14	290	‡1405	4.8	*17	23	111	4.8	0	†17	1	104	4
2000—Washington NFL	15	15	332	1318	4.0	11	33	313	9.5	0	11	0	66	4
2001—Washington NFL	16	16	*356	‡1432	4.0	5	28	205	7.3	0	5	1	32	6
2002—Washington NFL	12	12	207	820	4.0	7	23	142	6.2	1	8	0	48	4
2003—Carolina NFL	14	14	318	1444	4.5	8	14	159	11.4	0	8	0	48	3
2004—Carolina NFL	2	2	24	92	3.8	0	2	32	16.0	0	0	0	0	0
Pro totals (9 years)	115	91	1725	7326	4.2	53	162	1359	8.4	3	56	2	340	22

DAWKINS, BRIAN   S   EAGLES

PERSONAL: Born October 13, 1973, in Jacksonville, Fla. ... 6-0/210.
HIGH SCHOOL: Raines (Jacksonville, Fla.).
COLLEGE: Clemson.
TRANSACTIONS/CAREER NOTES: Selected by Philadelphia Eagles in second round (61st pick overall) of 1996 NFL draft. ... Signed by Eagles (July 17, 1996).
CHAMPIONSHIP GAME EXPERIENCE: Played in NFC championship game (2001-2004 seasons). ... Played in Super Bowl 39 (2004 season).
HONORS: Named defensive back on THE SPORTING NEWS college All-America second team (1995). ... Played in Pro Bowl (1999, 2001, 2002 and 2004 seasons). ... Named safety on THE SPORTING NEWS NFL All-Pro team (2001, 2002 and 2004).

Year Team	G	GS	TOTALS Tk.	Ast.	Sks.	INTERCEPTIONS No.	Yds.	Avg.	TD
1996—Philadelphia NFL	14	13	53	21	1.0	3	41	13.7	0
1997—Philadelphia NFL	15	15	61	13	0.0	3	76	25.3	1
1998—Philadelphia NFL	14	14	45	11	1.0	2	39	19.5	0
1999—Philadelphia NFL	16	16	58	20	1.5	4	127	31.7	1
2000—Philadelphia NFL	13	13	54	17	2.0	4	62	15.5	0
2001—Philadelphia NFL	15	15	58	12	1.5	2	15	7.5	0
2002—Philadelphia NFL	16	16	66	29	3.5	2	27	13.5	0
2003—Philadelphia NFL	7	7	28	7	0.5	1	0	0.0	0
2004—Philadelphia NFL	15	15	62	8	3.0	4	40	10.0	0
Pro totals (9 years)	125	124	485	138	13.5	25	427	17.1	2

DAWSON, PHIL   K   BROWNS

PERSONAL: Born January 23, 1975, in West Palm Beach, Fla. ... 5-11/200.
HIGH SCHOOL: Lake Highlands (Dallas).
COLLEGE: Texas.
TRANSACTIONS/CAREER NOTES: Signed as non-drafted free agent by Oakland Raiders (April 24, 1998). ... Claimed on waivers by New England Patriots (August 21, 1998). ... Released by Patriots (August 30, 1998). ... Re-signed by Patriots to practice squad (August 31, 1998). ... Granted free agency after 1998 season. ... Signed by Cleveland Browns (March 25, 1999). ... Granted free agency (March 1, 2002). ... Re-signed by Browns (April 26, 2002). ... On injured reserve with arm injury (December 9, 2003-remainder of season).

Year Team	G	FIELD GOALS 1-29	30-39	40-49	50+	Tot.	Pct.	Lg.	TOTALS XPM	XPA	Pts.
1999—Cleveland NFL	15	2-2	3-5	3-5	0-0	8-12	66.7	49	23	24	47
2000—Cleveland NFL	16	7-7	5-5	2-5	0-0	14-17	82.4	45	17	17	59
2001—Cleveland NFL	16	10-10	8-9	4-6	0-0	22-25	88.0	48	29	30	95
2002—Cleveland NFL	16	9-10	6-8	5-7	2-3	22-28	78.6	52	34	35	100
2003—Cleveland NFL	13	9-9	4-5	3-5	2-2	18-21	85.7	52	20	21	74
2004—Cleveland NFL	16	11-11	6-8	6-9	1-1	24-29	82.8	50	28	28	100
Pro totals (6 years)	92	48-49	32-40	23-37	5-6	108-132	81.8	52	151	155	475

DAYNE, RON   RB   BRONCOS

PERSONAL: Born March 14, 1978, in Berlin, N.J. ... 5-10/245.
HIGH SCHOOL: Overbrook (Berlin, N.J.).
COLLEGE: Wisconsin.
TRANSACTIONS/CAREER NOTES: Selected by New York Giants in first round (11th pick overall) of 2000 NFL draft. ... Signed by Giants (July 21, 2000). ... Inactive for 16 games (2003). ... Granted unconditional free agency (March 2, 2005). ... Signed by Denver Broncos (April 1, 2005).
CHAMPIONSHIP GAME EXPERIENCE: Played in NFC championship game (2000 season). ... Played in Super Bowl 35 (2000 season).
HONORS: Heisman Trophy winner (1999). ... Doak Walker Award winner (1999). ... Maxwell Award winner (1999). ... Named running back on THE SPORTING NEWS college All-America first team (1999). ... Named College Football Player of the Year by THE SPORTING NEWS (1999).
SINGLE GAME HIGHS (regular season): Attempts—25 (October 29, 2000, vs. Philadelphia); yards—111 (September 30, 2001, vs. New Orleans); and rushing touchdowns—2 (December 15, 2002, vs. Dallas).
STATISTICAL PLATEAUS: 100-yard rushing games: 2000 (1), 2001 (1). Total: 2.

			RUSHING				RECEIVING				TOTALS			
Year Team	G	GS	Att.	Yds.	Avg.	TD	No.	Yds.	Avg.	TD	TD	2pt.	Pts.	Fum.
2000—New York Giants NFL	16	4	228	770	3.4	5	3	11	3.7	0	5	0	30	1
2001—New York Giants NFL	16	7	180	690	3.8	7	8	67	8.4	0	7	1	44	2
2002—New York Giants NFL	16	1	125	428	3.4	3	11	49	4.5	0	3	0	18	1
2003—New York Giants NFL	Did not play.													
2004—New York Giants NFL	14	2	52	179	3.4	1	1	7	7.0	0	1	0	6	0
Pro totals (4 years)	62	14	585	2067	3.5	16	23	134	5.8	0	16	1	98	4

DEARTH, JAMES   TE/LS   JETS

PERSONAL: Born January 22, 1976, in Fort Ord, Calif. ... 6-4/270.
HIGH SCHOOL: Scurry-Rosser (Scurry, Texas).
COLLEGE: Tarleton State.
TRANSACTIONS/CAREER NOTES: Selected by Cleveland Browns in sixth round (191st pick overall) of 1999 NFL draft. ... Signed by Browns (July 22, 1999). ... Released by Browns (September 3, 1999). ... Re-signed by Browns to practice squad (November 23, 1999). ... Activated (December 14, 1999). ... Assigned by Browns to Scottish Claymores in 2000 NFL Europe enhancement allocation program (February 11, 2000). ... Released by Browns (April 18, 2000). ... Signed by Titans (July 14, 2000). ... Released by Titans (August 22, 2000). ... Re-signed by Titans to practice squad (November 8, 2000). ... Granted free agency following 2000 season. ... Signed by New York Jets (January 24, 2001).
PLAYING EXPERIENCE: Cleveland NFL, 1999; New York Jets NFL, 2001-2004. ... Games/Games started: 1999 (2/0), 2001 (16/0), 2002 (16/0), 2003 (16/0), 2004 (16/0). Total: 66/0.
SINGLE GAME HIGHS (regular season): Receptions—1 (December 16, 2001, vs. Cincinnati); yards—9 (November 11, 2001, vs. Kansas City); and touchdown receptions—1 (December 16, 2001, vs. Cincinnati).

DEESE, DERRICK   T   BUCCANEERS

PERSONAL: Born May 17, 1970, in Culver City, Calif. ... 6-3/289.
HIGH SCHOOL: Culver City (Calif.).
JUNIOR COLLEGE: El Camino Junior College (Calif.).
COLLEGE: Southern California.
TRANSACTIONS/CAREER NOTES: Signed as non-drafted free agent by San Francisco 49ers (May 8, 1992). ... On injured reserve with elbow injury (August 4, 1992-entire season). ... Inactive for six games (1993). ... On injured reserve with broken wrist (October 23, 1993-remainder of season). ... Granted free agency (February 17, 1995). ... Tendered offer sheet by St. Louis Rams (April 20, 1995). ... Offer matched by 49ers (April 21, 1995). ... Granted unconditional free agency (February 16, 1996). ... Re-signed by 49ers (June 4, 1996). ... Granted unconditional free agency (February 14, 1997). ... Re-signed by 49ers (April 22, 1997). ... Released by 49ers (February 26, 2004). ... Signed by Tampa Bay Buccaneers (March 4, 2004).
PLAYING EXPERIENCE: San Francisco NFL, 1994-2003; Tampa Bay NFL, 2004. ... Games/Games started: 1994 (16/15), 1995 (2/2), 1996 (16/0), 1997 (16/13), 1998 (16/16), 1999 (16/16), 2000 (13/13), 2001 (16/16), 2002 (14/14), 2003 (11/11), 2004 (16/16). Total: 152/132.
CHAMPIONSHIP GAME EXPERIENCE: Played in NFC championship game (1994 and 1997 seasons). ... Member of Super Bowl championship team (1994 season).

DELHOMME, JAKE   QB   PANTHERS

PERSONAL: Born January 10, 1975, in Breaux Bridge, La. ... 6-2/215.
HIGH SCHOOL: Teurlings (La.).
COLLEGE: Louisiana-Lafayette.
TRANSACTIONS/CAREER NOTES: Signed as non-drafted free agent by New Orleans Saints (June 10, 1997). ... Released by Saints (August 18, 1997). ... Re-signed by Saints to practice sqaud (November 19, 1997). ... Assigned by Saints to Amsterdam Admirals in 1998 NFL Europe enhancement allocation program (February 18, 1998). ... Inactive for five games (1998). ... Released by Saints (October 14, 1998). ... Re-signed by Saints to practice squad (October 15, 1998). ... Assigned by Saints to Frankfurt Galaxy in 1999 NFL Europe enhancement allocation program (February 22, 1999). ... Released by Saints (September 5, 1999). ... Re-signed by Saints (November 23, 1999). ... Granted free agency (March 1, 2002). ... Re-signed by Saints (April 19, 2002). ... Granted unconditional free agency (February 28, 2003). ... Signed by Carolina Panthers (March 5, 2003).
CHAMPIONSHIP GAME EXPERIENCE: Played in NFC championship game (2003 season). ... Played in Super Bowl 38 (2003 season).
POST SEASON RECORDS: Holds Super Bowl record for longest pass completion (to Muhsin Muhammad)—85 yards (February 1, 2004, vs. New England).
SINGLE GAME HIGHS (regular season): Attempts—50 (January 2, 2005, vs. New Orleans); completions—31 (October 19, 2003, vs. Tennessee); passing yards—362 (October 19, 2003, vs. Dallas); and touchdown passes—4 (December 26, 2004, vs. Tampa Bay).
STATISTICAL PLATEAUS: 300-yard passing games: 2003 (2), 2004 (4). Total: 6.
MISCELLANEOUS: Regular-season record as starting NFL quarterback: 18-15 (.545). ... Post-season record as NFL starting quarterback: 3-1 (.750).

D

Year	Team	G	GS	Att.	Cmp.	Pct.	Yds.	TD	Int.	Avg.	Skd.	Rat.	Att.	Yds.	Avg.	TD	TD	2pt.	Pts.
1999—New Orleans NFL		2	2	76	42	55.3	521	3	5	6.86	6	62.4	11	72	6.5	2	2	0	12
2000—New Orleans NFL		Did not play.																	
2002—New Orleans NFL		4	0	10	8	80.0	113	0	0	11.30	0	113.8	4	-2	-0.5	0	0	0	0
2003—Carolina NFL		16	15	449	266	59.2	3219	19	16	7.17	23	80.6	42	39	0.9	1	1	0	6
2004—Carolina NFL		16	16	533	310	58.2	3886	29	15	7.29	33	87.3	25	71	2.8	1	1	0	6
Pro totals (4 years)		38	33	1068	626	58.6	7739	51	36	7.25	62	83.0	82	180	2.2	4	4	0	24

DELOACH, JERRY — DE — TEXANS

PERSONAL: Born July 17, 1977, in Sacramento, Calif. ... 6-2/335.
HIGH SCHOOL: Valley (Calif.).
COLLEGE: California.
TRANSACTIONS/CAREER NOTES: Singed as non-drafted free agent by Washington Redskins (April 28, 2000). ... Traded by Redskins to Houston Texans for QB Danny Wuerffel (March 4, 2002). ... Re-signed by Texans (March 21, 2003). ... Granted free agency (March 3, 2004). ... Re-signed by Texans (April 28, 2004). ... Granted unconditional free agency (March 2, 2005). ... Re-signed by Texans (March 10, 2005).

Year	Team	G	GS	Tk.	Ast.	Sks.
2001—Washington NFL		15	4	9	2	1.0
2002—Houston NFL		16	16	24	8	1.0
2003—Houston NFL		16	16	37	14	0.0
2004—Houston NFL		15	3	17	8	0.0
Pro totals (4 years)		62	39	87	32	2.0

DELOATCH, CURTIS — CB — GIANTS

PERSONAL: Born October 4, 1981, in Murfreesboro, N.C. ... 6-2/217.
HIGH SCHOOL: Hertford County (Ahoskie, N.C.).
COLLEGE: North Carolina A&T.
TRANSACTIONS/CAREER NOTES: Signed as non-drafted free agent by New York Giants (May 7, 2004).

Year	Team	G	GS	Tk.	Ast.	Sks.	No.	Yds.	Avg.	TD
				TOTALS			**INTERCEPTIONS**			
2004—New York Giants NFL		16	0	15	2	0.0	0	0	0.0	0

DEMAR, ENOCH — T — BROWNS

PERSONAL: Born September 7, 1980, in Indianapolis, Ind. ... 6-4/320.
HIGH SCHOOL: Arsenal Tech (Indianapolis, Ind.).
COLLEGE: Indiana.
TRANSACTIONS/CAREER NOTES: Signed as non-drafted free agent by Cleveland Browns (May 2, 2003).
PLAYING EXPERIENCE: Cleveland NFL, 2003-2004. ... Games/Games started: 2003 (5/2), 2004 (15/11). Total: 20/13.

DEMPS, WILL — S

PERSONAL: Born November 7, 1979, in Charelston, S.C. ... 6-0/205. ... Full name: Will Henry Demps.
HIGH SCHOOL: Highlands (Palmdale, Calif.).
COLLEGE: San Diego State.
TRANSACTIONS/CAREER NOTES: Signed as non-drafted free agent by Baltimore Ravens (April 26, 2002). ... Granted free agency (March 2, 2005).

Year	Team	G	GS	Tk.	Ast.	Sks.	No.	Yds.	Avg.	TD
				TOTALS			**INTERCEPTIONS**			
2002—Baltimore NFL		14	10	43	6	1.0	1	18	18.0	0
2003—Baltimore NFL		16	9	31	8	0.0	2	57	28.5	0
2004—Baltimore NFL		16	16	64	19	2.5	1	0	0.0	0
Pro totals (3 years)		46	35	138	33	3.5	4	75	18.8	0

DEMULLING, RICK — G — LIONS

PERSONAL: Born July 21, 1977, in Cheney, Wash. ... 6-4/304. ... Full name: Rick Elwood DeMulling.
HIGH SCHOOL: Cheney (Wash.).
COLLEGE: Idaho.
TRANSACTIONS/CAREER NOTES: Selected by Indianapolis Colts in seventh round (220th pick overall) of 2001 NFL draft. ... Signed by Colts (June 19, 2001). ... Granted free agency (March 3, 2004). ... Re-signed by Colts (April 16, 2004). ... Granted unconditional free agency (March 2, 2005). ... Signed by Detriot Lions (March 16, 2005).
PLAYING EXPERIENCE: Indianapolis NFL, 2001-2004. ... Games/Games started: 2001 (7/0), 2002 (14/14), 2003 (16/16), 2004 (11/11). Total: 48/41.
CHAMPIONSHIP GAME EXPERIENCE: Played in AFC championship game (2003 season).

DENNEY, RYAN — DE — BILLS

PERSONAL: Born June 15, 1977, in Denver, Colo. ... 6-7/275.
HIGH SCHOOL: Horizon (Thornton, Colo.).
COLLEGE: Brigham Young.
TRANSACTIONS/CAREER NOTES: Selected by Buffalo Bills in second round (61st pick overall) of 2002 NFL draft. ... Signed by Bills (July 26, 2002).

Year Team	G	GS	TOTALS Tk.	Ast.	Sks.	INTERCEPTIONS No.	Yds.	Avg.	TD
2002—Buffalo NFL	8	0	6	3	0.0	0	0	0.0	0
2003—Buffalo NFL	16	13	27	16	3.5	0	0	0.0	0
2004—Buffalo NFL	16	5	12	20	3.0	0	0	0.0	0
Pro totals (3 years)	40	18	45	39	6.5	0	0	0.0	0

DENNIS, PAT — CB

PERSONAL: Born June 30, 1978, in Shreveport, La. ... 6-0/203. ... Full name: Patrick Dennis.
HIGH SCHOOL: Southwood (Shreveport, La.).
COLLEGE: Louisiana-Monroe.
TRANSACTIONS/CAREER NOTES: Selected after junior season by Kansas City Chiefs in fifth round (162nd pick overall) of 2000 NFL draft. ... Signed by Chiefs (July 20, 2000). ... On injured reserve with knee injury (September 1-October 3, 2001). ... Claimed on waivers by Dallas Cowboys (October 3, 2001). ... Claimed on waivers by Houston Texans (September 2, 2002). ... On injured reserve with knee injury (October 22, 2002-remainder of season). ... Granted free agency (February 28, 2003). ... Re-signed by Texans (March 18, 2003). ... Granted unconditional free agency (March 3, 2004). ... Re-signed by Texans (March 30, 2004). ... Released by Texans (April 27, 2004). ... Signed by Washington Redskins (October 13, 2004). ... Granted unconditional free agency (March 2, 2005).

Year Team	G	GS	TOTALS Tk.	Ast.	Sks.	INTERCEPTIONS No.	Yds.	Avg.	TD
2000—Kansas City NFL	16	13	0	0	0.0	1	0	0.0	0
2001—Dallas NFL	11	0	0	0	0.0	0	0	0.0	0
2002—Houston NFL	3	0	0	0	0.0	0	0	0.0	0
2004—Washington NFL	11	0	1	0	0.0	0	0	0.0	0
Pro totals (4 years)	41	13	1	0	0.0	1	0	0.0	0

DETMER, KOY — QB — EAGLES

PERSONAL: Born July 5, 1973, in San Antonio, Texas. ... 6-1/195. ... Full name: Koy Dennis Detmer. ... Brother of Ty Detmer, quarterback, Atlanta Falcons.
HIGH SCHOOL: Mission (Texas).
COLLEGE: Colorado.
TRANSACTIONS/CAREER NOTES: Selected by Philadelphia Eagles in seventh round (207th pick overall) of 1997 NFL draft. ... Signed by Eagles (June 4, 1997). ... On injured reserve with knee injury (August 22, 1997-entire season). ... Granted free agency (February 11, 2000). ... Re-signed by Eagles (April 17, 2000).
CHAMPIONSHIP GAME EXPERIENCE: Played in NFC championship game (2001-2004 seasons). ... Played in Super Bowl 39 (2004 season).
SINGLE GAME HIGHS (regular season): Attempts—43 (December 20, 1998, vs. Dallas); completions—24 (December 20, 1998, vs. Dallas); yards—231 (December 20, 1998, vs. Dallas); and touchdown passes—3 (December 19, 1999, vs. New England).
MISCELLANEOUS: Regular-season record as starting NFL quarterback: 3-5 (.375).

Year Team	G	GS	PASSING Att.	Cmp.	Pct.	Yds.	TD	Int.	Avg.	Skd.	Rat.	RUSHING Att.	Yds.	Avg.	TD	TOTALS TD	2pt.	Pts.
1997—Philadelphia NFL	Did not play.																	
1998—Philadelphia NFL	8	5	181	97	53.6	1011	5	5	5.59	5	67.7	7	20	2.9	0	0	0	0
1999—Philadelphia NFL	1	1	29	10	34.5	181	3	2	6.24	0	62.6	2	-2	-1.0	0	0	0	0
2000—Philadelphia NFL	16	0	1	0	0.0	0	0	1	0.00	0	0.0	1	8	8.0	0	0	0	0
2001—Philadelphia NFL	16	0	14	5	35.7	51	0	1	3.64	0	17.3	8	6	0.8	0	0	0	0
2002—Philadelphia NFL	14	1	28	19	67.9	224	2	0	8.00	1	115.8	2	4	2.0	1	1	0	6
2003—Philadelphia NFL	16	0	5	3	60.0	32	0	0	6.40	0	78.8	0	0	0.0	0	0	0	0
2004—Philadelphia NFL	16	1	40	18	45.0	207	0	2	5.18	2	40.3	10	-7	-0.7	0	0	0	0
Pro totals (7 years)	87	8	298	152	51.0	1706	10	11	5.72	9	64.2	30	29	1.0	1	1	0	6

DETMER, TY — QB — FALCONS

PERSONAL: Born October 30, 1967, in San Marcos, Texas. ... 6-0/189. ... Full name: Ty Hubert Detmer. ... Brother of Koy Detmer, quarterback, Philadelphia Eagles.
HIGH SCHOOL: Southwest (San Antonio).
COLLEGE: Brigham Young.
TRANSACTIONS/CAREER NOTES: Selected by Green Bay Packers in ninth round (230th pick overall) of 1992 NFL draft. ... Signed by Packers (July 22, 1992). ... Active for two games (1992); did not play. ... Active for five games (1994); did not play. ... On injured reserve with thumb injury (November 8, 1995-remainder of season). ... Granted unconditional free agency (February 16, 1996). ... Signed by Philadelphia Eagles (March 1, 1996). ... Granted unconditional free agency (February 13, 1998). ... Signed by San Francisco 49ers (March 12, 1998). ... Traded by 49ers with fourth-round pick (LB Wali Rainer) in 1999 draft to Cleveland Browns for fourth- (traded to Indianapolis) and fifth-round (traded to Miami) picks in 1999 draft (February 23, 1999). ... On injured reserve with Achilles' tendon injury (August 16, 2000-entire season). ... Traded by Browns to Detroit Lions for undisclosed pick in 2002 draft (September 2, 2001). ... Granted unconditional free agency (March 3, 2004). ... Signed by Atlanta Falcons (March 30, 2004). ... Granted unconditional free agency (March 2, 2005). ... Re-signed by Falcons (March 28, 2005).
CHAMPIONSHIP GAME EXPERIENCE: Member of Falcons for NFC championship game (2004 season); inactive.
HONORS: Heisman Trophy winner (1990). ... Maxwell Award winner (1990). ... Davey O'Brien Award winner (1990 and 1991). ... Named quarterback on THE SPORTING NEWS college All-America first team (1990 and 1991).
SINGLE GAME HIGHS (regular season): Attempts—51 (December 30, 2001, vs. Chicago); completions—31 (Decmeber 30, 2001, vs. Chicago); yards—342 (October 27, 1996, vs. Carolina); and touchdown passes—4 (October 20, 1996, vs. Miami).
STATISTICAL PLATEAUS: 300-yard passing games: 1996 (3), 2001 (1). Total: 4.
MISCELLANEOUS: Regular-season record as starting NFL quarterback: 11-14 (.440). ... Postseason record as starting NFL quarterback: 0-1.

Year Team	G	GS	PASSING Att.	Cmp.	Pct.	Yds.	TD	Int.	Avg.	Skd.	Rat.	RUSHING Att.	Yds.	Avg.	TD	TOTALS TD	2pt.	Pts.
1992_Green Bay NFL	Did not play.																	
1993_Green Bay NFL	3	0	5	3	60.0	26	0	0	5.20	0	73.7	1	-2	-2.0	0	0	0	0
1994_Green Bay NFL	Did not play.																	

Year Team	G	GS	Att.	Cmp.	Pct.	Yds.	TD	Int.	Avg.	Skd.	Rat.	Att.	Yds.	Avg.	TD	TD	2pt.	Pts.
					PASSING								**RUSHING**				**TOTALS**	
1995_Green Bay NFL	4	0	16	8	50.0	81	1	1	5.06	0	59.6	3	3	1.0	0	0	0	0
1996_Philadelphia NFL	13	11	401	238	59.4	2911	15	13	7.26	27	80.8	31	59	1.9	1	1	0	6
1997_Philadelphia NFL	8	7	244	134	54.9	1567	7	6	6.42	19	73.9	14	46	3.3	1	1	0	6
1998_San Francisco NFL	16	1	38	24	63.2	312	4	3	8.21	5	91.1	8	7	0.9	0	0	0	0
1999_Cleveland NFL	5	2	91	47	51.6	548	4	2	6.02	4	75.7	6	38	6.3	1	1	0	6
2000_Cleveland NFL	Did not play.																	
2001_Detroit NFL	4	4	151	92	60.9	906	3	10	6.00	12	56.9	9	26	2.9	0	0	0	0
2002_Detroit NFL	Did not play.																	
2003_Detroit NFL	1	0	0	0	0.0	0	0	0	0.00	0	0.0	0	0	0.0	0	0	0	0
2004_Detroit NFL	Did not play.																	
Pro totals (8 years)	54	25	946	546	57.7	6351	34	35	6.71	67	74.7	72	177	2.5	3	3	0	18

DEVRIES, JARED   DE   LIONS

PERSONAL: Born June 11, 1976, in Aplington, Iowa. ... 6-4/275.
HIGH SCHOOL: Aplington-Parkersburg (Aplington, Iowa).
COLLEGE: Iowa.
TRANSACTIONS/CAREER NOTES: Selected by Detroit Lions in third round (70th pick overall) of 1999 NFL draft. ... Signed by Lions (July 28, 1999). ... On physically unable to perform list with blood clot (July 24-October 27, 2001). ... Granted free agency (March 1, 2002). ... Re-signed by Lions (April 16, 2002). ... On injured reserve with foot injury (December 11, 2002-remainder of season). ... Granted unconditional free agency (February 28, 2003). ... Re-signed by Lions (March 5, 2003).
HONORS: Named defensive tackle on THE SPORTING NEWS college All-America third team (1997). ... Named defensive tackle on THE SPORTING NEWS college All-America first team (1998).

Year Team	G	GS	Tk.	Ast.	Sks.
			TOTALS		
1999—Detroit NFL	2	0	0	0	0.0
2000—Detroit NFL	15	1	14	8	0.0
2001—Detroit NFL	11	0	9	4	0.0
2002—Detroit NFL	10	0	5	5	1.0
2003—Detroit NFL	13	2	8	6	1.0
2004—Detroit NFL	15	0	16	9	3.0
Pro totals (6 years)	66	3	52	32	5.0

DIAMOND, LORENZO   TE

PERSONAL: Born December 15, 1978, in Biloxi, Miss. ... 6-3/260.
HIGH SCHOOL: Biloxi (Miss.).
COLLEGE: Auburn.
TRANSACTIONS/CAREER NOTES: Signed as non-drafted free agent by Arizona Cardinals (April 28, 2003). ... Released by Cardinals (August 30, 2003). ... Re-signed by Cardinals to practice squad (September 1, 2003). ... Activated (December 20, 2003). ... Released by Cardinals (December 15, 2004). ... Re-signed by Cardinals to practice squad (December 16, 2004). ... Activated (January 4, 2005). ... Released by Cardinals (May 18, 2005).
SINGLE GAME HIGHS (regular season): Receptions—1 (October 10, 2004, vs. San Francisco); yards—8 (October 10, 2004, vs. San Francisco); touchdown receptions—0.

Year Team	G	GS	No.	Yds.	Avg.	TD	TD	2pt.	Pts.	Fum.
			RECEIVING				**TOTALS**			
2004—Arizona NFL	5	4	3	19	6.3	0	0	0	0	0

DIEDRICK, DAHRRAN   RB   REDSKINS

PERSONAL: Born January 11, 1979, in Montego Bay, Jamaica. ... 6-0/225.
HIGH SCHOOL: Cedarbrae Collegiate Institute (Scarborough, Ontario).
COLLEGE: Nebraska.
TRANSACTIONS/CAREER NOTES: Signed as non-drafted free agent by San Diego Chargers (May 2, 2003). ... Released by Chargers (August 31, 2003). ... Signed by Green Bay Packers to practice squad (September 24, 2003). ... Released by Packers (October 20, 2003). ... Re-signed by Packers to practice squad (November 13, 2003). ... Activated (January 27, 2004). ... Released by Packers (August 29, 2004). ... Signed by Washington Redskins to practice squad (October 29, 2004). ... Activated (December 29, 2004). ... Assigned by Redskins to Rhein Fire in 2005 NFL Europe enhancement allocation program (February 14, 2005).

Year Team	G	GS	Att.	Yds.	Avg.	TD	TD	2pt.	Pts.	Fum.
			RUSHING				**TOTALS**			
2004—Washington NFL	1	0	0	0	0.0	0	0	0	0	0

DIEHL, DAVID   G   GIANTS

PERSONAL: Born September 15, 1980, in Chicago, Ill. ... 6-5/315. ... Full name: David Michael Diehl.
HIGH SCHOOL: Brother Rice (Oak Lawn, Ill.).
COLLEGE: Illinois.
TRANSACTIONS/CAREER NOTES: Selected by New York Giants in fifth round (160th pick overall) of 2003 NFL draft. ... Signed by Giants (June 12, 2003).
PLAYING EXPERIENCE: New York Giants NFL, 2003-2004. ... Games/Games started: 2003 (16/16), 2004 (16/16). Total: 32/32.

DIELMAN, KRIS   G   CHARGERS

PERSONAL: Born February 3, 1981, in Goshen, Ind. ... 6-4/310.
HIGH SCHOOL: Troy (Ohio).
COLLEGE: Indiana.
TRANSACTIONS/CAREER NOTES: Signed as non-drafted free agent by San Diego Chargers (May 2, 2003). ... Waived by Chargers (August 26, 2003). ... Re-signed by Chargers to practice squad (September 2, 2003). ... Activated (October 16, 2003).
PLAYING EXPERIENCE: San Diego NFL, 2003-2004. ... Games/Games started: 2003 (6/0), 2004 (15/0). Total: 21/0.

DIEM, RYAN   G   COLTS

PERSONAL: Born July 1, 1979, in Carol Stream, Ill. ... 6-6/331.
HIGH SCHOOL: Glenbard North (Carol Stream, Ill.).
COLLEGE: Northern Illinois.
TRANSACTIONS/CAREER NOTES: Selected by Indianapolis Colts in fourth round (118th pick overall) of 2001 NFL draft. ... Signed by Colts (July 19, 2001). ... Granted free agency (March 3, 2004). ... Re-signed by Colts (April 20, 2004).
PLAYING EXPERIENCE: Indianapolis NFL, 2001-2004. ... Games/Games started: 2001 (15/8), 2002 (16/16), 2003 (13/13), 2004 (16/16). Total: 60/53.
CHAMPIONSHIP GAME EXPERIENCE: Played in AFC championship game (2003 season).

DIGGS, NA'IL   LB   PACKERS

PERSONAL: Born July 8, 1978, in Phoenix, Ariz. ... 6-4/237. ... Full name: Na'il Ronald Diggs.
HIGH SCHOOL: Dorsey (Los Angeles).
COLLEGE: Ohio State.
TRANSACTIONS/CAREER NOTES: Selected after junior season by Green Bay Packers in fourth round (98th pick overall) of 2000 NFL draft. ... Signed by Packers (June 19, 2000). ... Granted free agency (February 28, 2003). ... Tendered offer sheet by Detroit Lions (March 21, 2003). ... Offer matched by Packers (March 28, 2003).

				TOTALS			INTERCEPTIONS			
Year Team	G	GS	Tk.	Ast.	Sks.	No.	Yds.	Avg.	TD
2000—Green Bay NFL	13	12	24	9	0.0	0	0	0.0	0
2001—Green Bay NFL	16	16	51	16	2.0	0	0	0.0	0
2002—Green Bay NFL	16	16	65	19	3.0	2	62	31.0	0
2003—Green Bay NFL	16	16	76	11	1.0	2	13	6.5	0
2004—Green Bay NFL	14	14	61	19	1.0	0	0	0.0	0
Pro totals (5 years)	75	74	277	74	7.0	4	75	18.8	0

DILFER, TRENT   QB   BROWNS

PERSONAL: Born March 13, 1972, in Santa Cruz, Calif. ... 6-4/225. ... Full name: Trent Farris Dilfer.
HIGH SCHOOL: Aptos (Calif.).
COLLEGE: Fresno State.
TRANSACTIONS/CAREER NOTES: Selected after junior season by Tampa Bay Buccaneers in first round (sixth pick overall) of 1994 NFL draft. ... Signed by Buccaneers (August 3, 1994). ... Granted unconditional free agency (January 25, 2000). ... Signed by Baltimore Ravens (March 8, 2000). ... Granted unconditional free agency (March 2, 2001). ... Signed by Seattle Seahawks (August 3, 2001). ... Granted unconditional free agency (March 1, 2002). ... Re-signed by Seahawks (March 5, 2002). ... On injured reserve with knee and Achillies' injuries (October 29, 2002-remainder of season). ... Traded by Seahawks to Cleveland Browns for fourth-round pick (traded to Carolina) in 2005 draft (March 7, 2005).
CHAMPIONSHIP GAME EXPERIENCE: Member of Buccaneers for NFC championship game (1999 season); inactive. ... Played in AFC championship game (2000 season). ... Member of Super Bowl championship team (2000 season).
HONORS: Played in Pro Bowl (1997 season).
SINGLE GAME HIGHS (regular season): Attempts—48 (November 26, 1995, vs. Green Bay); completions—30 (November 17, 1996, vs. San Diego); yards—352 (September 15, 2002, vs. Arizona); and touchdown passes—4 (September 21, 1997, vs. Miami).
STATISTICAL PLATEAUS: 300-yard passing games: 1995 (1), 1996 (1), 1999 (1), 2002 (1). Total: 4.
MISCELLANEOUS: Regular-season record as starting NFL quarterback: 53-43 (.552). ... Postseason record as starting NFL quarterback: 5-1 (.833).

			PASSING								RUSHING				TOTALS		
Year Team	G	GS	Att.	Cmp.	Pct.	Yds.	TD	Int.	Avg.	Skd.	Rat.	Att.	Yds.	Avg.	TD	TD	2pt.	Pts.
1994—Tampa Bay NFL	5	2	82	38	46.3	433	1	6	5.28	8	36.3	2	27	13.5	0	0	0	0
1995—Tampa Bay NFL	16	16	415	224	54.0	2774	4	18	6.68	47	60.1	23	115	5.0	2	2	0	12
1996—Tampa Bay NFL	16	16	482	267	55.4	2859	12	19	5.93	28	64.8	32	124	3.9	0	0	0	0
1997—Tampa Bay NFL	16	16	386	217	56.2	2555	21	11	6.62	32	82.8	33	99	3.0	1	1	0	6
1998—Tampa Bay NFL	16	16	429	225	52.4	2729	21	15	6.36	27	74.0	40	141	3.5	2	2	0	12
1999—Tampa Bay NFL	10	10	244	146	59.8	1619	11	11	6.64	26	75.8	35	144	4.1	0	0	0	0
2000—Baltimore NFL	11	8	226	134	59.3	1502	12	11	6.65	23	76.6	20	75	3.8	0	0	0	0
2001—Seattle NFL	7	4	122	73	59.8	1014	7	4	8.31	10	92.0	11	17	1.5	0	0	0	0
2002—Seattle NFL	6	6	168	94	56.0	1182	4	6	7.04	7	71.1	10	27	2.7	0	0	0	0
2003—Seattle NFL	5	0	8	4	50.0	31	1	1	3.88	1	59.9	2	-1	-0.5	0	0	0	0
2004—Seattle NFL	5	2	58	25	43.1	333	1	3	5.74	4	46.1	10	14	1.4	0	0	0	0
Pro totals (11 years)	113	96	2620	1447	55.2	17031	95	105	6.50	213	70.6	218	782	3.6	5	5	0	30

DILGER, KEN   TE

PERSONAL: Born February 2, 1971, in Mariah Hill, Ind. ... 6-5/250. ... Full name: Kenneth Ray Dilger. ... Name pronounced: DIL-gur.
HIGH SCHOOL: Heritage Hills (Lincoln City, Ind.).
COLLEGE: Illinois.

TRANSACTIONS/CAREER NOTES: Selected by Indianapolis Colts in second round (48th pick overall) of 1995 NFL draft. ... Signed by Colts (July 15, 1995). ... Released by Colts (February 21, 2002). ... Signed by Tampa Bay Buccaneers (April 17, 2002). ... Released by Buccaneers (March 2, 2004). ... Re-signed by Buccaneers (March 24, 2004). ... Granted unconditional free agency (March 2, 2005).
CHAMPIONSHIP GAME EXPERIENCE: Played in AFC championship game (1995 season). ... Played in NFC championship game (2002 season). ... Member of Super Bowl championship team (2002 season).
HONORS: Played in Pro Bowl (2001 season).
SINGLE GAME HIGHS (regular season): Receptions—8 (September 10, 2000, vs. Oakland); yards—156 (September 8, 1996, vs. New York Jets); and touchdown receptions—3 (December 14, 1997, vs. Miami).
STATISTICAL PLATEAUS: 100-yard receiving games: 1995 (1), 1996 (1), 1997 (1). Total: 3.

			RECEIVING				TOTALS			
Year Team	G	GS	No.	Yds.	Avg.	TD	TD	2pt.	Pts.	Fum.
1995—Indianapolis NFL	16	13	42	635	15.1	4	4	0	24	0
1996—Indianapolis NFL	16	16	42	503	12.0	4	4	0	24	1
1997—Indianapolis NFL	14	14	27	380	14.1	3	3	0	18	0
1998—Indianapolis NFL	16	16	31	303	9.8	1	1	1	8	0
1999—Indianapolis NFL	15	15	40	479	12.0	2	2	0	12	1
2000—Indianapolis NFL	16	16	47	538	11.4	3	3	0	18	1
2001—Indianapolis NFL	16	16	32	343	10.7	1	1	1	8	2
2002—Tampa Bay NFL	16	15	34	329	9.7	2	2	0	12	1
2003—Tampa Bay NFL	15	15	22	244	11.1	1	1	0	6	1
2004—Tampa Bay NFL	16	14	39	345	8.8	3	3	1	20	0
Pro totals (10 years)	156	150	356	4099	11.5	24	24	3	150	7

DILLON, COREY   RB   PATRIOTS

PERSONAL: Born October 24, 1974, in Seattle, Wash. ... 6-1/225.
HIGH SCHOOL: Franklin (Seattle).
JUNIOR COLLEGE: Garden City (Kan.) Community College, then Dixie College (Utah).
COLLEGE: Washington.
TRANSACTIONS/CAREER NOTES: Selected after junior season by Cincinnati Bengals in second round (43rd pick overall) of 1997 NFL draft. ... Signed by Bengals (July 21, 1997). ... Granted free agency (February 11, 2000). ... Re-signed by Bengals (August 9, 2000). ... Designated by Bengals as transition player (February 12, 2001). ... Re-signed by Bengals (May 11, 2001). ... Traded by Bengals to New England Patriots for second-round pick (S Madieu Williams) in 2004 draft (April 19, 2004).
CHAMPIONSHIP GAME EXPERIENCE: Played in AFC championship game (2004 season). ... Member of Super Bowl championship team (2004 season).
HONORS: Named running back on THE SPORTING NEWS college All-America second team (1996). ... Played in Pro Bowl (1999-2001 seasons). ... Named to play in Pro Bowl (2004 season); replaced by Jerome Bettis due to injury.
SINGLE GAME HIGHS (regular season): Attempts—39 (December 4, 1997, vs. Tennessee); yards—278 (October 22, 2000, vs. Denver); and rushing touchdowns—4 (December 4, 1997, vs. Tennessee).
STATISTICAL PLATEAUS: 100-yard rushing games: 1997 (4), 1998 (4), 1999 (5), 2000 (5), 2001 (4), 2002 (5), 2003 (1), 2004 (9). Total: 37.
MISCELLANEOUS: Selected by San Diego Padres organization in 34th round of free agent draft (June 3, 1993); did not sign. ... Holds Cincinnati Bengals all-time record for most yards rushing (8,061).

			RUSHING				RECEIVING				KICKOFF RETURNS				TOTALS			
Year Team	G	GS	Att.	Yds.	Avg.	TD	No.	Yds.	Avg.	TD	No.	Yds.	Avg.	TD	TD	2pt.	Pts.	Fum.
1997—Cincinnati NFL	16	6	233	1129	4.8	10	27	259	9.6	0	6	182	30.3	0	10	0	60	1
1998—Cincinnati NFL	15	15	262	1130	4.3	4	28	178	6.4	1	0	0	0.0	0	5	0	30	2
1999—Cincinnati NFL	15	15	263	1200	4.6	5	31	290	9.4	1	1	4	4.0	0	6	0	36	3
2000—Cincinnati NFL	16	16	315	1435	4.6	7	18	158	8.8	0	0	0	0.0	0	7	0	42	4
2001—Cincinnati NFL	16	16	§340	1315	3.9	10	34	228	6.7	3	0	0	0.0	0	13	0	78	5
2002—Cincinnati NFL	16	16	314	1311	4.2	7	43	298	6.9	0	0	0	0.0	0	7	0	42	5
2003—Cincinnati NFL	13	11	138	541	3.9	2	11	71	6.5	0	0	0	0.0	0	2	0	12	0
2004—New England NFL	15	14	345	1635	4.7	12	15	103	6.9	1	0	0	0.0	0	13	1	80	5
Pro totals (8 years)	122	109	2210	9696	4.4	57	207	1585	7.7	6	7	186	26.6	0	63	1	380	25

DINAPOLI, GENNARO   C

PERSONAL: Born May 25, 1975, in Manhasset, N.Y. ... 6-3/287. ... Full name: Gennaro L. DiNapoli. ... Name pronounced: den-ah-POLE-e.
HIGH SCHOOL: Cazenovia (N.Y.), then Milford (Conn.) Academy.
COLLEGE: Virginia Tech.
TRANSACTIONS/CAREER NOTES: Selected by Oakland Raiders in fourth round (109th pick overall) of 1998 NFL draft. ... Signed by Raiders (July 24, 1998). ... Active for four games (1998); did not play. ... Traded by Raiders to Tennessee Titans for undisclosed pick (August 27, 2000). ... Granted unconditional free agency (March 1, 2002). ... Re-signed by Titans (April 19, 2002). ... Released by Titans (February 27, 2003). ... Signed by Dallas Cowboys (August 7, 2003). ... On injured reserve with ankle injury (October 29, 2003-remainder of season). ... Granted unconditional free agency (March 3, 2004). ... Re-signed by Cowboys (March 8, 2004). ... On physically unable to perform list with leg injury (August 31, 2004-entire season). ... Released by Cowboys (February 22, 2005).
PLAYING EXPERIENCE: Oakland NFL, 1999; Tennessee NFL, 2001-2002; Dallas NFL, 2003-2004. ... Games/Games started: 1999 (11/9), 2001 (5/2), 2002 (16/16), 2003 (7/0), Total: 39/27.
CHAMPIONSHIP GAME EXPERIENCE: Played in AFC championship game (2002 season).

DINGLE, ADRIAN   DE   CHARGERS

PERSONAL: Born June 25, 1977, in Holly Hill, S.C. ... 6-3/296. ... Full name: Adrian Kennell Dingle.
HIGH SCHOOL: Holly Hill (S.C.)-Roberts.
COLLEGE: Clemson.
TRANSACTIONS/CAREER NOTES: Selected by San Diego Chargers in fifth round (139th pick overall) of 1999 NFL draft. ... Signed by Chargers (July 23, 1999). ... On physically unable to perform list with knee injury (August 31-November 17, 1999). ... Active for two games (1999); did

not play. ... Granted free agency (March 1, 2002). ... Re-signed by Chargers (March 29, 2002). ... Granted unconditional free agency (February 28, 2003). ... Re-signed by Chargers (March 11, 2003).

					TOTALS			INTERCEPTIONS			
Year Team	G	GS	Tk.	Ast.	Sks.		No.	Yds.	Avg.	TD	
1999—San Diego NFL		Did not play.									
2000—San Diego NFL	14	1	15	1	2.5		0	0	0.0	0	
2001—San Diego NFL	14	0	10	1	1.0		0	0	0.0	0	
2002—San Diego NFL	16	3	24	1	4.0		0	0	0.0	0	
2003—San Diego NFL	16	15	31	6	6.0		0	0	0.0	0	
2004—San Diego NFL	10	2	3	3	1.0		1	1	1.0	0	
Pro totals (5 years)	70	21	83	12	14.5		1	1	1.0	0	

DINKINS, DARNELL — TE — RAVENS

PERSONAL: Born January 20, 1977, in Pittsburgh, Pa. ... 6-3/255. ... Full name: Darnell Joseph Dinkins.
HIGH SCHOOL: Schenley (Pittsburgh).
COLLEGE: Pittsburgh.
TRANSACTIONS/CAREER NOTES: Signed as non-drafted free agent by New York Giants (January 31, 2002). ... Assigned by Giants to Rhein Fire in 2002 NFL Europe enhancement allocation program (February 12, 2002). ... On injured reserve with foot injury (November 1, 2002-remainder of season). ... Waived by Giants (August 31, 2003). ... Re-signed by Giants to practice squad (September 1, 2003). ... Activated (November 15, 2003). ... Released by Giants (July 28, 2004). ... Signed by Baltimore Ravens to practice squad (October 4, 2004). ... Activated (October 29, 2004). ... Granted free agency (March 2, 2005). ... Re-signed by Ravens (March 16, 2005).
SINGLE GAME HIGHS (regular season): Receptions—3 (November 21, 2004, vs. Dallas); yards—40 (November 21, 2004, vs. Dallas); and touchdown receptions—1 (November 21, 2004, vs. Dallas).

			RECEIVING				TOTALS			
Year Team	G	GS	No.	Yds.	Avg.	TD	TD	2pt.	Pts.	Fum.
2002—New York Giants NFL	2	0	0	0	0.0	0	0	0	0	0
2003—New York Giants NFL	7	0	2	16	8.0	0	0	0	0	0
2004—Baltimore NFL	10	4	9	94	10.4	1	1	0	6	0
Pro totals (3 years)	19	4	11	110	10.0	1	1	0	6	0

DISHMAN, CHRIS — G

PERSONAL: Born February 27, 1974, in Cozad, Neb. ... 6-3/375.
HIGH SCHOOL: Cozad (Neb.).
COLLEGE: Nebraska.
TRANSACTIONS/CAREER NOTES: Selected by Arizona Cardinals in fourth round (106th pick overall) of 1997 NFL draft. ... Signed by Cardinals (July 9, 1997). ... Granted free agency (February 11, 2000). ... Re-signed by Cardinals (April 28, 2000) ... Granted unconditional free agency (March 2, 2001). ... Re-signed by Cardinals (March 5, 2001). ... Granted unconditional free agency (March 3, 2004). ... Signed by St. Louis Rams (August 5, 2004). ... On injured reserve with knee injury (December 28, 2004-remainder of season). ... Granted unconditional free agency (March 2, 2005).
PLAYING EXPERIENCE: Arizona NFL, 1997-2003; St. Louis NFL, 2004. ... Games/Games started: 1997 (8/0), 1998 (12/11), 1999 (13/10), 2000 (15/12), 2001 (16/5), 2002 (14/14), 2003 (14/2), 2004 (7/5). Total: 99/59.

DIXON, DAVID — G

PERSONAL: Born January 5, 1969, in Papakura, New Zealand. ... 6-5/343. ... Full name: David Tukatahi Dixon.
HIGH SCHOOL: Pukekohe (New Zealand).
JUNIOR COLLEGE: Ricks College (Idaho).
COLLEGE: Arizona State.
TRANSACTIONS/CAREER NOTES: Selected by New England Patriots in ninth-round (232nd pick overall) of 1992 draft. ... Signed by Patriots for 1992 season. ... Released by Patriots (August 1992). ... Signed by Minnesota Vikings to practice squad (October 20, 1992). ... Released by Vikings (August 23, 1993). ... Signed by Dallas Cowboys to practice squad (September 8, 1993). ... Granted free agency after 1993 season. ... Signed by Vikings (July 12, 1994). ... Granted free agency (February 14, 1997). ... Re-signed by Vikings (May 1, 1997). ... Granted unconditional free agency (February 13, 1998). ... Re-signed by Vikings (February 17, 1998). ... On physically unable to perform list with knee injury (August 1-10, 1999). ... Granted unconditional free agency (March 2, 2005).
PLAYING EXPERIENCE: Minnesota NFL, 1994-2004. ... Games/Games started: 1994 (1/0), 1995 (15/6), 1996 (13/6), 1997 (13/13), 1998 (16/16), 1999 (16/16), 2000 (16/16), 2001 (15/14), 2002 (15/15), 2003 (16/16), 2004 (16/16). Total: 152/134.
CHAMPIONSHIP GAME EXPERIENCE: Played in NFC championship game (1998 and 2000 seasons).

DIXON, TONY — S

PERSONAL: Born June 18, 1979, in Tuscaloosa, Ala. ... 6-1/210.
HIGH SCHOOL: Pickens County (Reform, Ala.).
COLLEGE: Alabama.
TRANSACTIONS/CAREER NOTES: Selected by Dallas Cowboys in second round (56th pick overall) of 2001 NFL draft. ... Signed by Cowboys (July 21, 2001). ... Granted unconditional free agency (March 2, 2005).

				TOTALS			INTERCEPTIONS			
Year Team	G	GS	Tk.	Ast.	Sks.		No.	Yds.	Avg.	TD
2001—Dallas NFL	8	0	5	2	1.0		0	0	0.0	0
2002—Dallas NFL	16	7	31	9	2.0		1	0	0.0	0
2003—Dallas NFL	16	0	0	0	0.0		0	0	0.0	0
2004—Dallas NFL	16	7	28	2	3.0		0	0	0.0	0
Pro totals (4 years)	56	14	64	13	6.0		1	0	0.0	0

DOCKERY, DERRICK — G — REDSKINS

PERSONAL: Born September 7, 1980, in Garland, Texas. ... 6-6/345.
HIGH SCHOOL: Lakeview Centennial (Lakeview, Texas).
COLLEGE: Texas.
TRANSACTIONS/CAREER NOTES: Selected by Washington Redskins in third round (81st pick overall) of 2003 NFL draft. ... Signed by Redskins (July 28, 2003).
PLAYING EXPERIENCE: Washington NFL, 2003-2004. ... Games/Games started: 2003 (16/13), 2004 (16/16). Total: 32/29.

DOCKETT, DARNELL — DT — CARDINALS

PERSONAL: Born May 27, 1981, in Burtonville, Md. ... 6-4/301.
HIGH SCHOOL: Paint Branch (Burtonsville, Md.).
COLLEGE: Florida State.
TRANSACTIONS/CAREER NOTES: Selected by Arizona Cardinals in third round (64th pick overall) of 2004 NFL draft. ... Signed by Cardinals (August 4, 2004).
HONORS: Named defensive lineman on THE SPORTING NEWS Freshman All-America first team (2000). ... Named defensive tackle on THE SPORTING NEWS college All-America second team (2003).

Year Team	G	GS	TOTALS Tk.	Ast.	Sks.	INTERCEPTIONS No.	Yds.	Avg.	TD
2004—Arizona NFL	16	15	35	5	3.5	1	20	20.0	0

DOERING, CHRIS — WR

PERSONAL: Born May 19, 1973, in Gainesville, Fla. ... 6-4/201. ... Full name: Christopher Paul Doering. ... Name pronounced: DOOR-ing.
HIGH SCHOOL: P.K. Yonge (Gainesville, Fla.).
COLLEGE: Florida.
TRANSACTIONS/CAREER NOTES: Selected by Jacksonville Jaguars in sixth round (185th pick overall) of 1996 NFL draft. ... Signed by Jaguars (June 5, 1996). ... Claimed on waivers by New York Jets (August 20, 1996). ... Released by Jets (August 25, 1996). ... Signed by Indianapolis Colts to practice squad (August 27, 1996). ... Activated (December 20, 1996). ... Released by Colts (August 24, 1997). ... Re-signed by Colts to practice squad (August 25, 1997). ... Activated (December 5, 1997). ... Claimed on waivers by Cincinnati Bengals (February 25, 1998). ... Released by Bengals (September 2, 1998). ... Signed by Denver Broncos (February 3, 1999). ... Released by Broncos (August 7, 2000). ... Re-signed by Broncos (August 6, 2001). ... Released by Broncos (August 28, 2001). ... Signed by Washington Redskins (February 21, 2002). ... Granted free agency (February 28, 2003). ... Signed by Pittsburgh Steelers (May 20, 2003). ... Granted unconditional free agency (March 3, 2004). ... Re-signed by Steelers (March 4, 2004). ... Released by Steelers (September 18, 2004). ... Re-signed by Steelers (November 24, 2004). ... Released by Steelers (December 31, 2004).
SINGLE GAME HIGHS (regular season): Receptions—4 (November 17, 2003, vs. San Francisco); yards—62 (November 9, 2003, vs. Arizona); and touchdown receptions—1 (November 9, 2003, vs. Arizona).

Year Team	G	GS	RECEIVING No.	Yds.	Avg.	TD	TOTALS TD	2pt.	Pts.	Fum.
1996—Indianapolis NFL	1	0	1	10	10.0	0	0	0	0	0
1997—Indianapolis NFL	2	0	2	12	6.0	0	0	0	0	0
1999—Denver NFL	3	0	3	22	7.3	0	0	0	0	0
2002—Washington NFL	15	3	18	192	10.7	2	2	1	14	1
2003—Pittsburgh NFL	16	0	18	240	13.3	1	1	0	6	0
2004—Pittsburgh NFL	3	0	0	0	0.0	0	0	0	0	0
Pro totals (6 years)	40	3	42	476	11.3	3	3	1	20	1

DOERING, JASON — S

PERSONAL: Born April 22, 1978, in Rhinelander, Wis. ... 6-0/201. ... Full name: Jason James Doering.
HIGH SCHOOL: Rhinelander (Wis.).
COLLEGE: Wisconsin.
TRANSACTIONS/CAREER NOTES: Selected by Indianapolis Colts in sixth round (193rd pick overall) of 2001 NFL draft. ... Signed by Colts (June 7, 2001). ... Granted unconditional free agency (March 3, 2004). ... Signed by New York Giants (May 20, 2004). ... Released by Giants (September 5, 2004). ... Signed by Washington Redskins (November 2, 2004). ... On injured reserve with ankle injury (December 13, 2004-remainder of season). ... Granted unconditional free agency (March 2, 2005).
CHAMPIONSHIP GAME EXPERIENCE: Played in AFC championship game (2003 season).

Year Team	G	GS	TOTALS Tk.	Ast.	Sks.	INTERCEPTIONS No.	Yds.	Avg.	TD
2001—Indianapolis NFL	16	1	10	1	0.0	0	0	0.0	0
2002—Indianapolis NFL	15	6	24	12	0.0	0	0	0.0	0
2003—Indianapolis NFL	16	0	6	0	0.0	0	0	0.0	0
2004—Washington NFL	6	0	0	0	0.0	0	0	0.0	0
Pro totals (4 years)	53	7	40	13	0.0	0	0	0.0	0

DORENBOS, JON — C/LS — BILLS

PERSONAL: Born July 21, 1980, in Humble, Texas. ... 6-0/250. ... Name pronounced: DORN-bahs.
HIGH SCHOOL: Pacifica (Garden Grove, Calif.).
JUNIOR COLLEGE: Golden West (Huntington Beach, Calif.).
COLLEGE: Texas-El Paso.

TRANSACTIONS/CAREER NOTES: Signed as non-drafted free agent by Buffalo Bills (April 28, 2003). ... On injured reserve with knee injury (December 22, 2004-remainder of season).
PLAYING EXPERIENCE: Buffalo NFL, 2003-2004. ... Games/Games started: 2003 (16/0), 2004 (13/0). Total: 29/0.

DORSEY, KEN — QB — 49ERS

PERSONAL: Born April 22, 1981, in Orinda, Calif. ... 6-4/218. ... Full name: Kenneth Simon Dorsey.
HIGH SCHOOL: Miramonte (Orinda, Calif.).
COLLEGE: Miami (Fla.).
TRANSACTIONS/CAREER NOTES: Selected by San Francisco 49ers in seventh round (241st pick overall) of 2003 NFL draft. ... Signed by 49ers (July 23, 2003).
SINGLE GAME HIGHS (regular season): Attempts—38 (December 18, 2004, vs. Washington); completions—20 (December 18, 2004, vs. Washington); yards—206 (December 18, 2004, vs. Washington); and touchdown passes—3 (December 12, 2004, vs. Arizona).
MISCELLANEOUS: Regular-season record as starting NFL quarterback: 1-6 (.143).

					PASSING						RUSHING				TOTALS		
Year Team	G	GS	Att.	Cmp.	Pct.	Yds.	TD	Int.	Avg.	Skd.	Rat.	Att.	Yds.	Avg.	TD	TD	2pt.	Pts.
2003—San Francisco NFL	Did not play.																
2004—San Francisco NFL	9	7	226	123	54.4	1231	6	9	5.45	13	62.4	5	7	1.4	0	0	0	0
Pro totals (1 year)	9	7	226	123	54.4	1231	6	9	5.45	13	62.4	5	7	1.4	0	0	0	0

DORSEY, NAT — T — VIKINGS

PERSONAL: Born September 9, 1983, in New Orleans, La. ... 6-7/322. ... Full name: Nathaniel Willie Dorsey III.
HIGH SCHOOL: St. Augustine (New Orleans, La.).
COLLEGE: Georgia Tech.
TRANSACTIONS/CAREER NOTES: Selected after junior season by Minnesota Vikings in fourth round (115th pick overall) of 2004 NFL draft. ... Signed by Vikings (July 29, 2004).
PLAYING EXPERIENCE: Minnesota NFL, 2004. ... Games/Games started: 2004 (13/7). Total: 13/7.
HONORS: Named offensive tackle on THE SPORTING NEWS Freshman All-America first team (2001).

DOSS, MIKE — S — COLTS

PERSONAL: Born March 24, 1981, in Canton, Ohio. ... 5-10/207.
HIGH SCHOOL: McKinley (Canton, Ohio).
COLLEGE: Ohio State.
TRANSACTIONS/CAREER NOTES: Selected by Indianapolis Colts in second round (58th pick overall) of 2003 NFL draft. ... Signed by Colts (July 31, 2003).
CHAMPIONSHIP GAME EXPERIENCE: Played in AFC championship game (2003 season).

			TOTALS			INTERCEPTIONS			
Year Team	G	GS	Tk.	Ast.	Sks.	No.	Yds.	Avg.	TD
2003—Indianapolis NFL	15	15	68	29	0.0	1	15	15.0	0
2004—Indianapolis NFL	10	9	41	7	1.0	2	32	16.0	0
Pro totals (2 years)	25	24	109	36	1.0	3	47	15.7	0

DOUGLAS, HUGH — DE — EAGLES

PERSONAL: Born August 23, 1971, in Mansfield, Ohio. ... 6-2/281.
HIGH SCHOOL: Mansfield (Ohio).
COLLEGE: Central State.
TRANSACTIONS/CAREER NOTES: Selected after junior season by New York Jets in first round (16th pick overall) of 1995 NFL draft. ... Signed by Jets (June 8, 1995). ... Traded by Jets to Philadelphia Eagles for second- (traded to Pittsburgh) and fifth-round (LB Casey Dailey) picks in 1998 draft (March 13, 1998). ... On injured reserve with bicep injury (October 20, 1999-remainder of season). ... Granted unconditional free agency (February 28, 2003). ... Signed by Jacksonville Jaguars (March 16, 2003). ... Released by Jaguars (August 30, 2004). ... Signed by Eagles (August 30, 2004). ... Granted unconditional free agency (March 2, 2005). ... Re-signed by Eagles (March 3, 2005).
CHAMPIONSHIP GAME EXPERIENCE: Played in NFC championship game (2001, 2002 and 2004 seasons). ... Member of Eagles for Super Bowl 39 (2004 season); did not play.
HONORS: Named defensive end on THE SPORTING NEWS NFL All-Pro team (2000). ... Played in Pro Bowl (2000-2002 seasons).

			TOTALS			INTERCEPTIONS			
Year Team	G	GS	Tk.	Ast.	Sks.	No.	Yds.	Avg.	TD
1995—New York Jets NFL..	15	3	25	8	10.0	0	0	0.0	0
1996—New York Jets NFL..	10	10	28	8	8.0	0	0	0.0	0
1997—New York Jets NFL..	15	15	31	8	4.0	0	0	0.0	0
1998—Philadelphia NFL..	15	13	37	9	12.5	0	0	0.0	0
1999—Philadelphia NFL..	4	2	5	3	2.0	0	0	0.0	0
2000—Philadelphia NFL..	16	15	44	12	15.0	1	9	9.0	0
2001—Philadelphia NFL..	15	15	39	8	9.5	0	0	0.0	0
2002—Philadelphia NFL..	16	16	45	8	12.5	0	0	0.0	0
2003—Jacksonville NFL	16	16	22	5	3.5	0	0	0.0	0
2004—Philadelphia NFL..	16	3	15	0	3.0	0	0	0.0	0
Pro totals (10 years)	138	108	291	69	80.0	1	9	9.0	0

DOUGLAS, MARQUES   DE   49ERS

PERSONAL: Born March 5, 1977, in Greensboro, N.C. ... 6-2/290. ... Full name: Marques Lamont Douglas.
HIGH SCHOOL: Dudley (Greensboro, N.C.).
COLLEGE: Howard.
TRANSACTIONS/CAREER NOTES: Signed by Baltimore Ravens as non-drafted free agent (April 23, 1999). ... Released by Ravens (September 4, 1999). ... Re-signed by Ravens (December 22, 1999). ... Claimed on waivers by New Orleans Saints (August 28, 2000). ... Released by Saints (September 14, 2000). ... Re-signed by Saints (September 20, 2000). ... On injured reserve with knee injury (October 12, 2000-remainder of season). ... Released by Saints (September 2, 2001). ... Re-signed by Saints to practice squad (September 3, 2001). ... Signed by Baltimore Ravens off Saints practice squad (November 28, 2001). ... Re-signed by Ravens (March 23, 2003). ... Granted free agency (March 3, 2004). ... Re-signed by Ravens (April 16, 2004). ... Granted unconditional free agency (March 2, 2005). ... Signed by San Francisco 49ers (April 7, 2005).

			TOTALS		
Year Team	G	GS	Tk.	Ast.	Sks.
2000—New Orleans NFL	1	0	1	0	0.0
2001—Baltimore NFL	2	0	1	1	1.0
2002—Baltimore NFL	5	1	6	4	1.0
2003—Baltimore NFL	16	16	52	11	4.5
2004—Baltimore NFL	16	15	49	23	5.5
Pro totals (5 years)	40	32	109	39	12.0

DOWNING, ERIC   DT

PERSONAL: Born September 16, 1978, in Ahoskie, N.C. ... 6-3/315. ... Full name: Eric Lamont Downing.
HIGH SCHOOL: John F. Kennedy (Paterson, N.J.).
JUNIOR COLLEGE: Coffeyville (Kan.) Community College.
COLLEGE: Syracuse.
TRANSACTIONS/CAREER NOTES: Selected by Kansas City Chiefs in third round (75th pick overall) of 2001 NFL draft. ... Signed by Chiefs (May 23, 2001). ... Granted free agency (March 3, 2004). ... Re-signed by Chiefs (March 24, 2004). ... Released by Chiefs (September 5, 2004). ... Signed by San Diego Chargers (September 22, 2004). ... On injured reserve with knee injury (January 1, 2005-remainder of season). ... Granted unconditional free agency (March 2, 2005).

			TOTALS		
Year Team	G	GS	Tk.	Ast.	Sks.
2001—Kansas City NFL	15	9	13	6	1.5
2002—Kansas City NFL	13	4	10	4	0.5
2003—Kansas City NFL	14	0	7	3	0.0
2004—San Diego NFL	3	0	1	0	0.0
Pro totals (4 years)	45	13	31	13	2.0

DRAFT, CHRIS   LB   PANTHERS

PERSONAL: Born February 26, 1976, in Anaheim, Calif. ... 5-11/232.
HIGH SCHOOL: Valencia (Placentia, Calif.).
COLLEGE: Stanford.
TRANSACTIONS/CAREER NOTES: Selected by Chicago Bears in sixth round (157th pick overall) of 1998 NFL draft. ... Signed by Bears (June 16, 1998). ... Released by Bears (August 30, 1998). ... Re-signed by Bears to practice squad (August 31, 1998). ... Activated (December 2, 1998). ... Released by Bears (August 30, 1999). ... Signed by San Francisco 49ers to practice squad (September 29, 1999). ... Activated (November 19, 1999). ... Released by 49ers (February 10, 2000). ... Signed by Atlanta Falcons (February 14, 2000). ... Released by Falcons (April 1, 2005). ... Signed by Carolina Panthers (April 20, 2005).
CHAMPIONSHIP GAME EXPERIENCE: Played in NFC championship game (2004 season).

			TOTALS			INTERCEPTIONS			
Year Team	G	GS	Tk.	Ast.	Sks.	No.	Yds.	Avg.	TD
1998—Chicago NFL	1	0	0	0	0.0	0	0	0.0	0
1999—San Francisco NFL	7	0	0	0	0.0	0	0	0.0	0
2000—Atlanta NFL	13	8	41	15	1.0	0	0	0.0	0
2001—Atlanta NFL	13	10	53	19	0.0	0	0	0.0	0
2002—Atlanta NFL	15	5	49	15	3.5	2	12	6.0	0
2003—Atlanta NFL	16	16	102	20	2.0	1	4	4.0	0
2004—Atlanta NFL	14	13	42	15	0.0	1	33	33.0	0
Pro totals (7 years)	79	52	287	84	6.5	4	49	12.3	0

DRIVER, DONALD   WR   PACKERS

PERSONAL: Born February 2, 1975, in Houston, Texas. ... 6-0/192. ... Full name: Donald Jerome Driver.
HIGH SCHOOL: Milby (Houston).
COLLEGE: Alcorn State.
TRANSACTIONS/CAREER NOTES: Selected by Green Bay Packers in seventh round (213th pick overall) of 1999 NFL draft. ... Signed by Packers (June 2, 1999). ... Granted free agency (March 1, 2002). ... Re-signed by Packers (April 16, 2002).
HONORS: Played in Pro Bowl (2002 season).
SINGLE GAME HIGHS (regular season): Receptions—11 (December 24, 2004, vs. Minnesota); yards—162 (December 24, 2004, vs. Minnesota); and touchdown receptions—2 (October 17, 2004, vs. Detroit).
STATISTICAL PLATEAUS: 100-yard receiving games: 2002 (3), 2003 (1), 2004 (4). Total: 8.

Year Team	G	GS	RUSHING				RECEIVING				TOTALS			
			Att.	Yds.	Avg.	TD	No.	Yds.	Avg.	TD	TD	2pt.	Pts.	Fum.
1999—Green Bay NFL	6	0	0	0	0.0	0	3	31	10.3	1	1	0	6	0
2000—Green Bay NFL	16	2	1	4	4.0	0	21	322	15.3	1	1	1	8	0
2001—Green Bay NFL	13	2	3	38	12.7	1	13	167	12.8	1	2	0	12	0
2002—Green Bay NFL	16	16	8	70	8.8	0	70	1064	15.2	9	9	0	54	1
2003—Green Bay NFL	15	15	5	51	10.2	0	52	621	11.9	2	2	0	12	0
2004—Green Bay NFL	16	11	3	4	1.3	0	84	1208	14.4	9	9	1	56	2
Pro totals (6 years)	82	46	20	167	8.4	1	243	3413	14.0	23	24	2	148	3

DROUGHNS, REUBEN — RB — BROWNS

PERSONAL: Born August 21, 1978, in Chicago, Ill. ... 5-11/207.
HIGH SCHOOL: Anaheim (Calif.).
JUNIOR COLLEGE: Merced (Calif.) College.
COLLEGE: Oregon.
TRANSACTIONS/CAREER NOTES: Selected by Detroit Lions in third round (81st pick overall) of 2000 NFL draft. ... Signed by Lions (July 15, 2000). ... On injured reserve with shoulder injury (August 22, 2000-entire season). ... Released by Lions (September 12, 2001). ... Signed by Miami Dolphins to practice squad (September 18, 2001). ... Signed by Lions off Dolphins practice squad (October 9, 2001). ... Granted free agency (March 1, 2002). ... Signed by Denver Broncos (April 1, 2002). ... Granted free agency (February 28, 2003). ... Re-signed by Broncos (April 24, 2003). ... Granted unconditional free agency (March 3, 2004). ... Re-signed by Broncos (March 19, 2004). ... Traded by Broncos to Cleveland Browns for DE Ebenezer Ekuban and DT Michael Myers (March 30, 2005).
SINGLE GAME HIGHS (regular season): Attempts—38 (October 17, 2004, vs. Oakland); yards—193 (October 10, 2004, vs. Carolina); and rushing touchdowns—2 (December 25, 2004, vs. Tennessee).
STATISTICAL PLATEAUS: 100-yard rushing games: 2004 (6). Total: 6.

Year Team	G	GS	RUSHING				RECEIVING				KICKOFF RETURNS				TOTALS			
			Att.	Yds.	Avg.	TD	No.	Yds.	Avg.	TD	No.	Yds.	Avg.	TD	TD	2pt.	Pts.	Fum.
2000—Detroit NFL	Did not play.																	
2001—Detroit NFL	9	3	30	72	2.4	0	4	21	5.3	1	0	0	0.0	0	1	0	6	0
2002—Denver NFL	16	0	4	11	2.8	1	5	53	10.6	1	20	516	25.8	0	2	0	12	0
2003—Denver NFL	15	4	6	14	2.3	0	9	87	9.7	2	12	293	24.4	0	2	0	12	0
2004—Denver NFL	16	15	275	1240	4.5	6	32	241	7.5	2	14	344	24.6	0	8	0	48	5
Pro totals (4 years)	56	22	315	1337	4.2	7	50	402	8.0	6	46	1153	25.1	0	13	0	78	5

DRUMMOND, EDDIE — WR

PERSONAL: Born April 12, 1980, in Pittsburgh, Pa. ... 5-9/190.
HIGH SCHOOL: Linsley (Pittsburgh).
COLLEGE: Penn State.
TRANSACTIONS/CAREER NOTES: Signed as non-drafted free agent by Detroit Lions (April 26, 2002). ... On injured reserve with shoulder injury (December 22, 2004-remainder of season). ... Granted free agency (March 2, 2005).
HONORS: Named punt returner on THE SPORTING NEWS NFL All-Pro team (2004). ... Named to play in Pro Bowl (2004 season); replaced by Allen Rossum due to injury.
RECORDS: Shares NFL single-season record for most kick returns for a touchdown—4 (2004).
SINGLE GAME HIGHS (regular season): Receptions—1 (December 8, 2002, vs. Arizona); yards—1 (December 8, 2002, vs. Arizona); and touchdown receptions—0.

Year Team	G	GS	RUSHING				RECEIVING				PUNT RETURNS				KICKOFF RETURNS				TOTALS		
			Att.	Yds.	Avg.	TD	No.	Yds.	Avg.	TD	No.	Yds.	Avg.	TD	No.	Yds.	Avg.	TD	TD	2pt.	Pts.
2002—Det. NFL	9	0	4	38	9.5	0	2	-3	-1.5	0	18	138	7.7	1	40	1039	26.0	0	1	0	6
2003—Det. NFL	6	0	1	1	1.0	0	0	0	0.0	0	12	151	12.6	1	21	469	22.3	0	1	0	6
2004—Det. NFL	11	1	1	9	9.0	0	0	0	0.0	0	24	316	*13.2	*2	41	1092	26.6	‡2	4	0	24
Pro totals (3 years)	26	1	6	48	8.0	0	2	-3	-1.5	0	54	605	11.2	4	102	2600	25.5	2	6	0	36

DUCKETT, DAMANE — DT — GIANTS

PERSONAL: Born January 21, 1981, in Waterbury, Conn. ... 6-6/300. ... Full name: Damane Jerrel Duckett.
HIGH SCHOOL: North Davidson (Lexington, N.C.).
COLLEGE: East Carolina.
TRANSACTIONS/CAREER NOTES: Signed as non-drafted free agent by Carolina Panthers (April 30, 2004). ... Released by Panthers (November 4, 2004). ... Re-signed by Panthers to practice squad (November 6, 2004). ... Signed by New York Giants off Panthers practice squad (December 2, 2004).

Year Team	G	GS	TOTALS		
			Tk.	Ast.	Sks.
2004—Carolina NFL	2	0	0	0	0.0
—New York Giants NFL	4	1	2	3	1.0
Pro totals (1 year)	6	1	2	3	1.0

DUCKETT, T.J. — RB — FALCONS

PERSONAL: Born February 17, 1981, in Kalamazoo, Mich. ... 6-0/254.
HIGH SCHOOL: Loy Norrix (Kalamazoo, Mich.).
COLLEGE: Michigan State.
TRANSACTIONS/CAREER NOTES: Selected after junior season by Atlanta Falcons in first round (18th pick overall) of 2002 NFL draft. ... Signed by Falcons (August 3, 2002).

SINGLE GAME HIGHS (regular season): Attempts—27 (December 20, 2003, vs. Tampa Bay); yards—100 (September 28, 2003, vs. Carolina); and rushing touchdowns—4 (December 12, 2004, vs. Oakland).
STATISTICAL PLATEAUS: 100-yard rushing games: 2003 (1). Total: 1.

Year Team			RUSHING				RECEIVING				TOTALS			
	G	GS	Att.	Yds.	Avg.	TD	No.	Yds.	Avg.	TD	TD	2pt.	Pts.	Fum.
2002—Atlanta NFL	11	4	130	507	3.9	4	9	61	6.8	0	4	0	24	0
2003—Atlanta NFL	16	10	197	779	4.0	11	11	94	8.5	0	11	0	66	3
2004—Atlanta NFL	13	0	104	509	4.9	8	3	15	5.0	0	8	0	48	2
Pro totals (3 years)	40	14	431	1795	4.2	23	23	170	7.4	0	23	0	138	5

DUDLEY, RICKEY · TE

PERSONAL: Born July 15, 1972, in Henderson, Texas. ... 6-6/255.
HIGH SCHOOL: Henderson (Texas).
COLLEGE: Ohio State.
TRANSACTIONS/CAREER NOTES: Selected by Oakland Raiders in first round (ninth pick overall) of 1996 NFL draft. ... Signed by Raiders (July 12, 1996). ... Granted unconditional free agency (March 2, 2001). ... Signed by Cleveland Browns (March 30, 2001). ... On injured reserve with foot injury (October 9, 2001-remainder of season). ... Released by Browns (September 1, 2002). ... Signed by Tampa Bay Buccaneers (September 17, 2002). ... Granted unconditional free agency (February 28, 2003). ... Re-signed by Buccaneers (April 25, 2003). ... Received injury settlement and released by Buccaneers (August 31, 2003). ... Re-signed by Buccaneers (November 11, 2003). ... Granted unconditional free agency (March 3, 2004). ... Re-signed by Buccaneers (March 5, 2004). ... On injured reserve with hand injury (September 29, 2004-remainder of season). ... Granted unconditional free agency (March 2, 2005).
CHAMPIONSHIP GAME EXPERIENCE: Played in AFC championship game (2000 season). ... Played in NFC championship game (2002 season). ... Member of Super Bowl championship team (2002 season).
SINGLE GAME HIGHS (regular season): Receptions—6 (November 8, 1998, vs. Baltimore); yards—116 (November 9, 1997, vs. New Orleans); and touchdown receptions—2 (December 24, 2000, vs. Carolina).
STATISTICAL PLATEAUS: 100-yard receiving games: 1997 (2), 1998 (1). Total: 3.
MISCELLANEOUS: Member of Ohio State basketball team (1991-92 through 1993-94).

Year Team			RECEIVING				TOTALS			
	G	GS	No.	Yds.	Avg.	TD	TD	2pt.	Pts.	Fum.
1996—Oakland NFL	16	15	34	386	11.4	4	4	0	24	1
1997—Oakland NFL	16	16	48	787	16.4	7	7	0	42	0
1998—Oakland NFL	16	15	36	549	15.3	5	5	1	32	1
1999—Oakland NFL	16	16	39	555	14.2	9	9	0	54	0
2000—Oakland NFL	16	16	29	350	12.1	4	4	0	24	1
2001—Cleveland NFL	4	4	9	115	12.8	0	0	0	0	0
2002—Tampa Bay NFL	14	3	16	192	12.0	3	3	0	18	0
2003—Tampa Bay NFL	7	2	7	42	6.0	1	1	0	6	0
2004—Tampa Bay NFL	3	0	3	48	16.0	0	0	0	0	0
Pro totals (9 years)	108	87	221	3024	13.7	33	33	1	200	3

DUGAN, JEFF · TE · VIKINGS

PERSONAL: Born April 8, 1981, in Allison Park, Pa. ... 6-4/258. ... Full name: Jeffery Steven Dugan.
HIGH SCHOOL: Central Catholic (Allison Park, Pa.).
COLLEGE: Maryland.
TRANSACTIONS/CAREER NOTES: Selected by Minnesota Vikings in seventh round (220th pick overall) of 2004 NFL draft. ... Signed by Vikings (July 26, 2004).

Year Team			RECEIVING				TOTALS			
	G	GS	No.	Yds.	Avg.	TD	TD	2pt.	Pts.	Fum.
2004—Minnesota NFL	14	2	0	0	0.0	0	0	0	0	0

DUNCAN, JAMIE · LB

PERSONAL: Born July 20, 1975, in Wilmington, Del. ... 6-1/238. ... Full name: Jamie Robert Duncan.
HIGH SCHOOL: Christiana (Newark, Del.).
COLLEGE: Vanderbilt.
TRANSACTIONS/CAREER NOTES: Selected by Tampa Bay Buccaneers in third round (84th pick overall) of 1998 NFL draft. ... Signed by Buccaneers (July 10, 1998). ... Granted unconditional free agency (March 1, 2002). ... Signed by St. Louis Rams (March 7, 2002). ... Released by Rams (April 26, 2004). ... Signed by Atlanta Falcons (April 30, 2004). ... Granted unconditional free agency (March 2, 2005).
CHAMPIONSHIP GAME EXPERIENCE: Played in NFC championship game (1999 season). ... Member of Falcons for NFC championship game (2004 season); inactive.
HONORS: Named inside linebacker on THE SPORTING NEWS college All-America second team (1997).

Year Team			TOTALS			INTERCEPTIONS			
	G	GS	Tk.	Ast.	Sks.	No.	Yds.	Avg.	TD
1998—Tampa Bay NFL	14	6	30	6	0.0	0	0	0.0	0
1999—Tampa Bay NFL	15	0	0	0	0.0	0	0	0.0	0
2000—Tampa Bay NFL	15	15	48	17	0.0	4	55	13.8	1
2001—Tampa Bay NFL	15	15	66	21	2.0	1	9	9.0	0
2002—St. Louis NFL	16	12	47	16	0.0	0	0	0.0	0
2003—St. Louis NFL	16	6	17	10	1.0	1	0	0.0	0
2004—Atlanta NFL	4	2	6	0	0.0	0	0	0.0	0
Pro totals (7 years)	95	56	214	70	3.0	6	64	10.7	1

DUNN, JASON   TE   CHIEFS

PERSONAL: Born November 15, 1973, in Harrodsburg, Ky. ... 6-6/276. ... Full name: Jason Adam Dunn.
HIGH SCHOOL: Harrodsburg (Ky.).
COLLEGE: Eastern Kentucky.
TRANSACTIONS/CAREER NOTES: Selected by Philadelphia Eagles in second round (54th pick overall) of 1996 NFL draft. ... Signed by Eagles (July 17, 1996). ... On injured reserve with knee injury (December 1, 1998-remainder of season). ... Granted free agency (February 12, 1999). ... Re-signed by Eagles for 1999 season. ... Released by Eagles (June 17, 1999). ... Signed by Kansas City Chiefs (July 11, 2000). ... Granted unconditional free agency (March 2, 2001). ... Re-signed by Chiefs (March 26, 2001). ... On injured reserve with elbow injury (January 4, 2001-remainder of season). ... Granted unconditional free agency (March 3, 2004). ... Re-signed by Chiefs (March 18, 2004).
SINGLE GAME HIGHS (regular season): Receptions—4 (November 15, 1998, vs. Washington); yards—58 (September 22, 1996, vs. Atlanta); and touchdown receptions—1 (November 7, 2004, vs. Tampa Bay).

| | | | RECEIVING | | | | TOTALS | | | |
Year Team	G	GS	No.	Yds.	Avg.	TD	TD	2pt.	Pts.	Fum.
1996—Philadelphia NFL	16	12	15	332	22.1	2	2	0	12	0
1997—Philadelphia NFL	15	4	7	93	13.3	2	2	0	12	0
1998—Philadelphia NFL	10	10	18	132	7.3	0	0	0	0	1
2000—Kansas City NFL	14	2	2	26	13.0	0	0	0	0	0
2001—Kansas City NFL	15	5	4	54	13.5	1	1	0	6	0
2002—Kansas City NFL	11	4	2	16	8.0	0	0	0	0	0
2003—Kansas City NFL	16	4	5	35	7.0	3	3	0	18	0
2004—Kansas City NFL	16	0	17	120	7.1	3	3	0	18	0
Pro totals (8 years)	113	41	70	808	11.5	11	11	0	66	1

DUNN, WARRICK   RB   FALCONS

PERSONAL: Born January 5, 1975, in Baton Rouge, La. ... 5-9/180. ... Full name: Warrick De'Mon Dunn.
HIGH SCHOOL: Catholic (Baton Rouge, La.).
COLLEGE: Florida State.
TRANSACTIONS/CAREER NOTES: Selected by Tampa Bay Buccaneers in first round (12th pick overall) of 1997 NFL draft. ... Signed by Buccaneers (July 24, 1997). ... Granted unconditional free agency (March 1, 2002). ... Signed by Atlanta Falcons (March 15, 2002). ... On injured reserve with foot injury (November 25, 2003-remainder of season).
CHAMPIONSHIP GAME EXPERIENCE: Played in NFC championship game (1999 and 2004 seasons).
HONORS: Named NFL Rookie of the Year by The Sporting News (1997). ... Played in Pro Bowl (1997 and 2000 seasons).
SINGLE GAME HIGHS (regular season): Attempts—30 (December 22, 2002, vs. Detroit); yards—210 (December 3, 2000, vs. Dallas); and rushing touchdowns—3 (December 18, 2000, vs. St. Louis).
STATISTICAL PLATEAUS: 100-yard rushing games: 1997 (5), 1998 (2), 2000 (3), 2002 (4), 2003 (2), 2004 (4). Total: 20. 100-yard receiving games: 1997 (1), 1999 (1), 2001 (1), 2003 (1). Total: 4.

| | | | RUSHING | | | | RECEIVING | | | | KICKOFF RETURNS | | | | TOTALS | | | |
Year Team	G	GS	Att.	Yds.	Avg.	TD	No.	Yds.	Avg.	TD	No.	Yds.	Avg.	TD	TD	2pt.	Pts.	Fum.
1997—Tampa Bay NFL	16	10	224	978	4.4	4	39	462	11.8	3	6	129	21.5	0	7	0	42	4
1998—Tampa Bay NFL	16	14	245	1026	4.2	2	44	344	7.8	0	1	25	25.0	0	2	0	12	1
1999—Tampa Bay NFL	15	15	195	616	3.2	0	64	589	9.2	2	8	156	19.5	0	2	0	12	3
2000—Tampa Bay NFL	16	14	248	1133	4.6	8	44	422	9.6	1	0	0	0.0	0	9	0	54	1
2001—Tampa Bay NFL	13	12	158	447	2.8	3	68	557	8.2	3	0	0	0.0	0	6	0	36	2
2002—Atlanta NFL	15	14	230	927	4.0	7	50	377	7.5	2	0	0	0.0	0	9	0	54	4
2003—Atlanta NFL	11	6	125	672	5.4	3	37	336	9.1	2	0	0	0.0	0	5	0	30	2
2004—Atlanta NFL	16	16	265	1106	4.2	9	29	294	10.1	0	0	0	0.0	0	9	0	54	3
Pro totals (8 years)	118	101	1690	6905	4.1	36	375	3381	9.0	13	15	310	20.7	0	49	0	294	20

DWIGHT, TIM   WR   PATRIOTS

PERSONAL: Born July 13, 1975, in Iowa City, Iowa. ... 5-8/180. ... Full name: Timothy John Dwight Jr.
HIGH SCHOOL: Iowa City (Iowa) High.
COLLEGE: Iowa.
TRANSACTIONS/CAREER NOTES: Selected by Atlanta Falcons in fourth round (114th pick overall) of 1998 NFL draft. ... Signed by Falcons (June 25, 1998). ... Granted free agency (March 2, 2001). ... Re-signed by Falcons (April 21, 2001). ... Traded by Falcons with first-(RB LaDainian Tomlinson) and third-round (DB Tay Cody) picks in 2001 draft and second-round pick in 2002 draft to San Diego Chargers for first-round pick (QB Michael Vick) in 2001 draft (April 20, 2001). ... On injured reserve with collapsed lung (November 26, 2003-remainder of season). ... Released by Chargers (February 22, 2005). ... Signed by New England Patriots (March 13, 2005).
CHAMPIONSHIP GAME EXPERIENCE: Played in NFC championship game (1998 season). ... Played in Super Bowl 33 (1998 season).
HONORS: Named kick returner on THE SPORTING NEWS college All-America second team (1996). ... Named kick returner on THE SPORTING NEWS college All-America first team (1997).
POST SEASON RECORDS: Holds Super Bowl career record for highest kickoff return average (minimum four returns)—42.0. ... Shares Super Bowl single-game record for most touchdowns by kickoff return—1 (January 31, 1999, vs. Denver).
SINGLE GAME HIGHS (regular season): Receptions—7 (January 3, 2000, vs. San Francisco); yards—162 (January 3, 2000, vs. San Francisco); and touchdown receptions—2 (January 3, 2000, vs. San Francisco).
STATISTICAL PLATEAUS: 100-yard receiving games: 1999 (2). Total: 2.

| | | | RUSHING | | | | RECEIVING | | | | PUNT RETURNS | | | | KICKOFF RETURNS | | | | TOTALS | | |
Year Team	G	GS	Att.	Yds.	Avg.	TD	No.	Yds.	Avg.	TD	No.	Yds.	Avg.	TD	No.	Yds.	Avg.	TD	TD	2pt.	Pts.
1998—Atl. NFL	12	0	8	19	2.4	0	4	94	23.5	1	31	263	8.5	0	36	973	27.0	1	2	0	12
1999—Atl. NFL	12	8	5	28	5.6	1	32	669	*20.9	7	20	220	11.0	∞1	44	944	21.5	0	9	0	54
2000—Atl. NFL	14	1	5	8	1.6	0	26	406	15.6	3	33	309	9.4	1	32	680	21.3	0	4	0	24
2001—S.D. NFL	10	2	2	24	12.0	1	25	406	16.2	0	24	271	11.3	1	0	0	0.0	0	2	0	12
2002—S.D. NFL	16	14	12	108	9.0	1	50	623	12.5	2	19	231	12.2	0	8	166	20.8	0	3	0	18
2003—S.D. NFL	9	3	9	88	9.8	0	14	193	13.8	0	2	0	0.0	0	22	488	22.2	0	0	0	0
2004—S.D. NFL	12	0	4	54	13.5	0	2	31	15.5	1	1	6	6.0	0	50	1222	24.4	1	2	0	12
Pro totals (7 years)	85	28	45	329	7.3	3	153	2422	15.8	14	130	1300	10.0	2	192	4473	23.3	2	22	0	132

D

DYSON, ANDRE   CB   SEAHAWKS

PERSONAL: Born May 25, 1979, in Logan, Utah. ... 5-10/183. ... Brother of Kevin Dyson, wide receiver with Tennessee Titans (1998-2002) and Carolina Panthers (2003).
HIGH SCHOOL: Clearfield (Utah).
COLLEGE: Utah.
TRANSACTIONS/CAREER NOTES: Selected by Tennessee Titans in second round (60th pick overall) of 2001 NFL draft. ... Signed by Titans (July 24, 2001). ... Granted unconditional free agency (March 2, 2005). ... Signed by Seattle Seahawks (April 26, 2005).
CHAMPIONSHIP GAME EXPERIENCE: Played in AFC championship game (2002 season).

Year Team	G	GS	TOTALS			INTERCEPTIONS			
			Tk.	Ast.	Sks.	No.	Yds.	Avg.	TD
2001—Tennessee NFL	14	12	54	4	0.0	3	36	12.0	0
2002—Tennessee NFL	16	16	56	5	1.0	3	27	9.0	1
2003—Tennessee NFL	16	16	54	11	0.0	4	62	15.5	†2
2004—Tennessee NFL	16	16	35	6	0.0	6	135	22.5	0
Pro totals (4 years)	62	60	199	26	1.0	16	260	16.3	3

EARL, GLENN   DB   TEXANS

PERSONAL: Born June 10, 1981, in Lisle, Ill. ... 6-1/215.
HIGH SCHOOL: Naperville North (Lisle, Ill.).
COLLEGE: Notre Dame.
TRANSACTIONS/CAREER NOTES: Selected by Houston Texans in fourth round (122nd pick overall) of 2004 NFL draft. ... Signed by Texans (July 30, 2004).

Year Team	G	GS	TOTALS			INTERCEPTIONS			
			Tk.	Ast.	Sks.	No.	Yds.	Avg.	TD
2004—Houston NFL	12	9	35	9	0.0	0	0	0.0	0

EASLICK, DOUG   FB   BENGALS

PERSONAL: Born December 4, 1980, in Mount Holly, N.J. ... 5-11/243. ... Full name: Arthur Doug Easlick.
HIGH SCHOOL: Cherokee (Marlton, N.J.).
COLLEGE: Virginia Tech.
TRANSACTIONS/CAREER NOTES: Signed as non-drafted free agent by Miami Dolphins (April 30, 2004). ... Released by Dolphins (October 2, 2004). ... Re-signed by Dolphins to practice squad (October 5, 2004). ... Released by Dolphins (October 12, 2004). ... Signed by Cincinnati Bengals (December 22, 2004). ... Activated (January 3, 2005).

Year Team	G	GS	RECEIVING				TOTALS			
			No.	Yds.	Avg.	TD	TD	2pt.	Pts.	Fum.
2004—Miami NFL	3	1	1	4	4.0	0	0	0	0	0

EASON, NICHOLAS   DT   BROWNS

PERSONAL: Born May 29, 1980, in Lyons, Ga. ... 6-3/301.
HIGH SCHOOL: Toombs County (Lyons, Ga.).
COLLEGE: Clemson.
TRANSACTIONS/CAREER NOTES: Drafted by Denver Broncos in fourth round (114th pick overall) in 2003 NFL draft. ... Signed by Broncos (July 23, 2003). ... On injured reserve with Achilles injury (August 29, 2003-entire season). ... Assigned by Broncos to Scottish Claymores in NFL Europe enhancement allocation program (February 9, 2004). ... Released by Broncos (September 5, 2004). ... Re-signed by Broncos to practice squad (September 6, 2004). ... Released by Broncos from practice squad (September 24, 2004). ... Signed by Cleveland Browns to practice squad (October 6, 2004). ... Activated (November 24, 2005).

Year Team	G	GS	TOTALS		
			Tk.	Ast.	Sks.
2004—Cleveland NFL	1	0	1	1	0.0

EASY, OMAR   FB   CHIEFS

PERSONAL: Born October 29, 1977, in Spanish Town, Jamaica. ... 6-2/245. ... Full name: Omar Xavier Easy.
HIGH SCHOOL: Everett (Mass.).
COLLEGE: Penn State.
TRANSACTIONS/CAREER NOTES: Selected by Kansas City Chiefs in fourth round (107th pick overall) of 2002 NFL draft. ... Signed by Chiefs (June 11, 2002).
SINGLE GAME HIGHS (regular season): Attempts—4 (December 19, 2004, vs. Denver); yards—1 (December 19, 2004, vs. Denver); and rushing touchdowns—0.

Year Team	G	GS	RUSHING				RECEIVING				TOTALS			
			Att.	Yds.	Avg.	TD	No.	Yds.	Avg.	TD	TD	2pt.	Pts.	Fum.
2002—Kansas City NFL	7	0	0	0	0.0	0	3	23	7.7	1	1	0	6	0
2003—Kansas City NFL	15	0	0	0	0.0	0	3	19	6.3	0	0	0	0	0
2004—Kansas City NFL	15	0	4	1	0.3	0	0	0	0.0	0	0	0	0	0
Pro totals (3 years)	37	0	4	1	0.3	0	6	42	7.0	1	1	0	6	0

EATON, CHAD   DT

PERSONAL: Born April 6, 1972, in Exeter, N.H. ... 6-5/303. ... Full name: Chad Everett Eaton.
HIGH SCHOOL: Rogers (Puyallup, Wash.).
COLLEGE: Washington State.
TRANSACTIONS/CAREER NOTES: Selected by Arizona Cardinals in seventh round (241st pick overall) of 1995 NFL draft. ... Signed by Cardinals (July 24, 1995). ... Released by Cardinals (August 14, 1995). ... Signed by New York Jets (August 15, 1995). ... Released by Jets (August 27, 1995). ... Signed by Cleveland Browns to practice squad (September 28, 1995). ... Activated (December 15, 1995); did not play. ... Browns franchise moved to Baltimore and renamed Ravens for 1996 season (March 11, 1996). ... Released by Ravens (August 19, 1996). ... Signed by New England Patriots to practice squad (August 27, 1996). ... Activated (November 28, 1996). ... Granted unconditional free agency (March 2, 2001). ... Signed by Seattle Seahawks (March 9, 2001). ... On injured reserve with knee injury (August 26, 2003-remainder of season). ... Released by Seahawks (February 27, 2004). ... Signed by Dallas Cowboys (August 25, 2004). ... Released by Cowboys (October 30, 2004).
CHAMPIONSHIP GAME EXPERIENCE: Played in AFC championship game (1996 season). ... Played in Super Bowl 31 (1996 season).
HONORS: Named defensive lineman on THE SPORTING NEWS college All-America second team (1994).

			TOTALS		
Year Team	G	GS	Tk.	Ast.	Sks.
1995—Cleveland NFL	Did not play.				
1996—New England NFL	4	0	3	1	1.0
1997—New England NFL	16	1	13	8	1.0
1998—New England NFL	15	14	49	31	6.0
1999—New England NFL	16	16	38	18	3.0
2000—New England NFL	14	13	59	19	2.5
2001—Seattle NFL	16	16	44	13	1.0
2002—Seattle NFL	16	16	48	25	1.0
2003—Seattle NFL	Did not play.				
2004—Dallas NFL	6	1	5	4	0.0
Pro totals (8 years)	103	77	259	119	15.5

ECHEMANDU, ADIMCHINOBE   RB   BROWNS

PERSONAL: Born November 21, 1980, in Lagos, Nigeria. ... 5-10/226.
HIGH SCHOOL: Hawthorne (Calif.).
COLLEGE: California.
TRANSACTIONS/CAREER NOTES: Selected by Cleveland Browns in seventh round (208th pick overall) of 2004 NFL draft. ... Signed by Browns (July 29, 2004). ... On reserve/non-football injury list with ankle injury (August 30-November 16, 2004).
SINGLE GAME HIGHS (regular season): Attempts—5 (December 12, 2004, vs. Buffalo); yards—13 (December 12, 2004, vs. Buffalo); and rushing touchdowns—0.

			RUSHING				RECEIVING				KICKOFF RETURNS				TOTALS			
Year Team	G	GS	Att.	Yds.	Avg.	TD	No.	Yds.	Avg.	TD	No.	Yds.	Avg.	TD	TD	2pt.	Pts.	Fum.
2004—Cleveland NFL	4	0	8	25	3.1	0	3	25	8.3	0	0	0	0.0	0	0	0	0	1

EDINGER, PAUL   K   VIKINGS

PERSONAL: Born January 17, 1978, in Frankfort, Mich. ... 5-8/175. ... Full name: Paul E. Edinger.
HIGH SCHOOL: Kathleen (Lakeland, Fla.).
COLLEGE: Michigan State.
TRANSACTIONS/CAREER NOTES: Selected by Chicago Bears in sixth round (174th pick overall) of 2000 NFL draft. ... Signed by Bears (June 8, 2000). ... Granted free agency (February 28, 2003). ... Tendered offer sheet by Minnesota Vikings (March 9, 2003). ... Offer matched by Bears (March 12, 2003). ... Released by Bears (May 22, 2005). ... Signed by Minnesota Vikings (May 24, 2005).

		FIELD GOALS							TOTALS		
Year Team	G	1-29	30-39	40-49	50+	Tot.	Pct.	Lg.	XPM	XPA	Pts.
2000—Chicago NFL	16	6-6	7-9	6-10	2-2	21-27	77.8	54	21	21	84
2001—Chicago NFL	16	6-7	7-8	13-16	0-0	26-31	83.9	48	34	34	112
2002—Chicago NFL	16	4-4	5-6	8-10	5-8	22-28	78.6	∞53	29	29	95
2003—Chicago NFL	16	5-5	9-13	9-14	3-4	26-36	72.2	54	27	27	105
2004—Chicago NFL	16	6-7	2-5	4-7	3-5	15-24	62.5	53	22	22	67
Pro totals (5 years)	80	27-29	30-41	40-57	13-19	110-146	75.3	54	133	133	463

EDWARDS, ANTUAN   S

PERSONAL: Born May 26, 1977, in Starkville, Miss. ... 6-1/210. ... Full name: Antuan Minye' Edwards. ... Name pronounced: AN-twan.
HIGH SCHOOL: Starkville (Miss.).
COLLEGE: Clemson.
TRANSACTIONS/CAREER NOTES: Selected by Green Bay Packers in first round (25th pick overall) of 1999 NFL draft. ... Signed by Packers (June 7, 1999). ... On injured reserve with knee injury (October 3, 2001-remainder of season). ... On injured reserve with hamstring injury (December 6, 2003-remainder of season). ... Granted unconditional free agency (March 3, 2004). ... Signed by Miami Dolphins (April 12, 2004). ... Claimed on waivers by St. Louis Rams (November 11, 2004). ... Granted unconditional free agency (March 2, 2005).

			TOTALS			INTERCEPTIONS				PUNT RETURNS				TOTALS			
Year Team	G	GS	Tk.	Ast.	Sks.	No.	Yds.	Avg.	TD	No.	Yds.	Avg.	TD	TD	2pt.	Pts.	Fum.
1999—Green Bay NFL	16	1	26	4	0.0	4	26	6.5	1	10	90	9.0	0	1	0	6	1
2000—Green Bay NFL	13	3	21	4	0.0	2	4	2.0	0	0	0	0.0	0	0	0	0	0
2001—Green Bay NFL	3	0	2	0	0.0	0	0	0.0	0	0	0	0.0	0	0	0	0	0
2002—Green Bay NFL	12	4	25	14	1.0	0	0	0.0	0	1	0	0.0	0	0	0	0	0

E

Year Team	G	GS	TOTALS Tk.	Ast.	Sks.	INTERCEPTIONS No.	Yds.	Avg.	TD	PUNT RETURNS No.	Yds.	Avg.	TD	TOTALS TD	2pt.	Pts.	Fum.
2003—Green Bay NFL	10	10	42	8	1.0	1	5	5.0	0	0	0	0.0	0	0	0	0	0
2004—Miami NFL	8	8	24	12	1.0	0	0	0.0	0	0	0	0.0	0	0	0	0	0
—St. Louis NFL	6	5	23	6	0.0	0	0	0.0	0	0	0	0.0	0	0	0	0	0
Pro totals (6 years)	68	31	163	48	3.0	7	35	5.0	1	11	90	8.2	0	1	0	6	1

EDWARDS, DONNIE — LB — CHARGERS

PERSONAL: Born April 6, 1973, in San Diego, Calif. ... 6-2/227. ... Full name: Donnie Lewis Edwards Jr.
HIGH SCHOOL: Chula Vista (San Diego).
COLLEGE: UCLA.
TRANSACTIONS/CAREER NOTES: Selected by Kansas City Chiefs in fourth round (98th pick overall) of 1996 NFL draft. ... Signed by Chiefs (July 24, 1996). ... Released by Chiefs (March 1, 2002). ... Signed by San Diego Chargers (April 25, 2002).
HONORS: Played in Pro Bowl (2002).

Year Team	G	GS	TOTALS Tk.	Ast.	Sks.	INTERCEPTIONS No.	Yds.	Avg.	TD
1996—Kansas City NFL	15	1	8	3	0.0	1	22	22.0	0
1997—Kansas City NFL	16	16	80	20	2.5	2	15	7.5	0
1998—Kansas City NFL	15	15	80	44	6.0	0	0	0.0	0
1999—Kansas City NFL	16	16	98	25	3.0	5	50	10.0	1
2000—Kansas City NFL	16	16	114	18	1.0	2	45	22.5	1
2001—Kansas City NFL	16	16	98	32	2.0	0	0	0.0	0
2002—San Diego NFL	16	16	100	29	0.0	5	95	19.0	1
2003—San Diego NFL	16	16	124	38	0.5	2	27	13.5	0
2004—San Diego NFL	16	16	105	46	1.0	5	49	9.8	1
Pro totals (9 years)	142	128	807	255	16.0	22	303	13.8	4

EDWARDS, DWAN — DT — RAVENS

PERSONAL: Born May 16, 1981, in Billings, Mont. ... 6-3/315. ... Full name: Dwan Sedaine Edwards. ... Name pronounced: Duh-wan.
HIGH SCHOOL: Columbus (Mont.).
COLLEGE: Oregon State.
TRANSACTIONS/CAREER NOTES: Selected by Baltimore Ravens in second round (51st pick overall) of 2004 NFL draft. ... Signed by Ravens (July 26, 2004).

Year Team	G	GS	TOTALS Tk.	Ast.	Sks.
2004—Baltimore NFL	4	0	1	0	0.0

E

EDWARDS, ERIC — TE — CARDINALS

PERSONAL: Born August 4, 1980, in Monroe, La. ... 6-5/256.
HIGH SCHOOL: Ouachita Christian (Monroe, La.).
COLLEGE: Louisiana State.
TRANSACTIONS/CAREER NOTES: Signed as non-drafted free agent by Arizona Cardinals (April 27, 2004).
SINGLE GAME HIGHS (regular season): Receptions—3 (December 12, 2004, vs. San Francisco); yards—39 (December 12, 2004, vs. San Francisco); and touchdown receptions—0.

Year Team	G	GS	RECEIVING No.	Yds.	Avg.	TD	KICKOFF RETURNS No.	Yds.	Avg.	TD	TOTALS TD	2pt.	Pts.	Fum.
2004—Arizona NFL	16	1	5	51	10.2	0	3	40	13.3	0	0	0	0	0

EDWARDS, KALIMBA — DE — LIONS

PERSONAL: Born December 26, 1979, in East Point, Ga. ... 6-6/265.
HIGH SCHOOL: Tri-Cities (Atlanta).
COLLEGE: South Carolina.
TRANSACTIONS/CAREER NOTES: Selected by Detroit Lions in second round (35th pick overall) of 2002 NFL draft. ... Signed by Lions (July 23, 2002). ... On injured reserve with groin injury (December 23, 2003-remainder of season.)
HONORS: Named linebacker on THE SPORTING NEWS college All-America first team (2001).

Year Team	G	GS	TOTALS Tk.	Ast.	Sks.	INTERCEPTIONS No.	Yds.	Avg.	TD
2002—Detroit NFL	16	4	23	8	6.5	0	0	0.0	0
2003—Detroit NFL	15	0	15	1	2.0	0	0	0.0	0
2004—Detroit NFL	16	0	18	4	4.5	0	0	0.0	0
Pro totals (3 years)	47	4	56	13	13.0	0	0	0.0	0

EDWARDS, MARC — FB

PERSONAL: Born November 17, 1974, in Cincinnati, Ohio. ... 6-0/249. ... Full name: Marc Alexander Edwards.
HIGH SCHOOL: Norwood (Cincinnati).
COLLEGE: Notre Dame.
TRANSACTIONS/CAREER NOTES: Selected by San Francisco 49ers in second round (55th pick overall) of 1997 NFL draft. ... Signed by 49ers (July 23, 1997). ... On physically unable to perform list with back injury (July 17-August 10, 1998). ... Traded by 49ers to Cleveland Browns

for fourth-round pick (DB Pierson Prioleau) in 1999 draft (April 18, 1999). ... Granted unconditional free agency (March 2, 2001). ... Signed by New England Patriots (March 19, 2001). ... Granted unconditional free agency (February 28, 2003). ... Signed by Jacksonville Jaguars (March 16, 2003). ... Released by Jaguars (March 3, 2005).

CHAMPIONSHIP GAME EXPERIENCE: Played in NFC championship game (1997 season). ... Played in AFC championship game (2001 season). ... Member of Super Bowl championship team (2001 season).

SINGLE GAME HIGHS (regular season): Attempts—7 (September 15, 2002, vs. New York Jets); yards—41 (September 27, 1998, vs. Atlanta); and rushing touchdowns—1 (December 2, 2001, vs. New York Jets).

Year—Team	G	GS	RUSHING Att.	Yds.	Avg.	TD	RECEIVING No.	Yds.	Avg.	TD	KICKOFF RETURNS No.	Yds.	Avg.	TD	TOTALS TD	2pt.	Pts.	Fum.
1997—San Francisco NFL	15	1	5	17	3.4	0	6	48	8.0	0	1	30	30.0	0	0	0	0	0
1998—San Francisco NFL	16	10	22	94	4.3	1	22	218	9.9	2	0	0	0.0	0	3	0	18	0
1999—Cleveland NFL	16	14	6	35	5.8	0	27	212	7.9	2	0	0	0.0	0	2	0	12	1
2000—Cleveland NFL	16	8	2	9	4.5	0	16	128	8.0	2	1	24	24.0	0	2	0	12	2
2001—New England NFL	16	13	51	141	2.8	1	25	166	6.6	2	1	23	23.0	0	3	0	18	3
2002—New England NFL	16	10	31	96	3.1	0	23	196	8.5	0	3	27	9.0	0	0	0	0	1
2003—Jacksonville NFL	16	16	7	13	1.9	1	31	226	7.3	0	2	44	22.0	0	1	0	6	0
2004—Jacksonville NFL	13	5	0	0	0.0	0	7	41	5.9	0	1	8	8.0	0	0	0	0	0
Pro totals (8 years)	124	77	124	405	3.3	3	157	1235	7.9	8	9	156	17.3	0	11	0	66	7

EDWARDS, MARIO — CB — DOLPHINS

PERSONAL: Born December 1, 1975, in Gautier, Miss. ... 6-0/199. ... Full name: Mario L. Edwards.
HIGH SCHOOL: Pascagoula (Miss.).
COLLEGE: Florida State.
TRANSACTIONS/CAREER NOTES: Selected by Dallas Cowboys in sixth round (180th pick overall) of 2000 NFL draft. ... Signed by Cowboys (July 14, 2000). ... Granted free agency (February 28, 2003). ... Re-signed by Cowboys (April 15, 2003). ... Granted unconditional free agency (March 3, 2004). ... Signed by Tampa Bay Buccaneers (April 4, 2004). ... Released by Buccaneers (March 1, 2005). ... Signed by Miami Dolphins (April 4, 2005).

Year—Team	G	GS	TOTALS Tk.	Ast.	Sks.	INTERCEPTIONS No.	Yds.	Avg.	TD
2000—Dallas NFL	11	1	5	0	0.0	0	0	0.0	0
2001—Dallas NFL	16	15	42	7	0.0	1	71	71.0	1
2002—Dallas NFL	15	15	53	4	0.0	2	29	14.5	0
2003—Dallas NFL	16	16	37	5	0.0	1	27	27.0	1
2004—Tampa Bay NFL	15	3	19	1	0.0	0	0	0.0	0
Pro totals (5 years)	73	50	156	17	0.0	4	127	31.8	2

EDWARDS, RON — DT — BILLS

PERSONAL: Born July 12, 1979, in Columbus, Ohio. ... 6-3/320.
HIGH SCHOOL: Klein Forest (Houston).
COLLEGE: Texas A&M.
TRANSACTIONS/CAREER NOTES: Selected by Buffalo Bills in third round (76th pick overall) of 2001 NFL draft. ... Signed by Bills (June 1, 2001). ... On injured reserve with shoulder injury (November 12, 2003-remainder of season). ... Granted free agency (March 3, 2004). ... Re-signed by Bills (2004).

Year—Team	G	GS	TOTALS Tk.	Ast.	Sks.
2001—Buffalo NFL	7	3	7	3	0.0
2002—Buffalo NFL	16	16	25	15	2.5
2003—Buffalo NFL	5	0	5	2	0.5
2004—Buffalo NFL	16	2	12	9	4.0
Pro totals (4 years)	44	21	49	29	7.0

EDWARDS, STEVE — T — BEARS

PERSONAL: Born February 20, 1979, in Chicago, Ill. ... 6-5/330.
HIGH SCHOOL: Mount Carmel (Chicago).
JUNIOR COLLEGE: West Hills Community College (Calif.).
COLLEGE: Central Florida.
TRANSACTIONS/CAREER NOTES: Signed as non-drafted free agent by Philadelphia Eagles (April 23, 2002). ... Released by Eagles (September 1, 2002). ... Re-signed by Eagles to practice squad (September 3, 2002). ... Signed by Chicago Bears off Eagles practice squad (October 9, 2002). ... Granted free agency (March 2, 2005). ... Re-signed by Bears (March 31, 2005).
PLAYING EXPERIENCE: Chicago NFL, 2002-2004. ... Games/Games started: 2002 (1/0), 2003 (16/16), 2004 (15/8). Total: 32/24.

EDWARDS, TROY — WR — JAGUARS

PERSONAL: Born April 7, 1977, in Shreveport, La. ... 5-10/195.
HIGH SCHOOL: Huntington (Shreveport, La.).
COLLEGE: Louisiana Tech.
TRANSACTIONS/CAREER NOTES: Selected by Pittsburgh Steelers in first round (13th pick overall) of 1999 NFL draft. ... Signed by Steelers (July 28, 1999). ... Traded by Steelers to St. Louis Rams for sixth-round pick (TE Matt Kranchick) in 2004 draft (September 1, 2002). ... Released by Rams (August 31, 2003). ... Signed by Jacksonville Jaguars (September 23, 2003). ... Granted unconditional free agency (March 2, 2005). ... Re-signed by Jaguars (March 15, 2005).
CHAMPIONSHIP GAME EXPERIENCE: Played in AFC championship game (2001 season).

E

HONORS: Fred Biletnikoff Award winner (1998). ... Named wide receiver on THE SPORTING NEWS college All-America second team (1998).
SINGLE GAME HIGHS (regular season): Receptions—7 (November 28, 1999, vs. Cincinnati); yards—111 (September 28, 2003, vs. Houston); and touchdown receptions—1 (December 5, 2004, vs. Pittsburgh).
STATISTICAL PLATEAUS: 100-yard receiving games: 2003 (1). Total: 1.

Year Team	G	GS	RUSHING				RECEIVING				PUNT RETURNS				KICKOFF RETURNS				TOTALS		
			Att.	Yds.	Avg.	TD	No.	Yds.	Avg.	TD	No.	Yds.	Avg.	TD	No.	Yds.	Avg.	TD	TD	2pt.	Pts.
1999—Pit. NFL	16	6	0	0	0.0	0	61	714	11.7	5	25	234	9.4	0	13	234	18.0	0	5	0	30
2000—Pit. NFL	14	1	3	4	1.3	0	18	215	11.9	0	0	0	0.0	0	15	298	19.9	0	0	0	0
2001—Pit. NFL	16	0	5	28	5.6	1	19	283	14.9	0	10	83	8.3	0	20	462	23.1	0	2	0	12
2002—StL. NFL	14	0	3	21	7.0	0	18	157	8.7	2	0	0	0.0	0	10	211	21.1	0	2	0	12
2003—Jac. NFL	13	11	3	-9	-3.0	0	35	487	13.9	3	0	0	0.0	0	1	20	20.0	0	3	0	18
2004—Jac. NFL	16	4	2	2	1.0	0	50	533	10.7	1	3	26	8.7	0	15	335	22.3	0	1	0	6
Pro totals (6 years)	89	22	16	46	2.9	1	201	2389	11.9	11	38	343	9.0	0	74	1560	21.1	0	13	0	78

EKUBAN, EBENEZER — DE — BRONCOS

PERSONAL: Born May 29, 1976, in Ghana, Africa. ... 6-3/275. ... Full name: Ebenezer Ekuban Jr. ... Name pronounced: ECK-you-bon.
HIGH SCHOOL: Bladensburg (Md.).
COLLEGE: North Carolina.
TRANSACTIONS/CAREER NOTES: Selected by Dallas Cowboys in first round (20th pick overall) of 1999 NFL draft. ... Signed by Cowboys (July 27, 1999). ... On injured reserve with back injury (December 21, 2001-remainder of season). ... Granted unconditional free agency (March 3, 2004). ... Signed by Cleveland Browns (March 11, 2004). ... Traded by Browns with DT Michael Myers to Denver Broncos for RB Reuben Droughns (March 30, 2005).

Year Team	G	GS	TOTALS		
			Tk.	Ast.	Sks.
1999—Dallas NFL	16	2	20	3	2.5
2000—Dallas NFL	12	2	22	7	6.5
2001—Dallas NFL	1	1	1	1	0.0
2002—Dallas NFL	16	15	26	5	1.0
2003—Dallas NFL	15	14	19	8	2.5
2004—Cleveland NFL	16	11	29	10	8.0
Pro totals (6 years)	76	45	117	34	20.5

ELAM, JASON — K — BRONCOS

PERSONAL: Born March 8, 1970, in Ft. Walton Beach, Fla. ... 5-11/200. ... Name pronounced: EE-lum.
HIGH SCHOOL: Brookwood (Snellville, Ga.).
COLLEGE: Hawaii.
TRANSACTIONS/CAREER NOTES: Selected by Denver Broncos in third round (70th pick overall) of 1993 NFL draft. ... Signed by Broncos (July 12, 1993). ... Designated by Broncos as franchise player (February 21, 2002). ... Granted free agency (March 1, 2002). ... Re-signed by Broncos (July 25, 2002).
CHAMPIONSHIP GAME EXPERIENCE: Played in AFC championship game (1997 and 1998 seasons). ... Member of Super Bowl championship team (1997 and 1998 seasons).
HONORS: Named kicker on THE SPORTING NEWS college All-America second team (1989 and 1991). ... Played in Pro Bowl (1995, 1998 and 2001 seasons).
RECORDS: Holds NFL career record for most consecutive PATs made—371 (1993-2002). ... Holds NFL career record for highest PAT percentage—99.56. ... Shares NFL career record for longest field goal—63 (October 25, 1998, vs. Jacksonville).
MISCELLANEOUS: Denver Broncos all-time scoring leader (1,442 points).

Year Team	G	FIELD GOALS							TOTALS		
		1-29	30-39	40-49	50+	Tot.	Pct.	Lg.	XPM	XPA	Pts.
1993—Denver NFL	16	11-12	7-7	4-10	4-6	26-35	74.3	54	§41	§42	119
1994—Denver NFL	16	11-11	11-11	7-12	1-3	30-37	81.1	†54	29	29	119
1995—Denver NFL	16	7-9	14-15	5-7	5-7	31-38	81.6	§56	39	39	132
1996—Denver NFL	16	10-10	4-5	6-10	1-3	21-28	75.0	51	§46	§46	109
1997—Denver NFL	15	10-11	10-12	3-8	3-5	26-36	72.2	53	§46	§46	124
1998—Denver NFL	16	3-3	13-14	4-6	3-4	23-27	85.2	*63	§58	§58	§127
1999—Denver NFL	16	9-9	7-8	8-11	5-8	29-36	80.6	*55	29	29	116
2000—Denver NFL	13	7-7	6-7	4-9	1-1	18-24	75.0	51	*49	*49	103
2001—Denver NFL	16	11-11	8-8	10-13	2-4	*31-36	86.1	50	31	31	124
2002—Denver NFL	16	10-10	7-9	5-11	4-6	26-§36	72.2	55	42	43	120
2003—Denver NFL	16	10-11	6-6	9-11	2-3	27-31	87.1	51	39	39	120
2004—Denver NFL	16	10-10	7-8	9-12	3-4	29-*34	85.3	52	42	42	129
Pro totals (12 years)	188	109-114	100-110	74-120	34-54	317-398	79.6	63	491	493	1442

ELLING, AARON — K — VIKINGS

PERSONAL: Born May 31, 1978, in Waconia, Minn. ... 6-2/201.
HIGH SCHOOL: Lander Valley (Lander, Wy.).
COLLEGE: Wyoming.
TRANSACTIONS/CAREER NOTES: Signed as non-drafted free agent by Seattle Seahawks (May 7, 2002). ... Released by Seahawks (August 30, 2002). ... Signed by Minnesota Vikings (March 21, 2003). ... Released by Vikings (September 1, 2004). ... Signed by Tennessee Titans (September 10, 2004). ... Released by Titans (September 14, 2004). ... Signed by Vikings (September 17, 2004). ... On injured reserve with ankle injury (November 10, 2004-remainder of season).

E

Year Team	G	FIELD GOALS							TOTALS		
		1-29	30-39	40-49	50+	Tot.	Pct.	Lg.	XPM	XPA	Pts.
2003—Minnesota NFL	16	7-7	6-8	4-7	1-3	18-25	72.0	51	48	48	102
2004—Tennessee NFL	1	1-1	0-1	0-0	0-0	1-2	50.0	22	2	2	5
—Minnesota NFL	7	0-0	0-0	0-0	0-0	0-0	0.0	0	0	0	0
Pro totals (2 years)	24	8-8	6-9	4-7	1-3	19-27	70.4	51	50	50	107

ELLIS, ED   T

PERSONAL: Born October 13, 1975, in New Haven, Conn. ... 6-5/325. ... Full name: Edward Key Ellis.
HIGH SCHOOL: Hamden (Conn.).
COLLEGE: Buffalo.
TRANSACTIONS/CAREER NOTES: Selected by New England Patriots in fourth round (125th pick overall) of 1997 NFL draft. ... Signed by Patriots (June 19, 1997). ... Granted free agency (February 11, 2000). ... Assigned by Patriots to Barcelona Dragons in 2000 NFL Europe enhancement allocation program (February 18, 2000). ... Re-signed by Patriots (March 13, 2000). ... Released by Patriots (July 17, 2000). ... Signed by Washington Redskins (July 20, 2000). ... Granted unconditional free agency (March 2, 2001). ... Signed by San Diego Chargers (April 2, 2001). ... Released by Chargers (February 27, 2003). ... Signed by Denver Broncos (April 24, 2003). ... Released by Broncos (August 31, 2003). ... Signed by San Diego Chargers (December 17, 2003). ... Granted unconditional free agency (March 3, 2004). ... Signed by New York Giants (April 6, 2004). ... On injured reserve with neck injury (August 11, 2004-entire season). ... Granted unconditional free agency (March 2, 2005).
PLAYING EXPERIENCE: New England NFL, 1997-1999; Washington NFL, 2000; San Diego NFL, 2001-2003; New York Giants NFL, 2004. ... Games/Games started: 1997 (1/0), 1998 (7/0), 1999 (2/1), 2000 (12/0), 2001 (16/2), 2002 (15/3), 2003 (2/1), Total: 55/7.

ELLIS, GREG   DE   COWBOYS

PERSONAL: Born August 14, 1975, in Wendell, N.C. ... 6-6/271. ... Full name: Gregory Lemont Ellis.
HIGH SCHOOL: East Wake (Wendell, N.C.).
COLLEGE: North Carolina.
TRANSACTIONS/CAREER NOTES: Selected by Dallas Cowboys in first round (eighth pick overall) of 1998 NFL draft. ... Signed by Cowboys (July 13, 1998). ... On injured reserve with leg injury (December 16, 1999-remainder of season).
HONORS: Named defensive end on THE SPORTING NEWS college All-America second team (1996 and 1997).

Year Team	G	GS	TOTALS			INTERCEPTIONS			
			Tk.	Ast.	Sks.	No.	Yds.	Avg.	TD
1998—Dallas NFL	16	16	27	12	3.0	0	0	0.0	0
1999—Dallas NFL	13	13	37	7	7.5	1	87	87.0	1
2000—Dallas NFL	16	16	39	13	3.0	0	0	0.0	0
2001—Dallas NFL	16	16	45	16	6.0	0	0	0.0	0
2002—Dallas NFL	15	15	50	17	7.5	1	0	0.0	0
2003—Dallas NFL	16	15	35	14	8.0	0	0	0.0	0
2004—Dallas NFL	16	16	44	15	9.0	0	0	0.0	0
Pro totals (7 years)	108	107	277	94	44.0	2	87	43.5	1

ELLIS, SHAUN   DE   JETS

PERSONAL: Born June 24, 1977, in Anderson, S.C. ... 6-5/285. ... Full name: MeShaunda Pizarrur Ellis.
HIGH SCHOOL: Westside (Anderson, S.C.).
COLLEGE: Tennessee.
TRANSACTIONS/CAREER NOTES: Selected by New York Jets in first round (12th pick overall) of 2000 NFL draft. ... Signed by Jets (July 10, 2000).
HONORS: Played in Pro Bowl (2003 season).

Year Team	G	GS	TOTALS			INTERCEPTIONS			
			Tk.	Ast.	Sks.	No.	Yds.	Avg.	TD
2000—New York Jets NFL	16	3	38	15	8.5	1	1	1.0	0
2001—New York Jets NFL	16	16	28	12	5.0	0	0	0.0	0
2002—New York Jets NFL	16	16	31	10	4.0	0	0	0.0	0
2003—New York Jets NFL	16	16	48	21	12.5	0	0	0.0	0
2004—New York Jets NFL	15	15	39	18	11.0	0	0	0.0	0
Pro totals (5 years)	79	66	184	76	41.0	1	1	1.0	0

ELLISS, LUTHER   DT   BRONCOS

PERSONAL: Born March 22, 1973, in Mancos, Colo. ... 6-5/318.
HIGH SCHOOL: Mancos (Colo.).
COLLEGE: Utah.
TRANSACTIONS/CAREER NOTES: Selected by Detroit Lions in first round (20th pick overall) of 1995 NFL draft. ... Signed by Lions (July 19, 1995). ... On injured reserve with ankle injury (December 19, 2002-remainder of season). ... On active/non-football injury list (July 23-November 15, 2003). ... Released by Lions (March 2, 2004). ... Signed by Denver Broncos (March 22, 2004). ... On injured reserve with back injury (December 17, 2004-remainder of season). ... Granted unconditional free agency (March 2, 2005). ... Re-signed by Broncos (April 1, 2005).
HONORS: Named defensive lineman on THE SPORTING NEWS college All-America first team (1994). ... Played in Pro Bowl (1999 and 2000 seasons).

Year Team	G	GS	TOTALS		
			Tk.	Ast.	Sks.
1995—Detroit NFL	16	16	9	10	0.0
1996—Detroit NFL	14	14	26	23	6.5

Year Team	G	GS	TOTALS					
			Tk.	Ast.	Sks.			
1997—Detroit NFL	16	16	35	28	8.5			
1998—Detroit NFL	16	16	38	12	3.0			
1999—Detroit NFL	15	14	31	16	3.5			
2000—Detroit NFL	16	16	23	16	3.0			
2001—Detroit NFL	14	13	26	5	0.0			
2002—Detroit NFL	14	14	19	7	2.5			
2003—Detroit NFL	5	0	0	0	0.0			
2004—Denver NFL	8	0	6	1	2.0			
Pro totals (10 years)	134	119	213	118	29.0			

EMMONS, CARLOS — LB — GIANTS

PERSONAL: Born September 3, 1973, in Greenwood, Miss. ... 6-5/250. ... Name pronounced: EM-mins.
HIGH SCHOOL: Greenwood (Miss.).
COLLEGE: Arkansas State.
TRANSACTIONS/CAREER NOTES: Selected by Pittsburgh Steelers in seventh round (242nd pick overall) of 1996 NFL draft. ... Signed by Steelers (July 16, 1996). ... Granted free agency (February 12, 1999). ... Re-signed by Steelers (April 23, 1999). ... Granted unconditional free agency (February 11, 2000). ... Signed by Philadelphia Eagles (March 23, 2000). ... On injured reserve with fibula injury (December 23, 2003-remainder of season). ... Granted unconditional free agency (March 3, 2004). ... Signed by New York Giants (March 5, 2004).
CHAMPIONSHIP GAME EXPERIENCE: Played in AFC championship game (1997 season). ... Played in NFC championship game (2001 and 2002 seasons).

Year Team	G	GS	TOTALS			INTERCEPTIONS			
			Tk.	Ast.	Sks.	No.	Yds.	Avg.	TD
1996—Pittsburgh NFL	15	0	5	2	2.5	0	0	0.0	0
1997—Pittsburgh NFL	5	0	1	0	0.0	0	0	0.0	0
1998—Pittsburgh NFL	15	14	46	17	3.5	1	2	2.0	0
1999—Pittsburgh NFL	16	16	51	16	6.0	1	22	22.0	0
2000—Philadelphia NFL	16	13	55	23	0.5	2	8	4.0	0
2001—Philadelphia NFL	16	15	61	18	1.0	0	0	0.0	0
2002—Philadelphia NFL	13	13	51	9	3.5	0	0	0.0	0
2003—Philadelphia NFL	15	15	65	20	0.0	0	0	0.0	0
2004—New York Giants NFL	15	15	62	35	1.0	0	0	0.0	0
Pro totals (9 years)	126	101	397	140	18.0	4	32	8.0	0

ENA, JUSTIN — LB — TITANS

E

PERSONAL: Born November 20, 1977, in Shelton, Wash. ... 6-3/247.
HIGH SCHOOL: Shelton (Calif.).
COLLEGE: Brigham Young.
TRANSACTIONS/CAREER NOTES: Signed as non-drafted free agent by Philadelphia Eagles (April 23, 2002). ... Claimed on waivers by Tennessee Titans (September 6, 2004).
CHAMPIONSHIP GAME EXPERIENCE: Played in NFC championship game (2002 and 2003 seasons).

Year Team	G	GS	TOTALS			INTERCEPTIONS			
			Tk.	Ast.	Sks.	No.	Yds.	Avg.	TD
2002—Philadelphia NFL	9	0	1	0	0.0	0	0	0.0	0
2003—Philadelphia NFL	16	0	0	0	0.0	0	0	0.0	0
2004—Tennessee NFL	16	5	17	4	0.0	0	0	0.0	0
Pro totals (3 years)	41	5	18	4	0.0	0	0	0.0	0

ENGELBERGER, JOHN — DE — 49ERS

PERSONAL: Born October 18, 1976, in Heidelberg, Germany. ... 6-4/268. ... Full name: John Albert Engelberger.
HIGH SCHOOL: Robert E. Lee (Springfield, Va.).
COLLEGE: Virginia Tech.
TRANSACTIONS/CAREER NOTES: Selected by San Francisco 49ers in second round (35th pick overall) of 2000 NFL draft. ... Signed by 49ers (July 18, 2000). ... Granted unconditional free agency (March 3, 2004). ... Re-signed by 49ers (March 4, 2004).

Year Team	G	GS	TOTALS		
			Tk.	Ast.	Sks.
2000—San Francisco NFL	16	13	21	9	3.0
2001—San Francisco NFL	15	14	30	1	4.0
2002—San Francisco NFL	15	0	9	1	0.0
2003—San Francisco NFL	16	16	26	3	4.5
2004—San Francisco NFL	16	15	25	20	6.0
Pro totals (5 years)	78	58	111	34	17.5

ENGRAM, BOBBY — WR — SEAHAWKS

PERSONAL: Born January 7, 1973, in Camden, S.C. ... 5-10/188. ... Full name: Simon Engram III.
HIGH SCHOOL: Camden (S.C.).
COLLEGE: Penn State.
TRANSACTIONS/CAREER NOTES: Selected by Chicago Bears in second round (52nd pick overall) of 1996 NFL draft. ... Signed by Bears (July 17, 1996). ... Granted free agency (February 12, 1999). ... Re-signed by Bears (April 16, 1999). ... Granted unconditional free agency (February

11, 2000). ... Re-signed by Bears (April 26, 2000). ... On injured reserve with knee injury (September 19, 2000-remainder of season). ... Released by Bears (August 28, 2001). ... Signed by Seattle Seahawks (August 30, 2001). ... Granted unconditional free agency (February 28, 2003). ... Re-signed by Seahawks (March 5, 2003).
HONORS: Named wide receiver on THE SPORTING NEWS college All-America second team (1994 and 1995).
SINGLE GAME HIGHS (regular season): Receptions—13 (December 26, 1999, vs. St. Louis); yards—143 (December 26, 1999, vs. St. Louis); and touchdown receptions—2 (November 23, 2003, vs. Baltimore).
STATISTICAL PLATEAUS: 100-yard receiving games: 1998 (3), 1999 (2). Total: 5.

				RECEIVING			PUNT RETURNS				KICKOFF RETURNS				TOTALS			
Year Team	G	GS	No.	Yds.	Avg.	TD	No.	Yds.	Avg.	TD	No.	Yds.	Avg.	TD	TD	2pt.	Pts.	Fum.
1996—Chicago NFL	16	2	33	389	11.8	6	31	282	9.1	0	25	580	23.2	0	6	0	36	2
1997—Chicago NFL	11	11	45	399	8.9	2	1	4	4.0	0	2	27	13.5	0	2	1	14	1
1998—Chicago NFL	16	16	64	987	15.4	5	0	0	0.0	0	0	0	0.0	0	5	0	30	1
1999—Chicago NFL	16	14	88	947	10.8	4	0	0	0.0	0	0	0	0.0	0	4	0	24	2
2000—Chicago NFL	3	3	16	109	6.8	0	0	0	0.0	0	0	0	0.0	0	0	0	0	1
2001—Seattle NFL	16	4	29	400	13.8	0	6	96	16.0	0	1	6	6.0	0	0	0	0	0
2002—Seattle NFL	15	6	50	619	12.4	0	21	224	10.7	0	0	0	0.0	0	1	0	6	2
2003—Seattle NFL	16	7	52	637	12.3	6	31	320	10.3	1	1	18	18.0	0	7	0	42	5
2004—Seattle NFL	13	7	36	499	13.9	2	10	118	11.8	0	0	0	0.0	0	2	0	12	1
Pro totals (9 years)	122	70	413	4986	12.1	25	100	1044	10.4	2	29	631	21.8	0	27	1	164	15

EPHRAIM, ALONZO   C

PERSONAL: Born November 9, 1981, in Birmingham, Ala. ... 6-4/312. ... Full name: Alonzo Brandon Ephraim.
HIGH SCHOOL: Wenonah (Ala.).
COLLEGE: Alabama.
TRANSACTIONS/CAREER NOTES: Signed as non-drafted free agent by Philadelphia Eagles (April 28, 2003). ... Released by Eagles (April 28, 2005).
PLAYING EXPERIENCE: Philadelphia NFL, 2003-2004. ... Games/Games started: 2003 (16/0), 2004 (14/2). Total: 30/2.
CHAMPIONSHIP GAME EXPERIENCE: Played in NFC championship game (2003 and 2004 seasons). ... Member of Eagles for Super Bowl 39 (2004 season); did not play.

EUHUS, TIM   TE   BILLS

PERSONAL: Born October 2, 1980, in Eugene, Ore. ... 6-5/249.
HIGH SCHOOL: Churchill (Eugene, Ore.).
COLLEGE: Oregon State.
TRANSACTIONS/CAREER NOTES: Selected by Buffalo Bills in fourth round (109th pick overall) of 2004 NFL draft. ... Signed by Bills (May 18, 2004). ... On injured reserve with knee injury (December 14, 2004-remainder of season).
SINGLE GAME HIGHS (regular season): Receptions—4 (December 5, 2004, vs. Miami); yards—32 (December 5, 2004, vs. Miami); and touchdown receptions—1 (December 5, 2004, vs. Miami).

			RECEIVING				TOTALS			
Year Team	G	GS	No.	Yds.	Avg.	TD	TD	2pt.	Pts.	Fum.
2004—Buffalo NFL	12	5	11	98	8.9	2	2	0	12	0

EVANS, DEMETRIC   DE   REDSKINS

PERSONAL: Born September 3, 1979, in Haynesville, La. ... 6-3/300. ... Full name: Demetric Untrell Evans.
HIGH SCHOOL: Haynesville (La.).
COLLEGE: Georgia.
TRANSACTIONS/CAREER NOTES: Signed as non-drafted free agent by Dallas Cowboys (April 27, 2001). ... Released by Cowboys (August 31, 2003). ... Signed by Washington Redskins (June 15, 2004). ... Granted free agency (March 2, 2005). ... Re-signed by Redskins (April 14, 2005).

			TOTALS		
Year Team	G	GS	Tk.	Ast.	Sks.
2001—Dallas NFL	16	0	0	0	1.0
2002—Dallas NFL	4	0	0	0	0.0
2004—Washington NFL	12	8	17	9	2.5
Pro totals (3 years)	32	8	17	9	3.5

EVANS, HEATH   FB   DOLPHINS

PERSONAL: Born December 30, 1978, in West Palm Beach, Fla. ... 6-0/245. ... Full name: Bryan Heath Evans.
HIGH SCHOOL: Kings Academy (Miami).
COLLEGE: Auburn.
TRANSACTIONS/CAREER NOTES: Selected by Seattle Seahawks in third round (82nd pick overall) of 2001 NFL draft. ... Signed by Seahawks (July 26, 2001). ... Granted free agency (March 3, 2004). ... Re-signed by Seahawks (April 4, 2004). ... Granted unconditional free agency (March 2, 2005). ... Signed by Miami Dolphins (March 17, 2005).
SINGLE GAME HIGHS (regular season): Attempts—6 (September 26, 2004, vs. San Francisco); yards—22 (December 29, 2002, vs. San Diego); and rushing touchdowns—0.

			RUSHING				RECEIVING				KICKOFF RETURNS				TOTALS			
Year Team	G	GS	Att.	Yds.	Avg.	TD	No.	Yds.	Avg.	TD	No.	Yds.	Avg.	TD	TD	2pt.	Pts.	Fum.
2001—Seattle NFL	16	0	2	11	5.5	0	0	0	0.0	0	3	40	13.3	0	0	0	0	0
2002—Seattle NFL	16	1	17	53	3.1	0	8	41	5.1	0	6	84	14.0	0	0	0	0	1
2003—Seattle NFL	14	0	7	24	3.4	0	2	34	17.0	0	1	14	14.0	0	0	0	0	0
2004—Seattle NFL	15	0	7	20	2.9	0	2	12	6.0	0	3	51	17.0	0	0	0	0	1
Pro totals (4 years)	61	1	33	108	3.3	0	12	87	7.3	0	13	189	14.5	0	0	0	0	2

E

EVANS, JOSH — DT

PERSONAL: Born September 6, 1972, in Langdale, Ala. ... 6-3/280. ... Full name: Mijoshki Antwon Evans.
HIGH SCHOOL: Lanett (Ala.).
COLLEGE: Alabama-Birmingham.
TRANSACTIONS/CAREER NOTES: Signed as non-drafted free agent by Dallas Cowboys (April 27, 1995). ... Released by Cowboys (August 22, 1995). ... Signed by Houston Oilers to practice squad (September 1, 1995). ... Activated (November 10, 1995). ... On injured reserve with knee injury (November 29, 1996-remainder of season). ... Oilers franchise moved to Tennessee for 1997 season. ... Granted free agency (February 13, 1998). ... Re-signed by Oilers (July 25, 1998). ... Oilers franchise renamed Tennessee Titans for 1999 season (December 26, 1998). ... On suspended list for violating league substance abuse policy (September 6-October 4, 1999). ... On suspended list for violating league substance abuse policy (March 1, 2000-April 13, 2001). ... Granted unconditional free agency (March 1, 2002). ... Signed by New York Jets (July 17, 2002). ... On suspended list for violating league substance abuse policy (June 27-November 17, 2003). ... On injured reserve with back injury (September 22, 2004-remainder of season). ... Granted unconditional free agency (March 2, 2005). ... Re-signed by Jets (April 5, 2005). ... Announced retirement (April 27, 2005).
CHAMPIONSHIP GAME EXPERIENCE: Played in AFC championship game (1999 season). ... Played in Super Bowl 34 (1999 season).

				TOTALS		
Year Team		G	GS	Tk.	Ast.	Sks.
1995—Houston NFL		7	0	2	1	0.0
1996—Houston NFL		8	0	4	7	0.0
1997—Tennessee NFL		15	0	23	3	2.0
1998—Tennessee NFL		14	11	30	13	3.5
1999—Tennessee NFL		11	10	21	5	3.5
2000—Tennessee NFL		Did not play.				
2001—Tennessee NFL		16	16	41	12	5.5
2002—New York Jets NFL		16	16	40	7	6.0
2003—New York Jets NFL		6	0	10	4	1.0
2004—New York Jets NFL		1	0	0	1	0.0
Pro totals (9 years)		94	53	171	53	21.5

EVANS, LEE — WR — BILLS

PERSONAL: Born March 11, 1981, in Bedford, Ohio. ... 5-10/197.
HIGH SCHOOL: Bedford (Ohio).
COLLEGE: Wisconsin.
TRANSACTIONS/CAREER NOTES: Selected by Buffalo Bills in first round (13th pick overall) of 2004 NFL draft. ... Signed by Bills (July 31, 2004).
HONORS: Named wide receiver on THE SPORTING NEWS college All-America second team (2001).
SINGLE GAME HIGHS (regular season): Receptions—8 (December 26, 2004, vs. San Francisco); yards—110 (December 5, 2004, vs. Miami); and touchdown receptions—2 (December 26, 2004, vs. San Francisco).
STATISTICAL PLATEAUS: 100-yard receiving games: 2004 (2). Total: 2.

			RUSHING				RECEIVING				TOTALS			
Year Team	G	GS	Att.	Yds.	Avg.	TD	No.	Yds.	Avg.	TD	TD	2pt.	Pts.	Fum.
2004—Buffalo NFL	16	11	5	85	17.0	0	48	843	17.6	9	9	0	54	1

EVANS, TROY — LB — TEXANS

PERSONAL: Born December 3, 1977, in Bay City, Mich. ... 6-1/237. ... Full name: Troy Lyn Evans.
HIGH SCHOOL: Lakota (Cincinnati).
COLLEGE: Cincinnati.
TRANSACTIONS/CAREER NOTES: Signed as non-drafted free agent by St. Louis Rams (April 25, 2001). ... Released by Rams (August 27, 2001). ... Re-signed by Rams to practice squad (November 21, 2001). ... Granted free agency following 2001 season. ... Signed by Houston Texans (February 12, 2002). ... Released by Texans (September 23, 2002). ... Re-signed by Texans (October 30, 2002). ... Re-signed by Texans (April 1, 2003). ... On injured reserve with ankle injury (December 15, 2004-remainder of season). ... Granted free agency (March 2, 2005). ... Re-signed by Texans (April 12, 2005).

				TOTALS			INTERCEPTIONS			
Year Team		G	GS	Tk.	Ast.	Sks.	No.	Yds.	Avg.	TD
2002—Houston NFL		12	0	0	0	0.0	0	0	0.0	0
2003—Houston NFL		15	0	2	0	0.0	0	0	0.0	0
2004—Houston NFL		13	0	0	1	0.0	0	0	0.0	0
Pro totals (3 years)		40	0	2	1	0.0	0	0	0.0	0

FABINI, JASON — T — JETS

PERSONAL: Born August 25, 1974, in Fort Wayne, Ind. ... 6-7/304.
HIGH SCHOOL: Bishop Dwenger (Fort Wayne, Ind.).
COLLEGE: Cincinnati.
TRANSACTIONS/CAREER NOTES: Selected by New York Jets in fourth round (111th pick overall) of 1998 NFL draft. ... Signed by Jets (July 13, 1998). ... On injured reserve with knee injury (November 16, 1999-remainder of season). ... Granted free agency (March 2, 2001). ... Re-signed by Jets (May 30, 2001).
PLAYING EXPERIENCE: New York Jets NFL, 1998-2004. ... Games/Games started: 1998 (16/16), 1999 (9/9), 2000 (16/16), 2001 (16/16), 2002 (16/16), 2003 (16/16), 2004 (16/16). Total: 105/105.
CHAMPIONSHIP GAME EXPERIENCE: Played in AFC championship game (1998 season).

F

FAGGINS, DEMARCUS   CB   TEXANS

PERSONAL: Born June 13, 1979, in Irving, Texas. ... 5-10/180. ... Full name: Demarcus Faggins.
HIGH SCHOOL: Irving (Texas).
JUNIOR COLLEGE: Navarro College (Texas).
COLLEGE: Kansas State.
TRANSACTIONS/CAREER NOTES: Selected by Houston Texans in sixth round (173rd pick overall) of 2002 NFL draft. ... Signed by Texans (July 13, 2002). ... Waived by Texans (August 31, 2003). ... Re-signed by Texans to practice squad (September 1, 2003). ... Activated (November 9, 2003).

			TOTALS			INTERCEPTIONS			
Year Team	G	GS	Tk.	Ast.	Sks.	No.	Yds.	Avg.	TD
2002—Houston NFL	2	0	0	0	0.0	0	0	0.0	0
2003—Houston NFL	8	1	12	1	0.0	0	0	0.0	0
2004—Houston NFL	16	2	35	4	0.0	3	47	15.7	1
Pro totals (3 years)	26	3	47	5	0.0	3	47	15.7	1

FAINE, JEFF   C   BROWNS

PERSONAL: Born April 6, 1981, in Milwaukie, Ore. ... 6-3/300. ... Full name: Jeffrey Kalei Faine.
HIGH SCHOOL: Seminole (Sanford, Fla.).
COLLEGE: Notre Dame.
TRANSACTIONS/CAREER NOTES: Selected after junior season by Cleveland Browns in first round (21st pick overall) of 2003 NFL draft. ... Signed by Browns (July 28, 2003). ... On injured reserve with ankle injury (November 26, 2003-remainder of season). ... On injured reserve with ankle injury (December 14, 2004-remainder of season).
PLAYING EXPERIENCE: Cleveland NFL, 2003-2004. ... Games/Games started: 2003 (9/9), 2004 (13/13). Total: 22/22.

FANECA, ALAN   G   STEELERS

PERSONAL: Born December 7, 1976, in New Orleans, La. ... 6-5/307. ... Full name: Alan Joseph Faneca Jr.
HIGH SCHOOL: John Curtis Christian (New Orleans), then Lamar (Houston).
COLLEGE: Louisiana State.
TRANSACTIONS/CAREER NOTES: Selected after junior season by Pittsburgh Steelers in first round (26th pick overall) of 1998 NFL draft. ... Signed by Steelers (July 29, 1998).
PLAYING EXPERIENCE: Pittsburgh NFL, 1998-2004. ... Games/Games started: 1998 (16/12), 1999 (15/14), 2000 (16/16), 2001 (15/15), 2002 (16/16), 2003 (16/16), 2004 (16/16). Total: 110/105.
CHAMPIONSHIP GAME EXPERIENCE: Played in AFC championship game (2001 and 2004 seasons).
HONORS: Named guard on THE SPORTING NEWS college All-America first team (1997). ... Named guard on THE SPORTING NEWS NFL All-Pro team (2001, 2002 and 2004). ... Played in Pro Bowl (2001-2004 seasons).

FARGAS, JUSTIN   RB   RAIDERS

PERSONAL: Born January 25, 1980, in Encino, Calif. ... 6-1/220.
HIGH SCHOOL: Notre Dame (Sherman Oaks, Calif.).
COLLEGE: Southern California.
TRANSACTIONS/CAREER NOTES: Selected by Oakland Raiders in third round (96th pick overall) of 2003 NFL draft. ... Signed by Raiders (July 24, 2003). ... On injured reserve with knee injury (November 19, 2003-remainder of season).
SINGLE GAME HIGHS (regular season): Attempts—16 (November 9, 2003, vs. New York Jets); yards—62 (November 9, 2003, vs. New York Jets); and rushing touchdowns—1 (October 10, 2004, vs. Indianapolis).

			RUSHING				RECEIVING				KICKOFF RETURNS				TOTALS			
Year Team	G	GS	Att.	Yds.	Avg.	TD	No.	Yds.	Avg.	TD	No.	Yds.	Avg.	TD	TD	2pt.	Pts.	Fum.
2003—Oakland NFL	10	1	40	203	5.1	0	2	2	1.0	0	16	315	19.7	0	0	0	0	1
2004—Oakland NFL	12	0	35	126	3.6	1	11	68	6.2	0	0	0	0.0	0	1	0	6	1
Pro totals (2 years)	22	1	75	329	4.4	1	13	70	5.4	0	16	315	19.7	0	1	0	6	2

FARRIOR, JAMES   LB   STEELERS

PERSONAL: Born January 6, 1975, in Richmond, Va. ... 6-2/243. ... Full name: James Alfred Farrior.
HIGH SCHOOL: Matoaca (Ettrick, Va.).
COLLEGE: Virginia.
TRANSACTIONS/CAREER NOTES: Selected by New York Jets in first round (eighth pick overall) of 1997 NFL draft. ... Signed by Jets (July 20, 1997). ... Granted unconditional free agency (March 1, 2002). ... Signed by Pittsburgh Steelers (April 12, 2002).
CHAMPIONSHIP GAME EXPERIENCE: Played in AFC championship game (1998 and 2004 seasons).
HONORS: Named linebacker on THE SPORTING NEWS NFL All-Pro team (2004). ... Played in Pro Bowl (2004 season).

			TOTALS			INTERCEPTIONS			
Year Team	G	GS	Tk.	Ast.	Sks.	No.	Yds.	Avg.	TD
1997—New York Jets NFL	16	15	53	18	1.5	0	0	0.0	0
1998—New York Jets NFL	12	2	17	10	0.0	0	0	0.0	0
1999—New York Jets NFL	16	4	30	8	2.0	0	0	0.0	0
2000—New York Jets NFL	16	6	46	10	1.0	1	0	0.0	0
2001—New York Jets NFL	16	16	107	36	1.0	2	84	42.0	0
2002—Pittsburgh NFL	14	14	55	22	0.0	0	0	0.0	0
2003—Pittsburgh NFL	16	16	94	43	0.0	1	9	9.0	0
2004—Pittsburgh NFL	16	16	67	28	3.0	4	113	28.3	1
Pro totals (8 years)	122	89	469	175	8.5	8	206	25.8	1

F

FARRIS, JIMMY   WR   REDSKINS

PERSONAL: Born April 13, 1978, in Lewiston, Idaho. ... 6-0/200.
HIGH SCHOOL: Lewiston (Idaho).
COLLEGE: Montana.
TRANSACTIONS/CAREER NOTES: Signed as non-drafted free agent by San Francisco 49ers (April 26, 2001). ... Released by 49ers (September 2, 2001). ... Re-signed by 49ers to practice squad (September 4, 2001). ... Signed by New England Patriots off 49ers practice squad (January 11, 2002). ... Released by Patriots (August 27, 2002). ... Signed by Atlanta Falcons to practice squad (November 27, 2002). ... Activated (January 7, 2003). ... Released by Falcons (April 25, 2005). ... Signed by Washington Redskins (May 5, 2005).
CHAMPIONSHIP GAME EXPERIENCE: Member of Falcons for NFC championship game (2004 season); inactive.
SINGLE GAME HIGHS (regular season): Receptions—2 (September 14, 2003, vs. Washington); yards—58 (September 14, 2003, vs. Washington); and touchdown receptions—1 (October 5, 2003, vs. Minnesota).

| | | | RECEIVING | | | | TOTALS | | | |
Year Team	G	GS	No.	Yds.	Avg.	TD	TD	2pt.	Pts.	Fum.
2003—Atlanta NFL	16	0	6	100	16.7	2	2	0	12	0
2004—Atlanta NFL	14	0	0	0	0.0	0	0	0	0	0
Pro totals (2 years)	30	0	6	100	16.7	2	2	0	12	0

FATAFEHI, MARIO   DT   BRONCOS

PERSONAL: Born January 27, 1979, in Chicago, Ill. ... 6-2/300.
HIGH SCHOOL: Ferrington (Honolulu, Hawaii).
JUNIOR COLLEGE: Snow College (Utah).
COLLEGE: Kansas State.
TRANSACTIONS/CAREER NOTES: Selected by Arizona Cardinals in fifth round (133rd pick overall) of 2001 NFL draft. ... Signed by Cardinals (June 5, 2001). ... On injured reserve with hand injury (November 30, 2001-remainder of season). ... Released by Cardinals (October 5, 2002). ... Signed by Carolina Panthers (November 1, 2002). ... Waived by Panthers (July 14, 2003). ... Signed by Denver Broncos (July 28, 2003).

| | | | TOTALS | | |
Year Team	G	GS	Tk.	Ast.	Sks.
2001—Arizona NFL	7	1	4	4	0.0
2002—Carolina NFL	6	0	0	0	0.0
2003—Denver NFL	16	9	22	9	2.5
2004—Denver NFL	16	16	14	7	2.5
Pro totals (4 years)	45	26	40	20	5.0

FAULK, KEVIN   RB   PATRIOTS

PERSONAL: Born June 5, 1976, in Lafayette, La. ... 5-8/202. ... Full name: Kevin Tony Faulk.
HIGH SCHOOL: Carencro (Lafayette, La.).
COLLEGE: Louisiana State.
TRANSACTIONS/CAREER NOTES: Selected by New England Patriots in second round (46th pick overall) of 1999 NFL draft. ... Signed by Patriots (July 28, 1999). ... On injured reserve with broken ankle (December 15, 1999-remainder of season). ... Granted unconditional free agency (March 3, 2004). ... Re-signed by Patriots (March 10, 2004).
CHAMPIONSHIP GAME EXPERIENCE: Played in AFC championship game (2001, 2003 and 2004 seasons). ... Member of Super Bowl championship team (2001, 2003 and 2004 seasons).
HONORS: Named kick returner on THE SPORTING NEWS college All-America second team (1998).
SINGLE GAME HIGHS (regular season): Attempts—23 (November 23, 2003, vs. Houston); yards—96 (October 26, 2003, vs. Cleveland); and rushing touchdowns—1 (December 12, 2004, vs. Cincinnati).
STATISTICAL PLATEAUS: 100-yard receiving games: 2002 (1), 2003 (1). Total: 2.

| | | | RUSHING | | | | RECEIVING | | | | PUNT RETURNS | | | | KICKOFF RETURNS | | | | TOTALS | | |
Year Team	G	GS	Att.	Yds.	Avg.	TD	No.	Yds.	Avg.	TD	No.	Yds.	Avg.	TD	No.	Yds.	Avg.	TD	TD	2pt.	Pts.
1999—N.E. NFL	11	2	67	227	3.4	1	12	98	8.2	1	10	90	9.0	0	39	943	24.2	0	2	0	12
2000—N.E. NFL	16	9	164	570	3.5	4	51	465	9.1	1	6	58	9.7	0	38	816	21.5	0	5	1	32
2001—N.E. NFL	15	1	41	169	4.1	1	30	189	6.3	2	4	27	6.8	0	33	662	20.1	0	3	0	18
2002—N.E. NFL	15	0	52	271	5.2	2	37	379	10.2	3	8	65	8.1	0	26	725	§27.9	†2	7	0	42
2003—N.E. NFL	15	8	178	638	3.6	0	48	440	9.2	0	5	66	13.2	0	10	207	20.7	0	0	0	0
2004—N.E. NFL	11	1	54	255	4.7	2	26	248	9.5	1	20	133	6.7	0	4	73	18.3	0	3	0	18
Pro totals (6 years)	83	21	556	2130	3.8	10	204	1819	8.9	8	53	439	8.3	0	150	3426	22.8	2	20	1	122

FAULK, MARSHALL   RB   RAMS

PERSONAL: Born February 26, 1973, in New Orleans, La. ... 5-10/211. ... Full name: Marshall William Faulk.
HIGH SCHOOL: G. W. Carver (New Orleans).
COLLEGE: San Diego State.
TRANSACTIONS/CAREER NOTES: Selected after junior season by Indianapolis Colts in first round (second pick overall) of 1994 NFL draft. ... Signed by Colts (July 24, 1994). ... Traded by Colts to St. Louis Rams for second- (LB Mike Peterson) and fifth-round (DE Brad Scioli) picks in 1999 draft (April 15, 1999).
CHAMPIONSHIP GAME EXPERIENCE: Member of Colts for AFC championship game (1995 season); inactive due to injury. ... Played in NFC championship game (1999 and 2001 seasons). ... Member of Super Bowl championship team (1999 season). ... Played in Super Bowl 36 (2001 season).
HONORS: Named running back on THE SPORTING NEWS college All-America first team (1991-1993). ... Named NFL Rookie of the Year by THE SPORTING NEWS (1994). ... Played in Pro Bowl (1994, 1995, 1998, 1999, 2001 and 2002 seasons). ... Named Outstanding Player of Pro Bowl (1994 season). ... Named running back on THE SPORTING NEWS NFL All-Pro team (1999-2001). ... Named NFL Player of the Year by THE SPORTING NEWS (2000 and 2001). ... Named to play in Pro Bowl (2000 season); replaced by Stephen Davis due to injury.

RECORDS: Shares NFL single-game record for most two-point conversions—2 (October 15, 2000).
SINGLE GAME HIGHS (regular season): Attempts—32 (October 20, 2002, vs. Seattle); yards—220 (December 24, 2000, vs. New Orleans); and rushing touchdowns—4 (December 10, 2000, vs. Minnesota).
STATISTICAL PLATEAUS: 100-yard rushing games: 1994 (4), 1995 (1), 1996 (1), 1997 (4), 1998 (4), 1999 (7), 2000 (4), 2001 (5), 2002 (3), 2003 (5), 2004 (3). Total: 41. 100-yard receiving games: 1994 (1), 1998 (3), 1999 (1), 2000 (2), 2001 (1). Total: 8.
MISCELLANEOUS: Holds Rams franchise all-time records for most rushing touchdowns (58) and most touchdowns (84). ... Active NFL leader for career rushing touchdowns (100).

Year Team	G	GS	RUSHING Att.	Yds.	Avg.	TD	RECEIVING No.	Yds.	Avg.	TD	TOTALS TD	2pt.	Pts.	Fum.
1994—Indianapolis NFL	16	16	314	1282	4.1	11	52	522	10.0	1	▲12	0	72	5
1995—Indianapolis NFL	16	16	289	1078	3.7	11	56	475	8.5	3	14	0	84	8
1996—Indianapolis NFL	13	13	198	587	3.0	7	56	428	7.6	0	7	0	42	2
1997—Indianapolis NFL	16	16	264	1054	4.0	7	47	471	10.0	1	8	0	48	5
1998—Indianapolis NFL	16	15	324	1319	4.1	6	86	908	10.6	4	10	0	60	3
1999—St. Louis NFL	16	16	253	1381	*5.5	7	87	1048	12.0	5	12	1	74	2
2000—St. Louis NFL	14	14	253	1359	*5.4	*18	81	830	10.2	8	*26	2	*160	0
2001—St. Louis NFL	14	14	260	1382	*5.3	‡12	83	765	9.2	9	*21	1	*128	3
2002—St. Louis NFL	14	10	212	953	4.5	8	80	537	6.7	2	10	0	60	4
2003—St. Louis NFL	11	11	209	818	3.9	10	45	290	6.4	1	11	0	66	0
2004—St. Louis NFL	14	14	195	774	4.0	3	50	310	6.2	1	4	†2	28	2
Pro totals (11 years)	160	155	2771	11987	4.3	100	723	6584	9.1	35	135	6	822	34

FAULK, TREV   LB   RAMS

PERSONAL: Born August 6, 1981, in Lafayette, La. ... 6-3/254. ... Full name: Treverance Faulk.
HIGH SCHOOL: Lafayette (La.).
COLLEGE: Louisiana State.
TRANSACTIONS/CAREER NOTES: Signed as non-drafted free agent by Denver Broncos (April 22, 2002). ... Released by Broncos (August 26, 2002). ... Signed by Arizona Cardinals to practice squad (December 11, 2002). ... Signed by St. Louis Rams off Cardinals practice squad (December 31, 2003).

Year Team	G	GS	TOTALS Tk.	Ast.	Sks.	INTERCEPTIONS No.	Yds.	Avg.	TD
2004—St. Louis NFL	13	2	15	8	0.0	0	0	0.0	0

FAURIA CHRISTIAN   TE   PATRIOTS

PERSONAL: Born September 22, 1971, in Northridge, Calif. ... 6-4/250. ... Name pronounced: FOUR-ee-ah.
HIGH SCHOOL: Crespi Carmelite (Encino, Calif.).
COLLEGE: Colorado.
TRANSACTIONS/CAREER NOTES: Selected by Seattle Seahawks in second round (39th pick overall) of 1995 NFL draft. ... Signed by Seahawks (July 17, 1995). ... Granted free agency (February 13, 1998). ... Re-signed by Seahawks (April 20, 1998). ... Granted unconditional free agency (February 12, 1999). ... Re-signed by Seahawks (March 5, 1999). ... Granted unconditional free agency (March 1, 2002). ... Signed by New England Patriots (March 22, 2002).
CHAMPIONSHIP GAME EXPERIENCE: Played in AFC championship game (2003 and 2004 seasons). ... Member of Super Bowl championship team (2003 and 2004 seasons).
SINGLE GAME HIGHS (regular season): Receptions—6 (December 26, 1999, vs. Kansas City); yards—84 (December 26, 1999, vs. Kansas City); and touchdown receptions—2 (September 14, 2003, vs. Philadelphia).

Year Team	G	GS	RECEIVING No.	Yds.	Avg.	TD	TOTALS TD	2pt.	Pts.	Fum.
1995—Seattle NFL	14	9	17	181	10.6	1	1	0	6	0
1996—Seattle NFL	10	9	18	214	11.9	1	1	0	6	0
1997—Seattle NFL	16	3	10	110	11.0	0	0	0	0	0
1998—Seattle NFL	16	15	37	377	10.2	2	2	0	12	1
1999—Seattle NFL	16	16	35	376	10.7	0	0	0	0	1
2000—Seattle NFL	15	10	28	237	8.5	2	2	0	12	1
2001—Seattle NFL	16	11	21	188	9.0	1	1	1	8	2
2002—New England NFL	16	13	27	253	9.4	7	7	1	44	0
2003—New England NFL	16	12	28	285	10.2	2	2	0	12	0
2004—New England NFL	16	10	16	195	12.2	2	2	0	12	0
Pro totals (10 years)	151	108	237	2416	10.2	18	18	2	112	5

FAVORS GREG   LB   JAGUARS

PERSONAL: Born September 30, 1974, in Atlanta, Ga. ... 6-1/244. ... Full name: Gregory Bernard Favors.
HIGH SCHOOL: Southside (Atlanta).
COLLEGE: Mississippi State.
TRANSACTIONS/CAREER NOTES: Selected by Kansas City Chiefs in fourth round (120th pick overall) of 1998 NFL draft. ... Signed by Chiefs (July 17, 1998). ... Claimed on waivers by Tennessee Titans (September 8, 1999). ... Granted free agency (March 2, 2001). ... Re-signed by Titans (May 9, 2001). ... Granted unconditional free agency (March 1, 2002). ... Signed by Indianapolis Colts (April 9, 2002). ... Released by Colts (November 4, 2002). ... Signed by Buffalo Bills (November 19, 2002). ... Granted unconditional free agency (February 28, 2003). ... Signed by Carolina Panthers (March 25, 2003). ... Granted unconditional free agency (March 3, 2004). ... Signed by Jacksonville Jaguars (March 23, 2004).
CHAMPIONSHIP GAME EXPERIENCE: Played in AFC championship game (1999 season). ... Played in Super Bowl 34 (1999 season) and Super Bowl 38 (2003 season).

F

Year Team	G	GS	TOTALS			INTERCEPTIONS			
			Tk.	Ast.	Sks.	No.	Yds.	Avg.	TD
1998—Kansas City NFL	16	4	17	2	2.0	0	0	0.0	0
1999—Tennessee NFL	15	0	0	0	0.0	0	0	0.0	0
2000—Tennessee NFL	16	16	28	9	5.5	0	0	0.0	0
2001—Tennessee NFL	16	12	30	17	1.5	1	0	0.0	0
2002—Buffalo NFL	6	0	0	0	0.0	0	0	0.0	0
2003—Carolina NFL	16	12	56	20	0.0	0	0	0.0	0
2004—Jacksonville NFL	15	11	25	11	5.5	0	0	0.0	0
Pro totals (7 years)	100	55	156	59	14.5	1	0	0.0	0

FAVRE, BRETT   QB   PACKERS

PERSONAL: Born October 10, 1969, in Gulfport, Miss. ... 6-2/224. ... Full name: Brett Lorenzo Favre. ... Name pronounced: FARVE.
HIGH SCHOOL: Hancock North Central (Kiln, Miss.).
COLLEGE: Southern Miss.
TRANSACTIONS/CAREER NOTES: Selected by Atlanta Falcons in second round (33rd pick overall) of 1991 NFL draft. ... Signed by Falcons (July 18, 1991). ... Traded by Falcons to Green Bay Packers for first-round pick (OT Bob Whitfield) in 1992 draft (February 11, 1992). ... Granted free agency (February 17, 1994). ... Re-signed by Packers (July 14, 1994).
CHAMPIONSHIP GAME EXPERIENCE: Played in NFC championship game (1995-1997 seasons). ... Member of Super Bowl championship team (1996 season). ... Played in Super Bowl 32 (1997 season).
HONORS: Played in Pro Bowl (1992, 1993, 1995 and 1996 seasons). ... Named NFL Player of the Year by THE SPORTING NEWS (1995 and 1996). ... Named quarterback on THE SPORTING NEWS NFL All-Pro team (1995-97). ... Named to play in Pro Bowl (1997 season); replaced by Chris Chandler due to injury. ... Named to play in Pro Bowl (2001 season); replaced by Donovan McNabb due to injury. ... Named to play in Pro Bowl (2002 season); replaced by Donovan McNabb due to injury. ... Named to play in Pro Bowl (2003 season); replaced by Matt Hasselbeck due to injury.
RECORDS: Shares NFL record for longest pass completion (to Robert Brooks)—99 yards, touchdown (September 11, 1995, at Chicago). ... Shares NFL career record for most seasons with 3,000 or more yards passing—13.
SINGLE GAME HIGHS (regular season): Attempts—61 (October 14, 1996, vs. San Francisco); completions—36 (December 5, 1993, vs. Chicago); yards—402 (December 5, 1993, vs. Chicago); and touchdown passes—5 (September 27, 1998, vs. Carolina).
STATISTICAL PLATEAUS: 300-yard passing games: 1993 (1), 1994 (4), 1995 (7), 1996 (2), 1997 (2), 1998 (4), 1999 (6), 2000 (2), 2001 (4), 2002 (3), 2003 (1), 2004 (5). Total: 41.
MISCELLANEOUS: Regular-season record as starting NFL quarterback: 135-70 (.659). ... Postseason record as starting NFL quarterback: 11-9 (.550). ... Active NFL leader for passing yards (49,734) and touchdown passes (376). ... Holds Green Bay Packers all-time records for most yards passing (49,734) and most touchdown passes (376).

Year Team	G	GS	PASSING									RUSHING				TOTALS		
			Att.	Cmp.	Pct.	Yds.	TD	Int.	Avg.	Skd.	Rat.	Att.	Yds.	Avg.	TD	TD	2pt.	Pts.
1991—Atlanta NFL	2	0	5	0	0.0	0	0	2	0.00	1	0.0	0	0	0.0	0	0	0	0
1992—Green Bay NFL	15	13	471	∞302	64.1	3227	18	13	6.85	34	85.3	47	198	4.2	1	1	0	6
1993—Green Bay NFL	16	16	‡522	‡318	60.9	3303	19	*24	6.33	30	72.2	58	216	3.7	1	1	0	6
1994—Green Bay NFL	16	16	582	363	62.4	3882	33	14	6.67	31	90.7	42	202	4.8	2	2	0	12
1995—Green Bay NFL	16	16	570	359	63.0	*4413	*38	13	‡7.74	33	‡99.5	39	181	4.6	3	3	0	18
1996—Green Bay NFL	16	16	‡543	‡325	59.9	‡3899	*39	13	7.18	40	95.8	49	136	2.8	2	2	0	12
1997—Green Bay NFL	16	16	513	‡304	59.3	‡3867	*35	16	7.54	25	92.6	58	187	3.2	1	1	0	6
1998—Green Bay NFL	16	16	‡551	*347	*63.0	*4212	31	‡23	7.64	38	87.8	40	133	3.3	1	1	0	6
1999—Green Bay NFL	16	16	*595	341	57.3	4091	22	23	6.88	35	74.7	28	142	5.1	0	0	0	0
2000—Green Bay NFL	16	16	‡580	338	58.3	3812	20	16	6.57	33	78.0	27	108	4.0	0	0	0	0
2001—Green Bay NFL	16	16	510	314	61.6	3921	32	15	7.69	22	94.1	38	56	1.5	1	1	0	6
2002—Green Bay NFL	16	16	‡551	‡341	61.9	3658	∞27	16	6.64	26	85.6	25	73	2.9	0	0	0	0
2003—Green Bay NFL	16	16	471	308	‡65.4	3361	*32	21	7.14	19	90.4	18	15	0.8	0	0	0	0
2004—Green Bay NFL	16	16	540	346	64.1	4088	30	17	7.57	12	92.4	16	36	2.3	0	0	0	0
Pro totals (14 years)	209	205	7004	4306	61.5	49734	376	226	7.10	379	87.4	485	1683	3.5	12	12	0	72

FEAGLES, JEFF   P   GIANTS

PERSONAL: Born March 7, 1966, in Anaheim, Calif. ... 6-1/215. ... Full name: Jeffrey Allan Feagles.
HIGH SCHOOL: Gerard Catholic (Phoenix).
JUNIOR COLLEGE: Scottsdale (Ariz.) Community College.
COLLEGE: Miami (Fla.).
TRANSACTIONS/CAREER NOTES: Signed as non-drafted free agent by New England Patriots (May 1, 1988). ... Claimed on waivers by Philadelphia Eagles (June 5, 1990). ... Granted unconditional free agency (February 1-April 1, 1992). ... Re-signed by Eagles for 1992 season. ... Granted unconditional free agency (February 17, 1994). ... Signed by Phoenix Cardinals (March 2, 1994). ... Cardinals franchise renamed Arizona Cardinals for 1994 season. ... Granted unconditional free agency (February 13, 1998). ... Signed by Seattle Seahawks (March 4, 1998). ... Granted unconditional free agency (February 28, 2003). ... Signed by New York Giants (March 7, 2003).
HONORS: Played in Pro Bowl (1995 season).

Year Team	G	PUNTING					
		No.	Yds.	Avg.	Net avg.	In. 20	Blk.
1988—New England NFL	16	▲91	3482	38.3	34.1	24	0
1989—New England NFL	16	63	2392	38.0	31.3	13	1
1990—Philadelphia NFL	16	72	3026	42.0	35.5	20	2
1991—Philadelphia NFL	16	*87	3640	41.8	34.0	*29	1
1992—Philadelphia NFL	16	‡82	‡3459	42.2	36.9	‡26	0
1993—Philadelphia NFL	16	83	3323	40.0	35.3	*31	0
1994—Arizona NFL	16	*98	‡3997	40.8	36.0	‡33	0
1995—Arizona NFL	16	72	3150	43.8	‡38.2	20	0
1996—Arizona NFL	16	76	3328	43.8	36.4	23	1
1997—Arizona NFL	16	91	4028	44.3	36.8	24	1
1998—Seattle NFL	16	81	3568	44.0	36.5	27	0

Year Team	G	No.	Yds.	Avg.	Net avg.	In. 20	Blk.
				PUNTING			
1999—Seattle NFL	16	84	3425	40.8	35.2	34	0
2000—Seattle NFL	16	74	2960	40.0	36.9	24	▲1
2001—Seattle NFL	16	85	3730	43.9	36.4	26	1
2002—Seattle NFL	16	61	2542	41.7	37.0	22	0
2003—New York Giants NFL	16	90	3641	40.5	33.9	31	1
2004—New York Giants NFL	16	74	3069	41.5	34.6	23	2
Pro totals (17 years)	272	1364	56760	41.6	35.6	430	11

FEELEY, A.J.   QB   DOLPHINS

PERSONAL: Born May 16, 1977, in Caldwell, Idaho. ... 6-3/225. ... Full name: Adam Joshua Feeley.

HIGH SCHOOL: Ontario (Ore.).

COLLEGE: Oregon.

TRANSACTIONS/CAREER NOTES: Selected by Philadelphia Eagles in fifth round (155th pick overall) of 2001 NFL draft. ... Signed by Eagles (June 6, 2001). ... Released by Eagles (September 26, 2002). ... Re-signed by Eagles to practice squad (September 28, 2002). ... Activated (October 8, 2002). ... Inactive for all 16 games (2003). ... Traded by Eagles to Miami Dolphins for second-round pick (WR Reggie Brown) in 2005 draft (March 3, 2004).

CHAMPIONSHIP GAME EXPERIENCE: Member of Eagles for NFC championship game (2001-2003 seasons); inactive.

SINGLE GAME HIGHS (regular season): Attempts—51 (December 5, 2004, vs. Buffalo); completions—25 (December 26, 2004, vs. Cleveland); passing yards—303 (December 5, 2004, vs. Buffalo); and touchdown passes—3 (December 5, 2004, vs. Buffalo).

STATISTICAL PLATEAUS: 300-yard passing games: 2004 (1). Total: 1.

MISCELLANEOUS: Regular-season record as starting NFL quarterback: 7-6 (.538).

Year Team	G	GS	Att.	Cmp.	Pct.	Yds.	TD	Int.	Avg.	Skd.	Rat.	Att.	Yds.	Avg.	TD	TD	2pt.	Pts.
					PASSING							RUSHING				TOTALS		
2001—Philadelphia NFL	1	0	14	10	71.4	143	2	1	10.21	0	114.0	0	0	0.0	0	0	0	0
2002—Philadelphia NFL	6	5	154	86	55.8	1011	6	5	6.56	7	75.4	12	6	0.5	0	0	0	0
2003—Philadelphia NFL			Did not play.															
2004—Miami NFL	11	8	356	191	53.7	1893	11	15	5.32	23	61.7	14	13	0.9	1	1	0	6
Pro totals (3 years)	18	13	524	287	54.8	3047	19	21	5.81	30	67.3	26	19	0.7	1	1	0	6

FEELY, JAY   K   GIANTS

PERSONAL: Born May 23, 1976, in Odessa, Fla. ... 5-10/206.

HIGH SCHOOL: Tampa Jesuit (Fla.).

COLLEGE: Michigan.

TRANSACTIONS/CAREER NOTES: Signed as non-drafted free agent by Atlanta Falcons (April 12, 2001). ... Granted free agency (March 3, 2004). ... Re-signed by Falcons (May 20, 2004). ... Granted unconditional free agency (March 2, 2005). ... Signed by New York Giants (March 8, 2005).

CHAMPIONSHIP GAME EXPERIENCE: Played in NFC championship game (2004 season).

Year Team	G	1-29	30-39	40-49	50+	Tot.	Pct.	Lg.	XPM	XPA	Pts.
			FIELD GOALS							TOTALS	
2001—Atlanta NFL	16	9-9	14-15	4-9	2-4	‡29-∞37	78.4	†55	28	28	115
2002—Atlanta NFL	16	8-10	12-14	11-13	1-3	†32-*40	80.0	52	42	43	‡138
2003—Atlanta NFL	16	6-6	9-11	4-7	0-3	19-27	70.4	46	32	33	89
2004—Atlanta NFL	16	8-8	7-9	3-6	0-0	18-23	78.3	47	40	40	94
Pro totals (4 years)	64	31-33	42-49	22-35	3-10	98-127	77.2	55	142	144	436

FERGUSON, JASON   DT   COWBOYS

PERSONAL: Born November 28, 1974, in Nettleton, Miss. ... 6-3/305. ... Full name: Jason O. Ferguson.

HIGH SCHOOL: Nettleton (Miss.).

JUNIOR COLLEGE: Itawamba Community College (Miss.).

COLLEGE: Georgia.

TRANSACTIONS/CAREER NOTES: Selected by New York Jets in seventh round (229th pick overall) of 1997 NFL draft. ... Signed by Jets (April 30, 1997). ... On suspended list for violating league substance abuse policy (November 24-December 22, 1999). ... Granted free agency (February 11, 2000). ... Re-signed by Jets (May 24, 2000). ... Granted unconditional free agency (March 2, 2001). ... Re-signed by Jets (March 11, 2001). ... On injured reserve with shoulder injury (September 3, 2001-entire season). ... Granted unconditional free agency (March 2, 2005). ... Signed by Dallas Cowboys (March 3, 2005).

CHAMPIONSHIP GAME EXPERIENCE: Played in AFC championship game (1998 season).

Year Team	G	GS	Tk.	Ast.	Sks.
			TOTALS		
1997—New York Jets NFL	13	1	23	8	3.5
1998—New York Jets NFL	16	16	42	21	4.0
1999—New York Jets NFL	9	9	23	10	1.0
2000—New York Jets NFL	15	11	34	11	1.0
2001—New York Jets NFL			Did not play.		
2002—New York Jets NFL	16	16	42	21	3.0
2003—New York Jets NFL	16	16	52	23	4.5
2004—New York Jets NFL	16	14	38	21	3.5
Pro totals (7 years)	101	83	254	115	20.5

F

FERGUSON, NICK   S   BRONCOS

PERSONAL: Born November 27, 1974, in Miami, Fla. ... 5-11/201.
HIGH SCHOOL: Jackson (Miami).
COLLEGE: Georgia Tech.
TRANSACTIONS/CAREER NOTES: Signed as non-drafted free agent by Cincinnati Bengals (April 23, 1996). ... Released by Bengals (August 5, 1996). ... Signed by Sasketchewan Roughriders of CFL (September 27, 1996). ... Traded by Roughriders to Winnipeg Blue Bombers (May 9, 1997). ... Signed by Chicago Bears (February 12, 1999). ... Assigned by Bears to Rhein Fire in 1999 NFL Europe enhancement allocation program (February 22, 1999). ... Released by Bears (August 30, 1999). ... Signed by Buffalo Bills (July 6, 2000). ... Released by Bills (August 27, 2000). ... Re-signed by Bills to practice squad (August 28, 2000). ... Signed by New York Jets off Bills practice squad (November 7, 2000). ... Granted free agency (February 28, 2003). ... Signed by Denver Broncos (April 2, 2003). ... On injured reserve with forearm injury (December 24, 2003-remainder of season).

				TOTALS			INTERCEPTIONS			
Year Team	G	GS	Tk.	Ast.	Sks.	No.	Yds.	Avg.	TD
1996—Saskatchewan CFL	5	0	...	...	0.0	0	0	0.0	0
1997—Winnipeg CFL	15	0	...	...	0.0	2	35	17.5	0
1998—Winnipeg CFL	16	0	...	...	0.0	1	0	0.0	0
1999—Winnipeg CFL	3	0	...	...	0.0	0	0	0.0	0
2000—New York Jets NFL	7	0	5	4	0.0	1	20	20.0	0
2001—New York Jets NFL	16	1	10	3	0.0	0	0	0.0	0
2002—New York Jets NFL	16	0	7	2	0.0	0	0	0.0	0
2003—Denver NFL	15	10	53	11	1.0	0	0	0.0	0
2004—Denver NFL	16	1	10	5	0.0	0	0	0.0	0
CFL totals (4 years)	39	0	...	...	0.0	3	35	11.7	0
NFL totals (5 years)	70	12	85	25	1.0	1	20	20.0	0
Pro totals (9 years)	109	12	...	...	1.0	4	55	13.8	0

FERGUSON, ROBERT   WR   PACKERS

PERSONAL: Born December 17, 1979, in Houston, Texas. ... 6-1/210.
HIGH SCHOOL: Spring Woods (Houston).
JUNIOR COLLEGE: Tyler (Texas) Junor College.
COLLEGE: Texas A&M.
TRANSACTIONS/CAREER NOTES: Selected after junior season by Green Bay Packers in second round (41st pick overall) of 2001 NFL draft. ... Signed by Packers (July 23, 2001).
SINGLE GAME HIGHS (regular season): Receptions—7 (December 7, 2003, vs. Chicago); yards—105 (December 8, 2002, vs. Minnesota); and touchdown receptions—2 (December 14, 2003, vs. San Diego).
STATISTICAL PLATEAUS: 100-yard receiving games: 2002 (1). Total: 1.

			RECEIVING				KICKOFF RETURNS				TOTALS			
Year Team	G	GS	No.	Yds.	Avg.	TD	No.	Yds.	Avg.	TD	TD	2pt.	Pts.	Fum.
2001—Green Bay NFL	1	0	0	0	0.0	0	2	32	16.0	0	0	0	0	0
2002—Green Bay NFL	16	1	22	293	13.3	3	6	113	18.8	0	3	0	18	0
2003—Green Bay NFL	15	12	38	520	13.7	4	7	148	21.1	0	4	0	24	0
2004—Green Bay NFL	13	5	24	367	15.3	1	21	526	25.0	0	1	1	8	1
Pro totals (4 years)	45	18	84	1180	14.0	8	36	819	22.8	0	8	1	50	1

FIEDLER, JAY   QB   JETS

F

PERSONAL: Born December 29, 1971, in Oceanside, N.Y. ... 6-2/225. ... Full name: Jay Brian Fiedler.
HIGH SCHOOL: Oceanside (N.Y.).
COLLEGE: Dartmouth.
TRANSACTIONS/CAREER NOTES: Signed as non-drafted free agent by Philadelphia Eagles (April 29, 1994). ... Inactive for all 16 games (1994). ... Claimed on waivers by Cincinnati Bengals (July 31, 1996). ... Released by Bengals (August 25, 1996). ... Played for Amsterdam Admirals of World League (1997). ... Signed by Minnesota Vikings (April 3, 1998). ... Released by Vikings (August 30, 1998). ... Re-signed by Vikings (September 15, 1998). ... Granted free agency (February 12, 1999). ... Signed by Jacksonville Jaguars (April 16, 1999). ... Granted unconditional free agency (February 11, 2000). ... Signed by Miami Dolphins (February 17, 2000). ... On physically unable to perform list with hip injury (July 26-31, 2002). ... On injured reserve with neck injury (November 23, 2004-remainder of season). ... Released by Dolphins (February 23, 2005). ... Signed by New York Jets (March 11, 2005).
CHAMPIONSHIP GAME EXPERIENCE: Member of Vikings for NFC championship game (1998 season); inactive. ... Member of Jaguars for AFC championship game (1999 season); did not play.
SINGLE GAME HIGHS (regular season): Attempts—45 (September 29, 2002, vs. Kansas City); completions—30 (December 24, 2000, vs.New England); yards—328 (December 28, 2003, vs. New York Jets); and touchdown passes—3 (November 27, 2003, vs. Dallas).
STATISTICAL PLATEAUS: 300-yard passing games: 1999 (1), 2001 (1), 2002 (1), 2003 (1). Total: 4.
MISCELLANEOUS: Regular-season record as starting NFL quarterback: 37-23 (.617). ... Postseason record as starting NFL quarterback: 1-2 (.333).

					PASSING							RUSHING				TOTALS		
Year Team	G	GS	Att.	Cmp.	Pct.	Yds.	TD	Int.	Avg.	Skd.	Rat.	Att.	Yds.	Avg.	TD	TD	2pt.	Pts.
1994—Philadelphia NFL	Did not play.																	
1995—Philadelphia NFL	Did not play.																	
1996—	Did not play.																	
1998—Minnesota NFL	5	0	7	3	42.9	41	0	1	5.86	0	22.6	4	-6	-1.5	0	0	0	0
1999—Jacksonville NFL	8	1	94	61	64.9	656	2	2	6.98	7	83.5	13	26	2.0	0	0	0	0
2000—Miami NFL	15	15	357	204	57.1	2402	14	14	6.73	23	74.5	54	267	4.9	1	1	0	6
2001—Miami NFL	16	16	450	273	60.7	3290	20	19	7.31	27	80.3	73	321	4.4	4	4	0	24
2002—Miami NFL	11	10	292	179	61.3	2024	14	9	6.93	13	85.2	28	99	3.5	3	3	0	18
2003—Miami NFL	12	11	314	179	57.0	2138	11	13	6.81	19	72.4	34	88	2.6	3	3	0	18
2004—Miami NFL	8	7	190	101	53.2	1186	7	8	6.24	25	67.1	12	59	4.9	0	0	0	0
Pro totals (7 years)	75	60	1704	1000	58.7	11737	68	66	6.89	114	76.9	218	854	3.9	11	11	0	66

FIELDS, MARK   LB   PANTHERS

PERSONAL: Born November 9, 1972, in Los Angeles, Calif. ... 6-2/244. ... Full name: Mark Lee Fields.
HIGH SCHOOL: Washington (Cerritos, Calif.).
JUNIOR COLLEGE: Los Angeles Southwest Community College.
COLLEGE: Washington State.
TRANSACTIONS/CAREER NOTES: Selected by New Orleans Saints in first round (13th pick overall) of 1995 NFL draft. ... Signed by Saints (July 20, 1995). ... Released by Saints (March 30, 2001). ... Signed by St. Louis Rams (April 10, 2001). ... Released by Rams (March 7, 2002). ... Signed by Carolina Panthers (March 21, 2002). ... On reserve/non-football injury list (August 18, 2003-entire season).
CHAMPIONSHIP GAME EXPERIENCE: Played in NFC championship game (2001 season). ... Played in Super Bowl 36 (2001 season).
HONORS: Played in Pro Bowl (2000 and 2004 seasons).

				TOTALS			INTERCEPTIONS			
Year Team	G	GS	Tk.	Ast.	Sks.	No.	Yds.	Avg.	TD
1995—New Orleans NFL	16	3	31	9	1.0	0	0	0.0	0
1996—New Orleans NFL	16	15	85	22	2.0	0	0	0.0	0
1997—New Orleans NFL	16	15	88	20	8.0	0	0	0.0	0
1998—New Orleans NFL	15	15	82	27	6.0	0	0	0.0	0
1999—New Orleans NFL	14	14	63	18	4.0	2	0	0.0	0
2000—New Orleans NFL	16	14	63	21	2.0	0	0	0.0	0
2001—St. Louis NFL	14	12	48	15	0.0	1	30	30.0	0
2002—Carolina NFL	15	15	76	27	7.5	1	37	37.0	0
2003—Carolina NFL			Did not play.						
2004—Carolina NFL	14	10	50	12	4.0	1	14	14.0	0
Pro totals (9 years)	136	113	586	171	34.5	5	81	16.2	0

FINN, JIM   FB   GIANTS

PERSONAL: Born December 2, 1976, in Teaneck, N.J. ... 6-0/245.
HIGH SCHOOL: Bergen Catholic (Oradell, N.J.).
COLLEGE: Pennsylvania.
TRANSACTIONS/CAREER NOTES: Selected by Chicago Bears in seventh round (253rd pick overall) of 1999 NFL draft. ... Signed by Bears (June 3, 1999). ... Released by Bears (August 30, 1999). ... Re-signed by Bears to practice squad (September 21, 1999). ... Released by Bears (October 11, 1999). ... Signed by Indianapolis Colts (January 25, 2000). ... Granted free agency (February 28, 2003). ... Signed by New York Giants (March 11, 2003). ... Granted unconditional free agency (March 2, 2005). ... Re-signed by Giants (March 28, 2005).
SINGLE GAME HIGHS (regular season): Attempts—3 (October 31, 2004, vs. Minnesota); yards—8 (November 3, 2002, vs. Tennessee); and rushing touchdowns—0.

			RUSHING				RECEIVING				KICKOFF RETURNS				TOTALS			
Year Team	G	GS	Att.	Yds.	Avg.	TD	No.	Yds.	Avg.	TD	No.	Yds.	Avg.	TD	TD	2pt.	Pts.	Fum.
2000—Indianapolis NFL	16	1	1	1	1.0	0	4	13	3.3	1	0	0	0.0	0	1	0	6	1
2001—Indianapolis NFL	15	0	0	0	0.0	0	0	0	0.0	0	3	29	9.7	0	0	0	0	0
2002—Indianapolis NFL	12	2	5	8	1.6	0	6	31	5.2	0	0	0	0.0	0	0	0	0	2
2003—New York Giants NFL	15	9	0	0	0.0	0	14	115	8.2	0	1	19	19.0	0	0	0	0	0
2004—New York Giants NFL	16	9	3	7	2.3	0	15	112	7.5	0	1	16	16.0	0	0	0	0	0
Pro totals (5 years)	74	21	9	16	1.8	0	39	271	6.9	1	5	64	12.8	0	1	0	6	3

FINNERAN, BRIAN   WR   FALCONS

PERSONAL: Born January 31, 1976, in Mission Viejo, Calif. ... 6-5/210.
HIGH SCHOOL: Santa Margarita (Mission Viejo, Calif.).
COLLEGE: Villanova.
TRANSACTIONS/CAREER NOTES: Signed as non-drafted free agent by Seattle Seahawks (April 21, 1998). ... Released by Seahawks (August 24, 1998). ... Selected by Barcelona Dragons in 1999 NFL Europe draft (February 18, 1999). ... Signed by Philadelphia Eagles (July 6, 1999). ... Released by Eagles (October 12, 1999). ... Signed by Atlanta Falcons to practice squad (December 13, 1999). ... Granted free agency (February 28, 2003). ... Re-signed by Falcons (March 23, 2003).
CHAMPIONSHIP GAME EXPERIENCE: Played in NFC championship game (2004 season).
HONORS: Won Walter Payton Award (1997).
SINGLE GAME HIGHS (regular season): Receptions—6 (November 10, 2002, vs. Pittsburgh); yards—114 (December 1, 2002, vs. Minnesota); and touchdown receptions—2 (September 22, 2002, vs. Cincinnati).
STATISTICAL PLATEAUS: 100-yard receiving games: 2002 (2). Total: 2.

			RECEIVING				TOTALS			
Year Team	G	GS	No.	Yds.	Avg.	TD	TD	2pt.	Pts.	Fum.
1999—Philadelphia NFL	3	0	2	21	10.5	0	0	0	0	0
2000—Atlanta NFL	11	0	7	60	8.6	0	0	0	0	0
2001—Atlanta NFL	16	1	23	491	21.3	3	3	0	18	0
2002—Atlanta NFL	16	16	56	838	15.0	6	6	0	36	2
2003—Atlanta NFL	12	10	26	368	14.2	2	2	0	12	0
2004—Atlanta NFL	12	1	23	258	11.2	2	2	0	12	1
Pro totals (6 years)	70	28	137	2036	14.9	13	13	0	78	3

FISHER, BRYCE   DE   SEAHAWKS

PERSONAL: Born May 12, 1977, in Renton, Wash. ... 6-3/272.
HIGH SCHOOL: Seattle Prep.
COLLEGE: Air Force.

F

TRANSACTIONS/CAREER NOTES: Selected by Buffalo Bills in seventh round (248th pick overall) of 1999 NFL draft. ... Signed by Bills (July 27, 1999). ... On military reserve list (August 30, 1999-entire season). ... On military reserve list (August 27, 2000-entire season). ... Claimed on waivers by St. Louis Rams (September 3, 2002). ... Granted free agency (March 3, 2004). ... Re-signed by Rams (April 22, 2004). ... Granted unconditional free agency (March 2, 2005). ... Signed by Seattle Seahawks (March 21, 2005).

			TOTALS		
Year Team	G	GS	Tk.	Ast.	Sks.
1999—Buffalo NFL	Did not play.				
2001—Buffalo NFL	13	2	19	13	3.0
2002—St. Louis NFL	4	0	2	1	0.0
2003—St. Louis NFL	16	1	21	3	2.0
2004—St. Louis NFL	16	14	35	11	8.5
Pro totals (4 years)	49	17	77	28	13.5

FISHER, LEVAR LB SAINTS

PERSONAL: Born July 2, 1979, in Beaufort, N.C. ... 6-1/239.
HIGH SCHOOL: East Carteret (Beaufort, N.C.).
COLLEGE: North Carolina State.
TRANSACTIONS/CAREER NOTES: Selected by Arizona Cardinals in second round (49th pick overall) of 2002 NFL draft. ... Signed by Cardinals (July 22, 2002). ... On injured reserve with knee injury (December 18, 2002-remainder of season). ... Released by Cardinals (September 16, 2004). ... Signed by New Orleans Saints (March 17, 2005).
HONORS: Named linebacker on THE SPORTING NEWS college All-America third team (2001). ... Named linebacker on THE SPORTING NEWS college All-America second team (2000).

			TOTALS			INTERCEPTIONS			
Year Team	G	GS	Tk.	Ast.	Sks.	No.	Yds.	Avg.	TD
2002—Arizona NFL	7	0	18	2	0.0	0	0	0.0	0
2003—Arizona NFL	16	15	50	8	1.0	0	0	0.0	0
2004—Arizona NFL	Did not play.								
Pro totals (2 years)	23	15	68	10	1.0	0	0	0.0	0

FISHER, TONY RB PACKERS

PERSONAL: Born October 12, 1979, in Euclid, Ohio. ... 6-1/222. ... Full name: Antoine Maurice Fisher.
HIGH SCHOOL: Euclid (Ohio).
COLLEGE: Notre Dame.
TRANSACTIONS/CAREER NOTES: Signed as non-drafted free agent by Green Bay Packers (April 25, 2002). ... Granted unconditional free agency by Packers (March 3, 2004). ... Re-signed by Packers (April 16, 2004).
SINGLE GAME HIGHS (regular season): Attempts—25 (December 8, 2002, vs. Minnesota); yards—96 (December 8, 2002, vs. Minnesota); and rushing touchdowns—1 (October 5, 2003, vs. Seattle).

			RUSHING				RECEIVING				KICKOFF RETURNS				TOTALS			
Year Team	G	GS	Att.	Yds.	Avg.	TD	No.	Yds.	Avg.	TD	No.	Yds.	Avg.	TD	TD	2pt.	Pts.	Fum.
2002—Green Bay NFL	15	1	70	283	4.0	2	18	70	3.9	0	2	42	21.0	0	2	0	12	2
2003—Green Bay NFL	15	0	40	200	5.0	1	21	206	9.8	2	0	0	0.0	0	3	0	18	0
2004—Green Bay NFL	16	0	65	224	3.4	0	38	277	7.3	2	0	0	0.0	0	2	0	12	1
Pro totals (3 years)	46	1	175	707	4.0	3	77	553	7.2	4	2	42	21.0	0	7	0	42	3

FISHER, TRAVIS CB RAMS

F

PERSONAL: Born September 12, 1979, in Tallahassee, Fla. ... 5-10/189.
HIGH SCHOOL: Godby (Tallahassee, Fla.).
JUNIOR COLLEGE: Coffeyville (Kan.) Community College.
COLLEGE: Central Florida.
TRANSACTIONS/CAREER NOTES: Selected by St. Louis Rams in second round (64th pick overall) of 2002 NFL draft. ... Signed by Rams (June 21, 2002).

			TOTALS			INTERCEPTIONS			
Year Team	G	GS	Tk.	Ast.	Sks.	No.	Yds.	Avg.	TD
2002—St. Louis NFL	14	11	54	7	0.0	2	0	0.0	0
2003—St. Louis NFL	15	15	51	5	0.0	4 †205	51.3	†2
2004—St. Louis NFL	10	10	32	3	0.0	1	30	30.0	0
Pro totals (3 years)	39	36	137	15	0.0	7	235	33.6	2

FISK, JASON DT BROWNS

PERSONAL: Born September 4, 1972, in Davis, Calif. ... 6-3/295.
HIGH SCHOOL: Davis (Calif.).
COLLEGE: Stanford.
TRANSACTIONS/CAREER NOTES: Selected by Minnesota Vikings in seventh round (243rd pick overall) of 1995 NFL draft. ... Signed by Vikings (July 24, 1995). ... Granted unconditional free agency (February 12, 1999). ... Signed by Tennessee Titans (March 3, 1999). ... Granted unconditional free agency (March 1, 2002). ... Signed by San Diego Chargers (March 8, 2002). ... Released by Chargers (February 28, 2005). ... Signed by Cleveland Browns (March 14, 2005).
CHAMPIONSHIP GAME EXPERIENCE: Played in NFC championship game (1998 season). ... Played in AFC championship game (1999 season). ... Played in Super Bowl 34 (1999 season).

Year Team	G	GS	Tk.	Ast.	Sks.	No.	Yds.	Avg.	TD
			TOTALS			**INTERCEPTIONS**			
1995—Minnesota NFL	8	0	0	0	0.0	0	0	0.0	0
1996—Minnesota NFL	16	6	22	9	1.0	1	0	0.0	0
1997—Minnesota NFL	16	10	20	8	3.0	1	1	1.0	0
1998—Minnesota NFL	16	0	12	5	1.5	0	0	0.0	0
1999—Tennessee NFL	16	16	35	13	4.0	1	17	17.0	0
2000—Tennessee NFL	15	15	30	10	2.0	0	0	0.0	0
2001—Tennessee NFL	16	16	26	16	2.5	0	0	0.0	0
2002—San Diego NFL	16	14	28	10	3.0	0	0	0.0	0
2003—San Diego NFL	16	16	41	10	1.0	0	0	0.0	0
2004—San Diego NFL	15	1	19	11	1.0	0	0	0.0	0
Pro totals (10 years)	150	94	233	92	19.0	3	18	6.0	0

FITZGERALD, LARRY   WR   CARDINALS

PERSONAL: Born August 31, 1983, in Minneapolis, Minn. ... 6-3/223. ... Full name: Larry Darnell Fitzgerald.
HIGH SCHOOL: Academy of Holy Angels (Minn.), then Valley Forge Military Academy (Pa.).
COLLEGE: Pittsburgh.
TRANSACTIONS/CAREER NOTES: Selected after junior season by Arizona Cardinals in first round (third pick overall) of 2004 NFL draft. ... Signed by Cardinals (August 2, 2004).
HONORS: Fred Biletnikoff Award winner (2003). ... Walter Camp Award winner (2003). ... Named wide receiver on THE SPORTING NEWS Freshman All-America first team (2002). ... Named wide receiver on THE SPORTING NEWS college All-America first team (2003).
SINGLE GAME HIGHS (regular season): Receptions—7 (November 21, 2004, vs. Carolina); yards—94 (October 10, 2004, vs. San Francisco); and touchdown receptions—2 (December 26, 2004, vs. Seattle).

Year Team	G	GS	Att.	Yds.	Avg.	TD	No.	Yds.	Avg.	TD	TD	2pt.	Pts.	Fum.
			RUSHING				**RECEIVING**				**TOTALS**			
2004—Arizona NFL	16	16	8	14	1.8	0	58	780	13.4	8	8	0	48	1

FITZSIMMONS, CASEY   TE   LIONS

PERSONAL: Born October 10, 1980, in Wolf Point, Mont. ... 6-4/258.
HIGH SCHOOL: Chester (Mont.).
COLLEGE: Carroll (Mont.).
TRANSACTIONS/CAREER NOTES: Signed as non-drafted free agent by Detroit Lions (May 2, 2003).
SINGLE GAME HIGHS (regular season): Receptions—5 (November 9, 2003, vs. Chicago); yards—36 (December 28, 2003, vs. St. Louis); and touchdown receptions—1 (December 28, 2003, vs. St. Louis).

Year Team	G	GS	No.	Yds.	Avg.	TD	TD	2pt.	Pts.	Fum.
			RECEIVING				**TOTALS**			
2003—Detroit NFL	16	11	23	160	7.0	2	2	0	12	0
2004—Detroit NFL	16	2	10	103	10.3	0	0	0	0	0
Pro totals (2 years)	32	13	33	263	8.0	2	2	0	12	0

FLANAGAN, MIKE   C   PACKERS

PERSONAL: Born November 10, 1973, in Washington, DC. ... 6-5/297. ... Full name: Michael Christopher Flanagan.
HIGH SCHOOL: Rio Americano (Sacramento).
COLLEGE: UCLA.
TRANSACTIONS/CAREER NOTES: Selected by Green Bay Packers in third round (90th pick overall) of 1996 NFL draft. ... Signed by Packers (July 17, 1996). ... On injured reserve with leg injury (August 19, 1996-entire season). ... On physically unable to perform list with ankle injury (August 19, 1997-entire season). ... Traded by Packers to Carolina Panthers for an undisclosed draft pick (August 31, 1998); trade later voided because Flanagan failed physical (September 1, 1998). ... Granted free agency (February 12, 1999). ... Re-signed by Packers (March 25, 1999). ... On physically unable to perform list with knee injury (August 2-30, 2004). ... On injured reserve with knee injury (October 2, 2004-remainder of season).
PLAYING EXPERIENCE: Green Bay NFL, 1998-2004. ... Games/Games started: 1998 (2/0), 1999 (15/0), 2000 (16/2), 2001 (16/16), 2002 (16/13), 2003 (16/16), 2004 (3/3). Total: 84/50.
HONORS: Played in Pro Bowl (2003 season).

FLECK, P.J.   WR   49ERS

PERSONAL: Born November 29, 1980, in Sugar Grove, Ill. ... 5-10/191. ... Full name: P.J. John Fleck.
HIGH SCHOOL: Maple Park (Kaneland, Ill.).
COLLEGE: Northern Illinois.
TRANSACTIONS/CAREER NOTES: Signed as non-drafted free agent by San Francisco 49ers (May 3, 2004). ... Released by 49ers (September 5, 2004). ... Re-signed by 49ers to practice squad (September 6, 2004). ... Activated (December 29, 2004).

Year Team	G	GS	No.	Yds.	Avg.	TD	TD	2pt.	Pts.	Fum.
			RECEIVING				**TOTALS**			
2004—San Francisco NFL	1	0	0	0	0.0	0	0	0	0	0

FLEMING, TROY   RB   TITANS

PERSONAL: Born October 1, 1980, in Franklin, Tenn. ... 6-0/230. ... Full name: Troy Majors Fleming.
HIGH SCHOOL: Battle Ground Academy (Franklin, Tenn.).
COLLEGE: Tennessee.

F

TRANSACTIONS/CAREER NOTES: Selected by Tennessee Titans in sixth round (191st pick overall) of 2004 NFL draft. ... Signed by Titans (July 29, 2004).

SINGLE GAME HIGHS (regular season): Attempts—3 (January 2, 2005, vs. Detroit); yards—15 (December 19, 2004, vs. Oakland); and rushing touchdowns—0.

Year Team	G	GS	RUSHING Att.	Yds.	Avg.	TD	RECEIVING No.	Yds.	Avg.	TD	KICKOFF RETURNS No.	Yds.	Avg.	TD	TOTALS TD	2pt.	Pts.	Fum.
2004—Tennessee NFL	16	0	7	40	5.7	0	19	164	8.6	2	18	316	17.6	0	2	0	12	0

FLEMONS, RONALD   DE   DOLPHINS

PERSONAL: Born October 20, 1979, in San Antonio, Texas. ... 6-5/265.
HIGH SCHOOL: Marshall (San Antonio).
COLLEGE: Texas A&M.
TRANSACTIONS/CAREER NOTES: Selected by Atlanta Falcons in seventh round (226th pick overall) of 2001 NFL draft. ... Signed by Falcons (May 21, 2001). ... Released by Falcons (September 17, 2002). ... Re-signed by Falcons to practice squad (September 19, 2002). ... Released by Falcons (October 22, 2002). ... Signed by New Orleans Saints to practice squad (November 5, 2002). ... Signed off Saints practice squad by Falcons (November 21, 2002). ... Released by Falcons (August 30, 2003). ... Signed by Miami Dolphins (January 27, 2004). ... Released by Dolphins (September 5, 2004). ... Re-signed by Dolphins to practice squad (September 6, 2004). ... Activated (October 16, 2004). ... Released by Dolphins (October 27, 2004). ... Re-signed by Dolphins to practice squad (October 29, 2004). ... Activated (November 3, 2004). ... Released by Dolphins (November 19, 2004). ... Re-signed by Dolphins to practice squad (November 23, 2004).

Year Team	G	GS	TOTALS Tk.	Ast.	Sks.
2001—Atlanta NFL	1	0	0	0	0.0
2002—Atlanta NFL	4	0	0	0	0.5
2004—Miami NFL	1	0	1	0	0.0
Pro totals (3 years)	6	0	1	0	0.5

FLETCHER, JAMAR   CB   CHARGERS

PERSONAL: Born August 28, 1979, in St. Louis, Mo. ... 5-10/186. ... Full name: Jamar Mondell Fletcher.
HIGH SCHOOL: Hazelwood East (St. Louis).
COLLEGE: Wisconsin.
TRANSACTIONS/CAREER NOTES: Selected after junior season by Miami Dolphins in first round (26th pick overall) of 2001 NFL draft. ... Signed by Dolphins (July 25, 2001). ... On injured reserve with forearm injury (December 1, 2003-remainder of season). ... Traded by Dolphins to San Diego Chargers to complete March 15 trade that sent WR David Boston from San Diego to Miami (March 16, 2004).
HONORS: Named cornerback on THE SPORTING NEWS college All-America first team (1999). ... Named cornerback on THE SPORTING NEWS college All-America second team (2000). ... Jim Thorpe Award winner (2000).

Year Team	G	GS	TOTALS Tk.	Ast.	Sks.	INTERCEPTIONS No.	Yds.	Avg.	TD
2001—Miami NFL	14	2	8	2	0.0	0	0	0.0	0
2002—Miami NFL	16	4	35	2	0.0	2	30	15.0	0
2003—Miami NFL	11	0	5	3	0.0	0	0	0.0	0
2004—San Diego NFL	16	0	24	3	0.0	1	0	0.0	0
Pro totals (4 years)	57	6	72	10	0.0	3	30	10.0	0

FLETCHER, LONDON   LB   BILLS

PERSONAL: Born May 19, 1975, in Cleveland, Ohio. ... 5-10/245. ... Full name: London Levi Fletcher.
HIGH SCHOOL: Villa Angela-St. Joseph (Cleveland).
COLLEGE: John Carroll.
TRANSACTIONS/CAREER NOTES: Signed as non-drafted free agent by St. Louis Rams (April 28, 1998). ... Granted free agency (March 2, 2001). ... Re-signed by Rams (May 9, 2001). ... Granted unconditional free agency (March 1, 2002). ... Signed by Buffalo Bills (March 7, 2002).
CHAMPIONSHIP GAME EXPERIENCE: Played in NFC championship game (1999 and 2001 seasons). ... Member of Super Bowl championship team (1999 season). ... Played in Super Bowl 36 (2001 season).

Year Team	G	GS	TOTALS Tk.	Ast.	Sks.	INTERCEPTIONS No.	Yds.	Avg.	TD	KICKOFF RETURNS No.	Yds.	Avg.	TD	TOTALS TD	2pt.	Pts.	Fum.
1998—St. Louis NFL	16	1	11	1	0.0	0	0	0.0	0	5	72	14.4	0	0	0	0	1
1999—St. Louis NFL	16	16	66	24	0.0	0	0	0.0	0	2	13	6.5	0	0	0	2	0
2000—St. Louis NFL	16	15	106	27	5.5	4	33	8.3	0	1	17	17.0	0	0	1	2	0
2001—St. Louis NFL	16	16	90	29	4.5	2	18	9.0	0	0	0	0.0	0	0	0	0	0
2002—Buffalo NFL	16	16	98	51	3.0	0	0	0.0	0	0	0	0.0	0	0	0	0	0
2003—Buffalo NFL	16	16	98	35	2.0	0	0	0.0	0	0	0	0.0	0	0	0	0	0
2004—Buffalo NFL	16	16	94	50	3.5	0	0	0.0	0	4	86	21.5	0	0	0	0	0
Pro totals (7 years)	112	96	563	217	21.5	6	51	8.5	0	12	188	15.7	0	0	1	4	1

FLORENCE, DRAYTON   CB   CHARGERS

PERSONAL: Born December 19, 1980, in Waycross, Ga. ... 6-0/195. ... Full name: Drayton Florence Jr.
HIGH SCHOOL: Richland Northeast (Columbia, S.C.), then Vanguard (Ocala, Fla.).
COLLEGE: Tuskegee.
TRANSACTIONS/CAREER NOTES: Selected by San Diego Chargers in second round (46th pick overall) of 2003 NFL draft. ... Signed by Chargers (July 23, 2003).

Year Team	G	GS	Tk.	Ast.	Sks.	No.	Yds.	Avg.	TD	No.	Yds.	Avg.	TD	TD	2pt.	Pts.	Fum.
			TOTALS			INTERCEPTIONS				KICKOFF RETURNS				TOTALS			
2003—San Diego NFL	16	0	16	0	0.0	0	0	0.0	0	4	47	11.8	0	0	0	0	0
2004—San Diego NFL	13	5	28	4	0.0	4	54	13.5	0	0	0	0.0	0	0	0	0	1
Pro totals (2 years)	29	5	44	4	0.0	4	54	13.5	0	4	47	11.8	0	0	0	0	1

FLOWERS, ERIK   LB

PERSONAL: Born March 1, 1978, in San Antonio, Texas. ... 6-4/273. ... Full name: Erik Mathews Flowers.
HIGH SCHOOL: Theodore Roosevelt (San Antonio, Texas).
JUNIOR COLLEGE: Trinity Valley Community College (Texas).
COLLEGE: Arizona State.
TRANSACTIONS/CAREER NOTES: Selected by Buffalo Bills in first round (26th pick overall) of 2000 NFL draft. ... Signed by Bills (July 23, 2000). ... Claimed on waivers by Houston Texans (August 21, 2002). ... Claimed on waivers by Pittsburgh Steelers (September 3, 2003). ... Released by Steelers (September 16, 2003). ... Signed by St. Louis Rams (December 3, 2003). ... Granted unconditional free agency (March 2, 2005).

Year Team	G	GS	Tk.	Ast.	Sks.	No.	Yds.	Avg.	TD
			TOTALS			INTERCEPTIONS			
2000—Buffalo NFL	16	0	11	9	2.0	1	0	0.0	0
2001—Buffalo NFL	15	5	15	6	2.0	0	0	0.0	0
2002—Houston NFL	14	0	0	1	0.0	0	0	0.0	0
2003—St. Louis NFL	4	0	0	0	0.0	0	0	0.0	0
2004—St. Louis NFL	9	0	5	2	1.0	0	0	0.0	0
Pro totals (5 years)	58	5	31	18	5.0	1	0	0.0	0

FLOYD, ANTHONY   CB   COLTS

PERSONAL: Born February 1, 1981, in Youngstown, Ohio. ... 5-10/202.
COLLEGE: Louisville.
TRANSACTIONS/CAREER NOTES: Signed as non-drafted free agent by Indianapolis Colts (May 2, 2003). ... Waived by Colts (September 26, 2003). ... Re-signed by Colts (November 11, 2003).
CHAMPIONSHIP GAME EXPERIENCE: Played in AFC championship game (2003 season).

Year Team	G	GS	Tk.	Ast.	Sks.	No.	Yds.	Avg.	TD
			TOTALS			INTERCEPTIONS			
2003 Indianapolis NFL	6	0	10	3	0.0	0	0	0.0	0
2004—Indianapolis NFL	11	2	23	12	0.0	0	0	0.0	0
Pro totals (2 years)	17	2	33	15	0.0	0	0	0.0	0

FLOYD, MALCOM   WR   CHARGERS

PERSONAL: Born September 8, 1981, in Sacramento, Calif. ... 6-5/201. ... Brother of Malcolm Floyd, wide receiver with Houston/Tennessee Oilers (1994-97) and St. Louis Rams (1997).
HIGH SCHOOL: River City (Sacramento, Calif.).
COLLEGE: Wyoming.
TRANSACTIONS/CAREER NOTES: Signed as non-drafted free agent by San Diego Chargers (April 30, 2004). ... Released by Chargers (September 5, 2004). ... Re-signed by Chargers to practice squad (September 6, 2004). ... Activated (December 11, 2004).
SINGLE GAME HIGHS (regular season): Receptions—3 (January 2, 2005, vs. Kansas City); yards—49 (January 2, 2005, vs. Kansas City); and touchdown receptions—1 (January 2, 2005, vs. Kansas City).

Year Team	G	GS	No.	Yds.	Avg.	TD	TD	2pt.	Pts.	Fum.
			RECEIVING				TOTALS			
2004—San Diego NFL	4	2	3	49	16.3	1	1	0	6	0

FLUTIE, DOUG   QB   PATRIOTS

PERSONAL: Born October 23, 1962, in Manchester, Md. ... 5-10/180. ... Full name: Douglas Richard Flutie. ... Brother of Darren Flutie, wide receiver with San Diego Chargers (1998), B.C. Lions of CFL (1991-95), Edmonton Eskimos of CFL (1996 and 1997) and Hamilton Tiger-Cats of CFL (1998).
HIGH SCHOOL: Natick (Mass.).
COLLEGE: Boston College.
TRANSACTIONS/CAREER NOTES: Selected by New Jersey Generals in 1985 USFL territorial draft. ... Signed by Generals (February 4, 1985). ... Granted roster exemption (February 4-14, 1985). ... Activated (February 15, 1985). ... On developmental squad for three games with Generals (1985). ... Selected by Los Angeles Rams in 11th round (285th pick overall) of 1985 NFL draft. ... On developmental squad (June 10, 1995-remainder of season). ... Rights traded to Rams with fourth-round pick in 1987 draft to Chicago Bears for third- and sixth-round picks in 1987 draft (October 14, 1986). ... Signed by Bears (October 21, 1986). ... Granted roster exemption (October 21-November 3, 1986). ... Activated (November 4, 1986). ... Crossed picket line during players strike (October 13, 1987). ... Traded by Bears to New England Patriots for eighth-round pick in 1988 draft (October 13, 1987). ... Released by Patriots after 1989 season. ... Signed by B.C. Lions of CFL (June 1990). ... Granted free agency (February 1992). ... Signed by Calgary Stampeders of CFL (March 1992). ... Rights assigned to Toronto Argonauts of CFL (March 15, 1996). ... Signed by Buffalo Bills (January 16, 1998). ... Released by Bills (March 1, 2001). ... Signed by San Diego Chargers (March 9, 2001). ... Released by Chargers (March 11, 2005). ... Signed by New England Patriots (April 29, 2005).
CHAMPIONSHIP GAME EXPERIENCE: Member of CFL championship team (1992, 1996 and 1997). ... Named Most Valuable Player of Grey Cup, CFL championship game (1992, 1996 and 1997). ... Played in Grey Cup (1993 and 1995).
HONORS: Heisman Trophy winner (1984). ... Named College Football Player of the Year by THE SPORTING NEWS (1984). ... Named quarterback on THE SPORTING NEWS college All-America first team (1984). ... Most Outstanding Player of CFL (1991-1994, 1996 and 1997). ... Played in Pro Bowl (1998 season).

SINGLE GAME HIGHS (regular season): Attempts—53 (December 30, 2001, vs. Seattle); completions—34 (December 30, 2001, vs. Seattle); yards—377 (December 30, 2001, vs. Seattle); and touchdown passes—4 (October 30, 1988, vs. Chicago).
STATISTICAL PLATEAUS: 300-yard passing games: 1998 (2), 1999 (1), 2000 (1), 2001 (4). Total: 8.
MISCELLANEOUS: Regular-season record as starting NFL quarterback: 38-28 (.576). ... Postseason record as starting NFL quarterback: 0-2 (.000).

Year Team	G	GS	PASSING Att.	Cmp.	Pct.	Yds.	TD	Int.	Avg.	Skd.	Rat.	RUSHING Att.	Yds.	Avg.	TD	TOTALS TD	2pt.	Pts.
1985—New Jersey USFL	15	...	281	134	47.7	2109	13	14	7.51	...	67.8	65	465	7.2	6	6	0	36
1986—Chicago NFL	4	1	46	23	50.0	361	3	2	7.85	6	80.1	9	36	4.0	1	1	0	6
1987—Chicago NFL	1	0	0	0	0.0	0	0	0	0.00	0	0.0	0	0	0.0	0	0	0	0
—New England NFL	1	1	25	15	60.0	199	1	0	7.96	1	98.6	6	43	7.2	0	0	0	0
1988—New England NFL	11	9	179	92	51.4	1150	8	10	6.42	11	63.3	38	179	4.7	1	1	0	6
1989—New England NFL	5	3	91	36	39.6	493	2	4	5.42	6	46.6	16	87	5.4	0	0	0	0
1990—British Columbia CFL	16	...	392	207	52.8	2960	16	19	7.55	...	71.0	79	662	8.4	3	3	0	18
1991—British Columbia CFL	18	...	730	466	63.8	6619	38	24	9.07	...	96.7	120	610	5.1	14	14	1	86
1992—Calgary CFL	18	...	688	396	57.6	5945	32	30	8.64	...	83.4	96	669	7.0	11	11	0	66
1993—Calgary CFL	18	...	703	416	59.2	6092	44	17	8.67	...	98.3	74	373	5.0	11	11	0	66
1994—Calgary CFL	18	...	659	403	61.2	5726	48	19	8.69	...	101.5	96	760	7.9	8	8	0	48
1995—Calgary CFL	12	...	332	223	67.2	2788	16	5	8.40	...	102.8	46	288	6.3	5	5	0	30
1996—Toronto CFL	18	...	677	434	64.1	5720	29	17	8.45	...	94.5	101	756	7.5	9	9	0	54
1997—Toronto CFL	18	18	673	430	63.9	5505	47	24	8.18	...	97.8	92	542	5.9	9	9	0	54
1998—Buffalo NFL	13	10	354	202	57.1	2711	20	11	7.66	12	87.4	48	248	5.2	1	1	0	6
1999—Buffalo NFL	15	15	478	264	55.2	3171	19	16	6.63	26	75.1	88	476	5.4	1	1	0	6
2000—Buffalo NFL	11	5	231	132	57.1	1700	8	3	7.36	10	86.5	36	161	4.5	1	1	0	6
2001—San Diego NFL	16	16	521	294	56.4	3464	15	18	6.65	25	72.0	53	192	3.6	1	1	0	6
2002—San Diego NFL	1	0	11	3	27.3	64	0	0	5.82	0	51.3	1	6	6.0	0	0	0	0
2003—San Diego NFL	7	5	167	91	54.5	1097	9	4	6.57	8	82.8	33	168	5.1	2	2	0	12
2004—San Diego NFL	2	1	38	20	52.6	276	1	0	7.26	1	85.0	5	39	7.8	2	2	0	12
USFL totals (1 year)	15	...	281	134	47.7	2109	13	14	7.51	...	67.8	65	465	7.2	6	6	0	36
CFL totals (8 years)	136	18	4854	2975	61.3	41355	270	155	8.52	...	93.9	704	4660	6.6	70	70	1	422
NFL totals (11 years)	87	66	2141	1172	54.7	14686	86	68	6.86	106	76.4	333	1635	4.9	10	10	0	60
Pro totals (20 years)	238	...	7276	4281	58.8	58150	369	237	7.99	...	87.7	1102	6760	6.1	86	86	1	518

FLYNN, MIKE   C   RAVENS

PERSONAL: Born June 15, 1974, in Doylestown, Pa. ... 6-3/305. ... Full name: Michael Patrick Flynn.
HIGH SCHOOL: Cathedral (Springfield, Mass.).
COLLEGE: Maine.
TRANSACTIONS/CAREER NOTES: Signed as non-drafted free agent by Baltimore Ravens (April 25, 1997). ... Released by Ravens (August 24, 1997). ... Signed by Tampa Bay Buccaneers to practice squad (August 27, 1997). ... Released by Buccaneers (September 2, 1997). ... Signed by Jacksonville Jaguars to practice squad (November 4, 1997). ... Signed by Ravens off Jaguars practice squad (December 3, 1997). ... Granted free agency (March 2, 2001). ... Re-signed by Ravens (March 13, 2001).
PLAYING EXPERIENCE: Baltimore NFL, 1998-2004. ... Games/Games started: 1998 (2/0), 1999 (12/0), 2000 (16/16), 2001 (16/16), 2002 (15/15), 2003 (16/16), 2004 (9/5). Total: 86/68.
CHAMPIONSHIP GAME EXPERIENCE: Played in AFC championship game (2000 season). ... Member of Super Bowl championship team (2000 season).

FOLAU, SPENCER   T   SAINTS

PERSONAL: Born April 5, 1973, in Nuku'alofa, Tonga. ... 6-5/310. ... Full name: Spencer Sione Folau. ... Name pronounced: fah-LOWE.
HIGH SCHOOL: Sequoia (Redwood City, Calif.).
COLLEGE: Idaho.
TRANSACTIONS/CAREER NOTES: Signed as non-drafted free agent by Baltimore Ravens (April 26, 1996). ... Released by Ravens (August 25, 1996). ... Re-signed by Ravens to practice squad (October 29, 1996). ... Assigned by Ravens to Rhein Fire in 1997 World League enhancement allocation program (February 1997). ... Released by Ravens (October 28, 1998). ... Re-signed by Ravens (November 3, 1998). ... Granted free agency (February 11, 2000). ... Tendered offer sheet by New England Patriots (April 10, 2000). ... Offer matched by Ravens (April 12, 2000). ... Released by Ravens (March 1, 2001). ... Signed by Miami Dolphins (July 28, 2001). ... Granted unconditional free agency (March 1, 2002). ... Signed by New Orleans Saints (April 1, 2002). ... On injured reserve with knee injury (December 19, 2003-remainder of season). ... Granted unconditional free agency (March 3, 2004). ... Re-signed by Saints (March 17, 2004).
PLAYING EXPERIENCE: Baltimore NFL, 1997-2000; Miami NFL, 2001; New Orleans NFL, 2002-2004. ... Games/Games started: 1997 (10/0), 1998 (3/3), 1999 (7/1), 2000 (11/4), 2001 (16/15), 2002 (16/16), 2003 (14/1), 2004 (16/3). Total: 93/43.
CHAMPIONSHIP GAME EXPERIENCE: Played in AFC championship game (2000 season). ... Member of Super Bowl championship team (2000 season).

FOLEY, STEVE   LB   CHARGERS

PERSONAL: Born September 11, 1975, in Little Rock, Ark. ... 6-4/265.
HIGH SCHOOL: Hall (Little Rock, Ark.).
COLLEGE: Louisiana-Monroe.
TRANSACTIONS/CAREER NOTES: Selected by Cincinnati Bengals in third round (75th pick overall) of 1998 NFL draft. ... Signed by Bengals (July 19, 1998). ... On injured reserve with shoulder injury (September 1, 2002-entire season). ... Released by Bengals (August 31, 2003). ... Signed by Houston Texans (September 2, 2003). ... Granted unconditional free agency (March 3, 2004). ... Signed by San Diego Chargers (March 4, 2004).

Year Team	G	GS	TOTALS Tk.	Ast.	Sks.	INTERCEPTIONS No.	Yds.	Avg.	TD
1998—Cincinnati NFL	10	1	11	1	2.0	0	0	0.0	0
1999—Cincinnati NFL	16	16	34	3	3.5	0	0	0.0	0

F

Year Team	G	GS	TOTALS Tk.	Ast.	Sks.	INTERCEPTIONS No.	Yds.	Avg.	TD
2000—Cincinnati NFL	16	16	34	9	4.0	1	1	1.0	0
2001—Cincinnati NFL	12	12	25	14	0.0	0	0	0.0	0
2002—Cincinnati NFL	Did not play.								
2003—Houston NFL	13	3	21	5	1.0	0	0	0.0	0
2004—San Diego NFL	16	16	48	17	10.0	2	4	2.0	0
Pro totals (6 years)	83	64	173	49	20.5	3	5	1.7	0

FONOTI, TONIU   G   CHARGERS

PERSONAL: Born November 26, 1981, in American Samoa. ... 6-4/350. ... Full name: Toniuolevaiavea Satele Fonoti.
HIGH SCHOOL: Kahuku (Hauula, Hawaii).
COLLEGE: Nebraska.
TRANSACTIONS/CAREER NOTES: Selected after junior season by San Diego Chargers in second round (39th pick overall) of 2002 NFL draft. ... Signed by Chargers (July 30, 2002). ... On injured reserve with foot injury (August 31, 2003-entire season).
PLAYING EXPERIENCE: San Diego NFL, 2002-2004. ... Games/Games started: 2002 (15/14), 2004 (16/16), Total: 31/30.

FONTENOT, JERRY   C

PERSONAL: Born November 21, 1966, in Lafayette, La. ... 6-3/300. ... Full name: Jerry Paul Fontenot.
HIGH SCHOOL: Lafayette (La.).
COLLEGE: Texas A&M.
TRANSACTIONS/CAREER NOTES: Selected by Chicago Bears in third round (65th pick overall) of 1989 NFL draft. ... Signed by Bears (July 27, 1989). ... Granted free agency (March 1, 1993). ... Re-signed by Bears (June 16, 1993). ... Granted free agency (February 16, 1996). ... Re-signed by Bears (July 10, 1996). ... Granted unconditional free agency (February 14, 1997). ... Signed by New Orleans Saints (May 28, 1997). ... On injured reserve with knee injury (October 14, 1998-remainder of season). ... Granted unconditional free agency (February 12, 1999). ... Re-signed by Saints (February 15, 1999). ... Granted unconditional free agency (February 28, 2003). ... Re-signed by Saints (June 18, 2003). ... Granted unconditional free agency (March 3, 2004). ... Re-signed by Saints (May 13, 2004). ... Released by Saints (September 5, 2004). ... Signed by Cincinnati Bengals (September 16, 2004). ... Granted unconditional free agency (March 2, 2005).
PLAYING EXPERIENCE: Chicago NFL, 1989-1996; New Orleans NFL, 1997-2003; Cincinnati NFL, 2004. ... Games/Games started: 1989 (16/0), 1990 (16/2), 1991 (16/7), 1992 (16/16), 1993 (16/16), 1994 (16/16), 1995 (16/16), 1996 (16/16), 1997 (16/16), 1998 (4/4), 1999 (16/16), 2000 (16/16), 2001 (16/16), 2002 (16/16), 2003 (16/16), 2004 (11/6). Total: 239/195.

FOOTE, LARRY   LB   STEELERS

PERSONAL: Born June 12, 1980, in Detroit, Mich. ... 6-0/239. ... Full name: Lawrence Edward Foote Jr.
HIGH SCHOOL: Pershing (Detroit).
COLLEGE: Michigan.
TRANSACTIONS/CAREER NOTES: Selected by Pittsburgh Steelers in fourth round (128th pick overall) of 2002 NFL draft. ... Signed by Steelers (July 18, 2002). ... Granted free agency (March 2, 2005). ... Re-signed by Steelers (March 7, 2005).
CHAMPIONSHIP GAME EXPERIENCE: Played in AFC championship game (2004 season).
HONORS: Named linebacker on THE SPORTING NEWS college All-America second team (2001).

Year Team	G	GS	TOTALS Tk.	Ast.	Sks.	INTERCEPTIONS No.	Yds.	Avg.	TD
2002—Pittsburgh NFL	14	3	11	7	0.0	0	0	0.0	0
2003—Pittsburgh NFL	16	0	0	0	0.0	0	0	0.0	0
2004—Pittsburgh NFL	16	16	53	16	3.0	1	1	1.0	0
Pro totals (3 years)	46	19	64	23	3.0	1	1	1.0	0

FORDHAM, TODD   T   PANTHERS

PERSONAL: Born October 9, 1973, in Atlanta, Ga. ... 6-5/319. ... Full name: Lindsey Todd Fordham.
HIGH SCHOOL: Tift County (Tifton, Ga.).
COLLEGE: Florida State.
TRANSACTIONS/CAREER NOTES: Signed as non-drafted free agent by Jacksonville Jaguars (April 21, 1997). ... Released by Jaguars (August 24, 1997). ... Re-signed by Jaguars to practice squad (August 25, 1997). ... Activated (September 23, 1997). ... On injured reserve with knee injury (August 31, 1999-entire season). ... Granted free agency (February 11, 2000). ... Re-signed by Jaguars (February 24, 2000). ... Granted unconditional free agency (March 2, 2001). ... Signed by Denver Broncos (April 13, 2001). ... Released by Broncos (September 2, 2001). ... Signed by Jaguars (October 2, 2001). ... Granted unconditional free agency (March 1, 2002). ... Re-signed by Jaguars (April 16, 2002). ... Granted unconditional free agency (February 28, 2003). ... Signed by Pittsburgh Steelers (March 18, 2003). ... Traded by Steelers to Carolina Panthers for seventh-round pick (DE Shaun Nua) in 2005 draft (September 5, 2004).
PLAYING EXPERIENCE: Jacksonville NFL, 1997-2002; Pittsburgh NFL, 2003; Carolina NFL, 2004. ... Games/Games started: 1997 (1/0), 1998 (11/1), 2000 (16/8), 2001 (12/12), 2002 (16/9), 2003 (11/6), 2004 (15/7), Total: 82/43.

FOREMAN, JAY   LB   RAIDERS

PERSONAL: Born February 18, 1976, in Eden Prairie, Minn. ... 6-1/240. ... Full name: Jamal A. Foreman. ... Son of Chuck Foreman, running back with Minnesota Vikings (1973-79) and New England Patriots (1980).
HIGH SCHOOL: Eden Prairie (Minn.).
COLLEGE: Nebraska.
TRANSACTIONS/CAREER NOTES: Selected by Buffalo Bills in fifth round (156th pick overall) of 1999 NFL draft. ... Signed by Bills (July 27, 1999). ... Granted free agency (March 1, 2002). ... Re-signed by Bills (April 17, 2002). ... Traded by Bills to Houston Texans for KR/PR Charlie Rogers (April 17, 2002). ... Granted unconditional free agency (February 28, 2003). ... Re-signed by Texans (March 4, 2003). ... On injured reserve with ankle injury (December 6, 2004-remainder of season). ... Released by Texans (March 14, 2005). ... Signed by Oakland Raiders (May 12, 2005).

F

Year Team	G	GS	TOTALS			INTERCEPTIONS			
			Tk.	Ast.	Sks.	No.	Yds.	Avg.	TD
1999—Buffalo NFL	7	0	0	0	0.0	0	0	0.0	0
2000—Buffalo NFL	15	3	32	18	0.0	0	0	0.0	0
2001—Buffalo NFL	16	16	69	28	2.5	0	0	0.0	0
2002—Houston NFL	16	16	101	36	0.0	0	0	0.0	0
2003—Houston NFL	16	16	101	35	2.0	0	0	0.0	0
2004—Houston NFL	11	11	53	26	0.0	0	0	0.0	0
Pro totals (6 years)	81	62	356	143	4.5	0	0	0.0	0

FORNEY, KYNAN   G   FALCONS

PERSONAL: Born September 8, 1978, in Nacogdoches, Texas. ... 6-3/307.
HIGH SCHOOL: Nacogdoches (Texas).
JUNIOR COLLEGE: Trinity Valley Community College (Texas).
COLLEGE: Hawaii.
TRANSACTIONS/CAREER NOTES: Selected by Atlanta Falcons in seventh round (219th pick overall) of 2001 NFL draft. ... Signed by Falcons (May 21, 2001). ... Granted free agency (March 3, 2004). ... Re-signed by Falcons (April 6, 2004).
PLAYING EXPERIENCE: Atlanta NFL, 2001-2004. ... Games/Games started: 2001 (12/8), 2002 (14/12), 2003 (16/16), 2004 (16/16). Total: 58/52.
CHAMPIONSHIP GAME EXPERIENCE: Played in NFC championship game (2004 season).

FORSEY, BROCK   RB   REDSKINS

PERSONAL: Born February 11, 1980, in Meridian, Idaho. ... 5-11/203.
HIGH SCHOOL: Centennial (Meridian, Idaho).
COLLEGE: Boise State.
TRANSACTIONS/CAREER NOTES: Selected by Chicago Bears in sixth round (206th pick overall) of 2003 NFL draft. ... Signed by Bears (June 19, 2003). ... Released by Bears (September 4, 2004). ... Signed by Miami Dolphins (September 29, 2004). ... Released by Dolphins (December 4, 2004). ... Re-signed by Dolphins (December 7, 2004). ... Released by Dolphins (April 28, 2005). ... Signed by Washington Redskins (May 5, 2005).
SINGLE GAME HIGHS (regular season): Attempts—27 (November 30, 2003, vs. Arizona); yards—134 (November 30, 2003, vs. Arizona); and rushing touchdowns—1 (November 30, 2003, vs. Arizona).
STATISTICAL PLATEAUS: 100-yard rushing games: 2003 (1). Total: 1.

Year Team	G	GS	RUSHING				RECEIVING				KICKOFF RETURNS				TOTALS			
			Att.	Yds.	Avg.	TD	No.	Yds.	Avg.	TD	No.	Yds.	Avg.	TD	TD	2pt.	Pts.	Fum.
2003—Chicago NFL	9	2	50	191	3.8	2	3	37	12.3	0	0	0	0.0	0	2	0	12	0
2004—Miami NFL	7	0	19	53	2.8	0	0	0	0.0	0	0	0	0.0	0	0	0	0	1
Pro totals (2 years)	16	2	69	244	3.5	2	3	37	12.3	0	0	0	0.0	0	2	0	12	1

FOSTER, DESHAUN   RB   PANTHERS

PERSONAL: Born January 10, 1980, in Charlotte, N.C. ... 6-0/222. ... Full name: DeShaun Xavier Foster.
HIGH SCHOOL: Tustin (Calif.).
COLLEGE: UCLA.
TRANSACTIONS/CAREER NOTES: Selected by Carolina Panthers in second round (34th pick overall) of 2002 NFL draft. ... Signed by Panthers (July 30, 2002). ... On injured reserve with knee injury (October 25, 2002-remainder of season). ... On injured reserve with clavicle injury (October 27, 2004-remainder of season).
CHAMPIONSHIP GAME EXPERIENCE: Played in NFC championship game (2003 season). ... Played Super Bowl 38 (2003 season).
HONORS: Named running back on THE SPORTING NEWS college All-America second team (2001).
SINGLE GAME HIGHS (regular season): Attempts—32 (September 19, 2004, vs. Kansas City); yards—174 (September 19, 2004, vs. Kansas City; and rushing touchdowns—1 (October 3, 2004, vs. Atlanta).
STATISTICAL PLATEAUS: 100-yard rushing games: 2004 (1). Total: 1.

Year Team	G	GS	RUSHING				RECEIVING				KICKOFF RETURNS				TOTALS			
			Att.	Yds.	Avg.	TD	No.	Yds.	Avg.	TD	No.	Yds.	Avg.	TD	TD	2pt.	Pts.	Fum.
2002—Carolina NFL	Did not play.																	
2003—Carolina NFL	14	2	113	429	3.8	0	26	207	8.0	2	0	0	0.0	0	2	0	12	3
2004—Carolina NFL	4	3	59	255	4.3	2	9	76	8.4	0	2	16	8.0	0	2	0	12	0
Pro totals (2 years)	18	5	172	684	4.0	2	35	283	8.1	2	2	16	8.0	0	4	0	24	3

FOSTER, GEORGE   T   BRONCOS

PERSONAL: Born June 9, 1980, in Macon, Ga. ... 6-5/338.
HIGH SCHOOL: Southeast (Macon, Ga.).
COLLEGE: Georgia.
TRANSACTIONS/CAREER NOTES: Selected by Denver Broncos in first round (20th pick overall) of 2003 NFL draft. ... Signed by Broncos (July 24, 2003).
PLAYING EXPERIENCE: Denver NFL, 2003-2004. ... Games/Games started: 2003 (1/0), 2004 (16/16). Total: 17/16.

FOWLER, MELVIN   G/C

PERSONAL: Born March 31, 1979, in Brooklyn, N.Y. ... 6-3/305. ... Full name: Melvin Thaddeus Fowler Jr.
HIGH SCHOOL: Half Hollow Hills (Long Island, N.Y.).
COLLEGE: Maryland.

F

TRANSACTIONS/CAREER NOTES: Selected by Cleveland Browns in third round (76th pick overall) of 2002 NFL draft. ... Signed by Browns (July 22, 2002). ... Granted free agency (March 2, 2005).
PLAYING EXPERIENCE: Cleveland NFL, 2002-2004. ... Games/Games started: 2002 (1/1), 2003 (14/10), 2004 (15/3). Total: 30/14.

FOWLER, RYAN — LB — COWBOYS

PERSONAL: Born May 20, 1982, in Redington Shores, Fla. ... 6-3/243.
HIGH SCHOOL: Seminole (Redington Shores, Fla.).
COLLEGE: Duke.
TRANSACTIONS/CAREER NOTES: Signed as non-drafted free agent by Dallas Cowboys (April 30, 2004). ... Released by Cowboys (May 25, 2004). ... Re-signed by Cowboys (August 4, 2004). ... Released by Cowboys (September 5, 2004). ... Re-signed by Cowboys to practice squad (September 7, 2004). ... Activated (October 15, 2004).
HONORS: Named linebacker on THE SPORTING NEWS Freshman All-America third team (2000).

Year Team	G	GS	TOTALS Tk.	Ast.	Sks.	INTERCEPTIONS No.	Yds.	Avg.	TD
2004—Dallas NFL	2	0	0	0	0.0	0	0	0.0	0

FOX, KEYARON — LB — CHIEFS

PERSONAL: Born January 24, 1982, in Atlanta, Ga. ... 6-3/235. ... Full name: Keyaron James Fox. ... Name pronounced: key-AIR-un.
HIGH SCHOOL: Westlake (Atlanta, Ga.).
COLLEGE: Georgia Tech.
TRANSACTIONS/CAREER NOTES: Selected by Kansas City Chiefs in third round (93rd pick overall) of 2004 NFL draft. ... Signed by Chiefs (July 1, 2004).

Year Team	G	GS	TOTALS Tk.	Ast.	Sks.	INTERCEPTIONS No.	Yds.	Avg.	TD
2004—Kansas City NFL	12	0	0	0	0.0	0	0	0.0	0

FOX, VERNON — S — LIONS

PERSONAL: Born October 9, 1979, in Las Vegas, Nev. ... 5-9/200. ... Full name: Vernon Lee Fox III.
HIGH SCHOOL: Caimarron-Memorial (Las Vegas).
COLLEGE: Fresno State.
TRANSACTIONS/CAREER NOTES: Signed as non-drafted free agent by San Diego Chargers (April 26, 2002). ... Released by Chargers (August 31, 2004). ... Signed by Detroit Lions to practice squad (September 14, 2004). ... Released by Lions (September 18, 2004). ... Re-signed by Lions (September 22, 2004). ... Granted free agency (March 2, 2005). ... Re-signed by Lions (April 20, 2005).

Year Team	G	GS	TOTALS Tk.	Ast.	Sks.	INTERCEPTIONS No.	Yds.	Avg.	TD
2002—San Diego NFL	16	3	17	6	0.0	1	25	25.0	0
2003—San Diego NFL	12	2	18	4	0.0	0	0	0.0	0
2004—Detroit NFL	14	0	0	0	0.0	0	0	0.0	0
Pro totals (3 years)	42	5	35	10	0.0	1	25	25.0	0

FRALEY, HANK — C/G — EAGLES

PERSONAL: Born September 21, 1977, in Gaithersburg, Md. ... 6-2/300.
HIGH SCHOOL: Gaithersburg (Md.).
COLLEGE: Robert Morris.
TRANSACTIONS/CAREER NOTES: Signed as non-drafted free agent by Pittsburgh Steelers (April 21, 2000). ... Claimed on waivers by Philadelphia Eagles (August 28, 2000). ... Inactive for all 16 games (2000).
PLAYING EXPERIENCE: Philadelphia NFL, 2001-2004. ... Games/Games started: 2001 (16/15), 2002 (16/16), 2003 (16/16), 2004 (16/16). Total: 64/63.
CHAMPIONSHIP GAME EXPERIENCE: Played in NFC championship game (2001-2004 seasons). ... Played in Super Bowl 39 (2004 season).

FRANCIS, CARLOS — WR — RAIDERS

PERSONAL: Born January 3, 1981, in Fort Worth, Texas. ... 5-9/190. ... Full name: Carlos Miguel Francis.
HIGH SCHOOL: Southwest (Fort Worth, Texas).
COLLEGE: Texas Tech.
TRANSACTIONS/CAREER NOTES: Selected by Oakland Raiders in fourth round (98th pick overall) of 2004 NFL draft. ... Signed by Raiders (July 29, 2004). ... On injured reserve with knee injury (October 28, 2004-remainder of season).

Year Team	G	GS	RUSHING Att.	Yds.	Avg.	TD	RECEIVING No.	Yds.	Avg.	TD	KICKOFF RETURNS No.	Yds.	Avg.	TD	TOTALS TD	2pt.	Pts.	Fum.
2004—Oakland NFL	5	0	0	0	0.0	0	0	0	0.0	0	14	259	18.5	0	0	0	0	1

FRANKLIN, AUBRAYO — DT — RAVENS

PERSONAL: Born August 27, 1980, in Johnson City, Tenn. ... 6-1/320. ... Full name: Aubrayo Razyo Franklin.
HIGH SCHOOL: Science Hill (Johnson City, Tenn.).
JUNIOR COLLEGE: Itawamba Community College (Miss.).
COLLEGE: Tennessee.

F

TRANSACTIONS/CAREER NOTES: Selected by Baltimore Ravens in fifth round (146th pick overall) of 2003 NFL draft. ... Signed by Ravens (July 19, 2003).

Year Team			TOTALS		
	G	GS	Tk.	Ast.	Sks.
2003—Baltimore NFL	1	0	1	0	0.0
2004—Baltimore NFL	6	0	2	0	0.0
Pro totals (2 years)	7	0	3	0	0.0

FRANKS, BUBBA — TE — PACKERS

PERSONAL: Born January 6, 1978, in Riverside, Calif. ... 6-6/265. ... Full name: Daniel Lamont Franks.
HIGH SCHOOL: Big Springs (Texas).
COLLEGE: Miami (Fla.).
TRANSACTIONS/CAREER NOTES: Selected after junior season by Green Bay Packers in first round (14th pick overall) of 2000 NFL draft. ... Signed by Packers (July 19, 2000).
HONORS: Named tight end on THE SPORTING NEWS college All-America first team (1999). ... Played in Pro Bowl (2001-2003 seasons).
SINGLE GAME HIGHS (regular season): Receptions—9 (September 22, 2002, vs. Detroit); yards—62 (September 22, 2002, vs. Detroit); and touchdown receptions—2 (October 11, 2004, vs. Tennessee).

Year Team			RECEIVING				TOTALS			
	G	GS	No.	Yds.	Avg.	TD	TD	2pt.	Pts.	Fum.
2000—Green Bay NFL	16	13	34	363	10.7	1	1	0	6	1
2001—Green Bay NFL	16	14	36	322	8.9	9	9	0	54	0
2002—Green Bay NFL	16	15	54	442	8.2	7	7	0	42	0
2003—Green Bay NFL	16	15	30	241	8.0	4	4	∞2	28	0
2004—Green Bay NFL	16	14	34	361	10.6	7	7	0	42	0
Pro totals (5 years)	80	71	188	1729	9.2	28	28	2	172	1

FRANZ, TODD — S — PACKERS

PERSONAL: Born April 12, 1976, in Enid, Okla. ... 6-0/202. ... Full name: Stephen Todd Franz.
HIGH SCHOOL: Weatherford (Okla.).
COLLEGE: Tulsa.
TRANSACTIONS/CAREER NOTES: Selected by Detroit Lions in fifth round (145th pick overall) of 2000 NFL draft. ... Signed by Lions (July 15, 2000). ... Claimed on waivers by New Orleans Saints (August 28, 2000). ... Released by Saints (October 10, 2000). ... Signed by Cleveland Browns (November 14, 2000). ... Released by Browns (August 4, 2001). ... Signed by New York Jets (January 15, 2002). ... Claimed on waivers by Green Bay Packers (July 22, 2002). ... Released by Packers (September 1, 2002). ... Re-signed by Packers to practice squad (September 4, 2002). ... Released by Packers (September 9, 2002). ... Re-signed by Packers to practice squad (October 9, 2002). ... Activated (October 12, 2002). ... Released by Packers (October 23, 2002). ... Re-signed by Packers to practice squad (October 24, 2002). ... Released by Packers (November 13, 2002). ... Signed by Washington Redskins to practice squad (November 19, 2002). ... Activated (December 17, 2002). ... Did not receive qualifying offer from Redskins (March 2, 2005). ... Signed by Packers (March 15, 2005).

Year Team			TOTALS			INTERCEPTIONS			
	G	GS	Tk.	Ast.	Sks.	No.	Yds.	Avg.	TD
2000—New Orleans NFL	5	0	0	0	0.0	0	0	0.0	0
—Cleveland NFL	2	0	2	0	0.0	0	0	0.0	0
2002—Green Bay NFL	2	0	2	1	0.0	0	0	0.0	0
2003—Washington NFL	16	1	21	5	0.0	0	0	0.0	0
2004—Washington NFL	16	0	3	1	0.0	1	22	22.0	0
Pro totals (4 years)	41	1	28	7	0.0	1	22	22.0	0

FRAZIER, LANCE — CB — COWBOYS

F

PERSONAL: Born May 23, 1981, in Boynton Beach, Fla. ... 5-10/183. ... Full name: Lance Antonio Frazier.
HIGH SCHOOL: Spanish River (Delray Beach, Fla.).
COLLEGE: West Virginia.
TRANSACTIONS/CAREER NOTES: Signed as non-drafted free agent by Baltimore Ravens (April 30, 2004). ... Released by Ravens (September 6, 2004). ... Signed by Dallas Cowboys (October 12, 2004).

Year Team			TOTALS			INTERCEPTIONS				PUNT RETURNS				TOTALS		
	G	GS	Tk.	Ast.	Sks.	No.	Yds.	Avg.	TD	No.	Yds.	Avg.	TD	TD	2pt.	Pts.	Fum.
2004—Dallas NFL	12	8	34	6	0.0	2	2	1.0	0	24	229	9.5	0	0	0	0	2

FREEMAN, ARTURO — S — PACKERS

PERSONAL: Born October 27, 1976, in Orangeburg, S.C. ... 6-1/210. ... Full name: Arturo C. Freeman.
HIGH SCHOOL: Orangeburg-Wilkinson (Orangeburg, S.C.).
COLLEGE: South Carolina.
TRANSACTIONS/CAREER NOTES: Selected by Miami Dolphins in fifth round (152nd pick overall) of 2000 NFL draft. ... Signed by Dolphins (July 11, 2000). ... Granted free agency (February 28, 2003). ... Re-signed by Dolphins (March 2, 2003). ... Released by Dolphins (February 23, 2005). ... Signed by Green Bay Packers (April 15, 2005).

Year Team			TOTALS			INTERCEPTIONS			
	G	GS	Tk.	Ast.	Sks.	No.	Yds.	Avg.	TD
2000—Miami NFL	8	0	0	0	0.0	0	0	0.0	0
2001—Miami NFL	16	4	25	7	1.0	1	0	0.0	0
2002—Miami NFL	16	16	56	16	1.5	0	0	0.0	0
2003—Miami NFL	16	0	17	5	1.0	0	0	0.0	0
2004—Miami NFL	16	9	19	9	0.0	4	59	14.8	0
Pro totals (5 years)	72	29	117	37	3.5	5	59	11.8	0

FREENEY, DWIGHT — DE — COLTS

PERSONAL: Born February 19, 1980, in Hartford, Conn. ... 6-1/268. ... Full name: Dwight Jason Freeney.
HIGH SCHOOL: Bloomfield (Conn.).
COLLEGE: Syracuse.
TRANSACTIONS/CAREER NOTES: Selected by Indianapolis Colts in first round (11th pick overall) of 2002 NFL draft. ... Signed by Colts (July 28, 2002).
CHAMPIONSHIP GAME EXPERIENCE: Played in AFC championship game (2003) season.
HONORS: Named defensive end on THE SPORTING NEWS college All-America first team (2001). ... Played in Pro Bowl (2003 and 2004 seasons). ... Named defensive end on THE SPORTING NEWS NFL All-Pro team (2004).

| | | | | TOTALS | |
Year Team	G	GS	Tk.	Ast.	Sks.
2002—Indianapolis NFL	16	8	45	1	13.0
2003—Indianapolis NFL	15	13	28	4	11.0
2004—Indianapolis NFL	16	16	33	3	*16.0
Pro totals (3 years)	47	37	106	8	40.0

FREITAS, MAKOA — T/G — COLTS

PERSONAL: Born November 23, 1979, in Honolulu, Hawaii. ... 6-4/307. ... Full name: Rockne Makoa Freitas. ... Son of Rocky Freitas, offensive tackle with Detroit Lions (1968-77) and Tampa Bay Buccaneers (1978).
HIGH SCHOOL: Kamehameha (Honolulu, Hawaii).
COLLEGE: Arizona.
TRANSACTIONS/CAREER NOTES: Selected by Indianapolis Colts in sixth round (208th pick overall) of 2003 NFL draft. ... Signed by Colts (July 25, 2003). ... Released by Colts (August 31, 2003). ... Re-signed by Colts (September 26, 2003).
PLAYING EXPERIENCE: Indianapolis NFL, 2003-2004. ... Games/Games started: 2003 (12/6), 2004 (16/0). Total: 28/6.
CHAMPIONSHIP GAME EXPERIENCE: Member of Colts for AFC championship game (2003 season); did not play.

FREROTTE, GUS — QB — DOLPHINS

PERSONAL: Born July 31, 1971, in Kittanning, Pa. ... 6-3/237. ... Full name: Gustave Joseph Frerotte.
HIGH SCHOOL: Ford City (Pa.) Junior-Senior.
COLLEGE: Tulsa.
TRANSACTIONS/CAREER NOTES: Selected by Washington Redskins in seventh round (197th pick overall) of 1994 NFL draft. ... Signed by Redskins (July 19, 1994). ... Granted free agency (February 14, 1997). ... Re-signed by Redskins (July 18, 1997). ... On injured reserve with hip injury (December 2, 1997-remainder of season). ... Released by Redskins (February 11, 1999). ... Signed by Detroit Lions (March 3, 1999). ... Granted unconditional free agency (February 11, 2000). ... Signed by Denver Broncos (March 7, 2000). ... Granted unconditional free agency (March 2, 2001). ... Re-signed by Broncos (March 13, 2001). ... On injured reserve with shoulder injury (December 19, 2001-remainder of season). ... Granted unconditional free agency (March 1, 2002). ... Signed by Cincinnati Bengals (May 1, 2002). ... Granted unconditional free agency (February 28, 2003). ... Signed by Minnesota Vikings (March 19, 2003). ... Granted unconditional free agency (March 2, 2005). ... Signed by Miami Dolphins (March 17, 2005).
HONORS: Played in Pro Bowl (1996 season).
SINGLE GAME HIGHS (regular season): Attempts—58 (November 19, 2000, vs. San Diego); completions—36 (November 19, 2000, vs. San Diego); yards—462 (November 19, 2000, vs. San Diego); and touchdown passes—5 (November 19, 2000, vs. San Diego).
STATISTICAL PLATEAUS: 300-yard passing games: 1995 (1), 1996 (1), 1999 (2), 2000 (1). Total: 5.
MISCELLANEOUS: Regular-season record as starting NFL quarterback: 27-36-1 (.430). ... Postseason record as starting NFL quarterback: 0-2 (.000).

| | | | PASSING | | | | | | | | RUSHING | | | | TOTALS | | |
Year Team	G	GS	Att.	Cmp.	Pct.	Yds.	TD	Int.	Avg.	Skd.	Rat.	Att.	Yds.	Avg.	TD	TD	2pt.	Pts.
1994—Washington NFL	4	4	100	46	46.0	600	5	5	6.00	3	61.3	4	1	0.3	0	0	0	0
1995—Washington NFL	16	11	396	199	50.3	2751	13	13	6.95	23	70.2	22	16	0.7	1	1	0	6
1996—Washington NFL	16	16	470	270	57.4	3453	12	11	7.35	22	79.3	28	16	0.6	0	0	0	0
1997—Washington NFL	13	13	402	204	50.7	2682	17	12	6.67	23	73.8	24	65	2.7	2	2	0	12
1998—Washington NFL	3	2	54	25	46.3	283	1	3	5.24	12	45.5	3	20	6.7	0	0	0	0
1999—Detroit NFL	9	6	288	175	60.8	2117	9	7	7.35	28	83.6	15	33	2.2	0	0	0	0
2000—Denver NFL	10	6	232	138	59.5	1776	9	8	7.66	12	82.1	22	64	2.9	1	1	0	6
2001—Denver NFL	4	1	48	30	62.5	308	3	0	6.42	3	101.7	10	9	0.9	1	1	0	6
2002—Cincinnati NFL	4	3	85	44	51.8	437	1	5	5.14	10	46.1	4	22	5.5	0	0	0	0
2003—Minnesota NFL	16	2	65	38	58.5	690	7	2	10.62	5	118.1	12	-2	-0.2	0	0	0	0
2004—Minnesota NFL	16	0	1	0	0.0	0	0	0	0.00	0	39.6	0	0	0.0	0	0	0	0
Pro totals (11 years)	111	64	2141	1169	54.6	15097	77	66	7.05	141	76.1	144	244	1.7	5	5	0	30

FRIEDMAN, LENNIE — G — REDSKINS

PERSONAL: Born October 13, 1976, in Livingston, N.J. ... 6-3/283. ... Full name: Leonard Lebrecht Friedman.
HIGH SCHOOL: West Milford (N.J.).
COLLEGE: Duke.
TRANSACTIONS/CAREER NOTES: Selected by Denver Broncos in second round (61st pick overall) of 1999 NFL draft. ... Signed by Broncos (June 14, 1999). ... On injured reserve with knee injury (August 31, 1999-entire season). ... Assigned by Broncos to Barcelona Dragons in 2000 NFL Europe enhancement allocation program (February 18, 2000). ... Released by Broncos (February 25, 2003). ... Signed by Washington Redskins (March 3, 2003).
PLAYING EXPERIENCE: Denver NFL, 1999-2002; Washington NFL, 2003-2004. ... Games/Games started: 2000 (15/8), 2001 (15/14), 2002 (2/0), 2003 (16/8), 2004 (5/2), Total: 53/32.

F

FROST, DERRICK   P   BROWNS

PERSONAL: Born November 25, 1980, in St. Louis, Mo. ... 6-4/210.
HIGH SCHOOL: Clayton (Mo.).
COLLEGE: Northern Iowa.
TRANSACTIONS/CAREER NOTES: Signed as non-drafted free agent by Philadelphia Eagles (May 2, 2003). ... Claimed on waivers by Baltimore Ravens (May 27, 2003). ... Released by Ravens (August 30, 2003). ... Signed by Cleveland Browns (December 10, 2003). ... Inactive for three games (2003).

			PUNTING				
Year Team	G	No.	Yds.	Avg.	Net avg.	In. 20	Blk.
2004—Cleveland NFL	16	85	3404	40.0	35.4	24	0

FUAMATU-MA'AFALA, CHRIS   RB   JAGUARS

PERSONAL: Born March 4, 1977, in Honolulu, Hawaii. ... 6-0/252. ... Name pronounced: fu-ah-MAH-tu ma-ah-FAH-la.
HIGH SCHOOL: St. Louis (Honolulu).
COLLEGE: Utah.
TRANSACTIONS/CAREER NOTES: Selected after junior season by Pittsburgh Steelers in sixth round (178th pick overall) of 1998 NFL draft. ... Signed by Steelers (July 10, 1998). ... On injured reserve with broken foot (Decemeber 20, 2000-remainder of season). ... Granted free agency (March 2, 2001). ... Tendered offer sheet by New England Patriots (April 14, 2001). ... Offer matched by Steelers (April 19, 2001). ... Released by Steelers (August 31, 2003). ... Signed by Jacksonville Jaguars (September 3, 2003). ... Granted unconditional free agency (March 2, 2005). Re-signed by Jaguars (March 15, 2005).
CHAMPIONSHIP GAME EXPERIENCE: Played in AFC championship game (2001 season).
SINGLE GAME HIGHS (regular season): Attempts—26 (December 23, 2001, vs. Detroit); yards—126 (December 23, 2001, vs. Detroit); and rushing touchdowns—1 (October 10, 2004, vs. San Diego).
STATISTICAL PLATEAUS: 100-yard rushing games: 2001 (1). Total: 1.

			RUSHING				RECEIVING				TOTALS			
Year Team	G	GS	Att.	Yds.	Avg.	TD	No.	Yds.	Avg.	TD	TD	2pt.	Pts.	Fum.
1998—Pittsburgh NFL	12	0	7	30	4.3	2	9	84	9.3	1	3	0	18	0
1999—Pittsburgh NFL	9	0	1	4	4.0	0	0	0	0.0	0	0	0	0	0
2000—Pittsburgh NFL	7	1	21	149	7.1	1	11	107	9.7	0	1	0	6	0
2001—Pittsburgh NFL	16	5	120	453	3.8	3	16	127	7.9	1	4	0	24	0
2002—Pittsburgh NFL	8	0	23	115	5.0	0	2	12	6.0	0	0	0	0	0
2003—Jacksonville NFL	13	0	35	144	4.1	1	1	2	2.0	0	1	0	6	0
2004—Jacksonville NFL	7	1	20	69	3.5	1	4	19	4.8	0	1	0	6	0
Pro totals (7 years)	72	7	227	964	4.2	8	43	351	8.2	2	10	0	60	0

FUJITA, SCOTT   LB   CHIEFS

PERSONAL: Born April 28, 1979, in Ventura, Calif. ... 6-5/250.
HIGH SCHOOL: Rio Mesa (Calif.).
COLLEGE: California.
TRANSACTIONS/CAREER NOTES: Selected by Kansas City Chiefs in fifth round (143rd pick overall) of 2002 NFL draft. ... Signed by Chiefs (June 21, 2002). ... Granted free agency (March 2, 2005). ... Re-signed by Chiefs (April 8, 2005).

			TOTALS			INTERCEPTIONS			
Year Team	G	GS	Tk.	Ast.	Sks.	No.	Yds.	Avg.	TD
2002—Kansas City NFL	16	9	50	5	1.0	0	0	0.0	0
2003—Kansas City NFL	16	16	98	16	4.0	1	8	8.0	0
2004—Kansas City NFL	16	16	67	23	4.5	0	0	0.0	0
Pro totals (3 years)	48	41	215	44	9.5	1	8	8.0	0

FULLER, COREY   CB   RAVENS

PERSONAL: Born May 1, 1971, in Tallahassee, Fla. ... 5-10/220.
HIGH SCHOOL: James S. Rickards (Tallahassee, Fla.).
COLLEGE: Florida State.
TRANSACTIONS/CAREER NOTES: Selected by Minnesota Vikings in second round (55th pick overall) of 1995 NFL draft. ... Signed by Vikings (July 24, 1995). ... Granted unconditional free agency (February 12, 1999). ... Signed by Cleveland Browns (February 18, 1999). ... Released by Browns (February 26, 2003). ... Signed by Baltimore Ravens (March 4, 2003).
CHAMPIONSHIP GAME EXPERIENCE: Played in NFC championship game (1998 season).

			TOTALS			INTERCEPTIONS			
Year Team	G	GS	Tk.	Ast.	Sks.	No.	Yds.	Avg.	TD
1995—Minnesota NFL	16	10	57	9	0.5	1	0	0.0	0
1996—Minnesota NFL	16	14	53	11	0.0	3	3	1.0	0
1997—Minnesota NFL	16	16	82	9	0.0	2	24	12.0	0
1998—Minnesota NFL	16	16	70	9	1.0	4	36	9.0	0
1999—Cleveland NFL	16	16	64	13	0.0	0	0	0.0	0
2000—Cleveland NFL	15	15	37	5	0.0	3	0	0.0	0
2001—Cleveland NFL	16	16	72	15	0.0	3	82	27.3	1
2002—Cleveland NFL	13	12	57	5	0.0	1	0	0.0	0
2003—Baltimore NFL	14	10	30	4	0.0	0	0	0.0	0
2004—Baltimore NFL	14	2	10	3	0.0	0	0	0.0	0
Pro totals (10 years)	152	127	502	83	1.5	17	145	8.5	1

FULLER, CURTIS   S   PANTHERS

PERSONAL: Born July 25, 1978, in Fort Worth, Texas. ... 5-10/188.
HIGH SCHOOL: Christian (Fort Worth, Texas).
JUNIOR COLLEGE: Trinity Valley Community College (Texas).
COLLEGE: Texas Christian.
TRANSACTIONS/CAREER NOTES: Selected by Seattle Seahawks in fourth round (127th pick overall) of 2001 NFL draft. ... Signed by Seahawks (June 8, 2001). ... Claimed on waivers by Green Bay Packers (September 1, 2003). ... Released by Packers (September 5, 2004). ... Re-signed by Packers (October 27, 2004). ... Claimed on waivers by Carolina Panthers (November 3, 2004).

				TOTALS			INTERCEPTIONS			
Year Team	G	GS	Tk.	Ast.	Sks.	No.	Yds.	Avg.	TD
2001—Seattle NFL	10	1	12	2	0.0	0	0	0.0	0
2002—Seattle NFL	16	1	22	11	0.0	1	3	3.0	0
2003—Green Bay NFL	9	0	2	3	0.0	0	0	0.0	0
2004—Green Bay NFL	1	0	0	0	0.0	0	0	0.0	0
—Carolina NFL	6	0	0	0	0.0	0	0	0.0	0
Pro totals (4 years)	42	2	36	16	0.0	1	3	3.0	0

FURREY, MIKE   WR   RAMS

PERSONAL: Born May 12, 1977, in Grove City, Ohio. ... 6-0/185. ... Full name: Michael Thomas Furrey.
HIGH SCHOOL: Hilliard (Ohio).
COLLEGE: Northern Iowa.
TRANSACTIONS/CAREER NOTES: Signed as non-drafted free agent by Indianapolis Colts (April 20, 2000). ... Released by Colts (August 27, 2000). ... Signed by New York Jets (July 27, 2002). ... Waived by Jets (October 3, 2002). ... Signed by St. Louis Rams (April 29, 2003).
SINGLE GAME HIGHS (regular season): Receptions—4 (December 14, 2003, vs. Seattle); yards—45 (December 14, 2003, vs. Seattle); and touchdown receptions—0.

			RUSHING				RECEIVING				PUNT RETURNS				KICKOFF RETURNS				TOTALS		
Year Team	G	GS	Att.	Yds.	Avg.	TD	No.	Yds.	Avg.	TD	No.	Yds.	Avg.	TD	No.	Yds.	Avg.	TD	TD	2pt.	Pts.
2003—StL. NFL	13	0	3	5	1.7	0	20	189	9.5	0	11	119	10.8	0	7	140	20.0	0	0	0	0
2004—StL. NFL	8	0	0	0	0.0	0	1	8	8.0	0	0	0	0.0	0	8	157	19.6	0	0	0	0
Pro totals (2 years)	21	0	3	5	1.7	0	21	197	9.4	0	11	119	10.8	0	15	297	19.8	0	0	0	0

GABRIEL, DOUG   WR   RAIDERS

PERSONAL: Born August 27, 1980, in Miami, Fla. ... 6-2/215. ... Full name: Douglas Gabriel.
HIGH SCHOOL: Dr. Phillips (Orlando).
JUNIOR COLLEGE: Mississippi Gulf Coast Junior College.
COLLEGE: Central Florida.
TRANSACTIONS/CAREER NOTES: Selected by Oakland Raiders in fifth round (167th pick overall) of 2003 NFL draft. ... Signed by Raiders (July 24, 2003).
SINGLE GAME HIGHS (regular season): Receptions—4 (November 28, 2004, vs. Denver); yards—81 (September 12, 2004, vs. Pittsburgh); and touchdown receptions—1 (December 19, 2004, vs. Tennessee).

			RUSHING				RECEIVING				KICKOFF RETURNS				TOTALS			
Year Team	G	GS	Att.	Yds.	Avg.	TD	No.	Yds.	Avg.	TD	No.	Yds.	Avg.	TD	TD	2pt.	Pts.	Fum.
2003—Oakland NFL	12	0	0	0	0.0	0	1	17	17.0	0	29	646	22.3	1	1	0	6	0
2004—Oakland NFL	16	5	2	7	3.5	0	33	551	16.7	2	53	1140	21.5	0	2	0	12	2
Pro totals (2 years)	28	5	2	7	3.5	0	34	568	16.7	2	82	1786	21.8	1	3	0	18	2

GAFFNEY, JABAR   WR   TEXANS

PERSONAL: Born December 1, 1980, in San Antonio, Texas. ... 6-1/205. ... Full name: Derrick Jabar Gaffney.
HIGH SCHOOL: Raines (Jacksonville, Fla.).
COLLEGE: Florida.
TRANSACTIONS/CAREER NOTES: Selected after sophomore season by Houston Texans in second round (33rd pick overall) of 2002 NFL draft. ... Signed by Texans (July 19, 2002).
HONORS: Named College Football Freshman of the Year by THE SPORTING NEWS (2000). ... Named wide receiver on THE SPORTING NEWS college All-America first team (2001).
SINGLE GAME HIGHS (regular season): Receptions—6 (November 7, 2004, vs. Denver); yards—109 (December 19, 2004, vs. Chicago); and touchdown receptions—1 (October 17, 2004, vs. Tennessee).
STATISTICAL PLATEAUS: 100-yard receiving games: 2004 (1). Total: 1.

			RUSHING				RECEIVING				PUNT RETURNS				TOTALS			
Year Team	G	GS	Att.	Yds.	Avg.	TD	No.	Yds.	Avg.	TD	No.	Yds.	Avg.	TD	TD	2pt.	Pts.	Fum.
2002—Houston NFL	16	14	0	0	0.0	0	41	483	11.8	1	3	-3	-1.0	0	1	1	8	1
2003—Houston NFL	16	11	1	13	13.0	0	34	402	11.8	2	4	22	5.5	0	2	0	12	0
2004—Houston NFL	16	12	4	30	7.5	0	41	632	15.4	2	0	0	0.0	0	2	0	12	1
Pro totals (3 years)	48	37	5	43	8.6	0	116	1517	13.1	5	7	19	2.7	0	5	1	32	2

GAGE, JUSTIN   WR   BEARS

PERSONAL: Born January 25, 1981, in Indianapolis, Ind. ... 6-4/210.
HIGH SCHOOL: Jefferson City (Mo.).
COLLEGE: Missouri.

TRANSACTIONS/CAREER NOTES: Selected by Chicago Bears in fifth round (143rd pick overall) of 2003 NFL draft. ... Signed by Bears (July 18, 2003).

SINGLE GAME HIGHS (regular season): Receptions—4 (October 24, 2004, vs. Tampa Bay); yards—100 (November 30, 2003, vs. Arizona); and touchdown receptions—1 (December 21, 2003, vs. Washington).

STATISTICAL PLATEAUS: 100-yard receiving games: 2003 (1). Total: 1.

					RECEIVING				TOTALS		
Year Team	G	GS	No.	Yds.	Avg.	TD	TD	2pt.	Pts.	Fum.
2003—Chicago NFL	10	3	17	338	19.9	2	2	0	12	1
2004—Chicago NFL	16	2	12	156	13.0	0	0	0	0	0
Pro totals (2 years)	26	5	29	494	17.0	2	2	0	12	1

GAINES, MICHAEL TE PANTHERS

PERSONAL: Born March 30, 1980, in Tallahassee, Fla. ... 6-3/280.
HIGH SCHOOL: Florida (Tallahassee, Fla.).
COLLEGE: Central Florida.
TRANSACTIONS/CAREER NOTES: Selected by Carolina Panthers in seventh round (232nd pick overall) of 2004 NFL draft. ... Signed by Panthers (July 12, 2004).
SINGLE GAME HIGHS (regular season): Receptions—2 (October 10, 2004, vs. Denver); yards—18 (October 10, 2004, vs. Denver); and touchdown receptions—0.

					RECEIVING				TOTALS		
Year Team	G	GS	No.	Yds.	Avg.	TD	TD	2pt.	Pts.	Fum.
2004—Carolina NFL	15	6	4	34	8.5	0	0	0	0	0

GALLERY, ROBERT T RAIDERS

PERSONAL: Born July 26, 1980, in Manchester, Iowa. ... 6-7/325.
HIGH SCHOOL: East Buchanan (Masonville, Iowa).
COLLEGE: Iowa.
TRANSACTIONS/CAREER NOTES: Selected by Oakland Raiders in first round (second pick overall) of 2004 NFL draft. ... Signed by Raiders (July 29, 2004).
PLAYING EXPERIENCE: Oakland NFL, 2004. ... Games/Games started: 2004 (16/15). Total: 16/15.
HONORS: Outland Award winner (2003). ... Named offensive tackle on THE SPORTING NEWS Freshman All-America first team (2003).

GALLOWAY, JOEY WR BUCCANEERS

PERSONAL: Born November 20, 1971, in Bellaire, Ohio. ... 5-11/197.
HIGH SCHOOL: Bellaire (Ohio).
COLLEGE: Ohio State.
TRANSACTIONS/CAREER NOTES: Selected by Seattle Seahawks in first round (eighth pick overall) of 1995 NFL draft. ... Signed by Seahawks (July 20, 1995). ... On did not report list (September 4-November 9, 1999). ... Designated by Seahawks as franchise player (February 11, 2000). ... Traded by Seahawks to Dallas Cowboys for first-round pick (RB Shaun Alexander) in 2000 draft and first round pick (traded to San Francisco) in 2001 draft (February 12, 2000). ... On injured reserve with knee injury (September 8, 2000-remainder of season). ... Traded by Cowboys to Tampa Bay Buccaneers for WR Keyshawn Johnson (March 19, 2004). ... Granted unconditional free agency (March 2, 2005). ... Re-signed by Buccaneers (March 8, 2005).
SINGLE GAME HIGHS (regular season): Receptions—9 (December 26, 2004, vs. Carolina); yards—146 (December 30, 2001, vs. San Francisco); and touchdown receptions—3 (October 26, 1997, vs. Oakland).
STATISTICAL PLATEAUS: 100-yard receiving games: 1995 (3), 1996 (2), 1997 (3), 1998 (4), 2001 (1), 2002 (3), 2003 (2). Total: 18.

			RUSHING				RECEIVING				PUNT RETURNS				KICKOFF RETURNS				TOTALS		
Year Team	G	GS	Att.	Yds.	Avg.	TD	No.	Yds.	Avg.	TD	No.	Yds.	Avg.	TD	No.	Yds.	Avg.	TD	TD	2pt.	Pts.
1995—Sea. NFL	16	16	11	154	14.0	1	67	1039	15.5	7	36	360	10.0	†1	2	30	15.0	0	9	0	54
1996—Sea. NFL	16	16	15	127	8.5	0	57	987	17.3	7	15	158	10.5	▲1	0	0	0.0	0	8	0	48
1997—Sea. NFL	15	15	9	72	8.0	0	72	1049	14.6	▲12	0	0	0.0	0	0	0	0.0	0	12	0	72
1998—Sea. NFL	16	16	9	26	2.9	0	65	1047	16.1	▲10	25	251	10.0	†2	0	0	0.0	0	12	0	72
1999—Sea. NFL	8	4	1	-1	-1.0	0	22	335	15.2	1	3	54	18.0	0	0	0	0.0	0	1	0	6
2000—Dal. NFL	1	1	0	0	0.0	0	4	62	15.5	1	1	2	2.0	0	0	0	0.0	0	1	0	6
2001—Dal. NFL	16	16	3	32	10.7	0	52	699	13.4	3	1	6	6.0	0	0	0	0.0	0	3	0	18
2002—Dal. NFL	16	16	4	31	7.8	0	61	908	14.9	6	15	181	12.1	0	0	0	0.0	0	6	0	36
2003—Dal. NFL	15	13	4	22	5.5	0	34	672	*19.8	2	20	178	8.9	0	2	38	19.0	0	2	0	12
2004—T.B. NFL	10	7	2	19	9.5	0	33	416	12.6	5	20	142	7.1	1	0	0	0.0	0	6	0	36
Pro totals (10 years)	129	120	58	482	8.3	1	467	7214	15.4	54	136	1332	9.8	5	4	68	17.0	0	60	0	360

GAMBLE, CHRIS CB PANTHERS

PERSONAL: Born March 11, 1983, in Boston, Mass. ... 6-1/181.
HIGH SCHOOL: Dillard (Sunrise, Fla.).
COLLEGE: Ohio State.
TRANSACTIONS/CAREER NOTES: Selected after junior season by Carolina Panthers in first round (28th pick overall) of 2004 NFL draft. ... Signed by Panthers (August 2, 2004).
HONORS: Named cornerback on THE SPORTING NEWS college All-America second team (2002 and 2003).

			TOTALS			INTERCEPTIONS				PUNT RETURNS				KICKOFF RETURNS				TOTALS			
Year Team	G	GS	Tk.	Ast.	Sks.	No.	Yds.	Avg.	TD	No.	Yds.	Avg.	TD	No.	Yds.	Avg.	TD	TD	2pt.	Pts.	Fum.
2004—Car. NFL	16	16	60	6	0.0	∞6	15	2.5	0	9	69	7.7	0	0	0	0.0	0	0	0	0	1

GAMMON, KENDALL　　　　　TE　　　　　CHIEFS

PERSONAL: Born October 23, 1968, in Wichita, Kan. ... 6-4/255. ... Full name: Kendall Robert Gammon.
HIGH SCHOOL: Rose Hill (Kan.).
COLLEGE: Pittsburg State.
TRANSACTIONS/CAREER NOTES: Selected by Pittsburgh Steelers in 11th round (291st pick overall) of 1992 NFL draft. ... Signed by Steelers (July 14, 1992). ... Released by Steelers (August 30, 1993). ... Re-signed by Steelers (August 31, 1993). ... Granted unconditional free agency (February 17, 1995). ... Re-signed by Steelers (May 8, 1995). ... Released by Steelers (August 26, 1996). ... Signed by New Orleans Saints (August 28, 1996). ... Granted unconditional free agency (February 11, 2000). ... Signed by Kansas City Chiefs (February 23, 2000). ... Granted unconditional free agency (February 28, 2003). ... Re-signed by Chiefs (March 23, 2003). ... Granted unconditional free agency (March 3, 2004). ... Re-signed by Chiefs (March 3, 2004). ... Granted unconditional free agency (March 2, 2005). ... Re-signed by Chiefs (March 29, 2005).
CHAMPIONSHIP GAME EXPERIENCE: Played in AFC championship game (1994 and 1995 seasons). ... Played in Super Bowl 30 (1995 season).
HONORS: Played in Pro Bowl (2004 season).

| | | | RECEIVING | | | | TOTALS | | |
Year　Team	G	GS	No.	Yds.	Avg.	TD	TD	2pt.	Pts.	Fum.
1992—Pittsburgh NFL	16	0	0	0	0.0	0	0	0	0	0
1993—Pittsburgh NFL	16	0	0	0	0.0	0	0	0	0	0
1994—Pittsburgh NFL	16	0	0	0	0.0	0	0	0	0	0
1995—Pittsburgh NFL	16	0	0	0	0.0	0	0	0	0	0
1996—New Orleans NFL	16	0	0	0	0.0	0	0	0	0	0
1997—New Orleans NFL	16	0	0	0	0.0	0	0	0	0	0
1998—New Orleans NFL	16	0	0	0	0.0	0	0	0	0	0
1999—New Orleans NFL	16	0	0	0	0.0	0	0	0	0	0
2000—Kansas City NFL	16	0	0	0	0.0	0	0	0	0	0
2001—Kansas City NFL	16	0	0	0	0.0	0	0	0	0	0
2002—Kansas City NFL	16	0	0	0	0.0	0	0	0	0	0
2003—Kansas City NFL	16	0	0	0	0.0	0	0	0	0	0
2004—Kansas City NFL	16	0	0	0	0.0	0	0	0	0	0
Pro totals (13 years)	208	0	0	0	0.0	0	0	0	0	0

GANDY, MIKE　　　　　T/G　　　　　BILLS

PERSONAL: Born January 3, 1979, in Rockford, Ill. ... 6-4/310. ... Full name: Michael Joseph Gandy.
HIGH SCHOOL: Garland (Texas).
COLLEGE: Notre Dame.
TRANSACTIONS/CAREER NOTES: Selected by Chicago Bears in third round (68th pick overall) of 2001 NFL draft. ... Signed by Bears (July 20, 2001). ... Inactive for all 16 games (2001). ... Granted free agency (March 3, 2004). ... Re-signed by Bears (March 19, 2004). ... Released by Bears (November 8, 2004). ... Signed by Buffalo Bills (March 4, 2005).
PLAYING EXPERIENCE: Chicago NFL, 2002-2004. ... Games/Games started: 2002 (13/11), 2003 (14/14), 2004 (5/5). Total: 32/30.
HONORS: Named guard on THE SPORTING NEWS college All-America first team (2000).

GANDY, WAYNE　　　　　T　　　　　SAINTS

PERSONAL: Born February 10, 1971, in Haines City, Fla. ... 6-4/315. ... Full name: Wayne Lamar Gandy.
HIGH SCHOOL: Haines City (Fla.).
COLLEGE: Auburn.
TRANSACTIONS/CAREER NOTES: Selected by Los Angeles Rams in first round (15th pick overall) of 1994 NFL draft. ... Signed by Rams (July 23, 1994). ... Rams franchise moved to St. Louis (April 12, 1995). ... Granted unconditional free agency (February 12, 1999). ... Signed by Pittsburgh Steelers (April 6, 1999). ... Granted unconditional free agency (February 28, 2003). ... Signed by New Orleans Saints (March 2, 2003).
PLAYING EXPERIENCE: Los Angeles Rams NFL, 1994; St. Louis NFL, 1995-1998; Pittsburgh NFL, 1999-2002; New Orleans NFL, 2003-2004. ... Games/Games started: 1994 (16/9), 1995 (16/16), 1996 (16/16), 1997 (16/16), 1998 (16/16), 1999 (16/16), 2000 (16/16), 2001 (15/15), 2002 (16/16), 2003 (16/16), 2004 (16/16). Total: 175/168.
CHAMPIONSHIP GAME EXPERIENCE: Played in AFC championship game (2001 season).
HONORS: Named offensive lineman on THE SPORTING NEWS college All-America first team (1993).

GANNON, RICH　　　　　QB　　　　　RAIDERS

PERSONAL: Born December 20, 1965, in Philadelphia, Pa. ... 6-3/210. ... Full name: Richard Joseph Gannon.
HIGH SCHOOL: St. Joseph's Prep (Philadelphia).
COLLEGE: Delaware.
TRANSACTIONS/CAREER NOTES: Selected by New England Patriots in fourth round (98th pick overall) of 1987 NFL draft. ... Rights traded by Patriots to Minnesota Vikings for fourth- (WR Sammy Martin) and 11th-round (traded) picks in 1988 draft (May 6, 1987). ... Signed by Vikings (July 30, 1987). ... Active for 13 games (1989); did not play. ... Granted free agency (February 1, 1990). ... Re-signed by Vikings (July 30, 1990). ... Granted free agency (February 1, 1991). ... Re-signed by Vikings (July 25, 1991). ... Granted free agency (February 1, 1992). ... Re-signed by Vikings (August 8, 1992). ... Traded by Vikings to Washington Redskins for conditional draft pick (August 20, 1993). ... Granted unconditional free agency (February 17, 1994). ... Signed by Kansas City Chiefs (March 29, 1995). ... Released by Chiefs (February 15, 1996). ... Re-signed by Chiefs (April 3, 1996). ... Granted unconditional free agency (February 12, 1999). ... Signed by Oakland Raiders (February 16, 1999). ... On injured reserve with shoulder injury (November 12, 2003-remainder of season). ... On injured reserve with neck injury (October 20, 2004-remainder of season).
CHAMPIONSHIP GAME EXPERIENCE: Member of Vikings for NFC championship game (1987 season); did not play. ... Played in AFC championship game (2000 and 2002 seasons). ... Played in Super Bowl 37 (2002 season).

HONORS: Played in Pro Bowl (1999-2002 seasons). ... Named quarterback on THE SPORTING NEWS NFL All-Pro team (2000 and 2002). ... Named Outstanding Player of Pro Bowl (2000 and 2001). ... Named NFL Player of the Year by THE SPORTING NEWS (2002).
RECORDS: Holds NFL single-season record for most completions—418 (2002); and most games with 300 or more yards passing—10 (2002). ... Shares NFL record for most consecutive games with 300 or more yards passing—6 (September 15-October 27, 2002). ... Holds NFL single-game record for most consecutive completions—21 (November 11, 2002, vs. Denver).
POST SEASON RECORDS: Holds Super Bowl single-game record for most passes intercepted—5 (January 26, 2003, vs. Tampa Bay).
SINGLE GAME HIGHS (regular season): Attempts—64 (September 15, 2002, vs. Pittsburgh); completions—43 (September 15, 2002, vs. Pittsburgh); yards—403 (September 15, 2002, vs. Pittsburgh); and touchdown passes—5 (December 24, 2000, vs. Carolina).
STATISTICAL PLATEAUS: 300-yard passing games: 1991 (1), 1992 (1), 1997 (1), 1998 (1), 1999 (2), 2000 (2), 2001 (4), 2002 (10), 2003 (1), 2004 (1). Total: 24.
MISCELLANEOUS: Regular-season record as starting NFL quarterback: 76-56 (.576). ... Postseason record as starting NFL quarterback: 4-3 (.571).

Year Team	G	GS	PASSING Att.	Cmp.	Pct.	Yds.	TD	Int.	Avg.	Skd.	Rat.	RUSHING Att.	Yds.	Avg.	TD	TOTALS TD	2pt.	Pts.
1987—Minnesota NFL	4	0	6	2	33.3	18	0	1	3.00	0	2.8	0	0	0.0	0	0	0	0
1988—Minnesota NFL	3	0	15	7	46.7	90	0	0	6.00	3	66.0	4	29	7.3	0	0	0	0
1989—Minnesota NFL	Did not play.																	
1990—Minnesota NFL	14	12	349	182	52.1	2278	16	16	6.53	34	68.9	52	268	5.2	1	1	0	6
1991—Minnesota NFL	15	11	354	211	59.6	2166	12	6	6.12	19	81.5	43	236	5.5	2	2	0	12
1992—Minnesota NFL	12	12	279	159	57.0	1905	12	13	6.83	25	72.9	45	187	4.2	0	0	0	0
1993—Washington NFL	8	4	125	74	59.2	704	3	7	5.63	16	59.6	21	88	4.2	1	1	0	6
1994—	Did not play.																	
1995—Kansas City NFL	2	0	11	7	63.6	57	0	0	5.18	0	76.7	8	25	3.1	1	1	0	6
1996—Kansas City NFL	4	3	90	54	60.0	491	6	1	5.46	5	92.4	12	81	6.8	0	0	0	0
1997—Kansas City NFL	9	6	175	98	56.0	1144	7	4	6.54	13	79.8	33	109	3.3	2	2	0	12
1998—Kansas City NFL	12	10	354	206	58.2	2305	10	6	6.51	25	80.1	44	168	3.8	3	3	0	18
1999—Oakland NFL	16	16	515	304	59.0	3840	24	14	7.46	49	86.5	46	298	6.5	2	2	0	12
2000—Oakland NFL	16	16	473	284	60.0	3430	28	11	7.25	28	92.4	89	529	5.9	4	4	1	26
2001—Oakland NFL	16	16	549	§361	§65.8	3828	§27	9	6.97	27	§95.5	63	231	3.7	2	2	1	14
2002—Oakland NFL	16	16	*618	*418	67.6	*4689	26	10	7.59	36	97.3	50	156	3.1	3	3	0	18
2003—Oakland NFL	7	7	225	125	55.6	1274	6	4	5.66	17	73.5	6	18	3.0	0	0	0	0
2004—Oakland NFL	3	3	68	41	60.3	524	3	2	7.71	5	86.9	5	26	5.2	0	0	0	0
Pro totals (16 years)	157	132	4206	2533	60.2	28743	180	104	6.83	302	84.7	521	2449	4.7	21	21	2	130

GARCIA, JEFF   QB   LIONS

PERSONAL: Born February 24, 1970, in Gilroy, Calif. ... 6-1/200.
HIGH SCHOOL: Gilroy (Calif.).
JUNIOR COLLEGE: Gavilan College (Calif.).
COLLEGE: San Jose State.
TRANSACTIONS/CAREER NOTES: Signed by Calgary Stampeders of CFL (1994). ... Granted free agency (February 16, 1997). ... Re-signed by Stampeders (April 30, 1997). ... Signed as non-drafted free agent by San Francisco 49ers (February 16, 1999). ... Released by 49ers (March 2, 2004). ... Signed by Cleveland Browns (March 9, 2004). ... On injured reserve with knee injury (December 13, 2004-remainder of season). ... Released by Browns (February 23, 2005). ... Signed by Detroit Lions (March 12, 2005).
CHAMPIONSHIP GAME EXPERIENCE: Played in Grey Cup (1995). ... Member of CFL Championship team (1998). ... Named Most Valuable Player of Grey Cup, CFL championship game (1998).
HONORS: Played in Pro Bowl (2000-2002 seasons).
RECORDS: Shares NFL record for longest pass completion (to Andre Davis)—99 yards, touchdown (October 17, 2004 vs. Cincinnati).
SINGLE GAME HIGHS (regular season): Attempts—55 (December 8, 2002, vs. Dallas); completions—36 (December 8, 2002, vs. Dallas); passing yards—437 (December 5, 1999, vs. Cincinnati); and touchdown passes—4 (October 17, 2004, vs. Cincinnati).
STATISTICAL PLATEAUS: 300-yard passing games: 1999 (3), 2000 (6), 2001 (3), 2002 (1), 2003 (1), 2004 (1). Total: 15.
MISCELLANEOUS: Regular-season record as starting NFL quarterback: 38-43 (.469). ... Postseason record as starting NFL quarterback: 1-2 (.333).

Year Team	G	GS	PASSING Att.	Cmp.	Pct.	Yds.	TD	Int.	Avg.	Skd.	Rat.	RUSHING Att.	Yds.	Avg.	TD	TOTALS TD	2pt.	Pts.
1994—Calgary CFL	7	...	3	2	66.7	10	0	0	3.33	...	71.5	2	3	1.5	0	0	...	0
1995—Calgary CFL	18	...	364	230	63.2	3358	25	7	9.23	...	108.1	61	396	6.5	5	5	...	30
1996—Calgary CFL	18	...	537	315	58.7	4225	25	16	7.87	...	86.9	92	657	7.1	6	6	...	36
1997—Calgary CFL	17	...	566	354	62.5	4573	33	14	8.08	...	97.0	135	727	5.4	7	7	1	44
1998—Calgary CFL	18	...	554	348	62.8	4276	28	15	7.72	...	92.2	94	575	6.1	6	6	...	36
1999—San Francisco NFL	13	10	375	225	60.0	2544	11	11	6.78	15	77.9	45	231	5.1	2	2	0	12
2000—San Francisco NFL	16	16	561	‡355	63.3	‡4278	‡31	10	7.63	24	97.6	72	414	5.8	4	4	0	24
2001—San Francisco NFL	16	16	504	316	62.7	3538	32	12	7.02	26	94.8	72	254	3.5	5	5	0	30
2002—San Francisco NFL	16	16	528	328	62.1	3344	21	10	6.33	17	85.6	73	353	4.8	3	3	1	20
2003—San Francisco NFL	13	13	392	225	57.4	2704	18	13	6.90	21	80.1	56	319	5.7	7	7	0	42
2004—Cleveland NFL	11	10	252	144	57.1	1731	10	9	6.87	24	76.7	35	169	4.8	2	2	0	12
CFL totals (5 years)	78	...	2024	1249	61.7	16442	111	52	8.12	...	94.9	384	2358	6.1	24	24	1	146
NFL totals (6 years)	85	81	2612	1593	61.0	18139	123	65	6.94	127	87.2	353	1740	4.9	23	23	1	140
Pro totals (11 years)	163	...	4636	2842	61.3	34581	234	117	7.46	...	90.6	737	4098	5.6	47	47	2	286

GARDNER, BARRY   LB   JETS

PERSONAL: Born December 13, 1976, in Harvey, Ill. ... 6-1/245. ... Full name: Barry Allan Gardner.
HIGH SCHOOL: Thornton (Harvey, Ill.).
COLLEGE: Northwestern.
TRANSACTIONS/CAREER NOTES: Selected by Philadelphia Eagles in second round (35th pick overall) of 1999 NFL draft. ... Signed by Eagles (July 25, 1999). ... Granted unconditional free agency (February 28, 2003). ... Signed by Cleveland Browns (March 14, 2003). ... Granted unconditional free agency (March 2, 2005). ... Signed by New York Jets (March 11, 2005).
CHAMPIONSHIP GAME EXPERIENCE: Played in NFC championship game (2001 and 2002 seasons).

G

Year Team	G	GS	TOTALS			INTERCEPTIONS			
			Tk.	Ast.	Sks.	No.	Yds.	Avg.	TD
1999—Philadelphia NFL	16	5	27	10	0.0	0	0	0.0	0
2000—Philadelphia NFL	16	13	42	15	1.0	0	0	0.0	0
2001—Philadelphia NFL	16	0	10	5	0.0	0	0	0.0	0
2002—Philadelphia NFL	16	0	19	9	1.0	0	0	0.0	0
2003—Cleveland NFL	16	0	13	6	0.0	0	0	0.0	0
2004—Cleveland NFL	14	5	17	10	0.0	1	30	30.0	0
Pro totals (6 years)	94	23	128	55	2.0	1	30	30.0	0

GARDNER, GILBERT — LB — COLTS

PERSONAL: Born May 9, 1982, in Angleton, Texas. ... 6-1/228. ... Full name: Gilbert Ravelle Gardner II.
HIGH SCHOOL: Angleton (Texas).
COLLEGE: Purdue.
TRANSACTIONS/CAREER NOTES: Selected by Indianapolis Colts in third round (69th pick overall) of 2004 NFL draft. ... Signed by Colts (July 29, 2004).

Year Team	G	GS	TOTALS			INTERCEPTIONS			
			Tk.	Ast.	Sks.	No.	Yds.	Avg.	TD
2004—Indianapolis NFL	11	0	4	2	0.0	0	0	0.0	0

GARDNER, RICH — CB — TITANS

PERSONAL: Born February 1, 1981, in Carbondale, Ill. ... 5-10/199. ... Full name: Richard James Gardner.
HIGH SCHOOL: Hales Franciscan (Chicago, Ill.).
COLLEGE: Penn State.
TRANSACTIONS/CAREER NOTES: Selected by Tennessee Titans in third round (92nd pick overall) of 2004 NFL draft. ... Signed by Titans (July 29, 2004).

Year Team	G	GS	TOTALS			INTERCEPTIONS			
			Tk.	Ast.	Sks.	No.	Yds.	Avg.	TD
2004—Tennessee NFL	15	1	8	1	0.0	1	-1	-1.0	0

GARDNER, ROD — WR — REDSKINS

PERSONAL: Born October 26, 1977, in Jacksonville, Fla. ... 6-2/213. ... Full name: Roderick F. Gardner.
HIGH SCHOOL: Raines (Jacksonville, Fla.).
COLLEGE: Clemson.
TRANSACTIONS/CAREER NOTES: Selected by Washington Redskins in first round (15th pick overall) of 2001 NFL draft. ... Signed by Redskins (August 2, 2001).
SINGLE GAME HIGHS (regular season): Receptions—10 (September 27, 2004, vs. Dallas); yards—208 (October 21, 2001, vs. Carolina); and touchdown receptions—2 (October 31, 2004, vs. Green Bay).
STATISTICAL PLATEAUS: 100-yard receiving games: 2001 (1), 2002 (2), 2003 (1), 2004 (2). Total: 6.

Year Team	G	GS	RECEIVING				TOTALS			
			No.	Yds.	Avg.	TD	TD	2pt.	Pts.	Fum.
2001—Washington NFL	16	16	46	741	16.1	4	4	0	24	1
2002—Washington NFL	16	15	71	1006	14.2	8	8	0	48	1
2003—Washington NFL	16	16	59	600	10.2	5	5	0	30	1
2004—Washington NFL	16	14	51	650	12.7	5	5	0	30	0
Pro totals (4 years)	64	61	227	2997	13.2	22	22	0	132	3

GARDNER, TALMAN — WR — SAINTS

PERSONAL: Born March 10, 1980, in New Orleans, La. ... 6-1/210.
HIGH SCHOOL: McDonough (New Orleans).
COLLEGE: Florida State.
TRANSACTIONS/CAREER NOTES: Selected by New Orleans Saints in seventh round (231st pick overall) of 2003 NFL draft. ... Signed by Saints (July 23, 2003). ... Released by Saints (August 31, 2003). ... Re-signed by Saints to practice squad (September 3, 2003). ... Activated (October 4, 2003).
SINGLE GAME HIGHS (regular season): Receptions—2 (November 23, 2003, vs. Philadelphia); yards—23 (September 26, 2004, vs. St. Louis); and touchdown receptions—0.

Year Team	G	GS	RUSHING				RECEIVING				KICKOFF RETURNS				TOTALS		
			Att.	Yds.	Avg.	TD	No.	Yds.	Avg.	TD	No.	Yds.	Avg.	TD	TD	2pt.	Pts. Fum.
2003—New Orleans NFL	10	1	0	0	0.0	0	3	29	9.7	0	0	0	0.0	0	0	0	0 0
2004—New Orleans NFL	11	1	0	0	0.0	0	1	23	23.0	0	0	0	0.0	0	0	0	0 0
Pro totals (2 years)	21	2	0	0	0.0	0	4	52	13.0	0	0	0	0.0	0	0	0	0 0

GARDOCKI, CHRIS — P — STEELERS

PERSONAL: Born February 7, 1970, in Stone Mountain, Ga. ... 6-1/192. ... Full name: Christopher Allen Gardocki.
HIGH SCHOOL: Redan (Stone Mountain, Ga.).
COLLEGE: Clemson.
TRANSACTIONS/CAREER NOTES: Selected after junior season by Chicago Bears in third round (78th pick overall) of 1991 NFL draft. ... Signed by Bears (June 24, 1991). ... On injured reserve with groin injury (August 27-November 27, 1991). ... Granted unconditional free agency

(February 17, 1995). ... Signed by Indianapolis Colts (February 24, 1995). ... Granted unconditional free agency (February 12, 1999). ... Signed by Cleveland Browns (February 16, 1999). ... Granted unconditional free agency (March 3, 2004). ... Signed by Pittsburgh Steelers (March 6, 2004).

CHAMPIONSHIP GAME EXPERIENCE: Played in AFC championship game (1995 and 2004 seasons).
HONORS: Named kicker on THE SPORTING NEWS college All-America second team (1990). ... Named punter on THE SPORTING NEWS NFL All-Pro team (1996). ... Played in Pro Bowl (1996 season).
RECORDS: Holds NFL career record for most consecutive punts without a block—1,045.

					PUNTING			
Year Team	G	No.	Yds.	Avg.	Net avg.	In. 20	Blk.
1991—Chicago NFL	4	0	0	0.0	0.0	0	0
1992—Chicago NFL	16	79	3393	42.9	36.2	19	0
1993—Chicago NFL	16	80	3080	38.5	36.6	28	0
1994—Chicago NFL	16	76	2871	37.8	32.3	23	0
1995—Indianapolis NFL	16	63	2681	42.6	33.3	16	0
1996—Indianapolis NFL	16	68	3105	45.7	§39.0	23	0
1997—Indianapolis NFL	16	67	3034	45.3	36.2	18	0
1998—Indianapolis NFL	16	79	3583	45.4	37.1	23	0
1999—Cleveland NFL	16	§106	*4645	43.8	34.6	20	0
2000—Cleveland NFL	16	*108	*4919	45.5	37.3	25	0
2001—Cleveland NFL	16	*99	§4249	42.9	34.6	25	0
2002—Cleveland NFL	16	81	3388	41.8	35.3	27	0
2003—Cleveland NFL	16	72	3019	41.9	34.8	18	0
2004—Pittsburgh NFL	16	67	2879	43.0	37.4	24	0
Pro totals (14 years)	212	1045	44846	42.9	35.7	289	0

GARMON, KELVIN   G

PERSONAL: Born October 26, 1976, in Fort Worth, Texas. ... 6-2/350.
HIGH SCHOOL: Haltom (Fort Worth, Texas).
COLLEGE: Baylor.
TRANSACTIONS/CAREER NOTES: Selected by Dallas Cowboys in seventh round (243rd pick overall) of 1999 NFL draft. ... Signed by Cowboys (August 8, 1999). ... On non-football injury list with leg injury (August 31, 1999-entire season). ... Active for one game (2000); did not play. ... Traded by Cowboys to San Diego Chargers for conditional seventh-round pick (traded to Detroit) in 2003 draft (October 13, 2002). ... Granted unconditional free agency (March 3, 2004). ... Signed by Cleveland Browns (March 23, 2004). ... On injured reserve with knee injury (November 9, 2004-remainder of season). ... Released by Browns (March 28, 2005).
PLAYING EXPERIENCE: Dallas NFL, 1999-2002; San Diego NFL, 2002-2003; Cleveland NFL, 2004. ... Games/Games started: 2001 (16/16), 2002 (12/10), 2003 (16/16), 2004 (8/8), Total: 52/50.

GARNER, CHARLIE   RB   BUCCANEERS

PERSONAL: Born February 13, 1972, in Fairfax, Va. ... 5-10/190.
HIGH SCHOOL: Jeb Stuart (Falls Church, Va.).
JUNIOR COLLEGE: Scottsdale (Ariz.) Community College.
COLLEGE: Tennessee.
TRANSACTIONS/CAREER NOTES: Selected by Philadelphia Eagles in second round (42nd pick overall) of 1994 NFL draft. ... Signed by Eagles (July 18, 1994). ... Granted free agency (February 14, 1997). ... Re-signed by Eagles (June 16, 1997). ... Granted unconditional free agency (February 13, 1998). ... Re-signed by Eagles (February 23, 1998). ... On injured reserve with rib injury (December 10, 1998-remainder of season). ... Released by Eagles (April 20, 1999). ... Signed by San Francisco 49ers (July 19, 1999). ... Granted unconditional free agency (March 2, 2001). ... Signed by Oakland Raiders (April 13, 2001). ... Granted unconditional free agency (March 3, 2004). ... Signed by Tampa Bay Buccaneers (March 9, 2004). ... On injured reserve with knee injury (September 29, 2004-remainder of season).
CHAMPIONSHIP GAME EXPERIENCE: Played in AFC championship game (2002 season). ... Played in Super Bowl 36 (2002 season).
HONORS: Played in Pro Bowl (2000 season).
SINGLE GAME HIGHS (regular season): Attempts—36 (September 24, 2000, vs. Dallas); yards—201 (September 24, 2000, vs. Dallas); and rushing touchdowns—3 (October 8, 1995, vs. Washington).
STATISTICAL PLATEAUS: 100-yard rushing games: 1994 (2), 1995 (1), 1997 (1), 1998 (1), 1999 (3), 2000 (3), 2002 (3). Total: 14. 100-yard receiving games: 2000 (1), 2003 (1). Total: 2.

			RUSHING				RECEIVING				KICKOFF RETURNS				TOTALS			
Year Team	G	GS	Att.	Yds.	Avg.	TD	No.	Yds.	Avg.	TD	No.	Yds.	Avg.	TD	TD	2pt.	Pts.	Fum.
1994—Philadelphia NFL	10	8	109	399	3.7	3	8	74	9.3	0	0	0	0.0	0	3	0	18	3
1995—Philadelphia NFL	15	3	108	588	*5.4	6	10	61	6.1	0	29	590	20.3	0	6	0	36	2
1996—Philadelphia NFL	15	1	66	346	5.2	1	14	92	6.6	0	6	117	19.5	0	1	0	6	1
1997—Philadelphia NFL	16	2	116	547	4.7	3	24	225	9.4	0	0	0	0.0	0	3	0	18	1
1998—Philadelphia NFL	10	3	96	381	4.0	4	19	110	5.8	0	0	0	0.0	0	4	0	24	1
1999—San Francisco NFL	16	15	241	1229	5.1	4	56	535	9.6	2	0	0	0.0	0	6	0	36	4
2000—San Francisco NFL	16	15	258	1142	4.4	7	68	647	9.5	3	0	0	0.0	0	10	0	60	4
2001—Oakland NFL	16	16	211	839	4.0	1	72	578	8.0	2	0	0	0.0	0	3	0	18	2
2002—Oakland NFL	16	15	182	962	5.3	7	91	941	10.3	4	0	0	0.0	0	11	0	66	0
2003—Oakland NFL	14	9	120	553	4.6	3	48	386	8.0	1	0	0	0.0	0	4	0	24	1
2004—Tampa Bay NFL	3	3	30	111	3.7	0	9	62	6.9	0	0	0	0.0	0	0	0	0	0
Pro totals (11 years)	147	90	1537	7097	4.6	39	419	3711	8.9	12	35	707	20.2	0	51	0	306	19

GARRARD, DAVID   QB   JAGUARS

PERSONAL: Born February 14, 1978, in East Orange, N.J. ... 6-2/244. ... Full name: David Douglas Garrard.
HIGH SCHOOL: Southern Durham (N.C.).
COLLEGE: East Carolina.

G

TRANSACTIONS/CAREER NOTES: Selected by Jacksonville Jaguars in fourth round (108th pick overall) of 2002 NFL draft. ... Signed by Jaguars (July 22, 2002).
SINGLE GAME HIGHS (regular season): Attempts—36 (November 14, 2004, vs. Detroit); completions—19 (November 14, 2004, vs. Detroit); yards—198 (November 14, 2004, vs. Detroit); and touchdown passes—2 (November 14, 2004, vs. Detroit).
MISCELLANEOUS: Regular-season record as starting NFL quarterback: 1-2 (.333).

				PASSING								RUSHING				TOTALS		
Year Team	G	GS	Att.	Cmp.	Pct.	Yds.	TD	Int.	Avg.	Skd.	Rat.	Att.	Yds.	Avg.	TD	TD	2pt.	Pts.
2002—Jacksonville NFL	4	1	46	23	50.0	231	1	2	5.02	7	53.8	25	139	5.6	2	2	0	12
2003—Jacksonville NFL	2	0	12	9	75.0	86	1	0	7.17	0	122.2	0	0	0.0	0	0	0	0
2004—Jacksonville NFL	4	2	72	38	52.8	374	2	1	5.19	6	71.2	12	76	6.3	1	1	0	6
Pro totals (3 years)	10	3	130	70	53.8	691	4	3	5.32	13	69.7	37	215	5.8	3	3	0	18

GARRETT, KEVIN — CB — RAMS

PERSONAL: Born July 29, 1980, in San Benito, Texas. ... 5-10/194.
HIGH SCHOOL: Sweeney (Brazoria, Texas).
COLLEGE: Southern Methodist.
TRANSACTIONS/CAREER NOTES: Selected by St. Louis Rams in fifth round (172nd pick overall) of 2003 NFL draft. ... Signed by Rams (July 22, 2003).

			TOTALS			INTERCEPTIONS			
Year Team	G	GS	Tk.	Ast.	Sks.	No.	Yds.	Avg.	TD
2003—St. Louis NFL	9	0	0	0	0.0	0	0	0.0	0
2004—St. Louis NFL	14	1	8	2	0.0	0	0	0.0	0
Pro totals (2 years)	23	1	8	2	0.0	0	0	0.0	0

GARZA, ROBERTO — G/C — BEARS

PERSONAL: Born March 26, 1979, in Rio Hondo, Texas. ... 6-2/296. ... Full name: Robert Garza.
HIGH SCHOOL: Rio Hondo (Texas).
COLLEGE: Texas A&M-Kingsville.
TRANSACTIONS/CAREER NOTES: Selected by Atlanta Falcons in fourth round (99th pick overall) of 2001 NFL draft. ... Signed by Falcons (May 21, 2001). ... On injured reserve with knee injury (December 16, 2003-remainder of season). ... Granted free agency (March 3, 2004). ... Re-signed by Falcons (March 25, 2004). ... Granted unconditional free agency (March 2, 2005). ... Signed by Chicago Bears (March 21, 2005).
PLAYING EXPERIENCE: Atlanta NFL, 2001-2004. ... Games/Games started: 2001 (16/4), 2002 (6/4), 2003 (14/8), 2004 (16/15). Total: 52/31.
CHAMPIONSHIP GAME EXPERIENCE: Played in NFC championship game (2004 season).

GATES, ANTONIO — TE — CHARGERS

PERSONAL: Born June 18, 1980, in Detroit, Mich. ... 6-4/260.
HIGH SCHOOL: Detroit Central (Mich.).
COLLEGE: Kent State.
TRANSACTIONS/CAREER NOTES: Signed as non-drafted free agent by San Diego Chargers (May 2, 2003).
HONORS: Named tight end on THE SPORTING NEWS NFL All-Pro team (2004). ... Played in Pro Bowl (2004 season).
SINGLE GAME HIGHS (regular season): Receptions—8 (November 21, 2004, vs. Oakland); yards—123 (September 12, 2004, vs. Houston); and touchdown receptions—3 (November 7, 2004, vs. New Orleans).
STATISTICAL PLATEAUS: 100-yard receiving games: 2003 (1), 2004 (2). Total: 3.

			RECEIVING				TOTALS			
Year Team	G	GS	No.	Yds.	Avg.	TD	TD	2pt.	Pts.	Fum.
2003—San Diego NFL	15	11	24	389	16.2	2	2	0	12	1
2004—San Diego NFL	15	15	81	964	11.9	13	13	0	78	0
Pro totals (2 years)	30	26	105	1353	12.9	15	15	0	90	1

GAY, RANDALL — CB — PATRIOTS

PERSONAL: Born May 5, 1982, in Baton Rouge, La. ... 5-11/186. ... Full name: Randall Jerome Gay.
HIGH SCHOOL: Brusly (La.).
COLLEGE: Louisiana State.
TRANSACTIONS/CAREER NOTES: Signed as non-drafted free agent by New England Patriots (April 29, 2004).
CHAMPIONSHIP GAME EXPERIENCE: Played in AFC championship game (2004 season). ... Member of Super Bowl championship team (2004 season).

			TOTALS			INTERCEPTIONS			
Year Team	G	GS	Tk.	Ast.	Sks.	No.	Yds.	Avg.	TD
2004—New England NFL	15	9	29	5	0.0	2	23	11.5	0

GBAJA-BIAMILA, AKBAR — DE — RAIDERS

PERSONAL: Born May 6, 1979, in Los Angeles, Calif. ... 6-5/270. ... Brother of Kabeer Gbaja-Biamila, defensive end, Green Bay Packers.
HIGH SCHOOL: Crenshaw (Los Angeles, Calif.).
COLLEGE: San Diego State.
TRANSACTIONS/CAREER NOTES: Signed as non-drafted free agent by Oakland Raiders (April 29, 2003).

G

Year Team	G	GS	TOTALS Tk.	Ast.	Sks.
2003—Oakland NFL	13	0	4	3	1.0
2004—Oakland NFL	14	0	10	3	1.0
Pro totals (2 years)	27	0	14	6	2.0

GBAJA-BIAMILA, KABEER DE PACKERS

PERSONAL: Born September 24, 1977, in Los Angeles, Calif. ... 6-4/252. ... Full name: Muhammed-Kabeer Olarewaja Gbaja-Biamila. ... Brother of Akbar Gbaja-Biamila, defensive end, Oakland Raiders.
HIGH SCHOOL: Crenshaw (Los Angeles).
COLLEGE: San Diego State.
TRANSACTIONS/CAREER NOTES: Selected by Green Bay Packers in fifth round (149th pick overall) of 2000 NFL draft. ... Signed by Packers (July 17, 2000). ... Released by Packers (August 27, 2000). ... Re-signed by Packers to practice squad (August 28, 2000). ... Activated (October 10, 2000). ... Granted free agency (February 28, 2003). ... Re-signed by Packers (April 2, 2003).
HONORS: Played in Pro Bowl (2003 season).

			TOTALS			INTERCEPTIONS			
Year Team	G	GS	Tk.	Ast.	Sks.	No.	Yds.	Avg.	TD
2000—Green Bay NFL	7	0	3	1	1.5	0	0	0.0	0
2001—Green Bay NFL	16	0	19	5	13.5	0	0	0.0	0
2002—Green Bay NFL	15	11	35	11	12.0	1	72	72.0	1
2003—Green Bay NFL	16	16	36	11	10.0	0	0	0.0	0
2004—Green Bay NFL	16	15	33	14	13.5	0	0	0.0	0
Pro totals (5 years)	70	42	126	42	50.5	1	72	72.0	1

GEATHERS, ROBERT DE BENGALS

PERSONAL: Born August 11, 1983, in Georgetown, S.C. ... 6-2/271. ... Full name: Robert L. Geathers.
HIGH SCHOOL: Carvers Bay (Georgetown, S.C.).
COLLEGE: Georgia.
TRANSACTIONS/CAREER NOTES: Selected by Cincinnati Bengals in fourth round (117th pick overall) of 2004 NFL draft. ... Signed by Bengals (July 30, 2004).

			TOTALS			INTERCEPTIONS			
Year Team	G	GS	Tk.	Ast.	Sks.	No.	Yds.	Avg.	TD
2004—Cincinnati NFL	14	1	7	6	3.5	1	36	36.0	1

GEORGE, EDDIE RB

PERSONAL: Born September 24, 1973, in Philadelphia, Pa. ... 6-3/235. ... Full name: Edward Nathan George.
HIGH SCHOOL: Abington (Philadelphia), then Fork Union (Va.) Military Academy.
COLLEGE: Ohio State.
TRANSACTIONS/CAREER NOTES: Selected by Houston Oilers in first round (14th pick overall) of 1996 NFL draft. ... Signed by Oilers (July 20, 1996). ... Oilers franchise moved to Tennessee for 1997 season. ... Oilers franchise renamed Tennessee Titans for 1999 season (December 26, 1998). ... On physically unable to perform list with toe injury (July 28-31, 2001). ... Released by Titans (July 21, 2004). ... Signed by Dallas Cowboys (July 23, 2004). ... Granted unconditional free agency (March 2, 2005).
CHAMPIONSHIP GAME EXPERIENCE: Played in AFC championship game (1999 and 2002 seasons). ... Played in Super Bowl 34 (1999 season).
HONORS: Heisman Trophy winner (1995). ... Maxwell Award winner (1995). ... Doak Walker Award winner (1995). ... Named running back on THE SPORTING NEWS college All-America first team (1995). ... Named NFL Rookie of the Year by THE SPORTING NEWS (1996). ... Played in Pro Bowl (1997-2000 seasons).
SINGLE GAME HIGHS (regular season): Attempts—36 (November 19, 2000, vs. Cleveland); yards—216 (August 31, 1997, vs. Oakland); and rushing touchdowns—3 (December 17, 2000, vs. Cleveland).
STATISTICAL PLATEAUS: 100-yard rushing games: 1996 (4), 1997 (8), 1998 (6), 1999 (5), 2000 (6), 2001 (1), 2002 (4), 2003 (2). Total: 36. 100-yard receiving games: 2000 (1). Total: 1.
MISCELLANEOUS: Holds Titans franchise all-time record for most yards rushing (10,009) and most touchdowns (74).

			RUSHING				RECEIVING				TOTALS			
Year Team	G	GS	Att.	Yds.	Avg.	TD	No.	Yds.	Avg.	TD	TD	2pt.	Pts.	Fum.
1996—Houston NFL	16	16	335	1368	4.1	8	23	182	7.9	0	8	0	48	3
1997—Tennessee NFL	16	16	357	1399	3.9	6	7	44	6.3	1	7	1	44	4
1998—Tennessee NFL	16	16	348	1294	3.7	5	37	310	8.4	1	6	1	38	7
1999—Tennessee NFL	16	16	320	1304	4.1	9	47	458	9.7	4	13	0	78	5
2000—Tennessee NFL	16	16	*403	1509	3.7	14	50	453	9.1	2	16	0	96	5
2001—Tennessee NFL	16	16	315	939	3.0	5	37	279	7.5	0	5	0	30	8
2002—Tennessee NFL	16	16	343	1165	3.4	12	36	255	7.1	2	14	1	86	1
2003—Tennessee NFL	16	16	312	1031	3.3	5	22	163	7.4	0	5	0	30	1
2004—Dallas NFL	13	8	132	432	3.3	4	9	83	9.2	0	4	0	24	3
Pro totals (9 years)	141	136	2865	10441	3.6	68	268	2227	8.3	10	78	3	474	37

GIBSON, AARON G/T

PERSONAL: Born September 27, 1977, in Indianapolis, Ind. ... 6-6/370.
HIGH SCHOOL: Decatur Central (Indianapolis).
COLLEGE: Wisconsin.

TRANSACTIONS/CAREER NOTES: Selected by Detroit Lions in first round (27th pick overall) of 1999 NFL draft. ... Signed by Lions (July 24, 1999). ... On injured reserve with shoulder injury (August 31, 1999-entire season). ... On injured reserve with shoulder injury (December 4, 2000-remainder of season). ... Claimed on waivers by Dallas Cowboys (October 31, 2001). ... Released by Cowboys (September 18, 2002). ... Signed by Chicago Bears (November 26, 2002). ... Granted unconditional free agency (March 2, 2005).
PLAYING EXPERIENCE: Detroit NFL, 1999-2001; Dallas NFL, 2001-2002; Chicago NFL, 2003-2004. ... Games/Games started: 2000 (10/10), 2001 (1/0), 2002 (7/5), 2003 (16/16), 2004 (4/3), Total: 38/34.
HONORS: Named offensive tackle on THE SPORTING NEWS college All-America second team (1998).

GILBERT, TONY — LB — JAGUARS

PERSONAL: Born October 16, 1979, in Macon, Ga. ... 6-1/244. ... Full name: Antonio C. Gilbert.
HIGH SCHOOL: Central (Macon, Ga.).
COLLEGE: Georgia.
TRANSACTIONS/CAREER NOTES: Selected by Arizona Cardinals in sixth round (210th pick overall) of 2003 NFL draft. ... Signed by Cardinals (June 2, 2003). ... Released by Cardinals (August 31, 2003). ... Re-signed by Cardinals to practice squad (September 1, 2003). ... Signed by Jacksonville Jaguars off Cardinals practice squad (October 29, 2003). ... Assigned by Jaguars to Rhein Fire in 2005 NFL Europe enhancement allocation program (February 14, 2005).

			TOTALS			INTERCEPTIONS			
Year Team	G	GS	Tk.	Ast.	Sks.	No.	Yds.	Avg.	TD
2003—Jacksonville NFL	8	0	0	0	0.0	0	0	0.0	0
2004—Jacksonville NFL	16	0	0	0	0.0	0	0	0.0	0
Pro totals (2 years)	24	0	0	0	0.0	0	0	0.0	0

GILDON, JASON — LB

PERSONAL: Born July 31, 1972, in Altus, Okla. ... 6-4/255. ... Full name: Jason Larue Gildon.
HIGH SCHOOL: Altus (Okla.).
COLLEGE: Oklahoma State.
TRANSACTIONS/CAREER NOTES: Selected by Pittsburgh Steelers in third round (88th pick overall) of 1994 NFL draft. ... Signed by Steelers (July 15, 1994). ... Granted free agency (February 14, 1997). ... Re-signed by Steelers (July 21, 1997). ... Granted unconditional free agency (February 13, 1998). ... Re-signed by Steelers (April 7, 1998). ... Designated by Steelers as franchise player (February 21, 2002). ... Re-signed by Steelers (February 25, 2002). ... Released by Steelers (June 2, 2004). ... Signed by Buffalo Bills (July 19, 2004). ... Released by Bills (September 5, 2004). ... Signed by Jacksonville Jaguars (October 27, 2004). ... Granted unconditional free agency (March 2, 2005).
CHAMPIONSHIP GAME EXPERIENCE: Played in AFC championship game (1994, 1995, 1997 and 2001 seasons). ... Played in Super Bowl 30 (1995 season).
HONORS: Played in Pro Bowl (2000-2002 seasons).
MISCELLANEOUS: Holds Pittsburgh Steelers all-time record for most sacks (77).

			TOTALS			INTERCEPTIONS			
Year Team	G	GS	Tk.	Ast.	Sks.	No.	Yds.	Avg.	TD
1994—Pittsburgh NFL	16	1	4	0	2.0	0	0	0.0	0
1995—Pittsburgh NFL	16	0	8	4	3.0	0	0	0.0	0
1996—Pittsburgh NFL	14	13	47	12	7.0	0	0	0.0	0
1997—Pittsburgh NFL	16	16	41	12	5.0	0	0	0.0	0
1998—Pittsburgh NFL	16	16	42	12	11.0	0	0	0.0	0
1999—Pittsburgh NFL	16	16	42	15	8.5	0	0	0.0	0
2000—Pittsburgh NFL	16	16	58	19	13.5	0	0	0.0	0
2001—Pittsburgh NFL	16	16	43	13	12.0	1	0	0.0	0
2002—Pittsburgh NFL	16	16	45	22	9.0	0	0	0.0	0
2003—Pittsburgh NFL	16	16	42	19	6.0	1	1	1.0	0
2004—Jacksonville NFL	9	0	11	1	3.0	0	0	0.0	0
Pro totals (11 years)	167	126	383	129	80.0	2	1	0.5	0

GILMORE, BRYAN — WR — DOLPHINS

PERSONAL: Born January 21, 1978, in Lufkin, Texas. ... 6-0/195.
HIGH SCHOOL: Lufkin (Texas).
COLLEGE: Midwestern State.
TRANSACTIONS/CAREER NOTES: Signed as non-drafted free agent by Arizona Cardinals (April 17, 2000). ... Released by Cardinals (August 27, 2000). ... Re-signed by Cardinals to practice squad (August 28, 2000). ... Activated (December 15, 2000). ... Assigned by Cardinals to Barcelona Dragons in 2001 NFL Europe enhancement allocation program (February 19, 2001). ... Released by Cardinals (September 2, 2001). ... Re-signed by Cardinals to practice squad (September 3, 2001). ... Activated (November 29, 2001). ... On injured reserve with ankle injury (October 30, 2002-remainder of season). ... Claimed on waivers by Miami Dolphins (August 24, 2004).
SINGLE GAME HIGHS (regular season): Receptions—3 (January 2, 2005, vs. Baltimore); yards—57 (October 3, 2004, vs. New York Jets); and touchdown receptions—1 (December 5, 2004, vs. Buffalo).

			RECEIVING				KICKOFF RETURNS				TOTALS			
Year Team	G	GS	No.	Yds.	Avg.	TD	No.	Yds.	Avg.	TD	TD	2pt.	Pts.	Fum.
2000—Arizona NFL	1	0	0	0	0.0	0	0	0	0.0	0	0	0	0	0
2001—Arizona NFL	2	0	0	0	0.0	0	0	0	0.0	0	0	0	0	0
2002—Arizona NFL	7	0	1	14	14.0	0	0	0	0.0	0	0	0	0	0
2003—Arizona NFL	14	10	17	208	12.2	2	0	0	0.0	0	2	0	12	0
2004—Miami NFL	16	2	15	206	13.7	1	5	114	22.8	0	1	0	6	1
Pro totals (5 years)	40	12	33	428	13.0	3	5	114	22.8	0	3	0	18	1

G

GILMORE, JOHN   TE   BEARS

PERSONAL: Born September 21, 1979, in Marquette, Mich. ... 6-4/262. ... Full name: John Henry Gilmore.
HIGH SCHOOL: Wilson (West Lawn, Pa.).
COLLEGE: Penn State.
TRANSACTIONS/CAREER NOTES: Selected by New Orleans Saints in sixth round (196th pick overall) of 2002 NFL draft. ... Signed by Saints (July 22, 2002). ... Released by Saints (September 1, 2002). ... Signed by Chicago Bears to practice squad (September 3, 2002). ... Activated (October 25, 2002). ... Granted free agency (March 2, 2005). ... Re-signed by Bears (April 6, 2005).
SINGLE GAME HIGHS (regular season): Receptions—3 (December 15, 2002, vs. New York Jets); yards—32 (December 22, 2002, vs. Carolina); and touchdown receptions—0.

			RECEIVING				KICKOFF RETURNS				TOTALS			
Year Team	G	GS	No.	Yds.	Avg.	TD	No.	Yds.	Avg.	TD	TD	2pt.	Pts.	Fum.
2002—Chicago NFL	8	4	10	130	13.0	0	0	0	0.0	0	0	0	0	0
2003—Chicago NFL	15	1	0	0	0.0	0	3	25	8.3	0	0	0	0	0
2004—Chicago NFL	16	1	1	11	11.0	0	0	0	0.0	0	0	0	0	0
Pro totals (3 years)	39	6	11	141	12.8	0	3	25	8.3	0	0	0	0	0

GIVENS, DAVID   WR

PERSONAL: Born August 16, 1980, in Youngstown, Ohio. ... 6-0/215. ... Full name: David Lamar Givens.
HIGH SCHOOL: Humble (Texas).
COLLEGE: Notre Dame.
TRANSACTIONS/CAREER NOTES: Selected by New England Patriots in seventh round (253rd pick overall) of 2002 NFL draft. ... Signed by Patriots (July 21, 2002). ... Granted free agency (March 2, 2005).
CHAMPIONSHIP GAME EXPERIENCE: Played in AFC championship game (2003 and 2004 seasons). ... Member of Super Bowl championship team (2003 and 2004 seasons).
SINGLE GAME HIGHS (regular season): Receptions—8 (October 31, 2004, vs. Pittsburgh); yards—120 (September 19, 2004, vs. Arizona); and touchdown receptions—2 (October 31, 2004, vs. Pittsburgh).
STATISTICAL PLATEAUS: 100-yard receiving games: 2004 (4). Total: 4.

			RUSHING				RECEIVING				KICKOFF RETURNS				TOTALS			
Year Team	G	GS	Att.	Yds.	Avg.	TD	No.	Yds.	Avg.	TD	No.	Yds.	Avg.	TD	TD	2pt.	Pts.	Fum.
2002—New England NFL	12	0	0	0	0.0	0	9	92	10.2	1	0	0	0.0	0	1	0	6	1
2003—New England NFL	13	5	0	0	0.0	0	34	510	15.0	6	2	31	15.5	0	6	0	36	0
2004—New England NFL	15	12	0	0	0.0	0	56	874	15.6	3	0	0	0.0	0	3	0	18	0
Pro totals (3 years)	40	17	0	0	0.0	0	99	1476	14.9	10	2	31	15.5	0	10	0	60	1

GLEASON, STEVE   S   SAINTS

PERSONAL: Born March 19, 1977, in Spokane, Wash. ... 5-11/212. ... Full name: Stephen Gleason.
HIGH SCHOOL: Gonzaga (Wash.) Prep.
COLLEGE: Washington State.
TRANSACTIONS/CAREER NOTES: Signed as non-drafted free agent by Indianapolis Colts (April 16, 2000). ... Released by Colts (August 27, 2000). ... Signed by New Orleans Saints to practice squad (November 21, 2000). ... Activated (December 3, 2000). ... Released by Saints (September 2, 2001). ... Re-signed by Saints (November 23, 2001). ... Granted free agency (March 3, 2004). ... Re-signed by Saints (May 5, 2004). ... Granted unconditional free agency (March 2, 2005). ... Re-signed by Saints (March 22, 2005).

			TOTALS			INTERCEPTIONS			
Year Team	G	GS	Tk.	Ast.	Sks.	No.	Yds.	Avg.	TD
2000—New Orleans NFL	3	0	0	0	0.0	0	0	0.0	0
2001—New Orleans NFL	7	0	0	0	0.0	0	0	0.0	0
2002—New Orleans NFL	14	0	1	1	0.0	0	0	0.0	0
2003—New Orleans NFL	16	0	0	0	0.0	0	0	0.0	0
2004—New Orleans NFL	15	0	0	2	0.0	0	0	0.0	0
Pro totals (5 years)	55	0	1	3	0.0	0	0	0.0	0

GLENN, AARON   CB   COWBOYS

G

PERSONAL: Born July 16, 1972, in Humble, Texas. ... 5-9/185. ... Full name: Aaron DeVon Glenn.
HIGH SCHOOL: Nimitz (Irving, Texas).
JUNIOR COLLEGE: Navarro College (Texas).
COLLEGE: Texas A&M.
TRANSACTIONS/CAREER NOTES: Selected by New York Jets in first round (12th pick overall) of 1994 NFL draft. ... Signed by Jets (July 21, 1994). ... Selected by Houston Texans from Jets in NFL expansion draft (February 18, 2002). ... On injured reserve with groin injury (December 10, 2003-remainder of season). ... Released by Texans (April 26, 2005). ... Signed by Dallas Cowboys (April 27, 2005).
CHAMPIONSHIP GAME EXPERIENCE: Played in AFC championship game (1998 season).
HONORS: Named defensive back on THE SPORTING NEWS college All-America first team (1993). ... Played in Pro Bowl (1997 and 2002 seasons). ... Named to play in Pro Bowl (1998 season); replaced by Charles Woodson due to injury. ... Named cornerback on the THE SPORTING NEWS NFL All-Pro team (2002).
MISCELLANEOUS: Holds Houston Texans all-time record for most interceptions (11).

			TOTALS			INTERCEPTIONS				KICKOFF RETURNS				TOTALS			
Year Team	G	GS	Tk.	Ast.	Sks.	No.	Yds.	Avg.	TD	No.	Yds.	Avg.	TD	TD	2pt.	Pts.	Fum.
1994—New York Jets NFL	15	15	58	9	0.0	0	0	0.0	0	27	582	21.6	0	0	0	0	2
1995—New York Jets NFL	16	16	42	10	0.0	1	17	17.0	0	1	12	12.0	0	0	0	0	0
1996—New York Jets NFL	16	16	38	6	0.0	4	113	28.2	†2	1	6	6.0	0	2	0	12	0
1997—New York Jets NFL	16	16	54	11	0.0	1	5	5.0	0	28	741§26.5	▲1	1	0	6	1

Year Team	G	GS	Tk.	Ast.	Sks.	No.	Yds.	Avg.	TD	No.	Yds.	Avg.	TD	TD	2pt.	Pts.	Fum.
			TOTALS			INTERCEPTIONS				KICKOFF RETURNS				TOTALS			
1998—New York Jets NFL	13	13	47	1	0.0	6	23	3.8	0	24	585	24.4	0	1	0	6	1
1999—New York Jets NFL	16	16	46	5	0.0	3	20	6.7	0	27	601	22.3	0	0	0	0	0
2000—New York Jets NFL	16	16	28	9	0.0	4	34	8.5	0	3	51	17.0	0	0	0	0	0
2001—New York Jets NFL	13	12	28	5	0.0	5	82	16.4	1	0	0	0.0	0	1	0	6	1
2002—Houston NFL	16	16	56	11	1.0	5	181	36.2	▲2	0	0	0.0	0	2	0	12	0
2003—Houston NFL	11	11	29	6	0.0	1	0	0.0	0	0	0	0.0	0	0	0	0	0
2004—Houston NFL	16	16	55	8	0.0	5	40	8.0	0	0	0	0.0	0	0	0	0	2
Pro totals (11 years)	164	163	481	81	1.0	35	515	14.7	5	111	2578	23.2	1	7	0	42	7

GLENN, JASON   LB

PERSONAL: Born August 20, 1979, in Aldine, Texas. ... 6-0/231.
HIGH SCHOOL: Nimitz (Aldine, Texas).
COLLEGE: Texas A&M.
TRANSACTIONS/CAREER NOTES: Selected by Detroit Lions in sixth round (173rd pick overall) of 2001 NFL draft. ... Signed by Lions (July 20, 2001). ... Claimed on waivers by New York Jets (September 3, 2001). ... Granted free agency (March 3, 2004). ... Re-signed by Jets (May 5, 2004). ... Granted unconditional free agency (March 2, 2005).

Year Team	G	GS	Tk.	Ast.	Sks.	No.	Yds.	Avg.	TD
			TOTALS			INTERCEPTIONS			
2001—New York Jets NFL	15	0	0	0	0.0	0	0	0.0	0
2002—New York Jets NFL	16	0	0	0	0.0	0	0	0.0	0
2003—New York Jets NFL	14	1	29	11	0.0	0	0	0.0	0
2004—New York Jets NFL	10	0	3	0	0.0	0	0	0.0	0
Pro totals (4 years)	55	1	32	11	0.0	0	0	0.0	0

GLENN, TARIK   T   COLTS

PERSONAL: Born May 25, 1976, in Cleveland, Ohio. ... 6-5/332.
HIGH SCHOOL: Bishop O'Dowd (Oakland).
COLLEGE: California.
TRANSACTIONS/CAREER NOTES: Selected by Indianapolis Colts in first round (19th pick overall) of 1997 NFL draft. ... Signed by Colts (August 11, 1997). ... Granted free agency (March 1, 2002). ... Re-signed by Colts (March 15, 2002).
PLAYING EXPERIENCE: Indianapolis NFL, 1997-2004. ... Games/Games started. 1997 (16/16), 1998 (16/16), 1999 (16/16), 2000 (16/16), 2001 (16/16), 2002 (16/16), 2003 (10/10), 2004 (16/16). Total: 122/122.
CHAMPIONSHIP GAME EXPERIENCE: Played in AFC championship game (2003 season).
HONORS: Named offensive tackle on THE SPORTING NEWS college All-America second team (1996). ... Played in Pro Bowl (2004 season).

GLENN, TERRY   WR   COWBOYS

PERSONAL: Born July 23, 1974, in Columbus, Ohio. ... 5-11/193.
HIGH SCHOOL: Brookhaven (Columbus, Ohio).
COLLEGE: Ohio State.
TRANSACTIONS/CAREER NOTES: Selected after junior season by New England Patriots in first round (seventh pick overall) of 1996 NFL draft. ... Signed by Patriots (July 12, 1996). ... On injured reserve with fractured ankle (December 18, 1998-remainder of season). ... On suspended list for violating league substance abuse policy (Sepetmber 9-October 7, 2001). ... On reserve/left squad list (August 15-September 13, 2001). ... Traded by Patriots to Green Bay Packers for fourth-round pick (DE Jarvis Green) in 2002 draft and conditional pick in 2003 draft (March 8, 2002). ... Traded by Packers to Dallas Cowboys for undisclosed draft pick (February 28, 2003). ... On injured reserve with foot injury (October 30, 2004-remainder of season).
CHAMPIONSHIP GAME EXPERIENCE: Played in AFC championship game (1996 season). ... Played in Super Bowl 31 (1996 season).
HONORS: Fred Biletnikoff Award winner (1995). ... Named wide receiver on THE SPORTING NEWS college All-America first team (1995). ... Played in Pro Bowl (1999 season).
SINGLE GAME HIGHS (regular season): Receptions—13 (October 3, 1999, vs. Cleveland); yards—214 (October 3, 1999, vs. Cleveland); and touchdown receptions—3 (October 19, 2003, vs. Detroit).
STATISTICAL PLATEAUS: 100-yard receiving games: 1996 (2), 1997 (1), 1998 (4), 1999 (4), 2000 (1), 2001 (1), 2002 (1), 2003 (2), 2004 (1). Total: 17.

Year Team	G	GS	Att.	Yds.	Avg.	TD	No.	Yds.	Avg.	TD	TD	2pt.	Pts.	Fum.
			RUSHING				RECEIVING				TOTALS			
1996—New England NFL	15	15	5	42	8.4	0	90	1132	12.6	6	6	0	36	1
1997—New England NFL	9	9	0	0	0.0	0	27	431	16.0	2	2	0	12	1
1998—New England NFL	10	9	2	-1	-0.5	0	50	792	15.8	3	3	0	18	0
1999—New England NFL	14	13	0	0	0.0	0	69	1147	16.6	4	4	0	24	2
2000—New England NFL	16	15	4	39	9.8	0	79	963	12.2	6	6	0	36	0
2001—New England NFL	4	1	0	0	0.0	0	14	204	14.6	1	1	0	6	0
2002—Green Bay NFL	15	14	0	0	0.0	0	56	817	14.6	2	2	0	12	1
2003—Dallas NFL	16	14	3	55	18.3	0	52	754	14.5	5	5	0	30	2
2004—Dallas NFL	6	6	1	-3	-3.0	0	24	400	16.7	2	2	0	12	0
Pro totals (9 years)	105	96	15	132	8.8	0	461	6640	14.4	31	31	0	186	7

GLOVER, LA'ROI   DT   COWBOYS

PERSONAL: Born July 4, 1974, in San Diego, Calif. ... 6-2/282. ... Full name: La'Roi Damon Glover. ... Name pronounced: la-ROY.
HIGH SCHOOL: Point Loma (San Diego).
COLLEGE: San Diego State.

G

TRANSACTIONS/CAREER NOTES: Selected by Oakland Raiders in fifth round (166th pick overall) of 1996 NFL draft. ... Signed by Raiders (July 12, 1996). ... Assigned by Raiders to Barcelona Dragons in 1997 World League enhancement allocation program (February 19, 1997). ... Claimed on waivers by New Orleans Saints (August 25, 1997). ... Granted unconditional free agency (March 1, 2002). ... Signed by Dallas Cowboys (March 12, 2002).

HONORS: Named defensive tackle on THE SPORTING NEWS NFL All-Pro team (2000 and 2002). ... Played in Pro Bowl (2000-2004 seasons).

			TOTALS			INTERCEPTIONS			
Year Team	G	GS	Tk.	Ast.	Sks.	No.	Yds.	Avg.	TD
1996—Oakland NFL	2	0	2	0	0.0	0	0	0.0	0
1997—New Orleans NFL	15	2	24	9	6.5	0	0	0.0	0
1998—New Orleans NFL	16	15	59	8	10.0	1	0	0.0	0
1999—New Orleans NFL	16	16	46	16	8.5	0	0	0.0	0
2000—New Orleans NFL	16	16	53	14	*17.0	0	0	0.0	0
2001—New Orleans NFL	16	16	36	11	8.0	0	0	0.0	0
2002—Dallas NFL	16	16	39	11	6.5	1	7	7.0	0
2003—Dallas NFL	16	16	33	16	5.0	0	0	0.0	0
2004—Dallas NFL	16	16	31	10	7.0	0	0	0.0	0
Pro totals (9 years)	129	113	323	95	68.5	2	7	3.5	0

GLYMPH, JUNIOR · DE · FALCONS

PERSONAL: Born September 2, 1980, in Hackensack, N.J. ... 6-5/270. ... Full name: Clarence Glymph.
HIGH SCHOOL: Newberry (S.C.).
COLLEGE: Carson-Newman.
TRANSACTIONS/CAREER NOTES: Signed as non-drafted free agent by Green Bay Packers (April 30, 2004). ... Released by Packers (July 29, 2004). ... Signed by Atlanta Falcons (2004). ... Released by Falcons (September 4, 2004). ... Re-signed by Falcons to practice squad (September 6, 2004). ... Activated (October 16, 2004).

			TOTALS		
Year Team	G	GS	Tk.	Ast.	Sks.
2004—Atlanta NFL	3	0	4	0	1.0

GODFREY, RANDALL · LB · CHARGERS

PERSONAL: Born April 6, 1973, in Valdosta, Ga. ... 6-2/245. ... Full name: Randall Euralentris Godfrey.
HIGH SCHOOL: Lowndes County (Valdosta, Ga.).
COLLEGE: Georgia.
TRANSACTIONS/CAREER NOTES: Selected by Dallas Cowboys in second round (49th pick overall) of 1996 NFL draft. ... Signed by Cowboys (July 17, 1996). ... Granted free agency (February 12, 1999). ... Re-signed by Cowboys (June 25, 1999). ... Granted unconditional free agency (February 11, 2000). ... Signed by Tennessee Titans (February 16, 2000). ... Released by Titans (June 18, 2003). ... Signed by Seattle Seahawks (June 23, 2003). ... Granted unconditional free agency (March 3, 2004). ... Signed by San Diego Chargers (March 9, 2004).
CHAMPIONSHIP GAME EXPERIENCE: Played in AFC championship game (2002 season).

			TOTALS			INTERCEPTIONS			
Year Team	G	GS	Tk.	Ast.	Sks.	No.	Yds.	Avg.	TD
1996—Dallas NFL	16	6	25	3	0.0	0	0	0.0	0
1997—Dallas NFL	16	16	66	31	1.0	0	0	0.0	0
1998—Dallas NFL	16	16	70	16	3.0	1	0	0.0	0
1999—Dallas NFL	16	16	81	15	1.0	1	10	10.0	0
2000—Tennessee NFL	16	16	98	23	3.0	2	25	12.5	1
2001—Tennessee NFL	14	14	62	16	1.0	1	5	5.0	0
2002—Tennessee NFL	8	5	25	7	1.0	0	0	0.0	0
2003—Seattle NFL	15	14	45	14	0.0	1	7	7.0	0
2004—San Diego NFL	15	15	68	19	2.0	0	0	0.0	0
Pro totals (9 years)	132	118	540	144	12.0	6	47	7.8	1

GOFF, MIKE · G · CHARGERS

PERSONAL: Born January 6, 1976, in Spring Valley, Ill. ... 6-5/311. ... Full name: Michael J. Goff.
HIGH SCHOOL: Lasalle-Peru (Peru, Ill.).
COLLEGE: Iowa.
TRANSACTIONS/CAREER NOTES: Selected by Cincinnati Bengals in third round (78th pick overall) of 1998 NFL draft. ... Signed by Bengals (July 20, 1998). ... Granted unconditional free agency (March 3, 2004). ... Signed by San Diego Chargers (March 5, 2004).
PLAYING EXPERIENCE: Cincinnati NFL, 1998-2003; San Diego NFL, 2004. ... Games/Games started: 1998 (10/5), 1999 (14/1), 2000 (16/16), 2001 (16/16), 2002 (13/13), 2003 (16/16), 2004 (16/16). Total: 101/83.

GOINGS, NICK · RB · PANTHERS

PERSONAL: Born January 26, 1978, in Columbus, Ohio. ... 6-0/225. ... Full name: Nick Aaron Goings.
HIGH SCHOOL: Dublin Scioto (Ohio).
COLLEGE: Pittsburgh.
TRANSACTIONS/CAREER NOTES: Signed as non-drafted free agent by Carolina Panthers (April 23, 2001). ... Granted free agency (March 3, 2004). ... Re-signed by Panthers (April 8, 2004).
CHAMPIONSHIP GAME EXPERIENCE: Played in NFC championship game (2003 sesaon). ... Played in Super Bowl 38 (2003 season).
SINGLE GAME HIGHS (regular season): Attempts—36 (December 5, 2004, vs. New Orleans); yards—127 (December 26, 2004, vs. Tampa Bay); and rushing touchdowns—3 (November 21, 2004, vs. Arizona).
STATISTICAL PLATEAUS: 100-yard rushing games: 2004 (5). Total: 5.

G

Year Team			RUSHING				RECEIVING				TOTALS			
Year Team	G	GS	Att.	Yds.	Avg.	TD	No.	Yds.	Avg.	TD	TD	2pt.	Pts.	Fum.
2001—Carolina NFL	13	2	66	197	3.0	0	8	39	4.9	0	0	0	0	1
2002—Carolina NFL	14	2	50	188	3.8	0	18	91	5.1	0	0	1	2	2
2003—Carolina NFL	15	0	10	69	6.9	0	12	97	8.1	1	1	0	6	0
2004—Carolina NFL	16	8	217	821	3.8	6	45	394	8.8	1	7	0	42	1
Pro totals (4 years)	58	12	343	1275	3.7	6	83	621	7.5	2	8	1	50	4

GOLD, IAN   LB   BRONCOS

PERSONAL: Born August 23, 1978, in Ann Arbor, Mich. ... 6-0/223. ... Full name: Ian Maurice Gold.
HIGH SCHOOL: Belleville (Mich.).
COLLEGE: Michigan.
TRANSACTIONS/CAREER NOTES: Selected by Denver Broncos in second round (40th pick overall) of 2000 NFL draft. ... Signed by Broncos (July 23, 2000). ... On injured reserve with knee injury (October 14, 2003-remainder of season). ... Granted unconditional free agency (March 3, 2004). ... Signed by Tampa Bay Buccaneers (April 28, 2004). ... Released by Buccaneers (March 1, 2005). ... Signed by Broncos (March 3, 2005).
HONORS: Played in Pro Bowl (2001 season).

Year Team			TOTALS			INTERCEPTIONS			
Year Team	G	GS	Tk.	Ast.	Sks.	No.	Yds.	Avg.	TD
2000—Denver NFL	16	0	16	3	2.0	0	0	0.0	0
2001—Denver NFL	16	0	21	3	3.0	0	0	0.0	0
2002—Denver NFL	16	16	85	14	6.5	0	0	0.0	0
2003—Denver NFL	6	6	26	1	0.0	2	14	7.0	1
2004—Tampa Bay NFL	16	13	54	17	0.5	1	31	31.0	0
Pro totals (5 years)	70	35	202	38	12.0	3	45	15.0	1

GOLDBERG, ADAM   T   VIKINGS

PERSONAL: Born August 12, 1980, in Edina, Minn. ... 6-7/310.
HIGH SCHOOL: Edina (Minn.).
COLLEGE: Wyoming.
TRANSACTIONS/CAREER NOTES: Signed as non-drafted free agent by Minnesota Vikings (May 1, 2003). ... Released by Vikings (August 31, 2003). ... Re-signed by Vikings to practice squad (September 1, 2003). ... Activated (January 14, 2004).
PLAYING EXPERIENCE: Minnesota NFL, 2004. ... Games/Games started: 2004 (13/6). Total: 13/6.

GONZALEZ, JOAQUIN   T   COLTS

PERSONAL: Born September 7, 1979, in Miami, Fla. ... 6-5/315. ... Full name: Joaquin Antonio Gonzalez.
HIGH SCHOOL: Columbus (Miami).
COLLEGE: Miami (Fla.).
TRANSACTIONS/CAREER NOTES: Selected by Cleveland Browns in seventh round (227th pick overall) of 2002 NFL draft. ... Signed by Browns (July 16, 2002). ... Did not receive qualifying offer from Browns (March 2, 2005). ... Signed by Indianapolis Colts (March 28, 2005).
PLAYING EXPERIENCE: Cleveland NFL, 2002-2004. ... Games/Games started: 2002 (9/0), 2003 (16/3), 2004 (16/11). Total: 41/14.
HONORS: Named offensive tackle on THE SPORTING NEWS college All-America second team (2001).

GONZALEZ, TONY   TE   CHIEFS

PERSONAL: Born February 27, 1976, in Torrance, Calif. ... 6-5/251. ... Full name: Anthony Gonzalez.
HIGH SCHOOL: Huntington Beach (Calif.).
COLLEGE: California.
TRANSACTIONS/CAREER NOTES: Selected by Kansas City Chiefs in first round (13th pick overall) of 1997 NFL draft. ... Signed by Chiefs (July 29, 1997). ... Designated by Chiefs as franchise player (February 21, 2002). ... Re-signed by Chiefs (August 30, 2002).
HONORS: Named tight end on THE SPORTING NEWS college All-America first team (1996). ... Named tight end on THE SPORTING NEWS NFL All-Pro team (1999-2003). ... Played in Pro Bowl (1999-2000 and 2002-2004 seasons). ... Named to play in Pro Bowl (2001 season); replaced by Ken Dilger due to injury.
SINGLE GAME HIGHS (regular season): Receptions—14 (January 2, 2005, vs. San Diego); yards—147 (December 4, 2000, vs. New England); and touchdown receptions—3 (September 29, 2002, vs. Miami).
STATISTICAL PLATEAUS: 100-yard receiving games: 2000 (6), 2001 (1), 2002 (1), 2003 (1), 2004 (6). Total: 15.
MISCELLANEOUS: Holds Kansas City Chiefs all-time record for most receptions (570).

G

Year Team			RECEIVING				TOTALS			
Year Team	G	GS	No.	Yds.	Avg.	TD	TD	2pt.	Pts.	Fum.
1997—Kansas City NFL	16	0	33	368	11.2	2	2	1	14	0
1998—Kansas City NFL	16	16	59	621	10.5	2	2	0	12	3
1999—Kansas City NFL	15	15	76	849	11.2	11	11	0	66	2
2000—Kansas City NFL	16	16	93	1203	12.9	9	9	0	54	0
2001—Kansas City NFL	16	16	73	917	12.6	6	6	1	38	0
2002—Kansas City NFL	16	16	63	773	12.3	7	7	0	42	0
2003—Kansas City NFL	16	16	71	916	12.9	10	10	0	60	0
2004—Kansas City NFL	16	16	*102	1258	12.3	7	7	0	42	0
Pro totals (8 years)	127	111	570	6905	12.1	54	54	2	328	5

GOOCH, JEFF
LB — BUCCANEERS

PERSONAL: Born October 31, 1974, in Nashville, Tenn. ... 5-11/226. ... Full name: Jeffery Lance Gooch.
HIGH SCHOOL: Overton (Nashville).
COLLEGE: Austin Peay.
TRANSACTIONS/CAREER NOTES: Signed as non-drafted free agent by Tampa Bay Buccaneers (April 23, 1996). ... On injured reserve with knee injury (December 17, 1996-remainder of season). ... Granted free agency (February 12, 1999). ... Re-signed by Buccaneers (April 13, 1999). ... Traded by Buccaneers to St. Louis Rams for fifth-round pick in 2001 draft (March 19, 2001); trade voided because Gooch failed physical (March 23, 2001). ... Released by Buccaneers (February 26, 2002). ... Signed by Detroit Lions (April 16, 2002). ... Granted unconditional free agency (March 3, 2004). ... Signed by Tampa Bay Buccaneers (March 10, 2004).
CHAMPIONSHIP GAME EXPERIENCE: Played in NFC championship game (1999 season).

				TOTALS			INTERCEPTIONS			
Year Team	G	GS	Tk.	Ast.	Sks.	No.	Yds.	Avg.	TD
1996—Tampa Bay NFL	15	0	4	2	0.0	0	0	0.0	0
1997—Tampa Bay NFL	14	5	18	8	0.0	0	0	0.0	0
1998—Tampa Bay NFL	16	16	35	18	1.0	0	0	0.0	0
1999—Tampa Bay NFL	15	0	3	1	0.0	0	0	0.0	0
2000—Tampa Bay NFL	16	0	6	1	0.0	0	0	0.0	0
2001—Tampa Bay NFL	13	0	6	5	0.5	0	0	0.0	0
2002—Detroit NFL	16	2	24	9	0.0	1	3	3.0	0
2003—Detroit NFL	16	0	11	3	0.0	0	0	0.0	0
2004—Tampa Bay NFL	16	1	18	6	0.5	0	0	0.0	0
Pro totals (9 years)	137	24	125	53	2.0	1	3	3.0	0

GOODMAN, ANDRE'
CB — LIONS

PERSONAL: Born August 11, 1978, in Greenville, S.C. ... 5-10/185.
HIGH SCHOOL: Eastwood (Greenville, S.C.).
COLLEGE: South Carolina.
TRANSACTIONS/CAREER NOTES: Selected by Detroit Lions in third round (68th pick overall) of 2002 NFL draft. ... Signed by Lions (July 16, 2002). ... On injured reserve with shoulder injury (September 25, 2003-remainder of season). ... Granted free agency (March 2, 2005). ... Re-signed by Lions (April 15, 2005).

				TOTALS			INTERCEPTIONS			
Year Team	G	GS	Tk.	Ast.	Sks.	No.	Yds.	Avg.	TD
2002—Detroit NFL	14	6	34	8	0.0	1	2	2.0	0
2003—Detroit NFL	3	3	11	0	0.0	0	0	0.0	0
2004—Detroit NFL	11	4	19	5	0.0	1	0	0.0	0
Pro totals (3 years)	28	13	64	13	0.0	2	2	1.0	0

GOODSPEED, JOEY
FB — RAMS

PERSONAL: Born February 22, 1978, in Berwyn, Ill. ... 6-1/247. ... Full name: Joey Allen Goodspeed.
HIGH SCHOOL: Oswego (Ill.).
COLLEGE: Notre Dame.
TRANSACTIONS/CAREER NOTES: Signed as non-drafted free agent by Pittsburgh Steelers (April 18, 2000). ... Released by Steelers (August 21, 2000). ... Re-signed by Steelers to practice squad (October 18, 2000). ... Granted free agency following 2000 season. ... Signed by New Orleans Saints (February 10, 2001). ... Released by Saints (September 1, 2001). ... Signed by San Diego Chargers (February 14, 2002). ... Re-signed by Chargers (April 4, 2003). ... Waived by Chargers (August 31, 2003). ... Signed by St. Louis Rams (October 28, 2003). ... Released by Rams (November 7, 2003). ... Re-signed by Rams (November 11, 2003). ... Granted free agency (March 2, 2005). ... Re-signed by Rams (March 21, 2005).
SINGLE GAME HIGHS (regular season): Attempts—2 (December 5, 2004, vs. San Francisco); yards—4 (December 5, 2004, vs. San Francisco); and rushing touchdowns—1 (October 3, 2004, vs. San Francisco).

			RUSHING				RECEIVING				TOTALS			
Year Team	G	GS	Att.	Yds.	Avg.	TD	No.	Yds.	Avg.	TD	TD	2pt.	Pts.	Fum.
2002—San Diego NFL	12	0	0	0	0.0	0	0	0	0.0	0	0	0	0	0
2003—St. Louis NFL	8	4	0	0	0.0	0	0	0	0.0	0	0	0	0	0
2004—St. Louis NFL	16	5	3	6	2.0	1	11	71	6.5	0	1	0	6	1
Pro totals (3 years)	36	9	3	6	2.0	1	11	71	6.5	0	1	0	6	1

GOODWIN, JONATHAN
G — JETS

PERSONAL: Born December 2, 1978, in Columbia, S.C. ... 6-3/318. ... Full name: Jonathan Scott Goodwin.
HIGH SCHOOL: Lower Richland (S.C.).
COLLEGE: Michigan.
TRANSACTIONS/CAREER NOTES: Selected by New York Jets in fifth round (154th pick overall) of 2002 NFL draft. ... Signed by Jets (July 24, 2002). ... Granted free agency (March 2, 2005). ... Re-signed by Jets (April 5, 2005).
PLAYING EXPERIENCE: New York Jets NFL, 2002-2004. ... Games/Games started: 2002 (12/0), 2003 (15/0), 2004 (15/3). Total: 42/3.
HONORS: Named guard on THE SPORTING NEWS college All-America third team (2001).

GORDON, AMON
DT — BROWNS

PERSONAL: Born October 13, 1981, in San Diego, Calif. ... 6-2/305.
HIGH SCHOOL: Mira Mesa (San Diego, Calif.).
COLLEGE: Stanford.

G

TRANSACTIONS/CAREER NOTES: Selected after junior season by Cleveland Browns in fifth round (161st pick overall) of 2004 NFL draft. ... Signed by Browns (July 29, 2004).

Year Team				G	GS	Tk.	Ast.	Sks.
			TOTALS					
2004—Cleveland NFL				6	0	5	2	0.0

GORDON, LAMAR — RB — DOLPHINS

PERSONAL: Born January 7, 1980, in Milwaukee, Wis. ... 6-1/228.
HIGH SCHOOL: Cudahy (Milwaukee).
COLLEGE: North Dakota State.
TRANSACTIONS/CAREER NOTES: Selected by St. Louis Rams in third round (84th pick overall) of 2002 NFL draft. ... Signed by Rams (July 2, 2002). ... Traded by Rams to Miami Dolphins for third-round pick (S Oshiomogho Atogwe) in 2005 draft (September 9, 2004). ... On injured reserve with shoulder injury (September 28, 2004-remainder of season).
SINGLE GAME HIGHS (regular season): Attempts—21 (September 28, 2003, vs. Arizona); yards—92 (October 13, 2003, vs. Atlanta); and rushing touchdowns—1 (September 28, 2003, vs. Arizona).

Year Team	G	GS	RUSHING				RECEIVING				KICKOFF RETURNS				TOTALS			
			Att.	Yds.	Avg.	TD	No.	Yds.	Avg.	TD	No.	Yds.	Avg.	TD	TD	2pt.	Pts.	Fum.
2002—St. Louis NFL	13	5	65	228	3.5	1	30	278	9.3	2	6	104	17.3	0	3	0	18	4
2003—St. Louis NFL	10	4	71	298	4.2	1	8	59	7.4	0	0	0	0.0	0	1	0	6	1
2004—Miami NFL	3	2	35	64	1.8	0	13	74	5.7	0	0	0	0.0	0	0	0	0	1
Pro totals (3 years)	26	11	171	590	3.5	2	51	411	8.1	2	6	104	17.3	0	4	0	24	6

GORIN, BRANDON — T — PATRIOTS

PERSONAL: Born July 17, 1978, in Muncie, Ind. ... 6-6/308. ... Full name: Brandon Michael Gorin.
HIGH SCHOOL: Southside (Ind.).
COLLEGE: Purdue.
TRANSACTIONS/CAREER NOTES: Selected by San Diego Chargers in seventh round (201st pick overall) of 2001 NFL draft. ... Signed by Chargers (June 21, 2001). ... Released by Chargers (August 25, 2002). ... Signed by New England Patriots (September 5, 2002).
PLAYING EXPERIENCE: New England NFL, 2003-2004. ... Games/Games started: 2003 (6/0), 2004 (14/10). Total: 20/10.
CHAMPIONSHIP GAME EXPERIENCE: Played in AFC championship game (2003 and 2004 seasons). ... Member of Patriots for Super Bowl 38 (2003 season); did not play. ... Member of Super Bowl championship team (2004 season).

GOWIN, TOBY — P — FALCONS

PERSONAL: Born March 30, 1975, in Jacksonville, Texas. ... 5-10/167. ... Name pronounced: GO-in.
HIGH SCHOOL: Jacksonville (Texas).
COLLEGE: North Texas.
TRANSACTIONS/CAREER NOTES: Signed as non-drafted free agent by Dallas Cowboys (April 24, 1997). ... Granted free agency (February 11, 2000). ... Tendered offer sheet by New Orleans Saints (April 6, 2000). ... Cowboys declined to match offer (April 6, 2000). ... Granted unconditional free agency (February 28, 2003). ... Signed by Cowboys (March 3, 2003). ... Released by Cowboys (March 10, 2004). ... Signed by New York Jets (March 31, 2004). ... Granted unconditional free agency (March 2, 2005). ... Signed by Atlanta Falcons (March 8, 2005).

Year Team	G	No.	Yds.	Avg.	Net avg.	In. 20	Blk.
				PUNTING			
1997—Dallas NFL	16	86	3592	41.8	35.4	26	0
1998—Dallas NFL	16	77	3342	43.4	36.6	31	∞1
1999—Dallas NFL	16	81	3500	43.2	35.1	24	0
2000—New Orleans NFL	16	74	3043	41.1	32.3	22	0
2001—New Orleans NFL	16	76	3180	41.8	35.8	24	0
2002—New Orleans NFL	15	61	2553	41.9	36.9	15	0
2003—Dallas NFL	16	‡94	‡3665	39.0	34.9	25	0
2004—New York Jets NFL	16	80	3057	38.2	33.5	22	0
Pro totals (8 years)	127	629	25932	41.2	35.0	189	1

GRAGG, SCOTT — T — 49ERS

PERSONAL: Born February 28, 1972, in Silverton, Ore. ... 6-8/315.
HIGH SCHOOL: Silverton (Ore.) Union.
COLLEGE: Montana.
TRANSACTIONS/CAREER NOTES: Selected by New York Giants in second round (54th pick overall) of 1995 NFL draft. ... Signed by Giants (July 23, 1995). ... Granted free agency (February 13, 1998). ... Re-signed by Giants (September 4, 1998). ... Released by Giants (March 28, 2000). ... Signed by San Francisco 49ers (July 19, 2000). ... Granted unconditional free agency (March 2, 2001). ... Re-signed by 49ers (April 5, 2001).
PLAYING EXPERIENCE: New York Giants NFL, 1995-1999; San Francisco NFL, 2000-2004. ... Games/Games started: 1995 (13/0), 1996 (16/16), 1997 (16/16), 1998 (16/16), 1999 (16/16), 2000 (16/16), 2001 (16/16), 2002 (16/16), 2003 (15/14), 2004 (16/16). Total: 156/142.

G

GRAHAM, DANIEL — TE — PATRIOTS

PERSONAL: Born November 16, 1978, in Torrance, Calif. ... 6-3/257.
HIGH SCHOOL: Thomas Jefferson (Denver).
COLLEGE: Colorado.

TRANSACTIONS/CAREER NOTES: Selected by New England Patriots in first round (21st pick overall) of 2002 NFL draft. ... Signed by Patriots (July 21, 2002). ... On injured reserve with rib injury (December 24, 2002-remainder of season).
CHAMPIONSHIP GAME EXPERIENCE: Played in AFC championship game (2003 and 2004 seasons). ... Member of Super Bowl championship team (2003 and 2004 seasons).
HONORS: Named tight end on THE SPORTING NEWS college All-America first team (2001).
SINGLE GAME HIGHS (regular season): Receptions—7 (September 9, 2004, vs. Indianapolis); yards—110 (October 26, 2003, vs. Cleveland); and touchdown receptions—2 (September 19, 2004, vs. Arizona).
STATISTICAL PLATEAUS: 100-yard receiving games: 2003 (1). Total: 1.

				RECEIVING				TOTALS			
Year Team	G	GS	No.	Yds.	Avg.	TD	TD	2pt.	Pts.	Fum.
2002—New England NFL	12	6	15	150	10.0	1	1	0	6	0
2003—New England NFL	14	9	38	409	10.8	4	4	0	24	0
2004—New England NFL	14	14	30	364	12.1	7	7	0	42	0
Pro totals (3 years)	40	29	83	923	11.1	12	12	0	72	0

GRAHAM, EARNEST   RB   BUCCANEERS

PERSONAL: Born January 15, 1980, in Naples, Fla. ... 5-9/215.
HIGH SCHOOL: Mariner (Fort Myers, Fla.).
COLLEGE: Florida.
TRANSACTIONS/CAREER NOTES: Signed as non-drafted free agent by Tampa Bay Buccaneers (April 28, 2003). ... Released by Buccaneers (August 22, 2003). ... Re-signed by Buccaneers to practice squad (December 3, 2003). ... Released by Buccaneers (December 9, 2003). ... Re-signed by Buccaneers (January 14, 2004). ... Released by Buccaneers (September 5, 2004). ... Re-signed by Buccaneers to practice squad (September 7, 2004). ... Activated (October 27, 2004).
SINGLE GAME HIGHS (regular season): Attempts—4 (November 21, 2004, vs. San Francisco); yards—27 (November 21, 2004, vs. San Francisco); and rushing touchdowns—0.

			RUSHING				KICKOFF RETURNS				TOTALS			
Year Team	G	GS	Att.	Yds.	Avg.	TD	No.	Yds.	Avg.	TD	TD	2pt.	Pts.	Fum.
2004—Tampa Bay NFL	9	0	13	73	5.6	0	3	52	17.3	0	0	0	0	0

GRAHAM, SHAYNE   K   BENGALS

PERSONAL: Born December 9, 1977, in Radford, Va. ... 6-0/197. ... Full name: Michael Shayne Graham.
HIGH SCHOOL: Pulaski County (Va.).
COLLEGE: Virginia Tech.
TRANSACTIONS/CAREER NOTES: Signed as non-drafted free agent by New Orleans Saints (June 30, 2000). ... Released by Saints (August 22, 2000). ... Signed by Seattle Seahawks (April 27, 2001). ... Released by Seahawks (September 2, 2001). ... Signed by Buffalo Bills (November 27, 2001). ... Released by Bills (April 24, 2002). ... Signed by Seattle Seahawks (May 13, 2002). ... Released by Seahawks (August 13, 2002). ... Signed by Carolina Panthers (September 28, 2002). ... Claimed on waivers by Cincinnati Bengals (September 1, 2003). ... Granted free agency (March 3, 2004). ... Tendered offer sheet by Jacksonville Jaguars (March 5, 2004). ... Offer matched by Bengals (March 11, 2004).

		FIELD GOALS							TOTALS		
Year Team	G	1-29	30-39	40-49	50+	Tot.	Pct.	Lg.	XPM	XPA	Pts.
2001—Buffalo NFL	6	4-4	0-0	2-4	0-0	6-8	75.0	41	7	7	25
2002—Carolina NFL	11	3-5	2-3	6-8	2-2	13-18	72.2	50	21	21	60
2003—Cincinnati NFL	16	5-5	10-10	7-8	0-2	22-25	88.0	48	40	40	106
2004—Cincinnati NFL	16	7-7	10-12	7-8	3-4	27-31	87.1	53	41	41	122
Pro totals (4 years)	49	19-21	22-25	22-28	5-8	68-82	82.9	53	109	109	313

GRAMATICA, BILL   K

PERSONAL: Born July 10, 1978, in Buenos Aires, Argentina. ... 5-10/189. ... Full name: Guillermo Gramatica. ... Brother of Martin Gramatica, kicker, Tampa Bay Buccaneers (1999-2004) and Indianapolis Colts (2004).
HIGH SCHOOL: LaBelle (Fla.).
COLLEGE: South Florida.
TRANSACTIONS/CAREER NOTES: Selected by Arizona Cardinals in fourth round (98th pick overall) of 2001 NFL draft. ... Signed by Cardinals (June 4, 2001). ... On injured reserve with knee injury (December 18, 2001-remainder of season). ... On injured reserve with back injury (November 18, 2003-remainder of season). ... Granted unconditional free agency (March 3, 2004). ... Signed by New York Giants (May 14, 2004). ... Released by Giants (August 31, 2004). ... Signed by Miami Dolphins (November 6, 2004). ... Released by Dolphins (November 9, 2004).

G

		FIELD GOALS							TOTALS		
Year Team	G	1-29	30-39	40-49	50+	Tot.	Pct.	Lg.	XPM	XPA	Pts.
2001—Arizona NFL	13	8-8	3-4	4-7	1-1	16-20	80.0	50	25	25	73
2002—Arizona NFL	16	6-7	2-2	6-8	1-4	15-21	71.4	50	29	29	74
2003—Arizona NFL	4	1-1	2-2	0-0	0-1	3-4	75.0	38	6	6	15
2004—Miami NFL	1	2-2	1-1	0-0	0-0	3-3	100.0	30	0	1	9
Pro totals (4 years)	34	17-18	8-9	10-15	2-6	37-48	77.1	50	60	61	171

GRAMATICA, MARTIN   K

PERSONAL: Born November 27, 1975, in Buenos Aires, Argentina. ... 5-8/170. ... Name pronounced: mar-TEEN gruh-MAT-ee-ka. ... Brother of Bill Gramatica, kicker, Arizona Cardinals (2001-03) and Miami Dolphins (2004).
HIGH SCHOOL: La Belle (Fla.).
COLLEGE: Kansas State.

TRANSACTIONS/CAREER NOTES: Selected by Tampa Bay Buccaneers in third round (80th pick overall) of 1999 NFL draft. ... Signed by Buccaneers (July 29, 1999). ... Released by Buccaneers (November 30, 2004). ... Signed by Indianapolis Colts (December 8, 2004). ... Granted unconditional free agency (March 2, 2005).
CHAMPIONSHIP GAME EXPERIENCE: Played in NFC championship game (1999 and 2002 seasons). ... Member of Super Bowl championship team (2002 season).
HONORS: Named kicker on THE SPORTING NEWS college All-America first team (1997). ... Named kicker on THE SPORTING NEWS college All-America second team (1998). ... Won Lou Groza Award (1997). ... Played in Pro Bowl (2000 season).
MISCELLANEOUS: Tampa Bay Buccaneers all-time scoring leader (592 points).

				FIELD GOALS						TOTALS		
Year Team	G	1-29	30-39	40-49	50+	Tot.	Pct.	Lg.	XPM	XPA	Pts.
1999—Tampa Bay NFL	16	8-8	10-12	6-8	3-4	∍27-∞32	84.4	∞53	25	25	106
2000—Tampa Bay NFL	16	8-8	8-10	7-9	5-7	28-34	82.4	*55	42	42	126
2001—Tampa Bay NFL	14	9-10	9-9	5-7	0-3	23-29	79.3	49	28	28	97
2002—Tampa Bay NFL	16	7-8	14-15	6-10	5-6	†32-39	82.1	∞53	32	32	128
2003—Tampa Bay NFL	16	9-9	3-6	3-8	1-3	16-26	61.5	50	33	34	81
2004—Tampa Bay NFL	11	6-7	3-6	1-5	1-1	11-19	57.9	53	21	22	54
—Indianapolis NFL	4	0-0	0-0	0-0	0-0	0-0	0.0	0	0	0	0
Pro totals (6 years)	93	47-50	47-58	28-47	15-24	137-179	76.5	55	181	183	592

GRANT CHARLES   DE   SAINTS

PERSONAL: Born September 3, 1978, in Colquitt, Ga. ... 6-3/290.
HIGH SCHOOL: Miller County (Colquitt, Ga.).
COLLEGE: Georgia.
TRANSACTIONS/CAREER NOTES: Selected by New Orleans Saints in first round (25th pick overall) of 2002 NFL draft. ... Signed by Saints (July 27, 2002).

			TOTALS			INTERCEPTIONS			
Year Team	G	GS	Tk.	Ast.	Sks.	No.	Yds.	Avg.	TD
2002—New Orleans NFL	16	6	30	7	7.0	0	0	0.0	0
2003—New Orleans NFL	16	16	48	13	10.0	0	0	0.0	0
2004—New Orleans NFL	16	16	67	13	10.5	1	8	8.0	0
Pro totals (3 years)	48	38	145	33	27.5	1	8	8.0	0

GRANT, CIE   LB   SAINTS

PERSONAL: Born November 27, 1979, in New Philadelphia, Ohio. ... 6-0/228. ... Full name: Willie Grant.
HIGH SCHOOL: New Philadelphia (Ohio).
COLLEGE: Ohio State.
TRANSACTIONS/CAREER NOTES: Selected by New Orleans Saints in third round (86th pick overall) of 2003 NFL draft. ... Signed by Saints (July 25, 2003). ... On injured reserve with knee injury (August 31, 2004-entire season).

			TOTALS			INTERCEPTIONS			
Year Team	G	GS	Tk.	Ast.	Sks.	No.	Yds.	Avg.	TD
2003—New Orleans NFL	7	0	1	0	0.0	0	0	0.0	0
2004—New Orleans NFL		Did not play.							
Pro totals (1 year)	7	0	1	0	0.0	0	0	0.0	0

GRANT DELAWRENCE   DE   RAIDERS

PERSONAL: Born November 18, 1979, in Compton, Calif. ... 6-3/280. ... Full name: DeLawrence Grant Jr.
HIGH SCHOOL: Centennial (Compton, Calif.).
JUNIOR COLLEGE: El Camino College (Calif.).
COLLEGE: Oregon State.
TRANSACTIONS/CAREER NOTES: Selected by Oakland Raiders in third round (89th pick overall) of 2001 NFL draft. ... Signed by Raiders (July 22, 2001). ... Released by Raiders (March 3, 2005). ... Re-signed by Raiders (April 7, 2005).
CHAMPIONSHIP GAME EXPERIENCE: Played in AFC championship game (2002 season). ... Played in Super Bowl 37 (2002 season).
HONORS: Named defensive end on THE SPORTING NEWS college All-America second team (2000).

			TOTALS		
Year Team	G	GS	Tk.	Ast.	Sks.
2001—Oakland NFL	2	0	0	0	0.0
2002—Oakland NFL	16	14	21	5	3.0
2003—Oakland NFL	13	4	8	10	1.0
2004—Oakland NFL	9	9	14	6	2.0
Pro totals (4 years)	40	27	43	21	6.0

G

GRANT, DEON   S   JAGUARS

PERSONAL: Born March 14, 1979, in Augusta, Ga. ... 6-2/210.
HIGH SCHOOL: Josey (Augusta, Ga.).
COLLEGE: Tennessee.
TRANSACTIONS/CAREER NOTES: Selected after junior season by Carolina Panthers in second round (57th pick overall) of 2000 NFL draft. ... Signed by Panthers (July 13, 2000). ... On injured reserve with hip injury (August 20, 2000-entire season). ... Granted unconditional free agency (March 3, 2004). ... Signed by Jacksonville Jaguars (March 10, 2004).
CHAMPIONSHIP GAME EXPERIENCE: Played in NFC championship game (2003 season). ... Played in Super Bowl 38 (2003 season).
HONORS: Named free safety on THE SPORTING NEWS college All-America first team (1999).

Year Team	G	GS	TOTALS			INTERCEPTIONS			
			Tk.	Ast.	Sks.	No.	Yds.	Avg.	TD
2000—Carolina NFL	Did not play.								
2001—Carolina NFL	16	16	59	12	1.0	5	96	19.2	0
2002—Carolina NFL	16	16	54	14	0.0	3	16	5.3	0
2003—Carolina NFL	16	16	65	12	1.0	3	25	8.3	0
2004—Jacksonville NFL	16	16	50	15	1.0	2	4	2.0	0
Pro totals (4 years)	64	64	228	53	3.0	13	141	10.8	0

GRASMANIS, PAUL — DT — EAGLES

PERSONAL: Born August 2, 1974, in Grand Rapids, Mich. ... 6-3/298. ... Full name: Paul Ryan Grasmanis.
HIGH SCHOOL: Jenison (Mich.).
COLLEGE: Notre Dame.
TRANSACTIONS/CAREER NOTES: Selected by Chicago Bears in fourth round (116th pick overall) of 1996 NFL draft. ... Signed by Bears (June 13, 1996). ... Granted free agency (February 12, 1999). ... Re-signed by Bears (April 13, 1999). ... Released by Bears (September 5, 1999). ... Signed by St. Louis Rams (September 7, 1999). ... Inactive for one game with Rams (1999). ... Released by Rams (September 13, 1999). ... Signed by Denver Broncos (November 1, 1999). ... Granted unconditional free agency (February 11, 2000). ... Signed by Philadelphia Eagles (March 3, 2000). ... Granted unconditional free agency (March 2, 2001). ... Re-signed by Eagles (April 24, 2001). ... On injured reserve with Achilles injury (September 16, 2003-remainder of season). ... Granted unconditional free agency (March 3, 2004). ... Re-signed by Eagles (March 11, 2004).
CHAMPIONSHIP GAME EXPERIENCE: Played in NFC championship game (2001 and 2002 seasons). ... Member of Eagles for NFC championship game (2004 season); inactive. ... Member of Eagles for Super Bowl 39 (2004 season); inactive.

Year Team	G	GS	TOTALS		
			Tk.	Ast.	Sks.
1996—Chicago NFL	14	3	8	3	0.0
1997—Chicago NFL	16	0	9	5	0.5
1998—Chicago NFL	15	0	15	2	1.0
1999—Denver NFL	5	0	5	2	0.0
2000—Philadelphia NFL	16	0	30	5	3.5
2001—Philadelphia NFL	14	2	14	5	2.0
2002—Philadelphia NFL	16	3	20	11	4.0
2003—Philadelphia NFL	2	1	4	2	1.0
2004—Philadelphia NFL	4	0	10	0	0.0
Pro totals (9 years)	102	9	115	35	12.0

GRAY, BOBBY — S — BEARS

PERSONAL: Born April 30, 1978, in Houston, Texas. ... 6-0/210. ... Full name: Bobby Wayne Gray.
HIGH SCHOOL: Aldine (Texas).
COLLEGE: Louisiana Tech.
TRANSACTIONS/CAREER NOTES: Selected by Chicago Bears in fifth round (140th pick overall) of 2002 NFL draft. ... Signed by Bears (July 19, 2002). ... On injured reserve with wrist injury (September 23, 2002-remainder of season). ... Granted free agency (March 2, 2005). ... Re-signed by Bears (March 8, 2005).

Year Team	G	GS	TOTALS			INTERCEPTIONS			
			Tk.	Ast.	Sks.	No.	Yds.	Avg.	TD
2002—Chicago NFL	3	0	4	1	0.0	0	0	0.0	0
2003—Chicago NFL	16	9	41	11	1.0	0	0	0.0	0
2004—Chicago NFL	10	4	16	4	0.0	1	31	31.0	0
Pro totals (3 years)	29	13	61	16	1.0	1	31	31.0	0

GRAY, CHRIS — G/C

PERSONAL: Born June 19, 1970, in Birmingham, Ala. ... 6-4/308. ... Full name: Christopher William Gray.
HIGH SCHOOL: Homewood (Ala.).
COLLEGE: Auburn.
TRANSACTIONS/CAREER NOTES: Selected by Miami Dolphins in fifth round (132nd pick overall) of 1993 NFL draft. ... Signed by Dolphins (July 12, 1993). ... On injured reserve with ankle injury (November 15, 1995-remainder of season). ... On injured reserve with broken leg (November 19, 1996-remainder of season). ... Released by Dolphins (August 12, 1997). ... Signed by Chicago Bears (September 9, 1997). ... Granted unconditional free agency (February 13, 1998). ... Signed by Seattle Seahawks (February 20, 1998). ... Granted unconditional free agency (March 2, 2005).
PLAYING EXPERIENCE: Miami NFL, 1993-1996; Chicago NFL, 1997; Seattle NFL, 1998-2004. ... Games/Games started: 1993 (5/0), 1994 (16/2), 1995 (10/10), 1996 (11/11), 1997 (8/2), 1998 (15/8), 1999 (16/10), 2000 (16/16), 2001 (16/16), 2002 (16/16), 2003 (16/16), 2004 (16/16). Total: 161/123.

G

GREEN, AHMAN — RB — PACKERS

PERSONAL: Born February 16, 1977, in Omaha, Neb. ... 6-0/218.
HIGH SCHOOL: North (Omaha, Neb.), then Central Christian (Omaha, Neb.).
COLLEGE: Nebraska.
TRANSACTIONS/CAREER NOTES: Selected after junior season by Seattle Seahawks in third round (76th pick overall) of 1998 NFL draft. ... Signed by Seahawks (July 18, 1998). ... Traded by Seahawks with fifth-round pick (WR/KR Joey Jamison) in 2000 draft to Green Bay Packers for CB Fred Vinson and sixth-round pick (DT Tim Watson) in 2000 draft (April 14, 2000). ... Granted free agency (March 2, 2001). ... Re-signed by Packers (July 24, 2001).

HONORS: Named running back on THE SPORTING NEWS college All-America second team (1997). ... Played in Pro Bowl (2001, 2003 and 2004 seasons). ... Named to play in Pro Bowl (2002 season); replaced by Michael Bennett due to injury.
SINGLE GAME HIGHS (regular season): Attempts—33 (September 13, 2004, vs. Carolina); yards—218 (December 3, 2003, vs. Denver); and rushing touchdowns—3 (October 20, 2002, vs. Washington).
STATISTICAL PLATEAUS: 100-yard rushing games: 1998 (1), 2000 (3), 2001 (7), 2002 (4), 2003 (10), 2004 (4). Total: 29.

Year Team	G	GS	RUSHING Att	Yds	Avg.	TD	RECEIVING No.	Yds	Avg.	TD	KICKOFF RETURNS No.	Yds	Avg.	TD	TOTALS TD	2pt	Pts.	Fum.
1998—Seattle NFL	16	0	35	209	6.0	1	3	2	0.7	0	27	620	23.0	0	1	0	6	1
1999—Seattle NFL	14	0	26	120	4.6	0	0	0	0.0	0	36	818	22.7	0	0	0	0	2
2000—Green Bay NFL	16	11	263	1175	4.5	10	73	559	7.7	3	0	0	0.0	0	13	0	78	6
2001—Green Bay NFL	16	16	304	1387	4.6	9	62	594	9.6	2	0	0	0.0	0	11	0	66	5
2002—Green Bay NFL	14	14	286	1240	4.3	7	57	393	6.9	2	0	0	0.0	0	9	0	54	4
2003—Green Bay NFL	16	16	‡355	‡1883	5.3	‡15	50	367	7.3	5	0	0	0.0	0	‡20	0	120	7
2004—Green Bay NFL	15	15	259	1163	4.5	7	40	275	6.9	1	0	0	0.0	0	8	0	48	7
Pro totals (7 years)	107	72	1528	7177	4.7	49	285	2190	7.7	13	63	1438	22.8	0	62	0	372	32

GREEN, BARRETT — LB — GIANTS

PERSONAL: Born October 29, 1977, in West Palm Beach, Fla. ... 6-0/225. ... Son of Joe Green, defensive back with New York Giants (1970 and 1971).
HIGH SCHOOL: Suncoast (West Palm Beach, Fla.).
COLLEGE: West Virginia.
TRANSACTIONS/CAREER NOTES: Selected by Detroit Lions in second round (50th pick overall) of 2000 NFL draft. ... Signed by Lions (July 15, 2000). ... Granted unconditional free agency (March 3, 2004). ... Signed by New York Giants (March 8, 2004). ... On injured reserve with knee injury (December 20, 2004-remainder of season).

Year Team	G	GS	TOTALS Tk.	Ast.	Sks.	INTERCEPTIONS No.	Yds.	Avg.	TD
2000—Detroit NFL	9	0	0	0	0.0	0	0	0.0	0
2001—Detroit NFL	14	10	51	24	1.0	0	0	0.0	0
2002—Detroit NFL	15	14	50	23	1.0	0	0	0.0	0
2003—Detroit NFL	16	16	65	29	3.0	0	0	0.0	0
2004—New York Giants NFL	10	9	26	12	0.0	0	0	0.0	0
Pro totals (5 years)	64	49	192	88	5.0	0	0	0.0	0

GREEN, BRANDON — DE

PERSONAL: Born September 5, 1980, in Victoria, Texas. ... 6-2/264. ... Full name: James Brandon Green.
HIGH SCHOOL: Industrial (Vanderbilt, Texas).
COLLEGE: Rice.
TRANSACTIONS/CAREER NOTES: Selected by Jacksonville Jaguars in sixth round (176th pick overall) of 2003 NFL draft. ... Signed by Jaguars (July 25, 2003). ... On injured reserve with knee injury (September 19, 2003-remainder of season). ... On injured reserve with knee injury (October 27, 2004-remainder of season). ... Released by Jaguars (April 26, 2005).

Year Team	G	GS	TOTALS Tk.	Ast.	Sks.	INTERCEPTIONS No.	Yds.	Avg.	TD
2004—Jacksonville NFL	3	0	2	1	0.0	0	0	0.0	0

GREEN, HOWARD — DT — SAINTS

PERSONAL: Born January 12, 1979, in Donaldsonville, La. ... 6-2/320. ... Full name: Howard Green Jr.
HIGH SCHOOL: Donaldsonville (La.).
JUNIOR COLLEGE: Southwest Mississippi College.
COLLEGE: Louisiana State.
TRANSACTIONS/CAREER NOTES: Selected by Houston Texans in sixth round (190th pick overall) of 2002 NFL draft. ... Signed by Texans (June 19, 2002). ... Claimed on waivers by Baltimore Ravens (September 3, 2002). ... Released by Ravens (October 29, 2002). ... Signed by Texans to practice squad (October 31, 2002). ... Activated (December 18, 2002). ... Re-signed by Texans (March 24, 2003). ... Released by Texans (August 25, 2003). ... Signed by New Orleans Saints to practice squad (October 3, 2003). ... Activated (December 6, 2003).

Year Team	G	GS	TOTALS Tk.	Ast.	Sks.
2002—Baltimore NFL	1	0	0	0	0.0
2003—New Orleans NFL	4	0	0	0	0.0
2004—New Orleans NFL	14	12	18	10	0.0
Pro totals (3 years)	19	12	18	10	0.0

G

GREEN, JAMAAL — DE — EAGLES

PERSONAL: Born June 5, 1980, in Camden, N.J. ... 6-2/272. ... Full name: Jamaal Hakeem Green.
HIGH SCHOOL: Woodrow Wilson (Camden, N.J.).
COLLEGE: Miami (Fla.).
TRANSACTIONS/CAREER NOTES: Selected by Philadelphia Eagles in fourth round (131st pick overall) of 2003 NFL draft. ... Signed by Eagles (May 29, 2003). ... On injured reserve with ankle injury (August 24, 2003-entire season).
CHAMPIONSHIP GAME EXPERIENCE: Member of Eagles for NFC championship game (2004 season); inactive. ... Member of Eagles for Super Bowl 39 (2004 season); inactive.

Year Team	G	GS	TOTALS		
			Tk.	Ast.	Sks.
2003—Philadelphia NFL	Did not play.				
—Houston NFL	Did not play.				
2004—Philadelphia NFL	8	0	2	0	1.0
Pro totals (1 year)	8	0	2	0	1.0

GREEN, JARVIS · DE

PERSONAL: Born January 12, 1979, in Thibodaux, La. ... 6-3/290. ... Full name: Jarvis Pernell Green.
HIGH SCHOOL: Donaldsonville (La.).
COLLEGE: Louisiana State.
TRANSACTIONS/CAREER NOTES: Selected by New England Patriots in fourth round (126th pick overall) of 2002 NFL draft. ... Signed by Patriots (July 18, 2002). ... Granted free agency (March 2, 2005).
CHAMPIONSHIP GAME EXPERIENCE: Played in AFC championship game (2003 and 2004 seasons). ... Member of Super Bowl championship team (2003 and 2004 seasons).

Year Team	G	GS	TOTALS		
			Tk.	Ast.	Sks.
2002—New England NFL	15	4	14	7	2.5
2003—New England NFL	16	7	9	8	2.0
2004—New England NFL	16	1	15	6	4.0
Pro totals (3 years)	47	12	38	21	8.5

GREEN, LOUIS · LB · BRONCOS

PERSONAL: Born September 23, 1979, in Vicksburg, Miss. ... 6-3/228. ... Full name: Louis Edward Green.
HIGH SCHOOL: Jefferson County (Lorman, Miss.).
COLLEGE: Alcorn State.
TRANSACTIONS/CAREER NOTES: Signed as non-drafted free agent by Baltimore Ravens (June 2, 2002). ... Released by Ravens (August 26, 2002). ... Signed by Denver Broncos (January 7, 2003). ... Assigned by Broncos to Amsterdam Admirals in 2003 NFL Europe enhancement allocation program (February 3, 2003). ... Released by Broncos (August 31, 2003). ... Re-signed by Broncos to practice squad (November 19, 2003). ... Released by Broncos from practice squad (December 24, 2003). ... Re-signed by Broncos to practice squad (December 29, 2003). ... Released by Broncos (September 5, 2004). ... Re-signed by Broncos to practice squad (September 6, 2004). ... Activated (September 11, 2004). ... Released by Broncos and re-signed to practice squad (September 13, 2004). ... Activated (November 30, 2004).
PLAYING EXPERIENCE: Denver NFL, 2004. ... Games/Games started: 2004 (6/0). Total: 6/0.

GREEN, MIKE · S · BEARS

PERSONAL: Born December 6, 1976, in Ruston, La. ... 6-0/195.
HIGH SCHOOL: Ruston (La.).
COLLEGE: Northwestern State.
TRANSACTIONS/CAREER NOTES: Selected by Chicago Bears in seventh round (254th pick overall) of 2000 NFL draft. ... Signed by Bears (May 30, 2000). ... On injured reserve with groin injury (December 23, 2003-remainder of season).

Year Team	G	GS	TOTALS			INTERCEPTIONS			
			Tk.	Ast.	Sks.	No.	Yds.	Avg.	TD
2000—Chicago NFL	7	0	0	0	0.0	0	0	0.0	0
2001—Chicago NFL	16	2	53	4	3.0	0	0	0.0	0
2002—Chicago NFL	16	16	91	27	1.0	0	0	0.0	0
2003—Chicago NFL	10	8	36	7	0.5	1	3	3.0	0
2004—Chicago NFL	16	16	84	23	1.5	2	0	0.0	0
Pro totals (5 years)	65	42	264	61	6.0	3	3	1.0	0

GREEN, RODERICK · LB · RAVENS

PERSONAL: Born April 26, 1982, in Brenham, Texas. ... 6-2/250.
HIGH SCHOOL: Brenham (Texas).
JUNIOR COLLEGE: Blinn (Texas).
COLLEGE: Central Missouri State.
TRANSACTIONS/CAREER NOTES: Selected by Baltimore Ravens in fifth round (153rd pick overall) of 2004 NFL draft. ... Signed by Ravens (July 29, 2004).

Year Team	G	GS	TOTALS			INTERCEPTIONS			
			Tk.	Ast.	Sks.	No.	Yds.	Avg.	TD
2004—Baltimore NFL	9	0	1	0	0.0	0	0	0.0	0

GREEN, TRENT · QB · CHIEFS

PERSONAL: Born July 9, 1970, in St. Louis, Mo. ... 6-3/217. ... Full name: Trent Jason Green.
HIGH SCHOOL: Vianney (St. Louis).
COLLEGE: Indiana.
TRANSACTIONS/CAREER NOTES: Selected by San Diego Chargers in eighth round (222nd pick overall) of 1993 NFL draft. ... Signed by Chargers (July 15, 1993). ... Inactive for all 16 games (1993). ... Released by Chargers (August 22, 1994). ... Signed by Washington Redskins (April 5, 1995). ... Inactive for all 16 games (1995). ... Inactive for all 16 games (1996). ... Granted free agency (February 14, 1997). ... Re-

G

signed by Redskins (June 6, 1997). ... Granted unconditional free agency (February 12, 1999). ... Signed by St. Louis Rams (February 16, 1999). ... On injured reserve with knee injury (August 30, 1999-entire season). ... Traded by Rams with fifth-round pick (RB Derrick Blaylock) in 2001 draft to Kansas City Chiefs for first-round pick (DT Damione Lewis) in 2001 draft (April 20, 2001).

HONORS: Played in Pro Bowl (2003 season).
RECORDS: Shares NFL record for longest pass completion (to Marc Boerigter)—99 yards, touchdown (December 22, 2002, vs. San Diego).
SINGLE GAME HIGHS (regular season): Attempts—54 (September 20, 1998, vs. Seattle); completions—34 (December 7, 2003, vs. Denver); yards—431 (November 5, 2000, vs. Carolina); and touchdown passes—5 (September 29, 2002, vs. Miami).
STATISTICAL PLATEAUS: 300-yard passing games: 1998 (2), 2000 (3), 2001 (3), 2002 (4), 2003 (5), 2004 (8). Total: 25.
MISCELLANEOUS: Regular-season record as starting NFL quarterback: 42-41 (.506). ... Post-season record as starting NFL quarterback: 0-1 (.000).

					PASSING							RUSHING				TOTALS		
Year Team	G	GS	Att.	Cmp.	Pct.	Yds.	TD	Int.	Avg.	Skd.	Rat.	Att.	Yds.	Avg.	TD	TD	2pt.	Pts.
1993—San Diego NFL	Did not play.																	
1994—	Did not play.																	
1995—Washington NFL	Did not play.																	
1996—Washington NFL	Did not play.																	
1997—Washington NFL	1	0	1	0	0.0	0	0	0	0.00	0	39.6	0	0	0.0	0	0	0	0
1998—Washington NFL	15	14	509	278	54.6	3441	23	11	6.76	49	81.8	42	117	2.8	2	2	0	12
1999—St. Louis NFL	Did not play.																	
2000—St. Louis NFL	8	5	240	145	60.4	2063	16	5	8.60	24	‡101.8	20	69	3.5	1	1	0	6
2001—Kansas City NFL	16	16	523	296	56.6	3783	17	*24	7.23	39	71.1	35	158	4.5	0	0	1	2
2002—Kansas City NFL	16	16	470	287	61.1	3690	26	13	*7.85	26	92.6	31	225	7.3	1	1	1	8
2003—Kansas City NFL	16	16	523	330	63.1	4039	24	12	7.72	20	92.6	26	83	3.2	2	2	0	12
2004—Kansas City NFL	16	16	*556	§369	66.4	§4591	27	17	8.26	32	95.2	25	85	3.4	0	0	0	0
Pro totals (7 years)	88	83	2822	1705	60.4	21607	133	82	7.66	190	87.9	179	737	4.1	6	6	2	40

GREEN, WILLIAM RB BROWNS

PERSONAL: Born December 17, 1979, in Atlantic City, N.J. ... 6-0/215.
HIGH SCHOOL: Holy Spirit (Atlantic City, N.J.).
COLLEGE: Boston College.
TRANSACTIONS/CAREER NOTES: Selected after junior season by Cleveland Browns in first round (16th pick overall) of 2002 NFL draft. ... Signed by Browns (July 27, 2002). ... Suspended one game for conduct detrimental to team (November 9, 2003). ... On suspended list for violating league substance abuse policy (November 13, 2003-remainder of season).
HONORS: Named running back on THE SPORTING NEWS college All-America first team (2001).
SINGLE GAME HIGHS (regular season): Attempts—33 (October 5, 2003, vs. Pittsburgh); yards—178 (December 29, 2002, vs. Atlanta); and rushing touchdowns—2 (December 29, 2002, vs. Atlanta).
STATISTICAL PLATEAUS: 100-yard rushing games: 2002 (3), 2003 (2), 2004 (1). Total: 6.

			RUSHING				RECEIVING				TOTALS			
Year Team	G	GS	Att.	Yds.	Avg.	TD	No.	Yds.	Avg.	TD	TD	2pt.	Pts.	Fum.
2002—Cleveland NFL	16	10	243	887	3.7	6	16	113	7.1	0	6	0	36	4
2003—Cleveland NFL	7	7	142	559	3.9	1	10	50	5.0	0	1	0	6	5
2004—Cleveland NFL	15	12	163	585	3.6	2	14	84	6.0	0	2	0	12	3
Pro totals (3 years)	38	29	548	2031	3.7	9	40	247	6.2	0	9	0	54	12

GREENWOOD, MORLON LB TEXANS

PERSONAL: Born July 17, 1978, in Jamaica, West Indies. ... 6-0/238. ... Full name: Morlon O'Neil Greenwood.
HIGH SCHOOL: Freeport (N.Y.).
COLLEGE: Syracuse.
TRANSACTIONS/CAREER NOTES: Selected by Miami Dolphins in third round (88th pick overall) of 2001 NFL draft. ... Signed by Dolphins (July 23, 2001). ... Granted free agency (March 3, 2004). ... Re-signed by Dolphins (April 19, 2004). ... Granted unconditional free agency (March 2, 2005). ... Signed by Houston Texans (March 3, 2005).

			TOTALS			INTERCEPTIONS			
Year Team	G	GS	Tk.	Ast.	Sks.	No.	Yds.	Avg.	TD
2001—Miami NFL	14	12	30	28	1.5	0	0	0.0	0
2002—Miami NFL	16	13	33	18	1.0	0	0	0.0	0
2003—Miami NFL	16	11	43	23	0.5	0	0	0.0	0
2004—Miami NFL	16	15	61	40	0.0	0	0	0.0	0
Pro totals (4 years)	62	51	167	109	3.0	0	0	0.0	0

GREER, JABARI CB BILLS

G

PERSONAL: Born February 2, 1982, in Jackson, Tenn. ... 5-11/169. ... Full name: Jabari Amin Greer.
HIGH SCHOOL: South Side (Jackson, Tenn.).
COLLEGE: Tennessee.
TRANSACTIONS/CAREER NOTES: Signed as non-drafted free agent by Buffalo Bills (April 26, 2004).

			TOTALS			INTERCEPTIONS			
Year Team	G	GS	Tk.	Ast.	Sks.	No.	Yds.	Avg.	TD
2004—Buffalo NFL	12	1	12	0	1.0	0	0	0.0	0

GREGG, KELLY DT RAVENS

PERSONAL: Born November 1, 1976, in Wichita, Kan. ... 6-0/310.
HIGH SCHOOL: Edmond (Okla.).
COLLEGE: Oklahoma.

TRANSACTIONS/CAREER NOTES: Selected by Cincinnati Bengals in sixth round (173rd pick overall) of 1999 NFL draft. ... Signed by Bengals (June 23, 1999). ... Released by Bengals (September 6, 1999). ... Re-signed by Bengals to practice squad (September 7, 1999). ... Signed by Philadelphia Eagles off Bengals practice squad (December 7, 1999). ... Released by Eagles (September 12, 2000). ... Signed by Baltimore Ravens to practice squad (September 13, 2000). ... Assigned by Ravens to Rhein Fire in 2001 NFL Europe enhancement allocation program (February 19, 2001).

			TOTALS		
Year Team	G	GS	Tk.	Ast.	Sks.
1999—Philadelphia NFL	3	0	2	0	0.0
2000—Baltimore NFL	Did not play.				
2001—Baltimore NFL	8	1	7	3	1.0
2002—Baltimore NFL	16	16	45	11	2.0
2003—Baltimore NFL	16	15	63	17	3.0
2004—Baltimore NFL	14	14	44	17	1.5
Pro totals (5 years)	57	46	161	48	7.5

GREGORY, DAMIAN   DT   BUCCANEERS

PERSONAL: Born January 21, 1977, in Ann Arbor, Mich. ... 6-2/305. ... Full name: Damian K. Gregory.
HIGH SCHOOL: Sexton (Lansing, Mich.).
COLLEGE: Illinois State.
TRANSACTIONS/CAREER NOTES: Signed as non-drafted free agent by Miami Dolphins (April 27, 2000). ... On injured reserve with knee injury (August 22, 2000-remainder of season). ... On non-football injury list after spleen surgery (October 16, 2001-remainder of season). ... Claimed on waivers by Cleveland Browns (March 1, 2002). ... Released by Browns (September 1, 2002). ... Re-signed by Browns to practice squad (September 4, 2002). ... Activated (November 14, 2002). ... Released by Browns (November 26, 2002). ... Re-signed by Browns to practice squad (November 28, 2002). ... Signed by Oakland Raiders (March 23, 2003). ... Released by Raiders (May 29, 2003). ... Signed by Tampa Bay Buccaneers (February 26, 2004). ... On injured reserve with knee injury (October 20, 2004-remainder of season).

			TOTALS		
Year Team	G	GS	Tk.	Ast.	Sks.
2001—Miami NFL	2	0	0	0	0.0
2002—Cleveland NFL	1	0	0	0	0.0
2004—Tampa Bay NFL	6	0	3	0	0.0
Pro totals (3 years)	9	0	3	0	0.0

GREISEN, NICK   LB

PERSONAL: Born August 10, 1979, in Sturgeon Bay, Wis. ... 6-1/245.
HIGH SCHOOL: Sturgeon Bay (Wis.).
COLLEGE: Wisconsin.
TRANSACTIONS/CAREER NOTES: Selected by New York Giants in fifth round (152nd pick overall) of 2002 NFL draft. ... Signed by Giants (July 23, 2002). ... Granted free agency (March 2, 2005).

			TOTALS			INTERCEPTIONS			
Year Team	G	GS	Tk.	Ast.	Sks.	No.	Yds.	Avg.	TD
2002—New York Giants NFL	8	1	3	0	1.0	0	0	0.0	0
2003—New York Giants NFL	15	0	0	1	0.0	0	0	0.0	0
2004—New York Giants NFL	15	7	53	19	2.0	0	0	0.0	0
Pro totals (3 years)	38	8	56	20	3.0	0	0	0.0	0

GRIESE, BRIAN   QB   BUCCANEERS

PERSONAL: Born March 18, 1975, in Miami, Fla. ... 6-3/214. ... Full name: Brian David Griese. ... Name pronounced: GREE-see. ... Son of Bob Griese, Hall of Fame quarterback with Miami Dolphins (1967-80).
HIGH SCHOOL: Columbus (Miami).
COLLEGE: Michigan.
TRANSACTIONS/CAREER NOTES: Selected by Denver Broncos in third round (91st pick overall) of 1998 NFL draft. ... Signed by Broncos (July 22, 1998). ... Granted free agency (March 2, 2001). ... Re-signed by Broncos (April 11, 2001). ... Waived by Broncos (June 2, 2003). ... Signed by Miami Dolphins (June 9, 2003). ... Released by Dolphins (March 2, 2004). ... Signed by Tampa Bay Buccaneers (March 19, 2004).
CHAMPIONSHIP GAME EXPERIENCE: Member of Broncos for AFC championship game (1998 season); inactive. ... Member of Super Bowl championship team (1998 season); inactive.
HONORS: Played in Pro Bowl (2000 season).
SINGLE GAME HIGHS (regular season): Attempts—53 (September 30, 2002, vs. Baltimore); completions—36 (December 12, 2004, vs. San Diego); yards—392 (December 12, 2004, vs. San Diego); and touchdown passes—3 (December 26, 2004, vs. Carolina).
STATISTICAL PLATEAUS: 300-yard passing games: 1999 (2), 2000 (5), 2001 (1), 2002 (4), 2004 (3). Total: 15.
MISCELLANEOUS: Regular-season record as starting NFL quarterback: 34-32 (.515).

			PASSING								RUSHING				TOTALS		
Year Team	G	GS	Att.	Cmp.	Pct.	Yds.	TD	Int.	Avg.	Skd.	Rat.	Att.	Yds.	Avg.	TD	TD	2pt.	Pts.
1998—Denver NFL	1	0	3	1	33.3	2	0	1	0.67	0	2.8	4	-4	-1.0	0	0	0	0
1999—Denver NFL	14	13	452	261	57.7	3032	14	14	6.71	27	75.6	46	138	3.0	2	2	0	12
2000—Denver NFL	10	10	336	216	§64.3	2688	19	4	§8.00	17	*102.9	29	102	3.5	1	1	0	6
2001—Denver NFL	15	15	451	275	61.0	2827	23	19	6.27	38	71.5	50	173	3.5	1	1	0	6
2002—Denver NFL	13	13	436	291	66.7	3214	15	11	7.37	34	85.6	37	107	2.9	1	1	0	6
2003—Miami NFL	5	5	130	74	56.9	813	5	6	6.25	12	69.2	5	15	3.0	0	0	0	0
2004—Tampa Bay NFL	11	10	336	233	*69.3	2632	20	12	7.83	26	97.5	30	17	0.6	0	0	0	0
Pro totals (7 years)	69	66	2144	1351	63.0	15208	96	71	7.09	154	85.3	201	548	2.7	5	5	0	30

GRIFFIN, CORNELIUS   DT   REDSKINS

PERSONAL: Born December 3, 1976, in Brundidge, Ala. ... 6-3/300.
HIGH SCHOOL: Pike County (Brundidge, Ala.).
JUNIOR COLLEGE: Pearl River Community College (Miss.).
COLLEGE: Alabama.
TRANSACTIONS/CAREER NOTES: Selected by New York Giants in second round (42nd pick overall) of 2000 NFL draft. ... Signed by Giants (July 25, 2000). ... Granted unconditional free agency (March 3, 2004). ... Signed by Washington Redskins (March 4, 2004).
CHAMPIONSHIP GAME EXPERIENCE: Played in NFC championship game (2000 season). ... Played in Super Bowl 35 (2000 season).

| | | | TOTALS | | |
Year Team	G	GS	Tk.	Ast.	Sks.
2000—New York Giants NFL	15	0	20	4	5.0
2001—New York Giants NFL	16	16	47	16	2.5
2002—New York Giants NFL	14	14	32	17	4.0
2003—New York Giants NFL	15	15	39	16	1.0
2004—Washington NFL	15	15	55	15	6.0
Pro totals (5 years)	75	60	193	68	18.5

GRIFFIN, QUENTIN   RB   BRONCOS

PERSONAL: Born January 12, 1981, in Houston, Texas. ... 5-7/195.
HIGH SCHOOL: Aldine-Nimitz (Aldine, Texas).
COLLEGE: Oklahoma.
TRANSACTIONS/CAREER NOTES: Selected by Denver Broncos in fourth round (108th pick overall) of 2003 NFL draft. ... Signed by Broncos (July 24, 2003). ... On injured reserve with knee injury (October 27, 2004-remainder of season).
SINGLE GAME HIGHS (regular season): Attempts—28 (December 21, 2003, vs. Indianapolis); yards—156 (September 12, 2004, vs. Kansas City); and rushing touchdowns—2 (September 12, 2004, vs. Kansas City).
STATISTICAL PLATEAUS: 100-yard rushing games: 2003 (1), 2004 (1). Total: 2.

| | | | RUSHING | | | | RECEIVING | | | | KICKOFF RETURNS | | | | TOTALS | | | |
Year Team	G	GS	Att.	Yds.	Avg.	TD	No.	Yds.	Avg.	TD	No.	Yds.	Avg.	TD	TD	2pt.	Pts.	Fum.
2003—Denver NFL	10	1	94	345	3.7	0	8	61	7.6	0	0	0	0.0	0	0	0	0	3
2004—Denver NFL	6	4	85	311	3.7	2	10	68	6.8	1	4	52	13.0	0	3	0	18	3
Pro totals (2 years)	16	5	179	656	3.7	2	18	129	7.2	1	4	52	13.0	0	3	0	18	6

GRIFFITH, JUSTIN   FB   FALCONS

PERSONAL: Born April 13, 1981, in Magee, Miss. ... 5-11/232. ... Full name: Justin Montrel Griffith.
HIGH SCHOOL: Magee (Sanatorium, Miss.).
COLLEGE: Mississippi State.
TRANSACTIONS/CAREER NOTES: Selected by Atlanta Falcons in fourth round (121st pick overall) of 2003 NFL draft. ... Signed by Falcons (July 21, 2003).
SINGLE GAME HIGHS (regular season): Attempts—9 (December 28, 2003, vs. Jacksonville); yards—38 (December 28, 2003, vs. Jacksonville); and rushing touchdowns—0.

| | | | RUSHING | | | | RECEIVING | | | | TOTALS | | | |
Year Team	G	GS	Att.	Yds.	Avg.	TD	No.	Yds.	Avg.	TD	TD	2pt.	Pts.	Fum.
2003—Atlanta NFL	16	11	38	168	4.4	0	21	122	5.8	2	2	0	12	0
2004—Atlanta NFL	12	11	9	39	4.3	0	22	220	10.0	1	1	0	6	0
Pro totals (2 years)	28	22	47	207	4.4	0	43	342	8.0	3	3	0	18	0

GRIFFITH, ROBERT   S   CARDINALS

PERSONAL: Born November 30, 1970, in Lanham, Md. ... 5-11/200. ... Full name: Robert Otis Griffith.
HIGH SCHOOL: Mount Miguel (Spring Valley, Calif.).
COLLEGE: San Diego State.
TRANSACTIONS/CAREER NOTES: Signed by Sacramento Gold Miners of CFL to practice squad (August 8, 1993). ... Granted free agency after 1993 season. ... Signed as non-drafted free agent by Minnesota Vikings (April 21, 1994). ... Granted free agency (February 14, 1997). ... Re-signed by Vikings (May 7, 1997). ... Granted unconditional free agency (March 1, 2002). ... Signed by Cleveland Browns (March 6, 2002). ... Released by Browns (February 28, 2005). ... Signed by Arizona Cardinals (March 8, 2005).
CHAMPIONSHIP GAME EXPERIENCE: Played in NFC championship game (1998 and 2000 seasons).
HONORS: Named safety on THE SPORTING NEWS NFL All-Pro team (1998). ... Played in Pro Bowl (2000 season).

G

| | | | TOTALS | | | INTERCEPTIONS | | | |
Year Team	G	GS	Tk.	Ast.	Sks.	No.	Yds.	Avg.	TD
1994—Minnesota NFL	15	0	8	3	0.0	0	0	0.0	0
1995—Minnesota NFL	16	1	30	8	0.5	0	0	0.0	0
1996—Minnesota NFL	14	14	78	17	2.0	4	67	16.8	0
1997—Minnesota NFL	16	16	90	25	0.0	2	26	13.0	0
1998—Minnesota NFL	16	16	74	15	0.0	5	25	5.0	0
1999—Minnesota NFL	16	16	94	26	0.0	3	0	0.0	0
2000—Minnesota NFL	16	16	75	29	1.0	1	25	25.0	0
2001—Minnesota NFL	10	9	47	16	0.0	2	25	12.5	0
2002—Cleveland NFL	12	12	62	11	0.0	3	0	0.0	0
2003—Cleveland NFL	16	16	74	19	0.0	2	3	1.5	0
2004—Cleveland NFL	16	16	92	26	1.0	1	18	18.0	0
Pro totals (11 years)	163	132	724	195	8.5	23	189	8.2	0

GROCE, DEJUAN CB RAMS

PERSONAL: Born February 17, 1980, in Garfield Heights, Ohio. ... 5-10/192.
HIGH SCHOOL: St. Edward (Garfield Heights, Ohio).
COLLEGE: Nebraska.
TRANSACTIONS/CAREER NOTES: Selected by St. Louis Rams in fourth round (107th pick overall) of 2003 NFL draft. ... Signed by Rams (July 22, 2003).

			TOTALS			INTERCEPTIONS				PUNT RETURNS				TOTALS			
Year Team	G	GS	Tk.	Ast.	Sks.	No.	Yds.	Avg.	TD	No.	Yds.	Avg.	TD	TD	2pt.	Pts.	Fum.
2003—St. Louis NFL	16	1	11	0	0.0	1	7	7.0	0	19	135	7.1	0	0	0	0	5
2004—St. Louis NFL	11	4	27	0	0.0	0	0	0.0	0	0	0	0.0	0	0	0	0	0
Pro totals (2 years)	27	5	38	0	0.0	1	7	7.0	0	19	135	7.1	0	0	0	0	5

GROSS, JORDAN T PANTHERS

PERSONAL: Born July 20, 1980, in Fruitland, Idaho. ... 6-4/300.
HIGH SCHOOL: Fruitland (Idaho).
COLLEGE: Utah.
TRANSACTIONS/CAREER NOTES: Selected by Carolina Panthers in first round (eighth pick overall) of 2003 NFL draft. ... Signed by Panthers (July 26, 2003).
PLAYING EXPERIENCE: Carolina NFL, 2003-2004. ... Games/Games started: 2003 (16/16), 2004 (16/16). Total: 32/32.
CHAMPIONSHIP GAME EXPERIENCE: Played in NFC championship game (2003 season). ... Played in Super Bowl 38 (2003 season).

GROSSMAN, REX QB BEARS

PERSONAL: Born August 23, 1980, in Bloomington, Ind. ... 6-1/218.
HIGH SCHOOL: Bloomington South (Bloomington, Ind.).
COLLEGE: Florida.
TRANSACTIONS/CAREER NOTES: Selected after junior season by Chicago Bears in first round (22nd pick overall) of 2003 NFL draft. ... Signed by Bears (July 25, 2003). ... On injured reserve with knee injury (September 28, 2004-remainder of season).
SINGLE GAME HIGHS (regular season): Attempts—35 (September 12, 2004, vs. Detroit); completions—21 (September 26, 2004, vs. Minnesota); yards—249 (December 21, 2003, vs. Washington); and touchdown passes—2 (December 21, 2003, vs. Washington).
MISCELLANEOUS: Reguar-season record as starting NFL quarterback: 3-3 (.500).

			PASSING								RUSHING				TOTALS		
Year Team	G	GS	Att.	Cmp.	Pct.	Yds.	TD	Int.	Avg.	Skd.	Rat.	Att.	Yds.	Avg.	TD	TD	2pt.	Pts.
2003—Chicago NFL	3	3	72	38	52.8	437	2	1	6.07	4	74.8	3	-1	-0.3	0	0	0	0
2004—Chicago NFL	3	3	84	47	56.0	607	1	3	7.23	5	67.9	11	48	4.4	1	1	0	6
Pro totals (2 years)	6	6	156	85	54.5	1044	3	4	6.69	9	71.1	14	47	3.4	1	1	0	6

GROVE, JAKE C RAIDERS

PERSONAL: Born January 22, 1980, in Johnson City, Tenn. ... 6-4/300. ... Full name: Charles Jacob Grove.
HIGH SCHOOL: Jefferson Forest (Forest, Va.).
COLLEGE: Virginia Tech.
TRANSACTIONS/CAREER NOTES: Selected by Oakland Raiders in second round (45th pick overall) of 2004 NFL draft. ... Signed by Raiders (July 30, 2004).
PLAYING EXPERIENCE: Oakland NFL, 2004. ... Games/Games started: 2004 (9/8). Total: 9/8.
HONORS: Named center on THE SPORTING NEWS college All-America first team (2003).

GURODE, ANDRE G COWBOYS

PERSONAL: Born March 6, 1978, in Houston, Texas. ... 6-4/314.
HIGH SCHOOL: North Shore (Houston).
COLLEGE: Colorado.
TRANSACTIONS/CAREER NOTES: Selected by Dallas Cowboys in second round (37th pick overall) of 2002 NFL draft. ... Signed by Cowboys (July 26, 2002).
PLAYING EXPERIENCE: Dallas NFL, 2002-2004. ... Games/Games started: 2002 (14/14), 2003 (16/15), 2004 (14/13). Total: 44/42.
HONORS: Named guard on THE SPORTING NEWS college All-America first team (2001).

G

GUTIERREZ, BROCK C

PERSONAL: Born September 25, 1973, in Charlotte, Mich. ... 6-3/304.
HIGH SCHOOL: Charlotte (Mich.).
COLLEGE: Central Michigan.
TRANSACTIONS/CAREER NOTES: Signed as non-drafted free agent by Cincinnati Bengals (April 23, 1996). ... Active for two games (1996). ... Released by Bengals (August 30, 1998). ... Re-signed by Bengals (November 4, 1998). ... Released by Bengals (November 17, 1998). ... Signed by Jacksonville Jaguars to practice squad (November 30, 1998). ... Signed by Bengals off Jaguars practice squad (December 15, 1998). ... Granted free agency (February 11, 2000). ... Re-signed by Bengals (March 17, 2000). ... Released by Bengals (May 27, 2003). ... Signed by San Francisco 49ers (August 16, 2003). ... Granted unconditional free agency (March 3, 2004). ... Re-signed by 49ers (March 31, 2004). ... Granted unconditional free agency (March 2, 2005).
PLAYING EXPERIENCE: Cincinnati NFL, 1997-2002; San Francisco NFL, 2003-2004. ... Games/Games started: 1997 (5/0), 1998 (1/0), 1999 (16/0), 2000 (16/7), 2001 (14/0), 2002 (16/1), 2003 (12/0), 2004 (16/15). Total: 96/23.

HAAYER, ADAM   T   CARDINALS

PERSONAL: Born February 22, 1977, in Wyoming, Minn. ... 6-6/308.
HIGH SCHOOL: Forest Lake (Minn.).
COLLEGE: Minnesota.
TRANSACTIONS/CAREER NOTES: Selected by Tennessee Titans in sixth round (199th pick overall) of 2001 NFL draft. ... Signed by Titans (July 6, 2001). ... On injured reserve with knee injury (August 25, 2001-entire season). ... Claimed on waivers by Minnesota Vikings (August 27, 2002). ... Released by Vikings (August 31, 2003). ... Re-signed by Vikings to practice squad (September 1, 2003). ... Activated (January 7, 2004). ... Did not receive qualifying offer from Vikings (March 2, 2005). ... Signed by Arizona Cardinals (April 25, 2005).
PLAYING EXPERIENCE: Minnesota NFL, 2002-2004. ... Games/Games started: 2002 (4/0), 2004 (4/1). Total: 8/1.

HADDAD, DREW   WR   BILLS

PERSONAL: Born August 15, 1978, in Cleveland, Ohio. ... 5-11/187.
HIGH SCHOOL: St. Ignatius (Westlake, Ohio).
COLLEGE: Buffalo.
TRANSACTIONS/CAREER NOTES: Selected by Buffalo Bills in seventh round (233rd pick overall) of 2000 NFL draft. ... Signed by Bills (July 17, 2000). ... Released by Bills (August 27, 2000). ... Re-signed by Bills to practice squad (August 28, 2000). ... Released by Bills (November 22, 2000). ... Signed by Indianapolis Colts to practice squad (December 7, 2000). ... Activated (January 17, 2001). ... On injured reserve with hamstring injury (October 8, 2001-remainder of season). ... Released by Colts (August 26, 2003). ... Signed by Bills (June 18, 2004). ... Released by Bills (September 5, 2004). ... Re-signed by Bills to practice squad (September 6, 2004). ... Activated (October 15, 2004). ... Released by Bills (November 5, 2004). ... Re-signed by Bills to practice squad (November 9, 2004).
SINGLE GAME HIGHS (regular season): Receptions—1 (November 3, 2002, vs. Tennessee); yards—11 (November 3, 2002, vs. Tennessee); and touchdown receptions—0.

			RECEIVING				PUNT RETURNS				KICKOFF RETURNS				TOTALS		
Year — Team	G	GS	No.	Yds.	Avg.	TD	No.	Yds.	Avg.	TD	No.	Yds.	Avg.	TD	TD 2pt.	Pts. Fum.	
2002—Indianapolis NFL	1	0	1	11	11.0	0	0	0	0.0	0	2	19	9.5	0	0	0	0 0
2004—Buffalo NFL	1	0	0	0	0.0	0	0	0	0.0	0	0	0	0.0	0	0	0	0 0
Pro totals (2 years)	2	0	1	11	11.0	0	0	0	0.0	0	2	19	9.5	0	0	0	0 0

HADNOT, REX   G/C   DOLPHINS

PERSONAL: Born January 28, 1982, in Lufkin, Texas. ... 6-2/323. ... Full name: Rex Hadnot Jr.
HIGH SCHOOL: Lufkin (Texas).
COLLEGE: Houston.
TRANSACTIONS/CAREER NOTES: Selected by Miami Dolphins in sixth round (174th pick overall) of 2004 NFL draft. ... Signed by Dolphins (July 30, 2004).
PLAYING EXPERIENCE: Miami NFL, 2004. ... Games/Games started: 2004 (14/7). Total: 14/7.

HAGGAN, MARIO   LB   BILLS

PERSONAL: Born March 3, 1980, in Clarksdale, Miss. ... 6-3/248. ... Full name: Mario Marcell Haggan.
HIGH SCHOOL: Clarksdale (Miss.).
COLLEGE: Mississippi State.
TRANSACTIONS/CAREER NOTES: Selected by Buffalo Bills in seventh round (228th pick overall) of 2003 NFL draft. ... Signed by Bills (July 22, 2003). ... Released by Bills (September 4, 2003). ... Re-signed by Bills to practice squad (September 8, 2003). ... Activated (November 14, 2003).

			TOTALS			INTERCEPTIONS			
Year — Team	G	GS	Tk.	Ast.	Sks.	No.	Yds.	Avg.	TD
2003—Buffalo NFL	1	0	0	0	0.0	0	0	0.0	0
2004—Buffalo NFL	16	0	1	1	0.0	0	0	0.0	0
Pro totals (2 years)	17	0	1	1	0.0	0	0	0.0	0

HAGGANS, CLARK   LB   STEELERS

PERSONAL: Born January 10, 1977, in Torrance, Calif. ... 6-4/243. ... Full name: Clark Cromwell Haggans.
HIGH SCHOOL: Peninsula (Torrance, Calif.).
COLLEGE: Colorado State.
TRANSACTIONS/CAREER NOTES: Selected by Pittsburgh Steelers in fifth round (137th pick overall) of 2000 NFL draft. ... Signed by Steelers (July 7, 2000). ... Granted free agency (February 28, 2003). ... Re-signed by Steelers (April 21, 2003). ... Granted unconditional free agency (March 3, 2004). ... Re-signed by Steelers (March 6, 2004).
CHAMPIONSHIP GAME EXPERIENCE: Played in AFC championship game (2001 and 2004 seasons).

			TOTALS			INTERCEPTIONS			
Year — Team	G	GS	Tk.	Ast.	Sks.	No.	Yds.	Avg.	TD
2000—Pittsburgh NFL	2	0	0	0	0.0	0	0	0.0	0
2001—Pittsburgh NFL	16	1	3	2	0.0	0	0	0.0	0
2002—Pittsburgh NFL	16	1	17	9	6.5	0	0	0.0	0
2003—Pittsburgh NFL	16	2	11	5	1.0	0	0	0.0	0
2004—Pittsburgh NFL	13	13	30	8	6.0	0	0	0.0	0
Pro totals (5 years)	63	17	61	24	13.5	0	0	0.0	0

H

HAKIM, AZ-ZAHIR WR

PERSONAL: Born June 3, 1977, in Los Angeles, Calif. ... 5-10/189. ... Full name: Az-Zahir Ali Hakim. ... Name pronounced: oz-za-HERE ha-KEEM.
HIGH SCHOOL: Fairfax (Los Angeles).
COLLEGE: San Diego State.
TRANSACTIONS/CAREER NOTES: Selected by St. Louis Rams in fourth round (96th pick overall) of 1998 NFL draft. ... Signed by Rams (July 13, 1998). ... Granted free agency (March 2, 2001). ... Re-signed by Rams (May 23, 2001). ... Granted unconditional free agency (March 1, 2002). ... Signed by Detroit Lions (March 7, 2002). ... On injured reserve with hip injury (November 20, 2002-remainder of season). ... Released by Lions (April 25, 2005).
CHAMPIONSHIP GAME EXPERIENCE: Played in NFC championship game (1999 and 2001 seasons). ... Member of Super Bowl championship team (1999 season). ... Played in Super Bowl 36 (2001 season).
HONORS: Named punt returner on THE SPORTING NEWS NFL All-Pro team (2000).
SINGLE GAME HIGHS (regular season): Receptions—9 (September 8, 2002, vs. Miami); yards—147 (November 5, 2000, vs. Carolina); and touchdown receptions—3 (October 3, 1999, vs. Cincinnati).
STATISTICAL PLATEAUS: 100-yard receiving games: 1999 (1), 2000 (3), 2002 (1), 2004 (2). Total: 7.

				RUSHING				RECEIVING				PUNT RETURNS				KICKOFF RETURNS				TOTALS	
Year Team	G	GS	Att.	Yds.	Avg.	TD	No.	Yds.	Avg.	TD	No.	Yds.	Avg.	TD	No.	Yds.	Avg.	TD	TD	2pt.	Pts.
1998—StL. NFL	9	4	2	30	15.0	1	20	247	12.4	1	0	0	0.0	0	0	0	0.0	0	2	0	12
1999—StL. NFL	15	0	4	44	11.0	0	36	677	18.8	8	∞44	461	10.5	∞1	2	35	17.5	0	9	0	54
2000—StL. NFL	16	4	5	19	3.8	0	53	734	13.8	4	32	‡489	‡15.3	1	1	2	2.0	0	5	0	30
2001—StL. NFL	16	2	11	50	4.5	0	39	374	9.6	3	36	330	9.2	0	0	0	0.0	0	3	0	18
2002—Det. NFL	10	10	4	3	0.8	0	37	541	14.6	3	10	148	14.8	1	0	0	0.0	0	4	0	24
2003—Det. NFL	14	12	3	51	17.0	0	49	449	9.2	4	9	85	9.4	0	0	0	0.0	0	4	1	26
2004—Det. NFL	12	5	1	0	0.0	0	31	533	17.2	3	0	0	0.0	0	0	0	0.0	0	3	0	18
Pro totals (7 years)	92	37	30	197	6.6	1	265	3555	13.4	26	131	1513	11.5	3	3	37	12.3	0	30	1	182

HALEY, JERMAINE DT

PERSONAL: Born February 23, 1973, in Fresno, Calif. ... 6-4/325.
HIGH SCHOOL: Hanford (Calif.).
JUNIOR COLLEGE: Butte College (Calif.).
TRANSACTIONS/CAREER NOTES: Signed by Toronto Argonauts of CFL (May 1998). ... Selected by Miami Dolphins in seventh round (232nd pick overall) of 1999 NFL draft. ... Signed by Dolphins (March 2, 2000). ... Granted free agency (February 28, 2003). ... Tendered offer sheet by Washington Redskins (April 18, 2003). ... Dolphins declined to match offer (April 25, 2003). ... On injured reserve with hand injury (November 24, 2003-remainder of season). ... Released by Redskins (February 22, 2005).

			TOTALS			INTERCEPTIONS			
Year Team	G	GS	Tk.	Ast.	Sks.	No.	Yds.	Avg.	TD
1998—Toronto CFL	16	...	...	...	7.0	0	0	0.0	0
1999—Toronto CFL	15	0	...	...	3.0	1	0	0.0	0
2000—Miami NFL	15	4	15	7	1.5	0	0	0.0	0
2001—Miami NFL	12	5	10	8	0.5	0	0	0.0	0
2002—Miami NFL	16	0	13	14	0.5	1	0	0.0	0
2003—Washington NFL	6	5	11	2	0.0	0	0	0.0	0
2004—Washington NFL	13	1	7	1	1.0	0	0	0.0	0
CFL totals (2 years)	31	0	...	...	10.0	1	0	0.0	0
NFL totals (5 years)	62	15	56	32	3.5	1	0	0.0	0
Pro totals (7 years)	93	15	...	...	13.5	2	0	0.0	0

HALL, CARLOS DE CHIEFS

PERSONAL: Born January 16, 1979, in Marianna, Ark. ... 6-4/261.
HIGH SCHOOL: Lee (Mariana, Ark.).
COLLEGE: Arkansas.
TRANSACTIONS/CAREER NOTES: Selected by Tennessee Titans in seventh round (240th pick overall) of 2002 NFL draft. ... Signed by Titans (July 9, 2002). ... Traded by Titans to Kansas City Chiefs for fifth-round pick (OT Daniel Loper) in 2005 draft (April 5, 2005).
CHAMPIONSHIP GAME EXPERIENCE: Played in AFC championship game (2002 season).

			TOTALS		
Year Team	G	GS	Tk.	Ast.	Sks.
2002—Tennessee NFL	15	13	27	15	8.0
2003—Tennessee NFL	16	4	29	8	3.0
2004—Tennessee NFL	14	14	26	15	2.5
Pro totals (3 years)	45	31	82	38	13.5

HALL, CORY S

PERSONAL: Born December 5, 1976, in Bakersfield, Calif. ... 6-0/213.
HIGH SCHOOL: South (Bakersfield, Calif.).
COLLEGE: Fresno State.
TRANSACTIONS/CAREER NOTES: Selected by Cincinnati Bengals in third round (65th pick overall) of 1999 NFL draft. ... Signed by Bengals (May 7, 1999). ... Granted free agency (March 1, 2002). ... Re-signed by Bengals (April 23, 2002). ... On injured reserve with shoulder injury (December 17, 2002-remainder of season). ... Granted unconditional free agency (February 28, 2003). ... Signed by Atlanta Falcons (March 3, 2003). ... Released by Falcons (February 28, 2005).
CHAMPIONSHIP GAME EXPERIENCE: Played in NFC championship game (2004 season).

H

| Year Team | G | GS | TOTALS | | | INTERCEPTIONS | | | |
			Tk.	Ast.	Sks.	No.	Yds.	Avg.	TD
1999—Cincinnati NFL	16	12	36	13	0.0	1	0	0.0	0
2000—Cincinnati NFL	16	6	36	5	4.0	1	12	12.0	0
2001—Cincinnati NFL	16	15	31	16	0.0	0	0	0.0	0
2002—Cincinnati NFL	14	14	43	15	2.0	1	2	2.0	0
2003—Atlanta NFL	11	10	26	5	0.0	0	0	0.0	0
2004—Atlanta NFL	14	13	42	11	0.0	0	0	0.0	0
Pro totals (6 years)	87	70	214	65	6.0	3	14	4.7	0

HALL, DANTE — WR — CHIEFS

PERSONAL: Born September 20, 1978, in Lufkin, Texas. ... 5-8/187. ... Full name: Damieon Dante Hall.
HIGH SCHOOL: Nimitz (Irving, Texas).
COLLEGE: Texas A&M.
TRANSACTIONS/CAREER NOTES: Selected by Kansas City Chiefs in fifth round (153rd pick overall) of 2000 NFL draft. ... Signed by Chiefs (July 6, 2000). ... Assigned by Chiefs to Scottish Claymores in 2001 NFL Europe enhancement allocation program (February 19, 2001).
HONORS: Played in Pro Bowl (2002-2003 seasons). ... Named punt returner on THE SPORTING NEWS NFL All-Pro team (2003).
RECORDS: Shares NFL single-season record for most kick returns for a touchdown—4 (2003).
POST SEASON RECORDS: Shares NFL postseason single-game record for most touchdowns by kickoff return—1 (January 11, 2004, vs. Indianapolis).
SINGLE GAME HIGHS (regular season): Receptions—11 (December 7, 2003, vs. Denver); yards—143 (December 15, 2002, vs. Denver); and touchdown receptions—2 (December 15, 2002, vs. Denver).
STATISTICAL PLATEAUS: 100-yard receiving games: 2002 (1), 2003 (2). Total: 3.

| Year Team | G | GS | RUSHING | | | | RECEIVING | | | | PUNT RETURNS | | | | KICKOFF RETURNS | | | | TOTALS | | |
			Att.	Yds.	Avg.	TD	No.	Yds.	Avg.	TD	No.	Yds.	Avg.	TD	No.	Yds.	Avg.	TD	TD	2pt.	Pts.
2000—K.C. NFL	5	0	0	0	0.0	0	0	0	0.0	0	6	37	6.2	0	17	358	21.1	0	0	0	0
2001—K.C. NFL	13	0	2	10	5.0	0	0	0	0.0	0	32	235	7.3	0	43	969	22.5	0	0	0	0
2002—K.C. NFL	16	0	11	54	4.9	0	20	322	16.1	3	29	390	13.4	†2	57	1354	23.8	1	6	0	36
2003—K.C. NFL	16	2	16	73	4.6	0	40	423	10.6	1	29	472	*16.3	†2	57	§1478	25.9	†2	5	0	30
2004—K.C. NFL	16	6	8	56	7.0	0	25	230	9.2	0	23	232	10.1	0	*68	*1718	25.3	2	2	0	12
Pro totals (5 years)	66	8	37	193	5.2	0	85	975	11.5	4	119	1366	11.5	4	242	5877	24.3	5	13	0	78

HALL, DEANGELO — CB — FALCONS

PERSONAL: Born November 19, 1983, in Chesapeake, Va. ... 5-10/197. ... Full name: DeAngelo Eugene Hall.
HIGH SCHOOL: Deep Creek (Chesapeake, Va.).
COLLEGE: Virginia Tech.
TRANSACTIONS/CAREER NOTES: Selected after junior season by Atlanta Falcons in first round (eighth pick overall) of 2004 NFL draft. ... Signed by Falcons (August 3, 2004).
CHAMPIONSHIP GAME EXPERIENCE: Played in NFC championship game (2004 season).
HONORS: Named cornerback on THE SPORTING NEWS Freshman All-America fourth team (2001). ... Named cornerback on THE SPORTING NEWS college All-America second team (2003).

| Year Team | G | GS | TOTALS | | | INTERCEPTIONS | | | | PUNT RETURNS | | | | TOTALS | | | |
			Tk.	Ast.	Sks.	No.	Yds.	Avg.	TD	No.	Yds.	Avg.	TD	TD	2pt.	Pts.	Fum.
2004—Atlanta NFL	10	9	30	6	0.5	2	50	25.0	1	0	0	0.0	0	1	0	6	0

HALL, JAMES — DE — LIONS

PERSONAL: Born February 4, 1977, in New Orleans, La. ... 6-2/280.
HIGH SCHOOL: St. Augustine (La.).
COLLEGE: Michigan.
TRANSACTIONS/CAREER NOTES: Signed as non-drafted free agent by Detroit Lions (April 28, 2000). ... Granted free agency (February 28, 2003). ... Re-signed by Lions (May 28, 2003).
HONORS: Named linebacker on THE SPORTING NEWS college All-America third team (1999).

| Year Team | G | GS | TOTALS | | | INTERCEPTIONS | | | |
			Tk.	Ast.	Sks.	No.	Yds.	Avg.	TD
2000—Detroit NFL	5	0	1	0	1.0	0	0	0.0	0
2001—Detroit NFL	15	0	25	8	4.0	0	0	0.0	0
2002—Detroit NFL	16	14	34	15	2.0	0	0	0.0	0
2003—Detroit NFL	16	16	48	14	4.5	0	0	0.0	0
2004—Detroit NFL	16	16	38	10	11.5	1	30	30.0	0
Pro totals (5 years)	68	46	146	47	23.0	1	30	30.0	0

HALL, JOHN — K — REDSKINS

PERSONAL: Born March 17, 1974, in Port Charlotte, Fla. ... 6-3/240.
HIGH SCHOOL: Port Charlotte (Fla.).
COLLEGE: Wisconsin.
TRANSACTIONS/CAREER NOTES: Signed as non-drafted free agent by New York Jets (April 25, 1997). ... Granted free agency (February 11, 2000). ... Re-signed by Jets (April 13, 2000). ... Granted unconditional free agency (February 28, 2003). ... Signed by Washington Redskins (March 2, 2003). ... On injured reserve with quadriceps injury (December 16, 2004-remainder of season).
CHAMPIONSHIP GAME EXPERIENCE: Played in AFC championship game (1998 season).

H

Year	Team	G	FIELD GOALS							TOTALS		
			1-29	30-39	40-49	50+	Tot.	Pct.	Lg.	XPM	XPA	Pts.
1997—New York Jets NFL	16	11-12	11-17	2-6	4-6	28-†41	68.3	†55	36	36	120
1998—New York Jets NFL	16	9-9	9-13	6-10	1-3	25-35	71.4	54	45	46	120
1999—New York Jets NFL	16	3-4	17-17	7-12	0-0	27-33	81.8	48	27	29	108
2000—New York Jets NFL	15	8-9	6-8	6-12	1-3	21-32	65.6	51	30	30	93
2001—New York Jets NFL	16	9-9	5-7	7-9	3-6	24-31	77.4	53	32	32	104
2002—New York Jets NFL	16	9-9	9-11	6-10	0-1	24-31	77.4	46	35	37	107
2003—Washington NFL	16	8-8	7-9	6-9	4-7	25-33	75.8	54	26	27	101
2004—Washington NFL	8	4-4	3-3	1-3	0-1	8-11	72.7	46	13	13	37
Pro totals (8 years)	119	61-64	67-85	41-71	13-27	182-247	73.7	55	244	250	790

HALL, LAMONT   TE   SAINTS

PERSONAL: Born November 16, 1974, in Clover, S.C. ... 6-4/260. ... Full name: James Lamont Hall.
HIGH SCHOOL: Clover (S.C.).
COLLEGE: Clemson.
TRANSACTIONS/CAREER NOTES: Signed as non-drafted free agent by Tampa Bay Buccaneers (April 24, 1998). ... Released by Buccaneers (August 25, 1998). ... Re-signed by Buccaneers to practice squad (October 21, 1998). ... Granted free agency following 1998 season. ... Selected by Rhein Fire in 1999 NFL Europe draft (February 18, 1999). ... Signed by Green Bay Packers (July 7, 1999). ... Traded by Packers with QB Aaron Brooks to New Orleans Saints for LB K.D. Williams and third-round pick (traded to San Francisco) in 2001 draft (July 31, 2000). ... Granted free agency (March 1, 2002). ... Re-signed by Saints (May 31, 2002). ... Granted unconditional free agency (February 28, 2003). ... Signed by Atlanta Falcons (April 1, 2003). ... Released by Falcons (September 1, 2003). ... Signed by New Orleans Saints (May 10, 2004). ... Granted unconditional free agency (March 2, 2005). ... Re-signed by Saints (March 22, 2005).
SINGLE GAME HIGHS (regular season): Receptions—2 (October 22, 2000, vs. Atlanta); yards—20 (October 22, 2000, vs. Atlanta); and touchdown receptions—1 (October 24, 2004, vs. Oakland).

Year	Team	G	GS	RECEIVING				TOTALS			
				No.	Yds.	Avg.	TD	TD	2pt.	Pts.	Fum.
1998—Tampa Bay NFL		Did not play.									
1999—Green Bay NFL	14	0	3	33	11.0	0	0	0	0	0
2000—New Orleans NFL	16	5	5	33	6.6	1	1	0	6	0
2001—New Orleans NFL	16	6	2	15	7.5	0	0	0	0	1
2002—New Orleans NFL	16	1	2	6	3.0	0	0	0	0	0
2004—New Orleans NFL	16	2	1	4	4.0	1	1	0	6	0
Pro totals (5 years)	78	14	13	91	7.0	2	2	0	12	1

HALL, TRAVIS   DE

PERSONAL: Born August 3, 1972, in Kenai, Alaska. ... 6-5/295.
HIGH SCHOOL: West Jordan (Utah).
COLLEGE: Brigham Young.
TRANSACTIONS/CAREER NOTES: Selected by Atlanta Falcons in sixth round (181st pick overall) of 1995 NFL draft. ... Signed by Falcons (June 30, 1995). ... Released by Falcons (February 28, 2005).
CHAMPIONSHIP GAME EXPERIENCE: Played in NFC championship game (1998 season). ... Member of Falcons for NFC championship game (2004 season); inactive. ... Played in Super Bowl 33 (1998 season).

Year	Team	G	GS	TOTALS		
				Tk.	Ast.	Sks.
1995—Atlanta NFL	1	0	0	0	0.0
1996—Atlanta NFL	14	13	44	7	6.0
1997—Atlanta NFL	16	16	61	17	10.5
1998—Atlanta NFL	14	13	39	10	4.5
1999—Atlanta NFL	16	15	36	9	4.5
2000—Atlanta NFL	16	16	45	18	4.5
2001—Atlanta NFL	16	16	39	12	2.5
2002—Atlanta NFL	11	1	14	11	1.0
2003—Atlanta NFL	15	2	32	7	5.0
2004—Atlanta NFL	15	0	23	6	3.0
Pro totals (10 years)	134	92	333	97	41.5

HALLEN, BOB   C/G   CHARGERS

PERSONAL: Born March 9, 1975, in Mentor, Ohio. ... 6-3/305. ... Full name: Robert Joseph Hallen.
HIGH SCHOOL: Mentor (Ohio).
COLLEGE: Kent State.
TRANSACTIONS/CAREER NOTES: Selected by Atlanta Falcons in second round (53rd pick overall) of 1998 NFL draft. ... Signed by Falcons (June 3, 1998). ... Granted unconditional free agency (March 1, 2002). ... Signed by San Diego Chargers (May 2, 2002). ... On injured reserve with pectoral injury (October 8, 2003-remainder of season). ... Granted unconditional free agency (March 3, 2004). ... Signed by New England Patriots (May 11, 2004). ... Released by Patriots (September 8, 2004). ... Signed by Chargers (October 27, 2004). ... Granted unconditional free agency (March 2, 2005). ... Re-signed by Chargers (March 17, 2005).
PLAYING EXPERIENCE: Atlanta NFL, 1998-2001; San Diego NFL, 2002-2004. ... Games/Games started: 1998 (12/0), 1999 (16/14), 2000 (16/5), 2001 (15/12), 2002 (13/11), 2003 (3/2), 2004 (2/0). Total: 77/44.
CHAMPIONSHIP GAME EXPERIENCE: Played in NFC championship game (1998 season). ... Played in Super Bowl 33 (1998 season).

H

HAMBRICK, TROY   RB   CARDINALS

PERSONAL: Born November 6, 1976, in Lacoochee, Fla. ... 6-1/233.
HIGH SCHOOL: Pasco (Fla.).
COLLEGE: Savannah State.
TRANSACTIONS/CAREER NOTES: Signed as non-drafted free agent by Dallas Cowboys (June 1, 2000). ... Released by Cowboys (August 27, 2000). ... Re-signed by Cowboys to practice squad (August 29, 2000). ... Activated (December 8, 2000). ... Released by Cowboys (May 13, 2004). ... Signed by Oakland Raiders (May 17, 2004). ... Traded by Raiders with DE Peppi Zellner to Arizona Cardinals for an undisclosed 2005 draft choice (August 31, 2004). ... On injured reserve with foot injury (November 24, 2004-remainder of season). ... Granted unconditional free agency (March 2, 2005). ... Re-signed by Cardinals (March 7, 2005).
SINGLE GAME HIGHS (regular season): Attempts—33 December 14, 2003, vs. Washington; yards—189 (December 14, 2001, vs. Washington); and rushing touchdowns—2 (December 14, 2003, vs. Washington).
STATISTICAL PLATEAUS: 100-yard rushing games: 2001 (2), 2003 (3). Total: 5.

				RUSHING				RECEIVING				TOTALS			
Year Team	G	GS	Att.	Yds.	Avg.	TD	No.	Yds.	Avg.	TD	TD	2pt.	Pts.	Fum.
2000—Dallas NFL	3	0	6	28	4.7	0	0	0	0.0	0	0	0	0	0
2001—Dallas NFL	16	11	113	579	5.1	2	4	62	15.5	0	2	0	12	1
2002—Dallas NFL	16	0	79	317	4.0	1	21	99	4.7	0	1	0	6	2
2003—Dallas NFL	16	16	275	972	3.5	5	17	99	5.8	0	5	0	30	4
2004—Arizona NFL	10	0	63	283	4.5	1	4	16	4.0	1	2	0	12	0
Pro totals (5 years)	61	27	536	2179	4.1	9	46	276	6.0	1	10	0	60	7

HAMILTON, BEN   C/G   BRONCOS

PERSONAL: Born August 18, 1977, in Minneapolis, Minn. ... 6-4/283. ... Son of Wes Hamilton, guard with Minnesota Vikings (1976-84).
HIGH SCHOOL: Wayzata (Minn.).
COLLEGE: Minnesota.
TRANSACTIONS/CAREER NOTES: Selected by Denver Broncos in fourth round (113th pick overall) of 2001 NFL draft. ... Signed by Broncos (July 10, 2001). ... Granted free agency (March 3, 2004). ... Re-signed by Broncos (May 7, 2004). ... Granted unconditional free agency (March 2, 2005). ... Re-signed by Broncos (March 3, 2005).
PLAYING EXPERIENCE: Denver NFL, 2002-2004. ... Games/Games started: 2002 (16/16), 2003 (16/16), 2004 (16/16). Total: 48/48.
HONORS: Named center on THE SPORTING NEWS college All-America first team (1999 and 2000).

HAMILTON, BOBBY   DE   RAIDERS

PERSONAL: Born July 1, 1971, in Denver, Colo. ... 6-5/285.
HIGH SCHOOL: East Marion (Columbia, Miss.).
COLLEGE: Southern Miss.
TRANSACTIONS/CAREER NOTES: Signed as non-drafted free agent by Seattle Seahawks (April 19, 1994). ... On injured reserve with knee injury (August 17, 1994-entire season). ... Assigned by Seahawks to Amsterdam Admirals in 1995 World League enhancement allocation draft. ... Released by Seahawks (August 15, 1995). ... Signed by New York Jets (June, 1996). ... Released by Jets (August 24, 1996). ... Re-signed by Jets to practice squad (August 26, 1996). ... Activated (September 4, 1996). ... Granted unconditional free agency (February 11, 2000). ... Signed by New England Patriots (July 16, 2000). ... Granted unconditional free agency (March 3, 2004). ... Signed by Oakland Raiders (May 19, 2004). ... Granted unconditional free agency (March 2, 2005). ... Re-signed by Raiders (March 14, 2005).
CHAMPIONSHIP GAME EXPERIENCE: Played in AFC championship game (1998, 2001 and 2003 seasons). ... Member of Super Bowl championship team (2001 and 2003 seasons).

			TOTALS			INTERCEPTIONS			
Year Team	G	GS	Tk.	Ast.	Sks.	No.	Yds.	Avg.	TD
1994—Seattle NFL	Did not play.								
1996—New York Jets NFL	15	11	32	17	4.5	0	0	0.0	0
1997—New York Jets NFL	16	0	13	11	1.0	0	0	0.0	0
1998—New York Jets NFL	16	1	13	8	0.0	0	0	0.0	0
1999—New York Jets NFL	7	0	4	2	0.0	0	0	0.0	0
2000—New England NFL	16	16	41	38	1.5	0	0	0.0	0
2001—New England NFL	16	15	31	21	7.0	0	0	0.0	0
2002—New England NFL	16	15	34	21	2.0	1	0	0.0	0
2003—New England NFL	16	16	30	16	0.0	0	0	0.0	0
2004—Oakland NFL	16	15	35	22	1.0	0	0	0.0	0
Pro totals (9 years)	134	89	233	156	17.0	1	0	0.0	0

HAMILTON, DERRICK   WR   49ERS

PERSONAL: Born November 30, 1981, in Dillon, S.C. ... 6-4/203. ... Full name: Derrick T. Hamilton.
HIGH SCHOOL: Dillon (S.C.).
COLLEGE: Clemson.
TRANSACTIONS/CAREER NOTES: Selected after junior season by San Francisco 49ers in third round (77th pick overall) of 2004 NFL draft. ... Signed by 49ers (July 30, 2004).
HONORS: Named wide receiver on THE SPORTING NEWS Freshman All-America second team (2001).

			RUSHING				RECEIVING				PUNT RETURNS				KICKOFF RETURNS				TOTALS		
Year Team	G	GS	Att.	Yds.	Avg.	TD	No.	Yds.	Avg.	TD	No.	Yds.	Avg.	TD	No.	Yds.	Avg.	TD	TD	2pt.	Pts.
2004—S.F. NFL	2	0	0	0	0.0	0	0	0	0.0	0	0	0	0.0	0	0	0	0.0	0	0	0	0

H

HAMILTON, LAWRENCE   WR   CARDINALS

PERSONAL: Born August 31, 1980, in Marshall, Texas. ... 6-3/204.
HIGH SCHOOL: Marshall (Texas).
COLLEGE: Stephen F. Austin.
TRANSACTIONS/CAREER NOTES: Signed as non-drafted free agent by Arizona Cardinals (April 28, 2003). ... Claimed on waivers by Cincinnati Bengals (August 6, 2003). ... Released by Bengals (October 16, 2003). ... Re-signed by Bengals to practice squad (October 17, 2003). ... Signed by New York Jets off Bengals practice squad (December 8, 2003). ... Claimed on waivers by Arizona Cardinals (August 24, 2004). ... Released by Cardinals (September 5, 2004). ... Re-signed by Cardinals to practice squad (September 6, 2004). ... Activated (December 15, 2004).

| | | | RECEIVING | | | | TOTALS | | | |
Year Team	G	GS	No.	Yds.	Avg.	TD	TD	2pt.	Pts.	Fum.
2003—Cincinnati NFL	5	1	0	0	0.0	0	0	0	0	0
2004—Arizona NFL	1	0	0	0	0.0	0	0	0	0	0
Pro totals (2 years)	6	1	0	0	0.0	0	0	0	0	0

HAMLIN, KEN   S   SEAHAWKS

PERSONAL: Born January 20, 1981, in Memphis, Tenn. ... 6-2/209.
HIGH SCHOOL: Fraysar (Memphis, Tenn.).
COLLEGE: Arkansas.
TRANSACTIONS/CAREER NOTES: Selected after junior season by Seattle Seahawks in second round (42nd pick overall) of 2003 NFL draft. ... Signed by Seahawks (July 24, 2003).

| | | | TOTALS | | | INTERCEPTIONS | | | |
Year Team	G	GS	Tk.	Ast.	Sks.	No.	Yds.	Avg.	TD
2003—Seattle NFL	16	14	76	20	0.0	1	2	2.0	0
2004—Seattle NFL	16	16	63	16	2.0	4	48	12.0	0
Pro totals (2 years)	32	30	139	36	2.0	5	50	10.0	0

HAMPTON, CASEY   DT   STEELERS

PERSONAL: Born September 3, 1977, in Galveston, Texas. ... 6-1/325.
HIGH SCHOOL: Ball (Galveston, Texas).
COLLEGE: Texas.
TRANSACTIONS/CAREER NOTES: Selected by Pittsburgh Steelers in first round (19th pick overall) of 2001 NFL draft. ... Signed by Steelers (July 21, 2001). ... On injured reserve with knee injury (October 20, 2004-remainder of season).
CHAMPIONSHIP GAME EXPERIENCE: Played in AFC championship game (2001 season).
HONORS: Named defensive tackle on THE SPORTING NEWS college All-America second team (1999). ... Named defensive tackle on THE SPORTING NEWS college All-America first team (2000). ... Played in Pro Bowl (2003 season).

| | | | TOTALS | | |
Year Team	G	GS	Tk.	Ast.	Sks.
2001—Pittsburgh NFL	16	11	10	13	1.0
2002—Pittsburgh NFL	16	15	24	17	2.0
2003—Pittsburgh NFL	16	16	27	12	1.0
2004—Pittsburgh NFL	6	6	8	7	0.0
Pro totals (4 years)	54	48	69	49	4.0

HAMPTON, WILLIAM   CB   PANTHERS

PERSONAL: Born March 7, 1975, in Little Rock, Ark. ... 5-10/190.
HIGH SCHOOL: McClellan (Little Rock, Ark.).
COLLEGE: Murray State.
TRANSACTIONS/CAREER NOTES: Signed as non-drafted free agent by Denver Broncos (January 25, 2000). ... Released by Broncos (August 21, 2000). ... Signed by Philadelphia Eagles to practice squad (August 31, 2000). ... Released by Eagles (August 31, 2002). ... Signed by Carolina Panthers (January 13, 2003). ... On injured reserve with knee injury (October 13, 2004-remainder of season).
CHAMPIONSHIP GAME EXPERIENCE: Played in NFC championship game (2001 season). ... Member of Panthers for NFC championship game (2003 season); inactive. ... Member of Panthers for Super Bowl 38 (2003 season); inactive.

| | | | TOTALS | | | INTERCEPTIONS | | | |
Year Team	G	GS	Tk.	Ast.	Sks.	No.	Yds.	Avg.	TD
2000—Philadelphia NFL	Did not play.								
2001—Philadelphia NFL	13	0	6	0	0.0	1	33	33.0	1
2003—Carolina NFL	5	0	2	0	0.0	0	0	0.0	0
2004—Carolina NFL	4	0	0	0	0.0	0	0	0.0	0
Pro totals (3 years)	22	0	8	0	0.0	1	33	33.0	1

HAND, NORMAN   DT

H

PERSONAL: Born September 4, 1972, in Queens, N.Y. ... 6-3/310. ... Full name: Norman L. Hand.
HIGH SCHOOL: Walterboro (S.C.).
JUNIOR COLLEGE: Itawamba Community College (Miss.).
COLLEGE: Mississippi.
TRANSACTIONS/CAREER NOTES: Selected by Miami Dolphins in fifth round (158th pick overall) of 1995 NFL draft. ... Signed by Dolphins (May 17, 1995). ... Inactive for all 16 games (1995). ... Claimed on waivers by San Diego Chargers (August 25, 1997). ... Granted free agency

(February 13, 1998). ... Re-signed by Chargers (July 14, 1998). ... Designated by Chargers as franchise player (February 11, 2000). ... Free agency status changed from franchise to unconditional (February 16, 2000). ... Signed by New Orleans Saints (February 23, 2000). ... On injured reserve with foot injury (January 4, 2002-remainder of season). ... Traded by Saints to Seattle Seahawks for sixth-round pick (WR Kareem Kelly) in 2003 draft (April 27, 2003). ... On injured reserve with arm injury (November 14, 2003-remainder of season). ... Released by Seahawks (March 29, 2004). ... Signed by New York Giants (April 7, 2004). ... On injured reserve with groin injury (December 25, 2004-remainder of season). ... Released by Giants (March 14, 2005).

				TOTALS			INTERCEPTIONS			
Year Team	G	GS	Tk.	Ast.	Sks.	No.	Yds.	Avg.	TD	
1995—Miami NFL	Did not play.									
1996—Miami NFL	9	0	2	3	0.5	0	0	0.0	0	
1997—San Diego NFL	15	1	16	3	1.0	0	0	0.0	0	
1998—San Diego NFL	16	16	42	7	6.0	2	47	23.5	0	
1999—San Diego NFL	14	14	41	14	4.0	0	0	0.0	0	
2000—New Orleans NFL	15	15	44	10	3.0	0	0	0.0	0	
2001—New Orleans NFL	13	13	25	11	3.5	0	0	0.0	0	
2002—New Orleans NFL	16	13	30	9	2.5	0	0	0.0	0	
2003—Seattle NFL	6	4	4	6	1.0	0	0	0.0	0	
2004—New York Giants NFL	11	11	11	4	1.0	0	0	0.0	0	
Pro totals (9 years)	115	87	215	67	22.5	2	47	23.5	0	

HANKTON, CORTEZ   WR   JAGUARS

PERSONAL: Born January 20, 1981, in New Orleans, La. ... 6-0/200.
HIGH SCHOOL: St. Augustine (New Orleans, La.).
COLLEGE: Texas Southern.
TRANSACTIONS/CAREER NOTES: Signed as non-drafted free agent by Jacksonville Jaguars (April 28, 2003).
SINGLE GAME HIGHS (regular season): Receptions—4 (December 7, 2003, vs. Houston); yards—49 (December 7, 2003, vs. Houston); and touchdown receptions—1 (October 17, 2004, vs. Kansas City).

			RECEIVING				TOTALS			
Year Team	G	GS	No.	Yds.	Avg.	TD	TD	2pt.	Pts.	Fum.
2003—Jacksonville NFL	16	0	17	166	9.8	0	0	0	0	0
2004—Jacksonville NFL	12	0	9	81	9.0	2	2	0	12	0
Pro totals (2 years)	28	0	26	247	9.5	2	2	0	12	0

HANKTON, KARL   WR   PANTHERS

PERSONAL: Born July 24, 1970, in New Orleans, La. ... 6-2/202.
HIGH SCHOOL: De La Salle (New Orleans), then Valley Forge Military Academy (Wayne, Penn.).
COLLEGE: Trinity (Ill.).
TRANSACTIONS/CAREER NOTES: Signed as non-drafted free agent by Washington Redskins (April 1, 1997). ... Released by Redskins (February 25, 1998). ... Signed by Philadelphia Eagles (April 9, 1998). ... Released by Eagles (August 31, 1998). ... Re-signed by Eagles to practice squad (September 2, 1998). ... Released by Eagles (August 31, 1998). ... Re-signed by Eagles to practice squad (September 25, 1998). ... Activated (September 25, 1998). ... Released by Eagles (September 7, 1999). ... Signed by Carolina Panthers (February 29, 2000). ... Granted free agency (March 2, 2001).
CHAMPIONSHIP GAME EXPERIENCE: Played in NFC championship game (2003 season). ... Played in Super Bowl 38 (2003 season).
SINGLE GAME HIGHS (regular season): Receptions—2 (September 13, 2004, vs. Green Bay); yards—38 (October 13, 2002, vs. Dallas); and touchdown receptions—0.

			RECEIVING				TOTALS			
Year Team	G	GS	No.	Yds.	Avg.	TD	TD	2pt.	Pts.	Fum.
1998—Philadelphia NFL	10	0	0	0	0.0	0	0	0	0	0
2000—Carolina NFL	16	0	4	38	9.5	0	0	0	0	0
2001—Carolina NFL	11	0	0	0	0.0	0	0	0	0	0
2002—Carolina NFL	16	1	9	146	16.2	0	0	0	0	0
2003—Carolina NFL	14	0	2	27	13.5	0	0	0	0	0
2004—Carolina NFL	15	0	2	25	12.5	0	0	0	0	0
Pro totals (6 years)	82	1	17	236	13.9	0	0	0	0	0

HANNAM, RYAN   TE   SEAHAWKS

PERSONAL: Born February 24, 1980, in St. Ansgar, Iowa. ... 6-2/248.
HIGH SCHOOL: St. Ansgar (Iowa).
COLLEGE: Northern Iowa.
TRANSACTIONS/CAREER NOTES: Selected by Seattle Seahawks in fifth round (169th pick overall) of 2002 NFL draft. ... Signed by Seahawks (July 25, 2002). ... On injured reserve with knee injury (October 31, 2003-remainder of season). ... Granted free agency (March 2, 2005). ... Re-signed by Seahawks (March 15, 2005).
SINGLE GAME HIGHS (regular season): Receptions—2 (January 2, 2005, vs. Atlanta); yards—44 (December 12, 2004, vs. Minnesota); and touchdown receptions—1 (November 10, 2002, vs. Arizona).

			RECEIVING				KICKOFF RETURNS				TOTALS			
Year Team	G	GS	No.	Yds.	Avg.	TD	No.	Yds.	Avg.	TD	TD	2pt.	Pts.	Fum.
2002—Seattle NFL	14	0	1	16	16.0	1	0	0	0.0	0	1	0	6	0
2003—Seattle NFL	5	0	0	0	0.0	0	1	17	17.0	0	0	0	0	0
2004—Seattle NFL	16	0	8	110	13.8	0	0	0	0.0	0	0	0	0	0
Pro totals (3 years)	35	0	9	126	14.0	1	1	17	17.0	0	1	0	6	0

H

HANSON, CHRIS   P   JAGUARS

PERSONAL: Born October 25, 1976, in Riverdale, Ga. ... 6-1/223.
HIGH SCHOOL: East Coweta (Ga.).
COLLEGE: Marshall.
TRANSACTIONS/CAREER NOTES: Signed as non-drafted free agent by Cleveland Browns (April 23, 1999). ... Claimed on waivers by Green Bay Packers (September 1, 1999). ... Released by Packers (September 14, 1999). ... Re-signed by Packers to practice squad (September 16, 1999). ... Released by Packers (October 12, 1999). ... Signed by Miami Dolphins (February 8, 2000). ... Assigned by Dolphins to Barcelona Dragons in 2000 NFL Europe enhancement allocation program (February 18, 2000). ... On injured reserve with knee injury (July 21, 2000-entire season). ... Released by Dolphins (August 15, 2001). ... Signed by Jacksonville Jaguars (August 18, 2001). ... On injured reserve with leg injury (October 10, 2003-remainder of season).
HONORS: Played in Pro Bowl (2002 season).

				PUNTING			
Year Team	G	No.	Yds.	Avg.	Net avg.	In. 20	Blk.
1999—Green Bay NFL	1	4	157	39.2	38.5	0	0
2000—Miami NFL	Did not play.						
2001—Jacksonville NFL	16	82	3577	43.6	37.1	24	0
2002—Jacksonville NFL	16	81	3583	§44.2	§37.6	27	0
2003—Jacksonville NFL	5	23	1001	43.5	31.1	4	1
2004—Jacksonville NFL	16	84	3592	42.8	35.5	28	0
Pro totals (5 years)	54	274	11910	43.5	36.3	83	1

HANSON, JASON   K   LIONS

PERSONAL: Born June 17, 1970, in Spokane, Wash. ... 5-11/182. ... Full name: Jason Douglas Hanson.
HIGH SCHOOL: Mead (Spokane, Wash.).
COLLEGE: Washington State.
TRANSACTIONS/CAREER NOTES: Selected by Detroit Lions in second round (56th pick overall) of 1992 NFL draft. ... Signed by Lions (July 23, 1992). ... Designated by Lions as transition player (February 15, 1994).
HONORS: Named kicker on THE SPORTING NEWS college All-America first team (1989). ... Named kicker on THE SPORTING NEWS NFL All-Pro team (1993). ... Played in Pro Bowl (1997 and 1999 season).
MISCELLANEOUS: Detroit Lions all-time scoring leader (1,336 points).

				FIELD GOALS							TOTALS		
Year Team	G	1-29	30-39	40-49	50+	Tot.	Pct.	Lg.		XPM	XPA	Pts.	
1992—Detroit NFL	16	5-5	10-10	4-6	2-5	21-26	80.8	52		30	30	93	
1993—Detroit NFL	16	9-9	15-15	7-12	3-7	‡34-‡43	79.1	53		28	28	‡130	
1994—Detroit NFL	16	6-7	7-7	5-8	0-5	18-27	66.7	49		39	40	93	
1995—Detroit NFL	16	6-6	16-17	5-10	1-1	28-34	82.4	56		*48	†48	132	
1996—Detroit NFL	16	4-4	4-5	3-5	1-3	12-17	70.6	51		36	36	72	
1997—Detroit NFL	16	10-10	8-9	5-5	3-5	26-29	89.7	†55		39	40	117	
1998—Detroit NFL	16	8-8	7-7	13-15	1-3	29-33	87.9	51		27	29	114	
1999—Detroit NFL	16	8-8	4-4	10-12	4-8	26-∞32	81.3	52		28	29	106	
2000—Detroit NFL	16	8-9	10-12	4-7	2-2	24-30	80.0	54		29	29	101	
2001—Detroit NFL	16	3-3	8-8	6-12	4-7	21-30	70.0	54		23	23	86	
2002—Detroit NFL	16	8-8	8-9	7-8	0-3	23-28	82.1	49		31	31	100	
2003—Detroit NFL	16	7-7	6-6	5-6	4-4	22-23	‡95.7	54		26	27	92	
2004—Detroit NFL	16	9-9	10-11	5-8	0-0	24-28	85.7	48		28	28	100	
Pro totals (13 years)	208	91-93	113-120	79-114	25-53	308-380	81.1	56		412	418	1336	

HANSON, JOSELIO   CB   49ERS

PERSONAL: Born August 13, 1981, in Inglewood, Calif. ... 5-9/175.
HIGH SCHOOL: St. Bernard (Playa del Rey, Calif.).
JUNIOR COLLEGE: El Camino (Torrance, Calif.).
COLLEGE: Texas Tech.
TRANSACTIONS/CAREER NOTES: Signed as non-drafted free agent by San Francisco 49ers (May 2, 2003). ... Released by 49ers (August 31, 2003). ... Re-signed by 49ers (January 16, 2004). ... Released by 49ers (September 25, 2004). ... Re-signed by 49ers (September 28, 2004).

			TOTALS			INTERCEPTIONS			
Year Team	G	GS	Tk.	Ast.	Sks.	No.	Yds.	Avg.	TD
2004—San Francisco NFL	13	3	18	2	1.0	0	0	0.0	0

HAPE, PATRICK   TE   BRONCOS

PERSONAL: Born June 6, 1974, in Killen, Ala. ... 6-4/262. ... Full name: Patrick Stephen Hape.
HIGH SCHOOL: Brooks (Killen, Ala.).
COLLEGE: Alabama.
TRANSACTIONS/CAREER NOTES: Selected by Tampa Bay Buccaneers in fifth round (137th pick overall) of 1997 NFL draft. ... Signed by Buccaneers (July 20, 1997). ... Granted free agency (February 11, 2000). ... Re-signed by Buccaneers (July 23, 2000). ... Granted unconditional free agency (March 2, 2001). ... Signed by Denver Broncos (March 14, 2001). ... Granted unconditional free agency (March 3, 2004). ... Re-signed by Broncos (April 15, 2004). ... Granted unconditional free agency (March 2, 2005). ... Re-signed by Broncos (April 1, 2005).
CHAMPIONSHIP GAME EXPERIENCE: Played in NFC championship game (1999 season).
SINGLE GAME HIGHS (regular season): Receptions—2 (January 2, 2005, vs. Indianapolis); yards—35 (December 16, 2001, vs. Kansas City); and touchdown receptions—1 (January 2, 2005, vs. Indianapolis). ... Rushing attempts—2 (September 10, 2001, vs. New York Giants); yards—1 (August 31, 1997, vs. San Francisco); and rushing touchdowns—0.

H

Year Team	G	GS	RECEIVING				TOTALS			
			No.	Yds.	Avg.	TD	TD	2pt.	Pts.	Fum.
1997—Tampa Bay NFL	14	3	4	22	5.5	1	1	0	6	1
1998—Tampa Bay NFL	16	2	4	27	6.8	0	0	1	2	1
1999—Tampa Bay NFL	15	1	5	12	2.4	1	1	0	6	0
2000—Tampa Bay NFL	16	2	6	39	6.5	0	0	0	0	0
2001—Denver NFL	15	8	15	96	6.4	3	3	0	18	0
2002—Denver NFL	16	0	6	26	4.3	2	2	0	12	0
2003—Denver NFL	16	0	3	30	10.0	0	0	0	0	0
2004—Denver NFL	16	5	8	35	4.4	4	4	0	24	0
Pro totals (8 years)	124	21	51	287	5.6	11	11	1	68	2

HARDWICK, NICK　　　　C　　　　CHARGERS

PERSONAL: Born September 12, 1981, in Franklin, Ind. ... 6-4/295. ... Full name: Nicholas Adam Hardwick.
HIGH SCHOOL: Lawrence North (Indianapolis, Ind.).
COLLEGE: Purdue.
TRANSACTIONS/CAREER NOTES: Selected by San Diego Chargers in third round (66th pick overall) of 2004 NFL draft. ... Signed by Chargers (July 28, 2004).
PLAYING EXPERIENCE: San Diego NFL, 2004. ... Games/Games started: 2004 (14/14). Total: 14/14.

HARDY, KEVIN　　　　LB

PERSONAL: Born July 24, 1973, in Evansville, Ind. ... 6-4/259. ... Full name: Kevin Lamont Hardy.
HIGH SCHOOL: Harrison (Evansville, Ind.).
COLLEGE: Illinois.
TRANSACTIONS/CAREER NOTES: Selected by Jacksonville Jaguars in first round (second pick overall) of 1996 NFL draft. ... Signed by Jaguars (July 17, 1996). ... On injured reserve with knee injury (December 11, 2001-remainder of season). ... Granted unconditional free agency (March 1, 2002). ... Signed by Dallas Cowboys (April 14, 2002). ... Granted unconditional free agency (February 28, 2003). ... Signed by Cincinnati Bengals (March 7, 2003). ... Released by Bengals (May 3, 2005).
CHAMPIONSHIP GAME EXPERIENCE: Played in AFC championship game (1996 and 1999 seasons).
HONORS: Butkus Award winner (1995). ... Named linebacker on THE SPORTING NEWS college All-America first team (1995). ... Named linebacker on THE SPORTING NEWS NFL All-Pro team (1999). ... Played in Pro Bowl (1999 season).

Year Team	G	GS	TOTALS			INTERCEPTIONS			
			Tk.	Ast.	Sks.	No.	Yds.	Avg.	TD
1996—Jacksonville NFL	16	15	64	22	5.5	2	19	9.5	0
1997—Jacksonville NFL	13	11	48	7	2.5	0	0	0.0	0
1998—Jacksonville NFL	16	16	87	25	1.5	2	40	20.0	0
1999—Jacksonville NFL	16	16	74	24	10.5	0	0	0.0	0
2000—Jacksonville NFL	16	16	72	14	3.0	1	0	0.0	0
2001—Jacksonville NFL	9	9	57	12	5.5	0	0	0.0	0
2002—Dallas NFL	16	15	60	15	2.0	0	0	0.0	0
2003—Cincinnati NFL	16	16	59	33	1.5	0	0	0.0	0
2004—Cincinnati NFL	16	14	42	27	4.0	0	0	0.0	0
Pro totals (9 years)	134	128	563	179	36.0	5	59	11.8	0

HARGROVE, ANTHONY　　　　DE　　　　RAMS

PERSONAL: Born July 20, 1983, in Brooklyn, N.Y. ... 6-3/269. ... Full name: Anthony La'Ron Hargrove.
HIGH SCHOOL: Port Charlotte (Punta Gorde, Fla.).
COLLEGE: Georgia Tech.
TRANSACTIONS/CAREER NOTES: Selected after junior season by St. Louis Rams in third round (91st pick overall) of 2004 NFL draft. ... Signed by Rams (July 27, 2004).

Year Team	G	GS	TOTALS		
			Tk.	Ast.	Sks.
2004—St. Louis NFL	15	2	21	6	1.0

HARPER, ALAN　　　　DT　　　　JETS

PERSONAL: Born September 6, 1979, in Fontana, Calif. ... 6-1/285.
HIGH SCHOOL: Fontana (Calif.).
COLLEGE: Fresno State.
TRANSACTIONS/CAREER NOTES: Selected by New York Jets in fourth round (121st pick overall) of 2002 NFL draft. ... Signed by Jets (July 25, 2002). ... Inactive for all 16 games (2002). ... Assigned by Jets to Scottish Claymores in 2004 NFL Europe enhancement allocation program (February 9, 2004). ... Released by Jets (September 5, 2004). ... Re-signed by Jets to practice squad (September 6, 2004). ... Activated (September 27, 2004).
HONORS: Named defensive tackle on THE SPORTING NEWS college All-America second team (2001).

Year Team	G	GS	TOTALS			INTERCEPTIONS			
			Tk.	Ast.	Sks.	No.	Yds.	Avg.	TD
2004—New York Jets NFL	11	0	3	2	0.0	0	0	0.0	0

HARPER, DEVERON　　　　CB

PERSONAL: Born November 15, 1977, in Orangeburg, S.C. ... 5-11/200. ... Full name: Deveron Alfredo Harper.
HIGH SCHOOL: Orangeburg-Wilkinson (Orangeburg, S.C.).
COLLEGE: Notre Dame.

TRANSACTIONS/CAREER NOTES: Signed as non-drafted free agent by Carolina Panthers (April 17, 2000). ... Released by Panthers (August 1, 2002). ... Selected by Scottish Claymores in 2003 NFL Europe draft (February 5, 2003). ... Signed by New Orleans Saints (July 14, 2003). ... Released by Saints (October 12, 2004).

Year Team	G	GS	TOTALS			INTERCEPTIONS			
			Tk.	Ast.	Sks.	No.	Yds.	Avg.	TD
2000—Carolina NFL	16	0	0	0	0.0	0	0	0.0	0
2001—Carolina NFL	8	1	3	0	0.0	0	0	0.0	0
2003—New Orleans NFL	14	0	2	1	0.0	0	0	0.0	0
2004—New Orleans NFL	5	0	2	0	0.0	0	0	0.0	0
Pro totals (4 years)	43	1	7	1	0.0	0	0	0.0	0

HARPER, NICK   CB   COLTS

PERSONAL: Born September 10, 1974, in Baldwin, Ga. ... 5-10/182. ... Full name: Nicholas Necosi Harper.
HIGH SCHOOL: Baldwin (Milledgeville, Ga.).
COLLEGE: Fort Valley State.
TRANSACTIONS/CAREER NOTES: Signed as non-drafted free agent by Indianapolis Colts (January 16, 2001). ... Granted free agency (March 3, 2004). ... Re-signed by Colts (April 23, 2004). ... Granted unconditional free agency (March 2, 2005). ... Re-signed by Colts (April 15, 2005).
CHAMPIONSHIP GAME EXPERIENCE: Played in AFC championship game (2003 season).

Year Team	G	GS	TOTALS			INTERCEPTIONS			
			Tk.	Ast.	Sks.	No.	Yds.	Avg.	TD
2001—Indianapolis NFL	13	2	19	4	0.0	2	17	8.5	0
2002—Indianapolis NFL	16	1	35	5	0.0	0	0	0.0	0
2003—Indianapolis NFL	16	13	82	13	0.0	4	121	30.3	1
2004—Indianapolis NFL	14	14	58	19	0.0	3	12	4.0	0
Pro totals (4 years)	59	30	194	41	0.0	9	150	16.7	1

HARRINGTON, JOEY   QB   LIONS

PERSONAL: Born October 21, 1978, in Portland, Ore. ... 6-4/220. ... Full name: John Joseph Harrington.
HIGH SCHOOL: Central Catholic (Portland, Ore.).
COLLEGE: Oregon.
TRANSACTIONS/CAREER NOTES: Selected by Detroit Lions in first round (third pick overall) of 2002 NFL draft. ... Signed by Lions (July 23, 2002).
HONORS: Named quarterback on THE SPORTING NEWS college All-America second team (2001).
SINGLE GAME HIGHS (regular season): Attempts—55 (September 14, 2003, vs. Green Bay); completions—33 (January 2, 2005, vs. Tennessee); yards—361 (December 19, 2004, vs. Minnesota); and touchdown passes—4 (September 7, 2003, vs. Arizona).
STATISTICAL PLATEAUS: 300-yard passing games: 2002 (1), 2004 (2). Total: 3.
MISCELLANEOUS: Regular-season record as starting NFL quarterback: 14-30 (.318).

Year Team	G	GS	PASSING									RUSHING				TOTALS		
			Att.	Cmp.	Pct.	Yds.	TD	Int.	Avg.	Skd.	Rat.	Att.	Yds.	Avg.	TD	TD	2pt.	Pts.
2002—Detroit NFL	14	12	429	215	50.1	2294	12	16	5.35	8	59.9	7	4	0.6	0	0	0	0
2003—Detroit NFL	16	16	554	309	55.8	2880	17	†22	5.20	9	63.9	30	86	2.9	0	0	0	0
2004—Detroit NFL	16	16	489	274	56.0	3047	19	12	6.23	36	77.5	48	175	3.6	0	0	0	0
Pro totals (3 years)	46	44	1472	798	54.2	8221	48	50	5.58	53	67.2	85	265	3.1	0	0	0	0

HARRIS, AL   CB   PACKERS

PERSONAL: Born December 7, 1974, in Pompano Beach, Fla. ... 6-1/185. ... Full name: Alshinard Harris.
HIGH SCHOOL: Ely (Pompano Beach, Fla.).
JUNIOR COLLEGE: Trinity Valley Community College (Texas).
COLLEGE: Texas A&M-Kingsville.
TRANSACTIONS/CAREER NOTES: Selected by Tampa Bay Buccaneers in sixth round (169th pick overall) of 1997 NFL draft. ... Signed by Buccaneers (July 1, 1997). ... Released by Buccaneers (August 24, 1997). ... Re-signed by Buccaneers to practice squad (August 26, 1997). ... Claimed on waivers by Philadelphia Eagles (August 31, 1998). ... Traded by Eagles to Green Bay Packers for second-round pick (traded to San Diego) in 2003 draft (March 1, 2003).
CHAMPIONSHIP GAME EXPERIENCE: Played in NFC championship game (2001 and 2002 seasons).

Year Team	G	GS	TOTALS			INTERCEPTIONS			
			Tk.	Ast.	Sks.	No.	Yds.	Avg.	TD
1998—Philadelphia NFL	16	7	40	1	0.0	0	0	0.0	0
1999—Philadelphia NFL	16	6	32	6	0.0	4	‡151	37.7	1
2000—Philadelphia NFL	16	4	25	2	0.0	0	1	0.0	0
2001—Philadelphia NFL	16	2	20	2	0.0	2	22	11.0	0
2002—Philadelphia NFL	16	2	22	2	0.0	1	0	0.0	0
2003—Green Bay NFL	16	16	46	2	0.0	3	89	29.7	1
2004—Green Bay NFL	16	16	56	6	0.0	1	29	29.0	0
Pro totals (7 years)	112	53	241	21	0.0	11	292	26.5	2

HARRIS, ARLEN   RB   RAMS

PERSONAL: Born April 22, 1980, in Chester, Pa. ... 5-10/212. ... Full name: Arlen Quincy Harris.
HIGH SCHOOL: Downingtown (Pa.).
COLLEGE: Virginia.
TRANSACTIONS/CAREER NOTES: Signed as non-drafted free agent by St. Louis Rams (April 27, 2003).

SINGLE GAME HIGHS (regular season): Attempts—34 (September 7, 2003, vs. Pittsburgh); yards—85 (October 19, 2003, vs. Green Bay); and rushing touchdowns—3 (October 26, 2003, vs. Pittsburgh).

			RUSHING				RECEIVING				PUNT RETURNS				KICKOFF RETURNS				TOTALS		
Year Team	G	GS	Att.	Yds.	Avg.	TD	No.	Yds.	Avg.	TD	No.	Yds.	Avg.	TD	No.	Yds.	Avg.	TD	TD	2pt.	Pts.
2003—StL. NFL	16	2	85	255	3.0	4	15	102	6.8	0	7	36	5.1	0	51	1175	23.0	0	4	0	24
2004—StL. NFL	14	1	20	63	3.2	0	4	44	11.0	0	0	0	0.0	0	47	951	20.2	0	0	0	0
Pro totals (2 years) ..	30	3	105	318	3.0	4	19	146	7.7	0	7	36	5.1	0	98	2126	21.7	0	4	0	24

HARRIS, JOEY — RB — PANTHERS

PERSONAL: Born December 18, 1980, in Houston, Texas. ... 5-10/205. ... Full name: Joseph Andreas Harris.
HIGH SCHOOL: Klein Oak (Texas).
COLLEGE: Purdue.
TRANSACTIONS/CAREER NOTES: Signed as non-drafted free agent by Carolina Panthers (April 30, 2004). ... Released by Panthers (September 5, 2004). ... Re-signed by Panthers to practice squad (September 7, 2004). ... Activated (October 13, 2004). ... On injured reserve with hamstring injury (November 19, 2004-remainder of season).
SINGLE GAME HIGHS (regular season): Attempts—9 (October 31, 2004, vs. Seattle); yards—45 (October 31, 2004, vs. Seattle); and rushing touchdowns—0.

			RUSHING				TOTALS			
Year Team	G	GS	Att.	Yds.	Avg.	TD	TD	2pt.	Pts.	Fum.
2004—Carolina NFL...	4	0	15	53	3.5	0	0	0	0	0

HARRIS, KWAME — T — 49ERS

PERSONAL: Born March 15, 1982, in Jamaica. ... 6-7/310.
HIGH SCHOOL: Newark (Del.).
COLLEGE: Stanford.
TRANSACTIONS/CAREER NOTES: Selected after junior season by San Francisco 49ers in first round (26th pick overall) of 2003 NFL draft. ... Signed by 49ers (July 25, 2003).
PLAYING EXPERIENCE: San Francisco NFL, 2003-2004. ... Games/Games started: 2003 (14/5), 2004 (14/7). Total: 28/12.

HARRIS, NAPOLEON — LB — VIKINGS

PERSONAL: Born February 25, 1979, in Chicago, Ill. ... 6-2/255. ... Full name: Napoleon Bill Harris.
HIGH SCHOOL: Thornton (Harvey, Ill.).
COLLEGE: Northwestern.
TRANSACTIONS/CAREER NOTES: Selected by Oakland Raiders in first round (23rd pick overall) of 2002 NFL draft. ... Signed by Raiders (July 19, 2002). ... Traded by Raiders with first- (WR Troy Williamson) and seventh- (CB Adrian Ward) round picks in 2005 draft to Minnesota Vikings for WR Randy Moss (March 2, 2005).
CHAMPIONSHIP GAME EXPERIENCE: Played in AFC championship game (2002 season). ... Played in Super Bowl 37 (2002 season).

			TOTALS			INTERCEPTIONS			
Year Team	G	GS	Tk.	Ast.	Sks.	No.	Yds.	Avg.	TD
2002—Oakland NFL..	15	13	59	22	0.5	0	0	0.0	0
2003—Oakland NFL..	16	16	75	34	2.0	0	0	0.0	0
2004—Oakland NFL..	14	9	46	14	0.0	0	0	0.0	0
Pro totals (3 years)	45	38	180	70	2.5	0	0	0.0	0

HARRIS, NICK — P — LIONS

PERSONAL: Born July 23, 1978, in Phoenix, Ariz. ... 6-2/218.
HIGH SCHOOL: Westview (Phoenix).
COLLEGE: California.
TRANSACTIONS/CAREER NOTES: Selected by Denver Broncos in fourth round (120th pick overall) of 2001 NFL draft. ... Signed by Broncos (May 22, 2001). ... Claimed on waivers by Cincinnati Bengals (August 29, 2001). ... Waived by Bengals (October 7, 2003). ... Signed by Detroit Lions (October 15, 2003).

		PUNTING					
Year Team	G	No.	Yds.	Avg.	Net avg.	In. 20	Blk.
2001—Cincinnati NFL..	16	84	3372	40.1	33.9	21	1
2002—Cincinnati NFL..	15	65	2608	40.1	31.4	11	1
2003—Cincinnati NFL..	5	28	1084	38.7	30.0	5	0
—Detroit NFL..	11	63	2531	40.2	33.1	11	1
2004—Detroit NFL..	16	92	3765	40.9	34.2	32	1
Pro totals (4 years)	63	332	13360	40.2	33.0	80	4

HARRIS, QUENTIN — S — CARDINALS

PERSONAL: Born January 26, 1977, in Wilkes-Barre, Pa. ... 6-1/214. ... Full name: Quentin Hugh Harris.
HIGH SCHOOL: Wilkes-Barre (Pa.).
COLLEGE: Syracuse.
TRANSACTIONS/CAREER NOTES: Signed as non-drafted free agent by Arizona Cardinals (April 22, 2002). ... Released by Cardinals (September 1, 2002). ... Re-signed by Cardinals to practice squad (September 3, 2002). ... Activated (November 14, 2002). ... Granted free agency (March 2, 2005). ... Re-signed by Cardinals (April 7, 2005).

Year Team	G	GS	TOTALS Tk.	Ast.	Sks.	INTERCEPTIONS No.	Yds.	Avg.	TD
2002—Arizona NFL	6	0	0	0	0.0	0	0	0.0	0
2003—Arizona NFL	16	1	5	0	0.0	0	0	0.0	0
2004—Arizona NFL	16	4	21	2	1.0	1	-1	-1.0	0
Pro totals (3 years)	38	5	26	2	1.0	1	-1	-1.0	0

HARRIS, TOMMIE DT BEARS

PERSONAL: Born April 29, 1983, in Killeen, Texas. ... 6-3/300.
HIGH SCHOOL: Ellison (Killeen, Texas).
COLLEGE: Oklahoma.
TRANSACTIONS/CAREER NOTES: Selected after junior season by Chicago Bears in first round (14th pick overall) of 2004 NFL draft. ... Signed by Bears (July 28, 2004).
HONORS: Lombardi Award winner (2003). ... Named defensive tackle on THE SPORTING NEWS Freshman All-America first team (2001). ... Named defensive tackle on THE SPORTING NEWS college All-America second team (2002) and first team (2003).

Year Team	G	GS	TOTALS Tk.	Ast.	Sks.
2004—Chicago NFL	16	16	29	15	3.5

HARRIS, WALT CB REDSKINS

PERSONAL: Born August 10, 1974, in LaGrange, Ga. ... 5-11/192. ... Full name: Walter Lee Harris.
HIGH SCHOOL: La Grange (Ga.).
COLLEGE: Mississippi State.
TRANSACTIONS/CAREER NOTES: Selected by Chicago Bears in first round (13th pick overall) of 1996 NFL draft. ... Signed by Bears (July 11, 1996). ... On injured reserve with knee injury (December 22, 1998-remainder of season). ... On injured reserve with knee injury (December 22, 2000-remainder of season). ... Granted unconditional free agency (March 2, 2001). ... Re-signed by Bears (April 25, 2001). ... Granted unconditional free agency (March 1, 2002). ... Signed by Indianapolis Colts (March 15, 2002). ... Released by Colts (February 27, 2004). ... Signed by Washington Redskins (March 18, 2004).
CHAMPIONSHIP GAME EXPERIENCE: Played in AFC championship game (2003 season).

Year Team	G	GS	TOTALS Tk.	Ast.	Sks.	INTERCEPTIONS No.	Yds.	Avg.	TD
1996—Chicago NFL	15	13	84	14	0.0	2	0	0.0	0
1997—Chicago NFL	16	16	76	7	0.0	5	30	6.0	0
1998—Chicago NFL	14	14	64	5	0.0	4	41	10.3	1
1999—Chicago NFL	15	15	60	10	1.0	1	-1	-1.0	0
2000—Chicago NFL	12	12	33	9	0.0	2	35	17.5	1
2001—Chicago NFL	15	13	49	2	0.0	1	45	45.0	1
2002—Indianapolis NFL	15	15	35	9	0.0	2	0	0.0	0
2003—Indianapolis NFL	16	15	36	19	0.0	0	0	0.0	0
2004—Washington NFL	16	2	16	2	0.0	2	31	15.5	0
Pro totals (9 years)	134	115	453	77	1.0	19	181	9.5	3

HARRISON, JAMES LB STEELERS

PERSONAL: Born May 4, 1978, in Akron, Ohio. ... 6-0/242. ... Full name: James Harrison Jr.
HIGH SCHOOL: Coventry (Akron, Ohio).
COLLEGE: Kent State.
TRANSACTIONS/CAREER NOTES: Signed as non-drafted free agent by Pittsburgh Steelers (April 22, 2002). ... Released by Steelers (September 1, 2002). ... Re-signed by Steelers to practice squad (September 3, 2002). ... Activated (December 17, 2002). ... Released by Steelers (September 3, 2003). ... Re-signed by Steelers to practice squad (September 17, 2003). ... Released by Steelers from practice squad (October 7, 2003). ... Signed by Baltimore Ravens (2003). ... Assigned by Ravens to Rhein Fire in 2004 NFL Europe enhancement allocation program (February 9, 2004). ... Released by Ravens (June 17, 2004). ... Signed by Pittsburgh Steelers (July 26, 2004).
CHAMPIONSHIP GAME EXPERIENCE: Played in AFC championship game (2004 season).

Year Team	G	GS	TOTALS Tk.	Ast.	Sks.	INTERCEPTIONS No.	Yds.	Avg.	TD
2002—Pittsburgh NFL	1	0	0	0	0.0	0	0	0.0	0
2004—Pittsburgh NFL	16	4	20	2	1.0	0	0	0.0	0
Pro totals (2 years)	17	4	20	2	1.0	0	0	0.0	0

HARRISON, MARVIN WR COLTS

PERSONAL: Born August 25, 1972, in Philadelphia, Pa. ... 6-0/175. ... Full name: Marvin Daniel Harrison.
HIGH SCHOOL: Roman Catholic (Philadelphia).
COLLEGE: Syracuse.
TRANSACTIONS/CAREER NOTES: Selected by Indianapolis Colts in first round (19th pick overall) of 1996 NFL draft. ... Signed by Colts (July 8, 1996). ... On injured reserve with shoulder injury (December 2, 1998-remainder of season).
CHAMPIONSHIP GAME EXPERIENCE: Played in AFC championship game (2003 season).
HONORS: Named kick returner on THE SPORTING NEWS All-America first team (1995). ... Named wide receiver on THE SPORTING NEWS NFL All-Pro team (1999-2004). ... Played in Pro Bowl (1999-2004 seasons).
RECORDS: Holds NFL single-season record for most pass receptions—143 (2002).
SINGLE GAME HIGHS (regular season): Receptions—14 (November 17, 2002, vs. Dallas); yards—196 (September 26, 1999, vs. San Diego); and touchdown receptions—3 (November 25, 2004, vs. Detroit).

STATISTICAL PLATEAUS: 100-yard receiving games: 1996 (2), 1998 (2), 1999 (9), 2000 (8), 2001 (6), 2002 (10), 2003 (6), 2004 (4). Total: 47.

MISCELLANEOUS: Holds Colts franchise all-time records for most receptions (845), most yards receiving (11,185) and most touchdown receptions (98).

			RECEIVING				PUNT RETURNS				TOTALS			
Year Team	G	GS	No.	Yds.	Avg.	TD	No.	Yds.	Avg.	TD	TD	2pt.	Pts.	Fum.
1996—Indianapolis NFL	16	15	64	836	13.1	8	18	177	9.8	0	8	0	48	1
1997—Indianapolis NFL	16	15	73	866	11.9	6	0	0	0.0	0	6	2	40	2
1998—Indianapolis NFL	12	12	59	776	13.2	7	0	0	0.0	0	7	1	44	0
1999—Indianapolis NFL	16	16	115	*1663	14.5	§12	0	0	0.0	0	12	1	74	2
2000—Indianapolis NFL	16	16	†102	1413	13.9	§14	0	0	0.0	0	14	0	84	2
2001—Indianapolis NFL	16	16	109	§1524	14.0	§15	0	0	0.0	0	15	0	90	0
2002—Indianapolis NFL	16	16	*143	*1722	12.0	11	0	0	0.0	0	11	1	68	0
2003—Indianapolis NFL	15	15	94	1272	13.5	10	0	0	0.0	0	10	0	60	2
2004—Indianapolis NFL	16	16	86	1113	12.9	§15	0	0	0.0	0	15	0	90	1
Pro totals (9 years)	139	137	845	11185	13.2	98	18	177	9.8	0	98	5	598	10

HARRISON, RODNEY   S   PATRIOTS

PERSONAL: Born December 15, 1972, in Markham, Ill. ... 6-1/220. ... Full name: Rodney Scott Harrison.
HIGH SCHOOL: Marian Catholic (Chicago Heights, Ill.).
COLLEGE: Western Illinois.
TRANSACTIONS/CAREER NOTES: Selected after junior season by San Diego Chargers in fifth round (145th pick overall) of 1994 NFL draft. ... Signed by Chargers (June 29, 1994). ... Released by Chargers (February 27, 2003). ... Signed by New England Patriots (March 12, 2003).
CHAMPIONSHIP GAME EXPERIENCE: Played in AFC championship game (1994, 2003 and 2004 seasons). ... Played in Super Bowl 29 (1994 season). ... Member of Super Bowl championship team (2003 and 2004 seasons).
HONORS: Named safety on THE SPORTING NEWS NFL All-Pro team (1998 and 2001). ... Played in Pro Bowl (1998 and 2001 seasons).

			TOTALS			INTERCEPTIONS			
Year Team	G	GS	Tk.	Ast.	Sks.	No.	Yds.	Avg.	TD
1994—San Diego NFL	15	0	0	0	0.0	0	0	0.0	0
1995—San Diego NFL	11	0	21	3	0.0	5	22	4.4	0
1996—San Diego NFL	16	16	105	20	1.0	5	56	11.2	0
1997—San Diego NFL	16	16	96	36	4.0	2	75	37.5	1
1998—San Diego NFL	16	16	89	20	4.0	3	42	14.0	0
1999—San Diego NFL	6	6	30	11	1.0	1	0	0.0	0
2000—San Diego NFL	16	16	101	26	6.0	6	97	16.2	1
2001—San Diego NFL	14	14	91	17	3.5	2	51	25.5	0
2002—San Diego NFL	13	13	69	19	2.0	2	2	1.0	0
2003—New England NFL	16	16	93	32	3.0	3	0	0.0	0
2004—New England NFL	16	16	89	40	3.0	2	12	6.0	0
Pro totals (11 years)	155	129	784	229	27.5	31	357	11.5	2

HART, CLINTON   S   CHARGERS

PERSONAL: Born July 20, 1977, in Dade City, Fla. ... 6-0/205. ... Full name: Clinton Glenn Hart.
HIGH SCHOOL: South Sumter (Bushnell, Fla.).
JUNIOR COLLEGE: Central Florida Community College.
TRANSACTIONS/CAREER NOTES: Signed as non-drafted free agent by Philadelphia Eagles (January 29, 2002). ... Assigned by Eagles to 2002 NFL Europe enhancement allocation program (February 7, 2002). ... Re-signed by Eagles (January 30, 2003). ... Claimed on waivers by San Diego Chargers (September 15, 2004).
CHAMPIONSHIP GAME EXPERIENCE: Played in NFC championship game (2003 season).

			TOTALS			INTERCEPTIONS			
Year Team	G	GS	Tk.	Ast.	Sks.	No.	Yds.	Avg.	TD
2003—Philadelphia NFL	16	9	38	8	1.0	0	0	0.0	0
2004—San Diego NFL	14	0	5	4	0.0	1	13	13.0	0
Pro totals (2 years)	30	9	43	12	1.0	1	13	13.0	0

HARTINGS, JEFF   C   STEELERS

PERSONAL: Born September 7, 1972, in St. Henry, Ohio. ... 6-3/299. ... Full name: Jeffrey Allen Hartings.
HIGH SCHOOL: St. Henry (Ohio).
COLLEGE: Penn State.
TRANSACTIONS/CAREER NOTES: Selected by Detroit Lions in first round (23rd pick overall) of 1996 NFL draft. ... Signed by Lions (September 27, 1996). ... Granted unconditional free agency (March 2, 2001). ... Signed by Pittsburgh Steelers (March 8, 2001).
PLAYING EXPERIENCE: Detroit NFL, 1996-2000; Pittsburgh NFL, 2001-2004. ... Games/Games started: 1996 (11/10), 1997 (16/16), 1998 (13/13), 1999 (16/16), 2000 (16/16), 2001 (16/16), 2002 (13/11), 2003 (16/16), 2004 (16/16). Total: 133/130.
CHAMPIONSHIP GAME EXPERIENCE: Played in AFC championship game (2001 and 2004 seasons).
HONORS: Named offensive lineman on THE SPORTING NEWS college All-America second team (1994). ... Named offensive lineman on THE SPORTING NEWS college All-America first team (1995). ... Named center on THE SPORTING NEWS NFL All-Pro team (2004). ... Played in Pro Bowl (2004 season).

HARTS, SHAUNARD   S   CHIEFS

PERSONAL: Born August 4, 1978, in Pittsburg, Calif. ... 6-0/210.
HIGH SCHOOL: Pittsburg (Calif.).
COLLEGE: Boise State.

TRANSACTIONS/CAREER NOTES: Selected by Kansas City Chiefs in seventh round (212th pick overall) of 2001 NFL draft. ... Signed by Chiefs (July 3, 2001). ... Released by Chiefs (September 2, 2001). ... Re-signed by Chiefs to practice squad (September 3, 2001). ... Activated (December 22, 2001). ... Granted free agency (March 2, 2005). ... Re-signed by Chiefs (April 18, 2005).

				TOTALS			INTERCEPTIONS			
Year Team	G	GS	Tk.	Ast.	Sks.	No.	Yds.	Avg.	TD
2001—Kansas City NFL	3	0	0	0	0.0	0	0	0.0	0
2002—Kansas City NFL	16	11	71	9	2.0	0	0	0.0	0
2003—Kansas City NFL	16	0	11	5	0.0	2	39	19.5	1
2004—Kansas City NFL	16	6	37	7	0.0	0	0	0.0	0
Pro totals (4 years)	51	17	119	21	2.0	2	39	19.5	1

HARTSOCK, BEN — TE — COLTS

PERSONAL: Born July 5, 1980, in Chillicothe, Ohio. ... 6-4/262.
HIGH SCHOOL: Uniote (Chillicothe, Ohio).
COLLEGE: Ohio State.
TRANSACTIONS/CAREER NOTES: Selected by Indianapolis Colts in third round (68th pick overall) of 2004 NFL draft. ... Signed by Colts (July 30, 2004).
SINGLE GAME HIGHS (regular season): Receptions—2 (January 2, 2005, vs. Denver); yards—21 (December 26, 2004, vs. San Diego); and touchdown receptions—0.

			RECEIVING				TOTALS			
Year Team	G	GS	No.	Yds.	Avg.	TD	TD	2pt.	Pts.	Fum.
2004—Indianapolis NFL	16	3	4	33	8.3	0	0	0	0	0

HARTWELL, EDGERTON — LB — FALCONS

PERSONAL: Born May 27, 1978, in Las Vegas, Nev. ... 6-1/250.
HIGH SCHOOL: Cheyenne (Las Vegas, Nev.).
COLLEGE: Western Illinois.
TRANSACTIONS/CAREER NOTES: Selected by Baltimore Ravens in fourth round (126th pick overall) of 2001 NFL draft. ... Signed by Ravens (June 8, 2001). ... Granted free agency (March 3, 2004). ... Re-signed by Ravens (May 24, 2004). ... Granted unconditional free agency (March 2, 2005). ... Signed by Atlanta Falcons (March 22, 2005).

			TOTALS			INTERCEPTIONS			
Year Team	G	GS	Tk.	Ast.	Sks.	No.	Yds.	Avg.	TD
2001—Baltimore NFL	16	0	0	0	0.0	0	0	0.0	0
2002—Baltimore NFL	16	16	105	39	3.0	0	0	0.0	0
2003—Baltimore NFL	16	15	68	26	3.0	1	26	26.0	0
2004—Baltimore NFL	16	15	56	41	0.0	0	0	0.0	0
Pro totals (4 years)	64	46	229	106	6.0	1	26	26.0	0

HARTWIG, JUSTIN — C/G

PERSONAL: Born November 21, 1978, in Mankato, Minn. ... 6-4/305.
HIGH SCHOOL: Valley (West Des Moines, Iowa).
COLLEGE: Kansas.
TRANSACTIONS/CAREER NOTES: Selected by Tennessee Titans in sixth round (187th pick overall) of 2002 NFL draft. ... Signed by Titans (July 11, 2002). ... Granted free agency (March 2, 2005).
PLAYING EXPERIENCE: Tennessee NFL, 2002-2004. ... Games/Games started: 2002 (3/0), 2003 (16/16), 2004 (15/15). Total: 34/31.
CHAMPIONSHIP GAME EXPERIENCE: Member of Titans for AFC championship game (2002 season); inactive.

HASSELBECK, MATT — QB — SEAHAWKS

PERSONAL: Born September 25, 1975, in Westwood, Mass. ... 6-4/223. ... Full name: Matthew Michael Hasselbeck. ... Son of Don Hasselbeck, tight end with New England Patriots (1977-85); and brother of Tim Hasselbeck, quarterback, New York Giants.
HIGH SCHOOL: Xaverian Brothers (Westwood, Mass.).
COLLEGE: Boston College.
TRANSACTIONS/CAREER NOTES: Selected by Green Bay Packers in sixth round (187th pick overall) of 1998 NFL draft. ... Signed by Packers (July 17, 1998). ... Released by Packers (September 3, 1998). ... Re-signed by Packers to practice squad (September 5, 1998). ... Traded by Packers with first-round pick (G Steve Hutchinson) in 2001 draft to Seattle Seahawks for first-round pick (DE Jamal Reynolds) in 2001 draft (March 2, 2001).
HONORS: Played in Pro Bowl (2003 season).
SINGLE GAME HIGHS (regular season): Attempts—55 (December 1, 2002, vs. San Francisco); completions—36 (December 29, 2002, vs. San Diego); passing yards—449 (December 29, 2002, vs. San Diego); and touchdown passes—5 (November 23, 2003, vs. Baltimore).
STATISTICAL PLATEAUS: 300-yard passing games: 2002 (4), 2003 (4), 2004 (3). Total: 11.
MISCELLANEOUS: Regular-season record as starting NFL quarterback: 27-25 (.519). ... Post-season record as starting NFL quarterback: 0-2 (.000).

			PASSING								RUSHING				TOTALS		
Year Team	G	GS	Att.	Cmp.	Pct.	Yds.	TD	Int.	Avg.	Skd.	Rat.	Att.	Yds.	Avg.	TD	TD	2pt.	Pts.
1999—Green Bay NFL	16	0	10	3	30.0	41	1	0	4.10	1	77.5	6	15	2.5	0	0	0	0
2000—Green Bay NFL	16	0	19	10	52.6	104	1	0	5.47	1	86.3	4	-5	-1.2	0	0	0	0
2001—Seattle NFL	13	12	321	176	54.8	2023	7	8	6.30	28	70.9	40	141	3.5	0	0	0	0
2002—Seattle NFL	16	10	419	267	‡63.7	3075	15	10	7.34	26	87.8	40	202	5.1	1	1	1	8
2003—Seattle NFL	16	16	513	313	61.0	3841	26	15	7.49	42	88.8	36	125	3.5	2	2	0	12
2004—Seattle NFL	14	14	474	279	58.9	3382	22	15	7.14	30	83.1	27	90	3.3	1	1	0	6
Pro totals (6 years)	91	52	1756	1048	59.7	12466	72	48	7.10	138	83.7	153	568	3.7	4	4	1	26

H

HASSELBECK, TIM   QB   GIANTS

PERSONAL: Born April 6, 1978, in Norfolk, Mass. ... 6-1/211. ... Son of Don Hasselbeck, tight end with New England Patriots (1977-85); and brother of Matt Hasselbeck, quarterback, Seattle Seahawks.
HIGH SCHOOL: Xaverian Brothers (Westwood, Mass.).
COLLEGE: Boston College.
TRANSACTIONS/CAREER NOTES: Signed as non-drafted free agent by Buffalo Bills (April 24, 2001). ... Released by Bills (July 23, 2001). ... Signed by Baltimore Ravens (August 1, 2001). ... Released by Ravens (August 24, 2001). ... Signed by Philadelphia Eagles (February 6, 2002). ... Assigned by Eagles to Berlin Thunder in 2002 NFL Europe enhancement allocation program (February 12, 2002). ... Released by Eagles (September 1, 2002). ... Signed by Carolina Panthers to practice squad (October 22, 2002). ... Activated (October 25, 2002). ... Released by Panthers (October 29, 2002). ... Re-signed by Eagles to practice squad (November 19, 2002). ... Activated (November 27, 2002). ... Released by Eagles (August 31, 2003). ... Signed by Washington Redskins (October 23, 2003). ... Inactive for all 16 games (2004). ... Granted free agency (March 2, 2005). ... Re-signed by Redskins (April 19, 2005). ... Claimed on waivers by New York Giants (May 9, 2005).
CHAMPIONSHIP GAME EXPERIENCE: Member of Eagles for NFC championship game (2002 season); inactive.
SINGLE GAME HIGHS (regular season): Attempts—42 (November 30, 2003, vs. New Orleans); completions—22 (November 30, 2003, vs. New Orleans); yards—231 (November 30, 2003, vs. New Orleans); and touchdown passes—2 (December 21, 2003).
MISCELLANEOUS: Regular-season record as starting NFL quarterback: 1-4 (.200).

				PASSING								RUSHING				TOTALS		
Year Team	G	GS	Att.	Cmp.	Pct.	Yds.	TD	Int.	Avg.	Skd.	Rat.	Att.	Yds.	Avg.	TD	TD	2pt.	Pts.
2002_Philadelphia NFL	2	0	0	0	0.0	0	0	0	0.00	0	0.0	0	0	0.0	0	0	0	0
2003_Washington NFL	7	5	177	95	53.7	1012	5	7	5.72	9	63.6	15	41	2.7	0	0	0	0
2004_Washington NFL	Did not play.																	
Pro totals (2 years)	9	5	177	95	53.7	1012	5	7	5.72	9	63.6	15	41	2.7	0	0	0	0

HAWKINS, ARTRELL   CB

PERSONAL: Born November 24, 1976, in Johnstown, Pa. ... 5-10/190.
HIGH SCHOOL: Bishop McCort (Johnstown, Pa.).
COLLEGE: Cincinnati.
TRANSACTIONS/CAREER NOTES: Selected by Cincinnati Bengals in second round (43rd pick overall) of 1998 NFL draft. ... Signed by Bengals (May 14, 1998). ... Granted free agency (March 2, 2001). ... Re-signed by Bengals (April 4, 2001). ... Granted unconditional free agency (March 1, 2002). ... Re-signed by Bengals (March 18, 2002). ... Released by Bengals (March 5, 2004). ... Signed by Carolina Panthers (March 10, 2004). ... Released by Panthers (March 1, 2005).

			TOTALS			INTERCEPTIONS			
Year Team	G	GS	Tk.	Ast.	Sks.	No.	Yds.	Avg.	TD
1998—Cincinnati NFL	16	16	65	5	1.0	3	21	7.0	0
1999—Cincinnati NFL	14	13	61	7	0.0	0	0	0.0	0
2000—Cincinnati NFL	16	6	43	4	0.0	0	0	0.0	0
2001—Cincinnati NFL	14	13	49	10	0.0	3	26	8.7	0
2002—Cincinnati NFL	15	15	69	7	2.0	2	102	51.0	1
2003—Cincinnati NFL	14	9	50	5	0.0	1	8	8.0	0
2004—Carolina NFL	14	4	24	5	0.0	1	9	9.0	0
Pro totals (7 years)	103	76	361	43	3.0	10	166	16.6	1

HAWTHORNE, MICHAEL   S   RAMS

PERSONAL: Born January 26, 1977, in Sarasota, Fla. ... 6-3/204. ... Full name: Michael Seneca Hawthorne.
HIGH SCHOOL: Booker (Sarasota, Fla.).
COLLEGE: Purdue.
TRANSACTIONS/CAREER NOTES: Selected by New Orleans Saints in sixth round (195th pick overall) of 2000 NFL draft. ... Signed by Saints (June 23, 2000). ... On injured reserve with knee injury (December 22, 2002-remainder of season). ... Granted free agency (February 28, 2003). ... Re-signed by Saints (May 7, 2003). ... Waived by Saints (September 10, 2003). ... Signed by Green Bay Packers (September 15, 2003). ... Granted unconditional free agency (March 3, 2004). ... Re-signed by Packers (March 26, 2004). ... Released by Packers (March 4, 2005). ... Signed by St. Louis Rams (April 11, 2005).

			TOTALS			INTERCEPTIONS			
Year Team	G	GS	Tk.	Ast.	Sks.	No.	Yds.	Avg.	TD
2000—New Orleans NFL	11	1	6	1	0.0	0	0	0.0	0
2001—New Orleans NFL	11	2	15	3	0.0	0	0	0.0	0
2002—New Orleans NFL	6	4	25	9	0.0	1	0	0.0	0
2003—Green Bay NFL	14	2	22	6	1.0	2	8	4.0	0
2004—Green Bay NFL	16	5	26	8	0.0	0	0	0.0	0
Pro totals (5 years)	58	14	94	27	1.0	3	8	2.7	0

HAYES, GERALD   LB   CARDINALS

PERSONAL: Born October 10, 1980, in Paterson, N.J. ... 6-1/242.
HIGH SCHOOL: Passaic County Technical Institute (Passaic, N.J.).
COLLEGE: Pittsburgh.
TRANSACTIONS/CAREER NOTES: Selected by Arizona Cardinals in third round (70th pick overall) of 2003 NFL draft. ... Signed by Cardinals (June 24, 2003).

			TOTALS			INTERCEPTIONS			
Year Team	G	GS	Tk.	Ast.	Sks.	No.	Yds.	Avg.	TD
2003—Arizona NFL	12	2	19	2	0.0	0	0	0.0	0
2004—Arizona NFL	16	1	12	3	0.0	0	0	0.0	0
Pro totals (2 years)	28	3	31	5	0.0	0	0	0.0	0

H

HAYNES, MICHAEL   DE   BEARS

PERSONAL: Born September 13, 1980, in Brooklyn, N.Y. ... 6-3/274. ... Full name: Michael Washington Augustis Haynes Jr.
HIGH SCHOOL: Balboa (Panama City, Fla.).
COLLEGE: Penn State.
TRANSACTIONS/CAREER NOTES: Selected by Chicago Bears in first round (14th pick overall) of 2003 NFL draft. ... Signed by Bears (July 25, 2003).

Year Team	G	GS	TOTALS Tk.	Ast.	Sks.	INTERCEPTIONS No.	Yds.	Avg.	TD
2003—Chicago NFL	16	0	18	4	2.0	0	0	0.0	0
2004—Chicago NFL	16	4	25	6	2.0	1	45	45.0	1
Pro totals (2 years)	32	4	43	10	4.0	1	45	45.0	1

HAYNES, VERRON   RB   STEELERS

PERSONAL: Born February 17, 1979, in Woodstock, Ga. ... 5-9/222.
HIGH SCHOOL: North Springs (Atlanta).
COLLEGE: Georgia.
TRANSACTIONS/CAREER NOTES: Selected by Pittsburgh Steelers in fifth round (166th pick overall) of 2002 NFL draft. ... Signed by Steelers (July 24, 2002). ... On injured reserve with broken leg (December 17, 2002-remainder of season). ... On injured reserve with knee injury (December 10, 2003-remainder of season). ... Granted free agency (March 2, 2005). ... Re-signed by Steelers (April 26, 2005).
CHAMPIONSHIP GAME EXPERIENCE: Played in AFC championship game (2004 season).
SINGLE GAME HIGHS (regular season): Attempts—12 (November 7, 2004, vs. Philadelphia); yards—61 (December 26, 2004, vs. Baltimore); and rushing touchdowns—0.

Year Team	G	GS	RUSHING Att.	Yds.	Avg.	TD	RECEIVING No.	Yds.	Avg.	TD	TOTALS TD	2pt.	Pts.	Fum.
2002—Pittsburgh NFL	14	0	10	51	5.1	0	3	10	3.3	0	0	0	0	0
2003—Pittsburgh NFL	12	0	20	63	3.2	0	7	57	8.1	0	0	0	0	2
2004—Pittsburgh NFL	13	0	55	272	4.9	0	18	142	7.9	2	2	0	12	0
Pro totals (3 years)	39	0	85	386	4.5	0	28	209	7.5	2	2	0	12	2

HAYNESWORTH, ALBERT   DT   TITANS

PERSONAL: Born June 17, 1981, in Hartsville, S.C. ... 6-6/320. ... Full name: Albert Haynesworth III.
HIGH SCHOOL: Hartsville (S.C.).
COLLEGE: Tennessee.
TRANSACTIONS/CAREER NOTES: Selected after junior season by Tennessee Titans in first round (15th pick overall) of 2002 NFL draft. ... Signed by Titans (July 29, 2002).
CHAMPIONSHIP GAME EXPERIENCE: Played in AFC championship game (2002 season).

Year Team	G	GS	TOTALS Tk.	Ast.	Sks.
2002—Tennessee NFL	16	3	21	9	1.0
2003—Tennessee NFL	12	11	21	11	2.5
2004—Tennessee NFL	10	10	26	11	1.0
Pro totals (3 years)	38	24	68	31	4.5

HAYWARD, REGGIE   DE   JAGUARS

PERSONAL: Born March 14, 1979, in Chicago, Ill. ... 6-5/270.
HIGH SCHOOL: Thornridge (Dolton, Ill.).
COLLEGE: Iowa State.
TRANSACTIONS/CAREER NOTES: Selected by Denver Broncos in third round (87th pick overall) of 2001 NFL draft. ... Signed by Broncos (July 26, 2001). ... On injured reserve with hand injury (December 4, 2002-remainder of season). ... Granted free agency (March 3, 2004). ... Re-signed by Broncos (April 9, 2004). ... Granted unconditional free agency (March 2, 2005). ... Signed by Jacksonville Jaguars (March 2, 2005).

Year Team	G	GS	TOTALS Tk.	Ast.	Sks.	INTERCEPTIONS No.	Yds.	Avg.	TD
2001—Denver NFL	6	2	15	3	3.0	0	0	0.0	0
2002—Denver NFL	9	0	6	3	0.0	0	0	0.0	0
2003—Denver NFL	16	2	24	4	8.5	0	0	0.0	0
2004—Denver NFL	16	15	31	12	10.5	1	76	76.0	0
Pro totals (4 years)	47	19	76	22	22.0	1	76	76.0	0

HEAP, TODD   TE   RAVENS

PERSONAL: Born March 16, 1980, in Mesa, Ariz. ... 6-5/252. ... Full name: Todd Benjamin Heap.
HIGH SCHOOL: Mountain View (Mesa, Ariz.).
COLLEGE: Arizona State.
TRANSACTIONS/CAREER NOTES: Selected after junior season by Baltimore Ravens in first round (31st pick overall) of 2001 NFL draft. ... Signed by Ravens (July 28, 2001).
HONORS: Named tight end on THE SPORTING NEWS college All-America first team (2000). ... Played in Pro Bowl (2002 and 2003 seasons).
SINGLE GAME HIGHS (regular season): Receptions—9 (September 12, 2004, vs. Cleveland); yards—146 (December 29, 2002, vs. Pittsburgh); and touchdown receptions—2 (December 12, 2004, vs. New York Giants).
STATISTICAL PLATEAUS: 100-yard receiving games: 2002 (1), 2003 (1). Total: 2.

H

Year Team	G	GS	No.	Yds.	Avg.	TD	TD	2pt.	Pts.	Fum.
				RECEIVING				TOTALS		
2001—Baltimore NFL	12	7	16	206	12.9	1	1	0	6	1
2002—Baltimore NFL	16	16	68	836	12.3	6	6	1	38	0
2003—Baltimore NFL	16	16	57	693	12.2	3	3	*4	26	1
2004—Baltimore NFL	6	6	27	303	11.2	3	3	0	18	0
Pro totals (4 years)	50	45	168	2038	12.1	13	13	5	88	2

HEARD, RONNIE — S — FALCONS

PERSONAL: Born October 5, 1976, in Bay City, Texas. ... 6-3/215.
HIGH SCHOOL: Brazoswood (Clute, Texas).
COLLEGE: Mississippi.
TRANSACTIONS/CAREER NOTES: Signed as non-drafted free agent by San Francisco 49ers (April 20, 2000). ... Released by 49ers (August 27, 2000). ... Re-signed by 49ers to practice squad (August 29, 2000). ... Activated (October 16, 2000). ... Granted free agency (February 28, 2003). ... Released by 49ers (March 23, 2003). ... Re-signed by 49ers (May 16, 2003). ... Granted unconditional free agency (March 3, 2004). ... Re-signed by 49ers (March 4, 2004). ... Granted unconditional free agency (March 2, 2005). ... Signed by Atlanta Falcons (March 18, 2005).

Year Team	G	GS	Tk.	Ast.	Sks.	No.	Yds.	Avg.	TD
			TOTALS			INTERCEPTIONS			
2000—San Francisco NFL	13	3	13	3	2.0	0	0	0.0	0
2001—San Francisco NFL	16	0	24	6	1.0	0	0	0.0	0
2002—San Francisco NFL	12	6	34	8	0.0	4	60	15.0	0
2003—San Francisco NFL	12	1	7	4	0.5	1	0	0.0	0
2004—San Francisco NFL	16	14	56	12	0.0	1	14	14.0	0
Pro totals (5 years)	69	24	134	33	3.5	6	74	12.3	0

HEARST, GARRISON — RB

PERSONAL: Born January 4, 1971, in Lincolnton, Ga. ... 5-11/215. ... Full name: Gerald Garrison Hearst.
HIGH SCHOOL: Lincoln County (Lincolnton, Ga.).
COLLEGE: Georgia.
TRANSACTIONS/CAREER NOTES: Selected after junior season by Phoenix Cardinals in first round (third pick overall) of 1993 NFL draft. ... Signed by Cardinals (August 28, 1993). ... On injured reserve with knee injury (November 4, 1993-remainder of season). ... Cardinals franchise renamed Arizona Cardinals for 1994 season. ... On physically unable to perform list with knee injury (August 23-October 13, 1994). ... Granted free agency (February 16, 1996). ... Re-signed by Cardinals (May 23, 1996). ... Claimed on waivers by Cincinnati Bengals (August 21, 1996). ... Granted unconditional free agency (February 14, 1997). ... Signed by San Francisco 49ers (March 7, 1997). ... On physically unable to perform list with leg injury (July 30, 1999-entire season). ... On physically unable to perform list with leg injury (August 22-November 21, 2000). ... Granted unconditional free agency (March 1, 2002). ... Re-signed by 49ers (March 19, 2002). ... Released by 49ers (February 26, 2004). ... Signed by Denver Broncos (March 24, 2004). ... On injured reserve with hand injury (December 28, 2004-remainder of season). ... Granted unconditional free agency (March 2, 2005).
CHAMPIONSHIP GAME EXPERIENCE: Played in NFC championship game (1997 season).
HONORS: Doak Walker Award winner (1992). ... Named running back on THE SPORTING NEWS college All-America first team (1992). ... Named to play in Pro Bowl (1998 season); replaced by Emmitt Smith due to injury. ... Played in Pro Bowl (2001 season).
SINGLE GAME HIGHS (regular season): Attempts—31 (December 1, 2002, vs. Seattle); yards—198 (December 14, 1998, vs. Detroit); and rushing touchdowns—3 (December 1, 2002, vs. Seattle).
STATISTICAL PLATEAUS: 100-yard rushing games: 1995 (3), 1997 (3), 1998 (6), 2001 (4), 2002 (2), 2003 (1). Total: 19. 100-yard receiving games: 1998 (2), 2001 (1). Total: 3.

Year Team	G	GS	Att.	Yds.	Avg.	TD	No.	Yds.	Avg.	TD	TD	2pt.	Pts.	Fum.
			RUSHING				RECEIVING				TOTALS			
1993—Phoenix NFL	6	5	76	264	3.5	1	6	18	3.0	0	1	0	6	2
1994—Arizona NFL	8	0	37	169	4.6	1	6	49	8.2	0	1	0	6	0
1995—Arizona NFL	16	15	284	1070	3.8	1	29	243	8.4	1	2	0	12	12
1996—Cincinnati NFL	16	12	225	847	3.8	0	12	131	10.9	1	1	1	8	1
1997—San Francisco NFL	13	13	234	1019	4.4	4	21	194	9.2	2	6	0	36	2
1998—San Francisco NFL	16	16	310	1570	‡5.1	7	39	535	13.7	2	9	1	56	4
1999—San Francisco NFL			Did not play.											
2000—San Francisco NFL			Did not play.											
2001—San Francisco NFL	16	16	252	1206	4.8	4	41	347	8.5	1	5	0	30	1
2002—San Francisco NFL	16	16	215	972	4.5	8	48	317	6.6	1	9	1	56	4
2003—San Francisco NFL	12	12	178	768	4.3	3	25	211	8.4	1	4	0	24	2
2004—Denver NFL	7	0	20	81	4.1	1	2	20	10.0	0	1	0	6	0
Pro totals (10 years)	126	105	1831	7966	4.4	30	229	2065	9.0	9	39	3	240	28

HEIDEN, STEVE — TE — BROWNS

PERSONAL: Born September 21, 1976, in Rushford, Minn. ... 6-5/265. ... Full name: Steve Allen Heiden. ... Name pronounced: HIGH-den.
HIGH SCHOOL: Rushford-Peterson (Rushford, Minn.).
COLLEGE: South Dakota State.
TRANSACTIONS/CAREER NOTES: Selected by San Diego Chargers in third round (69th pick overall) of 1999 NFL draft. ... Signed by Chargers (July 22, 1999). ... Granted free agency (March 1, 2002). ... Re-signed by Chargers (April 3, 2002). ... Traded by Chargers to Cleveland Browns for seventh-round pick (traded to Dallas) in 2003 draft (September 1, 2002). ... On injured reserve with ankle injury (November 12, 2003-remainder of season).
SINGLE GAME HIGHS (regular season): Receptions—7 (November 28, 2004, vs. Cincinnati); yards—82 (November 28, 2004, vs. Cincinnati); and touchdown receptions—3 (November 28, 2004, vs. Cincinnati).

H

Year Team	G	GS	RECEIVING No.	Yds.	Avg.	TD	TOTALS TD	2pt.	Pts.	Fum.
1999—San Diego NFL	11	0	0	0	0.0	0	0	0	0	0
2000—San Diego NFL	15	3	6	32	5.3	1	1	0	6	0
2001—San Diego NFL	16	10	8	55	6.9	1	1	0	6	0
2002—Cleveland NFL	16	6	17	105	6.2	1	1	0	6	0
2003—Cleveland NFL	9	9	18	134	7.4	0	0	0	0	0
2004—Cleveland NFL	13	13	28	287	10.3	5	5	1	32	1
Pro totals (6 years)	80	41	77	613	8.0	8	8	1	50	1

HEINRICH, KEITH   TE

PERSONAL: Born March 19, 1979, in Houston, Texas. ... 6-5/255.
HIGH SCHOOL: Tomball (Texas).
COLLEGE: Sam Houston State.
TRANSACTIONS/CAREER NOTES: Selected by Carolina Panthers in sixth round (174th pick overall) of 2002 NFL draft. ... Signed by Panthers (July 12, 2002). ... On injured reserve with knee injury (October 17, 2002-remainder of season). ... Claimed on waivers by Cleveland Browns (August 28, 2003). ... Waived by Browns (August 31, 2003). ... Re-signed by Browns to practice squad (September 1, 2003). ... Activated (November 13, 2003). ... On physically unable to perform list with ankle injury (August 30-November 16, 2004). ... Granted free agency (March 2, 2005).
SINGLE GAME HIGHS (regular season): Receptions—5 (November 16, 2003, vs. Arizona); yards—45 (November 16, 2003, vs. Arizona); and touchdown receptions—1 (December 14, 2003, vs. Denver).

Year Team	G	GS	RECEIVING No.	Yds.	Avg.	TD	TOTALS TD	2pt.	Pts.	Fum.
2002—Carolina NFL	4	0	0	0	0.0	0	0	0	0	0
2003—Cleveland NFL	7	3	8	64	8.0	2	2	0	12	0
2004—Cleveland NFL	7	0	1	1	1.0	0	0	0	0	0
Pro totals (3 years)	18	3	9	65	7.2	2	2	0	12	0

HEITMANN, ERIC   G

PERSONAL: Born February 24, 1980, in Brookshire, Texas. ... 6-3/305.
HIGH SCHOOL: Katy (Texas).
COLLEGE: Stanford.
TRANSACTIONS/CAREER NOTES: Selected by San Francisco 49ers in seventh round (239th pick overall) of 2002 NFL draft. ... Signed by 49ers (July 21, 2002). ... Granted free agency (March 2, 2005).
PLAYING EXPERIENCE: San Francisco NFL, 2002-2004. ... Games/Games started: 2002 (16/12), 2003 (9/8), 2004 (16/16). Total: 41/36.
HONORS: Named guard on THE SPORTING NEWS college All-America second team (2001).

HELLER, WILL   TE   BUCCANEERS

PERSONAL: Born February 28, 1981, in Dunwoody, Ga. ... 6-6/250. ... Full name: Will Sanders Heller.
HIGH SCHOOL: Marist (Ga.).
COLLEGE: Georgia Tech.
TRANSACTIONS/CAREER NOTES: Signed as non-drafted free agent by Tampa Bay Buccaneers (April 28, 2003). ... On injured reserve with hip injury (December 14, 2004-remainder of season).
SINGLE GAME HIGHS (regular season): Receptions—3 (December 12, 2004, vs. San Diego); yards—22 (November 7, 2004, vs. Kansas City); and touchdown receptions—1 (October 18, 2004, vs. St. Louis).

Year Team	G	GS	RECEIVING No.	Yds.	Avg.	TD	TOTALS TD	2pt.	Pts.	Fum.
2003—Tampa Bay NFL	9	1	2	15	7.5	1	1	0	6	0
2004—Tampa Bay NFL	10	2	12	98	8.2	1	1	0	6	1
Pro totals (2 years)	19	3	14	113	8.1	2	2	0	12	1

HENDERSON, DEVERY   WR   SAINTS

PERSONAL: Born March 26, 1982, in Lafayette, La. ... 5-11/200. ... Full name: Devery Vaughn Henderson.
HIGH SCHOOL: Opelousas (La.).
COLLEGE: Louisiana State.
TRANSACTIONS/CAREER NOTES: Selected by New Orleans Saints in second round (50th pick overall) of 2004 NFL draft. ... Signed by Saints (August 6, 2004).

Year Team	G	GS	RECEIVING No.	Yds.	Avg.	TD	TOTALS TD	2pt.	Pts.	Fum.
2004—New Orleans NFL	1	0	0	0	0.0	0	0	0	0	0

HENDERSON, E.J.   LB   VIKINGS

PERSONAL: Born August 3, 1980, in Aberdeen, Md. ... 6-1/245. ... Full name: Eric N. Henderson.
HIGH SCHOOL: Aberdeen (Md.).
COLLEGE: Maryland.
TRANSACTIONS/CAREER NOTES: Selected by Minnesota Vikings in second round (40th pick overall) of 2003 NFL draft. ... Signed by Vikings (July 25, 2003).

Year Team	G	GS	Tk.	Ast.	Sks.	No.	Yds.	Avg.	TD
			TOTALS			**INTERCEPTIONS**			
2003—Minnesota NFL	16	0	15	2	0.0	0	0	0.0	0
2004—Minnesota NFL	14	14	66	28	1.0	0	0	0.0	0
Pro totals (2 years)	30	14	81	30	1.0	0	0	0.0	0

HENDERSON, JOHN — DT — JAGUARS

PERSONAL: Born January 9, 1979, in Nashville, Tenn. ... 6-7/328. ... Full name: John Nathan Henderson.
HIGH SCHOOL: Pearl-Cohn (Nashville, Tenn.).
COLLEGE: Tennessee.
TRANSACTIONS/CAREER NOTES: Selected by Jacksonville Jaguars in first round (ninth pick overall) of 2002 NFL draft. ... Signed by Jaguars (July 25, 2002).
CHAMPIONSHIP GAME EXPERIENCE: Played in Pro Bowl (2004 season).
HONORS: Named defensive tackle on THE SPORTING NEWS college All-America first team (2000 and 2001). ... Outland Trophy winner (2000).

Year Team	G	GS	Tk.	Ast.	Sks.
			TOTALS		
2002—Jacksonville NFL	16	13	45	9	6.5
2003—Jacksonville NFL	16	16	47	11	3.5
2004—Jacksonville NFL	16	16	62	13	5.5
Pro totals (3 years)	48	45	154	33	15.5

HENDERSON, WILLIAM — FB — PACKERS

PERSONAL: Born February 19, 1971, in Richmond, Va. ... 6-1/251. ... Full name: William Terrelle Henderson.
HIGH SCHOOL: Thomas Dale (Chester, Va.).
COLLEGE: North Carolina.
TRANSACTIONS/CAREER NOTES: Selected by Green Bay Packers in third round (66th pick overall) of 1995 NFL draft. ... Signed by Packers (July 17, 1995). ... Granted free agency (February 13, 1998). ... Re-signed by Packers (June 15, 1998). ... Granted unconditional free agency (February 12, 1999). ... Re-signed by Packers (April 6, 1999). ... Granted unconditional free agency (March 1, 2002). ... Re-signed by Packers (March 1, 2002).
CHAMPIONSHIP GAME EXPERIENCE: Played in NFC championship game (1995-1997 seasons). ... Member of Super Bowl championship team (1996 season). ... Played in Super Bowl 32 (1997 season).
SINGLE GAME HIGHS (regular season): Attempts—6 (December 29, 2002, vs. New York Jets); yards—40 (September 9, 1996, vs. Philadelphia); and rushing touchdowns—1 (September 8, 2002, vs. Atlanta).

Year Team	G	GS	Att.	Yds.	Avg.	TD	No.	Yds.	Avg.	TD	No.	Yds.	Avg.	TD	TD	2pt.	Pts.	Fum.
			RUSHING				**RECEIVING**				**KICKOFF RETURNS**				**TOTALS**			
1995—Green Bay NFL	15	1	7	35	5.0	0	3	21	7.0	0	0	0	0.0	0	0	0	0	0
1996—Green Bay NFL	16	11	39	130	3.3	0	27	203	7.5	1	2	38	19.0	0	1	0	6	1
1997—Green Bay NFL	16	14	31	113	3.6	0	41	367	9.0	1	0	0	0.0	0	1	0	6	1
1998—Green Bay NFL	16	10	23	70	3.0	2	37	241	6.5	1	0	0	0.0	0	3	0	18	1
1999—Green Bay NFL	16	13	7	29	4.1	2	30	203	6.8	1	2	23	11.5	0	3	0	18	1
2000—Green Bay NFL	16	6	2	16	8.0	0	35	234	6.7	1	5	80	16.0	0	1	0	6	1
2001—Green Bay NFL	16	8	6	11	1.8	0	21	193	9.2	0	6	62	10.3	0	0	0	0	0
2002—Green Bay NFL	15	12	7	27	3.9	1	26	168	6.5	3	0	0	0.0	0	4	0	24	0
2003—Green Bay NFL	16	12	0	0	0.0	0	24	214	8.9	3	3	33	11.0	0	3	0	18	0
2004—Green Bay NFL	16	8	0	0	0.0	0	34	239	7.0	3	2	16	8.0	0	3	0	18	0
Pro totals (10 years)	158	95	122	431	3.5	5	278	2083	7.5	14	20	252	12.6	0	19	0	114	5

HENDRICKS, TOMMY — LB

PERSONAL: Born October 23, 1978, in Houston, Texas. ... 6-2/235. ... Full name: Thomas Emmett Hendricks III.
HIGH SCHOOL: Scarborough (Texas), then Eiserhower (Houston).
COLLEGE: Michigan.
TRANSACTIONS/CAREER NOTES: Signed as non-drafted free agent by Miami Dolphins (April 25, 2000). ... Released by Dolphins (August 27, 2000). ... Re-signed by Dolphins (September 26, 2000). ... Released by Dolphins (October 2, 2000). ... Re-signed by Dolphins to practice squad (October 4, 2000). ... Activated (November 10, 2000). ... Granted unconditional free agency (March 3, 2004). ... Signed by Jacksonville Jaguars (March 6, 2004). ... Waived by Jaguars (March 22, 2005).

Year Team	G	GS	Tk.	Ast.	Sks.	No.	Yds.	Avg.	TD
			TOTALS			**INTERCEPTIONS**			
2000—Miami NFL	8	0	0	1	0.0	0	0	0.0	0
2001—Miami NFL	16	1	2	2	0.0	0	0	0.0	0
2002—Miami NFL	16	0	2	0	0.0	0	0	0.0	0
2003—Miami NFL	16	2	17	6	0.0	0	0	0.0	0
2004—Jacksonville NFL	15	1	11	5	0.0	0	0	0.0	0
Pro totals (5 years)	71	4	32	14	0.0	0	0	0.0	0

HENRY, ANTHONY — CB — COWBOYS

PERSONAL: Born November 3, 1976, in Fort Myers, Fla. ... 6-1/205. ... Full name: Anthony Daniel Henry.
HIGH SCHOOL: Estero (Fla.).
COLLEGE: South Florida.
TRANSACTIONS/CAREER NOTES: Selected by Cleveland Browns in fourth round (97th pick overall) of 2001 NFL draft. ... Signed by Browns (June 15, 2001). ... Granted unconditional free agency (March 2, 2005). ... Signed by Dallas Cowboys (March 2, 2005).

H

Year Team	G	GS	TOTALS			INTERCEPTIONS			
			Tk.	Ast.	Sks.	No.	Yds.	Avg.	TD
2001—Cleveland NFL	16	2	37	9	0.0	†10	177	17.7	1
2002—Cleveland NFL	16	10	57	5	0.0	2	4	2.0	0
2003—Cleveland NFL	14	13	39	15	0.0	1	19	19.0	0
2004—Cleveland NFL	15	14	67	9	0.0	4	83	20.8	0
Pro totals (4 years)	61	39	200	38	0.0	17	283	16.6	1

HENRY, LEONARD　　　　　RB　　　　　DOLPHINS

PERSONAL: Born January 5, 1978, in Clinton, N.C. ... 6-1/210.
HIGH SCHOOL: Clinton (N.C.).
COLLEGE: East Carolina.
TRANSACTIONS/CAREER NOTES: Selected by Miami Dolphins in seventh round (241st pick overall) of 2002 NFL draft. ... Signed by Dolphins (July 25, 2002). ... Released by Dolphins (September 1, 2002). ... Re-signed by Dolphins to practice squad (September 2, 2002). ... Activated (December 4, 2002). ... Assigned by Dolphins to Frankfurt Galaxy in 2004 NFL Europe enhancement allocation program (February 9, 2004). ... Released by Dolphins (September 9, 2004). ... Re-signed by Dolphins to practice squad (September 11, 2004). ... Activated (September 18, 2004). ... Released by Dolphins (December 7, 2004). ... Re-signed by Dolphins to practice squad (December 8, 2004).
HONORS: Named running back on THE SPORTING NEWS college All-America third team (2001).
SINGLE GAME HIGHS (regular season): Attempts—21 (September 26, 2004, vs. Pittsburgh); yards—85 (October 3, 2004, vs. New York Jets); and rushing touchdowns—0.

Year Team	G	GS	RUSHING				RECEIVING				TOTALS			
			Att.	Yds.	Avg.	TD	No.	Yds.	Avg.	TD	TD	2pt.	Pts.	Fum.
2004—Miami NFL	6	2	46	141	3.1	0	3	12	4.0	0	0	0	0	1

HENRY, TRAVIS　　　　　RB　　　　　BILLS

PERSONAL: Born October 29, 1978, in Frostproof, Fla. ... 5-9/215. ... Full name: Travis Deion Henry.
HIGH SCHOOL: Frostproof (Fla.).
COLLEGE: Tennessee.
TRANSACTIONS/CAREER NOTES: Selected by Buffalo Bills in second round (58th pick overall) of 2001 NFL draft. ... Signed by Bills (July 26, 2001).
HONORS: Played in Pro Bowl (2002 season).
SINGLE GAME HIGHS (regular season): Attempts—35 (December 1, 2002, vs. Miami); yards—169 (December 7, 2003, vs. New York Jets); and rushing touchdowns—3 (September 14, 2003, vs. Jacksonville).
STATISTICAL PLATEAUS: 100-yard rushing games: 2001 (2), 2002 (6), 2003 (5). Total: 13.

Year Team	G	GS	RUSHING				RECEIVING				TOTALS			
			Att.	Yds.	Avg.	TD	No.	Yds.	Avg.	TD	TD	2pt.	Pts.	Fum.
2001—Buffalo NFL	13	12	213	729	3.4	4	22	179	8.1	0	4	0	24	5
2002—Buffalo NFL	16	16	325	1438	4.4	13	43	309	7.2	1	14	0	84	11
2003—Buffalo NFL	15	15	331	1356	4.1	10	28	158	5.6	1	11	0	66	7
2004—Buffalo NFL	10	5	94	326	3.5	0	10	45	4.5	0	0	0	0	0
Pro totals (4 years)	54	48	963	3849	4.0	27	103	691	6.7	2	29	0	174	23

HENSON, DREW　　　　　QB　　　　　COWBOYS

PERSONAL: Born February 13, 1980, in San Diego, Calif. ... 6-4/233. ... Full name: Drew Daniel Henson.
HIGH SCHOOL: Brighton (Mich.).
COLLEGE: Michigan.
TRANSACTIONS/CAREER NOTES: Selected by Houston Texans in sixth round (192nd pick overall) of 2003 NFL draft. ... Traded by Texans to Dallas Cowboys for third-round pick (RB Vernand Morency) in 2005 draft (March 18, 2003).
SINGLE GAME HIGHS (regular season): Attempts—12 (November 25, 2004, vs. Chicago); completions—6 (November 21, 2004, vs. Baltimore); yards—47 (November 21, 2004, vs. Baltimore); and touchdown passes—1 (November 21, 2004, vs. Baltimore).
MISCELLANEOUS: Selected by New York Yankees organization in third round of free-agent draft (June 2, 1998). ... Regular-season record as starting NFL quarterback: 1-0 (1.000).

Year Team	G	GS	PASSING								RUSHING				TOTALS		
			Att.	Cmp.	Pct.	Yds.	TD	Int.	Avg.	Skd.	Rat.	Att.	Yds.	Avg.	TD	TD	2pt.	Pts.
2004—Dallas NFL	7	1	18	10	55.6	78	1	1	4.33	2	61.8	1	7	7.0	0	0	0	0

HENTRICH, CRAIG　　　　　P/K　　　　　TITANS

PERSONAL: Born May 18, 1971, in Alton, Ill. ... 6-3/213. ... Full name: Craig Anthony Hentrich. ... Name pronounced: HEN-trick.
HIGH SCHOOL: Alton-Marquette (Ill.).
COLLEGE: Notre Dame.
TRANSACTIONS/CAREER NOTES: Selected by New York Jets in eighth round (200th pick overall) of 1993 NFL draft. ... Signed by Jets (July 14, 1993). ... Released by Jets (August 24, 1993). ... Signed by Green Bay Packers to practice squad (September 7, 1993). ... Activated (January 14, 1994); did not play. ... Granted unconditional free agency (February 13, 1998). ... Signed by Tennessee Oilers (February 19, 1998). ... Oilers franchise renamed Tennessee Titans for 1999 season (December 26, 1998). ... Designated by Titans as transition player (February 20, 2003).
CHAMPIONSHIP GAME EXPERIENCE: Played in NFC championship game (1995-1997 seasons). ... Member of Super Bowl championship team (1996 season). ... Played in Super Bowl 32 (1997 season) and Super Bowl 34 (1999 season). ... Played in AFC championship game (1999 and 2002 seasons).
HONORS: Named punter on THE SPORTING NEWS NFL All-Pro team (1998). ... Played in Pro Bowl (1998 and 2003 seasons).

H

Year Team	G	PUNTING						KICKING					TOTALS	
		No.	Yds.	Avg.	Net avg.	In. 20	Blk.	50+	Tot.	Pct.	Lg.	XPM	XPA	Pts.
1993—Green Bay NFL	Did not play.													
1994—Green Bay NFL	16	81	3351	41.4	35.5	24	0	0-0	0-0	0.0	0	0	0	0
1995—Green Bay NFL	16	65	2740	42.2	34.6	26	2	0-0	3-5	60.0	49	5	5	14
1996—Green Bay NFL	16	68	2886	42.4	36.2	28	0	0-0	0-0	0.0	0	0	0	0
1997—Green Bay NFL	16	75	3378	45.0	36.0	26	0	0-0	0-0	0.0	0	0	0	0
1998—Tennessee NFL	16	69	3258	*47.2	*39.2	18	0	0-0	0-1	0.0	0	0	0	0
1999—Tennessee NFL	16	90	3824	42.5	38.1	35	0	0-0	0-0	0.0	0	0	0	0
2000—Tennessee NFL	16	76	3101	40.8	36.3	33	0	0-1	0-1	0.0	0	0	0	0
2001—Tennessee NFL	16	85	3567	42.0	37.0	28	0	0-0	0-0	0.0	0	0	0	0
2002—Tennessee NFL	16	65	2725	41.9	33.9	28	1	0-0	0-0	0.0	0	0	0	0
2003—Tennessee NFL	16	71	3117	43.9§	37.8	26	0	0-1	4-5	80.0	49	1	1	13
2004—Tennessee NFL	16	73	3117	42.7	38.0	20	0	1-3	1-3	33.3	50	0	0	3
Pro totals (11 years)	176	818	35064	42.9	36.7	292	3	1-5	8-15	53.3	50	6	6	30

HERNDON, KELLY   CB   SEAHAWKS

PERSONAL: Born November 3, 1976, in Bedford, Ohio. ... 5-10/180.
HIGH SCHOOL: Chamberlain (Ohio).
COLLEGE: Toledo.
TRANSACTIONS/CAREER NOTES: Signed as non-drafted free agent by San Francisco 49ers (April 23, 1999). ... Released by 49ers (September 6, 1999). ... Re-signed by 49ers (July 7, 2000). ... Released by 49ers (August 28, 2000). ... Signed by New York Giants (May 15, 2001). ... Released by Giants (September 2, 2001). ... Re-signed by Giants to practice squad (September 4, 2001). ... Released by Giants (September 18, 2001). ... Signed by Denver Broncos (October 24, 2001). ... Granted free agency (March 2, 2005). ... Tendered offer sheet by Seattle Seahawks (March 17, 2005). ... Broncos declined to match offer (March 25, 2005).

Year Team	G	GS	TOTALS			INTERCEPTIONS			
			Tk.	Ast.	Sks.	No.	Yds.	Avg.	TD
2002—Denver NFL	14	0	0	0	0.0	1	0	0.0	0
2003—Denver NFL	15	11	56	5	0.0	3	19	6.3	0
2004—Denver NFL	16	16	56	13	1.0	2	17	8.5	0
Pro totals (3 years)	45	27	112	18	1.0	6	36	6.0	0

HERNDON, STEVE   G   FALCONS

PERSONAL: Born May 25, 1977, in LaGrange, Ga. ... 6-4/292. ... Full name: Steven Marshall Herndon.
HIGH SCHOOL: Troup County (LaGrange, Ga.).
COLLEGE: Georgia.
TRANSACTIONS/CAREER NOTES: Signed as non-drafted free agent by Miami Dolphins (April 25, 2000). ... Released by Dolphins (August 22, 2000). ... Signed by Denver Broncos to practice squad (August 29, 2000). ... Assigned by Broncos to Barcelona Dragons in 2001 NFL Europe enhancement allocation program (February 17, 2001). ... Received no tender from Broncos (2004). ... Signed by Atlanta Falcons (March 8, 2004). ... Granted unconditional free agency (March 2, 2005). ... Re-signed by Falcons (March 8, 2005).
PLAYING EXPERIENCE: Denver NFL, 2001-2003; Atlanta NFL, 2004. ... Games/Games started: 2001 (5/3), 2002 (15/9), 2003 (2/0), 2004 (15/1). Total: 37/13.
CHAMPIONSHIP GAME EXPERIENCE: Played in NFC championship game (2004 season).

HERRING, KIM   SS   BENGALS

PERSONAL: Born September 10, 1975, in Detroit, Mich. ... 6-0/212. ... Full name: Kimani Masai Herring.
HIGH SCHOOL: Solon (Ohio).
COLLEGE: Penn State.
TRANSACTIONS/CAREER NOTES: Selected by Baltimore Ravens in second round (58th pick overall) of 1997 NFL draft. ... Signed by Ravens (July 18, 1997). ... On injured reserve with shoulder injury (December 2, 1998-remainder of season). ... Granted free agency (February 11, 2000). ... Re-signed by Ravens (April 18, 2000). ... Granted unconditional free agency (March 2, 2001). ... Signed by St. Louis Rams (March 22, 2001). ... On injured reserve with forearm injury (August 31, 2003-entire season). ... Released by Rams (March 1, 2004). ... Signed by Cincinnati Bengals (March 4, 2004).
CHAMPIONSHIP GAME EXPERIENCE: Member of Ravens for AFC Championship game (2000 season); inactive. ... Member of Super Bowl championship team (2000 season). ... Played in NFC championship game (2001 season). ... Played in Super Bowl 36 (2001 season).
HONORS: Named free safety on THE SPORTING NEWS college All-America first team (1996).

Year Team	G	GS	TOTALS			INTERCEPTIONS			
			Tk.	Ast.	Sks.	No.	Yds.	Avg.	TD
1997—Baltimore NFL	15	4	44	8	1.0	0	0	0.0	0
1998—Baltimore NFL	7	7	20	7	0.0	0	0	0.0	0
1999—Baltimore NFL	16	16	48	10	0.0	0	0	0.0	0
2000—Baltimore NFL	16	16	47	7	1.0	3	74	24.7	0
2001—St. Louis NFL	16	15	49	6	0.0	1	15	15.0	0
2002—St. Louis NFL	16	16	66	9	0.0	3	38	12.7	0
2003—St. Louis NFL	Did not play.								
2004—Cincinnati NFL	12	10	49	13	0.0	1	0	0.0	0
Pro totals (7 years)	98	84	323	60	2.0	8	127	15.9	0

HETHERINGTON, CHRIS   FB   RAIDERS

PERSONAL: Born November 27, 1972, in North Branford, Conn. ... 6-3/245. ... Full name: Christopher Raymond Hetherington.
HIGH SCHOOL: Avon (Conn.) Old Farms.
COLLEGE: Yale.

H

TRANSACTIONS/CAREER NOTES: Signed as non-drafted free agent by Cincinnati Bengals (April 23, 1996). ... Released by Bengals (August 21, 1996). ... Re-signed by Bengals to practice squad (August 26, 1996). ... Signed by Indianapolis Colts off Bengals practice squad (October 22, 1996). ... Released by Colts (August 24, 1998). ... Re-signed by Colts (August 31, 1998). ... Released by Colts (February 12, 1999). ... Signed by Carolina Panthers (March 5, 1999). ... Granted unconditional free agency (February 11, 2000). ... Re-signed by Panthers (February 23, 2000). ... Granted unconditional free agency (March 1, 2002). ... Signed by St. Louis Rams (April 30, 2002). ... Granted unconditional free agency (February 28, 2003). ... Signed by Oakland Raiders (March 19, 2003). ... Granted unconditional free agency (March 3, 2004). ... Re-signed by Raiders (March 4, 2004). ... Released by Raiders (September 5, 2004). ... Re-signed by Raiders (December 1, 2004). ... Granted unconditional free agency (March 2, 2005). ... Re-signed by Raiders (March 21, 2005).
SINGLE GAME HIGHS (regular season): Attempts—5 (December 10, 2000, vs. Kansas City); yards—29 (December 24, 2000, vs. Oakland); and rushing touchdowns—1 (December 10, 2000, vs. Kansas City).

Year Team	G	GS	RUSHING				RECEIVING				KICKOFF RETURNS				TOTALS			
			Att.	Yds.	Avg.	TD	No.	Yds.	Avg.	TD	No.	Yds.	Avg.	TD	TD	2pt.	Pts.	Fum.
1996—Indianapolis NFL	6	0	0	0	0.0	0	0	0	0.0	0	1	16	16.0	0	0	0	0	0
1997—Indianapolis NFL	16	0	0	0	0.0	0	0	0	0.0	0	2	23	11.5	0	0	0	0	0
1998—Indianapolis NFL	14	1	0	0	0.0	0	0	0	0.0	0	5	71	14.2	0	0	0	0	1
1999—Carolina NFL	14	0	2	7	3.5	0	0	0	0.0	0	1	16	16.0	0	0	0	0	0
2000—Carolina NFL	16	5	23	65	2.8	2	14	116	8.3	1	2	21	10.5	0	3	0	18	0
2001—Carolina NFL	16	1	5	12	2.4	0	23	124	5.4	0	4	31	7.8	0	0	0	0	0
2002—St. Louis NFL	6	4	1	0	0.0	0	1	2	2.0	0	0	0	0.0	0	0	0	0	0
2003—Oakland NFL	14	1	0	0	0.0	0	2	23	11.5	0	0	0	0.0	0	0	0	0	0
2004—Oakland NFL	5	2	1	4	4.0	0	3	28	9.3	0	1	23	23.0	0	0	0	0	1
Pro totals (9 years)	107	14	32	88	2.8	2	43	293	6.8	1	16	201	12.6	0	3	0	18	2

HICKS, ARTIS — T — EAGLES

PERSONAL: Born November 28, 1978, in Jackson, Tenn. ... 6-4/320. ... Full name: Artis Hicks Jr.
HIGH SCHOOL: Central Merry (Jackson, Tenn.).
COLLEGE: Memphis.
TRANSACTIONS/CAREER NOTES: Signed as non-drafted free agent by Philadelphia Eagles (April 23, 2002). ... Inactive for 16 games (2002).
PLAYING EXPERIENCE: Philadelphia NFL, 2003-2004. ... Games/Games started: 2003 (10/4), 2004 (14/13). Total: 24/17.
CHAMPIONSHIP GAME EXPERIENCE: Played in NFC championship game (2003 and 2004 seasons). ... Played in Super Bowl 39 (2004 season).

HICKS, ERIC — DE — CHIEFS

PERSONAL: Born June 17, 1976, in Erie, Pa. ... 6-6/280. ... Full name: Eric David Hicks.
HIGH SCHOOL: Mercyhurst (Erie, Pa.).
COLLEGE: Maryland.
TRANSACTIONS/CAREER NOTES: Signed as non-drafted free agent by Kansas City Chiefs (April 25, 1998). ... Granted unconditional free agency (March 3, 2004). ... Re-signed by Chiefs (March 5, 2004).

Year Team	G	GS	TOTALS		
			Tk.	Ast.	Sks.
1998—Kansas City NFL	3	0	0	0	0.0
1999—Kansas City NFL	16	16	28	9	4.0
2000—Kansas City NFL	13	11	37	9	14.0
2001—Kansas City NFL	16	16	44	9	3.5
2002—Kansas City NFL	16	15	40	14	9.0
2003—Kansas City NFL	16	16	37	12	5.0
2004—Kansas City NFL	16	16	27	6	5.0
Pro totals (7 years)	96	90	213	59	40.5

HICKS, MAURICE — RB — 49ERS

PERSONAL: Born July 22, 1978, in Emporia, Va. ... 5-11/200.
HIGH SCHOOL: Greensville County (Emporia, Va.).
COLLEGE: North Carolina A&T.
TRANSACTIONS/CAREER NOTES: Signed as non-drafted free agent by Chicago Bears (April 26, 2002). ... On reserve/non-football injury list (August 27, 2002-January 30, 2003). ... Assigned by Bears to Scottish Claymores in 2003 NFL Europe enhancement allocation program (February 6, 2003). ... Released by Bears (August 31, 2003). ... Signed by San Francisco 49ers (December 31, 2003). ... Assigned by 49ers to Scottish Claymores in 2004 NFL Europe enhancement allocation program (February 9, 2004). ... Released by 49ers (September 5, 2004). ... Re-signed by 49ers to practice squad (September 6, 2004). ... Activated (November 3, 2004).
SINGLE GAME HIGHS (regular season): Attempts—34 (December 12, 2004, vs. Arizona); yards—139 (December 12, 2004, vs. Arizona); and rushing touchdowns—1 (December 12, 2004, vs. Arizona).
STATISTICAL PLATEAUS: 100-yard rushing games: 2004 (1). Total: 1.

Year Team	G	GS	RUSHING				RECEIVING				KICKOFF RETURNS				TOTALS			
			Att.	Yds.	Avg.	TD	No.	Yds.	Avg.	TD	No.	Yds.	Avg.	TD	TD	2pt.	Pts.	Fum.
2004—San Francisco NFL	9	2	96	362	3.8	2	16	154	9.6	0	31	623	20.1	0	2	0	12	3

HILL, DARRELL — WR — CHIEFS

H

PERSONAL: Born June 19, 1979, in Chicago, Ill. ... 6-3/200.
HIGH SCHOOL: Mount Carmel (Chicago).
COLLEGE: Northern Illinois.
TRANSACTIONS/CAREER NOTES: Selected by Tennessee Titans in seventh round (225th pick overall) of 2002 NFL draft. ... Signed by Titans (July 22, 2002). ... Did not receive qualifying offer from Titans (March 2, 2005). ... Signed by Kansas City Chiefs (April 5, 2005).
CHAMPIONSHIP GAME EXPERIENCE: Member of Titans for AFC championship game (2002 season); inactive.

Year Team	G	GS	RECEIVING No.	Yds.	Avg.	TD	TOTALS TD	2pt.	Pts.	Fum.
2002—Tennessee NFL	7	0	0	0	0.0	0	0	0	0	0
2003—Tennessee NFL	12	0	0	0	0.0	0	0	0	0	0
2004—Tennessee NFL	14	0	0	0	0.0	0	0	0	0	0
Pro totals (3 years)	33	0	0	0	0.0	0	0	0	0	0

HILL, MARQUISE DE PATRIOTS

PERSONAL: Born August 7, 1982, in New Orleans, La. ... 6-6/300.
HIGH SCHOOL: De La Salle (New Orleans, La.).
COLLEGE: Louisiana State.
TRANSACTIONS/CAREER NOTES: Selected by New England Patriots in second round (63rd pick overall) of 2004 NFL draft. ... Signed by Patriots (June 23, 2004).
CHAMPIONSHIP GAME EXPERIENCE: Member of Patriots for AFC championship game (2004 season); inactive. ... Member of Patriots for Super Bowl 39 (2004 season); inactive.

Year Team	G	GS	TOTALS Tk.	Ast.	Sks.
2004—New England NFL	1	0	0	0	0.0

HILL, RENALDO CB RAIDERS

PERSONAL: Born November 12, 1978, in Detroit, Mich. ... 5-11/189.
HIGH SCHOOL: Chadsey (Mich.).
COLLEGE: Michigan State.
TRANSACTIONS/CAREER NOTES: Selected by Arizona Cardinals in seventh round (202nd pick overall) of 2001 NFL draft. ... Signed by Cardinals (May 29, 2001). ... Granted free agency (March 3, 2004). ... Re-signed by Cardinals (May 7, 2004). ... Granted unconditional free agency (March 2, 2005). ... Signed by Oakland Raiders (April 11, 2005).

Year Team	G	GS	TOTALS Tk.	Ast.	Sks.	INTERCEPTIONS No.	Yds.	Avg.	TD
2001—Arizona NFL	14	1	16	6	0.5	0	0	0.0	0
2002—Arizona NFL	14	7	52	4	1.0	2	4	2.0	0
2003—Arizona NFL	14	14	47	11	2.0	5	119	23.8	1
2004—Arizona NFL	13	10	38	7	1.0	1	2	2.0	0
Pro totals (4 years)	55	32	153	28	4.5	8	125	15.6	1

HILLENMEYER, HUNTER LB BEARS

PERSONAL: Born October 28, 1980, in Nashville, Tenn. ... 6-4/238.
HIGH SCHOOL: Montgomery Bell (Nashville).
COLLEGE: Vanderbilt.
TRANSACTIONS/CAREER NOTES: Selected by Green Bay Packers in fifth round (166th pick overall) of 2003 NFL draft. ... Signed by Packers (July 18, 2003). ... Waived by Packers (September 10, 2003). ... Signed by Chicago Bears to practice squad (September 13, 2003). ... Activated (October 1, 2003).

Year Team	G	GS	TOTALS Tk.	Ast.	Sks.	INTERCEPTIONS No.	Yds.	Avg.	TD
2003—Chicago NFL	13	0	0	0	0.0	0	0	0.0	0
2004—Chicago NFL	16	11	51	20	2.5	0	0	0.0	0
Pro totals (2 years)	29	11	51	20	2.5	0	0	0.0	0

HILLIARD, IKE WR BUCCANEERS

PERSONAL: Born April 5, 1976, in Patterson, La. ... 5-11/210. ... Full name: Isaac Jason Hilliard.
HIGH SCHOOL: Patterson (La.).
COLLEGE: Florida.
TRANSACTIONS/CAREER NOTES: Selected by New York Giants in first round (seventh pick overall) of 1997 NFL draft. ... Signed by Giants (July 19, 1997). ... On injured reserve with neck injury (September 30, 1997-remainder of season). ... On injured reserve with shoulder injury (November 1, 2002-remainder of season). ... Granted unconditional free agency (February 28, 2003). ... Re-signed by Giants (March 6, 2003). ... Released by Giants (March 3, 2005). ... Signed by Tampa Bay Buccaneers (May 6, 2005).
CHAMPIONSHIP GAME EXPERIENCE: Played in NFC championship game (2000 season). ... Played in Super Bowl 35 (2000 season).
SINGLE GAME HIGHS (regular season): Receptions—9 (October 26, 2003, vs. Minnesota); yards—141 (November 30, 1998, vs. San Francisco); and touchdown receptions—2 (October 26, 2003, vs. Minnesota).
STATISTICAL PLATEAUS: 100-yard receiving games: 1998 (1), 1999 (3), 2000 (1), 2001 (2), 2003 (1). Total: 8.

Year Team	G	GS	RECEIVING No.	Yds.	Avg.	TD	TOTALS TD	2pt.	Pts.	Fum.
1997—New York Giants NFL	2	2	2	42	21.0	0	0	0	0	0
1998—New York Giants NFL	16	16	51	715	14.0	2	2	0	12	2
1999—New York Giants NFL	16	16	72	996	13.8	3	3	0	18	0
2000—New York Giants NFL	14	14	55	787	14.3	8	8	0	48	0
2001—New York Giants NFL	14	14	52	659	12.7	6	6	0	36	0
2002—New York Giants NFL	7	7	27	386	14.3	2	2	0	12	0
2003—New York Giants NFL	13	12	60	608	10.1	6	6	0	36	2
2004—New York Giants NFL	16	15	49	437	8.9	0	0	0	0	3
Pro totals (8 years)	98	91	368	4630	12.6	27	27	0	162	7

H

HILLIARD, JASON T GIANTS

PERSONAL: Born June 29, 1981, in Jeffersonville, Ind. ... 6-6/328. ... Full name: Jason Bradley Hilliard.
HIGH SCHOOL: Jeffersonville (Ind.).
COLLEGE: Louisville.
TRANSACTIONS/CAREER NOTES: Signed as non-drafted free agent by Green Bay Packers (April 30, 2004). ... Released by Packers (August 28, 2004). ... Signed by New York Giants to practice squad (November 16, 2004). ... Activated (December 20, 2004).
PLAYING EXPERIENCE: New York Giants NFL, 2004. ... Games/Games started: 2004 (2/0). Total: 2/0.

HOBSON, VICTOR LB JETS

PERSONAL: Born February 3, 1980, in Mount Laurel, N.J. ... 6-0/252.
HIGH SCHOOL: St. Joseph's Prep (Philadelphia).
COLLEGE: Michigan.
TRANSACTIONS/CAREER NOTES: Selected by New York Jets in second round (53rd pick overall) of 2003 NFL draft. ... Signed by Jets (July 20, 2003).

Year Team	G	GS	TOTALS			INTERCEPTIONS			
			Tk.	Ast.	Sks.	No.	Yds.	Avg.	TD
2003—New York Jets NFL	16	1	32	16	2.0	1	26	26.0	0
2004—New York Jets NFL	12	10	30	15	0.0	1	2	2.0	0
Pro totals (2 years)	28	11	62	31	2.0	2	28	14.0	0

HOCHSTEIN, RUSS G PATRIOTS

PERSONAL: Born October 7, 1977, in Hartington, Neb. ... 6-4/305.
HIGH SCHOOL: Cedar Catholic (Hartington, Neb.).
COLLEGE: Nebraska.
TRANSACTIONS/CAREER NOTES: Selected by Tampa Bay Buccaneers in fifth round (151st pick overall) of 2001 NFL draft. ... Signed by Buccaneers (July 16, 2001). ... Inactive for 16 games (2001). ... Released by Buccaneers (September 17, 2002). ... Re-signed by Buccaneers (September 24, 2002). ... Released by Buccaneers (October 1, 2002). ... Re-signed by Buccaneers to practice squad (October 1, 2002). ... Released by Buccaneers (October 16, 2002). ... Signed by New England Patriots to practice squad (October 21, 2002). ... Activated (November 17, 2002). ... Released by Patriots (August 31, 2003). ... Re-signed by Patriots to practice squad (September 1, 2003). ... Activated (September 14, 2003).
PLAYING EXPERIENCE: New England NFL, 2002; Tampa Bay NFL, 2002; New England NFL, 2003-2004. ... Games/Games started: 2002 (1/0), 2003 (14/1), 2004 (16/2). Total: 31/3.
CHAMPIONSHIP GAME EXPERIENCE: Played in AFC championship game (2003 and 2004 seasons). ... Member of Super Bowl championship team (2003 and 2004 seasons).
HONORS: Named guard on THE SPORTING NEWS college All-America first team (2000).

HODEL, NATHAN TE/LS CARDINALS

PERSONAL: Born November 12, 1977, in Maryville, Ill. ... 6-2/256.
HIGH SCHOOL: East (Belleville, Ill.).
COLLEGE: Illinois.
TRANSACTIONS/CAREER NOTES: Signed as non-drafted free agent by Carolina Panthers (April 23, 2001). ... Released by Panthers (September 1, 2001). ... Re-signed by Panthers to practice squad (September 4, 2001). ... Released by Panthers (October 24, 2001). ... Signed by Arizona Cardinals to practice squad (October 26, 2001). ... Activated (December 27, 2001); did not play. ... Re-signed by Cardinals (March 26, 2004).
PLAYING EXPERIENCE: Arizona NFL, 2002-2004. ... Games/Games started: 2002 (16/0), 2003 (16/0), 2004 (16/0). Total: 48/0.

HODGE, SEDRICK LB SAINTS

PERSONAL: Born September 13, 1978, in Fayetteville, Ga. ... 6-4/246. ... Full name: Sedrick Jamaine Hodge.
HIGH SCHOOL: Westminster (Atlanta).
COLLEGE: North Carolina.
TRANSACTIONS/CAREER NOTES: Selected by New Orleans Saints in third round (70th pick overall) of 2001 NFL draft. ... Signed by Saints (June 6, 2001). ... Granted free agency (March 3, 2004). ... Re-signed by Saints (May 7, 2004). ... On suspended list for violating league substance abuse policy (September 5-October 4, 2004). ... Granted unconditional free agency (March 2, 2005). ... Re-signed by Saints (March 22, 2005).

Year Team	G	GS	TOTALS			INTERCEPTIONS			
			Tk.	Ast.	Sks.	No.	Yds.	Avg.	TD
2001—New Orleans NFL	16	0	6	2	0.0	0	0	0.0	0
2002—New Orleans NFL	16	16	58	17	0.0	0	0	0.0	0
2003—New Orleans NFL	9	9	29	5	1.0	0	0	0.0	0
2004—New Orleans NFL	9	6	17	7	0.0	0	0	0.0	0
Pro totals (4 years)	50	31	110	31	1.0	0	0	0.0	0

H

HOKE, CHRIS DT STEELERS

PERSONAL: Born April 6, 1976, in Long Beach, Calif. ... 6-3/296.
HIGH SCHOOL: Foothill (Santa Ana, Calif.).
COLLEGE: Brigham Young.

TRANSACTIONS/CAREER NOTES: Signed as non-drafted free agent by Pittsburgh Steelers (April 23, 2001). ... Inactive for 14 games (2001). ... Inactive for 13 games (2002). ... Inactive for 16 games (2003).

CHAMPIONSHIP GAME EXPERIENCE: Played in AFC championship game (2004 season).

| | | | | TOTALS | | |
Year	Team	G	GS	Tk.	Ast.	Sks.
2004—Pittsburgh NFL		14	10	13	11	1.0

HOLCOMB, KELLY   QB   BILLS

PERSONAL: Born July 9, 1973, in Fayetteville, Tenn. ... 6-2/212. ... Full name: Bryan Kelly Holcomb.

HIGH SCHOOL: Lincoln County (Fayetteville, Tenn.).

COLLEGE: Middle Tennessee State.

TRANSACTIONS/CAREER NOTES: Signed as non-drafted free agent by Tampa Bay Buccaneers (May 1, 1995). ... Released by Buccaneers (August 22, 1995). ... Re-signed by Buccaneers to practice squad (August 29, 1995). ... Released by Buccaneers (September 19, 1995). ... Re-signed by Buccaneers to practice squad (October 4, 1995). ... Released by Buccaneers (October 17, 1995). ... Re-signed by Buccaneers to practice squad (December 19, 1995). ... Played for Barcelona Dragons of World League (1996). ... Released by Buccaneers (August 19, 1996). ... Signed by Indianapolis Colts to practice squad (November 27, 1996). ... Activated (December 12, 1996). ... Active for all 16 games (1998); did not play. ... Granted free agency (February 11, 2000). ... Re-signed by Colts (February 26, 2000). ... Released by Colts (February 28, 2001) ... Signed by Cleveland Browns (March 2, 2001). ... Granted unconditional free agency (March 2, 2005). ... Signed by Buffalo Bills (March 4, 2005).

SINGLE GAME HIGHS (regular season): Attempts—44 (November 23, 2003, vs. Pittsburgh); completions—30 (November 28, 2004, vs. Cincinnati); yards—413 (November 28, 2004, vs. Cincinnati); and touchdown passes—5 (November 28, 2004, vs. Cincinnati).

STATISTICAL PLATEAUS: 300-yard passing games: 2002 (1), 2003 (1), 2004 (1). Total: 3.

MISCELLANEOUS: Regular-season record as starting NFL quarterback: 4-9 (.308). ... Postseason record as starting NFL quarterback: 0-1.

| | | | | PASSING | | | | | | | | RUSHING | | | | TOTALS | | |
Year	Team	G	GS	Att.	Cmp.	Pct.	Yds.	TD	Int.	Avg.	Skd.	Rat.	Att.	Yds.	Avg.	TD	TD	2pt.	Pts.
1995—Tampa Bay NFL		Did not play.																	
1996—Indianapolis NFL		Did not play.																	
1997—Indianapolis NFL		5	1	73	45	61.6	454	1	8	6.22	11	44.3	5	5	1.0	0	0	0	0
1998—Indianapolis NFL		Did not play.																	
1999—Indianapolis NFL		Did not play.																	
2000—Indianapolis NFL		Did not play.																	
2001—Cleveland NFL		4	0	12	7	58.3	114	1	0	9.50	0	118.1	1	0	0.0	0	0	0	0
2002—Cleveland NFL		5	2	106	64	60.4	790	8	4	7.45	5	92.9	8	9	1.1	0	0	0	0
2003—Cleveland NFL		10	8	302	193	63.9	1797	10	12	5.95	21	74.6	8	7	0.9	0	0	0	0
2004—Cleveland NFL		4	2	87	59	67.8	737	7	5	8.47	5	96.8	3	-2	-0.7	0	0	0	0
Pro totals (5 years)		28	13	580	368	63.4	3892	27	29	6.71	42	77.6	25	19	0.8	0	0	0	0

HOLCOMBE, ROBERT   RB   CHIEFS

PERSONAL: Born December 11, 1975, in Houston, Texas. ... 5-11/220. ... Full name: Robert Wayne Holcombe.

HIGH SCHOOL: Jeff Davis Senior (Houston), then Mesa (Ariz.).

COLLEGE: Illinois.

TRANSACTIONS/CAREER NOTES: Selected by St. Louis Rams in second round (37th pick overall) of 1998 NFL draft. ... Signed by Rams (July 2, 1998). ... Granted unconditional free agency (March 1, 2002). ... Signed by Tennessee Titans (May 28, 2002). ... Released by Titans (February 21, 2005). ... Signed by Kansas City Chiefs (April 7, 2005).

CHAMPIONSHIP GAME EXPERIENCE: Played in NFC championship game (1999 and 2001 seasons). ... Member of Super Bowl championship team (1999 season). ... Played in Super Bowl 36 (2001 season). ... Played in AFC championship game (2002 season).

SINGLE GAME HIGHS (regular season): Attempts—21 (September 27, 1998, vs. Arizona); yards—86 (January 2, 2000, vs. Philadelphia); and rushing touchdowns—2 (September 27, 1998, vs. Arizona).

| | | | | RUSHING | | | | RECEIVING | | | | KICKOFF RETURNS | | | | TOTALS | | | |
Year	Team	G	GS	Att.	Yds.	Avg.	TD	No.	Yds.	Avg.	TD	No.	Yds.	Avg.	TD	TD	2pt.	Pts.	Fum.
1998—St. Louis NFL		13	6	98	230	2.3	2	6	34	5.7	0	0	0	0.0	0	2	0	12	0
1999—St. Louis NFL		15	7	78	294	3.8	4	14	163	11.6	0	0	0	0.0	0	5	0	30	4
2000—St. Louis NFL		14	9	21	70	3.3	3	8	90	11.3	1	0	0	0.0	0	4	0	24	0
2001—St. Louis NFL		16	0	13	42	3.2	1	1	14	14.0	0	0	0	0.0	0	1	0	6	1
2002—Tennessee NFL		8	0	47	242	5.1	0	10	91	9.1	0	0	0	0.0	0	0	0	0	1
2003—Tennessee NFL		15	0	63	201	3.2	1	19	121	6.4	1	4	38	9.5	0	2	1	14	2
2004—Tennessee NFL		16	8	17	62	3.6	0	11	60	5.5	0	3	26	8.7	0	0	0	0	0
Pro totals (7 years)		97	30	337	1141	3.4	11	69	573	8.3	3	7	64	9.1	0	14	1	86	8

HOLDMAN, WARRICK   LB   REDSKINS

PERSONAL: Born November 22, 1975, in Alief, Texas. ... 6-1/235. ... Full name: Warrick Donte Holdman.

HIGH SCHOOL: Elsik (Alief, Texas).

COLLEGE: Texas A&M.

TRANSACTIONS/CAREER NOTES: Selected by Chicago Bears in fourth round (106th pick overall) of 1999 NFL draft. ... Signed by Bears (July 25, 1999). ... On injured reserve with knee injury (November 21, 2000-remainder of season). ... Granted free agency (March 1, 2002). ... Tendered offer sheet by Kansas City Chiefs (April 16, 2002). ... Offer matched by Bears (April 19, 2002). ... On injured reserve with knee injury (October 1, 2002-remainder of season). ... Released by Bears (March 3, 2004). ... Signed by Cleveland Browns (April 16, 2004). ... Granted unconditional free agency (March 2, 2005). ... Signed by Washington Redskins (May 11, 2005).

| | | | | TOTALS | | | INTERCEPTIONS | | | |
Year	Team	G	GS	Tk.	Ast.	Sks.	No.	Yds.	Avg.	TD
1999—Chicago NFL		16	5	47	13	2.0	0	0	0.0	0
2000—Chicago NFL		10	10	57	16	0.0	0	0	0.0	0
2001—Chicago NFL		16	15	95	14	1.5	1	0	0.0	0

H

Year Team	G	GS	TOTALS			INTERCEPTIONS			
			Tk.	Ast.	Sks.	No.	Yds.	Avg.	TD
2002—Chicago NFL	4	4	16	4	0.0	0	0	0.0	0
2003—Chicago NFL	13	13	57	14	0.0	0	0	0.0	0
2004—Cleveland NFL	16	14	49	27	0.5	0	0	0.0	0
Pro totals (6 years)	75	61	321	88	4.0	1	0	0.0	0

HOLLAND, DARIUS   DT

PERSONAL: Born November 10, 1973, in Petersburg, Va. ... 6-5/330. ... Full name: Darius Jerome Holland.
HIGH SCHOOL: Mayfield (Las Cruces, N.M.).
COLLEGE: Colorado.
TRANSACTIONS/CAREER NOTES: Selected by Green Bay Packers in third round (65th pick overall) of 1995 NFL draft. ... Signed by Packers (July 18, 1995). ... Granted free agency (February 13, 1998). ... Re-signed by Packers (April 10, 1998). ... Traded by Packers to Kansas City Chiefs for DE Vaughn Booker (May 13, 1998). ... Released by Chiefs (October 13, 1998). ... Signed by Detroit Lions (October 19, 1998). ... Granted unconditional free agency (February 12, 1999). ... Signed by Cleveland Browns (April 23, 1999). ... Granted unconditional free agency (February 11, 2000). ... Re-signed by Browns (February 15, 2000). ... Released by Browns (September 1, 2001). ... Signed by Minnesota Vikings (March 12, 2002). ... Granted unconditional free agency (February 28, 2003). ... Signed by Denver Broncos (July 28, 2003). ... Released by Broncos (September 11, 2004). ... Re-signed by Broncos (September 13, 2004). ... Released by Broncos (December 21, 2004).
CHAMPIONSHIP GAME EXPERIENCE: Played in NFC championship game (1995-1997 seasons). ... Member of Super Bowl championship team (1996 season). ... Played in Super Bowl 32 (1997 season).

Year Team	G	GS	TOTALS			INTERCEPTIONS			
			Tk.	Ast.	Sks.	No.	Yds.	Avg.	TD
1995—Green Bay NFL	14	4	9	8	1.5	0	0	0.0	0
1996—Green Bay NFL	16	0	9	1	0.0	0	0	0.0	0
1997—Green Bay NFL	12	1	5	7	0.0	0	0	0.0	0
1998—Kansas City NFL	6	0	0	0	0.0	0	0	0.0	0
—Detroit NFL	10	4	11	0	0.0	0	0	0.0	0
1999—Cleveland NFL	15	11	30	6	2.0	0	0	0.0	0
2000—Cleveland NFL	16	1	28	4	1.0	1	0	0.0	0
2002—Minnesota NFL	4	0	0	2	0.0	0	0	0.0	0
2003—Denver NFL	16	14	15	9	0.0	0	0	0.0	0
2004—Denver NFL	2	0	2	0	0.0	0	0	0.0	0
Pro totals (9 years)	111	35	109	37	4.5	1	0	0.0	0

HOLLAND, MONTRAE   G   SAINTS

PERSONAL: Born May 21, 1980, in Jefferson, Texas. ... 6-2/322.
HIGH SCHOOL: Jefferson (Ore City, Texas).
COLLEGE: Florida State.
TRANSACTIONS/CAREER NOTES: Selected by New Orleans Saints in fourth round (102nd pick overall) of 2003 NFL draft. ... Signed by Saints (July 25, 2003).
PLAYING EXPERIENCE: New Orleans NFL, 2003-2004. ... Games/Games started: 2003 (16/7), 2004 (13/13). Total: 29/20.

HOLLIDAY, VONNIE   DE   DOLPHINS

PERSONAL: Born December 11, 1975, in Camden, S.C. ... 6-5/290. ... Full name: Dimetry Giovonni Holliday.
HIGH SCHOOL: Camden (S.C.).
COLLEGE: North Carolina.
TRANSACTIONS/CAREER NOTES: Selected by Green Bay Packers in first round (19th pick overall) of 1998 NFL draft. ... Signed by Packers (June 15, 1998). ... Granted unconditional free agency (February 28, 2003). ... Signed by Kansas City Chiefs (April 7, 2003). ... On injured reserve with groin injury (December 24, 2004-remainder of season). ... Released by Chiefs (February 22, 2005). ... Signed by Miami Dolphins (March 5, 2005).

Year Team	G	GS	TOTALS			INTERCEPTIONS			
			Tk.	Ast.	Sks.	No.	Yds.	Avg.	TD
1998—Green Bay NFL	12	12	34	18	8.0	0	0	0.0	0
1999—Green Bay NFL	16	16	47	20	6.0	0	0	0.0	0
2000—Green Bay NFL	12	9	22	13	5.0	1	3	3.0	0
2001—Green Bay NFL	16	16	47	25	7.0	0	0	0.0	0
2002—Green Bay NFL	10	10	18	8	6.0	1	3	3.0	0
2003—Kansas City NFL	16	16	30	8	5.5	0	0	0.0	0
2004—Kansas City NFL	9	3	12	1	0.0	0	0	0.0	0
Pro totals (7 years)	91	82	210	93	37.5	2	6	3.0	0

HOLLINGS, TONY   RB   TEXANS

PERSONAL: Born December 1, 1981, in Macon, Ga. ... 5-10/218. ... Full name: Tony Terrell Hollings.
HIGH SCHOOL: Twigs County (Jeffersonville, Ga.).
COLLEGE: Georgia Tech.
TRANSACTIONS/CAREER NOTES: Selected after junior season by Houston Texans in 2003 NFL supplemental draft. Texans forfeited their second-round pick (33rd overall) in 2004 regular draft. ... Signed by Texans (July 24, 2003).
SINGLE GAME HIGHS (regular season): Attempts—18 (December 7, 2003, vs. Jacksonville); yards)—41 (September 21, 2003, vs. Kansas City); and rushing touchdowns—0.

H

Year Team	G	GS	RUSHING Att.	Yds.	Avg.	TD	RECEIVING No.	Yds.	Avg.	TD	KICKOFF RETURNS No.	Yds.	Avg.	TD	TOTALS TD	2pt.	Pts.	Fum.
2003—Houston NFL	14	1	38	102	2.7	0	2	25	12.5	0	8	142	17.8	0	0	0	0	2
2004—Houston NFL	7	0	11	47	4.3	0	5	46	9.2	0	1	23	23.0	0	0	0	0	0
Pro totals (2 years)	21	1	49	149	3.0	0	7	71	10.1	0	9	165	18.3	0	0	0	0	2

HOLLOWELL, T.J.   LB   GIANTS

PERSONAL: Born April 8, 1981, in Copperas Cove, Texas. ... 6-0/235. ... Full name: Thomas Anthony Hollowell.
HIGH SCHOOL: Copperas Cove (Texas).
COLLEGE: Nebraska.
TRANSACTIONS/CAREER NOTES: Signed as non-drafted free agent by New York Giants (May 7, 2004). ... Released by Giants (September 5, 2004). ... Re-signed by Giants to practice squad (September 7, 2004). ... Activated (October 13, 2004).

Year Team	G	GS	TOTALS Tk.	Ast.	Sks.	INTERCEPTIONS No.	Yds.	Avg.	TD
2004—New York Giants NFL	4	0	0	0	0.0	0	0	0.0	0

HOLMES, EARL   LB   LIONS

PERSONAL: Born April 28, 1973, in Tallahassee, Fla. ... 6-2/242. ... Full name: Earl L. Holmes.
HIGH SCHOOL: Florida A&M University (Tallahassee, Fla.).
COLLEGE: Florida A&M.
TRANSACTIONS/CAREER NOTES: Selected by Pittsburgh Steelers in fourth round (126th pick overall) of 1996 NFL draft. ... Signed by Steelers (July 16, 1996). ... Granted unconditional free agency (March 1, 2002). ... Signed by Cleveland Browns (April 5, 2002). ... Released by Browns (February 27, 2003). ... Signed by Detroit Lions (April 9, 2003).
CHAMPIONSHIP GAME EXPERIENCE: Played in AFC championship game (1997 and 2001 seasons).

Year Team	G	GS	TOTALS Tk.	Ast.	Sks.	INTERCEPTIONS No.	Yds.	Avg.	TD
1996—Pittsburgh NFL	3	1	9	1	1.0	0	0	0.0	0
1997—Pittsburgh NFL	16	16	67	29	4.0	0	0	0.0	0
1998—Pittsburgh NFL	14	14	55	25	1.5	1	36	36.0	0
1999—Pittsburgh NFL	16	16	89	26	0.0	0	0	0.0	0
2000—Pittsburgh NFL	16	16	87	41	1.0	0	0	0.0	0
2001—Pittsburgh NFL	16	16	85	33	2.0	0	0	0.0	0
2002—Cleveland NFL	16	15	96	32	0.0	0	0	0.0	0
2003—Detroit NFL	16	13	68	29	2.0	0	0	0.0	0
2004—Detroit NFL	16	14	78	33	0.0	0	0	0.0	0
Pro totals (9 years)	129	121	634	249	11.5	1	36	36.0	0

HOLMES, PRIEST   RB   CHIEFS

PERSONAL: Born October 7, 1973, in Fort Smith, Ark. ... 5-9/213. ... Full name: Priest Anthony Holmes.
HIGH SCHOOL: Marshall (Texas).
COLLEGE: Texas.
TRANSACTIONS/CAREER NOTES: Signed as non-drafted free agent by Baltimore Ravens (April 25, 1997). ... Granted free agency (February 11, 2000). ... Re-signed by Ravens (June 9, 2000). ... Granted unconditional free agency (March 2, 2001). ... Signed by Kansas City Chiefs (April 1, 2001). ... On injured reserve with knee injury (December 9, 2004-remainder of season).
CHAMPIONSHIP GAME EXPERIENCE: Played in AFC championship game (2000 season). ... Member of Super Bowl championship team (2000 season).
HONORS: Played in Pro Bowl (2001 and 2003 seasons). ... Named to play in Pro Bowl (2002 season); replaced by Travis Henry due to injury. ... Named running back on the THE SPORTING NEWS NFL All-Pro team (2002-2003).
RECORDS: Holds NFL single-season record for most touchdowns—27 (2003).
SINGLE GAME HIGHS (regular season): Attempts—36 (November 22, 1998, vs. Cincinnati); yards—227 (November 22, 1998, vs. Cincinnati); and rushing touchdowns—4 (October 24, 2004, vs. Atlanta).
STATISTICAL PLATEAUS: 100-yard rushing games: 1998 (4), 1999 (2), 2000 (1), 2001 (7), 2002 (9), 2003 (3), 2004 (5). Total: 31. 100-yard receiving games: 2001 (2), 2002 (1), 2003 (1). Total: 4.
MISCELLANEOUS: Holds Kansas City Chiefs all-time records for most yards rushing (5,482), most rushing touchdowns (70) and most touchdowns (76).

Year Team	G	GS	RUSHING Att.	Yds.	Avg.	TD	RECEIVING No.	Yds.	Avg.	TD	TOTALS TD	2pt.	Pts.	Fum.
1997—Baltimore NFL	7	0	0	0	0.0	0	0	0	0.0	0	0	0	0	0
1998—Baltimore NFL	16	13	233	1008	4.3	7	43	260	6.0	0	7	0	42	3
1999—Baltimore NFL	9	4	89	506	5.7	1	13	104	8.0	1	2	0	12	0
2000—Baltimore NFL	16	2	137	588	4.3	2	32	221	6.9	0	2	0	12	2
2001—Kansas City NFL	16	16	327	*1555	4.8	8	62	614	9.9	2	10	0	60	4
2002—Kansas City NFL	14	14	313	1615	5.2	*21	70	672	9.6	3	*24	0	*144	1
2003—Kansas City NFL	16	16	320	1420	4.4	*27	74	690	9.3	0	*27	0	§162	1
2004—Kansas City NFL	8	8	196	892	4.6	14	19	187	9.8	1	15	0	90	4
Pro totals (8 years)	102	73	1615	7584	4.7	80	313	2748	8.8	7	87	0	522	15

HOLT, TERRENCE   S   LIONS

PERSONAL: Born March 5, 1980, in Greensboro, N.C. ... 6-2/208. ... Brother of Torry Holt, wide receiver, St. Louis Rams.
HIGH SCHOOL: Eastern Guilford (Gibsonville, N.C.).
COLLEGE: North Carolina State.

H

TRANSACTIONS/CAREER NOTES: Selected by Detroit Lions in fifth round (137th pick overall) of 2003 NFL draft. ... Signed by Lions (July 10, 2003).

Year Team	G	GS	TOTALS Tk.	Ast.	Sks.	INTERCEPTIONS No.	Yds.	Avg.	TD	KICKOFF RETURNS No.	Yds.	Avg.	TD	TOTALS TD	2pt.	Pts.	Fum.
2003—Detroit NFL	11	2	19	4	0.0	3	42	14.0	0	0	0	0.0	0	0	0	0	1
2004—Detroit NFL	16	0	15	5	0.0	0	0	0.0	0	0	0	0.0	0	0	0	0	0
Pro totals (2 years)	27	2	34	9	0.0	3	42	14.0	0	0	0	0.0	0	0	0	0	1

HOLT, TORRY WR RAMS

PERSONAL: Born June 5, 1976, in Greensboro, N.C. ... 6-0/190. ... Full name: Torry Jabar Holt. ... Brother of Terrence Holt, safety, Detroit Lions.
HIGH SCHOOL: Eastern Guilford (Gibsonville, N.C.).
COLLEGE: North Carolina State.
TRANSACTIONS/CAREER NOTES: Selected by St. Louis Rams in first round (sixth pick overall) of 1999 NFL draft. ... Signed by Rams (June 5, 1999).
CHAMPIONSHIP GAME EXPERIENCE: Played in NFC championship game (1999 and 2001 seasons). ... Member of Super Bowl championship team (1999 season). ... Played in Super Bowl 36 (2001 season).
HONORS: Named wide receiver on THE SPORTING NEWS college All-America first team (1998). ... Named wide receiver on THE SPORTING NEWS NFL All-Pro team (2003). ... Played in Pro Bowl (2000, 2001, 2003 and 2004 seasons).
SINGLE GAME HIGHS (regular season): Receptions—12 (September 28, 2003, vs. Arizona); yards—203 (December 30, 2001, vs. Indianapolis); and touchdown receptions—2 (January 2, 2005, vs. New York Jets).
STATISTICAL PLATEAUS: 100-yard receiving games: 1999 (2), 2000 (8), 2001 (3), 2002 (4), 2003 (10), 2004 (6). Total: 33.

Year Team	G	GS	RUSHING Att.	Yds.	Avg.	TD	RECEIVING No.	Yds.	Avg.	TD	TOTALS TD	2pt.	Pts.	Fum.
1999—St. Louis NFL	16	15	3	25	8.3	0	52	788	15.2	6	6	0	36	4
2000—St. Louis NFL	16	15	2	7	3.5	0	82	*1635	*19.9	6	6	0	36	2
2001—St. Louis NFL	16	14	2	0	0.0	0	81	1363	16.8	7	7	0	42	2
2002—St. Louis NFL	16	11	2	18	9.0	0	91	1302	14.3	4	4	0	24	1
2003—St. Louis NFL	16	15	1	5	5.0	0	*117	*1696	14.5	12	12	0	72	1
2004—St. Louis NFL	16	16	0	0	0.0	0	∞94	1372	14.6	10	10	0	60	3
Pro totals (6 years)	96	86	10	55	5.5	0	517	8156	15.8	45	45	0	270	13

HOOD, RODERICK CB EAGLES

PERSONAL: Born October 3, 1981, in Columbus, Ga. ... 5-11/196.
HIGH SCHOOL: Carver (Columbus, Ga.).
COLLEGE: Auburn.
TRANSACTIONS/CAREER NOTES: Signed as non-drafted free agent by Philadelphia Eagles (April 28, 2003).
CHAMPIONSHIP GAME EXPERIENCE: Played in NFC championship game (2003 and 2004 seasons). ... Played in Super Bowl 39 (2004 season).

Year Team	G	GS	TOTALS Tk.	Ast.	Sks.	INTERCEPTIONS No.	Yds.	Avg.	TD	KICKOFF RETURNS No.	Yds.	Avg.	TD	TOTALS TD	2pt.	Pts.	Fum.
2003—Philadelphia NFL	14	0	5	0	0.0	1	5	5.0	0	0	0	0.0	0	0	0	0	1
2004—Philadelphia NFL	16	2	33	2	0.0	1	20	20.0	0	15	336	22.4	0	0	0	0	1
Pro totals (2 years)	30	2	38	2	0.0	2	25	12.5	0	15	336	22.4	0	0	0	0	2

HOOVER, BRAD FB PANTHERS

PERSONAL: Born November 11, 1976, in High Point, N.C. ... 6-0/245. ... Full name: Bradley R. Hoover.
HIGH SCHOOL: Ledford (Thomasville, N.C.).
COLLEGE: Western Carolina.
TRANSACTIONS/CAREER NOTES: Signed as non-drafted free agent by Carolina Panthers (April 17, 2000).
CHAMPIONSHIP GAME EXPERIENCE: Played in NFC championship game (2003 season). ... Played in Super Bowl 38 (2003 season).
SINGLE GAME HIGHS (regular season): Attempts—24 (October 24, 2004, vs. San Diego); yards—117 (November 27, 2000, vs. Green Bay); and rushing touchdowns—1 (November 27, 2000, vs. Green Bay).
STATISTICAL PLATEAUS: 100-yard rushing games: 2000 (1). Total: 1.

Year Team	G	GS	RUSHING Att.	Yds.	Avg.	TD	RECEIVING No.	Yds.	Avg.	TD	TOTALS TD	2pt.	Pts.	Fum.
2000—Carolina NFL	16	4	89	290	3.3	1	15	112	7.5	0	1	0	6	1
2001—Carolina NFL	16	7	17	71	4.2	0	26	185	7.1	0	0	0	0	1
2002—Carolina NFL	16	10	31	129	4.2	0	17	187	11.0	2	2	0	12	1
2003—Carolina NFL	16	9	6	21	3.5	0	12	72	6.0	1	1	0	6	1
2004—Carolina NFL	14	9	68	246	3.6	0	21	161	7.7	2	2	0	12	0
Pro totals (5 years)	78	39	211	757	3.6	1	91	717	7.9	5	6	0	36	4

HOPE, CHRIS S STEELERS

H

PERSONAL: Born September 29, 1980, in Rock Hill, S.C. ... 5-11/206.
HIGH SCHOOL: Rock Hill (S.C.).
COLLEGE: Florida State.
TRANSACTIONS/CAREER NOTES: Selected by Pittsburgh Steelers in third round (94th pick overall) of 2002 NFL draft. ... Signed by Steelers (July 12, 2002). ... Granted free agency (March 2, 2005). ... Re-signed by Steelers (April 15, 2005).

CHAMPIONSHIP GAME EXPERIENCE: Played in AFC championship game (2004 season).
HONORS: Named free safety on THE SPORTING NEWS college All-America second team (2000).

			TOTALS			INTERCEPTIONS			
Year Team	G	GS	Tk.	Ast.	Sks.	No.	Yds.	Avg.	TD
2002—Pittsburgh NFL	14	0	12	0	0.0	0	0	0.0	0
2003—Pittsburgh NFL	16	0	11	2	0.0	0	0	0.0	0
2004—Pittsburgh NFL	16	16	59	31	0.0	1	41	41.0	0
Pro totals (3 years)	46	16	82	33	0.0	1	41	41.0	0

HOPKINS, BRAD   T   TITANS

PERSONAL: Born September 5, 1970, in Columbia, S.C. ... 6-3/305. ... Full name: Bradley D. Hopkins.
HIGH SCHOOL: Moline (Ill.).
COLLEGE: Illinois.
TRANSACTIONS/CAREER NOTES: Selected by Houston Oilers in first round (13th pick overall) of 1993 NFL draft. ... Signed by Oilers (August 10, 1993). ... Granted unconditional free agency (February 14, 1997). ... Re-signed by Oilers (March 10, 1997). ... Oilers franchise moved to Tennessee for 1997 season. ... Oilers franchise renamed Tennessee Titans for 1999 season (December 26, 1998).
PLAYING EXPERIENCE: Houston NFL, 1993-1996; Tennessee NFL, 1997; Tennessee NFL, 1998-2004. ... Games/Games started: 1993 (16/11), 1994 (16/15), 1995 (16/16), 1996 (16/16), 1997 (16/16), 1998 (13/13), 1999 (16/16), 2000 (15/15), 2001 (14/14), 2002 (14/14), 2003 (16/16), 2004 (11/11). Total: 179/173.
CHAMPIONSHIP GAME EXPERIENCE: Played in AFC championship game (1999 and 2002 seasons). ... Played in Super Bowl 34 (1999 season).
HONORS: Played in Pro Bowl (2000 and 2003 seasons).

HOPSON, TYRONE   G   LIONS

PERSONAL: Born May 28, 1976, in Hopkinsville, Ky. ... 6-2/294. ... Full name: Tyrone Hopson Jr.
HIGH SCHOOL: Davies County (Owensboro, Ky.).
COLLEGE: Eastern Kentucky.
TRANSACTIONS/CAREER NOTES: Selected by San Francisco 49ers in fifth round (161st pick overall) of 1999 NFL draft. ... Signed by 49ers (July 26, 1999). ... On injured reserve with shoulder injury (October 20, 1999-remainder of season). ... Released by 49ers (August 27, 2000). ... Re-signed by 49ers to practice squad (August 29, 2000). ... Activated (November 14, 2000). ... Released by 49ers (September 2, 2001). ... Signed by Jacksonville Jaguars to practice squad (October 14, 2001). ... Released by Jaguars (October 22, 2001). ... Signed by Detroit Lions to practice squad (October 31, 2001). ... Activated (December 18, 2001).
PLAYING EXPERIENCE: San Francisco NFL, 1999-2000, Detroit NFL, 2002-2004. ... Games/Games started: 1999 (1/0), 2000 (2/1), 2002 (8/0), 2004 (11/0). Total: 22/1.

HORN, CHRIS   WR   CHIEFS

PERSONAL: Born July 13, 1977, in Caldwell, Idaho. ... 5-11/195. ... Full name: Christopher Michael Horn.
COLLEGE: Rocky Mountain (Mont.).
TRANSACTIONS/CAREER NOTES: Played with Billings Thunderbolts in Indoor Football League (2000). ... Played with Arizona Rattlers in Arena Football League (2001 and 2002). ... Signed by Kansas City Chiefs (April 10, 2003). ... Released by Chiefs (September 10, 2003). ... Re-signed by Chiefs (September 16, 2003). ... Released by Chiefs (September 23, 2003). ... Re-signed by Chiefs to practice squad (September 25, 2003). ... Activated (October 1, 2003). ... Released by Chiefs (October 8, 2003). ... Re-signed by Chiefs (October 15, 2003). ... Released by Chiefs (October 22, 2003). ... Re-signed by Chiefs (November 3, 2003). ... Released by Chiefs (November 11, 2003). ... Re-signed by Chiefs (November 19, 2003). ... Released by Chiefs (November 26, 2003). ... Re-signed by Chiefs (December 3, 2003). ... Released by Chiefs (December 8, 2003). ... Re-signed by Chiefs to practice squad (December 10, 2003). ... Assigned by Chiefs to Amsterdam Admirals in 2004 NFL Europe enhancement allocation program (February 13, 2004). ... Released by Chiefs (September 5, 2004). ... Re-signed by Chiefs to practice squad (September 6, 2004). ... Activated (September 25, 2004).
SINGLE GAME HIGHS (regular season): Receptions—5 (October 4, 2004, vs. Baltimore); yards—60 (October 4, 2004, vs. Baltimore); and touchdown receptions—1 (September 26, 2004, vs. Houston).

			RECEIVING				KICKOFF RETURNS				TOTALS			
Year Team	G	GS	No.	Yds.	Avg.	TD	No.	Yds.	Avg.	TD	TD	2pt.	Pts.	Fum.
2004—Kansas City NFL	14	0	15	178	11.9	1	4	44	11.0	0	1	0	6	0

HORN, JOE   WR   SAINTS

PERSONAL: Born January 16, 1972, in Tupelo, Miss. ... 6-1/213. ... Full name: Joseph Horn.
HIGH SCHOOL: Douglas Bird (Fayetteville, N.C.).
JUNIOR COLLEGE: Itawamba (Miss.).
COLLEGE: None.
TRANSACTIONS/CAREER NOTES: Signed by Memphis Mad Dogs of CFL (March 25, 1995). ... Selected by Kansas City Chiefs in fifth round (135th pick overall) of 1996 NFL draft. ... Signed by Chiefs (June 25, 1996). ... Granted free agency (February 12, 1999). ... Re-signed by Chiefs (June 16, 1999). ... Granted unconditional free agency (February 11, 2000). ... Signed by New Orleans Saints (February 13, 2000).
HONORS: Played in Pro Bowl (2000, 2002 and 2004 seasons). ... Named to play in Pro Bowl (2001 season); replaced by Torry Holt due to injury.
SINGLE GAME HIGHS (regular season): Receptions—13 (December 2, 2001, vs. Carolina); yards—180 (November 5, 2000, vs. San Francisco); and touchdown receptions—4 (December 14, 2003, vs. New York Giants).
STATISTICAL PLATEAUS: 100-yard receiving games: 2000 (5), 2001 (4), 2002 (6), 2003 (4), 2004 (5). Total: 24.

			RUSHING				RECEIVING				KICKOFF RETURNS				TOTALS			
Year Team	G	GS	Att.	Yds.	Avg.	TD	No.	Yds.	Avg.	TD	No.	Yds.	Avg.	TD	TD	2pt.	Pts.	Fum.
1995—Memphis CFL	17	17	...	...	0.0	...	71	1415	19.9	5	2	17	8.5	0	5	0	30	0
1996—Kansas City NFL	9	0	1	8	8.0	0	2	30	15.0	0	0	0	0.0	0	0	0	0	0

H

Year Team	G	GS	RUSHING				RECEIVING				KICKOFF RETURNS				TOTALS			
			Att.	Yds.	Avg.	TD	No.	Yds.	Avg.	TD	No.	Yds.	Avg.	TD	TD	2pt.	Pts.	Fum.
1997—Kansas City NFL.........	8	0	0	0	0.0	0	2	65	32.5	0	0	0	0.0	0	0	0	0	0
1998—Kansas City NFL.........	16	1	1	0	0.0	0	14	198	14.1	1	11	233	21.2	0	1	0	6	2
1999—Kansas City NFL.........	16	1	2	15	7.5	0	35	586	16.7	6	9	165	18.3	0	6	0	36	0
2000—New Orleans NFL	16	16	6	10	1.7	0	94	1340	14.3	8	0	0	0.0	0	8	0	48	1
2001—New Orleans NFL	16	16	1	4	4.0	0	83	1265	15.2	9	0	0	0.0	0	9	0	54	1
2002—New Orleans NFL	16	16	1	2	2.0	0	88	1312	14.9	7	0	0	0.0	0	7	1	44	1
2003—New Orleans NFL	15	14	2	15	7.5	0	78	973	12.5	10	0	0	0.0	0	10	0	60	2
2004—New Orleans NFL	16	16	0	0	0.0	0	∞94	1399	14.9	11	0	0	0.0	0	11	1	68	0
CFL totals (1 year)	17	17	...	...	0.0	...	71	1415	19.9	5	2	17	8.5	0	5	0	30	0
NFL totals (9 years)	128	80	14	54	3.9	0	490	7168	14.6	52	20	398	19.9	0	52	2	316	7
Pro totals (10 years)	145	97	...	...	3.9	...	561	8583	15.3	57	22	415	18.9	0	57	2	346	7

HORTON, JASON   CB   PACKERS

PERSONAL: Born February 16, 1980, in Ahoskie, N.C. ... 6-0/193. ... Full name: Jason Dennard Horton.
HIGH SCHOOL: Hertford County (Ahoskie, N.C.).
COLLEGE: North Carolina A&T.
TRANSACTIONS/CAREER NOTES: Signed as non-drafted free agent by Green Bay Packers (January 19, 2004). ... Played with Toronto Argonauts in Canadian Football League (2002-2003).

Year Team	G	GS	TOTALS			INTERCEPTIONS			
			Tk.	Ast.	Sks.	No.	Yds.	Avg.	TD
2004—Green Bay NFL	14	0	3	2	0.0	0	0	0.0	0

HOUSER, KEVIN   C/LS   SAINTS

PERSONAL: Born August 23, 1977, in Westlake, Ohio. ... 6-2/252. ... Full name: Kevin J. Houser.
HIGH SCHOOL: Westlake (Ohio).
COLLEGE: Ohio State.
TRANSACTIONS/CAREER NOTES: Selected by New Orleans Saints in seventh round (228th pick overall) of 2000 NFL draft. ... Signed by Saints (June 20, 2000).
PLAYING EXPERIENCE: New Orleans NFL, 2000-2004. ... Games/Games started: 2000 (16/0), 2001 (16/0), 2002 (16/0), 2003 (16/0), 2004 (16/0). Total: 80/0.

HOUSHMANDZADEH, T.J.   WR   BENGALS

PERSONAL: Born September 26, 1977, in Victorville, Calif. ... 6-1/197. ... Full name: Touraj Houshmandzadeh.
HIGH SCHOOL: Barstow (Calif.).
JUNIOR COLLEGE: Cerritos (Calif.).
COLLEGE: Oregon State.
TRANSACTIONS/CAREER NOTES: Selected by Cincinnati Bengals in seventh round (204th pick overall) of 2001 NFL draft. ... Signed by Bengals (July 18, 2001). ... Granted free agency (March 3, 2004). ... Re-signed by Bengals (April 14, 2004). ... Granted unconditional free agency (March 2, 2005). ... Re-signed by Bengals (March 3, 2005).
SINGLE GAME HIGHS (regular season): Receptions—12 (December 12, 2004, vs. New England); yards—171 (December 5, 2004, vs. Baltimore); and touchdown receptions—2 (November 28, 2004, vs. Cleveland).
STATISTICAL PLATEAUS: 100-yard receiving games: 2004 (3). Total: 3.

Year Team	G	GS	RUSHING				RECEIVING				PUNT RETURNS				KICKOFF RETURNS				TOTALS		
			Att.	Yds.	Avg.	TD	No.	Yds.	Avg.	TD	No.	Yds.	Avg.	TD	No.	Yds.	Avg.	TD	TD	2pt.	Pts.
2001—Cin. NFL	12	1	0	0	0.0	0	21	228	10.9	0	12	163	13.6	0	10	185	18.5	0	0	0	0
2002—Cin. NFL	16	5	0	0	0.0	0	41	492	12.0	1	24	117	4.9	0	13	288	22.2	0	1	0	6
2003—Cin. NFL	2	0	0	0	0.0	0	0	0	0.0	0	0	0	0.0	0	0	0	0.0	0	0	0	0
2004—Cin. NFL	16	13	6	51	8.5	0	73	978	13.4	4	11	88	8.0	0	10	227	22.7	0	4	0	24
Pro totals (4 years)	46	19	6	51	8.5	0	135	1698	12.6	5	47	368	7.8	0	33	700	21.2	0	5	0	30

HOVAN, CHRIS   DT   BUCCANEERS

PERSONAL: Born May 12, 1978, in Rocky River, Ohio. ... 6-2/296. ... Full name: Christopher James Hovan.
HIGH SCHOOL: St. Ignatius (Cleveland).
COLLEGE: Boston College.
TRANSACTIONS/CAREER NOTES: Selected by Minnesota Vikings in first round (25th pick overall) of 2000 NFL draft. ... Signed by Vikings (July 24, 2000). ... Granted unconditional free agency (March 2, 2005). ... Signed by Tampa Bay Buccaneers (April 1, 2005).
CHAMPIONSHIP GAME EXPERIENCE: Played in NFC championship game (2000 season).
HONORS: Named defensive end on THE SPORTING NEWS college All-America third team (1999).

Year Team	G	GS	TOTALS		
			Tk.	Ast.	Sks.
2000—Minnesota NFL	16	13	43	5	2.0
2001—Minnesota NFL	16	16	30	15	6.0
2002—Minnesota NFL	16	16	38	14	5.5
2003—Minnesota NFL	16	16	19	8	2.0
2004—Minnesota NFL	13	9	11	9	1.5
Pro totals (5 years)..	77	70	141	51	17.0

H

HOWARD, BRIAN   DT   RAMS

PERSONAL: Born September 9, 1981, in Seattle, Wash. ... 6-4/278. ... Full name: Brian Lewis Howard.
HIGH SCHOOL: Kent-Meridian (Kent, Wash.).
COLLEGE: Idaho.
TRANSACTIONS/CAREER NOTES: Signed as non-drafted free agent by St. Louis Rams (April 30, 2004).

Year Team	G	GS	TOTALS Tk.	Ast.	Sks.
2004—St. Louis NFL	15	1	2	5	0.0

HOWARD, DARREN   DE   SAINTS

PERSONAL: Born November 19, 1976, in St. Petersburg, Fla. ... 6-3/275.
HIGH SCHOOL: Boca Ciega (Fla.).
COLLEGE: Kansas State.
TRANSACTIONS/CAREER NOTES: Selected by New Orleans Saints in second round (33rd pick overall) of 2000 NFL draft. ... Signed by Saints (July 17, 2000). ... Designated by Saints as franchise player (February 24, 2004). ... Re-signed by Saints (May 4, 2004). ... Designated by Saints as franchise player (February 22, 2005). ... Re-signed by Saints (March 15, 2005).

Year Team	G	GS	TOTALS Tk.	Ast.	Sks.	INTERCEPTIONS No.	Yds.	Avg.	TD
2000—New Orleans NFL	16	16	37	15	11.0	1	46	46.0	0
2001—New Orleans NFL	16	16	36	18	6.0	1	37	37.0	0
2002—New Orleans NFL	16	16	35	13	8.0	0	0	0.0	0
2003—New Orleans NFL	8	8	27	2	5.0	0	0	0.0	0
2004—New Orleans NFL	13	12	37	9	11.0	0	0	0.0	0
Pro totals (5 years)	69	68	172	57	41.0	2	83	41.5	0

HOWARD, REGGIE   CB   DOLPHINS

PERSONAL: Born May 17, 1977, in Memphis, Tenn. ... 6-0/190. ... Full name: Reginald Clement Howard.
HIGH SCHOOL: Kirby (Memphis,Tenn.).
COLLEGE: Memphis.
TRANSACTIONS/CAREER NOTES: Signed as non-drafted free agent by Carolina Panthers (April 17, 2000). ... Released by Panthers (August 29, 2000)   Signed by New Orleans Saints to practice squad (September 1, 2000). ... Activated (October 22, 2000). ... Claimed on waivers by Panthers (October 25, 2000). ... Granted free agency (February 28, 2003). ... Re-signed by Panthers (May 2, 2003). ... Granted unconditional free agency (March 3, 2004). ... Signed by Miami Dolphins (March 5, 2004).
CHAMPIONSHIP GAME EXPERIENCE: Played in NFC championship game (2003 season). ... Played in Super Bowl 38 (2003 season).

Year Team	G	GS	TOTALS Tk.	Ast.	Sks.	INTERCEPTIONS No.	Yds.	Avg.	TD
2000—New Orleans NFL	1	0	0	0	0.0	0	0	0.0	0
—Carolina NFL	1	0	0	0	0.0	0	0	0.0	0
2001—Carolina NFL	11	0	15	0	1.0	1	16	16.0	0
2002—Carolina NFL	14	14	75	9	1.0	2	19	9.5	0
2003—Carolina NFL	15	15	52	10	0.5	2	2	1.0	0
2004—Miami NFL	15	3	16	7	0.0	0	0	0.0	0
Pro totals (5 years)	57	32	158	26	2.5	5	37	7.4	0

HOWELL, JOHN   S

PERSONAL: Born April 28, 1978, in North Platte, Neb. ... 6-0/210. ... Full name: John Thomas Howell.
HIGH SCHOOL: Mullen (Neb.).
COLLEGE: Colorado State.
TRANSACTIONS/CAREER NOTES: Selected by Tampa Bay Buccaneers in fourth round (117th pick overall) of 2001 NFL draft. ... Signed by Buccaneers (July 25, 2001). ... On injured reserve with hamstring injury (November 11, 2003-remainder of season). ... Granted free agency (March 3, 2004). ... Re-signed by Buccaneers (April 15, 2004). ... Granted unconditional free agency (March 2, 2005).
CHAMPIONSHIP GAME EXPERIENCE: Played in NFC championship game (2002 season). ... Member of Super Bowl championship team (2002 season).

Year Team	G	GS	TOTALS Tk.	Ast.	Sks.	INTERCEPTIONS No.	Yds.	Avg.	TD
2001—Tampa Bay NFL	14	1	16	8	0.0	0	0	0.0	0
2002—Tampa Bay NFL	16	1	14	1	0.0	0	0	0.0	0
2003—Tampa Bay NFL	8	0	3	0	0.0	0	0	0.0	0
2004—Tampa Bay NFL	16	6	15	2	0.0	0	0	0.0	0
Pro totals (4 years)	54	8	48	11	0.0	0	0	0.0	0

HOWRY, KEENAN   WR   VIKINGS

PERSONAL: Born June 17, 1981, in Los Angeles, Calif. ... 5-10/172. ... Full name: Keenan Rashaun Howry.
HIGH SCHOOL: Los Alamitos (Calif.).
COLLEGE: Oregon.
TRANSACTIONS/CAREER NOTES: Selected by Minnesota Vikings in seventh round (221st pick overall) of 2003 NFL draft. ... Signed by Vikings (July 21, 2003). ... On injured reserve with shoulder injury (October 13, 2004-remainder of season).
SINGLE GAME HIGHS (regular season): Receptions—2 (October 26, 2003, vs. New York Giants); yards—15 (October 26, 2003, vs. New York Giants); and touchdown receptions—0.

H

Year	Team	G	GS	RUSHING Att.	Yds.	Avg.	TD	RECEIVING No.	Yds.	Avg.	TD	PUNT RETURNS No.	Yds.	Avg.	TD	KICKOFF RETURNS No.	Yds.	Avg.	TD	TOTALS TD	2pt.	Pts.
2003—Min. NFL		16	1	0	0	0.0	0	2	15	7.5	0	35	247	7.1	0	12	271	22.6	0	0	0	0
2004—Min. NFL		3	0	0	0	0.0	0	1	3	3.0	0	2	33	16.5	0	2	45	22.5	0	0	0	0
Pro totals (2 years)		19	1	0	0	0.0	0	3	18	6.0	0	37	280	7.6	0	14	316	22.6	0	0	0	0

HUFF, ORLANDO   LB   CARDINALS

PERSONAL: Born August 14, 1978, in Mobile, Ala. ... 6-2/250.
HIGH SCHOOL: Upland (Calif.).
JUNIOR COLLEGE: Eastern Arizona Junior College.
COLLEGE: Fresno State.
TRANSACTIONS/CAREER NOTES: Selected by Seattle Seahawks in fourth round (104th pick overall) of 2001 NFL draft. ... Signed by Seahawks (July 9, 2001). ... Granted free agency (March 3, 2004). ... Granted unconditional free agency (March 2, 2005). ... Signed by Arizona Cardinals (March 15, 2005).

Year	Team	G	GS	TOTALS Tk.	Ast.	Sks.	INTERCEPTIONS No.	Yds.	Avg.	TD
2001—Seattle NFL		12	0	0	0	0.0	0	0	0.0	0
2002—Seattle NFL		16	7	38	13	0.0	1	0	0.0	0
2003—Seattle NFL		11	2	16	4	1.0	0	0	0.0	0
2004—Seattle NFL		16	14	41	10	1.0	0	0	0.0	0
Pro totals (4 years)		55	23	95	27	2.0	1	0	0.0	0

HULSEY, COREY   G/T   RAIDERS

PERSONAL: Born July 26, 1977, in Lula, Ga. ... 6-4/325. ... Full name: Corey Spear Hulsey.
HIGH SCHOOL: North Hall (Lula, Ga.).
COLLEGE: Clemson.
TRANSACTIONS/CAREER NOTES: Signed as non-drafted free agent by Buffalo Bills (April 19, 1999). ... Released by Bills (August 30, 1999). ... Re-signed by Bills (April 27, 2000). ... Released by Bills (August 27, 2000). ... Re-signed by Bills to practice squad (August 28, 2000). ... Released by Bills (September 1, 2002). ... Signed by Oakland Raiders (January 7, 2003). ... Waived by Raiders (August 26, 2003). ... Re-signed by Raiders (November 19, 2003). ... Released by Raiders (September 5, 2004). ... Re-signed by Raiders (November 5, 2004).
PLAYING EXPERIENCE: Buffalo NFL, 2001; Oakland NFL, 2003-2004. ... Games/Games started: 2001 (16/12), 2003 (4/0), 2004 (3/0). Total: 23/12.

HUNT, CLETIDUS   DT   PACKERS

PERSONAL: Born January 2, 1976, in Memphis, Tenn. ... 6-4/310. ... Full name: Cletidus Marquell Hunt.
HIGH SCHOOL: Whitehaven (Memphis, Tenn.).
JUNIOR COLLEGE: Northwest Mississippi Community College.
COLLEGE: Kentucky State.
TRANSACTIONS/CAREER NOTES: Selected by Green Bay Packers in third round (94th pick overall) of NFL draft. ... Signed by Packers (July 26, 1999). ... On suspended list for violating league substance abuse policy (July 20-October 14, 2001). ... Granted free agency (March 1, 2002). ... Re-signed by Packers (April 24, 2002). ... Designated by Packers as franchise player (February 20, 2003). ... Re-signed by Packers (March 5, 2003).

Year	Team	G	GS	TOTALS Tk.	Ast.	Sks.
1999—Green Bay NFL		11	1	10	10	0.5
2000—Green Bay NFL		16	11	18	10	5.0
2001—Green Bay NFL		12	4	15	10	0.0
2002—Green Bay NFL		14	14	31	5	5.5
2003—Green Bay NFL		16	16	27	9	4.0
2004—Green Bay NFL		16	14	18	14	2.0
Pro totals (6 years)		85	60	119	58	17.0

HUNTER, PETE   CB   COWBOYS

PERSONAL: Born May 25, 1980, in Atlantic City, N.J. ... 6-2/208. ... Full name: Ralph Hunter.
HIGH SCHOOL: Atlantic City (N.J.).
COLLEGE: Virginia Union.
TRANSACTIONS/CAREER NOTES: Selected by Dallas Cowboys in fifth round (168th pick overall) of 2002 NFL draft. ... Signed by Cowboys (July 25, 2002). ... On injured reserve with knee injury (September 30, 2004-remainder of season). ... Granted free agency (March 2, 2005). ... Re-signed by Cowboys (April 21, 2005).

Year	Team	G	GS	TOTALS Tk.	Ast.	Sks.	INTERCEPTIONS No.	Yds.	Avg.	TD
2002—Dallas NFL		11	2	18	2	0.0	1	16	16.0	0
2003—Dallas NFL		16	1	19	2	0.0	1	0	0.0	0
2004—Dallas NFL		3	3	6	0	1.0	1	2	2.0	0
Pro totals (3 years)		30	6	43	4	1.0	3	18	6.0	0

H

HUNTER, WAYNE   T   SEAHAWKS

PERSONAL: Born July 2, 1981, in Honolulu, Hawaii. ... 6-5/303.
HIGH SCHOOL: Radford (Honolulu, Hawaii).
COLLEGE: Hawaii.

TRANSACTIONS/CAREER NOTES: Selected after junior season by Seattle Seahawks in third round (73rd pick overall) of 2003 NFL draft.... Inactive for 16 games (2003).
PLAYING EXPERIENCE: Seattle NFL, 2004. ... Games/Games started: 2004 (1/0). Total: 1/0.

HUTCHINS, VON   CB   COLTS

PERSONAL: Born February 14, 1981, in Natchez, Miss. ... 5-9/181. ... Full name: Tahaya De'Von Hutchins.
HIGH SCHOOL: Cathedral (Natchez, Miss.).
COLLEGE: Mississippi.
TRANSACTIONS/CAREER NOTES: Selected by Indianapolis Colts in sixth round (173rd pick overall) of 2004 NFL draft. ... Signed by Colts (July 26, 2004).

			TOTALS			INTERCEPTIONS			
Year Team	G	GS	Tk.	Ast.	Sks.	No.	Yds.	Avg.	TD
2004—Indianapolis NFL	16	1	29	11	0.0	1	77	77.0	1

HUTCHINSON, CHAD   QB   BEARS

PERSONAL: Born February 21, 1977, in Boulder, Colo. ... 6-5/237. ... Full name: Chad Martin Hutchinson.
HIGH SCHOOL: Torrey Pines (Encinitas, Calif.).
COLLEGE: Stanford.
TRANSACTIONS/CAREER NOTES: Signed as non-drafted free agent by Dallas Cowboys (January 26, 2002). ... Assigned by Cowboys to Rhein Fire in 2004 NFL Europe enhancement allocation program (February 9, 2004). ... Released by Cowboys (July 27, 2004). ... Signed by Chicago Bears (September 28, 2004).
SINGLE GAME HIGHS (regular season): Attempts—40 (December 15, 2002, vs. New York Giants); completions—22 (November 3, 2002, vs. Detroit); yards—301 (November 24, 2002, vs. Jacksonville); and touchdown passes—3 (December 5, 2004, vs. Minnesota).
STATISTICAL PLATEAUS: 300-yard passing games: 2002 (1). Total: 1.
MISCELLANEOUS: Regular-season record as starting NFL quarterback: 3-11 (.214).

			PASSING								RUSHING				TOTALS		
Year Team	G	GS	Att.	Cmp.	Pct.	Yds.	TD	Int.	Avg.	Skd.	Rat.	Att.	Yds.	Avg.	TD	TD	2pt.	Pts.
2002—Dallas NFL	9	9	250	127	50.8	1555	7	8	6.22	34	66.3	18	74	4.1	0	0	0	0
2003—Dallas NFL	1	0	2	1	50.0	8	0	0	4.00	0	60.4	2	-3	-1.5	0	0	0	0
2004—Chicago NFL	5	5	161	92	57.1	903	4	3	5.61	23	73.6	6	14	2.3	0	0	0	0
Pro totals (3 years)	15	14	413	220	53.3	2466	11	11	5.97	57	69.1	26	85	3.3	0	0	0	0

HUTCHINSON, STEVE   G   SEAHAWKS

PERSONAL: Born November 1, 1977, in Fort Lauderdale, Fla. ... 6-5/313.
HIGH SCHOOL: Coral Springs (Fla.).
COLLEGE: Michigan.
TRANSACTIONS/CAREER NOTES: Selected by Seattle Seahawks in first round (17th pick overall) of 2001 NFL draft. ... Signed by Seahawks (July 25, 2001). ... On injured reserve with broken leg (November 12, 2002-remainder of season).
PLAYING EXPERIENCE: Seattle NFL, 2001-2004. ... Games/Games started: 2001 (16/16), 2002 (4/4), 2003 (16/16), 2004 (16/16). Total: 52/52.
HONORS: Named guard on THE SPORTING NEWS college All-America first team (2000). ... Named guard on THE SPORTING NEWS NFL All-Pro team (2003). ... Played in Pro Bowl (2003 and 2004 seasons).

HUTTON, TREVOR   G   COLTS

PERSONAL: Born February 28, 1980, in Hilo, Hawaii. ... 6-2/308.
HIGH SCHOOL: Righetti (Santa Maria, Calif.).
JUNIOR COLLEGE: Hancock.
COLLEGE: Utah State.
TRANSACTIONS/CAREER NOTES: Sigend as non-drafted free agent by Indianapolis Colts (April 30, 2004). ... Released by Colts (September 6, 2004). ... Re-signed by Colts to practice squad (September 6, 2004). ... Activated (November 17, 2004). ... Released by Colts (January 16, 2005). ... Re-signed by Colts (February 9, 2005). ... Assigned by Colts to Amsterdam Admirals in 2005 NFL Europe enhancement allocation program (February 14, 2005).
PLAYING EXPERIENCE: Indianapolis NFL, 2004. ... Games/Games started: 2004 (4/0). Total: 4/0.

HYMES, RANDY   WR

PERSONAL: Born August 7, 1979, in Galveston, Texas. ... 6-3/211.
HIGH SCHOOL: Hitchcock (Texas).
COLLEGE: Grambling State.
TRANSACTIONS/CAREER NOTES: Signed as non-drafted free agent by Baltimore Ravens (April 26, 2002). ... Released by Ravens (August 30, 2002). ... Re-signed by Ravens to practice squad (September 3, 2002). ... Activated (November 14, 2002). ... On injured reserve with knee injury (August 30, 2003-entire season). ... Granted free agency (March 2, 2005).
SINGLE GAME HIGHS (regular season): Receptions—5 (September 12, 2004, vs. Cleveland); yards—76 (December 29, 2002, vs. Pittsburgh); and touchdown receptions—1 (October 4, 2004, vs. Kansas City).

			RECEIVING				TOTALS			
Year Team	G	GS	No.	Yds.	Avg.	TD	TD	2pt.	Pts.	Fum.
2002—Baltimore NFL	7	2	6	123	20.5	0	0	0	0	0
2004—Baltimore NFL	14	7	26	323	12.4	2	2	0	12	0
Pro totals (2 years)	21	9	32	446	13.9	2	2	0	12	0

H

IDONIJE, ISRAEL — DL — BEARS

PERSONAL: Born November 17, 1980, in Brandon, MB. ... 6-7/290.
COLLEGE: Manitoba.
TRANSACTIONS/CAREER NOTES: Signed as non-drafted free agent by Cleveland Browns (May 2, 2003). ... Released by Browns (September 30, 2003). ... Signed by Chicago Bears to practice squad (November 18, 2003). ... Assigned by Bears to Berlin Thunder in 2004 NFL Europe enhancement allocation program (February 18, 2004).

				TOTALS	
Year Team	G	GS	Tk.	Ast.	Sks.
2004—Chicago NFL	15	0	10	3	1.0

IOANE, JUNIOR — DT — TEXANS

PERSONAL: Born July 21, 1977, in American Samoa. ... 6-4/332. ... Full name: Junior Burton Ioane.
HIGH SCHOOL: North Sanpete (Mount Pleasant, Utah).
JUNIOR COLLEGE: Snow College (Utah).
COLLEGE: Arizona State.
TRANSACTIONS/CAREER NOTES: Selected by Oakland Raiders in fourth round (107th pick overall) of 2000 NFL draft. ... Signed by Raiders (June 1, 2000). ... Inactive for all 16 games (2000). ... Claimed on waivers by Houston Texans (September 1, 2003).
CHAMPIONSHIP GAME EXPERIENCE: Played in AFC championship game (2002 season). ... Played in Super Bowl 37 (2002 season).

				TOTALS	
Year Team	G	GS	Tk.	Ast.	Sks.
2001—Oakland NFL	3	0	0	0	0.0
2002—Oakland NFL	6	0	2	1	1.0
2003—Houston NFL	13	4	19	10	0.5
2004—Houston NFL	3	0	1	0	0.0
Pro totals (4 years)	25	4	22	11	1.5

IRONS, GRANT — DE — RAIDERS

PERSONAL: Born July 7, 1979, in Middleburg Heights, Ohio. ... 6-6/285. ... Full name: Grant Michael Irons. ... Son of Gerald Irons, linebacker with Oakland Raiders (1970-1975) and Cleveland Browns (1976-1979).
HIGH SCHOOL: Woodlands (Texas).
COLLEGE: Notre Dame.
TRANSACTIONS/CAREER NOTES: Signed as non-drafted free agent by Buffalo Bills (April 26, 2002). ... Released by Bills (August 31, 2003). ... Signed by Oakland Raiders (December 18, 2003).

				TOTALS	
Year Team	G	GS	Tk.	Ast.	Sks.
2002—Buffalo NFL	15	0	5	3	2.5
2003—Oakland NFL	1	0	0	0	0.0
2004—Oakland NFL	8	2	10	2	1.0
Pro totals (3 years)	24	2	15	5	3.5

IRVIN, KEN — CB — VIKINGS

PERSONAL: Born July 11, 1972, in Rome, Ga. ... 5-11/182. ... Full name: Kenneth Irvin.
HIGH SCHOOL: Pepperell (Lindale, Ga.).
COLLEGE: Memphis.
TRANSACTIONS/CAREER NOTES: Selected by Buffalo Bills in fourth round (109th pick overall) of 1995 NFL draft. ... Signed by Bills (July 10, 1995). ... Granted free agency (February 13, 1998). ... Re-signed by Bills (April 17, 1998). ... Granted unconditional free agency (February 12, 1999). ... Re-signed by Bills (March 17, 1999). ... On injured reserve with foot injury (December 23, 1999-remainder of season). ... Released by Bills (February 28, 2002). ... Signed by New Orleans Saints (April 24, 2002). ... Granted unconditional free agency (February 28, 2003). ... Signed by Minnesota Vikings (March 20, 2003). ... On injured reserve with Achilles injury (September 14, 2004-remainder of season).

			TOTALS			INTERCEPTIONS			
Year Team	G	GS	Tk.	Ast.	Sks.	No.	Yds.	Avg.	TD
1995—Buffalo NFL	16	3	18	2	0.0	0	0	0.0	0
1996—Buffalo NFL	16	1	17	4	2.0	0	0	0.0	0
1997—Buffalo NFL	16	0	5	0	0.0	2	28	14.0	0
1998—Buffalo NFL	16	16	46	5	0.0	1	43	43.0	0
1999—Buffalo NFL	14	14	40	5	0.0	1	1	1.0	0
2000—Buffalo NFL	16	16	29	2	0.0	2	1	0.5	0
2001—Buffalo NFL	14	4	33	3	0.0	1	0	0.0	0
2002—New Orleans NFL	16	9	58	4	0.0	2	10	5.0	0
2003—Minnesota NFL	16	8	45	10	0.0	1	1	1.0	0
2004—Minnesota NFL			Did not play.						
Pro totals (9 years)	140	71	291	35	2.0	10	84	8.4	0

ISOM, JASEN — FB — 49ERS

PERSONAL: Born January 7, 1977, in Wheatley Heights, N.Y. ... 6-0/240.
HIGH SCHOOL: Half Hollow Hills (Wheatley Heights, N.Y.).
COLLEGE: Western Illinois.

TRANSACTIONS/CAREER NOTES: Signed as non-drafted free agent by San Francisco 49ers to practice squad (April 27, 2001). ... Waived by 49ers (September 1, 2001). ... Re-signed by 49ers (January 15, 2002). ... Waived by 49ers (August 30, 2002). ... Re-signed by 49ers to practice squad (October 16, 2002) ... Activated (January 30, 2003). ... Waived by 49ers (August 31, 2003). ... Re-signed by 49ers to practice squad (September 1, 2003). ... Activated (October 25, 2003). ... Waived by 49ers (October 27, 2003). ... Re-signed by 49ers to practice squad (October 29, 2003). ... Activated (December 10, 2003). ... On injured reserve with Achilles injury (October 13, 2004-remainder of season).

SINGLE GAME HIGHS (regular season): Attempts—1 (September 26, 2004, vs. Seattle); yards—0; and rushing touchdowns—0.

			RUSHING				TOTALS		
Year Team	G	GS	Att.	Yds.	Avg.	TD	TD	2pt.	Pts.	Fum.
2003—San Francisco NFL	2	0	0	0	0.0	0	0	0	0	0
2004—San Francisco NFL	5	1	1	0	0.0	0	0	0	0	0
Pro totals (2 years)	7	1	1	0	0.0	0	0	0	0	0

IVY, COREY CB RAMS

PERSONAL: Born March 29, 1977, in St. Louis, Mo. ... 5-8/188. ... Full name: Corey Terrell Ivy.
HIGH SCHOOL: Moore (Okla.).
JUNIOR COLLEGE: Northeastern Oklahoma.
COLLEGE: Oklahoma.
TRANSACTIONS/CAREER NOTES: Signed as non-drafted free agent by New England Patriots (May 13, 1999). ... Released by Patriots (September 5, 1999). ... Re-signed by Patriots to practice squad (December 29, 1999). ... Signed by Cleveland Browns (July 12, 2000). ... Released by Browns (August 27, 2000). ... Signed by Tampa Bay Buccaneers (June 4, 2001). ... Released by Buccaneers (September 2, 2001). ... Re-signed by Buccaneers to practice squad (September 3, 2001). ... Activated (November 10, 2001). ... Released by Buccaneers (December 4, 2001). ... Re-signed by Buccaneers to practice squad (December 5, 2001). ... Assigned by Buccaneers to Rhein Fire in 2002 NFL Europe enhancement allocation program (February 12, 2002). ... Did not receive qualifying offer from Buccaneers (March 2, 2005). ... Signed by St. Louis Rams (April 28, 2005).
CHAMPIONSHIP GAME EXPERIENCE: Played in NFC championship game (2002 season). ... Member of Super Bowl championship team (2002 season).

			TOTALS			INTERCEPTIONS			
Year Team	G	GS	Tk.	Ast.	Sks.	No.	Yds.	Avg.	TD
2001—Tampa Bay NFL	1	0	3	2	0.0	0	0	0.0	0
2002—Tampa Bay NFL	16	0	0	0	0.0	0	0	0.0	0
2003—Tampa Bay NFL	16	2	18	0	0.0	0	0	0.0	0
2004—Tampa Bay NFL	16	0	0	0	0.0	0	11	0.0	0
Pro totals (4 years)	49	2	21	2	0.0	0	11	0.0	0

IWUOMA, CHIDI CB STEELERS

PERSONAL: Born February 19, 1978, in Los Angeles, Calif. ... 5-8/184.
HIGH SCHOOL: Pasadena (Calif.).
COLLEGE: California.
TRANSACTIONS/CAREER NOTES: Signed as non-drafted free agent by Detroit Lions (April 27, 2000). ... Released by Lions (September 2, 2001). ... Re-signed by Lions to practice squad (September 4, 2001). ... Activated (September 8, 2001). ... Released by Lions (September 1, 2002). ... Signed by Pittsburgh Steelers (September 11, 2002). ... Granted free agency (March 3, 2004). ... Re-signed by Steelers (April 28, 2004).
CHAMPIONSHIP GAME EXPERIENCE: Member of Steelers for AFC championship game (2004 season); inactive.

			TOTALS			INTERCEPTIONS			
Year Team	G	GS	Tk.	Ast.	Sks.	No.	Yds.	Avg.	TD
2001—Detroit NFL	13	1	5	0	0.0	0	0	0.0	0
2002—Pittsburgh NFL	13	0	0	1	0.0	0	0	0.0	0
2003—Pittsburgh NFL	15	0	0	0	0.0	0	0	0.0	0
2004—Pittsburgh NFL	14	0	0	0	0.0	0	0	0.0	0
Pro totals (4 years)	55	1	5	1	0.0	0	0	0.0	0

IZZO, LARRY LB PATRIOTS

PERSONAL: Born September 26, 1974, in Fort Belvoir, Va. ... 5-10/228. ... Full name: Lawrence Alexander Izzo.
HIGH SCHOOL: McCullough (Houston).
COLLEGE: Rice.
TRANSACTIONS/CAREER NOTES: Signed as non-drafted free agent by Miami Dolphins (April 25, 1996). ... On injured reserve with foot injury (August 18, 1997-entire season). ... Granted free agency (February 12, 1999). ... Re-signed by Dolphins (March 31, 1999). ... Granted unconditional free agency (March 2, 2001). ... Signed by New England Patriots (March 6, 2001).
CHAMPIONSHIP GAME EXPERIENCE: Played in AFC championship game (2001, 2003 and 2004 seasons). ... Member of Super Bowl championship team (2001, 2003 and 2004 seasons).
HONORS: Played in Pro Bowl (2000, 2002 and 2004 seasons).

			TOTALS			INTERCEPTIONS			
Year Team	G	GS	Tk.	Ast.	Sks.	No.	Yds.	Avg.	TD
1996—Miami NFL	16	0	1	0	0.0	0	0	0.0	0
1997—Miami NFL		Did not play.							
1998—Miami NFL	13	0	0	0	0.0	0	0	0.0	0
1999—Miami NFL	16	0	0	0	0.0	0	0	0.0	0
2000—Miami NFL	16	0	4	0	0.0	0	0	0.0	0
2001—New England NFL	16	0	1	1	0.0	0	0	0.0	0
2002—New England NFL	15	0	1	0	0.0	0	0	0.0	0
2003—New England NFL	16	0	5	0	0.0	1	0	0.0	0
2004—New England NFL	16	0	1	0	0.0	0	0	0.0	0
Pro totals (8 years)	124	0	13	1	0.0	1	0	0.0	0

JACKSON, ALONZO — LB — STEELERS

PERSONAL: Born September 15, 1980, in Americus, Ga. ... 6-4/268.
HIGH SCHOOL: Americus (Ga.).
COLLEGE: Florida State.
TRANSACTIONS/CAREER NOTES: Selected by Pittsburgh Steelers in second round (59th pick overall) of 2003 NFL draft. ... Signed by Steelers (July 25, 2003).
CHAMPIONSHIP GAME EXPERIENCE: Member of Steelers for AFC championship game (2004 season); inactive.

Year Team	G	GS	TOTALS Tk.	Ast.	Sks.	INTERCEPTIONS No.	Yds.	Avg.	TD
2003—Pittsburgh NFL	2	0	0	0	0.0	0	0	0.0	0
2004—Pittsburgh NFL	7	0	2	1	0.0	0	0	0.0	0
Pro totals (2 years)	9	0	2	1	0.0	0	0	0.0	0

JACKSON, COREY — DL — BROWNS

PERSONAL: Born November 6, 1978, in Cassatt, S.C. ... 6-6/255.
HIGH SCHOOL: North Central (Kershaw, S.C.).
COLLEGE: Nevada.
TRANSACTIONS/CAREER NOTES: Signed as non-drafted free agent by Cleveland Browns (May 2, 2003). ... Released by Browns (August 26, 2003). ... Re-signed by Browns to practice squad (September 1, 2003). ... Released by Browns from practice squad (September 24, 2003). ... Re-signed by Browns to practice squad (December 10, 2003). ... Activated (January 2, 2004).

Year Team	G	GS	TOTALS Tk.	Ast.	Sks.
2004—Cleveland NFL	1	0	0	0	0.0

JACKSON, DARRELL — WR — SEAHAWKS

PERSONAL: Born December 6, 1978, in Dayton, Ohio. ... 6-0/201. ... Full name: Darrell Lamont Jackson.
HIGH SCHOOL: Tampa Catholic.
COLLEGE: Florida.
TRANSACTIONS/CAREER NOTES: Selected after junior season by Seattle Seahawks in third round (80th pick overall) of 2000 NFL draft. ... Signed by Seahawks (July 19, 2000). ... Granted free agency (February 28, 2003). ... Re-signed by Seahawks (April 25, 2003). ... Granted unconditional free agency (March 3, 2004). ... Re-signed by Seahawks (March 9, 2004).
SINGLE GAME HIGHS (regular season): Receptions—10 (December 12, 2004, vs. Minnesota); yards—174 (September 15, 2002, vs. Arizona); and touchdown receptions—2 (November 7, 2004, vs. San Francisco).
STATISTICAL PLATEAUS: 100-yard receiving games: 2001 (5), 2002 (2), 2003 (3), 2004 (5). Total: 15.

Year Team	G	GS	RUSHING Att.	Yds.	Avg.	TD	RECEIVING No.	Yds.	Avg.	TD	PUNT RETURNS No.	Yds.	Avg.	TD	TOTALS TD	2pt.	Pts.	Fum.
2000—Seattle NFL	16	10	1	-1	-1.0	0	53	713	13.5	6	0	0	0.0	0	6	0	36	2
2001—Seattle NFL	16	16	1	9	9.0	0	70	1081	15.4	8	0	0	0.0	0	8	0	48	0
2002—Seattle NFL	13	13	3	3	1.0	0	62	877	14.1	4	4	32	8.0	0	4	0	24	3
2003—Seattle NFL	16	16	0	0	0.0	0	68	1137	16.7	9	0	0	0.0	0	9	0	54	1
2004—Seattle NFL	16	16	0	0	0.0	0	87	1199	13.8	7	0	0	0.0	0	7	1	44	2
Pro totals (5 years)	77	71	5	11	2.2	0	340	5007	14.7	34	4	32	8.0	0	34	1	206	8

JACKSON, DEXTER — S — BUCCANEERS

PERSONAL: Born July 28, 1977, in Quincy, Fla. ... 6-0/205. ... Full name: Dexter Lamar Jackson.
HIGH SCHOOL: James A. Shanks (Quincy, Fla.).
COLLEGE: Florida State.
TRANSACTIONS/CAREER NOTES: Selected by Tampa Bay Buccaneers in fourth round (113th pick overall) of 1999 NFL draft. ... Signed by Buccaneers (July 29, 1999). ... Granted free agency (March 1, 2002). ... Re-signed by Buccaneers (April 26, 2002). ... Granted unconditional free agency (February 28, 2003). ... Signed by Arizona Cardinals (March 12, 2003). ... On injured reserve with back injury (September 5-14, 2004). ... Released by Cardinals (October 14, 2004). ... Signed by Buccaneers (November 16, 2004). ... Granted unconditional free agency (March 2, 2005). ... Re-signed by Buccaneers (April 1, 2005).
CHAMPIONSHIP GAME EXPERIENCE: Played in NFC championship game (1999 and 2002 seasons). ... Member of Super Bowl championship team (2002 season).
HONORS: Named Most Valuable Player of Super Bowl 37 (2002 season).

Year Team	G	GS	TOTALS Tk.	Ast.	Sks.	INTERCEPTIONS No.	Yds.	Avg.	TD
1999—Tampa Bay NFL	12	0	0	0	0.0	0	0	0.0	0
2000—Tampa Bay NFL	13	0	18	2	0.0	0	0	0.0	0
2001—Tampa Bay NFL	15	15	54	11	2.5	4	42	10.5	0
2002—Tampa Bay NFL	16	16	56	15	0.0	3	101	33.7	0
2003—Arizona NFL	16	16	73	13	0.0	6	122	20.3	0
2004—Tampa Bay NFL	6	1	14	2	0.0	0	0	0.0	0
Pro totals (6 years)	78	48	215	43	2.5	13	265	20.4	0

JACKSON, EDDIE — CB — PANTHERS

PERSONAL: Born December 19, 1980, in Americus, Ga. ... 6-0/190.
HIGH SCHOOL: Richardson (Texas).
COLLEGE: Arkansas.

TRANSACTIONS/CAREER NOTES: Signed as a non-drafted free agent by Carolina Panthers (April 30, 2004). ... Released by Panthers (September 5, 2004). ... Re-signed by Panthers to practice squad (September 7, 2004). ... Activated (October 27, 2004).

Year Team	G	GS	TOTALS Tk.	Ast.	Sks.	INTERCEPTIONS No.	Yds.	Avg.	TD
2004—Carolina NFL	10	0	7	1	0.0	0	0	0.0	0

JACKSON, FRISMAN — WR — BROWNS

PERSONAL: Born June 12, 1979, in Chicago, Ill. ... 6-3/220.
HIGH SCHOOL: Morgan Park (Chicago).
COLLEGE: Western Illinois.
TRANSACTIONS/CAREER NOTES: Signed as non-drafted free agent by Cleveland Browns (April 26, 2002). ... Released by Browns (September 5, 2004). ... Re-signed by Browns to practice squad (September 6, 2004). ... Activated (October 20, 2004).
SINGLE GAME HIGHS (regular season): Receptions—5 (November 14, 2004, vs. Pittsburgh); yards—61 (November 14, 2004, vs. Pittsburgh); and touchdown receptions—0.

Year Team	G	GS	RECEIVING No.	Yds.	Avg.	TD	KICKOFF RETURNS No.	Yds.	Avg.	TD	TOTALS TD	2pt.	Pts.	Fum.
2002—Cleveland NFL	7	0	1	6	6.0	0	3	58	19.3	0	0	0	0	0
2003—Cleveland NFL	5	0	2	29	14.5	0	0	0	0.0	0	0	0	0	0
2004—Cleveland NFL	10	0	13	168	12.9	0	4	70	17.5	0	0	0	0	1
Pro totals (3 years)	22	0	16	203	12.7	0	7	128	18.3	0	0	0	0	1

JACKSON, GRADY — DT — PACKERS

PERSONAL: Born January 21, 1973, in Greensboro, Ala. ... 6-2/340.
HIGH SCHOOL: Greensboro (Ala.) East.
JUNIOR COLLEGE: Hinds Community College (Miss.).
COLLEGE: Knoxville.
TRANSACTIONS/CAREER NOTES: Selected by Oakland Raiders in sixth round (193rd pick overall) of 1997 NFL draft. ... Signed by Raiders (July 18, 1997). ... Granted unconditional free agency (March 1, 2002). ... Signed by New Orleans Saints (April 11, 2002). ... Suspended one game for conduct detrimental to team (October 28, 2003). ... Claimed on waivers by Green Bay Packers (November 4, 2003).
CHAMPIONSHIP GAME EXPERIENCE: Played in AFC championship game (2000 season).

Year Team	G	GS	TOTALS Tk.	Ast.	Sks.
1997—Oakland NFL	5	0	4	2	0.0
1998—Oakland NFL	15	1	29	10	3.0
1999—Oakland NFL	15	0	25	9	4.0
2000—Oakland NFL	16	15	51	17	8.0
2001—Oakland NFL	16	16	52	17	4.0
2002—New Orleans NFL	15	15	31	12	5.5
2003—New Orleans NFL	7	6	20	5	3.5
—Green Bay NFL	8	1	16	7	2.5
2004—Green Bay NFL	10	10	17	6	1.0
Pro totals (8 years)	107	64	245	85	31.5

JACKSON, JAMES — RB

PERSONAL: Born August 4, 1976, in Belle Glade, Fla. ... 5-10/215. ... Full name: James Shurrate Jackson.
HIGH SCHOOL: Glades Central (Belle Glade, Fla.).
COLLEGE: Miami (Fla.).
TRANSACTIONS/CAREER NOTES: Selected by Cleveland Browns in third round (65th pick overall) of 2001 NFL draft. ... Signed by Browns (July 23, 2001). ... On injured reserve with ankle injury (December 20, 2001-remainder of season). ... On injured reserve with knee injury (December 9, 2003-remainder of season). ... Released by Browns (November 16, 2004). ... Signed by Green Bay Packers (November 23, 2004). ... Released by Packers (December 7, 2004).
SINGLE GAME HIGHS (regular season): Attempts—31 (September 23, 2001, vs. Detroit); yards—124 (September 23, 2001, vs. Detroit); and rushing touchdowns—2 (November 16, 2003, vs. Arizona).
STATISTICAL PLATEAUS: 100-yard rushing games: 2001 (1). Total: 1.

Year Team	G	GS	RUSHING Att.	Yds.	Avg.	TD	RECEIVING No.	Yds.	Avg.	TD	KICKOFF RETURNS No.	Yds.	Avg.	TD	TOTALS TD	2pt.	Pts.	Fum.
2001—Cleveland NFL	11	10	195	554	2.8	2	7	56	8.0	0	0	0	0.0	0	2	0	12	1
2002—Cleveland NFL	15	0	12	54	4.5	0	3	9	3.0	0	1	13	13.0	0	0	0	0	0
2003—Cleveland NFL	12	6	102	382	3.7	3	14	114	8.1	0	1	68	68.0	0	3	0	18	3
2004—Cleveland NFL	4	0	12	81	6.8	0	6	22	3.7	0	2	39	19.5	0	0	0	0	1
—Green Bay NFL	1	0	0	0	0.0	0	0	0	0.0	0	0	0	0.0	0	0	0	0	0
Pro totals (4 years)	43	16	321	1071	3.3	5	30	201	6.7	0	4	120	30.0	0	5	0	30	5

JACKSON, NATE — WR — BRONCOS

PERSONAL: Born June 4, 1979, in San Jose, Calif. ... 6-3/223.
HIGH SCHOOL: Pioneer (San Jose, Calif.)
COLLEGE: Menlo.
TRANSACTIONS/CAREER NOTES: Signed as non-drafted free agent by San Francisco 49ers (April 23, 2002). ... Waived by 49ers (August 21, 2002). ... Re-signed by 49ers (January 27, 2003). ... Traded by 49ers to Denver Broncos for conditional pick in 2004 draft (August 12, 2003).

... Released by Broncos (August 31, 2003). ... Re-signed by Broncos to practice squad (September 1, 2003). ... Activated (December 26, 2003). ... On injured reserve with ankle injury (December 7, 2004-remainder of season).
SINGLE GAME HIGHS (regular season): Receptions—4 (October 25, 2004, vs. Cincinnati); yards—33 (October 25, 2004, vs. Cincinnati); and touchdown receptions—0.

				RECEIVING				TOTALS			
Year Team	G	GS	No.	Yds.	Avg.	TD	TD	2pt.	Pts.	Fum.
2003—Denver NFL	1	0	0	0	0.0	0	0	0	0	0
2004—Denver NFL	12	0	8	73	9.1	0	0	0	0	0
Pro totals (2 years)	13	0	8	73	9.1	0	0	0	0	0

JACKSON, STEVEN — RB — RAMS

PERSONAL: Born July 22, 1983, in Las Vegas, Nev. ... 6-2/233. ... Full name: Steven Rashad Jackson.
HIGH SCHOOL: Eldorado (Las Vegas, Nev.).
COLLEGE: Oregon State.
TRANSACTIONS/CAREER NOTES: Selected after junior season by St. Louis Rams in first round (24th pick overall) of 2004 NFL draft. ... Signed by Rams (July 25, 2004).
SINGLE GAME HIGHS (regular season): Attempts—26 (December 5, 2004, vs. San Francisco); yards—148 (December 27, 2004, vs. Philadelphia); and rushing touchdowns—1 (January 2, 2005, vs. New York Jets).
STATISTICAL PLATEAUS: 100-yard rushing games: 2004 (2). Total: 2.

			RUSHING				RECEIVING				KICKOFF RETURNS				TOTALS			
Year Team	G	GS	Att.	Yds.	Avg.	TD	No.	Yds.	Avg.	TD	No.	Yds.	Avg.	TD	TD	2pt.	Pts.	Fum.
2004—St. Louis NFL	14	3	134	673	5.0	4	19	189	9.9	0	4	79	19.8	0	4	1	26	1

JACKSON, TERRY — FB — 49ERS

PERSONAL: Born January 10, 1976, in Gainesville, Fla. ... 6-0/232. ... Full name: Terrance Bernard Jackson. ... Brother of Willie Jackson Jr., wide receiver with six NFL teams (1994-2002).
HIGH SCHOOL: P.K. Yonge (Gainesville, Fla.).
COLLEGE: Florida.
TRANSACTIONS/CAREER NOTES: Selected by San Francisco 49ers in fifth round (157th pick overall) of 1999 NFL draft. ... Signed by 49ers (July 26, 1999). ... Granted free agency (March 1, 2002). ... Re-signed by 49ers (July 22, 2002). ... On injured reserve with knee injury (October 16, 2002-remainder of season). ... Granted unconditional free agency (March 2, 2005). ... Re-signed by 49ers (March 7, 2005).
SINGLE GAME HIGHS (regular season): Attempts—5 (December 12, 2004, vs. Arizona); yards—37 (December 2, 2001, vs. Buffalo); and rushing touchdowns—1 (January 6, 2002, vs. New Orleans).

			RUSHING				RECEIVING				KICKOFF RETURNS				TOTALS			
Year Team	G	GS	Att.	Yds.	Avg.	TD	No.	Yds.	Avg.	TD	No.	Yds.	Avg.	TD	TD	2pt.	Pts.	Fum.
1999—San Francisco NFL	16	0	15	75	5.0	0	3	6	2.0	0	0	0	0.0	0	0	0	0	1
2000—San Francisco NFL	15	1	5	6	1.2	0	5	48	9.6	1	1	9	9.0	0	2	1	14	0
2001—San Francisco NFL	16	1	22	138	6.3	1	12	91	7.6	2	0	0	0.0	0	3	0	18	1
2002—San Francisco NFL	5	0	0	0	0.0	0	0	0	0.0	0	4	67	16.8	0	0	0	0	0
2003—San Francisco NFL	16	0	0	0	0.0	0	0	0	0.0	0	0	0	0.0	0	0	0	0	0
2004—San Francisco NFL	16	0	26	101	3.9	0	21	139	6.6	0	2	22	11.0	0	0	0	0	3
Pro totals (6 years)	84	2	68	320	4.7	2	41	284	6.9	3	7	98	14.0	0	5	1	32	5

JACKSON, TYOKA — DT — RAMS

PERSONAL: Born November 22, 1971, in Washington, DC. ... 6-2/280. ... Name pronounced: tie-OH-kah.
HIGH SCHOOL: Bishop McNamara (Forestville, Md.).
COLLEGE: Penn State.
TRANSACTIONS/CAREER NOTES: Signed as non-drafted free agent by Atlanta Falcons (May 2, 1994). ... Released by Falcons (August 29, 1994). ... Re-signed by Falcons to practice squad (August 30, 1994). ... Signed by Miami Dolphins off Falcons practice squad (November 16, 1994). ... Released by Dolphins (August 27, 1995). ... Signed by Tampa Bay Buccaneers (December 27, 1995). ... Granted free agency (February 13, 1998). ... Re-signed by Buccaneers (June 22, 1998). ... Granted unconditional free agency (March 2, 2001). ... Signed by St. Louis Rams (May 1, 2001). ... Granted unconditional free agency (February 28, 2003). ... Re-signed by Rams (March 17, 2003).
CHAMPIONSHIP GAME EXPERIENCE: Member of Buccaneers for NFC championship game (1999 season); inactive. ... Played in NFC championship game (2001 season). ... Played in Super Bowl 36 (2001 season).

			TOTALS			INTERCEPTIONS			
Year Team	G	GS	Tk.	Ast.	Sks.	No.	Yds.	Avg.	TD
1994—Miami NFL	1	0	0	0	0.0	0	0	0.0	0
1995—			Did not play.						
1996—Tampa Bay NFL	13	2	9	2	0.0	0	0	0.0	0
1997—Tampa Bay NFL	12	0	5	2	2.5	0	0	0.0	0
1998—Tampa Bay NFL	16	12	21	6	3.0	0	0	0.0	0
1999—Tampa Bay NFL	6	1	5	2	1.0	0	0	0.0	0
2000—Tampa Bay NFL	16	1	4	3	2.0	0	0	0.0	0
2001—St. Louis NFL	16	0	12	7	3.0	0	0	0.0	0
2002—St. Louis NFL	16	0	14	3	3.5	0	0	0.0	0
2003—St. Louis NFL	16	3	19	4	5.5	1	11	11.0	0
2004—St. Louis NFL	14	0	21	3	4.0	0	0	0.0	0
Pro totals (10 years)	126	19	110	32	24.5	1	11	11.0	0

JACOBS, TAYLOR — WR — REDSKINS

PERSONAL: Born May 30, 1981, in Tallahassee, Fla. ... 6-0/198. ... Full name: Taylor Houser Jacobs.
HIGH SCHOOL: Florida A&M (Tallahassee, Fla.).
COLLEGE: Florida.

TRANSACTIONS/CAREER NOTES: Selected by Washington Redskins in second round (44th pick overall) of 2003 NFL draft. ... Signed by Redskins (July 28, 2003).
SINGLE GAME HIGHS (regular season): Receptions—5 (October 31, 2004, vs. Green Bay); yards—56 (January 2, 2005, vs. Minnesota); and touchdown receptions—1 (November 2, 2003, vs. Dallas).

				RUSHING				RECEIVING				TOTALS		
Year Team	G	GS	Att.	Yds.	Avg.	TD	No.	Yds.	Avg.	TD	TD	2pt.	Pts.	Fum.
2003—Washington NFL	8	0	0	0	0.0	0	3	37	12.3	1	1	0	6	0
2004—Washington NFL	15	4	1	-6	-6.0	0	16	178	11.1	0	0	1	2	0
Pro totals (2 years)	23	4	1	-6	-6.0	0	19	215	11.3	1	1	1	8	0

JACOX, KENDYL　　　　　C/G　　　　　SAINTS

PERSONAL: Born June 10, 1975, in Dallas, Texas. ... 6-2/325. ... Full name: Kendyl LaMarc Jacox. ... Name pronounced: JAY-cox.
HIGH SCHOOL: Carter (Dallas).
COLLEGE: Kansas State.
TRANSACTIONS/CAREER NOTES: Signed as non-drafted free agent by San Diego Chargers (April 20, 1998). ... On injured reserve with knee injury (December 4, 1999-remainder of season). ... Granted free agency (March 2, 2001). ... Re-signed by Chargers (April 10, 2001). ... Granted unconditional free agency (March 1, 2002). ... Signed by New Orleans Saints (May 28, 2002).
PLAYING EXPERIENCE: San Diego NFL, 1998-2001; New Orleans NFL, 2002-2004. ... Games/Games started: 1998 (16/6), 1999 (10/5), 2000 (15/3), 2001 (16/16), 2002 (16/16), 2003 (12/11), 2004 (13/13). Total: 98/70.

JAMES, BRADIE　　　　　LB　　　　　COWBOYS

PERSONAL: Born January 17, 1981, in Monroe, La. ... 6-2/245. ... Full name: Bradie Gene James.
HIGH SCHOOL: West Monroe (Monroe, La.).
COLLEGE: Louisiana State.
TRANSACTIONS/CAREER NOTES: Selected by Dallas Cowboys in fourth round (103rd pick overall) of 2003 NFL draft. ... Signed by Cowboys (July 26, 2003).

			TOTALS			INTERCEPTIONS			
Year Team	G	GS	Tk.	Ast.	Sks.	No.	Yds.	Avg.	TD
2003—Dallas NFL	14	0	3	0	0.0	0	0	0.0	0
2004—Dallas NFL	16	2	24	7	0.0	0	0	0.0	0
Pro totals (2 years)	30	2	27	7	0.0	0	0	0.0	0

JAMES, EDGERRIN　　　　　RB　　　　　COLTS

PERSONAL: Born August 1, 1978, in Immokalee, Fla. ... 6-0/214. ... Full name: Edgerrin Tyree James. ... Name pronounced: EDGE-rin.
HIGH SCHOOL: Immokalee (Fla.).
COLLEGE: Miami (Fla.).
TRANSACTIONS/CAREER NOTES: Selected after junior season by Indianapolis Colts in first round (fourth pick overall) of 1999 NFL draft. ... Signed by Colts (August 12, 1999). ... On injured reserve with knee injury (November 21, 2001-remainder of season). ... Designated by Colts as franchise player (February 22, 2005). ... Re-signed by Colts (March 16, 2005).
CHAMPIONSHIP GAME EXPERIENCE: Played in AFC championship game (2003 season).
HONORS: Named NFL Rookie of the Year by THE SPORTING NEWS (1999). ... Named running back on THE SPORTING NEWS NFL All-Pro team (1999, 2000 and 2004). ... Played in Pro Bowl (1999 and 2000 seasons). ... Named to play in Pro Bowl (2004 season); replaced by Corey Dillon due to injury.
SINGLE GAME HIGHS (regular season): Attempts—38 (October 15, 2000, vs. Seattle); yards—219 (October 15, 2000, vs. Seattle); and rushing touchdowns—3 (November 16, 2003, vs. New York Jets).
STATISTICAL PLATEAUS: 100-yard rushing games: 1999 (10), 2000 (9), 2001 (5), 2002 (2), 2003 (6), 2004 (8). Total: 40.
MISCELLANEOUS: Holds Colts franchise all-time record for most yards rushing (7,720).

				RUSHING				RECEIVING				TOTALS		
Year Team	G	GS	Att.	Yds.	Avg.	TD	No.	Yds.	Avg.	TD	TD	2pt.	Pts.	Fum.
1999—Indianapolis NFL	16	16	*369	*1553	4.2	▲13	62	586	9.5	4	†17	0	102	8
2000—Indianapolis NFL	16	16	387	*1709	4.4	13	63	594	9.4	5	§18	1	110	5
2001—Indianapolis NFL	6	6	151	662	4.4	3	24	193	8.0	0	3	1	20	3
2002—Indianapolis NFL	14	14	277	989	3.6	2	61	354	5.8	1	3	1	20	4
2003—Indianapolis NFL	13	13	310	1259	4.1	11	51	292	5.7	0	11	0	66	5
2004—Indianapolis NFL	16	16	334	1548	4.6	9	51	483	9.5	0	9	1	56	6
Pro totals (6 years)	81	81	1828	7720	4.2	51	312	2502	8.0	10	61	4	374	31

JAMES, JENO　　　　　G　　　　　DOLPHINS

PERSONAL: Born January 12, 1977, in Montgomery, Ala. ... 6-3/315. ... Full name: Jenorris James.
HIGH SCHOOL: Sidney Lanier (Montgomery, Ala.).
COLLEGE: Auburn.
TRANSACTIONS/CAREER NOTES: Selected by Carolina Panthers in sixth round (182nd pick overall) of 2000 NFL draft. ... Signed by Panthers (June 19, 2000). ... Granted free agency (February 28, 2003). ... Re-signed by Panthers (June 3, 2003). ... Granted unconditional free agency (March 3, 2004). ... Signed by Miami Dolphins (March 5, 2004).
PLAYING EXPERIENCE: Carolina NFL, 2000-2003; Miami NFL, 2004. ... Games/Games started: 2000 (16/4), 2001 (14/6), 2002 (9/2), 2003 (16/16), 2004 (14/14). Total: 69/42.
CHAMPIONSHIP GAME EXPERIENCE: Played in NFC championship game (2003 season). ... Played in Super Bowl 38 (2003 season).

JAMES, TORY CB BENGALS

PERSONAL: Born May 18, 1973, in New Orleans, La. ... 6-2/186. ... Full name: Tory Steven James.
HIGH SCHOOL: Archbishop Shaw (Marrero, La.).
COLLEGE: Louisiana State.
TRANSACTIONS/CAREER NOTES: Selected by Denver Broncos in second round (44th pick overall) of 1996 NFL draft. ... Signed by Broncos (July 22, 1996). ... On injured reserve with knee injury (August 18, 1997-entire season). ... Granted unconditional free agency (February 11, 2000). ... Signed by Oakland Raiders (February 28, 2000). ... Released by Raiders (February 27, 2003). ... Signed by Cincinnati Bengals (March 10, 2003).
CHAMPIONSHIP GAME EXPERIENCE: Played in AFC championship game (1998, 2000 and 2002 seasons). ... Member of Super Bowl championship team (1998 season). ... Played in Super Bowl 37 (2002 season).
HONORS: Played in Pro Bowl (2004 season).

Year Team	G	GS	TOTALS Tk.	Ast.	Sks.	INTERCEPTIONS No.	Yds.	Avg.	TD
1996—Denver NFL	16	2	22	1	0.0	2	15	7.5	0
1997—Denver NFL	Did not play.								
1998—Denver NFL	16	0	10	1	0.0	0	0	0.0	0
1999—Denver NFL	16	4	32	1	0.0	5	59	11.8	0
2000—Oakland NFL	16	1	26	3	0.0	2	25	12.5	0
2001—Oakland NFL	16	2	33	3	0.0	5	72	14.4	0
2002—Oakland NFL	14	13	41	4	0.0	4	35	8.8	0
2003—Cincinnati NFL	16	16	57	6	1.0	4	56	14.0	0
2004—Cincinnati NFL	16	16	58	5	0.0	8	66	8.3	0
Pro totals (8 years)	126	54	279	24	1.0	30	328	10.9	0

JAMESON, MICHAEL CB BROWNS

PERSONAL: Born July 14, 1979, in Killeen, Texas. ... 5-11/205.
HIGH SCHOOL: Ellison (Killeen, Texas).
COLLEGE: Texas A&M.
TRANSACTIONS/CAREER NOTES: Selected by Cleveland Browns in sixth round (165th pick overall) of 2001 NFL draft. ... Signed by Browns (May 24, 2001). ... On injured reserve with ankle injury (August 27, 2001-entire season). ... Released by Browns (September 1, 2002). ... Re-signed by Browns to practice squad (September 4, 2002). ... Activated (October 9, 2002).

Year Team	G	GS	TOTALS Tk.	Ast.	Sks.	INTERCEPTIONS No.	Yds.	Avg.	TD
2002—Cleveland NFL	11	1	8	2	1.0	1	0	0.0	0
2003—Cleveland NFL	15	0	2	1	0.0	0	0	0.0	0
2004—Cleveland NFL	16	0	8	5	0.0	0	0	0.0	0
Pro totals (3 years)	42	1	18	8	1.0	1	0	0.0	0

JAMMER, QUENTIN CB CHARGERS

PERSONAL: Born June 19, 1979, in Matagorda County, Texas. ... 6-0/204. ... Full name: Quentin T. Jammer.
HIGH SCHOOL: Angleton (Texas).
COLLEGE: Texas.
TRANSACTIONS/CAREER NOTES: Selected by San Diego Chargers in first round (fifth pick overall) of 2002 NFL draft. ... Signed by Chargers (September 11, 2002).
HONORS: Named cornerback on THE SPORTING NEWS college All-America first team (2001).

Year Team	G	GS	TOTALS Tk.	Ast.	Sks.	INTERCEPTIONS No.	Yds.	Avg.	TD
2002—San Diego NFL	14	4	56	8	0.0	0	0	0.0	0
2003—San Diego NFL	16	16	57	14	0.0	4	6	1.5	0
2004—San Diego NFL	16	16	53	9	0.0	1	12	12.0	0
Pro totals (3 years)	46	36	166	31	0.0	5	18	3.6	0

JANIKOWSKI, SEBASTIAN K RAIDERS

PERSONAL: Born March 2, 1978, in Walbrzych, Poland. ... 6-2/250.
HIGH SCHOOL: Seabreeze (Daytona, Fla.).
COLLEGE: Florida State.
TRANSACTIONS/CAREER NOTES: Selected after junior season by Oakland Raiders in first round (17th pick overall) of 2000 NFL draft. ... Signed by Raiders (July 20, 2000).
CHAMPIONSHIP GAME EXPERIENCE: Played in AFC championship game (2000 and 2002 seasons). ... Played in Super Bowl 37 (2002 season).
HONORS: Named kicker on THE SPORTING NEWS college All-America first team (1998 and 1999). ... Lou Groza Award winner (1998 and 1999).
RECORDS: Shares NFL record for most field goals made, one quarter (4), vs. Chicago (October 5, 2003, second quarter).

Year Team	G	FIELD GOALS 1-29	30-39	40-49	50+	Tot.	Pct.	Lg.	TOTALS XPM	XPA	Pts.
2000—Oakland NFL	14	7-7	6-7	8-14	1-4	22-32	68.8	▲54	46	46	112
2001—Oakland NFL	15	7-7	9-10	6-9	1-2	23-28	82.1	52	§42	▲42	111
2002—Oakland NFL	16	10-11	7-8	7-12	2-2	26-33	78.8	51	50	50	128
2003—Oakland NFL	16	6-6	6-6	9-10	1-3	22-25	88.0	55	28	29	94
2004—Oakland NFL	16	8-8	7-8	8-10	2-2	25-28	89.3	52	31	32	106
Pro totals (5 years)	77	38-39	35-39	38-55	7-13	118-146	80.8	55	197	199	551

JANSEN, JON — T — REDSKINS

PERSONAL: Born January 28, 1976, in Clawson, Mich. ... 6-6/305. ... Full name: Jonathan Ward Jansen.
HIGH SCHOOL: Clawson (Mich.).
COLLEGE: Michigan.
TRANSACTIONS/CAREER NOTES: Selected by Washington Redskins in second round (37th pick overall) of 1999 NFL draft. ... Signed by Redskins (July 9, 1999). ... On injured reserve with Achilles injury (August 11, 2004-entire season).
PLAYING EXPERIENCE: Washington NFL, 1999-2004. ... Games/Games started: 1999 (16/16), 2000 (16/16), 2001 (16/16), 2002 (16/16), 2003 (16/16), Total: 80/80.

JASPER, ED — DT

PERSONAL: Born January 18, 1973, in Tyler, Texas. ... 6-2/293. ... Full name: Edward Vidal Jasper.
HIGH SCHOOL: Troup (Texas).
COLLEGE: Texas A&M.
TRANSACTIONS/CAREER NOTES: Selected by Philadelphia Eagles in sixth round (198th pick overall) of 1997 NFL draft. ... Signed by Eagles (July 16, 1997). ... Released by Eagles (August 30, 1998). ... Re-signed by Eagles (September 17, 1998). ... Released by Eagles (October 23, 1998). ... Re-signed by Eagles (December 9, 1998). ... Released by Eagles (February 12, 1999). ... Signed by Atlanta Falcons (March 5, 1999). ... Released by Falcons (February 28, 2005).
CHAMPIONSHIP GAME EXPERIENCE: Played in NFC championship game (2004 season).

Year Team	G	GS	TOTALS Tk.	Ast.	Sks.
1997—Philadelphia NFL	10	1	5	3	1.0
1998—Philadelphia NFL	7	0	11	2	0.0
1999—Atlanta NFL	13	0	23	5	0.0
2000—Atlanta NFL	15	15	30	12	3.5
2001—Atlanta NFL	16	1	20	5	3.5
2002—Atlanta NFL	16	16	29	6	2.0
2003—Atlanta NFL	14	14	35	6	3.0
2004—Atlanta NFL	12	12	27	7	2.0
Pro totals (8 years)	103	59	180	46	15.0

JEFFERSON, JOSEPH — CB

PERSONAL: Born February 15, 1980, in Russellville, Ky. ... 6-1/202. ... Full name: Joseph Jefferson Jr.
HIGH SCHOOL: Logan County (Adairville, Ky.).
COLLEGE: Western Kentucky.
TRANSACTIONS/CAREER NOTES: Selected by Indianapolis Colts in third round (74th pick overall) of 2002 NFL draft. ... Signed by Colts (July 22, 2002). ... Granted free agency (March 2, 2005).

Year Team	G	GS	TOTALS Tk.	Ast.	Sks.	INTERCEPTIONS No.	Yds.	Avg.	TD	PUNT RETURNS No.	Yds.	Avg.	TD	KICKOFF RETURNS No.	Yds.	Avg.	TD	TOTALS TD	2pt.	Pts.	Fum.
2002—Ind. NFL	14	0	0	0	0.0	0	0	0.0	0	0	0	0.0	0	0	0	0.0	0	0	0	0	0
2004—Ind. NFL	9	3	19	4	0.0	1	0	0.0	0	0	0	0.0	0	0	0	0.0	0	0	0	0	0
Pro totals (2 years)	23	3	19	4	0.0	1	0	0.0	0	0	0	0.0	0	0	0	0.0	0	0	0	0	0

JENKINS, COREY — LB — DOLPHINS

PERSONAL: Born August 25, 1976, in Columbia, S.C. ... 6-0/222.
HIGH SCHOOL: Dreher (Columbia, S.C.).
JUNIOR COLLEGE: Garden City (Kan.) Community College.
COLLEGE: South Carolina.
TRANSACTIONS/CAREER NOTES: Selected by Miami Dolphins in sixth round (181st pick overall) of 2003 NFL draft. ... Signed by Dolphins (June 9, 2003). ... Claimed on waivers by Chicago Bears (September 15, 2004). ... Claimed on waivers by Dolphins (December 13, 2004).
MISCELLANEOUS: Selected by Boston Red Sox organization in first round (24th pick overall) of free-agent draft (June 1, 1995).

Year Team	G	GS	TOTALS Tk.	Ast.	Sks.	INTERCEPTIONS No.	Yds.	Avg.	TD
2003—Miami NFL	16	0	1	0	0.0	0	0	0.0	0
2004—Chicago NFL	4	0	0	0	0.0	0	0	0.0	0
—Miami NFL	3	0	0	0	0.0	0	0	0.0	0
Pro totals (2 years)	23	0	1	0	0.0	0	0	0.0	0

JENKINS, CULLEN — DL — PACKERS

PERSONAL: Born January 20, 1981, in Detroit, Mich. ... 6-3/292. ... Full name: Cullen Darome Jenkins.
HIGH SCHOOL: Belleville (Mich.).
COLLEGE: Central Michigan.
TRANSACTIONS/CAREER NOTES: Signed as a non-drafted free agent by Green Bay Packers (May 2, 2003). ... Released by Packers (August 26, 2003). ... Re-signed by Packers (January 19, 2004). ... Assigned by Packers to Cologne Centurions in 2004 NFL Europe enhancement allocation program (February 9, 2004).

Year Team	G	GS	TOTALS Tk.	Ast.	Sks.
2004—Green Bay NFL	16	6	13	5	4.5

JENKINS, KERRY   G

PERSONAL: Born September 6, 1973, in Tuscaloosa, Ala. ... 6-5/305.
HIGH SCHOOL: Holt (Ala.).
COLLEGE: Troy.
TRANSACTIONS/CAREER NOTES: Signed as non-drafted free agent by Chicago Bears (April 25, 1997). ... Released by Bears (August 24, 1997). ... Re-signed by Bears to practice squad (August 27, 1997). ... Signed by New York Jets off Bears practice squad (December 3, 1997). ... Granted free agency (March 2, 2001). ... Re-signed by Jets (May 30, 2001). ... Granted unconditional free agency (March 1, 2002). ... Signed by Tampa Bay Buccaneers (March 6, 2002). ... On injured reserve with neck injury (September 6-29, 2004). ... Released by Buccaneers (September 29, 2004).
PLAYING EXPERIENCE: New York Jets NFL, 1997-2001; Tampa Bay NFL, 2002-2004. ... Games/Games started: 1997 (2/2), 1998 (16/0), 1999 (16/16), 2000 (16/16), 2001 (16/16), 2002 (15/15), 2003 (16/11), Total: 97/76.
CHAMPIONSHIP GAME EXPERIENCE: Played in AFC championship game (1998 season). ... Played in NFC championship game (2002 season). ... Member of Super Bowl championship team (2002 season).

JENKINS, KRIS   DT   PANTHERS

PERSONAL: Born August 3, 1979, in Ypsilanti, Mich. ... 6-4/335. ... Full name: Kristopher Rudy-Charles Jenkins.
HIGH SCHOOL: Belleville (Ypsilanti, Mich.).
COLLEGE: Maryland.
TRANSACTIONS/CAREER NOTES: Selected by Carolina Panthers in second round (44th pick overall) of 2001 NFL draft. ... Signed by Panthers (July 13, 2001). ... On injured reserve with shoulder injury (October 13, 2004-remainder of season).
CHAMPIONSHIP GAME EXPERIENCE: Played in NFC championship game (2003 season). ... Played in Super Bowl 38 (2003 season).
HONORS: Named defensive tackle on THE SPORTING NEWS NFL All-Pro team (2003). ... Played in Pro Bowl (2002 and 2003 seasons).

				TOTALS		
Year Team	G	GS	Tk.	Ast.	Sks.
2001—Carolina NFL	16	11	27	7	2.0
2002—Carolina NFL	16	16	36	8	7.0
2003—Carolina NFL	16	16	39	7	5.0
2004—Carolina NFL	4	4	8	3	1.0
Pro totals (4 years)	52	47	110	25	15.0

JENKINS, MICHAEL   WR   FALCONS

PERSONAL: Born June 18, 1982, in Tampa, Fla. ... 6-4/217.
HIGH SCHOOL: Leto (Tampa, Fla.).
COLLEGE: Ohio State.
TRANSACTIONS/CAREER NOTES: Selected by Atlanta Falcons in first round (29th pick overall) of 2004 NFL draft. ... Signed by Falcons (July 28, 2004).
CHAMPIONSHIP GAME EXPERIENCE: Played in NFC championship game (2004 season).
SINGLE GAME HIGHS (regular season): Receptions—2 (January 2, 2005, vs. Seattle); yards—46 (October 31, 2004, vs. Denver); and touchdown receptions—0.

			RECEIVING				PUNT RETURNS				TOTALS			
Year Team	G	GS	No.	Yds.	Avg.	TD	No.	Yds.	Avg.	TD	TD	2pt.	Pts.	Fum.
2004—Atlanta NFL	16	0	7	119	17.0	0	0	0	0.0	0	0	0	0	0

JENNINGS, BRIAN   TE/LS   49ERS

PERSONAL: Born October 14, 1976, in Mesa, Ariz. ... 6-5/245. ... Full name: Brian Lewis Jennings.
HIGH SCHOOL: Red Mountain (Mesa, Ariz.).
COLLEGE: Arizona State.
TRANSACTIONS/CAREER NOTES: Selected by San Francisco 49ers in seventh round (230th pick overall) of 2000 NFL draft. ... Signed by 49ers (July 10, 2000). ... Granted free agency (February 28, 2003). ... Re-signed by 49ers (April 24, 2003). ... Granted unconditional free agency (March 3, 2004). ... Re-signed by 49ers (March 4, 2004).
PLAYING EXPERIENCE: San Francisco NFL, 2000-2004. ... Games/Games started: 2000 (16/0), 2001 (16/0), 2002 (16/0), 2003 (16/0), 2004 (16/0). Total: 80/0.
HONORS: Played in Pro Bowl (2004 season).

JENNINGS, JONAS   T   49ERS

PERSONAL: Born November 21, 1977, in College Park, Ga. ... 6-3/325.
HIGH SCHOOL: Tri-Cities (East Point, Ga.).
COLLEGE: Georgia.
TRANSACTIONS/CAREER NOTES: Selected by Buffalo Bills in third round (95th pick overall) of 2001 NFL draft. ... Signed by Bills (June 22, 2001). ... On injured reserve with toe injury (December 3, 2003-remainder of season). ... Granted unconditional free agency (March 2, 2005). ... Signed by San Francisco 49ers (March 3, 2005).
PLAYING EXPERIENCE: Buffalo NFL, 2001-2004. ... Games/Games started: 2001 (12/12), 2002 (15/15), 2003 (11/11), 2004 (14/14). Total: 52/52.

JERMAN, GREG   T

PERSONAL: Born January 24, 1979, in Hyannis, Mass. ... 6-5/310. ... Full name: Gregory Stephen Jerman.
HIGH SCHOOL: Franklin (El Paso, Texas).
COLLEGE: Baylor.

TRANSACTIONS/CAREER NOTES: Signed as non-drafted free agent by Miami Dolphins (April 25, 2002). ... Released by Dolphins (August 31, 2003). ... Re-signed by Dolphins to practice squad (September 1, 2003). ... Activated (September 6, 2003). ... Released by Dolphins (May 12, 2005).
PLAYING EXPERIENCE: Miami NFL, 2002-2004. ... Games/Games started: 2002 (2/0), 2003 (8/1), 2004 (1/0). Total: 11/1.

JIMOH, ADE   CB   REDSKINS

PERSONAL: Born April 18, 1980, in Los Angeles, Calif. ... 6-1/190.
HIGH SCHOOL: El Camino Real (Canoga Park, Calif.).
COLLEGE: Utah State.
TRANSACTIONS/CAREER NOTES: Signed as non-drafted free agent by Washington Redskins (May 2, 2003). ... On injured reserve with ankle injury (December 29, 2004-remainder of season).

			TOTALS			INTERCEPTIONS			
Year Team	G	GS	Tk.	Ast.	Sks.	No.	Yds.	Avg.	TD
2003—Washington NFL	16	0	5	1	0.0	0	0	0.0	0
2004—Washington NFL	15	0	6	0	0.0	0	0	0.0	0
Pro totals (2 years)	31	0	11	1	0.0	0	0	0.0	0

JOE, LEON   LB   CARDINALS

PERSONAL: Born October 26, 1981, in Fort Washington, Md. ... 6-1/235.
HIGH SCHOOL: Friendly (Clinton, Md.).
COLLEGE: Maryland.
TRANSACTIONS/CAREER NOTES: Selected by Chicago Bears in fourth round (112th pick overall) of 2004 NFL draft. ... Signed by Bears (June 9, 2004). ... Claimed on waivers by Arizona Cardinals (September 16, 2004).

			TOTALS			INTERCEPTIONS			
Year Team	G	GS	Tk.	Ast.	Sks.	No.	Yds.	Avg.	TD
2004—Chicago NFL	1	0	0	0	0.0	0	0	0.0	0
—Arizona NFL	4	0	0	0	0.0	0	0	0.0	0
Pro totals (1 year)	5	0	0	0	0.0	0	0	0.0	0

JOHNSON, AL   C   COWBOYS

PERSONAL: Born January 27, 1979, in Brussels, Wis. ... 6-5/296.
HIGH SCHOOL: Southern Door (Brussels, Wis.).
COLLEGE: Wisconsin.
TRANSACTIONS/CAREER NOTES: Selected by Dallas Cowboys in second round (38th pick overall) of 2003 NFL draft. ... Signed by Cowboys (July 25, 2003). ... On injured reserve with knee injury (August 26, 2003-entire season).
PLAYING EXPERIENCE: Dallas NFL, 2003-2004. ... Games/Games started: 2004 (16/15), Total: 16/15.

JOHNSON, ANDRE   WR   TEXANS

PERSONAL: Born July 11, 1981, in Miami, Fla. ... 6-3/219. ... Full name: Andre Lamont Johnson.
HIGH SCHOOL: Senior (Miami).
COLLEGE: Miami (Fla.).
TRANSACTIONS/CAREER NOTES: Selected after junior season by Houston Texans in first round (third pick overall) of 2003 NFL draft. ... Signed by Texans (July 22, 2003).
HONORS: Played in Pro Bowl (2004 season).
SINGLE GAME HIGHS (regular season): Receptions—12 (October 10, 2004, vs. Minnesota); yards—170 (October 10, 2004, vs. Minnesota); and touchdown receptions—2 (October 10, 2004, vs. Minnesota).
STATISTICAL PLATEAUS: 100-yard receiving games: 2003 (3), 2004 (4). Total: 7.
MISCELLANEOUS: Holds Houston Texans all-time records for most receptions (145) and most receiving yards (2,118).

			RUSHING				RECEIVING				KICKOFF RETURNS				TOTALS			
Year Team	G	GS	Att.	Yds.	Avg.	TD	No.	Yds.	Avg.	TD	No.	Yds.	Avg.	TD	TD	2pt.	Pts.	Fum.
2003—Houston NFL	16	16	5	-10	-2.0	0	66	976	14.8	4	0	0	0.0	0	4	0	24	0
2004—Houston NFL	16	16	4	12	3.0	0	79	1142	14.5	6	0	0	0.0	0	6	0	36	1
Pro totals (2 years)	32	32	9	2	0.2	0	145	2118	14.6	10	0	0	0.0	0	10	0	60	1

JOHNSON, BETHEL   WR   PATRIOTS

PERSONAL: Born February 11, 1979, in Corsicana, Texas. ... 5-11/200.
HIGH SCHOOL: Corsicana (Texas).
COLLEGE: Texas A&M.
TRANSACTIONS/CAREER NOTES: Selected by New England Patriots in second round (45th pick overall) of 2003 NFL draft. ... Signed by Patriots (July 21, 2003).
CHAMPIONSHIP GAME EXPERIENCE: Played in AFC championship game (2003 and 2004 seasons). ... Member of Super Bowl championship team (2003 and 2004 seasons).
SINGLE GAME HIGHS (regular season): Receptions—5 (November 23, 2003, vs. Houston); yards—65 (November 23, 2003, vs. Houston); and touchdown receptions—1 (November 7, 2004, vs. St. Louis).

Year Team	G	GS	RUSHING				RECEIVING				PUNT RETURNS				KICKOFF RETURNS				TOTALS		
			Att.	Yds.	Avg.	TD	No.	Yds.	Avg.	TD	No.	Yds.	Avg.	TD	No.	Yds.	Avg.	TD	TD	2pt.	Pts.
2003—N.E. NFL	15	5	1	-12	-12.0	0	16	209	13.1	2	1	2	2.0	0	30	847	§28.2	1	3	0	18
2004—N.E. NFL	13	1	2	8	4.0	0	10	174	17.4	1	4	8	2.0	0	41	1016	24.8	1	2	0	12
Pro totals (2 years)	28	6	3	-4	-1.3	0	26	383	14.7	3	5	10	2.0	0	71	1863	26.2	2	5	0	30

JOHNSON, BRAD   QB   VIKINGS

PERSONAL: Born September 13, 1968, in Marietta, Ga. ... 6-5/226. ... Full name: James Bradley Johnson.
HIGH SCHOOL: Charles D. Owen (Black Mountain, N.C.).
COLLEGE: Florida State.
TRANSACTIONS/CAREER NOTES: Selected by Minnesota Vikings in ninth round (227th pick overall) of 1992 NFL draft. ... Signed by Vikings (July 17, 1992). ... Active for one game (1992); did not play. ... Inactive for all 16 games (1993). ... Granted free agency (February 17, 1995). ... Assigned by Vikings to London Monarchs in 1995 World League enhancement allocation program (February 20, 1995). ... Re-signed by Vikings (March 27, 1995). ... On injured reserve with neck injury (December 5, 1997-remainder of season). ... Traded by Vikings to Washington Redskins for first- (QB Daunte Culpepper) and third-round (traded to Pittsburgh) picks in 1999 draft and second-round pick (DE Michael Boireau) in 2000 draft (February 15, 1999). ... Granted unconditional free agency (March 2, 2001). ... Signed by Tampa Bay Buccaneers (March 6, 2001). ... Released by Buccaneers (March 1, 2005). ... Signed by Vikings (March 16, 2005).
CHAMPIONSHIP GAME EXPERIENCE: Member of Vikings for NFC championship game (1998 season); did not play. ... Played in NFC championship game (2002 season). ... Member of Super Bowl championship team (2002 season).
HONORS: Played in Pro Bowl (1999 and 2002 seasons).
SINGLE GAME HIGHS (regular season): Attempts—61 (September 14, 2003, vs. Carolina); completions—40 (November 18, 2001, vs. Chicago); yards—471 (December 26, 1999, vs. San Francisco); and touchdown passes—5 (November 3, 2002, vs. Minnesota).
STATISTICAL PLATEAUS: 300-yard passing games: 1997 (2), 1998 (1), 1999 (4), 2001 (2), 2002 (1), 2003 (4), 2004 (1). Total: 15.
MISCELLANEOUS: Regular-season record as starting NFL quarterback: 58-41 (.586). ... Postseason record as starting NFL quarterback: 4-3 (.571).

Year Team	G	GS	PASSING								RUSHING				TOTALS		
			Att.	Cmp.	Pct.	Yds.	TD	Int.	Avg.	Skd.	Rat.	Att.	Yds.	Avg.	TD	TD	2pt.	Pts.
1992—Minnesota NFL	Did not play.																	
1993—Minnesota NFL	Did not play.																	
1994—Minnesota NFL	4	0	37	22	59.5	150	0	0	4.05	1	68.5	2	-2	-1.0	0	0	0	0
1995—Minnesota NFL	5	0	36	25	69.4	272	0	2	7.56	2	68.3	9	-9	-1.0	0	0	0	0
1996—Minnesota NFL	12	8	311	195	62.7	2258	17	10	7.26	15	89.4	34	90	2.6	1	1	0	6
1997—Minnesota NFL	13	13	452	275	60.8	3036	20	12	6.72	26	84.5	35	139	4.0	0	1	2	10
1998—Minnesota NFL	4	2	101	65	64.4	747	7	5	7.40	4	89.0	12	15	1.3	0	0	0	0
1999—Washington NFL	16	16	519	316	60.9	4005	24	13	7.72	29	90.0	26	31	1.2	2	2	0	12
2000—Washington NFL	12	11	365	228	62.5	2505	11	15	6.86	20	75.7	22	58	2.6	1	1	0	6
2001—Tampa Bay NFL	16	16	559	340	60.8	3406	13	11	6.09	44	77.7	39	120	3.1	3	3	0	18
2002—Tampa Bay NFL	13	13	451	281	62.3	3049	22	6	6.76	21	‡92.9	13	30	2.3	0	0	0	0
2003—Tampa Bay NFL	16	16	*570	‡354	62.1	3811	26	21	6.69	20	81.5	25	33	1.3	0	0	0	0
2004—Tampa Bay NFL	4	4	103	65	63.1	674	3	3	6.54	8	79.5	5	23	4.6	0	0	0	0
Pro totals (11 years)	115	99	3504	2166	61.8	23913	143	98	6.82	190	84.0	222	528	2.4	7	8	2	52

JOHNSON, BRYAN   FB   BEARS

PERSONAL: Born January 18, 1978, in Los Angeles, Calif. ... 6-1/242.
HIGH SCHOOL: Highland (Pocatello, Idaho).
COLLEGE: Boise State.
TRANSACTIONS/CAREER NOTES: Signed as non-drafted free agent by Washington Redskins (April 18, 2000). ... Released by Redskins (August 27, 2000). ... Re-signed by Redskins to practice squad (August 28, 2000). ... Re-signed by Redskins (April 29, 2003). ... Traded by Redskins to Chicago Bears for sixth-round pick (T Jim Molinaro) in 2004 draft (March 29, 2004). ... On injured reserve with foot injury (December 28, 2004-remainder of season).
SINGLE GAME HIGHS (regular season): Attempts—1 (September 28, 2003, vs. New England); yards—4 (September 28, 2003, vs. New England); and rushing touchdowns—0.

Year Team	G	GS	RUSHING				RECEIVING				TOTALS			
			Att.	Yds.	Avg.	TD	No.	Yds.	Avg.	TD	TD	2pt.	Pts.	Fum.
2000—Washington NFL	1	0	0	0	0.0	0	0	0	0.0	0	0	0	0	0
2001—Washington NFL	16	1	0	0	0.0	0	9	129	14.3	0	0	0	0	0
2002—Washington NFL	16	12	1	0	0.0	0	15	114	7.6	0	0	0	0	0
2003—Washington NFL	16	11	2	5	2.5	0	9	71	7.9	0	0	0	0	0
2004—Chicago NFL	12	6	0	0	0.0	0	14	55	3.9	2	2	0	12	0
Pro totals (5 years)	61	30	3	5	1.7	0	47	369	7.9	2	2	0	12	0

JOHNSON, BRYANT   WR   CARDINALS

PERSONAL: Born March 7, 1981, in Baltimore, Md. ... 6-2/214. ... Full name: Bryant Andrew Johnson.
HIGH SCHOOL: Baltimore City College (Baltimore).
COLLEGE: Penn State.
TRANSACTIONS/CAREER NOTES: Selected by Arizona Cardinals in first round (17th pick overall) of 2003 NFL draft. ... Signed by Cardinals (July 28, 2003).
SINGLE GAME HIGHS (regular season): Receptions—7 (October 24, 2004, vs. Seattle); yards—86 (September 21, 2003, vs. Green Bay); and touchdown receptions—1 (October 31, 2004, vs. Buffalo).

Year Team	G	GS	RECEIVING				PUNT RETURNS				KICKOFF RETURNS				TOTALS			
			No.	Yds.	Avg.	TD	No.	Yds.	Avg.	TD	No.	Yds.	Avg.	TD	TD	2pt.	Pts.	Fum.
2003—Arizona NFL	15	8	35	438	12.5	1	1	3	3.0	0	0	0	0.0	0	1	0	6	1
2004—Arizona NFL	16	11	49	537	11.0	1	0	0	0.0	0	6	135	22.5	0	1	0	6	1
Pro totals (2 years)	31	19	84	975	11.6	2	1	3	3.0	0	6	135	22.5	0	2	0	12	2

JOHNSON, CHAD — WR — BENGALS

PERSONAL: Born January 9, 1978, in Miami, Fla. ... 6-1/192.
HIGH SCHOOL: Miami Beach (Fla.).
JUNIOR COLLEGE: Santa Monica College (Calif.).
COLLEGE: Oregon State.
TRANSACTIONS/CAREER NOTES: Selected by Cincinnati Bengals in second round (36th pick overall) of 2001 NFL draft. ... Signed by Bengals (July 18, 2001).
HONORS: Played in Pro Bowl (2003 and 2004 seasons).
SINGLE GAME HIGHS (regular season): Receptions—10 (December 5, 2004, vs. Baltimore); yards—161 (December 5, 2004, vs. Baltimore); and touchdown receptions—3 (November 23, 2003, vs. San Diego).
STATISTICAL PLATEAUS: 100-yard receiving games: 2002 (5), 2003 (5), 2004 (3). Total: 13.

				RECEIVING				TOTALS		
Year Team	G	GS	No.	Yds.	Avg.	TD	TD	2pt.	Pts.	Fum.
2001—Cincinnati NFL	12	3	28	329	11.8	1	1	0	6	0
2002—Cincinnati NFL	16	14	69	1166	16.9	5	5	0	30	0
2003—Cincinnati NFL	16	14	90	§1355	15.1	10	10	0	60	0
2004—Cincinnati NFL	16	16	95	§1274	13.4	9	9	0	54	1
Pro totals (4 years)	60	47	282	4124	14.6	25	25	0	150	1

JOHNSON, DENNIS — DE

PERSONAL: Born December 4, 1979, in Danville, Ky. ... 6-5/269. ... Full name: Dennis Alan Johnson.
HIGH SCHOOL: Harrodsburg (Ky.).
COLLEGE: Kentucky.
TRANSACTIONS/CAREER NOTES: Selected after junior season by Arizona Cardinals in third round (98th pick overall) of 2002 NFL draft. ... Signed by Cardinals (June 12, 2002). ... Released by Cardinals (September 5, 2004). ... Signed by San Francisco 49ers (September 15, 2004). ... Released by 49ers (September 22, 2004).

			TOTALS		
Year Team	G	GS	Tk.	Ast.	Sks.
2002—Arizona NFL	13	0	10	6	0.0
2003—Arizona NFL	15	10	27	16	3.0
2004—San Francisco NFL	1	0	0	0	0.0
Pro totals (3 years)	29	10	37	22	3.0

JOHNSON, DIRK — P — EAGLES

PERSONAL: Born June 1, 1975, in Hoxie, Kan. ... 6-0/205. ... Full name: Dirk R. Johnson.
HIGH SCHOOL: Montrose (Colo.).
COLLEGE: Northern Colorado.
TRANSACTIONS/CAREER NOTES: Signed as non-drafted free agent by San Diego Chargers (May 4, 2001). ... Released by Chargers (August 27, 2001). ... Signed by New Orleans Saints (February 18, 2002). ... Assigned by Saints to Rhein Fire in 2002 NFL Europe enhancement allocation program (February 18, 2002). ... Released by Saints (September 1, 2002). ... Re-signed by Saints (September 6, 2002). ... Released by Saints (September 9, 2002). ... Signed by Philadelphia Eagles (February 10, 2003).
CHAMPIONSHIP GAME EXPERIENCE: Played in NFC championship game (2003 and 2004 seasons). ... Played in Super Bowl 39 (2004 season).

				PUNTING			
Year Team	G	No.	Yds.	Avg.	Net avg.	In. 20	Blk.
2002—New Orleans NFL	1	8	307	38.4	34.8	1	0
2003—Philadelphia NFL	16	79	3207	40.6	34.6	27	0
2004—Philadelphia NFL	16	72	3032	42.1	37.4	20	0
Pro totals (3 years)	33	159	6546	41.2	35.9	48	0

JOHNSON, DOUG — QB

PERSONAL: Born October 27, 1977, in Gainesville, Fla. ... 6-2/225.
HIGH SCHOOL: Buchholz (Gainesville, Fla.).
COLLEGE: Florida.
TRANSACTIONS/CAREER NOTES: Signed as non-drafted free agent by Atlanta Falcons (April 17, 2000). ... Granted unconditional free agency (March 3, 2004). ... Signed by Jacksonville Jaguars (April 28, 2004). ... Released by Jaguars (August 30, 2004). ... Signed by Tennessee Titans (September 8, 2004). ... Granted unconditional free agency (March 2, 2005).
SINGLE GAME HIGHS (regular season): Attempts—40 (October 5, 2003, vs. Minnesota); completions—28 (October 5, 2003, vs. Minnesota); yards—352 (October 5, 2003, vs. Minnesota); and touchdown passes—2 (November 23, 2003, vs. Tennessee).
STATISTICAL PLATEAUS: 300-yard passing games: 2003 (1). Total: 1.
MISCELLANEOUS: Regular-season record as starting NFL quarterback: 2-9 (.182).

			PASSING									RUSHING				TOTALS		
Year Team	G	GS	Att.	Cmp.	Pct.	Yds.	TD	Int.	Avg.	Skd.	Rat.	Att.	Yds.	Avg.	TD	TD	2pt.	Pts.
2000—Atlanta NFL	5	2	67	36	53.7	406	2	3	6.06	13	63.4	3	11	3.7	0	0	0	0
2001—Atlanta NFL	3	0	5	3	60.0	23	1	0	4.60	2	110.8	5	12	2.4	0	0	0	0
2002—Atlanta NFL	6	1	57	37	64.9	448	2	3	7.86	3	78.7	8	16	2.0	1	1	0	6
2003—Atlanta NFL	10	8	243	136	56.0	1655	8	12	6.81	19	67.5	14	21	1.5	1	1	0	6
2004—Tennessee NFL	2	0	12	6	50.0	68	0	0	5.67	1	67.4	2	-2	-1.0	0	0	0	0
Pro totals (5 years)	26	11	384	218	56.8	2600	13	18	6.77	38	69.4	32	58	1.8	2	2	0	12

JOHNSON, ELLIS — DT

PERSONAL: Born October 30, 1973, in Wildwood, Fla. ... 6-2/288. ... Full name: Ellis Bernard Johnson.
HIGH SCHOOL: Wildwood (Fla.).
COLLEGE: Florida.
TRANSACTIONS/CAREER NOTES: Selected by Indianapolis Colts in first round (15th pick overall) of 1995 NFL draft. ... Signed by Colts (June 7, 1995). ... On physically unable to perform list with knee injury (July 27-August 20, 2001). ... Released by Colts (August 28, 2002). ... Signed by Atlanta Falcons (September 1, 2002). ... Traded by Falcons to Denver Broncos for a fifth-round pick (LB Michael Boley) in 2005 draft (September 20, 2004). ... Granted unconditional free agency (March 2, 2005).
CHAMPIONSHIP GAME EXPERIENCE: Played in AFC championship game (1995 season).

Year Team	G	GS	TOTALS Tk.	Ast.	Sks.	INTERCEPTIONS No.	Yds.	Avg.	TD
1995—Indianapolis NFL	16	2	15	3	4.5	0	0	0.0	0
1996—Indianapolis NFL	12	6	14	8	0.0	0	0	0.0	0
1997—Indianapolis NFL	15	15	38	18	4.5	1	18	18.0	0
1998—Indianapolis NFL	16	16	38	17	8.0	0	0	0.0	0
1999—Indianapolis NFL	16	16	34	12	7.5	0	0	0.0	0
2000—Indianapolis NFL	13	13	29	11	5.0	1	-1	-1.0	0
2001—Indianapolis NFL	16	16	20	14	3.5	0	0	0.0	0
2002—Atlanta NFL	16	2	24	3	7.0	0	0	0.0	0
2003—Atlanta NFL	16	3	34	8	8.0	0	0	0.0	0
2004—Denver NFL	13	0	15	1	3.0	1	32	32.0	1
Pro totals (10 years)	**149**	**89**	**261**	**95**	**51.0**	**3**	**49**	**16.3**	**1**

JOHNSON, ERIC — S/LB

PERSONAL: Born April 30, 1976, in Carson, Calif. ... 6-0/210.
HIGH SCHOOL: Alhambra (Arizona).
COLLEGE: Nebraska.
TRANSACTIONS/CAREER NOTES: Signed as non-drafted free agent by Oakland Raiders (March 23, 2000). ... On injured reserve with broken leg (November 7, 2001-remainder of season). ... Granted unconditional free agency (March 3, 2004). ... Signed by Atlanta Falcons (March 9, 2004). ... Granted unconditional free agency (March 2, 2005).
CHAMPIONSHIP GAME EXPERIENCE: Played in AFC championship game (2002 season). ... Played in NFC championship game (2004 season). ... Played in Super Bowl 37 (2002 season).

Year Team	G	GS	TOTALS Tk.	Ast.	Sks.	INTERCEPTIONS No.	Yds.	Avg.	TD
2000—Oakland NFL	16	0	3	0	0.0	0	0	0.0	0
2001—Oakland NFL	7	0	0	0	0.0	0	0	0.0	0
2002—Oakland NFL	16	0	0	0	0.0	0	0	0.0	0
2003—Oakland NFL	16	2	7	2	0.0	1	3	3.0	0
2004—Atlanta NFL	16	0	0	0	0.0	0	0	0.0	0
Pro totals (5 years)	**71**	**2**	**10**	**2**	**0.0**	**1**	**3**	**3.0**	**0**

JOHNSON, ERIC — TE — 49ERS

PERSONAL: Born September 15, 1979, in Needham, Mass. ... 6-3/256.
HIGH SCHOOL: Needham (Mass.).
COLLEGE: Yale.
TRANSACTIONS/CAREER NOTES: Selected by San Francisco 49ers in seventh round (224th pick overall) of 2001 NFL draft. ... Signed by 49ers (July 24, 2001). ... Inactive for seven games (2003). ... On injured reserve with collarbone injury (October 25, 2003-remainder of season).
SINGLE GAME HIGHS (regular season): Receptions—13 (October 10, 2004, vs. Arizona); yards—162 (October 10, 2004, vs. Arizona); and touchdown receptions—1 (October 10, 2004, vs. Arizona).
STATISTICAL PLATEAUS: 100-yard receiving games: 2004 (2). Total: 2.

Year Team	G	GS	RECEIVING No.	Yds.	Avg.	TD	TOTALS TD	2pt.	Pts.	Fum.
2001—San Francisco NFL	16	14	40	362	9.1	3	3	1	20	1
2002—San Francisco NFL	12	10	36	321	8.9	0	0	0	0	0
2003—San Francisco NFL			Did not play.							
2004—San Francisco NFL	16	14	82	825	10.1	2	2	0	12	1
Pro totals (3 years)	**44**	**38**	**158**	**1508**	**9.5**	**5**	**5**	**1**	**32**	**2**

JOHNSON, JARRET — DE — RAVENS

PERSONAL: Born August 14, 1981, in Homestead, Fla. ... 6-3/285.
HIGH SCHOOL: Chiefland (Fla.).
COLLEGE: Alabama.
TRANSACTIONS/CAREER NOTES: Selected by Baltimore Ravens in fourth round (109th pick overall) of 2003 NFL draft. ... Signed by Ravens (July 26, 2003).

Year Team	G	GS	TOTALS Tk.	Ast.	Sks.	INTERCEPTIONS No.	Yds.	Avg.	TD
2003—Baltimore NFL	15	1	8	3	0.0	0	0	0.0	0
2004—Baltimore NFL	16	0	9	8	0.0	1	6	6.0	1
Pro totals (2 years)	**31**	**1**	**17**	**11**	**0.0**	**1**	**6**	**6.0**	**1**

JOHNSON, JEREMI FB BENGALS

PERSONAL: Born September 4, 1980, in Louisville, Ky. ... 5-11/265.
HIGH SCHOOL: Ballard (Louisville, Ky.).
COLLEGE: Western Kentucky.
TRANSACTIONS/CAREER NOTES: Selected by Cincinnati Bengals in fourth round (118th pick overall) of 2003 NFL draft. ... Signed by Bengals (July 27, 2003).
SINGLE GAME HIGHS (regular season): Attempts—5 (November 9, 2003, vs. Houston); yards—17 (November 23, 2003, vs. San Diego); and rushing touchdowns—1 (November 9, 2003, vs. Houston).

			RUSHING				RECEIVING				KICKOFF RETURNS				TOTALS		
Year Team	G	GS	Att.	Yds.	Avg.	TD	No.	Yds.	Avg.	TD	No.	Yds.	Avg.	TD	TD	2pt.	Pts. Fum.
2003—Cincinnati NFL	16	13	15	41	2.7	1	15	82	5.5	1	1	16	16.0	0	2	0	12 0
2004—Cincinnati NFL	16	6	3	5	1.7	0	16	53	3.3	1	0	0	0.0	0	1	0	6 1
Pro totals (2 years)	32	19	18	46	2.6	1	31	135	4.4	2	1	16	16.0	0	3	0	18 1

JOHNSON, KEVIN WR LIONS

PERSONAL: Born July 15, 1976, in Trenton, N.J. ... 5-11/195. ... Full name: Kevin L. Johnson.
HIGH SCHOOL: Hamilton West (Trenton, N.J.).
COLLEGE: Syracuse.
TRANSACTIONS/CAREER NOTES: Selected by Cleveland Browns in second round (32nd pick overall) of 1999 NFL draft. ... Signed by Browns (July 22, 1999). ... Claimed on waivers by Jacksonville Jaguars (November 12, 2003). ... Traded by Jaguars to Baltimore Ravens for fourth-round pick (WR Ernest Wilford) in 2004 draft (April 25, 2004). ... Released by Ravens (February 22, 2005). ... Signed by Detroit Lions (April 22, 2005).
SINGLE GAME HIGHS (regular season): Receptions—11 (September 21, 2003, vs. San Francisco); yards—153 (October 14, 2001, vs. Cincinnati); and touchdown receptions—2 (December 2, 2001, vs. Tennessee).
STATISTICAL PLATEAUS: 100-yard receiving games: 1999 (2), 2000 (1), 2001 (2), 2003 (1). Total: 6.

			RUSHING				RECEIVING				PUNT RETURNS				TOTALS		
Year Team	G	GS	Att.	Yds.	Avg.	TD	No.	Yds.	Avg.	TD	No.	Yds.	Avg.	TD	TD	2pt.	Pts. Fum.
1999—Cleveland NFL	16	16	1	-6	-6.0	0	66	986	14.9	8	19	128	6.7	0	8	0	48 1
2000—Cleveland NFL	16	16	0	0	0.0	0	57	669	11.7	0	0	0	0.0	0	0	0	0 0
2001—Cleveland NFL	16	16	0	0	0.0	0	84	1097	13.1	9	14	117	8.4	0	9	0	54 2
2002—Cleveland NFl	16	15	0	0	0.0	0	67	703	10.5	4	0	0	0.0	0	4	0	24 0
2003—Cleveland NFL	9	8	0	0	0.0	0	41	381	9.3	2	0	0	0.0	0	2	0	12 0
—Jacksonville NFL	6	1	0	0	0.0	0	17	253	14.9	1	0	0	0.0	0	1	0	6 0
2004—Baltimore NFL	16	5	1	0	0.0	0	35	373	10.7	1	0	0	0.0	0	1	0	6 1
Pro totals (6 years)	95	77	2	-6	-3.0	0	367	4462	12.2	25	33	245	7.4	0	25	0	150 4

JOHNSON, KEYSHAWN WR COWBOYS

PERSONAL: Born July 22, 1972, in Los Angeles, Calif. ... 6-4/214.
HIGH SCHOOL: Dorsey (Los Angeles).
JUNIOR COLLEGE: West Los Angeles College.
COLLEGE: Southern California.
TRANSACTIONS/CAREER NOTES: Selected by New York Jets in first round (first pick overall) of 1996 NFL draft. ... Signed by Jets (August 6, 1996). ... Traded by Jets to Tampa Bay Buccaneers for two first-round picks (LB John Abraham and TE Anthony Becht) in 2000 draft (April 12, 2000). ... Traded by Buccaneers to Dallas Cowboys for WR Joey Galloway (March 19, 2004).
CHAMPIONSHIP GAME EXPERIENCE: Played in AFC championship game (1998 season). ... Played in NFC championship game (2002 season). ... Member of Super Bowl championship team (2002 season).
HONORS: Named wide receiver on THE SPORTING NEWS college All-America first team (1995). ... Played in Pro Bowl (1998, 1999 and 2001 seasons). ... Named co-Outstanding Player of Pro Bowl (1998 season).
SINGLE GAME HIGHS (regular season): Receptions—12 (November 18, 2001, vs. Chicago); yards—194 (September 12, 1999, vs. New England); and touchdown receptions—2 (October 31, 2004, vs. Detroit).
STATISTICAL PLATEAUS: 100-yard receiving games: 1997 (1), 1998 (4), 1999 (2), 2000 (2), 2001 (4), 2002 (3), 2003 (2), 2004 (2). Total: 20.

			RECEIVING				TOTALS		
Year Team	G	GS	No.	Yds.	Avg.	TD	TD	2pt.	Pts.	Fum.
1996—New York Jets NFL	14	11	63	844	13.4	8	8	1	50	0
1997—New York Jets NFL	16	16	70	963	13.8	5	5	0	30	0
1998—New York Jets NFL	16	16	83	1131	13.6	▲10	11	0	66	0
1999—New York Jets NFL	16	16	89	1170	13.1	8	8	0	48	0
2000—Tampa Bay NFL	16	16	71	874	12.3	8	8	0	48	2
2001—Tampa Bay NFL	15	15	‡106	1266	11.9	1	1	0	6	2
2002—Tampa Bay NFL	16	16	76	1088	14.3	5	5	2	34	0
2003—Tampa Bay NFL	10	10	45	600	13.3	3	3	0	18	0
2004—Dallas NFL	16	16	70	981	14.0	6	6	0	36	1
Pro totals (9 years)	135	132	673	8917	13.2	54	55	3	336	5

JOHNSON, KYLE FB BRONCOS

PERSONAL: Born December 15, 1978, in Woodbridge, N.J. ... 6-0/242. ... Full name: Albert Kyle Johnson.
HIGH SCHOOL: Woodbridge (N.J.).
COLLEGE: Syracuse.
TRANSACTIONS/CAREER NOTES: Selected by Carolina Panthers in fifth round (145th pick overall) of 2002 NFL draft. ... Signed by Panthers (July 10, 2002). ... Released by Panthers (September 1, 2002). ... Signed by New York Giants to practice squad (September 3, 2002). ...

Released by Giants (October 23, 2002). ... Signed by Detroit Lions to practice squad (November 13, 2002). ... Signed off Lions' practice squad by Denver Broncos (December 10, 2002). ... Released by Broncos (August 26, 2003). ... Re-signed by Broncos to practice squad (September 10, 2003). ... Activated (October 14, 2003). ... Released by Broncos (November 18, 2003). ... Re-signed by Broncos to practice squad (December 24, 2003). ... Activated (December 28, 2003).

			RUSHING				RECEIVING				TOTALS			
Year Team	G	GS	Att.	Yds.	Avg.	TD	No.	Yds.	Avg.	TD	TD	2pt.	Pts.	Fum.
2004—Denver NFL	14	3	0	0	0.0	0	9	126	14.0	2	2	0	12	0

JOHNSON, LANDON — LB — BENGALS

PERSONAL: Born March 13, 1981, in Ector County, Texas. ... 6-1/227. ... Full name: Landon Tremone Johnson.
HIGH SCHOOL: Coronado (Lubbock, Texas).
COLLEGE: Purdue.
TRANSACTIONS/CAREER NOTES: Selected by Cincinnati Bengals in third round (96th pick overall) of 2004 NFL draft. ... Signed by Bengals (July 30, 2004).

			TOTALS			INTERCEPTIONS			
Year Team	G	GS	Tk.	Ast.	Sks.	No.	Yds.	Avg.	TD
2004—Cincinnati NFL	16	11	57	27	2.0	0	0	0.0	0

JOHNSON, LARRY — RB — CHIEFS

PERSONAL: Born November 19, 1979, in State College, Pa. ... 6-1/230. ... Full name: Larry Alphonso Johnson.
HIGH SCHOOL: State College (Pa.).
COLLEGE: Penn State.
TRANSACTIONS/CAREER NOTES: Selected by Kansas City Chiefs in first round (27th pick overall) of 2003 NFL draft. ... Signed by Chiefs (July 17, 2003).
SINGLE GAME HIGHS (regular season): Attempts—30 (December 19, 2004, vs. Denver); yards—151 (December 19, 2004, vs. Denver); and rushing touchdowns—2 (December 25, 2004, vs. Oakland).
STATISTICAL PLATEAUS: 100-yard rushing games: 2004 (3). Total: 3. 100-yard receiving games: 2004 (1). Total: 1.

			RUSHING				RECEIVING				TOTALS			
Year Team	G	GS	Att.	Yds.	Avg.	TD	No.	Yds.	Avg.	TD	TD	2pt.	Pts.	Fum.
2003—Kansas City NFL	6	0	20	85	4.3	1	1	2	2.0	0	1	0	6	0
2004—Kansas City NFL	10	3	120	581	4.8	9	22	278	12.6	2	11	0	66	0
Pro totals (2 years)	16	3	140	666	4.8	10	23	280	12.2	2	12	0	72	0

JOHNSON, RAYLEE — DE — BRONCOS

PERSONAL: Born June 1, 1970, in Chicago, Ill. ... 6-3/272. ... Full name: Raylee Terrell Johnson.
HIGH SCHOOL: Fordyce (Ark.).
COLLEGE: Arkansas.
TRANSACTIONS/CAREER NOTES: Selected by San Diego Chargers in fourth round (95th pick overall) of 1993 NFL draft. ... Signed by Chargers (July 15, 1993). ... Granted unconditional free agency (February 14, 1997). ... Re-signed by Chargers (March 11, 1997). ... On injured reserve with knee injury (August 22, 2000-entire season). ... On injured reserve with foot injury (November 29, 2003-remainder of season). ... Released by Chargers (March 2, 2004). ... Signed by Denver Broncos (March 22, 2004).
CHAMPIONSHIP GAME EXPERIENCE: Played in AFC championship game (1994 season). ... Played in Super Bowl 29 (1994 season).

			TOTALS		
Year Team	G	GS	Tk.	Ast.	Sks.
1993—San Diego NFL	9	0	0	1	0.0
1994—San Diego NFL	15	0	4	2	1.5
1995—San Diego NFL	16	1	14	1	3.0
1996—San Diego NFL	16	1	15	3	3.0
1997—San Diego NFL	16	0	16	3	2.5
1998—San Diego NFL	16	3	23	6	5.5
1999—San Diego NFL	16	16	33	8	10.5
2000—San Diego NFL			Did not play.		
2001—San Diego NFL	16	16	28	10	9.5
2002—San Diego NFL	16	16	32	8	6.5
2003—San Diego NFL	9	1	12	1	4.0
2004—Denver NFL	14	1	6	6	1.0
Pro totals (11 years)	159	55	183	49	47.0

JOHNSON, RUDI — RB — BENGALS

PERSONAL: Born October 1, 1979, in Petersburg, Va. ... 5-10/220. ... Full name: Rudi Ali Johnson.
HIGH SCHOOL: Thomas Dale (Ettrick, Va.).
JUNIOR COLLEGE: Butler County Community College (Kan.).
COLLEGE: Auburn.
TRANSACTIONS/CAREER NOTES: Selected by Cincinnati Bengals in fourth round (100th pick overall) of 2001 NFL draft. ... Signed by Bengals (July 17, 2001). ... Granted free agency (March 3, 2004). ... Re-signed by Bengals (May 11, 2004). ... Designated by Bengals as franchise player (February 22, 2005). ... Re-signed by Bengals (March 16, 2005).
HONORS: Named running back on THE SPORTING NEWS college All-America second team (2000). ... Played in Pro Bowl (2004 season).
SINGLE GAME HIGHS (regular season): Attempts—43 (November 9, 2003, vs. Houston); yards—202 (November 28, 2004, vs. Cleveland); and rushing touchdowns—3 (January 2, 2005, vs. Philadelphia).

STATISTICAL PLATEAUS: 100-yard rushing games: 2003 (4), 2004 (5). Total: 9.

			RUSHING				RECEIVING				KICKOFF RETURNS				TOTALS			
Year Team	G	GS	Att.	Yds.	Avg.	TD	No.	Yds.	Avg.	TD	No.	Yds.	Avg.	TD	TD	2pt.	Pts.	Fum.
2001—Cincinnati NFL.............	2	0	0	0	0.0	0	0	0	0.0	0	4	79	19.8	0	0	0	0	0
2002—Cincinnati NFL.............	7	0	17	67	3.9	0	6	34	5.7	0	13	277	21.3	0	0	0	0	0
2003—Cincinnati NFL.............	13	5	215	957	4.5	9	21	146	7.0	0	2	23	11.5	0	9	0	54	0
2004—Cincinnati NFL.............	16	16	361	1454	4.0	12	15	84	5.6	0	0	0	0.0	0	12	0	72	4
Pro totals (4 years)................	38	21	593	2478	4.2	21	42	264	6.3	0	19	379	19.9	0	21	0	126	4

JOHNSON, SPENCER — DT — VIKINGS

PERSONAL: Born December 12, 1981, in Waynesboro, Miss. ... 6-3/286.
HIGH SCHOOL: Southern Choctaw (Silas, Ala.).
COLLEGE: Auburn.
TRANSACTIONS/CAREER NOTES: Signed as non-drafted free agent by Minnesota Vikings (April 27, 2004).

			TOTALS		
Year Team	G	GS	Tk.	Ast.	Sks.
2004—Minnesota NFL	9	7	27	11	1.0

JOHNSON, TANK — DT — BEARS

PERSONAL: Born December 7, 1981, in Chandler, Ariz. ... 6-3/300. ... Full name: Terry Johnson.
HIGH SCHOOL: McClintock (Tempe, Ariz.).
COLLEGE: Washington.
TRANSACTIONS/CAREER NOTES: Selected by Chicago Bears in second round (47th pick overall) of 2004 NFL draft. ... Signed by Bears (June 28, 2004).

			TOTALS			INTERCEPTIONS			
Year Team	G	GS	Tk.	Ast.	Sks.	No.	Yds.	Avg.	TD
2004—Chicago NFL..................................	16	1	10	2	0.5	0	0	0.0	0

JOHNSON, TED — LB — PATRIOTS

PERSONAL: Born December 4, 1972, in Alameda, Calif. ... 6-4/253. ... Full name: Ted Curtis Johnson.
HIGH SCHOOL: Carlsbad (Calif.).
COLLEGE: Colorado.
TRANSACTIONS/CAREER NOTES: Selected by New England Patriots in second round (57th pick overall) of 1995 NFL draft. ... Signed by Patriots (July 18, 1995). ... On injured reserve with bicep injury (December 11, 1998-remainder of season).
CHAMPIONSHIP GAME EXPERIENCE: Played in AFC championship game (1996, 2001, 2003 and 2004 seasons). ... Played in Super Bowl 31 (1996 season). ... Member of Super Bowl championship team (2001, 2003 and 2004 seasons).
HONORS: Named linebacker on THE SPORTING NEWS college All-America second team (1994).

			TOTALS			INTERCEPTIONS			
Year Team	G	GS	Tk.	Ast.	Sks.	No.	Yds.	Avg.	TD
1995—New England NFL..............................	12	12	41	28	0.5	0	0	0.0	0
1996—New England NFL..............................	16	16	87	28	0.0	1	0	0.0	0
1997—New England NFL..............................	16	16	95	32	4.0	0	0	0.0	0
1998—New England NFL..............................	13	13	64	33	2.0	0	0	0.0	0
1999—New England NFL..............................	5	5	25	13	2.0	0	0	0.0	0
2000—New England NFL..............................	13	11	51	22	0.5	0	0	0.0	0
2001—New England NFL..............................	12	5	33	13	0.0	0	0	0.0	0
2002—New England NFL..............................	14	11	63	33	1.5	0	0	0.0	0
2003—New England NFL..............................	8	2	15	6	0.0	0	0	0.0	0
2004—New England NFL..............................	16	15	56	22	1.0	0	0	0.0	0
Pro totals (10 years).................................	125	106	530	230	11.5	1	0	0.0	0

JOHNSON, TEYO — TE — RAIDERS

PERSONAL: Born November 29, 1981, in San Diego, Calif. ... 6-6/260. ... Brother of Riall Johnson, linebacker with Cincinnati Bengals (2001-03).
HIGH SCHOOL: Mira Mesa (San Diego).
COLLEGE: Stanford.
TRANSACTIONS/CAREER NOTES: Selected after sophomore season by Oakland Raiders in second round (63rd pick overall) of 2003 NFL draft. ... Signed by Raiders (July 24, 2003).
SINGLE GAME HIGHS (regular season): Receptions—3 (December 25, 2004, vs. Kansas City); yards—52 (December 25, 2004, vs. Kansas City); and touchdown receptions—1 (December 19, 2004, vs. Tennessee).

			RECEIVING				TOTALS			
Year Team	G	GS	No.	Yds.	Avg.	TD	TD	2pt.	Pts.	Fum.
2003—Oakland NFL..................................	16	5	14	128	9.1	1	1	0	6	0
2004—Oakland NFL..................................	8	1	9	131	14.6	2	2	0	12	0
Pro totals (2 years)	24	6	23	259	11.3	3	3	0	18	0

JOHNSON, TIM — LB

PERSONAL: Born February 7, 1978, in Birmingham, Ala. ... 6-0/245.
HIGH SCHOOL: Fairfield (Ala.).
JUNIOR COLLEGE: East Mississippi Junior College.

COLLEGE: Youngstown State.
TRANSACTIONS/CAREER NOTES: Signed as non-drafted free agent by Baltimore Ravens (April 27, 2001). ... Released by Ravens (September 1, 2001). ... Re-signed by Ravens (September 5, 2001). ... Released by Ravens (September 10, 2001). ... Signed by Chicago Bears to practice squad (September 27, 2001). ... Released by Bears (October 30, 2001). ... Re-signed by Bears to practice squad (November 8, 2001). ... Assigned by Bears to Rhein Fire in 2002 NFL Europe enhancement allocation program (February 18, 2002). ... Released by Bears (September 1, 2002). ... Signed by Oakland Raiders to practice squad (September 3, 2002). ... Released by Raiders (September 18, 2002). ... Re-signed by Raiders to practice squad (September 24, 2002). ... Signed by Raiders (October 9, 2002). ... Re-signed by Raiders to practice squad (October 31, 2002). ... Activated (November 24, 2002). ... Granted free agency (March 2, 2005).
CHAMPIONSHIP GAME EXPERIENCE: Played in AFC championship game (2002 season). ... Played in Super Bowl 37 (2002 season).

				TOTALS			INTERCEPTIONS		
Year Team	G	GS	Tk.	Ast.	Sks.	No.	Yds.	Avg.	TD
2001—Baltimore NFL		Did not play.							
2002—Oakland NFL	6	0	0	0	0.0	0	0	0.0	0
2003—Oakland NFL	12	4	27	5	0.0	0	0	0.0	0
2004—Oakland NFL	16	0	12	10	0.5	1	8	8.0	0
Pro totals (3 years)	34	4	39	15	0.5	1	8	8.0	0

JOHNSON, TODD — SS — BEARS

PERSONAL: Born December 18, 1978, in Sarasota, Fla. ... 6-1/200. ... Full name: Todd Edward Johnson.
HIGH SCHOOL: Riverview (Sarasota, Fla.).
COLLEGE: Florida.
TRANSACTIONS/CAREER NOTES: Selected by Chicago Bears in fourth round (100th pick overall) of 2003 NFL draft. ... Signed by Bears (July 9, 2003). ... On injured reserve with jaw injury (September 9, 2003-entire season).

		INTERCEPTIONS			
Year Team	G	No.	Yds.	Avg.	TD
2003—Chicago NFL		Did not play.			
2004—Chicago NFL	16	0	0	0.0	0
Pro totals (1 year)	16	0	0	0.0	0

JOHNSON, TREVOR — DE — JETS

PERSONAL: Born February 26, 1981, in Gordon, Neb. ... 6-4/260.
HIGH SCHOOL: Northeast (Lincoln, Neb.).
COLLEGE: Nebraska.
TRANSACTIONS/CAREER NOTES: Selected by New York Jets in seventh round (234th pick overall) of 2004 NFL draft. ... Signed by Jets (May 28, 2004).

			TOTALS		
Year Team	G	GS	Tk.	Ast.	Sks.
2004—New York Jets NFL	16	0	9	4	0.0

JOHNSTONE, LANCE — DE — VIKINGS

PERSONAL: Born June 11, 1973, in Philadelphia, Pa. ... 6-4/250.
HIGH SCHOOL: Germantown (Philadelphia).
COLLEGE: Temple.
TRANSACTIONS/CAREER NOTES: Selected by Oakland Raiders in second round (57th pick overall) of 1996 NFL draft. ... Signed by Raiders for 1996 season. ... Granted unconditional free agency (March 2, 2001). ... Signed by Minnesota Vikings (March 30, 2001). ... Granted unconditional free agency (March 1, 2002). ... Re-signed by Vikings (March 28, 2002). ... Granted unconditional free agency (February 28, 2003). ... Re-signed by Vikings (March 20, 2003).
CHAMPIONSHIP GAME EXPERIENCE: Played in AFC championship game (2000 season).

			TOTALS			INTERCEPTIONS			
Year Team	G	GS	Tk.	Ast.	Sks.	No.	Yds.	Avg.	TD
1996—Oakland NFL	16	10	26	6	1.0	0	0	0.0	0
1997—Oakland NFL	14	6	20	11	3.5	0	0	0.0	0
1998—Oakland NFL	16	15	48	6	11.0	0	0	0.0	0
1999—Oakland NFL	16	16	45	7	10.0	1	0	0.0	0
2000—Oakland NFL	14	9	22	10	3.5	0	0	0.0	0
2001—Minnesota NFL	16	5	29	9	5.5	0	0	0.0	0
2002—Minnesota NFL	16	16	41	10	7.0	0	0	0.0	0
2003—Minnesota NFL	16	0	22	7	10.0	1	33	33.0	1
2004—Minnesota NFL	16	1	25	6	11.0	0	0	0.0	0
Pro totals (9 years)	140	78	278	72	62.5	2	33	16.5	1

JOLLEY, DOUG — TE — JETS

PERSONAL: Born January 2, 1979, in Sandy, Utah. ... 6-4/250.
HIGH SCHOOL: Dixie (St. George, Utah).
COLLEGE: Brigham Young.
TRANSACTIONS/CAREER NOTES: Selected by Oakland Raiders in second round (55th pick overall) of 2002 NFL draft. ... Signed by Raiders (July 23, 2002). ... Traded by Raiders with second-round pick (K Mike Nugent) and two sixth-round picks (RB Cedric Houston; traded to Jacksonville) in 2005 draft to New York Jets for first- (traded to Seattle) and seventh-round (traded to New England) picks in 2005 draft (April 21, 2005).
CHAMPIONSHIP GAME EXPERIENCE: Played in AFC championship game (2002 season). ... Played in Super Bowl 37 (2002 season).

SINGLE GAME HIGHS (regular season): Receptions—7 (September 28, 2003, vs. San Diego); yards—104 (December 8, 2002, vs. San Diego); and touchdown receptions—1 (October 31, 2004, vs. San Diego).
STATISTICAL PLATEAUS: 100-yard receiving games: 2002 (1). Total: 1.

				RECEIVING					TOTALS		
Year Team	G	GS	No.	Yds.	Avg.	TD	TD	2pt.	Pts.	Fum.
2002—Oakland NFL	16	4	32	409	12.8	2	2	0	12	0
2003—Oakland NFL	15	10	31	250	8.1	1	1	0	6	0
2004—Oakland NFL	16	13	27	313	11.6	2	2	0	12	0
Pro totals (3 years)	47	27	90	972	10.8	5	5	0	30	0

JONES, ADRIAN   T   JETS

PERSONAL: Born June 10, 1981, in Dallas, Texas. ... 6-4/296.
HIGH SCHOOL: Carter (Dallas, Texas).
COLLEGE: Kansas.
TRANSACTIONS/CAREER NOTES: Selected by New York Jets in fourth round (132nd pick overall) of 2004 NFL draft. ... Signed by Jets (July 29, 2004).
PLAYING EXPERIENCE: New York Jets NFL, 2004. ... Games/Games started: 2004 (12/0). Total: 12/0.

JONES, BRIAN   TE   JAGUARS

PERSONAL: Born August 23, 1981, in Bastrop, La. ... 6-3/235.
HIGH SCHOOL: Bastrop (La.).
COLLEGE: Arkansas-Pine Bluff.
TRANSACTIONS/CAREER NOTES: Signed as non-drafted free agent by Jacksonville Jaguars (April 25, 2004).
SINGLE GAME HIGHS (regular season): Receptions—2 (November 28, 2004, vs. Minnesota); yards—28 (November 28, 2004, vs. Minnesota); and touchdown receptions—1 (November 28, 2004, vs. Minnesota).

				RECEIVING					TOTALS		
Year Team	G	GS	No.	Yds.	Avg.	TD	TD	2pt.	Pts.	Fum.
2004—Jacksonville NFL	16	0	6	87	14.5	1	1	1	8	0

JONES, DARYL   WR

PERSONAL: Born February 2, 1979, in Dallas, Texas. ... 5-9/188. ... Full name: Daryl Lawrence Jones.
HIGH SCHOOL: Carter (Dallas).
COLLEGE: Miami (Fla.).
TRANSACTIONS/CAREER NOTES: Selected by New York Giants in seventh round (226th pick overall) of 2002 NFL draft. ... Signed by Giants (July 22, 2002). ... Released by Giants (August 31, 2003). ... Signed by Chicago Bears (December 23, 2003). ... Released by Bears (September 21, 2004).
SINGLE GAME HIGHS (regular season): Receptions—3 (December 8, 2002, vs. Washington); yards—41 (December 8, 2002, vs. Washington); and touchdown receptions—0.

			RECEIVING				PUNT RETURNS				KICKOFF RETURNS				TOTALS		
Year Team	G	GS	No.	Yds.	Avg.	TD	No.	Yds.	Avg.	TD	No.	Yds.	Avg.	TD	TD	2pt.	Pts. Fum.
2002—New York Giants NFL	13	6	8	90	11.3	0	6	28	4.7	0	10	195	19.5	0	0	0	0 1
2004—Chicago NFL	2	0	0	0	0.0	0	0	0	0.0	0	6	112	18.7	0	0	0	0 0
Pro totals (2 years)	15	6	8	90	11.3	0	6	28	4.7	0	16	307	19.2	0	0	0	0 1

JONES, DHANI   LB   EAGLES

PERSONAL: Born February 22, 1978, in San Diego, Calif. ... 6-1/240. ... Full name: Dhani Makalani Jones.
HIGH SCHOOL: Winston Churchill (Potomac, Md.).
COLLEGE: Michigan.
TRANSACTIONS/CAREER NOTES: Selected by New York Giants in sixth round (177th pick overall) of 2000 NFL draft. ... Signed by Giants (July 18, 2000). ... On injured reserve with knee injury (August 20, 2000-entire season). ... Granted free agency (February 28, 2003). ... Re-signed by Giants (April 28, 2003). ... Granted unconditional free agency (March 3, 2004). ... Signed by Philadelphia Eagles (March 9, 2004).
CHAMPIONSHIP GAME EXPERIENCE: Played in NFC championship game (2004 season). ... Played in Super Bowl 39 (2004 season).

			TOTALS			INTERCEPTIONS			
Year Team	G	GS	Tk.	Ast.	Sks.	No.	Yds.	Avg.	TD
2000—New York Giants NFL	Did not play.								
2001—New York Giants NFL	16	0	9	2	0.0	1	14	14.0	0
2002—New York Giants NFL	15	14	60	22	0.0	1	1	1.0	0
2003—New York Giants NFL	16	16	92	26	3.0	0	0	0.0	0
2004—Philadelphia NFL	16	15	45	22	0.5	1	0	0.0	0
Pro totals (4 years)	63	45	206	72	3.5	3	15	5.0	0

JONES, DONNIE   P   SEAHAWKS

PERSONAL: Born July 5, 1980, in Baton Rouge, La. ... 6-2/222. ... Full name: Donald Scott Jones Jr.
HIGH SCHOOL: Catholic (Baton Rouge, La.).
COLLEGE: Louisiana State.
TRANSACTIONS/CAREER NOTES: Selected by Seattle Seahawks in seventh round (224th pick overall) of 2004 NFL draft. ... Signed by Seahawks (June 17, 2004). ... Released by Seahawks (September 5, 2004). ... Re-signed by Seahawks to practice squad (September 6, 2004). ... Activated (October 15, 2004). ... Released by Seahawks (October 19, 2004). ... Re-signed by Seahawks to practice squad (October 20,

2004). ... Activated (October 23, 2004). ... Released by Seahawks (October 25, 2004). ... Re-signed by Seahawks to practice squad (October 26, 2004). ... Activated (October 29, 2004). ... Released by Seahawks (November 23, 2004). ... Re-signed by Seahawks to practice squad (November 24, 2004). ... Released by Seahawks (December 29, 2004). ... Re-signed by Seahawks to practice squad (January 4, 2005).

				PUNTING			
Year Team	G	No.	Yds.	Avg.	Net avg.	In. 20	Blk.
2004—Seattle NFL	7	26	988	38.0	32.2	6	1

JONES, FRED   LB

PERSONAL: Born October 18, 1977, in Subic Bay. ... 6-2/245. ... Full name: Fred Allen Jones.
HIGH SCHOOL: St. Augustine (San Diego).
COLLEGE: Colorado.
TRANSACTIONS/CAREER NOTES: Signed as non-drafted free agent by Buffalo Bills (April 23, 2000). ... Released by Bills (September 3, 2002). ... Selected by Frankfurt Galaxy in 2003 NFL Europe draft (February 5, 2003). ... Signed by Kansas City Chiefs (June 19, 2003). ... Granted unconditional free agency (March 2, 2005).

			TOTALS			INTERCEPTIONS			
Year Team	G	GS	Tk.	Ast.	Sks.	No.	Yds.	Avg.	TD
2000—Buffalo NFL	15	0	5	2	1.0	0	0	0.0	0
2001—Buffalo NFL	16	0	0	1	0.5	0	0	0.0	0
2003—Kansas City NFL	11	0	0	1	0.0	0	0	0.0	0
2004—Kansas City NFL	16	0	2	0	0.0	0	0	0.0	0
Pro totals (4 years)	58	0	7	4	1.5	0	0	0.0	0

JONES, FREDDIE   TE   PANTHERS

PERSONAL: Born September 16, 1974, in Cheverly, Md. ... 6-4/265. ... Full name: Freddie Ray Jones Jr.
HIGH SCHOOL: McKinley (Landover, Md.).
COLLEGE: North Carolina.
TRANSACTIONS/CAREER NOTES: Selected by San Diego Chargers in second round (45th pick overall) of 1997 NFL draft. ... Signed by Chargers (May 21, 1997). ... On injured reserve with leg injury (December 12, 1997-remainder of season). ... Granted free agency (February 11, 2000). ... Re-signed by Chargers (April 29, 2000). ... Released by Chargers (February 27, 2002). ... Signed by Arizona Cardinals (March 18, 2002). ... Granted unconditional free agency (March 2, 2005). ... Signed by Carolina Panthers (April 18, 2005).
SINGLE GAME HIGHS (regular season): Receptions—10 (October 29, 2000, vs. Oakland); yards—111 (October 29, 2000, vs. Oakland); and touchdown receptions—2 (November 26, 2000, vs. Kansas City).
STATISTICAL PLATEAUS: 100-yard receiving games: 2000 (1). Total: 1.

			RECEIVING				TOTALS			
Year Team	G	GS	No.	Yds.	Avg.	TD	TD	2pt.	Pts.	Fum.
1997—San Diego NFL	13	8	41	505	12.3	2	2	0	12	0
1998—San Diego NFL	16	16	57	602	10.6	3	3	1	20	1
1999—San Diego NFL	16	16	56	670	12.0	2	2	0	12	0
2000—San Diego NFL	16	16	71	766	10.8	5	5	0	30	3
2001—San Diego NFL	14	9	35	388	11.1	4	4	0	24	0
2002—Arizona NFL	16	16	44	358	8.1	1	1	0	6	0
2003—Arizona NFL	16	16	55	517	9.4	3	3	0	18	0
2004—Arizona NFL	16	15	45	426	9.5	2	2	0	12	0
Pro totals (8 years)	123	112	404	4232	10.5	22	22	1	134	4

JONES, GREG   RB   JAGUARS

PERSONAL: Born April 4, 1981, in Columbia, S.C. ... 6-1/250.
HIGH SCHOOL: Battery Creek (Beaufort, S.C.).
COLLEGE: Florida State.
TRANSACTIONS/CAREER NOTES: Selected by Jacksonville Jaguars in second round (55th pick overall) of 2004 NFL draft. ... Signed by Jaguars (July 30, 2004).
SINGLE GAME HIGHS (regular season): Attempts—16 (January 2, 2005, vs. Oakland); yards—38 (December 26, 2004, vs. Houston); and rushing touchdowns—1 (January 2, 2005, vs. Oakland).

			RUSHING				RECEIVING				KICKOFF RETURNS				TOTALS			
Year Team	G	GS	Att.	Yds.	Avg.	TD	No.	Yds.	Avg.	TD	No.	Yds.	Avg.	TD	TD	2pt.	Pts.	Fum.
2004—Jacksonville NFL	16	3	62	162	2.6	3	3	13	4.3	0	5	90	18.0	0	3	0	18	1

JONES, JULIUS   RB   COWBOYS

PERSONAL: Born August 14, 1981, in Big Stone Gap, Va. ... 5-10/205. ... Full name: Julius Andre Maurice Jones. ... Brother of Thomas Jones, running back, Chicago Bears.
HIGH SCHOOL: Powell Valley (Big Stone Gap, Va.).
COLLEGE: Notre Dame.
TRANSACTIONS/CAREER NOTES: Selected by Dallas Cowboys in second round (43rd pick overall) of 2004 NFL draft. ... Signed by Cowboys (July 30, 2004).
SINGLE GAME HIGHS (regular season): Attempts—33 (November 25, 2004, vs. Chicago); yards—198 (December 6, 2004, vs. Seattle); and rushing touchdowns—3 (December 6, 2004, vs. Seattle).
STATISTICAL PLATEAUS: 100-yard rushing games: 2004 (3). Total: 3.

			RUSHING				RECEIVING				PUNT RETURNS				KICKOFF RETURNS				TOTALS		
Year Team	G	GS	Att.	Yds.	Avg.	TD	No.	Yds.	Avg.	TD	No.	Yds.	Avg.	TD	No.	Yds.	Avg.	TD	TD	2pt.	Pts.
2004—Dal. NFL	8	7	197	819	4.2	7	17	109	6.4	0	0	0	0.0	0	0	0	0.0	0	7	0	42

JONES, KENYATTA   OL

PERSONAL: Born January 18, 1979, in Gainesville, Fla. ... 6-3/307. ... Full name: Kenyatta Lapoleon Jones.
HIGH SCHOOL: Eastside (Gainesville, Fla.).
COLLEGE: South Florida.
TRANSACTIONS/CAREER NOTES: Selected by New England Patriots in fourth round (96th pick overall) of 2001 NFL draft. ... Signed by Patriots (July 19, 2001). ... On physically unable to perform list with knee injury (August 26, 2003-October 25, 2003). ... Released by Patriots (October 25, 2003). ... Signed by Washington Redskins (November 25, 2003). ... On injured reserve with pectoral injury (December 3, 2003-remainder of season). ... Released by Redskins (October 22, 2004).
CHAMPIONSHIP GAME EXPERIENCE: Member of Patriots for AFC championship game (2001 season); inactive. ... Member of Super Bowl championship team (2001 season); inactive.

JONES, KEVIN   RB   LIONS

PERSONAL: Born August 21, 1982, in Chester, Pa. ... 5-11/221. ... Full name: Kevin S. Jones.
HIGH SCHOOL: Cardinal O'Hara (Chester, Pa.).
COLLEGE: Virginia Tech.
TRANSACTIONS/CAREER NOTES: Selected after junior season by Detroit Lions in first round (30th pick overall) of 2004 NFL draft. ... Signed by Lions (July 28, 2004).
HONORS: Named running back on THE SPORTING NEWS Freshman All-America second team (2001). ... Named running back on THE SPORTING NEWS college All-America first team (2003).
SINGLE GAME HIGHS (regular season): Attempts—33 (December 12, 2004, vs. Green Bay); yards—196 (December 5, 2004, vs. Arizona); and rushing touchdowns—1 (December 26, 2004, vs. Chicago).
STATISTICAL PLATEAUS: 100-yard rushing games: 2004 (4). Total: 4.

			RUSHING				RECEIVING				TOTALS			
Year Team	G	GS	Att.	Yds.	Avg.	TD	No.	Yds.	Avg.	TD	TD	2pt.	Pts.	Fum.
2004—Detroit NFL	15	14	241	1133	4.7	5	28	180	6.4	1	6	0	36	2

JONES, LEVI   T   BENGALS

PERSONAL: Born August 24, 1979, in Eloy, Ariz. ... 6-5/310. ... Full name: Levi J. Jones.
HIGH SCHOOL: Santa Cruz (Eloy, Ariz.).
COLLEGE: Arizona State.
TRANSACTIONS/CAREER NOTES: Selected by Cincinnati Bengals in first round (10th pick overall) of 2002 NFL draft. ... Signed by Bengals (July 25, 2002).
PLAYING EXPERIENCE: Cincinnati NFL, 2002-2004. ... Games/Games started: 2002 (16/14), 2003 (16/16), 2004 (16/16). Total: 48/46.

JONES, MARK   WR   GIANTS

PERSONAL: Born November 3, 1980, in Wallingford, Pa. ... 5-9/185. ... Full name: Mark Christopher Jones.
HIGH SCHOOL: Strath Haven (Wallingford, Pa.).
COLLEGE: Tennessee.
TRANSACTIONS/CAREER NOTES: Selected by Tampa Bay Buccaneers in seventh round (206th pick overall) of 2004 NFL draft. ... Signed by Buccaneers (July 29, 2004). ... Claimed on waivers by New York Giants (September 6, 2004).

			RECEIVING				PUNT RETURNS				TOTALS			
Year Team	G	GS	No.	Yds.	Avg.	TD	No.	Yds.	Avg.	TD	TD	2pt.	Pts.	Fum.
2004—New York Giants NFL	14	0	0	0	0.0	0	34	227	6.7	0	0	0	0	1

JONES, NATHAN   DB   COWBOYS

PERSONAL: Born June 13, 1982, in Scotch Plains, N.J. ... 5-10/184.
HIGH SCHOOL: Scotch Plains-Fanwood (N.J.).
COLLEGE: Rutgers.
TRANSACTIONS/CAREER NOTES: Selected by Dallas Cowboys in seventh round (205th pick overall) of 2004 NFL draft. ... Signed by Cowboys (July 29, 2004).

			TOTALS			INTERCEPTIONS				KICKOFF RETURNS				TOTALS			
Year Team	G	GS	Tk.	Ast.	Sks.	No.	Yds.	Avg.	TD	No.	Yds.	Avg.	TD	TD	2pt.	Pts.	Fum.
2004—Dallas NFL	16	1	29	2	1.0	0	0	0.0	0	2	43	21.5	0	0	0	0	0

JONES, RUSHEN   CB   VIKINGS

PERSONAL: Born August 4, 1980... 5-10/194.
HIGH SCHOOL: Whitehaven (Memphis, Tenn.).
COLLEGE: Vanderbilt.
TRANSACTIONS/CAREER NOTES: Signed as non-drafted free agent by Minnesota Vikings (May 2, 2003). ... Released by Vikings (October 13, 2004). ... Re-signed by Vikings (December 21, 2004).

			TOTALS			INTERCEPTIONS			
Year Team	G	GS	Tk.	Ast.	Sks.	No.	Yds.	Avg.	TD
2003—Minnesota NFL	11	0	0	0	0.0	0	0	0.0	0
2004—Minnesota NFL	5	0	1	0	0.0	0	0	0.0	0
Pro totals (2 years)	16	0	1	0	0.0	0	0	0.0	0

JONES, SEAN   DB   BROWNS

PERSONAL: Born March 2, 1982, in Atlanta, Ga. ... 6-2/212.
HIGH SCHOOL: Westlake (Atlanta, Ga.).
COLLEGE: Georgia.
TRANSACTIONS/CAREER NOTES: Selected after junior season by Cleveland Browns in second round (59th pick overall) of 2004 NFL draft. ... Signed by Browns (July 29, 2004). ... On physically unable to perform list with knee injury (August 30, 2004-entire season).

			TOTALS			INTERCEPTIONS				PUNT RETURNS				TOTALS		
Year	Team	G	GS	Tk.	Ast.	Sks.	No.	Yds.	Avg.	TD	No.	Yds.	Avg.	TD	TD	2pt.	Pts.	Fum.
2004—Cleveland NFL		Did not play.															

JONES, TEBUCKY   S   DOLPHINS

PERSONAL: Born October 6, 1974, in New Britain, Conn. ... 6-2/220. ... Full name: Tebucky Shermaine Jones.
HIGH SCHOOL: New Britain (Conn.).
COLLEGE: Syracuse.
TRANSACTIONS/CAREER NOTES: Selected by New England Patriots in first round (22nd pick overall) of 1998 NFL draft. ... Signed by Patriots (July 18, 1998). ... On injured reserve with knee injury (December 31, 1999-remainder of season). ... Designated by Patriots as franchise player (February 20, 2003). ... Traded by Patriots to New Orleans Saints for third- (traded to Miami) and seventh-round picks (DE Tully Banta-Cain) in 2003 draft and fourth-round pick (CB Dexter Reid) in 2004 draft (April 14, 2003). ... Released by Saints (March 15, 2005). ... Signed by Miami Dolphins (March 17, 2005).
CHAMPIONSHIP GAME EXPERIENCE: Played in AFC championship game (2001 season). ... Member of Super Bowl championship team (2001 season).

				TOTALS			INTERCEPTIONS			
Year	Team	G	GS	Tk.	Ast.	Sks.	No.	Yds.	Avg.	TD
1998—New England NFL		16	0	10	3	0.0	0	0	0.0	0
1999—New England NFL		12	2	12	0	0.0	0	0	0.0	0
2000—New England NFL		15	9	42	13	0.0	2	20	10.0	0
2001—New England NFL		16	12	41	16	1.0	1	-4	-4.0	0
2002—New England NFL		14	12	38	12	1.5	1	0	0.0	0
2003—New Orleans NFL		15	15	51	18	0.0	1	2	2.0	0
2004—New Orleans NFL		16	16	79	23	0.0	1	55	55.0	0
Pro totals (7 years)		104	66	273	85	2.5	6	73	12.2	0

JONES, TERRY   TE

PERSONAL: Born December 3, 1979, in Tuscaloosa, Ala. ... 6-3/260. ... Full name: Terry Jones Jr.
HIGH SCHOOL: Central (Tuscaloosa, Ala.).
COLLEGE: Alabama.
TRANSACTIONS/CAREER NOTES: Selected by Baltimore Ravens in fifth round (155th pick overall) of 2002 NFL draft. ... Signed by Ravens (July 26, 2002). ... Granted free agency (March 2, 2005).
SINGLE GAME HIGHS (regular season): Receptions—3 (December 26, 2004, vs. Pittsburgh); yards—38 (December 5, 2004, vs. Cincinnati); and touchdown receptions—1 (January 2, 2005, vs. Miami).

				RECEIVING				TOTALS			
Year	Team	G	GS	No.	Yds.	Avg.	TD	TD	2pt.	Pts.	Fum.
2002—Baltimore NFL		14	6	11	106	9.6	1	1	0	6	0
2003—Baltimore NFL		16	13	19	159	8.4	3	3	0	18	0
2004—Baltimore NFL		15	10	20	152	7.6	1	1	0	6	0
Pro totals (3 years)		45	29	50	417	8.3	5	5	0	30	0

JONES, THOMAS   RB   BEARS

PERSONAL: Born August 19, 1978, in Big Stone Gap, Va. ... 5-10/220. ... Full name: Thomas Quinn Jones. ... Brother of Julius Jones, running back, Dallas Cowboys.
HIGH SCHOOL: Powell Valley (Big Stone Gap, Va.).
COLLEGE: Virginia.
TRANSACTIONS/CAREER NOTES: Selected by Arizona Cardinals in first round (seventh pick overall) of 2000 NFL draft. ... Signed by Cardinals (July 21, 2000). ... On injured reserve with hand injury (November 26, 2002-remainder of season). ... Traded by Cardinals to Tampa Bay Buccaneers for WR Marquise Walker (June 13, 2003). ... Granted unconditional free agency (March 3, 2004). ... Signed by Chicago Bears (March 3, 2004).
HONORS: Named running back on THE SPORTING NEWS college All-America first team (1999).
SINGLE GAME HIGHS (regular season): Attempts—34 (December 14, 2003, vs. Houston); yards—173 (September 15, 2002, vs. Seattle); and rushing touchdowns—2 (January 2, 2005, vs. Green Bay).
STATISTICAL PLATEAUS: 100-yard rushing games: 2002 (1), 2003 (2), 2004 (4). Total: 7.

				RUSHING				RECEIVING				KICKOFF RETURNS				TOTALS			
Year	Team	G	GS	Att.	Yds.	Avg.	TD	No.	Yds.	Avg.	TD	No.	Yds.	Avg.	TD	TD	2pt.	Pts.	Fum.
2000—Arizona NFL		14	4	112	373	3.3	2	32	208	6.5	0	0	0	0.0	0	2	0	12	4
2001—Arizona NFL		16	2	112	380	3.4	5	21	151	7.2	0	0	0	0.0	0	5	0	30	2
2002—Arizona NFL		9	9	138	511	3.7	2	20	113	5.7	0	0	0	0.0	0	2	0	12	3
2003—Tampa Bay NFL		16	3	137	627	4.6	3	24	180	7.5	0	17	271	15.9	0	3	0	18	4
2004—Chicago NFL		14	14	240	948	4.0	7	56	427	7.6	0	0	0	0.0	0	7	0	42	2
Pro totals (5 years)		69	32	739	2839	3.8	19	153	1079	7.1	0	17	271	15.9	0	19	0	114	15

JONES, WALTER   T   SEAHAWKS

PERSONAL: Born January 19, 1974, in Aliceville, Ala. ... 6-5/315.
HIGH SCHOOL: Aliceville (Ala.).
JUNIOR COLLEGE: Holmes Junior College (Miss.).
COLLEGE: Florida State.
TRANSACTIONS/CAREER NOTES: Selected by Seattle Seahawks in first round (sixth pick overall) of 1997 NFL draft. ... Signed by Seahawks (August 6, 1997). ... Granted free agency (March 1, 2002). ... Re-signed by Seahawks (September 16, 2002). ... Designated by Seahawks as franchise player (February 20, 2003). ... Re-signed by Seahawks (September 2, 2003). ... Designated by Seahawks as franchise player (February 24, 2004). ... Re-signed by Seahawks (September 6, 2004).
PLAYING EXPERIENCE: Seattle NFL, 1997-2004. ... Games/Games started: 1997 (12/12), 1998 (16/16), 1999 (16/16), 2000 (16/16), 2001 (16/16), 2002 (14/14), 2003 (16/16), 2004 (16/16). Total: 122/122.
HONORS: Played in Pro Bowl (1999, 2001, 2003 and 2004 seasons). ... Named to play in Pro Bowl (2002 season); replaced by Chris Samuels due to injury. ... Named offensive tackle on THE SPORTING NEWS NFL All-Pro team (2004).

JORDAN, LAMONT   RB   RAIDERS

PERSONAL: Born November 11, 1978, in Forestville, Md. ... 5-10/230.
HIGH SCHOOL: Suitland (Forestville, Md.).
COLLEGE: Maryland.
TRANSACTIONS/CAREER NOTES: Selected by New York Jets in second round (49th pick overall) of 2001 NFL draft. ... Signed by Jets (July 25, 2001). ... Granted unconditional free agency (March 2, 2005). ... Signed by Oakland Raiders (March 3, 2005).
HONORS: Named running back on THE SPORTING NEWS college All-America third team (1999).
SINGLE GAME HIGHS (regular season): Attempts—18 (November 21, 2004, vs. Cleveland); yards—115 (November 1, 2004, vs. Miami); and rushing touchdowns—1 (November 1, 2004, vs. Miami).
STATISTICAL PLATEAUS: 100-yard rushing games: 2002 (1), 2004 (1). Total: 2.

Year Team	G	GS	RUSHING Att.	Yds.	Avg.	TD	RECEIVING No.	Yds.	Avg.	TD	KICKOFF RETURNS No.	Yds.	Avg.	TD	TOTALS TD	2pt.	Pts.	Fum.
2001—New York Jets NFL	16	0	39	292	7.5	1	7	44	6.3	1	3	62	20.7	0	2	0	12	0
2002—New York Jets NFL	14	0	84	316	3.8	3	17	160	9.4	0	5	112	22.4	0	3	0	18	4
2003—New York Jets NFL	16	0	46	190	4.1	4	11	101	9.2	0	11	209	19.0	0	4	0	24	0
2004—New York Jets NFL	16	0	93	479	5.2	2	15	112	7.5	0	14	284	20.3	0	2	0	12	1
Pro totals (4 years)	62	0	262	1277	4.9	10	50	417	8.3	1	33	667	20.2	0	11	0	66	5

JORDAN, LEANDER   T/G   CHARGERS

PERSONAL: Born September 15, 1977, in Pittsburgh, Pa. ... 6-4/316. ... Full name: Leander James Jordan.
HIGH SCHOOL: Garfield (Pittsburgh), then Peabody (Pittsburgh), then Brashear (Pittsburgh).
COLLEGE: Indiana (Pa.).
TRANSACTIONS/CAREER NOTES: Selected by Carolina Panthers in third round (82nd pick overall) of 2000 NFL draft. ... Signed by Panthers (June 8, 2000). ... Inactive for all 16 games (2000). ... Released by Panthers (September 1, 2002). ... Signed by Jacksonville Jaguars (October 15, 2002). ... Granted free agency (February 28, 2003). ... Re-signed by Jaguars (June 3, 2003). ... Granted unconditional free agency (March 3, 2004). ... Signed by San Diego Chargers (March 4, 2004).
PLAYING EXPERIENCE: Carolina NFL, 2001; Jacksonville NFL, 2003; San Diego NFL, 2004. ... Games/Games started: 2001 (13/5), 2003 (6/0), 2004 (5/0). Total: 24/5.

JORDAN, OMARI   DT   PANTHERS

PERSONAL: Born April 15, 1978, in Cleveland, Ohio. ... 6-4/315. ... Full name: Omari Jammile Jordan.
HIGH SCHOOL: Collingwood (Cleveland, Ohio).
JUNIOR COLLEGE: Vermilion (Minn.).
COLLEGE: Buffalo.
TRANSACTIONS/CAREER NOTES: Signed as non-drafted free agent by Baltimore Ravens (April 26, 2002). ... Released by Ravens (August 30, 2002). ... Signed by Buffalo Bills to practice squad (October 2, 2002). ... Released by Bills (August 20, 2003). ... Signed by Carolina Panthers to practice squad (December 17, 2003). ... Activated (February 11, 2004). ... Released by Panthers (November 16, 2004). ... Re-signed by Panthers (November 30, 2004).

Year Team	G	GS	TOTALS Tk.	Ast.	Sks.
2004—Carolina NFL	4	0	1	2	1.0

JOSEPH, WILLIAM   DT   GIANTS

PERSONAL: Born September 3, 1979, in Miami, Fla. ... 6-5/315.
HIGH SCHOOL: Edison (Miami).
COLLEGE: Miami (Fla.).
TRANSACTIONS/CAREER NOTES: Selected by New York Giants in first round (25th pick overall) of 2003 NFL draft. ... Signed by Giants (August 5, 2003).

Year Team	G	GS	TOTALS Tk.	Ast.	Sks.
2003—New York Giants NFL	14	0	5	2	1.0
2004—New York Giants NFL	15	4	20	5	2.0
Pro totals (2 years)	29	4	25	7	3.0

JOSUE, STEVE   LB

PERSONAL: Born April 5, 1980, in Miami, Fla. ... 6-2/230.
HIGH SCHOOL: North Miami (Fla.).
COLLEGE: Carson-Newman.
TRANSACTIONS/CAREER NOTES: Selected by Green Bay Packers in seventh round (257th pick overall) of 2003 NFL draft. ... Signed by Packers (July 18, 2003). ... Released by Packers (September 1, 2003). ... Re-signed by Packers to practice squad (September 2, 2003). ... Activated (January 26, 2004). ... Assigned by Packers to Amsterdam Admirals in 2004 NFL Europe enhancement allocation program (February 9, 2004). ... Released by Packers (September 5, 2004). ... Signed by Washington Redskins to practice squad (September 21, 2004). ... Released by Redskins (October 6, 2004). ... Signed by San Francisco 49ers to practice squad (November 3, 2004). ... Signed by Packers off 49ers practice squad (December 9, 2004). ... Released by Packers (April 26, 2005).

Year Team	G	GS	TOTALS			INTERCEPTIONS			
			Tk.	Ast.	Sks.	No.	Yds.	Avg.	TD
2004—Green Bay NFL	4	0	5	0	0.0	0	0	0.0	0

JOYCE, MATT   T

PERSONAL: Born March 30, 1972, in St. Petersburg, Fla. ... 6-7/300.
HIGH SCHOOL: New York Military Academy (Cornwall Hudson, N.Y.).
COLLEGE: Richmond.
TRANSACTIONS/CAREER NOTES: Signed as non-drafted free agent by Dallas Cowboys (May 2, 1994). ... Claimed on waivers by Cincinnati Bengals (August 28, 1994); released after failing physical. ... Signed by Cowboys to practice squad (September 5, 1994). ... Granted free agency after 1994 season. ... Signed by Seattle Seahawks (March 1, 1995). ... Released by Seahawks (August 25, 1996). ... Signed by Arizona Cardinals (December 3, 1996). ... Assigned by Cardinals to Scottish Claymores in 1997 World League enhancement allocation program (February 19, 1997). ... Granted free agency (February 12, 1999). ... Re-signed by Cardinals (April 1, 1999). ... Granted unconditional free agency (February 11, 2000). ... Re-signed by Cardinals (February 21, 2000). ... Released by Cardinals (March 16, 2001). ... Signed by Detroit Lions (April 26, 2001). ... On physically unable to perform list with shoulder injury (July 24-August 12, 2001). ... Granted unconditional free agency (March 1, 2002). ... Re-signed by Lions (March 14, 2002). ... Released by Lions (April 21, 2005).
PLAYING EXPERIENCE: Seattle NFL, 1995; Arizona NFL, 1996-2000; Detroit NFL, 2001-2004. ... Games/Games started: 1995 (16/13), 1996 (2/0), 1997 (9/6), 1998 (11/0), 1999 (15/15), 2000 (13/13), 2001 (16/12), 2002 (15/6), 2003 (13/3), 2004 (12/3). Total: 122/71.

JUE, BHAWOH   CB/S   CHARGERS

PERSONAL: Born May 24, 1979, in Monrovia, Liberia. ... 6-0/199. ... Full name: Bhawoh Papi Jue.
HIGH SCHOOL: Chantilly (Va.).
COLLEGE: Penn State.
TRANSACTIONS/CAREER NOTES: Selected by Green Bay Packers in third round (71st pick overall) of 2001 NFL draft. ... Signed by Packers (July 11, 2001). ... On injured reserve with hamstring injury (October 12, 2002-remainder of season). ... Granted free agency (March 3, 2004). ... Re-signed by Packers (April 23, 2004). ... Granted unconditional free agency (March 2, 2005). ... Signed by San Diego Chargers (March 3, 2005).

Year Team	G	GS	TOTALS			INTERCEPTIONS			
			Tk.	Ast.	Sks.	No.	Yds.	Avg.	TD
2001—Green Bay NFL	15	7	31	12	0.0	2	35	17.5	0
2002—Green Bay NFL	4	0	0	0	0.0	0	0	0.0	0
2003—Green Bay NFL	16	0	23	0	1.5	0	0	0.0	0
2004—Green Bay NFL	16	4	29	3	0.0	1	23	23.0	0
Pro totals (4 years)	51	11	83	15	1.5	3	58	19.3	0

JUNE, CATO   LB   COLTS

PERSONAL: Born November 18, 1979, in Riverside, Calif. ... 6-0/227.
HIGH SCHOOL: Anacostia (Washington, D.C.).
COLLEGE: Michigan.
TRANSACTIONS/CAREER NOTES: Selected by Indianapolis Colts in sixth round (198th pick overall) of 2003 NFL draft. ... Signed by Colts (July 24, 2003).
CHAMPIONSHIP GAME EXPERIENCE: Member of Colts for AFC championship game (2003 season); inactive.

Year Team	G	GS	TOTALS			INTERCEPTIONS			
			Tk.	Ast.	Sks.	No.	Yds.	Avg.	TD
2003—Indianapolis NFL	11	0	1	0	0.0	0	0	0.0	0
2004—Indianapolis NFL	16	16	79	25	0.0	2	71	35.5	0
Pro totals (2 years)	27	16	80	25	0.0	2	71	35.5	0

JUREVICIUS, JOE   WR   SEAHAWKS

PERSONAL: Born December 23, 1974, in Cleveland, Ohio. ... 6-5/230. ... Full name: Joe Michael Jurevicius. ... Name pronounced: jur-uh-VISH-us.
HIGH SCHOOL: Lake Catholic (Mentor, Ohio).
COLLEGE: Penn State.
TRANSACTIONS/CAREER NOTES: Selected by New York Giants in second round (55th pick overall) of 1998 NFL draft. ... Signed by Giants (July 28, 1998). ... Granted free agency (March 2, 2001). ... Re-signed by Giants for 2001 season. ... Granted unconditional free agency (March 1, 2002). ... Signed by Tampa Bay Buccaneers (April 9, 2002). ... On injured reserve with knee injury (December 2, 2003-remainder of season). ... On reserve/non-football injury list (July 29-October 23, 2004). ... Released by Buccaneers (March 1, 2005). ... Signed by Seattle Seahawks (March 25, 2005).

CHAMPIONSHIP GAME EXPERIENCE: Played in NFC championship game (2000 and 2002 seasons). ... Played in Super Bowl 35 (2000 season). ... Member of Super Bowl championship team (2002 season).
SINGLE GAME HIGHS (regular season): Receptions—8 (December 8, 2002, vs. Atlanta); yards—100 (December 8, 2002, vs. Atlanta); and touchdown receptions—2 (November 21, 2004, vs. San Francisco).
STATISTICAL PLATEAUS: 100-yard receiving games: 2002 (1). Total: 1.

Year Team	G	GS	No.	Yds.	Avg.	TD	TD	2pt.	Pts.	Fum.
				RECEIVING				TOTALS		
1998—New York Giants NFL	14	1	9	146	16.2	0	0	0	0	0
1999—New York Giants NFL	16	1	18	318	17.7	1	1	0	6	1
2000—New York Giants NFL	14	3	24	272	11.3	1	1	0	6	1
2001—New York Giants NFL	14	9	51	706	13.8	3	3	0	18	0
2002—Tampa Bay NFL	15	3	37	423	11.4	4	4	0	24	1
2003—Tampa Bay NFL	5	2	12	118	9.8	2	2	0	12	0
2004—Tampa Bay NFL	10	3	27	333	12.3	2	2	0	12	0
Pro totals (7 years)	88	22	178	2316	13.0	13	13	0	78	3

KACYVENSKI, ISAIAH — LB — SEAHAWKS

PERSONAL: Born October 3, 1977, in Syracuse, N.Y. ... 6-1/252. ... Name pronounced: kaz-uh-VEN-skee.
HIGH SCHOOL: Union Endicott (N.Y.).
COLLEGE: Harvard.
TRANSACTIONS/CAREER NOTES: Selected by Seattle Seahawks in fourth round (119th pick overall) of 2000 NFL draft. ... Signed by Seahawks (June 9, 2000). ... On injured reserve with ankle injury (December 4, 2002-remainder of season). ... Granted free agency (February 28, 2003). ... Re-signed by Seahawks (March 28, 2003). ... Granted unconditional free agency (March 3, 2004). ... Re-signed by Seahawks (March 10, 2004).

Year Team	G	GS	Tk.	Ast.	Sks.	No.	Yds.	Avg.	TD
				TOTALS			INTERCEPTIONS		
2000—Seattle NFL	16	0	10	3	0.0	1	0	0.0	0
2001—Seattle NFL	16	0	9	2	0.0	1	22	22.0	0
2002—Seattle NFL	9	9	52	20	0.0	1	27	27.0	0
2003—Seattle NFL	14	0	2	4	0.0	0	0	0.0	0
2004—Seattle NFL	16	13	62	19	1.0	0	0	0.0	0
Pro totals (5 years)	71	22	135	48	1.0	3	49	16.3	0

KADELA, DAVE — T — PANTHERS

PERSONAL: Born May 6, 1978, in Dearborn, Mich. ... 6-6/304. ... Full name: David Richard Kadela.
HIGH SCHOOL: Coffman (Ohio).
COLLEGE: Virginia Tech.
TRANSACTIONS/CAREER NOTES: Signed as non-drafted free agent by Atlanta Falcons (May 4, 2001). ... Claimed on waivers by Jacksonville Jaguars (August 28, 2001). ... Released by Jaguars (September 2, 2001). ... Signed by Falcons to practice squad (September 4, 2001). ...Activated (October 22, 2001). ... Released by Falcons (November 4, 2002). ... Signed by Jaguars (December 24, 2002). ... Released by Jaguars (August 25, 2003). ... Signed by Carolina Panthers (December 30, 2003). ... Assigned by Panthers to Berlin Thunder in 2004 NFL Europe enhancement allocation program (February 9, 2004).
PLAYING EXPERIENCE: Atlanta NFL, 2001; Carolina NFL, 2004. ... Games/Games started: 2001 (1/0), 2004 (1/0). Total: 2/0.

KAEDING, NATE — K — CHARGERS

PERSONAL: Born March 26, 1982, in Iowa City, Iowa. ... 6-0/187.
HIGH SCHOOL: Iowa City West (Coralville, Iowa).
COLLEGE: Iowa.
TRANSACTIONS/CAREER NOTES: Selected by San Diego Chargers in third round (65th pick overall) of 2004 NFL draft. ... Signed by Chargers (July 26, 2004).
HONORS: Named kicker on THE SPORTING NEWS Freshman All-America third team (2000). ... Named kicker on THE SPORTING NEWS college All-America first team (2002).

Year Team	G	1-29	30-39	40-49	50+	Tot.	Pct.	Lg.	XPM	XPA	Pts.
				FIELD GOALS					TOTALS		
2004—San Diego NFL	16	10-12	2-2	5-6	3-5	20-25	80.0	53	54	55	114

KAESVIHARN, KEVIN — S — BENGALS

PERSONAL: Born August 29, 1976, in Paramount, Calif. ... 6-1/194. ... Full name: Kevin Robert Kaesviharn.
HIGH SCHOOL: Lakeville (Minn.).
COLLEGE: Augustana (S.D.).
TRANSACTIONS/CAREER NOTES: Signed as non-drafted free agent by Green Bay Packers (April 25, 2001). ... Released by Packers (August 27, 2001). ... Signed by Cincinnati Bengals to practice squad (October 23, 2001). ... Activated (October 27, 2001). ... Released by Bengals (October 30, 2001). ... Re-signed by Bengals to practice squad (October 31, 2001). ... Activated (November 10, 2001). ... Granted free agency (March 3, 2004). ... Re-signed by Bengals (April 12, 2004).

Year Team	G	GS	Tk.	Ast.	Sks.	No.	Yds.	Avg.	TD
				TOTALS			INTERCEPTIONS		
2001—Cincinnati NFL	10	3	22	3	0.0	3	41	13.7	0
2002—Cincinnati NFL	16	6	43	7	0.0	2	17	8.5	0
2003—Cincinnati NFL	16	7	42	9	1.0	1	10	10.0	0
2004—Cincinnati NFL	15	6	44	14	0.0	0	0	0.0	0
Pro totals (4 years)	57	22	151	33	1.0	6	68	11.3	0

KALU, N.D. — DE — EAGLES

PERSONAL: Born August 3, 1975, in Baltimore, Md. ... 6-3/265. ... Full name: Ndukwe Dike Kalu. ... Name pronounced: EN-doo-kway ka-LOO.
HIGH SCHOOL: John Marshall (San Antonio).
COLLEGE: Rice.
TRANSACTIONS/CAREER NOTES: Selected by Philadelphia Eagles in fifth round (152nd pick overall) of 1997 NFL draft. ... Signed by Eagles (July 15, 1997). ... Released by Eagles (August 25, 1998). ... Signed by Washington Redskins (August 30, 1998). ... Granted free agency (February 11, 2000). ... Re-signed by Redskins (May 18, 2000). ... Granted unconditional free agency (March 2, 2001). ... Signed by Eagles (March 12, 2001). ... On injured reserve with knee injury (August 23, 2004-entire season).
CHAMPIONSHIP GAME EXPERIENCE: Played in NFC championship game (2001-2003 seasons).

Year Team	G	GS	TOTALS Tk.	Ast.	Sks.	INTERCEPTIONS No.	Yds.	Avg.	TD
1997—Philadelphia NFL	3	0	0	1	0.0	0	0	0.0	0
1998—Washington NFL	13	1	7	7	3.0	0	0	0.0	0
1999—Washington NFL	12	0	11	3	3.5	0	0	0.0	0
2000—Washington NFL	15	0	4	3	1.0	0	0	0.0	0
2001—Philadelphia NFL	14	1	12	1	3.0	0	0	0.0	0
2002—Philadelphia NFL	16	0	18	5	8.0	0	0	0.0	0
2003—Philadelphia NFL	16	16	39	8	5.5	1	15	15.0	1
2004—Philadelphia NFL	Did not play.								
Pro totals (7 years)	89	18	91	28	24.0	1	15	15.0	1

KAMPMAN, AARON — DE/DT — PACKERS

PERSONAL: Born November 30, 1979, in Cedar Rapids, Iowa. ... 6-4/284.
HIGH SCHOOL: Aplington-Parkersburg (Parkersburg, Iowa).
COLLEGE: Iowa.
TRANSACTIONS/CAREER NOTES: Selected by Green Bay Packers in fifth round (156th pick overall) of 2002 NFL draft. ... Signed by Packers (July 25, 2002). ... Granted free agency (March 2, 2005). ... Tendered offer sheet by Minnesota Vikings (April 10, 2005). ... Packers matched offer (April 20, 2005).

Year Team	G	GS	TOTALS Tk.	Ast.	Sks.	INTERCEPTIONS No.	Yds.	Avg.	TD
2002—Green Bay NFL	12	6	11	12	0.5	0	0	0.0	0
2003—Green Bay NFL	12	10	19	11	2.0	0	0	0.0	0
2004—Green Bay NFL	16	16	48	20	4.5	0	0	0.0	0
Pro totals (3 years)	40	32	78	43	7.0	0	0	0.0	0

KARNEY, MIKE — FB — SAINTS

PERSONAL: Born July 6, 1981, in San Jose, Calif. ... 5-11/258.
HIGH SCHOOL: Kentwood (Kent, Wash.).
COLLEGE: Arizona State.
TRANSACTIONS/CAREER NOTES: Selected by New Orleans Saints in fifth round (156th pick overall) of 2004 NFL draft. ... Signed by Saints (July 28, 2004).
SINGLE GAME HIGHS (regular season): Attempts—2 (January 2, 2005, vs. Carolina); yards—6 (January 2, 2005, vs. Carolina); and rushing touchdowns—0.

Year Team	G	GS	RUSHING Att.	Yds.	Avg.	TD	RECEIVING No.	Yds.	Avg.	TD	TOTALS TD	2pt.	Pts.	Fum.
2004—New Orleans NFL	16	8	3	7	2.3	0	6	42	7.0	0	0	0	0	0

KASAY, JOHN — K — PANTHERS

PERSONAL: Born October 27, 1969, in Athens, Ga. ... 5-10/198. ... Full name: John David Kasay. ... Name pronounced: CASEY.
HIGH SCHOOL: Clarke Central (Athens, Ga.).
COLLEGE: Georgia.
TRANSACTIONS/CAREER NOTES: Selected by Seattle Seahawks in fourth round (98th pick overall) of 1991 NFL draft. ... Signed by Seahawks (July 19, 1991). ... Granted free agency (February 17, 1994). ... Re-signed by Seahawks (July 19, 1994). ... Granted unconditional free agency (February 17, 1995). ... Signed by Carolina Panthers (February 20, 1995). ... On injured reserve with knee injury (December 14, 1999-remainder of season). ... On injured reserve with knee injury (August 14, 2000-entire season). ... On injured reserve with hernia (September 21, 2002-remainder of season).
CHAMPIONSHIP GAME EXPERIENCE: Played in NFC championship game (1996 and 2003 seasons). ... Played in Super Bowl 38 (2003 season).
HONORS: Played in Pro Bowl (1996 season).
POST SEASON RECORDS: Shares NFL postseason single-game record for most field goals made—5 (January 3, 2004, vs. Dallas).
MISCELLANEOUS: Carolina Panthers all-time scoring leader (843 points).

Year Team	G	FIELD GOALS 1-29	30-39	40-49	50+	Tot.	Pct.	Lg.	TOTALS XPM	XPA	Pts.
1991—Seattle NFL	16	6-7	11-14	6-7	2-3	25-31	80.6	54	27	28	102
1992—Seattle NFL	16	4-5	8-11	2-6	0-0	14-22	63.6	43	14	14	56
1993—Seattle NFL	16	6-6	10-11	4-6	3-5	23-28	82.1	55	29	29	98
1994—Seattle NFL	16	2-2	11-11	6-9	1-2	20-24	83.3	50	25	26	85
1995—Carolina NFL	16	6-6	10-14	9-12	1-1	26-33	78.8	52	27	28	105
1996—Carolina NFL	16	16-16	11-12	7-10	3-7	*37-*45	82.2	53	34	35	*145
1997—Carolina NFL	16	7-8	8-8	4-4	3-6	22-26	84.6	54	25	25	91

		FIELD GOALS							TOTALS		
Year Team	G	1-29	30-39	40-49	50+	Tot.	Pct.	Lg.	XPM	XPA	Pts.
1998—Carolina NFL	16	5-5	4-5	6-9	4-7	19-26	73.1	56	35	37	92
1999—Carolina NFL	13	9-9	6-6	5-6	2-4	22-25	88.0	52	33	33	99
2000—Carolina NFL	Did not play.										
2001—Carolina NFL	16	10-10	4-4	7-9	2-5	23-28	82.1	52	22	23	91
2002—Carolina NFL	2	2-2	0-0	0-2	0-1	2-5	40.0	27	5	5	11
2003—Carolina NFL	16	13-13	6-8	11-13	2-4	32-38	84.2	53	29	30	125
2004—Carolina NFL	14	11-11	4-4	1-2	3-5	19-22	86.4	54	27	28	84
Pro totals (13 years)	189	97-100	93-108	68-95	26-50	284-353	80.5	56	332	341	1184

KASHAMA, ALAIN　　　　　DE　　　　　BEARS

PERSONAL: Born December 8, 1979, in Montreal, Quebec. ... 6-4/270.
HIGH SCHOOL: Vieux Montreal (Montreal, Quebec).
COLLEGE: Michigan.
TRANSACTIONS/CAREER NOTES: Signed as non-drafted free agent by Chicago Bears (April 26, 2004). ... Released by Bears (October 25, 2004). ... Re-signed by Bears to practice squad (October 26, 2004). ... Activated (December 22, 2004).

			TOTALS		
Year Team	G	GS	Tk.	Ast.	Sks.
2004—Chicago NFL	3	0	0	1	0.0

KASPER, KEVIN　　　　　WR

PERSONAL: Born December 23, 1977, in Hinsdale, Ill. ... 6-1/197.
HIGH SCHOOL: Hinsdale South (Burr Ridge, Ill.).
COLLEGE: Iowa.
TRANSACTIONS/CAREER NOTES: Selected by Denver Broncos in sixth round (190th pick overall) of 2001 NFL draft. ... Signed by Broncos (May 17, 2001). ... Claimed on waivers by Seattle Seahawks (October 30, 2002). ... Claimed on waivers by Arizona Cardinals (November 23, 2002). ... Granted free agency (March 3, 2004). ... Re-signed by Cardinals (May 7, 2004). ... Released by Cardinals (September 4, 2004). ... Signed by New England Patriots (October 6, 2004). ... Released by Patriots (November 27, 2004). ... Re-signed by Patriots (November 30, 2004). ... Released by Patriots (December 3, 2004). ... Re-signed by Patriots (December 22, 2004). ... Granted unconditional free agency (March 2, 2005).
CHAMPIONSHIP GAME EXPERIENCE: Member of Patriots for AFC championship game (2004 season); inactive. ... Member of Patriots for Super Bowl 39 (2004 season), inactive.
SINGLE GAME HIGHS (regular season): Receptions—4 (December 29, 2002, vs. Denver); yards—54 (December 15, 2002, vs. St. Louis); and touchdown receptions—2 (December 21, 2002, vs. San Francisco).

			RUSHING				RECEIVING				KICKOFF RETURNS				TOTALS			
Year Team	G	GS	Att.	Yds.	Avg.	TD	No.	Yds.	Avg.	TD	No.	Yds.	Avg.	TD	TD 2pt.	Pts.	Fum.	
2001—Denver NFL	10	5	3	19	6.3	0	8	84	10.5	0	14	372	26.6	0	0	0	0	0
2002—Denver NFL	4	0	0	0	0.0	0	0	0	0.0	0	15	393	26.2	0	0	0	0	1
—Arizona NFL	6	4	3	19	6.3	0	15	180	12.0	3	32	722	22.6	0	3	0	18	0
—Seattle NFL	3	0	0	0	0.0	0	0	0	0.0	0	8	185	23.1	0	0	0	0	0
2003—Arizona NFL	7	0	1	-4	-4.0	0	1	23	23.0	0	5	136	27.2	0	0	0	0	0
2004—New England NFL	8	0	0	0	0.0	0	0	0	0.0	0	3	61	20.3	0	0	0	0	0
Pro totals (4 years)	38	9	7	34	4.9	0	24	287	12.0	3	77	1869	24.3	0	3	0	18	1

KASSELL, BRAD　　　　　LB

PERSONAL: Born January 7, 1980, in Llano, Texas. ... 6-3/242.
HIGH SCHOOL: Llano (Texas).
COLLEGE: North Texas.
TRANSACTIONS/CAREER NOTES: Signed as non-drafted free agent by Tennessee Titans (April 22, 2002). ... Released by Titans (September 1, 2002). ... Re-signed by Titans to practice squad (September 3, 2002). ... Activated (November 1, 2002). ... Granted free agency (March 2, 2005).
CHAMPIONSHIP GAME EXPERIENCE: Played in AFC championship game (2002 season).

			TOTALS			INTERCEPTIONS			
Year Team	G	GS	Tk.	Ast.	Sks.	No.	Yds.	Avg.	TD
2002—Tennessee NFL	9	0	0	0	0.0	0	0	0.0	0
2003—Tennessee NFL	16	4	23	4	0.0	0	0	0.0	0
2004—Tennessee NFL	15	14	75	27	0.0	0	0	0.0	0
Pro totals (3 years)	40	18	98	31	0.0	0	0	0.0	0

KEARSE, JEVON　　　　　DE　　　　　EAGLES

PERSONAL: Born September 3, 1976, in Fort Myers, Fla. ... 6-4/265. ... Name pronounced: juh-VAUGHN CURSE.
HIGH SCHOOL: North Fort Myers (Fla.).
COLLEGE: Florida.
TRANSACTIONS/CAREER NOTES: Selected after junior season by Tennessee Titans in first round (16th pick overall) of 1999 NFL draft. ... Signed by Titans (July 27, 1999). ... Granted unconditional free agency (March 3, 2004). ... Signed by Philadelphia Eagles (March 3, 2004).
CHAMPIONSHIP GAME EXPERIENCE: Played in AFC championship game (1999 and 2002 seasons). ... Played in NFC championship game (2004 season). ... Played in Super Bowl 34 (1999 season) and Super Bowl 39 (2004 season).
HONORS: Named outside linebacker on THE SPORTING NEWS college All-America second team (1998). ... Named defensive end on THE SPORTING NEWS NFL All-Pro team (1999). ... Played in Pro Bowl (1999-2001 seasons).
RECORDS: Holds NFL rookie-season record for most sacks—14.5 (1999).

Year Team	G	GS	TOTALS Tk.	Ast.	Sks.	INTERCEPTIONS No.	Yds.	Avg.	TD
1999—Tennessee NFL	16	16	48	9 §14.5		0	0	0.0	0
2000—Tennessee NFL	16	16	37	16 11.5		0	0	0.0	0
2001—Tennessee NFL	16	16	25	11 10.0		0	0	0.0	0
2002—Tennessee NFL	4	1	3	1 2.0		0	0	0.0	0
2003—Tennessee NFL	14	14	29	13 9.5		1	0	0.0	0
2004—Philadelphia NFL	14	14	27	4 7.5		0	0	0.0	0
Pro totals (6 years)	80	77	169	54 55.0		1	0	0.0	0

KEISEL, BRETT   DE   STEELERS

PERSONAL: Born September 19, 1978, in Provo, Utah. ... 6-5/285.
HIGH SCHOOL: Greybull (Wyo.).
JUNIOR COLLEGE: Snow College (Utah).
COLLEGE: Brigham Young.
TRANSACTIONS/CAREER NOTES: Selected by Pittsburgh Steelers in seventh round (242nd pick overall) of 2002 NFL draft. ... Signed by Steelers (July 17, 2002). ... Granted free agency (March 2, 2005). ... Re-signed by Steelers (April 12, 2005).
CHAMPIONSHIP GAME EXPERIENCE: Played in AFC championship game (2004 season).

Year Team	G	GS	TOTALS Tk.	Ast.	Sks.
2002—Pittsburgh NFL	5	0	0	0	0.0
2004—Pittsburgh NFL	13	0	3	3	0.0
Pro totals (2 years)	18	0	3	3	0.0

K

KELLEY, ETHAN   DT   PATRIOTS

PERSONAL: Born February 12, 1980, in Sugar Land, Texas. ... 6-2/310. ... Full name: Ethan Jeffery Arthur Kelley.
HIGH SCHOOL: Kempner (Sugar Land, Texas).
COLLEGE: Baylor.
TRANSACTIONS/CAREER NOTES: Selected by New England Patriots in seventh round (243rd pick overall) of 2003 NFL draft. ... Signed by Patriots (July 16, 2003). ... Released by Patriots (August 31, 2003). ... Re-signed by Patriots (September 2, 2003).
CHAMPIONSHIP GAME EXPERIENCE: Member of Patriots for AFC championship game (2004 season); did not play. ... Member of Patriots for Super Bowl 39 (2004 season); inactive.

Year Team	G	GS	TOTALS Tk.	Ast.	Sks.
2004—New England NFL	1	0	1	0	0.0

KELLY, BRIAN   CB   BUCCANEERS

PERSONAL: Born January 14, 1976, in Las Vegas, Nev. ... 5-11/193.
HIGH SCHOOL: Overland (Aurora, Colo.).
COLLEGE: Southern California.
TRANSACTIONS/CAREER NOTES: Selected by Tampa Bay Buccaneers in second round (45th pick overall) of 1998 NFL draft. ... Signed by Buccaneers (July 19, 1998). ... Granted free agency (March 2, 2001). ... Re-signed by Buccaneers (March 18, 2001). ... Granted unconditional free agency (March 1, 2002). ... Re-signed by Buccaneers (March 19, 2002). ... On injured reserve with pectoral injury (October 21, 2003-remainder of season).
CHAMPIONSHIP GAME EXPERIENCE: Played in NFC championship game (1999 and 2002 seasons). ... Member of Super Bowl championship team (2002 season).

Year Team	G	GS	TOTALS Tk.	Ast.	Sks.	INTERCEPTIONS No.	Yds.	Avg.	TD
1998—Tampa Bay NFL	16	3	25	2	0.0	1	4	4.0	0
1999—Tampa Bay NFL	16	3	29	5	0.0	1	26	26.0	0
2000—Tampa Bay NFL	16	3	44	4	0.0	1	9	9.0	1
2001—Tampa Bay NFL	16	11	40	10	1.5	0	0	0.0	0
2002—Tampa Bay NFL	16	16	58	8	1.0	†8	68	8.5	0
2003—Tampa Bay NFL	5	5	13	2	0.0	1	0	0.0	0
2004—Tampa Bay NFL	16	16	51	7	0.0	4	101	25.3	0
Pro totals (7 years)	101	57	260	38	2.5	16	208	13.0	1

KELLY, REGGIE   TE   BENGALS

PERSONAL: Born February 22, 1977, in Aberdeen, Miss. ... 6-4/255. ... Full name: Reginald Kuta Kelly.
HIGH SCHOOL: Aberdeen (Miss.).
COLLEGE: Mississippi State.
TRANSACTIONS/CAREER NOTES: Selected by Atlanta Falcons in second round (42nd pick overall) of 1999 NFL draft. ... Signed by Falcons (June 25, 1999). ... Granted unconditional free agency (February 28, 2003). ... Signed by Cincinnati Bengals (March 13, 2003).
SINGLE GAME HIGHS (regular season): Receptions—4 (December 5, 2004, vs. Baltimore); yards—83 (September 24, 2000, vs. St. Louis); and touchdown receptions—1 (September 28, 2003, vs. Cleveland).

Year Team	G	GS	RECEIVING No.	Yds.	Avg.	TD	TOTALS TD	2pt.	Pts.	Fum.
1999—Atlanta NFL	16	2	8	146	18.3	0	0	0	0	0
2000—Atlanta NFL	16	16	31	340	11.0	2	2	0	12	1
2001—Atlanta NFL	14	13	16	142	8.9	0	0	0	0	0

Year Team	G	GS	No.	RECEIVING Yds.	Avg.	TD	TD	TOTALS 2pt.	Pts.	Fum.
2002—Atlanta NFL	16	16	14	162	11.6	0	0	0	0	0
2003—Cincinnati NFL	12	11	13	81	6.2	1	1	0	6	0
2004—Cincinnati NFL	16	15	15	85	5.7	0	0	0	0	0
Pro totals (6 years)	90	73	97	956	9.9	3	3	0	18	1

KELLY, TOMMY   DT   RAIDERS

PERSONAL: Born December 27, 1980, in Jackson, Miss. ... 6-6/300. ... Full name: Tommy Terrell Kelly.
HIGH SCHOOL: Provine (Jackson, Miss.).
JUNIOR COLLEGE: Hinds (Miss.).
COLLEGE: Mississippi State.
TRANSACTIONS/CAREER NOTES: Signed as non-drafted free agent by Oakland Raiders (May 4, 2004).

Year Team	G	GS	TOTALS Tk.	Ast.	Sks.
2004—Oakland NFL	10	3	16	4	4.0

KELSAY, CHRIS   DE   BILLS

PERSONAL: Born October 31, 1979, in Auburn, Neb. ... 6-4/275.
HIGH SCHOOL: Auburn (Neb.).
COLLEGE: Nebraska.
TRANSACTIONS/CAREER NOTES: Selected by Buffalo Bills in second round (48th pick overall) of 2003 NFL draft. ... Signed by Bills (July 23, 2003).

Year Team	G	GS	TOTALS Tk.	Ast.	Sks.	INTERCEPTIONS No.	Yds.	Avg.	TD
2003—Buffalo NFL	16	0	12	7	0.0	0	0	0.0	0
2004—Buffalo NFL	16	10	22	15	4.5	1	3	3.0	0
Pro totals (2 years)	32	10	34	22	4.5	1	3	3.0	0

KEMOEATU, MAAKE   DT

PERSONAL: Born January 10, 1979, in Tonga. ... 6-5/340. ... Full name: Maake Tu'Amelie Kemoeatu. ... Brother of Chris Kemoeatu, rookie guard with Pittsburgh Steelers.
HIGH SCHOOL: Kahuku (Hawaii).
COLLEGE: Utah.
TRANSACTIONS/CAREER NOTES: Signed as non-drafted free agent by Baltimore Ravens (April 26, 2002). ... Granted free agency (March 2, 2005).

Year Team	G	GS	TOTALS Tk.	Ast.	Sks.
2002—Baltimore NFL	16	1	11	4	2.0
2003—Baltimore NFL	15	1	8	2	1.0
2004—Baltimore NFL	14	3	19	8	0.0
Pro totals (3 years)	45	5	38	14	3.0

KENDALL, PETE   C   JETS

PERSONAL: Born July 9, 1973, in Quincy, Mass. ... 6-5/280. ... Full name: Peter Marcus Kendall.
HIGH SCHOOL: Archbishop Williams (Weymouth, Mass.).
COLLEGE: Boston College.
TRANSACTIONS/CAREER NOTES: Selected by Seattle Seahawks in first round (21st pick overall) of 1996 NFL draft. ... Signed by Seahawks (July 21, 1996). ... Granted unconditional free agency (March 2, 2001). ... Signed by Arizona Cardinals (March 12, 2001). ... On injured reserve with foot injury (December 26, 2001-remainder of season). ... On injured reserve with ankle injury (December 27, 2002-remainder of season). ... Released by Cardinals (July 31, 2004). ... Signed by New York Jets (August 6, 2004).
PLAYING EXPERIENCE: Seattle NFL, 1996-2000; Arizona NFL, 2001-2003; New York Jets NFL, 2004. ... Games/Games started: 1996 (12/11), 1997 (16/16), 1998 (16/16), 1999 (16/16), 2000 (16/16), 2001 (11/11), 2002 (12/12), 2003 (13/13), 2004 (15/15). Total: 127/126.

KENNEDY, JIMMY   DT   RAMS

PERSONAL: Born November 15, 1979, in Yonkers, N.Y. ... 6-4/320. ... Full name: Jimmy Wayne Kennedy.
HIGH SCHOOL: Roosevelt (Yonkers, N.Y.).
COLLEGE: Penn State.
TRANSACTIONS/CAREER NOTES: Selected by St. Louis Rams in first round (12th pick overall) of 2003 NFL draft. ... Signed by Rams (July 28, 2003).

Year Team	G	GS	TOTALS Tk.	Ast.	Sks.
2003—St. Louis NFL	13	0	1	1	0.0
2004—St. Louis NFL	9	5	13	3	0.0
Pro totals (2 years)	22	5	14	4	0.0

KENNEDY, KENOY   S   LIONS

PERSONAL: Born November 15, 1977, in Dallas, Texas. ... 6-1/215. ... Full name: Kenoy Wayne Kennedy.
HIGH SCHOOL: Terrell (Texas).
COLLEGE: Arkansas.
TRANSACTIONS/CAREER NOTES: Selected by Denver Broncos in second round (45th pick overall) of 2000 NFL draft. ... Signed by Broncos (June 1, 2000). ... Granted unconditional free agency (March 2, 2005). ... Signed by Detroit Lions (March 7, 2005).

				TOTALS			INTERCEPTIONS			
Year Team	G	GS	Tk.	Ast.	Sks.	No.	Yds.	Avg.	TD	
2000—Denver NFL	13	0	5	2	0.0	1	0	0.0	0	
2001—Denver NFL	16	16	50	19	2.0	1	6	6.0	0	
2002—Denver NFL	15	15	53	14	0.0	0	0	0.0	0	
2003—Denver NFL	13	12	41	14	1.0	1	0	0.0	0	
2004—Denver NFL	16	16	66	16	2.0	1	21	21.0	0	
Pro totals (5 years)	73	59	215	65	5.0	4	27	6.8	0	

KENNISON, EDDIE   WR   CHIEFS

PERSONAL: Born January 20, 1973, in Lake Charles, La. ... 6-1/201. ... Full name: Eddie Joseph Kennison III.
HIGH SCHOOL: Washington-Marion (Lake Charles, La.).
COLLEGE: Louisiana State.
TRANSACTIONS/CAREER NOTES: Selected after junior season by St. Louis Rams in first round (18th pick overall) of 1996 NFL draft. ... Signed by Rams (July 27, 1996). ... Traded by Rams to New Orleans Saints for second-round pick (DB Dre' Bly) in 1999 draft (February 18, 1999). ... Traded by Saints to Chicago Bears for fifth-round pick (traded to Indianapolis) in 2000 draft (February 21, 2000). ... Granted unconditional free agency (March 2, 2001). ... Signed by Denver Broncos (April 5, 2001). ... Released by Broncos (November 14, 2001). ... Signed by Kansas City Chiefs (December 3, 2001).
SINGLE GAME HIGHS (regular season): Receptions—8 (December 5, 2004, vs. Oakland); yards—226 (December 15, 1996, vs. Atlanta); and touchdown receptions—3 (December 15, 1996, vs. Atlanta).
STATISTICAL PLATEAUS: 100-yard receiving games: 1996 (2), 1999 (1), 2000 (1), 2001 (1), 2002 (2), 2003 (1), 2004 (5). Total: 13.

			RUSHING				RECEIVING				PUNT RETURNS				KICKOFF RETURNS				TOTALS		
Year Team	G	GS	Att.	Yds.	Avg.	TD	No.	Yds.	Avg.	TD	No.	Yds.	Avg.	TD	No.	Yds.	Avg.	TD	TD	2pt.	Pts.
1996—StL. NFL	15	14	0	0	0.0	0	54	924	17.1	9	29	423	14.6	2	23	454	19.7	0	11	0	66
1997—StL. NFL	14	9	3	13	4.3	0	25	404	16.2	0	34	247	7.3	0	1	14	14.0	0	0	0	0
1998—StL. NFL	16	13	2	9	4.5	0	17	234	13.8	1	40	415	10.4	1	0	0	0.0	0	2	0	12
1999—N.O. NFL	16	16	3	20	6.7	0	61	835	13.7	4	35	258	7.4	0	0	0	0.0	0	4	1	26
2000—Chi. NFL	16	10	3	72	24.0	0	55	549	10.0	2	0	0	0.0	0	0	0	0.0	0	2	0	12
2001—Den. NFL	8	6	3	9	3.0	0	15	169	11.3	1	0	0	0.0	0	0	0	0.0	0	1	0	6
—K.C. NFL	5	1	2	13	6.5	0	16	322	20.1	0	0	0	0.0	0	0	0	0.0	0	0	1	2
2002—K.C. NFL	16	14	7	58	8.3	0	53	906	17.1	2	0	0	0.0	0	0	0	0.0	0	2	0	12
2003—K.C. NFL	16	16	2	9	4.5	0	56	853	15.2	5	3	70	23.3	0	0	0	0.0	0	5	0	30
2004—K.C. NFL	14	14	2	15	7.5	0	62	1086	17.5	8	0	0	0.0	0	1	36	36.0	0	8	1	50
Pro totals (9 years)	136	113	27	218	8.1	0	414	6282	15.2	32	141	1413	10.0	3	25	504	20.2	0	35	3	216

KERN, CHRIS   CB

PERSONAL: Born May 16, 1979, in Faribault, Minn. ... 5-11/196.
HIGH SCHOOL: Faribault (Minn.).
COLLEGE: Mount Union.
TRANSACTIONS/CAREER NOTES: Signed as non-drafted free agent by Detroit Lions (May 2, 2003). ... Released by Lions (July 21, 2003). ... Re-signed by Lions to practice squad (December 15, 2003). ... Assigned by Lions to Frankfurt Galaxy in 2004 NFL Europe enhancement allocation program (February 13, 2004). ... Released by Lions (September 22, 2004).

KERNEY, PATRICK   DE   FALCONS

PERSONAL: Born December 30, 1976, in Trenton, N.J. ... 6-5/273. ... Full name: Patrick Manning Kerney.
HIGH SCHOOL: Taft Prep (Watertown, Conn.).
COLLEGE: Virginia.
TRANSACTIONS/CAREER NOTES: Selected by Atlanta Falcons in first round (30th pick overall) of 1999 NFL draft. ... Signed by Falcons (June 25, 1999).
CHAMPIONSHIP GAME EXPERIENCE: Played in NFC championship game (2004 season).
HONORS: Named defensive end on THE SPORTING NEWS college All-America second team (1998). ... Played in Pro Bowl (2004 season).

				TOTALS			INTERCEPTIONS			
Year Team	G	GS	Tk.	Ast.	Sks.	No.	Yds.	Avg.	TD	
1999—Atlanta NFL	16	2	19	6	2.5	0	0	0.0	0	
2000—Atlanta NFL	16	16	30	15	2.5	1	8	8.0	0	
2001—Atlanta NFL	16	16	39	10	12.0	0	0	0.0	0	
2002—Atlanta NFL	16	16	45	13	10.5	0	0	0.0	0	
2003—Atlanta NFL	16	16	34	12	6.5	0	0	0.0	0	
2004—Atlanta NFL	16	15	55	11	13.0	1	0	0.0	0	
Pro totals (6 years)	96	81	222	67	47.0	2	8	4.0	0	

KEYS, ISAAC   LB   CARDINALS

PERSONAL: Born June 6, 1978, in St. Louis, Mo. ... 6-3/245.
HIGH SCHOOL: Hazelwood Central (St. Louis).
COLLEGE: Morehouse.

TRANSACTIONS/CAREER NOTES: Signed as non-drafted free agent by Minnesota Vikings (May 30, 2001). ... On injured reserve with shoulder injury (August 28, 2001-entire season). ... Released by Vikings (August 27, 2002). ... Signed by Green Bay Packers (January 3, 2003). ... Assigned by Packers to Scottish Claymores in 2003 NFL Europe enhancement allocation program (February 27, 2003). ... Released by Packers (August 29, 2003). ... Signed by Arizona Cardinals (April 2, 2004). ... Released by Cardinals (August 29, 2004). ... Re-signed by Cardinals to practice squad (September 6, 2004). ... Activated (December 15, 2004).

			TOTALS			INTERCEPTIONS			
Year Team	G	GS	Tk.	Ast.	Sks.	No.	Yds.	Avg.	TD
2004—Arizona NFL	3	0	0	0	0.0	0	0	0.0	0

KIEL, TERRENCE   S   CHARGERS

PERSONAL: Born November 24, 1980, in Lufkin, Texas. ... 5-11/207. ... Full name: Terrence Dewayne Kiel.
HIGH SCHOOL: Lufkin (Texas).
COLLEGE: Texas A&M.
TRANSACTIONS/CAREER NOTES: Selected by San Diego Chargers in second round (62nd pick overall) of 2003 NFL draft. ... Signed by Chargers (July 25, 2003).

			TOTALS			INTERCEPTIONS			
Year Team	G	GS	Tk.	Ast.	Sks.	No.	Yds.	Avg.	TD
2003—San Diego NFL	16	7	52	7	0.0	2	15	7.5	0
2004—San Diego NFL	16	16	71	25	1.0	2	31	15.5	0
Pro totals (2 years)	32	23	123	32	1.0	4	46	11.5	0

KIGHT, KELVIN   WR   PACKERS

PERSONAL: Born July 2, 1982, in Atlanta, Ga. ... 6-0/209. ... Full name: Kelvin Jerome Kight.
HIGH SCHOOL: Lithonia (Ga.).
COLLEGE: Florida.
TRANSACTIONS/CAREER NOTES: Signed as non-drafted free agent by St. Louis Rams (April 30, 2004). ... Claimed on waivers by Green Bay Packers (August 11, 2004). ... Released by Packers (September 5, 2004). ... Re-signed by Packers to practice squad (September 6, 2004). ... Activated (October 16, 2004). ... Released by Packers (November 19, 2004). ... Re-signed by Packers to practice squad (November 23, 2004). ... Activated (January 19, 2005).
PLAYING EXPERIENCE: Green Bay NFL, 2004. ... Games/Games started: 2004 (1/0). Total: 1/0.

KIMRIN, OLA   K   TITANS

PERSONAL: Born February 29, 1972, in Malmo, Sweden. ... 6-3/230.
HIGH SCHOOL: Borgaskolan (Malmo, Sweden).
COLLEGE: Texas-El Paso.
TRANSACTIONS/CAREER NOTES: Signed as non-drafted free agent by Denver Broncos (July 24, 2002). ... Released by Broncos (August 31, 2002). ... Signed by Dallas Cowboys (April 14, 2003). ... Released by Cowboys (August 23, 2003). ... Signed by Washington Redskins (July 31, 2004). ... Released by Redskins (September 5, 2004). ... Re-signed by Redskins to practice squad (September 17, 2004). ... Released by Redskins (September 21, 2004). ... Re-signed by Redskins (October 16, 2004). ... Released by Redskins (November 26, 2004). ... Signed by Tennessee Titans (March 10, 2005).

		FIELD GOALS							TOTALS		
Year Team	G	1-29	30-39	40-49	50+	Tot.	Pct.	Lg.	XPM	XPA	Pts.
2004—Washington NFL	5	3-3	2-3	1-3	0-1	6-10	60.0	41	6	6	24

KING, ANDRE   WR   BROWNS

PERSONAL: Born November 26, 1973, in Kingston, Jamaica. ... 5-11/195.
HIGH SCHOOL: Stranahan (Fla.).
COLLEGE: Miami (Fla.).
TRANSACTIONS/CAREER NOTES: Selected by Cleveland Browns in seventh round (245th pick overall) of 2001 NFL draft. ... Signed by Browns (July 18, 2001). ... Granted free agency (March 3, 2004). ... Re-signed by Browns (April 15, 2004).
SINGLE GAME HIGHS (regular season): Receptions—4 (December 16, 2001, vs. Jacksonville); yards—61 (December 30, 2001, vs. Tennessee); and touchdown receptions—0.

			RECEIVING				KICKOFF RETURNS				TOTALS			
Year Team	G	GS	No.	Yds.	Avg.	TD	No.	Yds.	Avg.	TD	TD	2pt.	Pts.	Fum.
2001—Cleveland NFL	7	0	11	149	13.5	0	14	279	19.9	0	0	0	0	1
2002—Cleveland NFL	11	1	5	41	8.2	0	8	155	19.4	0	0	0	0	0
2003—Cleveland NFL	15	0	9	88	9.8	0	9	172	19.1	0	1	0	6	0
2004—Cleveland NFL	9	2	5	49	9.8	0	5	95	19.0	0	0	0	0	0
Pro totals (4 years)	42	3	30	327	10.9	0	36	701	19.5	0	1	0	6	1

KING, AUSTIN   C   FALCONS

PERSONAL: Born April 11, 1981, in Cincinnati, Ohio. ... 6-5/303. ... Full name: Austin Patrick King.
HIGH SCHOOL: Purcell Marian (Cincinnati).
COLLEGE: Northwestern.
TRANSACTIONS/CAREER NOTES: Selected by Tampa Bay Buccaneers in fourth round (133rd pick overall) of 2003 NFL draft. ... Signed by Buccaneers (July 18, 2003). ... Released by Buccaneers (September 6, 2004). ... Signed by Atlanta Falcons to practice squad (September 8, 2004). ... Activated (December 7, 2004).
PLAYING EXPERIENCE: Atlanta NFL, 2004. ... Games/Games started: 2004 (4/0). Total: 4/0.
CHAMPIONSHIP GAME EXPERIENCE: Played in NFC championship game (2004 season).

KING, SHAUN — QB

PERSONAL: Born May 29, 1977, in St. Petersburg, Fla. ... 6-1/228. ... Full name: Shaun Earl King.
HIGH SCHOOL: Gibbs (St. Petersburg, Fla.).
COLLEGE: Tulane.
TRANSACTIONS/CAREER NOTES: Selected by Tampa Bay Buccaneers in second round (50th pick overall) of 1999 NFL draft. ... Signed by Buccaneers (August 1, 1999). ... Granted unconditional free agency (February 28, 2003). ... Re-signed by Buccaneers (April 4, 2003). ... Granted unconditional free agency (March 3, 2004). ... Signed by Arizona Cardinals (March 6, 2004). ... Released by Cardinals (March 9, 2005).
CHAMPIONSHIP GAME EXPERIENCE: Played in NFC championship game (1999 season). ... Member of Buccaneers for NFC championship game (2002 season); inactive. ... Member of Super Bowl championship team (2002 season); inactive.
SINGLE GAME HIGHS (regular season): Attempts—52 (November 21, 2004, vs. Carolina); completions—28 (November 21, 2004, vs. Carolina); passing yards—343 (November 21, 2004, vs. Carolina); and touchdown passes—4 (October 29, 2000, vs. Minnesota).
STATISTICAL PLATEAUS: 300-yard passing games: 2004 (1). Total: 1.
MISCELLANEOUS: Regular-season record as starting NFL quarterback: 14-10 (.583). ... Postseason record as starting NFL quarterback: 1-2 (.333).

Year Team	G	GS	PASSING Att.	Cmp.	Pct.	Yds.	TD	Int.	Avg.	Skd.	Rat.	RUSHING Att.	Yds.	Avg.	TD	TOTALS TD	2pt.	Pts.
1999—Tampa Bay NFL	6	5	146	89	61.0	875	7	4	5.99	11	82.4	18	38	2.1	0	0	0	0
2000—Tampa Bay NFL	16	16	428	233	54.4	2769	18	13	6.47	37	75.8	73	353	4.8	5	5	1	32
2001—Tampa Bay NFL	3	0	31	21	67.7	210	0	1	6.77	3	73.3	5	-12	-2.4	0	0	1	2
2002—Tampa Bay NFL	3	1	27	10	37.0	80	0	1	2.96	1	30.0	4	25	6.3	0	0	0	0
2003—Tampa Bay NFL	3	0	22	15	68.2	130	1	1	5.91	3	79.7	4	20	5.0	0	0	0	0
2004—Arizona NFL	3	2	84	47	56.0	502	1	4	5.98	6	57.7	9	30	3.3	0	0	0	0
Pro totals (6 years)	34	24	738	415	56.2	4566	27	24	6.19	61	73.4	113	454	4.0	5	5	2	34

KING, VICK — RB — JETS

PERSONAL: Born February 4, 1980, in Houma, La. ... 5-10/215. ... Full name: Vick Lee King.
HIGH SCHOOL: South LaFourche (Cutoff, La.).
COLLEGE: McNeese State.
TRANSACTIONS/CAREER NOTES: Signed as a non-drafted free agent by Tennessee Titans (April 26, 2004). ... Released by Titans (September 5, 2004). ... Signed by Miami Dolphins to practice squad (September 18, 2004). ... Released from Dolphins practice squad (October 29, 2004). ... Re-signed by Dolphins to practice squad (November 3, 2004). ... Activated (December 4, 2004). ... Released by Dolphins (April 28, 2005). ... Signed by New York Jets (May 17, 2005).
SINGLE GAME HIGHS (regular season): Attempts—3 (December 5, 2004, vs. Buffalo); yards—8 (December 5, 2004, vs. Buffalo); and rushing touchdowns—0.

Year Team	G	GS	RUSHING Att.	Yds.	Avg.	TD	TOTALS TD	2pt.	Pts.	Fum.
2004—Miami NFL	2	0	4	9	2.3	0	0	0	0	0

KINNEY, ERRON — TE — TITANS

PERSONAL: Born July 28, 1977, in Richmond, Va. ... 6-5/275. ... Full name: Erron Quincy Kinney.
HIGH SCHOOL: Patrick Henry (Ashland, Va.).
COLLEGE: Florida.
TRANSACTIONS/CAREER NOTES: Selected by Tennessee Titans in third round (68th pick overall) of 2000 NFL draft. ... Signed by Titans (July 17, 2000). ... Granted free agency (February 28, 2003). ... Re-signed by Titans (May 12, 2003).
CHAMPIONSHIP GAME EXPERIENCE: Played in AFC championship game (2002 season).
SINGLE GAME HIGHS (regular season): Receptions—7 (October 7, 2001, vs. Baltimore); yards—75 (October 7, 2001, vs. Baltimore); and touchdown receptions—2 (November 28, 2004, vs. Houston).

Year Team	G	GS	RECEIVING No.	Yds.	Avg.	TD	KICKOFF RETURNS No.	Yds.	Avg.	TD	TOTALS TD	2pt.	Pts.	Fum.
2000—Tennessee NFL	16	10	19	197	10.4	1	0	0	0.0	0	1	0	6	1
2001—Tennessee NFL	13	12	25	263	10.5	1	1	14	14.0	0	1	0	6	0
2002—Tennessee NFL	15	7	13	173	13.3	0	3	41	13.7	0	0	0	0	0
2003—Tennessee NFL	16	16	41	381	9.3	3	3	37	12.3	0	4	0	24	1
2004—Tennessee NFL	9	9	25	193	7.7	3	1	21	21.0	0	3	0	18	0
Pro totals (5 years)	69	54	123	1207	9.8	8	8	113	14.1	0	9	0	54	2

KIRCUS, DAVID — WR — LIONS

PERSONAL: Born February 19, 1980, in Mount Clemens, Mich. ... 6-1/185.
HIGH SCHOOL: Imlay City (Mich.).
COLLEGE: Grand Valley State.
TRANSACTIONS/CAREER NOTES: Selected by Detroit Lions in sixth round (175th pick overall) of 2003 NFL draft. ... Signed by Lions (July 17, 2003). ... Released by Lions (August 31, 2003). ... Re-signed by Lions to practice squad (September 1, 2003). ... Activated (November 18, 2003). ... Released by Lions (September 5, 2004). ... Re-signed by Lions to practice squad (September 6, 2004). ... Activated (September 13, 2004). ... Released by Lions (September 20, 2004). ... Re-signed by Lions to practice squad (September 22, 2004). ... Activated (October 23, 2004).
SINGLE GAME HIGHS (regular season): Receptions—2 (January 2, 2005, vs. Tennessee); yards—50 (October 31, 2004, vs. Dallas); and touchdown receptions—1 (October 31, 2004, vs. Dallas).

Year Team	G	GS	RECEIVING No.	Yds.	Avg.	TD	PUNT RETURNS No.	Yds.	Avg.	TD	KICKOFF RETURNS No.	Yds.	Avg.	TD	TOTALS TD	2pt.	Pts.	Fum.
2003—Detroit NFL	5	2	3	53	17.7	0	0	0	0.0	0	0	0	0.0	0	0	0	0	0
2004—Detroit NFL	7	0	3	68	22.7	1	0	0	0.0	0	0	0	0.0	0	1	0	6	0
Pro totals (2 years)	12	2	6	121	20.2	1	0	0	0.0	0	0	0	0.0	0	1	0	6	0

K

KIRSCHKE, TRAVIS — DT — STEELERS

PERSONAL: Born September 6, 1974, in Fullerton, Calif. ... 6-3/298.
HIGH SCHOOL: Esperanza (Anaheim, Calif.).
COLLEGE: UCLA.
TRANSACTIONS/CAREER NOTES: Signed as non-drafted free agent by Detroit Lions (April 24, 1997). ... Inactive for three games (1998). ... On injured reserve with abdominal injury (September 24, 1998-remainder of season). ... Granted free agency (February 11, 2000). ... Re-signed by Lions (April 25, 2000). ... Granted unconditional free agency (March 1, 2002). ... Re-signed by Lions (April 2, 2002). ... Granted unconditional free agency (February 28, 2003). ... Signed by San Francisco 49ers (April 8, 2003). ... Granted unconditional free agency (March 3, 2004). ... Signed by Pittsburgh Steelers (March 11, 2004).
CHAMPIONSHIP GAME EXPERIENCE: Played in AFC championship game (2004 season).

Year—Team	G	GS	TOTALS Tk.	Ast.	Sks.
1997—Detroit NFL	3	0	0	1	0.0
1999—Detroit NFL	15	7	12	8	2.0
2000—Detroit NFL	13	0	4	8	0.5
2001—Detroit NFL	16	2	11	8	0.0
2002—Detroit NFL	15	1	14	5	0.0
2003—San Francisco NFL	15	15	33	10	1.5
2004—Pittsburgh NFL	16	1	6	6	1.0
Pro totals (7 years)	93	26	80	46	5.0

KITNA, JON — QB — BENGALS

PERSONAL: Born September 21, 1972, in Tacoma, Wash. ... 6-2/220.
HIGH SCHOOL: Lincoln (Tacoma, Wash.).
COLLEGE: Central Washington.
TRANSACTIONS/CAREER NOTES: Signed as non-drafted free agent by Seattle Seahawks (April 25, 1996) ... Released by Seahawks (August 19, 1996) ... Re-signed by Seahawks to practice squad (August 20, 1996). ... Assigned by Seahawks to Barcelona Dragons in 1997 World League enhancement allocation program (April 7, 1997). ... Granted free agency (February 11, 2000). ... Re-signed by Seahawks (March 15, 2000). ... Granted unconditional free agency (March 2, 2001). ... Signed by Cincinnati Bengals (March 8, 2001).
SINGLE GAME HIGHS (regular season): Attempts—68 (December 30, 2001, vs. Pittsburgh); completions—35 (December 30, 2001, vs. Pittsburgh); yards—411 (December 30, 2001, vs. Pittsburgh); and touchdown passes—4 (November 23, 2003, vs. San Diego).
STATISTICAL PLATEAUS: 300-yard passing games: 2001 (3), 2002 (1), 2003 (1). Total: 5.
MISCELLANEOUS: Regular-season record as starting NFL quarterback: 36-43 (.456). ... Postseason record as starting NFL quarterback: 0-1.

Year—Team	G	GS	PASSING Att.	Cmp.	Pct.	Yds.	TD	Int.	Avg.	Skd.	Rat.	RUSHING Att.	Yds.	Avg.	TD	TOTALS TD	2pt.	Pts.
1997—Seattle NFL	3	1	45	31	68.9	371	1	2	8.24	3	82.7	10	9	0.9	1	1	0	6
1998—Seattle NFL	6	5	172	98	57.0	1177	7	8	6.84	11	72.3	20	67	3.4	1	1	0	6
1999—Seattle NFL	15	15	495	270	54.5	3346	23	16	6.76	32	77.7	35	56	1.6	0	0	0	0
2000—Seattle NFL	15	12	418	259	62.0	2658	18	19	6.36	33	75.6	48	127	2.6	1	1	0	6
2001—Cincinnati NFL	16	15	*581	313	53.9	3216	12	22	5.54	25	61.1	27	73	2.7	1	1	0	6
2002—Cincinnati NFL	14	12	473	294	62.2	3178	16	16	6.72	24	79.1	24	57	2.4	4	4	0	24
2003—Cincinnati NFL	16	16	520	324	62.3	3591	26	15	6.91	37	87.4	38	113	3.0	0	0	0	0
2004—Cincinnati NFL	4	3	104	61	58.7	623	5	4	5.99	6	75.9	10	42	4.2	0	0	0	0
Pro totals (8 years)	89	79	2808	1650	58.8	18160	108	102	6.47	171	75.7	212	544	2.6	8	8	0	48

KLECKO, DAN — DT — PATRIOTS

PERSONAL: Born January 12, 1981, in Colts Neck, N.J. ... 5-11/275. ... Son of Joe Klecko, defensive tackle with New York Jets (1977-87) and Indianapolis Colts (1988).
HIGH SCHOOL: Marlboro (N.J.).
COLLEGE: Temple.
TRANSACTIONS/CAREER NOTES: Selected by New England Patriots in fourth round (117th pick overall) of 2003 NFL draft. ... Signed by Patriots (July 15, 2003). ... On injured reserve with knee injury (October 30, 2004-remainder of season).
CHAMPIONSHIP GAME EXPERIENCE: Member of Patriots for AFC championship game (2003 season); inactive. ... Member of Patriots for Super Bowl 38 (2003 season); inactive.

Year—Team	G	GS	TOTALS Tk.	Ast.	Sks.
2003—New England NFL	13	1	12	5	1.5
2004—New England NFL	6	2	0	1	0.0
Pro totals (2 years)	19	3	12	6	1.5

KLEINSASSER, JIM — TE — VIKINGS

PERSONAL: Born January 31, 1977, in Carrington, N.D. ... 6-3/272.
HIGH SCHOOL: Carrington (N.D.).
COLLEGE: North Dakota.
TRANSACTIONS/CAREER NOTES: Selected by Minnesota Vikings in second round (44th pick overall) of 1999 NFL draft. ... Signed by Vikings (August 1, 1999). ... Designated by Vikings as franchise player (February 20, 2003). ... Re-signed by Vikings (March 23, 2003). ... On injured reserve with knee injury (September 22, 2004-remainder of season).
CHAMPIONSHIP GAME EXPERIENCE: Played in NFC championship game (2000 season).
SINGLE GAME HIGHS (regular season): Receptions—10 (November 30, 2003, vs. St. Louis); yards—79 (November 30, 2003, vs. St. Louis); and touchdown receptions—2 (September 14, 2003, vs. Chicago). Rushing attempts—5 (October 21, 2001, vs. Green Bay); yards—20 (October 21, 2001, vs. Green Bay); and rushing touchdowns—1 (October 21, 2001, vs. Green Bay).

Year Team	G	GS	RUSHING Att.	Yds.	Avg.	TD	RECEIVING No.	Yds.	Avg.	TD	TOTALS TD	2pt.	Pts.	Fum.
1999—Minnesota NFL	13	7	0	0	0.0	0	6	13	2.2	0	0	0	0	2
2000—Minnesota NFL	14	8	12	43	3.6	0	10	98	9.8	0	0	0	0	0
2001—Minnesota NFL	11	11	23	72	3.1	1	24	184	7.7	0	1	0	6	2
2002—Minnesota NFL	14	12	6	17	2.8	0	37	393	10.6	1	1	0	6	0
2003—Minnesota NFL	16	16	2	15	7.5	0	46	401	8.7	4	4	0	24	0
2004—Minnesota NFL	1	1	0	0	0.0	0	2	24	12.0	0	0	0	0	0
Pro totals (6 years)	69	55	43	147	3.4	1	125	1113	8.9	5	6	0	36	4

KLEMM, ADRIAN　　　　　　　T　　　　　　　PACKERS

PERSONAL: Born May 21, 1977, in Inglewood, Calif. ... 6-3/312. ... Full name: Adrian William Klemm.
HIGH SCHOOL: St. Monica (Santa Monica, Calif.).
COLLEGE: Hawaii.
TRANSACTIONS/CAREER NOTES: Selected by New England Patriots in second round (46th pick overall) of 2000 NFL draft. ... Signed by Patriots (July 12, 2000). ... On non-football injured list with knee injury (August 27-November 1, 2000). ... On injured reserve with leg injury (November 2, 2001-remainder of season). ... On injured reserve with knee injury (October 18, 2003-remainder of season). ... On injured reserve with foot injury (October 6, 2004-remainder of season). ... Granted unconditional free agency (March 2, 2005). ... Signed by Green Bay Packers (March 17, 2005).
PLAYING EXPERIENCE: New England NFL, 2000-2004. ... Games/Games started: 2000 (5/4), 2002 (16/3), 2003 (3/3), 2004 (2/0). Total: 26/10.

K

KNIGHT, ROGER　　　　　　LB

PERSONAL: Born October 11, 1978, in Queens Village, N.Y. ... 6-0/245. ... Full name: Roger Oliver Knight.
HIGH SCHOOL: Brooklyn Tech (N.Y.).
COLLEGE: Wisconsin.
TRANSACTIONS/CAREER NOTES: Selected by Pittsburgh Steelers in sixth round (182nd pick overall) of 2001 NFL draft. ... Signed by Steelers (June 6, 2001). ... Released by Steelers (August 31, 2001). ... Signed by New Orleans Saints (December 4, 2001). ... On injured reserve with knee injury (December 12, 2001-remainder of season). ... Granted free agency (March 2, 2005).

Year Team	G	GS	TOTALS Tk.	Ast.	Sks.	INTERCEPTIONS No.	Yds.	Avg.	TD
2001—New Orleans NFL	1	0	0	0	0.0	0	0	0.0	0
2002—New Orleans NFL	16	0	3	3	0.0	0	0	0.0	0
2003—New Orleans NFL	16	2	15	4	0.0	0	0	0.0	0
2004—New Orleans NFL	15	0	6	2	0.0	0	0	0.0	0
Pro totals (4 years)	48	2	24	9	0.0	0	0	0.0	0

KNIGHT, SAMMY　　　　　　S　　　　　　CHIEFS

PERSONAL: Born September 10, 1975, in Fontana, Calif. ... 6-0/215.
HIGH SCHOOL: Rubidoux (Riverside, Calif.).
COLLEGE: Southern California.
TRANSACTIONS/CAREER NOTES: Signed as non-drafted free agent by New Orleans Saints (April 25, 1997). ... Granted unconditional free agency (February 28, 2003). ... Signed by Miami Dolphins (May 13, 2003). ... Granted unconditional free agency (March 2, 2005). ... Signed by Kansas City Chiefs (March 11, 2005).
HONORS: Played in Pro Bowl (2001 season).

Year Team	G	GS	TOTALS Tk.	Ast.	Sks.	INTERCEPTIONS No.	Yds.	Avg.	TD
1997—New Orleans NFL	16	12	67	17	0.0	5	75	15.0	0
1998—New Orleans NFL	14	13	62	13	0.0	6	171	28.5	2
1999—New Orleans NFL	16	16	75	27	0.0	1	0	0.0	0
2000—New Orleans NFL	16	16	74	26	2.0	5	68	13.6	‡2
2001—New Orleans NFL	16	16	80	18	1.0	6	114	19.0	0
2002—New Orleans NFL	16	16	82	25	2.0	5	36	7.2	0
2003—Miami NFL	16	16	66	32	0.0	3	98	32.7	0
2004—Miami NFL	16	16	52	44	0.0	4	32	8.0	0
Pro totals (8 years)	126	121	558	202	5.0	35	594	17.0	4

KNORR, MICAH　　　　　　P/K　　　　　　JETS

PERSONAL: Born January 9, 1975, in Orange, Calif. ... 6-2/199.
HIGH SCHOOL: Orange (Calif.).
COLLEGE: Utah State.
TRANSACTIONS/CAREER NOTES: Signed as non-drafted free agent by Dallas Cowboys (April 18, 2000). ... Released by Cowboys (October 22, 2002). ... Signed by Denver Broncos (October 29, 2002). ... Released by Broncos (December 9, 2004). ... Signed by New York Jets (January 25, 2005).

Year Team	G	PUNTING No.	Yds.	Avg.	Net avg.	In. 20	Blk.
2000—Dallas NFL	14	58	2485	42.8	35.7	12	0
2001—Dallas NFL	16	78	3135	40.2	31.1	25	*3
2002—Dallas NFL	7	47	1928	41.0	35.1	11	0
—Denver NFL	8	24	906	37.8	34.1	8	0
2003—Denver NFL	16	68	2937	43.2	32.2	14	2
2004—Denver NFL	12	54	2243	41.5	34.2	12	1
Pro totals (5 years)	73	329	13634	41.4	33.5	82	6

KOLODZIEJ, ROSS   DT   CARDINALS

PERSONAL: Born May 11, 1978, in Stevens Point, Wis. ... 6-3/295.
HIGH SCHOOL: Stevens Point (Wis.).
COLLEGE: Wisconsin.
TRANSACTIONS/CAREER NOTES: Selected by New York Giants in seventh round (230th pick overall) of 2001 NFL draft. ... Signed by Giants (July 26, 2001). ... Released by Giants (September 1, 2002). ... Signed by San Francisco 49ers (September 8, 2002). ... Released by 49ers (October 14, 2002). ... Re-signed by 49ers (October 16, 2002). ... Released by 49ers (October 22, 2002). ... Signed by Giants (December 4, 2002). ... Did not receive qualifying offer from Giants (March 13, 2003). ... Signed by 49ers (April 7, 2003). ... Released by 49ers (September 30, 2003). ... Signed by Arizona Cardinals (April 2, 2004). ... Granted free agency (March 2, 2005). ... Re-signed by Cardinals (March 24, 2005).

| | | | | | TOTALS | | |
Year Team		G	GS	Tk.	Ast.	Sks.
2001—New York Giants NFL		9	1	0	0	0.0
2002—New York Giants NFL		1	0	0	0	0.0
2004—Arizona NFL		13	4	7	0	1.0
Pro totals (3 years)		**23**	**5**	**7**	**0**	**1.0**

KONRAD, ROB   FB   RAIDERS

PERSONAL: Born November 12, 1976, in Rochester, N.Y. ... 6-3/255. ... Full name: Robert L. Konrad.
HIGH SCHOOL: St. John's (Andover, Mass.).
COLLEGE: Syracuse.
TRANSACTIONS/CAREER NOTES: Selected by Miami Dolphins in second round (43rd pick overall) of 1999 NFL draft. ... Signed by Dolphins (July 27, 1999). ... On injured reserve with rib injury (January 12, 2002-remainder of 2001 playoffs). ... Granted unconditional free agency (February 28, 2003). ... Re-signed by Dolphins (March 1, 2003). ... On injured reserve with back injury (December 15, 2004-remainder of season). ... Released by Dolphins (March 14, 2005). ... Signed by Oakland Raiders (March 31, 2005).
SINGLE GAME HIGHS (regular season): Attempts—7 (September 3, 2000, vs. Seattle); yards—19 (December 10, 2001, vs. Indianapolis); and rushing touchdowns—1 (December 10, 2001, vs. Indianapolis).

| | | | RUSHING | | | | RECEIVING | | | | TOTALS | | |
Year Team	G	GS	Att.	Yds.	Avg.	TD	No.	Yds.	Avg.	TD	TD	2pt.	Pts.	Fum.
1999—Miami NFL	15	9	9	16	1.8	0	34	251	7.4	1	1	0	6	3
2000—Miami NFL	15	13	15	39	2.6	0	14	83	5.9	0	0	0	0	0
2001—Miami NFL	12	9	5	22	4.4	1	5	52	10.4	1	2	0	12	0
2002—Miami NFL	16	12	3	2	0.7	0	34	233	6.9	3	3	0	18	2
2003—Miami NFL	14	12	4	17	4.3	0	16	166	10.4	0	0	0	0	0
2004—Miami NFL	10	1	2	18	9.0	0	8	69	8.6	1	1	0	6	0
Pro totals (6 years)	**82**	**56**	**38**	**114**	**3.0**	**1**	**111**	**854**	**7.7**	**6**	**7**	**0**	**42**	**5**

KOOISTRA, SCOTT   T   BENGALS

PERSONAL: Born October 14, 1980, in Madison, Wis. ... 6-6/320. ... Full name: Daniel Scott Kooistra.
HIGH SCHOOL: Cary (N.C.).
COLLEGE: North Carolina State.
TRANSACTIONS/CAREER NOTES: Selected by Cincinnati Bengals in seventh round (215th pick overall) of 2003 NFL draft.
PLAYING EXPERIENCE: Cincinnati NFL, 2003-2004. ... Games/Games started: 2003 (8/0), 2004 (16/0). Total: 24/0.

KOPPEN, DANIEL   C   PATRIOTS

PERSONAL: Born September 12, 1979, in Dubuque, Iowa. ... 6-2/296.
HIGH SCHOOL: Whitehall (Pa.).
COLLEGE: Boston College.
TRANSACTIONS/CAREER NOTES: Selected by New England Patriots in fifth round (164th pick overall) of 2003 NFL draft. ... Signed by Patriots (July 21, 2003).
PLAYING EXPERIENCE: New England NFL, 2003-2004. ... Games/Games started: 2003 (16/15), 2004 (16/16). Total: 32/31.
CHAMPIONSHIP GAME EXPERIENCE: Played in AFC championship game (2003 and 2004 seasons). ... Member of Super Bowl championship team (2003 and 2004 seasons).

KOSIER, KYLE   T   LIONS

PERSONAL: Born November 27, 1978, in Peoria, Ariz. ... 6-5/309. ... Full name: Kyle Blaine Kosier.
HIGH SCHOOL: Cactus (Peoria, Ariz.).
COLLEGE: Arizona State.
TRANSACTIONS/CAREER NOTES: Selected by San Francisco 49ers in seventh round (248th pick overall) of 2002 NFL draft. ... Signed by 49ers (July 21, 2002). ... Granted free agency (March 2, 2005). ... Signed by Detroit Lions (April 21, 2005).
PLAYING EXPERIENCE: San Francisco NFL, 2002-2004. ... Games/Games started: 2002 (15/1), 2003 (16/12), 2004 (16/16). Total: 47/29.

KOUTOUVIDES, NIKO   LB   SEAHAWKS

PERSONAL: Born March 25, 1981, in Plainville, Conn. ... 6-2/238. ... Full name: Niko Stelios Koutouvides.
HIGH SCHOOL: Milford Academy (Conn.).
COLLEGE: Purdue.

K

TRANSACTIONS/CAREER NOTES: Selected by Seattle Seahawks in fourth round (116th pick overall) of 2004 NFL draft. ... Signed by Seahawks (July 15, 2004).

Year Team	G	GS	TOTALS			INTERCEPTIONS			
			Tk.	Ast.	Sks.	No.	Yds.	Avg.	TD
2004—Seattle NFL	16	2	38	8	1.0	0	0	0.0	0

KOZLOWSKI, BRIAN — TE

PERSONAL: Born October 4, 1970, in Rochester, N.Y. ... 6-3/250. ... Full name: Brian Scott Kozlowski.
HIGH SCHOOL: Webster (N.Y.).
COLLEGE: Connecticut.
TRANSACTIONS/CAREER NOTES: Signed as non-drafted free agent by New York Giants (May 1, 1993). ... Released by Giants (August 16, 1993). ... Re-signed by Giants to practice squad (December 8, 1993). ... Granted unconditional free agency (February 14, 1997). ... Signed by Atlanta Falcons (March 21, 1997). ... Granted unconditional free agency (February 13, 1998). ... Re-signed by Falcons (March 4, 1998). ... Granted unconditional free agency (March 2, 2001). ... Re-signed by Falcons (April 5, 2001). ... Granted unconditional free agency (March 1, 2002). ... Re-signed by Falcons (April 3, 2002). ... Granted unconditional free agency (February 28, 2003). ... Re-signed by Falcons (March 17, 2003). ... Granted unconditional free agency (March 3, 2004). ... Signed by Washington Redskins (April 13, 2004). ... Released by Redskins (October16, 2004). ... Re-signed by Redskins (October19, 2004). ... Granted unconditional free agency (March 2, 2005).
CHAMPIONSHIP GAME EXPERIENCE: Played in NFC championship game (1998 season). ... Played in Super Bowl 33 (1998 season).
SINGLE GAME HIGHS (regular season): Receptions—4 (September 23, 2001, vs. Carolina); yards—86 (September 23, 2001, vs. Carolina); and touchdown receptions—1 (November 11, 2001, vs. Dallas).

Year Team	G	GS	RECEIVING				KICKOFF RETURNS				TOTALS			
			No.	Yds.	Avg.	TD	No.	Yds.	Avg.	TD	TD	2pt.	Pts.	Fum.
1993—New York Giants NFL			Did not play.											
1994—New York Giants NFL	16	3	1	5	5.0	0	2	21	10.5	0	0	0	0	0
1995—New York Giants NFL	16	0	2	17	8.5	0	5	75	15.0	0	0	0	0	1
1996—New York Giants NFL	5	0	1	4	4.0	1	1	16	16.0	0	1	0	6	0
1997—Atlanta NFL	16	5	7	99	14.1	1	2	49	24.5	0	1	0	6	0
1998—Atlanta NFL	16	4	10	103	10.3	1	1	12	12.0	0	1	0	6	0
1999—Atlanta NFL	16	3	11	122	11.1	2	2	19	9.5	0	2	0	12	1
2000—Atlanta NFL	16	3	15	151	10.1	2	7	77	11.0	0	2	0	12	0
2001—Atlanta NFL	16	0	15	270	18.0	1	3	35	11.7	0	1	0	6	0
2002—Atlanta NFL	16	2	6	59	9.8	0	2	35	17.5	0	0	0	0	0
2003—Atlanta NFL	16	9	10	87	8.7	0	3	27	9.0	0	0	0	0	1
2004—Washington NFL	11	1	3	29	9.7	0	1	4	4.0	0	0	0	0	0
Pro totals (11 years)	160	30	81	946	11.7	8	29	370	12.8	0	8	0	48	3

KRAMER, JORDAN — LB — TITANS

PERSONAL: Born December 7, 1979, in Parma, Idaho. ... 6-1/230. ... Son of Jerry Kramer, guard, Green Bay Packers (1958-68).
HIGH SCHOOL: Parma (Idaho).
COLLEGE: Idaho.
TRANSACTIONS/CAREER NOTES: Signed as non-drafted free agent by San Diego Chargers (May 2, 2003). ... Waived by Chargers (August 31, 2003). ... Signed by Tennessee Titans to practice squad (October 1, 2003). ... Activated (November 13, 2003). ... Waived by Titans (November 18, 2003). ... Re-signed by Titans to practice squad (November 26, 2003). ... Activated (December 5, 2003). ... Released by Titans (September 5, 2004). ... Re-signed by Titans to practice squad (September 7, 2004). ... Activated (December 11, 2004).

Year Team	G	GS	TOTALS			INTERCEPTIONS			
			Tk.	Ast.	Sks.	No.	Yds.	Avg.	TD
2003—Tennessee NFL	2	0	0	0	0.0	0	0	0.0	0
2004—Tennessee NFL	4	0	0	0	0.0	0	0	0.0	0
Pro totals (2 years)	6	0	0	0	0.0	0	0	0.0	0

KRANCHICK, MATT — TE — STEELERS

PERSONAL: Born December 13, 1979, in Carlisle, Pa. ... 6-7/260. ... Full name: Matthew Alan Kranchick.
HIGH SCHOOL: Trinity (Carlisle, Pa.).
COLLEGE: Penn State.
TRANSACTIONS/CAREER NOTES: Selected by Pittsburgh Steelers in sixth round (194th pick overall) of 2004 NFL draft. ... Signed by Steelers (May 17, 2004).
CHAMPIONSHIP GAME EXPERIENCE: Member of Steelers for AFC championship game (2004 season); inactive.

Year Team	G	GS	RECEIVING				TOTALS		
			No.	Yds.	Avg.	TD	TD	2pt.	Pts.	Fum.
2004—Pittsburgh NFL	2	0	0	0	0.0	0	0	0	0	0

KRAUSE, RYAN — TE — CHARGERS

PERSONAL: Born June 16, 1981, in Omaha, Neb. ... 6-3/256.
HIGH SCHOOL: Millard (Omaha, Neb.).
COLLEGE: Nebraska-Omaha.
TRANSACTIONS/CAREER NOTES: Selected by San Diego Chargers in sixth round (169th pick overall) of 2004 NFL draft. ... Signed by Chargers (July 26, 2004).
SINGLE GAME HIGHS (regular season): Receptions—5 (January 2, 2005, vs. Kansas City); yards—81 (January 2, 2005, vs. Kansas City); and touchdown receptions—1 (January 2, 2005, vs. Kansas City).

Year Team	G	GS	RECEIVING				TOTALS		
			No.	Yds.	Avg.	TD	TD	2pt.	Pts.	Fum.
2004—San Diego NFL	1	1	5	81	16.2	1	1	0	6	0

KREIDER, DAN   FB   STEELERS

PERSONAL: Born March 11, 1977, in Lancaster, Pa. ... 5-11/255.
HIGH SCHOOL: Manheim Central (Pa.).
COLLEGE: New Hampshire.
TRANSACTIONS/CAREER NOTES: Signed as non-drafted free agent by Pittsburgh Steelers (April 21, 2000). ... On physically unable to per-form list with calf injury (July 20-September 2, 2001). ... Granted free agency (February 28, 2003). ... Re-signed by Steelers (April 20, 2003). ... Granted unconditional free agency (March 3, 2004). ... Re-signed by Steelers (March 3, 2004).
CHAMPIONSHIP GAME EXPERIENCE: Played in AFC championship game (2001 and 2004 seasons).
SINGLE GAME HIGHS (regular season): Attempts—3 (January 2, 2005, vs. Buffalo); yards—24 (December 3, 2000, vs. Oakland); and rush-ing touchdowns—1 (December 7, 2003, vs. Oakland).

			RUSHING				RECEIVING				KICKOFF RETURNS				TOTALS			
Year Team	G	GS	Att.	Yds.	Avg.	TD	No.	Yds.	Avg.	TD	No.	Yds.	Avg.	TD	TD	2pt.	Pts.	Fum.
2000—Pittsburgh NFL	10	7	2	24	12.0	0	5	42	8.4	0	1	0	0.0	0	0	0	0	0
2001—Pittsburgh NFL	13	1	7	29	4.1	1	2	5	2.5	0	0	0	0.0	0	1	0	6	0
2002—Pittsburgh NFL	16	13	6	16	2.7	0	18	122	6.8	1	1	18	18.0	0	1	1	8	1
2003—Pittsburgh NFL	16	12	7	29	4.1	1	9	107	11.9	0	3	29	9.7	0	1	0	6	0
2004—Pittsburgh NFL	16	9	4	18	4.5	0	10	75	7.5	1	0	0	0.0	0	1	0	6	0
Pro totals (5 years)	71	42	26	116	4.5	2	44	351	8.0	2	5	47	9.4	0	4	1	26	1

KRENZEL, CRAIG   QB   BEARS

PERSONAL: Born July 1, 1981, in Sterling Heights, Mich. ... 6-4/228.
HIGH SCHOOL: Henry Ford II (Sterling Heights, Mich.).
COLLEGE: Ohio State.
TRANSACTIONS/CAREER NOTES: Selected by Chicago Bears in fifth round (148th pick overall) of 2004 NFL draft. ... Signed by Bears (July 27, 2004). ... On injured reserve with ankle injury (December 7, 2004-remainder of season).
SINGLE GAME HIGHS (regular season): Attempts—28 (November 14, 2004, vs. Tennessee); completions—14 (November 21, 2004, vs. Indianapolis); yards—175 (November 21, 2004, vs. Indianapolis); and touchdown passes—1 (November 21, 2004, vs. Indianapolis).
MISCELLANEOUS: Regular-season record as starting NFL quarterback: 3-2 (.600).

			PASSING									RUSHING				TOTALS		
Year Team	G	GS	Att.	Cmp.	Pct.	Yds.	TD	Int.	Avg.	Skd.	Rat.	Att.	Yds.	Avg.	TD	TD	2pt.	Pts.
2004—Chicago NFL	6	5	127	59	46.5	718	3	6	5.65	23	52.5	18	41	2.3	0	0	1	2

KREUTZ, OLIN   C   BEARS

PERSONAL: Born June 9, 1977, in Honolulu, Hawaii. ... 6-2/292.
HIGH SCHOOL: St. Louis (Honolulu).
COLLEGE: Washington.
TRANSACTIONS/CAREER NOTES: Selected after junior season by Chicago Bears in third round (64th pick overall) of 1998 NFL draft. ... Signed by Bears (July 20, 1998). ... On injured reserve with knee injury (November 21, 2000-remainder of season). ... Granted free agency (March 2, 2001). ... Re-signed by Bears (April 18, 2001). ... Granted unconditional free agency (March 1, 2002). ... Re-signed by Bears (March 4, 2002).
PLAYING EXPERIENCE: Chicago NFL, 1998-2004. ... Games/Games started: 1998 (9/1), 1999 (16/16), 2000 (7/7), 2001 (16/16), 2002 (15/15), 2003 (16/16), 2004 (16/16). Total: 95/87.
HONORS: Named center on THE SPORTING NEWS college All-America first team (1997). ... Played in Pro Bowl (2001, 2002 and 2004 sea-sons). ... Named to play in Pro Bowl (2003 season); replaced by Mike Flanagan due to injury.

KRIEWALDT, CLINT   LB   STEELERS

PERSONAL: Born March 16, 1976, in Shiocton, Wis. ... 6-1/248.
HIGH SCHOOL: Shiocton (Wis.).
COLLEGE: Wisconsin-Stevens Point.
TRANSACTIONS/CAREER NOTES: Selected by Detroit Lions in sixth round (177th pick overall) of 1999 NFL draft. ... Signed by Lions (July 22, 1999). ... Granted free agency (March 1, 2002). ... Re-signed by Lions (April 16, 2002). ... Granted unconditional free agency (February 28, 2003). ... Signed by Pittsburgh Steelers (March 5, 2003).
CHAMPIONSHIP GAME EXPERIENCE: Played in AFC championship game (2004 season).

			TOTALS			INTERCEPTIONS			
Year Team	G	GS	Tk.	Ast.	Sks.	No.	Yds.	Avg.	TD
1999—Detroit NFL	12	0	2	0	0.0	1	2	2.0	0
2000—Detroit NFL	13	1	4	1	0.0	0	0	0.0	0
2001—Detroit NFL	14	1	11	10	0.0	0	0	0.0	0
2002—Detroit NFL	10	0	5	6	0.0	0	0	0.0	0
2003—Pittsburgh NFL	15	0	1	0	0.0	0	0	0.0	0
2004—Pittsburgh NFL	15	0	3	1	0.5	0	0	0.0	0
Pro totals (6 years)	79	2	26	18	0.5	1	2	2.0	0

KUEHL, RYAN   DT   GIANTS

PERSONAL: Born January 18, 1972, in Washington, DC. ... 6-5/280. ... Full name: Ryan Philip Kuehl.
HIGH SCHOOL: Walt Whitman (Bethesda, Md.).
COLLEGE: Virginia.

K

TRANSACTIONS/CAREER NOTES: Signed as non-drafted free agent by San Francisco 49ers (April 26, 1995). ... Released by 49ers (August 19, 1995). ...Re-signed by 49ers to practice squad (August 26, 1995). ... Signed by Washington Redskins (February 16, 1996). ... Released by Redskins (August 25, 1996). ... Re-signed by Redskins to practice squad (August 26, 1996). ... Activated (October 19, 1996). ... Released by Redskins (November 6, 1996). ... Re-signed by Redskins to practice squad (November 7, 1996). ... Activated (November 11, 1996). ... Released by Redskins (August 23, 1997). ... Re-signed by Redskins (September 9, 1997). ... Released by Redskins (August 30, 1998). ... Signed by Cleveland Browns (February 11, 1999). ... Granted unconditional free agency (February 28, 2003). ... Signed by New York Giants (March 6, 2003). ... On injured reserve with elbow injury (August 31, 2003-entire season).

Year Team	G	GS	Tk.	Ast.	Sks.
1996—Washington NFL	2	0	1	0	0.0
1997—Washington NFL	12	5	9	3	0.0
1999—Cleveland NFL	16	0	0	0	0.0
2000—Cleveland NFL	16	0	0	0	0.0
2001—Cleveland NFL	16	0	0	0	0.0
2002—Cleveland NFL	16	0	0	0	0.0
2003—New York Giants NFL	Did not play.				
2004—New York Giants NFL	16	0	0	0	0.0
Pro totals (7 years)	94	5	10	3	0.0

KURPEIKIS, JUSTIN — LB — PATRIOTS

PERSONAL: Born July 17, 1977, in Allison Park, Pa. ... 6-3/254. ... Full name: Justin William Kurpeikis.
HIGH SCHOOL: Central Catholic (Pittsburgh).
COLLEGE: Penn State.
TRANSACTIONS/CAREER NOTES: Signed as non-drafted free agent by Pittsburgh Steelers (April 23, 2001). ... Released by Steelers (October 22, 2002). ... Re-signed by Steelers (November 5, 2002). ... Released by Steelers (August 26, 2003). ... Signed by New England Patriots to practice squad (October 22, 2003). ... Released from Patriots practice squad (November 6, 2003). ... Re-signed by Patriots (February 6, 2004). ... Released by Patriots (September 5, 2004). ... Re-signed by Patriots to practice squad (September 6, 2004). ... Activated (November 22, 2004). ... Released by Patriots (December 21, 2004). ... Re-signed by Patriots to practice squad (December 22, 2004).
CHAMPIONSHIP GAME EXPERIENCE: Played in AFC championship game (2001 season).

Year Team	G	GS	TOTALS Tk.	Ast.	Sks.	INTERCEPTIONS No.	Yds.	Avg.	TD
2001—Pittsburgh NFL	3	0	0	0	0.0	0	0	0.0	0
2002—Pittsburgh NFL	6	0	0	0	0.0	0	0	0.0	0
2004—New England NFL	5	0	0	0	0.0	0	0	0.0	0
Pro totals (3 years)	14	0	0	0	0.0	0	0	0.0	0

KYLE, JASON — LB — PANTHERS

PERSONAL: Born May 12, 1972, in Tempe, Ariz. ... 6-3/242. ... Full name: Jason C. Kyle.
HIGH SCHOOL: McClintock (Tempe, Ariz.).
COLLEGE: Arizona State.
TRANSACTIONS/CAREER NOTES: Selected by Seattle Seahawks in fourth round (126th pick overall) of 1995 NFL draft. ... Signed by Seahawks (July 16, 1995). ... On injured reserve with shoulder injury (August 18, 1997-entire season). ... Granted free agency (February 13, 1998). ... Re-signed by Seahawks (April 16, 1998). ... Selected by Cleveland Browns from Seahawks in NFL expansion draft (February 9, 1999). ... On physically unable to perform list with knee injury (August 26, 1999-entire season). ... Released by Browns (August 27, 2000). ... Signed by St. Louis Rams (October 5, 2000). ... Released by Rams (October 16, 2000). ... Re-signed by Rams (October 24, 2000). ... Released by Rams (October 27, 2000). ... Signed by San Francisco 49ers (October 30, 2000). ... Granted unconditional free agency (March 2, 2001). ... Signed by Carolina Panthers (March 5, 2001). ... Granted unconditional free agency (March 3, 2004). ... Re-signed by Panthers (March 11, 2004).
CHAMPIONSHIP GAME EXPERIENCE: Played in NFC championship game (2003 season). ... Played in Super Bowl 38 (2003 season).

Year Team	G	GS	TOTALS Tk.	Ast.	Sks.	INTERCEPTIONS No.	Yds.	Avg.	TD
1995—Seattle NFL	16	0	0	0	0.0	0	0	0.0	0
1996—Seattle NFL	16	0	1	0	0.0	0	0	0.0	0
1998—Seattle NFL	16	0	0	0	0.0	0	0	0.0	0
1999—Cleveland NFL	Did not play.								
2000—San Francisco NFL	2	0	2	0	0.0	0	0	0.0	0
2001—Carolina NFL	16	0	0	0	0.0	0	0	0.0	0
2002—Carolina NFL	16	0	1	1	0.0	0	0	0.0	0
2003—Carolina NFL	16	0	0	0	0.0	0	0	0.0	0
2004—Carolina NFL	16	0	0	0	0.0	0	0	0.0	0
Pro totals (8 years)	114	0	4	1	0.0	0	0	0.0	0

LABINJO, MIKE — LB — EAGLES

PERSONAL: Born July 8, 1980, in Toronto, ON. ... 6-0/241.
HIGH SCHOOL: St. Michael's College HS (Toronto).
COLLEGE: Michigan State.
TRANSACTIONS/CAREER NOTES: Signed as non-drafted free agent by Philadelphia Eagles (April 27, 2004). ... Released by Eagles (September 5, 2004). ... Re-signed by Eagles to practice squad (September 6, 2004). ... Activated (December 14, 2004).

Year Team	G	GS	TOTALS Tk.	Ast.	Sks.	INTERCEPTIONS No.	Yds.	Avg.	TD
2004—Philadelphia NFL	3	0	10	0	0.0	0	0	0.0	0

LABOY, TRAVIS   DE   TITANS

PERSONAL: Born August 10, 1981, in Honolulu, Hawaii. ... 6-3/253.
HIGH SCHOOL: Marin Catholic (San Rafael, Calif.).
COLLEGE: Hawaii.
TRANSACTIONS/CAREER NOTES: Selected by Tennessee in second round (42nd pick overall) of 2004 NFL draft. ... Signed by Titans (July 31, 2004).

Year Team	G	GS	TOTALS Tk.	Ast.	Sks.	INTERCEPTIONS No.	Yds.	Avg.	TD
2004—Tennessee NFL	13	2	13	8	3.5	0	0	0.0	0

LAKE, ANTWAN   DE   FALCONS

PERSONAL: Born July 10, 1979, in Seaford, Del. ... 6-4/308.
HIGH SCHOOL: Cambridge South (Dorchester, Md.).
COLLEGE: West Virginia.
TRANSACTIONS/CAREER NOTES: Signed as non-drafted free agent by Detroit Lions (April 26, 2002). ... Released by Lions (August 31, 2003). ... Signed by Atlanta Falcons (December 31, 2003).
CHAMPIONSHIP GAME EXPERIENCE: Played in NFC championship game (2004 season).

Year Team	G	GS	TOTALS Tk.	Ast.	Sks.
2002—Detroit NFL	9	0	0	0	0.0
2004—Atlanta NFL	16	2	3	2	0.0
Pro totals (2 years)	25	2	3	2	0.0

LANDETA, SEAN   P

PERSONAL: Born January 6, 1962, in Baltimore, Md. ... 6-0/215. ... Full name: Sean Edward Landeta.
HIGH SCHOOL: Loch Raven (Baltimore).
COLLEGE: Towson.
TRANSACTIONS/CAREER NOTES: Selected by Philadelphia Stars in 14th round (161st pick overall) of 1983 USFL draft. ... Signed by Stars (January 24, 1983). ... Stars franchise moved to Baltimore (November 1, 1984). ... Granted free agency (August 1, 1985) ... Signed by New York Giants (August 5, 1985). ... On injured reserve with back injury (September 7, 1988-remainder of season). ... Granted free agency (February 1, 1990). ... Re-signed by Giants (July 23, 1990). ... On injured reserve with knee injury (November 25, 1992-remainder of season). ... Granted unconditional free agency (March 1, 1993). ... Re-signed by Giants (March 18, 1993). ... Released by Giants (November 9, 1993). ... Signed by Los Angeles Rams (November 12, 1993). ... Granted unconditional free agency (February 17, 1994). ... Re-signed by Rams (May 10, 1994). ... Granted unconditional free agency (February 17, 1995). ... Rams franchise moved to St. Louis (April 12, 1995). ... Re-signed by Rams (May 8, 1995). ... Released by Rams (March 18, 1997). ... Signed by Tampa Bay Buccaneers (October 9, 1997). ... Granted unconditional free agency (February 13, 1998). ... Signed by Green Packers (February 26, 1998). ... Granted unconditional free agency (February 12, 1999). ... Signed by Philadelphia Eagles (February 26, 1999). ... Granted unconditional free agency (March 1, 2002). ... Re-signed by Eagles (March 21, 2002). ... On injured reserve with calf injury (December 3, 2002-remainder of season). ... Granted unconditional free agency (February 28, 2003). ... Signed by Rams (March 18, 2003). ... Granted unconditional free agency (March 3, 2004). ... Re-signed by Rams (March 4, 2004). ... Released by Rams (November 26, 2004).
CHAMPIONSHIP GAME EXPERIENCE: Played in USFL championship game (1983-1985 seasons). ... Played in NFC championship game (1986, 1990 and 2001 seasons). ... Member of Super Bowl championship team (1986 and 1990 seasons).
HONORS: Named punter on THE SPORTING NEWS USFL All-Star team (1983 and 1984). ... Named punter on THE SPORTING NEWS NFL All-Pro team (1986, 1989 and 1990). ... Played in Pro Bowl (1986 and 1990 seasons).
RECORDS: Holds NFL career record for most punts—1,367.

Year Team	G	No.	Yds.	Avg.	Net avg.	In. 20	Blk.
1983—Philadelphia USFL	18	86	3601	41.9	36.5	31	0
1984—Philadelphia USFL	18	53	2171	41.0	*38.1	18	0
1985—Baltimore USFL	18	65	2718	41.8	33.2	18	0
—New York Giants NFL	16	81	3472	42.9	36.3	20	0
1986—New York Giants NFL	16	79	3539	‡44.8	‡37.1	24	0
1987—New York Giants NFL	12	65	2773	42.7	31.0	13	1
1988—New York Giants NFL	1	6	222	37.0	35.7	1	0
1989—New York Giants NFL	16	70	3019	43.1	*37.7	19	0
1990—New York Giants NFL	16	75	3306	‡44.1	37.2	†24	0
1991—New York Giants NFL	15	64	2768	43.3	35.2	16	0
1992—New York Giants NFL	11	53	2317	43.7	31.5	13	*2
1993—New York Giants NFL	8	33	1390	42.1	35.0	11	1
—Los Angeles Rams NFL	8	42	1825	43.5	32.8	7	0
1994—Los Angeles Rams NFL	16	78	3494	*44.8	34.2	23	0
1995—St. Louis NFL	16	83	3679	‡44.3	36.7	23	0
1996—St. Louis NFL	16	78	3491	44.8	36.1	23	0
1997—Tampa Bay NFL	10	54	2274	42.1	34.1	15	1
1998—Green Bay NFL	16	65	2788	42.9	37.1	30	0
1999—Philadelphia NFL	16	*107	‡4524	42.3	35.1	21	1
2000—Philadelphia NFL	16	86	3635	42.3	36.0	23	0
2001—Philadelphia NFL	16	‡97	4221	43.5	36.4	26	0
2002—Philadelphia NFL	12	52	2229	42.9	34.6	19	0
2003—St. Louis NFL	16	59	2525	42.8	32.9	14	0
2004—St. Louis NFL	10	40	1733	43.3	32.5	9	0
USFL totals (3 years)	54	204	8490	41.6	0.0	67	0
NFL totals (20 years)	279	1367	59224	43.3	35.3	374	6
Pro totals (22 years)	333	1571	67714	43.1	30.7	441	6

L

LANG, KENARD   DE   BROWNS

PERSONAL: Born January 31, 1975, in Orlando, Fla. ... 6-3/280. ... Full name: Kenard Dushun Lang.
HIGH SCHOOL: Maynard Evans (Orlando).
COLLEGE: Miami (Fla.).
TRANSACTIONS/CAREER NOTES: Selected by Washington Redskins in first round (17th pick overall) of 1997 NFL draft. ... Signed by Redskins (July 28, 1997). ... Granted unconditional free agency (March 1, 2002). ... Signed by Cleveland Browns (March 5, 2002).

Year Team	G	GS	TOTALS Tk.	Ast.	Sks.	INTERCEPTIONS No.	Yds.	Avg.	TD
1997—Washington NFL	11	11	26	9	1.5	0	0	0.0	0
1998—Washington NFL	16	16	46	8	7.0	0	0	0.0	0
1999—Washington NFL	16	9	34	3	6.0	0	0	0.0	0
2000—Washington NFL	16	0	16	0	3.0	0	0	0.0	0
2001—Washington NFL	16	16	52	15	4.0	1	14	14.0	0
2002—Cleveland NFL	15	14	33	13	5.5	1	71	71.0	0
2003—Cleveland NFL	15	15	47	13	8.0	1	0	0.0	0
2004—Cleveland NFL	16	15	49	13	7.0	0	0	0.0	0
Pro totals (8 years)	121	96	303	74	42.0	3	85	28.3	0

LARSON, KYLE   P   BENGALS

PERSONAL: Born September 2, 1980, in Kearney, Neb. ... 6-1/204.
HIGH SCHOOL: Kearney (Neb.).
COLLEGE: Nebraska.
TRANSACTIONS/CAREER NOTES: Signed as non-drafted free agent by Cincinnati Bengals (April 27, 2004).

Year Team	G	No.	PUNTING Yds.	Avg.	Net avg.	In. 20	Blk.
2004—Cincinnati NFL	16	83	3499	42.2	35.5	21	1

LASSITER, KWAMIE   S

PERSONAL: Born December 3, 1969, in Newport News, Va. ... 6-0/207.
HIGH SCHOOL: Menchville (Newport News, Va.).
JUNIOR COLLEGE: Butler County Community College (Kan.).
COLLEGE: Kansas.
TRANSACTIONS/CAREER NOTES: Signed as non-drafted free agent by Arizona Cardinals (April 28, 1995). ... On injured reserve with ankle injury (October 5, 1995-remainder of season). ... Granted free agency (February 13, 1998). ... Re-signed by Cardinals (May 21, 1998). ... Granted unconditional free agency (February 12, 1999). ... Re-signed by Cardinals (March 9, 1999). ... Granted free agency (March 1, 2002). ... Re-signed by Cardinals (May 1, 2002). ... Granted unconditional free agency (February 28, 2003). ... Signed by San Diego Chargers (June 9, 2003). ... On injured reserve with knee injury (November 19, 2003-remainder of season). ... Released by Chargers (September 5, 2004). ... Signed by St. Louis Rams (September 21, 2004). ... Released by Rams (October 22, 2004).

Year Team	G	GS	TOTALS Tk.	Ast.	Sks.	INTERCEPTIONS No.	Yds.	Avg.	TD
1995—Arizona NFL	5	0	5	2	0.0	0	0	0.0	0
1996—Arizona NFL	14	0	13	3	0.0	1	20	20.0	0
1997—Arizona NFL	16	1	24	15	3.0	1	10	10.0	0
1998—Arizona NFL	16	6	40	15	0.0	‡8	80	10.0	0
1999—Arizona NFL	16	16	69	34	0.0	2	110	55.0	1
2000—Arizona NFL	16	16	63	31	0.0	1	11	11.0	0
2001—Arizona NFL	16	16	83	28	1.0	9	80	8.9	0
2002—Arizona NFL	16	16	59	29	0.0	2	7	3.5	0
2003—San Diego NFL	10	10	51	8	0.0	1	38	38.0	1
2004—St. Louis NFL	4	0	6	1	0.0	0	0	0.0	0
Pro totals (10 years)	129	81	413	166	4.0	25	356	14.2	2

LAVALAIS, CHAD   DT   FALCONS

PERSONAL: Born April 15, 1979, in Marksville, La. ... 6-1/293. ... Full name: Chad Douglas Lavalais.
HIGH SCHOOL: Marksville (La.).
COLLEGE: Louisiana State.
TRANSACTIONS/CAREER NOTES: Selected by Atlanta Falcons in fifth round (142nd pick overall) of 2004 NFL draft. ... Signed by Falcons (July 28, 2004).
CHAMPIONSHIP GAME EXPERIENCE: Played in NFC championship game (2004 season).
HONORS: Named College Football Defensive Player of the Year by THE SPORTING NEWS (2003).

Year Team	G	GS	TOTALS Tk.	Ast.	Sks.	INTERCEPTIONS No.	Yds.	Avg.	TD
2004—Atlanta NFL	16	6	24	4	0.0	0	0	0.0	0

LAW, TY   CB

PERSONAL: Born February 10, 1974, in Aliquippa, Pa. ... 5-11/200. ... Full name: Tajuan Law.
HIGH SCHOOL: Aliquippa (Pa.).
COLLEGE: Michigan.

TRANSACTIONS/CAREER NOTES: Selected after junior season by New England Patriots in first round (23rd pick overall) of 1995 NFL draft. ... Signed by Patriots (July 20, 1995). ... On injured reserve with hand injury (December 29, 1999-remainder of season). ... On injured reserve with foot injury (January 1, 2005-remainder of season). ... Released by Patriots (February 22, 2005).
CHAMPIONSHIP GAME EXPERIENCE: Played in AFC championship game (1996, 2001 and 2003 seasons). ... Played in Super Bowl 31 (1996 season). ... Member of Super Bowl championship team (2001, 2003 and 2004 seasons).
HONORS: Named cornerback on THE SPORTING NEWS NFL All-Pro team (1998). ... Played in Pro Bowl (1998, 2001-2003 seasons). ... Named co-Outstanding Player of Pro Bowl (1998 season).
POST SEASON RECORDS: Shares Super Bowl single-game record for most interceptions returned for touchdown—1 (February 3, 2002 vs. St. Louis Rams).

				TOTALS			INTERCEPTIONS			
Year Team	G	GS	Tk.	Ast.	Sks.	No.	Yds.	Avg.	TD
1995—New England NFL	14	7	40	7	1.0	3	47	15.7	0
1996—New England NFL	13	12	56	6	0.0	3	45	15.0	0
1997—New England NFL	16	16	69	8	0.5	3	70	23.3	0
1998—New England NFL	16	16	60	10	0.0	*9	133	14.8	1
1999—New England NFL	13	13	50	9	0.5	2	20	10.0	1
2000—New England NFL	15	15	58	16	0.0	2	32	16.0	0
2001—New England NFL	16	16	60	10	1.0	3	91	30.3	†2
2002—New England NFL	16	16	60	17	1.0	4	33	8.3	0
2003—New England NFL	15	15	61	13	0.0	6	112	18.7	1
2004—New England NFL	7	7	23	5	0.0	1	0	0.0	0
Pro totals (10 years)	141	133	537	101	4.0	36	583	16.2	6

LAWRIE, NATE — TE — BUCCANEERS

PERSONAL: Born October 17, 1981, in Indianapolis, Ind. ... 6-5/262. ... Full name: Nathan Earl Lawrie.
HIGH SCHOOL: Roncalli (Indianapolis, Ind.).
COLLEGE: Yale.
TRANSACTIONS/CAREER NOTES: Selected by Tampa Bay Buccaneers in sixth round (181st pick overall) of 2004 NFL draft. ... Signed by Buccaneers (July 29, 2004). ... Released by Buccaneers (August 31, 2004). ... Signed by Philadelphia Eagles to practice squad (September 6, 2004). ... Released by Eagles from practice squad (September 22, 2004). ... Signed by Buccaneers to practice squad (September 29, 2004). ... Activated (December 14, 2004).
SINGLE GAME HIGHS (regular season): Receptions—1 (January 2, 2005, vs. Arizona); yards—15 (January 2, 2005, vs. Arizona); and touchdown receptions—0.

			RECEIVING				TOTALS			
Year Team	G	GS	No.	Yds.	Avg.	TD	TD	2pt.	Pts.	Fum.
2004—Tampa Bay NFL	2	0	1	15	15.0	0	0	0	0	0

LAYNE, GEORGE — FB

PERSONAL: Born October 9, 1978, in Alvin, Texas. ... 5-11/250.
HIGH SCHOOL: Alvin (Texas).
COLLEGE: Texas Christian.
TRANSACTIONS/CAREER NOTES: Selected after junior season by Kansas City Chiefs in fourth round (108th pick overall) of 2001 NFL draft. ... Signed by Chiefs (July 23, 2001). ... Released by Chiefs (September 2, 2001). ... Re-signed by Chiefs to practice squad (September 4, 2001). ... Signed by Atlanta Falcons off Chiefs practice squad (October 2, 2001). ... Released by Falcons (September 1, 2002). ... Signed by Falcons (November 12, 2002). ... Released by Falcons (September 2, 2003). ... Signed by Carolina Panthers to practice squad (September 10, 2003). ... Released by Panthers (October 1, 2003). ... Signed by Atlanta Falcons (November 26, 2003). ... On injured reserve with knee injury (December 16, 2003-remainder of season). ... Released by Falcons (September 1, 2004). ... Signed by San Diego Chargers (November 15, 2004). ... Released by Chargers (December 14, 2004). ... Signed by Falcons (December 22, 2004). ... On injured reserve with jaw injury (January 4, 2005-remainder of 2004 season playoffs). ... Granted free agency (March 2, 2005).
SINGLE GAME HIGHS (regular season): Attempts—1 (December 26, 2004, vs. New Orleans); yards—15 (December 14, 2003, vs. Indianapolis); and rushing touchdowns—0.

			RUSHING				RECEIVING				TOTALS			
Year Team	G	GS	Att.	Yds.	Avg.	TD	No.	Yds.	Avg.	TD	TD	2pt.	Pts.	Fum.
2001—Atlanta NFL	2	0	0	0	0.0	0	0	0	0.0	0	0	0	0	0
2002—Atlanta NFL	2	0	1	5	5.0	0	2	11	5.5	0	0	0	0	1
2003—Atlanta NFL	3	0	1	15	15.0	0	1	3	3.0	0	0	0	0	0
2004—San Diego NFL	2	0	0	0	0.0	0	0	0	0.0	0	0	0	0	0
—Atlanta NFL	2	0	1	12	12.0	0	1	6	6.0	0	0	0	0	0
Pro totals (4 years)	11	0	3	32	10.7	0	4	20	5.0	0	0	0	0	1

LEACH, MIKE — TE/LS — BRONCOS

PERSONAL: Born October 18, 1976, in Jefferson Township, N.J. ... 6-2/245.
HIGH SCHOOL: Jefferson Township (N.J.).
COLLEGE: William & Mary.
TRANSACTIONS/CAREER NOTES: Signed as non-drafted free agent by Tennessee Titans (April 20, 2000). ... Released by Titans (October 16, 2001). ... Signed by Chicago Bears (January 10, 2001). ... Released by Bears (August 26, 2002). ... Signed by Denver Broncos (November 4, 2002). ... Granted unconditional free agency (March 2, 2005). ... Re-signed by Broncos (March 10, 2005).
PLAYING EXPERIENCE: Tennessee NFL, 2000-2001; Denver NFL, 2002-2004. ... Games/Games started: 2000 (15/0), 2001 (4/0), 2002 (8/0), 2003 (16/0), 2004 (16/0). Total: 59/0.

LEACH, VONTA   RB   PACKERS

PERSONAL: Born November 6, 1981, in Lumberton, N.C. ... 6-0/246. ... Full name: Terzell Vonta Leach. ... Name pronounced: von-TAY.
HIGH SCHOOL: South Robeson (Rowland, N.C.).
COLLEGE: East Carolina.
TRANSACTIONS/CAREER NOTES: Signed as non-drafted free agent by Green Bay Packers (April 30, 2004). ... Released by Packers (September 6, 2004). ... Re-signed by Packers to practice squad (September 8, 2004). ... Activated (November 29, 2004).

				RUSHING				TOTALS		
Year Team	G	GS	Att.	Yds.	Avg.	TD	TD	2pt.	Pts.	Fum.
2004—Green Bay NFL	6	0	0	0	0.0	0	0	0	0	0

LEBER, BEN   LB   CHARGERS

PERSONAL: Born December 7, 1978, in Vermillion, S.D. ... 6-3/244.
HIGH SCHOOL: Vermillion (S.D.).
COLLEGE: Kansas State.
TRANSACTIONS/CAREER NOTES: Selected by San Diego Chargers in third round (71st pick overall) of 2002 NFL draft. ... Signed by Chargers (July 22, 2002).

			TOTALS			INTERCEPTIONS			
Year Team	G	GS	Tk.	Ast.	Sks.	No.	Yds.	Avg.	TD
2002—San Diego NFL	16	14	40	9	5.0	0	0	0.0	0
2003—San Diego NFL	16	16	69	11	3.0	0	0	0.0	0
2004—San Diego NFL	16	16	47	11	2.0	0	0	0.0	0
Pro totals (3 years)	48	46	156	31	10.0	0	0	0.0	0

LECHLER, SHANE   P   RAIDERS

PERSONAL: Born August 7, 1976, in Sealy, Texas. ... 6-2/225. ... Full name: Edward Shane Lechler.
HIGH SCHOOL: East Bernard (Texas).
COLLEGE: Texas A&M.
TRANSACTIONS/CAREER NOTES: Selected by Oakland Raiders in fifth round (142nd pick overall) of 2000 NFL draft. ... Signed by Raiders (July 22, 2000).
CHAMPIONSHIP GAME EXPERIENCE: Played in AFC championship game (2000 and 2002 seasons). ... Played in Super Bowl 37 (2002 season).
HONORS: Named punter on THE SPORTING NEWS college All-America second team (1997). ... Named punter on THE SPORTING NEWS college All-America first team (1998). ... Named punter on THE SPORTING NEWS college All-America third team (1999). ... Named punter on THE SPORTING NEWS NFL All-Pro team (2000 and 2004). ... Played in Pro Bowl (2001 and 2004 seasons).

			PUNTING				
Year Team	G	No.	Yds.	Avg.	Net avg.	In. 20	Blk.
2000—Oakland NFL	16	65	2984	45.9	*38.0	24	▲1
2001—Oakland NFL	16	73	3375	§46.2	35.6	23	1
2002—Oakland NFL	14	53	2251	42.5	32.7	18	0
2003—Oakland NFL	16	96	*4503	*46.9	37.2	27	0
2004—Oakland NFL	16	73	3409	*46.7	37.2	22	0
Pro totals (5 years)	78	360	16522	45.9	36.4	114	2

LECKEY, NICK   G   CARDINALS

PERSONAL: Born March 12, 1982, in Grapevine, Texas. ... 6-3/286.
HIGH SCHOOL: Grapevine (Texas).
COLLEGE: Kansas State.
TRANSACTIONS/CAREER NOTES: Selected by Arizona Cardinals in sixth round (167th pick overall) of 2004 NFL draft. ... Signed by Cardinals (July 29, 2004).
PLAYING EXPERIENCE: Arizona NFL, 2004. ... Games/Games started: 2004 (16/0). Total: 16/0.

LEE, ANDY   P   49ERS

PERSONAL: Born August 11, 1982, in Westminster, N.C. ... 6-0/206. ... Full name: Andy Paul Lee.
HIGH SCHOOL: West-Oak (Westminster, S.C.).
COLLEGE: Pittsburgh.
TRANSACTIONS/CAREER NOTES: Selected by San Francisco 49ers in sixth round (188th pick overall) of 2004 NFL draft. ... Signed by 49ers (July 29, 2004).

			PUNTING				
Year Team	G	No.	Yds.	Avg.	Net avg.	In. 20	Blk.
2004—San Francisco NFL	16	96	3990	41.6	35.3	25	0

LEE, CHARLES   WR

PERSONAL: Born November 19, 1977, in Miami, Fla. ... 6-3/227.
HIGH SCHOOL: Homestead (Fla.).
COLLEGE: Central Florida.

TRANSACTIONS/CAREER NOTES: Selected by Green Bay Packers in seventh round (242nd pick overall) of 2000 NFL draft. ... Signed by Packers (June 21, 2000). ... Released by Packers (September 1, 2002). ... Signed by Tampa Bay Buccaneers (October 1, 2002). ... Granted free agency (February 28, 2003). ... Re-signed by Buccaneers (May 22, 2003). ... Granted unconditional free agency (March 2, 2005).

SINGLE GAME HIGHS (regular season): Receptions—10 (December 20, 2003, vs. Atlanta); yards—95 (December 14, 2003, vs. Houston); and touchdown receptions—1 (December 20, 2003, vs. Atlanta).

				RUSHING				RECEIVING				TOTALS			
Year Team	G	GS	Att.	Yds.	Avg.	TD	No.	Yds.	Avg.	TD	TD	2pt.	Pts.	Fum.
2000—Green Bay NFL	15	1	0	0	0.0	0	10	134	13.4	0	0	0	0	0
2001—Green Bay NFL	7	0	0	0	0.0	0	3	32	10.7	1	1	0	6	0
2002—Tampa Bay NFL	1	0	0	0	0.0	0	0	0	0.0	0	0	0	0	0
2003—Tampa Bay NFL	8	5	2	14	7.0	0	33	432	13.1	2	2	0	12	0
2004—Tampa Bay NFL	7	3	0	0	0.0	0	15	207	13.8	0	0	0	0	1
Pro totals (5 years)	38	9	2	14	7.0	0	61	805	13.2	3	3	0	18	1

LEE, DONALD   TE   DOLPHINS

PERSONAL: Born August 31, 1980, in Maben, Miss. ... 6-3/255. ... Full name: Donald Tywon Lee.
HIGH SCHOOL: Maben (Miss.).
COLLEGE: Mississippi State.
TRANSACTIONS/CAREER NOTES: Selected by Miami Dolphins in fifth round (156th pick overall) of 2003 NFL draft. ... Signed by Dolphins (June 16, 2003).
SINGLE GAME HIGHS (regular season): Receptions—3 (January 2, 2005, vs. Baltimore); yards—48 (November 2, 2003, vs. Indianapolis); and touchdown receptions—1 (December 5, 2004, vs. Buffalo).

			RECEIVING				TOTALS			
Year Team	G	GS	No.	Yds.	Avg.	TD	TD	2pt.	Pts.	Fum.
2003—Miami NFL	16	5	7	110	15.7	1	1	0	6	0
2004—Miami NFL	16	10	13	110	8.5	1	1	0	6	2
Pro totals (2 years)	32	15	20	220	11.0	2	2	0	12	2

LEE, JAMES   DT   PACKERS

PERSONAL: Born March 12, 1980, in Salem, Ore. ... 6-5/325. ... Full name: James Franklin Lee.
HIGH SCHOOL: McKay (Salem, Ore.).
JUNIOR COLLEGE: College of the Redwoods (Calif.).
COLLEGE: Oregon State.
TRANSACTIONS/CAREER NOTES: Selected by Green Bay Packers in fifth round (147th pick overall) of 2003 NFL draft. ... Signed by Packers (June 4, 2003). ... On injured reserve with back injury (August 26, 2003-entire season). ... On injured reserve with knee injury (December 23, 2004-remainder of season).

			TOTALS		
Year Team	G	GS	Tk.	Ast.	Sks.
2004—Green Bay NFL	9	1	7	2	1.0

LEE, RESHARD   RB   BILLS

PERSONAL: Born October 12, 1980, in Brunswick, Ga. ... 5-10/220.
HIGH SCHOOL: Brunswick (Ga.).
COLLEGE: Middle Tennessee State.
TRANSACTIONS/CAREER NOTES: Signed as non-drafted free agent by Dallas Cowboys (May 1, 2003). ... Released by Cowboys (August 26, 2003). ... Re-signed by Cowboys to practice squad (December 12, 2003). ... Activated (January 5, 2004). ... Released by Cowboys (May 3, 2005). ... Signed by Buffalo Bills (May 13, 2005).
SINGLE GAME HIGHS (regular season): Attempts—6 (November 7, 2004, vs. Cincinnati); yards—39 (November 7, 2004, vs. Cincinnati); and rushing touchdowns—1 (September 12, 2004, vs. Minnesota).

			RUSHING				KICKOFF RETURNS				TOTALS			
Year Team	G	GS	Att.	Yds.	Avg.	TD	No.	Yds.	Avg.	TD	TD	2pt.	Pts.	Fum.
2004—Dallas NFL	14	0	27	128	4.7	1	41	964	23.5	0	1	0	6	0

LEFTWICH, BYRON   QB   JAGUARS

PERSONAL: Born January 14, 1980, in Washington, DC. ... 6-5/245. ... Full name: Byron A. Leftwich.
HIGH SCHOOL: H.D. Woodson (Washington, D.C.).
COLLEGE: Marshall.
TRANSACTIONS/CAREER NOTES: Selected by Jacksonville Jaguars in first round (seventh pick overall) of 2003 NFL draft. ... Signed by Jaguars (August 13, 2003).
SINGLE GAME HIGHS (regular season): Attempts—54 (October 10, 2004, vs. San Diego); completions—36 (October 10, 2004, vs. San Diego); yards—357 (October 10, 2004, vs. San Diego); and touchdown passes—2 (December 19, 2004, vs. Green Bay).
STATISTICAL PLATEAUS: 300-yard passing games: 2003 (1), 2004 (3). Total: 4.
MISCELLANEOUS: Regular-season record as starting NFL quarterback: 13-14 (.481).

			PASSING									RUSHING				TOTALS		
Year Team	G	GS	Att.	Cmp.	Pct.	Yds.	TD	Int.	Avg.	Skd.	Rat.	Att.	Yds.	Avg.	TD	TD	2pt.	Pts.
2003—Jacksonville NFL	15	13	418	239	57.2	2819	14	16	6.74	19	73.0	25	108	4.3	2	2	0	12
2004—Jacksonville NFL	14	14	441	267	60.5	2941	15	10	6.67	25	82.2	39	148	3.8	2	2	0	12
Pro totals (2 years)	29	27	859	506	58.9	5760	29	26	6.71	44	77.8	64	256	4.0	4	4	0	24

LEGREE, LANCE DT JETS

PERSONAL: Born December 22, 1977, in Charleston, S.C. ... 6-1/300.
HIGH SCHOOL: St. Stephens (S.C.).
COLLEGE: Notre Dame.
TRANSACTIONS/CAREER NOTES: Signed as non-drafted free agent by New York Giants (April 27, 2001). ... Granted unconditional free agency (March 2, 2005). ... Signed by New York Jets (March 4, 2005).

			TOTALS		
Year Team	G	GS	Tk.	Ast.	Sks.
2001—New York Giants NFL	13	2	15	4	0.0
2002—New York Giants NFL	15	10	18	12	0.0
2003—New York Giants NFL	16	2	15	5	2.0
2004—New York Giants NFL	15	7	22	14	2.0
Pro totals (4 years)	59	21	70	35	4.0

LEHAN, MICHAEL CB BROWNS

PERSONAL: Born November 25, 1979, in Hopkins, Minn. ... 6-0/190.
HIGH SCHOOL: Hopkins (Minn.).
COLLEGE: Minnesota.
TRANSACTIONS/CAREER NOTES: Selected by Cleveland Browns in fifth round (152nd pick overall) of 2003 NFL draft. ... Signed by Browns (August 1, 2003).

			TOTALS			INTERCEPTIONS			
Year Team	G	GS	Tk.	Ast.	Sks.	No.	Yds.	Avg.	TD
2003—Cleveland NFL	12	2	14	2	0.0	0	0	0.0	0
2004—Cleveland NFL	10	2	10	4	0.0	0	0	0.0	0
Pro totals (2 years)	22	4	24	6	0.0	0	0	0.0	0

LEHMAN, TEDDY LB LIONS

PERSONAL: Born November 18, 1981, in Tulsa, Okla. ... 6-2/238.
HIGH SCHOOL: Fort Gibson (Okla.).
COLLEGE: Oklahoma.
TRANSACTIONS/CAREER NOTES: Selected by Detroit Lions in second round (37th pick overall) of 2004 NFL draft. ... Signed by Lions (July 28, 2004).
HONORS: Chuck Bednarik Award winner (2003). ... Dick Butkus Award winner (2003). ... Named linebacker on THE SPORTING NEWS college All-America first team (2002 and 2003).

			TOTALS			INTERCEPTIONS			
Year Team	G	GS	Tk.	Ast.	Sks.	No.	Yds.	Avg.	TD
2004—Detroit NFL	16	16	73	24	1.0	1	1	1.0	0

LEHR, MATT C FALCONS

PERSONAL: Born April 25, 1979, in Jacksonville, Fla. ... 6-2/293. ... Full name: Matthew Steven Lehr.
HIGH SCHOOL: Woodbridge (Va.).
COLLEGE: Virginia Tech.
TRANSACTIONS/CAREER NOTES: Selected by Dallas Cowboys in fifth round (137th pick overall) of 2001 NFL draft. ... Signed by Cowboys (July 21, 2001). ... Granted free agency (March 3, 2004). ... Re-signed by Cowboys (April 14, 2004). ... Claimed on waivers by St. Louis Rams (December 29, 2004). ... Granted unconditional free agency (March 2, 2005). ... Signed by Atlanta Falcons (March 14, 2005).
PLAYING EXPERIENCE: Dallas NFL, 2001-2004. ... Games/Games started: 2001 (8/0), 2002 (12/4), 2003 (16/16), 2004 (7/2). Total: 43/22.

LEISLE, RODNEY DT SAINTS

PERSONAL: Born February 5, 1981, in Fresno, Calif. ... 6-3/315. ... Full name: Rodney Allen Leisle.
HIGH SCHOOL: Ridgeview (Bakersfield, Calif.).
COLLEGE: UCLA.
TRANSACTIONS/CAREER NOTES: Selected by New Orleans Saints in fifth round (139th pick overall) of 2004 NFL draft. ... Signed by Saints (July 29, 2004).
HONORS: Named defensive lineman on THE SPORTING NEWS Freshman All-America third team (2000).

			TOTALS			INTERCEPTIONS			
Year Team	G	GS	Tk.	Ast.	Sks.	No.	Yds.	Avg.	TD
2004—New Orleans NFL	2	0	1	0	0.0	0	0	0.0	0

LELIE, ASHLEY WR BRONCOS

PERSONAL: Born February 16, 1980, in Bellflower, Calif. ... 6-3/200.
HIGH SCHOOL: Radford (Honolulu, Hawaii).
COLLEGE: Hawaii.
TRANSACTIONS/CAREER NOTES: Selected after junior season by Denver Broncos in first round (19th pick overall) of 2002 NFL draft. ... Signed by Broncos (July 25, 2002).
HONORS: Named wide receiver on THE SPORTING NEWS college All-America third team (2001).

SINGLE GAME HIGHS (regular season): Receptions—8 (November 11, 2002, vs. Oakland); yards—115 (December 21, 2003, vs. Indianapolis); and touchdown receptions—1 (January 2, 2005, vs. Indianapolis).
STATISTICAL PLATEAUS: 100-yard receiving games: 2002 (1), 2003 (2), 2004 (1). Total: 4.

			RUSHING				RECEIVING				TOTALS		
Year Team	G	GS	Att.	Yds.	Avg.	TD	No.	Yds.	Avg.	TD	TD	2pt.	Pts.	Fum.
2002—Denver NFL	16	1	4	40	10.0	0	35	525	15.0	2	2	0	12	0
2003—Denver NFL	16	10	8	43	5.4	0	37	628	17.0	2	2	0	12	0
2004—Denver NFL	16	16	3	5	1.7	0	54	1084	*20.1	7	7	0	42	0
Pro totals (3 years)	48	27	15	88	5.9	0	126	2237	17.8	11	11	0	66	0

LEMONS, DEVIN LB REDSKINS

PERSONAL: Born March 20, 1979, in Bryan, Texas. ... 6-2/232.
HIGH SCHOOL: Pampa (Texas).
COLLEGE: Texas Tech.
TRANSACTIONS/CAREER NOTES: Signed as non-drafted free agent by Chicago Bears (April 2001). ... Released by Bears (September 1, 2001). ... Signed by Bears to practice squad (September 3, 2001). ... Released by Bears practice squad (October 9, 2001). ... Re-signed by Bears (January 22, 2002). ... Released by Bears (August 26, 2002). ... Signed by Miami Dolphins (January 15, 2003). ... Released by Dolphins (August 23, 2003). ... Signed by Washington Redskins (March 31, 2004). ... Released by Redskins (August 30, 2004). ... Re-signed by Redskins to practice squad (September 15, 2004). ... Activated (September 17, 2004). ... Released by Redskins (September 21, 2004). ... Re-signed by Redskins to practice squad (November 17, 2004). ... Activated (December 31, 2004).

			TOTALS			INTERCEPTIONS			
Year Team	G	GS	Tk.	Ast.	Sks.	No.	Yds.	Avg.	TD
2004—Washington NFL	1	0	0	0	0.0	0	0	0.0	0

LENON, PARIS LB PACKERS

PERSONAL: Born November 26, 1977, in Lynchburg, Va. ... 6-2/245. ... Full name: Paris Michael Lenon.
HIGH SCHOOL: Heritage (Lynchburg, Va.).
COLLEGE: Richmond.
TRANSACTIONS/CAREER NOTES: Signed as non-drafted free agent by Carolina Panthers (April 26, 2000). ... Released by Panthers (June 9, 2000). ... Signed by Green Bay Packers (April 26, 2001). ... Released by Packers (July 24, 2001). ... Signed by Seattle Seahawks (August 16, 2001). ... Released by Seahawks (August 27, 2001). ... Signed by Packers to practice squad (December 27, 2001). ... Assigned by Packers to Amsterdam Admirals in 2002 NFL Europe enhancement allocation program (February 12, 2002). ... Granted free agency (March 3, 2004). ... Re-signed by Packers (April 22, 2004). ... Granted free agency (March 2, 2005). ... Re-signed by Packers (April 13, 2005).

			TOTALS			INTERCEPTIONS			
Year Team	G	GS	Tk.	Ast.	Sks.	No.	Yds.	Avg.	TD
2002—Green Bay NFL	16	0	3	0	0.0	0	0	0.0	0
2003—Green Bay NFL	16	0	4	4	0.0	0	0	0.0	0
2004—Green Bay NFL	16	4	15	6	0.0	0	0	0.0	0
Pro totals (3 years)	48	4	22	10	0.0	0	0	0.0	0

LEPSIS, MATT T BRONCOS

PERSONAL: Born January 13, 1974, in Conroe, Texas. ... 6-4/290. ... Full name: Matthew Lepsis.
HIGH SCHOOL: Frisco (Texas).
COLLEGE: Colorado.
TRANSACTIONS/CAREER NOTES: Signed as non-drafted free agent by Denver Broncos (April 22, 1997). ... On non-football injury list with knee injury (July 16, 1997-entire season). ... Assigned by Broncos to Barcelona Dragons in 1998 NFL Europe enhancement allocation program (February 18, 1998). ... Granted free agency (March 2, 2001). ... Re-signed by Broncos (March 21, 2001).
PLAYING EXPERIENCE: Denver NFL, 1997-2004. ... Games/Games started: 1998 (16/0), 1999 (16/16), 2000 (16/16), 2001 (16/16), 2002 (16/15), 2003 (16/16), 2004 (16/16), Total: 112/95.
CHAMPIONSHIP GAME EXPERIENCE: Played in AFC championship game (1998 season). ... Member of Super Bowl championship team (1998 season).

LEVENS, DORSEY RB

PERSONAL: Born May 21, 1970, in Syracuse, N.Y. ... 6-1/230. ... Full name: Herbert Dorsey Levens.
HIGH SCHOOL: Nottingham (Syracuse, N.Y.).
COLLEGE: Georgia Tech.
TRANSACTIONS/CAREER NOTES: Selected by Green Bay Packers in fifth round (149th pick overall) of 1994 NFL draft. ... Signed by Packers (June 9, 1994). ... Granted free agency (February 14, 1997). ... Re-signed by Packers (June 20, 1997). ... Designated by Packers as franchise player (February 13, 1998). ... Signed by Packers (August 30, 1998). ... Released by Packers (February 28, 2002). ... Signed by Philadelphia Eagles (July 11, 2002). ... Granted unconditional free agency (February 28, 2003). ... Signed by New York Giants (April 7, 2003). ... Released by Giants (February 25, 2004). ... Re-signed by Eagles (August 23, 2004). ... Released by Eagles (September 5, 2004). ... Re-signed by Eagles (September 14, 2004). ... Granted unconditional free agency (March 2, 2005).
CHAMPIONSHIP GAME EXPERIENCE: Played in NFC championship game (1995-97, 2002 and 2004 seasons). ... Member of Super Bowl championship team (1996 season). ... Played in Super Bowl 32 (1997 season) and Super Bowl 39 (2004 season).
HONORS: Played in Pro Bowl (1997 season).
SINGLE GAME HIGHS (regular season): Attempts—33 (November 23, 1997, vs. Dallas); yards—190 (November 23, 1997, vs. Dallas); and rushing touchdowns—4 (January 2, 2000, vs. Arizona).
STATISTICAL PLATEAUS: 100-yard rushing games: 1997 (6), 1998 (1), 1999 (3). Total: 10.

L

Year—Team	G	GS	RUSHING				RECEIVING				KICKOFF RETURNS				TOTALS			
			Att.	Yds.	Avg.	TD	No.	Yds.	Avg.	TD	No.	Yds.	Avg.	TD	TD	2pt.	Pts.	Fum.
1994—Green Bay NFL	14	0	5	15	3.0	0	1	9	9.0	0	2	31	15.5	0	0	0	0	0
1995—Green Bay NFL	15	12	36	120	3.3	3	48	434	9.0	4	0	0	0.0	0	7	0	42	0
1996—Green Bay NFL	16	1	121	566	4.7	5	31	226	7.3	5	5	84	16.8	0	10	0	60	2
1997—Green Bay NFL	16	16	329	1435	4.4	7	53	370	7.0	5	0	0	0.0	0	12	1	74	5
1998—Green Bay NFL	7	4	115	378	3.3	1	27	162	6.0	0	0	0	0.0	0	1	0	6	0
1999—Green Bay NFL	14	14	279	1034	3.7	9	71	573	8.1	1	0	0	0.0	0	10	0	60	5
2000—Green Bay NFL	5	5	77	224	2.9	3	16	146	9.1	0	0	0	0.0	0	3	0	18	0
2001—Green Bay NFL	15	1	44	165	3.8	0	24	159	6.6	1	14	362	25.9	0	1	0	6	0
2002—Philadelphia NFL	16	0	75	411	5.5	1	19	124	6.5	1	1	24	24.0	0	2	0	12	1
2003—New York Giants NFL	11	0	68	197	2.9	3	5	39	7.8	0	0	0	0.0	0	3	0	18	0
2004—Philadelphia NFL	15	5	94	410	4.4	4	9	92	10.2	0	0	0	0.0	0	4	0	24	0
Pro totals (11 years)	144	58	1243	4955	4.0	36	304	2334	7.7	17	22	501	22.8	0	53	1	320	13

LEVERETTE, OTIS   DE   SEAHAWKS

PERSONAL: Born May 31, 1978, in Americus, Ga. ... 6-6/278. ... Full name: Otis Catrell Leverette.
HIGH SCHOOL: Americus (Ga.).
JUNIOR COLLEGE: Middle Georgia College.
COLLEGE: Alabama-Birmingham.
TRANSACTIONS/CAREER NOTES: Selected by Miami Dolphins in sixth round (187th pick overall) of 2001 NFL draft. ... Signed by Dolphins (July 12, 2001). ... Claimed on waivers by Washington Redskins (September 3, 2001). ... Claimed on waivers by San Diego Chargers (November 19, 2002). ... Granted free agency (March 3, 2004). ... Re-signed by Chargers (May 13, 2004). ... Released by Chargers (September 5, 2004). ... Claimed on waivers by San Francisco 49ers (September 6, 2004). ... Released by 49ers (November 9, 2004). ... Signed by Seattle Seahawks to practice squad (November 12, 2004).

Year—Team	G	GS	TOTALS			INTERCEPTIONS			
			Tk.	Ast.	Sks.	No.	Yds.	Avg.	TD
2001—Washington NFL	4	0	0	0	0.0	1	1	1.0	0
2002—Washington NFL	1	0	1	0	0.0	0	0	0.0	0
2003—San Diego NFL	7	0	17	6	1.0	0	0	0.0	0
2004—San Francisco NFL	5	1	7	0	1.0	0	0	0.0	0
Pro totals (4 years)	17	1	25	6	2.0	1	1	1.0	0

LEWIS, ALEX   LB   LIONS

PERSONAL: Born June 11, 1981, in Delran, N.J. ... 6-0/227.
HIGH SCHOOL: Delran (N.J.).
JUNIOR COLLEGE: SUNY-Morrisville (N.Y.).
COLLEGE: Wisconsin.
TRANSACTIONS/CAREER NOTES: Selected by Detroit Lions in fifth round (140th pick overall) of 2004 NFL draft. ... Signed by Lions (July 29, 2004).

Year—Team	G	GS	TOTALS			INTERCEPTIONS			
			Tk.	Ast.	Sks.	No.	Yds.	Avg.	TD
2004—Detroit NFL	15	1	35	14	2.0	1	33	33.0	0

LEWIS, CHAD   TE

PERSONAL: Born October 5, 1971, in Fort Dix, N.J. ... 6-6/252. ... Full name: Chad Wayne Lewis.
HIGH SCHOOL: Orem (Utah).
COLLEGE: Brigham Young.
TRANSACTIONS/CAREER NOTES: Signed as non-drafted free agent by Philadelphia Eagles (April 23, 1997). ... Released by Eagles (September 15, 1998). ... Signed by St. Louis Rams (December 9, 1998). ... Inactive for three games with Rams (1998). ... Claimed on waivers by Eagles (November 16, 1999). ... Granted free agency (February 11, 2000). ... Re-signed by Eagles (March 17, 2000). ... On injured reserve with foot injury (January 25, 2005-remainder of 2004 season playoffs). ... Granted unconditional free agency (March 2, 2005).
CHAMPIONSHIP GAME EXPERIENCE: Played in NFC championship game (2001-2004 seasons).
HONORS: Played in Pro Bowl (2000-2002 seasons).
SINGLE GAME HIGHS (regular season): Receptions—9 (December 24, 2000, vs. Cincinnati); yards—100 (December 10, 2000, vs. Cleveland); and touchdown receptions—2 (December 30, 2001, vs. New York Giants).
STATISTICAL PLATEAUS: 100-yard receiving games: 2000 (1). Total: 1.

Year—Team	G	GS	RECEIVING				TOTALS			
			No.	Yds.	Avg.	TD	TD	2pt.	Pts.	Fum.
1997—Philadelphia NFL	16	3	12	94	7.8	4	4	0	24	0
1998—Philadelphia NFL	2	0	0	0	0.0	0	0	0	0	0
1999—St. Louis NFL	6	0	1	12	12.0	0	0	0	0	0
—Philadelphia NFL	6	4	7	76	10.9	3	3	0	18	0
2000—Philadelphia NFL	16	16	69	735	10.7	3	3	0	18	0
2001—Philadelphia NFL	15	15	41	422	10.3	6	6	0	36	2
2002—Philadelphia NFL	16	16	42	398	9.5	3	3	2	22	2
2003—Philadelphia NFL	16	14	23	293	12.7	1	1	0	6	0
2004—Philadelphia NFL	15	9	29	267	9.2	3	3	0	18	0
Pro totals (8 years)	108	77	224	2297	10.3	23	23	2	142	4

LEWIS, DAMIONE — DT — RAMS

PERSONAL: Born March 1, 1978, in Sulphur Springs, Texas. ... 6-2/301. ... Full name: Damione Ramon Lewis.
HIGH SCHOOL: Sulphur Springs (Texas).
COLLEGE: Miami (Fla.).
TRANSACTIONS/CAREER NOTES: Selected by St. Louis Rams in first round (12th pick overall) of 2001 NFL draft. ... Signed by Rams (July 27, 2001). ... On injured reserve with foot injury (November 20, 2001-remainder of season).
HONORS: Named defensive tackle on THE SPORTING NEWS college All-America third team (2000).

				TOTALS			INTERCEPTIONS			
Year Team	G	GS	Tk.	Ast.	Sks.	No.	Yds.	Avg.	TD	
2001—St. Louis NFL	9	3	9	1	0.0	0	0	0.0	0	
2002—St. Louis NFL	16	2	14	6	4.0	0	0	0.0	0	
2003—St. Louis NFL	12	7	12	4	0.5	0	0	0.0	0	
2004—St. Louis NFL	16	10	26	10	5.0	0	0	0.0	0	
Pro totals (4 years)	53	22	61	21	9.5	0	0	0.0	0	

LEWIS, GREG — WR — EAGLES

PERSONAL: Born February 12, 1980, in Chicago, Ill. ... 6-0/180. ... Full name: Gregory Alan Lewis Jr.
HIGH SCHOOL: Rich South (Matteson, Ill.).
COLLEGE: Illinois.
TRANSACTIONS/CAREER NOTES: Signed as non-drafted free agent by Philadelphia Eagles (April 28, 2003).
CHAMPIONSHIP GAME EXPERIENCE: Played in NFC championship game (2003 and 2004 seasons). ... Played in Super Bowl 39 (2004 season).
SINGLE GAME HIGHS (regular season): Receptions—6 (January 2, 2005, vs. Cincinnati); yards—53 (January 2, 2005, vs. Cincinnati); and touchdown receptions—0.

			RUSHING				RECEIVING				TOTALS			
Year Team	G	GS	Att.	Yds.	Avg.	TD	No.	Yds.	Avg.	TD	TD	2pt.	Pts.	Fum.
2003—Philadelphia NFL	11	0	0	0	0.0	0	6	95	15.8	0	0	0	0	0
2004—Philadelphia NFL	16	3	4	16	4.0	0	17	183	10.8	0	0	0	0	0
Pro totals (2 years)	27	3	4	16	4.0	0	23	278	12.1	0	0	0	0	0

LEWIS, JAMAL — RB — RAVENS

PERSONAL: Born August 29, 1979, in Atlanta, Ga. ... 5-11/245. ... Full name: Jamal Lafitte Lewis.
HIGH SCHOOL: Douglass (Atlanta).
COLLEGE: Tennessee.
TRANSACTIONS/CAREER NOTES: Selected after junior season by Baltimore Ravens in first round (fifth pick overall) of 2000 NFL draft. ... Signed by Ravens (July 24, 2000). ... On injured reserve with knee injury (August 28, 2001-entire season). ... On suspended list for violating league substance abuse policy (November 17, 2001). ... Suspended by NFL for two games without pay and fined an additional two weeks' salary for violating league substance abuse policy (October 8, 2004).
CHAMPIONSHIP GAME EXPERIENCE: Played in AFC championship game (2000 season). ... Member of Super Bowl championship team (2000 season).
HONORS: Named College Football Freshman of the Year by THE SPORTING NEWS (1997). ... Named running back on THE SPORTING NEWS NFL All-Pro team (2003). ... Played in Pro Bowl (2003 season).
RECORDS: Holds NFL record for most yards rushing in a game—295 (September 14, 2003, vs. Cleveland).
SINGLE GAME HIGHS (regular season): Attempts—34 (January 2, 2005, vs. Miami); yards—295 (September 14, 2003, vs. Cleveland); and rushing touchdowns—3 (December 7, 2003, vs. Cincinnati).
STATISTICAL PLATEAUS: 100-yard rushing games: 2000 (5), 2002 (5), 2003 (12), 2004 (4). Total: 26. 100-yard receiving games: 2002 (1). Total: 1.
MISCELLANEOUS: Holds Baltimore Ravens all-time records for most yards rushing (5,763), most rushing touchdowns (33) and most touchdowns (34).

			RUSHING				RECEIVING				TOTALS			
Year Team	G	GS	Att.	Yds.	Avg.	TD	No.	Yds.	Avg.	TD	TD	2pt.	Pts.	Fum.
2000—Baltimore NFL	16	13	309	1364	4.4	6	27	296	11.0	0	6	1	38	6
2001—Baltimore NFL	Did not play.													
2002—Baltimore NFL	16	15	308	1327	4.3	6	47	442	9.4	1	7	0	42	8
2003—Baltimore NFL	16	16	387	*2066	5.3	14	26	205	7.9	0	14	0	84	8
2004—Baltimore NFL	12	12	235	1006	4.3	7	10	116	11.6	0	7	0	42	2
Pro totals (4 years)	60	56	1239	5763	4.7	33	110	1059	9.6	1	34	1	206	24

LEWIS, JERMAINE — WR/KR

PERSONAL: Born October 16, 1974, in Lanham, Md. ... 5-7/183. ... Full name: Jermaine Edward Lewis.
HIGH SCHOOL: Eleanor Roosevelt (Greenbelt, Md.).
COLLEGE: Maryland.
TRANSACTIONS/CAREER NOTES: Selected by Baltimore Ravens in fifth round (153rd pick overall) of 1996 NFL draft. ... Signed by Ravens (July 18, 1996). ... Selected by Houston Texans from Ravens in NFL expansion draft (February 18, 2002). ... Released by Texans (February 20, 2003). ... Signed by Jacksonville Jaguars (March 20, 2003). ... On injured reserve with knee injury (September 16, 2003-remainder of season). ... Released by Jaguars (December 13, 2004).
CHAMPIONSHIP GAME EXPERIENCE: Played in AFC championship game (2000 season). ... Member of Super Bowl championship team (2000 season).
HONORS: Named punt returner on THE SPORTING NEWS NFL All-Pro team (1998 and 2001). ... Played in Pro Bowl (1998 and 2001 seasons).

RECORDS: Shares NFL single-game records for most touchdowns by punt returns—2; (December 24, 2000, vs. New York Jets, and December 7, 1997, vs. Seattle) and most touchdowns by combined kick return—2 (December 7, 1997, vs. Seattle and also on December 24, 2000, vs. New York Jets).

SINGLE GAME HIGHS (regular season): Receptions—8 (September 21, 1997, vs. Tennessee); yards—124 (September 21, 1997, vs. Tennessee); and touchdown receptions—2 (December 5, 1999, vs. Tennessee).

STATISTICAL PLATEAUS: 100-yard receiving games: 1997 (2), 1998 (2). Total: 4.

			RUSHING				RECEIVING				PUNT RETURNS				KICKOFF RETURNS				TOTALS		
Year Team	G	GS	Att.	Yds.	Avg.	TD	No.	Yds.	Avg.	TD	No.	Yds.	Avg.	TD	No.	Yds.	Avg.	TD	TD	2pt.	Pts.
1996—Bal. NFL	16	1	1	-3	-3.0	0	5	78	15.6	1	36	339	9.4	0	41	883	21.5	0	1	0	6
1997—Bal. NFL	14	7	3	35	11.7	0	42	648	15.4	6	28	437	*15.6	2	41	905	22.1	0	8	0	48
1998—Bal. NFL	13	13	5	20	4.0	0	41	784	19.1	6	32	405	12.7	†2	6	145	24.2	0	8	0	48
1999—Bal. NFL	15	6	5	11	2.2	0	25	281	11.2	2	*57	452	7.9	0	8	158	19.8	0	2	0	12
2000—Bal. NFL	15	1	3	38	12.7	0	19	161	8.5	1	36	578	*16.1	†2	1	23	23.0	0	3	0	18
2001—Bal. NFL	15	2	9	33	3.7	0	4	32	8.0	0	*42	*519	12.4	0	42	1039	24.7	0	0	0	0
2002—Hou. NFL	12	1	3	8	2.7	0	2	41	20.5	0	36	280	7.8	0	46	961	20.9	0	0	0	0
2003—Jac. NFL	2	0	1	6	6.0	0	4	100	25.0	1	5	45	9.0	0	6	111	18.5	0	1	0	6
2004—Jac. NFL	9	0	0	0	0.0	0	1	4	4.0	0	23	227	9.9	0	21	386	18.4	0	0	0	0
Pro totals (9 years)	111	31	30	148	4.9	0	143	2129	14.9	17	295	3282	11.1	6	212	4611	21.8	0	23	0	138

LEWIS, KEITH   DB   49ERS

PERSONAL: Born October 20, 1981, in Sacramento, Calif. ... 6-0/202. ... Full name: Keith D'Andre Lewis.
HIGH SCHOOL: Valley (Sacramento, Calif.).
COLLEGE: Oregon.
TRANSACTIONS/CAREER NOTES: Selected by San Francisco 49ers in sixth round (198th pick overall) of 2004 NFL draft. ... Signed by 49ers (July 6, 2004).

			TOTALS			INTERCEPTIONS			
Year Team	G	GS	Tk.	Ast.	Sks.	No.	Yds.	Avg.	TD
2004—San Francisco NFL	16	0	0	1	0.0	0	0	0.0	0

LEWIS, KEVIN   LB   GIANTS

PERSONAL: Born October 6, 1978, in Orlando, Fla. ... 6-1/235.
HIGH SCHOOL: Jones (Orlando, Fla.).
COLLEGE: Duke.
TRANSACTIONS/CAREER NOTES: Signed by New York Giants as non-drafted free agent (April 20, 2000). ... Released by Giants (September 2, 2001). ... Re-signed by Giants to practice squad (September 3, 2001). ... Activated (November 4, 2001). ... Granted free agency (February 28, 2003). ... Re-signed by Giants (March 6, 2003).
CHAMPIONSHIP GAME EXPERIENCE: Member of Giants for Super Bowl 35 (2000 season); inactive.

			TOTALS			INTERCEPTIONS			
Year Team	G	GS	Tk.	Ast.	Sks.	No.	Yds.	Avg.	TD
2000—New York Giants NFL	6	0	1	0	0.0	0	0	0.0	0
2001—New York Giants NFL	9	0	0	0	0.0	0	0	0.0	0
2002—New York Giants NFL	15	2	10	3	1.0	0	0	0.0	0
2003—New York Giants NFL	16	0	1	2	0.0	0	0	0.0	0
2004—New York Giants NFL	16	16	62	26	1.0	0	0	0.0	0
Pro totals (5 years)	62	18	74	31	2.0	0	0	0.0	0

LEWIS, MICHAEL   WR   SAINTS

PERSONAL: Born November 14, 1971, in New Orleans, La. ... 5-8/173. ... Full name: Michael Lee Lewis.
HIGH SCHOOL: Grace King (Metairie, La.).
COLLEGE: None.
TRANSACTIONS/CAREER NOTES: Signed as non-drafted free agent by Philadelphia Eagles (July 14, 2000). ... Released by Eagles (August 21, 2000). ... Signed by New Orleans Saints (January 9, 2001). ... Assigned by Saints to Rhein Fire in 2001 NFL Europe enhancement allocation program (February 17, 2001). ... Released by Saints (October 30, 2001). ... Re-signed by Saints (December 21, 2001).
HONORS: Played in Pro Bowl (2002 season). ... Named kick returner on the THE SPORTING NEWS NFL All-Pro team (2002).
RECORDS: Holds NFL single-season record for most combined kick returns—114 (2002); and most yards from combined kick returns—2,432 (2002).
SINGLE GAME HIGHS (regular season): Receptions—4 (November 16, 2003, vs. Atlanta); yards—114 (November 24, 2002, vs. Cleveland); and touchdown receptions—1 (November 2, 2003, vs. Tampa Bay).
STATISTICAL PLATEAUS: 100-yard receiving games: 2002 (1). Total: 1.

			RECEIVING				PUNT RETURNS				KICKOFF RETURNS				TOTALS			
Year Team	G	GS	No.	Yds.	Avg.	TD	No.	Yds.	Avg.	TD	No.	Yds.	Avg.	TD	TD	2pt.	Pts.	Fum.
2001—New Orleans NFL	8	0	0	0	0.0	0	14	81	5.8	0	32	762	23.8	0	0	0	0	6
2002—New Orleans NFL	16	0	8	200	25.0	0	44	*625	14.2	1	*70	*1807	25.8	†2	3	0	18	6
2003—New Orleans NFL	13	0	12	226	18.8	0	30	275	9.2	0	45	1068	23.7	0	1	0	6	2
2004—New Orleans NFL	14	1	8	127	15.9	0	34	382	11.2	0	51	1215	23.8	1	1	0	6	1
Pro totals (4 years)	51	2	28	553	19.8	1	122	1363	11.2	1	198	4852	24.5	3	5	0	30	15

LEWIS, MICHAEL   S   EAGLES

PERSONAL: Born April 29, 1980, in Houston, Texas. ... 6-1/211.
HIGH SCHOOL: Lamar Consolidated (Richmond, Texas).
COLLEGE: Colorado.

TRANSACTIONS/CAREER NOTES: Selected by Philadelphia Eagles in second round (58th pick overall) of 2002 NFL draft. ... Signed by Eagles (June 25, 2002).
CHAMPIONSHIP GAME EXPERIENCE: Played in NFC championship game (2002, 2003 and 2004 seasons). ... Played in Super Bowl 39 (2004 season).
HONORS: Named safety on THE SPORTING NEWS college All-America third team (2001). ... Played in Pro Bowl (2004 season).

				TOTALS			INTERCEPTIONS			
Year Team	G	GS	Tk.	Ast.	Sks.	No.	Yds.	Avg.	TD
2002—Philadelphia NFL	14	4	33	5	1.0	1	0	0.0	0
2003—Philadelphia NFL	16	16	67	19	2.0	3	31	10.3	0
2004—Philadelphia NFL	16	16	76	14	0.0	1	0	0.0	0
Pro totals (3 years)	46	36	176	38	3.0	5	31	6.2	0

LEWIS, RAY   LB   RAVENS

PERSONAL: Born May 15, 1975, in Bartow, Fla. ... 6-1/245. ... Full name: Ray Anthony Lewis.
HIGH SCHOOL: Kathleen (Lakeland, Fla.).
COLLEGE: Miami (Fla.).
TRANSACTIONS/CAREER NOTES: Selected after junior season by Baltimore Ravens in first round (26th pick overall) of 1996 NFL draft. ... Signed by Ravens (July 15, 1996). ... On injured reserve with shoulder injury (November 26, 2002-remainder of season).
CHAMPIONSHIP GAME EXPERIENCE: Played in AFC championship game (2000 season). ... Member of Super Bowl championship team (2000 season).
HONORS: Named linebacker on THE SPORTING NEWS college All-America second team (1995). ... Played in Pro Bowl (1997, 1998, 2000, 2001 and 2003 seasons). ... Named linebacker on THE SPORTING NEWS NFL All-Pro team (1998-2001 and 2003-2004). ... Named to play in Pro Bowl (1999 season); replaced by Junior Seau due to personal reasons. ... Named Most Valuable Player of Super Bowl 35 (2000 season). ... Named to play in Pro Bowl (2004 season); replaced by Tedy Bruschi due to injury.

				TOTALS			INTERCEPTIONS			
Year Team	G	GS	Tk.	Ast.	Sks.	No.	Yds.	Avg.	TD
1996—Baltimore NFL	14	13	95	15	2.5	1	0	0.0	0
1997—Baltimore NFL	16	16	156	28	4.0	1	18	18.0	0
1998—Baltimore NFL	14	14	101	19	3.0	2	25	12.5	0
1999—Baltimore NFL	16	16	131	37	3.5	3	97	32.3	0
2000—Baltimore NFL	16	16	107	30	3.0	2	1	0.5	0
2001—Baltimore NFL	16	16	114	48	3.5	3	115	38.3	0
2002—Baltimore NFL	5	5	43	15	0.0	2	4	2.0	0
2003—Baltimore NFL	16	16	121	42	1.5	8	99	16.5	1
2004—Baltimore NFL	15	15	101	46	1.0	0	0	0.0	0
Pro totals (9 years)	128	127	969	280	22.0	20	359	18.0	1

LIGHT, MATT   T   PATRIOTS

PERSONAL: Born June 23, 1978, in Greenville, Ohio. ... 6-4/305. ... Full name: Matthew Charles Light.
HIGH SCHOOL: Greenville (Ohio).
COLLEGE: Purdue.
TRANSACTIONS/CAREER NOTES: Selected by New England Patriots in second round (48th pick overall) of 2001 NFL draft. ... Signed by Patriots (July 22, 2001).
PLAYING EXPERIENCE: New England NFL, 2001-2004. ... Games/Games started: 2001 (14/12), 2002 (16/16), 2003 (16/16), 2004 (16/16). Total: 62/60.
CHAMPIONSHIP GAME EXPERIENCE: Played in AFC championship game (2001, 2003 and 2004 seasons). ... Member of Super Bowl championship team (2001, 2003 and 2004 seasons).
HONORS: Named offensive tackle on THE SPORTING NEWS college All-America third team (2000).

LILJA, RYAN   C   COLTS

PERSONAL: Born October 15, 1981, in Kansas City, Mo. ... 6-2/285.
COLLEGE: Kansas State.
TRANSACTIONS/CAREER NOTES: Signed as non-drafted free agent by Kansas City Chiefs (April 27, 2004). ... Claimed on waivers by Indianapolis Colts (September 5, 2004).
PLAYING EXPERIENCE: Indianapolis NFL, 2004. ... Games/Games started: 2004 (7/6). Total: 7/6.

LINDELL, RIAN   K   BILLS

PERSONAL: Born January 20, 1977, in Vancouver, Wash. ... 6-3/235. ... Full name: Rian David Lindell.
HIGH SCHOOL: Mountain View (Vancouver, Wash.).
COLLEGE: Washington State.
TRANSACTIONS/CAREER NOTES: Signed as non-drafted free agent by Seattle Seahawks (September 26, 2000). ... Granted free agency (February 28, 2003). ... Signed by Buffalo Bills (March 24, 2003).

		FIELD GOALS							TOTALS		
Year Team	G	1-29	30-39	40-49	50+	Tot.	Pct.	Lg.	XPM	XPA	Pts.
2000—Seattle NFL	12	4-5	1-1	7-8	3-3	15-17	88.2	52	25	25	70
2001—Seattle NFL	16	7-8	4-5	6-14	3-5	20-32	62.5	54	33	33	93
2002—Seattle NFL	16	10-10	8-10	4-5	1-4	23-29	79.3	52	38	38	107
2003—Buffalo NFL	16	11-12	3-3	3-7	0-2	17-24	70.8	44	24	24	75
2004—Buffalo NFL	16	13-14	10-11	1-3	0-0	24-28	85.7	43	45	45	117
Pro totals (5 years)	76	45-49	26-30	21-37	7-14	99-130	76.2	54	165	165	462

LITTLE, EARL   S   PACKERS

PERSONAL: Born March 10, 1973, in Miami, Fla. ... 6-1/205. ... Full name: Earl Jerome Little.
HIGH SCHOOL: North Miami.
COLLEGE: Miami (Fla.).
TRANSACTIONS/CAREER NOTES: Signed as non-drafted free agent by Miami Dolphins (April 24, 1997). ... Released by Dolphins (August 24, 1997). ... Re-signed by Dolphins to practice squad (August 26, 1997). ... Released by Dolphins (August 29, 1997). ... Signed by New Orleans Saints to practice squad (October 1, 1997). ... Claimed on waivers by Cleveland Browns (October 25, 1999). ... Granted unconditional free agency (February 28, 2003). ... Re-signed by Browns (March 13, 2003). ... Released by Browns (April 1, 2005). ... Signed by Green Bay Packers (April 15, 2005).

Year Team	G	GS	TOTALS Tk.	Ast.	Sks.	INTERCEPTIONS No.	Yds.	Avg.	TD
1998—New Orleans NFL	16	0	0	0	0.0	0	0	0.0	0
1999—New Orleans NFL	1	0	0	0	0.0	0	0	0.0	0
—Cleveland NFL	9	0	5	0	0.0	1	0	0.0	0
2000—Cleveland NFL	16	0	24	2	0.0	1	7	7.0	0
2001—Cleveland NFL	16	16	65	17	1.0	5	33	6.6	0
2002—Cleveland NFL	13	9	42	19	0.0	4	17	4.3	0
2003—Cleveland NFL	16	16	42	18	0.0	6	41	6.8	0
2004—Cleveland NFL	16	11	37	11	0.0	1	28	28.0	0
Pro totals (7 years)	103	52	215	67	1.0	18	126	7.0	0

LITTLE, LEONARD   DE   RAMS

PERSONAL: Born October 19, 1974, in Asheville, N.C. ... 6-3/261. ... Full name: Leonard Antonio Little.
HIGH SCHOOL: Asheville (N.C.).
JUNIOR COLLEGE: Coffeyville (Kan.) Community College.
COLLEGE: Tennessee.
TRANSACTIONS/CAREER NOTES: Selected by St. Louis Rams in third round (65th pick overall) of 1998 NFL draft. ... Signed by Rams (July 2, 1998). ... On non-football injury list for personal reasons (November 17, 1998-November 16, 1999). ... On suspended list for violating league substance abuse policy (July 16-November 9, 1999). ... Granted free agency (March 2, 2001). ... Re-signed by Rams (April 20, 2001). ... Granted unconditional free agency (March 1, 2002). ... Re-signed by Rams (March 3, 2002).
CHAMPIONSHIP GAME EXPERIENCE: Played in NFC championship game (1999 and 2001 seasons). ... Member of Super Bowl championship team (1999 season). ... Played in Super Bowl 36 (2001 season).
HONORS: Played in Pro Bowl (2003 season).

Year Team	G	GS	TOTALS Tk.	Ast.	Sks.
1998—St. Louis NFL	6	0	1	1	0.5
1999—St. Louis NFL	6	0	1	0	0.0
2000—St. Louis NFL	14	0	13	4	5.0
2001—St. Louis NFL	13	0	23	3	14.5
2002—St. Louis NFL	16	15	37	7	12.0
2003—St. Louis NFL	12	12	41	6	12.5
2004—St. Louis NFL	16	16	36	10	7.0
Pro totals (7 years)	83	43	152	31	51.5

LITTLETON, JODY   LB   LIONS

PERSONAL: Born October 23, 1974, in Denver, Colo. ... 6-1/235.
HIGH SCHOOL: Brighton (Colo.).
COLLEGE: Baylor.
TRANSACTIONS/CAREER NOTES: Signed as non-drafted free agent by Atlanta Falcons (April 27, 1998). ... Released by Falcons (July 2, 1998). ... Signed by New York Giants (May 14, 2001). ... Released by Giants (August 27, 2001). ... Re-signed by Giants (January 15, 2002). ... Assigned by Giants to Frankfurt Galaxy in 2002 NFL Europe enhancement allocation program (February 12, 2002). ... Released by Giants (August 26, 2002). ... Signed by Chicago Bears (October 17, 2002). ... Released by Bears (October 30, 2002). ... Signed by Detroit Lions to practice squad (December 19, 2002). ... Assigned by Lions to Frankfurt Galaxy in 2003 NFL Europe enhancement allocation program (January 28, 2003). ... Released by Lions (August 31, 2003). ... Re-signed by Lions (December 8, 2003). ... On injured reserve with hamstring injury (November 9, 2004-remainder of season).

Year Team	G	GS	TOTALS Tk.	Ast.	Sks.	INTERCEPTIONS No.	Yds.	Avg.	TD
2002—Chicago NFL	2	0	0	0	0.0	0	0	0.0	0
2003—Detroit NFL	3	0	0	0	0.0	0	0	0.0	0
2004—Detroit NFL	8	0	0	0	0.0	0	0	0.0	0
Pro totals (3 years)	13	0	0	0	0.0	0	0	0.0	0

LIWIENSKI, CHRIS   G   VIKINGS

PERSONAL: Born August 2, 1975, in Sterling Heights, Mich. ... 6-5/325. ... Name pronounced: Loo-win-ski.
HIGH SCHOOL: Stevenson (Sterling Heights, Mich.).
COLLEGE: Indiana.
TRANSACTIONS/CAREER NOTES: Selected by Detroit Lions in seventh round (207th pick overall) of 1998 NFL draft. ... Signed by Lions (July 15, 1998). ... Released by Lions (August 24, 1998). ... Signed by Minnesota Vikings to practice squad (August 31, 1998). ... Activated (November 18, 1998). ... Released by Vikings (September 9, 1999). ... Re-signed by Vikings to practice squad (September 10, 1999). ... Activated (December 10, 1999); did not play.

PLAYING EXPERIENCE: Minnesota NFL, 1998-2004. ... Games/Games started: 1998 (1/0), 2000 (14/1), 2001 (16/16), 2002 (16/16), 2003 (16/16), 2004 (16/16). Total: 79/65.
CHAMPIONSHIP GAME EXPERIENCE: Member of Vikings for NFC championship game (1998 season); inactive. ... Played in NFC championship game (2000 season).

LLOYD, BRANDON   WR   49ERS

PERSONAL: Born July 5, 1981, in Kansas City, Mo. ... 6-0/192. ... Full name: Brandon Matthew Lloyd.
HIGH SCHOOL: Blue Springs (Mo.).
COLLEGE: Illinois.
TRANSACTIONS/CAREER NOTES: Selected after junior season by San Francisco 49ers in fourth round (124th pick overall) of 2003 NFL draft. ... Signed by 49ers (July 25, 2003).
SINGLE GAME HIGHS (regular season): Receptions—6 (October 17, 2004, vs. New York Jets); yards—93 (October 17, 2004, vs. New York Jets); and touchdown receptions—1 (December 18, 2004, vs. Washington).

			RUSHING				RECEIVING				PUNT RETURNS				KICKOFF RETURNS				TOTALS		
Year	Team	G	GS	Att.	Yds.	Avg.	TD	No.	Yds.	Avg.	TD	No.	Yds.	Avg.	TD	No.	Yds.	Avg.	TD	TD	2pt.	Pts.
2003—S.F. NFL		16	1	0	0	0.0	0	14	212	15.1	2	0	0	0.0	0	2	32	16.0	0	2	1	14
2004—S.F. NFL		13	13	0	0	0.0	0	43	565	13.1	6	0	0	0.0	0	0	0	0.0	0	6	1	38
Pro totals (2 years)		29	14	0	0	0.0	0	57	777	13.6	8	0	0	0.0	0	2	32	16.0	0	8	2	52

LOCKLEAR, SEAN   G   SEAHAWKS

PERSONAL: Born May 29, 1981, in Lumberton, S.C. ... 6-4/301.
HIGH SCHOOL: Lumberton (N.C.).
COLLEGE: North Carolina State.
TRANSACTIONS/CAREER NOTES: Selected by Seattle Seahawks in third round (84th pick overall) of 2004 NFL draft. ... Signed by Seahawks (July 30, 2004).
PLAYING EXPERIENCE: Seattle NFL, 2004. ... Games/Games started: 2004 (16/0). Total: 16/0.

LOEFFLER, CULLEN   C   VIKINGS

PERSONAL: Born January 27, 1981, in Washington, DC. ... 6-5/241. ... Full name: Cullen Crawford Loeffler.
HIGH SCHOOL: Tom Moore (Ingram, Texas).
COLLEGE: Texas.
TRANSACTIONS/CAREER NOTES: Signed as non-drafted free agent by Minnesota Vikings (May 3, 2004).
PLAYING EXPERIENCE: Minnesota NFL, 2004. ... Games/Games started: 2004 (16/0). Total: 16/0.

LOGAN, MIKE   S   STEELERS

PERSONAL: Born September 15, 1974, in Pittsburgh, Pa. ... 6-1/211. ... Full name: Michael V. Logan.
HIGH SCHOOL: McKeesport (Pa.).
COLLEGE: West Virginia.
TRANSACTIONS/CAREER NOTES: Selected by Jacksonville Jaguars in second round (50th pick overall) of 1997 NFL draft. ... Signed by Jaguars (May 23, 1997). ... On injured reserve with ankle injury (September 20, 1999-remainder of season). ... Granted free agency (February 11, 2000). ... Re-signed by Jaguars (March 10, 2000). ... Granted unconditional free agency (March 2, 2001). ... Signed by Pittsburgh Steelers (March 24, 2001). ... On injured reserve with knee injury (January 6, 2003-remainder of 2002 playoffs). ... Granted unconditional free agency (March 3, 2004). ... Re-signed by Steelers (March 22, 2004). ... On injured reserve with hamstring injury (October 20, 2004-remainder of season).
CHAMPIONSHIP GAME EXPERIENCE: Played in AFC championship game (2001 season).

				TOTALS			INTERCEPTIONS				PUNT RETURNS				KICKOFF RETURNS				TOTALS			
Year	Team	G	GS	Tk.	Ast.	Sks.	No.	Yds.	Avg.	TD	No.	Yds.	Avg.	TD	No.	Yds.	Avg.	TD	TD	2pt.	Pts.	Fum.
1997—Jac. NFL	11	0	5	0	0.0	0	0	0.0	0	0	0	0.0	0	10	236	23.6	0	0	0	0	0
1998—Jac. NFL	15	0	13	5	0.0	0	0	0.0	0	2	26	13.0	0	18	414	23.0	0	0	0	0	1
1999—Jac. NFL	2	0	0	1	0.0	0	0	0.0	0	1	7	7.0	0	1	25	25.0	0	0	0	0	0
2000—Jac. NFL	15	11	48	6	1.0	2	14	7.0	0	0	0	0.0	0	0	0	0.0	0	0	0	0	0
2001—Pit. NFL	16	1	20	3	2.0	2	2	1.0	0	0	0	0.0	0	1	9	9.0	0	0	0	0	0
2002—Pit. NFL	14	0	29	7	0.5	1	46	46.0	0	0	0	0.0	0	0	0	0.0	0	0	0	0	0
2003—Pit. NFL	16	15	70	23	1.0	0	0	0.0	0	0	0	0.0	0	0	0	0.0	0	0	0	0	0
2004—Pit. NFL	3	0	1	2	0.0	0	0	0.0	0	0	0	0.0	0	0	0	0.0	0	0	0	0	0
Pro totals (8 years)	92	27	186	47	4.5	5	62	12.4	0	3	33	11.0	0	30	684	22.8	0	0	0	0	1

LONG, RIEN   DT   TITANS

PERSONAL: Born August 7, 1981, in Los Angeles, Calif. ... 6-6/300. ... Full name: Rien M. Long.
HIGH SCHOOL: Anacortes (Wash.).
COLLEGE: Washington State.
TRANSACTIONS/CAREER NOTES: Selected after junior season by Tennessee Titans in fourth round (126th pick overall) of 2003 NFL draft. ... Signed by Titans (July 16, 2003).

			TOTALS		
Year	Team	G	GS	Tk.	Ast.	Sks.
2003—Tennessee NFL	8	0	2	1	1.0
2004—Tennessee NFL	15	3	21	5	5.0
Pro totals (2 years)	23	3	23	6	6.0

LONGWELL, RYAN   K   PACKERS

PERSONAL: Born August 16, 1974, in Seattle, Wash. ... 6-0/202. ... Full name: Ryan Walker Longwell.
HIGH SCHOOL: Bend (Ore.).
COLLEGE: California.
TRANSACTIONS/CAREER NOTES: Signed as non-drafted free agent by San Francisco 49ers (April 28, 1997). ... Claimed on waivers by Green Bay Packers (July 10, 1997).
CHAMPIONSHIP GAME EXPERIENCE: Played in NFC championship game (1997 season). ... Played in Super Bowl 32 (1997 season).
MISCELLANEOUS: Green Bay Packers all-time leading scorer (964 points).

		FIELD GOALS							TOTALS		
Year Team	G	1-29	30-39	40-49	50+	Tot.	Pct.	Lg.	XPM	XPA	Pts.
1997—Green Bay NFL	16	11-12	10-13	2-4	1-1	24-30	80.0	50	*48	*48	120
1998—Green Bay NFL	16	7-7	13-15	9-10	0-1	29-33	87.9	45	41	43	128
1999—Green Bay NFL	16	8-9	8-9	8-10	1-2	25-30	83.3	50	38	38	113
2000—Green Bay NFL	16	7-8	10-10	13-15	3-5	‡33-‡38	86.8	52	32	32	131
2001—Green Bay NFL	16	3-4	9-10	7-14	1-3	20-31	64.5	54	44	45	104
2002—Green Bay NFL	16	9-10	12-13	7-10	0-1	28-34	82.4	49	‡44	‡44	128
2003—Green Bay NFL	16	5-5	11-11	6-9	1-1	23-26	88.5	50	‡51	‡51	120
2004—Green Bay NFL	16	8-8	8-9	6-8	2-3	24-28	85.7	53	‡48	‡48	120
Pro totals (8 years)	128	58-63	81-90	58-80	9-17	206-250	82.4	54	346	349	964

LOOKER, DANE   WR

PERSONAL: Born April 5, 1976, in Puyallup, Wash. ... 6-0/194.
HIGH SCHOOL: Puyallup (Wash.).
COLLEGE: Washington.
TRANSACTIONS/CAREER NOTES: Signed as non-drafted free agent by St. Louis Rams (April 17, 2000). ... Traded by Rams to New England Patriots for undisclosed draft pick (August 7, 2000). ... Inactive for 10 games (2000). ... On injured reserve with leg injury (November 16, 2000-remainder of season). ... Released by Patriots (July 31, 2001). ... Signed by Rams (August 7, 2001). ... Released by Rams (August 27, 2001). ... Re-signed by Rams (February 12, 2002). ... Assigned by Rams to Berlin Thunder in 2002 NFL Europe enhancement allocation program (February 12, 2002). ... Released by Rams (September 1, 2002). ... Re-signed by Rams to practice squad (September 9, 2002). ... Activated (December 12, 2002). ... Granted free agency (March 2, 2005).
SINGLE GAME HIGHS (regular season): Receptions—5 (September 26, 2004, vs. New Orleans); yards—69 (September 26, 2004, vs. New Orleans); and touchdown receptions—1 (October 19, 2003, vs. Green Bay).

			RECEIVING				PUNT RETURNS				TOTALS		
Year Team	G	GS	No.	Yds.	Avg.	TD	No.	Yds.	Avg.	TD	TD	2pt.	Pts.	Fum.
2002—St. Louis NFL	3	0	0	0	0.0	0	0	0	0.0	0	0	0	0	0
2003—St. Louis NFL	16	2	47	495	10.5	3	2	47	23.5	0	3	0	18	1
2004—St. Louis NFL	14	0	13	183	14.1	0	0	0	0.0	0	0	0	0	1
Pro totals (3 years)	33	2	60	678	11.3	3	2	47	23.5	0	3	0	18	2

LOPIENSKI, TOM   RB

PERSONAL: Born June 12, 1979, in Parkersburg, W.Va. ... 6-0/246.
COLLEGE: Notre Dame.
TRANSACTIONS/CAREER NOTES: Signed as non-drafted free agent by Indianapolis Colts (May 5, 2003). ... Released by Colts (August 31, 2003). ... Re-signed by Colts (December 2, 2003). ... Released by Colts to practice squad (September 22, 2004). ... Signed by Tampa Bay Buccaneers off Colts practice squad (February 9, 2005). ... Released by Buccaneers (April 26, 2005).
CHAMPIONSHIP GAME EXPERIENCE: Played in AFC championship game (2003 season).

			RUSHING				TOTALS		
Year Team	G	GS	Att.	Yds.	Avg.	TD	TD	2pt.	Pts.	Fum.
2003—Indianapolis NFL	4	0	0	0	0.0	0	0	0	0	0
2004—Indianapolis NFL	2	0	0	0	0.0	0	0	0	0	0
Pro totals (2 years)	6	0	0	0	0.0	0	0	0	0	0

LORD, JAMMAL   DB   TEXANS

PERSONAL: Born January 10, 1981, in Brooklyn, N.Y. ... 6-2/220.
HIGH SCHOOL: Bayonne (N.J.).
COLLEGE: Nebraska.
TRANSACTIONS/CAREER NOTES: Selected by Houston Texans in sixth round (175th pick overall) of 2004 NFL draft. ... Signed by Texans (June 23, 2004). ... Released by Texans (September 5, 2004). ... Re-signed by Texans to practice squad (September 6, 2004). ... Activated (December 17, 2004).

			PASSING								RUSHING				TOTALS		
Year Team	G	GS	Att.	Cmp.	Pct.	Yds.	TD	Int.	Avg.	Skd.	Rat.	Att.	Yds.	Avg.	TD	TD	2pt.	Pts.
2004—Houston NFL	1	0	0	0	0.0	0	0	0	0.00	0	0.0	0	0	0.0	0	0	0	0

LOSMAN, J.P.   QB   BILLS

PERSONAL: Born March 12, 1981, in Venice, Calif. ... 6-2/217. ... Full name: Jonathan Paul Losman.
HIGH SCHOOL: Venice (Calif.).
COLLEGE: Tulane.
TRANSACTIONS/CAREER NOTES: Selected by Buffalo Bills in first round (22nd pick overall) of 2004 NFL draft. ... Signed by Bills (July 31, 2004).

					PASSING								RUSHING			TOTALS		
Year	Team	G	GS	Att.	Cmp.	Pct.	Yds.	TD	Int.	Avg.	Skd.	Rat.	Att.	Yds.	Avg.	TD	TD	2pt.	Pts.
2004—Buffalo NFL		4	0	5	3	60.0	32	0	1	6.40	1	39.2	2	15	7.5	0	0	0	0

LOTT, ANDRE   CB   REDSKINS

PERSONAL: Born May 31, 1979, in Memphis, Tenn. ... 5-10/196. ... Full name: Andre Marquette Lott.
HIGH SCHOOL: Melrose (Memphis, Tenn.).
COLLEGE: Tennessee.
TRANSACTIONS/CAREER NOTES: Selected by Washington Redskins in fifth round (159th pick overall) of 2002 NFL draft. ... Signed by Redskins (July 12, 2002). ... On injured reserve with pectoral injury (November 1, 2004-remainder of season). ... Granted free agency (March 2, 2005). ... Re-signed by Redskins (April 15, 2005).

				TOTALS			INTERCEPTIONS			
Year	Team	G	GS	Tk.	Ast.	Sks.	No.	Yds.	Avg.	TD
2002—Washington NFL		16	0	4	0	1.0	0	0	0.0	0
2003—Washington NFL		11	0	4	2	0.0	0	0	0.0	0
2004—Washington NFL		4	3	7	1	0.0	0	0	0.0	0
Pro totals (3 years)		31	3	15	3	1.0	0	0	0.0	0

LOVERNE, DAVID   G   LIONS

PERSONAL: Born May 22, 1976, in Concord, Calif. ... 6-3/299. ... Name pronounced: LAH-vern.
HIGH SCHOOL: De La Salle (Concord, Calif.).
COLLEGE: San Jose State.
TRANSACTIONS/CAREER NOTES: Selected by New York Jets in third round (90th pick overall) of 1999 NFL draft. ... Signed by Jets (July 1, 1999). ... Inactive for all 16 games (1999). ... Granted free agency (March 1, 2002). ... Re-signed by Jets (April 6, 2002). ... Traded by Jets with undisclosed draft pick to Washington Redskins for undisclosed draft pick (April 6, 2002). ... Traded by Redskins with fourth-round pick (DB DeJuan Groce) in 2003 draft to St. Louis Rams for RB Trung Canidate (February 28, 2003). ... Granted unconditional free agency (March 3, 2004). ... Signed by Detroit Lions (March 23, 2004).
PLAYING EXPERIENCE: New York Jets NFL, 2000-2001; Washington NFL, 2002; St. Louis NFL, 2003; Detroit NFL, 2004. ... Games/Games started: 2000 (16/0), 2001 (16/0), 2002 (15/11), 2003 (1/0), 2004 (15/13). Total: 63/24.

LOWE, OMARE   CB   SEAHAWKS

PERSONAL: Born April 20, 1978, in Seattle, Wash. ... 6-1/195.
HIGH SCHOOL: Tacoma (Wash.).
COLLEGE: Washington.
TRANSACTIONS/CAREER NOTES: Selected by Miami Dolphins in fifth round (161st pick overall) of 2002 NFL draft. ... Signed by Dolphins (July 25, 2002). ... Released by Dolphins (August 31, 2003). ... Signed by Tennessee Titans to practice squad (September 3, 2003). ... Released by Titans (September 19, 2003). ... Signed by New York Jets to practice squad (October 15, 2003). ... Activated (November 11, 2003). ... Granted free agency (March 3, 2004). ... Signed by New York Jets (March 22, 2004). ... Claimed on waivers by Minnesota Vikings (September 6, 2004). ... Released by Vikings (September 14, 2004). ... Signed by Vikings to practice squad (September 16, 2004). ... Released by Vikings practice squad (September 21, 2004). ... Signed by Redskins to practice squad (November 5, 2004). ... Released by Washington Redskins practice squad (November 11, 2004). ... Signed by New England Patriots to practice squad (November 16, 2004). ... Activated (November 28, 2004). ... Released by Patriots (November 30, 2004). ... Re-signed by Patriots to practice squad (December 2, 2004). ... Activated (December 20, 2004). ... Released by Patriots (December 22, 2004). ... Re-signed by Patriots (December 25, 2004). ... Signed by Patriots to practice squad (December 29, 2004). ... Signed by Seattle Seahawks (April 1, 2005).

				TOTALS			INTERCEPTIONS			
Year	Team	G	GS	Tk.	Ast.	Sks.	No.	Yds.	Avg.	TD
2002—Miami NFL		1	0	0	0	0.0	0	0	0.0	0
2003—New England NFL		2	0	0	0	0.0	0	0	0.0	0
2004—New England NFL		3	0	0	0	0.0	0	0	0.0	0
Pro totals (3 years)		6	0	0	0	0.0	0	0	0.0	0

LUCAS, JUSTIN   S   RAMS

PERSONAL: Born July 15, 1976, in Victoria, Texas. ... 5-10/211.
HIGH SCHOOL: Stroman (Victoria, Texas).
COLLEGE: Abilene Christian.
TRANSACTIONS/CAREER NOTES: Signed as non-drafted free agent by Arizona Cardinals (April 23, 1999). ... Released by Cardinals (September 5, 1999). ... Re-signed by Cardinals to practice squad (September 7, 1999). ... Activated (October 17, 1999). ... Released by Cardinals (October 19, 1999). ... Re-signed by Cardinals to practice squad (October 20, 1999). ... Activated (December 31, 1999). ... Granted free agency (February 28, 2003). ... Re-signed by Cardinals (April 3, 2003). ... On injured reserve with ankle injury (December 20, 2003-remainder of season). ... Granted unconditional free agency (March 3, 2004). ... Re-signed by Cardinals (March 26, 2004). ... Released by Cardinals (June 1, 2004). ... Signed by St. Louis Rams (June 4, 2004). ... Released by Rams (September 5, 2004). ... Re-signed by Rams (September 9, 2004).

				TOTALS			INTERCEPTIONS			
Year	Team	G	GS	Tk.	Ast.	Sks.	No.	Yds.	Avg.	TD
1999—Arizona NFL		2	0	0	0	0.0	0	0	0.0	0
2000—Arizona NFL		16	0	12	8	0.0	0	0	0.0	0
2001—Arizona NFL		13	4	26	5	0.0	0	0	0.0	0
2002—Arizona NFL		16	4	27	9	0.0	2	80	40.0	2
2003—Arizona NFL		11	0	20	2	0.0	0	0	0.0	0
2004—St. Louis NFL		7	0	1	1	0.0	0	0	0.0	0
Pro totals (6 years)		65	8	86	25	0.0	2	80	40.0	2

L

LUCAS, KEN   CB   PANTHERS

PERSONAL: Born January 23, 1979, in Cleveland, Miss. ... 6-0/205.
HIGH SCHOOL: East Side (Cleveland, Miss.).
COLLEGE: Mississippi.
TRANSACTIONS/CAREER NOTES: Selected by Seattle Seahawks in second round (40th pick overall) of 2001 NFL draft. ... Signed by Seahawks (July 26, 2001). ... Granted unconditional free agency (March 2, 2005). ... Signed by Carolina Panthers (March 3, 2005).

				TOTALS			INTERCEPTIONS			
Year Team	G	GS	Tk.	Ast.	Sks.	No.	Yds.	Avg.	TD
2001—Seattle NFL	16	8	42	5	0.0	1	0	0.0	0
2002—Seattle NFL	16	16	71	11	0.0	3	67	22.3	0
2003—Seattle NFL	14	7	52	10	0.0	1	27	27.0	0
2004—Seattle NFL	16	16	60	7	0.0	∞6	46	7.7	1
Pro totals (4 years)	62	47	225	33	0.0	11	140	12.7	1

LUCHEY, NICK   FB   PACKERS

PERSONAL: Born March 30, 1977, in Royal Oak, Mich. ... 6-2/273. ... Full name: James Nicolas Luchey. ... Formerly known as Nick Williams.
HIGH SCHOOL: Harrison (Farmington Hills, Mich.).
COLLEGE: Miami (Fla.).
TRANSACTIONS/CAREER NOTES: Selected by Cincinnati Bengals in fifth round (135th pick overall) of 1999 NFL draft. ... Signed by Bengals (May 19, 1999). ... On physically unable to perform list with knee injury (July 22-November 27, 2001). ... Granted free agency (March 1, 2002). ... Re-signed by Bengals (April 23, 2002). ... Granted unconditional free agency (February 28, 2003). ... Signed by Green Bay Packers (March 11, 2003).
SINGLE GAME HIGHS (regular season): Attempts—12 (December 22, 2002, vs. New Orleans); yards—59 (December 22, 2002, vs. New Orleans); and rushing touchdowns—2 (December 22, 2002, vs. New Orleans).

			RUSHING				RECEIVING				KICKOFF RETURNS				TOTALS			
Year Team	G	GS	Att.	Yds.	Avg.	TD	No.	Yds.	Avg.	TD	No.	Yds.	Avg.	TD	TD	2pt.	Pts.	Fum.
1999—Cincinnati NFL	11	0	10	30	3.0	0	10	96	9.6	0	8	109	13.6	0	0	0	0	1
2000—Cincinnati NFL	14	4	10	54	5.4	0	7	84	12.0	0	2	12	6.0	0	0	0	0	2
2001—Cincinnati NFL	4	2	0	0	0.0	0	0	0	0.0	0	0	0	0.0	0	0	0	0	0
2002—Cincinnati NFL	16	3	12	59	4.9	2	7	46	6.6	0	3	40	13.3	0	2	0	12	0
2003—Green Bay NFL	11	2	1	3	3.0	0	1	12	12.0	0	2	21	10.5	0	0	0	0	0
2004—Green Bay NFL	16	6	10	24	2.4	0	2	20	10.0	0	0	0	0.0	0	0	0	0	0
Pro totals (6 years)	72	17	43	170	4.0	2	27	258	9.6	0	15	182	12.1	0	2	0	12	3

LUCIER, WAYNE   C   GIANTS

PERSONAL: Born December 5, 1979, in Amesbury, Mass. ... 6-3/300. ... Name pronounced: loo-SEAR.
HIGH SCHOOL: St. John's (Salem, N.H.).
COLLEGE: Colorado.
TRANSACTIONS/CAREER NOTES: Selected by New York Giants in seventh round (249th pick overall) of 2003 NFL draft. ... Signed by Giants (July 16, 2003). ... On injured reserve with knee injury (December 2, 2003-remainder of season).
PLAYING EXPERIENCE: New York Giants NFL, 2003-2004. ... Games/Games started: 2003 (12/11), 2004 (15/9). Total: 27/20.

LUKE, TRIANDOS   WR   BRONCOS

PERSONAL: Born December 24, 1981, in Phenix City, Ala. ... 5-10/189.
HIGH SCHOOL: Central (Phenix City, Ala.).
COLLEGE: Alabama.
TRANSACTIONS/CAREER NOTES: Selected by Denver Broncos in sixth round (171st pick overall) of 2004 NFL draft. ... Signed by Broncos (June 11, 2004).
SINGLE GAME HIGHS (regular season): Receptions—5 (December 19, 2004, vs. Kansas City); yards—40 (December 19, 2004, vs. Kansas City); and touchdown receptions—0.

			RECEIVING				PUNT RETURNS				KICKOFF RETURNS				TOTALS			
Year Team	G	GS	No.	Yds.	Avg.	TD	No.	Yds.	Avg.	TD	No.	Yds.	Avg.	TD	TD	2pt.	Pts.	Fum.
2004—Denver NFL	10	0	6	52	8.7	0	19	135	7.1	0	15	306	20.4	0	0	0	0	2

LYMAN, DUSTIN   TE   BEARS

PERSONAL: Born August 5, 1976, in Boulder, Colo. ... 6-5/254.
HIGH SCHOOL: Fairview (Boulder, Colo.).
COLLEGE: Wake Forest.
TRANSACTIONS/CAREER NOTES: Selected by Chicago Bears in third round (87th pick overall) of 2000 NFL draft. ... Signed by Bears (June 15, 2000). ... On injured reserve with knee injury (December 10, 2002-remainder of season). ... On injured reserve with spleen injury (December 15, 2003-remainder of season).
SINGLE GAME HIGHS (regular season): Receptions—7 (December 1, 2002, vs. Green Bay); yards—58 (December 1, 2002, vs. Green Bay); and touchdown receptions—2 (December 1, 2002, vs. Green Bay).

			RECEIVING				TOTALS			
Year Team	G	GS	No.	Yds.	Avg.	TD	TD	2pt.	Pts.	Fum.
2000—Chicago NFL	14	7	1	4	4.0	0	0	0	0	0
2001—Chicago NFL	4	0	0	0	0.0	0	0	0	0	0
2002—Chicago NFL	12	3	14	121	8.6	2	2	0	12	0
2003—Chicago NFL	9	1	11	80	7.3	0	0	0	0	0
2004—Chicago NFL	16	10	11	73	6.6	1	1	0	6	0
Pro totals (5 years)	55	21	37	278	7.5	3	3	0	18	0

LYNCH, JAMES   FB

PERSONAL: Born June 17, 1982, in Washington, DC. ... 5-11/276.
HIGH SCHOOL: Dunbar (Washington, D.C.).
COLLEGE: Maryland.
TRANSACTIONS/CAREER NOTES: Signed as non-drafted free agent by Minnesota Vikings (April 28, 2003). ... Released by Vikings (September 9, 2003). ... Signed by Cincinnati Bengals to practice squad (September 30, 2003). ... Released by Bengals (September 23, 2004). ... Re-signed by Bengals to practice squad (September 27, 2004). ... Signed by Miami Dolphins off Bengals practice squad (December 17, 2004). ... Released by Dolphins (April 5, 2005).

			RUSHING					TOTALS		
Year Team	G	GS	Att.	Yds.	Avg.	TD	TD	2pt.	Pts.	Fum.
2004—Cincinnati NFL	1	0	0	0	0.0	0	0	0	0	0

LYNCH, JOHN   S   BRONCOS

PERSONAL: Born September 25, 1971, in Hinsdale, Ill. ... 6-2/220. ... Full name: John Terrence Lynch. ... Son of John Lynch, linebacker with Pittsburgh Steelers (1969).
HIGH SCHOOL: Torrey Pines (Encinitas, Calif.).
COLLEGE: Stanford.
TRANSACTIONS/CAREER NOTES: Selected by Tampa Bay Buccaneers in third round (82nd pick overall) of 1993 NFL draft. ... Signed by Buccaneers (June 1, 1993). ... On injured reserve with knee injury (December 12, 1995-remainder of season). ... Granted free agency (February 16, 1996). ... Re-signed by Buccaneers (July 13, 1996). ... Released by Buccaneers (March 11, 2004). ... Signed by Denver Broncos (March 22, 2004).
CHAMPIONSHIP GAME EXPERIENCE: Played in NFC championship game (1999 and 2002 seasons). ... Member of Super Bowl championship team (2002 season).
HONORS: Played in Pro Bowl (1997, 1999-2002 and 2004 seasons). ... Named safety on THE SPORTING NEWS NFL All-Pro team (1999 and 2000).

			TOTALS			INTERCEPTIONS			
Year Team	G	GS	Tk.	Ast.	Sks.	No.	Yds.	Avg.	TD
1993—Tampa Bay NFL	15	4	8	5	0.0	0	0	0.0	0
1994—Tampa Bay NFL	16	0	11	4	0.0	0	0	0.0	0
1995—Tampa Bay NFL	9	6	27	10	0.0	3	3	1.0	0
1996—Tampa Bay NFL	16	14	74	29	1.0	3	26	8.7	0
1997—Tampa Bay NFL	16	16	75	34	0.0	2	20	14.0	0
1998—Tampa Bay NFL	15	15	50	35	2.0	2	29	14.5	0
1999—Tampa Bay NFL	16	16	81	36	0.5	2	32	16.0	0
2000—Tampa Bay NFL	16	16	56	29	1.0	3	43	14.3	0
2001—Tampa Bay NFL	16	16	62	25	1.0	3	21	7.0	0
2002—Tampa Bay NFL	15	15	41	23	0.0	3	0	0.0	0
2003—Tampa Bay NFL	14	14	50	22	0.5	2	18	9.0	0
2004—Denver NFL	15	15	48	17	2.0	1	2	2.0	0
Pro totals (12 years)	179	147	583	269	8.0	24	202	8.4	0

MACKLIN, DAVID   CB   CARDINALS

PERSONAL: Born July 14, 1978, in Newport News, Va. ... 5-10/200. ... Full name: David Thurman Macklin.
HIGH SCHOOL: Menchville (Newport News, Va.).
COLLEGE: Penn State.
TRANSACTIONS/CAREER NOTES: Selected by Indianapolis Colts in third round (91st pick overall) of 2000 NFL draft. ... Signed by Colts (July 13, 2000). ... Granted free agency (February 28, 2003). ... Re-signed by Colts (April 15, 2003). ... Granted unconditional free agency (March 3, 2004). ... Signed by Arizona Cardinals (March 10, 2004).
CHAMPIONSHIP GAME EXPERIENCE: Played in AFC championship game (2003 season).

			TOTALS			INTERCEPTIONS			
Year Team	G	GS	Tk.	Ast.	Sks.	No.	Yds.	Avg.	TD
2000—Indianapolis NFL	16	2	23	4	0.0	2	35	17.5	0
2001—Indianapolis NFL	16	16	53	9	0.5	3	15	5.0	0
2002—Indianapolis NFL	16	15	47	9	0.0	1	30	30.0	0
2003—Indianapolis NFL	16	4	27	5	0.0	1	0	0.0	0
2004—Arizona NFL	16	16	59	12	0.5	4	18	4.5	0
Pro totals (5 years)	80	53	209	39	1.0	11	98	8.9	0

MADDOX, ANTHONY   DT   JAGUARS

PERSONAL: Born November 22, 1978, in Funston, Ga. ... 6-1/295.
HIGH SCHOOL: Monroe (Albany, Ga.).
JUNIOR COLLEGE: Jones County (Ellisville, Miss.).
COLLEGE: Delta State.
TRANSACTIONS/CAREER NOTES: Selected by Jacksonville Jaguars in fourth round (118th pick overall) of 2004 NFL draft. ... Signed by Jaguars (July 22, 2004). ... Released by Jaguars (September 5, 2004). ... Signed by Jaguars to practice squad (September 8, 2004). ... Activated (December 3, 2004).

			TOTALS		
Year Team	G	GS	Tk.	Ast.	Sks.
2004—Jacksonville NFL	2	0	0	1	0.0

M

MADDOX, TOMMY　　　　　QB　　　　　STEELERS

PERSONAL: Born September 2, 1971, in Shreveport, La. ... 6-4/219. ... Full name: Thomas Alfred Maddox.
HIGH SCHOOL: L.D. Bell (Hurst, Texas).
COLLEGE: UCLA.
TRANSACTIONS/CAREER NOTES: Selected after sophomore season by Denver Broncos in first round (25th pick overall) of 1992 NFL draft. ... Signed by Broncos (July 22, 1992). ... Traded by Broncos to Los Angeles Rams for fourth-round pick (LB Ken Brown) in 1995 draft (August 27, 1994). ... Granted free agency (February 17, 1995). ... Rams franchise moved to St. Louis (April 12, 1995). ... Re-signed by Rams (July 7, 1995). ... Released by Rams (August 27, 1995). ... Signed by New York Giants (August 30, 1995). ... Released by Giants (August 19, 1996). ... Signed by Atlanta Falcons (April 19, 1997). ... Released by Falcons (August 18, 1997). ... Signed by New Jersey Red Dogs of Arena League (November 9, 1999). ... Signed by Pittsburgh Steelers (June 12, 2001).
CHAMPIONSHIP GAME EXPERIENCE: Member of Steelers for AFC championship game (2001 and 2004 seasons); did not play.
SINGLE GAME HIGHS (regular season): Attempts—57 (December 8, 2002, vs. Houston); completions—31 September 28, 2003, vs. Tennessee); yards—473 (November 10, 2002 vs. Atlanta); and touchdown passes—4 (November 10, 2002, vs. Atlanta).
STATISTICAL PLATEAUS: 300-yard passing games: 2002 (2), 2003 (4). Total: 6.
MISCELLANEOUS: Regular-season record as starting NFL quarterback: 15-18-1 (.456). ... Postseason record as starting NFL quarterback: 1-1 (.500).

				PASSING								RUSHING				TOTALS		
Year　Team	G	GS	Att.	Cmp.	Pct.	Yds.	TD	Int.	Avg.	Skd.	Rat.	Att.	Yds.	Avg.	TD	TD	2pt.	Pts.
1992—Denver NFL	13	4	121	66	54.5	757	5	9	6.26	10	56.4	9	20	2.2	0	0	0	0
1993—Denver NFL	16	0	1	1	100.0	1	1	0	1.00	0	118.8	2	-2	-1.0	0	0	0	0
1994—L.A. Rams NFL	5	0	19	10	52.6	141	0	2	7.42	0	37.3	1	1	1.0	0	0	0	0
1995—New York Giants NFL	16	0	23	6	26.1	49	0	3	2.13	2	0.0	1	4	4.0	0	0	0	0
1996—			Did not play.															
1997—			Did not play.															
1998—			Did not play.															
1999—			Did not play.															
2000—			Did not play.															
2001—Pittsburgh NFL	5	0	9	7	77.8	154	1	1	17.11	1	116.2	6	9	1.5	1	1	0	6
2002—Pittsburgh NFL	15	11	377	234	62.1	2836	20	16	7.52	26	85.2	19	43	2.3	0	0	0	0
2003—Pittsburgh NFL	16	16	519	298	57.4	3414	18	§17	6.58	41	75.3	13	12	0.9	0	0	0	0
2004—Pittsburgh NFL	4	3	60	30	50.0	329	1	2	5.48	6	58.3	9	15	1.7	0	0	0	0
Pro totals (8 years)	90	34	1129	652	57.8	7681	46	50	6.80	86	73.7	60	102	1.7	1	1	0	6

MADISON, SAM　　　　　CB　　　　　DOLPHINS

M

PERSONAL: Born April 23, 1974, in Thomasville, Ga. ... 5-11/185. ... Full name: Samuel A. Madison Jr.
HIGH SCHOOL: Florida A&M High (Monticello, Fla.).
COLLEGE: Louisville.
TRANSACTIONS/CAREER NOTES: Selected by Miami Dolphins in second round (44th pick overall) of 1997 NFL draft. ... Signed by Dolphins (June 16, 1997).
HONORS: Named cornerback on THE SPORTING NEWS NFL All-Pro team (1999 and 2000). ... Played in Pro Bowl (1999, 2000 and 2002 seasons). ... Named to play in Pro Bowl (2001 season); replaced by Ryan McNeil due to injury.

			TOTALS			INTERCEPTIONS			
Year　Team	G	GS	Tk.	Ast.	Sks.	No.	Yds.	Avg.	TD
1997—Miami NFL	14	3	16	5	0.0	1	21	21.0	0
1998—Miami NFL	16	16	31	13	1.0	8	114	14.3	0
1999—Miami NFL	16	16	38	8	0.0	†7	164	23.4	1
2000—Miami NFL	16	16	29	10	0.0	5	80	16.0	0
2001—Miami NFL	13	13	18	7	0.0	2	0	0.0	0
2002—Miami NFL	16	16	24	10	0.0	3	15	5.0	0
2003—Miami NFL	16	16	47	3	0.0	3	82	27.3	1
2004—Miami NFL	16	16	34	13	0.0	0	0	0.0	0
Pro totals (8 years)	123	112	237	69	1.0	29	476	16.4	2

MAESE, JOE　　　　　C/LS　　　　　RAVENS

PERSONAL: Born December 2, 1978, in Morenci, Ariz. ... 6-0/245.
HIGH SCHOOL: Cortez (Ariz.).
JUNIOR COLLEGE: Phoenix College.
COLLEGE: New Mexico.
TRANSACTIONS/CAREER NOTES: Selected by Baltimore Ravens in sixth round (194th pick overall) in 2001 NFL draft. ... Signed by Ravens (June 14, 2001). ... On injured reserve with knee injury (January 3, 2002-remainder of season). ... Granted free agency (March 3, 2004). ... Re-signed by Ravens (2004). ... Granted unconditional free agency (March 2, 2005). ... Re-signed by Ravens (March 15, 2005).
PLAYING EXPERIENCE: Baltimore NFL, 2001-2004. ... Games/Games started: 2001 (15/0), 2002 (16/0), 2003 (16/0), 2004 (15/0). Total: 62/0.

MAHAN, SEAN　　　　　G　　　　　BUCCANEERS

PERSONAL: Born May 28, 1980, in Tulsa, Okla. ... 6-3/301. ... Full name: Sean Christopher Mahan.
HIGH SCHOOL: Jenks (Okla.).
COLLEGE: Notre Dame.
TRANSACTIONS/CAREER NOTES: Selected by Tampa Bay Buccaneers in fifth round (168th pick overall) of 2003 NFL draft. ... Signed by Buccaneers (July 18, 2003).
PLAYING EXPERIENCE: Tampa Bay NFL, 2003-2004. ... Games/Games started: 2003 (9/0), 2004 (16/8). Total: 25/8.

MAHE, RENO   RB   EAGLES

PERSONAL: Born June 3, 1980, in Los Angeles, Calif. ... 5-10/212. ... Full name: Sateki Reno Mahe Jr.
HIGH SCHOOL: Brighton (Salt Lake City, Utah).
JUNIOR COLLEGE: Dixie (Utah).
COLLEGE: Brigham Young.
TRANSACTIONS/CAREER NOTES: Signed as non-drafted free agent by Philadelphia Eagles (April 28, 2003).
CHAMPIONSHIP GAME EXPERIENCE: Played in NFC championship game (2003 and 2004 seasons). ... Played in Super Bowl 39 (2004 season).
SINGLE GAME HIGHS (regular season): Attempts—7 (January 2, 2005, vs. Cincinnati); yards—26 (January 2, 2005, vs. Cincinnati); and rushing touchdowns—0.

			RUSHING				RECEIVING				PUNT RETURNS				KICKOFF RETURNS				TOTALS		
Year Team	G	GS	Att.	Yds.	Avg.	TD	No.	Yds.	Avg.	TD	No.	Yds.	Avg.	TD	No.	Yds.	Avg.	TD	TD	2pt.	Pts.
2003—Phi. NFL	2	0	0	0	0.0	0	1	5	5.0	0	6	55	9.2	0	0	0	0.0	0	0	0	0
2004—Phi. NFL	11	0	23	91	4.0	0	14	123	8.8	0	19	109	5.7	0	3	44	14.7	0	0	0	0
Pro totals (2 years)	13	0	23	91	4.0	0	15	128	8.5	0	25	164	6.6	0	3	44	14.7	0	0	0	0

MALLARD, WESLY   LB   PATRIOTS

PERSONAL: Born November 21, 1978, in Hinesville, Ga. ... 6-1/230.
HIGH SCHOOL: Hardaway (Columbus, Ga.).
COLLEGE: Oregon.
TRANSACTIONS/CAREER NOTES: Selected by New York Giants in sixth round (188th pick overall) of 2002 NFL draft. ... On injured reserve with knee injury (December 24, 2003-remainder of season). ... On injured reserve with knee injury (October 13, 2004-remainder of season). ... Did not receive qualifying offer from Giants (March 2, 2005). ... Signed by New England Patriots (April 18, 2005).

			TOTALS			INTERCEPTIONS			
Year Team	G	GS	Tk.	Ast.	Sks.	No.	Yds.	Avg.	TD
2002—New York Giants NFL	15	0	0	1	0.0	0	0	0.0	0
2003—New York Giants NFL	15	0	1	0	0.0	0	0	0.0	0
2004—New York Giants NFL	4	0	2	0	0.0	0	0	0.0	0
Pro totals (3 years)	34	0	3	1	0.0	0	0	0.0	0

MANGUM, KRIS   TE   PANTHERS

PERSONAL: Born August 15, 1973, in Magee, Miss. ... 6-4/252. ... Full name: Kris Thomas Mangum. ... Son of John Mangum, defensive tackle with Boston Patriots (1966 and 1967) of AFL; and brother of John Mangum, cornerback with Chicago Bears (1990-98).
HIGH SCHOOL: Magee (Miss.).
COLLEGE: Mississippi.
TRANSACTIONS/CAREER NOTES: Selected by Carolina Panthers in seventh round (228th pick overall) of 1997 NFL draft. ... Signed by Panthers (May 20, 1997). ... Released by Panthers (September 2, 1997). ... Re-signed by Panthers to practice squad (September 4, 1997). ... Activated (December 5, 1997). ... Granted unconditional free agency (March 3, 2004). ... Re-signed by Panthers (March 4, 2004).
CHAMPIONSHIP GAME EXPERIENCE: Played in NFC championship game (2003 season). ... Played in Super Bowl 38 (2003 season).
SINGLE GAME HIGHS (regular season): Receptions—6 (January 2, 2005, vs. New Orleans); yards—56 (December 20, 1997, vs. St. Louis); and touchdown receptions—1 (December 18, 2004, vs. Atlanta).

			RECEIVING				TOTALS			
Year Team	G	GS	No.	Yds.	Avg.	TD	TD	2pt.	Pts.	Fum.
1997—Carolina NFL	2	1	4	56	14.0	0	0	0	0	0
1998—Carolina NFL	6	0	1	5	5.0	0	0	0	0	0
1999—Carolina NFL	11	0	1	6	6.0	0	0	0	0	0
2000—Carolina NFL	15	6	19	215	11.3	1	1	0	6	0
2001—Carolina NFL	16	10	15	89	5.9	2	2	0	12	0
2002—Carolina NFL	16	8	16	159	9.9	0	0	0	0	0
2003—Carolina NFL	16	11	17	199	11.7	0	0	0	0	0
2004—Carolina NFL	15	10	34	323	9.5	3	3	0	18	0
Pro totals (8 years)	97	46	107	1052	9.8	6	6	0	36	0

MANNELLY, PATRICK   T/LS   BEARS

PERSONAL: Born April 18, 1975, in Atlanta, Ga. ... 6-5/265. ... Full name: James Patrick Mannelly.
HIGH SCHOOL: Marist (Atlanta).
COLLEGE: Duke.
TRANSACTIONS/CAREER NOTES: Selected by Chicago Bears in sixth round (189th pick overall) of 1998 NFL draft. ... Signed by Bears (June 11, 1998).
PLAYING EXPERIENCE: Chicago NFL, 1998-2004. ... Games/Games started: 1998 (16/0), 1999 (16/0), 2000 (16/0), 2001 (15/0), 2002 (14/0), 2003 (16/0), 2004 (16/0). Total: 109/0.

MANNING, ELI   QB   GIANTS

PERSONAL: Born January 3, 1981, in New Orleans, La. ... 6-4/218. ... Full name: Elisha Nelson Manning. ... Son of Archie Manning, quarterback with New Orleans Saints (1971-82), Houston Oilers (1982-83) and Minnesota Vikings (1983-84). ... Brother of Peyton Manning, quarterback, Indianapolis Colts.
HIGH SCHOOL: Isadore Newman (New Orleans, La.).
COLLEGE: Mississippi.

M

TRANSACTIONS/CAREER NOTES: Selected by San Diego Chargers in first round (first pick overall) of 2004 NFL draft. ... Traded by Chargers to New York Giants for QB Phillip Rivers, a third-round pick (K Nate Kaeding) in 2004 draft and 2005 first- (LB Shawne Merriman) and fifth-round (traded to St. Louis) draft choices (April 24, 2004). ... Signed by Giants (July 29, 2004).
HONORS: Maxwell Award winner (2003). ... Johnny Unitas Award winner (2003). ... Named quarterback on THE SPORTING NEWS college All-America second team (2003).
SINGLE GAME HIGHS (regular season): Attempts—37 (December 26, 2004, vs. Cincinnati); completions—19 (December 26, 2004, vs. Cincinnati); yards—201 (December 26, 2004, vs. Cincinnati); and touchdown passes—3 (January 2, 2005, vs. Dallas).
MISCELLANEOUS: Regular-season record as starting NFL quarterback: 1-6 (.143).

				PASSING								RUSHING				TOTALS		
Year Team	G	GS	Att.	Cmp.	Pct.	Yds.	TD	Int.	Avg.	Skd.	Rat.	Att.	Yds.	Avg.	TD	TD	2pt.	Pts.
2004—New York Giants NFL	9	7	197	95	48.2	1043	6	9	5.29	13	55.4	6	35	5.8	0	0	0	0

MANNING, PEYTON QB COLTS

PERSONAL: Born March 24, 1976, in New Orleans, La. ... 6-5/230. ... Full name: Peyton Williams Manning. ... Son of Archie Manning, quarterback with New Orleans Saints (1971-82), Houston Oilers (1982-83) and Minnesota Vikings (1983-84). ... Brother of Eli Manning, quarterback, New York Giants.
HIGH SCHOOL: Isidore Newman (New Orleans, La.).
COLLEGE: Tennessee.
TRANSACTIONS/CAREER NOTES: Selected by Indianapolis Colts in first round (first pick overall) of 1998 NFL draft. ... Signed by Colts (July 28, 1998). ... Designated by Colts as franchise player (February 24, 2004). ... Re-signed by Colts (March 2, 2004).
CHAMPIONSHIP GAME EXPERIENCE: Played in AFC championship game (2003 season).
HONORS: Davey O'Brien Award winner (1997). ... Named quarterback on THE SPORTING NEWS college All-America second team (1997). ... Named quarterback on THE SPORTING NEWS NFL All-Pro team (2003 and 2004). ... Played in Pro Bowl (1999, 2000 and 2002-2004 seasons). ... Named Outstanding Player of Pro Bowl (2004 season). ... Named NFL Player of the Year by THE SPORTING NEWS (2003 and 2004).
RECORDS: Holds NFL rookie-season records for most passes attempted—575 (1998); most passes completed—326 (1998); and most yards passing—3,739 (1998). ... Holds NFL single-season records for most touchdown passes—49 (2004) and highest passer rating—121.1 (2004).
SINGLE GAME HIGHS (regular season): Attempts—54 (October 8, 2000, vs. New England); completions—37 (November 3, 2002, vs. Tennessee); yards—472 (October 31, 2004, vs. Kansas City); and touchdown passes—6 (November 25, 2004, vs. Detroit).
STATISTICAL PLATEAUS: 300-yard passing games: 1998 (4), 1999 (2), 2000 (5), 2001 (5), 2002 (4), 2003 (4), 2004 (6). Total: 30.
MISCELLANEOUS: Regular-season record as starting NFL quarterback: 66-46 (.589). ... Postseason record as starting NFL quarterback: 3-5 (.375).

				PASSING								RUSHING				TOTALS		
Year Team	G	GS	Att.	Cmp.	Pct.	Yds.	TD	Int.	Avg.	Skd.	Rat.	Att.	Yds.	Avg.	TD	TD	2pt.	Pts.
1998—Indianapolis NFL	16	16	*575	§326	56.7	§3739	26	*28	6.50	22	71.2	15	62	4.1	0	0	0	0
1999—Indianapolis NFL	16	16	533	§331	§62.1	§4135	§26	15	§7.76	14	§90.7	35	73	2.1	2	2	0	12
2000—Indianapolis NFL	16	16	571	*357	62.5	*4413	†33	15	7.73	20	94.7	37	116	3.1	1	1	0	6
2001—Indianapolis NFL	16	16	547	343	62.7	§4131	26	23	7.55	29	84.1	35	157	4.5	4	4	0	24
2002—Indianapolis NFL	16	16	591	392	66.3	4200	27	§19	7.11	23	88.8	38	148	3.9	2	2	0	12
2003—Indianapolis NFL	16	16	§566	*379	*67.0	*4267	§29	10	7.54	18	99.0	28	26	0.9	0	0	0	0
2004—Indianapolis NFL	16	16	497	336	§67.6	4557	*49	10	*9.17	13	*121.1	25	38	1.5	0	0	0	0
Pro totals (7 years)	112	112	3880	2464	63.5	29442	216	120	7.59	139	92.3	213	620	2.9	9	9	0	54

MANNING, RICKY CB PANTHERS

PERSONAL: Born November 18, 1980, in Fresno, Calif. ... 5-8/185. ... Full name: Ricky Manning Jr.
HIGH SCHOOL: Edison (Fresno, Calif.).
COLLEGE: UCLA.
TRANSACTIONS/CAREER NOTES: Selected by Carolina Panthers in third round (82nd pick overall) of 2003 NFL draft. ... Signed by Panthers (June 3, 2003).
CHAMPIONSHIP GAME EXPERIENCE: Played in NFC championship game (2003 season). ... Played in Super Bowl 38 (2003 season).
MISCELLANEOUS: Selected by Minnesota Twins organization in 22nd round of free-agent draft (1999).

			TOTALS			INTERCEPTIONS			
Year Team	G	GS	Tk.	Ast.	Sks.	No.	Yds.	Avg.	TD
2003—Carolina NFL	16	7	48	6	0.0	3	33	11.0	1
2004—Carolina NFL	16	16	50	10	0.0	4	46	11.5	0
Pro totals (2 years)	32	23	98	16	0.0	7	79	11.3	1

MANUEL, MARQUAND S

PERSONAL: Born July 11, 1979, in Miami, Fla. ... 6-0/209. ... Full name: Marquand Alexander Manuel.
HIGH SCHOOL: Miami Senior (Fla.).
COLLEGE: Florida.
TRANSACTIONS/CAREER NOTES: Selected by Cincinnati Bengals in sixth round (181st pick overall) of 2002 NFL draft. ... Signed by Bengals (May 13, 2002). ... Claimed on waivers by Seattle Seahawks (September 6, 2004). ... Granted free agency (March 2, 2005).

			TOTALS			INTERCEPTIONS			
Year Team	G	GS	Tk.	Ast.	Sks.	No.	Yds.	Avg.	TD
2002—Cincinnati NFL...	15	8	26	8	0.0	0	0	0.0	0
2003—Cincinnati NFL...	13	1	9	2	0.0	0	0	0.0	0
2004—Seattle NFL...	15	0	7	3	0.0	0	0	0.0	0
Pro totals (3 years)	43	9	42	13	0.0	0	0	0.0	0

MANUMALEUNA, BRANDON   TE   RAMS

PERSONAL: Born January 4, 1980, in Torrance, Calif. ... 6-2/288. ... Full name: Brandon Michael Manumaleuna.
HIGH SCHOOL: Narbonne (Calif.).
COLLEGE: Arizona.
TRANSACTIONS/CAREER NOTES: Selected by St. Louis Rams in fourth round (129th pick overall) of 2001 NFL draft. ... Signed by Rams (June 21, 2001). ... Granted free agency (March 3, 2004). ... Tendered offer sheet by Carolina Panthers (March 4, 2004). ... Offer matched by Rams (March 11, 2004).
CHAMPIONSHIP GAME EXPERIENCE: Played in NFC championship game (2001 season). ... Played in Super Bowl 36 (2001 season).
SINGLE GAME HIGHS (regular season): Receptions—4 (October 19, 2003, vs. Green Bay); yards—56 (October 13, 2003, vs. Atlanta); and touchdown receptions—1 (October 10, 2004, vs. Seattle).

			RECEIVING				TOTALS			
Year Team	G	GS	No.	Yds.	Avg.	TD	TD	2pt.	Pts.	Fum.
2001—St. Louis NFL	16	0	1	1	1.0	1	1	0	6	0
2002—St. Louis NFL	16	10	8	106	13.3	1	1	0	6	0
2003—St. Louis NFL	16	15	29	238	8.2	2	2	0	12	0
2004—St. Louis NFL	16	16	15	174	11.6	1	1	0	6	0
Pro totals (4 years)	64	41	53	519	9.8	5	5	0	30	0

MANUWAI, VINCE   G   JAGUARS

PERSONAL: Born July 12, 1980, in Honolulu, Hawaii. ... 6-2/312. ... Full name: Vincent Manuwai.
HIGH SCHOOL: Farrington (Honolulu, Hawaii).
COLLEGE: Hawaii.
TRANSACTIONS/CAREER NOTES: Selected by Jacksonville Jaguars in third round (72nd pick overall) of 2003 NFL draft. ... Signed by Jaguars (July 25, 2003).
PLAYING EXPERIENCE: Jacksonville NFL, 2003-2004. ... Games/Games started: 2003 (15/14), 2004 (16/16). Total: 31/30.

MARE, OLINDO   K   DOLPHINS

PERSONAL: Born June 6, 1973, in Hollywood, Fla. ... 5-10/195. ... Full name: Olindo Franco Mare. ... Name pronounced: o-LEND-o MAR-ray.
HIGH SCHOOL: Cooper City (Fla.).
JUNIOR COLLEGE: Valencia Community College (Fla.).
COLLEGE: Syracuse.
TRANSACTIONS/CAREER NOTES: Signed as non-drafted free agent by New York Giants (May 2, 1996). ... Released by Giants (August 25, 1996). ... Re-signed by Giants to practice squad (August 27, 1996). ... Granted free agency after 1996 season. ... Signed by Miami Dolphins (February 27, 1997). ... Granted free agency (February 11, 2000). ... Re-signed by Dolphins (June 15, 2000). ... Granted unconditional free agency (March 2, 2001). ... Re-signed by Dolphins (March 2, 2001).
HONORS: Named kicker on THE SPORTING NEWS NFL All-Pro team (1999). ... Played in Pro Bowl (1999 season).
RECORDS: Shares NFL single-season record for most field goals made—39 (1999).
MISCELLANEOUS: Miami Dolphins all-time leading scorer (840 points).

		FIELD GOALS							TOTALS		
Year Team	G	1-29	30-39	40-49	50+	Tot.	Pct.	Lg.	XPM	XPA	Pts.
1996—New York Giants NFL	Did not play.										
1997—Miami NFL	16	16-17	8-10	3-6	1-3	28-36	77.8	50	33	33	117
1998—Miami NFL	16	12-13	5-5	5-7	0-2	22-27	81.5	48	33	34	99
1999—Miami NFL	16	10-10	17-17	9-14	3-5	*39-*46	84.8	54	27	27	144
2000—Miami NFL	16	7-8	9-10	12-13	0-0	28-31	90.3	49	33	34	117
2001—Miami NFL	16	9-9	8-8	2-4	0-0	19-21	90.5	46	39	40	96
2002—Miami NFL	16	13-14	2-3	7-11	2-3	24-31	77.4	53	42	43	114
2003—Miami NFL	16	9-9	3-6	6-8	4-6	22-29	75.9	52	33	34	99
2004—Miami NFL	11	1-2	6-7	3-4	2-3	12-16	75.0	51	18	18	54
Pro totals (8 years)	123	77-82	58-66	47-67	12-22	194-237	81.9	54	258	263	840

MARION, BROCK   S

PERSONAL: Born June 11, 1970, in Bakersfield, Calif. ... 6-0/200. ... Full name: Brock Elliot Marion.
HIGH SCHOOL: West (Bakersfield, Calif.).
COLLEGE: Nevada.
TRANSACTIONS/CAREER NOTES: Selected by Dallas Cowboys in seventh round (196th overall) of 1993 NFL draft. ... Signed by Cowboys (July 14, 1993). ... Granted free agency (February 16, 1996). ... Re-signed by Cowboys (May 2, 1996). ... Granted unconditional free agency (February 14, 1997). ... Re-signed by Cowboys (April 7, 1997). ... Granted unconditional free agency (February 13, 1998). ... Signed by Miami Dolphins (March 3, 1998). ... Granted unconditional free agency (March 2, 2001). ... Re-signed by Dolphins (June 9, 2001). ... Released by Dolphins (February 28, 2002). ... Re-signed by Dolphins (March 10, 2002). ... Released by Dolphins (March 2, 2004). ... Signed by Detroit Lions (March 25, 2004). ... Released by Lions (April 25, 2005).
CHAMPIONSHIP GAME EXPERIENCE: Played in NFC championship game (1993-1995 seasons). ... Member of Super Bowl championship team (1993 and 1995 seasons).
HONORS: Played in Pro Bowl (2000, 2002 and 2003 seasons).

			TOTALS			INTERCEPTIONS				KICKOFF RETURNS				TOTALS			
Year Team	G	GS	Tk.	Ast.	Sks.	No.	Yds.	Avg.	TD	No.	Yds.	Avg.	TD	TD	2pt.	Pts.	Fum.
1993—Dallas NFL	15	0	11	5	0.0	1	2	2.0	0	0	0	0.0	0	0	0	0	0
1994—Dallas NFL	14	1	22	4	1.0	1	11	11.0	0	2	39	19.5	0	0	0	0	0
1995—Dallas NFL	16	16	64	16	0.0	6	40	6.7	1	1	16	16.0	0	1	0	6	0

M

Year Team	G	GS	TOTALS			INTERCEPTIONS				KICKOFF RETURNS				TOTALS			
			Tk.	Ast.	Sks.	No.	Yds.	Avg.	TD	No.	Yds.	Avg.	TD	TD	2pt.	Pts.	Fum.
1996—Dallas NFL	10	10	41	10	0.0	0	0	0.0	0	3	68	22.7	0	0	0	0	1
1997—Dallas NFL	16	16	100	17	0.0	0	0	0.0	0	10	311	31.1	0	0	0	0	0
1998—Miami NFL	16	16	71	27	0.0	0	0	0.0	0	6	109	18.2	0	0	0	0	0
1999—Miami NFL	16	16	53	33	1.0	2	30	15.0	0	*62	*1524	24.6	0	0	0	0	2
2000—Miami NFL	16	16	72	24	0.0	5	72	14.4	0	22	513	23.3	0	0	0	0	0
2001—Miami NFL	15	15	55	24	0.0	5	*227	45.4	†2	17	371	21.8	0	2	0	12	1
2002—Miami NFL	16	16	64	29	0.0	5	99	19.8	0	0	0	0.0	0	0	0	0	0
2003—Miami NFL	16	16	57	24	0.0	3	3	1.0	0	0	0	0.0	0	0	0	0	0
2004—Detroit NFL	16	16	66	22	0.0	3	43	14.3	0	0	0	0.0	0	0	0	0	0
Pro totals (12 years)	182	154	676	235	2.0	31	527	17.0	3	123	2951	24.0	0	3	0	18	4

MARSHALL, ALFONSO   CB   BEARS

PERSONAL: Born January 17, 1981, in Clewiston, Fla. ... 6-1/183. ... Full name: Alfonso Lanard Marshall.
HIGH SCHOOL: Clewiston (Fla.).
COLLEGE: Miami (Fla.).
TRANSACTIONS/CAREER NOTES: Selected by Chicago Bears in seventh round (215th pick overall) of 2004 NFL draft. ... Signed by Chicago Bears (July 23, 2004). ... Released by Bears (September 5, 2004). ... Signed by Bears to practice squad (September 6, 2004). ... Activated (September 21, 2004). ... On injured reserve with knee injury (November 15, 2004-remainder of season).

Year Team	G	GS	TOTALS			INTERCEPTIONS			
			Tk.	Ast.	Sks.	No.	Yds.	Avg.	TD
2004—Chicago NFL	7	0	0	1	0.0	0	0	0.0	0

MARSHALL, LEMAR   LB   REDSKINS

PERSONAL: Born December 17, 1976, in Cincinnati, Ohio. ... 6-2/227.
HIGH SCHOOL: St. Xavier (Cincinnati).
COLLEGE: Michigan State.
TRANSACTIONS/CAREER NOTES: Signed as non-drafted free agent by Tampa Bay Buccaneers (April 19, 1999). ... Released by Buccaneers (September 6, 1999). ... Signed by Philadelphia Eagles (January 12, 2000). ... Claimed on waivers by Buccaneers (August 22, 2000). ... Released by Buccaneers (August 28, 2000). ... Re-signed by Buccaneers to practice squad (November 22, 2000). ... Released by Buccaneers (December 14, 2000). ... Signed by Denver Broncos (January 29, 2001). ... Released by Broncos (September 1, 2001). ... Signed by Washington Redskins (December 26, 2001).

Year Team	G	GS	TOTALS			INTERCEPTIONS			
			Tk.	Ast.	Sks.	No.	Yds.	Avg.	TD
2002—Washington NFL	16	0	3	0	0.0	0	0	0.0	0
2003—Washington NFL	12	0	2	0	0.5	0	0	0.0	0
2004—Washington NFL	16	14	45	20	1.5	0	0	0.0	0
Pro totals (3 years)	44	14	50	20	2.0	0	0	0.0	0

M

MARSHALL, TORRANCE   LB

PERSONAL: Born June 12, 1977, in Miami, Fla. ... 6-2/255.
HIGH SCHOOL: Sunset (Miami).
JUNIOR COLLEGE: Kemper Military Junior College (Mo.), then Miami-Dade Community College.
COLLEGE: Oklahoma.
TRANSACTIONS/CAREER NOTES: Selected by Green Bay Packers in third round (72nd pick overall) of 2001 NFL draft. ... Signed by Packers (July 24, 2001). ... On suspended list for violating league substance abuse policy (September 7-30, 2003). ... Granted free agency (March 3, 2004). ... Re-signed by Packers (April 21, 2004). ... On injured reserve with hamstring injury (November 27, 2004-remainder of season). ... Granted unconditional free agency (March 2, 2005).
HONORS: Named linebacker on THE SPORTING NEWS college All-America third team (2000).

Year Team	G	GS	TOTALS			INTERCEPTIONS			
			Tk.	Ast.	Sks.	No.	Yds.	Avg.	TD
2001—Green Bay NFL	14	1	9	3	0.0	0	0	0.0	0
2002—Green Bay NFL	16	0	2	1	0.0	0	0	0.0	0
2003—Green Bay NFL	12	1	11	3	1.0	0	0	0.0	0
2004—Green Bay NFL	9	0	3	0	0.0	0	0	0.0	0
Pro totals (4 years)	51	2	25	7	1.0	0	0	0.0	0

MARTIN, CURTIS   RB   JETS

PERSONAL: Born May 1, 1973, in Pittsburgh, Pa. ... 5-11/210.
HIGH SCHOOL: Taylor-Allderdice (Pittsburgh).
COLLEGE: Pittsburgh.
TRANSACTIONS/CAREER NOTES: Selected after junior season by New England Patriots in third round (74th pick overall) of 1995 NFL draft. ... Signed by Patriots (July 18, 1995). ... Granted free agency (February 13, 1998). ... Tendered offer sheet by New York Jets (March 20, 1998). ... Patriots declined to match offer (March 25, 1998).
CHAMPIONSHIP GAME EXPERIENCE: Played in AFC championship game (1996 and 1998 seasons). ... Played in Super Bowl 31 (1996 season).
HONORS: Named NFL Rookie of the Year by THE SPORTING NEWS (1995). ... Played in Pro Bowl (1995, 1996, 1998 and 2001 seasons). ... Named running back on THE SPORTING NEWS NFL All-Pro team (2001 and 2004). ... Named to play in Pro Bowl (2004 season); replaced by Rudi Johnson due to injury.

SINGLE GAME HIGHS (regular season): Attempts—40 (September 14, 1997, vs. New York Jets); yards—203 (December 3, 2000, vs. Indianapolis); and rushing touchdowns—3 (November 11, 2001, vs. Kansas City).

STATISTICAL PLATEAUS: 100-yard rushing games: 1995 (9), 1996 (2), 1997 (3), 1998 (8), 1999 (6), 2000 (3), 2001 (7), 2002 (5), 2003 (4), 2004 (9). Total: 56.

MISCELLANEOUS: Holds New York Jets all-time records for most yards rushing (9,567) and most rushing touchdowns (53). ... Active NFL leader in career rushing yards (13,366).

Year Team	G	GS	RUSHING				RECEIVING				TOTALS			
			Att.	Yds.	Avg.	TD	No.	Yds.	Avg.	TD	TD	2pt.	Pts.	Fum.
1995—New England NFL	16	15	§368	§1487	4.0	14	30	261	8.7	1	15	1	92	5
1996—New England NFL	16	15	316	1152	3.6	§14	46	333	7.2	3	§17	1	104	4
1997—New England NFL	13	13	274	1160	4.2	4	41	296	7.2	1	5	0	30	3
1998—New York Jets NFL	15	15	369	1287	3.5	8	43	365	8.5	1	9	0	54	5
1999—New York Jets NFL	16	16	367	1464	4.0	5	45	259	5.8	0	5	0	30	2
2000—New York Jets NFL	16	16	316	1204	3.8	9	70	508	7.3	2	11	0	66	2
2001—New York Jets NFL	16	16	333	1513	4.5	10	53	320	6.0	0	10	0	60	2
2002—New York Jets NFL	16	16	261	1094	4.2	7	49	362	7.4	0	7	1	44	0
2003—New York Jets NFL	16	16	323	1308	4.0	2	42	262	6.2	0	2	0	12	2
2004—New York Jets NFL	16	16	*371	*1697	4.6	12	41	245	6.0	2	14	0	84	2
Pro totals (10 years)	156	154	3298	13366	4.1	85	460	3211	7.0	10	95	3	576	27

MARTIN, DAVID   TE   PACKERS

PERSONAL: Born March 13, 1979, in Fort Campbell, Ky. ... 6-4/262. ... Full name: David Earl Martin.

HIGH SCHOOL: Norview (Norfolk, Va.).

COLLEGE: Tennessee.

TRANSACTIONS/CAREER NOTES: Selected by Green Bay Packers in sixth round (198th pick overall) of 2001 NFL draft. ... Signed by Packers (June 15, 2001). ... Granted free agency (March 3, 2004). ... Re-signed by Packers (April 20, 2004). ... On injured reserve with knee injury (November 30, 2004-remainder of season). ... Granted unconditional free agency (March 2, 2005). ... Re-signed by Packers (March 16, 2005).

SINGLE GAME HIGHS (regular season): Receptions—3 (October 20, 2002, vs. Washington); yards—35 (November 14, 2004, vs. Minnesota); and touchdown receptions—1 (December 22, 2003, vs. Oakland).

Year Team	G	GS	RECEIVING				TOTALS			
			No.	Yds.	Avg.	TD	TD	2pt.	Pts.	Fum.
2001—Green Bay NFL	14	1	13	144	11.1	1	1	0	6	0
2002—Green Bay NFL	8	2	8	33	4.1	1	1	0	6	0
2003—Green Bay NFL	16	3	13	79	6.1	2	2	0	12	0
2004—Green Bay NFL	9	3	5	88	17.6	0	0	0	0	0
Pro totals (4 years)	47	9	39	344	8.8	4	4	0	24	0

MARTIN, JAMAR   FB   DOLPHINS

PERSONAL: Born April 12, 1980, in Canton, Ohio. ... 5-11/244.

HIGH SCHOOL: McKinley (Canton, Ohio).

COLLEGE: Ohio State.

TRANSACTIONS/CAREER NOTES: Selected by Dallas Cowboys in fourth round (129th pick overall) of 2002 NFL draft. ... Signed by Cowboys (July 25, 2002). ... On injured reserve with knee injury (August 27, 2002-remainder of season). ... Claimed on waivers by Miami Dolphins (September 6, 2004). ... Released by Dolphins (September 18, 2004). ... Re-signed by Dolphins (September 21, 2004).

SINGLE GAME HIGHS (regular season): Attempts—1 (December 28, 2003, vs. New Orleans); yards—3 (November 2, 2003, vs. Washington); and rushing touchdowns—0.

Year Team	G	GS	RUSHING				RECEIVING				TOTALS			
			Att.	Yds.	Avg.	TD	No.	Yds.	Avg.	TD	TD	2pt.	Pts.	Fum.
2003—Dallas NFL	14	1	4	7	1.8	0	2	9	4.5	0	0	0	0	0
2004—Miami NFL	9	1	0	0	0.0	0	4	15	3.8	0	0	0	0	1
Pro totals (2 years)	23	2	4	7	1.8	0	6	24	4.0	0	0	0	0	1

MARTIN, JAMIE   QB   RAMS

PERSONAL: Born February 8, 1970, in Orange, Calif. ... 6-2/205. ... Full name: Jamie Blane Martin.

HIGH SCHOOL: Arroyo Grande (Calif.).

COLLEGE: Weber State.

TRANSACTIONS/CAREER NOTES: Signed as non-drafted free agent by Los Angeles Rams (May 3, 1993). ... Released by Rams (August (24, 1993). ... Re-signed by Rams to practice squad (August 31, 1993). ... Activated (November 23, 1993). ... Inactive for five games (1993). ... Released by Rams (August 27, 1994). ... Re-signed by Rams (October 4, 1994). ... Released by Rams (October 12, 1994). ... Re-signed by Rams (November 15, 1994). ... Active for one game (1994); did not play. ... Assigned by Rams to Amsterdam Admirals of World Football League (1995). ... Rams franchise moved to St. Louis (April 12, 1995). ... On physically unable to perform list with broken collarbone (June 3, 1995-entire season). ... Released by Rams (August 17, 1997). ... Signed by Washington Redskins (December 2, 1997). ... Granted free agency (February 13, 1998). ... Signed by Jacksonville Jaguars (March 6, 1998). ... On injured reserve with knee injury (December 15, 1998-remainder of season). ... Granted unconditional free agency (February 12, 1999). ... Signed by Cleveland Browns (August 25, 1999). ... Granted unconditional free agency (February 11, 2000). ... Signed by Jaguars (February 22, 2000). ... Released by Jaguars (March 1, 2001). ... Re-signed by Jaguars (April 2, 2001). ... Released by Jaguars (September 2, 2001). ... Re-signed by Rams (September 3, 2001). ... Released by Rams (February 27, 2003). ... Signed by New York Jets (August 26, 2003). ... Released by Jets (September 2, 2003). ... Re-signed by Jets (September 8, 2003). ... Released by Jets (October 22, 2003). ... Re-signed by Rams (December 6, 2004). ... Granted unconditional free agency (March 2, 2005). ... Re-signed by Rams (April 20, 2005).

CHAMPIONSHIP GAME EXPERIENCE: Member of Rams for NFC championship game (2001 season); did not play. ... Member of Rams for Super Bowl 36 (2001 season); did not play.

HONORS: Walter Payton Award winner (1991).

SINGLE GAME HIGHS (regular season): Attempts—48 (December 22, 2002, vs. Seattle); completions—31 (December 22, 2002, vs. Seattle); yards—262 (September 29, 2002, vs. Dallas); and touchdown passes—3 (December 30, 2002, vs. San Francisco).
MISCELLANEOUS: Regular-season record as starting NFL quarterback: 0-3.

Year Team	G	GS	Att.	Cmp.	Pct.	Yds.	TD	Int.	Avg.	Skd.	Rat.	Att.	Yds.	Avg.	TD	TD	2pt.	Pts.
						PASSING							RUSHING				TOTALS	
1993—L.A.Rams NFL...............	Did not play.																	
1994—L.A. Rams NFL	Did not play.																	
1995—St. Louis NFL	Did not play.																	
1996—St. Louis NFL	6	0	34	23	67.6	241	3	2	7.09	0	92.9	7	14	2.0	0	0	0	0
1997—Washington NFL	Did not play.																	
1998—Jacksonville NFL............	4	1	45	27	60.0	355	2	0	7.89	0	99.8	5	8	1.6	0	0	0	0
1999—Cleveland NFL	Did not play.																	
2000—Jacksonville NFL............	5	0	33	22	66.7	307	2	1	9.30	0	104.0	7	-6	-0.9	0	0	0	0
2001—St. Louis NFL	5	0	3	3	100.0	22	0	0	7.33	0	97.2	8	-9	-1.1	0	0	0	0
2002—St. Louis NFL	5	2	195	124	63.6	1216	7	10	6.24	0	71.7	5	6	1.2	0	0	0	0
2004—St. Louis NFL	1	0	30	16	53.3	188	0	2	6.27	2	72.6	0	0	0.0	0	0	0	0
Pro totals (6 years)	26	3	340	215	63.2	2329	14	13	6.85	2	81.1	32	13	0.4	0	0	0	0

MARTIN, STEVE DT VIKINGS

PERSONAL: Born May 31, 1974, in St. Paul, Minn. ... 6-4/320. ... Full name: Steven Albert Martin.
HIGH SCHOOL: Jefferson City (Mo.).
COLLEGE: Missouri.
TRANSACTIONS/CAREER NOTES: Selected by Indianapolis Colts in fifth round (151st pick overall) of 1996 NFL draft. ... Signed by Colts (July 5, 1996). ... Claimed on waivers by Philadelphia Eagles (October 23, 1998). ... Granted free agency (February 12, 1999). ... Re-signed by Eagles (April 9, 1999). ... Granted unconditional free agency (February 11, 2000). ... Signed by Kansas City Chiefs (February 24, 2000). ... Released by Chiefs (September 1, 2001). ... Signed by New York Jets (September 3, 2001). ... Granted unconditional free agency (March 1, 2002). ... Signed by New England Patriots (April 3, 2002). ... Released by Patriots (December 19, 2002). ... Signed by Green Bay Packers (July 22, 2003). ... Released by Packers (August 31, 2003). ... Signed by Houston Texans (September 15, 2003). ... Granted unconditional free agency (March 3, 2004). ... Signed by Minnesota Vikings (March 6, 2004).

Year Team	G	GS	TOTALS Tk.	Ast.	Sks.
1996—Indianapolis NFL..	14	5	25	11	1.0
1997—Indianapolis NFL..	12	0	9	7	0.0
1998—Indianapolis NFL..	4	0	2	0	0.0
—Philadelphia NFL..	9	3	21	7	1.0
1999—Philadelphia NFL..	16	15	26	17	2.0
2000—Kansas City NFL..	16	0	8	5	0.0
2001—New York Jets NFL..	16	15	40	18	2.5
2002—New England NFL..	14	6	13	4	0.0
2003—Houston NFL	14	8	45	17	1.0
2004—Minnesota NFL	12	0	11	9	0.5
Pro totals (9 years)...	127	52	200	95	8.0

MARTIN, TERRANCE DE BENGALS

PERSONAL: Born July 6, 1979, in Toano, Va. ... 6-2/290.
HIGH SCHOOL: Lafayette (Toano, Va.).
COLLEGE: North Carolina State.
TRANSACTIONS/CAREER NOTES: Signed as non-drafted free agent by Houston Texans (May 12, 2003). ... Released by Texans (September 5, 2004). ... Signed by Cincinnati Bengals (November 3, 2004).

Year Team	G	GS	TOTALS Tk.	Ast.	Sks.
2003—Houston NFL	12	1	3	3	0.0
2004—Cincinnati NFL	2	0	1	0	0.0
Pro totals (2 years)..	14	1	4	3	0.0

MASLOWSKI, MIKE LB CHIEFS

PERSONAL: Born July 11, 1974, in Thorp, Wis. ... 6-1/243. ... Full name: Michael John Maslowski.
HIGH SCHOOL: Thorp (Wis.).
COLLEGE: Wisconsin-La Crosse.
TRANSACTIONS/CAREER NOTES: Signed as non-drafted free agent by San Diego Chargers (April 21, 1997). ... Released by Chargers (August 1997). ... Played for San Jose Sabercats of Arena League (1998). ... Signed by Kansas City Chiefs (January 12, 1999). ... Assigned by Chiefs to Barcelona Dragons in 1999 NFL Europe enhancement allocation program (February 22, 1999). ... On injured reserve with knee injury (December 22, 2001-remainder of season). ... Granted free agency (March 1, 2002). ... Tendered offer sheet by New England Patriots (March 7, 2002). ... Offer matched by Chiefs (March 14, 2002). ... On injured reserve with knee injury (September 5, 2004-entire season).

Year Team	G	GS	TOTALS Tk.	Ast.	Sks.	INTERCEPTIONS No.	Yds.	Avg.	TD
1999—Kansas City NFL...	15	0	0	0	0.0	0	0	0.0	0
2000—Kansas City NFL...	16	5	29	12	2.0	0	0	0.0	0
2001—Kansas City NFL...	8	0	5	1	1.0	0	0	0.0	0
2002—Kansas City NFL...	16	16	94	32	1.0	3	28	9.3	0
2003—Kansas City NFL...	10	10	46	14	0.0	0	0	0.0	0
2004—Kansas City NFL...	Did not play.								
Pro totals (5 years)...	65	31	174	59	4.0	3	28	9.3	0

M

MASON, DERRICK   WR   RAVENS

PERSONAL: Born January 17, 1974, in Detroit, Mich. ... 5-10/190. ... Full name: Derrick James Mason.
HIGH SCHOOL: Mumford (Detroit).
COLLEGE: Michigan State.
TRANSACTIONS/CAREER NOTES: Selected by Houston Oilers in fourth round (98th pick overall) of 1997 NFL draft. ... Oilers franchise moved to Tennessee for 1997 season. ... Signed by Oilers (July 19, 1997). ... Oilers franchise renamed Tennessee Titans for 1999 season (December 26, 1998). ... Granted free agency (February 11, 2000). ... Re-signed by Titans (June 1, 2000). ... Granted unconditional free agency (March 2, 2001). ... Re-signed by Titans (March 2, 2001). ... Released by Titans (February 21, 2005). ... Signed by Baltimore Ravens (March 2, 2005).
CHAMPIONSHIP GAME EXPERIENCE: Played in AFC championship game (1999 and 2002 seasons). ... Played in Super Bowl 34 (1999 season).
HONORS: Named kick returner on THE SPORTING NEWS NFL All-Pro team (2000). ... Played in Pro Bowl (2000 and 2003 seasons).
RECORDS: Holds NFL single-season record for most combined net yards—2,690 (2000).
SINGLE GAME HIGHS (regular season): Receptions—12 (October 3, 2004, vs. San Diego); yards—186 (January 6, 2002, vs. Cincinnati); and touchdown receptions—3 (October 12, 2003, vs. Houston).
STATISTICAL PLATEAUS: 100-yard receiving games: 2000 (1), 2001 (4), 2002 (3), 2003 (3), 2004 (2). Total: 13.

			RUSHING				RECEIVING				PUNT RETURNS				KICKOFF RETURNS				TOTALS		
Year—Team	G	GS	Att.	Yds.	Avg.	TD	No.	Yds.	Avg.	TD	No.	Yds.	Avg.	TD	No.	Yds.	Avg.	TD	TD	2pt.	Pts.
1997—Ten. NFL	16	2	1	-7	-7.0	0	14	186	13.3	0	13	95	7.3	0	26	551	21.2	0	0	0	0
1998—Ten. NFL	16	0	0	0	0.0	0	25	333	13.3	3	31	228	7.4	0	8	154	19.3	0	3	0	18
1999—Ten. NFL	13	0	0	0	0.0	0	8	89	11.1	0	26	225	8.7	1	41	805	19.6	0	1	0	6
2000—Ten. NFL	16	12	1	1	1.0	0	63	895	14.2	5	*51	*662	13.0	1	42	1132	§27.0	0	6	0	36
2001—Ten. NFL	15	15	0	0	0.0	0	73	1128	15.5	9	20	128	6.4	0	34	748	22.0	1	10	1	62
2002—Ten. NFL	14	14	0	0	0.0	0	79	1012	12.8	5	9	60	6.7	0	0	0	0.0	0	5	0	30
2003—Ten. NFL	16	16	3	11	3.7	0	95	1303	13.7	8	8	99	12.4	0	5	106	21.2	0	8	0	48
2004—Ten. NFL	16	16	1	-3	-3.0	0	96	1168	12.2	7	24	93	3.9	0	0	0	0.0	0	7	0	42
Pro totals (8 years)	122	75	6	2	0.3	0	453	6114	13.5	37	182	1590	8.7	2	156	3496	22.4	1	40	1	242

MASSEY, CHRIS   RB   RAMS

PERSONAL: Born August 21, 1979, in Charleston, W.Va. ... 6-0/245. ... Full name: Christopher Todd Massey.
HIGH SCHOOL: East Bank (W.Va.).
COLLEGE: Marshall.
TRANSACTIONS/CAREER NOTES: Selected by St. Louis Rams in seventh round (243rd pick overall) of 2002 NFL draft. ... Signed by Rams (June 28, 2002). ... Granted free agency (March 2, 2005). ... Re-signed by Rams (March 17, 2005).
SINGLE GAME HIGHS (regular season): Attempts—1 (September 28, 2003, vs. Arizona); yards—1 (September 28, 2003, vs. Arizona); and rushing touchdowns—0.

			RUSHING				TOTALS			
Year—Team	G	GS	Att.	Yds.	Avg.	TD	TD	2pt.	Pts.	Fum.
2002—St. Louis NFL	16	1	0	0	0.0	0	0	0	0	0
2003—St. Louis NFL	16	0	1	-1	-1.0	0	0	0	0	0
2004—St. Louis NFL	16	0	0	0	0.0	0	0	0	0	0
Pro totals (3 years)	48	1	1	-1	-1.0	0	0	0	0	0

M

MATHEWS, JASON   T

PERSONAL: Born February 9, 1971, in Orange, Texas. ... 6-5/285. ... Full name: Samuel Jason Mathews.
HIGH SCHOOL: Bridge City (Texas).
COLLEGE: Texas A&M.
TRANSACTIONS/CAREER NOTES: Selected by Indianapolis Colts in third round (67th pick overall) of 1994 NFL draft. ... Signed by Colts (July 23, 1994). ... Granted free agency (February 14, 1997). ... Re-signed by Colts (April 30, 1997). ... Granted unconditional free agency (February 13, 1998). ... Signed by Tampa Bay Buccaneers (May 7, 1998). ... Released by Buccaneers (August 30, 1998). ... Signed by Tennessee Oilers (September 1, 1998). ... Oilers franchise renamed Tennessee Titans for 1999 season (December 26, 1998). ... Granted unconditional free agency (March 2, 2005).
PLAYING EXPERIENCE: Indianapolis NFL, 1994-1997; Tennessee NFL, 1998-2004. ... Games/Games started: 1994 (10/0), 1995 (16/16), 1996 (16/15), 1997 (16/0), 1998 (3/0), 1999 (3/0), 2000 (16/1), 2001 (16/2), 2002 (16/2), 2003 (15/0), 2004 (15/7). Total: 142/43.
CHAMPIONSHIP GAME EXPERIENCE: Played in AFC championship game (1995, 1999 and 2002 seasons). ... Member of Titans for Super Bowl 34 (1999 season); did not play.

MATHIS, KEVIN   CB   FALCONS

PERSONAL: Born April 29, 1974, in Gainesville, Texas. ... 5-9/185.
HIGH SCHOOL: Gainesville (Texas).
COLLEGE: Texas A&M-Commerce.
TRANSACTIONS/CAREER NOTES: Signed as non-drafted free agent by Dallas Cowboys (April 24, 1997). ... Granted free agency (February 11, 2000). ... Re-signed by Cowboys (April 26, 2000). ... Traded by Cowboys to New Orleans Saints for LB Chris Bordano (April 26, 2000). ... Granted unconditional free agency (March 2, 2001). ... Re-signed by Saints (March 2, 2001). ... Released by Saints (July 24, 2002). ... Signed by Atlanta Falcons (September 17, 2002). ... Granted unconditional free agency (February 28, 2003). ... Re-signed by Falcons (March 31, 2003). ... Granted unconditional free agency (March 2, 2005). ... Re-signed by Falcons (March 11, 2005).
CHAMPIONSHIP GAME EXPERIENCE: Member of Falcons for NFC championship game (2004 season); inactive.

			TOTALS			INTERCEPTIONS				PUNT RETURNS				KICKOFF RETURNS				TOTALS		
Year—Team	G	GS	Tk.	Ast.	Sks.	No.	Yds.	Avg.	TD	No.	Yds.	Avg.	TD	No.	Yds.	Avg.	TD	TD	2pt.	Pts.	Fum.
1997—Dal. NFL	16	3	15	1	0.0	0	0	0.0	0	11	91	8.3	0	0	0	0.0	0	0	0	0	2
1998—Dal. NFL	13	4	28	4	1.0	2	0	0.0	0	2	3	1.5	0	25	621	24.8	0	0	0	0	2

Year Team	G	GS	TOTALS			INTERCEPTIONS				PUNT RETURNS				KICKOFF RETURNS				TOTALS			
			Tk.	Ast.	Sks.	No.	Yds.	Avg.	TD	No.	Yds.	Avg.	TD	No.	Yds.	Avg.	TD	TD	2pt.	Pts.	Fum.
1999—Dal. NFL	8	4	11	3	0.0	0	0	0.0	0	0	0	0.0	0	18	408	22.7	0	0	0	0	1
2000—N.O. NFL	16	16	58	15	0.0	1	0	0.0	0	1	5	5.0	0	8	187	23.4	0	0	0	0	0
2001—N.O. NFL	14	13	63	14	1.0	2	34	17.0	0	0	0	0.0	0	0	0	0.0	0	0	0	0	0
2002—Atl. NFL	11	0	15	1	0.0	3	21	7.0	0	0	0	0.0	0	0	0	0.0	0	0	0	0	0
2003—Atl. NFL	14	2	29	4	1.0	1	32	32.0	1	0	0	0.0	0	0	0	0.0	0	1	0	6	0
2004—Atl. NFL	15	12	59	5	0.0	2	101	50.5	†2	0	0	0.0	0	0	0	0.0	0	2	0	12	0
Pro totals (8 years)	107	54	278	47	3.0	11	188	17.1	3	14	99	7.1	0	51	1216	23.8	0	3	0	18	6

MATHIS, RASHEAN   S   JAGUARS

PERSONAL: Born August 27, 1980, in Jacksonville, Fla. ... 6-1/200.
HIGH SCHOOL: Englewood (Jacksonville, Fla.).
COLLEGE: Bethune-Cookman.
TRANSACTIONS/CAREER NOTES: Selected by Jacksonville Jaguars in second round (39th pick overall) of 2003 NFL draft. ... Signed by Jaguars (July 25, 2003).

Year Team	G	GS	TOTALS			INTERCEPTIONS				PUNT RETURNS				KICKOFF RETURNS				TOTALS			
			Tk.	Ast.	Sks.	No.	Yds.	Avg.	TD	No.	Yds.	Avg.	TD	No.	Yds.	Avg.	TD	TD	2pt.	Pts.	Fum.
2003—Jac. NFL	16	16	68	10	0.0	2	0	0.0	0	2	7	3.5	0	1	7	7.0	0	0	0	0	0
2004—Jac. NFL	16	16	52	10	0.0	5	42	8.4	0	1	8	8.0	0	0	0	0.0	0	0	0	0	0
Pro totals (2 years)	32	32	120	20	0.0	7	42	6.0	0	3	15	5.0	0	1	7	7.0	0	0	0	0	0

MATHIS, ROBERT   DE   COLTS

PERSONAL: Born February 26, 1981, in Atlanta, Ga. ... 6-2/235.
HIGH SCHOOL: McNair (Atlanta).
COLLEGE: Alabama A&M.
TRANSACTIONS/CAREER NOTES: Selected by Indianapolis Colts in fifth round (138th pick overall) of 2003 NFL draft. ... Signed by Colts (July 24, 2003).
CHAMPIONSHIP GAME EXPERIENCE: Played in AFC championship game (2003 season).

Year Team	G	GS	TOTALS		
			Tk.	Ast.	Sks.
2003—Indianapolis NFL	16	0	7	1	3.5
2004—Indianapolis NFL	16	1	22	1	10.5
Pro totals (2 years)	32	1	29	2	14.0

MATTHEWS, SHANE   QB   BILLS

PERSONAL: Born June 1, 1970, in Pascagoula, Miss. ... 6-3/199. ... Full name: Michael Shane Matthews.
HIGH SCHOOL: Pascagoula (Miss.).
COLLEGE: Florida.
TRANSACTIONS/CAREER NOTES: Signed as non-drafted free agent by Chicago Bears (April 29, 1993). ... Released by Bears (August 30, 1993). ... Re-signed by Bears to practice squad (September 1, 1993). ... Activated (October 8, 1993); did not play. ... Active for two games (1994); did not play. ... Released by Bears (September 15, 1995). ... Re-signed by Bears (February 12, 1996). ... Released by Bears (June 7, 1996). ... Re-signed by Bears (October 9, 1996). ... Granted unconditional free agency (February 14, 1997). ... Assigned by Bears to Rhein Fire in 1997 World League enhancement allocation program (February 19, 1997). ... Signed by Carolina Panthers (August 25, 1997). ... Released by Panthers (September 17, 1997). ... Re-signed by Panthers (October 16, 1997). ... Active for two games (1997); did not play. ... Granted unconditional free agency (February 13, 1998). ... Re-signed by Panthers (March 19, 1998). ... Active for 12 games (1998); did not play. ... Granted unconditional free agency (February 12, 1999). ... Signed by Bears (April 3, 1999). ... Granted unconditional free agency (February 11, 2000). ... Re-signed by Bears (July 18, 2000). ... Granted unconditional free agency (March 2, 2001). ... Re-signed by Bears (March 14, 2001). ... Released by Bears (October 13, 2001). ... Re-signed by Bears (October 13, 2001). ... Released by Bears (April 24, 2002). ... Signed by Washington Redskins (April 29, 2002). ... Granted unconditional free agency (February 28, 2003). ... Signed by Tampa Bay Buccaneers (March 14, 2003). ... Released by Buccaneers (April 28, 2003). ... Signed by Cincinnati Bengals (June 1, 2003). ... Granted free agency (March 3, 2004). ... Signed by Buffalo Bills (August 30, 2004). ... Granted unconditional free agency (March 2, 2005). ... Re-signed by Bills (April 20, 2005).
SINGLE GAME HIGHS (regular season): Attempts—50 (November 10, 2002, vs. Jacksonville); completions—30 (November 4, 2001, vs. Cleveland); yards—357 (November 4, 2001, vs. Cleveland); and touchdown passes—3 (September 8, 2002, vs. Arizona).
STATISTICAL PLATEAUS: 300-yard passing games: 2001 (1), 2002 (1). Total: 2.
MISCELLANEOUS: Regular-season record as starting NFL quarterback: 11-11 (.500).

Year Team	G	GS	PASSING									RUSHING				TOTALS		
			Att.	Cmp.	Pct.	Yds.	TD	Int.	Avg.	Skd.	Rat.	Att.	Yds.	Avg.	TD	TD	2pt.	Pts.
1993—Chicago NFL	Did not play.																	
1994—Chicago NFL	Did not play.																	
1995—Buffalo AFL	Did not play.																	
1996—Chicago NFL	2	0	17	13	76.5	158	1	0	9.29	0	124.1	1	2	2.0	1	1	0	6
1997—Carolina NFL	Did not play.																	
1998—Carolina NFL	Did not play.																	
1999—Chicago NFL	8	7	275	167	60.7	1645	10	6	5.98	0	80.6	14	31	2.2	0	0	0	0
2000—Chicago NFL	6	5	178	102	57.3	964	3	6	5.42	0	64.0	10	35	3.5	0	0	0	0
2001—Chicago NFL	5	3	129	84	65.1	694	5	6	5.38	0	72.3	4	5	1.3	0	0	0	0
2002—Washington NFL	8	7	237	124	52.3	1251	11	6	5.28	0	72.6	12	31	2.6	0	0	0	0
2003—	Did not play.																	
2004—Buffalo NFL	3	0	3	2	66.7	44	1	0	14.67	0	149.3	2	-3	-1.5	0	0	0	0
Pro totals (6 years)	32	22	839	492	58.6	4756	31	24	5.67	0	75.0	43	101	2.3	1	1	0	6

MAWAE, KEVIN   C   JETS

PERSONAL: Born January 23, 1971, in Savannah, Ga. ... 6-4/289. ... Full name: Kevin James Mawae. ... Name pronounced: ma-WHY.
HIGH SCHOOL: Leesville (La.).
COLLEGE: Louisiana State.
TRANSACTIONS/CAREER NOTES: Selected by Seattle Seahawks in second round (36th pick overall) of 1994 NFL draft. ... Signed by Seahawks (July 21, 1994). ... Granted free agency (February 14, 1997). ... Re-signed by Seahawks (May 5, 1997). ... Granted unconditional free agency (February 13, 1998). ... Signed by New York Jets (February 19, 1998).
PLAYING EXPERIENCE: Seattle NFL, 1994-1997; New York Jets NFL, 1998-2004. ... Games/Games started: 1994 (14/11), 1995 (16/16), 1996 (16/16), 1997 (16/16), 1998 (16/16), 1999 (16/16), 2000 (16/16), 2001 (16/16), 2002 (16/16), 2003 (16/16), 2004 (16/16). Total: 174/171.
CHAMPIONSHIP GAME EXPERIENCE: Played in AFC championship game (1998 season).
HONORS: Named center on THE SPORTING NEWS NFL All-Pro team (1999, 2001 and 2002). ... Played in Pro Bowl (1999-2004 seasons).

MAXWELL, JAMES   LB   GIANTS

PERSONAL: Born August 8, 1981, in Johnsonville, S.C. ... 6-4/242.
HIGH SCHOOL: Johnsonville (S.C.).
COLLEGE: Gardner-Webb.
TRANSACTIONS/CAREER NOTES: Signed as non-drafted free agent by New York Giants (May 7, 2004). ... Released by Giants (September 1, 2004). ... Signed by Giants to practice squad (September 7, 2004). ... Activated (September 15, 2004).

			TOTALS			INTERCEPTIONS			
Year Team	G	GS	Tk.	Ast.	Sks.	No.	Yds.	Avg.	TD
2004—New York Giants NFL	14	0	4	3	1.0	0	0	0.0	0

MAYBERRY, JERMANE   G/T   SAINTS

PERSONAL: Born August 29, 1973, in Floresville, Texas. ... 6-4/325. ... Full name: Jermane Timothy Mayberry.
HIGH SCHOOL: Floresville (Texas).
JUNIOR COLLEGE: Navarro College (Texas).
COLLEGE: Texas A&M-Kingsville.
TRANSACTIONS/CAREER NOTES: Selected by Philadelphia Eagles in first round (25th pick overall) of 1996 NFL draft. ... Signed by Eagles (June 13, 1996). ... On injured reserve with elbow injury (October 27, 2003-remainder of season). ... Granted unconditional free agency (March 2, 2005). ... Signed by New Orleans Saints (March 5, 2005).
PLAYING EXPERIENCE: Philadelphia NFL, 1996-2004. ... Games/Games started: 1996 (3/1), 1997 (16/16), 1998 (15/10), 1999 (13/5), 2000 (16/16), 2001 (16/15), 2002 (16/16), 2003 (5/5), 2004 (12/12). Total: 112/96.
CHAMPIONSHIP GAME EXPERIENCE: Played in NFC championship game (2001, 2002 and 2004 seasons). ... Played in Super Bowl 39 (2004 season).
HONORS: Played in Pro Bowl (2002 season).

M

MAYER, SHAWN   S   FALCONS

PERSONAL: Born March 4, 1979, in Hillsborough, N.J. ... 6-0/202. ... Full name: Shawn Arron Mayer.
HIGH SCHOOL: Hillsborough (N.J.).
COLLEGE: Penn State.
TRANSACTIONS/CAREER NOTES: Signed as non-drafted free agent by New England Patriots (May 2, 2003). ... Released by Patriots (August 31, 2003). ... Re-signed by Patriots to practice squad (September 1, 2003). ... Activated (October 18, 2003). ... Released by Patriots (November 7, 2003). ... Re-signed by Patriots to practice squad (November 10, 2003). ... Activated (November 22, 2003). ... Released by Patriots (October 6, 2004). ... Signed by Atlanta Falcons (January 31, 2005). ... Assigned by Falcons to Hamburg Sea Devils in 2005 NFL Europe enhancement allocation program (February 14, 2005). ...
CHAMPIONSHIP GAME EXPERIENCE: Played in AFC championship game (2003 season). ... Member of Super Bowl championship team (2003 season).

			TOTALS			INTERCEPTIONS			
Year Team	G	GS	Tk.	Ast.	Sks.	No.	Yds.	Avg.	TD
2003—New England NFL	9	0	3	0	0.0	0	0	0.0	0
2004—New England NFL	3	0	0	0	0.0	0	0	0.0	0
Pro totals (2 years)	12	0	3	0	0.0	0	0	0.0	0

MAYES, ADRIAN   SS   CARDINALS

PERSONAL: Born November 17, 1980, in Hattiesburg, Miss. ... 6-1/211.
HIGH SCHOOL: Forest Brook (Houston, Texas).
COLLEGE: Louisiana State.
TRANSACTIONS/CAREER NOTES: Signed as non-drafted free agent by Arizona Cardinals (April 27, 2004). ... Released by Cardinals (September 4, 2004). ... Re-signed by Cardinals to practice squad (September 6, 2004). ... Activated (November 2, 2004). ... Assigned by Cardinals to Berlin Thunder in 2005 NFL Europe enhancement allocation program (February 14, 2005).

			TOTALS			INTERCEPTIONS			
Year Team	G	GS	Tk.	Ast.	Sks.	No.	Yds.	Avg.	TD
2004—Arizona NFL	4	0	0	0	0.0	0	0	0.0	0

MAYNARD, BRAD   P   BEARS

PERSONAL: Born February 9, 1974, in Tipton, Ind. ... 6-1/186. ... Full name: Bradley Alan Maynard.
HIGH SCHOOL: Sheridan (Ind.).
COLLEGE: Ball State.
TRANSACTIONS/CAREER NOTES: Selected by New York Giants in third round (95th pick overall) of 1997 NFL draft. ... Signed by Giants (July 19, 1997). ... Granted free agency (February 11, 2000). ... Re-signed by Giants (June 8, 2000). ... Granted unconditional free agency (March 2, 2001). ... Signed by Chicago Bears (March 3, 2001).
CHAMPIONSHIP GAME EXPERIENCE: Played in NFC championship game (2000 season). ... Played in Super Bowl 35 (2000 season).
HONORS: Named punter on THE SPORTING NEWS college All-America second team (1996).

			PUNTING				
Year Team	G	No.	Yds.	Avg.	Net avg.	In. 20	Blk.
1997—New York Giants NFL	16	*111	*4531	40.8	34.6	*33	1
1998—New York Giants NFL	16	101	*4566	45.2	37.8	∞33	0
1999—New York Giants NFL	16	89	3651	41.0	35.1	‡31	0
2000—New York Giants NFL	16	79	3210	40.6	33.7	26	1
2001—Chicago NFL	16	87	3709	42.6	37.0	*36	0
2002—Chicago NFL	16	87	3679	42.3	37.4	26	0
2003—Chicago NFL	16	79	3258	41.2	34.6	23	2
2004—Chicago NFL	16	*108	*4638	42.9	38.7	34	0
Pro totals (8 years)	128	741	31242	42.2	36.2	242	4

MAYS, LEE   WR   STEELERS

PERSONAL: Born September 18, 1978, in Houston, Texas. ... 6-2/193.
HIGH SCHOOL: Westfield (Houston).
COLLEGE: Texas-El Paso.
TRANSACTIONS/CAREER NOTES: Selected by Pittsburgh Steelers in sixth round (202nd pick overall) of 2002 NFL draft. ... Signed by Steelers (July 18, 2002). ... Granted free agency (March 2, 2005). ... Re-signed by Steelers (April 8, 2005).
CHAMPIONSHIP GAME EXPERIENCE: Played in AFC championship game (2004 season).
SINGLE GAME HIGHS (regular season): Receptions—3 (December 5, 2004, vs. Jacksonville); yards—46 (December 12, 2004, vs. New York Jets); and touchdown receptions—0.

			RUSHING				RECEIVING				KICKOFF RETURNS				TOTALS			
Year Team	G	GS	Att.	Yds.	Avg.	TD	No.	Yds.	Avg.	TD	No.	Yds.	Avg.	TD	TD	2pt.	Pts.	Fum.
2002—Pittsburgh NFL	16	0	0	0	0.0	0	0	0	0.0	0	32	671	21.0	0	0	0	0	0
2003—Pittsburgh NFL	16	0	0	0	0.0	0	2	17	8.5	0	4	79	19.8	0	0	0	0	0
2004—Pittsburgh NFL	16	1	0	0	0.0	0	9	137	15.2	0	0	0	0.0	0	0	0	0	0
Pro totals (3 years)	48	1	0	0	0.0	0	11	154	14.0	0	36	750	20.8	0	0	0	0	0

MCADDLEY, JASON   WR   TITANS

M

PERSONAL: Born July 28, 1979, in Brooklyn, N.Y. ... 6-2/200.
HIGH SCHOOL: Oak Ridge (Tenn.).
COLLEGE: Alabama.
TRANSACTIONS/CAREER NOTES: Selected by Arizona Cardinals in fifth round (149th pick overall) of 2002 NFL draft. ... Signed by Cardinals (June 5, 2002). ... On injured reserve with hamstring injury (November 26, 2003-remainder of season). ... Released by Cardinals (August 22, 2004). ... Signed by Tennessee Titans (October 7, 2004).
SINGLE GAME HIGHS (regular season): Receptions—5 (December 8, 2002, vs. Detroit); yards—113 (November 10, 2002, vs. Seattle); and touchdown receptions—1 (November 17, 2002, vs. Philadelphia).
STATISTICAL PLATEAUS: 100-yard receiving games: 2002 (1). Total: 1.

			RUSHING				RECEIVING				KICKOFF RETURNS				TOTALS			
Year Team	G	GS	Att.	Yds.	Avg.	TD	No.	Yds.	Avg.	TD	No.	Yds.	Avg.	TD	TD	2pt.	Pts.	Fum.
2002—Tennessee NFL	9	8	0	0	0.0	0	25	362	14.5	1	2	45	22.5	0	1	0	6	0
2003—Tennessee NFL	2	0	0	0	0.0	0	4	53	13.3	0	0	0	0.0	0	0	0	0	0
2004—Tennessee NFL	11	1	0	0	0.0	0	2	38	19.0	0	38	849	22.3	0	0	0	0	1
Pro totals (3 years)	22	9	0	0	0.0	0	31	453	14.6	1	40	894	22.4	0	1	0	6	1

MCAFEE, FRED   RB   SAINTS

PERSONAL: Born June 20, 1968, in Philadelphia, Miss. ... 5-10/193. ... Full name: Fred Lee McAfee.
HIGH SCHOOL: Philadelphia (Miss.).
COLLEGE: Mississippi College.
TRANSACTIONS/CAREER NOTES: Selected by New Orleans Saints in sixth round (154th pick overall) of 1991 NFL draft. ... Signed by Saints (July 14, 1991). ... Released by Saints (August 26, 1991). ... Re-signed by Saints to practice squad (August 28, 1991). ... Activated (October 18, 1991). ... On injured reserve with shoulder injury (December 15, 1992-remainder of season). ... Granted free agency (February 17, 1994). ... Signed by Arizona Cardinals (August 2, 1994). ... Released by Cardinals (October 31, 1994). ... Signed by Pittsburgh Steelers (November 9, 1994). ... Granted unconditional free agency (February 16, 1996). ... Re-signed by Steelers (April 12, 1996). ... Granted unconditional free agency (February 12, 1999). ... Signed by Kansas City Chiefs (July 30, 1999). ... Released by Chiefs (August 31, 1999). ... Signed by Tampa Bay Buccaneers (December 28, 1999). ... Granted unconditional free agency (February 11, 2000). ... Signed by Saints (October 2, 2000). ... Granted unconditional free agency (March 2, 2001). ... Re-signed by Saints (June 6, 2001). ... Granted unconditional free agency (February 28, 2003). ... Re-signed by Saints (March 19, 2003). ... Granted unconditional free agency (March 3, 2004). ... Re-signed by Saints (October 12, 2004). ... Granted unconditional free agency (March 2, 2005). ... Re-signed by Saints (March 2, 2005).
CHAMPIONSHIP GAME EXPERIENCE: Played in AFC championship game (1994, 1995 and 1997 seasons). ... Played in Super Bowl 30 (1995 season). ... Played in NFC championship game (1999 season).
HONORS: Played in Pro Bowl (2002 season).

SINGLE GAME HIGHS (regular season): Attempts—28 (November 24, 1991, vs. Atlanta); yards—138 (November 24, 1991, vs. Atlanta); and rushing touchdowns—1 (September 10, 1995, vs. Houston).
STATISTICAL PLATEAUS: 100-yard rushing games: 1991 (1). Total: 1.

Year Team	G	GS	RUSHING				RECEIVING				KICKOFF RETURNS				TOTALS			
			Att.	Yds.	Avg.	TD	No.	Yds.	Avg.	TD	No.	Yds.	Avg.	TD	TD	2pt.	Pts.	Fum.
1991—New Orleans NFL	9	0	109	494	4.5	2	1	8	8.0	0	1	14	14.0	0	2	0	12	2
1992—New Orleans NFL	14	1	39	114	2.9	1	1	16	16.0	0	19	393	20.7	0	1	0	6	0
1993—New Orleans NFL	15	4	51	160	3.1	1	1	3	3.0	0	28	580	20.7	0	1	0	6	3
1994—Arizona NFL	7	0	2	-5	-2.5	1	1	4	4.0	0	7	113	16.1	0	1	0	6	1
—Pittsburgh NFL	6	0	16	56	3.5	1	0	0	0.0	0	0	0	0.0	0	1	0	6	0
1995—Pittsburgh NFL	16	1	39	156	4.0	1	15	88	5.9	0	5	56	11.2	0	1	0	6	0
1996—Pittsburgh NFL	14	0	7	17	2.4	0	5	21	4.2	0	0	0	0.0	0	0	0	0	0
1997—Pittsburgh NFL	14	0	13	41	3.2	0	2	44	22.0	0	0	0	0.0	0	0	0	0	1
1998—Pittsburgh NFL	14	0	18	111	6.2	0	9	27	3.0	0	1	10	10.0	0	1	0	6	0
1999—Tampa Bay NFL	1	0	0	0	0.0	0	0	0	0.0	0	0	0	0.0	0	0	0	0	0
2000—New Orleans NFL	12	0	2	37	18.5	0	0	0	0.0	0	10	251	25.1	0	0	0	0	0
2001—New Orleans NFL	16	0	1	2	2.0	0	0	0	0.0	0	6	144	24.0	0	0	0	0	0
2002—New Orleans NFL	11	0	1	11	11.0	0	0	0	0.0	0	2	69	34.5	0	0	0	0	0
2003—New Orleans NFL	14	0	1	13	13.0	0	0	0	0.0	0	9	140	15.6	0	0	0	0	1
2004—New Orleans NFL	11	0	2	54	27.0	0	0	0	0.0	0	8	137	17.1	0	0	0	0	0
Pro totals (14 years)	174	6	301	1261	4.2	7	35	211	6.0	0	96	1907	19.9	0	8	0	48	8

MCALISTER, CHRIS — CB — RAVENS

PERSONAL: Born June 14, 1977, in Pasadena, Calif. ... 6-1/206. ... Full name: Christopher James McAlister. ... Son of James McAlister, running back with Philadelphia Eagles (1975 and 1976) and New England Patriots (1978).
HIGH SCHOOL: Pasadena (Calif.).
JUNIOR COLLEGE: Mt. San Antonio College (Calif.).
COLLEGE: Arizona.
TRANSACTIONS/CAREER NOTES: Selected by Baltimore Ravens in first round (10th pick overall) of 1999 NFL draft. ... Signed by Ravens (July 23, 1999). ... Designated by Ravens as franchise player (February 20, 2003). ... Designated by Ravens as franchise player (February 24, 2004).
CHAMPIONSHIP GAME EXPERIENCE: Played in AFC championship game (2000 season). ... Member of Super Bowl championship team (2000 season).
HONORS: Named cornerback on THE SPORTING NEWS college All-America third team (1997). ... Named cornerback on THE SPORTING NEWS college All-America first team (1998). ... Named cornerback on THE SPORTING NEWS NFL All-Pro team (2004). ... Played in Pro Bowl (2003 season). ... Named to play in Pro Bowl (2004 season); replaced by Nate Clements due to injury.

Year Team	G	GS	TOTALS			INTERCEPTIONS				PUNT RETURNS				TOTALS			
			Tk.	Ast.	Sks.	No.	Yds.	Avg.	TD	No.	Yds.	Avg.	TD	TD	2pt.	Pts.	Fum.
1999—Baltimore NFL	16	12	45	2	0.0	5	28	5.6	0	0	0	0.0	0	0	0	0	0
2000—Baltimore NFL	16	16	35	6	0.0	4	*165	41.2	1	0	0	0.0	0	1	0	6	0
2001—Baltimore NFL	16	16	63	8	0.0	1	0	0.0	0	5	44	8.8	0	0	0	0	0
2002—Baltimore NFL	13	12	48	5	0.0	1	0	0.0	0	17	122	7.2	0	1	0	6	2
2003—Baltimore NFL	15	15	33	10	0.0	3	93	31.0	1	0	0	0.0	0	1	0	6	0
2004—Baltimore NFL	15	14	38	4	0.0	1	51	51.0	1	0	0	0.0	0	2	0	12	0
Pro totals (6 years)	91	85	262	35	0.0	15	337	22.5	3	22	166	7.5	0	5	0	30	2

MCALLISTER, DEUCE — RB — SAINTS

PERSONAL: Born December 27, 1978, in Lena, Miss. ... 6-1/232. ... Full name: Dulymus James McAllister.
HIGH SCHOOL: Morton (Miss.).
COLLEGE: Mississippi.
TRANSACTIONS/CAREER NOTES: Selected by New Orleans Saints in first round (23rd pick overall) of 2001 NFL draft. ... Signed by Saints (August 4, 2001).
HONORS: Played in Pro Bowl (2002 season). ... Named to play in Pro Bowl (2003 season); replaced by Shaun Alexander due to injury.
SINGLE GAME HIGHS (regular season): Attempts—32 (December 8, 2002, vs. Baltimore); yards—184 (November 23, 2003, vs. Philadelphia); and rushing touchdowns—3 (December 8, 2002, vs. Baltimore).
STATISTICAL PLATEAUS: 100-yard rushing games: 2002 (8), 2003 (9), 2004 (5). Total: 22.

Year Team	G	GS	RUSHING				RECEIVING				PUNT RETURNS				KICKOFF RETURNS				TOTALS		
			Att.	Yds.	Avg.	TD	No.	Yds.	Avg.	TD	No.	Yds.	Avg.	TD	No.	Yds.	Avg.	TD	TD	2pt.	Pts.
2001—N.O. NFL	16	4	16	91	5.7	1	15	166	11.1	1	4	24	6.0	0	45	1091	24.2	0	2	0	12
2002—N.O. NFL	15	15	‡325	‡1388	4.3	13	47	352	7.5	3	0	0	0.0	0	0	0	0.0	0	16	0	96
2003—N.O. NFL	16	16	351	1641	4.7	8	69	516	7.5	0	0	0	0.0	0	0	0	0.0	0	8	0	48
2004—N.O. NFL	14	14	269	1074	4.0	9	34	228	6.7	0	0	0	0.0	0	0	0	0.0	0	9	0	54
Pro totals (4 years)	61	49	961	4194	4.4	31	165	1262	7.6	4	4	24	6.0	0	45	1091	24.2	0	35	0	210

MCBRIAR, MAT

PERSONAL: Born July 8, 1979, in Melbourne, Australia. ... 6-1/202.
HIGH SCHOOL: Brighton Grammar (Melbourne).
COLLEGE: Hawaii.
TRANSACTIONS/CAREER NOTES: Signed as non-drafted free agent by Denver Broncos (April 28, 2003). ... Traded by Broncos to Seattle Seahawks for a conditional draft pick (August 22, 2003). ... Released by Seahawks (August 31, 2003). ... Signed by Dallas Cowboys to practice squad (December 24, 2003). ... Activated (January 5, 2004).

Year Team	G	PUNTING					
		No.	Yds.	Avg.	Net avg.	In. 20	Blk.
2004—Dallas NFL	16	75	3182	42.4	35.1	22	0

MCBRIDE, TOD   CB

PERSONAL: Born January 26, 1976, in Los Angeles, Calif. ... 6-1/208. ... Full name: Tod Anthony McBride.
HIGH SCHOOL: Walnut (Calif.).
COLLEGE: UCLA.
TRANSACTIONS/CAREER NOTES: Signed as non-drafted free agent by Seattle Seahawks (April 23, 1999). ... Claimed on waivers by Green Bay Packers (June 23, 1999). ... Granted free agency (March 1, 2002). ... Re-signed by Packers (April 24, 2002). ... Granted unconditional free agency (February 28, 2003). ... Signed by Atlanta Falcons (March 24, 2003). ... Released by Falcons (September 5, 2004). ... Signed by Seahawks (September 14, 2004). ... Released by Seahawks (October 13, 2004). ... Signed by St. Louis Rams (October 27, 2004). ... Released by Rams (November 22, 2004).

			TOTALS			INTERCEPTIONS			
Year Team	G	GS	Tk.	Ast.	Sks.	No.	Yds.	Avg.	TD
1999—Green Bay NFL	15	0	4	1	0.0	0	0	0.0	0
2000—Green Bay NFL	15	6	43	11	0.0	2	43	21.5	0
2001—Green Bay NFL	16	0	29	7	2.0	0	0	0.0	0
2002—Green Bay NFL	15	4	35	7	0.0	1	0	0.0	0
2003—Atlanta NFL	12	9	26	1	0.0	3	44	14.7	1
2004—St. Louis NFL	2	0	1	0	0.0	0	0	0.0	0
Pro totals (6 years)	75	19	138	27	2.0	6	87	14.5	1

MCCADAM, KEVIN   S   FALCONS

PERSONAL: Born March 6, 1979, in La Mesa, Calif. ... 6-1/219. ... Full name: Kevin Edward McCadam.
HIGH SCHOOL: El Capitan (Calif.).
JUNIOR COLLEGE: Grossmont College.
COLLEGE: Virginia Tech.
TRANSACTIONS/CAREER NOTES: Selected by Atlanta Falcons in fifth round (148th pick overall) of 2002 NFL draft. ... Signed by Falcons (June 19, 2002).
CHAMPIONSHIP GAME EXPERIENCE: Played in NFC championship game (2004 season).

			TOTALS			INTERCEPTIONS			
Year Team	G	GS	Tk.	Ast.	Sks.	No.	Yds.	Avg.	TD
2002—Atlanta NFL	11	1	3	0	0.0	0	0	0.0	0
2003—Atlanta NFL	12	3	12	1	1.0	0	0	0.0	0
2004—Atlanta NFL	16	2	12	2	0.0	0	0	0.0	0
Pro totals (3 years)	39	6	27	3	1.0	0	0	0.0	0

MCCANTS, DARNERIEN   WR   REDSKINS

PERSONAL: Born August 1, 1977, in Odenton, Md. ... 6-3/214.
HIGH SCHOOL: Arundel (Md.).
COLLEGE: Delaware State.
TRANSACTIONS/CAREER NOTES: Selected by Washington Redskins in fifth round (154th pick overall) of 2001 NFL draft. ... Signed by Redskins (July 25, 2001). ... Granted free agency (March 3, 2004). ... Re-signed by Redskins (March 30, 2004).
SINGLE GAME HIGHS (regular season): Receptions—6 (December 29, 2002, vs. Dallas); yards—79 (October 5, 2003, vs. Philadelphia); and touchdown receptions—1 (December 7, 2003, vs. New York Giants).

			RECEIVING				TOTALS			
Year Team	G	GS	No.	Yds.	Avg.	TD	TD	2pt.	Pts.	Fum.
2002—Washington NFL	9	1	21	256	12.2	2	2	0	12	1
2003—Washington NFL	15	1	27	360	13.3	6	6	∞2	40	0
2004—Washington NFL	5	1	5	71	14.2	0	0	0	0	0
Pro totals (3 years)	29	3	53	687	13.0	8	8	2	52	1

MCCARDELL, KEENAN   WR   CHARGERS

PERSONAL: Born January 6, 1970, in Houston, Texas. ... 6-1/191. ... Full name: Keenan Wayne McCardell. ... Name pronounced: mc-CAR-dell.
HIGH SCHOOL: Waltrip (Houston).
COLLEGE: Nevada-Las Vegas.
TRANSACTIONS/CAREER NOTES: Selected by Washington Redskins in 12th round (326th pick overall) of 1991 NFL draft. ... Signed by Redskins for 1991 season. ... On injured reserve with knee injury (August 20, 1991-entire season). ... Granted unconditional free agency (February 1, 1992). ... Signed by Cleveland Browns (March 24, 1992). ... Released by Browns (September 1, 1992). ... Re-signed by Browns to practice squad (September 3, 1992). ... Activated (October 6, 1992). ... Released by Browns (October 13, 1992). ... Re-signed by Browns to practice squad (October 14, 1992). ... Activated (November 14, 1992). ... Released by Browns (November 19, 1992). ... Re-signed by Browns to practice squad (November 20, 1992). ... Activated (December 26, 1992). ... Released by Browns (September 22, 1993). ... Signed by Chicago Bears to practice squad (November 2, 1993). ... Signed by Browns off Bears practice squad (November 24, 1993). ... Granted free agency (February 17, 1994). ... Re-signed by Browns (March 4, 1994). ... Granted unconditional free agency (February 16, 1996). ... Signed by Jacksonville Jaguars (March 2, 1996). ... Released by Jaguars (June 3, 2002). ... Signed by Tampa Bay Buccaneers (June 8, 2002). ... Placed by Buccaneers on reserve/did not report list (July 29, 2004). ... Traded by Buccaneers to San Diego Chargers for third- (OT Chris Colmer) and sixth-round (traded to Cleveland) picks in 2005 draft (October 19, 2004).
CHAMPIONSHIP GAME EXPERIENCE: Played in AFC championship game (1996 and 1999 seasons). ... Played in NFC championship game (2002 season). ... Member of Super Bowl championship team (2002 season).
HONORS: Played in Pro Bowl (1996 and 2003 seasons).
SINGLE GAME HIGHS (regular season): Receptions—16 (October 20, 1996, vs. St. Louis); yards—232 (October 20, 1996, vs. St. Louis); and touchdown receptions—2 (October 6, 2003, vs. Indianapolis).

STATISTICAL PLATEAUS: 100-yard receiving games: 1995 (1), 1996 (3), 1997 (4), 1998 (2), 1999 (3), 2000 (5), 2001 (2), 2002 (2), 2003 (4). Total: 26.

					RECEIVING			TOTALS			
Year Team	G	GS	No.	Yds.	Avg.	TD	TD	2pt.	Pts.	Fum.
1991—Washington NFL	Did not play.									
1992—Cleveland NFL	2	0	1	8	8.0	0	0	0	0	0
1993—Cleveland NFL	6	3	13	234	18.0	4	4	0	24	0
1994—Cleveland NFL	13	3	10	182	18.2	0	0	0	0	0
1995—Cleveland NFL	16	5	56	709	12.7	4	4	0	24	0
1996—Jacksonville NFL	16	15	85	1129	13.3	3	3	2	22	1
1997—Jacksonville NFL	16	16	85	1164	13.7	5	5	0	30	0
1998—Jacksonville NFL	15	15	64	892	13.9	6	6	1	38	0
1999—Jacksonville NFL	16	15	78	891	11.4	5	5	1	32	1
2000—Jacksonville NFL	16	16	94	1207	12.8	5	5	0	30	3
2001—Jacksonville NFL	16	16	93	1110	11.9	6	6	1	38	1
2002—Tampa Bay NFL	14	14	61	670	11.0	6	6	0	36	1
2003—Tampa Bay NFL	16	16	84	1174	14.0	8	9	0	54	1
2004—San Diego NFL	7	6	31	393	12.7	1	1	0	6	0
Pro totals (13 years)	169	140	755	9763	12.9	53	54	5	334	8

MCCAREINS, JUSTIN WR JETS

PERSONAL: Born December 11, 1978, in Evanston, Ill. ... 6-2/215.
HIGH SCHOOL: Naperville (Ill.) North.
COLLEGE: Northern Illinois.
TRANSACTIONS/CAREER NOTES: Selected by Tennessee Titans in fourth round (124th pick overall) of 2001 NFL draft. ... Signed by Titans (July 9, 2001). ... Traded by Titans to New York Jets for second-round pick (DE Travis LaBoy) in 2004 draft (March 5, 2004).
CHAMPIONSHIP GAME EXPERIENCE: Played in AFC championship game (2002 season).
SINGLE GAME HIGHS (regular season): Receptions—6 (January 2, 2005, vs. St. Louis); yards—92 (December 1, 2003, vs. New York Jets); and touchdown receptions—1 (December 19, 2004, vs. Seattle).

			RECEIVING				PUNT RETURNS				KICKOFF RETURNS				TOTALS			
Year Team	G	GS	No.	Yds.	Avg.	TD	No.	Yds.	Avg.	TD	No.	Yds.	Avg.	TD	TD	2pt.	Pts.	Fum.
2001—Tennessee NFL	4	1	3	88	29.3	0	2	29	14.5	0	4	70	17.5	0	0	0	0	0
2002—Tennessee NFL	16	1	19	301	15.8	2	6	44	7.3	0	13	300	23.1	0	2	0	12	0
2003—Tennessee NFL	16	10	47	813	§17.3	7	29	330	11.4	1	13	256	19.7	0	8	0	48	2
2004—New York Jets NFL	16	16	56	770	13.8	4	14	88	6.3	0	0	0	0.0	0	4	0	24	3
Pro totals (4 years)	52	28	125	1972	15.8	13	51	491	9.6	1	30	626	20.9	0	14	0	84	5

MCCLAIN, JIMMY LB

PERSONAL: Born July 23, 1980, in Enterprise, Ala. ... 6-0/231.
HIGH SCHOOL: Enterprise (Ala.).
COLLEGE: Troy.
TRANSACTIONS/CAREER NOTES: Signed as non-drafted free agent by Houston Texans (April 25, 2002). ... Waived by Texans (September 2, 2003). ... Re-signed by Texans (September 10, 2003). ... Released by Texans (November 17, 2003). ... Signed by Jacksonville Jaguars (January 27, 2004). ... Assigned by Jaguars to Scottish Claymores in 2004 NFL Europe enhancement allocation program (February 9, 2004). ... Released by Jaguars (September 6, 2004). ... Re-signed by Jaguars (November 10, 2004). ... Released by Jaguars (November 30, 2004).

			TOTALS			INTERCEPTIONS			
Year Team	G	GS	Tk.	Ast.	Sks.	No.	Yds.	Avg.	TD
2002—Houston NFL	15	0	1	1	0.0	0	0	0.0	0
2003—Houston NFL	9	0	0	0	0.0	0	0	0.0	0
2004—Jacksonville NFL	1	0	0	0	0.0	0	0	0.0	0
Pro totals (3 years)	25	0	1	1	0.0	0	0	0.0	0

MCCLEON, DEXTER CB CHIEFS

PERSONAL: Born October 9, 1973, in Meridian, Miss. ... 5-10/195. ... Full name: Dexter Keith McCleon.
HIGH SCHOOL: Meridian (Miss.).
COLLEGE: Clemson.
TRANSACTIONS/CAREER NOTES: Selected by St. Louis Rams in second round (40th pick overall) of 1997 NFL draft. ... Signed by Rams (July 3, 1997). ... Granted free agency (February 11, 2000). ... Re-signed by Rams (June 13, 2000). ... Released by Rams (February 27, 2003). ... Signed by Kansas City Chiefs (March 5, 2003).
CHAMPIONSHIP GAME EXPERIENCE: Played in NFC championship game (1999 and 2001 seasons). ... Member of Super Bowl championship team (1999 season). ... Played in Super Bowl 36 (2001 season).
MISCELLANEOUS: Selected by Minnesota Twins organization in 13th round of free-agent baseball draft (June 3, 1993); did not sign.

			TOTALS			INTERCEPTIONS			
Year Team	G	GS	Tk.	Ast.	Sks.	No.	Yds.	Avg.	TD
1997—St. Louis NFL	16	1	13	0	1.0	1	0	0.0	0
1998—St. Louis NFL	15	6	28	1	0.0	2	29	14.5	0
1999—St. Louis NFL	15	15	41	4	1.5	4	17	4.3	0
2000—St. Louis NFL	16	16	49	5	2.0	8	28	3.5	0
2001—St. Louis NFL	16	16	59	6	0.0	4	66	16.5	0
2002—St. Louis NFL	13	4	17	4	0.0	1	0	0.0	0
2003—Kansas City NFL	16	16	55	5	0.0	6	-3	-0.5	0
2004—Kansas City NFL	13	6	30	6	0.0	2	23	11.5	0
Pro totals (8 years)	120	80	292	31	4.5	28	160	5.7	0

M

MCCLOVER, DARRELL　　　　　LB　　　　　JETS

PERSONAL: Born August 25, 1981, in Coconut Creek, Fla. ... 6-2/226. ... Full name: Darrell A. McClover.
HIGH SCHOOL: Coconut Creek (Fla.).
COLLEGE: Miami (Fla.).
TRANSACTIONS/CAREER NOTES: Selected by New York Jets in seventh round (213th pick overall) of 2004 NFL draft. ... Signed by Jets (July 15, 2004).

Year　Team	G	GS	TOTALS			INTERCEPTIONS			
			Tk.	Ast.	Sks.	No.	Yds.	Avg.	TD
2004—New York Jets NFL	16	0	1	0	0.0	0	0	0.0	0

MCCLURE, TODD　　　　　C　　　　　FALCONS

PERSONAL: Born February 16, 1977, in Baton Rouge, La. ... 6-1/286.
HIGH SCHOOL: Central (Baton Rouge, La.).
COLLEGE: Louisiana State.
TRANSACTIONS/CAREER NOTES: Selected by Atlanta Falcons in seventh round (237th pick overall) of 1999 NFL draft. ... Signed by Falcons (June 25, 1999). ... On injured reserve with knee injury (August 30, 1999-entire season). ... Granted free agency (March 1, 2002). ... Re-signed by Falcons (May 28, 2002). ... Granted unconditional free agency (February 28, 2003). ... Re-signed by Falcons (April 16, 2003).
PLAYING EXPERIENCE: Atlanta NFL, 1999-2004. ... Games/Games started: 2000 (9/7), 2001 (15/15), 2002 (16/16), 2003 (16/16), 2004 (16/16), Total: 72/70.
CHAMPIONSHIP GAME EXPERIENCE: Played in NFC championship game (2004 season).

MCCOLLUM, ANDY　　　　　C　　　　　RAMS

PERSONAL: Born June 2, 1970, in Akron, Ohio. ... 6-4/300. ... Full name: Andrew Jon McCollum. ... Name pronounced: Mc-COL-umn.
HIGH SCHOOL: Revere (Richfield, Ohio).
COLLEGE: Toledo.
TRANSACTIONS/CAREER NOTES: Played with Milwaukee Mustangs of Arena League (1994). ... Signed as non-drafted free agent by Cleveland Browns (June 1994). ... Released by Browns (August 28, 1994). ... Re-signed by Browns to practice squad (August 30, 1994). ... Signed by New Orleans Saints off Browns practice squad (November 15, 1994). ... Inactive for five games (1994). ... Assigned by Saints to Barcelona Dragons in 1995 World League enhancement allocation program (February 20, 1995). ... Granted unconditional free agency (February 12, 1999). ... Signed by St. Louis Rams (April 13, 1999). ... Granted unconditional free agency (February 11, 2000). ... Re-signed by Rams (February 22, 2000). ... Granted unconditional free agency (February 28, 2003). ... Re-signed by Rams (April 4, 2003).
PLAYING EXPERIENCE: New Orleans NFL, 1995-1998; St. Louis NFL, 1999-2004. ... Games/Games started: 1995 (11/9), 1996 (16/16), 1997 (16/16), 1998 (16/5), 1999 (16/2), 2000 (16/16), 2001 (16/16), 2002 (16/16), 2003 (16/16), 2004 (16/16). Total: 155/128.
CHAMPIONSHIP GAME EXPERIENCE: Played in NFC championship game (1999 and 2001 seasons). ... Member of Super Bowl championship team (1999 season). ... Played in Super Bowl 36 (2001 season).

MCCOO, ERIC　　　　　RB　　　　　EAGLES

PERSONAL: Born September 6, 1980, in Red Bank, N.J. ... 5-10/210. ... Full name: Eric Franklin McCoo.
HIGH SCHOOL: Regional (Red Bank, N.J.).
COLLEGE: Penn State.
TRANSACTIONS/CAREER NOTES: Signed as non-drafted free agent by Chicago Bears (April 22, 2002). ... Released by Bears (August 31, 2002). ... Signed by Washington Redskins (January 6, 2003). ... Released by Redskins (April 28, 2003). ... Signed by Bears (May 1, 2003). ... Released by Bears (August 29, 2003). ... Signed by Philadelphia Eagles to practice squad (January 7, 2004). ... Assigned by Eagles to Berlin Thunder in 2004 NFL Europe enhancement allocation program (February 26, 2004). ... Released by Eagles (September 5, 2004). ... Re-signed by Eagles to practice squad (September 22, 2004). ... Activated (December 29, 2004).
SINGLE GAME HIGHS (regular season): Attempts—9 (January 2, 2005, vs. Cincinnati); yards—54 (January 2, 2005, vs. Cincinnati); and rushing touchdowns—0.

Year　Team	G	GS	RUSHING				RECEIVING				TOTALS			
			Att.	Yds.	Avg.	TD	No.	Yds.	Avg.	TD	TD	2pt.	Pts.	Fum.
2004—Philadelphia NFL	1	0	9	54	6.0	0	2	15	7.5	0	0	0	0	0

MCCOWN, JOSH　　　　　QB　　　　　CARDINALS

PERSONAL: Born July 4, 1979, in Jacksonville, Texas. ... 6-4/212. ... Full name: Joshua McCown. ... Brother of Luke McCown, quarterback, Tampa Bay Buccaneers.
HIGH SCHOOL: Jacksonville (Texas).
COLLEGE: Sam Houston State.
TRANSACTIONS/CAREER NOTES: Selected by Arizona Cardinals in third round (81st pick overall) of 2002 NFL draft. ... Signed by Cardinals (July 25, 2002). ... Granted free agency (March 2, 2005). ... Re-signed by Cardinals (March 30, 2005).
SINGLE GAME HIGHS (regular season): Attempts—44 (December 12, 2004, vs. San Francisco); completions—26 (December 12, 2004, vs. San Francisco); yards—307 (December 12, 2004, vs. San Francisco); and touchdown passes—3 (December 26, 2004, vs. Seattle).
STATISTICAL PLATEAUS: 300-yard passing games: 2004 (1). Total: 1.
MISCELLANEOUS: Regular-season record as starting NFL quarterback: 7-9 (.438).

Year　Team	G	GS	PASSING									RUSHING				TOTALS		
			Att.	Cmp.	Pct.	Yds.	TD	Int.	Avg.	Skd.	Rat.	Att.	Yds.	Avg.	TD	TD	2pt.	Pts.
2002—Arizona NFL	2	0	18	7	38.9	66	0	2	3.67	5	10.2	1	20	20.0	0	0	0	0
2003—Arizona NFL	10	3	166	95	57.2	1018	5	6	6.13	25	70.3	28	158	5.6	1	1	0	6
2004—Arizona NFL	14	13	408	233	57.1	2511	11	10	6.15	31	74.1	36	112	3.1	2	2	1	14
Pro totals (3 years)	26	16	592	335	56.6	3595	16	18	6.07	61	70.9	65	290	4.5	3	3	1	20

M

MCCOWN, LUKE QB BUCCANEERS

PERSONAL: Born July 12, 1981, in Jacksonville, Texas. ... 6-3/212. ... Brother of Josh McCown, quarterback, Arizona Cardinals.
HIGH SCHOOL: Jacksonville (Texas).
COLLEGE: Louisiana Tech.
TRANSACTIONS/CAREER NOTES: Selected by Cleveland Browns in fourth round (106th pick overall) of 2004 NFL draft. ... Signed by Browns (July 29, 2004). ... Traded by Browns to Tampa Bay Buccaneers for sixth-round pick (DT Andrew Hoffman) in 2005 draft (April 24, 2005).
SINGLE GAME HIGHS (regular season): Attempts—34 (December 5, 2004, vs. New England); completions—20 (December 5, 2004, vs. New England); yards—277 (December 5, 2004, vs. New England); and touchdown passes—2 (December 5, 2004, vs. New England).
MISCELLANEOUS: Regular-season record as starting NFL quarterback: 0-4 (.000).

			PASSING									RUSHING				TOTALS		
Year Team	G	GS	Att.	Cmp.	Pct.	Yds.	TD	Int.	Avg.	Skd.	Rat.	Att.	Yds.	Avg.	TD	TD	2pt.	Pts.
2004—Cleveland NFL	5	4	98	48	49.0	608	4	7	6.20	12	52.6	6	25	4.2	0	0	0	0

MCCRARY, FRED FB FALCONS

PERSONAL: Born September 19, 1972, in Naples, Fla. ... 6-0/247. ... Full name: Freddy Demetrius McCrary.
HIGH SCHOOL: Naples (Fla.).
COLLEGE: Mississippi State.
TRANSACTIONS/CAREER NOTES: Selected by Philadelphia Eagles in sixth round (208th pick overall) of 1995 NFL draft. ... Signed by Eagles (June 27, 1995). ... Released by Eagles (August 25, 1996). ... Signed by New Orleans Saints (March 5, 1997). ... Released by Saints (August 24, 1998). ... Signed by San Diego Chargers (March 26, 1999). ... Granted free agency (February 11, 2000). ... Re-signed by Chargers (May 22, 2000). ... Released by Chargers (February 25, 2003). ... Signed by New England Patriots (March 24, 2003). ... Released by Patriots (October 4, 2003). ... Re-signed by Patriots (October 7, 2003). ... On injured reserve with leg injury (November 20, 2003-remainder of season). ... Released by Patriots (August 24, 2004). ... Signed by Atlanta Falcons (December 14, 2004). ... Granted unconditional free agency (March 2, 2005). ... Re-signed by Falcons (March 11, 2005).
CHAMPIONSHIP GAME EXPERIENCE: Played in NFC championship game (2004 season).
SINGLE GAME HIGHS (regular season): Attempts—5 (September 24, 2000, vs. Seattle); yards—13 (November 23, 1997, vs. Atlanta); and rushing touchdowns—1 (September 10, 1995, vs. Arizona).

			RUSHING				RECEIVING				TOTALS			
Year Team	G	GS	Att.	Yds.	Avg.	TD	No.	Yds.	Avg.	TD	TD	2pt.	Pts.	Fum.
1995—Philadelphia NFL...................	13	4	3	1	0.3	1	9	60	6.7	0	1	0	6	0
1996—	Did not play.													
1997—New Orleans NFL..................	7	0	8	15	1.9	0	4	17	4.3	0	0	0	0	0
1998—	Did not play.													
1999—San Diego NFL.....................	16	14	0	0	0.0	0	37	201	5.4	1	1	0	6	0
2000—San Diego NFL.....................	15	12	7	8	1.1	0	18	141	7.8	2	2	0	12	1
2001—San Diego NFL.....................	16	12	2	3	1.5	0	13	71	5.5	0	0	0	0	0
2002—San Diego NFL.....................	16	16	2	1	0.5	0	22	96	4.4	3	3	0	18	1
2003—New England NFL................	6	3	3	3	1.0	0	2	12	6.0	0	0	0	0	0
2004—Atlanta NFL.........................	3	2	0	0	0.0	0	2	23	11.5	0	0	0	0	0
Pro totals (8 years).......................	92	63	25	31	1.2	1	107	621	5.8	6	7	0	42	2

MCCRAY, BOBBY DE JAGUARS

PERSONAL: Born November 1, 1981, in Miami, Fla. ... 6-5/251.
HIGH SCHOOL: Homestead (Miami, Fla.).
COLLEGE: Florida.
TRANSACTIONS/CAREER NOTES: Selected by Jacksonville Jaguars in seventh round (249th pick overall) of 2004 NFL draft. ... Signed by Jaguars (July 30, 2004).

			TOTALS		
Year Team	G	GS	Tk.	Ast.	Sks.
2004—Jacksonville NFL..	16	7	19	5	3.5

MCCREE, MARLON S PANTHERS

PERSONAL: Born March 17, 1977, in Orlando, Fla. ... 5-11/202. ... Full name: Marlon Tarron McCree.
HIGH SCHOOL: Atlantic (Daytona, Fla.).
COLLEGE: Kentucky.
TRANSACTIONS/CAREER NOTES: Selected by Jacksonville Jaguars in seventh round (233rd pick overall) of 2001 NFL draft. ... Signed by Jaguars (May 30, 2001). ... Waived by Jaguars (September 16, 2003). ... Claimed on waivers by Houston Texans (September 17, 2003). ... Granted free agency (March 3, 2004). ... Re-signed by Texans (April 30, 2004). ... Granted unconditional free agency (March 2, 2005). ... Signed by Carolina Panthers (March 10, 2005).

			TOTALS			INTERCEPTIONS			
Year Team	G	GS	Tk.	Ast.	Sks.	No.	Yds.	Avg.	TD
2001—Jacksonville NFL	13	11	33	13	1.0	1	10	10.0	0
2002—Jacksonville NFL	16	16	56	15	1.0	6	129	21.5	0
2003—Jacksonville NFL	2	0	1	1	0.0	0	0	0.0	0
—Houston NFL	13	11	34	16	0.0	1	95	95.0	1
2004—Houston NFL	16	1	22	2	0.0	1	24	24.0	0
Pro totals (4 years)	60	39	146	47	2.0	9	258	28.7	1

M

MCCUTCHEON, DAYLON   CB   BROWNS

PERSONAL: Born December 9, 1976, in Los Angeles, Calif. ... 5-10/190. ... Name pronounced: mc-CUTCH-in. ... Son of Lawrence McCutcheon, Director of Scouting, St. Louis Rams, and former running back with four NFL teams (1972-81).
HIGH SCHOOL: Bishop Amat (La Puente, Calif.).
COLLEGE: Southern California.
TRANSACTIONS/CAREER NOTES: Selected by Cleveland Browns in third round (62nd pick overall) of 1999 NFL draft. ... Signed by Browns (July 22, 1999). ... Granted free agency (March 1, 2002). ... Re-signed by Browns (June 11, 2002).
HONORS: Named cornerback on THE SPORTING NEWS college All-America second team (1998).

				TOTALS			INTERCEPTIONS			
Year Team	G	GS	Tk.	Ast.	Sks.	No.	Yds.	Avg.	TD
1999—Cleveland NFL	16	15	74	5	1.0	1	12	12.0	0
2000—Cleveland NFL	15	15	56	3	4.0	1	20	20.0	0
2001—Cleveland NFL	16	15	67	6	2.0	4	62	15.5	1
2002—Cleveland NFL	13	11	40	2	0.0	1	24	24.0	0
2003—Cleveland NFL	15	14	43	5	0.0	1	75	75.0	1
2004—Cleveland NFL	12	10	45	5	0.0	2	0	0.0	0
Pro totals (6 years)	87	80	325	26	7.0	10	193	19.3	2

MCDONALD, SHAUN   WR   RAMS

PERSONAL: Born June 13, 1981, in Phoenix, Ariz. ... 5-10/183. ... Full name: Shaun Terrance McDonald.
HIGH SCHOOL: Shadow Mountain (Phoenix).
COLLEGE: Arizona State.
TRANSACTIONS/CAREER NOTES: Selected after junior season by St. Louis Rams in fourth round (106th pick overall) of 2003 NFL draft. ... Signed by Rams (July 18, 2003).
SINGLE GAME HIGHS (regular season): Receptions—6 (November 29, 2004, vs. Green Bay); yards—79 (November 29, 2004, vs. Green Bay); and touchdown receptions—1 (October 24, 2004, vs. Miami).

			RUSHING				RECEIVING				PUNT RETURNS				TOTALS			
Year Team	G	GS	Att.	Yds.	Avg.	TD	No.	Yds.	Avg.	TD	No.	Yds.	Avg.	TD	TD	2pt.	Pts.	Fum.
2003—St. Louis NFL	8	1	2	7	3.5	0	10	62	6.2	0	0	0	0.0	0	0	0	0	1
2004—St. Louis NFL	16	0	4	0	0.0	0	37	494	13.4	3	30	143	4.8	0	3	0	18	4
Pro totals (2 years)	24	1	6	7	1.2	0	47	556	11.8	3	30	143	4.8	0	3	0	18	5

MCDOUGLE, JEROME   DE   EAGLES

PERSONAL: Born December 15, 1978, in Pompano Beach, Fla. ... 6-2/264. ... Full name: Jerome McDougle Jr. ... Brother of Stockar McDougle, offensive tackle, Miami Dolphins.
HIGH SCHOOL: Ely (Pompano Beach, Fla.).
JUNIOR COLLEGE: Hinds Community College (Miss.).
COLLEGE: Miami (Fla.).
TRANSACTIONS/CAREER NOTES: Selected by Philadelphia Eagles in first round (15th pick overall) of 2003 NFL draft. ... Signed by Eagles (July 31, 2003).
CHAMPIONSHIP GAME EXPERIENCE: Played in NFC championship game (2003 and 2004 seasons). ... Played in Super Bowl 39 (2004 season).

				TOTALS			INTERCEPTIONS			
Year Team	G	GS	Tk.	Ast.	Sks.	No.	Yds.	Avg.	TD
2003—Philadelphia NFL	8	0	6	4	0.0	0	0	0.0	0
2004—Philadelphia NFL	11	0	13	0	2.0	0	0	0.0	0
Pro totals (2 years)	19	0	19	4	2.0	0	0	0.0	0

MCDOUGLE, STOCKAR   T   DOLPHINS

PERSONAL: Born January 11, 1977, in Fort Lauderdale, Fla. ... 6-6/335. ... Brother of Jerome McDougle, defensive end, Philadelphia Eagles.
HIGH SCHOOL: Deerfield Beach (Fla.).
JUNIOR COLLEGE: Navarro College (Texas).
COLLEGE: Oklahoma.
TRANSACTIONS/CAREER NOTES: Selected by Detroit Lions in first round (20th pick overall) of 2000 NFL draft. ... Signed by Lions (July 15, 2000). ... Granted unconditional free agency (March 2, 2005). ... Signed by Miami Dolphins (March 15, 2005).
PLAYING EXPERIENCE: Detroit NFL, 2000-2004. ... Games/Games started: 2000 (8/8), 2001 (9/3), 2002 (12/11), 2003 (16/16), 2004 (16/16). Total: 61/54.

MCFARLAND, ANTHONY   DT   BUCCANEERS

PERSONAL: Born December 18, 1977, in Winnsboro, La. ... 6-0/300. ... Full name: Anthony Darelle McFarland.
HIGH SCHOOL: Winnsboro (La.).
COLLEGE: Louisiana State.
TRANSACTIONS/CAREER NOTES: Selected by Tampa Bay Buccaneers in first round (15th pick overall) of 1999 NFL draft. ... Signed by Buccaneers (August 3, 1999). ... On injured reserve with foot injury (December 17, 2002-remainder of season). ... On injured reserve with triceps injury (November 24, 2004-remainder of season).
CHAMPIONSHIP GAME EXPERIENCE: Played in NFC championship game (1999 season).
HONORS: Named defensive tackle on THE SPORTING NEWS college All-America second team (1998).

Year Team	G	GS	TOTALS Tk.	Ast.	Sks.	INTERCEPTIONS No.	Yds.	Avg.	TD
1999—Tampa Bay NFL	14	0	9	5	1.0	0	0	0.0	0
2000—Tampa Bay NFL	16	16	31	19	6.5	0	0	0.0	0
2001—Tampa Bay NFL	14	14	24	17	3.5	0	0	0.0	0
2002—Tampa Bay NFL	10	10	12	8	1.5	0	0	0.0	0
2003—Tampa Bay NFL	16	16	38	12	2.5	1	0	0.0	0
2004—Tampa Bay NFL	8	8	10	2	3.0	0	0	0.0	0
Pro totals (6 years)	78	64	124	63	18.0	1	0	0.0	0

MCFARLAND, DYLAN   T   BILLS

PERSONAL: Born July 11, 1980, in Kalispell, Mont. ... 6-5/290.
HIGH SCHOOL: Flathead (Kalispell, Mont.).
COLLEGE: Montana.
TRANSACTIONS/CAREER NOTES: Selected by Buffalo Bills in seventh round (207th pick overall) of 2004 NFL draft. ... Signed by Bills (May 25, 2004).
PLAYING EXPERIENCE: Buffalo NFL, 2004. ... Games/Games started: 2004 (2/0). Total: 2/0.

MCGAHEE, WILLIS   RB   BILLS

PERSONAL: Born October 20, 1981, in Miami, Fla. ... 6-0/228. ... Full name: Willis Andrew McGahee.
HIGH SCHOOL: Central (Miami).
COLLEGE: Miami (Fla.).
TRANSACTIONS/CAREER NOTES: Selected after sophomore season by Buffalo Bills in first round (23rd pick overall) of 2003 NFL draft. ... Signed by Bills (August 13, 2003). ... On reserve/non-football injury list with knee injury (August 13-November 5, 2003). ... Inactive for eight games (2003). ... Activated (November 5, 2003).
HONORS: Named running back on THE SPORTING NEWS college All-America first team (2002).
SINGLE GAME HIGHS (regular season): Attempts—37 (November 7, 2004, vs. New York Jets); yards—132 (November 7, 2004, vs. New York Jets); and rushing touchdowns—4 (November 28, 2004, vs. Seattle).
STATISTICAL PLATEAUS: 100-yard rushing games: 2004 (7). Total: 7.

Year Team	G	GS	RUSHING Att.	Yds.	Avg.	TD	RECEIVING No.	Yds.	Avg.	TD	TOTALS TD	2pt.	Pts.	Fum.
2004—Buffalo NFL	16	11	284	1128	4.0	13	22	169	7.7	0	13	0	78	4

MCGARRAHAN, SCOTT   S

PERSONAL: Born February 12, 1974, in Arlington, Texas. ... 6-1/200. ... Full name: John Scott McGarrahan. ... Name pronounced: ma-GAIR-a-han.
HIGH SCHOOL: Lamar (Arlington, Texas).
COLLEGE: New Mexico.
TRANSACTIONS/CAREER NOTES: Selected by Green Bay Packers in sixth round (156th pick overall) of 1998 NFL draft. ... Signed by Packers (July 17, 1998). ... On injured reserve with hamstring injury (December 29, 1999-remainder of season). ... Granted free agency (March 2, 2001). ... Re-signed by Packers (May 8, 2001). ... Released by Packers (September 1, 2001). ... Signed by Miami Dolphins (September 5, 2001). ... Granted unconditional free agency (March 1, 2002). ... Re-signed by Dolphins (March 21, 2002). ... Traded by Dolphins to Packers for 2006 conditional seventh-round pick (August 25, 2003). ... Released by Packers (August 31, 2003). ... Signed by Tennessee Titans (September 2, 2003). ... Granted unconditional free agency (March 3, 2004). ... Re-signed by Titans (July 30, 2004). ... Granted unconditional free agency (March 2, 2005).

Year Team	G	GS	TOTALS Tk.	Ast.	Sks.	INTERCEPTIONS No.	Yds.	Avg.	TD
1998—Green Bay NFL	15	0	8	3	0.0	0	0	0.0	0
1999—Green Bay NFL	13	0	2	0	0.0	0	0	0.0	0
2000—Green Bay NFL	16	0	8	1	0.5	0	0	0.0	0
2001—Miami NFL	16	0	0	0	0.0	0	0	0.0	0
2002—Miami NFL	14	0	1	1	1.0	0	0	0.0	0
2003—Tennessee NFL	16	2	20	7	1.0	0	0	0.0	0
2004—Tennessee NFL	16	1	21	6	0.5	1	11	11.0	0
Pro totals (7 years)	106	3	60	18	3.0	1	11	11.0	0

MCGEE, TERRENCE   CB   BILLS

PERSONAL: Born October 14, 1980, in Athens, Texas. ... 5-9/195.
HIGH SCHOOL: Athens (Texas).
COLLEGE: Northwestern State.
TRANSACTIONS/CAREER NOTES: Selected by Buffalo Bills in fourth round (111th pick overall) of 2003 NFL draft. ... Signed by Bills (July 23, 2003).
HONORS: Named kick returner on THE SPORTING NEWS NFL All-Pro team (2004). ... Played in Pro Bowl (2004 season).

Year Team	G	GS	INTERCEPTIONS No.	Yds.	Avg.	TD	PUNT RETURNS No.	Yds.	Avg.	TD	KICKOFF RETURNS No.	Yds.	Avg.	TD	TOTALS TD	2pt.	Pts.	Fum.
2003—Buffalo NFL	14	2	2	5	2.5	0	0	0	0.0	0	8	160	20.0	0	0	0	0	0
2004—Buffalo NFL	16	13	3	21	7.0	0	0	0	0.0	0	52	1370	§26.3	*3	3	0	18	2
Pro totals (2 years)	30	25	5	26	5.2	0	0	0	0.0	0	60	1530	25.5	3	3	0	18	2

MCGINEST, WILLIE | DE | PATRIOTS

PERSONAL: Born December 11, 1971, in Long Beach, Calif. ... 6-5/270. ... Full name: William Lee McGinest Jr.
HIGH SCHOOL: Polytechnic (Long Beach, Calif.).
COLLEGE: Southern California.
TRANSACTIONS/CAREER NOTES: Selected by New England Patriots in first round (fourth pick overall) of 1994 NFL draft. ... Signed by Patriots (May 17, 1994). ... Granted unconditional free agency (February 13, 1998). ... Re-signed by Patriots (February 12, 1998).
CHAMPIONSHIP GAME EXPERIENCE: Played in AFC championship game (1996, 2001, 2003 and 2004 seasons). ... Member of Super Bowl championship team (2001, 2003 and 2004 seasons). ... Played in Super Bowl 31 (1996 season).
HONORS: Played in Pro Bowl (1996 and 2003 seasons).

Year Team	G	GS	TOTALS Tk.	Ast.	Sks.	INTERCEPTIONS No.	Yds.	Avg.	TD
1994—New England NFL	16	7	29	14	4.5	0	0	0.0	0
1995—New England NFL	16	16	70	18	11.0	0	0	0.0	0
1996—New England NFL	16	16	49	18	9.5	1	46	46.0	1
1997—New England NFL	11	11	25	10	2.0	0	0	0.0	0
1998—New England NFL	9	8	21	8	3.5	0	0	0.0	0
1999—New England NFL	16	16	51	25	9.0	0	0	0.0	0
2000—New England NFL	14	14	45	18	6.0	0	0	0.0	0
2001—New England NFL	11	5	25	8	6.0	0	0	0.0	0
2002—New England NFL	16	10	42	21	5.5	1	2	2.0	0
2003—New England NFL	14	11	46	21	5.5	1	15	15.0	1
2004—New England NFL	16	16	35	16	9.5	1	27	27.0	0
Pro totals (11 years)	155	130	438	177	72.0	4	90	22.5	2

MCGRAW, JON | S | JETS

PERSONAL: Born April 2, 1979, in Manhattan, Kan. ... 6-3/206.
HIGH SCHOOL: Riley County (Manhattan, Kan.).
COLLEGE: Kansas State.
TRANSACTIONS/CAREER NOTES: Selected by New York Jets in second round (57th pick overall) of 2002 NFL draft. ... Signed by Jets (July 26, 2002). ... On injured reserve with shoulder injury (November 17, 2003-remainder of season).

Year Team	G	GS	TOTALS Tk.	Ast.	Sks.	INTERCEPTIONS No.	Yds.	Avg.	TD
2002—New York Jets NFL	15	1	20	8	0.0	1	0	0.0	0
2003—New York Jets NFL	6	6	19	11	0.0	0	0	0.0	0
2004—New York Jets NFL	12	1	22	6	0.0	2	0	0.0	0
Pro totals (3 years)	33	8	61	25	0.0	3	0	0.0	0

MCGRORTY, DUSTY | RB | RAMS

M

PERSONAL: Born May 9, 1981, in Seaside, Ore. ... 5-10/218. ... Full name: Dustin Scott McGrorty.
HIGH SCHOOL: Warrenton (Ore.).
COLLEGE: Southern Oregon.
TRANSACTIONS/CAREER NOTES: Signed as non-drafted free agent by St. Louis Rams (April 30, 2004). ... Released by Rams (September 5, 2004). ... Re-signed by Rams to practice squad (September 6, 2004). ... Activated (October 22, 2004). ... Released by Rams (October 25, 2004). ... Re-signed by Rams to practice squad (October 27, 2004).

Year Team	G	GS	RUSHING Att.	Yds.	Avg.	TD	TOTALS TD	2pt.	Pts.	Fum.
2004—St. Louis NFL	1	0	0	0	0.0	0	0	0	0	0

MCHUGH, SEAN | FB | PACKERS

PERSONAL: Born May 27, 1982, in Chargin Falls, Ohio. ... 6-5/262.
HIGH SCHOOL: Monsignor Bonner (Drexel Hill, Pa.).
COLLEGE: Penn State.
TRANSACTIONS/CAREER NOTES: Selected by Tennessee Titans in seventh round (241st pick overall) of 2004 NFL draft. ... Signed by Titans (July 22, 2004). ... Claimed on waivers by Green Bay Packers (September 6, 2004). ... Released by Packers (September 18, 2004). ... Re-signed by Packers to practice squad (September 22, 2004). ... Activated (December 21, 2004).

Year Team	G	GS	RUSHING Att.	Yds.	Avg.	TD	RECEIVING No.	Yds.	Avg.	TD	TOTALS TD	2pt.	Pts.	Fum.
2004—Green Bay NFL	1	0	0	0	0.0	0	0	0	0.0	0	0	0	0	0

MCINTOSH, DAMION | T | DOLPHINS

PERSONAL: Born March 25, 1977, in Kingston, Jamaica. ... 6-4/325. ... Full name: Damion Alexis McIntosh.
HIGH SCHOOL: McArthur (Hollywood, Fla.).
COLLEGE: Kansas State.
TRANSACTIONS/CAREER NOTES: Selected by San Diego Chargers in third round (83rd pick overall) of 2000 NFL draft. ... Signed by Chargers (July 20, 2000). ... Granted free agency (February 28, 2003). ... Re-signed by Chargers (April 16, 2003). ... Granted unconditional free agency (March 3, 2004). ... Signed by Miami Dolphins (March 16, 2004).
PLAYING EXPERIENCE: San Diego NFL, 2000-2003; Miami NFL, 2004. ... Games/Games started: 2000 (3/0), 2001 (15/14), 2002 (10/10), 2003 (13/13), 2004 (14/14). Total: 55/51.

MCKENZIE, KAREEM   T   GIANTS

PERSONAL: Born May 24, 1979, in Willingboro, N.J. ... 6-6/327. ... Full name: Kareem Michael McKenzie.
HIGH SCHOOL: Willingboro (N.J.).
COLLEGE: Penn State.
TRANSACTIONS/CAREER NOTES: Selected by New York Jets in third round (79th pick overall) of 2001 NFL draft. ... Signed by Jets (July 25, 2001). ... Granted free agency (March 3, 2004). ... Re-signed by Jets (May 10, 2004). ... Granted unconditional free agency (March 2, 2005). ... Signed by New York Giants (March 4, 2005).
PLAYING EXPERIENCE: New York Jets NFL, 2001-2004. ... Games/Games started: 2001 (8/0), 2002 (16/16), 2003 (16/16), 2004 (16/16). Total: 56/48.

MCKENZIE, MIKE   CB   SAINTS

PERSONAL: Born April 26, 1976, in Miami, Fla. ... 6-0/194. ... Full name: Michael Terrance McKenzie.
HIGH SCHOOL: Norland (Miami).
COLLEGE: Memphis.
TRANSACTIONS/CAREER NOTES: Selected after junior season by Green Bay Packers in third round (87th pick overall) of 1999 NFL draft. ... Signed by Packers (July 8, 1999). ... Placed on reserve/did not report list (August 2, 2004). ... Reinstated (September 15, 2004). ... Activated (September 18, 2004). ... Traded by Packers with a 2006 conditional draft pick to New Orleans Saints for QB J.T. O'Sullivan and second-round pick (S Nick Collins) in 2005 draft (October 4, 2004).

Year Team	G	GS	TOTALS Tk.	Ast.	Sks.	INTERCEPTIONS No.	Yds.	Avg.	TD
1999—Green Bay NFL	16	16	53	12	0.0	6	4	0.7	0
2000—Green Bay NFL	10	8	30	3	0.0	1	26	26.0	0
2001—Green Bay NFL	16	16	54	10	0.0	2	38	19.0	1
2002—Green Bay NFL	13	13	47	19	1.0	2	0	0.0	0
2003—Green Bay NFL	14	14	52	6	0.0	4	98	24.5	1
2004—Green Bay NFL	1	0	0	0	0.0	0	0	0.0	0
—New Orleans NFL	10	10	31	2	0.0	5	19	3.8	0
Pro totals (6 years)	80	77	267	52	1.0	20	185	9.3	2

MCKIE, JASON   FB   BEARS

PERSONAL: Born May 22, 1980, in Gulf Breeze, Fla. ... 5-11/240.
HIGH SCHOOL: Gulf Breeze (Fla.).
COLLEGE: Temple.
TRANSACTIONS/CAREER NOTES: Signed as non-drafted free agent by Philadelphia Eagles (April 23, 2002). ... Released by Eagles (September 1, 2002). ... Re-signed by Eagles to practice squad (September 3, 2002). ... Released by Eagles (September 17, 2002). ... Re-signed by Eagles to practice squad (September 25, 2002). ... Signed by Dallas Cowboys off Eagles practice squad (December 7, 2002). ... Released by Cowboys (August 17, 2003). ... Signed by Chicago Bears (August 19, 2003). ... Waived by Bears (August 31, 2003). ... Re-signed by Bears to practice squad (September 1, 2003). ... Activated (November 21, 2003).
SINGLE GAME HIGHS (regular season): Attempts—1 (September 12, 2004, vs. Detroit); yards—1 (September 12, 2004, vs. Detroit); and rushing touchdowns—0.

Year Team	G	GS	RUSHING Att.	Yds.	Avg.	TD	RECEIVING No.	Yds.	Avg.	TD	TOTALS TD	2pt.	Pts.	Fum.
2002—Dallas NFL	1	1	0	0	0.0	0	1	7	7.0	0	0	0	0	0
2003—Chicago NFL	6	0	0	0	0.0	0	0	0	0.0	0	0	0	0	0
2004—Chicago NFL	15	2	1	1	1.0	0	13	70	5.4	2	2	0	12	1
Pro totals (3 years)	22	3	1	1	1.0	0	14	77	5.5	2	2	0	12	1

MCKINLEY, ALVIN   DT   BROWNS

PERSONAL: Born June 9, 1978, in Kosciusko, Miss. ... 6-3/310. ... Full name: Alvin Jerome McKinley.
HIGH SCHOOL: Weir (Miss.).
JUNIOR COLLEGE: Holmes Junior College (Miss.).
COLLEGE: Mississippi State.
TRANSACTIONS/CAREER NOTES: Selected by Carolina Panthers in fourth round (120th pick overall) of 2000 NFL draft. ... Signed by Panthers (June 21, 2000). ... Claimed on waivers by Cleveland Browns (August 29, 2001). ... Released by Browns (September 1, 2001). ... Re-signed by Browns to practice squad (September 3, 2001). ... Activated (October 9, 2001). ... Granted free agency (February 28, 2003). ... Re-signed by Browns (March 7, 2003). ... On injured reserve with knee injury (November 12, 2003-remainder of season).

Year Team	G	GS	TOTALS Tk.	Ast.	Sks.
2000—Carolina NFL	7	0	9	0	0.0
2001—Cleveland NFL	7	0	6	6	0.0
2002—Cleveland NFL	13	0	7	4	0.0
2003—Cleveland NFL	9	0	9	14	0.0
2004—Cleveland NFL	16	2	29	20	3.0
Pro totals (5 years)	52	2	60	44	3.0

MCKINNEY, SETH   C   DOLPHINS

PERSONAL: Born June 12, 1979, in Buffalo, Texas. ... 6-3/305.
HIGH SCHOOL: Westlake (Austin, Texas).
JUNIOR COLLEGE: Lackawanna Junior College (Pa.).

M

COLLEGE: Texas A&M.
TRANSACTIONS/CAREER NOTES: Selected by Miami Dolphins in third round (90th pick overall) of 2002 NFL draft. ... Signed by Dolphins (July 28, 2002). ... Granted free agency (March 2, 2005). ... Re-signed by Dolphins (April 18, 2005).
PLAYING EXPERIENCE: Miami NFL, 2002-2004. ... Games/Games started: 2002 (16/2), 2003 (16/3), 2004 (16/16). Total: 48/21.
HONORS: Named center on THE SPORTING NEWS college All-America second team (2001).

MCKINNEY, STEVE — C — TEXANS

PERSONAL: Born October 15, 1975, in Galveston, Texas. ... 6-4/302. ... Full name: Stephen Michael McKinney.
HIGH SCHOOL: Clear Lake (Houston).
COLLEGE: Texas A&M.
TRANSACTIONS/CAREER NOTES: Selected by Indianapolis Colts in fourth round (93rd pick overall) of 1998 NFL draft. ... Signed by Colts (July 23, 1998). ... Granted free agency (March 2, 2001). ... Re-signed by Colts (May 9, 2001). ... Granted unconditional free agency (March 1, 2002). ... Signed by Houston Texans (March 6, 2002).
PLAYING EXPERIENCE: Indianapolis NFL, 1998-2001; Houston NFL, 2002-2004. ... Games/Games started: 1998 (16/16), 1999 (15/14), 2000 (16/16), 2001 (14/14), 2002 (16/16), 2003 (16/16), 2004 (16/16). Total: 109/108.

MCKINNIE, BRYANT — T — VIKINGS

PERSONAL: Born September 23, 1979, in Woodbury, N.J. ... 6-8/335. ... Full name: Bryant Douglas McKinnie.
HIGH SCHOOL: Woodbury (N.J.).
JUNIOR COLLEGE: Lackawanna Junior College (Pa.).
COLLEGE: Miami (Fla.).
TRANSACTIONS/CAREER NOTES: Selected by Minnesota Vikings in first round (seventh pick overall) of 2002 NFL draft. ... Signed by Vikings (November 2, 2002).
PLAYING EXPERIENCE: Minnesota NFL, 2002-2004. ... Games/Games started: 2002 (8/7), 2003 (16/16), 2004 (16/16). Total: 40/39.
HONORS: Named offensive tackle on THE SPORTING NEWS college All-America first team (2001). ... Outland Trophy winner (2001).

MCKINNON, RONALD — LB

PERSONAL: Born September 20, 1973, in Fort Rucker, Ala. ... 6-0/245.
HIGH SCHOOL: Elba (Ala.).
COLLEGE: North Alabama.
TRANSACTIONS/CAREER NOTES: Signed as non-drafted free agent by Arizona Cardinals (April 23, 1996). ... Granted free agency (February 12, 1999). ... Re-signed by Cardinals (June 14, 1999). ... Granted unconditional free agency (February 11, 2000). ... Re-signed by Cardinals (February 24, 2000). ... Granted unconditional free agency (March 2, 2005).
HONORS: Harlon Hill Trophy winner (1995).

				TOTALS			INTERCEPTIONS			
Year Team	G	GS	Tk.	Ast.	Sks.	No.	Yds.	Avg.	TD
1996—Arizona NFL	16	0	6	1	0.0	0	0	0.0	0
1997—Arizona NFL	16	16	61	36	1.0	3	40	13.3	0
1998—Arizona NFL	13	13	66	29	2.0	5	25	5.0	0
1999—Arizona NFL	16	16	94	47	1.0	1	0	0.0	0
2000—Arizona NFL	16	16	119	38	4.0	0	0	0.0	0
2001—Arizona NFL	16	16	98	49	2.0	1	24	24.0	1
2002—Arizona NFL	16	16	67	41	0.0	0	0	0.0	0
2003—Arizona NFL	16	16	80	25	2.0	0	0	0.0	0
2004—Arizona NFL	16	10	49	25	0.0	0	0	0.0	0
Pro totals (9 years)	141	119	640	291	12.0	10	89	8.9	1

MCMAHON, MIKE — QB — EAGLES

PERSONAL: Born February 8, 1979, in Pittsburgh, Pa. ... 6-2/215. ... Full name: Michael Edward McMahon.
HIGH SCHOOL: North Allegheny (Pa.).
COLLEGE: Rutgers.
TRANSACTIONS/CAREER NOTES: Selected by Detroit Lions in fifth round (149th pick overall) of 2001 NFL draft. ... Signed by Lions (June 7, 2001). ... Granted free agency (March 3, 2004). ... Re-signed by Lions (March 31, 2004). ... Granted unconditional free agency (March 2, 2005). ... Signed by Philadelphia Eagles (March 11, 2005).
SINGLE GAME HIGHS (regular season): Attempts—44 (December 29, 2002, vs. Minnesota); completions—19 (December 29, 2002, vs. Minnesota); yards—293 (December 29, 2002, vs. Minnesota); and touchdown passes—3 (December 29, 2002, vs. Minnesota).
MISCELLANEOUS: Regular-season record as starting NFL quarterback: 1-6 (.143).

					PASSING							RUSHING				TOTALS		
Year Team	G	GS	Att.	Cmp.	Pct.	Yds.	TD	Int.	Avg.	Skd.	Rat.	Att.	Yds.	Avg.	TD	TD	2pt.	Pts.
2001—Detroit NFL	8	3	115	53	46.1	671	3	1	5.83	21	69.9	27	145	5.4	1	1	1	8
2002—Detroit NFL	8	4	147	62	42.2	874	7	9	5.95	12	52.4	14	96	6.9	3	3	0	18
2003—Detroit NFL	3	0	31	9	29.0	87	0	2	2.81	2	12.7	5	32	6.4	0	0	0	0
2004—Detroit NFL	1	0	15	11	73.3	77	0	1	5.13	1	56.8	2	18	9.0	0	0	0	0
Pro totals (4 years)	20	7	308	135	43.8	1709	10	13	5.55	36	55.0	48	291	6.1	4	4	1	26

MCMICHAEL, RANDY — TE — DOLPHINS

PERSONAL: Born June 28, 1979, in Griffin, Ga. ... 6-3/250.
HIGH SCHOOL: Peach County (Fort Valley, Ga.).
COLLEGE: Georgia.

TRANSACTIONS/CAREER NOTES: Selected by Miami Dolphins in fourth round (114th pick overall) of 2002 NFL draft. ... Signed by Dolphins (July 25, 2002).
SINGLE GAME HIGHS (regular season): Receptions—9 (December 26, 2004, vs. Cleveland); yards—102 (October 19, 2003, vs. New England); and touchdown receptions—1 (November 28, 2004, vs. San Francisco).
STATISTICAL PLATEAUS: 100-yard receiving games: 2003 (1). Total: 1.

Year Team	G	GS	No.	Yds.	Avg.	TD	TD	2pt.	Pts.	Fum.
				RECEIVING					TOTALS	
2002—Miami NFL	16	16	39	485	12.4	4	4	0	24	1
2003—Miami NFL	16	16	49	598	12.2	2	3	0	18	0
2004—Miami NFL	16	16	73	791	10.8	4	4	1	26	2
Pro totals (3 years)	48	48	161	1874	11.6	10	11	1	68	3

MCMILLON, TODD   CB   BEARS

PERSONAL: Born September 26, 1974, in Bellflower, Calif. ... 5-11/188.
HIGH SCHOOL: Cerritus (Bellflower, Calif.).
COLLEGE: Northern Arizona.
TRANSACTIONS/CAREER NOTES: Signed as non-drafted free agent by Chicago Bears (February 16, 2000). ... Released by Bears (August 22, 2000). ... Re-signed by Bears to practice squad (August 29, 2000). ... Activated (November 15, 2000). ... Assigned by Bears to Frankfurt Galaxy in 2001 NFL Europe enhancement allocation program (February 19, 2001). ... Released by Bears (September 3, 2001). ... Re-signed by Bears to practice squad (September 5, 2001). ... Activated (November 13, 2001). ... On injured reserve with thumb injury (November 19, 2002-remainder of season). ... Granted free agency (February 28, 2003). ... Re-signed by Bears (April 22, 2003). ... Granted unconditional free agency (March 2, 2005). ... Re-signed by Bears (March 17, 2005).

Year Team	G	GS	Tk.	Ast.	Sks.	No.	Yds.	Avg.	TD
			TOTALS			INTERCEPTIONS			
2000—Chicago NFL	3	0	3	0	0.0	0	0	0.0	0
2001—Chicago NFL	8	0	1	0	0.0	0	0	0.0	0
2002—Chicago NFL	10	1	22	2	0.0	0	0	0.0	0
2003—Chicago NFL	13	0	3	0	0.0	0	0	0.0	0
2004—Chicago NFL	14	1	1	2	0.0	0	0	0.0	0
Pro totals (5 years)	48	2	30	4	0.0	0	0	0.0	0

MCMULLEN, BILLY   WR   EAGLES

PERSONAL: Born March 8, 1980, in Richmond, Va. ... 6-4/210. ... Full name: Wilbur Anthony McMullen Jr.
HIGH SCHOOL: Henrico (Richmond, Va.).
COLLEGE: Virginia.
TRANSACTIONS/CAREER NOTES: Selected by Philadelphia Eagles in third round (95th pick overall) of 2003 NFL draft. ... Signed by Eagles (July 24, 2003).
CHAMPIONSHIP GAME EXPERIENCE: Member of Eagles for NFC championship game (2003 season); inactive. ... Played in NFC championship game (2004 season). ... Member of Eagles for Super Bowl 39 (2004 season); inactive.
SINGLE GAME HIGHS (regular season): Receptions—2 (January 2, 2005, vs. Cincinnati); yards—19 (January 2, 2005, vs. Cincinnati); and touchdown receptions—0.

Year Team	G	GS	Att.	Yds.	Avg.	TD	No.	Yds.	Avg.	TD	TD	2pt.	Pts.	Fum.
			RUSHING				RECEIVING				TOTALS			
2003—Philadelphia NFL	5	0	0	0	0.0	0	1	2	2.0	0	0	0	0	0
2004—Philadelphia NFL	8	0	0	0	0.0	0	3	24	8.0	0	0	0	0	0
Pro totals (2 years)	13	0	0	0	0.0	0	4	26	6.5	0	0	0	0	0

MCNABB, DONOVAN   QB   EAGLES

PERSONAL: Born November 25, 1976, in Chicago, Ill. ... 6-2/240. ... Full name: Donovan Jamal McNabb.
HIGH SCHOOL: Mount Carmel (Ill.).
COLLEGE: Syracuse.
TRANSACTIONS/CAREER NOTES: Selected by Philadelphia Eagles in first round (second pick overall) of 1999 NFL draft. ... Signed by Eagles (July 30, 1999).
CHAMPIONSHIP GAME EXPERIENCE: Played in NFC championship game (2001-2004 seasons). ... Played in Super Bowl 39 (2004 season).
HONORS: Played in Pro Bowl (2000-2002 and 2004 seasons). ... Named to play in Pro Bowl (2003 season); replaced by Marc Bulger due to injury.
SINGLE GAME HIGHS (regular season): Attempts—55 (November 12, 2000, vs. Pittsburgh); completions—32 (December 5, 2004, vs. Green Bay); passing yards—464 (December 5, 2004, vs. Green Bay); and touchdown passes—5 (December 5, 2004, vs. Green Bay).
STATISTICAL PLATEAUS: 100-yard rushing games: 2000 (1), 2002 (2). Total: 3. 300-yard passing games: 2000 (2), 2001 (1), 2003 (2), 2004 (5). Total: 10.
MISCELLANEOUS: Regular-season record as starting NFL quarterback: 56-23 (.709). ... Postseason record as starting NFL quarterback: 7-5 (.583).

Year Team	G	GS	Att.	Cmp.	Pct.	Yds.	TD	Int.	Avg.	Skd.	Rat.	Att.	Yds.	Avg.	TD	TD	2pt.	Pts.
			PASSING									RUSHING				TOTALS		
1999—Philadelphia NFL	12	6	216	106	49.1	948	8	7	4.39	28	60.1	47	313	6.7	0	0	1	2
2000—Philadelphia NFL	16	16	569	330	58.0	3365	21	13	5.91	45	77.8	86	629	7.3	6	6	0	36
2001—Philadelphia NFL	16	16	493	285	57.8	3233	25	12	6.56	39	84.3	82	482	5.9	2	2	0	12
2002—Philadelphia NFL	10	10	361	211	58.4	2289	17	6	6.34	28	86.0	63	460	7.3	6	6	0	36
2003—Philadelphia NFL	16	16	478	275	57.5	3216	16	11	6.73	‡43	79.6	71	355	5.0	3	3	0	18
2004—Philadelphia NFL	15	15	469	300	64.0	3875	31	8	8.26	32	104.7	41	220	5.4	3	3	0	18
Pro totals (6 years)	85	79	2586	1507	58.3	16926	118	57	6.55	215	83.9	390	2459	6.3	20	20	1	122

MCNAIR, STEVE   QB   TITANS

PERSONAL: Born February 14, 1973, in Mt. Olive, Miss. ... 6-2/235. ... Full name: Steve LaTreal McNair.
HIGH SCHOOL: Mount Olive (Miss.).
COLLEGE: Alcorn State.
TRANSACTIONS/CAREER NOTES: Selected by Houston Oilers in first round (third pick overall) of 1995 NFL draft. ... Signed by Oilers (July 25, 1995). ... Oilers franchise moved to Tennessee for 1997 season. ... Oilers franchise renamed Tennessee Titans for 1999 season (December 26, 1998).
CHAMPIONSHIP GAME EXPERIENCE: Played in AFC championship game (1999 and 2002 seasons). ... Played in Super Bowl 34 (1999 season).
HONORS: Walter Payton Award winner (1994). ... Named to play in Pro Bowl (2000 season); replaced by Elvis Grbac due to injury. ... Played in Pro Bowl (2003 season).
SINGLE GAME HIGHS (regular season): Attempts—49 (December 20, 1998, vs. Green Bay); completions—32 (September 29, 2002, vs. Oakland); yards—421 (October 12, 2003, vs. Houston); and touchdown passes—5 (December 26, 1999, vs. Jacksonville).
STATISTICAL PLATEAUS: 300-yard passing games: 1996 (1), 1999 (1), 2001 (2), 2002 (2), 2003 (2). Total: 8.
MISCELLANEOUS: Regular-season record as starting NFL quarterback: 72-45 (.615). ... Postseason record as starting NFL quarterback: 5-4 (.556).

			PASSING									RUSHING				TOTALS		
Year Team	G	GS	Att.	Cmp.	Pct.	Yds.	TD	Int.	Avg.	Skd.	Rat.	Att.	Yds.	Avg.	TD	TD	2pt.	Pts.
1995—Houston NFL	4	2	80	41	51.3	569	3	1	7.11	6	81.7	11	38	3.5	0	0	0	0
1996—Houston NFL	9	4	143	88	61.5	1197	6	4	8.37	9	90.6	31	169	5.5	2	2	0	12
1997—Tennessee NFL	16	16	415	216	52.0	2665	14	13	6.42	31	70.4	101	674	*6.7	8	8	0	48
1998—Tennessee NFL	16	16	492	289	58.7	3228	15	10	6.56	33	80.1	77	559	7.3	4	4	0	24
1999—Tennessee NFL	11	11	331	187	56.5	2179	12	8	6.58	16	78.6	72	337	4.7	8	8	0	48
2000—Tennessee NFL	16	15	396	248	62.6	2847	15	13	7.19	24	83.2	72	403	5.6	0	0	0	0
2001—Tennessee NFL	15	15	431	264	61.3	3350	21	12	§7.77	37	90.2	75	414	5.5	5	5	0	30
2002—Tennessee NFL	16	16	492	301	61.2	3387	22	15	6.88	21	84.0	82	440	5.4	3	3	1	20
2003—Tennessee NFL	14	14	400	250	62.5	3215	24	7	*8.04	19	*100.4	38	138	3.6	4	4	1	26
2004—Tennessee NFL	8	8	215	129	60.0	1343	8	9	6.25	13	73.1	23	128	5.6	1	1	1	8
Pro totals (10 years)	125	117	3395	2013	59.3	23980	140	92	7.06	209	83.4	582	3300	5.7	35	35	3	216

MCQUARTERS, R.W.   CB

PERSONAL: Born December 21, 1976, in Tulsa, Okla. ... 5-10/195. ... Full name: Robert William McQuarters II.
HIGH SCHOOL: Washington (Okla.).
COLLEGE: Oklahoma State.
TRANSACTIONS/CAREER NOTES: Selected after junior season by San Francisco 49ers in first round (28th pick overall) of 1998 NFL draft. ... Signed by 49ers (July 28, 1998). ... On injured reserve with shoulder injury (November 30, 1999-remainder of season). ... Traded by 49ers to Chicago Bears for sixth-round pick (WR Cedrick Wilson) in 2001 draft (June 5, 2000). ... Released by Bears (May 23, 2005).

			TOTALS			INTERCEPTIONS				PUNT RETURNS				KICKOFF RETURNS				TOTALS			
Year Team	G	GS	Tk.	Ast.	Sks.	No.	Yds.	Avg.	TD	No.	Yds.	Avg.	TD	No.	Yds.	Avg.	TD	TD	2pt.	Pts.	Fum.
1998—S.F. NFL	16	7	45	4	0.0	0	0	0.0	0	*47	406	8.6	1	17	339	19.9	0	1	0	6	4
1999—S.F. NFL	11	4	25	3	0.0	1	25	25.0	0	18	90	5.0	0	26	568	21.8	0	0	0	0	1
2000—Chi. NFL	15	2	22	7	1.0	1	61	61.0	1	0	0	0.0	0	0	0	0.0	0	1	0	6	0
2001—Chi. NFL	16	16	65	14	1.0	3	47	15.7	0	12	96	8.0	0	0	0	0.0	0	1	0	6	0
2002—Chi. NFL	9	9	35	8	0.0	1	33	33.0	0	0	0	0.0	0	0	0	0.0	0	0	0	0	0
2003—Chi. NFL	16	6	38	8	0.0	2	72	36.0	0	37	452	12.2	1	0	0	0.0	0	1	0	6	1
2004—Chi. NFL	16	14	55	12	0.0	2	85	42.5	1	‡44	435	9.9	1	2	46	23.0	0	2	0	12	5
Pro totals (7 years)	99	58	285	56	2.0	10	323	32.3	2	158	1479	9.4	3	45	953	21.2	0	6	0	36	11

MEESTER, BRAD   C   JAGUARS

PERSONAL: Born March 23, 1977, in Iowa Falls, Iowa. ... 6-3/300. ... Full name: Brad Ley Meester.
HIGH SCHOOL: Aplington-Parkersburg (Aplington, Iowa).
COLLEGE: Northern Iowa.
TRANSACTIONS/CAREER NOTES: Selected by Jacksonville Jaguars in second round (60th pick overall) of 2000 NFL draft. ... Signed by Jaguars (May 16, 2000).
PLAYING EXPERIENCE: Jacksonville NFL, 2000-2004. ... Games/Games started: 2000 (16/16), 2001 (16/16), 2002 (16/16), 2003 (16/16), 2004 (16/16). Total: 80/80.

MEIER, ROB   DT   JAGUARS

PERSONAL: Born August 29, 1977, in Vancouver, BC. ... 6-5/293. ... Full name: Robert Jack Daniel Meier.
HIGH SCHOOL: Sentinel (West Vancouver, B.C.).
COLLEGE: Washington State.
TRANSACTIONS/CAREER NOTES: Selected by Jacksonville Jaguars in seventh round (241st pick overall) of 2000 NFL draft. ... Signed by Jaguars (May 17, 2000). ... On injured reserve with ankle injury (December 1, 2004-remainder of season).

			TOTALS		
Year Team	G	GS	Tk.	Ast.	Sks.
2000—Jacksonville NFL	16	0	10	1	0.5
2001—Jacksonville NFL	16	0	12	3	0.0
2002—Jacksonville NFL	16	7	20	3	2.0
2003—Jacksonville NFL	16	0	20	5	1.5
2004—Jacksonville NFL	11	8	15	7	0.5
Pro totals (5 years)	75	15	77	19	4.5

MEIER, SHAD   TE   SAINTS

PERSONAL: Born June 7, 1978, in St. Louis, Mo. ... 6-4/255.
HIGH SCHOOL: Pittsburgh (Kan.).
COLLEGE: Kansas State.
TRANSACTIONS/CAREER NOTES: Selected by Tennessee Titans in third round (90th pick overall) of 2001 NFL draft. ... Signed by Titans (July 24, 2001). ... Granted free agency (March 3, 2004). ... Re-signed by Titans (July 31, 2004). ... Granted unconditional free agency (March 2, 2005). ... Signed by New Orleans Saints (March 10, 2005).
CHAMPIONSHIP GAME EXPERIENCE: Played in AFC championship game (2002 season).
SINGLE GAME HIGHS (regular season): Receptions—9 (October 3, 2004, vs. San Diego); yards—53 (September 21, 2003, vs. New Orleans); and touchdown receptions—1 (October 31, 2004, vs. Cincinnati).

				RECEIVING				TOTALS		
Year Team	G	GS	No.	Yds.	Avg.	TD	TD	2pt.	Pts.	Fum.
2001—Tennessee NFL	11	1	3	31	10.3	0	0	0	0	0
2002—Tennessee NFL	12	0	1	17	17.0	1	1	0	6	0
2003—Tennessee NFL	15	6	13	159	12.2	0	0	0	0	1
2004—Tennessee NFL	14	7	25	127	5.1	2	2	0	12	1
Pro totals (4 years)	52	14	42	334	8.0	3	3	0	18	2

MELTON, TERRENCE   LB   SAINTS

PERSONAL: Born January 1, 1977, in Miami, Fla. ... 6-1/235. ... Full name: Terrence Lee Melton.
HIGH SCHOOL: North Shore (Houston, Texas).
COLLEGE: Rice.
TRANSACTIONS/CAREER NOTES: Signed as non-drafted free agent by Atlanta Falcons (March 2, 2004). ... Released by Falcons (September 5, 2004). ... Re-signed by Falcons to practice squad (September 6, 2004). ... Activated (September 11, 2004). ... Released by Falcons (September 13, 2004). ... Re-signed by Falcons to practice squad (September 15, 2004). ... Signed by New Orleans Saints off Falcons practice squad (December 2, 2004).

			TOTALS			INTERCEPTIONS			
Year Team	G	GS	Tk.	Ast.	Sks.	No.	Yds.	Avg.	TD
2004—Atlanta NFL	1	0	0	0	0.0	0	0	0.0	0
—New Orleans NFL	2	0	0	0	0.0	0	0	0.0	0
Pro totals (1 year)	3	0	0	0	0.0	0	0	0.0	0

METCALF, TERRENCE   G/T   BEARS

PERSONAL: Born January 28, 1978, in Clarksdale, Miss. ... 6-3/318. ... Full name: Terrence Orlando Metcalf.
HIGH SCHOOL: Clarksdale (Miss.).
COLLEGE: Mississippi.
TRANSACTIONS/CAREER NOTES: Selected by Chicago Bears in third round (93rd pick overall) of 2002 NFL draft. ... Signed by Bears (July 12, 2002). ... Granted free agency (March 2, 2005). ... Re-signed by Bears (April 18, 2005).
PLAYING EXPERIENCE: Chicago NFL, 2002-2004. ... Games/Games started: 2002 (5/0), 2003 (9/2), 2004 (13/5). Total: 27/7.
HONORS: Named guard on THE SPORTING NEWS college All-America second team (1999). ... Named offensive tackle on THE SPORTING NEWS college All-America third team (2001).

MIDDLEBROOKS, WILLIE   CB   BRONCOS

PERSONAL: Born February 12, 1979, in Miami, Fla. ... 6-1/200.
HIGH SCHOOL: Homestead (Fla.).
COLLEGE: Minnesota.
TRANSACTIONS/CAREER NOTES: Selected after junior season by Denver Broncos in first round (24th pick overall) of 2001 NFL draft. ... Signed by Broncos (July 27, 2001). ... On injured reserve with knee injury (December 17, 2004-remainder of season).

			TOTALS			INTERCEPTIONS			
Year Team	G	GS	Tk.	Ast.	Sks.	No.	Yds.	Avg.	TD
2001—Denver NFL	8	0	1	0	0.0	0	0	0.0	0
2002—Denver NFL	15	0	0	0	0.0	0	0	0.0	0
2003—Denver NFL	16	0	5	1	0.0	0	0	0.0	0
2004—Denver NFL	12	2	17	3	1.0	0	0	0.0	0
Pro totals (4 years)	51	2	23	4	1.0	0	0	0.0	0

MIDDLETON, FRANK   G   RAIDERS

PERSONAL: Born October 25, 1974, in Beaumont, Texas. ... 6-3/330. ... Full name: Frank Middleton Jr.
HIGH SCHOOL: West Brook (Beaumont, Texas).
JUNIOR COLLEGE: Fort Scott (Kan.) Community College.
COLLEGE: Arizona.
TRANSACTIONS/CAREER NOTES: Selected by Tampa Bay Buccaneers in third round (63rd pick overall) of 1997 NFL draft. ... Signed by Buccaneers (July 20, 1997). ... Granted free agency (February 11, 2000). ... Re-signed by Buccaneers (May 2, 2000). ... Granted unconditional free agency (March 2, 2001). ... Signed by Oakland Raiders (April 26, 2001). ... On injured reserve with quadriceps injury (December 17, 2003-remainder of season). ... On injured reserve with quadriceps injury (October 28, 2004-remainder of season).
PLAYING EXPERIENCE: Tampa Bay NFL, 1997-2000; Oakland NFL, 2001-2004. ... Games/Games started: 1997 (15/2), 1998 (16/16), 1999 (16/16), 2000 (16/16), 2001 (13/12), 2002 (16/16), 2003 (10/8), 2004 (7/7). Total: 109/93.
CHAMPIONSHIP GAME EXPERIENCE: Played in NFC championship game (1999 season). ... Played in AFC championship game (2002 season). ... Played in Super Bowl 37 (2002 season).

M

MIKELL, QUINTIN   S   EAGLES

PERSONAL: Born September 16, 1980, in New Orleans, La. ... 5-10/206.
HIGH SCHOOL: Willamette (Eugene, Ore.).
COLLEGE: Boise State.
TRANSACTIONS/CAREER NOTES: Signed as non-drafted free agent by Philadelphia Eagles (April 28, 2003).
CHAMPIONSHIP GAME EXPERIENCE: Played in NFC championship game (2003 and 2004 seasons). ... Played in Super Bowl 39 (2004 season).

			TOTALS			INTERCEPTIONS			
Year Team	G	GS	Tk.	Ast.	Sks.	No.	Yds.	Avg.	TD
2003—Philadelphia NFL	16	0	2	0	0.0	0	0	0.0	0
2004—Philadelphia NFL	14	0	6	0	0.0	1	0	0.0	0
Pro totals (2 years)	30	0	8	0	0.0	1	0	0.0	0

MILI, ITULA   TE   SEAHAWKS

PERSONAL: Born April 20, 1973, in Kahuku, Hawaii. ... 6-4/260. ... Name pronounced: EE-too-la MEE-lee.
HIGH SCHOOL: Kahuku (Hawaii).
COLLEGE: Brigham Young.
TRANSACTIONS/CAREER NOTES: Selected by Seattle Seahawks in sixth round (174th pick overall) of 1997 NFL draft. ... Signed by Seahawks (June 11, 1997). ... On physically unable to perform list with knee injury (August 18, 1997-entire season). ... On injured reserve with knee injury (December 25, 1998-remainder of season). ... Granted free agency (March 2, 2001). ... Re-signed by Seahawks (April 13, 2001). ... Granted unconditional free agency (March 1, 2002). ... Re-signed by Seahawks (March 14, 2002). ... Granted unconditional free agency (March 2, 2005). ... Re-signed by Seahawks (March 11, 2005).
SINGLE GAME HIGHS (regular season): Receptions—7 (December 29, 2002, vs. San Diego); yards—119 (December 29, 2002, vs. San Diego); and touchdown receptions—2 (October 26. 2003, vs. Cincinnati).
STATISTICAL PLATEAUS: 100-yard receiving games: 2002 (1). Total: 1.

			RECEIVING				TOTALS			
Year Team	G	GS	No.	Yds.	Avg.	TD	TD	2pt.	Pts.	Fum.
1997—Seattle NFL	Did not play.									
1998—Seattle NFL	7	0	1	20	20.0	0	0	0	0	0
1999—Seattle NFL	16	1	5	28	5.6	1	1	0	6	1
2000—Seattle NFL	16	6	28	288	10.3	3	3	0	18	1
2001—Seattle NFL	16	5	8	98	12.3	2	2	0	12	0
2002—Seattle NFL	16	12	43	508	11.8	2	2	0	12	1
2003—Seattle NFL	16	12	46	492	10.7	4	4	0	24	0
2004—Seattle NFL	15	4	23	240	10.4	1	1	0	6	0
Pro totals (7 years)	102	40	154	1674	10.9	13	13	0	78	3

MILLER, BILLY   TE   TEXANS

M

PERSONAL: Born April 24, 1977, in Los Angeles, Calif. ... 6-3/245. ... Full name: Billy RoShawn Miller.
HIGH SCHOOL: Westlake (Westlake Village, Calif.).
COLLEGE: Southern California.
TRANSACTIONS/CAREER NOTES: Selected by Denver Broncos in seventh round (218th pick overall) of 1999 NFL draft. ... Signed by Broncos (July 20, 1999). ... Released by Broncos (September 5, 1999). ... Re-signed by Broncos to practice squad (September 6, 1999). ... Activated (October 19, 1999). ... Released by Broncos (September 2, 2001). ... Signed by Houston Texans (February 8, 2002). ... Granted free agency (February 28, 2003). ... Re-signed by Texans (June 19, 2003).
SINGLE GAME HIGHS (regular season): Receptions—8 (December 15, 2002, vs. Baltimore); yards—78 (October 27, 2002, vs. Jacksonville); and touchdown receptions—1 (November 28, 2004, vs. Tennessee).

			RECEIVING				TOTALS			
Year Team	G	GS	No.	Yds.	Avg.	TD	TD	2pt.	Pts.	Fum.
1999—Denver NFL	10	0	5	59	11.8	0	0	0	0	0
2000—Denver NFL	12	0	1	7	7.0	0	0	0	0	0
2002—Houston NFL	16	7	51	613	12.0	3	3	0	18	0
2003—Houston NFL	16	6	40	355	8.9	3	3	0	18	0
2004—Houston NFL	16	8	17	178	10.5	1	1	0	6	1
Pro totals (5 years)	70	21	114	1212	10.6	7	7	0	42	1

MILLER, CALEB   LB   BENGALS

PERSONAL: Born September 3, 1980, in Guadalupe County, Texas. ... 6-3/225.
HIGH SCHOOL: Sulpher Springs (Texas).
COLLEGE: Arkansas.
TRANSACTIONS/CAREER NOTES: Selected by Cincinnati Bengals in third round (80th pick overall) of 2004 NFL draft. ... Signed by Bengals (July 30, 2004).

			TOTALS			INTERCEPTIONS			
Year Team	G	GS	Tk.	Ast.	Sks.	No.	Yds.	Avg.	TD
2004—Cincinnati NFL	13	3	17	11	0.0	0	0	0.0	0

MILLER, FRED   T   BEARS

PERSONAL: Born February 6, 1973, in Houston, Texas. ... 6-7/320. ... Full name: Fred J. Miller Jr.
HIGH SCHOOL: Aldine Eisenhower (Houston).
COLLEGE: Baylor.

TRANSACTIONS/CAREER NOTES: Selected by St. Louis Rams in fifth round (141st pick overall) of 1996 NFL draft. ... Signed by Rams (July 15, 1996). ... Granted free agency (February 12, 1999). ... Re-signed by Rams (May 24, 1999). ... Granted unconditional free agency (February 11, 2000). ... Signed by Tennessee Titans (February 16, 2000). ... Released by Titans (February 21, 2005). ... Signed by Chicago Bears (March 7, 2005).
PLAYING EXPERIENCE: St. Louis NFL, 1996-1999; Tennessee NFL, 2000-2004. ... Games/Games started: 1996 (14/0), 1997 (15/7), 1998 (15/15), 1999 (16/16), 2000 (16/16), 2001 (16/16), 2002 (16/16), 2003 (16/16), 2004 (16/16). Total: 140/118.
CHAMPIONSHIP GAME EXPERIENCE: Played in NFC championship game (1999 season). ... Member of Super Bowl championship team (1999 season). ... Played in AFC championship game (2002 season).

MILLER, JOSH   P   PATRIOTS

PERSONAL: Born July 14, 1970, in Queens, N.Y. ... 6-4/225.
HIGH SCHOOL: East Brunswick (N.J.).
JUNIOR COLLEGE: Scottsdale (Ariz.) Community College.
COLLEGE: Arizona.
TRANSACTIONS/CAREER NOTES: Signed as non-drafted free agent by Green Bay Packers (April 1993). ... Released by Packers before 1993 season. ... Signed by Baltimore Stallions of CFL (June 1994). ... Signed by Seattle Seahawks (May 29, 1996). ... Released by Seahawks (August 13, 1996). ... Signed by Pittsburgh Steelers (August 15, 1996). ... On injured reserve with shoulder injury (December 20, 2002-remainder of season). ... Released by Steelers (March 6, 2004). ... Signed by New England Patriots (March 15, 2004).
CHAMPIONSHIP GAME EXPERIENCE: Played in Grey Cup, CFL championship game (1994). ... Played in AFC championship game (1997, 2001 and 2004 seasons). ... Member of Super Bowl championship team (2004 season).
HONORS: Named punter on the Sporting News college All-America first team (1992).

				PUNTING			
Year Team	G	No.	Yds.	Avg.	Net avg.	In. 20	Blk.
1994—Baltimore CFL	18	117	5024	42.9	36.9	...	...
1995—Baltimore CFL	18	118	5629	47.7	42.2	...	...
1996—Pittsburgh NFL	12	55	2256	41.0	33.6	18	0
1997—Pittsburgh NFL	16	64	2729	42.6	35.0	17	0
1998—Pittsburgh NFL	16	81	3530	43.6	36.8	*34	0
1999—Pittsburgh NFL	16	84	3795	45.2	38.1	27	0
2000—Pittsburgh NFL	16	90	3944	43.8	37.5	*34	▲1
2001—Pittsburgh NFL	16	59	2505	42.5	34.9	23	1
2002—Pittsburgh NFL	14	55	2267	41.2	32.5	14	1
2003—Pittsburgh NFL	16	84	3521	41.9	36.0	27	1
2004—New England NFL	16	56	2350	42.0	33.7	19	0
CFL totals (2 years)	36	235	10653	45.3	0.0	...	...
NFL totals (9 years)	138	628	26897	42.8	35.7	213	4
Pro totals (11 years)	174	863	37550	43.5	26.0	...	...

MILLIGAN, HANIK   SS   CHARGERS

PERSONAL: Born November 3, 1979, in St. Croix, Virgin Islands. ... 6-3/200.
HIGH SCHOOL: Coconut Creek (North Fort Lauderdale, Fla.).
JUNIOR COLLEGE: Iowa Central Community College.
COLLEGE: Houston.
TRANSACTIONS/CAREER NOTES: Selected by San Diego Chargers in sixth round (188th pick overall) of 2003 NFL draft. ... Signed by Chargers (2003). ... On injured reserve with pectoral injury (August 26, 2003-entire season).

			INTERCEPTIONS			
Year Team	G	GS	No.	Yds.	Avg.	TD
2004—San Diego NFL	14	0	0	0	0.0	0

MILLOY, LAWYER   S   BILLS

PERSONAL: Born November 14, 1973, in St. Louis, Mo. ... 6-0/190.
HIGH SCHOOL: Lincoln (Tacoma, Wash.).
COLLEGE: Washington.
TRANSACTIONS/CAREER NOTES: Selected after junior season by New England Patriots in second round (36th pick overall) of 1996 NFL draft. ... Signed by Patriots (June 5, 1996). ... Released by Patriots (September 2, 2003). ... Signed by Buffalo Bills (September 4, 2003).
CHAMPIONSHIP GAME EXPERIENCE: Played in AFC championship game (1996 and 2001 seasons). ... Played in Super Bowl 31 (1996 season). ... Member of Super Bowl championship team (2001 season).
HONORS: Named defensive back on THE SPORTING NEWS college All-America first team (1995). ... Played in Pro Bowl (1998, 1999, 2001 and 2002 seasons). ... Named safety on THE SPORTING NEWS NFL All-Pro team (1999).

			TOTALS			INTERCEPTIONS			
Year Team	G	GS	Tk.	Ast.	Sks.	No.	Yds.	Avg.	TD
1996—New England NFL	16	10	54	30	1.0	2	14	7.0	0
1997—New England NFL	16	16	82	30	0.0	3	15	5.0	0
1998—New England NFL	16	16	79	41	1.0	6	54	9.0	1
1999—New England NFL	16	16	91	29	2.0	4	17	4.3	0
2000—New England NFL	16	16	90	31	0.0	2	2	1.0	0
2001—New England NFL	16	16	77	36	3.0	2	21	10.5	0
2002—New England NFL	16	16	61	30	0.0	0	0	0.0	0
2003—Buffalo NFL	16	16	70	35	3.0	0	0	0.0	0
2004—Buffalo NFL	11	11	39	23	4.0	2	20	10.0	0
Pro totals (9 years)	139	133	643	285	14.0	21	143	6.8	1

M

MINOR, TRAVIS   RB   DOLPHINS

PERSONAL: Born June 30, 1979, in New Orleans, La. ... 5-10/205. ... Full name: Travis D. Minor.
HIGH SCHOOL: Catholic (Baton, La.).
COLLEGE: Florida State.
TRANSACTIONS/CAREER NOTES: Selected by Miami Dolphins in third round (85th pick overall) of 2001 NFL draft. ... Signed by Dolphins (July 23, 2001). ... Granted free agency (March 3, 2004). ... Re-signed by Dolphins (April 21, 2004). ... Granted unconditional free agency (March 2, 2005). ... Re-signed by Dolphins (March 25, 2005).
SINGLE GAME HIGHS (regular season): Attempts—22 (November 28, 2004, vs. San Francisco); yards—90 (November 7, 2004, vs. Arizona); and rushing touchdowns—1 (December 20, 2004, vs. New England).

			RUSHING				RECEIVING				KICKOFF RETURNS				TOTALS			
Year Team	G	GS	Att.	Yds.	Avg.	TD	No.	Yds.	Avg.	TD	No.	Yds.	Avg.	TD	TD	2pt.	Pts.	Fum.
2001—Miami NFL	16	0	59	281	4.8	2	29	263	9.1	1	0	0	0.0	0	4	0	24	0
2002—Miami NFL	16	0	44	180	4.1	2	0	0	0.0	0	46	1071	23.3	0	2	0	12	0
2003—Miami NFL	16	0	41	193	4.7	1	4	13	3.3	0	34	727	21.4	0	1	0	6	0
2004—Miami NFL	11	4	109	388	3.6	3	13	75	5.8	0	0	0	0.0	0	3	0	18	0
Pro totals (4 years)	59	4	253	1042	4.1	8	46	351	7.6	1	80	1798	22.5	0	10	0	60	0

MINTER, MIKE   S   PANTHERS

PERSONAL: Born January 15, 1974, in Cleveland, Ohio. ... 5-10/195. ... Full name: Michael Christopher Minter.
HIGH SCHOOL: Lawton (Okla.).
COLLEGE: Nebraska.
TRANSACTIONS/CAREER NOTES: Selected by Carolina Panthers in second round (56th pick overall) of 1997 NFL draft. ... Signed by Panthers (June 12, 1997). ... Granted unconditional free agency (March 2, 2001). ... Re-signed by Panthers (March 3, 2001).
CHAMPIONSHIP GAME EXPERIENCE: Played in NFC championship game (2003 season). ... Played in Super Bowl 38 (2003 season).

			TOTALS			INTERCEPTIONS			
Year Team	G	GS	Tk.	Ast.	Sks.	No.	Yds.	Avg.	TD
1997—Carolina NFL	16	11	53	16	3.5	0	0	0.0	0
1998—Carolina NFL	6	4	19	7	0.0	1	7	7.0	0
1999—Carolina NFL	16	16	63	20	1.0	3	69	23.0	0
2000—Carolina NFL	16	16	86	30	2.0	2	38	19.0	1
2001—Carolina NFL	14	14	64	14	0.0	2	32	16.0	0
2002—Carolina NFL	16	16	62	20	1.0	4	125	31.2	1
2003—Carolina NFL	16	16	71	18	0.0	3	100	33.3	†2
2004—Carolina NFL	16	16	63	20	2.0	0	0	0.0	0
Pro totals (8 years)	116	109	481	145	9.5	15	371	24.7	4

MITCHELL, ANTHONY   S   BENGALS

PERSONAL: Born December 13, 1974, in Youngstown, Ohio. ... 6-1/198. ... Full name: Anthony Maurice Mitchell.
HIGH SCHOOL: West Lake (Atlanta, Ga.).
COLLEGE: Tuskegee.
TRANSACTIONS/CAREER NOTES: Signed as non-drafted free agent by Jacksonville Jaguars (April 26, 1999). ... Released by Jaguars (September 1, 1999). ... Signed by Baltimore Ravens to practice squad (September 7, 1999). ... Activated (December 7, 1999). ... Traded by Ravens to Jaguars for a 2004 conditional draft choice (August 26, 2003). ... Released by Jaguars (September 5, 2004). ... Signed by Cincinnati Bengals (October 6, 2004). ... Granted unconditional free agency (March 2, 2005). ... Re-signed by Bengals (March 22, 2005).
CHAMPIONSHIP GAME EXPERIENCE: Member of Super Bowl championship team (2000 season).

			TOTALS			INTERCEPTIONS			
Year Team	G	GS	Tk.	Ast.	Sks.	No.	Yds.	Avg.	TD
2000—Baltimore NFL	16	0	0	1	0.0	0	0	0.0	0
2001—Baltimore NFL	16	0	5	2	0.0	0	0	0.0	0
2002—Baltimore NFL	16	6	20	14	0.0	3	62	20.7	0
2003—Cincinnati NFL	16	1	8	2	0.0	0	0	0.0	0
2004—Cincinnati NFL	12	0	4	1	0.0	0	0	0.0	0
Pro totals (5 years)	76	7	37	20	0.0	3	62	20.7	0

MITCHELL, BRANDON   DE   FALCONS

PERSONAL: Born June 19, 1975, in Abbeville, La. ... 6-3/290. ... Full name: Brandon Pete Mitchell.
HIGH SCHOOL: Abbeville (La.).
COLLEGE: Texas A&M.
TRANSACTIONS/CAREER NOTES: Selected by New England Patriots in second round (59th pick overall) of 1997 NFL draft. ... Signed by Patriots (June 6, 1997). ... On injured reserve with ankle injury (October 30, 1998-remainder of season). ... Granted free agency (February 11, 2000). ... Re-signed by Patriots (July 16, 2000). ... On injured reserve with leg injury (December 6, 2000-remainder of season). ... Granted unconditional free agency (March 2, 2001). ... Re-signed by Patriots (April 16, 2001). ... Granted unconditional free agency (March 1, 2002). ... Signed by Seattle Seahawks (April 10, 2002). ... On injured reserve with calf injury (October 30, 2002-remainder of season). ... Granted unconditional free agency (March 2, 2005). ... Signed by Atlanta Falcons (April 5, 2005).
CHAMPIONSHIP GAME EXPERIENCE: Played in AFC championship game (2001 season). ... Member of Super Bowl championship team (2001 season).

			TOTALS		
Year Team	G	GS	Tk.	Ast.	Sks.
1997—New England NFL	12	0	6	3	0.0
1998—New England NFL	7	1	14	7	2.0
1999—New England NFL	16	16	23	25	3.0

M

Year Team	G	GS	TOTALS Tk.	Ast.	Sks.
2000—New England NFL	11	9	13	16	0.0
2001—New England NFL	16	11	26	17	1.0
2002—Seattle NFL	5	2	5	3	1.0
2003—Seattle NFL	14	6	20	4	3.0
2004—Seattle NFL	15	0	13	3	1.0
Pro totals (8 years)	96	45	120	78	11.0

MITCHELL, FREDDIE — WR

PERSONAL: Born November 28, 1978, in Lakeland, Fla. ... 6-0/195. ... Full name: Freddie Lee Mitchell II.
HIGH SCHOOL: Kathleen (Lakeland, Fla.).
COLLEGE: UCLA.
TRANSACTIONS/CAREER NOTES: Selected after junior season by Philadelphia Eagles in first round (25th pick overall) of 2001 NFL draft. ... Signed by Eagles (July 26, 2001). ... Released by Eagles (May 6, 2005).
CHAMPIONSHIP GAME EXPERIENCE: Played in NFC championship game (2001-2004 seasons). ... Played in Super Bowl 39 (2004 season).
HONORS: Named wide receiver on THE SPORTING NEWS college All-America first team (2000).
SINGLE GAME HIGHS (regular season): Receptions—6 (January 2, 2005, vs. Cincinnati); yards—76 (January 2, 2005, vs. Cincinnati); and touchdown receptions—1 (January 2, 2005, vs. Cincinnati).

Year Team	G	GS	RECEIVING No.	Yds.	Avg.	TD	TOTALS TD	2pt.	Pts.	Fum.
2001—Philadelphia NFL	15	1	21	283	13.5	1	1	0	6	0
2002—Philadelphia NFL	16	1	12	105	8.8	0	0	0	0	1
2003—Philadelphia NFL	16	6	35	498	14.2	2	2	0	12	0
2004—Philadelphia NFL	16	9	22	377	17.1	2	2	0	12	0
Pro totals (4 years)	63	17	90	1263	14.0	5	5	0	30	1

MITCHELL, JEFF — C — PANTHERS

PERSONAL: Born January 29, 1974, in Dallas, Texas. ... 6-4/300. ... Full name: Jeffrey Clay Mitchell.
HIGH SCHOOL: Countryside (Clearwater, Fla.).
COLLEGE: Florida.
TRANSACTIONS/CAREER NOTES: Selected by Baltimore Ravens in fifth round (134th pick overall) of 1997 NFL draft. ... Signed by Ravens (July 10, 1997). ... On injured reserve with knee injury (August 18, 1997-entire season). ... Granted free agency (February 11, 2000). ... Re-signed by Ravens (April 17, 2000). ... Granted unconditional free agency (March 2, 2001). ... Signed by Carolina Panthers (March 12, 2001).
PLAYING EXPERIENCE: Baltimore NFL, 1998-2000; Carolina NFL, 2001-2004. ... Games/Games started: 1998 (11/10), 1999 (16/16), 2000 (14/14), 2001 (15/15), 2002 (16/16), 2003 (15/15), 2004 (16/16). Total: 103/102.
CHAMPIONSHIP GAME EXPERIENCE: Played in AFC championship game (2000 and 2003 seasons). ... Member of Super Bowl championship team (2000 season). ... Played in Super Bowl 38 (2003 season).

MITCHELL, KAWIKA — LB — CHIEFS

M

PERSONAL: Born October 10, 1979, in Winter Springs, Fla. ... 6-1/253.
HIGH SCHOOL: Lake Howell (Casselberry, Fla.).
COLLEGE: South Florida.
TRANSACTIONS/CAREER NOTES: Selected by Kansas City Chiefs in second round (47th pick overall) of 2003 NFL draft. ... Signed by Chiefs (July 14, 2003).

Year Team	G	GS	TOTALS Tk.	Ast.	Sks.	INTERCEPTIONS No.	Yds.	Avg.	TD
2003—Kansas City NFL	12	6	14	3	0.0	1	3	3.0	0
2004—Kansas City NFL	15	12	57	14	1.0	0	0	0.0	0
Pro totals (2 years)	27	18	71	17	1.0	1	3	3.0	0

MITCHELL, MEL — CB — SAINTS

PERSONAL: Born February 10, 1979, in Rockledge, Fla. ... 6-1/222. ... Full name: Melvin Mitchell III.
HIGH SCHOOL: Rockledge (Fla.).
COLLEGE: Western Kentucky.
TRANSACTIONS/CAREER NOTES: Selected by New Orleans Saints in fifth round (150th pick overall) of 2002 NFL draft. ... Signed by Saints (July 25, 2002). ... On injured reserve with knee injury (August 31, 2003-entire season). ... Granted free agency (March 2, 2005). ... Re-signed by Saints (March 22, 2005).

Year Team	G	GS	TOTALS Tk.	Ast.	Sks.	INTERCEPTIONS No.	Yds.	Avg.	TD	KICKOFF RETURNS No.	Yds.	Avg.	TD	TOTALS TD	2pt.	Pts.	Fum.
2002—New Orleans NFL	16	0	0	0	0.0	0	0	0.0	0	0	0	0.0	0	0	0	0	0
2004—New Orleans NFL	15	0	3	0	0.0	0	0	0.0	0	0	0	0.0	0	1	0	6	0
Pro totals (2 years)	31	0	3	0	0.0	0	0	0.0	0	0	0	0.0	0	1	0	6	0

MITCHELL, QASIM — G — BEARS

PERSONAL: Born December 3, 1979, in Jacksonville, N.C. ... 6-6/355.
COLLEGE: North Carolina A&T.
TRANSACTIONS/CAREER NOTES: Signed as non-drafted free agent by Cleveland Browns (April 26, 2002) ... On injured reserve with lung injury (August 27, 2002-entire season). ... Re-signed by Browns to practice squad (September 1, 2003). ... Claimed on waivers by Chicago Bears (September 16, 2003). ... Signed by Bears to practice squad (September 17, 2003). ... Activated (November 14, 2003). ... On injured reserve with broken fibia (December 23, 2003-remainder of season).
PLAYING EXPERIENCE: Chicago NFL, 2003-2004. ... Games/Games started: 2003 (2/2), 2004 (16/14). Total: 18/16.

MIXON, KENNY   DE

PERSONAL: Born May 31, 1975, in Sun Valley, Calif. ... 6-4/271. ... Full name: Kenneth Jermaine Mixon.
HIGH SCHOOL: Pineville (La.).
COLLEGE: Louisiana State.
TRANSACTIONS/CAREER NOTES: Selected by Miami Dolphins in second round (49th pick overall) of 1998 NFL draft. ... Signed by Dolphins (July 21, 1998). ... Granted unconditional free agency (March 1, 2002). ... Signed by Minnesota Vikings (March 10, 2002). ... Released by Vikings (April 25, 2005).

			TOTALS			INTERCEPTIONS			
Year Team	G	GS	Tk.	Ast.	Sks.	No.	Yds.	Avg.	TD
1998—Miami NFL	16	16	22	13	2.0	0	0	0.0	0
1999—Miami NFL	11	2	4	6	0.0	0	0	0.0	0
2000—Miami NFL	16	16	25	19	2.5	0	0	0.0	0
2001—Miami NFL	16	16	26	18	2.0	1	56	56.0	1
2002—Minnesota NFL	16	16	45	26	4.5	1	6	6.0	0
2003—Minnesota NFL	16	16	45	8	5.0	0	0	0.0	0
2004—Minnesota NFL	14	14	28	18	2.5	0	0	0.0	0
Pro totals (7 years)	105	96	195	108	18.5	2	62	31.0	1

MOHR, CHRIS   P

PERSONAL: Born May 11, 1966, in Atlanta, Ga. ... 6-5/215. ... Full name: Christopher Garrett Mohr.
HIGH SCHOOL: Briarwood Academy (Warrenton, Ga.).
COLLEGE: Alabama.
TRANSACTIONS/CAREER NOTES: Selected by Tampa Bay Buccaneers in sixth round (146th pick overall) of 1989 NFL draft. ... Signed by Buccaneers (July 15, 1989). ... Released by Buccaneers (September 2, 1990). ... Signed by WLAF (January 31, 1991). ... Selected by Montreal Machine in first round (eighth punter) of 1991 WLAF positional draft. ... Signed by Buffalo Bills (June 6, 1991). ... Granted unconditional free agency (February 17, 1994). ... Re-signed by Bills (March 3, 1994). ... Granted unconditional free agency (February 14, 1997). ... Re-signed by Bills (March 4, 1997). ... Released by Bills (February 22, 2001). ... Signed by Atlanta Falcons (March 13, 2001). ... Re-signed by Falcons (March 13, 2003). ... Released by Falcons (March 8, 2005).
CHAMPIONSHIP GAME EXPERIENCE: Played in AFC championship game (1991-1993 seasons). ... Played in NFC championship game (2004 season). ... Played in Super Bowl 26 (1991 season), Super Bowl 27 (1992 season) and Super Bowl 28 (1993 season).
HONORS: Named punter on All-World League team (1991).

					PUNTING		
Year Team	G	No.	Yds.	Avg.	Net avg.	In. 20	Blk.
1989—Tampa Bay NFL	16	∞84	3311	39.4	32.1	10	2
1990—Tampa Bay NFL		Did not play.					
1991—Buffalo NFL	16	54	2085	38.6	36.1	12	0
1992—Buffalo NFL	15	60	2531	42.2	36.7	12	0
1993—Buffalo NFL	16	74	2991	40.4	36.0	19	0
1994—Buffalo NFL	16	67	2799	41.8	36.0	13	0
1995—Buffalo NFL	16	86	3473	40.4	36.2	23	0
1996—Buffalo NFL	16	§101	§4194	41.5	36.5	§27	0
1997—Buffalo NFL	16	90	3764	41.8	36.0	24	1
1998—Buffalo NFL	16	69	2882	41.8	33.2	18	0
1999—Buffalo NFL	16	73	2840	38.9	33.9	20	0
2000—Buffalo NFL	16	95	3661	38.5	31.4	19	▲1
2001—Atlanta NFL	16	69	2680	38.8	36.1	25	0
2002—Atlanta NFL	16	67	2804	41.9	*38.7	21	0
2003—Atlanta NFL	16	87	3473	39.9	36.0	19	0
2004—Atlanta NFL	16	76	3082	40.6	36.9	19	0
Pro totals (15 years)	239	1152	46570	40.4	35.4	281	4

MOLINARO, JIM   T   REDSKINS

PERSONAL: Born April 27, 1981, in Hatfield, Pa. ... 6-6/309. ... Full name: James Anthony Molinaro Jr.
HIGH SCHOOL: Catholic (Bethlehem, Pa.).
COLLEGE: Notre Dame.
TRANSACTIONS/CAREER NOTES: Selected by Washington Redskins in sixth round (180th pick overall) of 2004 NFL draft. ... Signed by Redskins (June 21, 2004).
PLAYING EXPERIENCE: Washington NFL, 2004. ... Games/Games started: 2004 (11/0). Total: 11/0.

MONDS, MARIO   DT

PERSONAL: Born November 10, 1976, in Fort Pierce, Fla. ... 6-2/325.
HIGH SCHOOL: Westwood (Fla.).
JUNIOR COLLEGE: Hutchinson (Kan.) Community College.
COLLEGE: Cincinnati.
TRANSACTIONS/CAREER NOTES: Selected by Washington Redskins in sixth round (186th pick overall) of 2001 NFL draft. ... Signed by Redskins (June 13, 2001). ... Claimed on waivers by Cincinnati Bengals (September 4, 2001). ... On non-football injury list with knee injury (August 19-November 11, 2002). ... Released by Bengals (November 14, 2002). ... Re-signed by Bengals to practice squad (November 15, 2002). ... Activated (December 31, 2002). ... Released by Bengals (August 18, 2003). ... Signed by New York Giants (January 6, 2004). ... Released by Giants (September 6, 2004). ... Re-signed by Giants to practice squad (September 7, 2004). ... Signed by Miami Dolphins off Giants practice squad (October 27, 2004). ... Released by Dolphins (April 28, 2005).

M

Year Team	G	GS	Tk.	Ast.	Sks.
2001—Miami NFL	2	0	0	0	0.0
2003—Miami NFL	Did not play.				
2004—Miami NFL	5	0	3	2	0.0
Pro totals (2 years)	7	0	3	2	0.0

MONK, QUINCY — LB — TEXANS

PERSONAL: Born January 30, 1979, in Jacksonville, N.C. ... 6-3/250. ... Full name: Quincy Omar Monk.
HIGH SCHOOL: White Oak (Jacksonville, N.C.).
COLLEGE: North Carolina.
TRANSACTIONS/CAREER NOTES: Selected by New York Giants in seventh round (245th pick overall) of 2002 NFL draft. ... Released by Giants (September 5, 2004). ... Signed by Houston Texans (December 15, 2004).

				TOTALS			INTERCEPTIONS		
Year Team	G	GS	Tk.	Ast.	Sks.	No.	Yds.	Avg.	TD
2002—New York Giants NFL	9	0	1	0	0.0	0	0	0.0	0
2003—New York Giants NFL	4	0	0	0	0.0	0	0	0.0	0
2004—Houston NFL	2	0	0	0	0.0	0	0	0.0	0
Pro totals (3 years)	15	0	1	0	0.0	0	0	0.0	0

MONTGOMERY, MONTY — CB

PERSONAL: Born December 8, 1973, in Dallas, Texas. ... 6-0/195. ... Full name: Delmonico Montgomery.
HIGH SCHOOL: Gladewater (Texas).
COLLEGE: Houston.
TRANSACTIONS/CAREER NOTES: Selected by Indianapolis Colts in fourth round (117th pick overall) of 1997 NFL draft. ... Signed by Colts (July 7, 1997). ... Released by Colts (September 15, 1999). ... Re-signed by Colts (September 17, 1999). ... Released by Colts (September 29, 1999). ... Signed by San Francisco 49ers (October 4, 1999). ... On injured reserve with broken arm (December 8, 1999-remainder of season). ... Granted unconditional free agency (March 2, 2001). ... Signed by Philadelphia Eagles (May 10, 2001). ... On injured reserve with shoulder injury (August 28, 2001-remainder of season). ... Released by Eagles (February 28, 2002). ... Signed by New Orleans Saints (July 27, 2004). ... Released by Saints (November 12, 2004). ... Re-signed by Saints (December 22, 2004). ... Granted unconditional free agency (March 2, 2005).

				TOTALS	
Year Team	G	GS	Tk.	Ast.	Sks.
1997—Indianapolis NFL	16	3	0	0	1.0
1998—Indianapolis NFL	16	5	0	0	2.0
1999—Indianapolis NFL	3	0	0	0	0.0
—San Francisco NFL	4	2	0	0	0.0
2000—San Francisco NFL	15	9	0	0	0.5
2004—New Orleans NFL	5	0	1	0	0.0
Pro totals (5 years)	59	19	1	0	3.5

MOORE, BRANDON — LB

PERSONAL: Born January 16, 1979, in East Meadow, N.Y. ... 6-1/242. ... Full name: Brandon T. Moore. ... Brother of Rob Moore, wide receiver with New York Jets (1990-95) and Arizona Cardinals (1996-2001).
HIGH SCHOOL: Baldwin (N.Y.).
COLLEGE: Oklahoma.
TRANSACTIONS/CAREER NOTES: Signed as non-drafted free agent by San Francisco 49ers (April 26, 2002). ... Released by 49ers (September 2, 2002). ... Signed by New England Patriots to practice squad (September 3, 2002). ... Signed by 49ers off Patriots practice squad (September 24, 2002). ... On injured reserve with ankle injury (December 10, 2004-remainder of season). ... Granted free agency (March 2, 2005).

				TOTALS			INTERCEPTIONS		
Year Team	G	GS	Tk.	Ast.	Sks.	No.	Yds.	Avg.	TD
2002—San Francisco NFL	13	2	7	1	0.0	0	0	0.0	0
2003—San Francisco NFL	15	1	3	0	0.0	0	0	0.0	0
2004—San Francisco NFL	12	1	11	2	1.0	0	0	0.0	0
Pro totals (3 years)	40	4	21	3	1.0	0	0	0.0	0

MOORE, BRANDON — G — JETS

PERSONAL: Born June 3, 1980, in Gary, Ind. ... 6-3/295.
HIGH SCHOOL: West Side (Gary, Ind.).
COLLEGE: Illinois.
TRANSACTIONS/CAREER NOTES: Signed as non-drafted free agent by New York Jets (April 26, 2002). ... Waived by Jets (August 26, 2002). ... Re-signed by Jets to practice squad (December 26, 2002). ... Assigned by Jets to Scottish Claymores in 2003 NFL Europe enhancement allocation program (January 28, 2003). ... Activated (October 23, 2003).
PLAYING EXPERIENCE: New York Jets NFL, 2003-2004. ... Games/Games started: 2003 (3/1), 2004 (13/13). Total: 16/14.

MOORE, CLARENCE — WR — RAVENS

PERSONAL: Born September 24, 1982, in Bellflower, Calif. ... 6-6/211. ... Full name: Clarence Kelly Moore.
HIGH SCHOOL: Cypress (Buena Park, Calif.).
COLLEGE: Northern Arizona.

M

Year Team	G	GS	RECEIVING				TOTALS			
			No.	Yds.	Avg.	TD	TD	2pt.	Pts.	Fum.
2004—Baltimore NFL	15	6	24	293	12.2	4	4	1	26	0

MOORE, DAVE   TE   BUCCANEERS

PERSONAL: Born November 11, 1969, in Morristown, N.J. ... 6-2/250. ... Full name: David Edward Moore.
HIGH SCHOOL: Roxbury (Succasunna, N.J.).
COLLEGE: Pittsburgh.
TRANSACTIONS/CAREER NOTES: Selected by Miami Dolphins in seventh round (191st pick overall) of 1992 NFL draft. ... Signed by Dolphins (July 15, 1992). ... Released by Dolphins (August 31, 1992). ... Re-signed by Dolphins to practice squad (September 1, 1992). ... Released by Dolphins (September 16, 1992). ... Re-signed by Dolphins to practice squad (October 21, 1992). ... Activated (October 24, 1992). ... Released by Dolphins (October 28, 1992). ... Re-signed by Dolphins to practice squad (October 28, 1992). ... Released by Dolphins (November 18, 1992). ... Signed by Tampa Bay Buccaneers to practice squad (November 24, 1992). ... Activated (December 4, 1992). ... Granted free agency (February 16, 1996). ... Re-signed by Buccaneers (May 31, 1996). ... Granted unconditional free agency (February 14, 1997). ... Re-signed by Buccaneers (February 18, 1997). ... Granted unconditional free agency (February 11, 2000). ... Re-signed by Buccaneers (March 20, 2000). ... Released by Buccaneers (February 27, 2002). ... Signed by Buffalo Bills (March 11, 2002). ... Released by Bills (March 3, 2004). ... Signed by Tampa Bay Buccaneers (March 3, 2004). ... Granted unconditional free agency (March 2, 2005). ... Re-signed by Buccaneers (March 4, 2005).
CHAMPIONSHIP GAME EXPERIENCE: Played in NFC championship game (1999 season).
SINGLE GAME HIGHS (regular season): Receptions—6 (November 2, 1997, vs. Indianapolis); yards—62 (November 3, 1996, vs. Chicago); and touchdown receptions—1 (November 30, 2003, vs. New York Giants).

Year Team	G	GS	RECEIVING				TOTALS			
			No.	Yds.	Avg.	TD	TD	2pt.	Pts.	Fum.
1992—Miami NFL	1	0	0	0	0.0	0	0	0	0	0
—Tampa Bay NFL	4	2	1	10	10.0	0	0	0	0	0
1993—Tampa Bay NFL	15	1	4	47	11.8	1	1	0	6	0
1994—Tampa Bay NFL	15	5	4	57	14.3	0	0	0	0	0
1995—Tampa Bay NFL	16	8	13	102	7.8	0	0	0	0	0
1996—Tampa Bay NFL	16	8	27	237	8.8	3	3	0	18	0
1997—Tampa Bay NFL	16	7	19	217	11.4	4	4	0	24	0
1998—Tampa Bay NFL	16	16	24	255	10.6	4	4	0	24	1
1999—Tampa Bay NFL	16	16	23	276	12.0	5	5	0	30	0
2000—Tampa Bay NFL	16	16	29	288	9.9	3	3	0	18	0
2001—Tampa Bay NFL	16	16	35	285	8.1	4	4	0	24	0
2002—Buffalo NFL	14	5	16	141	8.8	2	2	0	12	0
2003—Buffalo NFL	15	6	7	82	11.7	2	2	0	12	1
2004—Tampa Bay NFL	15	0	3	17	5.7	0	0	0	0	0
Pro totals (13 years)	191	106	205	2014	9.8	28	28	0	168	2

MOORE, EDDIE   LB   DOLPHINS

PERSONAL: Born July 5, 1980, in South Pittsburg, Tenn. ... 6-0/230. ... Full name: Eddie Deon Moore.
HIGH SCHOOL: Pittsburg (Tenn.).
COLLEGE: Tennessee.
TRANSACTIONS/CAREER NOTES: Selected by Miami Dolphins in second round (49th pick overall) of 2003 NFL draft. ... Signed by Dolphins (July 24, 2003). ... On injured reserve with foot injury (August 29, 2003-entire season). ... On injured reserve with knee injury (December 27, 2004-remainder of season).

Year Team	G	GS	TOTALS		
			Tk.	Ast.	Sks.
2003—Miami NFL	Did not play.				
2004—Miami NFL	13	3	18	7	0.0
Pro totals (1 year)	13	3	18	7	0.0

MOORE, LANGSTON   DT   BENGALS

PERSONAL: Born July 17, 1981, in Charleston, S.C. ... 6-1/303.
HIGH SCHOOL: James Island (Charleston, S.C.).
COLLEGE: South Carolina.
TRANSACTIONS/CAREER NOTES: Selected by Cincinnati Bengals in sixth round (174th pick overall) of 2003 NFL draft. ... On injured reserve with ankle injury (December 31, 2004-remainder of season).

Year Team	G	GS	TOTALS		
			Tk.	Ast.	Sks.
2004—Cincinnati NFL	15	8	22	9	1.0

MOORE, LARRY   C   BENGALS

PERSONAL: Born June 1, 1975, in San Diego, Calif. ... 6-3/300. ... Full name: Larry Maceo Moore.
HIGH SCHOOL: Monte Vista (Spring Valley, Calif.).
JUNIOR COLLEGE: Grossmont College (Calif.).
COLLEGE: Brigham Young.

TRANSACTIONS/CAREER NOTES: Signed as non-drafted free agent by Seattle Seahawks (April 25, 1997). ... Released by Seahawks (August 17, 1997). ... Signed by Washington Redskins to practice squad (August 26, 1997). ... Released by Redskins (September 3, 1997). ... Signed by Indianapolis Colts (January 29, 1998). ... Granted free agency (March 2, 2001). ... Re-signed by Colts (April 21, 2001). ... Granted unconditional free agency (March 1, 2002). ... Signed by Redskins (March 13, 2002). ... On injured reserve with foot injury (December 9, 2003-remainder of season). ... Released by Redskins (April 23, 2004). ... Signed by Cincinnati Bengals (April 30, 2004).
PLAYING EXPERIENCE: Indianapolis NFL, 1998-2001; Washington NFL, 2002-2003; Cincinnati NFL, 2004. ... Games/Games started: 1998 (6/5), 1999 (16/16), 2000 (16/16), 2001 (16/11), 2002 (16/16), 2003 (9/8), 2004 (13/1). Total: 92/73.

MOORE, MEWELDE   RB   VIKINGS

PERSONAL: Born July 24, 1982, in Hammond, La. ... 5-11/209. ... Full name: Mewelde Jaem Cadere Moore.
HIGH SCHOOL: Belaire (Baton Rouge, La.).
COLLEGE: Tulane.
TRANSACTIONS/CAREER NOTES: Selected by Minnesota Vikings in fourth round (119th pick overall) of 2004 NFL draft. ... Signed by Vikings (May 18, 2004).
HONORS: Named running back on THE SPORTING NEWS Freshman All-America second team (2000).
SINGLE GAME HIGHS (regular season): Attempts—20 (October 24, 2004, vs. Tennessee); yards—138 (October 24, 2004, vs. Tennessee); and rushing touchdowns—0.
STATISTICAL PLATEAUS: 100-yard rushing games: 2004 (2). Total: 2.

			RUSHING				RECEIVING				PUNT RETURNS				KICKOFF RETURNS				TOTALS		
Year Team	G	GS	Att.	Yds.	Avg.	TD	No.	Yds.	Avg.	TD	No.	Yds.	Avg.	TD	No.	Yds.	Avg.	TD	TD	2pt.	Pts.
2004—Min. NFL	10	3	65	379	5.8	0	27	238	8.8	0	4	28	7.0	0	20	386	19.3	0	0	0	0

MOORE, MICHAEL   G   FALCONS

PERSONAL: Born November 1, 1976, in Fayette, Ala. ... 6-2/318.
HIGH SCHOOL: Fayette (Ark.) County.
COLLEGE: Troy.
TRANSACTIONS/CAREER NOTES: Selected by Washington Redskins in fourth round (129th pick overall) of 2000 NFL draft. ... Signed by Redskins (June 5, 2000). ... Released by Redskins (September 2, 2001). ... Signed by Denver Broncos (December 24, 2001). ... Released by Broncos (September 1, 2002). ... Re-signed by Broncos (October 23, 2002). ... Released by Broncos (October 28, 2002). ... Re-signed by Broncos (December 4, 2002). ... Released by Broncos (December 10, 2002). ... Signed by Atlanta Falcons (January 17, 2003). ... Waived by Falcons (August 30, 2003). ... Re-signed by Falcons (November 4, 2003). ... On injured reserve with shoulder injury (September 15, 2004-remainder of season). ... Granted free agency (March 2, 2005). ... Re-signed by Falcons (March 3, 2005).
PLAYING EXPERIENCE: Washington NFL, 2000; Atlanta NFL, 2003-2004. ... Games/Games started: 2000 (5/1), 2003 (2/0), 2004 (1/1). Total: 8/2.

MOORE, RASHAD   DT   SEAHAWKS

PERSONAL: Born March 16, 1979, in Huntsville, Ala. ... 6-3/324. ... Full name: Glenn Rashad Moore.
HIGH SCHOOL: Johnson (Huntsville, Ala.).
COLLEGE: Tennessee.
TRANSACTIONS/CAREER NOTES: Selected by Seattle Seahawks in sixth round (183rd pick overall) of 2003 NFL draft. ... Signed by Seahawks (July 16, 2003).

			TOTALS		
Year Team	G	GS	Tk.	Ast.	Sks.
2003—Seattle NFL	13	6	20	10	1.0
2004—Seattle NFL	16	12	34	12	2.0
Pro totals (2 years)	29	18	54	22	3.0

MOOREHEAD, AARON   WR   COLTS

PERSONAL: Born November 5, 1980, in Aurora, Colo. ... 6-3/200.
COLLEGE: Illinois.
TRANSACTIONS/CAREER NOTES: Signed as non-drafted free agent by Indianapolis Colts (May 5, 2003).
CHAMPIONSHIP GAME EXPERIENCE: Member of Colts for AFC championship game (2003 season); inactive.
SINGLE GAME HIGHS (regular season): Receptions—5 (November 23, 2003, vs. Buffalo); yards—71 (November 23, 2003, vs. Buffalo); and touchdown receptions—0.

			RECEIVING				TOTALS			
Year Team	G	GS	No.	Yds.	Avg.	TD	TD	2pt.	Pts.	Fum.
2003—Indianapolis NFL	7	0	7	101	14.4	0	0	0	0	1
2004—Indianapolis NFL	7	0	1	7	7.0	0	0	0	0	0
Pro totals (2 years)	14	0	8	108	13.5	0	0	0	0	1

MOOREHEAD, KINDAL   DT   PANTHERS

PERSONAL: Born October 14, 1978, in Memphis, Tenn. ... 6-2/285.
HIGH SCHOOL: Melrose (Memphis, Tenn.).
COLLEGE: Alabama.
TRANSACTIONS/CAREER NOTES: Selected by Carolina Panthers in fifth round (145th pick overall) of 2003 NFL draft. ... Signed by Panthers (July 26, 2003).
CHAMPIONSHIP GAME EXPERIENCE: Member of Panthers for NFC championship game (2003 season); inactive. ... Member of Panthers for Super Bowl 38 (2003 season); inactive.

M

Year Team	G	GS	TOTALS Tk.	Ast.	Sks.	INTERCEPTIONS No.	Yds.	Avg.	TD
2003—Carolina NFL	14	0	6	4	0.0	0	0	0	0
2004—Carolina NFL	14	12	31	7	2.0	1	17	17.0	1
Pro totals (2 years)	28	12	37	11	2.0	1	17	17.0	1

MOORMAN, BRIAN P BILLS

PERSONAL: Born February 5, 1976, in Wichita, Kan. ... 6-0/175.
HIGH SCHOOL: Segdwick (Kan.).
COLLEGE: Pittsburg State.
TRANSACTIONS/CAREER NOTES: Signed as non-drafted free agent by Seattle Seahawks (February 24, 1999). ... Released by Seahawks (August 30, 1999). ... Re-signed by Seahawks (February 17, 2000). ... Assigned by Seahawks to Berlin Thunder in 2000 NFL Europe enhancement allocation program (February 18, 2000). ... Released by Seahawks (August 27, 2000). ... Signed by Buffalo Bills (July 20, 2001).

					PUNTING			
Year Team	G	No.	Yds.	Avg.	Net avg.	In. 20	Blk.
2001—Buffalo NFL	16	80	3262	40.8	33.8	16	0
2002—Buffalo NFL	16	66	2844	43.1	36.0	18	1
2003—Buffalo NFL	16	85	3788	44.6	37.1	20	0
2004—Buffalo NFL	16	77	3325	43.2	36.8	17	0
Pro totals (4 years)	64	308	13219	42.9	35.9	71	1

MORANT, JOHNNIE WR RAIDERS

PERSONAL: Born December 7, 1981, in Newark, N.J. ... 6-4/220. ... Full name: Johnnie E. Morant.
HIGH SCHOOL: Parsippany (N.J.).
COLLEGE: Syracuse.
TRANSACTIONS/CAREER NOTES: Selected by Oakland Raiders in fifth round (134th pick overall) of 2004 NFL draft. ... Signed by Raiders (July 29, 2004).
SINGLE GAME HIGHS (regular season): Receptions—1 (October 31, 2004, vs. San Diego); yards—20 (October 31, 2004, vs. San Diego); and touchdown receptions—0.

Year Team	G	GS	RECEIVING No.	Yds.	Avg.	TD	KICKOFF RETURNS No.	Yds.	Avg.	TD	TOTALS TD	2pt.	Pts.	Fum.
2004—Oakland NFL	4	0	1	20	20.0	0	0	0	0.0	0	0	0	0	0

MORELAND, EARTHWIND CB

PERSONAL: Born June 13, 1977, in Atlanta, Ga. ... 5-10/182. ... Full name: Earthwind C. Moreland.
HIGH SCHOOL: Grady (Atlanta).
COLLEGE: Georgia Southern.
TRANSACTIONS/CAREER NOTES: Signed as non-drafted free agent by Tampa Bay Buccaneers (April 16, 2000). ... Released by Buccaneers (August 27, 2000). ... Signed by New York Jets (August 29, 2000). ... Traded by Jets with sixth-round pick (TE John Gilmore) in 2002 draft to New Orleans Saints for RB Chad Morton (August 23, 2001). ... Claimed on waivers by Jacksonville Jaguars (September 3, 2001). ... Released by Jaguars (September 12, 2001). ... Re-signed by Jaguars to practice squad (September 18, 2001). ... Released by Jaguars (October 14, 2001). ... Signed by Cleveland Browns to practice squad (October 24, 2001). ... Activated (November 7, 2001). ... Assigned by Browns to Rhein Fire in 2002 NFL Europe enhancement allocation program (February 18, 2002). ... On injured reserve with groin injury (September 1, 2002-entire season). ... Granted free agency (February 28, 2003). ... Signed by Montreal Alouettes of CFL (April 14, 2003). ... Signed by New England Patriots (August 5, 2004). ... Released by Patriots (September 3, 2004). ... Signed by Minnesota Vikings to practice squad (September 8, 2004). ... Released by Vikings practice squad (September 21, 2004). ... Signed by Patriots to practice squad (September 22, 2004). ... Activated (November 7, 2004). ... Released by Patriots (February 23, 2005).
CHAMPIONSHIP GAME EXPERIENCE: Member of Patriots for AFC championship game (2004 season); inactive. ... Member of Patriots for Super Bowl 39 (2004 season); inactive.

Year Team	G	GS	TOTALS Tk.	Ast.	Sks.	INTERCEPTIONS No.	Yds.	Avg.	TD
2000—New York Jets NFL	1	0	0	0	0.0	0	0	0.0	0
2001—Cleveland NFL	2	0	0	0	0.0	0	0	0.0	0
2004—New England NFL	9	2	14	1	0.0	0	0	0.0	0
Pro totals (3 years)	12	2	14	1	0.0	0	0	0.0	0

MORENO, ZEKE LB TEXANS

PERSONAL: Born October 10, 1978, in Chula Vista, Calif. ... 6-2/235. ... Full name: Ezekiel Aaron Moreno.
HIGH SCHOOL: Castle Park (Chula Vista, Calif.).
COLLEGE: Southern California.
TRANSACTIONS/CAREER NOTES: Selected by San Diego Chargers in fifth round (139th pick overall) of 2001 NFL draft. ... Signed by Chargers (July 19, 2001). ... Granted free agency (March 3, 2004). ... Re-signed by Chargers (May 13, 2004). ... On injured reserve with shoulder injury (November 15, 2004-remainder of season). ... Granted unconditional free agency (March 2, 2005). ... Signed by Houston Texans (May 3, 2005).

Year Team	G	GS	TOTALS Tk.	Ast.	Sks.	INTERCEPTIONS No.	Yds.	Avg.	TD
2001—San Diego NFL	16	0	5	1	1.0	0	0	0.0	0
2002—San Diego NFL	16	3	28	4	0.0	1	8	8.0	0
2003—San Diego NFL	16	13	78	17	2.0	0	0	0.0	0
2004—San Diego NFL	9	0	6	2	0.0	0	0	0.0	0
Pro totals (4 years)	57	16	117	24	3.0	1	8	8.0	0

M

MOREY, SEAN   WR   STEELERS

PERSONAL: Born February 26, 1976, in Marshfield, Mass. ... 5-11/200. ... Full name: Sean Joseph Morey.
HIGH SCHOOL: Marshfield (Mass.).
COLLEGE: Brown.
TRANSACTIONS/CAREER NOTES: Selected by New England Patriots in seventh round (241st pick overall) of 1999 NFL draft. ... Signed by Patriots (June 10, 1999). ... Released by Patriots (September 15, 1999). ... Re-signed by Patriots to practice squad (September 16, 1999). ... Activated (December 7, 1999). ... Assigned by Patriots to Barcelona Dragons in 2000 NFL Europe enhancement allocation program (February 18, 2000). ... Released by Patriots (August 27, 2000). ... Re-signed by Patriots to practice squad (October 18, 2000). ... Released by Patriots (December 6, 2000). ... Signed by Patriots (January 3, 2001). ... Assigned by Patriots to Barcelona Dragons in 2001 NFL Europe enhancement allocation program (February 19, 2001). ... Released by Patriots (September 2, 2001). ... Signed by Philadelphia Eagles (January 8, 2002). ... Released by Eagles (September 1, 2002). ... Re-signed by Eagles and assigned to NFL Europe (January 30, 2003). ... Released by Eagles (September 5, 2004). ... Signed by Pittsburgh Steelers (September 6, 2004).
CHAMPIONSHIP GAME EXPERIENCE: Played in NFC championship game (2001 and 2003 seasons). ... Played in AFC championship game (2004 season).
SINGLE GAME HIGHS (regular season): Receptions—1 (November 28, 2004, vs. Washington); yards—8 (November 28, 2004, vs. Washington); and touchdown receptions—0.

			RECEIVING				KICKOFF RETURNS				TOTALS			
Year Team	G	GS	No.	Yds.	Avg.	TD	No.	Yds.	Avg.	TD	TD	2pt.	Pts.	Fum.
1999—New England NFL	2	0	0	0	0.0	0	0	0	0.0	0	0	0	0	0
2003—Philadelphia NFL	16	0	0	0	0.0	0	7	93	13.3	0	0	0	0	1
2004—Pittsburgh NFL	16	0	1	8	8.0	0	0	0	0.0	0	0	0	0	0
Pro totals (3 years)	34	0	1	8	8.0	0	7	93	13.3	0	0	0	0	1

MORGAN, DAN   LB   PANTHERS

PERSONAL: Born December 19, 1978, in Coral Springs, Fla. ... 6-2/245. ... Full name: Daniel Thomas Morgan Jr.
HIGH SCHOOL: Taravella (Coral Springs, Fla.).
COLLEGE: Miami (Fla.).
TRANSACTIONS/CAREER NOTES: Selected by Carolina Panthers in first round (11th pick overall) of 2001 NFL draft. ... Signed by Panthers (July 21, 2001). ... On injured reserve with shoulder injury (December 12, 2002-remainder of season). ... Inactive for five games (2003) due to concussion and hamstring injuries.
CHAMPIONSHIP GAME EXPERIENCE: Played in NFC championship game (2003 season). ... Played in Super Bowl 38 (2003 season).
HONORS: Named linebacker on THE SPORTING NEWS college All-America first team (2000). ... Butkus Award winner (2000). ... Bronko Nagurski Award winner (2000). ... Played in Pro Bowl (2004 season).

			TOTALS			INTERCEPTIONS			
Year Team	G	GS	Tk.	Ast.	Sks.	No.	Yds.	Avg.	TD
2001—Carolina NFL	11	11	45	22	1.0	1	10	10.0	0
2002—Carolina NFL	8	8	39	15	1.0	2	26	13.0	0
2003—Carolina NFL	11	11	46	20	0.0	0	0	0.0	0
2004—Carolina NFL	12	12	79	23	2.0	2	20	10.0	0
Pro totals (4 years)	42	42	209	80	4.0	5	56	11.2	0

MORGAN, QUINCY   WR   COWBOYS

PERSONAL: Born September 23, 1977, in Garland, Texas. ... 6-1/215.
HIGH SCHOOL: South Garland (Texas).
COLLEGE: Kansas State.
TRANSACTIONS/CAREER NOTES: Selected by Cleveland Browns in second round (33rd pick overall) of 2001 NFL draft. ... Signed by Browns (July 23, 2001). ... Traded by Browns to Dallas Cowboys for WR Antonio Bryant (October 19, 2004).
HONORS: Named wide receiver on THE SPORTING NEWS college All-America third team (2000).
SINGLE GAME HIGHS (regular season): Receptions—9 (September 8, 2002, vs. Kansas City); yards—151 (September 8, 2002, vs. Kansas City); and touchdown receptions—2 (December 8, 2002, vs. Jacksonville).
STATISTICAL PLATEAUS: 100-yard receiving games: 2002 (2), 2003 (1). Total: 3.

			RUSHING				RECEIVING				KICKOFF RETURNS				TOTALS			
Year Team	G	GS	Att.	Yds.	Avg.	TD	No.	Yds.	Avg.	TD	No.	Yds.	Avg.	TD	TD	2pt.	Pts.	Fum.
2001—Cleveland NFL	16	10	2	27	13.5	0	30	432	14.4	2	7	175	25.0	0	2	0	12	3
2002—Cleveland NFL	16	16	3	7	2.3	0	56	964	*17.2	7	0	0	0.0	0	7	1	44	2
2003—Cleveland NFL	16	15	3	-4	-1.3	0	38	516	13.6	3	2	67	33.5	0	3	0	18	0
2004—Cleveland NFL	6	5	0	0	0.0	0	9	144	16.0	0	0	0	0.0	0	3	0	18	1
—Dallas NFL	9	7	2	23	11.5	0	22	260	11.8	0	2	25	12.5	0	0	0	0	0
Pro totals (4 years)	63	53	10	53	5.3	0	155	2316	14.9	15	11	267	24.3	0	15	1	92	6

MORRIS, MAURICE   RB   SEAHAWKS

PERSONAL: Born December 1, 1979, in Chester, S.C. ... 5-11/202. ... Full name: Maurice Autora Morris.
HIGH SCHOOL: Chester (S.C.).
JUNIOR COLLEGE: Fresno City College.
COLLEGE: Oregon.
TRANSACTIONS/CAREER NOTES: Selected by Seattle Seahawks in second round (54th pick overall) of 2002 NFL draft. ... Signed by Seahawks (July 25, 2002).
SINGLE GAME HIGHS (regular season): Attempts—15 (November 10, 2002, vs. Arizona); yards—72 (November 10, 2002, vs. Arizona); and rushing touchdowns—0.

M

Year Team	G	GS	RUSHING Att.	Yds.	Avg.	TD	RECEIVING No.	Yds.	Avg.	TD	PUNT RETURNS No.	Yds.	Avg.	TD	KICKOFF RETURNS No.	Yds.	Avg.	TD	TOTALS TD	2pt.	Pts.
2002—Sea. NFL	11	0	32	153	4.8	0	3	25	8.3	0	0	0	0.0	0	34	821	24.1	1	1	0	6
2003—Sea. NFL	16	1	38	239	6.3	0	4	32	8.0	1	0	0	0.0	0	47	1007	21.4	0	1	0	6
2004—Sea. NFL	15	0	30	126	4.2	0	9	53	5.9	0	15	75	5.0	0	47	994	21.1	0	0	0	0
Pro totals (3 years)	42	1	100	518	5.2	0	16	110	6.9	1	15	75	5.0	0	128	2822	22.0	1	2	0	12

MORRIS, ROB　　　　　　　　　LB

PERSONAL: Born January 18, 1975, in Nampa, Idaho. ... 6-2/243. ... Full name: Robert Samuel Morris.
HIGH SCHOOL: Nampa (Idaho).
COLLEGE: Brigham Young.
TRANSACTIONS/CAREER NOTES: Selected by Indianapolis Colts in first round (28th pick overall) of 2000 NFL draft. ... Signed by Colts (July 26, 2000). ... On injured reserve with knee injury (October 25, 2000-remainder of season). ... Granted unconditional free agency (March 2, 2005).
CHAMPIONSHIP GAME EXPERIENCE: Played in AFC championship game (2003 season).
HONORS: Named linebacker on THE SPORTING NEWS college All-America second team (1999).

Year Team	G	GS	TOTALS Tk.	Ast.	Sks.	INTERCEPTIONS No.	Yds.	Avg.	TD
2000—Indianapolis NFL	7	0	8	3	0.0	0	0	0.0	0
2001—Indianapolis NFL	14	14	84	30	1.0	0	0	0.0	0
2002—Indianapolis NFL	16	16	76	24	3.0	0	0	0.0	0
2003—Indianapolis NFL	16	16	58	25	0.0	0	0	0.0	0
2004—Indianapolis NFL	15	14	53	23	3.0	1	17	17.0	0
Pro totals (5 years)	68	60	279	105	7.0	1	17	17.0	0

MORRIS, SAMMY　　　　　RB　　　　　DOLPHINS

PERSONAL: Born March 23, 1977, in San Antonio, Texas. ... 6-0/220. ... Full name: Samuel Morris III.
HIGH SCHOOL: John Jay (San Antonio).
COLLEGE: Texas Tech.
TRANSACTIONS/CAREER NOTES: Selected by Buffalo Bills in fifth round (156th pick overall) of 2000 NFL draft. ... Signed by Bills (June 21, 2000). ... Granted free agency (February 28, 2003). ... Re-signed by Bills (April 17, 2003). ... Granted unconditional free agency (March 3, 2004). ... Signed by Miami Dolphins (March 12, 2004).
SINGLE GAME HIGHS (regular season): Attempts—28 (October 24, 2004, vs. St. Louis); yards—91 (October 17, 2004, vs. Buffalo); and rushing touchdowns—2 (December 20, 2004, vs. New England).

Year Team	G	GS	RUSHING Att.	Yds.	Avg.	TD	RECEIVING No.	Yds.	Avg.	TD	KICKOFF RETURNS No.	Yds.	Avg.	TD	TOTALS TD	2pt.	Pts.	Fum.
2000—Buffalo NFL	12	8	93	341	3.7	5	37	268	7.2	1	1	17	17.0	0	6	0	36	2
2001—Buffalo NFL	16	1	20	72	3.6	0	7	36	5.1	0	0	0	0.0	0	0	0	0	1
2002—Buffalo NFL	16	0	2	5	2.5	0	3	48	16.0	0	1	0	0.0	0	0	0	0	0
2003—Buffalo NFL	9	0	19	70	3.7	1	14	100	7.1	0	6	146	24.3	0	1	0	6	0
2004—Miami NFL	13	8	132	523	4.0	6	22	124	5.6	0	1	27	27.0	0	6	0	36	1
Pro totals (5 years)	66	17	266	1011	3.8	12	83	576	6.9	1	9	190	21.1	0	13	0	78	4

MORROW, HAROLD　　　　　FB　　　　　RAVENS

PERSONAL: Born February 24, 1973, in Maplesville, Ala. ... 5-11/232. ... Full name: Harold Morrow Jr.
HIGH SCHOOL: Maplesville (Ala.).
COLLEGE: Auburn.
TRANSACTIONS/CAREER NOTES: Signed as non-drafted free agent by Dallas Cowboys (April 25, 1996). ... Claimed on waivers by Minnesota Vikings (August 26, 1996). ... Granted free agency (February 12, 1999). ... Re-signed by Vikings (April 23, 1999). ... Granted unconditional free agency (February 11, 2000). ... Re-signed by Vikings (March 7, 2000). ... Granted unconditional free agency (March 1, 2002). ... Re-signed by Vikings (March 6, 2002). ... Released by Vikings (February 27, 2003). ... Signed by Baltimore Ravens (March 6, 2003). ... Released by Ravens (September 5, 2004). ... Re-signed by Ravens (September 9, 2004). ... Released by Ravens (September 11, 2004). ... Re-signed by Ravens (September 16, 2004).
CHAMPIONSHIP GAME EXPERIENCE: Played in NFC championship game (1998 and 2000 seasons).
SINGLE GAME HIGHS (regular season): Attempts—5 (January 7, 2002, vs. Baltimore); yards—24 (December 30, 2001, vs. Green Bay); and rushing touchdowns—0.

Year Team	G	GS	RUSHING Att.	Yds.	Avg.	TD	TOTALS TD	2pt.	Pts.	Fum.
1996—Minnesota NFL	8	0	0	0	0.0	0	0	0	0	0
1997—Minnesota NFL	16	0	0	0	0.0	0	0	0	0	0
1998—Minnesota NFL	11	0	3	7	2.3	0	0	0	0	0
1999—Minnesota NFL	16	0	2	1	0.5	0	0	0	0	0
2000—Minnesota NFL	16	0	0	0	0.0	0	0	0	0	0
2001—Minnesota NFL	16	2	12	67	5.6	0	0	0	0	1
2002—Minnesota NFL	16	0	0	0	0.0	0	0	0	0	0
2003—Baltimore NFL	14	0	0	0	0.0	0	0	0	0	0
2004—Baltimore NFL	15	0	0	0	0.0	0	0	0	0	0
Pro totals (9 years)	128	2	17	75	4.4	0	0	0	0	1

MORTON, CHAD　　　　　RB/KR　　　　　REDSKINS

PERSONAL: Born April 4, 1977, in Torrance, Calif. ... 5-8/203. ... Brother of Johnnie Morton, wide receiver, Kansas City Chiefs.
HIGH SCHOOL: South Torrance (Calif.).
COLLEGE: Southern California.

M

TRANSACTIONS/CAREER NOTES: Selected by New Orleans Saints in fifth round (166th pick overall) of 2000 NFL draft. ... Signed by Saints (July 11, 2000). ... Traded by Saints to New York Jets for CB Earthwind Moreland and sixth-round pick (TE John Gilmore) in 2002 draft (August 23, 2001). ... Granted free agency (February 28, 2003). ... Tendered offer sheet by Washington Redskins (March 6, 2003). ... Jets ruled not to have matched offer sheet by arbitrator (April 7, 2003). ... On injured reserve with knee injury (November 1, 2004-remainder of season).
RECORDS: Shares NFL single-game record for most kickoff return touchdowns—2 (September 8, 2002, New York Jets at Buffalo).
SINGLE GAME HIGHS (regular season): Attempts—13 (December 7, 2003, vs. New York Giants); yards—56 (December 7, 2003, vs. New York Giants); and rushing touchdowns—0.

Year Team	G	GS	RUSHING Att	Yds	Avg.	TD	RECEIVING No.	Yds.	Avg.	TD	PUNT RETURNS No.	Yds.	Avg.	TD	KICKOFF RETURNS No.	Yds.	Avg.	TD	TOTALS TD	2pt.	Pts.
2000—N.O. NFL	16	3	36	136	3.8	0	30	213	7.1	0	30	278	9.3	0	44	1029	23.4	0	0	0	0
2001—NYJ NFL	9	0	0	0	0.0	0	0	0	0.0	0	13	113	8.7	0	12	247	20.6	0	0	0	0
2002—NYJ NFL	16	0	4	8	2.0	0	3	19	6.3	0	4	51	12.8	0	58	§1509	26.0	†2	2	0	12
2003—Was. NFL	15	2	48	216	4.5	0	15	187	12.5	1	19	188	9.9	0	44	1029	23.4	1	2	0	12
2004—Was. NFL	6	0	0	0	0.0	0	0	0	0.0	0	13	80	6.2	0	16	358	22.4	0	0	0	0
Pro totals (5 years)	62	5	88	360	4.1	0	48	419	8.7	1	79	710	9.0	0	174	4172	24.0	3	4	0	24

MORTON, CHRISTIAN   CB   FALCONS

PERSONAL: Born April 28, 1981, in St. Louis, Mo. ... 6-0/180.
HIGH SCHOOL: Riverview Gardens (St. Louis, Mo.).
COLLEGE: Illinois.
TRANSACTIONS/CAREER NOTES: Selected by New England Patriots in seventh round (233rd pick overall) of 2004 NFL draft. ... Signed by Patriots (July 25, 2004). ... Released by Patriots (September 5, 2004). ... Re-signed by Patriots to practice squad (September 6, 2004). ... Released by Patriots from practice squad (September 22, 2004). ... Signed by New Orleans Saints to practice squad (October 5, 2004). ... Released by Saints from practice squad (October 12, 2004). ... Signed by Cleveland Browns to practice squad (October 20, 2004). ... Released by Browns (November 24, 2004). ... Signed by Atlanta Falcons (December 7, 2004).
CHAMPIONSHIP GAME EXPERIENCE: Played in NFC championship game (2004 season).

Year Team	G	GS	TOTALS Tk.	Ast.	Sks.	INTERCEPTIONS No.	Yds.	Avg.	TD	KICKOFF RETURNS No.	Yds.	Avg.	TD	TOTALS TD	2pt.	Pts.	Fum.
2004—Atlanta NFL	2	0	2	0	0.0	0	0	0.0	0	0	0	0.0	0	0	0	0	0

MORTON, JOHNNIE   WR   CHIEFS

PERSONAL: Born October 7, 1971, in Inglewood, Calif. ... 6 0/185. ... Full name: Johnnie James Morton. ... Brother of Chad Morton, running back, Washington Redskins.
HIGH SCHOOL: South Torrance (Calif.).
COLLEGE: Southern California.
TRANSACTIONS/CAREER NOTES: Selected by Detroit Lions in first round (21st pick overall) of 1994 NFL draft. ... Signed by Lions (July 18, 1994). ... Released by Lions (March 14, 2002). ... Signed by Kansas City Chiefs (March 29, 2002).
HONORS: Named wide receiver on THE SPORTING NEWS college All-America first team (1993).
SINGLE GAME HIGHS (regular season): Receptions—10 (January 2, 2000, vs. Minnesota); yards—174 (September 22, 1996, vs. Chicago); and touchdown receptions—2 (January 2, 2000, vs. Minnesota).
STATISTICAL PLATEAUS: 100-yard receiving games: 1995 (1), 1996 (2), 1997 (3), 1998 (3), 1999 (5), 2001 (4), 2003 (1), 2004 (2). Total: 21.

Year Team	G	GS	RUSHING Att.	Yds.	Avg.	TD	RECEIVING No.	Yds.	Avg.	TD	KICKOFF RETURNS No.	Yds.	Avg.	TD	TOTALS TD	2pt.	Pts.	Fum.
1994—Detroit NFL	14	0	0	0	0.0	0	3	39	13.0	1	4	143	35.7	1	2	0	12	1
1995—Detroit NFL	16	13	3	33	11.0	0	44	590	13.4	8	18	390	21.7	0	8	0	48	1
1996—Detroit NFL	16	15	9	35	3.9	0	55	714	13.0	6	0	0	0.0	0	6	0	36	1
1997—Detroit NFL	16	16	3	33	11.0	0	80	1057	13.2	6	0	0	0.0	0	6	0	36	2
1998—Detroit NFL	16	16	1	11	11.0	0	69	1028	14.9	2	0	0	0.0	0	2	0	12	0
1999—Detroit NFL	16	12	0	0	0.0	0	80	1129	14.1	5	1	22	22.0	0	5	0	30	0
2000—Detroit NFL	16	16	4	25	6.3	0	61	788	12.9	3	0	0	0.0	0	3	1	20	1
2001—Detroit NFL	16	16	1	6	6.0	0	77	1154	15.0	4	1	4	4.0	0	4	0	24	1
2002—Kansas City NFL	14	14	10	124	12.4	0	29	397	13.7	1	0	0	0.0	0	1	0	6	0
2003—Kansas City NFL	16	16	8	94	11.8	0	50	740	14.8	4	0	0	0.0	0	4	0	24	0
2004—Kansas City NFL	13	12	7	43	6.1	0	55	795	14.5	3	0	0	0.0	0	3	0	18	2
Pro totals (11 years)	169	146	46	404	8.8	0	603	8431	14.0	43	24	559	23.3	1	44	1	266	9

MOSES, J.J.   WR   TEXANS

PERSONAL: Born September 12, 1979, in Waterloo, Iowa. ... 5-6/175. ... Full name: Jerry James Moses Jr.
HIGH SCHOOL: Waterloo (Iowa).
COLLEGE: Iowa State.
TRANSACTIONS/CAREER NOTES: Signed as non-drafted free agent by Kansas City Chiefs (April 26, 2001). ... Released by Chiefs (August 27, 2001). ... Signed by Green Bay Packers to practice squad (September 26, 2001). ... Released by Packers (October 3, 2001). ... Signed by Chiefs to practice squad (November 21, 2001). ... Assigned by Chiefs to Scottish Claymores in 2002 NFL Europe enhancement allocation program (February 12, 2002). ... Released by Chiefs (September 1, 2002). ... Signed by Packers to practice squad (November 13, 2002). ... Released by Packers (November 28, 2002). ... Re-signed by Packers to practice squad (December 2, 2002). ... Activated (December 15, 2002). ... Released by Packers (December 24, 2002). ... Signed by Houston Texans (February 2, 2003). ... Granted free agency (March 3, 2004). ... Re-signed by Texans (March 19, 2004).

Year Team	G	GS	RECEIVING No.	Yds.	Avg.	TD	PUNT RETURNS No.	Yds.	Avg.	TD	KICKOFF RETURNS No.	Yds.	Avg.	TD	TOTALS TD	2pt.	Pts.	Fum.
2002—Green Bay NFL	2	0	0	0	0.0	0	5	12	2.4	0	4	69	17.3	0	0	0	0	1
2003—Houston NFL	15	0	0	0	0.0	0	36	244	6.8	0	§58	1355	23.4	0	0	0	0	0
2004—Houston NFL	15	0	0	0	0.0	0	36	309	8.6	0	59	1303	22.1	0	0	0	0	1
Pro totals (3 years)	32	0	0	0	0.0	0	77	565	7.3	0	121	2727	22.5	0	0	0	0	2

M

PERSONAL: Born February 13, 1977, in Rand, W.Va. ... 6-4/210.
HIGH SCHOOL: DuPont (Belle, W.Va.).
COLLEGE: Marshall.
TRANSACTIONS/CAREER NOTES: Selected after sophomore season by Minnesota Vikings in first round (21st pick overall) of 1998 NFL draft. ... Signed by Minnesota Vikings (July 26, 1998). ... Traded by Vikings to Oakland Raiders for LB Napoleon Harris and first- (WR Troy Williamson) and seventh-round (CB Adrian Ward) picks in 2005 draft (March 2, 2005).
CHAMPIONSHIP GAME EXPERIENCE: Played in NFC championship game (1998 and 2000 seasons).
HONORS: Fred Biletnikoff Award winner (1997). ... Named wide receiver on THE SPORTING NEWS college All-America first team (1997). ... Named NFL Rookie of the Year by THE SPORTING NEWS (1998). ... Named wide receiver on THE SPORTING NEWS NFL All-Pro team (1998 and 2000). ... Played in Pro Bowl (1998 and 1999 seasons). Named to play in Pro Bowl (2002 season); replaced by Donald Driver due to injury. ... Named Outstanding Player of Pro Bowl (1999). ... Named to play in Pro Bowl (2000 season); replaced by Joe Horn due to injury. ... Named to play in Pro Bowl (2003 season); replaced by Laveranues Coles due to injury.
RECORDS: Holds NFL rookie-season record for most receiving touchdowns—17 (1998).
SINGLE GAME HIGHS (regular season): Receptions—12 (November 14, 1999, vs. Chicago); yards—204 (November 14, 1999, vs. Chicago); and touchdown receptions—3 (September 28, 2003, vs. San Francisco).
STATISTICAL PLATEAUS: 100-yard receiving games: 1998 (4), 1999 (7), 2000 (8), 2001 (4), 2002 (7), 2003 (8), 2004 (3). Total: 41.

Year Team	G	GS	RECEIVING				PUNT RETURNS				TOTALS			
			No.	Yds.	Avg.	TD	No.	Yds.	Avg.	TD	TD	2pt.	Pts.	Fum.
1998—Minnesota NFL	16	11	69	1313	‡19.0	*17	1	0	0.0	0	‡17	†2	106	2
1999—Minnesota NFL	16	16	80	‡1413	17.7	11	17	162	9.5	∞1	12	0	72	3
2000—Minnesota NFL	16	16	77	1437	18.7	*15	0	0	0.0	0	15	1	92	2
2001—Minnesota NFL	16	16	82	1233	15.0	10	0	0	0.0	0	10	0	60	0
2002—Minnesota NFL	16	16	‡106	‡1347	12.7	7	0	0	0.0	0	7	0	42	1
2003—Minnesota NFL	16	16	111	1632	14.7	*17	0	0	0.0	0	17	0	102	1
2004—Minnesota NFL	13	13	49	767	15.7	13	0	0	0.0	0	13	0	78	1
Pro totals (7 years)	109	104	574	9142	15.9	90	18	162	9.0	1	91	3	552	10

PERSONAL: Born June 1, 1979, in Miami, Fla. ... 5-10/185. ... Full name: Santana Terrell Moss.
HIGH SCHOOL: Carol City (Miami).
COLLEGE: Miami (Fla.).
TRANSACTIONS/CAREER NOTES: Selected by New York Jets in first round (16th pick overall) of 2001 NFL draft. ... Signed by Jets (July 28, 2001). ... Traded by Jets to Washington Redskins for WR Laveranues Coles (March 9, 2005).
HONORS: Named kick returner on THE SPORTING NEWS college All-America first team (2000). ... Named punt returner on the THE SPORTING NEWS NFL All-Pro team (2002).
SINGLE GAME HIGHS (regular season): Receptions—10 (November 2, 2003, vs. New York Giants); yards—157 (November 7, 2004, vs. Buffalo); and touchdown receptions—3 (November 2, 2003, vs. New York Giants).
STATISTICAL PLATEAUS: 100-yard receiving games: 2002 (1), 2003 (4), 2004 (2). Total: 7.

Year Team	G	GS	RUSHING				RECEIVING				PUNT RETURNS				TOTALS			
			Att.	Yds.	Avg.	TD	No.	Yds.	Avg.	TD	No.	Yds.	Avg.	TD	TD	2pt.	Pts.	Fum.
2001—New York Jets NFL	5	0	1	-6	-6.0	0	2	40	20.0	0	6	82	13.7	0	0	0	0	0
2002—New York Jets NFL	15	1	7	48	6.9	0	30	433	14.4	4	25	§413	§16.5	†2	6	0	36	2
2003—New York Jets NFL	16	12	10	67	6.7	0	74	1105	14.9	10	30	332	11.1	0	10	0	60	4
2004—New York Jets NFL	15	14	6	18	3.0	0	45	838	18.6	5	27	225	8.3	0	5	0	30	2
Pro totals (4 years)	51	27	24	127	5.3	0	151	2416	16.0	19	88	1052	12.0	2	21	0	126	8

PERSONAL: Born July 17, 1973, in Lucedale, Miss. ... 6-2/210. ... Full name: Eric Shannon Moulds.
HIGH SCHOOL: George County (Lucedale, Miss.).
COLLEGE: Mississippi State.
TRANSACTIONS/CAREER NOTES: Selected by Buffalo Bills in first round (24th pick overall) of 1996 NFL draft. ... Signed by Bills (July 16, 1996).
HONORS: Played in Pro Bowl (1998, 2000-2002 seasons).
POST SEASON RECORDS: Holds NFL postseason single-game record for most yards receiving—240 (January 2, 1999, vs. Miami).
SINGLE GAME HIGHS (regular season): Receptions—12 (October 22, 2000, vs. Minnesota); yards—196 (November 25, 2001, vs. Miami); and touchdown receptions—2 (December 8, 2002, vs. New England).
STATISTICAL PLATEAUS: 100-yard receiving games: 1998 (4), 1999 (3), 2000 (7), 2001 (2), 2002 (5), 2003 (2), 2004 (1). Total: 24.

Year Team	G	GS	RUSHING				RECEIVING				KICKOFF RETURNS				TOTALS			
			Att.	Yds.	Avg.	TD	No.	Yds.	Avg.	TD	No.	Yds.	Avg.	TD	TD	2pt.	Pts.	Fum.
1996—Buffalo NFL	16	5	12	44	3.7	0	20	279	14.0	2	52	1205	23.2	▲1	3	0	18	1
1997—Buffalo NFL	16	8	4	59	14.8	0	29	294	10.1	0	43	921	21.4	0	0	1	2	3
1998—Buffalo NFL	16	15	0	0	0.0	0	67	§1368	20.4	9	0	0	0.0	0	9	0	54	0
1999—Buffalo NFL	14	14	1	1	1.0	0	65	994	15.3	7	0	0	0.0	0	7	0	42	1
2000—Buffalo NFL	16	16	2	24	12.0	0	94	1326	14.1	5	0	0	0.0	0	5	0	30	1
2001—Buffalo NFL	16	16	3	3	1.0	0	67	904	13.5	5	0	0	0.0	0	5	1	32	1
2002—Buffalo NFL	16	15	1	7	7.0	0	100	1292	12.9	10	0	0	0.0	0	10	0	60	1
2003—Buffalo NFL	13	13	0	0	0.0	0	64	780	12.2	1	0	0	0.0	0	1	0	6	0
2004—Buffalo NFL	16	16	5	19	3.8	0	88	1043	11.9	5	1	2	2.0	0	5	0	30	1
Pro totals (9 years)	139	118	28	157	5.6	0	594	8280	13.9	44	96	2128	22.2	1	45	2	274	9

M

MRUCZKOWSKI, GENE

PERSONAL: Born June 6, 1980, in Cleveland, Ohio. ... 6-2/305. ... Brother of Scott Mruczkowski, rookie center with San Diego Chargers.
HIGH SCHOOL: Benedictine (Cleveland, Ohio).
COLLEGE: Purdue.
TRANSACTIONS/CAREER NOTES: Signed as non-drafted free agent by New England Patriots (May 16, 2003). ... Placed on reserve/non-football injury list with leg injury (August 26, 2003). ... On injured reserve with leg injury (November 25, 2003-remainder of season).
PLAYING EXPERIENCE: New England NFL, 2004. ... Games/Games started: 2004 (10/0). Total: 10/0.
CHAMPIONSHIP GAME EXPERIENCE: Played in AFC championship game (2004 season). ... Member of Super Bowl championship team (2004 season).

MUGHELLI, OVIE   FB   RAVENS

PERSONAL: Born June 10, 1980, in Boston, Mass. ... 6-1/255.
HIGH SCHOOL: Porter-Gaud (Charleston, S.C.).
COLLEGE: Wake Forest.
TRANSACTIONS/CAREER NOTES: Selected by Baltimore Ravens in fourth round (134th pick overall) of 2003 NFL draft. ... On injured reserve with hamstring injury (November 17, 2004-remainder of season).

| | | | RUSHING | | | | RECEIVING | | | | TOTALS | | |
Year Team	G	GS	Att.	Yds.	Avg.	TD	No.	Yds.	Avg.	TD	TD	2pt.	Pts.	Fum.
2003—Baltimore NFL	6	0	0	0	0.0	0	0	0	0.0	0	0	0	0	0
2004—Baltimore NFL	3	0	0	0	0.0	0	0	0	0.0	0	0	0	0	0
Pro totals (2 years)	9	0	0	0	0.0	0	0	0	0.0	0	0	0	0	0

MUHAMMAD, MUHSIN   WR   BEARS

PERSONAL: Born May 5, 1973, in Lansing, Mich. ... 6-2/217. ... Full name: Muhsin Muhammad II. ... Name pronounced: moo-SIN moo-HAH-med.
HIGH SCHOOL: Waverly (Lansing, Mich.).
COLLEGE: Michigan State.
TRANSACTIONS/CAREER NOTES: Selected by Carolina Panthers in second round (43rd pick overall) of 1996 NFL draft. ... Signed by Panthers (July 23, 1996). ... Released by Panthers (February 25, 2005). ... Signed by Chicago Bears (February 26, 2005).
CHAMPIONSHIP GAME EXPERIENCE: Played in NFC championship game (1996 and 2003 seasons). ... Played in Super Bowl 38 (2003 season).
HONORS: Played in Pro Bowl (1999 and 2004 seasons).
POST SEASON RECORDS: Holds Super Bowl record for longest pass completion (from Jake Delhomme)—85 yards (February 1, 2004, vs. New England).
SINGLE GAME HIGHS (regular season): Receptions—11 (November 27, 2000, vs. Green Bay); yards—192 (September 13, 1998, vs. New Orleans); and touchdown receptions—3 (November 14, 2004, vs. San Francisco).
STATISTICAL PLATEAUS: 100-yard receiving games: 1998 (3), 1999 (5), 2000 (5), 2001 (2), 2002 (3), 2003 (1), 2004 (7). Total: 26.
MISCELLANEOUS: Holds Carolina Panthers all-time records for most receptions (578) and most receiving yards (7,751). ... Shares Carolina Panthers all-time records for most touchdowns (44) and most receiving touchdowns (44).

| | | | RUSHING | | | | RECEIVING | | | | TOTALS | | |
Year Team	G	GS	Att.	Yds.	Avg.	TD	No.	Yds.	Avg.	TD	TD	2pt.	Pts.	Fum.
1996—Carolina NFL	9	5	1	-1	-1.0	0	25	407	16.3	1	1	0	6	0
1997—Carolina NFL	13	5	0	0	0.0	0	27	317	11.7	0	0	1	2	0
1998—Carolina NFL	16	16	0	0	0.0	0	68	941	13.8	6	6	1	38	2
1999—Carolina NFL	15	15	0	0	0.0	0	‡96	1253	13.1	8	8	0	48	1
2000—Carolina NFL	16	16	2	12	6.0	0	†102	1183	11.6	6	6	0	36	1
2001—Carolina NFL	11	11	0	0	0.0	0	50	585	11.7	1	1	0	6	2
2002—Carolina NFL	14	14	3	40	13.3	0	63	823	13.1	3	3	0	18	0
2003—Carolina NFL	15	15	2	-2	-1.0	0	54	837	15.5	3	3	0	18	3
2004—Carolina NFL	16	16	3	15	5.0	0	93	1405	15.1	16	16	0	96	3
Pro totals (9 years)	125	113	11	64	5.8	0	578	7751	13.4	44	44	2	268	12

MUHLBACH, DON   LS   LIONS

PERSONAL: Born August 17, 1981, in Newark, Ohio. ... 6-5/262. ... Full name: Don Lynn Muhlbach.
HIGH SCHOOL: Lufkin (Texas).
COLLEGE: Texas A&M.
TRANSACTIONS/CAREER NOTES: Signed as non-drafted free agent by Baltimore Ravens (April 30, 2004). ... Released by Ravens (August 30, 2004). ... Signed by Detroit Lions (November 9, 2004).
PLAYING EXPERIENCE: Detroit NFL, 2004. ... Games/Games started: 2004 (8/0). Total: 8/0.

MULITALO, EDWIN   G   RAVENS

PERSONAL: Born September 1, 1974, in Daly City, Calif. ... 6-3/345. ... Full name: Edwin Moliki Mulitalo. ... Name pronounced: moo-lih-TAHL-oh.
HIGH SCHOOL: Jefferson (Daly City, Calif.).
JUNIOR COLLEGE: Ricks College (Idaho).
COLLEGE: Arizona.
TRANSACTIONS/CAREER NOTES: Selected by Baltimore Ravens in fourth round (129th pick overall) of 1999 NFL draft. ... Signed by Ravens (July 29, 1999). ... Granted free agency (March 1, 2002). ... Re-signed by Ravens (June 17, 2002).
PLAYING EXPERIENCE: Baltimore NFL, 1999-2004. ... Games/Games started: 1999 (10/8), 2000 (16/16), 2001 (14/14), 2002 (16/15), 2003 (15/15), 2004 (15/15). Total: 86/83.
CHAMPIONSHIP GAME EXPERIENCE: Played in AFC championship game (2000 season). ... Member of Super Bowl championship team (2000 season).

M

MUNGRO, JAMES   RB

PERSONAL: Born February 13, 1978, in East Stroudsburg, Pa. ... 5-9/214. ... Full name: James Alevia Mungro II.
HIGH SCHOOL: East Stroudsburg (Pa.).
COLLEGE: Syracuse.
TRANSACTIONS/CAREER NOTES: Signed as non-drafted free agent by Detroit Lions (April 26, 2002). ... Claimed on waivers by Indianapolis Colts (September 3, 2002). ... On injured reserve with toe injury (December 2, 2003-remainder of season). ... Granted free agency (March 2, 2005).
SINGLE GAME HIGHS (regular season): Attempts—28 (November 10, 2002, vs. Philadelphia); yards—114 (November 10, 2002, vs. Philadelphia); and rushing touchdowns—2 (December 15, 2002, vs. Cleveland).
STATISTICAL PLATEAUS: 100-yard rushing games: 2002 (1). Total: 1.

			RUSHING				RECEIVING				KICKOFF RETURNS				TOTALS			
Year Team	G	GS	Att.	Yds.	Avg.	TD	No.	Yds.	Avg.	TD	No.	Yds.	Avg.	TD	TD	2pt.	Pts.	Fum.
2002—Indianapolis NFL.........	9	1	97	336	3.5	8	13	81	6.2	0	0	0	0.0	0	8	0	48	3
2003—Indianapolis NFL.........	7	0	24	60	2.5	2	1	-4	-4.0	0	2	7	3.5	0	2	1	14	0
2004—Indianapolis NFL.........	15	0	5	19	3.8	0	7	36	5.1	3	7	111	15.9	0	3	0	18	0
Pro totals (3 years)...............	31	1	126	415	3.3	10	21	113	5.4	3	9	118	13.1	0	13	1	80	3

MURPHY, FRANK   WR   BUCCANEERS

PERSONAL: Born February 11, 1977, in Jacksonville, Fla. ... 6-0/206.
HIGH SCHOOL: West Nassau (Callahan, Fla.).
JUNIOR COLLEGE: Itawamba Community College (Miss.), then Garden City (Kan.) Commmunity College.
COLLEGE: Kansas State.
TRANSACTIONS/CAREER NOTES: Selected by Chicago Bears in sixth round (170th pick overall) of 2000 NFL draft. ... Signed by Bears (May 31, 2000). ... Released by Bears (August 27, 2000). ... Signed by Tampa Bay Buccaneers to practice squad (August 28, 2000). ... Activated (November 22, 2000). ... Released by Buccaneers (September 1, 2002). ... Signed by Houston Texans (November 26, 2002). ... Released by Texans (December 8, 2002). ... Re-signed by Texans (March 24, 2003). ... Released by Texans (August 2003). ... Re-signed by Buccaneers (January 14, 2004). ... Assigned by Buccaneers to Berlin Thunder in 2004 NFL Europe enhancement allocation program (February 9, 2004). ... On injured reserve with Achilles injury (October 6, 2004-remainder of season).
SINGLE GAME HIGHS (regular season): Receptions—3 (January 6, 2002, vs. Philadelphia); yards—25 (January 6, 2002, vs. Philadelphia); and touchdown receptions—1 (October 21, 2001, vs. Pittsburgh).

			RECEIVING				KICKOFF RETURNS				TOTALS			
Year Team	G	GS	No.	Yds.	Avg.	TD	No.	Yds.	Avg.	TD	TD	2pt.	Pts.	Fum.
2000—Tampa Bay NFL....................................	1	0	0	0	0.0	0	2	24	12.0	0	0	0	0	0
2001—Tampa Bay NFL....................................	11	0	8	71	8.9	1	20	445	22.3	0	1	0	6	2
2002—Houston NFL..	5	0	0	0	0.0	0	1	0	0.0	0	0	0	0	1
2003—			Did not play.											
2004—Tampa Bay NFL....................................	3	0	0	0	0.0	0	8	208	26.0	0	0	0	0	0
Pro totals (4 years)..	20	0	8	71	8.9	1	31	677	21.8	0	1	0	6	3

MURPHY, MATT   TE   TEXANS

PERSONAL: Born February 23, 1980, in New Haven, Mich. ... 6-5/260.
HIGH SCHOOL: New Haven (Mich.).
COLLEGE: Maryland.
TRANSACTIONS/CAREER NOTES: Selected by Detroit Lions in seventh round (252nd pick overall) of 2002 NFL draft. ... Signed by Lions (July 18, 2002). ... Released by Lions (August 31, 2003). ... Re-signed by Lions to practice squad (September 1, 2003). ... Signed by Houston Texans off Lions practice squad (December 10, 2003). ... Released by Texans (September 5, 2004). ... Re-signed by Texans to practice squad (September 6, 2004). ... Activated (September 21, 2004).
SINGLE GAME HIGHS (regular season): Receptions—1 (December 29, 2002, vs. Minnesota); yards—8 (December 29, 2002, vs. Minnesota); and touchdown receptions—0.

			RECEIVING				TOTALS			
Year Team	G	GS	No.	Yds.	Avg.	TD	TD	2pt.	Pts.	Fum.
2002—Detroit NFL..	3	0	1	8	8.0	0	0	0	0	0
2003—Houston NFL..	1	0	0	0	0.0	0	0	0	0	0
2004—Houston NFL..	11	1	0	0	0.0	0	0	0	0	0
Pro totals (3 years)	15	1	1	8	8.0	0	0	0	0	0

MURPHY, NICK   P   CHIEFS

PERSONAL: Born October 22, 1979, in St. Louis, Mo. ... 5-11/188. ... Full name: Nicholas Jon Murphy.
HIGH SCHOOL: Desert Mountain (Scottsdale, Ariz.).
JUNIOR COLLEGE: Scottsdale (Ariz.).
COLLEGE: Arizona State.
TRANSACTIONS/CAREER NOTES: Signed as non-drafted free agent by Minnesota Vikings (April 22, 2002). ... Released by Vikings (August 26, 2002). ... Re-signed by Vikings (January 14, 2003). ... Assigned by Vikings to Barcelona Dragons in 2003 NFL Europe enhancement allocation program (February 4, 2003). ... Released by Vikings (August 25, 2003). ... Signed by Philadelphia Eagles and assigned to Scotland in 2004 NFL Europe enhancement allocation program (January 27, 2004). ... Released by Eagles (September 5, 2004). ... Signed by Baltimore Ravens (November 17, 2004). ... Released by Ravens (December 11, 2004). ... Signed by Kansas City Chiefs (December 21, 2004).

			PUNTING				
Year Team	G	No.	Yds.	Avg.	Net avg.	In. 20	Blk.
2004—Baltimore NFL.................................	3	18	777	43.2	36.6	6	0
—Kansas City NFL...............................	2	4	189	47.3	40.8	1	0
Pro totals (1 year)	5	22	966	43.9	37.3	7	0

MURPHY, ROB   C   49ERS

PERSONAL: Born January 18, 1977, in Buffalo, N.Y. ... 6-5/310. ... Full name: Robert Donald Murphy.
HIGH SCHOOL: Moeller (Cincinnati).
COLLEGE: Ohio State.
TRANSACTIONS/CAREER NOTES: Signed as non-drafted free agent by Cincinnati Bengals (July 9, 1999). ... Released by Bengals (August 30, 1999). ... Signed by Kansas City Chiefs (January 11, 2000). ... Allocated by Chiefs to Frankfurt Galaxy in 2000 NFL Europe enhancement allocation program (February 18, 2000). ... Released by Chiefs (September 18, 2000). ... Signed by Indianapolis Colts (April 22, 2001). ... Released by Colts (September 1, 2001). ... Re-signed by Colts to practice squad (September 3, 2001). ... Activated (March 23, 2003). ... Released by Colts (July 25, 2003). ... Signed by San Francisco 49ers (August 1, 2003). ... Waived by 49ers (August 31, 2003). ... Re-signed by 49ers (November 26, 2003).
PLAYING EXPERIENCE: Indianapolis NFL, 2002; San Francisco NFL, 2003-2004. ... Games/Games started: 2002 (9/0), 2003 (2/0), 2004 (15/0). Total: 26/0.

MUSTARD, CHAD   TE   BROWNS

PERSONAL: Born October 8, 1977, in Central City, Neb. ... 6-6/288.
HIGH SCHOOL: Scotus Central Catholic (Neb.).
COLLEGE: North Dakota.
TRANSACTIONS/CAREER NOTES: Signed as non-drafted free agent by Cleveland Browns (January 8, 2003). ... Assigned by Browns to 2003 NFL Europe enhancement allocation program (February 5, 2003). ... Waived by Browns (August 31, 2003). ... Re-signed by Browns to practice squad (October 1, 2003). ... Activated (October 11, 2003). ... Released by Browns (November 4, 2003). ... Re-signed by Browns to practice squad (November 5, 2003). ... Activated (November 12, 2003). ... Released by Browns (September 5, 2004). ... Re-signed by Browns (September 21, 2004). ... On injured reserve with foot injury (November 17, 2004-remainder of season).
SINGLE GAME HIGHS (regular season): Receptions—2 (November 23, 2003, vs. Pittsburgh); yards—17 (November 16, 2003, vs. Arizona); and touchdown receptions—0.

Year Team	G	GS	RECEIVING No.	Yds.	Avg.	TD	TOTALS TD	2pt.	Pts.	Fum.
2003—Cleveland NFL	10	0	4	29	7.3	0	0	0	0	0
2004—Cleveland NFL	7	0	1	9	9.0	0	0	0	0	0
Pro totals (2 years)	17	0	5	38	7.6	0	0	0	0	0

MYERS, MICHAEL   DT   BRONCOS

PERSONAL: Born January 20, 1976, in Vicksburg, Miss. ... 6-2/300.
HIGH SCHOOL: Vicksburg (Miss.).
JUNIOR COLLEGE: Hinds Community College (Miss.).
COLLEGE: Alabama.
TRANSACTIONS/CAREER NOTES: Selected by Dallas Cowboys in fourth round (100th pick overall) of 1998 NFL draft. ... Signed by Cowboys (July 10, 1998). ... Granted free agency (March 2, 2001). ... Re-signed by Cowboys (May 3, 2001). ... Granted unconditional free agency (March 1, 2002). ... Re-signed by Cowboys (April 19, 2002). ... Granted unconditional free agency (February 28, 2003). ... Re-signed by Cowboys (May 1, 2003). ... Released by Cowboys (October 7, 2003). ... Signed by Cleveland Browns (November 12, 2003). ... Granted unconditional free agency (March 3, 2004). ... Re-signed by Browns (March 18, 2004). ... Traded by Browns with DE Ebenezer Ekuban to Denver Broncos for RB Reuben Droughns (March 30, 2005).
HONORS: Named defensive tackle on THE SPORTING NEWS college All-America first team (1996).

Year Team	G	GS	TOTALS Tk.	Ast.	Sks.
1998—Dallas NFL	16	1	10	5	3.0
1999—Dallas NFL	6	0	4	4	0.0
2000—Dallas NFL	13	7	28	7	0.0
2001—Dallas NFL	16	16	37	18	3.5
2002—Dallas NFL	16	0	22	13	1.0
2003—Dallas NFL	1	1	0	1	0.0
—Cleveland NFL	7	1	8	6	3.0
2004—Cleveland NFL	16	7	22	12	1.0
Pro totals (7 years)	91	33	131	66	11.5

MYLES, REGGIE   CB   BENGALS

PERSONAL: Born October 10, 1979, in Pascagoula, Miss. ... 5-11/185.
HIGH SCHOOL: Pascagoula (Miss.).
COLLEGE: Alabama.
TRANSACTIONS/CAREER NOTES: Signed as non-drafted free agent by Cincinnati Bengals (April 23, 2002). ... Released by Bengals (September 1, 2002). ... Re-signed by Bengals to practice squad (September 2, 2002). ... Activated (November 2, 2002). ... Re-signed by Cincinnati Bengals (March 19, 2004). ... Granted free agency (March 2, 2005). ... Re-signed by Bengals (April 1, 2005).

Year Team	G	GS	TOTALS Tk.	Ast.	Sks.	INTERCEPTIONS No.	Yds.	Avg.	TD
2002—Cincinnati NFL	9	0	4	0	0.0	0	0	0.0	0
2003—Cincinnati NFL	16	0	4	0	0.0	0	0	0.0	0
2004—Cincinnati NFL	16	0	0	0	0.0	0	0	0.0	0
Pro totals (3 years)	41	0	8	0	0.0	0	0	0.0	0

M

NAEOLE, CHRIS   G   JAGUARS

PERSONAL: Born December 25, 1974, in Kailua, Hawaii. ... 6-3/320. ... Full name: Chris Kealoha Naeole. ... Name pronounced: NAY-oh-lee.
HIGH SCHOOL: Kahuka (Kaaava, Hawaii).
COLLEGE: Colorado.
TRANSACTIONS/CAREER NOTES: Selected by New Orleans Saints in first round (10th pick overall) of 1997 NFL draft. ... Signed by Saints (July 17, 1997). ... On injured reserve with ankle injury (October 17, 1997-remainder of season). ... Granted unconditional free agency (March 1, 2002). ... Signed by Jacksonville Jaguars (April 5, 2002).
PLAYING EXPERIENCE: New Orleans NFL, 1997-2001; Jacksonville NFL, 2002-2004. ... Games/Games started: 1997 (4/0), 1998 (16/16), 1999 (15/15), 2000 (16/16), 2001 (16/16), 2002 (16/16), 2003 (16/16), 2004 (16/16). Total: 115/111.
HONORS: Named guard on THE SPORTING NEWS college All-America second team (1996).

NALEN, TOM   C   BRONCOS

PERSONAL: Born May 13, 1971, in Foxboro, Mass. ... 6-3/286. ... Full name: Thomas Andrew Nalen.
HIGH SCHOOL: Foxboro (Mass.).
COLLEGE: Boston College.
TRANSACTIONS/CAREER NOTES: Selected by Denver Broncos in seventh round (218th pick overall) of 1994 NFL draft. ... Signed by Broncos (July 15, 1994). ... Released by Broncos (September 2, 1994). ... Re-signed by Broncos to practice squad (September 6, 1994). ... Activated (October 7, 1994). ... On injured reserve with knee injury (October 23, 2002-remainder of season).
PLAYING EXPERIENCE: Denver NFL, 1994-2004. ... Games/Games started: 1994 (7/1), 1995 (15/15), 1996 (16/16), 1997 (16/16), 1998 (16/16), 1999 (16/16), 2000 (16/16), 2001 (16/16), 2002 (7/7), 2003 (16/16), 2004 (16/16). Total: 157/151.
CHAMPIONSHIP GAME EXPERIENCE: Played in AFC championship game (1997 and 1998 seasons). ... Member of Super Bowl championship team (1997 and 1998 seasons).
HONORS: Played in Pro Bowl (1997-1999 and 2003 seasons). ... Named center on THE SPORTING NEWS NFL All-Pro team (1999 and 2000). ... Named to play in Pro Bowl (2000 season); replaced by Tim Ruddy due to injury.

NALL, CRAIG   QB   PACKERS

PERSONAL: Born April 21, 1979, in Alexandria, La. ... 6-3/228. ... Full name: Craig Matthew Nall.
HIGH SCHOOL: Alexandria (La.).
COLLEGE: Northwestern State.
TRANSACTIONS/CAREER NOTES: Selected by Green Bay Packers in fifth round (164th pick overall) of 2002 NFL draft. ... Signed by Packers (July 22, 2002). ... Assigned by Packers to NFL Europe in 2003 enhancement allocation program (February 26, 2003). ... Granted free agency (March 2, 2005). ... Re-signed by Packers (April 18, 2005).
SINGLE GAME HIGHS (regular season): Attempts—13 (January 2, 2005, vs. Chicago); completions—8 (December 5, 2004, vs. Philadelphia); yards—131 (January 2, 2005, vs. Chicago); and touchdown passes—2 (December 5, 2004, vs. Philadelphia).

				PASSING								RUSHING				TOTALS	
Year Team	G	GS	Att.	Cmp.	Pct.	Yds.	TD	Int.	Avg.	Skd.	Rat.	Att.	Yds.	Avg.	TD	TD	2pt.	Pts.
2003—Green Bay NFL	1	0	0	0	0.0	0	0	0	0.00	0	0.0	2	-2	-1.0	0	0	0	0
2004—Green Bay NFL	5	0	33	23	69.7	314	4	0	9.52	2	139.4	3	7	2.3	0	0	0	0
Pro totals (2 years)	6	0	33	23	69.7	314	4	0	9.52	2	139.4	5	5	1.0	0	0	0	0

NASH, KEYON   CB   RAIDERS

PERSONAL: Born March 11, 1979, in Colquitt, Ga. ... 6-3/215.
HIGH SCHOOL: Miller County (Ga.).
COLLEGE: Albany State (Ga.).
TRANSACTIONS/CAREER NOTES: Selected by Oakland Raiders in sixth round (189th pick overall) of 2002 NFL draft. ... Signed by Raiders (July 23, 2002). ... Released by Raiders (September 1, 2002). ... Re-signed by Raiders to practice squad (September 3, 2002). ... Activated (January 15, 2003). ... Released by Raiders (2003). ... Re-signed by Raiders to practice squad (January 22, 2003). ... Activated (March 3, 2004). ... Released by Raiders (September 5, 2004). ... Re-signed by Raiders to practice squad (September 7, 2004). ... Activated (December 24, 2004).
CHAMPIONSHIP GAME EXPERIENCE: Member of Raiders for AFC championship game (2002 season); inactive. ... Member of Raiders for Super Bowl 37 (2002 season); inactive.

		INTERCEPTIONS			
Year Team	G	No.	Yds.	Avg.	TD
2004—Oakland NFL	2	0	0	0.0	0

NATTIEL, MICHAEL   LB

PERSONAL: Born November 8, 1980, in Gainesville, Fla. ... 6-0/227. ... Full name: Michael Dondrill Nattiel.
HIGH SCHOOL: Newberry (Archer, Fla.).
COLLEGE: Florida.
TRANSACTIONS/CAREER NOTES: Selected by Minnesota Vikings in sixth round (190th pick overall) of 2003 NFL draft. ... Signed by Vikings (July 15, 2003). ... Released by Vikings (April 25, 2005).

			TOTALS			INTERCEPTIONS			
Year Team	G	GS	Tk.	Ast.	Sks.	No.	Yds.	Avg.	TD
2003—Minnesota NFL	16	0	15	2	0.0	1	80	80.0	1
2004—Minnesota NFL	16	0	11	3	0.0	0	0	0.0	0
Pro totals (2 years)	32	0	26	5	0.0	1	80	80.0	1

NAVARRE, JOHN — QB — CARDINALS

PERSONAL: Born September 9, 1980, in Cudahy, Wis. ... 6-6/250.
HIGH SCHOOL: Cudahy (Wis.).
COLLEGE: Michigan.
TRANSACTIONS/CAREER NOTES: Selected by Arizona Cardinals in seventh round (202nd pick overall) of 2004 NFL draft. ... Signed by Cardinals (July 28, 2004).
SINGLE GAME HIGHS (regular season): Attempts—40 (December 5, 2004, vs. Detroit); completions—18 (December 5, 2004, vs. Detroit); yards—168 (December 5, 2004, vs. Detroit); and touchdown passes—1 (December 5, 2004, vs. Detroit).
MISCELLANEOUS: Regular-season record as starting NFL quarterback: 0-1 (.000).

			PASSING								RUSHING				TOTALS		
Year Team	G	GS	Att.	Cmp.	Pct.	Yds.	TD	Int.	Avg.	Skd.	Rat.	Att.	Yds.	Avg.	TD	TD	2pt.	Pts.
2004—Arizona NFL	1	1	40	18	45.0	168	1	4	4.20	1	25.8	0	0	0.0	0	0	0	0

NAVIES, HANNIBAL — LB — PACKERS

PERSONAL: Born July 19, 1977, in Chicago, Ill. ... 6-3/249. ... Full name: Hannibal Carter Navies. ... Name pronounced: NAY-vees.
HIGH SCHOOL: St. Patrick (Chicago), then Berkeley (Oakland).
COLLEGE: Colorado.
TRANSACTIONS/CAREER NOTES: Selected by Carolina Panthers in fourth round (100th pick overall) of 1999 NFL draft. ... Signed by Panthers (July 21, 1999). ... On injured reserve with broken arm (October 23, 2001-remainder of season). ... Granted free agency (March 1, 2002). ... Re-signed by Panthers (May 10, 2002). ... Granted unconditional free agency (February 28, 2003). ... Signed by Green Bay Packers (March 19, 2003). ... Granted unconditional free agency (March 2, 2005). ... Re-signed by Packers (April 26, 2005).

			TOTALS			INTERCEPTIONS			
Year Team	G	GS	Tk.	Ast.	Sks.	No.	Yds.	Avg.	TD
1999—Carolina NFL	9	0	3	0	0.0	0	0	0.0	0
2000—Carolina NFL	13	1	19	1	2.0	1	0	0.0	0
2001—Carolina NFL	5	5	17	4	0.0	0	0	0.0	0
2002—Carolina NFL	12	9	21	11	0.0	0	0	0.0	0
2003—Green Bay NFL	16	16	69	17	1.0	0	0	0.0	0
2004—Green Bay NFL	15	14	37	10	0.5	0	0	0.0	0
Pro totals (6 years)	70	45	166	43	3.5	1	0	0.0	0

NEAL, LORENZO — FB — CHARGERS

PERSONAL: Born December 27, 1970, in Hanford, Calif. ... 5-11/255. ... Full name: Lorenzo LaVonne Neal.
HIGH SCHOOL: Lemoore (Calif.).
COLLEGE: Fresno State.
TRANSACTIONS/CAREER NOTES: Selected by New Orleans Saints in fourth round (89th pick overall) of 1993 NFL draft. ... Signed by Saints (July 15, 1993). ... On injured reserve with ankle injury (September 15, 1993-remainder of season). ... Granted free agency (February 16, 1996). ... Re-signed by Saints (July 1, 1996). ... Granted unconditional free agency (February 14, 1997). ... Signed by New York Jets (March 31, 1997). ... Traded by Jets to Tampa Bay Buccaneers for fifth-round pick (TE Blake Spence) in 1998 draft (March 12, 1998). ... Released by Buccaneers (February 11, 1999). ... Signed by Tennessee Titans (March 2, 1999). ... Released by Titans (March 1, 2001). ... Signed by Cincinnati Bengals (May 7, 2001). ... Granted unconditional free agency (February 28, 2003). ... Signed by San Diego Chargers (February 28, 2003).
CHAMPIONSHIP GAME EXPERIENCE: Played in AFC championship game (1999 season). ... Played in Super Bowl 34 (1999 season).
HONORS: Played in Pro Bowl (2002 season).
SINGLE GAME HIGHS (regular season): Attempts—14 (October 9, 1994, vs. Chicago); yards—89 (September 5, 1993, vs. Houston); and rushing touchdowns—1 (September 28, 2003, vs. Oakland).

			RUSHING				RECEIVING				KICKOFF RETURNS				TOTALS			
Year Team	G	GS	Att.	Yds.	Avg.	TD	No.	Yds.	Avg.	TD	No.	Yds.	Avg.	TD	TD	2pt.	Pts.	Fum.
1993—New Orleans NFL	2	2	21	175	8.3	1	0	0	0.0	0	0	0	0.0	0	1	0	6	1
1994—New Orleans NFL	16	7	30	90	3.0	1	2	9	4.5	0	1	17	17.0	0	1	0	6	1
1995—New Orleans NFL	16	7	5	3	0.6	0	12	123	10.3	1	2	28	14.0	0	1	0	6	2
1996—New Orleans NFL	16	11	21	58	2.8	1	31	194	6.3	1	0	0	0.0	0	2	0	12	1
1997—New York Jets NFL	16	10	10	28	2.8	0	8	40	5.0	1	2	22	11.0	0	1	0	6	0
1998—Tampa Bay NFL	16	1	5	25	5.0	0	5	14	2.8	1	0	0	0.0	0	1	0	6	0
1999—Tennessee NFL	16	14	2	1	0.5	1	7	27	3.9	2	2	15	7.5	0	3	0	18	0
2000—Tennessee NFL	16	5	1	-2	-2.0	0	9	31	3.4	2	1	15	15.0	0	2	0	12	0
2001—Cincinnati NFL	16	10	5	10	2.0	0	19	101	5.3	1	0	0	0.0	0	1	0	6	0
2002—Cincinnati NFL	16	8	9	31	3.4	0	21	133	6.3	1	5	52	10.4	0	1	0	6	0
2003—San Diego NFL	16	15	18	40	2.2	1	16	62	3.9	0	1	1	1.0	0	1	0	6	0
2004—San Diego NFL	16	10	16	53	3.3	0	13	66	5.1	0	1	12	12.0	0	0	0	0	1
Pro totals (12 years)	178	100	143	512	3.6	5	143	800	5.6	10	15	162	10.8	0	15	0	90	6

NEAL, STEPHEN — OL — PATRIOTS

PERSONAL: Born October 9, 1976, in San Diego, Calif. ... 6-4/305.
HIGH SCHOOL: San Diego (Calif.).
COLLEGE: Cal State Bakersfield.
TRANSACTIONS/CAREER NOTES: Signed as non-drafted free agent by New England Patriots (July 23, 2001). ... Released by Patriots (August 26, 2001). ... Signed by Philadelphia Eagles to practice squad (September 4, 2001). ... Signed by Patriots off Eagles practice squad (December 12, 2001). ... Inactive for three games (2001). ... On injured reserve with shoulder injury (October 23, 2002-remainder of season). ... Granted free agency (March 2, 2005). ... Re-signed by Patriots (March 8, 2005).
CHAMPIONSHIP GAME EXPERIENCE: Played in AFC championship game (2004 season). ... Member of Super Bowl championship team (2004 season).

N

NECE, RYAN　　　　　　　LB　　　　　　　BUCCANEERS

PERSONAL: Born February 24, 1979, in San Bernardino, Calif. ... 6-3/224. ... Full name: Ryan Clint Nece. ... Son of Ronnie Lott, Hall of Fame safety with San Francisco 49ers (1981-90), Los Angeles Raiders (1991-92) and New York Jets (1993-94).
HIGH SCHOOL: Pacific (San Bernardino, Calif.).
COLLEGE: UCLA.
TRANSACTIONS/CAREER NOTES: Signed as non-drafted free agent by Tampa Bay Buccaneers (April 22, 2002). ... On injured reserve with knee injury (October 29, 2002-remainder of season). ... Granted free agency (March 2, 2005). ... Re-signed by Buccaneers (March 5, 2005).

				TOTALS			INTERCEPTIONS			
Year　Team	G	GS	Tk.	Ast.	Sks.	No.	Yds.	Avg.	TD
2002—Tampa Bay NFL	8	0	1	1	0.0	0	0	0.0	0
2003—Tampa Bay NFL	15	10	44	11	0.0	1	2	2.0	0
2004—Tampa Bay NFL	16	0	0	1	0.0	1	2	2.0	0
Pro totals (3 years)	39	10	45	13	0.0	2	4	2.0	0

NED, LARRY　　　　　　　RB

PERSONAL: Born August 23, 1978, in Eunice, La. ... 5-11/217. ... Full name: Larry Lee Ned Jr.
HIGH SCHOOL: Rancho Verde (Calif.).
COLLEGE: San Diego State.
TRANSACTIONS/CAREER NOTES: Selected by Oakland Raiders in sixth round (197th pick overall) of 2002 NFL draft. ... Signed by Raiders (July 25, 2002). ... Released by Raiders (August 26, 2002). ... Signed by San Diego Chargers to practice squad (September 3, 2002). ... Released by Chargers (November 26, 2002). ... Signed by Minnesota Vikings to practice squad (December 10, 2002). ... Released by Vikings (August 31, 2003). ... Re-signed by Vikings to practice squad (September 1, 2003). ... Activated (December 9, 2003). ... Released by Vikings (February 2, 2005). ... Signed by Arizona Cardinals (March 3, 2005). ... Released by Cardinals (March 4, 2005).

			RUSHING				RECEIVING				TOTALS			
Year　Team	G	GS	Att.	Yds.	Avg.	TD	No.	Yds.	Avg.	TD	TD	2pt.	Pts.	Fum.
2003—Minnesota NFL	3	0	0	0	0.0	0	0	0	0.0	0	0	0	0	0
2004—Minnesota NFL	16	0	0	0	0.0	0	1	9	9.0	0	0	0	0	0
Pro totals (2 years)	19	0	0	0	0.0	0	1	9	9.0	0	0	0	0	0

NEDNEY, JOE　　　　　　　K　　　　　　　49ERS

PERSONAL: Born March 22, 1973, in San Jose, Calif. ... 6-5/225. ... Full name: Joseph Thomas Nedney. ... Name pronounced: NED-nee.
HIGH SCHOOL: Santa Teresa (San Jose, Calif.).
COLLEGE: San Jose State.
TRANSACTIONS/CAREER NOTES: Signed as non-drafted free agent by Green Bay Packers (April 1995). ... Released by Packers (August 27, 1995). ... Signed by Oakland Raiders to practice squad (August 29, 1995). ... Released by Raiders (September 6, 1995). ... Signed by Miami Dolphins to practice squad (September 21, 1995). ... Claimed on waivers by New York Jets (August 12, 1997). ... Released by Jets (August 25, 1997). ... Signed by Dolphins (October 3, 1997). ... Released by Dolphins (October 6, 1997). ... Signed by Arizona Cardinals (October 15, 1997). ... On injured reserve with knee injury (December 1, 1998-remainder of season). ... Released by Cardinals (February 12, 1999). ... Re-signed by Cardinals (March 31, 1999). ... Claimed on waivers by Baltimore Ravens (October 6, 1999). ... Inactive for four games with Ravens (1999). ... Released by Ravens (November 9, 1999). ... Signed by Raiders (December 14, 1999). ... Released by Raiders (August 27, 2000). ... Signed by Denver Broncos (September 12, 2000). ... Released by Broncos (October 2, 2000). ... Signed by Carolina Panthers (October 3, 2000). ... Granted unconditional free agency (March 2, 2001). ... Signed by Tennessee Titans (March 9, 2001). ... On injured reserve with ACL injury (September 11, 2003-remainder of season). ... On injured reserve with knee injury (September 8, 2004-entire season). ... Released by Tennessee Titans (February 21, 2005). ... Signed by San Francisco 49ers (March 10, 2005).
CHAMPIONSHIP GAME EXPERIENCE: Played in AFC championship game (2002 season).

		FIELD GOALS							TOTALS		
Year　Team	G	1-29	30-39	40-49	50+	Tot.	Pct.	Lg.	XPM	XPA	Pts.
1995—Miami NFL		Did not play.									
1996—Miami NFL	16	8-8	7-11	3-8	0-2	18-29	62.1	44	35	36	89
1997—Arizona NFL	10	4-4	4-4	3-7	0-2	11-17	64.7	45	19	19	52
1998—Arizona NFL	12	6-6	1-1	5-8	1-4	13-19	68.4	53	30	30	69
1999—Arizona NFL	1	0-0	0-0	0-0	0-0	0-0	0.0	0	0	0	0
—Oakland NFL	3	2-2	2-2	0-1	1-2	5-7	71.4	52	13	13	28
2000—Denver NFL	3	6-6	1-1	1-2	0-1	8-10	80.0	43	4	4	28
—Carolina NFL	12	11-11	6-7	7-8	2-2	26-28	92.9	52	20	20	98
2001—San Francisco NFL	16	6-6	5-5	8-15	1-2	20-28	71.4	51	34	35	94
2002—San Francisco NFL	16	9-9	10-12	5-8	1-2	25-31	80.6	53	36	36	111
2003—San Francisco NFL	1	0-0	0-0	0-0	1-1	1-1	100.0	50	0	1	3
2004—Tennessee NFL		Did not play.									
Pro totals (8 years)	90	52-52	36-43	32-57	7-18	127-170	74.7	53	191	194	572

NEIL, DAN　　　　　　　G

PERSONAL: Born October 21, 1973, in Houston, Texas. ... 6-2/285. ... Full name: Daniel Neil.
HIGH SCHOOL: Cypress Creek (Houston).
COLLEGE: Texas.
TRANSACTIONS/CAREER NOTES: Selected by Denver Broncos in third round (67th pick overall) of 1997 NFL draft. ... Signed by Broncos (July 17, 1997). ... Granted free agency (February 11, 2000). ... Re-signed by Broncos (April 28, 2000) ... Granted unconditional free agency (March 2, 2001). ... Re-signed by Broncos (March 2, 2001). ... Released by Broncos (February 24, 2005).
PLAYING EXPERIENCE: Denver NFL, 2004. ... Games/Games started: 1997 (3/0), 1998 (16/16), 1999 (15/15), 2000 (16/16), 2001 (15/15), 2002 (16/16), 2003 (14/14), 2004 (13/12). Total: 108/104.

CHAMPIONSHIP GAME EXPERIENCE: Member of Broncos for AFC championship game (1997 season); inactive. ... Member of Super Bowl championship team (1997 season); inactive. ... Played in AFC championship game (1998 season). ... Member of Super Bowl championship team (1998 season).
HONORS: Named guard on THE SPORTING NEWS college All-America first team (1996).

NELSON, BEN   WR   VIKINGS

PERSONAL: Born August 21, 1979, in Coon Rapids, Minn. ... 6-2/185.
HIGH SCHOOL: Anoka (Minn.).
COLLEGE: St. Cloud State.
TRANSACTIONS/CAREER NOTES: Signed as non-drafted free agent by Minnesota Vikings (April 26, 2003). ... Released by Vikings (August 31, 2003). ... Re-signed by Vikings to practice squad (September 1, 2003). ... Released by Vikings from practice squad (September 9, 2003). ... Re-signed by Vikings (January 7, 2004). ... Assigned by Vikings to Cologne Centurions in 2004 NFL Europe enhancement allocation program (February 13, 2004). ... Released by Vikings (September 5, 2004). ... Re-signed by Vikings to practice squad (September 6, 2004). ... Activated (November 2, 2004).

			RECEIVING				TOTALS			
Year Team	G	GS	No.	Yds.	Avg.	TD	TD	2pt.	Pts.	Fum.
2004—Minnesota NFL	3	0	0	0	0.0	0	0	0	0	0

NELSON, BRUCE   G   PANTHERS

PERSONAL: Born May 12, 1979, in Emmetsburg, Iowa. ... 6-5/301.
HIGH SCHOOL: Emmetsburg (Iowa).
COLLEGE: Iowa.
TRANSACTIONS/CAREER NOTES: Selected by Carolina Panthers in second round (50th pick overall) of 2003 NFL draft. ... Signed by Panthers (July 28, 2003). ... On physically unable to perform list with hip injury (July 30-November 29, 2004). ... On injured reserve with hip injury (November 29, 2004-remainder of season).
PLAYING EXPERIENCE: Carolina NFL, 2003-2004. ... Games/Games started: 2003 (14/1). Total: 14/1.
CHAMPIONSHIP GAME EXPERIENCE: Played in NFC championship game (2003 season). ... Played in Super Bowl 38 (2003 season).

NELSON, JIM   LB   RAVENS

PERSONAL: Born April 16, 1975, in Riverside, Calif. ... 6-1/234. ... Full name: James Robert Nelson.
HIGH SCHOOL: McDonough (Waldorf, Md.).
COLLEGE: Penn State.
TRANSACTIONS/CAREER NOTES: Signed as non-drafted free agent by San Francisco 49ers (April 24, 1998). ... Claimed on waivers by Green Bay Packers (July 20, 1998). ... Released by Packers (August 25, 1998). ... Re-signed by Packers to practice squad (September 14, 1998). ... Activated (December 29, 1998); did not play. ... Claimed on waivers by Minnesota Vikings (August 28, 2000). ... Granted free agency (March 1, 2002). ... Re-signed by Vikings (April 23, 2002). ... Granted unconditional free agency (February 28, 2003). ... Signed by Indianapolis Colts (March 22, 2003). ... Granted unconditional free agency (March 3, 2004). ... Re-signed by Colts (March 11, 2004). ... On injured reserve with clavicle injury (December 28, 2004-remainder of season). ... Granted unconditional free agency (March 2, 2005). ... Signed by Baltimore Ravens (April 20, 2005).
CHAMPIONSHIP GAME EXPERIENCE: Played in NFC championship game (2000 season). ... Played in AFC championship game (2003 season).

			TOTALS			INTERCEPTIONS			
Year Team	G	GS	Tk.	Ast.	Sks.	No.	Yds.	Avg.	TD
1998—Green Bay NFL	Did not play.								
1999—Green Bay NFL	16	0	7	1	0.0	1	0	0.0	0
2000—Minnesota NFL	16	0	3	3	0.0	0	0	0.0	0
2001—Minnesota NFL	16	2	21	16	0.0	0	0	0.0	0
2002—Minnesota NFL	16	1	7	2	0.0	0	0	0.0	0
2003—Indianapolis NFL	7	0	12	1	0.0	2	22	11.0	0
2004—Indianapolis NFL	15	1	40	12	0.0	1	0	0.0	0
Pro totals (6 years)	86	4	90	35	0.0	4	22	5.5	0

NELSON, RHETT   CB   CARDINALS

PERSONAL: Born February 16, 1980, in Minneapolis, Minn. ... 6-0/201.
COLLEGE: Colorado State.
TRANSACTIONS/CAREER NOTES: Signed as non-drafted free agent by Arizona Cardinals (April 28, 2003). ... Released by Cardinals (August 30, 2003). ... Signed by Minnesota Vikings to practice squad (September 9, 2003). ... Activated (November 12, 2003). ... Re-signed by Vikings to practice squad (September 28, 2004). ... Activated (December 15, 2004). ... Claimed on waivers by Cardinals (March 3, 2005).

			TOTALS			INTERCEPTIONS			
Year Team	G	GS	Tk.	Ast.	Sks.	No.	Yds.	Avg.	TD
2003—Minnesota NFL	3	0	0	0	0.0	0	0	0.0	0
2004—Minnesota NFL	4	0	2	0	0.0	0	0	0.0	0
Pro totals (2 years)	7	0	2	0	0.0	0	0	0.0	0

NESBIT, JAMAR   G/C   SAINTS

PERSONAL: Born December 17, 1976, in Heidelberg, Germany. ... 6-4/328. ... Full name: Jamar Kendric Nesbit.
HIGH SCHOOL: Summerville (S.C.).
COLLEGE: South Carolina.

N

TRANSACTIONS/CAREER NOTES: Signed as non-drafted free agent by Carolina Panthers (April 18, 1999). ... Granted free agency (March 1, 2002). ... Re-signed by Panthers (June 21, 2002). ... Granted unconditional free agency (February 28, 2003). ... Signed by Jacksonville Jaguars (May 5, 2003). ... Granted unconditional free agency (March 3, 2004). ... Signed by New Orleans Saints (March 25, 2004).
PLAYING EXPERIENCE: Carolina NFL, 1999-2002; Jacksonville NFL, 2003; New Orleans NFL, 2004. ... Games/Games started: 1999 (7/0), 2000 (16/16), 2001 (16/16), 2002 (14/13), 2003 (16/2), 2004 (16/4). Total: 85/51.

NEUFELD, RYAN   TE   BILLS

PERSONAL: Born November 22, 1975, in Morgan Hill, Calif. ... 6-4/250. ... Full name: Ryan Matthew Neufeld.
HIGH SCHOOL: Live Oak (Morgan Hill, Calif.).
COLLEGE: UCLA.
TRANSACTIONS/CAREER NOTES: Signed as non-drafted free agent by Dallas Cowboys (April 23, 1999). ... Released by Cowboys (September 5, 1999). ... Re-signed by Cowboys to practice squad (September 6, 1999). ... Activated (October 27, 1999). ... Assigned by Cowboys to Rhein Fire in 2000 NFL Europe enhancement allocation program (February 18, 2000). ... Released by Cowboys (August 27, 2000). ... Signed by Miami Dolphins to practice squad (August 30, 2000). ... Released by Dolphins (September 5, 2000). ... Signed by Jacksonville Jaguars to practice squad (September 13, 2000). ... Activated (October 12, 2000). ... Released by Jaguars (October 21, 2000). ... Re-signed by Jaguars (October 24, 2000). ... Released by Jaguars (August 25, 2001). ... Signed by Seattle Seahawks (January 23, 2002). ... Released by Seahawks (August 25, 2002). ... Signed by Buffalo Bills (January 22, 2003). ... Granted unconditional free agency (March 2, 2005). ... Re-signed by Buffalo (March 14, 2005).
SINGLE GAME HIGHS (regular season): Receptions—3 (January 2, 2005, vs. Pittsburgh); yards—40 (December 5, 2004, vs. Miami); and touchdown receptions—0.

				RECEIVING				TOTALS		
Year Team	G	GS	No.	Yds.	Avg.	TD	TD	2pt.	Pts.	Fum.
1999—Dallas NFL	6	0	0	0	0.0	0	0	0	0	0
2000—Jacksonville NFL	3	0	0	0	0.0	0	0	0	0	0
2003—Buffalo NFL	16	1	3	41	13.7	0	0	0	0	0
2004—Buffalo NFL	16	5	6	61	10.2	0	0	0	0	0
Pro totals (4 years)	41	6	9	102	11.3	0	0	0	0	0

NEWBERRY, JEREMY   C   49ERS

PERSONAL: Born March 23, 1976, in Antioch, Calif. ... 6-5/310. ... Full name: Jeremy David Newberry.
HIGH SCHOOL: Antioch (Calif.).
COLLEGE: California.
TRANSACTIONS/CAREER NOTES: Selected by after junior season San Francisco 49ers in second round (58th pick overall) of 1998 NFL draft. ... Signed by San Francisco 49ers (July 18, 1998). ... On physically unable to perform list with knee injury (July 17-November 7, 1998). ... Active for one game (1998); did not play. ... Granted unconditional free agency (March 1, 2002). ... Re-signed by 49ers (March 12, 2002). ... On injured reserve with back injury (December 9, 2004-remainder of season).
PLAYING EXPERIENCE: San Francisco NFL, 1999-2004. ... Games/Games started: 1999 (16/16), 2000 (16/16), 2001 (15/15), 2002 (16/16), 2003 (16/16), 2004 (2/1). Total: 81/80.
HONORS: Played in Pro Bowl (2001 and 2002 seasons).

NEWHOUSE, REGGIE   WR   CARDINALS

PERSONAL: Born February 16, 1981, in Dallas, Texas. ... 6-1/191. ... Son of Robert Newhouse, running back with Dallas Cowboys (1972-83).
HIGH SCHOOL: Lake Highlands (Dallas, Texas).
COLLEGE: Baylor.
TRANSACTIONS/CAREER NOTES: Signed as non-drafted free agent by Arizona Cardinals (April 28, 2003). ... Released by Cardinals (August 24, 2003). ... Re-signed by Cardinals to practice squad (November 26, 2003). ... Assigned by Cardinals to Cologne Centurions in 2004 NFL Europe enhancement allocation program (February 4, 2004). ... Released by Cardinals and re-signed to practice squad (November 2, 2004). ... Activated (November 30, 2004). ... Released by Cardinals (December 15, 2004). ... Re-signed by Cardinals to practice squad (December 16, 2004). ... Activated (January 4, 2005).
SINGLE GAME HIGHS (regular season): Receptions—1 (December 5, 2004, vs. Detroit); yards—5 (December 5, 2004, vs. Detroit); and touchdown receptions—0.

				RECEIVING				TOTALS		
Year Team	G	GS	No.	Yds.	Avg.	TD	TD	2pt.	Pts.	Fum.
2004—Arizona NFL	3	0	1	5	5.0	0	0	0	0	0

NEWMAN, KEITH   LB   VIKINGS

PERSONAL: Born January 19, 1977, in Tampa, Fla. ... 6-2/248. ... Full name: Keith Anthony Newman.
HIGH SCHOOL: Thomas Jefferson (Tampa).
COLLEGE: North Carolina.
TRANSACTIONS/CAREER NOTES: Selected by Buffalo Bills in fourth round (119th pick overall) of 1999 NFL draft. ... Signed by Bills (July 27, 1999). ... Granted free agency (March 1, 2002). ... Re-signed by Bills (May 21, 2002). ... Granted unconditional free agency (February 28, 2003). ... Signed by Atlanta Falcons (March 17, 2003). ... On suspended list for violation of league substance abuse policy (August 30-October 5, 2003). ... Released by Falcons (April 27, 2004). ... Signed by Minnesota Vikings (June 8, 2004). ... Granted unconditional free agency (March 2, 2005). ... Re-signed by Vikings (April 28, 2005).

			TOTALS			INTERCEPTIONS			
Year Team	G	GS	Tk.	Ast.	Sks.	No.	Yds.	Avg.	TD
1999—Buffalo NFL	3	0	0	1	0.0	0	0	0.0	0
2000—Buffalo NFL	16	16	44	18	8.0	0	0	0.0	0
2001—Buffalo NFL	16	16	62	21	3.5	0	0	0.0	0
2002—Buffalo NFL	16	10	21	13	3.0	0	0	0.0	0
2003—Minnesota NFL	12	11	35	6	2.0	1	29	29.0	0
2004—Minnesota NFL	15	14	36	12	3.5	0	0	0.0	0
Pro totals (6 years)	78	67	198	71	20.0	1	29	29.0	0

N

NEWMAN, TERENCE — CB — COWBOYS

PERSONAL: Born September 4, 1978, in Salina, Kan. ... 5-11/190.
HIGH SCHOOL: Central (Salina, Kan.).
COLLEGE: Kansas State.
TRANSACTIONS/CAREER NOTES: Selected by Dallas Cowboys in first round (fifth pick overall) of 2003 NFL draft. ... Signed by Cowboys (July 24, 2003).

Year Team	G	GS	TOTALS			INTERCEPTIONS			
			Tk.	Ast.	Sks.	No.	Yds.	Avg.	TD
2003—Dallas NFL	16	16	66	10	1.0	4	23	5.8	0
2004—Dallas NFL	16	16	66	4	0.0	4	31	7.8	0
Pro totals (2 years)	32	32	132	14	1.0	8	54	6.8	0

NEWSON, TONY — LB — RAMS

PERSONAL: Born September 11, 1979, in Las Vegas, Nev. ... 6-1/247. ... Full name: Tony Roderick Newson.
HIGH SCHOOL: Cheyenne (Las Vegas).
COLLEGE: Utah State.
TRANSACTIONS/CAREER NOTES: Signed as non-drafted free agent by Kansas City Chiefs (April 23, 2002). ... Released by Chiefs (September 1, 2002). ... Re-signed by Chiefs to practice squad (September 3, 2002). ... Activated (December 4, 2002). ... Released by Chiefs (August 31, 2003). ... Signed by St. Louis Rams (March 15, 2004). ... Released by Rams (September 6, 2004). ... Re-signed by Rams to practice squad (September 8, 2004). ... Activated (September 17, 2004). ... Released by Rams (October 19, 2004). ... Re-signed by Rams to practice squad (October 21, 2004). ... Released by Rams practice squad (December 7, 2004). ... Re-signed by Rams to practice squad (December 15, 2004).

Year Team	G	GS	TOTALS			INTERCEPTIONS			
			Tk.	Ast.	Sks.	No.	Yds.	Avg.	TD
2002—St. Louis NFL	4	0	0	0	0.0	0	0	0.0	0
2004—St. Louis NFL	3	0	0	0	0.0	0	0	0.0	0
Pro totals (2 years)	7	0	0	0	0.0	0	0	0.0	0

NGUYEN, DAT — LB — COWBOYS

PERSONAL: Born September 25, 1975, in Saigon, Vietnam. ... 5-11/238. ... Name pronounced: WIN.
HIGH SCHOOL: Rockport-Fulton (Rockport, Texas).
COLLEGE: Texas A&M.
TRANSACTIONS/CAREER NOTES: Selected by Dallas Cowboys in third round (85th pick overall) of 1999 NFL draft. ... Signed by Cowboys (July 26, 1999). ... Granted free agency (March 1, 2002). ... Re-signed by Cowboys (April 16, 2002).
HONORS: Lombardi Award winner (1998). ... Named inside linebacker on THE SPORTING NEWS college All-America first team (1998).

Year Team	G	GS	TOTALS			INTERCEPTIONS			
			Tk.	Ast.	Sks.	No.	Yds.	Avg.	TD
1999—Dallas NFL	16	0	26	5	1.0	1	6	6.0	0
2000—Dallas NFL	10	5	42	6	0.0	2	31	15.5	0
2001—Dallas NFL	16	16	91	22	0.0	0	0	0.0	0
2002—Dallas NFL	8	8	42	10	1.0	0	0	0.0	0
2003—Dallas NFL	16	16	90	31	2.0	0	0	0.0	0
2004—Dallas NFL	16	16	75	32	1.0	3	19	6.3	0
Pro totals (6 years)	82	61	366	106	5.0	6	56	9.3	0

NICKEY, DONNIE — S — TITANS

PERSONAL: Born April 25, 1980, in Akron, Ohio. ... 6-3/215.
HIGH SCHOOL: Jonathan Alder (Plain City, Ohio).
COLLEGE: Ohio State.
TRANSACTIONS/CAREER NOTES: Selected by Tennessee Titans in fifth round (154th pick overall) of 2003 NFL draft. ... Signed by Titans (July 16, 2003). ... Released by Titans (September 10, 2004). ... Re-signed by Titans (September 15, 2004).

Year Team	G	GS	TOTALS			INTERCEPTIONS			
			Tk.	Ast.	Sks.	No.	Yds.	Avg.	TD
2003—Tennessee NFL	12	0	0	0	0.0	0	0	0.0	0
2004—Tennessee NFL	15	6	28	4	0.0	0	0	0.0	0
Pro totals (2 years)	27	6	28	4	0.0	0	0	0.0	0

N

NIX, JOHN — DT

PERSONAL: Born November 24, 1976, in Lucedale, Miss. ... 6-1/313.
HIGH SCHOOL: George County (Miss.).
COLLEGE: Southern Miss.
TRANSACTIONS/CAREER NOTES: Selected by Dallas Cowboys in seventh round (240th pick overall) of 2001 NFL draft. ... Signed by Cowboys (July 20, 2001). ... Released by Cowboys (2003). ... Signed by San Francisco 49ers (August 26, 2003). ... Released by 49ers (August 31, 2003). ... Signed by Cleveland Browns (December 23, 2003). ... Assigned by Browns to Amsterdam Admirals in 2004 NFL Europe enhancement allocation program (February 9, 2004). ... Claimed on waivers by Arizona Cardinals (September 8, 2004). ... Released by Cardinals (October 6, 2004).

Year Team	G	GS	TOTALS		
			Tk.	Ast.	Sks.
2001—Dallas NFL	16	0	0	0	0.0
2002—Dallas NFL	14	0	0	0	0.0
2004—Arizona NFL	1	0	0	0	0.0
Pro totals (3 years)	31	0	0	0	0.0

NOBLE, BRANDON DT REDSKINS

PERSONAL: Born April 10, 1974, in San Rafael, Calif. ... 6-2/304. ... Full name: Brandon Patrick Noble.
HIGH SCHOOL: First Colonial (Virginia Beach, Va.).
COLLEGE: Penn State.
TRANSACTIONS/CAREER NOTES: Signed as non-drafted free agent by San Francisco 49ers (April 29, 1997). ... Released by 49ers (August 19, 1997). ... Re-signed by 49ers to practice squad (November 12, 1997). ... Released by 49ers (November 19, 1997). ... Re-signed by 49ers (January 13, 1998). ... Assigned by 49ers to Barcelona Dragons in 1998 NFL Europe enhancement allocation program (February 18, 1998). ... Released by 49ers (August 25, 1998). ... Re-signed by 49ers to practice squad (December 3, 1998). ... Granted free agency after 1998 season. ... Signed by Dallas Cowboys (February 2, 1999). ... Assigned by Cowboys to Barcelona Dragons in 1999 NFL Europe enhancement allocation program (February 22, 1999). ... Granted free agency (March 1, 2002). ... Re-signed by Cowboys (April 15, 2002). ... Granted unconditional free agency (February 28, 2003). ... Signed by Washington Redskins (March 1, 2003).

			TOTALS			INTERCEPTIONS			
Year Team	G	GS	Tk.	Ast.	Sks.	No.	Yds.	Avg.	TD
1999—Dallas NFL	16	0	0	0	3.0	0	0	0.0	0
2000—Dallas NFL	16	9	0	0	1.0	0	0	0.0	0
2001—Dallas NFL	16	16	0	0	3.5	0	0	0.0	0
2002—Dallas NFL	16	16	0	0	0.0	0	0	0.0	0
2004—Washington NFL	16	7	9	5	1.0	0	0	0.0	0
Pro totals (5 years)	80	48	9	5	8.5	0	0	0.0	0

NOLL, BEN T COWBOYS

PERSONAL: Born November 14, 1981, in Minneapolis, Minn. ... 6-4/300. ... Full name: Benjamin Richard Noll.
HIGH SCHOOL: Priory (St. Louis, Mo.).
COLLEGE: Pennsylvania.
TRANSACTIONS/CAREER NOTES: Signed as non-drafted free agent by St. Louis Rams (June 21, 2004). ... Released by Rams (September 5, 2004). ... Claimed on waivers by Dallas Cowboys (September 6, 2004).
PLAYING EXPERIENCE: Dallas NFL, 2004. ... Games/Games started: 2004 (1/1). Total: 1/1.

NORRIS, MORAN FB TEXANS

PERSONAL: Born June 16, 1978, in Houston, Texas. ... 6-1/254. ... Full name: Torrance Moran Norris.
HIGH SCHOOL: James Madison (Houston).
COLLEGE: Kansas.
TRANSACTIONS/CAREER NOTES: Selected by New Orleans Saints in fourth round (115th pick overall) of 2001 NFL draft. ... Signed by Saints (July 27, 2001). ... Claimed on waivers by Houston Texans (September 18, 2002). ... Granted free agency (March 3, 2004). ... Re-signed by Texans (April 19, 2004). ... Granted unconditional free agency (March 2, 2005). ... Re-signed by Texans (March 4, 2005).
SINGLE GAME HIGHS (regular season): Attempts—1 (December 5, 2004, vs. New York Jets); yards—0; and rushing touchdowns—0.

			RUSHING				RECEIVING				KICKOFF RETURNS				TOTALS			
Year Team	G	GS	Att.	Yds.	Avg.	TD	No.	Yds.	Avg.	TD	No.	Yds.	Avg.	TD	TD	2pt.	Pts.	Fum.
2001—New Orleans NFL	5	0	0	0	0.0	0	0	0	0.0	0	0	0	0.0	0	0	0	0	0
2002—Houston NFL	13	0	0	0	0.0	0	0	0	0.0	0	2	11	5.5	0	0	0	0	0
2003—Houston NFL	16	9	0	0	0.0	0	7	40	5.7	0	5	71	14.2	0	0	0	0	0
2004—Houston NFL	12	4	1	0	0.0	0	4	13	3.3	0	2	25	12.5	0	0	0	0	0
Pro totals (4 years)	46	13	1	0	0.0	0	11	53	4.8	0	9	107	11.9	0	0	0	0	0

NORTHCUTT, DENNIS WR BROWNS

PERSONAL: Born December 22, 1977, in Los Angeles, Calif. ... 5-11/175.
HIGH SCHOOL: Dorsey (Los Angeles).
COLLEGE: Arizona.
TRANSACTIONS/CAREER NOTES: Selected by Cleveland Browns in second round (32nd pick overall) of 2000 NFL draft. ... Signed by Browns (July 19, 2000). ... On non-football injury list with shoulder injury (July 23-September 30, 2001). ... Granted unconditional free agency (March 3, 2004). ... Re-signed by Browns (May 22, 2004).
HONORS: Named wide receiver on THE SPORTING NEWS college All-America second team (1999).
SINGLE GAME HIGHS (regular season): Receptions—9 (September 26, 2004, vs. New York Giants); yards—165 (October 6, 2002, vs. Baltimore); and touchdown receptions—2 (October 6, 2002, vs. Baltimore).
STATISTICAL PLATEAUS: 100-yard receiving games: 2002 (1), 2003 (1), 2004 (1). Total: 3.

			RUSHING				RECEIVING				PUNT RETURNS				TOTALS			
Year Team	G	GS	Att.	Yds.	Avg.	TD	No.	Yds.	Avg.	TD	No.	Yds.	Avg.	TD	TD	2pt.	Pts.	Fum.
2000—Cleveland NFL	15	8	9	33	3.7	0	39	422	10.8	0	27	289	10.7	0	0	0	0	1
2001—Cleveland NFL	12	7	3	26	8.7	0	18	211	11.7	0	15	86	5.7	0	0	0	0	3
2002—Cleveland NFL	13	0	8	104	13.0	1	38	601	15.8	5	25	367	14.7	†2	8	1	50	2
2003—Cleveland NFL	15	6	12	83	6.9	0	62	729	11.8	2	36	295	8.2	0	2	0	12	2
2004—Cleveland NFL	16	11	8	19	2.4	0	55	806	14.7	2	36	432	§12.0	0	2	0	12	2
Pro totals (5 years)	71	32	40	265	6.6	1	212	2769	13.1	9	139	1469	10.6	2	12	1	74	10

NUTTEN, TOM G

PERSONAL: Born June 8, 1971, in Toledo, Ohio. ... 6-5/280. ... Full name: Thomas Nutten. ... Name pronounced: NEW-ton.
HIGH SCHOOL: Champlain Regional (Lennoxville, Quebec).
COLLEGE: Western Michigan.

TRANSACTIONS/CAREER NOTES: Selected by Hamilton Tiger-Cats in first round (first pick overall) of 1995 CFL draft. ... Selected by Buffalo Bills in seventh round (221st pick overall) of 1995 NFL draft. ... Signed by Bills (June 12, 1995). ... Released by Bills (August 27, 1995). ... Re-signed by Bills to practice squad (August 29, 1995). ... Activated (October 10, 1995). ... Released by Bills (August 26, 1996). ... Signed by Denver Broncos (January 14, 1997). ... Released by Broncos (July 16, 1997). ... Signed by Tiger-Cats of CFL (July 28, 1997). ... Signed by St. Louis Rams (January 16, 1998). ... Assigned by Rams to Amsterdam Admirals in 1998 NFL Europe enhancement allocation program (February 18, 1998). ... On injured reserve with neck injury (November 17, 1998-remainder of season). ... Granted free agency (February 11, 2000). ... Re-signed by Rams (February 12, 2000). ... On injured reserve with broken leg (November 27, 2002-remainder of season). ... Granted unconditional free agency (February 28, 2003). ... Signed by New York Jets (March 7, 2003). ... Placed on reserve/retired list (August 18, 2003). ... Re-signed by Rams (August 20, 2004). ... Granted unconditional free agency (March 2, 2005).
PLAYING EXPERIENCE: Buffalo NFL, 1995; Hamilton CFL, 1997; St. Louis NFL, 1998-2004. ... Games/Games started: 1995 (1/0), 1997 (13/0), 1998 (4/2), 1999 (14/14), 2000 (16/16), 2001 (15/14), 2002 (11/11), 2004 (8/6), Total: 82/63.
CHAMPIONSHIP GAME EXPERIENCE: Played in NFC championship game (1999 and 2001 seasons). ... Member of Super Bowl championship team (1999 season). ... Played in Super Bowl 36 (2001 season).

OBEN, ROMAN — T — CHARGERS

PERSONAL: Born October 9, 1972, in Cameroon, West Africa. ... 6-4/305. ... Name pronounced: OH-bin.
HIGH SCHOOL: Gonzaga (Washington, D.C.), then Fork Union (Va.) Military Academy.
COLLEGE: Louisville.
TRANSACTIONS/CAREER NOTES: Selected by New York Giants in third round (66th pick overall) of 1996 NFL draft. ... Signed by Giants (July 20, 1996). ... Granted free agency (February 12, 1999). ... Re-signed by Giants (July 28, 1999). ... Granted unconditional free agency (February 11, 2000). ... Signed by Cleveland Browns (March 9, 2000). ... Released by Browns (February 25, 2002). ... Signed by Tampa Bay Buccaneers (May 20, 2002). ... Granted unconditional free agency (February 28, 2003). ... Re-signed by Buccaneers (March 31, 2003). ... Traded by Buccaneers to San Diego Chargers for fifth-round (traded to N.Y. Giants) pick in 2005 draft (June 9, 2004).
PLAYING EXPERIENCE: New York Giants NFL, 1996-1999; Cleveland NFL, 2000-2001; Tampa Bay NFL, 2002-2003; San Diego NFL, 2004. ... Games/Games started: 1996 (2/0), 1997 (16/16), 1998 (16/16), 1999 (16/16), 2000 (16/16), 2001 (16/14), 2002 (16/16), 2003 (15/13), 2004 (16/16). Total: 129/123.
CHAMPIONSHIP GAME EXPERIENCE: Played in NFC championship game (2002 season). ... Member of Super Bowl championship team (2002 season).

ODOM, ANTWAN — DE — TITANS

PERSONAL: Born September 24, 1981, in Mobile, Ala. ... 6-4/277.
HIGH SCHOOL: Alma (Bryant, Ala.).
COLLEGE: Alabama.
TRANSACTIONS/CAREER NOTES: Selected after junior season by Tennessee Titans in second round (57th pick overall) of 2004 NFL draft. ... Signed by Titans (July 31, 2004).

| | | | TOTALS | | |
Year Team	G	GS	Tk.	Ast.	Sks.
2004—Tennessee NFL	16	8	15	6	2.0

ODOM, JOE — LB — BEARS

PERSONAL: Born December 14, 1979, in Alton, Ill. ... 6-1/235. ... Full name: Joe Edward Odom.
HIGH SCHOOL: Civic Memorial (Bethalto, Ill.).
COLLEGE: Purdue.
TRANSACTIONS/CAREER NOTES: Selected by Chicago Bears in sixth round (191st pick overall) of 2003 NFL draft. ... Signed by Bears (June 9, 2003). ... On injured reserve with groin injury (November 21, 2003-remainder of season).

| | | | TOTALS | | | INTERCEPTIONS | | | |
Year Team	G	GS	Tk.	Ast.	Sks.	No.	Yds.	Avg.	TD
2003—Chicago NFL	10	3	14	6	0.0	0	0	0.0	0
2004—Chicago NFL	16	5	12	6	0.0	0	0	0.0	0
Pro totals (2 years)	26	8	26	12	0.0	0	0	0.0	0

O'DWYER, MATT — G — PACKERS

PERSONAL: Born September 1, 1972, in Lincolnshire, Ill. ... 6-5/305. ... Full name: Matthew Phillip O'Dwyer.
HIGH SCHOOL: Adlai E. Stevenson (Prairie View, Ill.).
COLLEGE: Northwestern.
TRANSACTIONS/CAREER NOTES: Selected by New York Jets in second round (33rd pick overall) of 1995 NFL draft. ... Signed by Jets (July 20, 1995). ... Granted unconditional free agency (February 12, 1999). ... Signed by Cincinnati Bengals (June 19, 1999). ... Suspended two games by NFL for involvement in bar fight (March 14, 2000). ... On injured reserve with broken ankle (November 20, 2000-remainder of season). ... Granted unconditional free agency (March 2, 2001). ... Re-signed by Bengals (March 2, 2001). ... On injured reserve with foot injury (December 9, 2003-remainder of season). ... Granted unconditional free agency (March 3, 2004). ... Signed by Tampa Bay Buccaneers (March 9, 2004). ... On physically unable to perform list with pectoral injury (August 31-November 30, 2004). ... Granted unconditional free agency (March 2, 2005). ... Signed by Green Bay Packers (March 24, 2005).
PLAYING EXPERIENCE: New York Jets NFL, 1995-1998; Cincinnati NFL, 1999-2003; Tampa Bay NFL, 2004. ... Games/Games started: 1995 (12/2), 1996 (16/16), 1997 (16/16), 1998 (16/16), 1999 (16/16), 2000 (10/10), 2001 (12/12), 2002 (16/16), 2003 (4/1), 2004 (4/0). Total: 122/105.
CHAMPIONSHIP GAME EXPERIENCE: Played in AFC championship game (1998 season).

OFFORD, WILLIE S

PERSONAL: Born December 22, 1978, in Palatka, Fla. ... 6-1/216.
HIGH SCHOOL: Palatka (Fla.).
COLLEGE: South Carolina.
TRANSACTIONS/CAREER NOTES: Selected by Minnesota Vikings in third round (70th pick overall) of 2002 NFL draft. ... Signed by Vikings (July 25, 2002). ... Granted free agency (March 2, 2005).

Year Team	G	GS	TOTALS Tk.	Ast.	Sks.	INTERCEPTIONS No.	Yds.	Avg.	TD
2002—Minnesota NFL	12	6	23	4	0.0	1	6	6.0	0
2003—Minnesota NFL	16	0	4	0	0.0	0	0	0.0	0
2004—Minnesota NFL	16	0	12	6	0.0	0	0	0.0	0
Pro totals (3 years)	44	6	39	10	0.0	1	6	6.0	0

OGBOGU, ERIC DE COWBOYS

PERSONAL: Born July 18, 1975, in Irvington, N.Y. ... 6-4/269. ... Name pronounced: a-BAH-goo.
HIGH SCHOOL: Archbishop Stepinac (White Plains, N.Y.).
COLLEGE: Maryland.
TRANSACTIONS/CAREER NOTES: Selected by New York Jets in sixth round (163rd pick overall) of 1998 NFL draft. ... Signed by Jets (July 2, 1998). ... On injured reserve with shoulder injury (August 7, 2000-entire season). ... Granted unconditional free agency (March 1, 2002). ... Signed by Cincinnati Bengals (April 29, 2002). ... Released by Bengals (May 27, 2003). ... Signed by Dallas Cowboys (August 11, 2003).
CHAMPIONSHIP GAME EXPERIENCE: Played in AFC championship game (1998 season).

Year Team	G	GS	TOTALS Tk.	Ast.	Sks.
1998—New York Jets NFL	12	0	5	3	0.0
1999—New York Jets NFL	14	0	9	4	1.0
2000—New York Jets NFL		Did not play.			
2001—New York Jets NFL	15	0	15	3	0.0
2002—Cincinnati NFL	12	0	1	2	0.0
2003—Dallas NFL	16	3	24	9	3.5
2004—Dallas NFL	15	1	10	4	4.5
Pro totals (6 years)	84	4	64	25	9.0

OGDEN, JONATHAN T RAVENS

PERSONAL: Born July 31, 1974, in Washington, DC. ... 6-9/345. ... Full name: Jonathan Phillip Ogden. ... Brother of Marques Ogden, offensive tackle with Jacksonville Jaguars (2003).
HIGH SCHOOL: St. Alban's (Washington, D.C.).
COLLEGE: UCLA.
TRANSACTIONS/CAREER NOTES: Selected by Baltimore Ravens in first round (fourth pick overall) of 1996 NFL draft. ... Signed by Ravens (July 15, 1996).
PLAYING EXPERIENCE: Baltimore NFL, 1996-2004. ... Games/Games started: 1996 (16/16), 1997 (16/16), 1998 (13/13), 1999 (16/16), 2000 (15/15), 2001 (16/16), 2002 (16/16), 2003 (16/16), 2004 (12/12). Total: 136/136.
CHAMPIONSHIP GAME EXPERIENCE: Played in AFC championship game (2000 season). ... Member of Super Bowl championship team (2000 season).
HONORS: Outland Trophy winner (1995). ... Named offensive lineman on THE SPORTING NEWS college All-America first team (1995). ... Named offensive tackle on the THE SPORTING NEWS NFL All-Pro team (1997 and 2000-2003). ... Played in Pro Bowl (1997-2004 seasons).

OGUNLEYE, ADEWALE DE BEARS

PERSONAL: Born August 9, 1977, in Brooklyn, N.Y. ... 6-4/260.
HIGH SCHOOL: Tottenville (Staten Island, N.Y.).
COLLEGE: Indiana.
TRANSACTIONS/CAREER NOTES: Signed as non-drafted free agent by Miami Dolphins (April 25, 2000). ... On non-football injury list with knee injury (August 22, 2000-entire season). ... Traded by Dolphins to Chicago Bears for WR Marty Booker and third-round (LB Channing Crowder) pick in 2005 draft (August 23, 2004). ... On injured reserve with ankle injury (December 28, 2004-remainder of season).
HONORS: Played in Pro Bowl (2003 season).

Year Team	G	GS	TOTALS Tk.	Ast.	Sks.
2001—Miami NFL	7	0	1	2	0.5
2002—Miami NFL	16	16	33	12	9.5
2003—Miami NFL	16	16	43	21	§15.0
2004—Chicago NFL	12	12	28	9	5.0
Pro totals (4 years)	51	44	105	44	30.0

OHALETE, IFEANYI CB/S CARDINALS

PERSONAL: Born May 22, 1979, in Springfield, Ill. ... 6-2/222.
HIGH SCHOOL: Los Alamitos (Calif.).
COLLEGE: Southern California.

TRANSACTIONS/CAREER NOTES: Signed as non-drafted free agent by Washington Redskins (April 25, 2001). ... On injured reserve with knee and ankle injuries (December 23, 2003-remainder of season). ... Granted free agency (March 3, 2004). ... Re-signed by Redskins (May 12, 2004). ... Claimed on waivers by Arizona Cardinals (August 18, 2004).

			TOTALS			INTERCEPTIONS			
Year Team	G	GS	Tk.	Ast.	Sks.	No.	Yds.	Avg.	TD
2001—Washington NFL	16	0	0	0	0.0	1	12	12.0	0
2002—Washington NFL	16	10	44	15	1.0	3	109	36.3	1
2003—Washington NFL	15	14	73	22	0.0	3	60	20.0	0
2004—Arizona NFL	16	13	51	13	0.0	0	0	0.0	0
Pro totals (4 years)	63	37	168	50	1.0	7	181	25.9	1

O'HARA, SHAUN G/C GIANTS

PERSONAL: Born June 23, 1977, in Chicago, Ill. ... 6-3/306.
HIGH SCHOOL: Hillsborough (N.J.).
COLLEGE: Rutgers.
TRANSACTIONS/CAREER NOTES: Signed as non-drafted free agent by Cleveland Browns (April 17, 2000). ... Granted free agency (February 28, 2003). ... Re-signed by Browns (June 6, 2003). ... Granted unconditional free agency (March 3, 2004). ... Signed by New York Giants (March 6, 2004).
PLAYING EXPERIENCE: Cleveland NFL, 2000-2003; New York Giants NFL, 2004. ... Games/Games started: 2000 (9/4), 2001 (16/4), 2002 (16/16), 2003 (14/14), 2004 (12/12). Total: 67/50.

OKEAFOR, CHIKE DE CARDINALS

PERSONAL: Born March 27, 1976, in Grand Rapids, Mich. ... 6-4/265. ... Full name: Chikeze Russell Okeafor. ... Name pronounced: chee-KAY oh-KEY-fer.
HIGH SCHOOL: West Lafayette (Ind.).
COLLEGE: Purdue.
TRANSACTIONS/CAREER NOTES: Selected by San Francisco 49ers in third round (89th pick overall) of 1999 NFL draft. ... Signed by 49ers (July 27, 1999). ... On non-football injury list with back injury (July 27-September 5, 1999). ... Granted free agency (March 1, 2002). ... Re-signed by 49ers (April 20, 2002). ... Granted unconditional free agency (February 28, 2003). ... Signed by Seattle Seahawks (April 4, 2003). ... Granted unconditional free agency (March 2, 2005). ... Signed by Arizona Cardinals (March 7, 2005).

			TOTALS			INTERCEPTIONS			
Year Team	G	GS	Tk.	Ast.	Sks.	No.	Yds.	Avg.	TD
1999—San Francisco NFL	12	0	10	0	1.0	0	0	0.0	0
2000—San Francisco NFL	15	0	22	9	2.0	0	0	0.0	0
2001—San Francisco NFL	14	3	23	10	2.5	0	0	0.0	0
2002—San Francisco NFL	16	16	32	11	6.0	0	0	0.0	0
2003—Seattle NFL	16	16	33	14	8.0	1	18	18.0	0
2004—Seattle NFL	16	16	41	12	8.5	0	0	0.0	0
Pro totals (6 years)	89	51	161	56	28.0	1	18	18.0	0

OKOBI, CHUKKY C/G STEELERS

PERSONAL: Born October 18, 1978, in Pittsburgh, Pa. ... 6-1/318. ... Full name: Chukwunweze Sonume Okobi.
HIGH SCHOOL: Trinity Prawling (N.Y.).
COLLEGE: Purdue.
TRANSACTIONS/CAREER NOTES: Selected by Pittsburgh Steelers in fifth round (146th pick overall) of 2001 NFL draft. ... Signed by Steelers (May 17, 2001). ... On physically unable to perform list with leg injury (July 20-August 14, 2001). ... Granted free agency (March 3, 2004). ... Re-signed by Steelers (March 16, 2004).
PLAYING EXPERIENCE: Pittsburgh NFL, 2001-2004. ... Games/Games started: 2001 (1/0), 2002 (13/5), 2003 (16/0), 2004 (16/0). Total: 46/5.
CHAMPIONSHIP GAME EXPERIENCE: Member of Steelers for AFC championship game (2001 season); inactive. ... Played in AFC championship game (2004 season).

OLIVEA, SHANE T CHARGERS

PERSONAL: Born October 7, 1981, in Cedarhurst, N.Y. ... 6-3/312.
HIGH SCHOOL: Lawrence (Cedarhurst, N.Y.).
COLLEGE: Ohio State.
TRANSACTIONS/CAREER NOTES: Selected by San Diego Chargers in seventh round (209th pick overall) of 2004 NFL draft. ... Signed by Chargers (June 25, 2004).
PLAYING EXPERIENCE: San Diego NFL, 2004. ... Games/Games started: 2004 (16/16). Total: 16/16.

OLSHANSKY, IGOR DT CHARGERS

PERSONAL: Born May 3, 1982, in Dnepropetrovsk, Ukraine. ... 6-6/309.
HIGH SCHOOL: St. Ignatius (San Francisco, Calif.).
COLLEGE: Oregon.
TRANSACTIONS/CAREER NOTES: Selected after junior season by San Diego Chargers in second round (35th pick overall) of 2004 NFL draft. ... Signed by Chargers (August 2, 2004).

			TOTALS			INTERCEPTIONS			
Year Team	G	GS	Tk.	Ast.	Sks.	No.	Yds.	Avg.	TD
2004—San Diego NFL	16	16	24	15	1.0	0	0	0.0	0

OLSON, BENJI — G — TITANS

PERSONAL: Born June 5, 1975, in Bremerton, Wash. ... 6-4/320. ... Full name: Benji Dempsey Olson.
HIGH SCHOOL: South Kitsap (Port Orchard, Wash.).
COLLEGE: Washington.
TRANSACTIONS/CAREER NOTES: Selected after junior season by Tennessee Oilers in fifth round (139th pick overall) of 1998 NFL draft. ... Signed by Oilers (June 29, 1998). ... Oilers franchise renamed Tennessee Titans for 1999 season (December 26, 1998). ... Granted free agency (March 2, 2001). ... Re-signed by Titans (July 25, 2001).
PLAYING EXPERIENCE: Tennessee NFL, 1998-2004. ... Games/Games started: 1998 (13/1), 1999 (16/16), 2000 (16/16), 2001 (16/16), 2002 (16/16), 2003 (16/16), 2004 (15/15). Total: 108/96.
CHAMPIONSHIP GAME EXPERIENCE: Played in AFC championship game (1999 and 2002 seasons). ... Played in Super Bowl 34 (1999 season).
HONORS: Named guard on THE SPORTING NEWS college All-America first team (1996).

O'NEAL, DELTHA — CB — BENGALS

PERSONAL: Born January 30, 1977, in Palo Alto, Calif. ... 5-11/191. ... Full name: Deltha Lee O'Neal III.
HIGH SCHOOL: West (Milpitas, Calif.).
COLLEGE: California.
TRANSACTIONS/CAREER NOTES: Selected by Denver Broncos in first round (15th pick overall) of 2000 NFL draft. ... Signed by Broncos (July 21, 2000). ... Traded by Broncos with first-round pick (RB Chris Perry) and fourth-round pick (DE Robert Geathers) in 2004 draft to Cincinnati Bengals for first-round pick (LB D.J. Williams) in 2004 draft (April 9, 2004).
HONORS: Named kick returner on THE SPORTING NEWS college All-America first team (1999). ... Named cornerback on THE SPORTING NEWS college All-America second team (1999). ... Played in Pro Bowl (2001 season).

			TOTALS			INTERCEPTIONS				PUNT RETURNS				KICKOFF RETURNS				TOTALS			
Year Team	G	GS	Tk.	Ast.	Sks.	No.	Yds.	Avg.	TD	No.	Yds.	Avg.	TD	No.	Yds.	Avg.	TD	TD	2pt.	Pts.	Fum.
2000—Den. NFL	16	0	3	0	0.0	0	0	0.0	0	34	354	10.4	0	46	1102	24.0	▲1	1	0	6	6
2001—Den. NFL	16	16	63	7	0.0	9	115	12.8	0	31	405	13.1	1	0	0	0.0	0	1	0	6	2
2002—Den. NFL	16	14	59	10	0.0	5	70	14.0	▲2	30	251	8.4	0	1	15	15.0	0	2	0	12	2
2003—Den. NFL	13	6	19	3	0.0	1	6	6.0	0	33	315	9.5	1	8	128	16.0	0	1	0	6	2
2004—Cin. NFL	12	10	35	5	1.0	4	60	15.0	1	7	33	4.7	0	1	15	15.0	0	1	0	6	0
Pro totals (5 years)	73	46	179	25	1.0	19	251	13.2	3	135	1358	10.1	0	56	1260	22.5	1	6	0	36	12

O'NEIL, KEITH — LB — COWBOYS

PERSONAL: Born August 26, 1980, in Rochester, Mich. ... 6-0/235.
HIGH SCHOOL: Sweet Home (Amherst, N.Y.).
COLLEGE: Northern Arizona.
TRANSACTIONS/CAREER NOTES: Signed as non-drafted free agent by Dallas Cowboys (May 1, 2003).

			TOTALS			INTERCEPTIONS			
Year Team	G	GS	Tk.	Ast.	Sks.	No.	Yds.	Avg.	TD
2003—Dallas NFL	15	0	0	0	0.0	0	0	0.0	0
2004—Dallas NFL	16	0	0	0	0.0	0	0	0.0	0
Pro totals (2 years)	31	0	0	0	0.0	0	0	0.0	0

ORR, RAHEEM — DE — GIANTS

PERSONAL: Born November 8, 1982, in Elizabeth, N.J. ... 6-4/260.
HIGH SCHOOL: Elizabeth (N.J.).
COLLEGE: Rutgers.
TRANSACTIONS/CAREER NOTES: Selected by Houston Texans in seventh round (210th pick overall) of 2004 NFL draft. ... Signed by Texans (June 8, 2004). ... Released by Texans (August 30, 2004). ... Signed by New York Giants (December 20, 2004).

			TOTALS		
Year Team	G	GS	Tk.	Ast.	Sks.
2004—New York Giants NFL	2	0	0	0	0.0

ORR, SHANTEE — LB — TEXANS

PERSONAL: Born May 28, 1981, in Detroit, Mich. ... 6-0/250. ... Full name: Shantee DeShJuan Orr.
HIGH SCHOOL: Denby (Detroit, Mich.).
COLLEGE: Michigan.
TRANSACTIONS/CAREER NOTES: Signed as non-drafted free agent by Green Bay Packers (May 2, 2003). ... Claimed on waivers by Houston Texans (July 30, 2003). ... Waived by Texans (August 31, 2003). ... Re-signed by Texans to practice squad (September 1, 2003). ... Activated (November 16, 2003). ... On injured reserve with fibula injury (December 22, 2003-remainder of season). ... Re-signed by Texans (March 26, 2004). ... Released by Texans (September 5, 2004). ... Re-signed by Texans to practice squad (September 6, 2004). ... Activated (December 6, 2004).

			TOTALS			INTERCEPTIONS			
Year Team	G	GS	Tk.	Ast.	Sks.	No.	Yds.	Avg.	TD
2003—Houston NFL	6	0	3	3	2.0	0	0	0.0	0
2004—Houston NFL	4	0	0	0	0.0	0	0	0.0	0
Pro totals (2 years)	10	0	3	3	2.0	0	0	0.0	0

O

OSGOOD, KASSIM — WR — CHARGERS

PERSONAL: Born May 20, 1980, in Boston, Mass. ... 6-5/209.
HIGH SCHOOL: North Salinas.
COLLEGE: San Diego State.
TRANSACTIONS/CAREER NOTES: Signed as non-drafted free agent by San Diego Chargers (May 2, 2003).
SINGLE GAME HIGHS (regular season): Receptions—4 (December 21, 2003, vs. Pittsburgh); yards—102 (December 21, 2003, vs. Pittsburgh); and touchdown receptions—1 (December 12, 2004, vs. Tampa Bay).
STATISTICAL PLATEAUS: 100-yard receiving games: 2003 (1). Total: 1.

				RECEIVING				TOTALS		
Year Team	G	GS	No.	Yds.	Avg.	TD	TD	2pt.	Pts.	Fum.
2003—San Diego NFL	16	2	13	278	21.4	2	2	0	12	0
2004—San Diego NFL	16	7	15	308	20.5	2	2	0	12	0
Pro totals (2 years)	32	9	28	586	20.9	4	4	0	24	0

O'SULLIVAN, J.T. — QB — PACKERS

PERSONAL: Born August 25, 1979, in Burbank, Calif. ... 6-2/220. ... Full name: John Thomas O'Sullivan.
HIGH SCHOOL: Jesuit (Folsom, Calif.).
COLLEGE: California-Davis.
TRANSACTIONS/CAREER NOTES: Selected by New Orleans Saints in sixth round (186th pick overall) of 2002 NFL draft. ... Signed by Saints (July 25, 2002). ... Assigned by Saints to Frankfurt Galaxy in 2004 NFL Europe enhancement allocation program (February 9, 2004). ... Traded by Saints with second-round pick (S Nick Collins) in 2005 draft to Green Bay Packers for CB Mike McKenzie and 2006 conditional draft pick (October 4, 2004). ... Granted free agency (March 2, 2005). ... Re-signed by Packers (April 22, 2005).

			PASSING								RUSHING				TOTALS	
Year Team	G	GS	Att.	Cmp.	Pct.	Yds.	TD	Int.	Avg.	Skd.	Rat.	Att.	Yds.	Avg.	TD	TD	2pt.	Pts.
2004—Green Bay NFL	1	0	0	0	0.0	0	0	0	0.00	0	0.0	2	-2	-1.0	0	0	0	0

OWENS, JOHN — TE — BEARS

PERSONAL: Born January 10, 1980, in Washington, DC. ... 6-3/270. ... Full name: John Wesley Owens.
HIGH SCHOOL: DeMatha (Hyattsville, Md.).
COLLEGE: Notre Dame.
TRANSACTIONS/CAREER NOTES: Selected by Detroit Lions in fifth round (138th pick overall) of 2002 NFL draft. ... Signed by Lions (July 22, 2002). ... Claimed on waivers by Chicago Bears (October 25, 2004). ... Granted free agency (March 2, 2005). ... Re-signed by Bears (April 12, 2005).
SINGLE GAME HIGHS (regular season): Receptions—2 (October 20, 2002, vs. Chicago); yards—19 (October 20, 2002, vs. Chicago); and touchdown receptions—0.

				RECEIVING				TOTALS		
Year Team	G	GS	No.	Yds.	Avg.	TD	TD	2pt.	Pts.	Fum.
2002—Detroit NFL	15	8	5	49	9.8	0	0	0	0	0
2003—Detroit NFL	7	1	0	0	0.0	0	0	0	0	0
2004—Chicago NFL	2	0	0	0	0.0	0	0	0	0	0
Pro totals (3 years)	24	9	5	49	9.8	0	0	0	0	0

OWENS, RICHARD — TE

PERSONAL: Born November 4, 1980, in Gainesville, Fla. ... 6-4/273.
HIGH SCHOOL: Middleburg (Fla.).
COLLEGE: Louisville.
TRANSACTIONS/CAREER NOTES: Signed as non-drafted free agent by Minnesota Vikings (May 3, 2004).
SINGLE GAME HIGHS (regular season): Receptions—3 (October 10, 2004, vs. Houston); yards—36 (September 20, 2004, vs. Philadelphia); and touchdown receptions—0.

				RECEIVING				TOTALS		
Year Team	G	GS	No.	Yds.	Avg.	TD	TD	2pt.	Pts.	Fum.
2004—Minnesota NFL	7	2	8	69	8.6	0	0	0	0	0

OWENS, TERRELL — WR — EAGLES

PERSONAL: Born December 7, 1973, in Alexander City, Ala. ... 6-3/226. ... Full name: Terrell Eldorado Owens. ... Name pronounced: TARE-el.
HIGH SCHOOL: Benjamin Russell (Alexander City, Ala.).
COLLEGE: Chattanooga.
TRANSACTIONS/CAREER NOTES: Selected by San Francisco 49ers in third round (89th pick overall) of 1996 NFL draft. ... Signed by 49ers (July 18, 1996). ... On physically unable to perform list with foot injury (July 17-August 11, 1997). ... Designated by 49ers as franchise player (February 12, 1999). ... Re-signed by 49ers (June 4, 1999). ... On injured reserve with fractured collarbone (December 24, 2003-remainder of season). ... Traded by 49ers to Baltimore Ravens for a 2004 second-round draft choice (March 4, 2004). Ravens later reacquired the pick. ... Traded by Ravens to Philadelphia Eagles as part of a three-way trade involving the San Francisco 49ers (March 16, 2004). The Ravens received a fifth-round draft choice from the Eagles as well as the 2004 second-round pick they sent to San Francisco in the March 4 trade. The 49ers received DE Brandon Whiting from Philadelphia.
CHAMPIONSHIP GAME EXPERIENCE: Played in NFC championship game (1997 season). ... Member of Eagles for NFC championship game (2004 season); inactive. ... Played in Super Bowl 39 (2004 season).
HONORS: Played in Pro Bowl (2000-2003 seasons). ... Named wide receiver on THE SPORTING NEWS NFL All-Pro team (2001, 2002 and 2004). ... Named to play in Pro Bowl (2004 season); replaced by Torry Holt due to injury.

RECORDS: Holds NFL record for most receptions in a game—20 (December 17, 2000, vs. Chicago).
POST SEASON RECORDS: Holds NFL single-game and career record for two-point conversions—2 (January 5, 2003 v. New York Giants).
SINGLE GAME HIGHS (regular season): Receptions—20 (December 17, 2000, vs. Chicago); yards—283 (December 17, 2000, vs. Chicago); and touchdown receptions—3 (November 15, 2004, vs. Dallas).
STATISTICAL PLATEAUS: 100-yard receiving games: 1996 (1), 1998 (2), 1999 (2), 2000 (5), 2001 (6), 2002 (5), 2003 (4), 2004 (7). Total: 32.

Year Team	G	GS	RUSHING				RECEIVING				TOTALS			
			Att.	Yds.	Avg.	TD	No.	Yds.	Avg.	TD	TD	2pt.	Pts.	Fum.
1996—San Francisco NFL	16	10	0	0	0.0	0	35	520	14.9	4	4	0	24	1
1997—San Francisco NFL	16	15	0	0	0.0	0	60	936	15.6	8	8	0	48	1
1998—San Francisco NFL	16	10	4	53	13.3	1	67	1097	16.4	14	15	1	92	1
1999—San Francisco NFL	14	14	0	0	0.0	0	60	754	12.6	4	4	0	24	1
2000—San Francisco NFL	14	13	3	11	3.7	0	97	1451	15.0	13	13	1	80	3
2001—San Francisco NFL	16	16	4	21	5.3	0	93	1412	15.2	*16	16	0	96	0
2002—San Francisco NFL	14	14	7	79	11.3	1	100	1300	13.0	*13	14	0	84	0
2003—San Francisco NFL	15	15	3	-2	-0.7	0	80	1102	13.8	9	9	0	54	0
2004—Philadelphia NFL	14	14	3	-5	-1.7	0	77	1200	15.6	14	14	0	84	2
Pro totals (9 years)	135	121	24	157	6.5	2	669	9772	14.6	95	97	2	586	9

PACE, CALVIN — DE — CARDINALS

PERSONAL: Born October 28, 1980, in Detroit, Mich. ... 6-4/262.
HIGH SCHOOL: Lithia Springs (Douglasville, Ga.).
COLLEGE: Wake Forest.
TRANSACTIONS/CAREER NOTES: Selected by Arizona Cardinals in first round (18th pick overall) of 2003 NFL draft. ... Signed by Cardinals (July 27, 2003).

Year Team	G	GS	TOTALS		
			Tk.	Ast.	Sks.
2003—Arizona NFL	16	16	25	7	1.0
2004—Arizona NFL	14	0	6	4	4.5
Pro totals (2 years)	30	16	31	11	5.5

PACE, ORLANDO — T — RAMS

PERSONAL: Born November 4, 1975, in Sandusky, Ohio. ... 6-7/325. ... Full name: Orlando Lamar Pace.
HIGH SCHOOL: Sandusky (Ohio).
COLLEGE: Ohio State.
TRANSACTIONS/CAREER NOTES: Selected after junior season by St. Louis Rams in first round (first pick overall) of 1997 NFL draft. ... Signed by Rams (August 16, 1997). ... Designated by Rams as franchise player (February 20, 2003). ... Re-signed by Rams (August 26, 2003). ... Designated by Rams as franchise player (February 24, 2004). ... Re-signed by Rams (September 6, 2004). ... Designated by Rams as franchise player (February 22, 2005). ... Re-signed by Rams (March 16, 2005).
PLAYING EXPERIENCE: St. Louis NFL, 1997-2004. ... Games/Games started: 1997 (13/9), 1998 (16/16), 1999 (16/16), 2000 (16/16), 2001 (16/16), 2002 (10/10), 2003 (16/16), 2004 (16/16). Total: 119/115.
CHAMPIONSHIP GAME EXPERIENCE: Played in NFC championship game (1999 and 2001 seasons). ... Member of Super Bowl championship team (1999 season). ... Played in Super Bowl 36 (2001 season).
HONORS: Lombardi Award winner (1995 and 1996). ... Named offensive tackle on THE SPORTING NEWS college All-America first team (1995 and 1996). ... Outland Trophy winner (1996). ... Named offensive tackle on THE SPORTING NEWS NFL All-Pro team (1999-2001 and 2003-2004). ... Played in Pro Bowl (1999, 2000, 2003 and 2004 seasons). ... Named to play in Pro Bowl (2001 season); replaced by Tra Thomas due to injury. ... Named to play in Pro Bowl (2002 season); replaced by Jon Runyan due to injury.

PAGEL, DEREK — S — JETS

PERSONAL: Born October 24, 1979, in Plainfield, Iowa. ... 6-1/208.
HIGH SCHOOL: Nashua-Plainfield (Plainfield, Iowa).
COLLEGE: Iowa.
TRANSACTIONS/CAREER NOTES: Selected by New York Jets in fifth round (140th pick overall) of 2003 NFL draft. ... Signed by Jets (July 14, 2003). ... On injured reserve with foot injury (November 9, 2004-remainder of season).

Year Team	G	GS	TOTALS			INTERCEPTIONS			
			Tk.	Ast.	Sks.	No.	Yds.	Avg.	TD
2003—New York Jets NFL	14	0	0	1	0.0	0	0	0.0	0
2004—New York Jets NFL	5	0	1	0	0.0	0	0	0.0	0
Pro totals (2 years)	19	0	1	1	0.0	0	0	0.0	0

PALEPOI, ANTON — DE — BRONCOS

PERSONAL: Born January 19, 1978, in American Samoa. ... 6-3/283. ... Full name: Anton Charles Palepoi.
HIGH SCHOOL: Hunter (Salt Lake City, Utah).
JUNIOR COLLEGE: Dixie College (Utah).
COLLEGE: Nevada-Las Vegas.
TRANSACTIONS/CAREER NOTES: Selected by Seattle Seahawks in second round (60th pick overall) of 2002 NFL draft. ... Signed by Seahawks (July 25, 2002). ... Released by Seahawks (September 14, 2004). ... Signed by Denver Broncos (September 22, 2004). ... Granted free agency (March 2, 2005). ... Re-signed by Broncos (April 21, 2005).

P

Year Team	G	GS	TOTALS		
			Tk.	Ast.	Sks.
2002—Seattle NFL	13	1	10	7	1.0
2003—Seattle NFL	7	0	1	2	0.0
2004—Seattle NFL	1	0	0	0	0.0
—Denver NFL	11	0	15	4	3.0
Pro totals (3 years)	32	1	26	13	4.0

PALMER, CARSON QB BENGALS

PERSONAL: Born December 27, 1979, in Fresno, Calif. ... 6-5/230.
HIGH SCHOOL: Santa Margarita (Rancho Santa Margarita, Calif.).
COLLEGE: Southern California.
TRANSACTIONS/CAREER NOTES: Selected by Cincinnati Bengals in first round (first pick overall) of 2003 NFL draft. ... Signed by Bengals (April 25, 2003).
HONORS: Heisman Trophy winner (2002). ... Named College Football Player of the Year by THE SPORTING NEWS (2002). ... Named quarterback on THE SPORTING NEWS college All-America first team (2002).
SINGLE GAME HIGHS (regular season): Attempts—52 (September 26, 2004, vs. Baltimore); completions—29 (December 5, 2004, vs. Baltimore); yards—382 (December 5, 2004, vs. Baltimore); and touchdown passes—4 (November 28, 2004, vs. Cleveland).
STATISTICAL PLATEAUS: 300-yard passing games: 2004 (2). Total: 2.
MISCELLANEOUS: Regular-season record as starting NFL quarterback: 6-7 (.462).

Year Team	G	GS	PASSING									RUSHING				TOTALS		
			Att.	Cmp.	Pct.	Yds.	TD	Int.	Avg.	Skd.	Rat.	Att.	Yds.	Avg.	TD	TD	2pt.	Pts.
2004—Cincinnati NFL	13	13	432	263	60.9	2897	18	18	6.71	25	77.3	18	47	2.6	1	1	0	6

PARKER, ERIC WR CHARGERS

PERSONAL: Born April 14, 1979, in Shorewood, Ill. ... 6-0/180. ... Full name: Eric Samuel Parker.
HIGH SCHOOL: Joliet Township (Shorewood, Ill.).
COLLEGE: Tennessee.
TRANSACTIONS/CAREER NOTES: Signed as non-drafted free agent by Houston Texans (April 25, 2002). ... Released by Texans (July 13, 2002). ... Signed by San Diego Chargers (July 23, 2002). ... Released by Chargers (September 1, 2002). ... Re-signed by Chargers to practice squad (September 3, 2002). ... Activated (September 26, 2002). ... Released by Chargers (October 12, 2002). ... Re-signed by Chargers (October 15, 2002). ... On injured reserve with shoulder injury (November 5, 2003-remainder of season). ... Re-signed by Chargers (May 19, 2004).
SINGLE GAME HIGHS (regular season): Receptions—7 (December 26, 2004, vs. Indianapolis); yards—118 (December 12, 2004, vs. Tampa Bay); and touchdown receptions—1 (December 26, 2004, vs. Indianapolis).
STATISTICAL PLATEAUS: 100-yard receiving games: 2004 (2). Total: 2.

Year Team	G	GS	RUSHING				RECEIVING				PUNT RETURNS				TOTALS			
			Att.	Yds.	Avg.	TD	No.	Yds.	Avg.	TD	No.	Yds.	Avg.	TD	TD	2pt.	Pts.	Fum.
2002—San Diego NFL	9	2	0	0	0.0	0	17	268	15.8	1	0	0	0.0	0	1	0	6	0
2003—San Diego NFL	8	4	3	21	7.0	0	18	244	13.6	3	23	207	9.0	0	3	0	18	1
2004—San Diego NFL	15	13	4	53	13.3	0	47	690	14.7	4	27	237	8.8	0	4	0	24	5
Pro totals (3 years)	32	19	7	74	10.6	0	82	1202	14.7	8	50	444	8.9	0	8	0	48	6

PARKER, SAMIE WR CHIEFS

PERSONAL: Born March 25, 1981, in Long Beach, Calif. ... 5-11/190. ... Full name: Samie Jabar Parker.
HIGH SCHOOL: Polytechnic (Long Beach, Calif.).
COLLEGE: Oregon.
TRANSACTIONS/CAREER NOTES: Selected by Kansas City Chiefs in fourth round (105th pick overall) of 2004 NFL draft. ... Signed by Chiefs (July 23, 2004).
SINGLE GAME HIGHS (regular season): Receptions—3 (January 2, 2005, vs. San Diego); yards—84 (December 19, 2004, vs. Denver); and touchdown receptions—1 (December 19, 2004, vs. Denver).

Year Team	G	GS	RECEIVING				TOTALS			
			No.	Yds.	Avg.	TD	TD	2pt.	Pts.	Fum.
2004—Kansas City NFL	4	0	9	137	15.2	1	1	0	6	0

PARKER, VAUGHN T

PERSONAL: Born June 5, 1971, in Buffalo, N.Y. ... 6-3/300. ... Full name: Vaughn Antoine Parker.
HIGH SCHOOL: Saint Joseph's Collegiate Institute (Buffalo).
COLLEGE: UCLA.
TRANSACTIONS/CAREER NOTES: Selected by San Diego Chargers in second round (63rd pick overall) of 1994 NFL draft. ... Signed by Chargers (July 12, 1994). ... Granted free agency (February 14, 1997). ... Re-signed by Chargers (June 6, 1997). ... On injured reserve with leg injury (December 12, 1998-remainder of season). ... Granted unconditional free agency (February 11, 2000). ... Re-signed by Chargers (February 11, 2000). ... On injured reserve with knee injury (September 24, 2003-remainder of season). ... Released by Chargers (March 2, 2004). ... Signed by Washington Redskins (October 25, 2004). ... Released by Redskins (February 22, 2005).
PLAYING EXPERIENCE: San Diego NFL, 1994-2003; Washington NFL, 2004. ... Games/Games started: 1994 (6/0), 1995 (15/7), 1996 (16/16), 1997 (16/16), 1998 (6/6), 1999 (15/15), 2000 (16/16), 2001 (16/16), 2002 (12/12), 2003 (3/3), 2004 (1/0). Total: 122/107.
CHAMPIONSHIP GAME EXPERIENCE: Played in AFC championship game (1994 season). ... Played in Super Bowl 29 (1994 season).

P

PARKER, WILLIE — RB — STEELERS

PERSONAL: Born November 11, 1980, in Clinton, N.C. ... 5-10/209. ... Full name: Willie Everette Parker.
HIGH SCHOOL: Clinton (N.C.).
COLLEGE: North Carolina.
TRANSACTIONS/CAREER NOTES: Signed as non-drafted free agent by Pittsburgh Steelers (April 26, 2004).
CHAMPIONSHIP GAME EXPERIENCE: Member of Steelers for AFC championship game (2004 season); inactive.
SINGLE GAME HIGHS (regular season): Attempts—19 (January 2, 2005, vs. Buffalo); yards—102 (January 2, 2005, vs. Buffalo); and rushing touchdowns—0.
STATISTICAL PLATEAUS: 100-yard rushing games: 2004 (1). Total: 1.

Year Team	G	GS	RUSHING Att.	Yds.	Avg.	TD	RECEIVING No.	Yds.	Avg.	TD	TOTALS TD	2pt.	Pts.	Fum.
2004—Pittsburgh NFL	8	0	32	186	5.8	0	3	16	5.3	0	0	0	0	0

PARRELLA, JOHN — DT — RAIDERS

PERSONAL: Born November 22, 1969, in Topeka, Kan. ... 6-3/300. ... Full name: John Lorin Parrella.
HIGH SCHOOL: Grand Island (Neb.) Central Catholic.
COLLEGE: Nebraska.
TRANSACTIONS/CAREER NOTES: Selected by Buffalo Bills in second round (55th pick overall) of 1993 NFL draft. ... Signed by Bills (July 12, 1993). ... Released by Bills (August 28, 1994). ... Signed by San Diego Chargers (September 12, 1994). ... Granted free agency (February 16, 1996). ... Re-signed by Chargers (June 14, 1996). ... Granted unconditional free agency (March 1, 2002). ... Signed by Oakland Raiders (March 7, 2002). ... On injured reserve with groin injury (December 10, 2003-remainder of season). ... Released by Raiders (March 2, 2005).
CHAMPIONSHIP GAME EXPERIENCE: Member of Bills for AFC championship game (1993 season); inactive. ... Member of Bills for Super Bowl 28 (1993 season); inactive. ... Played in AFC championship game (1994 and 2002 seasons). ... Played in Super Bowl 29 (1994 season). ... Played in Super Bowl 37 (2002 season).

Year Team	G	GS	TOTALS Tk.	Ast.	Sks.
1993—Buffalo NFL	10	0	1	1	1.0
1994—San Diego NFL	13	1	4	3	1.0
1995—San Diego NFL	16	1	9	4	2.0
1996—San Diego NFL	16	9	31	7	2.0
1997—San Diego NFL	16	16	32	7	3.5
1998—San Diego NFL	16	16	30	7	1.5
1999—San Diego NFL	16	16	45	9	5.5
2000—San Diego NFL	16	16	54	11	7.0
2001—San Diego NFL	16	16	61	6	2.0
2002—Oakland NFL	16	15	36	8	1.0
2003—Oakland NFL	5	5	14	4	0.0
2004—Oakland NFL	16	0	20	2	0.0
Pro totals (12 years)	172	111	337	69	26.5

PARRISH, TONY — S — 49ERS

PERSONAL: Born November 23, 1975, in Los Angeles, Calif. ... 6-0/210.
HIGH SCHOOL: Marina (Huntington Beach, Calif.).
COLLEGE: Washington.
TRANSACTIONS/CAREER NOTES: Selected by Chicago Bears in second round (35th pick overall) of 1998 NFL draft. ... Signed by Bears (July 20, 1998). ... Granted unconditional free agency (March 1, 2002). ... Signed by San Francisco 49ers (April 4, 2002).

Year Team	G	GS	TOTALS Tk.	Ast.	Sks.	INTERCEPTIONS No.	Yds.	Avg.	TD
1998—Chicago NFL	16	16	65	13	1.0	1	8	8.0	0
1999—Chicago NFL	16	16	87	13	0.0	1	41	41.0	0
2000—Chicago NFL	16	16	63	20	2.0	3	81	27.0	1
2001—Chicago NFL	16	16	56	11	1.0	3	36	12.0	0
2002—San Francisco NFL	16	16	63	9	0.0	7	204	29.1	0
2003—San Francisco NFL	16	16	51	15	0.5	†9	202	22.4	0
2004—San Francisco NFL	16	16	54	28	0.5	4	64	16.0	0
Pro totals (7 years)	112	112	439	109	5.0	28	636	22.7	1

PARRY, JOSH — FB — EAGLES

PERSONAL: Born April 5, 1978, in Sonora, Calif. ... 6-2/250. ... Full name: Joshua David Parry.
HIGH SCHOOL: Sonora (Calif.).
COLLEGE: San Jose State.
TRANSACTIONS/CAREER NOTES: Signed as non-drafted free agent by Philadelphia Eagles (April 23, 2001). ... Released by Eagles (August 24, 2001). ... Re-signed by Eagles (January 29, 2002). ... Assigned by Eagles to Frankfurt Galaxy in 2002 NFL Europe enhancement allocation program (February 7, 2002). ... Released by Eagles (August 31, 2003). ... Re-signed by Eagles (February 6, 2004). ... Released by Eagles (September 1, 2004). ... Re-signed by Eagles to practice squad (September 6, 2004). ... Released by Eagles from practice squad (September 22, 2004). ... Re-signed by Eagles (September 27, 2004).
CHAMPIONSHIP GAME EXPERIENCE: Played in NFC championship game (2004 season). ... Played in Super Bowl 39 (2004 season).

Year Team	G	GS	RECEIVING No.	Yds.	Avg.	TD	KICKOFF RETURNS No.	Yds.	Avg.	TD	TOTALS TD	2pt.	Pts.	Fum.
2004—Philadelphia NFL	13	4	9	75	8.3	0	2	24	12.0	0	0	0	0	0

P

PASHOS, TONY   T   RAVENS

PERSONAL: Born August 3, 1980, in Palos Heights, Ill. ... 6-6/337. ... Full name: Anthony George Pashos.
HIGH SCHOOL: Locksport Township (Ill.).
COLLEGE: Illinois.
TRANSACTIONS/CAREER NOTES: Selected by Baltimore Ravens in fifth round (173th pick overall) of 2003 NFL draft. ... Assigned by Ravens to Cologne Centurions in 2004 NFL Europe enhancement allocation program (February 9, 2004). ... Released by Ravens (September 6, 2004). ... Signed by Ravens to practice squad (September 7, 2004). ... Activated (September 11, 2004).
PLAYING EXPERIENCE: Baltimore NFL, 2004. ... Games/Games started: 2004 (6/0). Total: 6/0.

PASS, PATRICK   FB   PATRIOTS

PERSONAL: Born December 31, 1977, in Scottsdale, Ga. ... 5-10/217. ... Full name: Patrick D. Pass.
HIGH SCHOOL: Tucker (Ga.).
COLLEGE: Georgia.
TRANSACTIONS/CAREER NOTES: Selected by New England Patriots in seventh round (239th pick overall) of 2000 NFL draft. ... Signed by Patriots (June 29, 2000). ... Released by Patriots (August 27, 2000). ... Re-signed by Patriots to practice squad (August 29, 2000). ... Activated (September 16, 2000). ... Granted free agency (February 28, 2003). ... Re-signed by Patriots (May 22, 2003). ... Released by Patriots (August 31, 2003). ... Re-signed by Patriots (September 22, 2003). ... Granted unconditional free agency (March 3, 2004). ... Re-signed by Patriots (March 16, 2004). ... Granted unconditional free agency (March 2, 2005). ... Re-signed by Patriots (March 7, 2005).
CHAMPIONSHIP GAME EXPERIENCE: Played in AFC championship game (2001, 2003 and 2004 seasons). ... Member of Super Bowl championship team (2001, 2003 and 2004 seasons).
SINGLE GAME HIGHS (regular season): Attempts—12 (November 19, 2000, vs. Cincinnati); yards—39 (November 19, 2000, vs. Cincinnati); and rushing touchdowns—0.
MISCELLANEOUS: Selected by Florida Marlins organization in 44th round of free-agent draft (June 4, 1996).

			RUSHING				RECEIVING				KICKOFF RETURNS				TOTALS			
Year Team	G	GS	Att.	Yds.	Avg.	TD	No.	Yds.	Avg.	TD	No.	Yds.	Avg.	TD	TD	2pt.	Pts.	Fum.
2000—New England NFL........	5	2	18	58	3.2	0	4	17	4.3	0	0	0	0.0	0	0	0	0	0
2001—New England NFL........	16	0	1	7	7.0	0	6	66	11.0	1	10	222	22.2	0	1	0	6	0
2002—New England NFL........	15	0	4	27	6.8	0	0	0	0.0	0	7	123	17.6	0	0	0	0	0
2003—New England NFL........	13	1	6	27	4.5	0	4	21	5.3	0	11	254	23.1	0	0	0	0	0
2004—New England NFL........	14	4	39	141	3.6	0	28	215	7.7	0	6	115	19.2	0	0	0	0	1
Pro totals (5 years)	63	7	68	260	3.8	0	42	319	7.6	1	34	714	21.0	0	1	0	6	1

PATHON, JEROME   WR   SEAHAWKS

PERSONAL: Born December 16, 1975, in Cape Town, South Africa. ... 6-0/195. ... Name pronounced: PAY-thin.
HIGH SCHOOL: Carson Graham Secondary School (North Vancouver).
COLLEGE: Washington.
TRANSACTIONS/CAREER NOTES: Selected by Indianapolis Colts in second round (32nd pick overall) of 1998 NFL draft. ... Signed by Colts (July 26, 1998). ... On injured reserve with foot injury (November 19, 2001-remainder of season). ... Granted unconditional free agency (March 1, 2002). ... Signed by New Orleans Saints (April 15, 2002). ... Did not receive qualifying offer from Saints (March 2, 2005). ... Signed by Seattle Seahawks (April 21, 2005).
HONORS: Named wide receiver on THE SPORTING NEWS college All-America second team (1997).
SINGLE GAME HIGHS (regular season): Receptions—9 (September 23, 2001, vs. Buffalo); yards—168 (September 23, 2001, vs. Buffalo); and touchdown receptions—1 (September 19, 2004, vs. San Francisco).
STATISTICAL PLATEAUS: 100-yard receiving games: 2001 (1). Total: 1.

			RECEIVING				TOTALS			
Year Team	G	GS	No.	Yds.	Avg.	TD	TD	2pt.	Pts.	Fum.
1998—Indianapolis NFL	16	15	50	511	10.2	1	1	0	6	0
1999—Indianapolis NFL	12	2	14	163	11.6	0	0	0	0	0
2000—Indianapolis NFL	16	10	50	646	12.9	3	3	0	18	0
2001—Indianapolis NFL	4	3	24	330	13.8	2	2	0	12	0
2002—New Orleans NFL..	14	13	43	523	12.2	4	4	0	24	0
2003—New Orleans NFL..	16	12	44	578	13.1	4	4	0	24	1
2004—New Orleans NFL..	15	7	34	581	17.1	1	1	0	6	1
Pro totals (7 years)	93	62	259	3332	12.9	15	15	0	90	2

PATTEN, DAVID   WR   REDSKINS

PERSONAL: Born August 19, 1974, in Hopkins, S.C. ... 5-10/190.
HIGH SCHOOL: Lower Richland (Hopkins, S.C.).
COLLEGE: Western Carolina.
TRANSACTIONS/CAREER NOTES: Played for Albany Firebirds of Arena League (1996). ... Signed as non-drafted free agent by New York Giants (March 24, 1997). ... Released by Giants (August 24, 1997). ... Re-signed by Giants to practice squad (August 25, 1997). ... Activated (August 27, 1997). ... On injured reserve with knee injury (December 16, 1998-remainder of season). ... Granted free agency (February 11, 2000). ... Signed by Cleveland Browns (March 16, 2000). ... Granted unconditional free agency (March 2, 2001). ... Signed by New England Patriots (April 2, 2001). ... On injured reserve with knee injury (November 7, 2003-remainder of season). ... Granted unconditional free agency (March 2, 2005). ... Signed by Washington Redskins (March 3, 2005).
CHAMPIONSHIP GAME EXPERIENCE: Played in AFC championship game (2001 and 2004 seasons). ... Member of Super Bowl championship team (2001 and 2004 seasons).
SINGLE GAME HIGHS (regular season): Receptions—7 (September 29, 2002, vs. San Diego); yards—117 (October 21, 2001, vs. Indianapolis); and touchdown receptions—2 (October 6, 2002, vs. Miami).
STATISTICAL PLATEAUS: 100-yard receiving games: 2000 (2), 2001 (1), 2002 (2), 2004 (2). Total: 7.

P

Year	Team	G	GS	RECEIVING No.	Yds.	Avg.	TD	KICKOFF RETURNS No.	Yds.	Avg.	TD	TOTALS TD	2pt.	Pts.	Fum.
1997	New York Giants NFL	16	3	13	226	17.4	2	8	123	15.4	0	2	0	12	2
1998	New York Giants NFL	12	0	11	119	10.8	1	43	928	21.6	1	2	0	12	0
1999	New York Giants NFL	16	0	9	115	12.8	0	33	673	20.4	0	0	0	0	0
2000	Cleveland NFL	14	11	38	546	14.4	1	22	469	21.3	0	1	0	6	2
2001	New England NFL	16	14	51	749	14.7	4	2	44	22.0	0	5	0	30	1
2002	New England NFL	16	14	61	824	13.5	5	0	0	0.0	0	5	0	30	0
2003	New England NFL	6	5	9	140	15.6	0	0	0	0.0	0	0	0	0	0
2004	New England NFL	16	11	44	800	18.2	7	1	16	16.0	0	7	0	42	0
Pro totals (8 years)		112	58	236	3519	14.9	20	109	2253	20.7	1	22	0	132	5

PATTERSON, ELTON   DE   BENGALS

PERSONAL: Born June 13, 1981, in Tallahassee, Fla. ... 6-2/271.
HIGH SCHOOL: Rickards (Tallahassee, Fla.).
COLLEGE: Central Florida.
TRANSACTIONS/CAREER NOTES: Selected by Cincinnati Bengals in seventh round (259th pick overall) of 2003 NFL draft. ... Released by Bengals (September 5, 2004). ... Signed by Bengals to practice squad (September 6, 2004). ... Activated (September 23, 2004). ... Released by Bengals (October 5, 2004). ... Re-signed by Bengals to practice squad (October 6, 2004). ... Signed by Jacksonville Jaguars off Bengals practice squad (October 15, 2004). ... Did not receive qualifying offer from Jaguars (March 2, 2005). ... Signed by Bengals (April 25, 2005).

Year	Team	G	GS	TOTALS Tk.	Ast.	Sks.
2004	Cincinnati NFL	2	0	0	0	0.0
	Jacksonville NFL	6	0	3	4	1.0
Pro totals (1 year)		8	0	3	4	1.0

PAXTON, LONIE   C/LS   PATRIOTS

PERSONAL: Born March 13, 1978, in Anaheim, Calif. ... 6-2/260. ... Full name: Leonidas E. Paxton.
HIGH SCHOOL: Centennial (Carona, Calif.).
COLLEGE: Sacramento State.
TRANSACTIONS/CAREER NOTES: Signed as non-drafted free agent by New England Patriots (April 19, 2000). ... Granted free agency (February 28, 2003). ... Re-signed by Patriots (February 28, 2003). ... On injured reserve with leg injury (December 10, 2003-remainder of season).
PLAYING EXPERIENCE: New England NFL, 2000-2004. ... Games/Games started: 2000 (16/0), 2001 (16/0), 2002 (16/0), 2003 (13/0), 2004 (16/0). Total: 77/0.
CHAMPIONSHIP GAME EXPERIENCE: Played in AFC championship game (2001 and 2004 seasons). ... Member of Super Bowl championship team (2001 and 2004 seasons).

PAYNE, SETH   DT   TEXANS

PERSONAL: Born February 12, 1975, in Clifton Springs, N.Y. ... 6-4/315. ... Full name: Seth Copeland Payne.
HIGH SCHOOL: Victor (N.Y.) Central.
COLLEGE: Cornell.
TRANSACTIONS/CAREER NOTES: Selected by Jacksonville Jaguars in fourth round (114th pick overall) of 1997 NFL draft. ... Signed by Jaguars (May 23, 1997). ... On injured reserve with shoulder injury (November 17, 1998-remainder of season). ... Selected by Houston Texans from Jaguars in NFL expansion draft (February 18, 2002). ... On injured reserve with knee injury (September 15, 2003-remainder of season). ... Granted unconditional free agency (March 2, 2005). ... Re-signed by Texans (March 3, 2005).
CHAMPIONSHIP GAME EXPERIENCE: Played in AFC championship game (1999 season).

Year	Team	G	GS	TOTALS Tk.	Ast.	Sks.
1997	Jacksonville NFL	12	5	12	2	0.0
1998	Jacksonville NFL	6	1	7	4	0.0
1999	Jacksonville NFL	16	16	13	11	1.5
2000	Jacksonville NFL	16	14	22	11	2.0
2001	Jacksonville NFL	16	16	41	14	5.0
2002	Houston NFL	16	16	54	11	1.0
2003	Houston NFL	2	2	6	3	1.0
2004	Houston NFL	16	12	36	15	2.0
Pro totals (8 years)		100	82	191	71	12.5

PEARS, MORGAN   T   GIANTS

P

PERSONAL: Born May 4, 1980, in Los Angeles, Calif. ... 6-6/332. ... Full name: Morgan T. Pears.
HIGH SCHOOL: Kennedy (Denver, Colo.).
COLLEGE: Colorado State.
TRANSACTIONS/CAREER NOTES: Signed as non-drafted free agent by Miami Dolphins (May 1, 2003). ... Released by Dolphins (August 23, 2003). ... Signed by Pittsburgh Steelers to practice squad (September 30, 2003). ... Released by Steelers (August 27, 2004). ... Signed by New York Giants to practice squad (September 21, 2004). ... Activated (December 25, 2004).
PLAYING EXPERIENCE: New York Giants NFL, 2004. ... Games/Games started: 2004 (2/0). Total: 2/0.

PEARSON, MIKE   T   JAGUARS

PERSONAL: Born August 22, 1980, in Tampa, Fla. ... 6-7/297. ... Full name: Michael Wayne Pearson.
HIGH SCHOOL: Armwood (Seffner, Fla.).
COLLEGE: Florida.
TRANSACTIONS/CAREER NOTES: Selected after junior season by Jacksonville Jaguars in second round (40th pick overall) of 2002 NFL draft. ... Signed by Jaguars (July 24, 2002). ... On injured reserve with knee injury (October 5, 2004-remainder of season).
PLAYING EXPERIENCE: Jacksonville NFL, 2002-2004. ... Games/Games started: 2002 (16/11), 2003 (16/16), 2004 (4/4). Total: 36/31.
HONORS: Named offensive tackle on THE SPORTING NEWS college All-America first team (2001).

PEDERSON, DOUG   QB

PERSONAL: Born January 31, 1968, in Bellingham, Wash. ... 6-3/222. ... Full name: Douglas Irvin Pederson.
HIGH SCHOOL: Ferndale (Wash.).
COLLEGE: Louisiana-Monroe.
TRANSACTIONS/CAREER NOTES: Signed as non-drafted free agent by Miami Dolphins (April 30, 1991). ... Released by Dolphins (August 16, 1991). ... Selected by New York/New Jersey Knights in fifth round (49th pick overall) of 1992 World League draft. ... Re-signed by Dolphins (June 1, 1992). ... Released by Dolphins (August 31, 1992). ... Re-signed by Dolphins to practice squad (September 1, 1992). ... Released by Dolphins (October 7, 1992). ... Re-signed by Dolphins (March 3, 1993). ... Released by Dolphins (August 30, 1993). ... Re-signed by Dolphins to practice squad (August 31, 1993). ... Activated (October 22, 1993). ... Released by Dolphins (December 15, 1993). ... Re-signed by Dolphins (April 15, 1994). ... Inactive for all 16 games (1994). ... Selected by Carolina Panthers from Dolphins in NFL expansion draft (February 15, 1995). ... Released by Panthers (May 22, 1995). ... Signed by Dolphins (July 11, 1995). ... Released by Dolphins (August 21, 1995). ... Re-signed by Dolphins (October 10, 1995). ... Inactive for two games with Dolphins (1995). ... Released by Dolphins (October 25, 1995). ... Signed by Green Bay Packers (November 22, 1995). ... Inactive for five games with Packers (1995). ... Granted unconditional free agency (February 14, 1997). ... Re-signed by Packers (February 20, 1997). ... Granted unconditional free agency (February 12, 1999). ... Signed by Philadelphia Eagles (February 17, 1999). ... Released by Eagles (August 27, 2000). ... Signed by Cleveland Browns (September 1, 2000). ... Released by Browns (February 22, 2001). ... Signed by Packers (March 13, 2001). ... Granted unconditional free agency (March 1, 2002). ... Re-signed by Packers (April 2, 2002). ... Granted unconditional free agency (February 28, 2003). ... Re-signed by Packers (April 29, 2003). ... Granted unconditional free agency (March 3, 2004). ... Re-signed by Packers (April 28, 2004). ... On injured reserve with back and rib injuries (October 7, 2004-remainder of season). ... Granted unconditional free agency (March 2, 2005).
CHAMPIONSHIP GAME EXPERIENCE: Member of Packers for NFC championship game (1995-97 seasons); inactive. ... Member of Super Bowl championship team (1996 season); inactive. ... Member of Packers for Super Bowl 32 (1997 season); inactive.
SINGLE GAME HIGHS (regular season): Attempts—40 (December 10, 2000, vs. Philadelphia); completions—29 (December 10, 2000, vs. Philadelphia); yards—309 (December 10, 2000, vs. Philadelphia); and touchdown passes—2 (October 17, 1999, vs. Chicago).
STATISTICAL PLATEAUS: 300-yard passing games: 2000 (1). Total: 1.
MISCELLANEOUS: Regular-season record as starting NFL quarterback: 3-14 (.176).

Year Team	G	GS	PASSING Att.	Cmp.	Pct.	Yds.	TD	Int.	Avg.	Skd.	Rat.	RUSHING Att.	Yds.	Avg.	TD	TOTALS TD	2pt.	Pts.
1993—Miami NFL	7	0	8	4	50.0	41	0	0	5.13	1	65.1	2	-1	-0.5	0	0	0	0
1994—Miami NFL	Did not play.																	
1995—Miami NFL	Did not play.																	
—Green Bay NFL	Did not play.																	
1996—Green Bay NFL	1	0	0	0	0.0	0	0	0	0.00	0	0.0	0	0	0.0	0	0	0	0
1997—Green Bay NFL	1	0	0	0	0.0	0	0	0	0.00	0	0.0	3	-4	-1.3	0	0	0	0
1998—Green Bay NFL	12	0	24	14	58.3	128	2	0	5.33	1	100.7	8	-4	-0.5	0	0	0	0
1999—Philadelphia NFL	16	9	227	119	52.4	1276	7	9	5.62	20	62.9	20	33	1.7	0	0	0	0
2000—Cleveland NFL	11	8	210	117	55.7	1047	2	8	4.99	17	56.6	18	68	3.8	0	0	0	0
2001—Green Bay NFL	16	0	0	0	0.0	0	0	0	0.00	0	0.0	1	-1	-1.0	0	0	0	0
2002—Green Bay NFL	16	0	28	19	67.9	134	1	0	4.79	1	90.5	1	-1	-1.0	0	0	0	0
2003—Green Bay NFL	16	0	2	2	100.0	16	0	0	8.00	0	100.0	6	-5	-0.8	0	0	0	0
2004—Green Bay NFL	4	0	23	11	47.8	120	0	2	5.22	0	27.4	2	15	7.5	0	0	0	0
Pro totals (10 years)	100	17	522	286	54.8	2762	12	19	5.29	40	62.3	61	100	1.6	0	0	0	0

PEEK, ANTWAN   LB   TEXANS

PERSONAL: Born October 29, 1979, in Cincinnati, Ohio. ... 6-3/238.
HIGH SCHOOL: Woodward (Cincinnati).
COLLEGE: Cincinnati.
TRANSACTIONS/CAREER NOTES: Selected by Houston Texans in third round (67th pick overall) of 2003 NFL draft. ... Signed by Texans (July 23, 2003). ... On injured reserve with shoulder injury (December 28, 2004-remainder of season).

Year Team	G	GS	TOTALS Tk.	Ast.	Sks.	INTERCEPTIONS No.	Yds.	Avg.	TD
2003—Houston NFL	10	4	19	4	1.0	0	0	0.0	0
2004—Houston NFL	14	1	8	5	2.0	1	20	20.0	0
Pro totals (2 years)	24	5	27	9	3.0	1	20	20.0	0

PEELLE, JUSTIN   TE   CHARGERS

PERSONAL: Born March 15, 1979, in Fresno, Calif. ... 6-4/255. ... Full name: Justin Morris Peelle.
HIGH SCHOOL: Dublin (Calif.).
COLLEGE: Oregon.
TRANSACTIONS/CAREER NOTES: Selected by San Diego Chargers in fourth round (103rd pick overall) of 2002 NFL draft. ... Signed by Chargers (July 18, 2002). ... Granted free agency (March 2, 2005). ... Re-signed by Chargers (March 28, 2005).
SINGLE GAME HIGHS (regular season): Receptions—4 (September 21, 2003, vs. Baltimore); yards—29 (December 21, 2003, vs. Pittsburgh); and touchdown receptions—1 (October 31, 2004, vs. Oakland).

Year Team	G	GS	RECEIVING No.	Yds.	Avg.	TD	TOTALS TD	2pt.	Pts.	Fum.
2002—San Diego NFL	15	2	3	15	5.0	0	0	0	0	0
2003—San Diego NFL	15	9	16	133	8.3	1	1	0	6	0
2004—San Diego NFL	16	4	10	84	8.4	2	2	0	12	1
Pro totals (3 years)	46	15	29	232	8.0	3	3	0	18	1

PEETE, RODNEY   QB

PERSONAL: Born March 16, 1966, in Mesa, Ariz. ... 6-0/230. ... Son of Willie Peete, former running backs coach and scout with Chicago Bears.
HIGH SCHOOL: Sahuaro (Tucson, Ariz.), then Shawnee Mission South (Overland Park, Kan.).
COLLEGE: Southern California.
TRANSACTIONS/CAREER NOTES: Selected by Detroit Lions in sixth round (141st pick overall) of 1989 NFL draft. ... Signed by Lions (July 13, 1989). ... On injured reserve with Achilles' tendon injury (October 30, 1991-remainder of season). ... Granted free agency (February 1, 1992). ... Re-signed by Lions (July 30, 1992). ... Granted unconditional free agency (February 17, 1994). ... Signed by Dallas Cowboys (May 4, 1994). ... Granted unconditional free agency (February 17, 1995). ... Signed by Philadelphia Eagles (April 22, 1995). ... Granted unconditional free agency (February 16, 1996). ... Re-signed by Eagles (March 14, 1996). ... On injured reserve with knee injury (October 3, 1996-remainder of season). ... Granted unconditional free agency (February 14, 1997). ... Re-signed by Eagles (April 1, 1997). ... Traded by Eagles to Washington Redskins for sixth-round pick (C John Romero) in 2000 draft (April 28, 1999). ... Released by Redskins (April 18, 2000). ... Signed by Oakland Raiders (July 13, 2000). ... Released by Raiders (September 2, 2001). ... Re-signed by Raiders (September 29, 2001). ... Granted unconditional free agency (March 1, 2002). ... Signed by Carolina Panthers (March 28, 2002). ... Granted unconditional free agency (February 28, 2003). ... Re-signed by Panthers (March 5, 2003). ... Released by Panthers (February 28, 2005).
CHAMPIONSHIP GAME EXPERIENCE: Member of Cowboys for NFC championship game (1994 season); did not play. ... Member of Raiders for AFC Championship game (2000 season); inactive. ... Member of Panthers for NFC championship game (2003 season); did not play. ... Member of Panthers for Super Bowl 38 (2003 season); did not play.
HONORS: Named quarterback on THE SPORTING NEWS college All-America second team (1988).
SINGLE GAME HIGHS (regular season): Attempts—45 (October 8, 1995, vs. Washington); completions—30 (October 8, 1995, vs. Washington); yards—323 (September 27, 1992, vs. Tampa Bay); and touchdown passes—4 (December 16, 1990, vs. Chicago).
STATISTICAL PLATEAUS: 300-yard passing games: 1990 (1), 1992 (1), 2002 (3). Total: 5.
MISCELLANEOUS: Selected by Toronto Blue Jays organization in 30th round of free-agent baseball draft (June 4, 1984); did not sign. ... Selected by Oakland Athletics organization in 14th round of free-agent baseball draft (June 1, 1988); did not sign. ... Selected by Athletics organization in 13th round of free-agent baseball draft (June 5, 1989); did not sign. ... Regular-season record as starting NFL quarterback: 45-42 (.517). ... Postseason record as starting NFL quarterback: 1-1 (.500).

Year Team	G	GS	PASSING Att.	Cmp.	Pct.	Yds.	TD	Int.	Avg.	Skd.	Rat.	RUSHING Att.	Yds.	Avg.	TD	TOTALS TD	2pt.	Pts.
1989—Detroit NFL	8	8	195	103	52.8	1479	5	9	7.58	27	67.0	33	148	4.5	4	4	0	24
1990—Detroit NFL	11	11	271	142	52.4	1974	13	8	7.28	27	79.8	47	363	7.7	6	6	0	36
1991—Detroit NFL	8	8	194	116	59.8	1339	5	9	6.90	11	69.9	25	125	5.0	2	2	0	12
1992—Detroit NFL	10	10	213	123	57.7	1702	9	9	7.99	28	80.0	21	83	4.0	0	0	0	0
1993—Detroit NFL	10	10	252	157	62.3	1670	6	14	6.63	34	66.4	45	165	3.7	1	1	0	6
1994—Dallas NFL	7	1	56	33	58.9	470	4	1	8.39	4	102.5	9	-2	-0.2	0	0	0	0
1995—Philadelphia NFL	15	12	375	215	57.3	2326	8	14	6.20	33	67.3	32	147	4.6	1	1	0	6
1996—Philadelphia NFL	5	5	134	80	59.7	992	3	5	7.40	11	74.6	20	31	1.6	1	1	0	6
1997—Philadelphia NFL	5	3	118	68	57.6	869	4	4	7.36	17	78.0	8	37	4.6	0	0	0	0
1998—Philadelphia NFL	5	4	129	71	55.0	758	2	4	5.88	16	64.7	5	30	6.0	1	1	0	6
1999—Washington NFL	3	0	17	8	47.1	107	2	1	6.29	2	82.2	2	-1	-0.5	0	0	0	0
2000—Oakland NFL		Did not play.																
2001—Oakland NFL	1	0	0	0	0.0	0	0	0	0.00	0	0.0	0	0	0.0	0	0	0	0
2002—Carolina NFL	14	14	381	223	58.5	2630	15	14	6.90	31	77.4	22	14	0.6	0	0	0	0
2003—Carolina NFL	1	1	10	4	40.0	19	0	0	1.90	3	47.9	0	0	0.0	0	0	0	0
2004—Carolina NFL	1	0	1	1	100.0	3	0	0	3.00	0	79.2	1	-1	-1.0	0	0	0	0
Pro totals (15 years)	104	87	2346	1344	57.3	16338	76	92	6.96	244	73.3	270	1139	4.2	16	16	0	96

PEKO, TUPE   C/G

PERSONAL: Born September 19, 1978, in Whittier, Calif. ... 6-4/305. ... Full name: Siitupe Peko.
HIGH SCHOOL: La Serna (Calif.).
JUNIOR COLLEGE: Cerritos College (Calif.).
COLLEGE: Michigan State.
TRANSACTIONS/CAREER NOTES: Selected by New York Jets in seventh round (217th pick overall) in 2001 NFL draft. ... Signed by Jets (June 22, 2001). ... Released by Jets (September 2, 2001). ... Re-signed by Jets to practice squad (September 3, 2001). ... Released by Jets (September 26, 2001). ... Signed by Seattle Seahawks to practice squad (October 16, 2001). ... Released by Seahawks (September 2, 2002). ... Signed by Indianapolis Colts to practice squad (September 3, 2002). ... Activated (October 5, 2002). ... Re-signed to Colts (March 9, 2004). ... Granted free agency (March 2, 2005).
PLAYING EXPERIENCE: Indianapolis NFL, 2004. ... Games/Games started: 2003 (16/1), 2004 (11/8). Total: 27/9.
CHAMPIONSHIP GAME EXPERIENCE: Played in AFC championship game (2003 season).

PENNINGTON, CHAD   QB   JETS

PERSONAL: Born June 26, 1976, in Knoxville, Tenn. ... 6-3/225. ... Full name: James Chad Pennington.
HIGH SCHOOL: Webb (Knoxville, Tenn.).
COLLEGE: Marshall.
TRANSACTIONS/CAREER NOTES: Selected by New York Jets in first round (18th pick overall) of 2000 NFL draft. ... Signed by Jets (July 13, 2000).
HONORS: Named quarterback on THE SPORTING NEWS college All-America third team (1999).
SINGLE GAME HIGHS (regular season): Attempts—45 (November 2, 2003, vs. New York Giants); completions—31 (October 10, 2004, vs. Buffalo); yards—324 (October 20, 2002, vs. Minnesota); and touchdown passes—4 (November 2, 2003, vs. New York Giants).

P

STATISTICAL PLATEAUS: 300-yard passing games: 2002 (1), 2004 (1). Total: 2.
MISCELLANEOUS: Regular-season record as starting NFL quarterback: 20-14 (.588). ... Postseason record as starting NFL quarterback: 2-2 (.500).

| | | | | PASSING | | | | | | | | RUSHING | | | | TOTALS | |
Year Team	G	GS	Att.	Cmp.	Pct.	Yds.	TD	Int.	Avg.	Skd.	Rat.	Att.	Yds.	Avg.	TD	TD	2pt.	Pts.
2000—New York Jets NFL	2	0	5	2	40.0	67	1	0	13.40	1	127.1	1	0	0.0	0	0	0	0
2001—New York Jets NFL	2	0	20	10	50.0	92	1	0	4.60	1	79.6	1	11	11.0	0	0	0	0
2002—New York Jets NFL	15	12	399	275	*68.9	3120	22	6	7.82	22	*104.2	29	49	1.7	2	2	0	12
2003—New York Jets NFL	10	9	297	189	63.6	2139	13	12	7.20	25	82.9	21	42	2.0	2	2	0	12
2004—New York Jets NFL	13	13	370	242	65.4	2673	16	9	7.22	18	91.0	34	126	3.7	1	1	0	6
Pro totals (5 years)	42	34	1091	718	65.8	8091	53	27	7.42	67	93.7	86	228	2.7	5	5	0	30

PEPPERS, JULIUS　　　　　DE　　　　　PANTHERS

PERSONAL: Born January 18, 1980, in Wilson, N.C. ... 6-6/283. ... Full name: Julius Frazier Peppers.
HIGH SCHOOL: Southern Nash (Bailey, N.C.).
COLLEGE: North Carolina.
TRANSACTIONS/CAREER NOTES: Selected after junior season by Carolina Panthers in first round (second pick overall) of 2002 NFL draft. ... Signed by Panthers (July 22, 2002). ... On suspended list for violating league substance abuse policy (December 4, 2002-remainder of season).
CHAMPIONSHIP GAME EXPERIENCE: Played in NFC championship game (2003 season). ... Played in Super Bowl 38 (2003 season).
HONORS: Lombardi Award winner (2001). ... Named defensive end on THE SPORTING NEWS college All-America first team (2001). ... Named defensive end on THE SPORTING NEWS NFL All-Pro team (2004). ... Played in Pro Bowl (2004 season).

| | | | TOTALS | | | INTERCEPTIONS | | | |
Year Team	G	GS	Tk.	Ast.	Sks.	No.	Yds.	Avg.	TD
2002—Carolina NFL	12	12	29	7	12.0	1	21	21.0	0
2003—Carolina NFL	16	16	39	7	7.0	0	0	0.0	0
2004—Carolina NFL	16	16	53	12	11.0	2	143	71.5	1
Pro totals (3 years)	44	44	121	26	30.0	3	164	54.7	1

PERRY, CHRIS　　　　　RB　　　　　BENGALS

PERSONAL: Born December 27, 1981, in Advance, N.C. ... 6-0/224.
HIGH SCHOOL: Fork Union Military (Va.).
COLLEGE: Michigan.
TRANSACTIONS/CAREER NOTES: Selected by Cincinnati Bengals in first round (26th pick overall) of 2004 NFL draft. ... Signed by Bengals (August 10, 2004). ... On injured reserve with abdomen injury (December 29, 2004-remainder of season).
HONORS: Doak Walker Award winner (2003). ... Named running back on THE SPORTING NEWS college All-America first team (2003).
SINGLE GAME HIGHS (regular season): Attempts—2 (October 17, 2004, vs. Cleveland); yards—1 (October 17, 2004, vs. Cleveland); and rushing touchdowns—0.

| | | | RUSHING | | | | RECEIVING | | | | TOTALS | | |
Year Team	G	GS	Att.	Yds.	Avg.	TD	No.	Yds.	Avg.	TD	TD	2pt.	Pts.	Fum.
2004—Cincinnati NFL	2	0	2	1	0.5	0	3	33	11.0	0	0	0	0	0

PERRY, ED　　　　　TE　　　　　DOLPHINS

PERSONAL: Born September 1, 1974, in Richmond, Va. ... 6-4/265. ... Full name: Edward Lewis Perry.
HIGH SCHOOL: Highlands Springs (Va.).
COLLEGE: James Madison.
TRANSACTIONS/CAREER NOTES: Selected by Miami Dolphins in sixth round (177th pick overall) of 1997 NFL draft. ... Signed by Dolphins (June 13, 1997). ... Granted free agency (February 11, 2000). ... Re-signed by Dolphins (April 28, 2000). ... On injured reserve with shoulder injury (November 23, 2000-remainder of season). ... Granted unconditional free agency (March 2, 2001). ... Re-signed by Dolphins (March 16, 2001). ... Granted unconditional free agency (March 2, 2005). ... Re-signed by Dolphins (March 2, 2005).
SINGLE GAME HIGHS (regular season): Receptions—4 (September 13, 1998, vs. Buffalo); yards—59 (November 23, 1998, vs. New England); and touchdown receptions—1 (December 27, 1999, vs. New York Jets).

| | | | RECEIVING | | | | TOTALS | | | |
Year Team	G	GS	No.	Yds.	Avg.	TD	TD	2pt.	Pts.	Fum.
1997—Miami NFL	16	4	11	45	4.1	1	1	0	6	0
1998—Miami NFL	14	5	25	255	10.2	0	0	0	0	0
1999—Miami NFL	16	1	3	8	2.7	1	1	0	6	0
2000—Miami NFL	10	0	0	0	0.0	0	0	0	0	0
2001—Miami NFL	16	0	0	0	0.0	0	0	0	0	1
2002—Miami NFL	16	0	0	0	0.0	0	0	0	0	0
2004—Miami NFL	16	0	0	0	0.0	0	0	0	0	0
Pro totals (7 years)	104	10	39	308	7.9	2	2	0	12	1

PERRYMAN, RAY　　　　　S　　　　　JAGUARS

PERSONAL: Born November 27, 1978, in Phoenix, Ariz. ... 5-11/195. ... Full name: Raymond Perryman.
HIGH SCHOOL: South Mountain (Phoenix).
COLLEGE: Northern Arizona.
TRANSACTIONS/CAREER NOTES: Selected by Oakland Raiders in fifth round (158th pick overall) of 2001 NFL draft. ... Signed by Raiders (July 21, 2001). ... Released by Raiders (September 2, 2001). ... Re-signed by Raiders to practice squad (September 4, 2001). ... Activated (January 17, 2002). ... Assigned by Raiders to Amsterdam Admirals in 2002 NFL Europe enhancement allocation program (February 12, 2002). ...

P

Released by Raiders (September 1, 2002). ... Signed by Baltimore Ravens to practice squad (November 19, 2002). ... Activated (November 27, 2002). ... Re-signed by Ravens (March 23, 2003). ... Waived by Ravens (August 25, 2003). ... Signed by Jacksonville Jaguars to practice squad (October 30, 2003). ... Activated (November 27, 2003). ... Re-signed by Jaguars (March 22, 2004). ... Released by Jaguars (October 14, 2004). ... Re-signed by Jaguars (January 25, 2005). ... Assigned by Jaguars to Frankfurt Galaxy in 2005 NFL Europe enhancement allocation program (February 14, 2005).

				TOTALS			INTERCEPTIONS			
Year Team	G	GS	Tk.	Ast.	Sks.	No.	Yds.	Avg.	TD
2002—Baltimore NFL	2	0	0	0	0.0	0	0	0.0	0
2003—Jacksonville NFL	4	0	0	0	0.0	0	0	0.0	0
2004—Jacksonville NFL	4	0	0	0	0.0	0	0	0.0	0
Pro totals (3 years)	10	0	0	0	0.0	0	0	0.0	0

PETERMAN, STEPHEN　　　G　　　COWBOYS

PERSONAL: Born January 11, 1982, in Gulfport, Miss. ... 6-4/300. ... Full name: Stephen Frederick Peterman.
HIGH SCHOOL: St. Stanislaus (Waveland, Miss.).
COLLEGE: Louisiana State.
TRANSACTIONS/CAREER NOTES: Selected by Dallas Cowboys in third round (83rd pick overall) of 2004 NFL draft. ... Signed by Cowboys (July 29, 2004). ... On injured reserve with knee injury (September 3, 2004-entire season).
HONORS: Named guard on THE SPORTING NEWS college All-America first team (2003).

PETERS, JASON　　　TE　　　BILLS

PERSONAL: Born January 22, 1982, in Queen City, Texas. ... 6-4/328.
HIGH SCHOOL: Queen City (Texas).
COLLEGE: Arkansas.
TRANSACTIONS/CAREER NOTES: Signed as non-drafted free agent by Buffalo Bills (April 26, 2004). ... Released by Bills (August 31, 2004). ... Re-signed by Bills to practice squad (September 6, 2004). ... Activated (November 12, 2004).

			RECEIVING				TOTALS			
Year Team	G	GS	No.	Yds.	Avg.	TD	TD	2pt.	Pts.	Fum.
2004—Buffalo NFL	5	1	0	0	0.0	0	1	0	6	0

PETERSON, ADRIAN　　　RB　　　BEARS

PERSONAL: Born July 1, 1979, in Gainesville, Fla. ... 5-10/210. ... Brother of Mike Peterson, linebacker with Jacksonville Jaguars.
HIGH SCHOOL: Sante Fe (Alachua, Fla.).
COLLEGE: Georgia Southern.
TRANSACTIONS/CAREER NOTES: Selected by Chicago Bears in sixth round (199th pick overall) of 2002 NFL draft. ... Signed by Bears (July 25, 2002). ... On injured reserve with ankle injury (November 14, 2003-remainder of season).
SINGLE GAME HIGHS (regular season): Attempts—16 (October 19, 2003, vs. Seattle); yards—55 (October 19, 2003, vs. Seattle); and rushing touchdowns—1 (December 15, 2002, vs. New York Jets).

			RUSHING				RECEIVING				KICKOFF RETURNS				TOTALS			
Year Team	G	GS	Att.	Yds.	Avg.	TD	No.	Yds.	Avg.	TD	No.	Yds.	Avg.	TD	TD	2pt.	Pts.	Fum.
2002—Chicago NFL	9	0	19	101	5.3	1	3	18	6.0	0	2	37	18.5	0	1	0	6	0
2003—Chicago NFL	6	1	22	70	3.2	0	1	5	5.0	0	0	0	0.0	0	0	0	0	0
2004—Chicago NFL	14	0	6	19	3.2	0	2	30	15.0	0	3	57	19.0	0	0	0	0	0
Pro totals (3 years)	29	1	47	190	4.0	1	6	53	8.8	0	5	94	18.8	0	1	0	6	0

PETERSON, JULIAN　　　LB　　　49ERS

PERSONAL: Born July 28, 1978, in Temple Hills, Md. ... 6-3/235. ... Full name: Julian Thomas Peterson.
HIGH SCHOOL: Crossland (Temple Hills, Md.).
JUNIOR COLLEGE: Valley Forge Junior College (Pa.).
COLLEGE: Michigan State.
TRANSACTIONS/CAREER NOTES: Selected by San Francisco 49ers in first round (16th pick overall) of 2000 NFL draft. ... Signed by 49ers (July 27, 2000). ... Designated by 49ers as franchise player (February 24, 2004). ... Re-signed by 49ers (August 25, 2004). ... On injured reserve with Achilles injury (October 13, 2004-remainder of season). ... Designated by 49ers as franchise player (February 22, 2005). ... Re-signed by 49ers (March 25, 2005).
HONORS: Named linebacker on THE SPORTING NEWS NFL All-Pro team (2003). ... Played in Pro Bowl (2002 and 2003 seasons).

				TOTALS			INTERCEPTIONS			
Year Team	G	GS	Tk.	Ast.	Sks.	No.	Yds.	Avg.	TD
2000—San Francisco NFL	13	7	29	17	4.0	2	33	16.5	0
2001—San Francisco NFL	14	14	37	15	3.0	0	0	0.0	0
2002—San Francisco NFL	16	16	78	18	2.0	1	2	2.0	0
2003—San Francisco NFL	16	16	69	26	7.0	2	31	15.5	0
2004—San Francisco NFL	5	5	24	3	2.5	0	0	0.0	0
Pro totals (5 years)	64	58	237	79	18.5	5	66	13.2	0

P

PETERSON, KENNY　　　DT/DE　　　PACKERS

PERSONAL: Born November 21, 1978, in Canton, Ohio. ... 6-3/295.
HIGH SCHOOL: McKinley (Canton, Ohio).
COLLEGE: Ohio State.

TRANSACTIONS/CAREER NOTES: Selected by Green Bay Packers in third round (79th pick overall) of 2003 NFL draft. ... Signed by Packers (July 19, 2003).

			TOTALS		
Year Team	G	GS	Tk.	Ast.	Sks.
2003—Green Bay NFL	9	0	5	3	0.0
2004—Green Bay NFL	9	0	9	2	0.0
Pro totals (2 years)	18	0	14	5	0.0

PETERSON, MIKE — LB — JAGUARS

PERSONAL: Born June 17, 1976, in Gainesville, Fla. ... 6-1/230. ... Full name: Porter Michael Peterson. ... Brother of Adrian Peterson, running back with Chicago Bears.
HIGH SCHOOL: Santa Fe (Alachua, Fla.).
COLLEGE: Florida.
TRANSACTIONS/CAREER NOTES: Selected by Indianapolis Colts in second round (36th pick overall) of 1999 NFL draft. ... Signed by Colts (July 28, 1999). ... Granted unconditional free agency (February 28, 2003). ... Signed by Jacksonville Jaguars (March 13, 2003).
HONORS: Named outside linebacker on THE SPORTING NEWS college All-America first team (1998).

			TOTALS			INTERCEPTIONS			
Year Team	G	GS	Tk.	Ast.	Sks.	No.	Yds.	Avg.	TD
1999—Indianapolis NFL	16	13	71	21	3.0	0	0	0.0	0
2000—Indianapolis NFL	16	16	103	55	0.0	2	8	4.0	0
2001—Indianapolis NFL	9	9	46	19	1.5	2	18	9.0	0
2002—Indianapolis NFL	16	16	103	33	0.0	3	96	32.0	0
2003—Jacksonville NFL	16	16	73	29	1.0	3	8	2.7	0
2004—Jacksonville NFL	16	16	93	33	5.0	0	0	0.0	0
Pro totals (6 years)	89	86	489	190	10.5	10	130	13.0	0

PETERSON, TODD — K — FALCONS

PERSONAL: Born February 4, 1970, in Washington, DC. ... 5-11/180. ... Full name: Joseph Todd Peterson.
HIGH SCHOOL: Valdosta (Ga.) State.
COLLEGE: Georgia.
TRANSACTIONS/CAREER NOTES: Selected by New York Giants in seventh round (177th pick overall) of 1993 NFL draft. ... Signed by Giants (July 19, 1993). ... Released by Giants (August 24, 1993). ... Signed by New England Patriots to practice squad (November 30, 1993). ... Released by Patriots (December 6, 1993). ... Signed by Atlanta Falcons (May 3, 1994). ... Released by Falcons (August 29, 1994). ... Signed by Arizona Cardinals (October 12, 1994). ... Released by Cardinals (October 24, 1994). ... Signed by Seattle Seahawks (January 17, 1995). ... Granted free agency (February 13, 1998). ... Re-signed by Seahawks for 1998 season. ... Granted unconditional free agency (February 12, 1999). ... Re-signed by Seahawks (March 2, 1999). ... Released by Seahawks (August 27, 2000). ... Signed by Kansas City Chiefs (October 11, 2000). ... Granted unconditional free agency (March 1, 2002). ... Signed by Pittsburgh Steelers (March 25, 2002). ... On injured reserve with rib injury (November 19, 2002-remainder of season). ... Released by Steelers (February 27, 2003). ... Signed by San Francisco 49ers (October 28, 2003). ... Granted unconditional free agency (March 3, 2004). ... Re-signed by 49ers (March 23, 2004). ... Granted unconditional free agency (March 2, 2005). ... Signed by Atlanta Falcons (March 7, 2005).

		FIELD GOALS							TOTALS		
Year Team	G	1-29	30-39	40-49	50+	Tot.	Pct.	Lg.	XPM	XPA	Pts.
1993—New England NFL	Did not play.										
1994—Arizona NFL	2	1-1	1-1	0-2	0-0	2-4	50.0	35	4	4	10
1995—Seattle NFL	16	6-6	9-10	8-10	0-2	23-28	82.1	49	§40	§40	109
1996—Seattle NFL	16	11-13	7-7	8-11	2-3	28-34	82.4	54	27	27	111
1997—Seattle NFL	16	9-9	7-10	5-7	1-2	22-28	78.6	52	37	37	103
1998—Seattle NFL	16	7-7	4-5	5-5	3-7	19-24	79.2	51	41	41	98
1999—Seattle NFL	16	11-11	8-11	14-16	1-2	34-40	85.0	51	32	32	134
2000—Kansas City NFL	11	6-6	7-9	2-5	0-0	15-20	75.0	42	25	25	70
2001—Kansas City NFL	16	9-11	9-10	8-12	1-2	27-35	77.1	51	27	28	108
2002—Pittsburgh NFL	10	3-4	6-10	3-7	0-0	12-21	57.1	46	25	26	61
2003—San Francisco NFL	8	5-7	3-3	4-4	0-1	12-15	80.0	48	22	23	58
2004—San Francisco NFL	16	4-4	7-8	5-6	2-4	18-22	81.8	51	23	23	77
Pro totals (11 years)	143	72-79	68-84	62-85	10-23	212-271	78.2	54	303	306	939

PETERSON, WILL — CB — GIANTS

PERSONAL: Born June 15, 1979, in Uniontown, Pa. ... 6-0/200. ... Full name: William James Peterson Jr.
HIGH SCHOOL: Laurel Highlands (Pa.).
COLLEGE: Western Illinois.
TRANSACTIONS/CAREER NOTES: Selected by New York Giants in third round (78th pick overall) of 2001 NFL draft. ... Signed by Giants (July 26, 2001). ... On injured reserve with back injury (November 11, 2003-remainder of season). ... Granted free agency (March 3, 2004). ... Re-signed by Giants (March 15, 2004).

			TOTALS			INTERCEPTIONS			
Year Team	G	GS	Tk.	Ast.	Sks.	No.	Yds.	Avg.	TD
2001—New York Giants NFL	16	5	47	5	0.0	1	0	0.0	0
2002—New York Giants NFL	12	12	36	4	0.0	2	1	0.5	0
2003—New York Giants NFL	5	5	24	6	0.0	0	0	0.0	0
2004—New York Giants NFL	16	15	61	8	0.0	2	9	4.5	0
Pro totals (4 years)	49	37	168	23	0.0	5	10	2.0	0

P

PETITGOUT, LUKE — T — GIANTS

PERSONAL: Born June 16, 1976, in Milford, Del. ... 6-6/310. ... Full name: Lucas George Petitgout. ... Name pronounced: pet-ee-GOO.
HIGH SCHOOL: Sussex Central (Georgetown, Del.).
COLLEGE: Notre Dame.
TRANSACTIONS/CAREER NOTES: Selected by New York Giants in first round (19th pick overall) of 1999 NFL draft. ... Signed by Giants (July 29, 1999). ... Granted unconditional free agency (February 28, 2003). ... Re-signed by Giants (February 28, 2003). ... On injured reserve with back injury (December 17, 2003-remainder of season).
PLAYING EXPERIENCE: New York Giants NFL, 1999-2004. ... Games/Games started: 1999 (15/8), 2000 (16/16), 2001 (16/16), 2002 (16/16), 2003 (10/10), 2004 (16/16). Total: 89/82.
CHAMPIONSHIP GAME EXPERIENCE: Played in NFC championship game (2000 season). ... Played in Super Bowl 35 (2000 season).

PHIFER, ROMAN — LB

PERSONAL: Born March 5, 1968, in Plattsburgh, N.Y. ... 6-2/248. ... Full name: Roman Zubinsky Phifer.
HIGH SCHOOL: South Mecklenburg (Charlotte).
COLLEGE: UCLA.
TRANSACTIONS/CAREER NOTES: Selected by Los Angeles Rams in second round (31st pick overall) of 1991 NFL draft. ... Signed by Rams (July 19, 1991). ... On injured reserve with broken leg (November 26, 1991-remainder of season). ... Granted unconditional free agency (February 17, 1995). ... Re-signed by Rams (March 22, 1995). ... Rams franchise moved to St. Louis (April 12, 1995). ... Granted unconditional free agency (February 12, 1999). ... Signed by New York Jets (March 9, 1999). ... Released by Jets (February 22, 2001). ... Signed by New England Patriots (August 3, 2001). ... Granted unconditional free agency (March 1, 2002). ... Re-signed by Patriots (June 21, 2002). ... Released by Patriots (February 28, 2005).
CHAMPIONSHIP GAME EXPERIENCE: Played in AFC championship game (2001, 2003 and 2004 seasons). ... Member of Super Bowl championship team (2001, 2003 and 2004 seasons).

Year Team	G	GS	TOTALS Tk.	Ast.	Sks.	INTERCEPTIONS No.	Yds.	Avg.	TD
1991—Los Angeles Rams NFL	12	5	21	3	2.0	0	0	0.0	0
1992—Los Angeles Rams NFL	16	14	51	15	0.0	1	3	3.0	0
1993—Los Angeles Rams NFL	16	16	96	21	0.0	0	0	0.0	0
1994—Los Angeles Rams NFL	16	15	79	17	1.5	2	7	3.5	0
1995—St. Louis NFL	16	16	87	28	3.0	3	52	17.3	0
1996—St. Louis NFL	15	15	104	18	1.5	0	0	0.0	0
1997—St. Louis NFL	16	15	57	18	2.0	0	0	0.0	0
1998—St. Louis NFL	13	13	57	14	6.5	1	41	41.0	0
1999—New York Jets NFL	16	12	36	14	4.5	2	20	10.0	0
2000—New York Jets NFL	16	10	32	13	4.0	0	0	0.0	0
2001—New England NFL	16	16	71	21	2.0	1	14	14.0	0
2002—New England NFL	14	14	69	40	0.5	0	0	0.0	0
2003—New England NFL	16	15	67	33	0.0	0	0	0.0	0
2004—New England NFL	13	1	30	10	1.5	1	26	26.0	0
Pro totals (14 years)	**211**	**177**	**857**	**265**	**29.0**	**11**	**163**	**14.8**	**0**

PHILLIPS, JERMAINE — S — BUCCANEERS

PERSONAL: Born March 27, 1979, in Roswell, Ga. ... 6-1/214.
HIGH SCHOOL: Roswell (Ga.).
COLLEGE: Georgia.
TRANSACTIONS/CAREER NOTES: Selected by Tampa Bay Buccaneers in fifth round (157th pick overall) of 2002 NFL draft. ... Signed by Buccaneers (July 22, 2002). ... On injured reserve with arm injury (December 22, 2004-remainder of season).
CHAMPIONSHIP GAME EXPERIENCE: Played in NFC championship game (2002 season). ... Member of Super Bowl championship team (2002 season).

Year Team	G	GS	TOTALS Tk.	Ast.	Sks.	INTERCEPTIONS No.	Yds.	Avg.	TD
2002—Tampa Bay NFL	16	0	0	1	0.0	0	0	0.0	0
2003—Tampa Bay NFL	14	8	30	9	0.0	1	41	41.0	0
2004—Tampa Bay NFL	9	9	31	11	1.0	1	0	0.0	0
Pro totals (3 years)	**39**	**17**	**61**	**21**	**1.0**	**2**	**41**	**20.5**	**0**

PHILLIPS, SHAUN — DE — CHARGERS

PERSONAL: Born May 13, 1981, in Willingboro, N.J. ... 6-3/262. ... Full name: Shaun Jamal Phillips.
HIGH SCHOOL: Willingboro (N.J.).
COLLEGE: Purdue.
TRANSACTIONS/CAREER NOTES: Selected by San Diego Chargers in fourth round (98th pick overall) of 2004 NFL draft. ... Signed by Chargers (July 22, 2004).

Year Team	G	GS	TOTALS Tk.	Ast.	Sks.	INTERCEPTIONS No.	Yds.	Avg.	TD
2004—San Diego NFL	16	0	14	4	4.0	1	0	0.0	0

P

PICKETT, CODY — QB — 49ERS

PERSONAL: Born June 30, 1980, in Caldwell, Idaho. ... 6-3/227.
HIGH SCHOOL: Caldwell (Idaho).
COLLEGE: Washington.

TRANSACTIONS/CAREER NOTES: Selected by San Francisco 49ers in seventh round (217th pick overall) of 2004 NFL draft. ... Signed by 49ers (July 23, 2004).
SINGLE GAME HIGHS (regular season): Attempts—10 (December 26, 2004, vs. Buffalo); completions—4 (December 26, 2004, vs. Buffalo); yards—55 (December 26, 2004, vs. Buffalo); and touchdown passes—0.

Year Team	G	GS	Att.	Cmp.	Pct.	Yds.	TD	Int.	Avg.	Skd.	Rat.	Att.	Yds.	Avg.	TD	TD	2pt.	Pts.
						PASSING							RUSHING				TOTALS	
2004—San Francisco NFL	2	0	10	4	40.0	55	0	2	5.50	2	18.8	1	5	5.0	0	0	0	0

PICKETT, RYAN — DT — RAMS

PERSONAL: Born October 8, 1979, in Zephyrhills, Fla. ... 6-2/310.
HIGH SCHOOL: Zephyrhills (Fla.).
COLLEGE: Ohio State.
TRANSACTIONS/CAREER NOTES: Selected after junior season by St. Louis Rams in first round (29th pick overall) of 2001 NFL draft. ... Signed by Rams (July 29, 2001).
CHAMPIONSHIP GAME EXPERIENCE: Played in NFC championship game (2001 season). ... Played in Super Bowl 36 (2001 season).

Year Team	G	GS	Tk.	Ast.	Sks.
			TOTALS		
2001—St. Louis NFL	11	0	10	9	0.5
2002—St. Louis NFL	16	14	45	22	0.5
2003—St. Louis NFL	16	13	30	12	1.0
2004—St. Louis NFL	16	16	42	4	2.0
Pro totals (4 years)	59	43	127	47	4.0

PIERCE, ANTONIO — LB — GIANTS

PERSONAL: Born October 26, 1978, in Ontario, Calif. ... 6-1/240.
HIGH SCHOOL: Paramount (Calif.).
JUNIOR COLLEGE: Mount San Antonio College (Calif.).
COLLEGE: Arizona.
TRANSACTIONS/CAREER NOTES: Signed as non-drafted free agent by Washington Redskins (April 25, 2001). ... Granted free agency (March 3, 2004). ... Re-signed by Redskins (April 22, 2004). ... Granted unconditional free agency (March 2, 2005). ... Signed by New York Giants (March 3, 2005)

Year Team	G	GS	Tk.	Ast.	Sks.	No.	Yds.	Avg.	TD
			TOTALS			INTERCEPTIONS			
2001—Washington NFL	16	7	42	8	1.0	1	0	0.0	0
2002—Washington NFL	8	1	8	4	0.0	0	0	0.0	0
2003—Washington NFL	15	0	6	0	0.0	0	0	0.0	0
2004—Washington NFL	16	16	84	26	1.0	2	94	47.0	1
Pro totals (4 years)	55	24	140	38	2.0	3	94	31.3	1

PIERCE, BRETT — TE — COWBOYS

PERSONAL: Born January 7, 1981, in Vancouver, Wash. ... 6-5/250.
HIGH SCHOOL: Columbia River (Vancouver, Wash.).
COLLEGE: Stanford.
TRANSACTIONS/CAREER NOTES: Signed as non-drafted free agent by Baltimore Ravens (April 30, 2004). ... Released by Ravens (September 6, 2004). ... Signed by Dallas Cowboys off Ravens practice squad (October 2, 2004). ... Re-signed by Ravens to practice squad (September 7, 2005).

Year Team	G	GS	No.	Yds.	Avg.	TD	TD	2pt.	Pts.	Fum.
			RECEIVING				TOTALS			
2004—Dallas NFL	8	1	0	0	0.0	0	0	0	0	0

PIERCE, TERRY — LB — BRONCOS

PERSONAL: Born June 21, 1981, in Fort Worth, Texas. ... 6-1/251.
HIGH SCHOOL: Western Hills (Fort Worth, Texas).
COLLEGE: Kansas State.
TRANSACTIONS/CAREER NOTES: Selected after junior season by Denver Broncos in second round (51st pick overall) of 2003 NFL draft. ... Signed by Broncos (July 24, 2003). ... On injured reserve with pectoral injury (November 18, 2003-remainder of season).

Year Team	G	GS	Tk.	Ast.	Sks.	No.	Yds.	Avg.	TD
			TOTALS			INTERCEPTIONS			
2003—Denver NFL	3	0	1	1	0.0	0	0	0.0	0
2004—Denver NFL	15	0	3	0	0.0	0	0	0.0	0
Pro totals (2 years)	18	0	4	1	0.0	0	0	0.0	0

PIERSON, SHURRON — DE/LB — BEARS

PERSONAL: Born May 31, 1982, in Inverness, Fla. ... 6-2/250. ... Full name: Shurron Torian Pierson.
HIGH SCHOOL: Wildwood (Fla.).
COLLEGE: South Florida.

P

TRANSACTIONS/CAREER NOTES: Selected after junior season by Oakland Raiders in fourth round (129th pick overall) of 2003 NFL draft. ... Signed by Raiders (July 24, 2003). ... Released by Raiders (August 31, 2003). ... Re-signed by Raiders to practice squad (September 2, 2003). ... Activated (November 12, 2003). ... Assigned by Raiders to WLD* in 2004 NFL Europe enhancement allocation program (February 9, 2004). ... Traded by Raiders to Chicago Bears for conditional pick in 2005 draft (August 30, 2004). ... Released by Bears (September 5, 2004). ... Signed by Bears to practice squad (September 6, 2004). ... Activated (September 21, 2004).

			TOTALS		
Year Team	G	GS	Tk.	Ast.	Sks.
2003—Chicago NFL	6	0	0	0	0.0
2004—Chicago NFL	6	0	1	1	0.0
Pro totals (2 years)	12	0	1	1	0.0

PILE, WILLIE SS CHIEFS

PERSONAL: Born May 25, 1980, in New York, N.Y. ... 6-2/206. ... Full name: Willie Marquis Pile.
HIGH SCHOOL: West Potomac (Alexandria, Va.).
COLLEGE: Virginia Tech.
TRANSACTIONS/CAREER NOTES: Selected by Kansas City Chiefs in seventh round (252nd pick overall) of 2003 NFL draft. ... Signed by Chiefs (May 12, 2003). ... Released by Chiefs (August 31, 2003). ... Re-signed by Chiefs to practice squad (December 10, 2003). ... Activated (January 27, 2004). ... Assigned by Chiefs to Amsterdam Admirals in 2004 NFL Europe enhancement allocation program (February 9, 2004).

			TOTALS			INTERCEPTIONS			
Year Team	G	GS	Tk.	Ast.	Sks.	No.	Yds.	Avg.	TD
2004—Kansas City NFL	16	5	23	5	0.0	0	0	0.0	0

PILLER, ZACH G TITANS

PERSONAL: Born May 2, 1976, in St. Petersburg, Fla. ... 6-5/321. ... Full name: Zachary Paul Piller.
HIGH SCHOOL: Lincoln (Tallahassee, Fla.).
COLLEGE: Florida.
TRANSACTIONS/CAREER NOTES: Selected by Tennessee Titans in third round (81st pick overall) of 1999 NFL draft. ... Signed by Titans (July 22, 1999). ... Granted unconditional free agency (February 28, 2003). ... Re-signed by Titans (March 3, 2003). ... On injured reserve with biceps injury (October 7, 2004-remainder of season).
PLAYING EXPERIENCE: Tennessee NFL, 1999-2004. ... Games/Games started: 1999 (8/0), 2000 (16/0), 2001 (14/9), 2002 (13/13), 2003 (16/16), 2004 (1/1). Total: 68/39.
CHAMPIONSHIP GAME EXPERIENCE: Member of Titans for AFC championship game (1999 season); inactive. ... Member of Titans for Super Bowl 34 (1999 season); inactive. ... Played in AFC championship game (2002 season).

PINKNEY, CLEVELAND DT PANTHERS

PERSONAL: Born September 14, 1977, in Sumter, S.C. ... 6-1/300. ... Full name: Cleveland Pinkney III.
HIGH SCHOOL: Sumter (S.C.).
JUNIOR COLLEGE: Copiah-Lincoln (Wesson, Miss.).
COLLEGE: South Carolina.
TRANSACTIONS/CAREER NOTES: Signed as non-drafted free agent by Tampa Bay Buccaneers (April 14, 2003). ... Released by Buccaneers (November 14, 2003). ... Re-signed by Buccaneers to practice squad (November 14, 2003). ... Activated (December 13, 2003). ... Claimed on waivers by Atlanta Falcons (September 6, 2004). ... Claimed on waivers by Carolina Panthers (November 4, 2004).

			TOTALS		
Year Team	G	GS	Tk.	Ast.	Sks.
2003—Tampa Bay NFL	4	0	3	2	1.0
2004—Atlanta NFL	3	0	5	0	0.0
—Carolina NFL	2	0	0	0	0.0
Pro totals (2 years)	9	0	8	2	1.0

PINKSTON, TODD WR EAGLES

PERSONAL: Born April 23, 1977, in Forest, Miss. ... 6-3/180.
HIGH SCHOOL: Forest (Miss.).
COLLEGE: Southern Miss.
TRANSACTIONS/CAREER NOTES: Selected by Philadelphia Eagles in second round (36th pick overall) of 2000 NFL draft. ... Signed by Eagles (July 16, 2000).
CHAMPIONSHIP GAME EXPERIENCE: Played in NFC championship game (2001-2004 seasons). ... Played in Super Bowl 39 (2004 season).
SINGLE GAME HIGHS (regular season): Receptions—7 (December 8, 2002, vs. Seattle); yards—121 (December 21, 2003, vs. San Francisco); and touchdown receptions—2 (September 22, 2002, vs. Dallas).
STATISTICAL PLATEAUS: 100-yard receiving games: 2003 (1), 2004 (2). Total: 3.

			RECEIVING				TOTALS			
Year Team	G	GS	No.	Yds.	Avg.	TD	TD	2pt.	Pts.	Fum.
2000—Philadelphia NFL	16	1	10	181	18.1	0	0	0	0	0
2001—Philadelphia NFL	15	15	42	586	14.0	4	4	0	24	0
2002—Philadelphia NFL	15	15	60	798	13.3	7	7	0	42	2
2003—Philadelphia NFL	16	15	36	575	16.0	2	2	0	12	1
2004—Philadelphia NFL	16	16	36	676	‡18.8	1	1	0	6	0
Pro totals (5 years)	78	62	184	2816	15.3	14	14	0	84	3

PINNER, ARTOSE   RB   LIONS

PERSONAL: Born January 5, 1978, in Hopkinsville, Ky. ... 5-10/235. ... Full name: Artose Deonce Pinner.
HIGH SCHOOL: Hopkinsville (Ky.).
COLLEGE: Kentucky.
TRANSACTIONS/CAREER NOTES: Selected by Detroit Lions in fourth round (99th pick overall) of 2003 NFL draft. ... Signed by Lions (July 21, 2003). ... On non-football injury list with leg injury (July 23-November 23, 2003). ... Activated (November 24, 2003).
SINGLE GAME HIGHS (regular season): Attempts—23 (October 10, 2004, vs. Atlanta); yards—68 (October 10, 2004, vs. Atlanta); and rushing touchdowns—1 (October 24, 2004, vs. New York Giants).

				RUSHING				RECEIVING				TOTALS		
Year Team	G	GS	Att.	Yds.	Avg.	TD	No.	Yds.	Avg.	TD	TD	2pt.	Pts.	Fum.
2003—Detroit NFL	3	2	39	99	2.5	0	5	40	8.0	0	0	0	0	0
2004—Detroit NFL	9	2	57	174	3.1	2	11	72	6.5	0	2	0	12	0
Pro totals (2 years)	12	4	96	273	2.8	2	16	112	7.0	0	2	0	12	0

PINNOCK, ANDREW   FB   CHARGERS

PERSONAL: Born March 12, 1980, in Hartford, Conn. ... 5-10/260.
HIGH SCHOOL: Bloomfield (Conn.).
COLLEGE: South Carolina.
TRANSACTIONS/CAREER NOTES: Selected by San Diego Chargers in seventh round (229th pick overall) of 2003 NFL draft. ... Signed by Chargers (June 19, 2003). ... On suspended list (November 9-December 13, 2004). ... Inactive for 10 games (2004). ... Activated (December 20, 2004).
SINGLE GAME HIGHS (regular season): Attempts—9 (January 2, 2005, vs. Kansas City); yards—26 (January 2, 2005, vs. Kansas City); and rushing touchdowns—0.

				RUSHING				RECEIVING				TOTALS		
Year Team	G	GS	Att.	Yds.	Avg.	TD	No.	Yds.	Avg.	TD	TD	2pt.	Pts.	Fum.
2003—San Diego NFL	16	0	0	0	0.0	0	0	0	0.0	0	0	0	0	0
2004—San Diego NFL	1	0	9	26	2.9	0	3	26	8.7	0	0	0	0	1
Pro totals (2 years)	17	0	9	26	2.9	0	3	26	8.7	0	0	0	0	1

PIPPENS, JERRELL   S   BEARS

PERSONAL: Born June 30, 1980, in Philadelphia, Pa. ... 6-2/195.
HIGH SCHOOL: West Catholic (Philadelphia, Pa.).
COLLEGE: Nebraska.
TRANSACTIONS/CAREER NOTES: Signed as non-drafted free agent by San Diego Chargers (May 7, 2004). ... Released by Chargers (September 5, 2004). ... Re-signed by Chargers to practice squad (September 7, 2004). ... Activated (October 26, 2004). ... Claimed on waivers by Chicago Bears (December 21, 2004).

			TOTALS			INTERCEPTIONS			
Year Team	G	GS	Tk.	Ast.	Sks.	No.	Yds.	Avg.	TD
2004—San Diego NFL	7	0	0	0	0.0	0	0	0.0	0
—Chicago NFL	2	0	0	0	0.0	0	0	0.0	0
Pro totals (1 year)	9	0	0	0	0.0	0	0	0.0	0

PITTMAN, BRYAN   C/LS   TEXANS

PERSONAL: Born January 20, 1977, in Tacoma, Wash. ... 6-3/275.
HIGH SCHOOL: Thomas Jefferson (Federal Way, Wa.).
JUNIOR COLLEGE: Walla Walla (Wash.).
COLLEGE: Washington.
TRANSACTIONS/CAREER NOTES: Signed as non-drafted free agent by Cleveland Browns (April 9, 2003). ... Released by Browns (May 19, 2003). ... Re-signed by Browns (July 25, 2003). ... Released by Browns (August 28, 2003). ... Signed by Houston Texans to practice squad (September 1, 2003). ... Activated (September 7, 2003).
PLAYING EXPERIENCE: Houston NFL, 2003-2004. ... Games/Games started: 2003 (16/0), 2004 (16/0). Total: 32/0.

PITTMAN, KAVIKA   DE   PANTHERS

PERSONAL: Born October 9, 1974, in Frankfurt, Germany. ... 6-6/273. ... Name pronounced: kuh-VEE-kuh.
HIGH SCHOOL: Leesville (La.).
COLLEGE: McNeese State.
TRANSACTIONS/CAREER NOTES: Selected by Dallas Cowboys in second round (37th pick overall) of 1996 NFL draft. ... Signed by Cowboys (July 16, 1996). ... Granted unconditional free agency (February 11, 2000). ... Signed by Denver Broncos (February 22, 2000). ... On injured reserve with calf injury (December 19, 2001-remainder of season). ... Waived by Broncos (February 25, 2003). ... Signed by Carolina Panthers (May 22, 2003). ... On injured reserve with knee injury (September 18, 2003-remainder of season). ... Granted unconditional free agency (March 3, 2004). ... Re-signed by Panthers (March 22, 2004). ... On injured reserve with knee injury (August 22, 2004-entire season).

			TOTALS		
Year Team	G	GS	Tk.	Ast.	Sks.
1996—Dallas NFL	15	0	2	0	0.0
1997—Dallas NFL	15	0	4	1	1.0
1998—Dallas NFL	15	15	37	4	6.0
1999—Dallas NFL	16	16	33	10	3.0
2000—Denver NFL	15	15	26	2	7.0

P

		TOTALS				
Year Team		G	GS	Tk.	Ast.	Sks.
2001—Denver NFL		14	14	28	6	1.0
2002—Denver NFL		16	15	29	9	0.0
2003—Carolina NFL		2	0	0	0	0.0
2004—Carolina NFL		Did not play.				
Pro totals (8 years)		108	75	159	32	18.0

PITTMAN, MICHAEL　　　　RB　　　　BUCCANEERS

PERSONAL: Born August 14, 1975, in New Orleans, La. ... 6-0/218.
HIGH SCHOOL: Mira Mesa (San Diego).
COLLEGE: Fresno State.
TRANSACTIONS/CAREER NOTES: Selected by Arizona Cardinals in fourth round (95th pick overall) of 1998 NFL draft. ... Signed by Cardinals (May 20, 1998). ... Granted free agency (March 2, 2001). ... Re-signed by Cardinals (May 11, 2001). ... On suspended list (September 9-23, 2001). ... Granted unconditional free agency (March 1, 2002). ... Signed by Tampa Bay Buccaneers (March 25, 2002).
CHAMPIONSHIP GAME EXPERIENCE: Played in NFC championship game (2002 season). ... Member of Super Bowl championship team (2002 season).
SINGLE GAME HIGHS (regular season): Attempts—30 (October 26, 2003, vs. Dallas); yards—133 (November 14, 1999, vs. Detroit); and rushing touchdowns—3 (November 7, 2004, vs. Kansas City).
STATISTICAL PLATEAUS: 100-yard rushing games: 1999 (1), 2000 (1), 2003 (2), 2004 (4). Total: 8. 100-yard receiving games: 2004 (1). Total: 1.

			RUSHING				RECEIVING				PUNT RETURNS				KICKOFF RETURNS				TOTALS		
Year Team	G	GS	Att.	Yds.	Avg.	TD	No.	Yds.	Avg.	TD	No.	Yds.	Avg.	TD	No.	Yds.	Avg.	TD	TD	2pt.	Pts.
1998—Ari. NFL	15	0	29	91	3.1	0	0	0	0.0	0	0	0	0.0	0	4	84	21.0	0	0	0	0
1999—Ari. NFL	12	2	64	289	4.5	2	16	196	12.3	0	4	16	4.0	0	2	31	15.5	0	2	0	12
2000—Ari. NFL	16	11	184	719	3.9	4	73	579	7.9	2	0	0	0.0	0	0	0	0.0	0	6	0	36
2001—Ari. NFL	15	14	241	846	3.5	5	42	264	6.3	0	0	0	0.0	0	6	161	26.8	0	5	0	30
2002—T.B. NFL	16	15	204	718	3.5	1	59	477	8.1	0	0	0	0.0	0	0	0	0.0	0	1	0	6
2003—T.B. NFL	16	13	187	751	4.0	0	75	597	8.0	2	0	0	0.0	0	0	0	0.0	0	2	0	12
2004—T.B. NFL	13	13	219	926	4.2	7	41	391	9.5	3	0	0	0.0	0	0	0	0.0	0	10	0	60
Pro totals (7 years)	103	68	1128	4340	3.8	19	306	2504	8.2	7	4	16	4.0	0	12	276	23.0	0	26	0	156

PITTS, CHESTER　　　　G/T　　　　TEXANS

PERSONAL: Born June 26, 1979, in Inglewood, Calif. ... 6-4/329. ... Full name: Chester Morise Pitts II.
HIGH SCHOOL: California Academy for Math and Science (Los Angeles).
COLLEGE: San Diego State.
TRANSACTIONS/CAREER NOTES: Selected by Houston Texans in second round (50th pick overall) of 2002 NFL draft. ... Signed by Texans (July 16, 2002).
PLAYING EXPERIENCE: Houston NFL, 2002-2004. ... Games/Games started: 2002 (16/16), 2003 (16/16), 2004 (16/16). Total: 48/48.

PLAYER, SCOTT　　　　P　　　　CARDINALS

PERSONAL: Born December 17, 1969, in St. Augustine, Fla. ... 6-1/213.
HIGH SCHOOL: St. Augustine (Fla.).
JUNIOR COLLEGE: Florida Community College.
COLLEGE: Florida State.
TRANSACTIONS/CAREER NOTES: Played with Birmingham Barracudas of CFL (1995). ... Granted free agency (March 7, 1996). ... Signed as non-drafted free agent by Arizona Cardinals (April 23, 1996). ... Released by Cardinals (August 19, 1996). ... Signed by New York Giants (February 14, 1997). ... Assigned by Giants to Frankfurt Galaxy in 1997 World League enhancement allocation program (February 18, 1997). ... Released by Giants (August 24, 1997). ... Signed by New York Jets to practice squad (August 26, 1997). ... Released by Jets (August 28, 1997). ... Re-signed by Cardinals (March 3, 1998). ... Granted free agency (March 2, 2001). ... Re-signed by Cardinals (July 13, 2001).
HONORS: Played in Pro Bowl (2000 season).

		PUNTING				
Year Team	G	No.	Yds.	Avg.	Net avg.	In. 20	Blk.
1995—Birmingham CFL	18	143	6247	43.7	36.5	...	...
1996—	Did not play.					
1998—Arizona NFL	16	81	3378	41.7	35.9	12	∞1
1999—Arizona NFL	16	94	3948	42.0	36.7	18	0
2000—Arizona NFL	16	65	2871	44.2	37.3	17	0
2001—Arizona NFL	12	67	2779	41.5	33.8	17	0
2002—Arizona NFL	16	88	3864	43.9	35.0	28	1
2003—Arizona NFL	16	82	3511	42.8	34.4	19	1
2004—Arizona NFL	16	98	4230	43.2	36.4	32	1
CFL totals (1 year)	18	143	6247	43.7	0.0	...	...
NFL totals (7 years)	108	575	24581	42.7	35.7	143	4
Pro totals (8 years)	126	718	30828	42.9	28.6	...	...

P　　PLUMMER, AHMED　　　　CB　　　　49ERS

PERSONAL: Born March 26, 1976, in Wyoming, Ohio. ... 6-0/191. ... Full name: Ahmed Kamil Plummer.
HIGH SCHOOL: Wyoming (Ohio).
COLLEGE: Ohio State.

Year Team	G	GS	TOTALS			INTERCEPTIONS			
			Tk.	Ast.	Sks.	No.	Yds.	Avg.	TD
2000—San Francisco NFL	16	14	66	9	0.0	0	0	0.0	0
2001—San Francisco NFL	15	1?	58	6	0.0	7	45	6.4	0
2002—San Francisco NFL	15	15	52	11	0.0	1	0	0.0	0
2003—San Francisco NFL	15	15		8	0.0	4	85	21.3	1
2004—San Francisco NFL	6	6		7	0.0	0	0	0.0	0
Pro totals (5 years)	67	65		41	0.0	12	130	10.8	1

PLUMMER, JAKE   QB   BRONCOS

PERSONAL: Born December 19, 1974, in Boise, Idaho. ... 6-2/212. ... Full name: Jason Steven Plummer.
HIGH SCHOOL: Capital (Boise, Idaho).
COLLEGE: Arizona State.
TRANSACTIONS/CAREER NOTES: Selected by Arizona Cardinals in second round (42nd pick overall) of 1997 NFL draft. ... Signed by Cardinals (July 14, 1997). ... Granted unconditional free agency (February 28, 2003). ... Signed by Denver Broncos (March 5, 2003).
HONORS: Named quarterback on THE SPORTING NEWS college All-America second team (1996).
SINGLE GAME HIGHS (regular season): Attempts—57 (January 2, 2000, vs. Green Bay); completions—35 (January 2, 2000, vs. Green Bay); yards—499 (October 31, 2004, vs. Atlanta); and touchdown passes—4 (November 7, 2004, vs. Houston).
STATISTICAL PLATEAUS: 300-yard passing games: 1997 (2), 1998 (2), 1999 (1), 2000 (1), 2001 (1), 2004 (2). Total: 9.
MISCELLANEOUS: Regular-season record as starting NFL quarterback: 49-60 (.450). ... Postseason record as starting NFL quarterback: 1-3 (.250).

Year Team	G	GS	PASSING									RUSHING				TOTALS			
			Att.	Cmp.	Pct.	Yds.	TD	Int.	Avg.	Skd.	Rat.	Att.	Yds.	Avg.	TD	TD	2pt.	Pts.
1997—Arizona NFL	10	9	296	157	53.0	2203	15	15	7.44	52	73.1	39	216	5.5	2	2	1	14
1998—Arizona NFL	16	16	547	324	59.2	3737	17	20	6.83	49	75.0	51	217	4.3	4	4	0	24
1999—Arizona NFL	12	11	381	201	52.8	2111	9	*24	5.54	27	50.8	39	121	3.1	2	2	0	12
2000—Arizona NFL	14	14	475	270	56.8	2946	13	‡21	6.20	22	66.0	37	183	4.9	0	0	0	0
2001—Arizona NFL	16	16	525	304	57.9	3653	18	14	6.96	29	79.6	35	163	4.7	0	0	1	2
2002—Arizona NFL	16	16	530	284	53.6	2972	18	20	5.61	36	65.7	46	283	6.2	2	2	0	12
2003—Denver NFL	11	11	302	189	62.6	2182	15	7	7.23	14	91.2	37	205	5.5	3	3	0	18
2004—Denver NFL	16	16	521	303	58.2	4089	27	†20	7.85	15	84.5	62	202	3.3	1	1	0	6
Pro totals (8 years)	111	109	3577	2032	56.8	23893	132	141	6.68	244	73.1	346	1590	4.6	14	14	2	88

POLAMALU, TROY   S   STEELERS

PERSONAL: Born April 19, 1981, in Garden Grove, Calif. ... 5-10/212. ... Full name: Troy Aumua Polamalu.
HIGH SCHOOL: Douglas (Winston, Ore.).
COLLEGE: Southern California.
TRANSACTIONS/CAREER NOTES: Selected by Pittsburgh Steelers in first round (16th pick overall) of 2003 NFL draft. ... Signed by Steelers (July 28, 2003).
CHAMPIONSHIP GAME EXPERIENCE: Played in AFC championship game (2004 season).
HONORS: Played in Pro Bowl (2004 season).

Year Team	G	GS	TOTALS			INTERCEPTIONS			
			Tk.	Ast.	Sks.	No.	Yds.	Avg.	TD
2003—Pittsburgh NFL	16	0	17	6	2.0	0	0	0.0	0
2004—Pittsburgh NFL	16	16	66	28	1.0	5	58	11.6	1
Pro totals (2 years)	32	16	83	34	3.0	5	58	11.6	1

POLITE, LOUSAKA   FB   COWBOYS

PERSONAL: Born September 14, 1981, in North Braddock, Pa. ... 6-0/246. ... Full name: Lousaka Romon Polite.
HIGH SCHOOL: Woodland Hills (North Braddock, Pa.).
COLLEGE: Pittsburgh.
TRANSACTIONS/CAREER NOTES: Signed as non-drafted free agent by Dallas Cowboys (April 30, 2004). ... Released by Cowboys (September 5, 2004). ... Re-signed by Cowboys to practice squad (November 3, 2004). ... Activated (December 28, 2004).

Year Team	G	GS	RUSHING				RECEIVING				TOTALS			
			Att.	Yds.	Avg.	TD	No.	Yds.	Avg.	TD	TD	2pt.	Pts.	Fum.
2004—Dallas NFL	1	0	0	0	0.0	0	1	4	4.0	0	0	0	0	0

POLK, CARLOS   LB   CHARGERS

PERSONAL: Born February 22, 1977, in Memphis, Tenn. ... 6-2/250. ... Full name: Carlos Devonn Polk.
HIGH SCHOOL: Guilford (Rockford, Ill.).
COLLEGE: Nebraska.
TRANSACTIONS/CAREER NOTES: Selected by San Diego Chargers in fourth round (112th pick overall) of 2001 NFL draft. ... Signed by Chargers (June 20, 2001). ... On injured reserve with shoulder injury (November 14, 2001-remainder of season). ... Granted free agency (March 3, 2004). ... Re-signed by Chargers (April 27, 2004). ... On injured reserve with shoulder injury (September 21, 2004-remainder of season). ... Granted unconditional free agency (March 2, 2005). ... Re-signed by Chargers (March 17, 2005).
HONORS: Named linebacker on THE SPORTING NEWS college All-America third team (2000).

P

Year Team	G	GS	TOTALS Tk.	Ast.	Sks.	INTERCEPTIONS No.	Yds.	Avg.	TD
2001—San Diego NFL	6	0	0	0	0.0	0	0	0.0	0
2002—San Diego NFL	15	0	3	1	1.0	0	0	0.0	0
2003—San Diego NFL	16	0	5	1	0.0	0	0	0.0	0
2004—San Diego NFL	1	0	0	0	0.0	0	0	0.0	0
Pro totals (4 years)	38	0	8	2	1.0	0	0	0.0	0

POLK, DASHON — LB — TEXANS

PERSONAL: Born March 13, 1977, in Pacoima, Calif. ... 6-2/240. ... Full name: DaShon Lamor Polk.
HIGH SCHOOL: Taft (Woodlands Hills, Calif.).
COLLEGE: Arizona.
TRANSACTIONS/CAREER NOTES: Selected by Buffalo Bills in seventh round (251st pick overall) of 2000 NFL draft. ... Signed by Bills (June 22, 2000). ... Granted free agency (February 28, 2003). ... Re-signed by Bills (April 10, 2003). ... Granted unconditional free agency (March 3, 2004). ... Signed by Houston Texans (March 16, 2004).

Year Team	G	GS	TOTALS Tk.	Ast.	Sks.	INTERCEPTIONS No.	Yds.	Avg.	TD
2000—Buffalo NFL	5	0	0	0	0.0	0	0	0.0	0
2001—Buffalo NFL	16	1	13	6	0.0	0	0	0.0	0
2002—Buffalo NFL	16	0	8	10	0.0	0	0	0.0	0
2003—Buffalo NFL	16	0	1	3	0.0	0	0	0.0	0
2004—Houston NFL	16	4	18	12	1.0	0	0	0.0	0
Pro totals (5 years)	69	5	40	31	1.0	0	0	0.0	0

POLLARD, MARCUS — TE — LIONS

PERSONAL: Born February 8, 1972, in Valley, Ala. ... 6-3/247. ... Full name: Marcus LaJuan Pollard.
HIGH SCHOOL: Valley (Ala.).
JUNIOR COLLEGE: Seward County Community College, Kan. (did not play football).
COLLEGE: Bradley.
TRANSACTIONS/CAREER NOTES: Signed as non-drafted free agent by Indianapolis Colts (January 24, 1995). ... Released by Colts (August 22, 1995). ... Re-signed by Colts to practice squad (August 28, 1995). ... Activated (October 10, 1995). ... Granted free agency (February 13, 1998). ... Tendered offer sheet by Philadelphia Eagles (March 4, 1998). ... Offer matched by Colts (March 9, 1998). ... Designated by Colts as franchise player (February 22, 2001). ... Released by Colts (March 2, 2005). ... Signed by Detroit Lions (March 7, 2005).
CHAMPIONSHIP GAME EXPERIENCE: Played in AFC championship game (1995 and 2003 seasons).
SINGLE GAME HIGHS (regular season): Receptions—7 (November 3, 2002, vs. Tennessee); yards—126 (November 18, 2001, vs. New Orleans); and touchdown receptions—2 (November 8, 2004, vs. Minnesota).
STATISTICAL PLATEAUS: 100-yard receiving games: 2001 (2). Total: 2.

Year Team	G	GS	RECEIVING No.	Yds.	Avg.	TD	TOTALS TD	2pt.	Pts.	Fum.
1995—Indianapolis NFL	8	0	0	0	0.0	0	0	0	0	0
1996—Indianapolis NFL	16	4	6	86	14.3	1	1	0	6	0
1997—Indianapolis NFL	16	6	10	116	11.6	0	0	1	2	0
1998—Indianapolis NFL	16	11	24	309	12.9	4	4	†2	28	0
1999—Indianapolis NFL	16	10	34	374	11.0	4	4	0	24	2
2000—Indianapolis NFL	16	14	30	439	14.6	3	3	1	20	0
2001—Indianapolis NFL	16	16	47	739	15.7	8	8	0	48	0
2002—Indianapolis NFL	15	15	43	478	11.1	6	6	1	38	1
2003—Indianapolis NFL	14	13	40	541	13.5	3	3	0	18	1
2004—Indianapolis NFL	13	13	29	309	10.7	6	6	0	36	0
Pro totals (10 years)	146	102	263	3391	12.9	35	35	5	220	4

POLLARD, ROBERT — DE — CHARGERS

PERSONAL: Born June 28, 1981, in Metairie, La. ... 6-2/278. ... Son of Robert Pollard, defensive end with New Orleans Saints (1971-77) and St. Louis Cardinals (1978-81).
HIGH SCHOOL: Westbrook (Beaumont, Texas).
COLLEGE: Texas Christian.
TRANSACTIONS/CAREER NOTES: Signed as non-drafted free agent by San Diego Chargers (April 30, 2004). ... Released by Chargers (August 31, 2004). ... Signed by Chargers to practice squad (September 6, 2004). ... Released by Chargers from practice squad (October 12, 2004). ... Re-signed by Chargers to practice squad (October 19, 2004). ... Activated (January 1, 2005).

Year Team	G	GS	TOTALS Tk.	Ast.	Sks.
2004—San Diego NFL	1	0	0	0	0.0

POLLEY, TOMMY — LB — RAVENS

PERSONAL: Born January 18, 1978, in Baltimore, Md. ... 6-3/240.
HIGH SCHOOL: Dunbar (Baltimore).
COLLEGE: Florida State.
TRANSACTIONS/CAREER NOTES: Selected by St. Louis Rams in second round (42nd pick overall) of 2001 NFL draft. ... Signed by Rams (July 23, 2001). ... Granted unconditional free agency (March 2, 2005). ... Signed by Baltimore Ravens (April 11, 2005).
CHAMPIONSHIP GAME EXPERIENCE: Played in NFC championship game (2001 season). ... Played in Super Bowl 36 (2001 season).
HONORS: Named linebacker on THE SPORTING NEWS college All-America third team (2000).

P

Year Team	G	GS	TOTALS			INTERCEPTIONS			
			Tk.	Ast.	Sks.	No.	Yds.	Avg.	TD
2001—St. Louis NFL	16	11	61	17	0.0	0	0	0.0	0
2002—St. Louis NFL	12	11	42	15	0.0	0	0	0.0	0
2003—St. Louis NFL	14	14	58	12	0.0	4	32	8.0	0
2004—St. Louis NFL	15	13	65	13	2.0	0	0	0.0	0
Pro totals (4 years)	57	49	226	57	2.0	4	32	8.0	0

PONDER, WILLIE   WR   GIANTS

PERSONAL: Born February 14, 1980, in Tulsa, Okla. ... 6-0/205. ... Full name: Willie Columbus Ponder Jr.
HIGH SCHOOL: Central (Tulsa, Okla.).
JUNIOR COLLEGE: Coffeyville (Kan).
COLLEGE: Southeast Missouri State.
TRANSACTIONS/CAREER NOTES: Selected by New York Giants in sixth round (199th pick overall) of 2003 NFL draft. ... Signed by Giants (June 12, 2003).
SINGLE GAME HIGHS (regular season): Receptions—2 (December 28, 2003, vs. Carolina); yards—18 (December 28, 2003, vs. Carolina); and touchdown receptions—0.

Year Team	G	GS	RECEIVING				KICKOFF RETURNS				TOTALS			
			No.	Yds.	Avg.	TD	No.	Yds.	Avg.	TD	TD	2pt.	Pts.	Fum.
2003—New York Giants NFL	4	0	7	35	5.0	0	0	0	0.0	0	0	0	0	0
2004—New York Giants NFL	11	0	1	3	3.0	0	36	967	*26.9	1	1	0	6	1
Pro totals (2 years)	15	0	8	38	4.8	0	36	967	26.9	1	1	0	6	1

PONTBRIAND, RYAN   C/LS   BROWNS

PERSONAL: Born October 1, 1979, in Houston, Texas. ... 6-2/255. ... Full name: Ryan David Pontbriand. ... Name pronounced: pownt-bree-AWND.
HIGH SCHOOL: W.P. Clements (Sugar Land, Texas).
COLLEGE: Rice.
TRANSACTIONS/CAREER NOTES: Selected by Cleveland Browns in fifth round (142nd pick overall) of 2003 NFL draft. ... Signed by Browns (July 27, 2003).
PLAYING EXPERIENCE: Cleveland NFL, 2003-2004. ... Games/Games started: 2003 (16/0), 2004 (16/0). Total: 32/0.

POOLE, NATHAN   WR   SAINTS

PERSONAL: Born February 1, 1977, in Danville, Va. ... 6-2/204.
HIGH SCHOOL: George Washington (Danville, Va.).
COLLEGE: Marshall.
TRANSACTIONS/CAREER NOTES: Signed as non-drafted free agent by Arizona Cardinals (April 23, 2001). ... Released by Cardinals (September 1, 2001). ... Re-signed by Cardinals to practice squad (December 3, 2001). ... Released by Cardinals (August 26, 2002). ... Re-signed by Cardinals to practice squad (October 30, 2002). ... Activated (November 6, 2002). ... Granted free agency (March 3, 2003). ... Re-signed by Cardinals (April 2, 2003). ... Waived by Cardinals (August 30, 2003). ... Re-signed by Cardinals (September 12, 2003). ... Did not receive qualifying offer from Cardinals (March 2, 2005). ... Signed by New Orleans Saints (May 18, 2005).
SINGLE GAME HIGHS (regular season): Receptions—6 (December 8, 2002, vs. Detroit); yards—86 (December 28, 2003, vs. Minnesota); and touchdown receptions—1 (December 28, 2003, vs. Minnesota).

Year Team	G	GS	RECEIVING				TOTALS			
			No.	Yds.	Avg.	TD	TD	2pt.	Pts.	Fum.
2002—Arizona NFL	5	1	13	108	8.3	1	1	0	6	0
2003—Arizona NFL	15	1	13	177	13.6	1	1	0	6	0
2004—Arizona NFL	9	1	5	70	14.0	0	0	0	0	0
Pro totals (3 years)	29	3	31	355	11.5	2	2	0	12	0

POOLE, TYRONE   CB   PANTHERS

PERSONAL: Born February 3, 1972, in LaGrange, Ga. ... 5-8/188.
HIGH SCHOOL: La Grange (Ga.).
COLLEGE: Fort Valley State.
TRANSACTIONS/CAREER NOTES: Selected by Carolina Panthers in first round (22nd pick overall) of 1995 NFL draft. ... Signed by Panthers (July 15, 1995). ... Traded by Panthers to Indianapolis Colts for second-round pick (OT Chris Terry) in 1999 draft (July 22, 1998). ... Released by Colts (March 1, 2001). ... Signed by Denver Broncos (May 22, 2001). ... On reserve/left squad list (August 9, 2001-February 27, 2002). ... Granted unconditional free agency (February 28, 2003). ... Signed by New England Patriots (March 4, 2003). ... On injured reserve with knee injury (December 18, 2004-remainder of season).
CHAMPIONSHIP GAME EXPERIENCE: Played in NFC championship game (1996 season). ... Played in AFC championship game (2003 season). ... Member of Super Bowl championship team (2003 and 2004 seasons).

Year Team	G	GS	TOTALS			INTERCEPTIONS				PUNT RETURNS				TOTALS			
			Tk.	Ast.	Sks.	No.	Yds.	Avg.	TD	No.	Yds.	Avg.	TD	TD	2pt.	Pts.	Fum.
1995—Carolina NFL	16	13	59	9	2.0	2	8	4.0	0	0	0	0.0	0	0	0	0	0
1996—Carolina NFL	15	15	57	11	0.0	1	35	35.0	0	3	26	8.7	0	0	0	0	0
1997—Carolina NFL	16	16	48	4	1.0	2	0	0.0	0	26	191	7.3	0	0	0	0	3
1998—Indianapolis NFL	15	15	52	9	0.0	1	0	0.0	0	12	107	8.9	0	0	0	0	0
1999—Indianapolis NFL	15	14	34	5	1.0	3	85	28.3	0	0	0	0.0	0	0	0	0	0
2000—Indianapolis NFL	15	12	38	12	0.0	1	1	1.0	0	0	0	0.0	0	0	0	0	0
2002—Denver NFL	16	4	41	10	1.0	0	0	0.0	0	4	24	6.0	0	0	0	0	1
2003—New England NFL	16	16	47	12	0.0	6	81	13.5	0	11	75	6.8	0	0	0	0	1
2004—New England NFL	5	4	12	1	0.0	1	21	21.0	0	2	6	3.0	0	0	0	0	1
Pro totals (9 years)	129	109	388	73	5.0	17	231	13.6	0	58	429	7.4	0	0	0	0	6

P

POOLE, WILL   CB   DOLPHINS

PERSONAL: Born July 24, 1981, in St. Albans, N.Y. ... 5-10/193.
HIGH SCHOOL: Christ the King (St. Albans, N.Y.).
JUNIOR COLLEGE: Ventura (Calif.).
COLLEGE: Southern California.
TRANSACTIONS/CAREER NOTES: Selected by Miami Dolphins in fourth round (102nd pick overall) of 2004 NFL draft. ... Signed by Dolphins (July 31, 2004).

			TOTALS			INTERCEPTIONS			
Year Team	G	GS	Tk.	Ast.	Sks.	No.	Yds.	Avg.	TD
2004—Miami NFL	15	1	26	5	1.0	0	0	0.0	0

POPE, DERRICK   LB   DOLPHINS

PERSONAL: Born May 4, 1982, in Galveston, Texas. ... 5-11/233.
HIGH SCHOOL: Butler (Huntsville, Ala.).
COLLEGE: Alabama.
TRANSACTIONS/CAREER NOTES: Selected by Miami Dolphins in seventh round (222nd pick overall) of 2004 NFL draft. ... Signed by Dolphins (July 30, 2004).

			TOTALS			INTERCEPTIONS			
Year Team	G	GS	Tk.	Ast.	Sks.	No.	Yds.	Avg.	TD
2004—Miami NFL	16	3	22	15	2.0	0	0	0.0	0

POPE, KENDYLL   LB   COLTS

PERSONAL: Born March 9, 1981, in Fort White, Fla. ... 6-1/220.
HIGH SCHOOL: Columbia (Fort White, Fla.).
COLLEGE: Florida State.
TRANSACTIONS/CAREER NOTES: Selected by Indianapolis Colts in fourth round (107th pick overall) of 2004 NFL draft. ... Signed by Colts (July 28, 2004). ... On physically unable to perform list with hip injury (August 2-November 9, 2004). ... On reserve/non-football injury list with hip injury (November 9-30, 2004). ... Activated (November 30, 2004).
HONORS: Named linebacker on THE SPORTING NEWS Freshman All-America first team (2000).

			TOTALS			INTERCEPTIONS			
Year Team	G	GS	Tk.	Ast.	Sks.	No.	Yds.	Avg.	TD
2004—Indianapolis NFL	2	0	0	0	0.0	0	0	0.0	0

POPE, MONSANTO   DT   BRONCOS

PERSONAL: Born January 27, 1978, in Norfolk, Va. ... 6-3/300.
HIGH SCHOOL: Hopewell (Va.).
COLLEGE: Virginia.
TRANSACTIONS/CAREER NOTES: Selected by Denver Broncos in seventh round (231st pick overall) of 2002 NFL draft. ... Signed by Broncos (June 14, 2002). ... Granted free agency (March 2, 2005). ... Re-signed by Broncos (April 1, 2005).

			TOTALS		
Year Team	G	GS	Tk.	Ast.	Sks.
2002—Denver NFL	14	1	15	3	4.0
2003—Denver NFL	16	5	13	5	1.0
2004—Denver NFL	16	15	19	5	1.0
Pro totals (3 years)	46	21	47	13	6.0

PORTER, JERRY   WR   RAIDERS

PERSONAL: Born July 14, 1978, in Washington, DC. ... 6-2/220.
HIGH SCHOOL: Coolidge (Washington, D.C.).
COLLEGE: West Virginia.
TRANSACTIONS/CAREER NOTES: Selected by Oakland Raiders in second round (47th pick overall) of 2000 NFL draft. ... Signed by Raiders (July 22, 2000).
CHAMPIONSHIP GAME EXPERIENCE: Played in AFC championship game (2000 and 2002 seasons). ... Played in Super Bowl 37 (2002 season).
SINGLE GAME HIGHS (regular season): Receptions—8 (December 19, 2004, vs. Tennessee); yards—148 (December 19, 2004, vs. Tennessee); and touchdown receptions—3 (December 19, 2004, vs. Tennessee).
STATISTICAL PLATEAUS: 100-yard receiving games: 2002 (1), 2004 (3). Total: 4.

			RUSHING				RECEIVING				TOTALS			
Year Team	G	GS	Att.	Yds.	Avg.	TD	No.	Yds.	Avg.	TD	TD	2pt.	Pts.	Fum.
2000—Oakland NFL	12	0	0	0	0.0	0	1	6	6.0	0	0	0	0	0
2001—Oakland NFL	15	1	2	13	6.5	0	19	220	11.6	0	0	0	0	0
2002—Oakland NFL	16	13	4	6	1.5	0	51	688	13.5	9	9	2	58	0
2003—Oakland NFL	10	1	1	10	10.0	0	28	361	12.9	1	1	0	6	1
2004—Oakland NFL	16	16	1	-4	-4.0	0	64	998	15.6	9	9	0	54	2
Pro totals (5 years)	69	31	8	25	3.1	0	163	2273	13.9	19	19	2	118	3

P

PORTER, JOEY   LB   STEELERS

PERSONAL: Born March 22, 1977, in Bakersfield, Calif. ... 6-3/250. ... Full name: Joey Eugene Porter.
HIGH SCHOOL: Foothills (Calif.).
COLLEGE: Colorado State.
TRANSACTIONS/CAREER NOTES: Selected by Pittsburgh Steelers in third round (73rd pick overall) of 1999 NFL draft. ... Signed by Steelers (July 30, 1999). ... Granted free agency (March 1, 2002). ... Re-signed by Steelers (April 29, 2002).
CHAMPIONSHIP GAME EXPERIENCE: Played in AFC championship game (2001 and 2004 season).
HONORS: Played in Pro Bowl (2002 and 2004 seasons). ... Named linebacker on the THE SPORTING NEWS NFL All-Pro team (2002).

			TOTALS			INTERCEPTIONS			
Year Team	G	GS	Tk.	Ast.	Sks.	No.	Yds.	Avg.	TD
1999—Pittsburgh NFL	16	0	10	0	2.0	0	0	0.0	0
2000—Pittsburgh NFL	16	16	41	18	10.5	1	0	0.0	0
2001—Pittsburgh NFL	15	15	47	14	9.0	0	0	0.0	0
2002—Pittsburgh NFL	16	16	61	28	9.0	4	153	38.2	0
2003—Pittsburgh NFL	14	14	50	16	5.0	0	0	0.0	0
2004—Pittsburgh NFL	15	15	37	17	7.0	1	3	3.0	0
Pro totals (6 years)	92	76	246	93	42.5	6	156	26.0	0

PORTIS, CLINTON   RB   REDSKINS

PERSONAL: Born September 1, 1981, in Laurel, Miss. ... 5-11/205. ... Full name: Clinton Earl Portis.
HIGH SCHOOL: Gainesville (Fla.).
COLLEGE: Miami (Fla.).
TRANSACTIONS/CAREER NOTES: Selected after junior season by Denver Broncos in second round (51st pick overall) of 2002 NFL draft. ... Signed by Broncos (July 25, 2002). ... Traded by Broncos to Washington Redskins for CB Champ Bailey and a second-round pick (RB Tatum Bell) in 2004 NFL draft (March 4, 2004). ... On injured reserve with pectoral injury (December 29, 2004-remainder of season).
HONORS: Named NFL Rookie of the Year by THE SPORTING NEWS (2002). ... Played in Pro Bowl (2003 season).
SINGLE GAME HIGHS (regular season): Attempts—38 (December 14, 2003, vs. Cleveland); yards—228 (December 29, 2002, vs. Arizona); and rushing touchdowns—5 (December 7, 2003, vs. Kansas City).
STATISTICAL PLATEAUS: 100-yard rushing games: 2002 (8), 2003 (10), 2004 (5). Total: 23.

			RUSHING				RECEIVING				TOTALS			
Year Team	G	GS	Att.	Yds.	Avg.	TD	No.	Yds.	Avg.	TD	TD	2pt.	Pts.	Fum.
2002—Denver NFL	16	12	273	1508	§5.5	15	33	364	11.0	2	17	0	102	5
2003—Denver NFL	13	13	290	1591	*5.5	14	38	314	8.3	0	14	1	86	3
2004—Washington NFL	15	15	343	1315	3.8	5	40	235	5.9	2	7	0	42	5
Pro totals (3 years)	44	40	906	4414	4.9	34	111	913	8.2	4	38	1	230	13

PORTIS, MARICO   G   TITANS

PERSONAL: Born November 29, 1979, in Birmingham, Ala. ... 6-2/313. ... Full name: Marico Jermond Portis.
HIGH SCHOOL: Vigor (Pritchard, Ala.).
COLLEGE: Alabama.
TRANSACTIONS/CAREER NOTES: Signed as non-drafted free agent by Tennessee Titans (April 28, 2003). ... Released by Titans (August 29, 2003). ... Re-signed by Titans to practice squad (September 1, 2003). ... Released by Titans from practice squad (November 4, 2003). ... Re-signed by Titans to practice squad (November 12, 2003). ... Released by Titans from practice squad (December 9, 2003). ... Re-signed by Titans to practice squad (December 17, 2003). ... Released by Titans from practice squad (December 23, 2003). ... Re-signed by Titans to practice squad (January 6, 2004). ... Re-signed by Titans (March 26, 2004). ... Released by Titans (September 5, 2004). ... Re-signed by Titans to practice squad (September 14, 2004). ... Activated (December 31, 2004).
PLAYING EXPERIENCE: Tennessee NFL, 2004. ... Games/Games started: 2004 (1/0). Total: 1/0.

POSEY, JEFF   LB   BILLS

PERSONAL: Born August 14, 1975, in Bassfield, Miss. ... 6-4/241.
HIGH SCHOOL: Greenville (Miss.).
JUNIOR COLLEGE: Pearl River Community College (Miss.).
COLLEGE: Southern Miss.
TRANSACTIONS/CAREER NOTES: Signed as non-drafted free agent by San Francisco 49ers (May 2, 1997) ... Released by 49ers (August 19, 1997). ... Re-signed by 49ers to practice squad (August 25, 1997). ... Granted free agency (March 2, 2001). ... Signed by Philadelphia Eagles (June 18, 2001). ... Released by Eagles (August 31, 2001). ... Signed by Carolina Panthers (October 23, 2001). ... Claimed on waivers by Jacksonville Jaguars (November 21, 2001). ... Granted unconditional free agency (March 1, 2002). ... Signed by Houston Texans (April 19, 2002). ... Granted unconditional free agency (February 28, 2003). ... Signed by Buffalo Bills (February 28, 2003).

			TOTALS			INTERCEPTIONS			
Year Team	G	GS	Tk.	Ast.	Sks.	No.	Yds.	Avg.	TD
1998—San Francisco NFL	16	0	7	2	0.5	0	0	0.0	0
1999—San Francisco NFL	16	6	10	5	2.0	0	0	0.0	0
2000—San Francisco NFL	16	9	22	11	0.5	0	0	0.0	0
2001—Carolina NFL	4	0	2	0	0.0	0	0	0.0	0
—Jacksonville NFL	7	5	5	1	1.0	0	0	0.0	0
2002—Houston NFL	16	9	45	15	8.0	1	0	0.0	0
2003—Buffalo NFL	16	16	38	26	5.5	0	0	0.0	0
2004—Buffalo NFL	16	15	39	27	1.0	1	3	3.0	0
Pro totals (7 years)	107	60	168	87	17.5	2	3	1.5	0

P

POTEAT, HANK — CB — PATRIOTS

PERSONAL: Born August 30, 1977, in Harrisburg, Pa. ... 5-9/192. ... Full name: Henry Major Poteat II.
HIGH SCHOOL: Harrisburg (Pa.).
COLLEGE: Pittsburgh.
TRANSACTIONS/CAREER NOTES: Selected by Pittsburgh Steelers in third round (77th pick overall) of 2000 NFL draft. ... Signed by Steelers (July 21, 2000). ... Granted free agency (February 28, 2003). ... Re-signed by Steelers (April 21, 2003). ... Released by Steelers (August 31, 2003). ... Signed by Tampa Bay Buccaneers (October 21, 2003). ... Released by Buccaneers (November 12, 2003). ... Signed by Carolina Panthers (December 30, 2003). ... Released by Panthers (August 24, 2004). ... Signed by New England Patriots (January 10, 2005).
CHAMPIONSHIP GAME EXPERIENCE: Member of Steelers for AFC championship game (2001 season); inactive. ... Played in AFC championship game (2004 season). ... Member of Super Bowl championship team (2004 season).

Year Team	G	GS	TOTALS Tk.	Ast.	Sks.	INTERCEPTIONS No.	Yds.	Avg.	TD	PUNT RETURNS No.	Yds.	Avg.	TD	KICKOFF RETURNS No.	Yds.	Avg.	TD	TOTALS TD	2pt.	Pts.	Fum.
2000—Pit. NFL	15	0	0	0	0.0	0	0	0.0	0	36	467	13.0	1	24	465	19.4	0	1	0	6	3
2001—Pit. NFL	13	0	1	0	0.0	0	0	0.0	0	36	292	8.1	0	16	250	15.6	0	0	0	0	4
2002—Pit. NFL	13	0	8	0	0.0	0	0	0.0	0	4	29	7.3	0	5	103	20.6	0	0	0	0	0
2003—T.B. NFL	1	0	0	0	0.0	0	0	0.0	0	0	0	0.0	0	0	0	0.0	0	0	0	0	0
2004—N.E. NFL	Did not play.																				
Pro totals (4 years)	42	0	9	0	0.0	0	0	0.0	0	76	788	10.4	1	45	818	18.2	0	1	0	6	8

POWELL, CARL — DE — BENGALS

PERSONAL: Born January 4, 1974, in Detroit, Mich. ... 6-2/285. ... Full name: Carl Demetris Powell.
HIGH SCHOOL: Northern (Detroit).
JUNIOR COLLEGE: Grand Rapids (Mich.) Community College.
COLLEGE: Louisville.
TRANSACTIONS/CAREER NOTES: Selected by Indianapolis Colts in fifth round (156th pick overall) of 1997 NFL draft. ... Signed by Colts (July 3, 1997). ... Released by Colts (August 28, 1998). ... Selected by Rhein Fire in 1999 NFL Europe draft (February 23, 1999). ... Signed by Baltimore Ravens (July 21, 2000). ... Released by Ravens (November 13, 2000). ... Signed by Chicago Bears (March 5, 2001). ... Granted unconditional free agency (March 1, 2002). ... Signed by Washington Redskins (March 28, 2002). ... Granted unconditional free agency (February 28, 2003). ... Signed by Cincinnati Bengals (March 2, 2003). ... Granted unconditional free agency (March 2, 2005). ... Re-signed by Bengals (April 5, 2005).

Year Team	G	GS	TOTALS Tk.	Ast.	Sks.	INTERCEPTIONS No.	Yds.	Avg.	TD
1997—Indianapolis NFL	11	0	3	0	0.0	0	0	0.0	0
2000—Baltimore NFL	2	0	0	0	0.0	0	0	0.0	0
2001—Chicago NFL	16	0	8	1	0.0	0	0	0.0	0
2002—Washington NFL	15	4	21	10	3.0	0	0	0.0	0
2003—Cincinnati NFL	16	3	10	10	0.5	0	0	0.0	0
2004—Cincinnati NFL	10	2	16	6	2.0	1	-2	-2.0	0
Pro totals (6 years)	70	9	58	27	5.5	1	-2	-2.0	0

PRICE, MARCUS — T

PERSONAL: Born March 3, 1972, in Port Arthur, Texas. ... 6-4/310. ... Full name: Marcus Raymond Price.
HIGH SCHOOL: Lincoln (Port Arthur, Texas).
COLLEGE: Louisiana State.
TRANSACTIONS/CAREER NOTES: Selected by Jacksonville Jaguars in sixth round (172nd pick overall) of 1995 NFL draft. ... Signed by Jaguars (June 1, 1995). ... On injured reserve with ankle injury (August 19, 1995-entire season). ... Released by Jaguars (August 25, 1996). ... Signed by Denver Broncos to practice squad (December 3, 1996). ... Released by Broncos (December 30, 1996). ... Signed by Jaguars (January 31, 1997). ... Released by Jaguars (August 19, 1997). ... Re-signed by Jaguars to practice squad (October 28, 1997). ... Signed by San Diego Chargers off Jaguars practice squad (November 24, 1997). ... Released by Chargers (September 21, 1999). ... Signed by New Orleans Saints (March 23, 2000). ... Released by Saints (December 3, 2000). ... Re-signed by Saints (December 5, 2000). ... Granted unconditional free agency (March 1, 2002). ... Signed by Buffalo Bills (March 13, 2002). ... Granted unconditional free agency (March 2, 2005).
PLAYING EXPERIENCE: San Diego NFL, 1997-1998; New Orleans NFL, 2000-2001; Buffalo NFL, 2004. ... Games/Games started: 1997 (2/0), 1998 (10/0), 2000 (7/0), 2001 (12/0), 2002 (16/3), 2003 (16/4), 2004 (14/3). Total: 77/10.

PRICE, PEERLESS — WR — FALCONS

PERSONAL: Born October 27, 1976, in Dayton, Ohio. ... 5-11/190. ... Full name: Peerless LeCross Price.
HIGH SCHOOL: Meadowdale (Dayton, Ohio).
COLLEGE: Tennessee.
TRANSACTIONS/CAREER NOTES: Selected by Buffalo Bills in second round (53rd pick overall) of 1999 NFL draft. ... Signed by Bills (July 30, 1999). ... Designated by Bills as franchise player (February 19, 2003). ... Traded by Bills to Atlanta Falcons for first-round pick (RB Willis McGahee) in 2003 draft (March 7, 2003).
CHAMPIONSHIP GAME EXPERIENCE: Played in NFC championship game (2004 season).
SINGLE GAME HIGHS (regular season): Receptions—13 (September 15, 2002, vs. Minnesota); yards—185 (September 15, 2002, vs. Minnesota); and touchdown receptions—2 (October 31, 2004, vs. Denver).
STATISTICAL PLATEAUS: 100-yard receiving games: 1999 (1), 2000 (1), 2001 (3), 2002 (5), 2003 (1). Total: 11.

Year Team	G	GS	RUSHING Att.	Yds.	Avg.	TD	RECEIVING No.	Yds.	Avg.	TD	PUNT RETURNS No.	Yds.	Avg.	TD	KICKOFF RETURNS No.	Yds.	Avg.	TD	TOTALS TD	2pt.	Pts.
1999—Buf. NFL	16	4	1	-7	-7.0	0	31	393	12.7	3	1	16	16.0	0	1	27	27.0	0	3	0	18
2000—Buf. NFL	16	16	2	32	16.0	0	52	762	14.7	3	5	27	5.4	0	0	0	0.0	0	3	0	18
2001—Buf. NFL	16	16	6	97	16.2	0	55	895	16.3	7	19	110	5.8	0	0	0	0.0	0	7	0	42
2002—Buf. NFL	16	16	3	-13	-4.3	0	94	1252	13.3	9	0	0	0.0	0	0	0	0.0	0	9	0	54
2003—Atl. NFL	16	15	2	3	1.5	0	64	838	13.1	3	0	0	0.0	0	0	0	0.0	0	3	0	18
2004—Atl. NFL	16	15	3	34	11.3	0	45	575	12.8	3	0	0	0.0	0	0	0	0.0	0	3	0	18
Pro totals (6 years)	96	82	17	146	8.6	0	341	4715	13.8	28	25	153	6.1	0	1	27	27.0	0	28	0	168

PRIOLEAU, PIERSON S REDSKINS

PERSONAL: Born August 6, 1977, in Charleston, S.C. ... 5-11/188. ... Full name: Pierson Olin Prioleau. ... Name pronounced: pray-LOW.
HIGH SCHOOL: Macedonia (Saint Stephens, S.C.).
COLLEGE: Virginia Tech.
TRANSACTIONS/CAREER NOTES: Selected by San Francisco 49ers in fourth round (110th pick overall) of 1999 NFL draft. ... Signed by 49ers (July 27, 1999). ... Released by 49ers (September 2, 2001). ... Signed by Buffalo Bills (November 7, 2001). ... Granted free agency (March 1, 2002). ... Re-signed by Bills (April 16, 2002). ... Released by Bills (March 14, 2005). ... Signed by Washington Redskins (March 16, 2005).
HONORS: Named strong safety on THE SPORTING NEWS college All-America third team (1997).

				TOTALS			INTERCEPTIONS			
Year Team	G	GS	Tk.	Ast.	Sks.	No.	Yds.	Avg.	TD
1999—San Francisco NFL	14	5	32	8	0.0	0	0	0.0	0
2000—San Francisco NFL	13	6	36	10	0.0	1	13	13.0	0
2001—Buffalo NFL	6	2	23	8	1.0	0	0	0.0	0
2002—Buffalo NFL	16	16	64	22	1.0	0	0	0.0	0
2003—Buffalo NFL	16	6	21	12	0.5	0	0	0.0	0
2004—Buffalo NFL	16	2	15	7	0.0	0	0	0.0	0
Pro totals (6 years)	81	37	191	67	2.5	1	13	13.0	0

PRITCHETT, KELVIN DT

PERSONAL: Born October 24, 1969, in Atlanta, Ga. ... 6-3/330. ... Full name: Kelvin Bratodd Pritchett.
HIGH SCHOOL: Therrell (Atlanta).
COLLEGE: Mississippi.
TRANSACTIONS/CAREER NOTES: Selected by Dallas Cowboys in first round (20th pick overall) of 1991 NFL draft. ... Rights traded by Cowboys to Detroit Lions for second- (LB Dixon Edwards), third- (G James Richards) and fourth-round (DE Tony Hill) picks in 1991 draft (April 21, 1991). ... Granted free agency (February 17, 1994). ... Re-signed by Lions (August 12, 1994). ... Granted unconditional free agency (February 17, 1995). ... Signed by Jacksonville Jaguars (March 11, 1995). ... On injured reserve with knee injury (November 4, 1997-remainder of season). ... Granted unconditional free agency (February 12, 1999). ... Signed by Lions (April 22, 1999). ... Granted unconditional free agency (February 11, 2000). ... Re-signed by Lions (May 12, 2000). ... Granted unconditional free agency (March 2, 2001). ... Re-signed by Lions (July 11, 2001). ... Granted unconditional free agency (March 1, 2002). ... Re-signed by Lions (March 26, 2002). ... Granted unconditional free agency (February 28, 2003). ... Re-signed by Lions (March 13, 2003). ... Granted unconditional free agency (March 3, 2004). ... Re-signed by Lions (March 4, 2004). ... Granted unconditional free agency (March 2, 2005).
CHAMPIONSHIP GAME EXPERIENCE: Played in NFC championship game (1991 season). ... Played in AFC championship game (1996 season).

				TOTALS			INTERCEPTIONS			
Year Team	G	GS	Tk.	Ast.	Sks.	No.	Yds.	Avg.	TD
1991—Detroit NFL	16	0	20	6	1.5	0	0	0.0	0
1992—Detroit NFL	16	15	38	21	6.5	0	0	0.0	0
1993—Detroit NFL	16	5	33	9	4.0	0	0	0.0	0
1994—Detroit NFL	16	15	41	33	5.5	0	0	0.0	0
1995—Jacksonville NFL	16	16	41	22	1.5	0	0	0.0	0
1996—Jacksonville NFL	13	4	16	7	2.0	0	0	0.0	0
1997—Jacksonville NFL	8	5	20	12	3.0	0	0	0.0	0
1998—Jacksonville NFL	15	9	25	8	3.0	0	0	0.0	0
1999—Detroit NFL	16	2	16	4	1.0	0	0	0.0	0
2000—Detroit NFL	15	0	8	8	2.5	1	78	78.0	0
2001—Detroit NFL	16	1	10	7	0.0	0	0	0.0	0
2002—Detroit NFL	16	3	28	14	0.0	0	0	0.0	0
2003—Detroit NFL	13	0	8	1	0.0	0	0	0.0	0
2004—Detroit NFL	16	0	10	7	1.0	0	0	0.0	0
Pro totals (14 years)	208	75	314	159	31.5	1	78	78.0	0

PRITCHETT, STANLEY FB

PERSONAL: Born December 22, 1973, in Atlanta, Ga. ... 6-2/250. ... Full name: Stanley Jerome Pritchett.
HIGH SCHOOL: Frederick Douglass (College Park, Ga.).
COLLEGE: South Carolina.
TRANSACTIONS/CAREER NOTES: Selected by Miami Dolphins in fourth round (118th pick overall) of 1996 NFL draft. ... Signed by Dolphins (July 10, 1996). ... Granted free agency (February 12, 1999). ... Re-signed by Dolphins (April 13, 1999). ... Granted unconditional free agency (February 11, 2000). ... Signed by Philadelphia Eagles (March 9, 2000). ... Released by Eagles (September 2, 2001). ... Signed by Chicago Bears (October 17, 2001). ... Granted unconditional free agency (February 28, 2003). ... Re-signed by Bears (March 1, 2003). ... Granted unconditional free agency (March 3, 2004). ... Re-signed by Bears (March 3, 2004). ... Released by Bears (May 6, 2004). ... Signed by Atlanta Falcons (July 17, 2004). ... On injured reserve with thumb injury (December 22, 2004-remainder of season). ... Granted unconditional free agency (March 2, 2005).
SINGLE GAME HIGHS (regular season): Attempts—17 (December 12, 1999, vs. New York Jets); yards—68 (December 12, 1999, vs. New York Jets); and rushing touchdowns—1 (October 19, 2003, vs. Seattle).

			RUSHING				RECEIVING				TOTALS			
Year Team	G	GS	Att.	Yds.	Avg.	TD	No.	Yds.	Avg.	TD	TD	2pt.	Pts.	Fum.
1996—Miami NFL	16	16	7	27	3.9	0	33	354	10.7	2	2	0	12	3
1997—Miami NFL	6	5	3	7	2.3	0	5	35	7.0	0	0	0	0	0
1998—Miami NFL	16	12	6	19	3.2	1	17	97	5.7	0	1	0	6	0
1999—Miami NFL	14	7	47	158	3.4	1	43	312	7.3	4	5	0	30	0
2000—Philadelphia NFL	16	2	58	225	3.9	1	25	193	7.7	0	1	0	6	1
2001—Chicago NFL	7	0	0	0	0.0	0	0	0	0.0	0	0	0	0	0
2002—Chicago NFL	16	2	1	2	2.0	0	19	165	8.7	1	1	0	6	0
2003—Chicago NFL	16	11	21	93	4.4	2	18	83	4.6	0	2	0	12	0
2004—Atlanta NFL	14	2	6	18	3.0	0	2	5	2.5	1	1	0	6	0
Pro totals (9 years)	121	57	149	549	3.7	5	162	1244	7.7	8	13	0	78	4

P

PROEHL, RICKY   WR   PANTHERS

PERSONAL: Born March 7, 1968, in Bronx, N.Y. ... 6-0/190. ... Full name: Richard Scott Proehl.
HIGH SCHOOL: Hillsborough (Belle Mead, N.J.).
COLLEGE: Wake Forest.
TRANSACTIONS/CAREER NOTES: Selected by Phoenix Cardinals in third round (58th pick overall) of 1990 NFL draft. ... Signed by Cardinals (July 23, 1990). ... Granted free agency (March 1, 1993). ... Tendered offer sheet by New England Patriots (April 13, 1993). ... Offer matched by Cardinals (April 19, 1993). ... Cardinals franchise renamed Arizona Cardinals for 1994 season. ... Traded by Cardinals to Seattle Seahawks for fourth-round pick (traded to New York Jets) in 1995 draft (April 3, 1995). ... Released by Seahawks (March 7, 1997). ... Signed by Chicago Bears (April 10, 1997). ... Granted unconditional free agency (February 13, 1998). ... Signed by St. Louis Rams (February 25, 1998). ... Granted unconditional free agency (March 1, 2002). ... Re-signed by Rams (April 9, 2002). ... Granted unconditional free agency (February 28, 2003). ... Signed by Carolina Panthers (March 17, 2003). ... Granted unconditional free agency (March 3, 2004). ... Re-signed by Panthers (May 1, 2004).
CHAMPIONSHIP GAME EXPERIENCE: Played in NFC championship game (1999, 2001 and 2003 seasons). ... Member of Super Bowl championship team (1999 season). ... Played in Super Bowl 36 (2001 season) and Super Bowl 38 (2003 season).
SINGLE GAME HIGHS (regular season): Receptions—11 (November 16, 1997, vs. New York Jets); yards—164 (November 27, 1997, vs. Detroit); and touchdown receptions—2 (January 6, 2002, vs. Atlanta).
STATISTICAL PLATEAUS: 100-yard receiving games: 1990 (2), 1991 (1), 1992 (3), 1993 (1), 1997 (3), 1998 (1), 2001 (1), 2003 (1). Total: 13.

Year Team	G	GS	RUSHING Att.	Yds.	Avg.	TD	RECEIVING No.	Yds.	Avg.	TD	TOTALS TD	2pt.	Pts.	Fum.
1990—Phoenix NFL	16	2	1	4	4.0	0	56	802	14.3	4	4	0	24	0
1991—Phoenix NFL	16	16	3	21	7.0	0	55	766	13.9	2	2	0	12	0
1992—Phoenix NFL	16	15	3	23	7.7	0	60	744	12.4	3	3	0	18	5
1993—Phoenix NFL	16	16	8	47	5.9	0	65	877	13.5	7	7	0	42	1
1994—Arizona NFL	16	16	0	0	0.0	0	51	651	12.8	5	5	0	30	2
1995—Seattle NFL	8	0	0	0	0.0	0	5	29	5.8	0	0	0	0	0
1996—Seattle NFL	16	7	0	0	0.0	0	23	309	13.4	2	2	0	12	0
1997—Chicago NFL	15	10	0	0	0.0	0	58	753	13.0	7	7	1	44	2
1998—St. Louis NFL	16	11	1	14	14.0	0	60	771	12.9	3	3	1	20	0
1999—St. Louis NFL	15	2	0	0	0.0	0	33	349	10.6	0	0	0	0	0
2000—St. Louis NFL	12	4	0	0	0.0	0	31	441	14.2	4	4	0	24	0
2001—St. Louis NFL	16	3	1	5	5.0	0	40	563	14.1	5	5	1	32	0
2002—St. Louis NFL	16	2	0	0	0.0	0	43	466	10.8	4	4	0	24	0
2003—Carolina NFL	16	2	0	0	0.0	0	27	389	14.4	4	4	0	24	0
2004—Carolina NFL	16	3	1	9	9.0	0	34	497	14.6	0	0	0	0	0
Pro totals (15 years)	226	109	18	123	6.8	0	641	8407	13.1	50	50	3	306	10

PRUITT, ETRIC   DB   FALCONS

PERSONAL: Born August 16, 1981, in Theodore, Ala. ... 6-0/196.
HIGH SCHOOL: Theodore (Ala.).
COLLEGE: Southern Miss.
TRANSACTIONS/CAREER NOTES: Selected by Atlanta Falcons in sixth round (186th pick overall) of 2004 NFL draft. ... Signed by Falcons (July 13, 2004). ... Released by Falcons (September 11, 2004). ... Re-signed by Falcons (September 13, 2004). ... Released by Falcons (October 6, 2004). ... Re-signed by Falcons to practice squad (October 7, 2004). ... Activated (October 25, 2004).
CHAMPIONSHIP GAME EXPERIENCE: Member of Falcons for NFC championship game (2004 season); inactive.

Year Team	G	GS	TOTALS Tk.	Ast.	Sks.	INTERCEPTIONS No.	Yds.	Avg.	TD	PUNT RETURNS No.	Yds.	Avg.	TD	TOTALS TD	2pt.	Pts.	Fum.
2004—Atlanta NFL	3	0	0	0	0.0	0	0	0.0	0	0	0	0.0	0	0	0	0	0

PRYCE, TREVOR   DE   BRONCOS

PERSONAL: Born August 3, 1975, in Brooklyn, N.Y. ... 6-5/295.
HIGH SCHOOL: Lake Howell (Casselberry, Fla.).
COLLEGE: Clemson.
TRANSACTIONS/CAREER NOTES: Selected by Denver Broncos in first round (28th pick overall) of 1997 NFL draft. ... Signed by Broncos (July 24, 1997).
CHAMPIONSHIP GAME EXPERIENCE: Played in AFC championship game (1997 and 1998 seasons). ... Member of Super Bowl championship team (1997 and 1998 seasons).
HONORS: Played in Pro Bowl (1999, 2000 and 2002 seasons). ... Named to play in Pro Bowl (2001 season); replaced by Gary Walker due to injury.

Year Team	G	GS	TOTALS Tk.	Ast.	Sks.	INTERCEPTIONS No.	Yds.	Avg.	TD
1997—Denver NFL	8	3	16	8	2.0	0	0	0.0	0
1998—Denver NFL	16	15	31	12	8.5	1	1	1.0	0
1999—Denver NFL	15	15	33	13	13.0	1	0	0.0	0
2000—Denver NFL	16	16	34	12	12.0	0	0	0.0	0
2001—Denver NFL	16	16	34	7	7.0	0	0	0.0	0
2002—Denver NFL	16	16	40	6	9.0	0	0	0.0	0
2003—Denver NFL	16	16	27	9	8.5	0	0	0.0	0
2004—Denver NFL	2	1	1	1	0.0	0	0	0.0	0
Pro totals (8 years)	105	98	216	68	60.0	2	1	0.5	0

P

PUCILLO, MIKE — G — BILLS

PERSONAL: Born July 14, 1979, in Cleveland, Ohio. ... 6-4/311. ... Full name: Michael Pucillo.
HIGH SCHOOL: Brandon (Fla.).
COLLEGE: Auburn.
TRANSACTIONS/CAREER NOTES: Selected by Buffalo Bills in seventh round (215th pick overall) of 2002 NFL draft. ... Signed by Bills (July 17, 2002).
PLAYING EXPERIENCE: Buffalo NFL, 2003-2004. ... Games/Games started: 2003 (13/12), 2004 (2/0). Total: 15/12.

PUTZIER, JEB — TE — BRONCOS

PERSONAL: Born January 20, 1979, in Eagle, Idaho. ... 6-4/256.
HIGH SCHOOL: Eagle (Idaho).
COLLEGE: Boise State.
TRANSACTIONS/CAREER NOTES: Selected by Denver Broncos in sixth round (191st pick overall) of 2002 NFL draft. ... Signed by Broncos (June 14, 2002). ... Granted free agency (March 2, 2005). ... Tendered offer sheet by New York Jets (March 4, 2005). ... Broncos matched offer sheet (March 10, 2005).
SINGLE GAME HIGHS (regular season): Receptions—5 (September 26, 2004, vs. San Diego); yards—67 (January 2, 2005, vs. Indianapolis); and touchdown receptions—1 (November 7, 2004, vs. Houston).

			RECEIVING				TOTALS			
Year Team	G	GS	No.	Yds.	Avg.	TD	TD	2pt.	Pts.	Fum.
2002—Denver NFL	3	1	0	0	0.0	0	0	0	0	0
2003—Denver NFL	4	0	4	34	8.5	0	0	0	0	0
2004—Denver NFL	16	5	36	572	15.9	2	2	0	12	0
Pro totals (3 years)	23	6	40	606	15.2	2	2	0	12	0

PYATT, BRAD — WR — COLTS

PERSONAL: Born April 16, 1980, in Arvada, Colo. ... 5-11/195.
COLLEGE: Northern Colorado.
TRANSACTIONS/CAREER NOTES: Signed as non-drafted free agent by Indianapolis Colts (July 23, 2003). ... On injured reserve with concussion (November 9, 2003-remainder of season). ... Re-signed by Colts (January 7, 2004). ... Granted free agency (March 3, 2004). ... Re-signed by Colts (March 12, 2004).
SINGLE GAME HIGHS (regular season): Receptions—2 (January 2, 2005, vs. Denver); yards—12 (January 2, 2005, vs. Denver); and touchdown receptions—0.

			RECEIVING				PUNT RETURNS				KICKOFF RETURNS				TOTALS			
Year Team	G	GS	No.	Yds.	Avg.	TD	No.	Yds.	Avg.	TD	No.	Yds.	Avg.	TD	TD	2pt.	Pts.	Fum.
2003—Indianapolis NFL	8	0	1	2	2.0	0	12	110	9.2	0	19	544	28.6	0	0	0	0	2
2004—Indianapolis NFL	8	0	2	12	6.0	0	8	47	5.9	0	10	230	23.0	0	0	0	0	0
Pro totals (2 years)	16	0	3	14	4.7	0	20	157	7.9	0	29	774	26.7	0	0	0	0	2

QUARLES, SHELTON — LB — BUCCANEERS

PERSONAL: Born September 11, 1971, in Nashville, Tenn. ... 6-1/225. ... Full name: Shelton Eugene Quarles.
HIGH SCHOOL: Whites Creek (Tenn.).
COLLEGE: Vanderbilt.
TRANSACTIONS/CAREER NOTES: Signed as non-drafted free agent by Miami Dolphins (April 29, 1994). ... Released by Dolphins (August 15, 1994). ... Signed by B.C. Lions of CFL (December 1, 1994). ... Granted free agency (February 16, 1997). ... Signed by Tampa Bay Buccaneers (March 21, 1997). ... Granted unconditional free agency (February 28, 2003). ... Re-signed by Buccaneers (March 7, 2003).
CHAMPIONSHIP GAME EXPERIENCE: Played in NFC championship game (1999 and 2002 seasons). ... Member of Super Bowl championship team (2002 season).
HONORS: Played in Pro Bowl (2002).

			TOTALS			INTERCEPTIONS			
Year Team	G	GS	Tk.	Ast.	Sks.	No.	Yds.	Avg.	TD
1997—Tampa Bay NFL	16	0	1	3	0.0	0	0	0.0	0
1998—Tampa Bay NFL	16	0	9	3	1.0	0	0	0.0	0
1999—Tampa Bay NFL	16	14	23	12	0.0	0	0	0.0	0
2000—Tampa Bay NFL	14	13	35	15	2.0	1	5	5.0	0
2001—Tampa Bay NFL	16	16	28	16	2.0	1	98	98.0	1
2002—Tampa Bay NFL	16	16	74	39	1.0	2	29	14.5	1
2003—Tampa Bay NFL	11	11	57	23	0.0	0	0	0.0	0
2004—Tampa Bay NFL	15	15	72	32	3.5	0	0	0.0	0
Pro totals (8 years)	120	85	299	143	9.5	4	132	33.0	2

QUINN, JONATHAN — QB

PERSONAL: Born February 27, 1975, in Turlock, Calif. ... 6-6/240. ... Full name: Jonathan Ryan Quinn.
HIGH SCHOOL: McGavock (Nashville).
COLLEGE: Middle Tennessee State.
TRANSACTIONS/CAREER NOTES: Selected by Jacksonville Jaguars in third round (86th pick overall) of 1998 NFL draft. ... Signed by Jaguars (May 19, 1998). ... Active for one game (1999); did not play. ... Assigned by Jaguars to Berlin Thunder in 2001 NFL Europe enhancement allocation program (February 19, 2001). ... Granted unconditional free agency (March 1, 2002). ... Signed by Kansas City Chiefs (May 1, 2002). ... Granted unconditional free agency (March 3, 2004). ... Signed by Chicago Bears (March 4, 2004). ... Released by Bears (February 22, 2005).

CHAMPIONSHIP GAME EXPERIENCE: Member of Jaguars for AFC championship game (1999 season); inactive.
SINGLE GAME HIGHS (regular season): Attempts—43 (October 3, 2004, vs. Philadelphia); completions—26 (October 3, 2004, vs. Philadelphia); yards—225 (November 18, 2001, vs. Pittsburgh); and touchdown passes—1 (October 3, 2004, vs. Philadelphia).
MISCELLANEOUS: Regular-season record as starting NFL quarterback: 1-5 (.167).

				PASSING									RUSHING				TOTALS	
Year Team	G	GS	Att.	Cmp.	Pct.	Yds.	TD	Int.	Avg.	Skd.	Rat.	Att.	Yds.	Avg.	TD	TD	2pt.	Pts.
1998—Jacksonville NFL	4	2	64	34	53.1	387	2	3	6.05	9	62.4	11	77	7.0	1	1	0	6
1999—Jacksonville NFL	Did not play.																	
2000—Jacksonville NFL	2	0	0	0	0.0	0	0	0	0.00	0	0.0	2	-2	-1.0	0	0	0	0
2001—Kansas City NFL	6	1	61	32	52.5	361	1	1	5.92	6	69.1	8	42	5.3	0	0	0	0
2002—Kansas City NFL	1	0	0	0	0.0	0	0	0	0.00	0	0.0	1	-1	-1.0	0	0	0	0
2003—Kansas City NFL	Did not play.																	
2004—Chicago NFL	5	3	98	51	52.0	413	1	3	4.21	15	53.7	3	35	11.7	0	0	0	0
Pro totals (5 years)	18	6	223	117	52.5	1161	4	7	5.21	30	60.4	25	151	6.0	1	1	0	6

RABACH, CASEY   G/C   REDSKINS

PERSONAL: Born September 24, 1977, in Sturgeon Bay, Wis. ... 6-4/301.
HIGH SCHOOL: Sturgeon Bay (Wis.).
COLLEGE: Wisconsin.
TRANSACTIONS/CAREER NOTES: Selected by Baltimore Ravens in third round (92nd pick overall) of 2001 NFL draft. ... Signed by Ravens (July 21, 2001). ... Active for two games (2001); did not play. ... Granted free agency (March 3, 2004). ... Re-signed by Ravens (March 5, 2004). ... Granted unconditional free agency (March 2, 2005). ... Signed by Washington Redskins (March 2, 2005).
PLAYING EXPERIENCE: Baltimore NFL, 2001-2004. ... Games/Games started: 2002 (12/5), 2003 (14/2), 2004 (16/16), Total: 42/23.

RACKERS, NEIL   K   CARDINALS

PERSONAL: Born August 16, 1976, in St. Louis, Mo. ... 6-0/206. ... Full name: Neil W. Rackers.
HIGH SCHOOL: Aquinas-Mercy (Florissant, Mo.).
COLLEGE: Illinois.
TRANSACTIONS/CAREER NOTES: Selected by Cincinnati Bengals in sixth round (169th pick overall) of 2000 NFL draft. ... Signed by Bengals (July 21, 2000). ... Granted free agency (February 28, 2003). ... Re-signed by Bengals (April 15, 2003). ... Released by Bengals (September 1, 2003). ... Signed by Arizona Cardinals (November 11, 2003).

				FIELD GOALS						TOTALS		
Year Team	G	1-29	30-39	40-49	50+	Tot.	Pct.	Lg.		XPM	XPA	Pts.
2000—Cincinnati NFL	16	5-5	5-9	2-7	0-0	12-21	57.1	45		21	21	57
2001—Cincinnati NFL	16	4-6	8-11	4-9	1-2	17-28	60.7	52		23	24	74
2002—Cincinnati NFL	16	7-7	3-3	3-5	2-3	15-18	83.3	54		30	32	75
2003—Arizona NFL	7	5-5	1-4	3-3	0-0	9-12	75.0	49		8	8	35
2004—Arizona NFL	16	6-6	5-7	6-7	5-9	22-29	75.9	*55		28	28	94
Pro totals (5 years)	71	27-29	22-34	18-31	8-14	75-108	69.4	55		110	113	335

RACKLEY, DEREK   TE/LS   FALCONS

PERSONAL: Born July 18, 1977, in Apple Valley, Minn. ... 6-4/250.
HIGH SCHOOL: Apple Valley (Minn.).
COLLEGE: Minnesota.
TRANSACTIONS/CAREER NOTES: Signed as non-drafted free agent by Atlanta Falcons (April 17, 2000). ... Granted free agency (February 28, 2003). ... Re-signed by Falcons (March 25, 2003).
PLAYING EXPERIENCE: Atlanta NFL, 2000-2004. ... Games/Games started: 2000 (16/0), 2001 (16/0), 2002 (16/0), 2003 (16/1), 2004 (16/0). Total: 80/1.
CHAMPIONSHIP GAME EXPERIENCE: Played in NFC championship game (2004 season).
SINGLE GAME HIGHS (regular season): Receptions—1 (December 30, 2001, vs. Miami); yards—1 (December 30, 2001, vs. Miami); and touchdown receptions—1 (December 30, 2001, vs. Miami).

RAINER, WALI   LB   LIONS

PERSONAL: Born April 19, 1977, in Rockingham, N.C. ... 6-2/240. ... Full name: Wali Rashid Rainer.
HIGH SCHOOL: West Charlotte (N.C.).
COLLEGE: Virginia.
TRANSACTIONS/CAREER NOTES: Selected by Cleveland Browns in fourth round (124th pick overall) of 1999 NFL draft. ... Signed by Browns (July 22, 1999). ... Granted free agency (March 1, 2002). ... Re-signed by Browns (April 20, 2002). ... Traded by Browns with third-round pick (traded to Washington) in 2002 draft to Jacksonville Jaguars for third-round pick (C Melvin Fowler) in 2002 draft (April 20, 2002). ... Granted unconditional free agency (February 28, 2003). ... Signed by Detroit Lions (April 7, 2003). ... Granted unconditional free agency (March 2, 2005). ... Re-signed by Lions (April 6, 2005).

			TOTALS			INTERCEPTIONS			
Year Team	G	GS	Tk.	Ast.	Sks.	No.	Yds.	Avg.	TD
1999—Cleveland NFL	16	15	108	29	1.0	0	0	0.0	0
2000—Cleveland NFL	16	16	86	33	1.0	1	5	5.0	0
2001—Cleveland NFL	14	14	50	28	1.0	0	0	0.0	0
2002—Jacksonville NFL	16	14	66	20	1.0	0	0	0.0	0
2003—Detroit NFL	16	0	8	3	0.0	0	0	0.0	0
2004—Detroit NFL	16	0	3	4	0.0	0	0	0.0	0
Pro totals (6 years)	94	59	321	117	4.0	1	5	5.0	0

RAIOLA, DOMINIC C LIONS

PERSONAL: Born December 30, 1978, in Honolulu, Hawaii. ... 6-1/295.
HIGH SCHOOL: St. Louis (Honolulu, Hawaii).
COLLEGE: Nebraska.
TRANSACTIONS/CAREER NOTES: Selected by Detroit Lions in second round (50th pick overall) of 2001 NFL draft. ... Signed by Lions (July 23, 2001). ... Granted unconditional free agency (March 2, 2005). ... Re-signed by Lions (March 11, 2005).
PLAYING EXPERIENCE: Detroit NFL, 2001-2004. ... Games/Games started: 2001 (16/0), 2002 (16/16), 2003 (16/16), 2004 (16/16). Total: 64/48.
HONORS: Named center on THE SPORTING NEWS college All-America second team (2000).

RAMSEY, PATRICK QB REDSKINS

PERSONAL: Born February 14, 1979, in Ruston, La. ... 6-2/223. ... Full name: Patrick Allen Ramsey.
HIGH SCHOOL: Ruston (La.).
COLLEGE: Tulane.
TRANSACTIONS/CAREER NOTES: Selected by Washington Redskins in first round (32nd pick overall) of 2002 NFL draft. ... Signed by Redskins (August 7, 2002). ... On injured reserve with foot injury (December 8, 2003-remainder of season).
SINGLE GAME HIGHS (regular season): Attempts—50 (October 5, 2003, vs. Philadelphia); completions—29 (December 12, 2004, vs. Philadelphia); yards—356 (September 14, 2003, vs. Atlanta); and touchdown passes—3 (December 5, 2004, vs. New York Giants).
STATISTICAL PLATEAUS: 300-yard passing games: 2002 (1), 2003 (2). Total: 3.
MISCELLANEOUS: Regular-season record as starting NFL quarterback: 9-14 (.391).

Year Team	G	GS	PASSING									RUSHING				TOTALS		
			Att.	Cmp.	Pct.	Yds.	TD	Int.	Avg.	Skd.	Rat.	Att.	Yds.	Avg.	TD	TD	2pt.	Pts.
2002—Washington NFL	10	5	227	117	51.5	1539	9	8	6.78	18	71.8	13	-1	-0.1	1	1	0	6
2003—Washington NFL	11	11	337	179	53.1	2166	14	9	6.43	30	75.8	15	62	4.1	1	1	0	6
2004—Washington NFL	9	7	272	169	62.1	1665	10	11	6.12	23	74.8	10	19	1.9	0	0	0	0
Pro totals (3 years)	30	23	836	465	55.6	5370	33	28	6.42	71	74.4	38	80	2.1	2	2	0	12

RANDALL, CURTIS LB SEAHAWKS

PERSONAL: Born August 6, 1979, in Columbus, Ga. ... 6-3/225.
HIGH SCHOOL: Central Catholic (Morgan City, La.).
COLLEGE: Louisiana Tech.
TRANSACTIONS/CAREER NOTES: Signed as non-drafted free agent by Jacksonville Jaguars (April 28, 2003). ... Released by Jaguars (August 31, 2003). ... Re-signed by Jaguars to practice squad (November 28, 2003). ... Activated (December 31, 2003). ... Released by Jaguars (June 15, 2004). ... Signed by Carolina Panthers (August 17, 2004). ... Released by Panthers (August 30, 2004). ... Signed by Seattle Seahawks to practice squad (October 26, 2004). ... Activated (November 19, 2004). ... On injured reserve with hamstring injury (December 22, 2004-remainder of season).

Year Team	G	GS	TOTALS			INTERCEPTIONS			
			Tk.	Ast.	Sks.	No.	Yds.	Avg.	TD
2004—Seattle NFL	4	0	0	0	0.0	0	0	0.0	0

RANDLE EL, ANTWAAN WR STEELERS

PERSONAL: Born August 17, 1979, in Riverdale, Ill. ... 5-10/192.
HIGH SCHOOL: Thornton (Riverdale, Ill.).
COLLEGE: Indiana.
TRANSACTIONS/CAREER NOTES: Selected by Pittsburgh Steelers in second round (62nd pick overall) of 2002 NFL draft. ... Signed by Steelers (July 23, 2002).
CHAMPIONSHIP GAME EXPERIENCE: Played in AFC championship game (2004 season).
POST SEASON RECORDS: Shares NFL career and single-game record for most punt returns for touchdown—1 (January 5, 2003 v. Cleveland).
SINGLE GAME HIGHS (regular season): Receptions—8 (December 8, 2002, vs. Houston); yards—149 (December 18, 2004, vs. New York Giants); and touchdown receptions—1 (January 2, 2005, vs. Buffalo).
STATISTICAL PLATEAUS: 100-yard receiving games: 2004 (1). Total: 1.

Year Team	G	GS	RUSHING				RECEIVING				PUNT RETURNS				KICKOFF RETURNS				TOTALS		
			Att.	Yds.	Avg.	TD	No.	Yds.	Avg.	TD	No.	Yds.	Avg.	TD	No.	Yds.	Avg.	TD	TD	2pt.	Pts.
2002—Pit. NFL	16	0	19	134	7.1	0	47	489	10.4	2	§37	257	6.9	0	32	733	22.9	1	3	0	18
2003—Pit. NFL	16	1	15	75	5.0	0	37	364	9.8	1	†45	§542	12.0	†2	24	466	19.4	0	3	0	18
2004—Pit. NFL	16	7	8	34	4.3	0	43	601	14.0	3	42	347	8.3	0	21	527	25.1	0	3	0	18
Pro totals (3 years)	48	8	42	243	5.8	0	127	1454	11.4	6	124	1146	9.2	2	77	1726	22.4	1	9	0	54

RANSOM, DERRICK DT JAGUARS

PERSONAL: Born September 13, 1976, in Indianapolis, Ind. ... 6-3/306. ... Full name: Derrick Wayne Ransom Jr.
HIGH SCHOOL: Lawrence Central (Indianapolis).
COLLEGE: Cincinnati.
TRANSACTIONS/CAREER NOTES: Selected by Kansas City Chiefs in sixth round (181st pick overall) of 1998 NFL draft. ... Signed by Chiefs (June 3, 1998). ... Granted free agency (March 2, 2001). ... Re-signed by Chiefs (April 3, 2001). ... Granted unconditional free agency (March 1, 2002). ... Re-signed by Chiefs (April 3, 2002). ... Released by Chiefs (August 31, 2003). ... Signed by Arizona Cardinals (September 16, 2003). ... Granted unconditional free agency (March 3, 2004). ... Signed by Jacksonville Jaguars (June 15, 2004). ... Released by Jaguars (September 5, 2004). ... Re-signed by Jaguars (October 14, 2004).

Year Team	G	GS	Tk.	Ast.	Sks.
			TOTALS		
1998—Kansas City NFL	7	0	1	0	0.0
1999—Kansas City NFL	10	0	1	0	1.0
2000—Kansas City NFL	10	0	2	0	0.0
2001—Kansas City NFL	16	16	41	13	3.0
2002—Kansas City NFL	13	10	20	5	0.0
2003—Arizona NFL	5	0	1	2	0.0
2004—Jacksonville NFL	10	0	4	4	0.5
Pro totals (7 years)	71	26	70	24	4.5

RASBY, WALTER   TE   STEELERS

R

PERSONAL: Born September 7, 1972, in Washington, N.C. ... 6-3/252. ... Full name: Walter Herbert Rasby.
HIGH SCHOOL: Washington (N.C.).
COLLEGE: Wake Forest.
TRANSACTIONS/CAREER NOTES: Signed as non-drafted free agent by Pittsburgh Steelers (April 29, 1994). ... Released by Steelers (August 27, 1995). ... Signed by Carolina Panthers (October 17, 1995). ... Granted free agency (February 14, 1997). ... Re-signed by Panthers (June 3, 1997). ... On injured reserve with knee injury (December 10, 1997-remainder of season). ... Granted unconditional free agency (February 13, 1998). ... Signed by Detroit Lions (April 13, 1998). ... Granted unconditional free agency (March 2, 2001). ... Signed by Washington Redskins (April 10, 2001). ... Released by Redskins (February 26, 2003). ... Signed by New Orleans Saints (May 14, 2003). ... Granted unconditional free agency (March 3, 2004). ... Signed by Redskins (March 10, 2004). ... Released by Redskins (October 19, 2004). ... Signed by Pittsburgh Steelers (December 7, 2004). ... Granted unconditional free agency (March 2, 2005). ... Re-signed by Steelers (April 13, 2005).
CHAMPIONSHIP GAME EXPERIENCE: Played in AFC championship game (1994 and 2004 seasons). ... Played in NFC championship game (1996 season).
SINGLE GAME HIGHS (regular season): Receptions—5 (October 4, 1998, vs. Chicago); yards—45 (January 6, 2002, vs. Arizona); and touchdown receptions—1 (January 6, 2002, vs. Arizona).

Year Team	G	GS	No.	Yds.	Avg.	TD	TD	2pt.	Pts.	Fum.
			RECEIVING				**TOTALS**			
1994—Pittsburgh NFL	2	0	0	0	0.0	0	0	0	0	0
1995—Carolina NFL	9	2	5	47	9.4	0	0	1	2	0
1996—Carolina NFL	16	1	0	0	0.0	0	0	0	0	0
1997—Carolina NFL	14	2	1	1	1.0	0	0	0	0	0
1998—Detroit NFL	16	16	15	119	7.9	1	1	0	6	0
1999—Detroit NFL	16	6	3	19	6.3	1	1	0	6	0
2000—Detroit NFL	16	8	10	78	7.8	1	1	0	6	0
2001—Washington NFL	16	11	10	128	12.8	2	2	0	12	0
2002—Washington NFL	13	9	9	85	9.4	0	0	0	0	0
2003—New Orleans NFL	16	7	6	55	9.2	0	0	0	0	0
2004—Washington NFL	6	6	5	52	10.4	0	0	0	0	0
—Pittsburgh NFL	4	2	0	0	0.0	0	0	0	0	0
Pro totals (11 years)	144	70	64	584	9.1	5	5	1	32	0

RASHEED, SALEEM   LB   49ERS

PERSONAL: Born June 15, 1981, in Birmingham, Ala. ... 6-2/229.
HIGH SCHOOL: Shades Valley (Birmingham, Ala.).
COLLEGE: Alabama.
TRANSACTIONS/CAREER NOTES: Selected after junior season by San Francisco in third round (69th pick overall) of 2002 NFL draft. ... Signed by 49ers (July 21, 2002). ... Granted free agency (March 2, 2005). ... Re-signed by 49ers (May 5, 2005).

Year Team	G	GS	Tk.	Ast.	Sks.	No.	Yds.	Avg.	TD
			TOTALS			**INTERCEPTIONS**			
2002—San Francisco NFL	6	0	6	0	1.0	0	0	0.0	0
2003—San Francisco NFL	16	1	3	3	0.0	0	0	0.0	0
2004—San Francisco NFL	14	2	13	5	0.0	0	0	0.0	0
Pro totals (3 years)	36	3	22	8	1.0	0	0	0.0	0

RASMUSSEN, KEMP   DE

PERSONAL: Born May 25, 1979, in Rochester, Mich. ... 6-3/265. ... Full name: Kemp Alan Rasmussen.
HIGH SCHOOL: Lampeer West (Hadley, Mich.).
COLLEGE: Indiana.
TRANSACTIONS/CAREER NOTES: Signed as non-drafted free agent by Carolina Panthers (April 29, 2002). ... Granted free agency (March 2, 2005).
CHAMPIONSHIP GAME EXPERIENCE: Played in NFC championship game (2003 season). ... Played in Super Bowl 38 (2003 season).

Year Team	G	GS	Tk.	Ast.	Sks.
			TOTALS		
2002—Carolina NFL	10	0	2	1	0.0
2003—Carolina NFL	13	0	4	0	1.0
2004—Carolina NFL	12	0	1	1	0.0
Pro totals (3 years)	35	0	7	2	1.0

RATLIFF, KEIWAN   CB   BENGALS

PERSONAL: Born April 19, 1981, in Youngstown, Ohio. ... 5-11/190.
HIGH SCHOOL: Whitehall-Yearling (Columbus, Ohio).
COLLEGE: Florida.

TRANSACTIONS/CAREER NOTES: Selected by Cincinnati Bengals in second round (49th pick overall) of 2004 NFL draft. ... Signed by Bengals (August 5, 2004).
HONORS: Named cornerback on THE SPORTING NEWS college All-America first team (2003).

Year Team	G	GS	TOTALS Tk.	Ast.	Sks.	INTERCEPTIONS No.	Yds.	Avg.	TD	PUNT RETURNS No.	Yds.	Avg.	TD	TD	TOTALS 2pt.	Pts.	Fum.
2004—Cincinnati NFL	16	5	27	8	0.0	0	0	0.0	0	17	207	12.2	0	0	0	0	2

RATTAY, TIM   QB   49ERS

PERSONAL: Born March 15, 1977, in Elyria, Ohio. ... 6-0/200.
HIGH SCHOOL: Phoenix (Ariz.) Christian.
JUNIOR COLLEGE: Scottsdale (Ariz.) Community College.
COLLEGE: Louisiana Tech.
TRANSACTIONS/CAREER NOTES: Selected by San Francisco 49ers in seventh round (212th pick overall) of 2000 NFL draft. ... Signed by 49ers (July 16, 2000). ... Granted free agency (February 28, 2003). ... Re-signed by 49ers (April 7, 2003). ... On injured reserve with foot injury (December 30, 2004-remainder of season).
SINGLE GAME HIGHS (regular season): Attempts—57 (October 10, 2004, vs. Arizona); completions—38 (October 10, 2004, vs. Arizona); yards—417 (October 10, 2004, vs. Arizona); and touchdown passes—3 (November 2, 2003, vs. St. Louis).
STATISTICAL PLATEAUS: 300-yard passing games: 2004 (1). Total: 1.
MISCELLANEOUS: Regular-season record as starting NFL quarterback: 3-9 (.250).

Year Team	G	GS	PASSING Att.	Cmp.	Pct.	Yds.	TD	Int.	Avg.	Skd.	Rat.	RUSHING Att.	Yds.	Avg.	TD	TOTALS TD	2pt.	Pts.
2000—San Francisco NFL	1	0	1	1	100.0	-4	0	0	-4.00	0	79.2	2	-1	-0.5	0	0	0	0
2001—San Francisco NFL	3	0	2	2	100.0	21	0	0	10.50	0	110.4	5	-3	-0.6	0	0	0	0
2002—San Francisco NFL	4	0	43	26	60.5	232	2	0	5.40	5	90.5	5	0	0.0	0	0	0	0
2003—San Francisco NFL	11	3	118	73	61.9	856	7	2	7.25	7	96.6	8	0	0.0	0	0	0	0
2004—San Francisco NFL	9	9	325	198	60.9	2169	10	10	6.67	37	78.1	12	55	4.6	0	0	1	2
Pro totals (5 years)	28	12	489	300	61.3	3274	19	12	6.70	49	83.8	32	51	1.6	0	0	1	2

RAYBURN, SAM   DT   EAGLES

PERSONAL: Born October 20, 1980, in Chickasha, Okla. ... 6-3/303. ... Full name: Sam Branson Rayburn.
HIGH SCHOOL: Chickasha (Okla.).
COLLEGE: Tulsa.
TRANSACTIONS/CAREER NOTES: Signed as non-drafted free agent by Philadelphia Eagles (April 28, 2003).
CHAMPIONSHIP GAME EXPERIENCE: Played in NFC championship game (2003 and 2004 seasons). ... Played in Super Bowl 39 (2004 season).

Year Team	G	GS	TOTALS Tk.	Ast.	Sks.
2003—Philadelphia NFL	10	0	9	0	2.0
2004—Philadelphia NFL	16	2	28	2	6.0
Pro totals (2 years)	26	2	37	2	8.0

RAYMER, CORY   C   REDSKINS

PERSONAL: Born March 3, 1973, in Fond du Lac, Wis. ... 6-3/300.
HIGH SCHOOL: Goodrich (Fond du Lac, Wis.).
COLLEGE: Wisconsin.
TRANSACTIONS/CAREER NOTES: Selected by Washington Redskins in second round (37th pick overall) of 1995 NFL draft. ... Signed by Redskins (July 24, 1995). ... On injured reserve with back injury (November 25, 1996-remainder of season). ... Granted unconditional free agency (February 12, 1999). ... Re-signed by Redskins (March 16, 1999). ... Granted unconditional free agency (February 11, 2000). ... Re-signed by Redskins (February 26, 2000). ... On injured reserve with knee injury (September 28, 2000-remainder of season). ... Granted unconditional free agency (March 1, 2002). ... Signed by San Diego Chargers (March 8, 2002). ... On injured reserve with Achilles injury (September 26, 2002-remainder of season). ... Released by Chargers (March 2, 2004). ... Signed by Washington Redskins (March 11, 2004).
PLAYING EXPERIENCE: Washington NFL, 1995-2001; San Diego NFL, 2002-2003; Washington NFL, 2004. ... Games/Games started: 1995 (3/2), 1996 (6/5), 1997 (6/3), 1998 (16/16), 1999 (16/16), 2001 (16/16), 2002 (3/3), 2003 (15/8), 2004 (15/14), Total: 96/83.
HONORS: Named offensive lineman on THE SPORTING NEWS college All-America first team (1994).

REAGOR, MONTAE   DT   COLTS

PERSONAL: Born June 29, 1977, in Waxahachie, Texas. ... 6-3/285. ... Full name: Willie Montae Reagor. ... Name pronounced: MON-tay RAY-ger.
HIGH SCHOOL: Waxahachie (Texas).
COLLEGE: Texas Tech.
TRANSACTIONS/CAREER NOTES: Selected by Denver Broncos in second round (58th pick overall) of 1999 NFL draft. ... Signed by Broncos (July 13, 1999). ... Granted unconditional free agency (February 28, 2003). ... Signed by Indianapolis Colts (March 3, 2003).
CHAMPIONSHIP GAME EXPERIENCE: Played in AFC championship game (2003 season).
HONORS: Named defensive end on THE SPORTING NEWS college All-America second team (1997). ... Named defensive end on THE SPORTING NEWS college All-America first team (1998).

Year Team	G	GS	TOTALS Tk.	Ast.	Sks.	INTERCEPTIONS No.	Yds.	Avg.	TD
1999—Denver NFL	8	0	9	1	0.0	0	0	0.0	0
2000—Denver NFL	13	0	8	1	2.0	0	0	0.0	0
2001—Denver NFL	8	0	4	0	1.0	0	0	0.0	0

Year Team	G	GS	TOTALS			INTERCEPTIONS			
			Tk.	Ast.	Sks.	No.	Yds.	Avg.	TD
2002—Denver NFL	15	1	12	8	1.0	1	31	31.0	0
2003—Indianapolis NFL	13	12	18	8	0.5	0	0	0.0	0
2004—Indianapolis NFL	16	16	35	8	5.0	0	0	0.0	0
Pro totals (6 years)	73	29	86	26	9.5	1	31	31.0	0

REDDING, CORY DE LIONS

PERSONAL: Born November 15, 1980, in Houston, Texas. ... 6-4/290. ... Full name: Cory B. Redding.
HIGH SCHOOL: North Shore (Houston).
COLLEGE: Texas.
TRANSACTIONS/CAREER NOTES: Selected by Detroit Lions in third round (66th pick overall) of 2003 NFL draft. ... Signed by Lions (July 22, 2003).

Year Team	G	GS	TOTALS			INTERCEPTIONS			
			Tk.	Ast.	Sks.	No.	Yds.	Avg.	TD
2003—Detroit NFL	9	0	6	1	0.0	0	0	0.0	0
2004—Detroit NFL	16	16	34	6	3.0	0	0	0.0	0
Pro totals (2 years)	25	16	40	7	3.0	0	0	0.0	0

REDMOND, J.R. RB

PERSONAL: Born September 28, 1977, in Los Angeles, Calif. ... 5-11/215. ... Full name: Joseph Robert Redmond.
HIGH SCHOOL: Carson (Calif.).
COLLEGE: Arizona State.
TRANSACTIONS/CAREER NOTES: Selected by New England Patriots in third round (76th pick overall) of 2000 NFL draft. ... Signed by Patriots (July 23, 2000). ... Released by Patriots (August 24, 2003). ... Signed by Oakland Raiders (November 19, 2003). ... Granted unconditional free agency (March 2, 2005).
CHAMPIONSHIP GAME EXPERIENCE: Played in AFC championship game (2001 season). ... Member of Super Bowl championship team (2001 season).
SINGLE GAME HIGHS (regular season): Attempts—24 (November 5, 2000, vs. Buffalo); yards—97 (October 22, 2000, vs. Indianapolis); and rushing touchdowns—1 (November 5, 2000 vs. Buffalo).

Year Team	G	GS	RUSHING				RECEIVING				KICKOFF RETURNS				TOTALS			
			Att.	Yds.	Avg.	TD	No.	Yds.	Avg.	TD	No.	Yds.	Avg.	TD	TD	2pt.	Pts.	Fum.
2000—New England NFL	12	5	125	406	3.2	1	20	126	6.3	2	1	25	25.0	0	3	0	18	2
2001—New England NFL	12	0	35	119	3.4	0	13	132	10.2	0	2	57	28.5	0	0	0	0	0
2002—New England NFL	9	0	4	2	0.5	0	2	5	2.5	0	1	12	12.0	0	0	0	0	0
2003—Oakland NFL	1	0	9	30	3.3	0	1	6	6.0	0	0	0	0.0	0	0	0	0	0
2004—Oakland NFL	16	1	21	119	5.7	0	32	233	7.3	0	8	153	19.1	0	0	0	0	2
Pro totals (5 years)	50	6	194	676	3.5	1	68	502	7.4	2	12	247	20.6	0	3	0	18	4

REED, ED S RAVENS

PERSONAL: Born September 11, 1978, in St. Rose, La. ... 5-11/200. ... Full name: Edward Earl Reed.
HIGH SCHOOL: Destrehan (St. Rose, La.).
COLLEGE: Miami (Fla.).
TRANSACTIONS/CAREER NOTES: Selected by Baltimore Ravens in first round (24th pick overall) of 2002 NFL draft. ... Signed by Ravens (August 3, 2002).
HONORS: Named free safety on THE SPORTING NEWS college All-America first team (2001). ... Named safety on THE SPORTING NEWS NFL All-Pro team (2003 and 2004). ... Played in Pro Bowl (2003 and 2004 seasons).
RECORDS: Holds NFL single-season record for most yards on interception returns—358 (2004). ... Holds NFL record for longest interception return—106 yards, vs. Cleveland (November 7, 2004).
MISCELLANEOUS: Holds Baltimore Ravens all-time record for most interceptions (21).

Year Team	G	GS	TOTALS			INTERCEPTIONS				PUNT RETURNS				TOTALS			
			Tk.	Ast.	Sks.	No.	Yds.	Avg.	TD	No.	Yds.	Avg.	TD	TD	2pt.	Pts.	Fum.
2002—Baltimore NFL	16	16	67	13	1.0	5	167	33.4	0	0	0	0.0	0	1	0	6	1
2003—Baltimore NFL	16	15	58	12	1.0	▲7	132	18.9	1	5	33	6.6	0	3	0	18	1
2004—Baltimore NFL	16	16	64	14	2.0	*9	*358	39.8	1	0	0	0.0	0	2	0	12	1
Pro totals (3 years)	48	47	189	39	4.0	21	657	31.3	2	5	33	6.6	0	6	0	36	3

REED, JAMES DT

PERSONAL: Born February 3, 1977, in Saginaw, Mich. ... 6-0/286. ... Full name: James Reed Jr.
HIGH SCHOOL: Saginaw (Mich.).
COLLEGE: Iowa State.
TRANSACTIONS/CAREER NOTES: Selected by New York Jets in seventh round (206th pick overall) of 2001 NFL draft. ... Signed by Jets (June 28, 2001). ... Granted free agency (March 3, 2004). ... Re-signed by Jets (March 27, 2004). ... Granted unconditional free agency (March 2, 2005).

Year Team	G	GS	TOTALS		
			Tk.	Ast.	Sks.
2001—New York Jets NFL	16	2	19	9	1.0
2002—New York Jets NFL	16	0	12	4	0.0
2003—New York Jets NFL	16	0	18	13	1.0
2004—New York Jets NFL	16	0	13	6	2.0
Pro totals (4 years)	64	2	62	32	4.0

REED, JEFF — K — STEELERS

PERSONAL: Born April 9, 1979, in Charlotte, N.C. ... 5-11/232. ... Full name: Jeffrey Montgomery Reed.
HIGH SCHOOL: East Mecklenburg (Charlotte, N.C.).
COLLEGE: North Carolina.
TRANSACTIONS/CAREER NOTES: Signed as non-drafted free agent by New Orleans Saints (April 23, 2002). ... Released by Saints (August 26, 2002). ... Signed by Pittsburgh Steelers (November 19, 2002). ... Granted free agency (March 2, 2005). ... Re-signed by Steelers (March 10, 2005).
CHAMPIONSHIP GAME EXPERIENCE: Played in AFC championship game (2004 season).

		FIELD GOALS							TOTALS		
Year Team	G	1-29	30-39	40-49	50+	Tot.	Pct.	Lg.	XPM	XPA	Pts.
2002—Pittsburgh NFL	6	5-5	5-5	6-7	1-2	17-19	89.5	50	10	11	61
2003—Pittsburgh NFL	16	9-12	6-7	7-12	1-1	23-32	71.9	51	31	32	100
2004—Pittsburgh NFL	16	9-10	12-13	5-8	2-2	28-33	84.8	51	40	40	124
Pro totals (3 years)	38	23-27	23-25	18-27	4-5	68-84	81.0	51	81	83	285

REED, JOSH — WR — BILLS

PERSONAL: Born May 1, 1980, in Lafayette, La. ... 5-10/208. ... Full name: Joshua Blake Reed.
HIGH SCHOOL: Rayne (La.).
COLLEGE: Louisiana State.
TRANSACTIONS/CAREER NOTES: Selected after junior season by Buffalo Bills in second round (36th pick overall) of 2002 NFL draft. ... Signed by Bills (July 25, 2002).
HONORS: Named wide receiver on THE SPORTING NEWS college All-America first team (2001). ... Fred Biletnikoff Award winner (2001).
SINGLE GAME HIGHS (regular season): Receptions—8 (October 26, 2003, vs. Kansas City); yards—110 (September 15, 2002, vs. Minnesota); and touchdown receptions—1 (December 7, 2003, vs. New York Jets).
STATISTICAL PLATEAUS: 100-yard receiving games: 2002 (1), 2003 (1). Total: 2.

			RUSHING				RECEIVING				PUNT RETURNS				KICKOFF RETURNS				TOTALS		
Year Team	G	GS	Att.	Yds.	Avg.	TD	No.	Yds.	Avg.	TD	No.	Yds.	Avg.	TD	No.	Yds.	Avg.	TD	TD	2pt.	Pts.
2002—Buf. NFL	16	2	0	0	0.0	0	37	509	13.8	2	0	0	0.0	0	0	0	0.0	0	2	0	12
2003—Buf. NFL	16	16	3	38	12.7	0	58	588	10.1	2	0	0	0.0	0	0	0	0.0	0	2	0	12
2004—Buf. NFL	12	1	2	-1	-0.5	0	16	153	9.6	0	1	7	7.0	0	0	0	0.0	0	0	0	0
Pro totals (3 years)	44	19	5	37	7.4	0	111	1250	11.3	4	1	7	7.0	0	0	0	0.0	0	4	0	24

REED, J.R. — CB — EAGLES

PERSONAL: Born February 11, 1982, in Tampa, Fla. ... 5-11/202. ... Full name: Herbert Lee Reed Jr.
HIGH SCHOOL: Hillsborough (Tampa, Fla.).
COLLEGE: South Florida.
TRANSACTIONS/CAREER NOTES: Selected by Philadelphia Eagles in fourth round (129th pick overall) of 2004 NFL draft. ... Signed by Eagles (July 27, 2004).
CHAMPIONSHIP GAME EXPERIENCE: Played in NFC championship game (2004 season). ... Played in Super Bowl 39 (2004 season).

			TOTALS			INTERCEPTIONS				KICKOFF RETURNS				TOTALS			
Year Team	G	GS	Tk.	Ast.	Sks.	No.	Yds.	Avg.	TD	No.	Yds.	Avg.	TD	TD	2pt.	Pts.	Fum.
2004—Philadelphia NFL	14	1	12	0	0.0	0	0	0.0	0	33	761	23.1	0	0	0	0	0

REED, RAYSHUN — CB — 49ERS

PERSONAL: Born April 10, 1981, in Columbus, Ga. ... 5-10/185. ... Full name: Brandon Rayshun Reed.
HIGH SCHOOL: Russell County (Ga.).
COLLEGE: Troy.
TRANSACTIONS/CAREER NOTES: Signed as non-drafted free agent by San Francisco 49ers (May 2, 2004). ... Released by 49ers (September 5, 2004). ... Re-signed by 49ers to practice squad (September 7, 2004). ... Activated (October 30, 2004).

			TOTALS			INTERCEPTIONS			
Year Team	G	GS	Tk.	Ast.	Sks.	No.	Yds.	Avg.	TD
2004—San Francisco NFL	7	1	4	0	0.0	0	0	0.0	0

REESE, IKE — LB — FALCONS

PERSONAL: Born October 16, 1973, in Jacksonville, N.C. ... 6-2/222. ... Full name: Isaiah Reese.
HIGH SCHOOL: Woodward (Cincinnati), then Aiken (Cincinnati).
COLLEGE: Michigan State.
TRANSACTIONS/CAREER NOTES: Selected by Philadelphia Eagles in fifth round (142nd pick overall) of 1998 NFL draft. ... Signed by Eagles (July 14, 1998). ... Granted free agency (March 2, 2001). ... Re-signed by Eagles (March 20, 2001). ... Granted unconditional free agency (March 2, 2005). ... Signed by Atlanta Falcons (March 9, 2005).
CHAMPIONSHIP GAME EXPERIENCE: Member of Eagles for NFC championship game (2001 season); inactive. ... Played in NFC championship game (2002-2004 seasons). ... Played in Super Bowl 39 (2004 season).
HONORS: Played in Pro Bowl (2004 season).

			TOTALS			INTERCEPTIONS			
Year Team	G	GS	Tk.	Ast.	Sks.	No.	Yds.	Avg.	TD
1998—Philadelphia NFL	16	0	3	1	0.0	0	0	0.0	0
1999—Philadelphia NFL	16	0	15	6	3.0	0	0	0.0	0

Year Team	G	GS	TOTALS Tk.	Ast.	Sks.	INTERCEPTIONS No.	Yds.	Avg.	TD
2000—Philadelphia NFL	16	0	4	1	0.0	0	0	0.0	0
2001—Philadelphia NFL	16	0	13	5	0.0	0	0	0.0	0
2002—Philadelphia NFL	16	3	42	7	1.5	0	0	0.0	0
2003—Philadelphia NFL	16	1	25	1	1.0	0	0	0.0	0
2004—Philadelphia NFL	16	1	33	3	1.0	2	22	11.0	0
Pro totals (7 years)	112	5	135	24	6.5	2	22	11.0	0

REESE, IZELL — S

PERSONAL: Born May 7, 1974, in Dothan, Ala. ... 6-2/195.
HIGH SCHOOL: Northview (Dothan, Ala.).
COLLEGE: Alabama-Birmingham.
TRANSACTIONS/CAREER NOTES: Selected by Dallas Cowboys in sixth round (188th pick overall) of 1998 NFL draft. ... Signed by Cowboys (July 15, 1998). ... On injured reserve with neck injury (November 19, 1999-remainder of season). ... Granted free agency (March 2, 2001). ... Re-signed by Cowboys (April 30, 2001). ... Granted unconditional free agency (March 1, 2002). ... Signed by Denver Broncos (April 1, 2002). ... Granted unconditional free agency (February 28, 2003). ... Signed by Buffalo Bills (March 21, 2003). ... On injured reserve with calf injury (December 17, 2003-remainder of season). ... Granted unconditional free agency (March 2, 2005).

Year Team	G	GS	TOTALS Tk.	Ast.	Sks.	INTERCEPTIONS No.	Yds.	Avg.	TD
1998—Dallas NFL	16	0	4	0	0.0	1	6	6.0	0
1999—Dallas NFL	8	4	17	5	0.0	3	28	9.3	0
2000—Dallas NFL	16	7	32	15	0.0	2	60	30.0	0
2001—Dallas NFL	16	4	24	1	3.0	1	42	42.0	0
2002—Denver NFL	15	15	41	10	0.5	0	0	0.0	0
2003—Buffalo NFL	13	9	23	10	0.0	0	0	0.0	0
2004—Buffalo NFL	9	9	18	18	0.0	1	33	33.0	0
Pro totals (7 years)	93	48	159	59	3.5	8	169	21.1	0

REESE, MARCUS — LB

PERSONAL: Born June 15, 1981, in San Jose, Calif. ... 6-1/233. ... Full name: Marcus Harrison Reese.
HIGH SCHOOL: Oak Grove (San Jose, Calif.).
COLLEGE: UCLA.
TRANSACTIONS/CAREER NOTES: Signed as non-drafted free agent by San Francisco 49ers (May 2, 2003). ... Released by 49ers (August 26, 2003). ... Re-signed by 49ers to practice squad (September 2, 2003). ... Released by 49ers (September 16, 2003). ... Signed by Chicago Bears to practice squad (November 25, 2003). ... Activated (December 30, 2004). ... Assigned by Bears to Cologne Centurions in 2004 NFL Europe enhancement allocation program (February 18, 2004).

Year Team	G	GS	TOTALS Tk.	Ast.	Sks.	INTERCEPTIONS No.	Yds.	Avg.	TD
2004—Chicago NFL	11	2	6	2	0.0	0	0	0.0	0

REEVES, JACQUES — CB — COWBOYS

PERSONAL: Born October 8, 1982, in Lancaster, Texas. ... 5-11/190. ... Full name: Jacques D. Reeves.
HIGH SCHOOL: Lancaster (Texas).
COLLEGE: Purdue.
TRANSACTIONS/CAREER NOTES: Selected by Dallas Cowboys in seventh round (223rd pick overall) of 2004 NFL draft. ... Signed by Cowboys (July 27, 2004).

Year Team	G	GS	TOTALS Tk.	Ast.	Sks.	INTERCEPTIONS No.	Yds.	Avg.	TD	KICKOFF RETURNS No.	Yds.	Avg.	TD	TOTALS TD	2pt.	Pts.	Fum.
2004—Dallas NFL	15	1	12	1	0.0	0	0	0.0	0	13	199	15.3	0	0	0	0	0

REID, DEXTER — DB — PATRIOTS

PERSONAL: Born March 18, 1981, in Norfolk, Va. ... 5-11/203.
HIGH SCHOOL: Granby (Norfolk, Va.).
COLLEGE: North Carolina.
TRANSACTIONS/CAREER NOTES: Selected by New England Patriots in fourth round (113th pick overall) of 2004 NFL draft. ... Signed by Patriots (June 22, 2004).
CHAMPIONSHIP GAME EXPERIENCE: Played in AFC championship game (2004 season). ... Member of Super Bowl championship team (2004 season).
HONORS: Named defensive back on THE SPORTING NEWS Freshman All-America third team (2000).

Year Team	G	GS	TOTALS Tk.	Ast.	Sks.	INTERCEPTIONS No.	Yds.	Avg.	TD
2004—New England NFL	13	2	4	6	0.0	0	0	0.0	0

REUBER, ALAN — G — CARDINALS

PERSONAL: Born January 26, 1981, in Plano, Texas. ... 6-6/323. ... Full name: Alan Michael Reuber.
HIGH SCHOOL: Plano (Texas).
COLLEGE: Texas A&M.

TRANSACTIONS/CAREER NOTES: Signed as non-drafted free agent by Minnesota Vikings (May 3, 2004). ... Claimed on waivers by Arizona Cardinals (August 31, 2004).
PLAYING EXPERIENCE: Arizona NFL, 2004. ... Games/Games started: 2004 (3/0). Total: 3/0.

REYES, TUTAN   T   PANTHERS

PERSONAL: Born October 28, 1977, in Queens, N.Y. ... 6-3/305.
HIGH SCHOOL: August Martin (Queens, N.Y.).
COLLEGE: Mississippi.
TRANSACTIONS/CAREER NOTES: Selected by New Orleans Saints in fifth round (131st pick overall) of 2000 NFL draft. ... Signed by Saints (July 14, 2000). ... Inactive for all 16 games (2000). ... Released by Saints (September 10, 2002). ... Re-signed by Saints to practice squad (September 11, 2002). ... Claimed on waivers by Tampa Bay Buccaneers (October 1, 2002). ... Released by Buccaneers (November 6, 2002). ... Re-signed by Buccaneers to practice squad (November 7, 2002). ... Activated (November 18, 2002). ... Claimed on waivers by Carolina Panthers (November 26, 2002). ... Granted free agency (February 28, 2003). ... Re-signed by Panthers (March 4, 2003). ... Granted unconditional free agency (March 3, 2004). ... Re-signed by Panthers (March 4, 2004).
PLAYING EXPERIENCE: New Orleans NFL, 2001; Carolina NFL, 2004. ... Games/Games started: 2001 (1/0), 2004 (14/12). Total: 15/12.
CHAMPIONSHIP GAME EXPERIENCE: Member of Panthers for NFC championship game (2003 season); inactive. ... Member of Panthers for Super Bowl 38 (2003 season); inactive.

REYNOLDS, ROBERT   LB   TITANS

PERSONAL: Born May 20, 1981, in Bowling Green, Ky. ... 6-3/242.
HIGH SCHOOL: Bowling Green (Ky.).
COLLEGE: Ohio State.
TRANSACTIONS/CAREER NOTES: Selected by Tennessee Titans in fifth round (165th pick overall) of 2004 NFL draft. ... Signed by Titans (July 27, 2004).

			TOTALS			INTERCEPTIONS			
Year Team	G	GS	Tk.	Ast.	Sks.	No.	Yds.	Avg.	TD
2004—Tennessee NFL	14	1	2	3	0.0	0	0	0.0	0

RHODES, DOMINIC   RB   COLTS

PERSONAL: Born January 17, 1979, in Waco, Texas. ... 5-9/203. ... Full name: Dominic Dondrell Rhodes.
HIGH SCHOOL: Cooper (Texas).
JUNIOR COLLEGE: Tyler Junior College.
COLLEGE: Midwestern State.
TRANSACTIONS/CAREER NOTES: Signed as non-drafted free agent by Indianapolis Colts (April 22, 2001). ... On injured reserve with knee injury (August 26, 2002-entire season).
CHAMPIONSHIP GAME EXPERIENCE: Played in AFC championship game (2003 season).
SINGLE GAME HIGHS (regular season): Attempts—34 (November 4, 2001, vs. Buffalo); yards—177 (December 16, 2001, vs. Atlanta); and rushing touchdowns—2 (December 16, 2001, vs. Atlanta).
STATISTICAL PLATEAUS: 100-yard rushing games: 2001 (5). Total: 5.

			RUSHING				RECEIVING				KICKOFF RETURNS				TOTALS			
Year Team	G	GS	Att.	Yds.	Avg.	TD	No.	Yds.	Avg.	TD	No.	Yds.	Avg.	TD	TD	2pt.	Pts.	Fum.
2001—Indianapolis NFL	Did not play.																	
2003—Indianapolis NFL	11	0	37	157	4.2	0	6	62	10.3	1	16	411	25.7	0	1	0	6	0
2004—Indianapolis NFL	16	0	53	254	4.8	1	2	24	12.0	0	48	1188	24.8	1	2	0	12	2
Pro totals (2 years)	27	0	90	411	4.6	1	8	86	10.8	1	64	1599	25.0	1	3	0	18	2

RICARD, ALAN   FB   RAVENS

PERSONAL: Born January 17, 1977, in Independence, La. ... 5-11/237.
HIGH SCHOOL: Amite (La.).
COLLEGE: Louisiana-Monroe.
TRANSACTIONS/CAREER NOTES: Signed as non-drafted free agent by Dallas Cowboys (April 30, 1999). ... Released by Cowboys (August 4, 1999). ... Signed by Baltimore Ravens (July 21, 2000). ... Released by Ravens (August 26, 2000). ... Re-signed by Ravens (August 29, 2000).
SINGLE GAME HIGHS (regular season): Attempts—4 (December 21, 2003, vs. Cleveland); yards—36 (September 14, 2003, vs. Cleveland); and rushing touchdowns—1 (December 29, 2002, vs. Pittsburgh).

			RUSHING				RECEIVING				TOTALS			
Year Team	G	GS	Att.	Yds.	Avg.	TD	No.	Yds.	Avg.	TD	TD	2pt.	Pts.	Fum.
2001—Baltimore NFL	5	0	0	0	0.0	0	0	0	0.0	0	0	0	0	0
2002—Baltimore NFL	16	8	14	58	4.1	2	10	60	6.0	0	3	0	18	0
2003—Baltimore NFL	16	13	19	79	4.2	0	9	62	6.9	0	1	0	6	0
2004—Baltimore NFL	16	9	10	36	3.6	0	11	39	3.5	0	0	0	0	0
Pro totals (4 years)	53	30	43	173	4.0	2	30	161	5.4	0	4	0	24	0

RICE, JERRY   WR   BRONCOS

PERSONAL: Born October 13, 1962, in Crawford, Miss. ... 6-2/200. ... Full name: Jerry Lee Rice.
HIGH SCHOOL: Crawford MS Moor (Crawford, Miss.).
COLLEGE: Mississippi Valley State.

TRANSACTIONS/CAREER NOTES: Selected by Birmingham Stallions in first round (first pick overall) of 1985 USFL draft. ... Selected by San Francisco 49ers in first round (16th pick overall) of 1985 NFL draft. ... Signed by 49ers (July 23, 1985). ... Granted free agency (February 1, 1992). ... Re-signed by 49ers (August 25, 1992). ... On injured reserve with knee injury (December 23, 1997-remainder of season). ... Released by 49ers (June 4, 2001). ... Signed by Oakland Raiders (June 5, 2001). ... Traded by Raiders to Seattle Seahawks for conditional seventh-round pick in 2005 draft (October 19, 2004). ... Released by Seahawks (February 25, 2005). ... Signed by Denver Broncos (May 25, 2005).

CHAMPIONSHIP GAME EXPERIENCE: Played in NFC championship game (1988-1990 and 1992-1994 seasons). ... Member of Super Bowl championship team (1988, 1989 and 1994 seasons). ... Played in AFC championship game (2002 season). ... Played in Super Bowl 37 (2002 season).

HONORS: Named wide receiver on THE SPORTING NEWS college All-America first team (1984). ... Named wide receiver on THE SPORTING NEWS NFL All-Pro team (1986-1996). ... Played in Pro Bowl (1986, 1987, 1989-1993, 1995, 1998 and 2002 seasons). ... Named NFL Player of the Year by THE SPORTING NEWS (1987 and 1990). ... Named Most Valuable Player of Super Bowl 23 (1988 season). ... Named to play in Pro Bowl (1988 season); replaced by J.T. Smith due to injury. ... Named to play in Pro Bowl (1994 season); replaced by Herman Moore due to injury. ... Named Outstanding Player of Pro Bowl (1995 season). ... Named to play in Pro Bowl (1996 season); replaced by Irving Fryar due to injury.

RECORDS: Holds NFL career records for most touchdowns—208; most touchdown receptions—197; most total yards—23,546; receiving yards—22,895; most pass receptions—1,549; most seasons with 1,000 or more yards receiving—14; most games with 100 or more yards receiving—77; most consecutive games with one or more receptions—274 (December 9, 1985-September 12, 2004); most consecutive games with one or more touchdown receptions—13 (December 19, 1986-December 27, 1987); and most seasons with 50 or more receptions—17. ... Holds NFL single-season record for most yards receiving—1,848 (1995); and most touchdown receptions—22 (1987). ... Shares NFL single-game record for most touchdown receptions—5 (October 14, 1990, at Atlanta).

POST SEASON RECORDS: Holds Super Bowl career records for most points—48; most touchdowns—8; most touchdown receptions—7; most receptions—28; most combined yards—527; and most yards receiving—512; ;most points by a non-kicker—132. ... Holds Super Bowl single-game records for most touchdowns receptions—3 (January 28, 1990, vs. Denver and January 29, 1995, vs. San Diego); and most yards receiving—215 (January 22, 1989, vs. Cincinnati). ... Shares Super Bowl single-game records for most points—18; most touchdowns—3 (January 28, 1990, vs. Denver and January 29, 1995, vs. San Diego); and most receptions—11 (January 22, 1989, vs. Cincinnati). ... Holds NFL postseason career records for most touchdown receptions—22; most receptions—137; most yards receiving—2,042; and most games with 100 or more yards receiving—8; most points by a non-kicker—132. ... Holds NFL postseason record for most consecutive games with one or more receptions—28 (1985-present). ... Shares NFL postseason career record for most consecutive games with 100 or more yards receiving—3 (1988-89). ... Shares NFL postseason single-game record for most touchdown receptions—3 (January 28, 1990, vs. Denver; January 1, 1989, vs. Minnesota; and January 29, 1995, vs. San Diego).

SINGLE GAME HIGHS (regular season): Receptions—16 (November 20, 1994, vs. Los Angeles Rams); yards—289 (December 18, 1995, vs. Minnesota); and touchdown receptions—5 (October 14, 1990, vs. Atlanta).

STATISTICAL PLATEAUS: 100-yard receiving games: 1985 (2), 1986 (6), 1987 (4), 1988 (5), 1989 (8), 1990 (7), 1991 (4), 1992 (3), 1993 (5), 1994 (5), 1995 (9), 1996 (3), 1999 (2), 2001 (2), 2002 (5), 2003 (2), 2004 (2). Total: 77.

MISCELLANEOUS: Active NFL leader for career receptions (1,549), receiving yards (22,895), touchdown receptions (197) and touchdowns (208). ... Holds San Francisco 49ers all-time records for most yards receiving (19,247), most touchdowns (187), most receptions (1,281) and most touchdown receptions (176).

Year Team	G	GS	Att.	Yds.	Avg.	TD	No.	Yds.	Avg.	TD	TD	2pt.	Pts.	Fum.
			RUSHING				RECEIVING				TOTALS			
1985—San Francisco NFL	16	4	6	26	4.3	1	49	927	18.9	3	4	0	24	1
1986—San Francisco NFL	16	15	10	72	7.2	1	†86	*1570	18.3	*15	16	0	96	2
1987—San Francisco NFL	12	12	8	51	6.4	1	65	1078	16.6	*22	*23	0	*138	2
1988—San Francisco NFL	16	16	13	107	8.2	1	64	1306	20.4	9	10	0	60	2
1989—San Francisco NFL	16	16	5	33	6.6	0	82	*1483	18.1	*17	17	0	102	0
1990—San Francisco NFL	16	16	2	0	0.0	0	*100	*1502	15.0	*13	13	0	78	1
1991—San Francisco NFL	16	16	1	2	2.0	0	80	1206	15.1	*14	14	0	84	1
1992—San Francisco NFL	16	16	9	58	6.4	1	84	1201	14.3	10	11	0	66	2
1993—San Francisco NFL	16	16	3	69	23.0	1	98	*1503	15.3	†15	*16	0	96	3
1994—San Francisco NFL	16	16	7	93	13.3	2	112	*1499	13.4	13	15	1	92	1
1995—San Francisco NFL	16	16	5	36	7.2	1	122	*1848	15.1	15	17	1	104	3
1996—San Francisco NFL	16	16	11	77	7.0	1	*108	1254	11.6	8	9	0	54	0
1997—San Francisco NFL	2	1	1	-10	-10.0	0	7	78	11.1	1	1	0	6	0
1998—San Francisco NFL	16	16	0	0	0.0	0	82	1157	14.1	9	9	†2	58	2
1999—San Francisco NFL	16	16	2	13	6.5	0	67	830	12.4	5	5	0	30	0
2000—San Francisco NFL	16	16	1	-2	-2.0	0	75	805	10.7	7	7	0	42	3
2001—Oakland NFL	16	15	0	0	0.0	0	83	1139	13.7	9	9	0	54	1
2002—Oakland NFL	16	16	3	20	6.7	0	92	1211	13.2	7	7	0	42	1
2003—Oakland NFL	16	15	0	0	0.0	0	63	869	13.8	2	2	0	12	2
2004—Oakland NFL	6	5	0	0	0.0	0	5	67	13.4	0	0	0	0	0
—Seattle NFL	11	9	0	0	0.0	0	25	362	14.5	3	3	0	18	0
Pro totals (20 years)	303	284	87	645	7.4	10	1549	22895	14.8	197	208	4	1256	27

RICE, SIMEON — DE — BUCCANEERS

PERSONAL: Born February 24, 1974, in Chicago, Ill. ... 6-5/268. ... Name pronounced: simm-ee-ON.

HIGH SCHOOL: Mount Carmel (Chicago).

COLLEGE: Illinois.

TRANSACTIONS/CAREER NOTES: Selected by Arizona Cardinals in first round (third pick overall) of 1996 NFL draft. ... Signed by Cardinals (August 19, 1996). ... Designated by Cardinals as franchise player (February 11, 2000). ... Re-signed by Cardinals (September 7, 2000). ... Granted unconditional free agency (March 2, 2001). ... Signed by Tampa Bay Buccaneers (March 23, 2001).

CHAMPIONSHIP GAME EXPERIENCE: Played in NFC championship game (2002 season). ... Member of Super Bowl championship team (2002 season).

HONORS: Played in Pro Bowl (1999 and 2002 seasons). ... Named linebacker on THE SPORTING NEWS college All-America second team (1995). ... Named defensive end of THE SPORTING NFL All-Pro team (2002, 2003). ... Named to play in Pro Bowl (2003 season); replaced by Kabeer Gbaja-Biamila due to disciplinary problems.

Year Team	G	GS	Tk.	Ast.	Sks.	No.	Yds.	Avg.	TD
			TOTALS			INTERCEPTIONS			
1996—Arizona NFL	16	15	42	10	12.5	0	0	0.0	0
1997—Arizona NFL	16	15	33	14	5.0	1	0	0.0	0
1998—Arizona NFL	16	16	34	5	10.0	0	0	0.0	0

Year	Team	G	GS	TOTALS			INTERCEPTIONS			
				Tk.	Ast.	Sks.	No.	Yds.	Avg.	TD
1999—Arizona NFL		16	16	38	11	16.5	0	0	0.0	0
2000—Arizona NFL		15	11	30	3	7.5	0	0	0.0	0
2001—Tampa Bay NFL		16	16	39	5	11.0	0	0	0.0	0
2002—Tampa Bay NFL		16	16	41	9	‡15.5	1	30	30.0	0
2003—Tampa Bay NFL		16	16	45	5	15.0	2	12	6.0	0
2004—Tampa Bay NFL		16	16	35	5	12.0	0	0	0.0	0
Pro totals (9 years)		143	137	337	67	105.0	4	42	10.5	0

RICHARD, KRIS   CB

PERSONAL: Born October 28, 1978, in Los Angeles, Calif. ... 5-11/190.
HIGH SCHOOL: Serra (Gardena, Calif.).
COLLEGE: Southern California.
TRANSACTIONS/CAREER NOTES: Selected by Seattle Seahawks in third round (85th pick overall) of 2002 NFL draft. ... Signed by Seahawks (July 25, 2002). ... On injured reserve with hernia (December 17, 2002-remainder of season). ... Granted free agency (March 2, 2005).

Year	Team	G	GS	TOTALS			INTERCEPTIONS				PUNT RETURNS				TOTALS			
				Tk.	Ast.	Sks.	No.	Yds.	Avg.	TD	No.	Yds.	Avg.	TD	TD	2pt.	Pts.	Fum.
2002—Seattle NFL		7	0	3	0	0.0	0	0	0.0	0	0	0	0.0	0	0	0	0	0
2003—Seattle NFL		15	1	9	2	1.0	0	0	0.0	0	1	0	0.0	0	0	0	0	1
2004—Seattle NFL		16	0	21	3	0.0	0	0	0.0	0	4	31	7.8	0	0	0	0	0
Pro totals (3 years)		38	1	33	5	1.0	0	0	0.0	0	5	31	6.2	0	0	0	0	1

RICHARDSON, DAMIEN   SS   PANTHERS

PERSONAL: Born April 3, 1976, in Los Angeles. ... 6-1/210. ... Full name: Damien A. Richardson.
HIGH SCHOOL: Clovis West (Fresno, Calif.).
COLLEGE: Arizona State.
TRANSACTIONS/CAREER NOTES: Selected by Carolina Panthers in sixth round (165th pick overall) of 1998 NFL draft. ... Signed by Panthers (July 24, 1998). ... Granted free agency (March 2, 2001). ... Re-signed by Panthers (March 2, 2001). ... Granted unconditional free agency (March 1, 2002). ... Re-signed by Panthers (March 25, 2002). ... On injured reserve with neck injury (August 31, 2004-entire season).

Year	Team	G	GS	TOTALS			INTERCEPTIONS			
				Tk.	Ast.	Sks.	No.	Yds.	Avg.	TD
1998—Carolina NFL		14	7	0	0	0.0	0	0	0.0	0
1999—Carolina NFL		15	0	0	0	1.0	1	27	27.0	0
2000—Carolina NFL		16	1	0	0	0.0	0	0	0.0	0
2001—Carolina NFL		16	2	0	0	0.0	0	0	0.0	0
2002—Carolina NFL		16	0	0	0	0.0	0	0	0.0	0
2004—Carolina NFL				Did not play.						
Pro totals (5 years)		77	10	0	0	1.0	1	27	27.0	0

RICHARDSON, DAVID   CB   JAGUARS

PERSONAL: Born September 9, 1981, in Inglewood, Calif. ... 6-0/202.
HIGH SCHOOL: St. Bernard (Playa del Rey, Calif.).
COLLEGE: Cal Poly.
TRANSACTIONS/CAREER NOTES: Signed as non-drafted free agent by Jacksonville Jaguars (April 25, 2004).

Year	Team	G	GS	TOTALS			INTERCEPTIONS			
				Tk.	Ast.	Sks.	No.	Yds.	Avg.	TD
2004—Jacksonville NFL		2	0	0	0	0.0	0	0	0.0	0

RICHARDSON, KYLE   P   BROWNS

PERSONAL: Born March 2, 1973, in Farmington, Mo. ... 6-2/210. ... Full name: Kyle Davis Richardson.
HIGH SCHOOL: Farmington (Mo.).
COLLEGE: Arkansas State.
TRANSACTIONS/CAREER NOTES: Played for Rhein Fire of World League (1996). ... Signed as non-drafted free agent by Miami Dolphins (September 3, 1997). ... Released by Dolphins (September 8, 1997). ... Re-signed by Dolphins (September 18, 1997). ... Released by Dolphins (October 7, 1997). ... Signed by Seattle Seahawks (November 12, 1997). ... Released by Seahawks (November 25, 1997). ... Signed by Baltimore Ravens (March 25, 1998). ... Granted free agency (March 2, 2001). ... Re-signed by Ravens for 2001 season. ... Granted unconditional free agency (March 1, 2002). ... Signed by Minnesota Vikings (April 21, 2002). ... Granted unconditional free agency (February 28, 2003). ... Signed by Philadelphia Eagles (May 12, 2003). ... Released by Eagles (August 24, 2003). ... Signed by Cincinnati Bengals (October 7, 2003). ... On injured reserve with biceps injury (August 30, 2004-entire season). ... Granted unconditional free agency (March 2, 2005). ... Signed by Cleveland Browns (March 4, 2005).
CHAMPIONSHIP GAME EXPERIENCE: Played in AFC championship game (2000 season). ... Member of Super Bowl championship team (2000 season).

Year	Team	G	PUNTING					
			No.	Yds.	Avg.	Net avg.	In. 20	Blk.
1997—Miami NFL		3	11	480	43.6	33.1	0	0
—Seattle NFL		2	8	324	40.5	23.8	2	†2
1998—Baltimore NFL		16	90	3948	43.9	38.3	25	*2
1999—Baltimore NFL		16	103	4355	42.3	35.5	*39	1
2000—Baltimore NFL		16	86	3457	40.2	33.9	*35	0
2001—Baltimore NFL		16	85	3309	38.9	33.6	§29	§2

Year	Team				PUNTING			
		G	No.	Yds.	Avg.	Net avg.	In. 20	Blk.
2002—Minnesota NFL		16	62	2474	39.9	35.3	21	1
2003—Cincinnati NFL		11	49	1961	40.0	33.5	9	0
2004—Cincinnati NFL		Did not play.						
Pro totals (7 years)		96	494	20308	41.1	34.9	160	8

RICHARDSON, TONY   FB   CHIEFS

PERSONAL: Born December 17, 1971, in Frankfurt, Germany. ... 6-1/238. ... Full name: Antonio Richardson.
HIGH SCHOOL: Daleville (Ala.).
COLLEGE: Auburn.
TRANSACTIONS/CAREER NOTES: Signed as non-drafted free agent by Dallas Cowboys (April 28, 1994). ... Released by Cowboys (August 28, 1994). ... Re-signed by Cowboys to practice squad (August 30, 1994). ... Granted free agency after 1994 season. ... Signed by Kansas City Chiefs (February 28, 1995). ... On injured reserve with wrist injury (December 11, 1996-remainder of season). ... On injured reserve with shoulder injury (December 17, 2002-remainder of season).
HONORS: Played in Pro Bowl (2003 and 2004 seasons).
SINGLE GAME HIGHS (regular season): Attempts—23 (December 17, 2000, vs. Denver); yards—156 (December 17, 2000, vs. Denver); and rushing touchdowns—2 (November 4, 2001, vs. San Diego).
STATISTICAL PLATEAUS: 100-yard rushing games: 2000 (1). Total: 1.

Year	Team	G	GS	RUSHING				RECEIVING				TOTALS			
				Att.	Yds.	Avg.	TD	No.	Yds.	Avg.	TD	TD	2pt.	Pts.	Fum.
1995—Kansas City NFL		14	1	8	18	2.3	0	0	0	0.0	0	0	0	0	0
1996—Kansas City NFL		13	0	4	10	2.5	0	2	18	9.0	1	1	0	6	0
1997—Kansas City NFL		14	0	2	11	5.5	0	3	6	2.0	3	3	0	18	0
1998—Kansas City NFL		14	1	20	45	2.3	2	2	13	6.5	0	2	0	12	0
1999—Kansas City NFL		16	16	84	387	4.6	0	24	141	5.9	0	1	0	6	1
2000—Kansas City NFL		16	16	147	697	4.7	3	58	468	8.1	3	6	0	36	3
2001—Kansas City NFL		14	7	66	191	2.9	7	30	265	8.8	0	7	0	42	0
2002—Kansas City NFL		14	12	22	81	3.7	2	18	125	6.9	1	3	0	18	1
2003—Kansas City NFL		16	10	24	60	2.5	0	12	76	6.3	0	0	0	0	0
2004—Kansas City NFL		16	16	12	56	4.7	0	19	118	6.2	0	0	0	0	0
Pro totals (10 years)		147	79	389	1556	4.0	15	168	1230	7.3	8	23	0	138	5

RICHEY, WADE   K

PERSONAL: Born May 19, 1976, in Lafayette, La. ... 6-3/205. ... Full name: Wade Edward Richey.
HIGH SCHOOL: Carencro (Lafayette, La.).
COLLEGE: Louisiana State.
TRANSACTIONS/CAREER NOTES: Signed as non-drafted free agent by Seattle Seahawks (April 21, 1998). ... Claimed on waivers by San Francisco 49ers (August 26, 1998). ... Granted free agency (March 2, 2001). ... Tendered offer sheet by San Diego Chargers (April 13, 2001). ... 49ers declined to match offer (April 18, 2001). ... Released by Chargers (December 2, 2002). ... Signed by Baltimore Ravens (August 20, 2003). ... Granted unconditional free agency (March 3, 2004). ... Re-signed by Ravens (March 16, 2004). ... Granted unconditional free agency (March 2, 2005).

Year	Team	G	FIELD GOALS							TOTALS		
			1-29	30-39	40-49	50+	Tot.	Pct.	Lg.	XPM	XPA	Pts.
1998—San Francisco NFL		16	9-10	3-4	6-13	0-0	18-27	66.7	46	49	51	103
1999—San Francisco NFL		16	8-8	7-8	5-6	1-1	21-23	*91.3	52	30	31	93
2000—San Francisco NFL		16	6-7	6-8	3-6	0-1	15-22	68.2	47	43	‡45	88
2001—San Diego NFL		16	13-15	4-7	3-7	1-3	21-32	65.6	51	26	26	89
2002—San Diego NFL		12	0-0	0-0	0-0	0-0	0-0	0.0	0	0	0	0
2003—Baltimore NFL		15	0-0	0-0	0-0	1-2	1-2	50.0	§56	0	0	3
2004—Baltimore NFL		12	0-0	0-0	0-0	0-0	0-0	0.0	0	0	0	0
Pro totals (7 years)		103	36-40	20-27	17-32	3-7	76-106	71.7	56	148	153	376

RIEMERSMA, JAY   TE

PERSONAL: Born May 17, 1973, in Evansville, Ind. ... 6-5/256. ... Full name: Allen Jay Riemersma. ... Name pronounced: REEM-urz-muh.
HIGH SCHOOL: Zeeland (Mich.).
COLLEGE: Michigan.
TRANSACTIONS/CAREER NOTES: Selected by Buffalo Bills in seventh round (244th pick overall) of 1996 NFL draft. ... Signed by Bills (July 9, 1996). ... Released by Bills (August 25, 1996). ... Re-signed by Bills to practice squad (August 26, 1996). ... Activated (October 15, 1996); did not play. ... Granted free agency (February 12, 1999). ... Re-signed by Bills (April 26, 1999). ... Granted unconditional free agency (February 11, 2000). ... Re-signed by Bills (February 15, 2000). ... On physically unable to perform list with hamstring injury (July 25-28, 2002). ... Released by Bills (February 27, 2003). ... Signed by Pittsburgh Steelers (March 19, 2003). ... On injured reserve with Achilles injury (December 7, 2004-remainder of season). ... Released by Steelers (February 25, 2005).
SINGLE GAME HIGHS (regular season): Receptions—8 (December 30, 2001, vs. New York Jets); yards—86 (November 7, 1999, vs. Washington); and touchdown receptions—2 (September 10, 2000, vs. Green Bay).

Year	Team	G	GS	RECEIVING				TOTALS			
				No.	Yds.	Avg.	TD	TD	2pt.	Pts.	Fum.
1996—Buffalo NFL		Did not play.									
1997—Buffalo NFL		16	8	26	208	8.0	2	2	1	14	1
1998—Buffalo NFL		16	4	25	288	11.5	6	6	0	36	0
1999—Buffalo NFL		14	11	37	496	13.4	4	4	0	24	0
2000—Buffalo NFL		12	12	31	372	12.0	5	5	0	30	1
2001—Buffalo NFL		16	15	53	590	11.1	3	3	0	18	0
2002—Buffalo NFL		16	15	32	350	10.9	0	0	0	0	0
2003—Pittsburgh NFL		11	7	10	138	13.8	1	1	0	6	0
2004—Pittsburgh NFL		11	2	7	82	11.7	2	2	0	12	0
Pro totals (8 years)		112	74	221	2524	11.4	23	23	1	140	2

RILEY, KARON   LB

PERSONAL: Born August 23, 1978, in Detroit, Mich. ... 6-2/268.
HIGH SCHOOL: Martin Luther King (Detroit).
COLLEGE: Minnesota.
TRANSACTIONS/CAREER NOTES: Selected by Chicago Bears in fourth round (103rd pick overall) of 2001 NFL draft. ... Signed by Bears (June 18, 2001). ... Released by Bears (September 1, 2002). ... Signed by Atlanta Falcons to practice squad (September 3, 2002). ... Activated (October 14, 2002). ... Released by Falcons (November 12, 2002). ... Re-signed by Falcons to practice squad (November 13, 2002). ... Activated (November 25, 2002). ... Granted free agency (March 3, 2004). ... Re-signed by Falcons (May 20, 2004). ... Granted unconditional free agency (March 2, 2005).
HONORS: Named defensive end on THE SPORTING NEWS college All-America third team (2000).

| | | | | TOTALS | | | INTERCEPTIONS | | |
Year	Team	G	GS	Tk.	Ast.	Sks.	No.	Yds.	Avg.	TD
2001—Chicago NFL		5	0	1	0	0.0	0	0	0.0	0
2002—Atlanta NFL		3	0	0	0	0.0	0	0	0.0	0
2003—Atlanta NFL		16	0	6	4	0.0	0	0	0.0	0
2004—Atlanta NFL		1	0	0	0	0.0	0	0	0.0	0
Pro totals (4 years)		25	0	7	4	0.0	0	0	0.0	0

RILEY, VICTOR   T   TEXANS

PERSONAL: Born November 4, 1974, in Lexington, S.C. ... 6-5/340. ... Full name: Victor Allan Riley.
HIGH SCHOOL: Swansea (S.C.).
COLLEGE: Auburn.
TRANSACTIONS/CAREER NOTES: Selected by Kansas City Chiefs in first round (27th pick overall) of 1998 NFL draft. ... Signed by Chiefs (July 2, 1998). ... Granted unconditional free agency (March 1, 2002). ... Signed by New Orleans Saints (April 4, 2002). ... Granted unconditional free agency (March 2, 2005). ... Signed by Houston Texans (May 13, 2005).
PLAYING EXPERIENCE: Kansas City NFL, 1998-2001; Houston NFL, 2002-2003; New Orleans NFL, 2004. ... Games/Games started: 1998 (16/15), 1999 (16/16), 2000 (16/16), 2001 (7/5), 2002 (14/2), 2003 (16/16), 2004 (16/15). Total: 101/85.

RIMPF, BRIAN   T   RAVENS

PERSONAL: Born February 11, 1981, in Raleigh, N.C. ... 6-6/319.
HIGH SCHOOL: Leesville Road (Raleigh, N.C.).
COLLEGE: East Carolina.
TRANSACTIONS/CAREER NOTES: Selected by Baltimore Ravens in seventh round (246th pick overall) of 2004 NFL draft. ... Signed by Ravens (July 29, 2004). ... Released by Ravens (September 6, 2004). ... Signed by Ravens to practice squad (September 7, 2004). ... Activated (December 15, 2004).
PLAYING EXPERIENCE: Baltimore NFL, 2004. ... Games/Games started: 2004 (1/0). Total: 1/0.

RITCHIE, JON   FB   EAGLES

PERSONAL: Born September 4, 1974, in Mechanicsburg, Pa. ... 6-2/250.
HIGH SCHOOL: Cumberland Valley (Mechanicsburg, Pa.).
COLLEGE: Stanford.
TRANSACTIONS/CAREER NOTES: Selected by Oakland Raiders in third round (63rd pick overall) of 1998 NFL draft. ... Signed by Raiders (July 18, 1998). ... Granted unconditional free agency (February 28, 2003). ... Signed by Philadelphia Eagles (March 7, 2003). ... On injured reserve with knee injury (September 27, 2004-remainder of season). ... Granted unconditional free agency (March 2, 2005). ... Re-signed by Eagles (April 6, 2005).
CHAMPIONSHIP GAME EXPERIENCE: Played in AFC championship game (2000, 2002 and 2003 seasons). ... Played in Super Bowl 37 (2002 season).
SINGLE GAME HIGHS (regular season): Attempts—2 (September 12, 1999, vs. Green Bay); yards—14 (November 15, 1998, vs. Seattle); and rushing touchdowns—0.

| | | | | RUSHING | | | | RECEIVING | | | | TOTALS | | | |
Year	Team	G	GS	Att.	Yds.	Avg.	TD	No.	Yds.	Avg.	TD	TD	2pt.	Pts.	Fum.
1998—Oakland NFL		15	10	9	23	2.6	0	29	225	7.8	0	0	0	0	2
1999—Oakland NFL		16	14	5	12	2.4	0	45	408	9.1	1	1	0	6	0
2000—Oakland NFL		13	12	0	0	0.0	0	26	173	6.7	0	0	0	0	0
2001—Oakland NFL		15	10	0	0	0.0	0	19	154	8.1	2	2	0	12	0
2002—Oakland NFL		16	2	0	0	0.0	0	10	66	6.6	1	1	0	6	1
2003—Philadelphia NFL		16	7	1	1	1.0	0	17	86	5.1	3	3	0	18	0
2004—Philadelphia NFL		3	0	0	0	0.0	0	4	36	9.0	0	0	0	0	0
Pro totals (7 years)		94	55	15	36	2.4	0	150	1148	7.7	7	7	0	42	3

RIVERA, MARCO   G   COWBOYS

PERSONAL: Born April 26, 1972, in Brooklyn, N.Y. ... 6-4/307. ... Full name: Marco Anthony Rivera.
HIGH SCHOOL: Elmont (N.Y.) Memorial.
COLLEGE: Penn State.
TRANSACTIONS/CAREER NOTES: Selected by Green Bay Packers in sixth round (208th pick overall) of 1996 NFL draft. ... Signed by Packers (July 15, 1996). ... Inactive for all 16 games (1996). ... Assigned by Packers to Scottish Claymores in 1997 World League enhancement allocation program (February 19, 1997). ... Granted free agency (February 12, 1999). ... Re-signed by Packers (March 24, 1999). ... Granted unconditional free agency (March 2, 2005). ... Signed by Dallas Cowboys (March 3, 2005).

PLAYING EXPERIENCE: Green Bay NFL, 1997-2004. ... Games/Games started: 1997 (14/0), 1998 (15/15), 1999 (16/16), 2000 (16/16), 2001 (16/16), 2002 (16/16), 2003 (16/16), 2004 (16/16). Total: 125/111.
CHAMPIONSHIP GAME EXPERIENCE: Member of Packers for NFC championship game (1996 season); inactive. ... Member of Super Bowl championship team (1996 season); inactive. ... Played in NFC championship game (1997 season). ... Played in Super Bowl 32 (1997 season).
HONORS: Played in Pro Bowl (2002-2004 seasons).

RIVERS, MARCELLUS — TE — TEXANS

PERSONAL: Born October 26, 1978, in Oklahoma City, Okla. ... 6-4/250.
HIGH SCHOOL: Douglass (Oklahoma City, Okla.).
COLLEGE: Oklahoma State.
TRANSACTIONS/CAREER NOTES: Signed as non-drafted free agent by New York Giants (April 27, 2001). ... Granted free agency (March 3, 2004). ... Re-signed by Giants (April 19, 2004). ... Granted unconditional free agency (March 2, 2005). ... Signed by Houston Texans (May 18, 2005).
SINGLE GAME HIGHS (regular season): Receptions—4 (October 19, 2003, vs. Philadelphia); yards—49 (October 12, 2003, vs. New England); and touchdown receptions—1 (December 18, 2004, vs. Pittsburgh).

Year Team	G	GS	RECEIVING No.	Yds.	Avg.	TD	TOTALS TD	2pt.	Pts.	Fum.
2001—New York Giants NFL	16	0	3	11	3.7	2	2	0	12	0
2002—New York Giants NFL	15	0	2	25	12.5	1	1	1	8	0
2003—New York Giants NFL	12	6	17	155	9.1	0	0	0	0	0
2004—New York Giants NFL	16	3	5	36	7.2	1	1	0	6	1
Pro totals (4 years)	59	9	27	227	8.4	4	4	1	26	1

RIVERS, PHILIP — QB — CHARGERS

PERSONAL: Born December 8, 1981, in Decatur, Ala. ... 6-5/228.
HIGH SCHOOL: Athens (Ala.).
TRANSACTIONS/CAREER NOTES: Selected by New York Giants in first round (fourth pick overall) of 2004 NFL draft. ... Traded by Giants with a third-round pick (K Nate Kaeding) in 2004 draft and 2005 first- (LB Shawne Merriman) and fifth-round (traded to St. Louis) draft choices to San Diego Chargers for QB Eli Manning (April 24, 2004). ... Signed by Chargers (August 16, 2004).
HONORS: Named running back on THE SPORTING NEWS Freshman All-America first team (2000).
SINGLE GAME HIGHS (regular season): Attempts—8 (January 2, 2005, vs. Kansas City); completions—5 (January 2, 2005, vs. Kansas City); yards—33 (January 2, 2005, vs. Kansas City); and touchdown passes—1 (January 2, 2005, vs. Kansas City).

Year Team	G	GS	PASSING Att.	Cmp.	Pct.	Yds.	TD	Int.	Avg.	Skd.	Rat.	RUSHING Att.	Yds.	Avg.	TD	TOTALS TD	2pt.	Pts.
2004—San Diego NFL	2	0	8	5	62.5	33	1	0	4.13	1	110.9	4	-5	-1.2	0	0	0	0

ROAF, WILLIE — T — CHIEFS

PERSONAL: Born April 18, 1970, in Pine Bluff, Ark. ... 6-5/320. ... Full name: William Layton Roaf.
HIGH SCHOOL: Pine Bluff (Ark.).
COLLEGE: Louisiana Tech.
TRANSACTIONS/CAREER NOTES: Selected by New Orleans Saints in first round (eighth pick overall) of 1993 NFL draft. ... Signed by Saints (July 15, 1993). ... Designated by Saints as transition player (February 15, 1994). ... On injured reserve with knee injury (November 28, 2001-remainder of season). ... Traded by Saints to Kansas City Chiefs for third-round pick (traded to New England) in 2003 draft (March 26, 2002).
PLAYING EXPERIENCE: New Orleans NFL, 1993-2001; Kansas City NFL, 2002-2004. ... Games/Games started: 1993 (16/16), 1994 (16/16), 1995 (16/16), 1996 (13/13), 1997 (16/16), 1998 (15/15), 1999 (16/16), 2000 (16/16), 2001 (7/7), 2002 (16/16), 2003 (16/16), 2004 (16/16). Total: 179/179.
HONORS: Named offensive tackle on THE SPORTING NEWS college All-America second team (1992). ... Named offensive tackle on THE SPORTING NEWS NFL All-Pro team (1994-1996). ... Played in Pro Bowl (1994-1997, 1999, 2000 and 2002 seasons). ... Named to play in Pro Bowl (1998 season); replaced by Bob Whitfield due to injury. ... Named to play in Pro Bowl (2003 season); replaced by Brad Hopkins due to injury. ... Named to play in Pro Bowl (2004 season); replaced by Marvel Smith due to injury.

ROBBINS, FRED — DT — GIANTS

PERSONAL: Born March 25, 1977, in Pensacola, Fla. ... 6-4/325. ... Full name: Fredrick Robbins.
HIGH SCHOOL: Tate (Gonzalez, Fla.).
COLLEGE: Wake Forest.
TRANSACTIONS/CAREER NOTES: Selected by Minnesota Vikings in second round (55th pick overall) of 2000 NFL draft. ... Signed by Vikings (July 21, 2000). ... Granted unconditional free agency (March 3, 2004). ... Signed by New York Giants (March 5, 2004).
CHAMPIONSHIP GAME EXPERIENCE: Member of Vikings for NFC championship game (2000 season); inactive.

Year Team	G	GS	TOTALS Tk.	Ast.	Sks.	INTERCEPTIONS No.	Yds.	Avg.	TD
2000—Minnesota NFL	8	0	1	2	1.0	0	0	0.0	0
2001—Minnesota NFL	16	12	17	10	2.0	0	0	0.0	0
2002—Minnesota NFL	16	15	19	14	0.0	0	0	0.0	0
2003—Minnesota NFL	16	12	21	8	0.5	0	0	0.0	0
2004—New York Giants NFL	15	15	31	9	5.0	1	13	13.0	0
Pro totals (5 years)	71	54	89	43	8.5	1	13	13.0	0

ROBERTS, TERRELL   CB   BENGALS

PERSONAL: Born April 7, 1981, in Berkeley, Calif. ... 5-10/197.
HIGH SCHOOL: El Cerrito (Richmond, Calif.).
COLLEGE: Oregon State.
TRANSACTIONS/CAREER NOTES: Signed as non-drafted free agent by Cincinnati Bengals (May 2, 2003).

		TOTALS			INTERCEPTIONS				KICKOFF RETURNS				TOTALS			
Year Team	G	GS	Tk.	Ast.	Sks.	No.	Yds.	Avg.	TD	No.	Yds.	Avg.	TD	TD	2pt.	Pts.	Fum.
2003—Cincinnati NFL	12	0	13	3	1.0	1	6	6.0	0	7	128	18.3	0	0	0	0	0
2004—Cincinnati NFL	11	1	8	1	0.0	0	0	0.0	0	0	0	0.0	0	0	0	0	0
Pro totals (2 years)	23	1	21	4	1.0	1	6	6.0	0	7	128	18.3	0	0	0	0	0

ROBERTSON, DEWAYNE   DT   JETS

PERSONAL: Born October 16, 1981, in Memphis, Tenn. ... 6-1/317.
HIGH SCHOOL: Melrose (Memphis, Tenn.).
COLLEGE: Kentucky.
TRANSACTIONS/CAREER NOTES: Selected after junior season by New York Jets in first round (fourth pick overall) of 2003 NFL draft. ... Signed by Jets (July 20, 2003).

			TOTALS		
Year Team	G	GS	Tk.	Ast.	Sks.
2003—New York Jets NFL	16	16	34	9	1.5
2004—New York Jets NFL	16	16	39	14	3.0
Pro totals (2 years)	32	32	73	23	4.5

ROBERTSON, JAMAL   RB   PANTHERS

PERSONAL: Born January 10, 1977, in Washington, DC. ... 5-10/210.
HIGH SCHOOL: Stebbins (Dayton, Ohio).
COLLEGE: Ohio Northern.
TRANSACTIONS/CAREER NOTES: Signed by Calgary Stampeders of CFL (June 7, 2001). ... Released by Stampeders (June 23, 2001). ... Re-signed by Stampeders to practice squad (June 24, 2001). ... Signed as non-drafted free agent by San Francisco 49ers (January 23, 2002). ... Assigned by 49ers to Rhein Fire in 2002 NFL Europe enhancement allocation program (February 12, 2002). ... On injured reserve with hamstring injury (December 30, 2002-remainder of season). ... Released by 49ers (November 2, 2004). ... Signed by Carolina Panthers (November 13, 2004). ... Granted free agency (March 2, 2005). ... Re-signed by Panthers (March 15, 2005).
SINGLE GAME HIGHS (regular season): Attempts—9 (September 19, 2004, vs. New Orleans); yards—46 (December 7, 2003, vs. Arizona); and rushing touchdowns—1 (September 19, 2004, vs. New Orleans).

			RUSHING				RECEIVING				KICKOFF RETURNS				TOTALS			
Year Team	G	GS	Att.	Yds.	Avg.	TD	No.	Yds.	Avg.	TD	No.	Yds.	Avg.	TD	TD	2pt.	Pts.	Fum.
2002—San Francisco NFL	6	0	0	0	0.0	0	0	0	0.0	0	11	242	22.0	0	0	0	0	0
2003—San Francisco NFL	9	0	32	136	4.3	0	0	0	0.0	0	0	0	0.0	0	0	0	0	0
2004—San Francisco NFL	7	0	16	71	4.4	1	4	34	8.5	0	25	560	22.4	0	1	0	6	3
—Carolina NFL	5	0	0	0	0.0	0	0	0	0.0	0	6	180	30.0	0	0	0	0	0
Pro totals (3 years)	27	0	48	207	4.3	1	4	34	8.5	0	42	982	23.4	0	1	0	6	3

ROBINSON, BRYAN   DT   BENGALS

PERSONAL: Born June 22, 1974, in Toledo, Ohio. ... 6-4/296. ... Full name: Bryan Keith Robinson.
HIGH SCHOOL: Woodward (Cincinnati).
JUNIOR COLLEGE: College of the Desert (Palm Desert, Calif.).
COLLEGE: Fresno State.
TRANSACTIONS/CAREER NOTES: Signed as non-drafted free agent by St. Louis Rams (April 29, 1997). ... Claimed on waivers by Chicago Bears (August 31, 1998). ... Granted free agency (February 11, 2000). ... Re-signed by Bears (April 19, 2000). ... Designated by Bears as transition player (February 22, 2001). ... Released by Bears (September 5, 2004). ... Signed by Miami Dolphins (September 7, 2004). ... Granted unconditional free agency (March 2, 2005). ... Signed by Cincinnati Bengals (March 14, 2005).

			TOTALS		
Year Team	G	GS	Tk.	Ast.	Sks.
1997—St. Louis NFL	11	0	10	0	1.0
1998—Chicago NFL	11	5	11	7	0.5
1999—Chicago NFL	16	16	38	4	5.0
2000—Chicago NFL	16	16	42	9	4.5
2001—Chicago NFL	16	16	38	10	4.5
2002—Chicago NFL	15	13	28	6	1.0
2003—Chicago NFL	16	16	23	6	1.0
2004—Miami NFL	16	13	24	17	0.0
Pro totals (8 years)	117	95	214	59	17.5

ROBINSON, DUNTA   CB   TEXANS

PERSONAL: Born April 11, 1982, in Athens, Ga. ... 5-10/174.
HIGH SCHOOL: Clarke Central (Athens, Ga.).
COLLEGE: South Carolina.

Year Team	G	GS	TOTALS			INTERCEPTIONS			
			Tk.	Ast.	Sks.	No.	Yds.	Avg.	TD
2004—Houston NFL	16	16	74	14	3.0	6	146	24.3	0

ROBINSON, JEFF   TE   COWBOYS

PERSONAL: Born February 20, 1970, in Spokane, Wash. ... 6-4/250. ... Full name: Jeffrey William Robinson.
HIGH SCHOOL: Joel E. Ferris (Spokane, Wash.).
COLLEGE: Idaho.
TRANSACTIONS/CAREER NOTES: Selected by Denver Broncos in fourth round (98th pick overall) of 1993 NFL draft. ... Signed by Broncos (July 13, 1993). ... Granted free agency (February 16, 1996). ... Re-signed by Broncos (March 28, 1996). ... Granted unconditional free agency (February 14, 1997). ... Signed by St. Louis Rams (March 14, 1997). ... Granted unconditional free agency (March 1, 2002). ... Signed by Dallas Cowboys (March 5, 2002). ... On injured reserve with knee injury (August 27, 2002-entire season).
CHAMPIONSHIP GAME EXPERIENCE: Played in NFC championship game (1999 and 2001 seasons). ... Member of Super Bowl championship team (1999 season). ... Played in Super Bowl 36 (2001 season).
SINGLE GAME HIGHS (regular season): Receptions—2 (November 18, 2001, vs. New England); yards—34 (December 10, 2000, vs. Minnesota); and touchdown receptions—1 (November 21, 2004, vs. Baltimore).
MISCELLANEOUS: Played defensive line (1993-98).

Year Team	G	GS	RECEIVING				TOTALS			
			No.	Yds.	Avg.	TD	TD	2pt.	Pts.	Fum.
1993—Denver NFL	16	0	0	0	0.0	0	0	0	0	1
1994—Denver NFL	16	0	0	0	0.0	0	0	0	0	0
1995—Denver NFL	16	0	0	0	0.0	0	0	0	0	0
1996—Denver NFL	16	0	0	0	0.0	0	0	0	0	0
1997—St. Louis NFL	16	0	0	0	0.0	0	0	0	0	0
1998—St. Louis NFL	16	0	1	4	4.0	1	1	0	6	0
1999—St. Louis NFL	16	9	6	76	12.7	2	2	0	12	0
2000—St. Louis NFL	16	2	5	52	10.4	0	0	0	0	0
2001—St. Louis NFL	16	6	11	108	9.8	1	1	0	6	0
2002—Dallas NFL	Did not play.									
2003—Dallas NFL	16	0	2	8	4.0	2	2	0	12	0
2004—Dallas NFL	16	0	2	2	1.0	2	2	0	12	0
Pro totals (11 years)	176	17	27	250	9.3	8	8	0	48	1

ROBINSON, KOREN   WR   SEAHAWKS

PERSONAL: Born March 19, 1980, in Belmont, N.C. ... 6-1/205.
HIGH SCHOOL: South Point (N.C.).
COLLEGE: North Carolina State.
TRANSACTIONS/CAREER NOTES: Selected after sophomore season by Seattle Seahawks in first round (ninth pick overall) of 2001 NFL draft. ... Signed by Seahawks (July 27, 2001). ... On suspended list (November 28-December 24, 2004).
SINGLE GAME HIGHS (regular season): Receptions—9 (October 17, 2004, vs. New England); yards—168 (November 24, 2002, vs. Kansas City); and touchdown receptions—1 (November 7, 2004, vs. San Francisco).
STATISTICAL PLATEAUS: 100-yard receiving games: 2002 (5), 2003 (1), 2004 (1). Total: 7.

Year Team	G	GS	RUSHING				RECEIVING				TOTALS			
			Att.	Yds.	Avg.	TD	No.	Yds.	Avg.	TD	TD	2pt.	Pts.	Fum.
2001—Seattle NFL	16	13	4	13	3.3	0	39	536	13.7	1	1	0	6	2
2002—Seattle NFL	16	16	8	56	7.0	0	78	1240	15.9	5	5	0	30	2
2003—Seattle NFL	15	15	4	15	3.8	0	65	896	13.8	4	5	0	30	1
2004—Seattle NFL	10	8	1	3	3.0	0	31	495	16.0	2	2	0	12	0
Pro totals (4 years)	57	52	17	87	5.1	0	213	3167	14.9	12	13	0	78	5

ROBINSON, MARCUS   WR   VIKINGS

PERSONAL: Born February 27, 1975, in Ft. Valley, Ga. ... 6-3/215.
HIGH SCHOOL: Peach County (Fort Valley, Ga.).
COLLEGE: South Carolina.
TRANSACTIONS/CAREER NOTES: Selected by Chicago Bears in fourth round (108th pick overall) of 1997 NFL draft. ... Signed by Bears (July 11, 1997). ... Inactive for four games (1997). ... On injured reserve with thumb injury (September 24, 1997-remainder of season). ... Assigned by Bears to Rhein Fire in 1998 NFL Europe enhancement allocation program (February 18, 1998). ... On injured reserve with back injury (December 4, 2000-remainder of season). ... On injured reserve with knee injury (October 23, 2001-remainder of season). ... Released by Bears (April 16, 2003). ... Signed by Baltimore Ravens (May 1, 2003). ... Granted unconditional free agency (March 3, 2004). ... Signed by Minnesota Vikings (March 8, 2004).
SINGLE GAME HIGHS (regular season): Receptions—11 (December 19, 1999, vs. Detroit); yards—170 (December 19, 1999, vs. Detroit); and touchdown receptions—4 (November 23, 2003, vs. Seattle).
STATISTICAL PLATEAUS: 100-yard receiving games: 1999 (5), 2000 (1), 2001 (1), 2003 (2), 2004 (1). Total: 10.

Year Team	G	GS	RECEIVING				TOTALS			
			No.	Yds.	Avg.	TD	TD	2pt.	Pts.	Fum.
1997—Chicago NFL	Did not play.									
1998—Chicago NFL	3	0	4	44	11.0	1	1	0	6	0
1999—Chicago NFL	16	11	84	1400	16.7	9	9	0	54	0
2000—Chicago NFL	11	11	55	738	13.4	5	5	0	30	1
2001—Chicago NFL	5	4	23	269	11.7	2	2	0	12	0
2002—Chicago NFL	16	2	21	244	11.6	3	3	0	18	0
2003—Baltimore NFL	15	5	31	451	14.5	6	6	0	36	0
2004—Minnesota NFL	16	7	47	657	14.0	8	8	0	48	1
Pro totals (7 years)	82	40	265	3803	14.4	34	34	0	204	2

RODGERS, DERRICK   LB   SAINTS

PERSONAL: Born October 14, 1971, in Memphis, Tenn. ... 6-0/230. ... Full name: Derrick Andre Rodgers.
HIGH SCHOOL: St. Augustine (New Orleans).
JUNIOR COLLEGE: Riverside (Calif.) Community College.
COLLEGE: Arizona State.
TRANSACTIONS/CAREER NOTES: Selected by Miami Dolphins in third round (92nd pick overall) of 1997 NFL draft. ... Signed by Dolphins (July 8, 1997). ... Granted free agency (February 11, 2000). ... Re-signed by Dolphins (April 28, 2000). ... Granted unconditional free agency (March 2, 2001). ... Re-signed by Dolphins (March 3, 2001). ... On injured reserve with shoulder injury (December 27, 2001-remainder of season). ... Traded by Dolphins to New Orleans Saints for seventh-round pick (traded to Atlanta) in 2004 draft (May 27, 2003). ... On suspended list for violating league personal conduct policy (August 31-September 8, 2003). ... Granted unconditional free agency (March 3, 2004). ... Re-signed by Saints (March 3, 2004). ... On injured reserve with back injury (December 2, 2004-remainder of season).

| | | | | TOTALS | | | INTERCEPTIONS | | | |
Year Team	G	GS	Tk.	Ast.	Sks.	No.	Yds.	Avg.	TD
1997—Miami NFL	15	14	56	24	5.0	0	0	0.0	0
1998—Miami NFL	16	16	26	21	2.5	0	0	0.0	0
1999—Miami NFL	16	15	21	15	0.0	1	5	5.0	0
2000—Miami NFL	16	14	52	23	0.5	0	0	0.0	0
2001—Miami NFL	14	14	40	26	1.0	0	0	0.0	0
2002—Miami NFL	16	15	45	29	0.0	2	28	14.0	0
2003—New Orleans NFL	15	15	56	18	0.0	1	40	40.0	1
2004—New Orleans NFL	8	8	44	11	0.0	0	0	0.0	0
Pro totals (8 years)	116	111	340	167	9.0	4	73	18.3	1

ROETHLISBERGER, BEN   QB   STEELERS

PERSONAL: Born March 2, 1981, in Lima, Ohio. ... 6-5/241.
HIGH SCHOOL: Findlay (Ohio).
COLLEGE: Miami (Ohio).
TRANSACTIONS/CAREER NOTES: Selected after junior season by Pittsburgh Steelers in first round (11th pick overall) of 2004 NFL draft. ... Signed by Steelers (August 4, 2004).
CHAMPIONSHIP GAME EXPERIENCE: Played in AFC championship game (2004 season).
HONORS: Named quarterback on THE SPORTING NEWS Freshman All-America third team (2001). ... Named NFL Rookie of the Year by THE SPORTING NEWS (2004).
SINGLE GAME HIGHS (regular season): Attempts—28 (December 18, 2004, vs. New York Giants); completions—21 (October 17, 2004, vs. Dallas); yards—316 (December 18, 2004, vs. New York Giants); and touchdown passes—2 (December 26, 2004, vs. Baltimore).
STATISTICAL PLATEAUS: 300-yard passing games: 2004 (1). Total: 1.
MISCELLANEOUS: Regular-season record as starting NFL quarterback: 13-0 (1.000). ... Postseason record as starting NFL quarterback: 1-1 (.500).

| | | | PASSING | | | | | | | | RUSHING | | | | TOTALS | | |
Year Team	G	GS	Att.	Cmp.	Pct.	Yds.	TD	Int.	Avg.	Skd.	Rat.	Att.	Yds.	Avg.	TD	TD	2pt.	Pts.
2004—Pittsburgh NFL	14	13	295	196	66.4	2621	17	11	8.88	30	98.1	56	144	2.6	1	1	0	6

ROGERS, CHARLES   WR   LIONS

PERSONAL: Born May 23, 1981, in Saginaw, Mich. ... 6-3/202.
HIGH SCHOOL: Saginaw (Mich.).
COLLEGE: Michigan State.
TRANSACTIONS/CAREER NOTES: Selected after junior season by Detroit Lions in first round (second pick overall) of 2003 NFL draft. ... Signed by Lions (July 23, 2003). ... On injured reserve with collarbone injury (December 2, 2003-remainder of season). ... On injured reserve with collarbone injury (September 14, 2004-remainder of season).
SINGLE GAME HIGHS (regular season): Receptions—6 (September 21, 2003, vs. Minnesota); yards—62 (September 28, 2003, vs. Denver); and touchdown receptions—2 (September 7, 2003, vs. Arizona).

| | | | RUSHING | | | | RECEIVING | | | | PUNT RETURNS | | | | TOTALS | | | |
Year Team	G	GS	Att.	Yds.	Avg.	TD	No.	Yds.	Avg.	TD	No.	Yds.	Avg.	TD	TD	2pt.	Pts.	Fum.
2003—Detroit NFL	5	5	2	17	8.5	0	22	243	11.0	3	0	0	0.0	0	3	0	18	0
2004—Detroit NFL	1	1	0	0	0.0	0	0	0	0.0	0	0	0	0.0	0	0	0	0	0
Pro totals (2 years)	6	6	2	17	8.5	0	22	243	11.0	3	0	0	0.0	0	3	0	18	0

ROGERS, JACOB   T   COWBOYS

PERSONAL: Born August 17, 1981, in Oxnard, Calif. ... 6-6/305.
HIGH SCHOOL: Oxnard (Calif.).
COLLEGE: Southern California.
TRANSACTIONS/CAREER NOTES: Selected by Dallas Cowboys in second round (52nd pick overall) of 2004 NFL draft. ... Signed by Cowboys (July 31, 2004).
PLAYING EXPERIENCE: Dallas NFL, 2004. ... Games/Games started: 2004 (2/0). Total: 2/0.
HONORS: Named offensive tackle on THE SPORTING NEWS college All-America second team (2003).

ROGERS, NICK   LB

PERSONAL: Born May 31, 1979, in East Point, Ga. ... 6-2/251. ... Full name: Nicholas Quixote Rogers.
HIGH SCHOOL: St. Pius X (East Point, Ga.).
COLLEGE: Georgia Tech.

TRANSACTIONS/CAREER NOTES: Selected by Minnesota Vikings in sixth round (177th pick overall) of 2002 NFL draft. ... Signed by Vikings (July 16, 2002). ... Released by Vikings (September 5, 2004). ... Claimed on waivers by Green Bay Packers (September 6, 2004). ... Released by Packers (October 16, 2004). ... Re-signed by Packers (October 19, 2004). ... Released by Packers (November 23, 2004). ... Re-signed by Packers (November 27, 2004). ... Claimed on waivers by Indianapolis Colts (December 22, 2004). ... Granted free agency (March 2, 2005).

Year Team	G	GS	TOTALS Tk.	Ast.	Sks.	INTERCEPTIONS No.	Yds.	Avg.	TD
2002—Minnesota NFL	16	11	33	9	2.0	0	0	0.0	0
2003—Minnesota NFL	16	5	11	2	0.0	0	0	0.0	0
2004—Green Bay NFL	10	0	0	0	0.0	0	0	0.0	0
—Indianapolis NFL	1	0	3	1	0.0	0	0	0.0	0
Pro totals (3 years)	43	16	47	12	2.0	0	0	0.0	0

ROGERS, SHAUN DT LIONS

R

PERSONAL: Born March 12, 1979, in Houston, Texas. ... 6-4/345.
HIGH SCHOOL: LaPorte (Texas).
COLLEGE: Texas.
TRANSACTIONS/CAREER NOTES: Selected by Detroit Lions in second round (61st pick overall) of 2001 NFL draft. ... Signed by Lions (July 23, 2001). ... On physically unable to perform list with ankle injury (July 24-August 6, 2001). ... On physically unable to perform list with thumb injury (July 25-August 19, 2002).
HONORS: Played in Pro Bowl (2004 season).

Year Team	G	GS	TOTALS Tk.	Ast.	Sks.
2001—Detroit NFL	16	16	62	19	3.0
2002—Detroit NFL	14	12	26	22	2.5
2003—Detroit NFL	16	16	41	17	4.0
2004—Detroit NFL	16	16	49	19	4.0
Pro totals (4 years)	62	60	178	77	13.5

ROGERS, TYRONE DE

PERSONAL: Born March 9, 1974, in Montgomery, Ala. ... 6-5/280.
HIGH SCHOOL: Robert E. Lee (Montgomery, Ala.).
COLLEGE: Alabama State.
TRANSACTIONS/CAREER NOTES: Signed as non-drafted free agent by Cleveland Browns (April 23, 1999). ... Released by Browns (September 5, 1999). ... Re-signed by Browns to practice squad (September 6, 1999). ... Activated (November 23, 1999). ... Granted unconditional free agency (March 3, 2004). ... Signed by Green Bay Packers (July 23, 2004). ... Released by Packers (September 5, 2004). ... Re-signed by Browns (September 21, 2004). ... Granted unconditional free agency (March 2, 2005).

Year Team	G	GS	TOTALS Tk.	Ast.	Sks.
1999—Cleveland NFL	3	0	3	0	0.0
2000—Cleveland NFL	16	0	9	4	2.0
2001—Cleveland NFL	16	10	31	9	6.0
2002—Cleveland NFL	14	5	19	7	3.0
2003—Cleveland NFL	8	3	9	4	1.0
2004—Cleveland NFL	14	0	17	5	1.5
Pro totals (6 years)	71	18	88	29	13.5

ROGERS, VICTOR T LIONS

PERSONAL: Born November 10, 1978, in Seattle, Wash. ... 6-6/331.
HIGH SCHOOL: Decatur (Federal Way, Wash.).
COLLEGE: Colorado.
TRANSACTIONS/CAREER NOTES: Selected by Detroit Lions in seventh round (259th pick overall) of 2002 NFL draft.. ... Signed by Lions (July 18, 2002). ... On injured reserve with knee injury (August 27, 2002-entire season). ... On injured reserve with ankle injury (October 31, 2003-remainder of season). ... Granted free agency (March 2, 2005). ... Re-signed by Lions (April 20, 2005).
PLAYING EXPERIENCE: Detroit NFL, 2004. ... Games/Games started: 2004 (1/0). Total: 1/0.

ROLLE, SAMARI CB RAVENS

PERSONAL: Born August 10, 1976, in Miami, Fla. ... 6-0/175. ... Full name: Samari Toure Rolle. ... Name pronounced: suh-MARI ROLL.
HIGH SCHOOL: Miami Beach.
COLLEGE: Florida State.
TRANSACTIONS/CAREER NOTES: Selected by Tennessee Oilers in second round (46th pick overall) of 1998 NFL draft. ... Signed by Oilers (July 24, 1998). ... Oilers franchise renamed Tennessee Titans for 1999 season (December 26, 1998). ... Granted free agency (March 2, 2001). ... Re-signed by Titans (July 28, 2001). ... On physically unable to perform list with knee injury (July 28-August 14, 2001). ... Released by Titans (February 21, 2005). ... Signed by Baltimore Ravens (March 7, 2005).
CHAMPIONSHIP GAME EXPERIENCE: Played in AFC championship game (1999 and 2002 seasons). ... Played in Super Bowl 34 (1999 season).
HONORS: Named cornerback on THE SPORTING NEWS NFL All-Pro team (2000). ... Played in Pro Bowl (2000 season).

Year Team	G	GS	TOTALS Tk.	Ast.	Sks.	INTERCEPTIONS No.	Yds.	Avg.	TD
1998—Tennessee NFL	15	1	22	3	2.0	0	0	0.0	0
1999—Tennessee NFL	16	16	59	10	3.0	4	65	16.3	0

Year Team	G	GS	TOTALS			INTERCEPTIONS			
			Tk.	Ast.	Sks.	No.	Yds.	Avg.	TD
2000—Tennessee NFL	15	15	35	4	1.5	▲7	140	20.0	1
2001—Tennessee NFL	14	14	51	5	2.0	3	3	1.0	0
2002—Tennessee NFL	16	16	39	9	0.0	2	0	0.0	0
2003—Tennessee NFL	13	13	23	8	0.0	6	141	23.5	0
2004—Tennessee NFL	12	11	27	1	0.0	1	0	0.0	0
Pro totals (7 years)	101	86	256	40	8.5	23	349	15.2	1

ROMAN, MARK　　　　S　　　　PACKERS

PERSONAL: Born March 26, 1977, in New Iberia, La. ... 5-11/200. ... Full name: Mark Emery Roman.
HIGH SCHOOL: New Iberia (La.).
COLLEGE: Louisiana State.
TRANSACTIONS/CAREER NOTES: Selected by Cincinnati Bengals in second round (34th pick overall) of 2000 NFL draft. ... Signed by Bengals (August 7, 2000). ... On injured reserve with finger injury (December 20, 2001-remainder of season). ... On injured reserve with knee injury (December 23, 2002-remainder of season). ... Granted unconditional free agency (March 3, 2004). ... Signed by Green Bay Packers (March 24, 2004).

Year Team	G	GS	TOTALS			INTERCEPTIONS			
			Tk.	Ast.	Sks.	No.	Yds.	Avg.	TD
2000—Cincinnati NFL	8	2	15	1	0.0	0	0	0.0	0
2001—Cincinnati NFL	13	8	44	7	2.0	1	0	0.0	0
2002—Cincinnati NFL	13	1	23	7	0.0	0	0	0.0	0
2003—Cincinnati NFL	16	16	55	19	0.5	1	1	1.0	0
2004—Green Bay NFL	16	15	52	19	3.5	0	0	0.0	0
Pro totals (5 years)	66	42	189	53	6.0	2	1	0.5	0

ROMERO, DARIO　　　　DT　　　　DOLPHINS

PERSONAL: Born April 13, 1978, in Spokane, Wash. ... 6-3/305.
HIGH SCHOOL: Lewis and Clark (Spokane, Wash.).
COLLEGE: Eastern Washington.
TRANSACTIONS/CAREER NOTES: Signed by Miami Dolphins as non-drafted free agent (February 27, 2002). ... Inactive for 16 games (2002). ... Granted free agency (March 2, 2005). ... Re-signed by Dolphins (March 28, 2005).

Year Team	G	GS	TOTALS		
			Tk.	Ast.	Sks.
2003—Miami NFL	8	1	3	2	0.0
2004—Miami NFL	14	1	15	6	3.5
Pro totals (2 years)	22	2	18	8	3.5

ROMO, TONY　　　　QB　　　　COWBOYS

PERSONAL: Born April 21, 1980, in San Diego, Calif. ... 6-2/227.
HIGH SCHOOL: Burlington (Wis.).
COLLEGE: Eastern Illinois.
TRANSACTIONS/CAREER NOTES: Signed as non-drafted free agent by Dallas Cowboys (May 1, 2003). ... Inactive for all 16 games (2003).

Year Team	G	GS	PASSING									RUSHING				TOTALS		
			Att.	Cmp.	Pct.	Yds.	TD	Int.	Avg.	Skd.	Rat.	Att.	Yds.	Avg.	TD	TD	2pt.	Pts.
2004—Dallas NFL	6	0	0	0	0.0	0	0	0	0.00	0	0.0	0	0	0.0	0	0	0	0

ROSENFELS, SAGE　　　　QB　　　　DOLPHINS

PERSONAL: Born March 6, 1978, in Maquoketa, Iowa. ... 6-4/222.
HIGH SCHOOL: Maquoketa (Iowa).
COLLEGE: Iowa State.
TRANSACTIONS/CAREER NOTES: Selected by Washington Redskins in fourth round (109th pick overall) of 2001 NFL draft. ... Signed by Redskins (July 26, 2001). ... Traded by Redskins to Miami Dolphins for undisclosed pick in 2003 draft (August 22, 2002). ... Granted free agency (March 3, 2004). ... Re-signed by Dolphins (April 20, 2004). ... Granted unconditional free agency (March 2, 2005). ... Re-signed by Dolphins (March 11, 2005).
SINGLE GAME HIGHS (regular season): Attempts—38 (January 2, 2005, vs. Baltimore); completions—16 (January 2, 2005, vs. Baltimore); yards—264 (January 2, 2005, vs. Baltimore); and touchdown passes—1 (January 2, 2005, vs. Baltimore).
MISCELLANEOUS: Regular-season record as starting NFL quarterback: 0-1 (.000).

Year Team	G	GS	PASSING									RUSHING				TOTALS		
			Att.	Cmp.	Pct.	Yds.	TD	Int.	Avg.	Skd.	Rat.	Att.	Yds.	Avg.	TD	TD	2pt.	Pts.
2002—Miami NFL	4	0	3	0	0.0	0	0	0	0.00	0	39.6	2	-9	-4.5	0	0	0	0
2003—Miami NFL	2	0	6	4	66.7	50	1	0	8.33	0	131.9	1	-1	-1.0	0	0	0	0
2004—Miami NFL	3	1	39	16	41.0	264	1	3	6.77	3	41.0	0	0	0.0	0	0	0	0
Pro totals (3 years)	9	1	48	20	41.7	314	2	3	6.54	3	51.9	3	-10	-3.3	0	0	0	0

ROSENTHAL, MIKE　　　　　T　　　　　VIKINGS

PERSONAL: Born June 10, 1977, in Pittsburgh, Pa. ... 6-7/318. ... Full name: Michael Paul Rosenthal.
HIGH SCHOOL: Penn (Mishawaka, Ind.).
COLLEGE: Notre Dame.
TRANSACTIONS/CAREER NOTES: Selected by New York Giants in fifth round (149th pick overall) of 1999 NFL draft. ... Signed by Giants (July 26, 1999). ... Granted free agency (March 1, 2002). ... Re-signed by Giants (April 24, 2002). ... Granted unconditional free agency (February 28, 2003). ... Signed by Minnesota Vikings (March 20, 2003). ... On injured reserve with foot injury (September 22, 2004-remainder of season).
PLAYING EXPERIENCE: New York Giants NFL, 1999-2002; Minnesota NFL, 2003-2004. ... Games/Games started: 1999 (9/7), 2000 (8/2), 2001 (7/0), 2002 (16/16), 2003 (16/16), 2004 (2/2). Total: 58/43.
CHAMPIONSHIP GAME EXPERIENCE: Played in NFC championship game (2000 season). ... Played in Super Bowl 35 (2000 season).

R

ROSS, DEREK　　　　　CB

PERSONAL: Born January 5, 1980, in Rock Hill, S.C. ... 5-10/197.
HIGH SCHOOL: Northwestern (Rock Hill, S.C.).
COLLEGE: Ohio State.
TRANSACTIONS/CAREER NOTES: Selected after junior season by Dallas Cowboys in third round (75th pick overall) of 2002 NFL draft. ... Signed by Cowboys (July 26, 2002). ... Claimed on waivers by Atlanta Falcons (December 3, 2003). ... Claimed on waivers by Minnesota Vikings (August 24, 2004). ... Released by Vikings (September 5, 2004). ... Re-signed by Vikings (October 13, 2004). ... Released by Vikings (December 21, 2004).

			TOTALS			INTERCEPTIONS				KICKOFF RETURNS				TOTALS		
Year　Team	G	GS	Tk.	Ast.	Sks.	No.	Yds.	Avg.	TD	No.	Yds.	Avg.	TD	TD	2pt.	Pts.	Fum.
2002—Dallas NFL	14	9	51	5	0.0	5	17	3.4	0	0	0	0.0	0	0	0	0	0
2003—Dallas NFL	8	0	2	1	0.0	1	0	0.0	0	18	434	24.1	0	0	0	0	2
—Atlanta NFL	2	0	2	0	0.0	0	0	0.0	0	0	0	0.0	0	0	0	0	0
2004—Minnesota NFL	9	0	9	0	0.0	0	0	0.0	0	2	33	16.5	0	0	0	0	0
Pro totals (3 years)	33	9	64	6	0.0	6	17	2.8	0	20	467	23.4	0	0	0	0	2

ROSS, MICAH　　　　　WR　　　　　PANTHERS

PERSONAL: Born January 13, 1976, in Jacksonville, Fla. ... 6-2/219. ... Full name: Micah David Ross.
HIGH SCHOOL: Andrew Jackson (Fla.).
COLLEGE: Jacksonville.
TRANSACTIONS/CAREER NOTES: Signed as non-drafted free agent by Jacksonville Jaguars (August 17, 2001). ... Released by Jaguars (August 28, 2001). ... Re-signed by Jaguars to practice squad (October 31, 2001). ... Activated (December 8, 2001). ... Re-signed by Jaguars (March 24, 2003). ... Waived by Jaguars (October 3, 2003). ... Signed by San Diego Chargers (November 5, 2003). ... Re-signed by Chargers (March 3, 2004). ... Released by Chargers (October 26, 2004). ... Signed by Carolina Panthers (October 28, 2004).

			RECEIVING				TOTALS			
Year　Team	G	GS	No.	Yds.	Avg.	TD	TD	2pt.	Pts.	Fum.
2001—Jacksonville NFL	5	0	0	0	0.0	0	0	0	0	1
2002—Jacksonville NFL	16	0	0	0	0.0	0	0	0	0	1
2003—Jacksonville NFL	1	0	0	0	0.0	0	0	0	0	0
—San Diego NFL	6	0	0	0	0.0	0	0	0	0	0
2004—San Diego NFL	7	0	0	0	0.0	0	0	0	0	0
—Carolina NFL	10	0	0	0	0.0	0	0	0	0	0
Pro totals (4 years)	45	0	0	0	0.0	0	0	0	0	1

ROSS, OLIVER　　　　　G　　　　　CARDINALS

PERSONAL: Born September 27, 1974, in Culver City, Calif. ... 6-5/322.
HIGH SCHOOL: Washington (Los Angeles).
JUNIOR COLLEGE: Southwestern College (Calif.).
COLLEGE: Iowa State.
TRANSACTIONS/CAREER NOTES: Selected by Dallas Cowboys in fifth round (138th pick overall) of 1998 NFL draft. ... Signed by Cowboys (July 16, 1998). ... Assigned by Cowboys to Rhein Fire in 1999 NFL Europe enhancement allocation program (February 22, 1999). ... Released by Cowboys (September 5, 1999). ... Signed by Philadelphia Eagles to practice squad (September 8, 1999). ... Activated (September 14, 1999); did not play. ... Assigned by Eagles to Amsterdam Admirals in 2000 NFL Europe enhancement allocation program (February 18, 2000). ... Released by Eagles (August 27, 2000). ... Signed by Chicago Bears to practice squad (September 4, 2000). ... Released by Bears (September 7, 2000). ... Signed by Steelers to practice squad (November 22, 2000). ... Activated (December 13, 2000). ... Granted free agency (March 1, 2002). ... Tendered offer sheet by Cleveland Browns (March 13, 2002). ... Offer matched by Steelers (March 15, 2002). ... Granted unconditional free agency (March 2, 2005). ... Signed by Arizona Cardinals (March 4, 2005).
PLAYING EXPERIENCE: Dallas NFL, 1998; Philadelphia NFL, 1999; Pittsburgh NFL, 2001-2004. ... Games/Games started: 1998 (2/0), 2001 (16/7), 2002 (16/1), 2003 (16/11), 2004 (16/16), Total: 66/35.
CHAMPIONSHIP GAME EXPERIENCE: Played in AFC championship game (2001 and 2004 seasons).

ROSSUM, ALLEN　　　　　CB　　　　　FALCONS

PERSONAL: Born October 22, 1975, in Dallas, Texas. ... 5-8/178.
HIGH SCHOOL: Skyline (Dallas).
COLLEGE: Notre Dame.
TRANSACTIONS/CAREER NOTES: Selected by Philadelphia Eagles in third round (85th pick overall) of 1998 NFL draft. ... Signed by Eagles (July 14, 1998). ... Traded by Eagles to Green Bay Packers for fifth-round pick (TE Tony Stewart) in 2001 draft (August 21, 2000). ... Granted

free agency (March 2, 2001). ... Re-signed by Packers (April 23, 2001). ... Granted unconditional free agency (March 1, 2002). ... Signed by Atlanta Falcons (March 13, 2002). ... Granted unconditional free agency (March 2, 2005). ... Re-signed by Falcons (March 7, 2005).
CHAMPIONSHIP GAME EXPERIENCE: Played in NFC championship game (2004 season).
HONORS: Played in Pro Bowl (2004 season).

				PUNT RETURNS				KICKOFF RETURNS				TOTALS		
Year Team	G	GS	No.	Yds.	Avg.	TD	No.	Yds.	Avg.	TD	TD	2pt.	Pts.	Fum.
1998—Philadelphia NFL	15	2	22	187	8.5	0	44	1080	24.5	0	0	0	0	4
1999—Philadelphia NFL	16	0	28	250	8.9	0	54	1347	24.9	1	1	0	6	6
2000—Green Bay NFL	16	0	29	248	8.6	0	50	1288	25.8	1	1	0	6	4
2001—Green Bay NFL	6	0	11	109	9.9	∞1	23	431	18.7	0	1	0	6	0
2002—Atlanta NFL	14	0	24	288	12.0	0	53	1164	22.0	1	1	0	6	1
2003—Atlanta NFL	16	0	39	*545	14.0	1	62	1291	20.8	0	1	0	6	3
2004—Atlanta NFL	16	1	37	‡457	12.4	1	‡58	‡1250	21.6	0	1	0	6	2
Pro totals (7 years)	99	3	190	2084	11.0	3	344	7851	22.8	3	6	0	36	20

ROUEN, TOM — P — PANTHERS

PERSONAL: Born June 9, 1968, in Hinsdale, Ill. ... 6-3/225. ... Full name: Thomas Francis Rouen Jr. ... Name pronounced: RUIN.
HIGH SCHOOL: Heritage (Littleton, Colo.).
COLLEGE: Colorado.
TRANSACTIONS/CAREER NOTES: Signed as non-drafted free agent by New York Giants (April 29, 1991). ... Released by Giants (August 19, 1991). ... Selected by Ohio Glory in fourth round (44th pick overall) of 1992 World League draft. ... Signed by Los Angeles Rams (July 1992). ... Released by Rams (August 24, 1992). ... Signed by Denver Broncos (April 29, 1993). ... Granted unconditional free agency (February 14, 1997). ... Re-signed by Broncos (March 6, 1997). ... Granted unconditional free agency (February 11, 2000). ... Re-signed by Broncos (February 24, 2000). ... Released by Broncos (October 29, 2002). ... Signed by Giants (November 1, 2002). ... Released by Giants (November 19, 2002). ... Signed by Pittsburgh Steelers (December 20, 2002). ... Granted unconditional free agency (February 28, 2003). ... Signed by Seattle Seahawks (July 22, 2003) ... Granted unconditional free agency (March 3, 2004). ... Re-signed by Seahawks (March 18, 2004). ... On injured reserve with hamstring injury (October 29, 2004-remainder of season). ... Granted unconditional free agency (March 2, 2005). ... Signed by Carolina Panthers (April 20, 2005).
CHAMPIONSHIP GAME EXPERIENCE: Played in AFC championship game (1997 and 1998 seasons). ... Member of Super Bowl championship team (1997 and 1998 seasons).
HONORS: Named punter on THE SPORTING NEWS college All-America second team (1989).

				PUNTING			
Year Team	G	No.	Yds.	Avg.	Net avg.	In. 20	Blk.
1993—Denver NFL	16	67	3017	45.0	37.1	17	1
1994—Denver NFL	16	76	3250	42.9	▲37.1	23	0
1995—Denver NFL	16	52	2192	42.2	37.6	22	1
1996—Denver NFL	16	65	2714	41.8	36.2	16	0
1997—Denver NFL	16	60	2598	43.3	38.1	22	0
1998—Denver NFL	16	66	3097	46.9	37.6	14	1
1999—Denver NFL	16	84	3908	*46.5	35.6	19	0
2000—Denver NFL	16	61	2455	40.2	32.3	18	▲1
2001—Denver NFL	16	81	3668	45.3	36.5	25	1
2002—Denver NFL	8	29	1239	42.7	31.7	6	2
—New York Giants NFL	2	8	333	41.6	33.0	1	0
—Pittsburgh NFL	2	7	316	45.1	38.7	1	0
2003—Seattle NFL	16	67	2762	41.2	37.1	29	2
2004—Seattle NFL	4	26	1093	42.0	37.8	10	0
Pro totals (12 years)	176	749	32650	43.6	36.3	223	9

ROYAL, ROBERT — TE — REDSKINS

PERSONAL: Born May 15, 1979, in New Orleans, La. ... 6-4/257. ... Full name: Robert Shelton Royal Jr.
HIGH SCHOOL: Karr (New Orleans).
COLLEGE: Louisiana State.
TRANSACTIONS/CAREER NOTES: Selected by Washington Redskins in fifth round (160th pick overall) of 2002 NFL draft. ... Signed by Redskins (July 22, 2002). ... On injured reserve with ankle injury (September 1, 2002-entire season). ... On injured reserve with hip injury (October 14, 2003-remainder of season).
SINGLE GAME HIGHS (regular season): Receptions—2 (October 5, 2003, vs. Philadelphia); yards—24 (September 4, 2003, vs. New York Jets); and touchdown receptions—1 (January 2, 2005, vs. Minnesota).

				RECEIVING				TOTALS		
Year Team	G	GS	No.	Yds.	Avg.	TD	TD	2pt.	Pts.	Fum.
2003—Washington NFL	6	6	5	48	9.6	0	0	0	0	1
2004—Washington NFL	14	9	8	70	8.8	4	4	0	24	0
Pro totals (2 years)	20	15	13	118	9.1	4	4	0	24	1

ROYE, ORPHEUS — DT/DE — BROWNS

PERSONAL: Born January 21, 1973, in Miami, Fla. ... 6-4/320. ... Full name: Orpheus Michael Roye. ... Name pronounced: OR-fee-us ROY.
HIGH SCHOOL: Miami Springs.
JUNIOR COLLEGE: Jones County Junior College (Miss.).
COLLEGE: Florida State.
TRANSACTIONS/CAREER NOTES: Selected by Pittsburgh Steelers in sixth round (200th pick overall) of 1996 NFL draft. ... Signed by Steelers (July 16, 1996). ... Granted free agency (February 12, 1999). ... Re-signed by Steelers (April 23, 1999). ... Granted unconditional free agency (February 11, 2000). ... Signed by Cleveland Browns (February 12, 2000). ... On injured reserve with knee injury (December 11, 2001-remainder of season).

Year Team	G	GS	TOTALS			INTERCEPTIONS			
			Tk.	Ast.	Sks.	No.	Yds.	Avg.	TD
1996—Pittsburgh NFL	13	1	1	2	0.0	0	0	0.0	0
1997—Pittsburgh NFL	16	0	3	1	1.0	0	0	0.0	0
1998—Pittsburgh NFL	16	9	29	13	3.5	0	0	0.0	0
1999—Pittsburgh NFL	16	16	41	17	4.5	1	2	2.0	0
2000—Cleveland NFL	16	16	42	13	2.0	0	0	0.0	0
2001—Cleveland NFL	12	10	18	7	0.0	1	0	0.0	0
2002—Cleveland NFL	16	16	38	17	0.5	0	0	0.0	0
2003—Cleveland NFL	16	15	42	15	1.5	0	0	0.0	0
2004—Cleveland NFL	15	14	30	8	1.0	0	0	0.0	0
Pro totals (9 years)	136	97	244	93	14.0	2	2	1.0	0

R

RUCKER, MIKE — DE — PANTHERS

PERSONAL: Born February 28, 1975, in St. Joseph, Mo. ... 6-5/275. ... Full name: Michael Dean Rucker.
HIGH SCHOOL: Benton (St. Joseph, Mo.).
COLLEGE: Nebraska.
TRANSACTIONS/CAREER NOTES: Selected by Carolina Panthers in second round (38th pick overall) of 1999 NFL draft. ... Signed by Panthers (July 13, 1999).
CHAMPIONSHIP GAME EXPERIENCE: Played in NFC championship game (2003 season). ... Played in Super Bowl 38 (2003 season).
HONORS: Played in Pro Bowl (2003 season).

Year Team	G	GS	TOTALS		
			Tk.	Ast.	Sks.
1999—Carolina NFL	16	0	24	6	3.0
2000—Carolina NFL	16	1	33	6	2.5
2001—Carolina NFL	16	16	44	12	9.0
2002—Carolina NFL	16	15	58	10	10.0
2003—Carolina NFL	14	14	48	11	12.0
2004—Carolina NFL	16	16	35	3	3.5
Pro totals (6 years)	94	62	242	48	40.0

RUEGAMER, GREY — G/C — PACKERS

PERSONAL: Born June 11, 1976, in Las Vegas, Nev. ... 6-4/305. ... Full name: Christopher Grey Ruegamer.
HIGH SCHOOL: Bishop Gorman (Las Vegas, Nev.).
COLLEGE: Arizona State.
TRANSACTIONS/CAREER NOTES: Selected by Miami Dolphins in third round (72nd pick overall) of 1999 NFL draft. ... Signed by Dolphins (July 27, 1999). ... Active for one game (1999); did not play. ... Released by Dolphins (August 27, 2000). ... Signed by Pittsburgh Steelers to practice squad (August 29, 2000). ... Signed by New England Patriots off Steelers practice squad (November 16, 2000). ... Granted free agency (March 1, 2002). ... Re-signed by Patriots (April 19, 2002). ... Granted unconditional free agency (February 28, 2003). ... Signed by Green Bay Packers (April 8, 2003). ... Released by Packers (March 1, 2005). ... Re-signed by Packers (March 15, 2005).
PLAYING EXPERIENCE: Miami NFL, 1999; New England NFL, 2000-2002; Green Bay NFL, 2003-2004. ... Games/Games started: 2000 (6/0), 2001 (14/1), 2002 (13/2), 2003 (15/0), 2004 (15/11), Total: 63/14.
CHAMPIONSHIP GAME EXPERIENCE: Played in AFC championship game (2001 season). ... Member of Super Bowl championship team (2001 season).

RUFF, ORLANDO — LB — SAINTS

PERSONAL: Born September 28, 1976, in Charleston, S.C. ... 6-3/253. ... Full name: Orlando Bernarda Ruff.
HIGH SCHOOL: Fairfield Central (Winnsboro, S.C.).
COLLEGE: Furman.
TRANSACTIONS/CAREER NOTES: Signed as non-drafted free agent by San Diego Chargers (April 20, 1999). ... Granted free agency (March 1, 2002). ... Re-signed by Chargers (April 3, 2002). ... Granted unconditional free agency (February 28, 2003). ... Signed by New Orleans Saints (March 3, 2003).

Year Team	G	GS	TOTALS			INTERCEPTIONS			
			Tk.	Ast.	Sks.	No.	Yds.	Avg.	TD
1999—San Diego NFL	14	0	5	2	0.0	0	0	0.0	0
2000—San Diego NFL	16	14	54	14	0.0	1	18	18.0	0
2001—San Diego NFL	16	15	59	15	1.0	0	0	0.0	0
2002—San Diego NFL	16	0	4	0	0.0	0	0	0.0	0
2003—New Orleans NFL	16	9	47	19	0.0	1	7	7.0	0
2004—New Orleans NFL	14	8	53	21	0.0	1	0	0.0	0
Pro totals (6 years)	92	46	222	71	1.0	3	25	8.3	0

RUMPH, MIKE — CB — 49ERS

PERSONAL: Born November 8, 1979, in Boynton Beach, Fla. ... 6-2/205. ... Full name: Michael Jamaine Rumph.
HIGH SCHOOL: Atlantic (Delray Beach, Fla.).
COLLEGE: Miami (Fla.).
TRANSACTIONS/CAREER NOTES: Selected by San Francisco 49ers in first round (27th pick overall) of 2002 NFL draft. ... Signed by 49ers (July 23, 2002). ... On injured reserve with arm injury (October 16, 2004-remainder of season).

Year Team	G	GS	TOTALS			INTERCEPTIONS			
			Tk.	Ast.	Sks.	No.	Yds.	Avg.	TD
2002—San Francisco NFL	16	1	36	5	0.0	0	0	0.0	0
2003—San Francisco NFL	15	13	53	9	2.0	3	19	6.3	0
2004—San Francisco NFL	2	2	4	1	0.0	0	0	0.0	0
Pro totals (3 years)	33	16	93	15	2.0	3	19	6.3	0

RUNYAN, JON   T   EAGLES

PERSONAL: Born November 27, 1973, in Flint, Mich. ... 6-7/330. ... Full name: Jon Daniel Runyan.
HIGH SCHOOL: Carman-Ainsworth (Flint, Mich.).
COLLEGE: Michigan.
TRANSACTIONS/CAREER NOTES: Selected after junior season by Houston Oilers in fourth round (109th pick overall) of 1996 NFL draft. ... Signed by Oilers (July 20, 1996). ... Oilers franchise moved to Tennessee for 1997 season. ... Oilers franchise renamed Tennessee Titans for 1999 season (December 26, 1998). ... Granted free agency (February 12, 1999). ... Re-signed by Titans (June 23, 1999). ... Granted unconditional free agency (February 11, 2000). ... Signed by Philadelphia Eagles (February 14, 2000).
PLAYING EXPERIENCE: Houston NFL, 1996; Tennessee NFL, 1997; Tennessee NFL, 1998-1999; Philadelphia NFL, 2000-2004. ... Games/Games started: 1996 (10/0), 1997 (16/16), 1998 (16/16), 1999 (16/16), 2000 (16/16), 2001 (16/16), 2002 (16/16), 2003 (16/16), 2004 (16/16). Total: 138/128.
CHAMPIONSHIP GAME EXPERIENCE: Played in AFC championship game (1999 season). ... Played in Super Bowl 34 (1999 season) and Super Bowl 39 (2004 season). ... Played in NFC championship game (2001-2004 seasons).
HONORS: Named offensive lineman on THE SPORTING NEWS college All-America second team (1995). ... Played in Pro Bowl (2002 season).

RUSSELL, BRIAN   S   BROWNS

PERSONAL: Born February 5, 1978, in West Covina, Calif. ... 6-2/204. ... Full name: Brian William Russell.
HIGH SCHOOL: Bishop Amat (West Covina, Calif.).
COLLEGE: San Diego State.
TRANSACTIONS/CAREER NOTES: Signed as non-drafted free agent by Minnesota Vikings (April 23, 2001). ... Released by Vikings (September 1, 2001). ... Re-signed by Vikings to practice squad (September 3, 2001). ... Activated (January 14, 2002). ... Granted free agency (March 3, 2004). ... Re-signed by Vikings (May 3, 2004). ... Granted free agency (March 2, 2005). ... Signed by Cleveland Browns (April 9, 2005).

Year Team	G	GS	TOTALS			INTERCEPTIONS			
			Tk.	Ast.	Sks.	No.	Yds.	Avg.	TD
2002—Minnesota NFL	16	2	10	4	0.0	1	18	18.0	0
2003—Minnesota NFL	16	10	72	15	1.0	†9	185	20.6	0
2004—Minnesota NFL	16	16	58	20	0.0	1	41	41.0	0
Pro totals (3 years)	48	34	140	39	1.0	11	244	22.2	0

RUSSELL, CLIFF   WR   BENGALS

PERSONAL: Born February 8, 1979, in Ewa Beach, Hawaii. ... 5-11/193. ... Full name: Clifford Russell.
HIGH SCHOOL: Campbell (Ewa Beach, Hawaii).
COLLEGE: Utah.
TRANSACTIONS/CAREER NOTES: Selected by Washington Redskins in third round (87th pick overall) of 2002 NFL draft. ... Signed by Redskins (July 23, 2002). ... Released by Redskins (August 30, 2004). ... Signed by Cincinnati Bengals to practice squad (September 6, 2004). ... Activated (September 29, 2004).
SINGLE GAME HIGHS (regular season): Receptions—2 (December 27, 2003, vs. Philadelphia); yards—21 (October 17, 2004, vs. Cleveland); and touchdown receptions—0.

Year Team	G	GS	RUSHING				RECEIVING				KICKOFF RETURNS				TOTALS			
			Att.	Yds.	Avg.	TD	No.	Yds.	Avg.	TD	No.	Yds.	Avg.	TD	TD	2pt.	Pts.	Fum.
2003—Washington NFL	3	0	0	0	0.0	0	2	10	5.0	0	0	0	0.0	0	0	0	0	0
2004—Cincinnati NFL	13	1	3	15	5.0	0	1	21	21.0	0	39	872	22.4	0	0	0	0	2
Pro totals (2 years)	16	1	3	15	5.0	0	3	31	10.3	0	39	872	22.4	0	0	0	0	2

RYAN, SEAN   TE   COWBOYS

PERSONAL: Born March 27, 1980, in Buffalo, N.Y. ... 6-5/257.
HIGH SCHOOL: St. Joseph (Buffalo, N.Y.).
COLLEGE: Boston College.
TRANSACTIONS/CAREER NOTES: Selected by Dallas Cowboys in fifth round (144th pick overall) of 2004 NFL draft. ... Signed by Cowboys (July 29, 2004). ... Released by Cowboys (September 6, 2004). ... Re-signed by Cowboys to practice squad (September 8, 2004). ... Activated (November 24, 2004).

Year Team	G	GS	RECEIVING				TOTALS			
			No.	Yds.	Avg.	TD	TD	2pt.	Pts.	Fum.
2004—Dallas NFL	6	1	0	0	0.0	0	0	0	0	0

SAIPAIA, BLAINE   OL   RAMS

PERSONAL: Born August 25, 1978, in Oxnard, Calif. ... 6-3/310.
HIGH SCHOOL: Channel Islands (Oxnard, Calif.).
COLLEGE: Colorado State.
TRANSACTIONS/CAREER NOTES: Signed as non-drafted free agent by New Orleans Saints (2000). ... Released by Saints (late 2000/early 2001). ... Re-signed by Saints (February 9, 2001). ... Released by Saints (August 28, 2001). ... Signed by Tennessee Titans

(February 1, 2002). ... Released by Titans (May 28, 2002). ... Signed by Denver Broncos to practice squad (November 11, 2003). ... Released by Broncos from practice squad (November 26, 2003). ... Signed by Oakland Raiders (2004). ... Released by Raiders (September 5, 2004). ... Signed by St. Louis Rams (September 8, 2004).
PLAYING EXPERIENCE: Oakland NFL, 2003; St. Louis NFL, 2004. ... Games/Games started: 2003 (1/0); 2004 (8/5). Total: 9/5.

SALAAM, EPHRAIM   T   JAGUARS

PERSONAL: Born June 19, 1976, in Chicago, Ill. ... 6-7/295. ... Full name: Ephraim Mateen Salaam. ... Name pronounced: EFF-rum sah-LAHM.
HIGH SCHOOL: Florin (Sacramento).
COLLEGE: San Diego State.
TRANSACTIONS/CAREER NOTES: Selected by Atlanta Falcons in seventh round (199th pick overall) of 1998 NFL draft. ... Signed by Falcons (June 3, 1998). ... Granted free agency (March 2, 2001). ... Re-signed by Falcons (April 6, 2001). ... Granted unconditional free agency (March 1, 2002). ... Signed by Denver Broncos (April 15, 2002). ... Waived by Broncos (March 2, 2004). ... Signed by Jacksonville Jaguars (March 26, 2004).
PLAYING EXPERIENCE: Atlanta NFL, 1998-2001; Denver NFL, 2002-2003; Jacksonville NFL, 2004. ... Games/Games started: 1998 (16/16), 1999 (16/16), 2000 (14/10), 2001 (14/13), 2002 (16/16), 2003 (14/14), 2004 (15/12). Total: 105/97.
CHAMPIONSHIP GAME EXPERIENCE: Played in NFC championship game (1998 season). ... Played in Super Bowl 33 (1998 season).

SALAVE'A, JOE   DT   REDSKINS

PERSONAL: Born March 23, 1975, in Leone, American Samoa. ... 6-3/295. ... Full name: Joe Fagaone Salave'a. ... Name pronounced: sala-VAY-uh.
HIGH SCHOOL: Oceanside (Calif.).
COLLEGE: Arizona.
TRANSACTIONS/CAREER NOTES: Selected by Tennessee Oilers in fourth round (107th pick overall) of 1998 NFL draft. ... Signed by Oilers (June 30, 1998). ... Oilers franchise renamed Tennessee Titans for 1999 season (December 26, 1998). ... Granted free agency (March 2, 2001). ... Re-signed by Titans (April 25, 2001). ... Granted unconditional free agency (March 1, 2002). ... Re-signed by Titans (May 9, 2002). ... Released by Titans (August 31, 2002). ... Signed by Baltimore Ravens (January 6, 2003). ... Released by Ravens (August 31, 2003). ... Signed by San Diego Chargers (October 15, 2003). ... Granted unconditional free agency (March 3, 2004). ... Signed by Washington Redskins (March 26, 2004). ... Granted unconditional free agency (March 2, 2005). ... Re-signed by Redskins (March 2, 2005).
CHAMPIONSHIP GAME EXPERIENCE: Played in AFC championship game (1999 season). ... Played in Super Bowl 34 (1999 season).
HONORS: Named defensive tackle on THE SPORTING NEWS college All-America third team (1997).

| | | | TOTALS | | |
Year Team	G	GS	Tk.	Ast.	Sks.
1998—Tennessee NFL	13	0	8	1	1.0
1999—Tennessee NFL	10	0	5	1	0.0
2000—Tennessee NFL	15	1	16	4	4.0
2001—Tennessee NFL	11	0	4	5	0.0
2003—San Diego NFL	9	1	2	3	0.0
2004—Washington NFL	15	9	17	3	2.0
Pro totals (6 years)	73	11	52	17	7.0

SAM, P.K.   WR   PATRIOTS

PERSONAL: Born February 26, 1983, in Buford, Ga. ... 6-3/210.
HIGH SCHOOL: Buford (Ga.).
COLLEGE: Florida State.
TRANSACTIONS/CAREER NOTES: Selected after junior season by New England Patriots in fifth round (164th pick overall) of 2004 NFL draft. ... Signed by Patriots (July 24, 2004). ... On injured reserve with groin injury (October 20, 2004-remainder of season).

| | | | RECEIVING | | | | PUNT RETURNS | | | | KICKOFF RETURNS | | | | TOTALS | | |
Year Team	G	GS	No.	Yds.	Avg.	TD	No.	Yds.	Avg.	TD	No.	Yds.	Avg.	TD	TD	2pt.	Pts.	Fum.
2004—New England NFL	2	0	0	0	0.0	0	0	0	0.0	0	0	0	0.0	0	0	0	0	0

SAMPSON, KEVIN   T   CHIEFS

PERSONAL: Born June 19, 1981, in Westwood, N.J. ... 6-4/312. ... Full name: Kevin M. Sampson.
HIGH SCHOOL: Westwood (N.J.).
COLLEGE: Syracuse.
TRANSACTIONS/CAREER NOTES: Selected by Kansas City Chiefs in seventh round (231st pick overall) of 2004 NFL draft. ... Signed by Chiefs (June 16, 2004).
PLAYING EXPERIENCE: Kansas City NFL, 2004. ... Games/Games started: 2004 (6/0). Total: 6/0.

SAMS, B.J.   KR   RAVENS

PERSONAL: Born October 29, 1980, in New Orleans, La. ... 5-10/185. ... Full name: Bradley Jamar Sams.
HIGH SCHOOL: Mandeville (La.).
COLLEGE: McNeese State.
TRANSACTIONS/CAREER NOTES: Signed as non-drafted free agent by Baltimore Ravens (April 30, 2004).
SINGLE GAME HIGHS (regular season): Attempts—1 (December 12, 2004, vs. New York Giants); yards—8 (September 26, 2004, vs. Cincinnati); and rushing touchdowns—1 (October 24, 2004, vs. Buffalo).

Year	Team	G	GS	RUSHING				RECEIVING				PUNT RETURNS				KICKOFF RETURNS				TOTALS		
				Att.	Yds.	Avg.	TD	No.	Yds.	Avg.	TD	No.	Yds.	Avg.	TD	No.	Yds.	Avg.	TD	TD	2pt.	Pts.
2004—Bal. NFL		16	1	4	19	4.8	1	1	2	2.0	0	*55	*575	10.5	2	59	1251	21.2	0	3	0	18

SAMUEL, ASANTE   CB   PATRIOTS

PERSONAL: Born January 6, 1981, in Fort Lauderdale, Fla. ... 5-10/185.
HIGH SCHOOL: Boyd Anderson (Lauderdale Lake, Fla.).
COLLEGE: Central Florida.
TRANSACTIONS/CAREER NOTES: Selected by New England Patriots in fourth round (120th pick overall) of 2003 NFL draft. ... Signed by Patriots (July 15, 2003).
CHAMPIONSHIP GAME EXPERIENCE: Played in AFC championship game (2003 and 2004 seasons). ... Member of Super Bowl championship team (2003 and 2004 seasons).

Year Team	G	GS	TOTALS			INTERCEPTIONS			
			Tk.	Ast.	Sks.	No.	Yds.	Avg.	TD
2003—New England NFL	16	1	27	5	0.0	2	55	27.5	1
2004—New England NFL	13	8	37	2	0.0	1	34	34.0	1
Pro totals (2 years)	29	9	64	7	0.0	3	89	29.7	2

SAMUELS, CHRIS   T   REDSKINS

PERSONAL: Born July 28, 1977, in Mobile, Ala. ... 6-5/310.
HIGH SCHOOL: Shaw (Mobile, Ala.).
COLLEGE: Alabama.
TRANSACTIONS/CAREER NOTES: Selected by Washington Redskins in first round (third pick overall) of 2000 NFL draft. ... Signed by Redskins (July 18, 2000).
PLAYING EXPERIENCE: Washington NFL, 2000-2004. ... Games/Games started: 2000 (16/16), 2001 (16/16), 2002 (15/15), 2003 (13/13), 2004 (16/16). Total: 76/76.
HONORS: Outland Trophy winner (1999). ... Named offensive tackle on THE SPORTING NEWS college All-America first team (1999). ... Played in Pro Bowl (2001 and 2002 seasons).

SANDERS, BOB   DB   COLTS

PERSONAL: Born February 24, 1981, in Erie, Pa. ... 5-8/206. ... Full name: Demond Sanders.
HIGH SCHOOL: Catherdral Prep (Erie, Pa.).
COLLEGE: Iowa.
TRANSACTIONS/CAREER NOTES: Selected by Indianapolis Colts in second round (44th pick overall) of 2004 NFL draft. ... Signed by Colts (August 30, 2004).

Year Team	G	GS	TOTALS			INTERCEPTIONS			
			Tk.	Ast.	Sks.	No.	Yds.	Avg.	TD
2004—Indianapolis NFL	6	4	25	4	0.0	0	0	0.0	0

SANDERS, DARNELL   TE   BEARS

PERSONAL: Born March 16, 1979, in Cleveland, Ohio. ... 6-6/270.
HIGH SCHOOL: Warrensville Heights (Ohio).
COLLEGE: Ohio State.
TRANSACTIONS/CAREER NOTES: Selected after junior season by Cleveland Browns in fourth round (122nd pick overall) of 2002 NFL draft. ... Signed by Browns (July 8, 2002). ... Claimed on waivers by Atlanta Falcons (September 6, 2004). ... Claimed on waivers by Chicago Bears (February 8, 2005).
SINGLE GAME HIGHS (regular season): Receptions—3 (November 30, 2003, vs. Seattle); yards—23 (November 9, 2003, vs. Kansas City); and touchdown receptions—1 (October 19, 2003, vs. San Diego).

Year Team	G	GS	RECEIVING				TOTALS			
			No.	Yds.	Avg.	TD	TD	2pt.	Pts.	Fum.
2002—Cleveland NFL	10	3	3	23	7.7	1	1	0	6	0
2003—Cleveland NFL	16	12	15	95	6.3	1	1	0	6	1
2004—Atlanta NFL	2	0	0	0	0.0	0	0	0	0	0
Pro totals (3 years)	28	15	18	118	6.6	2	2	0	12	1

SANDERS, DEION   CB

PERSONAL: Born August 9, 1967, in Fort Myers, Fla. ... 6-1/198. ... Full name: Deion Luwynn Sanders.
HIGH SCHOOL: North Fort Myers (Fla.).
COLLEGE: Florida State.
TRANSACTIONS/CAREER NOTES: Selected by Atlanta Falcons in first round (fifth pick overall) of 1989 NFL draft. ... Signed by Falcons (September 7, 1989). ... On reserve/did not report list (July 27-August 13, 1990). ... Granted roster exemption for one game (September 1992). ... On reserve/did not report list (July 23-October 14, 1993). ... Designated by Falcons as transition player (February 15, 1994). ... Free agency status changed by Falcons from transitional to unconditional (April 28, 1994). ... Signed by San Francisco 49ers (September 15, 1994). ... Granted unconditional free agency (February 17, 1995). ... Signed by Dallas Cowboys (September 9, 1995). ... On reserve/did not report list (July 16-August 29, 1997). ... Released by Cowboys (June 2, 2000). ... Signed by Washington Redskins (June 5, 2000). ... Announced retirement (July 27, 2001). ... Claimed on waivers by San Diego Chargers (December 24, 2002). ... Granted unconditional free agency (February 28, 2003). ... Signed by Baltimore Ravens (September 1, 2004). ... Granted unconditional free agency (March 2, 2005).

S

CHAMPIONSHIP GAME EXPERIENCE: Played in NFC championship game (1994 and 1995 seasons). ... Member of Super Bowl championship team (1994 and 1995 seasons).

HONORS: Named defensive back on THE SPORTING NEWS college All-America first team (1986-1988). ... Jim Thorpe Award winner (1988). ... Named cornerback on THE SPORTING NEWS NFL All-Pro team (1991-1999). ... Played in Pro Bowl (1991-1994 and 1998 seasons). ... Named kick returner on THE SPORTING NEWS NFL All-Pro team (1992). ... Named to play in Pro Bowl (1996 season); replaced by Darrell Green due to injury. ... Named to play in Pro Bowl (1997 season); replaced by Cris Dishman due to injury. ... Named to play in Pro Bowl (1999 season); replaced by Troy Vincent due to injury.

Year Team	G	GS	TOTALS Tk.	Ast.	Sks.	INTERCEPTIONS No.	Yds.	Avg.	TD	PUNT RETURNS No.	Yds.	Avg.	TD	KICKOFF RETURNS No.	Yds.	Avg.	TD	TOTALS TD	2pt.	Pts.	Fum.
1989—Atl. NFL	15	10	0	0	0.0	5	52	10.4	0	28	307	11.0	†1	35	725	20.7	0	1	0	6	2
1990—Atl. NFL	16	16	0	0	0.0	3	153	*51.0	2	29	250	8.6	†1	39	851	21.8	0	3	0	18	4
1991—Atl. NFL	15	15	0	0	1.0	∞6	119	19.8	∞1	21	170	8.1	0	26	576	22.2	†1	2	0	12	1
1992—Atl. NFL	13	12	0	0	0.0	3	105	‡35.0	0	13	41	3.2	0	40	*1067	‡26.7	*2	3	0	18	3
1993—Atl. NFL	11	10	0	0	0.0	‡7	91	13.0	0	2	21	10.5	0	7	169	24.1	0	1	0	6	0
1994—S.F. NFL	14	12	0	0	0.0	6	*303	*50.5	†3	0	0	0.0	0	0	0	0.0	0	3	0	18	0
1995—Dal. NFL	9	9	0	0	0.0	2	34	17.0	0	1	54	54.0	0	1	15	15.0	0	0	0	0	0
1996—Dal. NFL	16	15	0	0	0.0	2	3	1.5	0	1	4	4.0	0	0	0	0.0	0	2	0	12	2
1997—Dal. NFL	13	12	0	0	0.0	2	81	40.5	1	33	407	12.3	∞1	1	18	18.0	0	2	0	12	1
1998—Dal. NFL	11	11	0	0	0.0	5	153	30.6	1	24	375	*15.6	†2	1	16	16.0	0	3	0	18	1
1999—Dal. NFL	14	14	0	0	0.0	3	2	0.7	0	30	344	11.5	∞1	4	87	21.7	0	1	0	6	1
2000—Was. NFL	16	15	0	0	0.0	4	91	22.7	0	25	185	7.4	0	1	-1	-1.0	0	0	0	0	3
2004—Bal. NFL	9	2	7	1	0.0	3	87	29.0	1	5	41	8.2	0	0	0	0.0	0	1	0	6	0
Pro totals (13 years)	172	153	7	1	1.0	51	1274	25.0	9	212	2199	10.4	6	155	3523	22.7	3	22	0	132	18

SANDERS, LEWIS   CB/S   TEXANS

PERSONAL: Born June 22, 1978, in Staten Island, N.Y. ... 6-1/210. ... Full name: Lewis Lindell Sanders.
HIGH SCHOOL: St. Peter's (Staten Island, N.Y.).
COLLEGE: Maryland.
TRANSACTIONS/CAREER NOTES: Selected after junior season by Cleveland Browns in fourth round (95th pick overall) of 2000 NFL draft. ... Signed by Browns (June 3, 2000). ... On injured reserve with leg injury (August 27, 2001-entire season). ... Granted free agency (February 28, 2003). ... Re-signed by Browns (March 25, 2003). ... On injured reserve with groin injury (December 9, 2003-remainder of season). ... Granted unconditional free agency (March 3, 2004). ... Signed by Jacksonville Jaguars (March 9, 2004). ... Released by Jaguars (August 31, 2004). ... Re-signed by Browns (September 1, 2004). ... Granted unconditional free agency (March 2, 2005). ... Signed by Houston Texans (March 8, 2005).
HONORS: Named cornerback on THE SPORTING NEWS college All-America third team (1999).

Year Team	G	GS	TOTALS Tk.	Ast.	Sks.	INTERCEPTIONS No.	Yds.	Avg.	TD
2000—Cleveland NFL	11	1	9	6	0.0	1	0	0.0	0
2002—Cleveland NFL	16	2	26	1	1.0	1	25	25.0	0
2003—Cleveland NFL	9	1	4	3	0.0	0	0	0.0	0
2004—Cleveland NFL	16	5	19	4	0.0	2	36	18.0	0
Pro totals (4 years)	52	9	58	14	1.0	4	61	15.3	0

SANDS, TERDELL   DT   RAIDERS

PERSONAL: Born October 31, 1979, in Chattanooga, Tenn. ... 6-7/335. ... Full name: Terdell Duane Sands.
HIGH SCHOOL: Howard (Chattanooga, Tenn.).
COLLEGE: Chattanooga.
TRANSACTIONS/CAREER NOTES: Selected by Kansas City Chiefs in seventh round (243rd pick overall) of 2001 NFL draft. ... Signed by Chiefs (July 19, 2001). ... On non-football injury list with foot injury (August 28, 2001-remainder of season). ... Assigned by Chiefs to Berlin Thunder in 2002 NFL Europe enhancement allocation program (February 12, 2002). ... Released by Chiefs (September 7, 2002). ... Re-signed by Chiefs to practice squad (September 10, 2002). ... Released by Chiefs (September 17, 2002). ... Signed by Green Bay Packers to practice squad (November 20, 2002). ... Waived by Packers (August 26, 2003). ... Re-signed by Packers to practice squad (September 2, 2003). ... Released by Packers (September 16, 2003). ... Re-signed by Packers to practice squad (October 1, 2003). ... Activated (October 15, 2003). ... Claimed on waivers by Oakland Raiders (November 12, 2003).

Year Team	G	GS	TOTALS Tk.	Ast.	Sks.
2003—Green Bay NFL	1	0	1	0	0.0
—Oakland NFL	3	1	2	1	0.0
2004—Oakland NFL	15	0	17	5	0.0
Pro totals (2 years)	19	1	20	6	0.0

SANDY, JUSTIN   S   TITANS

PERSONAL: Born February 22, 1982, in Wayne, Neb. ... 6-0/214. ... Full name: Justin Michael Sandy.
HIGH SCHOOL: East (Sioux City, Iowa).
COLLEGE: Northern Iowa.
TRANSACTIONS/CAREER NOTES: Signed as non-drafted free agent by Tennessee Titans (April 28, 2004). ... Released by Titans (September 1, 2004). ... Re-signed by Titans to practice squad (September 7, 2004). ... Activated (November 19, 2004). ... On injured reserve with foot injury (November 29, 2004-remainder of season).

Year Team	G	GS	TOTALS Tk.	Ast.	Sks.	INTERCEPTIONS No.	Yds.	Avg.	TD
2004—Tennessee NFL	1	0	1	0	0.0	0	0	0.0	0

SAPP, BENNY — CB

PERSONAL: Born January 20, 1981, in Fort Lauderdale, Fla. ... 5-9/190. ... Full name: Benjamin Lee Sapp.
HIGH SCHOOL: Anderson (Fort Lauderdale, Fla.).
COLLEGE: Northern Iowa.
TRANSACTIONS/CAREER NOTES: Signed as non-drafted free agent by Kansas City Chiefs (April 27, 2004).

			TOTALS			INTERCEPTIONS			
Year Team	G	GS	Tk.	Ast.	Sks.	No.	Yds.	Avg.	TD
2004—Kansas City NFL	15	1	8	1	0.0	1	0	0.0	0

SAPP, CECIL — RB — BRONCOS

PERSONAL: Born December 12, 1978, in Miami, Fla. ... 5-11/229.
HIGH SCHOOL: Palmetto (Miami, Fla.).
COLLEGE: Colorado State.
TRANSACTIONS/CAREER NOTES: Signed as non-drafted free agent by Denver Broncos (April 28, 2003). ... Waived by Broncos (August 31, 2003). ... Re-signed by Broncos to practice squad (September 1, 2003). ... Activated (December 26, 2003). ... Released by Broncos (September 5, 2004). ... Re-signed by Broncos to practice squad (September 6, 2004). ... Activated (October 27, 2004).
SINGLE GAME HIGHS (regular season): Attempts—12 (December 28, 2003, vs. Green Bay); yards—32 (January 2, 2005, vs. Indianapolis); and rushing touchdowns—0.

			RUSHING				TOTALS			
Year Team	G	GS	Att.	Yds.	Avg.	TD	TD	2pt.	Pts.	Fum.
2003—Denver NFL	1	0	12	31	2.6	0	0	0	0	0
2004—Denver NFL	5	0	4	32	8.0	0	0	0	0	0
Pro totals (2 years)	6	0	16	63	3.9	0	0	0	0	0

SAPP, GEROME — S — COLTS

PERSONAL: Born February 8, 1981, in Houston, Texas. ... 6-1/216. ... Full name: Gerome Daren Sapp.
HIGH SCHOOL: Lamar (Houston).
COLLEGE: Notre Dame.
TRANSACTIONS/CAREER NOTES: Selected by Baltimore Ravens in sixth round (182nd pick overall) of 2003 NFL draft. ... Signed by Ravens (July 7, 2003). ... Released by Ravens (September 16, 2004). ... Signed by Indianapolis Colts (September 21, 2004).

			TOTALS			INTERCEPTIONS			
Year Team	G	GS	Tk.	Ast.	Sks.	No.	Yds.	Avg.	TD
2003—Baltimore NFL	14	0	0	0	0.0	0	0	0.0	0
2004—Indianapolis NFL	13	0	13	2	0.0	0	0	0.0	0
Pro totals (2 years)	27	0	13	2	0.0	0	0	0.0	0

SAPP, WARREN — DT — RAIDERS

PERSONAL: Born December 19, 1972, in Orlando, Fla. ... 6-2/300. ... Full name: Warren Carlos Sapp.
HIGH SCHOOL: Apopka (Fla.).
COLLEGE: Miami (Fla.).
TRANSACTIONS/CAREER NOTES: Selected after junior season by Tampa Bay Buccaneers in first round (12th pick overall) of 1995 NFL draft. ... Signed by Buccaneers (April 27, 1995). ... Granted unconditional free agency (March 3, 2004). ... Signed by Oakland Raiders (March 21, 2004).
CHAMPIONSHIP GAME EXPERIENCE: Played in NFC championship game (1999 and 2002 seasons). ... Member of Super Bowl championship team (2002 season).
HONORS: Lombardi Award winner (1994). ... Bronko Nagurski Award winner (1994). ... Named defensive lineman on THE SPORTING NEWS college All-America first team (1994). ... Played in Pro Bowl (1997-2000 seasons). ... Named defensive tackle on THE SPORTING NEWS NFL All-Pro team (1999-2002). ... Named to play in Pro Bowl (2001 season); replaced by Ted Washington due to injury. ... Named to play in Pro Bowl (2002 season); replaced by Kris Jenkins due to injury. ... Named to play in Pro Bowl (2003 season); replaced by Corey Simon due to injury.

			TOTALS			INTERCEPTIONS			
Year Team	G	GS	Tk.	Ast.	Sks.	No.	Yds.	Avg.	TD
1995—Tampa Bay NFL	16	8	17	10	3.0	1	5	5.0	1
1996—Tampa Bay NFL	15	14	41	10	9.0	0	0	0.0	0
1997—Tampa Bay NFL	15	15	47	11	10.5	0	0	0.0	0
1998—Tampa Bay NFL	16	16	28	17	7.0	0	0	0.0	0
1999—Tampa Bay NFL	15	15	27	14	12.5	0	0	0.0	0
2000—Tampa Bay NFL	16	15	43	9	16.5	0	0	0.0	0
2001—Tampa Bay NFL	16	16	28	8	6.0	0	0	0.0	0
2002—Tampa Bay NFL	16	16	40	7	7.5	2	0	0.0	0
2003—Tampa Bay NFL	15	15	37	7	5.0	0	0	0.0	0
2004—Oakland NFL	16	16	31	11	2.5	0	0	0.0	0
Pro totals (10 years)	156	146	339	104	79.5	3	5	1.7	1

SATURDAY, JEFF — C — COLTS

PERSONAL: Born June 8, 1975, in Atlanta, Ga. ... 6-2/295. ... Full name: Jeffrey Bryant Saturday.
HIGH SCHOOL: Shamrock (Tucker, Ga.).
COLLEGE: North Carolina.

S

TRANSACTIONS/CAREER NOTES: Signed as non-drafted free agent by Baltimore Ravens (April 27, 1998). ... Released by Ravens (June 12, 1998). ... Signed by Indianapolis Colts (January 7, 1999). ... Granted free agency (March 1, 2002). ... Re-signed by Colts (April 3, 2002). ... Granted unconditional free agency (February 28, 2003). ... Re-signed by Colts (February 28, 2003).
PLAYING EXPERIENCE: Indianapolis NFL, 1999-2004. ... Games/Games started: 1999 (13/2), 2000 (16/16), 2001 (16/16), 2002 (16/16), 2003 (16/16), 2004 (14/14). Total: 91/80.
CHAMPIONSHIP GAME EXPERIENCE: Played in AFC championship game (2003 season).

SAUERBRUN, TODD   P   BRONCOS

PERSONAL: Born January 4, 1973, in Setauket, N.Y. ... 5-10/215. ... Name pronounced: SOUR-brun.
HIGH SCHOOL: Ward Melville (Setauket, N.Y.).
COLLEGE: West Virginia.
TRANSACTIONS/CAREER NOTES: Selected by Chicago Bears in second round (56th pick overall) of 1995 NFL draft. ... Signed by Bears (July 20, 1995). ... Granted free agency (February 13, 1998). ... Re-signed by Bears (May 19, 1998). ... On injured reserve with knee injury (September 23, 1998-remainder of season). ... Granted unconditional free agency (February 11, 2000). ... Signed by Kansas City Chiefs (March 27, 2000). ... Released by Chiefs (March 13, 2001). ... Signed by Carolina Panthers (April 24, 2001). ... Designated by Panthers as franchise player (February 19, 2003). ... Re-signed by Panthers (April 25, 2003). ... Traded by Panthers to Denver Broncos for P Jason Baker and seventh-round pick in 2006 draft (May 18, 2005).
CHAMPIONSHIP GAME EXPERIENCE: Played in NFC championship game (2003 season). ... Played in Super Bowl 38 (2003 season).
HONORS: Named punter on THE SPORTING NEWS college All-America first team (1994). ... Named punter on THE SPORTING NEWS NFL All-Pro team (2001-2003). ... Played in Pro Bowl (2001-2003 seasons).

					PUNTING		
Year Team	G	No.	Yds.	Avg.	Net avg.	In. 20	Blk.
1995—Chicago NFL	15	55	2080	37.8	31.1	16	0
1996—Chicago NFL	16	78	3491	44.8	34.9	15	0
1997—Chicago NFL	16	95	4059	42.7	32.8	26	0
1998—Chicago NFL	3	15	741	49.4	42.1	6	0
1999—Chicago NFL	16	85	3478	40.9	35.4	20	0
2000—Kansas City NFL	16	82	3656	44.6	35.8	28	0
2001—Carolina NFL	16	93	*4419	*47.5	*38.9	35	1
2002—Carolina NFL	16	‡104	*4735	*45.5	37.5	‡31	1
2003—Carolina NFL	16	77	3433	‡44.6	35.6	22	3
2004—Carolina NFL	16	76	3351	∞44.1	37.5	25	1
Pro totals (10 years)	146	760	33443	44.0	35.9	224	6

SAVAGE, JOSH   DE   BUCCANEERS

PERSONAL: Born September 28, 1980, in Ozark, Ala. ... 6-4/276.
HIGH SCHOOL: Hillcrest (Salt Lake City, Utah).
COLLEGE: Utah.
TRANSACTIONS/CAREER NOTES: Signed as non-drafted free agent by Tampa Bay Buccaneers (April 30, 2004).

			TOTALS		
Year Team	G	GS	Tk.	Ast.	Sks.
2004—Tampa Bay NFL	6	0	0	1	0.0

SCANLON, RICH   LB   CHIEFS

PERSONAL: Born December 23, 1980, in Oradell, N.J. ... 6-2/249. ... Full name: Richard James Scanlon.
HIGH SCHOOL: Bergen Catholic (Oradell, N.J.).
COLLEGE: Syracuse.
TRANSACTIONS/CAREER NOTES: Signed as non-drafted free agent by Kansas City Chiefs (April 27, 2004). ... Released by Chiefs (September 3, 2004). ... Re-signed by Chiefs to practice squad (September 6, 2004). ... Activated (November 10, 2004). ... Assigned by Chiefs to Berlin Thunder in 2005 NFL Europe enhancement allocation program (February 14, 2005).

			TOTALS			INTERCEPTIONS			
Year Team	G	GS	Tk.	Ast.	Sks.	No.	Yds.	Avg.	TD
2004—Kansas City NFL	6	0	0	0	0.0	0	0	0.0	0

SCHAUB, MATT   QB   FALCONS

PERSONAL: Born June 25, 1981, in Pittsburgh, Pa. ... 6-5/237. ... Full name: Matthew Rutledge Schaub. ... Name pronounced: Shob.
HIGH SCHOOL: West Chester East (West Chester, Pa.).
COLLEGE: Virginia.
TRANSACTIONS/CAREER NOTES: Selected by Atlanta Falcons in third round (90th pick overall) of 2004 NFL draft. ... Signed by Falcons (July 28, 2004).
CHAMPIONSHIP GAME EXPERIENCE: Played in NFC championship game (2004 season).
SINGLE GAME HIGHS (regular season): Attempts—41 (December 26, 2004, vs. New Orleans); completions—17 (December 26, 2004, vs. New Orleans); yards—188 (December 26, 2004, vs. New Orleans); and touchdown passes—1 (January 2, 2005, vs. Seattle).
MISCELLANEOUS: Regular-season record as starting NFL quarterback: 0-1 (.000).

			PASSING									RUSHING				TOTALS		
Year Team	G	GS	Att.	Cmp.	Pct.	Yds.	TD	Int.	Avg.	Skd.	Rat.	Att.	Yds.	Avg.	TD	TD	2pt.	Pts.
2004—Atlanta NFL	6	1	70	33	47.1	330	1	4	4.71	4	42.0	8	26	3.3	0	0	0	0

SCHIFINO, JAKE   WR   PATRIOTS

PERSONAL: Born November 15, 1979, in Pittsburgh, Pa. ... 6-1/201. ... Full name: Vernon Martin Schifino.
HIGH SCHOOL: Penn Hills (Pa.).
COLLEGE: Akron.
TRANSACTIONS/CAREER NOTES: Selected by Tennessee Titans in fifth round (151st pick overall) of 2002 NFL draft. ... Signed by Titans (July 19, 2002). ... On injured reserve with hamstring injury (August 22, 2002-entire season). ... Released by Titans (October 5, 2004). ... Signed by New England Patriots (January 6, 2005).

			RECEIVING				KICKOFF RETURNS				TOTALS		
Year Team	G	GS	No.	Yds.	Avg.	TD	No.	Yds.	Avg.	TD	TD	2pt.	Pts.	Fum.
2003—Tennessee NFL	13	0	0	0	0.0	0	35	703	20.1	0	0	0	0	0
2004—Tennessee NFL	1	0	0	0	0.0	0	0	0	0.0	0	0	0	0	0
Pro totals (2 years)	14	0	0	0	0.0	0	35	703	20.1	0	0	0	0	0

SCHLESINGER, CORY   FB   LIONS

PERSONAL: Born June 23, 1972, in Columbus, Neb. ... 6-0/247.
HIGH SCHOOL: Columbus (Neb.).
COLLEGE: Nebraska.
TRANSACTIONS/CAREER NOTES: Selected by Detroit Lions in sixth round (192nd pick overall) of 1995 NFL draft. ... Signed by Lions (July 19, 1995). ... Granted unconditional free agency (March 2, 2001). ... Re-signed by Lions (March 2, 2001).
SINGLE GAME HIGHS (regular season): Attempts—10 (September 12, 1999, vs. Seattle); yards—50 (September 12, 1999, vs. Seattle); and rushing touchdowns—1 (September 22, 2002, vs. Green Bay).

			RUSHING				RECEIVING				TOTALS		
Year Team	G	GS	Att.	Yds.	Avg.	TD	No.	Yds.	Avg.	TD	TD	2pt.	Pts.	Fum.
1995—Detroit NFL	16	2	1	1	1.0	0	1	2	2.0	0	0	0	0	0
1996—Detroit NFL	16	1	0	0	0.0	0	0	0	0.0	0	0	0	0	0
1997—Detroit NFL	16	2	7	11	1.6	0	5	69	13.8	1	1	0	6	0
1998—Detroit NFL	15	2	5	17	3.4	0	3	16	5.3	1	1	0	6	0
1999—Detroit NFL	16	11	43	124	2.9	0	21	151	7.2	1	1	0	6	4
2000—Detroit NFL	16	8	1	3	3.0	0	12	73	6.1	0	0	0	0	0
2001—Detroit NFL	16	13	47	154	3.3	3	60	466	7.8	0	3	0	18	1
2002—Detroit NFL	16	14	49	139	2.8	2	35	263	7.5	0	2	0	12	2
2003—Detroit NFL	16	10	9	16	1.8	0	34	247	7.3	2	2	0	12	0
2004—Detroit NFL	13	11	4	7	1.8	0	10	91	9.1	3	3	0	18	0
Pro totals (10 years)	156	74	166	472	2.8	5	181	1378	7.6	8	13	0	78	7

SCHNECK, MIKE   C/LS   STEELERS

PERSONAL: Born August 4, 1977, in Whitefish Bay, Wis. ... 6-0/237. ... Full name: Mike Louis Schneck.
HIGH SCHOOL: Whitefish Bay (Wis.).
COLLEGE: Wisconsin.
TRANSACTIONS/CAREER NOTES: Signed as non-drafted free agent by Pittsburgh Steelers (April 23, 1999); contract voided by NFL because he did not meet eligibility requirements. ... Re-signed by Steelers (July 12, 1999). ... Granted free agency (March 1, 2002). ... Re-signed by Steelers (April 23, 2002). ... Granted unconditional free agency (March 3, 2004). ... Re-signed by Steelers (March 30, 2004).
PLAYING EXPERIENCE: Pittsburgh NFL, 1999-2004. ... Games/Games started: 1999 (16/0), 2000 (16/0), 2001 (16/0), 2002 (12/0), 2003 (16/0), 2004 (16/0). Total: 92/0.
CHAMPIONSHIP GAME EXPERIENCE: Played in AFC championship game (2001 and 2004 seasons).

SCHOBEL, AARON   DE   BILLS

PERSONAL: Born September 1, 1977, in Columbus, Texas. ... 6-4/262. ... Brother of Matt Schobel, tight end, Cincinnati Bengals.
HIGH SCHOOL: Columbus (Texas).
COLLEGE: Texas Christian.
TRANSACTIONS/CAREER NOTES: Selected by Buffalo Bills in second round (46th pick overall) of 2001 NFL draft. ... Signed by Bills (July 26, 2001).
HONORS: Named defensive end on THE SPORTING NEWS college All-America second team (2000).

			TOTALS			INTERCEPTIONS			
Year Team	G	GS	Tk.	Ast.	Sks.	No.	Yds.	Avg.	TD
2001—Buffalo NFL	16	11	31	11	6.5	0	0	0.0	0
2002—Buffalo NFL	16	16	34	18	8.5	0	0	0.0	0
2003—Buffalo NFL	16	16	38	22	11.5	1	6	6.0	0
2004—Buffalo NFL	16	16	46	27	8.0	0	0	0.0	0
Pro totals (4 years)	64	59	149	78	34.5	1	6	6.0	0

SCHOBEL, BO   DE   TITANS

PERSONAL: Born March 24, 1981, in Columbus, Texas. ... 6-5/264. ... Full name: Robert Edward Schobel.
HIGH SCHOOL: Columbus (Texas).
COLLEGE: Texas Christian.
TRANSACTIONS/CAREER NOTES: Selected by Tennessee Titans in fourth round (103rd pick overall) of 2004 NFL draft. ... Signed by Titans (July 30, 2004). ... On physically unable to perform list with foot injury (August 31-November 29, 2004). ... Activated (November 29, 2004).

Year Team	G	GS	TOTALS		
			Tk.	Ast.	Sks.
2004—Tennessee NFL	5	2	14	1	0.0

SCHOBEL, MATT — TE — BENGALS

PERSONAL: Born November 4, 1978, in Columbus, Texas. ... 6-5/257. ... Full name: Matthew Thomas Schobel. ... Brother of Aaron Schobel, defensive end, Buffalo Bills.
HIGH SCHOOL: Columbus (Texas).
COLLEGE: Texas Christian.
TRANSACTIONS/CAREER NOTES: Selected by Cincinnati Bengals in third round (67th pick overall) of 2002 NFL draft. ... Signed by Bengals (May 10, 2002).
SINGLE GAME HIGHS (regular season): Receptions—4 (September 19, 2004, vs. Miami); yards—97 (September 7, 2003, vs. Denver); and touchdown receptions—1 (December 19, 2004, vs. Buffalo).

Year Team	G	GS	RECEIVING				TOTALS			
			No.	Yds.	Avg.	TD	TD	2pt.	Pts.	Fum.
2002—Cincinnati NFL	16	10	27	212	7.9	2	2	0	12	0
2003—Cincinnati NFL	15	1	24	332	13.8	2	2	0	12	2
2004—Cincinnati NFL	16	1	21	201	9.6	4	4	0	24	1
Pro totals (3 years)	47	12	72	745	10.3	8	8	0	48	3

SCHROEDER, BILL — WR

S

PERSONAL: Born January 9, 1971, in Eau Claire, Wis. ... 6-3/200. ... Full name: William Fredrich Schroeder. ... Name pronounced: SHRAY-der.
HIGH SCHOOL: Sheboygan (Wis.) South.
COLLEGE: Wisconsin-La Crosse.
TRANSACTIONS/CAREER NOTES: Selected by Green Bay Packers in sixth round (181st pick overall) of 1994 NFL draft. ... Signed by Packers (May 10, 1994). ... Released by Packers (August 28, 1994). ... Re-signed by Packers to practice squad (August 30, 1994). ... Activated (December 29, 1994). ... Traded by Packers with TE Jeff Wilner to New England Patriots for C Mike Arthur (August 11, 1995). ... On injured reserve with foot injury (August 27, 1995-entire season). ... Released by Patriots (August 14, 1996). ... Re-signed by Packers to practice squad (August 28, 1996). ... Assigned by Packers to Rhein Fire in 1997 World League enhancement allocation program (February 19, 1997). ... On injured reserve with broken collarbone (December 9, 1998-remainder of season). ... Granted unconditional free agency (March 1, 2002). ... Signed by Detroit Lions (March 14, 2002). ... Released by Lions (March 2, 2004). ... Signed by Tampa Bay Buccaneers (July 20, 2004). ... Released by Buccaneers (November 30, 2004).
CHAMPIONSHIP GAME EXPERIENCE: Member of Packers for NFC championship game (1997 season); inactive. ... Member of Packers for Super Bowl 32 (1997 season); inactive.
SINGLE GAME HIGHS (regular season): Receptions—8 (December 17, 2000, vs. Minnesota); yards—158 (October 10, 1999, vs. Tampa Bay); and touchdown receptions—2 (November 17, 2002, vs. New York Jets).
STATISTICAL PLATEAUS: 100-yard receiving games: 1998 (1), 1999 (1), 2000 (3), 2001 (5), 2002 (1), 2004 (1). Total: 12.

Year Team	G	GS	RECEIVING				PUNT RETURNS				KICKOFF RETURNS				TOTALS			
			No.	Yds.	Avg.	TD	No.	Yds.	Avg.	TD	No.	Yds.	Avg.	TD	TD	2pt.	Pts.	Fum.
1994—Green Bay NFL	Did not play.																	
1995—New England NFL	Did not play.																	
1996—Green Bay NFL	Did not play.																	
1997—Green Bay NFL	15	1	2	15	7.5	1	33	342	10.4	0	24	562	23.4	0	1	0	6	4
1998—Green Bay NFL	13	3	31	452	14.6	1	2	5	2.5	0	0	0	0.0	0	1	0	6	1
1999—Green Bay NFL	16	16	74	1051	14.2	5	0	0	0.0	0	1	10	10.0	0	5	0	30	3
2000—Green Bay NFL	16	16	65	999	15.4	4	0	0	0.0	0	0	0	0.0	0	4	0	24	1
2001—Green Bay NFL	14	14	53	918	‡17.3	9	0	0	0.0	0	0	0	0.0	0	9	0	54	1
2002—Detroit NFL	14	13	36	595	16.5	5	0	0	0.0	0	0	0	0.0	0	5	1	32	0
2003—Detroit NFL	16	13	36	397	11.0	2	0	0	0.0	0	0	0	0.0	0	2	0	12	0
2004—Tampa Bay NFL	7	2	7	156	22.3	1	6	21	3.5	0	2	29	14.5	0	1	0	6	2
Pro totals (8 years)	111	78	304	4583	15.1	28	41	368	9.0	0	27	601	22.3	0	28	1	170	12

SCHULTERS, LANCE — S — TITANS

PERSONAL: Born May 27, 1975, in Guyana. ... 6-2/202.
HIGH SCHOOL: Canarsie (Brooklyn, N.Y.).
JUNIOR COLLEGE: Nassau Community College (N.Y.).
COLLEGE: Hofstra.
TRANSACTIONS/CAREER NOTES: Selected by San Francisco 49ers in fourth round (119th pick overall) of 1998 NFL draft. ... Signed by 49ers (July 18, 1998). ... On injured reserve with knee injury (December 21, 2000-remainder of season). ... Granted free agency (March 2, 2001). ... Re-signed by 49ers (March 2, 2001). ... On physically unable to perform list with knee injury (July 29-August 6, 2001). ... Granted unconditional free agency (March 1, 2002). ... Signed by Tennessee Titans (April 11, 2002).
CHAMPIONSHIP GAME EXPERIENCE: Played in AFC championship game (2002 season).
HONORS: Played in Pro Bowl (1999 season).

Year Team	G	GS	TOTALS			INTERCEPTIONS			
			Tk.	Ast.	Sks.	No.	Yds.	Avg.	TD
1998—San Francisco NFL	15	0	12	3	0.0	0	0	0.0	0
1999—San Francisco NFL	13	13	53	9	0.0	6	127	21.2	1
2000—San Francisco NFL	12	12	61	30	0.5	0	0	0.0	0
2001—San Francisco NFL	16	16	52	9	1.0	3	0	0.0	0
2002—Tennessee NFL	16	16	71	13	2.0	6	56	9.3	0
2003—Tennessee NFL	16	16	65	20	1.0	0	0	0.0	0
2004—Tennessee NFL	3	3	12	2	1.0	0	0	0.0	0
Pro totals (7 years)	91	76	326	86	5.5	15	183	12.2	1

SCHWEIGERT, STUART   DB   RAIDERS

PERSONAL: Born June 21, 1981, in Saginaw, Mich. ... 6-1/210. ... Full name: Stuart Eric Schweigert.
HIGH SCHOOL: Heritage (Saginaw, Mich.).
COLLEGE: Purdue.
TRANSACTIONS/CAREER NOTES: Selected by Oakland Raiders in third round (67th pick overall) of 2004 NFL draft. ... Signed by Raiders (July 30, 2004).
HONORS: Named defensive back on THE SPORTING NEWS Freshman All-America first team (2000). ... Named safety on THE SPORTING NEWS college All-America fourth team (2001) and second team (2003).

			TOTALS			INTERCEPTIONS			
Year Team	G	GS	Tk.	Ast.	Sks.	No.	Yds.	Avg.	TD
2004—Oakland NFL	16	3	29	7	0.0	0	0	0.0	0

SCIFRES, MIKE   P/K   CHARGERS

PERSONAL: Born October 8, 1980, in Metairie, La. ... 6-2/236. ... Full name: Michael Scifres.
HIGH SCHOOL: Destrehan (Norco, La.).
COLLEGE: Western Illinois.
TRANSACTIONS/CAREER NOTES: Selected by San Diego Chargers in fifth round (149th pick overall) of 2003 NFL draft. ... Signed by Chargers (July 19, 2003).

				PUNTING			
Year Team	G	No.	Yds.	Avg.	Net avg.	In. 20	Blk.
2003—San Diego NFL	6	0	0	0.0	0.0	0	0
2004—San Diego NFL	16	69	2974	43.1	§38.4	29	0
Pro totals (2 years)	22	69	2974	43.1	38.4	29	0

SCIOLI, BRAD   DE

PERSONAL: Born September 6, 1976, in Bridgeport, Pa. ... 6-3/280. ... Full name: Brad Elliott Scioli. ... Name pronounced: SHE-o-lee.
HIGH SCHOOL: Upper Merion (King of Prussia, Pa.).
COLLEGE: Penn State.
TRANSACTIONS/CAREER NOTES: Selected by Indianapolis Colts in fifth round (138th pick overall) of 1999 NFL draft. ... Signed by Colts (July 22, 1999). ... Granted free agency (March 1, 2002). ... Re-signed by Colts (April 16, 2002). ... Granted unconditional free agency (February 28, 2003). ... Re-signed by Colts (March 9, 2003). ... Released by Colts (March 7, 2005).
CHAMPIONSHIP GAME EXPERIENCE: Played in AFC championship game (2003 season).

			TOTALS		
Year Team	G	GS	Tk.	Ast.	Sks.
1999—Indianapolis NFL	11	0	1	0	0.0
2000—Indianapolis NFL	16	2	7	3	2.0
2001—Indianapolis NFL	13	12	22	10	4.0
2002—Indianapolis NFL	16	13	39	11	7.0
2003—Indianapolis NFL	16	0	10	2	0.0
2004—Indianapolis NFL	9	0	7	5	2.0
Pro totals (6 years)	81	27	86	31	15.0

SCIULLO, STEVE   G   EAGLES

PERSONAL: Born August 27, 1980, in Pittsburgh, Pa. ... 6-5/325. ... Full name: Steven William Sciullo.
HIGH SCHOOL: Shaler Area (Pittsburgh).
COLLEGE: Marshall.
TRANSACTIONS/CAREER NOTES: Selected by Indianapolis Colts in fourth round (122nd pick overall) of 2003 NFL draft. ... Signed by Colts (July 25, 2003). ... Claimed on waivers by Philadelphia Eagles (September 8, 2004).
PLAYING EXPERIENCE: Philadelphia NFL, 2003-2004. ... Games/Games started: 2003 (13/13), 2004 (15/5). Total: 28/18.
CHAMPIONSHIP GAME EXPERIENCE: Played in AFC championship game (2003 season). ... Played in NFC championship game (2004 season). ... Played in Super Bowl 39 (2004 season).

SCOBEE, JOSH   K   JAGUARS

PERSONAL: Born June 23, 1982, in Longview, Texas. ... 6-1/190.
HIGH SCHOOL: Longview (Texas).
COLLEGE: Louisiana Tech.
TRANSACTIONS/CAREER NOTES: Selected by Jacksonville Jaguars in fifth round (137th pick overall) of 2004 NFL draft. ... Signed by Jaguars (July 30, 2004).

		FIELD GOALS							TOTALS		
Year Team	G	1-29	30-39	40-49	50+	Tot.	Pct.	Lg.	XPM	XPA	Pts.
2004—Jacksonville NFL	16	10-10	8-11	5-7	1-3	24-31	77.4	53	21	21	93

SCOBEY, JOSH   RB   CARDINALS

PERSONAL: Born December 11, 1979, in Oklahoma City, Okla. ... 6-0/216.
HIGH SCHOOL: Del City (Oklahoma City, Okla.).
JUNIOR COLLEGE: Northeastern A&M Community College (Okla.).

COLLEGE: Kansas State.

TRANSACTIONS/CAREER NOTES: Selected by Arizona Cardinals in sixth round (185th pick overall) of 2002 NFL draft. ... Signed by Cardinals (May 31, 2002). ... On injured reserve with thumb injury (September 1, 2002-remainder of season).

SINGLE GAME HIGHS (regular season): Attempts—9 (December 19, 2004, vs. St. Louis); yards—23 (December 19, 2004, vs. St. Louis); and rushing touchdowns—0.

Year Team	G	GS	RUSHING				RECEIVING				KICKOFF RETURNS				TOTALS			
			Att.	Yds.	Avg.	TD	No.	Yds.	Avg.	TD	No.	Yds.	Avg.	TD	TD	2pt.	Pts.	Fum.
2003—Arizona NFL	15	0	0	0	0.0	0	1	9	9.0	0	*73	*1684	23.1	1	1	0	6	0
2004—Arizona NFL	12	0	27	89	3.3	0	18	191	10.6	0	32	723	22.6	0	0	0	0	1
Pro totals (2 years)	27	0	27	89	3.3	0	19	200	10.5	0	105	2407	22.9	1	1	0	6	1

SCOTT, BART   LB

PERSONAL: Born August 18, 1980, in Detroit, Mich. ... 6-2/235. ... Full name: Bart Edward Scott.

HIGH SCHOOL: Southeastern (Detroit).

COLLEGE: Southern Illinois.

TRANSACTIONS/CAREER NOTES: Signed as non-drafted free agent by Baltimore Ravens (April 25, 2002). ... Granted free agency (March 2, 2005).

Year Team	G	GS	TOTALS			INTERCEPTIONS			
			Tk.	Ast.	Sks.	No.	Yds.	Avg.	TD
2002—Baltimore NFL	16	0	2	2	0.0	1	0	0.0	0
2003—Baltimore NFL	16	0	7	0	0.0	0	0	0.0	0
2004—Baltimore NFL	13	0	5	7	0.0	0	0	0.0	0
Pro totals (3 years)	45	0	14	9	0.0	1	0	0.0	0

SCOTT, BRYAN   CB   FALCONS

PERSONAL: Born April 13, 1981, in Washington, DC. ... 6-1/219. ... Full name: Bryan Anderson Scott.

HIGH SCHOOL: Central Bucks (Pa.).

COLLEGE: Penn State.

TRANSACTIONS/CAREER NOTES: Selected by Atlanta Falcons in second round (55th pick overall) of 2003 NFL draft. ... Signed by Falcons (July 10, 2003).

CHAMPIONSHIP GAME EXPERIENCE: Played in NFC championship game (2004 season).

Year Team	G	GS	TOTALS			INTERCEPTIONS			
			Tk.	Ast.	Sks.	No.	Yds.	Avg.	TD
2003—Atlanta NFL	15	7	49	7	0.0	2	3	1.5	0
2004—Atlanta NFL	16	16	76	11	2.5	1	22	22.0	0
Pro totals (2 years)	31	23	125	18	2.5	3	25	8.3	0

SCOTT, CHAD   CB   PATRIOTS

PERSONAL: Born September 6, 1974, in Capitol Heights, Md. ... 6-1/202. ... Full name: Chad Oliver Scott.

HIGH SCHOOL: Suitland (Forestville, Md.).

COLLEGE: Maryland.

TRANSACTIONS/CAREER NOTES: Selected by Pittsburgh Steelers in first round (24th pick overall) of 1997 NFL draft. ... Signed by Steelers (July 16, 1997). ... On injured reserve with knee injury (July 20, 1998-remainder of season). ... On injured reserve with hand injury (December 2, 2003-remainder of season). ... Released by Steelers (February 25, 2005). ... Signed by New England Patriots (April 26, 2005).

CHAMPIONSHIP GAME EXPERIENCE: Played in AFC championship game (1997, 2001 and 2004 seasons).

Year Team	G	GS	TOTALS			INTERCEPTIONS			
			Tk.	Ast.	Sks.	No.	Yds.	Avg.	TD
1997—Pittsburgh NFL	13	9	45	2	0.0	2	-4	-2.0	0
1998—Pittsburgh NFL		Did not play.							
1999—Pittsburgh NFL	13	12	49	1	0.0	1	16	16.0	0
2000—Pittsburgh NFL	16	16	64	6	0.0	5	49	9.8	0
2001—Pittsburgh NFL	15	15	71	9	0.0	5	204	40.8	†2
2002—Pittsburgh NFL	15	15	64	17	0.0	2	30	15.0	1
2003—Pittsburgh NFL	12	12	44	12	0.0	3	50	16.7	1
2004—Pittsburgh NFL	7	7	27	2	0.0	1	23	23.0	0
Pro totals (7 years)	91	86	364	49	0.0	19	368	19.4	4

SCOTT, DARRION   DE   VIKINGS

PERSONAL: Born October 25, 1981, in Charleston, W.Va. ... 6-3/289.

HIGH SCHOOL: Capital (Charleston, W.Va.).

COLLEGE: Ohio State.

TRANSACTIONS/CAREER NOTES: Selected by Minnesota Vikings in third round (88th pick overall) of 2004 NFL draft. ... Signed by Vikings (July 29, 2004).

Year Team	G	GS	TOTALS		
			Tk.	Ast.	Sks.
2004—Minnesota NFL	12	0	12	11	0.0

SCOTT, DEQUINCY　　　　　　　　DT　　　　　　　　CHARGERS

PERSONAL: Born March 5, 1978, in La Place, La. ... 6-1/260. ... Full name: Dequincy Scott.
HIGH SCHOOL: East St. John (LaPlace, La.).
COLLEGE: Southern Miss.
TRANSACTIONS/CAREER NOTES: Signed as non-drafted free agent by San Diego Chargers (April 30, 2001). ... Released by Chargers (September 2, 2001). ... Re-signed by Chargers to practice squad (September 4, 2001). ... Released by Chargers from practice squad (December 14, 2001). ... Re-signed by Chargers to practice squad (December 18, 2001). ... Released by Chargers from practice squad (December 21, 2001). ... Re-signed by Chargers (January 10, 2002). ... Granted free agency (March 2, 2005). ... Re-signed by Chargers (April 19, 2005).

| | | | | TOTALS | |
Year　Team	G	GS	Tk.	Ast.	Sks.
2002—San Diego NFL	10	0	8	0	2.0
2003—San Diego NFL	16	0	14	4	6.5
2004—San Diego NFL	14	2	14	5	1.5
Pro totals (3 years)	40	2	36	9	10.0

SCOTT, GREG　　　　　　　　DE　　　　　　　　BENGALS

PERSONAL: Born October 2, 1979, in Franklin, Va. ... 6-4/258.
HIGH SCHOOL: Southampton (Courtland, Va.).
COLLEGE: Hampton.
TRANSACTIONS/CAREER NOTES: Selected by Washington Redskins in seventh round (234th pick overall) of 2002 NFL draft. ... Signed by Redskins (July 16, 2002). ... Claimed on waivers by Cincinnati Bengals (August 27, 2003). ... Released by Bengals (September 1, 2003). ... Re-signed by Bengals to practice squad (September 3, 2003). ... Released by Bengals (September 5, 2004). ... Re-signed by Bengals to practice squad (September 6, 2004). ... Activated (October 29, 2004). ... Released by Bengals (November 2, 2004). ... Re-signed by Bengals to practice squad (November 4, 2004). ... Activated (November 29, 2004). ... Assigned by Bengals to Rhein Fire in 2005 NFL Europe enhancement allocation program (February 14, 2005).

| | | | | TOTALS | | | INTERCEPTIONS | | | |
Year　Team	G	GS	Tk.	Ast.	Sks.	No.	Yds.	Avg.	TD
2002—Cincinnati NFL	2	0	0	0	0.0	0	0	0.0	0
2004—Cincinnati NFL	1	0	0	0	0.0	0	0	0.0	0
Pro totals (2 years)	3	0	0	0	0.0	0	0	0.0	0

SCOTT, IAN　　　　　　　　DT　　　　　　　　BEARS

PERSONAL: Born November 8, 1981, in Greenville, S.C. ... 6-2/305. ... Full name: Josef Ian Scott.
HIGH SCHOOL: Gainesville (Fla.).
COLLEGE: Florida.
TRANSACTIONS/CAREER NOTES: Selected after junior season by Chicago Bears in fourth round (116th pick overall) of 2003 NFL draft. ... Signed by Bears (July 24, 2003).

| | | | | TOTALS | |
Year　Team	G	GS	Tk.	Ast.	Sks.
2003—Chicago NFL	6	0	2	0	0.0
2004—Chicago NFL	14	13	34	10	2.0
Pro totals (2 years)	20	13	36	10	2.0

SCOTT, JAKE　　　　　　　　T　　　　　　　　COLTS

PERSONAL: Born April 16, 1981, in Lewiston, Idaho. ... 6-5/280.
HIGH SCHOOL: Lewiston (Idaho).
COLLEGE: Idaho.
TRANSACTIONS/CAREER NOTES: Selected by Indianapolis Colts in fifth round (141st pick overall) of 2004 NFL draft. ... Signed by Colts (July 27, 2004).
PLAYING EXPERIENCE: Indianapolis NFL, 2004. ... Games/Games started: 2004 (12/9). Total: 12/9.

SCOTT, LYNN　　　　　　　　S　　　　　　　　COWBOYS

PERSONAL: Born June 23, 1977, in Turpin, Okla. ... 6-0/211.
HIGH SCHOOL: Turpin (Okla.).
COLLEGE: Northwestern Oklahoma State.
TRANSACTIONS/CAREER NOTES: Signed as non-drafted free agent by Dallas Cowboys (April 27, 2001). ... Re-signed by Cowboys (March 13, 2003). ... Granted free agency (March 3, 2004). ... Re-signed by Cowboys (April 15, 2004). ... Granted unconditional free agency (March 2, 2005). ... Re-signed by Cowboys (March 14, 2005).

| | | | | TOTALS | | | INTERCEPTIONS | | | |
Year　Team	G	GS	Tk.	Ast.	Sks.	No.	Yds.	Avg.	TD
2001—Dallas NFL	14	0	2	0	0.0	0	0	0.0	0
2002—Dallas NFL	14	0	6	4	0.0	0	0	0.0	0
2003—Dallas NFL	16	0	3	0	0.0	0	0	0.0	0
2004—Dallas NFL	16	9	28	9	1.0	1	2	2.0	0
Pro totals (4 years)	60	9	39	13	1.0	1	2	2.0	0

S

SEARS, COREY   DE   TEXANS

PERSONAL: Born April 15, 1973, in San Antonio, Texas. ... 6-3/314. ... Full name: Corey Alexander Sears.
HIGH SCHOOL: Judson (Converse, Texas).
JUNIOR COLLEGE: Navarro College (Texas).
COLLEGE: Mississippi State.
TRANSACTIONS/CAREER NOTES: Signed as non-drafted free agent by Baltimore Ravens (April 29, 1996). ... On injured reserve with knee injury (August 20-November 6, 1996). ... Released by Ravens (November 6, 1996). ... Signed by St. Louis Rams (April 24, 1998). ... Claimed on waivers by San Francisco 49ers (August 26, 1998). ... Released by 49ers (August 28, 1998). ... Signed by Rams to practice squad (September 1, 1998). ... Activated (November 30, 1998). ... Claimed on waivers by Arizona Cardinals (September 6, 1999). ... Released by Cardinals (February 19, 2001). ... Signed by Houston Texans (February 8, 2002). ... Granted unconditional free agency (February 28, 2003). ... Re-signed by Texans (March 11, 2003). ... Granted unconditional free agency (March 3, 2004). ... Re-signed by Texans (March 22, 2004). ... Granted unconditional free agency (March 2, 2005). ... Re-signed by Texans (March 8, 2005).

				TOTALS		
Year Team		G	GS	Tk.	Ast.	Sks.
1998—St. Louis NFL		4	0	4	0	0.0
1999—Arizona NFL		9	1	6	2	0.0
2000—Arizona NFL		8	2	9	9	0.0
2002—Houston NFL		16	0	13	8	1.0
2003—Houston NFL		16	12	26	11	1.0
2004—Houston NFL		15	0	5	5	0.0
Pro totals (6 years)		68	15	63	35	2.0

SEAU, JUNIOR   LB   DOLPHINS

PERSONAL: Born January 19, 1969, in San Diego, Calif. ... 6-3/250. ... Full name: Tiaina Seau Jr. ... Name pronounced: SAY-ow.
HIGH SCHOOL: Oceanside (Calif.).
COLLEGE: Southern California.
TRANSACTIONS/CAREER NOTES: Selected after junior season by San Diego Chargers in first round (fifth pick overall) of 1990 NFL draft. ... Signed by Chargers (August 27, 1990). ... Traded by Chargers to Miami Dolphins for fifth-round pick (RB Michael Turner) in 2004 draft (April 16, 2003). ... On injured reserve with pectoral injury (November 3, 2004-remainder of season).
CHAMPIONSHIP GAME EXPERIENCE: Played in AFC championship game (1994 season). ... Played in Super Bowl 29 (1994 season).
HONORS: Named linebacker on THE SPORTING NEWS college All-America first team (1989). ... Played in Pro Bowl (1991-2001 seasons). ... Named inside linebacker on THE SPORTING NEWS NFL All-Pro team (1992-1996, 1998 and 2000). ... Named to play in Pro Bowl (2002 season); replaced by Jason Gildon due to injury.

				TOTALS			INTERCEPTIONS			
Year Team		G	GS	Tk.	Ast.	Sks.	No.	Yds.	Avg.	TD
1990—San Diego NFL		16	15	61	24	1.0	0	0	0.0	0
1991—San Diego NFL		16	16	111	18	7.0	0	0	0.0	0
1992—San Diego NFL		15	15	79	23	4.5	2	51	25.5	0
1993—San Diego NFL		16	16	108	21	0.0	2	58	29.0	0
1994—San Diego NFL		16	16	124	31	5.5	0	0	0.0	0
1995—San Diego NFL		16	16	111	19	2.0	2	5	2.5	0
1996—San Diego NFL		15	15	110	28	7.0	2	18	9.0	0
1997—San Diego NFL		15	15	84	13	7.0	2	33	16.5	0
1998—San Diego NFL		16	16	92	23	3.5	0	0	0.0	0
1999—San Diego NFL		14	14	75	24	3.5	1	16	16.0	0
2000—San Diego NFL		16	16	103	20	3.5	2	2	1.0	0
2001—San Diego NFL		16	16	84	11	1.0	1	2	2.0	0
2002—San Diego NFL		13	13	60	24	1.5	1	25	25.0	0
2003—Miami NFL		15	15	66	30	3.0	0	0	0.0	0
2004—Miami NFL		8	8	31	26	1.0	0	0	0.0	0
Pro totals (15 years)		223	222	1299	335	51.0	15	210	14.0	0

SEIDMAN, MIKE   TE   PANTHERS

PERSONAL: Born February 11, 1981, in Westlake, Calif. ... 6-4/261. ... Full name: Michael H. Seidman.
HIGH SCHOOL: Westlake (Calif.).
COLLEGE: UCLA.
TRANSACTIONS/CAREER NOTES: Selected by Carolina Panthers in third round (76th pick overall) of 2003 NFL draft. ... Signed by Panthers (July 26, 2003). ... On injured reserve with knee injury (December 2, 2003-remainder of season).
SINGLE GAME HIGHS (regular season): Receptions—2 (January 2, 2005, vs. New Orleans); yards—34 (January 2, 2005, vs. New Orleans); and touchdown receptions—1 (December 26, 2004, vs. Tampa Bay).

				RECEIVING				KICKOFF RETURNS				TOTALS		
Year Team		G	GS	No.	Yds.	Avg.	TD	No.	Yds.	Avg.	TD	TD	2pt.	Pts.	Fum.
2003—Carolina NFL		12	5	5	35	7.0	0	2	24	12.0	0	0	0	0	0
2004—Carolina NFL		16	6	13	123	9.5	2	2	20	10.0	0	2	1	14	0
Pro totals (2 years)		28	11	18	158	8.8	2	4	44	11.0	0	2	1	14	0

SEIGLER, RICHARD   LB   49ERS

PERSONAL: Born October 19, 1980, in Las Vegas, Nev. ... 6-2/238. ... Full name: Richard Joseph Seigler.
HIGH SCHOOL: Chaparral (Las Vegas, Nev.).
COLLEGE: Oregon State.

S

Year Team	G	GS	TOTALS Tk.	Ast.	Sks.	INTERCEPTIONS No.	Yds.	Avg.	TD
2004—San Francisco NFL	7	0	0	1	0.0	0	0	0.0	0

SELLERS, MIKE   FB   REDSKINS

PERSONAL: Born July 21, 1975, in Lacy, Wash. ... 6-3/260.
HIGH SCHOOL: North Thurston (Lacey, Wash.).
JUNIOR COLLEGE: Walla Walla Community College.
COLLEGE: None.
TRANSACTIONS/CAREER NOTES: Signed by Edmonton Eskimos of CFL (March 21, 1995). ... Tranferred by Eskimos to reserve list (August 23, 1995). ... Transferred by Eskimos to injured list (October 12, 1995). ... Transferred by Eskimos to active roster (December 18, 1995). ... Signed as non-drafted free agent by Washington Redskins (February 11, 1998). ... Granted free agency (March 2, 2001). ... Signed by Cleveland Browns (March 15, 2001). ... Released by Browns (November 27, 2001). ... Signed by Winnipeg Blue Bombers of CFL (May 7, 2002). ... Granted unconditional free agency (March 2, 2005). ... Signed by Redskins (March 7, 2005).
SINGLE GAME HIGHS (regular season): Attempts—1 (September 24, 2000, vs. New York Giants); yards—2 (September 24, 2000, vs. New York Giants); and rushing touchdowns—0; receptions—3 (December 27, 1998, vs. Dallas); yards—18 (December 27, 1998, vs. Dallas); and touchdown receptions—0.

Year Team	G	GS	RECEIVING No.	Yds.	Avg.	TD	KICKOFF RETURNS No.	Yds.	Avg.	TD	TOTALS TD	2pt.	Pts.	Fum.
1996—Edmonton CFL	17	...	...	...	0.0	...	...	...	0.0	...	...	...	...	...
1997—Edmonton CFL	16	...	...	...	0.0	...	...	...	0.0	...	...	...	...	...
1998—Washington NFL	14	1	3	18	6.0	0	2	33	16.5	0	0	0	0	0
1999—Washington NFL	16	2	7	105	15.0	2	3	32	10.7	0	2	0	12	1
2000—Washington NFL	14	6	8	78	9.8	2	3	32	10.7	0	2	0	12	0
2001—Cleveland NFL	9	7	7	73	10.4	2	4	75	18.8	0	2	0	12	0
2004—Washington NFL	16	1	1	14	14.0	0	4	56	14.0	0	0	0	0	0
CFL totals (2 years)	33	...	...	...	0.0	...	...	...	0.0	...	...	...	...	...
NFL totals (5 years)	69	17	26	288	11.1	6	16	228	14.3	0	6	0	36	1
Pro totals (7 years)	102	...	...	...	11.1	...	...	...	14.3	...	...	...	...	...

SEYMOUR, RICHARD   DT   PATRIOTS

PERSONAL: Born October 6, 1979, in Gadsden, S.C. ... 6-6/310.
HIGH SCHOOL: Lower Richland (S.C.).
COLLEGE: Georgia.
TRANSACTIONS/CAREER NOTES: Selected by New England Patriots in first round (sixth pick overall) of 2001 NFL draft. ... Signed by Patriots (July 24, 2001).
CHAMPIONSHIP GAME EXPERIENCE: Played in AFC championship game (2001 and 2003 seasons). ... Member of Patriots for AFC championship game (2004 season); inactive. ... Member of Super Bowl championship team (2001, 2003 and 2004 seasons).
HONORS: Named defensive tackle on THE SPORTING NEWS college All-America second team (2000). ... Named defensive tackle on THE SPORTING NEWS NFL All-Pro team (2003 and 2004). ... Played in Pro Bowl (2002 and 2003 seasons). ... Named to play in Pro Bowl (2004 season); replaced by John Henderson due to injury.

Year Team	G	GS	TOTALS Tk.	Ast.	Sks.	INTERCEPTIONS No.	Yds.	Avg.	TD
2001—New England NFL	13	10	25	20	3.0	0	0	0.0	0
2002—New England NFL	16	16	33	23	5.5	1	6	6.0	0
2003—New England NFL	15	14	34	22	8.0	0	0	0.0	0
2004—New England NFL	15	15	25	15	5.0	0	0	0.0	0
Pro totals (4 years)	59	55	117	80	21.5	1	6	6.0	0

SHABAZZ, SIDDEEQ   S

PERSONAL: Born February 5, 1981, in Frankfurt, Germany. ... 5-11/200. ... Full name: Siddeeq Muneer Shabazz.
HIGH SCHOOL: Gadsden (Anthony, N.M.).
COLLEGE: New Mexico State.
TRANSACTIONS/CAREER NOTES: Selected by Oakland Raiders in seventh round (246th pick overall) of 2003 NFL draft. ... Signed by Raiders (July 24, 2003). ... Claimed on waivers by Atlanta Falcons (October 2, 2003). ... Claimed on waivers by Cincinnati Bengals (April 28, 2005). ... Released by Bengals (May 27, 2005).
CHAMPIONSHIP GAME EXPERIENCE: Played in NFC championship game (2004 season).

Year Team	G	GS	TOTALS Tk.	Ast.	Sks.	INTERCEPTIONS No.	Yds.	Avg.	TD
2003—Oakland NFL	4	0	0	0	0.0	0	0	0.0	0
—Atlanta NFL	7	0	1	0	0.0	0	0	0.0	0
2004—Atlanta NFL	15	0	1	0	0.0	0	0	0.0	0
Pro totals (2 years)	26	0	2	0	0.0	0	0	0.0	0

SHAFFER, KEVIN   T

PERSONAL: Born March 2, 1980, in Salisbury, Md. ... 6-5/290.
HIGH SCHOOL: Conestoga (Md.).
COLLEGE: Tulsa.

TRANSACTIONS/CAREER NOTES: Selected by Atlanta Falcons in seventh round (244th pick overall) of 2002 NFL draft. ... Signed by Falcons (June 14, 2002). ... Granted free agency (March 2, 2005).
PLAYING EXPERIENCE: Atlanta NFL, 2002-2004. ... Games/Games started: 2002 (6/0), 2003 (16/8), 2004 (15/15). Total: 37/23.

SHANLE, SCOTT — LB — COWBOYS

PERSONAL: Born November 23, 1979, in Genoa, Neb. ... 6-2/237.
HIGH SCHOOL: St. Edward (Neb.).
COLLEGE: Nebraska.
TRANSACTIONS/CAREER NOTES: Selected by St. Louis Rams in seventh round (251st pick overall) of 2003 NFL draft. ... Signed by Rams (July 23, 2003). ... On suspended list for violating league substance abuse policy (September 26-October 27, 2003). ... Claimed on waivers by Dallas Cowboys (December 10, 2003).

			TOTALS			INTERCEPTIONS			
Year Team	G	GS	Tk.	Ast.	Sks.	No.	Yds.	Avg.	TD
2003—St. Louis NFL	5	0	0	0	0.0	0	0	0.0	0
2004—Dallas NFL	16	3	17	6	0.0	0	0	0.0	0
Pro totals (2 years)	21	3	17	6	0.0	0	0	0.0	0

SHARPER, DARREN — S — VIKINGS

PERSONAL: Born November 3, 1975, in Richmond, Va. ... 6-2/210. ... Full name: Darren Mallory Sharper. ... Brother of Jamie Sharper, linebacker, Seattle Seahawks.
HIGH SCHOOL: Hermitage (Richmond, Va.).
COLLEGE: William & Mary.
TRANSACTIONS/CAREER NOTES: Selected by Green Bay Packers in second round (60th pick overall) of 1997 NFL draft. ... Signed by Packers (July 11, 1997). ... Released by Packers (March 10, 2005). ... Signed by Minnesota Vikings (March 12, 2005).
CHAMPIONSHIP GAME EXPERIENCE: Played in NFC championship game (1997 season). ... Played in Super Bowl 32 (1997 season).
HONORS: Named safety on THE SPORTING NEWS NFL All-Pro team (2000 and 2002). ... Played in Pro Bowl (2000 and 2002 seasons).

			TOTALS			INTERCEPTIONS				PUNT RETURNS				TOTALS			
Year Team	G	GS	Tk.	Ast.	Sks.	No.	Yds.	Avg.	TD	No.	Yds.	Avg.	TD	TD	2pt.	Pts.	Fum.
1997—Green Bay NFL	14	0	12	1	0.0	2	70	35.0	∞2	7	32	4.6	0	3	0	18	1
1998—Green Bay NFL	16	16	53	20	0.0	0	0	0.0	0	0	0	0.0	0	0	0	0	0
1999—Green Bay NFL	16	16	84	29	1.0	3	12	4.0	0	0	0	0.0	0	0	0	0	0
2000—Green Bay NFL	16	16	72	20	1.0	*9	109	12.1	0	0	0	0.0	0	0	0	0	0
2001—Green Bay NFL	16	16	71	24	2.0	6	78	13.0	0	1	18	18.0	0	0	0	0	1
2002—Green Bay NFL	13	13	51	17	0.0	7	*233	33.3	1	1	0	0.0	0	1	0	6	0
2003—Green Bay NFL	15	15	71	13	2.0	5	78	15.6	0	0	0	0.0	0	0	0	0	0
2004—Green Bay NFL	15	13	59	13	0.0	4	97	24.3	†2	1	9	9.0	0	3	0	18	0
Pro totals (8 years)	121	105	473	137	6.0	36	677	18.8	5	10	59	5.9	0	7	0	42	2

SHARPER, JAMIE — LB — SEAHAWKS

PERSONAL: Born November 23, 1974, in Richmond, Va. ... 6-3/239. ... Full name: Harry Jamie Sharper Jr. ... Brother of Darren Sharper, safety, Minnesota Vikings.
HIGH SCHOOL: Hermitage (Richmond, Va.).
COLLEGE: Virginia.
TRANSACTIONS/CAREER NOTES: Selected by Baltimore Ravens in second round (34th pick overall) of 1997 NFL draft. ... Signed by Ravens (July 23, 1997). ... Granted free agency (February 11, 2000). ... Re-signed by Ravens (June 16, 2000). ... Granted unconditional free agency (March 2, 2001). ... Re-signed by Ravens (April 3, 2001). ... Selected by Houston Texans from Ravens in NFL expansion draft (February 18, 2002). ... Released by Texans (April 1, 2005). ... Signed by Seattle Seahawks (April 21, 2005).
CHAMPIONSHIP GAME EXPERIENCE: Played in AFC championship game (2000 season). ... Member of Super Bowl championship team (2000 season).

			TOTALS			INTERCEPTIONS			
Year Team	G	GS	Tk.	Ast.	Sks.	No.	Yds.	Avg.	TD
1997—Baltimore NFL	16	15	52	14	3.0	1	4	4.0	0
1998—Baltimore NFL	16	16	45	9	1.0	0	0	0.0	0
1999—Baltimore NFL	16	16	69	17	4.0	0	0	0.0	0
2000—Baltimore NFL	16	16	59	13	0.0	1	45	45.0	0
2001—Baltimore NFL	16	16	77	31	6.0	0	0	0.0	0
2002—Houston NFL	16	16	95	42	5.5	0	0	0.0	0
2003—Houston NFL	16	16	107	59	4.0	0	0	0.0	0
2004—Houston NFL	16	16	98	41	2.0	0	0	0.0	0
Pro totals (8 years)	128	127	602	226	25.5	2	49	24.5	0

SHAW, BOBBY — WR

PERSONAL: Born April 23, 1975, in San Francisco, Calif. ... 6-1/185.
HIGH SCHOOL: Galileo (San Francisco).
COLLEGE: California.
TRANSACTIONS/CAREER NOTES: Selected by Seattle Seahawks in sixth round (169th pick overall) of 1998 NFL draft. ... Signed by Seahawks (June 5, 1998). ... Released by Seahawks (August 30, 1998). ... Re-signed by Seahawks to practice squad (August 31, 1998). ... Activated (November 4, 1998); did not play. ... Released by Seahawks (November 18, 1998). ... Signed by Pittsburgh Steelers (November 20, 1998). ... Granted free agency (March 2, 2001). ... Re-signed by Steelers (March 2, 2001). ... Granted unconditional free agency (March 1, 2002). ... Signed by Jacksonville Jaguars (April 3, 2002). ... Granted unconditional free agency (February 28, 2003). ... Signed by Buffalo Bills (March 17, 2003). ... Released by Bills (October 13, 2004). ... Signed by San Diego Chargers (October 19, 2004). ... Granted unconditional free agency (March 2, 2005).

CHAMPIONSHIP GAME EXPERIENCE: Played in AFC championship game (2001 season).
HONORS: Named wide receiver on THE SPORTING NEWS college All-America first team (1997).
SINGLE GAME HIGHS (regular season): Receptions—8 (September 28, 2003, vs. Philadelphia); yards—131 (January 2, 2000, vs. Tennessee); and touchdown receptions—1 (December 14, 2003, vs. Tennessee).
STATISTICAL PLATEAUS: 100-yard receiving games: 1999 (1), 2001 (1). Total: 2.

			RUSHING				RECEIVING				PUNT RETURNS				KICKOFF RETURNS				TOTALS		
Year Team	G	GS	Att.	Yds.	Avg.	TD	No.	Yds.	Avg.	TD	No.	Yds.	Avg.	TD	No.	Yds.	Avg.	TD	TD	2pt.	Pts.
1998—Sea. NFL	Did not play.																				
1999—Pit. NFL	13	1	0	0	0.0	0	28	387	13.8	3	4	53	13.3	0	0	0	0.0	0	3	0	18
2000—Pit. NFL	16	0	0	0	0.0	0	40	672	16.8	4	2	17	8.5	0	0	-8	0.0	0	4	0	24
2001—Pit. NFL	16	0	0	0	0.0	0	24	409	17.0	2	4	45	11.3	0	1	2	2.0	0	2	0	12
2002—Jac. NFL	16	10	0	0	0.0	0	44	525	11.9	1	25	310	12.4	1	3	53	17.7	0	2	0	12
2003—Buf. NFL	16	7	0	0	0.0	0	56	732	13.1	4	0	0	0.0	0	0	0	0.0	0	4	0	24
2004—Buf. NFL	4	0	0	0	0.0	0	5	59	11.8	0	0	0	0.0	0	0	0	0.0	0	0	0	0
—S.D. NFL	7	0	1	1	1.0	0	0	0	0.0	0	0	0	0.0	0	0	0	0.0	0	0	0	0
Pro totals (6 years)	88	18	1	1	1.0	0	197	2784	14.1	14	35	425	12.1	1	4	47	11.8	0	15	0	90

SHAW, JOSH   DT   DOLPHINS

PERSONAL: Born September 7, 1979, in Fort Lauderdale, Fla. ... 6-2/290.
HIGH SCHOOL: Dillard (Fort Lauderdale, Fla.).
COLLEGE: Michigan State.
TRANSACTIONS/CAREER NOTES: Selected by San Francisco 49ers in fifth round (172nd pick overall) of 2002 NFL draft. ... Signed by 49ers (July 26, 2002). ... On non-football injury list with knee injury (August 27-November 12, 2002). ... Signed by San Francisco 49ers (February 4, 2004). ... Released by 49ers (September 7, 2004). ... Signed by Miami Dolphins to practice squad (October 20, 2004). ... Activated (November 19, 2004).

			TOTALS			INTERCEPTIONS			
Year Team	G	GS	Tk.	Ast.	Sks.	No.	Yds.	Avg.	TD
2002—Miami NFL	3	0	0	0	1.0	0	0	0.0	0
2004—Miami NFL	5	0	3	1	0.0	0	0	0.0	0
Pro totals (2 years)	8	0	3	1	1.0	0	0	0.0	0

SHAW, TERRANCE   CB

PERSONAL: Born January 11, 1973, in Marshall, Texas. ... 6-0/200. ... Full name: Terrance Bernard Shaw.
HIGH SCHOOL: Marshall (Texas).
COLLEGE: Stephen F. Austin.
TRANSACTIONS/CAREER NOTES: Selected by San Diego Chargers in second round (34th pick overall) of 1995 NFL draft. ... Signed by Chargers (June 15, 1995). ... Released by Chargers (March 21, 2000). ... Signed by Miami Dolphins (June 13, 2000). ... Granted unconditional free agency (March 2, 2001). ... Signed by New England Patriots (March 22, 2001). ... Released by Patriots (February 25, 2002). ... Signed by Oakland Raiders (March 21, 2002). ... Granted unconditional free agency (March 3, 2004). ... Signed by Carolina Panthers (April 22, 2004). ... Released by Panthers (September 5, 2004). ... Signed by Minnesota Vikings (September 14, 2004). ... Released by Vikings (February 22, 2005).
CHAMPIONSHIP GAME EXPERIENCE: Played in AFC championship game (2001 and 2002 seasons). ... Member of Super Bowl championship team (2001 season). ... Played in Super Bowl 37 (2002 season).

			TOTALS			INTERCEPTIONS			
Year Team	G	GS	Tk.	Ast.	Sks.	No.	Yds.	Avg.	TD
1995—San Diego NFL	16	14	53	5	0.0	1	31	31.0	0
1996—San Diego NFL	16	16	72	13	0.0	3	78	26.0	0
1997—San Diego NFL	16	16	66	5	0.0	1	11	11.0	0
1998—San Diego NFL	13	13	35	5	0.0	2	0	0.0	0
1999—San Diego NFL	8	8	21	3	0.0	0	0	0.0	0
2000—Miami NFL	11	3	15	3	0.0	1	0	0.0	0
2001—New England NFL	13	2	19	2	0.0	0	0	0.0	0
2002—Oakland NFL	16	7	30	4	0.0	2	-2	-1.0	0
2003—Oakland NFL	16	8	52	12	0.0	0	0	0.0	0
2004—Minnesota NFL	15	4	27	4	0.0	1	22	22.0	0
Pro totals (10 years)	140	91	390	56	0.0	11	140	12.7	0

SHEA, AARON   TE   BROWNS

PERSONAL: Born December 5, 1976, in Ottawa, Ill. ... 6-3/255. ... Full name: Aaron T. Shea.
HIGH SCHOOL: Ottawa (Ill.).
COLLEGE: Michigan.
TRANSACTIONS/CAREER NOTES: Selected by Cleveland Browns in fourth round (110th pick overall) of 2000 NFL draft. ... Signed by Browns (July 13, 2000). ... On injured reserve with shoulder injury (December 27, 2001-remainder of season). ... On injured reserve with ankle injury (November 19, 2002-remainder of season). ... Granted free agency (February 28, 2003). ... Re-signed by Browns (April 25, 2003). ... On injured reserve with arm injury (October 7, 2003-remainder of season).
SINGLE GAME HIGHS (regular season): Receptions—6 (October 24, 2004, vs. Philadelphia); yards—76 (October 15, 2000, vs. Denver); and touchdown receptions—1 (November 21, 2004, vs. New York Jets).

			RECEIVING				TOTALS			
Year Team	G	GS	No.	Yds.	Avg.	TD	TD	2pt.	Pts.	Fum.
2000—Cleveland NFL	15	8	30	302	10.1	2	2	0	12	1
2001—Cleveland NFL	12	5	14	86	6.1	0	0	0	0	0
2002—Cleveland NFL	7	3	7	49	7.0	0	0	0	0	0
2003—Cleveland NFL	4	2	2	9	4.5	0	0	0	0	0
2004—Cleveland NFL	15	8	26	252	9.7	4	4	0	24	0
Pro totals (5 years)	53	26	79	698	8.8	6	6	0	36	1

SHELTON, DAIMON   FB   BILLS

PERSONAL: Born September 15, 1972, in Duarte, Calif. ... 6-0/262.
HIGH SCHOOL: Duarte (Calif.).
JUNIOR COLLEGE: Fresno (Calif.) City College.
COLLEGE: Sacramento State.
TRANSACTIONS/CAREER NOTES: Selected by Jacksonville Jaguars in sixth round (184th pick overall) of 1997 NFL draft. ... Signed by Jaguars (May 23, 1997). ... Granted free agency (February 11, 2000). ... Re-signed by Jaguars (March 21, 2000). ... Granted unconditional free agency (March 2, 2001). ... Signed by Chicago Bears (May 23, 2001). ... Granted unconditional free agency (March 1, 2002). ... Re-signed by Bears (April 2, 2002). ... On suspended list for violating league substance abuse policy (September 1-27, 2002). ... Waived by Bears (August 31, 2003). ... Signed by Buffalo Bills (January 28, 2004).
CHAMPIONSHIP GAME EXPERIENCE: Played in AFC championship game (1999 season).
SINGLE GAME HIGHS (regular season): Attempts—13 (October 18, 1998, vs. Buffalo); yards —44 (October 18, 1998, vs. Buffalo); and rushing touchdowns—1 (November 1, 1998, vs. Baltimore).

			RUSHING				RECEIVING				TOTALS		
Year Team	G	GS	Att.	Yds.	Avg.	TD	No.	Yds.	Avg.	TD	TD	2pt.	Pts.	Fum.
1997—Jacksonville NFL	13	0	6	4	0.7	0	0	0	0.0	0	0	0	0	1
1998—Jacksonville NFL	14	8	30	95	3.2	1	10	79	7.9	0	1	0	6	0
1999—Jacksonville NFL	16	9	1	2	2.0	0	12	87	7.3	0	0	0	0	0
2000—Jacksonville NFL	16	9	2	3	1.5	0	4	48	12.0	0	0	0	0	0
2001—Chicago NFL	16	9	0	0	0.0	0	12	76	6.3	1	1	0	6	2
2002—Chicago NFL	12	8	0	0	0.0	0	7	34	4.9	0	0	0	0	0
2003—Chicago NFL	Did not play.													
2004—Buffalo NFL	16	12	0	0	0.0	0	17	114	6.7	0	0	0	0	0
Pro totals (7 years)	103	55	39	104	2.7	1	62	438	7.1	1	2	0	12	3

SHELTON, L.J.   T

PERSONAL: Born March 21, 1976, in Rochester Hills, Mich. ... 6-6/335. ... Full name: Lonnie Jewel Shelton. ... Son of Lonnie Shelton, forward with New York Knicks (1976-77 and 1977-78), Seattle SuperSonics (1978-79 through 1982-83) and Cleveland Cavaliers (1983-84 through 1985-86).
HIGH SCHOOL: Rochester (Rochester Hills, Mich.).
COLLEGE: Eastern Michigan.
TRANSACTIONS/CAREER NOTES: Selected by Arizona Cardinals in first round (21st pick overall) of 1999 NFL draft. ... Signed by Cardinals (September 24, 1999). ... On injured reserve with knee injury (December 14, 2004-remainder of season). ... Released by Cardinals (May 18, 2005).
PLAYING EXPERIENCE: Arizona NFL, 1999-2004. ... Games/Games started: 1999 (9/7), 2000 (14/14), 2001 (16/16), 2002 (16/16), 2003 (15/15), 2004 (12/9). Total: 82/77.

SHEPPARD, LITO   CB   EAGLES

PERSONAL: Born April 8, 1981, in Jacksonville, Fla. ... 5-10/194. ... Full name: Lito Decorian Sheppard.
HIGH SCHOOL: Raines (Jacksonville).
COLLEGE: Florida.
TRANSACTIONS/CAREER NOTES: Selected after junior season by Philadelphia Eagles in first round (26th pick overall) of 2002 NFL draft. ... Signed by Eagles (July 24, 2002).
CHAMPIONSHIP GAME EXPERIENCE: Member of Eagles for NFC championship game (2002 season); inactive. ... Played in NFC championship game (2003 and 2004 seasons). ... Played in Super Bowl 39 (2004 season).
HONORS: Named cornerback on THE SPORTING NEWS college All-America second team (2000 and 2001). ... Played in Pro Bowl (2004 season).

			TOTALS			INTERCEPTIONS				PUNT RETURNS				KICKOFF RETURNS				TOTALS		
Year Team	G	GS	Tk.	Ast.	Sks.	No.	Yds.	Avg.	TD	No.	Yds.	Avg.	TD	No.	Yds.	Avg.	TD	TD	2pt.	Pts.	Fum.
2002—Phi. NFL	12	0	5	2	0.0	0	0	0.0	0	0	0	0.0	0	0	0	0.0	0	0	0	0	0
2003—Phi. NFL	16	9	44	6	0.0	1	34	34.0	0	4	15	3.8	0	0	0	0.0	0	0	0	0	0
2004—Phi. NFL	15	15	52	4	1.0	5	172	34.4	†2	2	42	21.0	0	0	0	0.0	0	2	0	12	0
Pro totals (3 years)	43	24	101	12	1.0	6	206	34.3	2	6	57	9.5	0	0	0	0.0	0	2	0	12	0

SHIANCOE, VISANTHE   TE   GIANTS

PERSONAL: Born June 18, 1980, in Laurel, Md. ... 6-4/250. ... Full name: Vishante Shiancoe.
HIGH SCHOOL: Blair (Laurel, Md.).
COLLEGE: Morgan State.
TRANSACTIONS/CAREER NOTES: Selected by New York Giants in third round (91st pick overall) of 2003 NFL draft. ... Signed by Giants (July 24, 2003).
SINGLE GAME HIGHS (regular season): Receptions—3 (December 21, 2003, vs. Dallas); yards—20 (December 21, 2003, vs. Dallas); and touchdown receptions—1 (January 2, 2005, vs. Dallas).

			RECEIVING				TOTALS		
Year Team	G	GS	No.	Yds.	Avg.	TD	TD	2pt.	Pts.	Fum.
2003—New York Giants NFL	16	7	10	56	5.6	2	2	0	12	0
2004—New York Giants NFL	16	7	5	25	5.0	1	1	0	6	0
Pro totals (2 years)	32	14	15	81	5.4	3	3	0	18	0

SHIELDS, WILL　　　　　　　　　G　　　　　　　　　CHIEFS

PERSONAL: Born September 15, 1971, in Fort Riley, Kan. ... 6-3/320. ... Full name: Will Herthie Shields.
HIGH SCHOOL: Lawton (Okla.).
COLLEGE: Nebraska.
TRANSACTIONS/CAREER NOTES: Selected by Kansas City Chiefs in the third round (74th pick overall) of 1993 NFL draft. ... Signed by Chiefs (May 3, 1993). ... Designated by Chiefs as franchise player (February 11, 2000).
PLAYING EXPERIENCE: Kansas City NFL, 1993-2004. ... Games/Games started: 1993 (16/15), 1994 (16/16), 1995 (16/16), 1996 (16/16), 1997 (16/16), 1998 (16/16), 1999 (16/16), 2000 (16/16), 2001 (16/16), 2002 (16/16), 2003 (16/16), 2004 (16/16). Total: 192/191.
CHAMPIONSHIP GAME EXPERIENCE: Played in AFC championship game (1993 season).
HONORS: Named guard on THE SPORTING NEWS college All-America second team (1991). ... Named guard on THE SPORTING NEWS college All-America first team (1992). ... Named guard on THE SPORTING NEWS NFL All-Pro team (1999, 2002 and 2003). ... Played in Pro Bowl (1995-2004 seasons).

SHIPP, MARCEL　　　　　　　　RB　　　　　　　　CARDINALS

PERSONAL: Born August 8, 1978, in Paterson, N.J. ... 5-11/230.
HIGH SCHOOL: Milford (Conn.), then Passaic (N.J.).
COLLEGE: Massachusetts.
TRANSACTIONS/CAREER NOTES: Signed as non-drafted free agent by Arizona Cardinals (April 23, 2001). ... On injured reserve with leg injury (September 1, 2004-entire season).
SINGLE GAME HIGHS (regular season): Attempts—35 (October 26, 2003, vs. San Francisco); yards—165 (October 26, 2003, vs. San Francisco); and rushing touchdowns—2 (December 15, 2002, vs. St. Louis).
STATISTICAL PLATEAUS: 100-yard rushing games: 2002 (1), 2003 (2). Total: 3.

			RUSHING				RECEIVING				KICKOFF RETURNS				TOTALS			
Year—Team	G	GS	Att.	Yds.	Avg.	TD	No.	Yds.	Avg.	TD	No.	Yds.	Avg.	TD	TD	2pt.	Pts.	Fum.
2001—Arizona NFL	11	0	0	0	0.0	0	0	0	0.0	0	6	118	19.7	0	0	0	0	0
2002—Arizona NFL	15	6	188	834	4.4	6	38	413	10.9	3	6	120	20.0	0	9	0	54	4
2003—Arizona NFL	16	11	228	830	3.6	0	30	184	6.1	0	0	0	0.0	0	0	0	0	3
2004—Arizona NFL	Did not play.																	
Pro totals (3 years)	42	17	416	1664	4.0	6	68	597	8.8	3	12	238	19.8	0	9	0	54	7

SHIVERS, JASON　　　　　　　DB　　　　　　　　BEARS

PERSONAL: Born November 4, 1982, in Phoenix, Ariz. ... 6-0/201.
HIGH SCHOOL: South Mountain (Phoenix, Ariz.).
COLLEGE: Arizona State.
TRANSACTIONS/CAREER NOTES: Selected after junior season by St. Louis Rams in fifth round (134th pick overall) of 2004 NFL draft. ... Signed by Rams (June 10, 2004). ... Released by Rams (September 16, 2004). ... Re-signed by Rams to practice squad (September 18, 2004). ... Claimed on waivers by Chicago Bears (December 14, 2004).
HONORS: Named free safety on THE SPORTING NEWS Freshman All-America first team (2001).

			TOTALS			INTERCEPTIONS			
Year　Team	G	GS	Tk.	Ast.	Sks.	No.	Yds.	Avg.	TD
2004—Chicago NFL	1	0	0	0	0.0	0	0	0.0	0

SHOATE, JEFF　　　　　　　　DB　　　　　　　　BRONCOS

PERSONAL: Born March 23, 1981, in San Diego, Calif. ... 5-10/189.
HIGH SCHOOL: Serra (San Diego, Calif.).
COLLEGE: San Diego State.
TRANSACTIONS/CAREER NOTES: Selected by Denver Broncos in fifth round (152nd pick overall) of 2004 NFL draft. ... Signed by Broncos (July 27, 2004).

			TOTALS			INTERCEPTIONS			
Year　Team	G	GS	Tk.	Ast.	Sks.	No.	Yds.	Avg.	TD
2004—Denver NFL	7	0	0	0	0.0	0	0	0.0	0

SHOCKEY, JEREMY　　　　　　TE　　　　　　　　GIANTS

PERSONAL: Born August 18, 1980, in Ada, Okla. ... 6-5/253. ... Full name: Jeremy Charles Shockey.
HIGH SCHOOL: Ada (Okla.).
JUNIOR COLLEGE: Northeastern A&M Community College (Okla.).
COLLEGE: Miami (Fla.).
TRANSACTIONS/CAREER NOTES: Selected after junior season by New York Giants in first round (14th pick overall) of 2002 NFL draft. ... Signed by Giants (July 29, 2002).
HONORS: Played in Pro Bowl (2002 season). ... Named to play in Pro Bowl (2003 season); replaced by Bubba Franks due to injury.
SINGLE GAME HIGHS (regular season): Receptions—11 (October 5, 2003, vs. Miami); yards—116 (December 22, 2002, vs. Indianapolis); and touchdown receptions—1 (December 18, 2004, vs. Pittsburgh).
STATISTICAL PLATEAUS: 100-yard receiving games: 2002 (2), 2003 (1). Total: 3.

			RECEIVING				TOTALS			
Year　Team	G	GS	No.	Yds.	Avg.	TD	TD	2pt.	Pts.	Fum.
2002—New York Giants NFL	15	14	74	894	12.1	2	2	0	12	3
2003—New York Giants NFL	9	9	48	535	11.1	2	2	0	12	1
2004—New York Giants NFL	15	15	61	666	10.9	6	6	0	36	1
Pro totals (3 years)	39	38	183	2095	11.4	10	10	0	60	5

S

SHORT, BRANDON LB PANTHERS

PERSONAL: Born July 11, 1977, in McKeesport, Pa. ... 6-3/253. ... Full name: Brandon Darnell Short.
HIGH SCHOOL: McKeesport (Pa.).
COLLEGE: Penn State.
TRANSACTIONS/CAREER NOTES: Selected by New York Giants in fourth round (105th pick overall) of 2000 NFL draft. ... Signed by Giants (July 25, 2000). ... Granted unconditional free agency (March 3, 2004). ... Signed by Carolina Panthers (April 2, 2004).
CHAMPIONSHIP GAME EXPERIENCE: Played in NFC championship game (2000 season). ... Played in Super Bowl 35 (2000 season).
HONORS: Named linebacker on THE SPORTING NEWS college All-America second team (1999).

Year Team	G	GS	TOTALS Tk.	Ast.	Sks.	INTERCEPTIONS No.	Yds.	Avg.	TD
2000—New York Giants NFL	11	0	3	0	0.0	0	0	0.0	0
2001—New York Giants NFL	16	16	45	15	1.0	1	21	21.0	0
2002—New York Giants NFL	16	15	62	25	3.0	1	32	32.0	0
2003—New York Giants NFL	16	12	49	26	3.0	0	0	0.0	0
2004—Carolina NFL	16	2	29	11	0.0	0	0	0.0	0
Pro totals (5 years)	75	45	188	77	7.0	2	53	26.5	0

SHORT, JASON LB EAGLES

PERSONAL: Born July 15, 1978, in Painesville, Ohio. ... 6-4/254. ... Full name: Jason Michael Short.
HIGH SCHOOL: Riverside (Painesville, Ohio).
COLLEGE: Eastern Michigan.
TRANSACTIONS/CAREER NOTES: Signed as non-drafted free agent by Philadelphia Eagles (July 10, 2003). ... Released by Eagles (August 31, 2003). ... Re-signed by Eagles to practice squad (December 23, 2003). ... Activated (February 6, 2004). ... On injured reserve with leg injury (December 14, 2004-remainder of season).

Year Team	G	GS	TOTALS Tk.	Ast.	Sks.	INTERCEPTIONS No.	Yds.	Avg.	TD
2004—Philadelphia NFL	11	0	0	0	0.0	0	0	0.0	0

SIAVII, JUNIOR DT CHIEFS

PERSONAL: Born November 14, 1978, in Pago Pago, American Samoa. ... 6-5/336. ... Full name: Saousoalii Poe Siavii Jr.
HIGH SCHOOL: Tafune (Pago Pago, American Samoa).
JUNIOR COLLEGE: Dixie College (Utah), then Butte College (Calif.).
COLLEGE: Oregon.
TRANSACTIONS/CAREER NOTES: Selected by Kansas City Chiefs in second round (36th pick overall) of 2004 NFL draft. ... Signed by Chiefs (July 21, 2004).

Year Team	G	GS	TOTALS Tk.	Ast.	Sks.
2004—Kansas City NFL	12	0	8	1	1.0

SIDNEY, DAINON CB

PERSONAL: Born May 30, 1975, in Atlanta, Ga. ... 6-0/197. ... Full name: Dainon Tarquinius Sidney. ... Name pronounced: DAY-nun.
HIGH SCHOOL: Riverdale (Ga.).
COLLEGE: Alabama-Birmingham.
TRANSACTIONS/CAREER NOTES: Selected by Tennessee Oilers in third round (77th pick overall) of 1998 NFL draft. ... Signed by Oilers (July 21, 1998). ... Oilers franchise renamed Tennessee Titans for 1999 season (December 26, 1998). ... Granted free agency (March 2, 2001). ... On injured reserve with knee injury (September 26, 2001-remainder of season). ... Granted unconditional free agency (March 1, 2002). ... Re-signed by Titans (March 12, 2002). ... Granted unconditional free agency (February 28, 2003). ... Signed by Buffalo Bills (April 10, 2003). ... Granted unconditional free agency (March 3, 2004). ... Signed by Detroit Lions (March 8, 2004). ... On injured reserve with Achilles injury (August 18, 2004-entire season). ... Granted unconditional free agency (March 2, 2005).
CHAMPIONSHIP GAME EXPERIENCE: Played in AFC championship game (1999 and 2002 seasons). ... Played in Super Bowl 34 (1999 season).

Year Team	G	GS	TOTALS Tk.	Ast.	Sks.	INTERCEPTIONS No.	Yds.	Avg.	TD
1998—Tennessee NFL	16	1	15	1	0.0	0	0	0.0	0
1999—Tennessee NFL	16	2	33	5	0.0	3	12	4.0	0
2000—Tennessee NFL	11	2	16	3	0.0	3	19	6.3	0
2001—Tennessee NFL	1	1	0	0	0.0	0	0	0.0	0
2002—Tennessee NFL	4	0	0	0	0.0	0	0	0.0	0
2003—Buffalo NFL	2	0	2	0	0.0	0	0	0.0	0
2004—Detroit NFL	Did not play.								
Pro totals (6 years)	50	6	66	9	0.0	6	31	5.2	0

SIMMONS, ANTHONY LB

PERSONAL: Born June 20, 1976, in Spartanburg, S.C. ... 6-0/240.
HIGH SCHOOL: Spartanburg (S.C.).
COLLEGE: Clemson.

TRANSACTIONS/CAREER NOTES: Selected after junior season by Seattle Seahawks in first round (15th pick overall) of 1998 NFL draft. ... Signed by Seahawks (July 18, 1998). ... Granted unconditional free agency (February 28, 2003). ... Re-signed by Seahawks (March 4, 2003). ... On injured reserve with wrist injury (November 19, 2004-remainder of season). ... Released by Seahawks (March 4, 2005).

HONORS: Named inside linebacker on THE SPORTING NEWS college All-America first team (1996 and 1997).

				TOTALS			INTERCEPTIONS			
Year Team	G	GS	Tk.	Ast.	Sks.	No.	Yds.	Avg.	TD
1998—Seattle NFL	12	4	31	10	0.0	1	36	36.0	1
1999—Seattle NFL	16	16	57	35	0.0	0	0	0.0	0
2000—Seattle NFL	16	16	119	28	4.0	2	15	7.5	0
2001—Seattle NFL	16	16	103	20	2.0	0	0	0.0	0
2002—Seattle NFL	7	7	35	11	1.0	2	19	9.5	0
2003—Seattle NFL	13	13	80	20	3.0	3	38	12.7	0
2004—Seattle NFL	7	7	30	12	0.0	1	23	23.0	1
Pro totals (7 years)	87	79	455	136	10.0	9	131	14.6	2

SIMMONS, BRIAN   LB   BENGALS

PERSONAL: Born June 21, 1975, in New Bern, N.C. ... 6-3/244. ... Full name: Brian Eugene Simmons.
HIGH SCHOOL: New Bern (N.C.).
COLLEGE: North Carolina.
TRANSACTIONS/CAREER NOTES: Selected by Cincinnati Bengals in first round (17th pick overall) of 1998 NFL draft. ... Signed by Bengals (July 27, 1998). ... On injured reserve with knee injury (November 9, 2000-remainder of season).
HONORS: Named outside linebacker on THE SPORTING NEWS college All-America second team (1996). ... Named outside linebacker on THE SPORTING NEWS college All-America third team (1997).

				TOTALS			INTERCEPTIONS			
Year Team	G	GS	Tk.	Ast.	Sks.	No.	Yds.	Avg.	TD
1998—Cincinnati NFL	14	12	62	16	3.0	1	18	18.0	0
1999—Cincinnati NFL	16	16	90	20	3.0	0	0	0.0	0
2000—Cincinnati NFL	1	1	7	2	1.0	0	0	0.0	0
2001—Cincinnati NFL	16	16	52	32	6.5	1	5	5.0	0
2002—Cincinnati NFL	16	15	65	21	3.0	1	51	51.0	1
2003—Cincinnati NFL	16	16	73	30	1.5	2	14	7.0	0
2004—Cincinnati NFL	15	15	76	31	1.0	2	61	30.5	1
Pro totals (7 years)	94	91	425	152	19.0	7	149	21.3	2

SIMMONS, JASON   CB   TEXANS

PERSONAL: Born March 30, 1976, in Inglewood, Calif. ... 5-9/199. ... Full name: Jason Lawrence Simmons.
HIGH SCHOOL: Leuzinger (Lawndale, Calif.).
COLLEGE: Arizona State.
TRANSACTIONS/CAREER NOTES: Selected by Pittsburgh Steelers in fifth round (137th pick overall) of 1998 NFL draft. ... Signed by Steelers (July 14, 1998). ... Granted free agency (March 2, 2001). ... Re-signed by Steelers (April 26, 2001). ... Granted unconditional free agency (March 1, 2002). ... Signed by Houston Texans (April 8, 2002). ... Granted unconditional free agency (February 28, 2003). ... Re-signed by Texans (March 21, 2003). ... Granted unconditional free agency (March 3, 2004). ... Re-signed by Texans (March 11, 2004). ... Granted unconditional free agency (March 2, 2005). ... Re-signed by Texans (March 8, 2005).
CHAMPIONSHIP GAME EXPERIENCE: Played in AFC championship game (2001 season).

				TOTALS			INTERCEPTIONS			
Year Team	G	GS	Tk.	Ast.	Sks.	No.	Yds.	Avg.	TD
1998—Pittsburgh NFL	6	0	7	1	0.0	0	0	0.0	0
1999—Pittsburgh NFL	16	0	3	1	0.0	0	0	0.0	0
2000—Pittsburgh NFL	15	0	12	1	0.0	0	0	0.0	0
2001—Pittsburgh NFL	12	0	4	1	0.0	0	0	0.0	0
2002—Houston NFL	15	0	7	1	1.0	0	0	0.0	0
2003—Houston NFL	16	2	18	4	0.0	0	0	0.0	0
2004—Houston NFL	10	6	32	6	0.0	1	0	0.0	0
Pro totals (7 years)	90	8	83	15	1.0	1	0	0.0	0

SIMMONS, KENDALL   G   STEELERS

PERSONAL: Born March 11, 1979, in Ripley, Miss. ... 6-3/313. ... Full name: Henry Alexander Kendall Simmons.
HIGH SCHOOL: Ripley (Miss.).
COLLEGE: Auburn.
TRANSACTIONS/CAREER NOTES: Selected by Pittsburgh Steelers in first round (30th pick overall) of 2002 NFL draft. ... Signed by Steelers (July 26, 2002). ... On injured reserve with knee injury (August 24, 2004-entire season).
PLAYING EXPERIENCE: Pittsburgh NFL, 2002-2004. ... Games/Games started: 2002 (14/14), 2003 (16/16), Total: 30/30.

SIMMS, CHRIS   QB   BUCCANEERS

PERSONAL: Born August 29, 1980, in Franklin Lakes, N.J. ... 6-4/220. ... Full name: Christopher David Simms. ... Son of Phil Simms, quarterback with New York Giants (1979-93).
HIGH SCHOOL: Ramapo (N.J.).
COLLEGE: Texas.
TRANSACTIONS/CAREER NOTES: Selected by Tampa Bay Buccaneers in third round (97th pick overall) of 2003 NFL draft. ... Signed by Buccaneers (July 18, 2003). ... Inactive for all 16 games (2003).

SINGLE GAME HIGHS (regular season): Attempts—32 (January 2, 2005, vs. Arizona); completions—21 (September 19, 2004, vs. Seattle); yards—224 (January 2, 2005, vs. Arizona); and touchdown passes—1 (January 2, 2005, vs. Arizona).
MISCELLANEOUS: Regular-season record as starting NFL quarterback: 1-1 (.500).

				PASSING								RUSHING				TOTALS		
Year Team	G	GS	Att.	Cmp.	Pct.	Yds.	TD	Int.	Avg.	Skd.	Rat.	Att.	Yds.	Avg.	TD	TD	2pt.	Pts.
2004—Tampa Bay NFL	5	2	73	42	57.5	467	1	3	6.40	10	64.1	7	14	2.0	0	0	0	0

SIMON, COREY — DT — EAGLES

PERSONAL: Born March 2, 1977, in Boynton Beach, Fla. ... 6-2/293.
HIGH SCHOOL: Ely (Pompano Beach, Fla.).
COLLEGE: Florida State.
TRANSACTIONS/CAREER NOTES: Selected by Philadelphia Eagles in first round (sixth pick overall) of 2000 NFL draft. ... Signed by Eagles (July 28, 2000). ... Designated by Eagles as franchise player (February 22, 2005).
CHAMPIONSHIP GAME EXPERIENCE: Played in NFC championship game (2001-2004 seasons). ... Played in Super Bowl 39 (2004 season).
HONORS: Named defensive tackle on THE SPORTING NEWS college All-America first team (1999). ... Played in Pro Bowl (2003 season).

			TOTALS		
Year Team	G	GS	Tk.	Ast.	Sks.
2000—Philadelphia NFL	16	16	38	13	9.5
2001—Philadelphia NFL	16	16	39	11	7.5
2002—Philadelphia NFL	14	14	32	7	2.0
2003—Philadelphia NFL	16	16	32	8	7.5
2004—Philadelphia NFL	16	16	26	6	5.5
Pro totals (5 years)	78	78	167	45	32.0

SIMONEAU, MARK — LB — EAGLES

PERSONAL: Born January 16, 1977, in Phillipsburg, Kan. ... 6-0/245.
HIGH SCHOOL: Smith Center (Kan.).
COLLEGE: Kansas State.
TRANSACTIONS/CAREER NOTES: Selected by Atlanta Falcons in third round (67th pick overall) of 2000 NFL draft. ... Signed by Falcons (May 17, 2000). ... Granted free agency (February 28, 2003). ... Traded by Falcons to Philadelphia Eagles for sixth-round pick (DB Waine Bacon) in 2003 draft and fourth-round pick (traded to Indianapolis) in 2004 draft (March 4, 2003).
CHAMPIONSHIP GAME EXPERIENCE: Played in NFC championship game (2003 season). ... Member of Eagles for NFC championship game (2004 season); inactive. ... Played in Super Bowl 39 (2004 season).
HONORS: Named linebacker on THE SPORTING NEWS college All-America first team (1999).

			TOTALS			INTERCEPTIONS			
Year Team	G	GS	Tk.	Ast.	Sks.	No.	Yds.	Avg.	TD
2000—Atlanta NFL	14	4	36	11	0.5	0	0	0.0	0
2001—Atlanta NFL	16	5	25	6	0.0	0	0	0.0	0
2002—Atlanta NFL	15	0	6	1	0.0	0	0	0.0	0
2003—Philadelphia NFL	16	16	79	22	2.0	0	0	0.0	0
2004—Philadelphia NFL	14	13	35	14	1.5	0	0	0.0	0
Pro totals (5 years)	75	38	181	54	4.0	0	0	0.0	0

SIMS, BARRY — T — RAIDERS

PERSONAL: Born December 1, 1974, in Park City, Utah. ... 6-5/300.
HIGH SCHOOL: Park City (Utah).
JUNIOR COLLEGE: Dixie College (Utah).
COLLEGE: Utah.
TRANSACTIONS/CAREER NOTES: Signed as non-drafted free agent by Oakland Raiders (July, 1999).
PLAYING EXPERIENCE: Oakland NFL, 1999-2004. ... Games/Games started: 1999 (16/10), 2000 (16/8), 2001 (15/15), 2002 (15/15), 2003 (16/16), 2004 (16/16). Total: 94/80.
CHAMPIONSHIP GAME EXPERIENCE: Played in AFC championship game (2000 and 2002 seasons). ... Played in Super Bowl 37 (2002 season).

SIMS, RYAN — DT — CHIEFS

PERSONAL: Born May 4, 1980, in Spartanburg, S.C. ... 6-4/315. ... Full name: Ryan O'Neal Sims.
HIGH SCHOOL: Paul M. Dorman (Spartanburg, S.C.).
COLLEGE: North Carolina.
TRANSACTIONS/CAREER NOTES: Selected by Kansas City Chiefs in first round (sixth pick overall) of 2002 NFL draft. ... Signed by Chiefs (August 28, 2002). ... On injured reserve with elbow injury (October 17, 2002-remainder of season).

			TOTALS			INTERCEPTIONS			
Year Team	G	GS	Tk.	Ast.	Sks.	No.	Yds.	Avg.	TD
2002—Kansas City NFL	6	2	5	1	0.0	0	0	0.0	0
2003—Kansas City NFL	16	16	35	4	3.0	1	8	8.0	0
2004—Kansas City NFL	15	13	13	2	2.0	0	0	0.0	0
Pro totals (3 years)	37	31	53	7	5.0	1	8	8.0	0

S

SINGLETON, AL   LB   COWBOYS

PERSONAL: Born August 7, 1975, in Newark, N.J. ... 6-2/236. ... Full name: Alshermond Glendale Singleton.
HIGH SCHOOL: Irvington (N.J.).
COLLEGE: Temple.
TRANSACTIONS/CAREER NOTES: Selected by Tampa Bay Buccaneers in fourth round (128th pick overall) of 1997 NFL draft. ... Signed by Buccaneers (July 17, 1997). ... Granted unconditional free agency (February 28, 2003). ... Signed by Dallas Cowboys (March 13, 2003). ... On injured reserve with abdomen injury (December 23, 2004-remainder of season).
CHAMPIONSHIP GAME EXPERIENCE: Member of Buccaneers for NFC championship game (1999 season); inactive. ... Played in NFC championship game (2002 season). ... Member of Super Bowl championship team (2002 season).

				TOTALS			INTERCEPTIONS			
Year Team	G	GS	Tk.	Ast.	Sks.	No.	Yds.	Avg.	TD
1997—Tampa Bay NFL	12	0	0	0	0.0	0	0	0.0	0
1998—Tampa Bay NFL	15	0	11	4	0.0	0	0	0.0	0
1999—Tampa Bay NFL	15	0	13	8	0.5	1	7	7.0	0
2000—Tampa Bay NFL	13	1	16	6	0.0	0	0	0.0	0
2001—Tampa Bay NFL	16	0	17	4	1.0	0	0	0.0	0
2002—Tampa Bay NFL	16	14	40	18	1.0	1	0	0.0	0
2003—Dallas NFL	16	15	32	9	1.0	2	42	21.0	1
2004—Dallas NFL	13	12	31	14	0.0	0	0	0.0	0
Pro totals (8 years)	116	42	160	63	3.5	4	49	12.3	1

SIRMON, PETER   LB   TITANS

PERSONAL: Born February 18, 1977, in Walla Walla, Wash. ... 6-2/237. ... Full name: Peter Anton Sirmon.
HIGH SCHOOL: Walla Walla (Wash.).
COLLEGE: Oregon.
TRANSACTIONS/CAREER NOTES: Selected by Tennessee Titans in fourth round (128th pick overall) of 2000 NFL draft. ... Signed by Titans (July 11, 2000). ... Granted free agency (February 28, 2003). ... Re-signed by Titans (April 17, 2003). ... On injured reserve with knee injury (August 12, 2004-entire season).
CHAMPIONSHIP GAME EXPERIENCE: Played in AFC championship game (2002 season).

				TOTALS			INTERCEPTIONS			
Year Team	G	GS	Tk.	Ast.	Sks.	No.	Yds.	Avg.	TD
2000—Tennessee NFL	5	0	0	0	0.0	0	0	0.0	0
2001—Tennessee NFL	16	0	0	0	0.0	0	0	0.0	0
2002—Tennessee NFL	16	11	72	21	2.0	3	88	29.3	1
2003—Tennessee NFL	14	14	63	23	0.0	0	0	0.0	0
2004—Tennessee NFL	Did not play.								
Pro totals (4 years)	51	25	135	44	2.0	3	88	29.3	1

SLAUGHTER, CHAD   T   RAIDERS

PERSONAL: Born June 4, 1978, in Dallas, Texas. ... 6-8/340.
HIGH SCHOOL: Kimball (Dallas).
COLLEGE: Alcorn State.
TRANSACTIONS/CAREER NOTES: Signed as non-drafted free agent by Dallas Cowboys (April 18, 2000). ... Claimed on waivers by New York Jets (August 22, 2000). ... Inactive for 16 games (2000). ... Claimed on waivers by Cowboys (August, 2001). ... Released by Cowboys (2001). ... Signed by Oakland Raiders to practice squad (February 7, 2002). ... Activated (February 24, 2002). ... Inactive for 16 games (2002). ... Granted restricted free agency (March 3, 2004). ... Re-signed by Raiders (March 19, 2004).
PLAYING EXPERIENCE: Oakland NFL, 2003-2004. ... Games/Games started: 2003 (6/1), 2004 (10/0). Total: 16/1.

SLAUGHTER, T.J.   LB

PERSONAL: Born February 20, 1977, in Birmingham, Ala. ... 6-0/233. ... Full name: Tavaris Jermell Slaughter.
HIGH SCHOOL: John Carroll (Birmingham, Ala.).
COLLEGE: Southern Miss.
TRANSACTIONS/CAREER NOTES: Selected by Jacksonville Jaguars in third round (92nd pick overall) of 2000 NFL draft. ... Signed by Jaguars (May 16, 2000). ... On suspended list for violating league substance abuse policy (September 6-October 7, 2002). ... On injured reserve with knee injury (December 8, 2001-remainder of season). ... Granted free agency (February 28, 2003). ... Re-signed by Jaguars (May 15, 2003). ... Released by Jaguars (October 28, 2003). ... Signed by Green Bay Packers (November 11, 2003). ... Released by Packers (December 9, 2003). ... Signed by Baltimore Ravens (December 17, 2003). ... Granted unconditional free agency (March 2, 2005).

				TOTALS			INTERCEPTIONS			
Year Team	G	GS	Tk.	Ast.	Sks.	No.	Yds.	Avg.	TD
2000—Jacksonville NFL	16	7	38	16	0.0	0	0	0.0	0
2001—Jacksonville NFL	9	8	41	13	1.0	0	0	0.0	0
2002—Jacksonville NFL	11	11	39	20	0.0	0	0	0.0	0
2003—Jacksonville NFL	6	3	16	3	1.0	0	0	0.0	0
—Green Bay NFL	1	0	0	0	0.0	0	0	0.0	0
—Baltimore NFL	1	0	0	0	0.0	0	0	0.0	0
2004—Baltimore NFL	14	1	2	1	0.0	0	0	0.0	0
Pro totals (5 years)	58	30	136	53	2.0	0	0	0.0	0

SMART, IAN   RB   BUCCANEERS

PERSONAL: Born October 28, 1980, in Jamaica, N.Y. ... 5-8/192.
HIGH SCHOOL: North Babylon (N.Y.).
COLLEGE: CW Post.
TRANSACTIONS/CAREER NOTES: Signed as non-drafted free agent by New York Jets (May 3, 2003). ... Released by Jets (August 25, 2003). ... Re-signed by Jets (January 6, 2004). ... Released by Jets (September 4, 2004). ... Signed by Tampa Bay Buccaneers to practice squad (September 22, 2004). ... Activated (November 24, 2004).
SINGLE GAME HIGHS (regular season): Attempts—1 (December 19, 2004, vs. New Orleans); yards—25 (December 5, 2004, vs. Atlanta); and rushing touchdowns—0.

			RUSHING				RECEIVING				KICKOFF RETURNS				TOTALS		
Year Team	G	GS	Att.	Yds.	Avg.	TD	No.	Yds.	Avg.	TD	No.	Yds.	Avg.	TD	TD 2pt.	Pts. Fum.	
2004—Tampa Bay NFL	4	0	2	26	13.0	0	2	10	5.0	0	8	167	20.9	0	0 0	0 0	

SMART, ROD   RB   PANTHERS

PERSONAL: Born January 9, 1977, in Lakeland, Fla. ... 5-11/201.
HIGH SCHOOL: Lakeland (Fla.).
COLLEGE: Western Kentucky.
TRANSACTIONS/CAREER NOTES: Signed as non-drafted free agent by San Diego Chargers (May 19, 2000). ... Released by Chargers (June 9, 2000). ... Signed by Philadelphia Eagles to practice squad (October 2, 2001). ... Activated (November 19, 2001). ... On injured reserve with foot injury (January 8, 2002-remainder of season). ... Claimed on waivers by Carolina Panthers (September 2, 2002). ... Granted free agency (March 3, 2004). ... Re-signed by Panthers (March 17, 2004). ... On injured reserve with knee injury (November 3, 2004-remainder of season).
CHAMPIONSHIP GAME EXPERIENCE: Played in NFC championship game (2003 season). ... Played in Super Bowl 38 (2003 season).
SINGLE GAME HIGHS (regular season): Attempts—9 (December 21, 2003, vs. Detroit); yards—24 (December 21, 2003, vs. Detroit); and rushing touchdowns—0.

			RUSHING				RECEIVING				KICKOFF RETURNS				TOTALS			
Year Team	G	GS	Att.	Yds.	Avg.	TD	No.	Yds.	Avg.	TD	No.	Yds.	Avg.	TD	TD	2pt.	Pts.	Fum.
2001—Philadelphia NFL	6	0	2	6	3.0	0	0	0	0.0	0	0	0	0.0	0	0	0	0	0
2002—Carolina NFL	16	0	1	2	2.0	0	0	0	0.0	0	0	0	0.0	0	0	0	0	0
2003—Carolina NFL	16	0	20	49	2.5	0	3	11	3.7	0	41	947	23.1	1	1	0	6	2
2004—Carolina NFL	3	0	3	4	1.3	0	1	5	5.0	0	8	169	21.1	0	0	0	0	1
Pro totals (4 years)	41	0	26	61	2.3	0	4	16	4.0	0	49	1116	22.8	1	1	0	6	3

SMILEY, JUSTIN   G   49ERS

PERSONAL: Born November 11, 1981, in Ellabell, Ga. ... 6-3/301.
HIGH SCHOOL: Southeast Bulloch (Ellabell, Ga.).
COLLEGE: Alabama.
TRANSACTIONS/CAREER NOTES: Selected after junior season by San Francisco 49ers in second round (46th pick overall) of 2004 NFL draft. ... Signed by 49ers (July 30, 2004).
PLAYING EXPERIENCE: San Francisco NFL, 2004. ... Games/Games started: 2004 (16/9). Total: 16/9.
HONORS: Named guard on THE SPORTING NEWS Freshman All-America third team (2001).

SMITH, AARON   DE   STEELERS

PERSONAL: Born April 9, 1976, in Colorado Springs, Colo. ... 6-5/298. ... Full name: Aaron Douglas Smith.
HIGH SCHOOL: Sierra (Colorado Springs, Colo.).
COLLEGE: Northern Colorado.
TRANSACTIONS/CAREER NOTES: Selected by Pittsburgh Steelers in fourth round (109th pick overall) of 1999 NFL draft. ... Signed by Steelers (August 3, 1999). ... Granted free agency (March 1, 2002). ... Re-signed by Steelers (July 25, 2002).
CHAMPIONSHIP GAME EXPERIENCE: Played in AFC championship game (2001 and 2004 seasons).
HONORS: Played in Pro Bowl (2004 season).

			TOTALS		
Year Team	G	GS	Tk.	Ast.	Sks.
1999—Pittsburgh NFL	6	0	1	1	0.0
2000—Pittsburgh NFL	16	15	27	15	4.0
2001—Pittsburgh NFL	16	16	23	6	8.0
2002—Pittsburgh NFL	16	16	53	17	5.5
2003—Pittsburgh NFL	16	16	36	9	2.0
2004—Pittsburgh NFL	16	15	31	13	8.0
Pro totals (6 years)	86	78	171	61	27.5

SMITH, ANTONIO   DE   CARDINALS

PERSONAL: Born October 21, 1981, in Oklahoma City, Okla. ... 6-3/274.
HIGH SCHOOL: John Marshall (Oklahoma City, Okla.).
COLLEGE: Oklahoma State.
TRANSACTIONS/CAREER NOTES: Selected by Arizona Cardinals in fifth round (135th pick overall) of 2004 NFL draft. ... Signed by Cardinals (July 27, 2004). ... Released by Cardinals (September 5, 2004). ... Re-signed by Cardinals to practice squad (September 6, 2004). ... Activated (December 15, 2004). ... Assigned by Cardinals to Hamburg Sea Devils in 2005 NFL Europe enhancement allocation program (February 14, 2005).

Year Team	G	GS	Tk.	Ast.	Sks.
			TOTALS		
2004—Arizona NFL	2	0	0	0	0.0

SMITH, ANTOWAIN RB SAINTS

PERSONAL: Born March 14, 1972, in Millbrook, Ala. ... 6-2/232. ... Full name: Antowain Drurell Smith. ... Name pronounced: AN-twan.
HIGH SCHOOL: Elmore (Ala.).
JUNIOR COLLEGE: East Mississippi Junior College.
COLLEGE: Houston.
TRANSACTIONS/CAREER NOTES: Selected by Buffalo Bills in first round (23rd pick overall) of 1997 NFL draft. ... Signed by Bills (July 11, 1997). ... Released by Bills (May 18, 2001). ... Signed by New England Patriots (June 7, 2001). ... Granted unconditional free agency (March 1, 2002). ... Re-signed by Patriots (March 1, 2002). ... Granted unconditional free agency (March 3, 2004). ... Signed by Tennessee Titans (July 22, 2004). ... Granted unconditional free agency (March 2, 2005). ... Signed by New Orleans Saints (April 1, 2005).
CHAMPIONSHIP GAME EXPERIENCE: Played in AFC championship game (2001 and 2003 seasons). ... Member of Super Bowl championship team (2001 and 2003 seasons).
SINGLE GAME HIGHS (regular season): Attempts—31 (October 11, 1998, vs. Indianapolis); yards—156 (December 22, 2001, vs. Miami); and rushing touchdowns—3 (December 23, 2000, vs. Seattle).
STATISTICAL PLATEAUS: 100-yard rushing games: 1997 (1), 1998 (3), 1999 (2), 2000 (1), 2001 (4), 2002 (1), 2003 (1). Total: 13.

Year Team	G	GS	Att.	Yds.	Avg.	TD	No.	Yds.	Avg.	TD	TD	2pt.	Pts.	Fum.
			RUSHING				**RECEIVING**				**TOTALS**			
1997—Buffalo NFL	16	0	194	840	4.3	8	28	177	6.3	0	8	0	48	4
1998—Buffalo NFL	16	14	300	1124	3.7	8	5	11	2.2	0	8	0	48	5
1999—Buffalo NFL	14	11	165	614	3.7	6	2	32	16.0	0	6	0	36	4
2000—Buffalo NFL	11	3	101	354	3.5	4	3	20	6.7	0	4	0	24	1
2001—New England NFL	16	15	287	1157	4.0	12	19	192	10.1	1	13	0	78	4
2002—New England NFL	16	15	252	982	3.9	6	31	243	7.8	2	8	1	50	2
2003—New England NFL	13	6	182	642	3.5	4	14	92	6.6	0	3	0	18	1
2004—Tennessee NFL	13	4	137	509	3.7	4	22	169	7.7	0	4	0	24	2
Pro totals (8 years)	115	68	1618	6222	3.8	51	124	936	7.5	3	54	1	326	23

SMITH, BRADY DE FALCONS

PERSONAL: Born June 5, 1973, in Royal Oak, Mich. ... 6-5/274. ... Full name: Brady McKay Smith. ... Son of Steve Smith, offensive tackle with four NFL teams (1966-74).
HIGH SCHOOL: Barrington (Ill.).
COLLEGE: Colorado State.
TRANSACTIONS/CAREER NOTES: Selected by New Orleans Saints in third round (70th pick overall) of 1996 NFL draft. ... Signed by Saints (July 12, 1996). ... Granted free agency (February 12, 1999). ... Re-signed by Saints (April 14, 1999). ... Granted unconditional free agency (February 11, 2000). ... Signed by Atlanta Falcons (February 19, 2000).
CHAMPIONSHIP GAME EXPERIENCE: Played in NFC championship game (2004 season).

Year Team	G	GS	Tk.	Ast.	Sks.	No.	Yds.	Avg.	TD
			TOTALS			**INTERCEPTIONS**			
1996—New Orleans NFL	16	4	15	2	2.0	0	0	0.0	0
1997—New Orleans NFL	16	2	22	8	5.0	0	0	0.0	0
1998—New Orleans NFL	14	5	10	2	6.0	0	0	0.0	0
1999—New Orleans NFL	16	16	26	7	6.0	0	0	0.0	0
2000—Atlanta NFL	15	14	29	5	4.5	0	0	0.0	0
2001—Atlanta NFL	15	15	26	8	8.0	0	0	0.0	0
2002—Atlanta NFL	14	14	26	13	6.5	0	0	0.0	0
2003—Atlanta NFL	16	14	24	1	4.0	0	0	0.0	0
2004—Atlanta NFL	16	16	25	5	6.0	1	1	1.0	0
Pro totals (9 years)	138	100	203	51	42.0	1	1	1.0	0

SMITH, BRENT G/T JETS

PERSONAL: Born November 21, 1973, in Dallas, Texas. ... 6-5/305. ... Full name: Gary Brent Smith.
HIGH SCHOOL: Pontotoc (Miss.).
COLLEGE: Mississippi State.
TRANSACTIONS/CAREER NOTES: Selected by Miami Dolphins in third round (96th pick overall) of 1997 NFL draft. ... Signed by Dolphins (July 8, 1997). ... Active for two games (1997); did not play. ... Granted free agency (February 11, 2000). ... Re-signed by Dolphins (June 9, 2000). ... On injured reserve with knee injury (July 28, 2001-entire season). ... On injured reserve with knee injury (August 27, 2002-entire season). ... Granted unconditional free agency (February 28, 2003). ... Signed by New York Jets (May 6, 2003). ... Granted unconditional free agency (March 3, 2004). ... Re-signed by Jets (March 5, 2004). ... Released by Jets (September 10, 2004). ... Re-signed by Jets (September 15, 2004). ... Released by Jets (November 9, 2004).
PLAYING EXPERIENCE: Miami NFL, 1998-2000; New York Jets NFL, 2003-2004. ... Games/Games started: 1998 (8/7), 1999 (13/4), 2000 (16/2), 2003 (16/16), 2004 (4/1). Total: 57/30.

SMITH, COREY DE

PERSONAL: Born November 2, 1979, in Richmond, Va. ... 6-2/250. ... Full name: Corey Dominique Smith.
HIGH SCHOOL: John Marshall (Richmond, Va.).
COLLEGE: North Carolina State.
TRANSACTIONS/CAREER NOTES: Signed as non-drafted free agent by Tampa Bay Buccaneers (April 22, 2002). ... On injured reserve with knee injury (November 28, 2002-remainder of season). ... Released by Buccaneers (August 31, 2003). ... Re-signed by Buccaneers to prac-

tice squad (December 9, 2003). ... Activated (December 22, 2003). ... Assigned by Buccaneers to Berlin Thunder in 2004 NFL Europe enhancement allocation program (February 9, 2004). ... Released by Buccaneers (September 5, 2004). ... Re-signed by Buccaneers to practice squad (September 7, 2004). ... Activated (October 20, 2004). ... Released by Buccaneers (December 15, 2004). ... Re-signed by Buccaneers to practice squad (December 17, 2004). ... Released by Buccaneers (December 22, 2004).

| | | | TOTALS | | |
Year Team	G	GS	Tk.	Ast.	Sks.
2002—Tampa Bay NFL	6	0	1	0	1.0
2003—Tampa Bay NFL	1	0	0	0	0.0
2004—Tampa Bay NFL	4	0	2	0	0.0
—San Francisco NFL	1	0	0	0	0.0
Pro totals (3 years)	12	0	3	0	1.0

SMITH, DARRIN — LB

PERSONAL: Born April 15, 1970, in Miami, Fla. ... 6-1/236. ... Full name: Darrin Andrew Smith.
HIGH SCHOOL: Miami Norland.
COLLEGE: Miami (Fla.).
TRANSACTIONS/CAREER NOTES: Selected by Dallas Cowboys in second round (54th pick overall) of 1993 NFL draft. ... Signed by Cowboys (July 21, 1993). ... On reserve/did not report list (July 20-October 14, 1995). ... Granted free agency (February 16, 1996). ... Re-signed by Cowboys (June 17, 1996). ... Granted unconditional free agency (February 14, 1997). ... Signed by Philadelphia Eagles (April 19, 1997). ... On injured reserve with ankle injury (November 19, 1997-remainder of season). ... Granted unconditional free agency (February 13, 1998). ... Signed by Seattle Seahawks (February 19, 1998). ... Released by Seahawks (February 10, 2000). ... Signed by New Orleans Saints (July 16, 2000). ... Granted unconditional free agency (March 2, 2001). ... Re-signed by Saints (April 10, 2001). ... Released by Saints (September 5, 2004). ... Re-signed by Saints (December 1, 2004). ... Granted unconditional free agency (March 2, 2005).
CHAMPIONSHIP GAME EXPERIENCE: Played in NFC championship game (1993 and 1995 seasons). ... Member of Super Bowl championship team (1993 and 1995 seasons).

| | | | TOTALS | | | INTERCEPTIONS | | | |
Year Team	G	GS	Tk.	Ast.	Sks.	No.	Yds.	Avg.	TD
1993—Dallas NFL	16	13	49	44	1.0	0	0	0.0	0
1994—Dallas NFL	16	16	46	21	4.0	2	13	6.5	1
1995—Dallas NFL	9	9	40	6	3.0	0	0	0.0	0
1996—Dallas NFL	16	16	54	27	1.0	0	0	0.0	0
1997—Philadelphia NFL	7	7	9	4	1.0	0	0	0.0	0
1998—Seattle NFL	13	12	59	21	5.0	3	56	18.7	▲2
1999—Seattle NFL	15	15	65	25	1.0	1	0	0.0	0
2000—New Orleans NFL	16	11	61	30	2.0	2	56	28.0	1
2001—New Orleans NFL	16	16	49	17	1.5	0	0	0.0	0
2002—New Orleans NFL	15	15	63	33	3.5	2	21	10.5	0
2003—New Orleans NFL	14	10	44	16	1.0	1	9	9.0	0
2004—New Orleans NFL	3	0	0	0	0.0	0	0	0.0	0
Pro totals (12 years)	156	140	539	244	24.0	11	155	14.1	4

SMITH, DARYL — LB — JAGUARS

PERSONAL: Born April 14, 1982, in Albany, Ga. ... 6-2/234.
HIGH SCHOOL: Dougherty County (Albany, Ga.).
COLLEGE: Georgia Tech.
TRANSACTIONS/CAREER NOTES: Selected by Jacksonville Jaguars in second round (39th pick overall) of 2004 NFL draft. ... Signed by Jaguars (July 30, 2004).
HONORS: Named linebacker on THE SPORTING NEWS Freshman All-America first team (2000).

| | | | TOTALS | | | INTERCEPTIONS | | | |
Year Team	G	GS	Tk.	Ast.	Sks.	No.	Yds.	Avg.	TD
2004—Jacksonville NFL	15	13	41	7	2.0	1	0	0.0	0

SMITH, DEREK — LB — 49ERS

PERSONAL: Born January 18, 1975, in American Fork, Utah. ... 6-2/245. ... Full name: Derek Mecham Smith.
HIGH SCHOOL: American Fork (Utah).
JUNIOR COLLEGE: Snow College (Utah).
COLLEGE: Arizona State.
TRANSACTIONS/CAREER NOTES: Selected by Washington Redskins in third round (80th pick overall) of 1997 NFL draft. ... Signed by Redskins (July 11, 1997). ... Granted free agency (February 11, 2000). ... Re-signed by Redskins (April 11, 2000). ... Granted unconditional free agency (March 2, 2001). ... Signed by San Francisco 49ers (March 23, 2001).

| | | | TOTALS | | | INTERCEPTIONS | | | |
Year Team	G	GS	Tk.	Ast.	Sks.	No.	Yds.	Avg.	TD
1997—Washington NFL	16	16	59	28	2.0	0	0	0.0	0
1998—Washington NFL	16	15	78	25	0.5	0	0	0.0	0
1999—Washington NFL	16	16	66	28	1.0	1	0	0.0	0
2000—Washington NFL	16	14	71	17	1.0	0	0	0.0	0
2001—San Francisco NFL	14	14	78	30	3.0	1	0	0.0	0
2002—San Francisco NFL	16	16	83	29	1.0	0	0	0.0	0
2003—San Francisco NFL	16	16	85	27	3.5	0	0	0.0	0
2004—San Francisco NFL	14	14	80	29	1.5	0	0	0.0	0
Pro totals (8 years)	124	121	600	213	13.5	2	0	0.0	0

SMITH, DWIGHT   S   SAINTS

PERSONAL: Born August 13, 1978, in Detroit, Mich. ... 5-10/201.
HIGH SCHOOL: Central (Detroit).
COLLEGE: Akron.
TRANSACTIONS/CAREER NOTES: Selected by Tampa Bay Buccaneers in third round (84th pick overall) of 2001 NFL draft. ... Signed by Buccaneers (July 17, 2001). ... Granted unconditional free agency (March 2, 2005). ... Signed by New Orleans Saints (March 7, 2005).
CHAMPIONSHIP GAME EXPERIENCE: Played in NFC championship game (2002 season). ... Member of Super Bowl championship team (2002 season).
HONORS: Named cornerback on THE SPORTING NEWS college All-America third team (2000).
POST SEASON RECORDS: Holds single-game Super Bowl record for most interceptions returned for touchdown—2 (January 26, 2003, vs. Oakland). ... Shares NFL single-game record for most interceptions returned for touchdown—2 (January 26, 2003, vs. Oakland).

			TOTALS			INTERCEPTIONS				KICKOFF RETURNS				TOTALS		
Year Team	G	GS	Tk.	Ast.	Sks.	No.	Yds.	Avg.	TD	No.	Yds.	Avg.	TD	TD	2pt.	Pts. Fum.
2001—Tampa Bay NFL	15	0	4	1	0.0	0	0	0.0	0	16	355	22.2	0	0	0	0	2
2002—Tampa Bay NFL	16	2	24	2	0.0	4	39	9.8	0	4	93	23.2	0	0	0	0	1
2003—Tampa Bay NFL	16	16	55	12	0.0	5	3	0.6	0	0	0	0.0	0	0	0	0	0
2004—Tampa Bay NFL	16	16	72	11	0.0	3	13	4.3	0	0	0	0.0	0	0	0	0	0
Pro totals (4 years)	63	34	155	26	0.0	12	55	4.6	0	20	448	22.4	0	0	0	0	3

SMITH, EMMITT   RB

PERSONAL: Born May 15, 1969, in Pensacola, Fla. ... 5-10/216. ... Full name: Emmitt J. Smith III.
HIGH SCHOOL: Escambia (Pensacola, Fla.).
COLLEGE: Florida.
TRANSACTIONS/CAREER NOTES: Selected after junior season by Dallas Cowboys in first round (17th pick overall) of 1990 NFL draft. ... Signed by Cowboys (September 4, 1990). ... Granted roster exemption (September 4-8, 1990). ... Granted free agency (March 1, 1993). ... Re-signed by Cowboys (September 16, 1993). ... Released by Cowboys (February 27, 2003). ... Signed by Arizona Cardinals (March 26, 2003). ... Announced retirement (February 3, 2005).
CHAMPIONSHIP GAME EXPERIENCE: Played in NFC championship game (1992-1995 seasons). ... Member of Super Bowl championship team (1992, 1993 and 1995 seasons).
HONORS: Named running back on THE SPORTING NEWS college All-America first team (1989). ... Played in Pro Bowl (1990-1992, 1995, 1998 and 1999 seasons). ... Named running back on THE SPORTING NEWS NFL All-Pro team (1992-1995). ... Named NFL Player of the Year by THE SPORTING NEWS (1993). ... Named Most Valuable Player of Super Bowl 28 (1993 season). ... Named to play in Pro Bowl (1993 season); replaced by Rodney Hampton due to injury. ... Named Sportsman of the Year by THE SPORTING NEWS (1994). ... Named to play in Pro Bowl (1994 season); replaced by Ricky Watters due to injury.
RECORDS: Holds NFL career record for most rushing attempts—4,409; most yards rushing—18,355; most rushing touchdowns—164; most 100-yard rushing games—78; most consecutive seasons with 1,000 or more yards rushing—11 (1991-2001); and most seasons with 1,000 or more yards rushing—11 (1991-2001).
POST SEASON RECORDS: Holds NFL postseason career record for most rushing touchdowns—19. ... Holds NFL postseason career record for most yards rushing—1,586. ... Shares NFL postseason career record for most games with 100 or more yards rushing—7. ... Holds Super Bowl career record for most rushing touchdowns—5.
SINGLE GAME HIGHS (regular season): Attempts—35 (November 7, 1994, vs. New York Giants); yards—237 (October 31, 1993, vs. Philadelphia); and rushing touchdowns—4 (September 4, 1995, vs. New York Giants).
STATISTICAL PLATEAUS: 100-yard rushing games: 1990 (3), 1991 (8), 1992 (7), 1993 (7), 1994 (6), 1995 (11), 1996 (4), 1997 (2), 1998 (7), 1999 (9), 2000 (6), 2001 (4), 2002 (2), 2004 (2). Total: 78. 100-yard receiving games: 1990 (1), 1993 (1). Total: 2.
MISCELLANEOUS: Holds Dallas Cowboys all-time records for most yards rushing (17,162), most touchdowns (164), most rushing touchdowns (153) and most points (986).

			RUSHING				RECEIVING				TOTALS			
Year Team	G	GS	Att.	Yds.	Avg.	TD	No.	Yds.	Avg.	TD	TD	2pt.	Pts.	Fum.
1990—Dallas NFL	16	15	241	937	3.9	11	24	228	9.5	0	11	0	66	7
1991—Dallas NFL	16	16	*365	*1563	4.3	12	49	258	5.3	1	13	0	78	8
1992—Dallas NFL	16	16	‡373	*1713	4.6	*18	59	335	5.7	1	*19	0	114	4
1993—Dallas NFL	14	13	283	*1486	*5.3	9	57	414	7.3	1	10	0	60	4
1994—Dallas NFL	15	15	*368	1484	4.0	*21	50	341	6.8	1	*22	0	132	1
1995—Dallas NFL	16	16	*377	*1773	4.7	*25	62	375	6.0	0	*25	0	*150	7
1996—Dallas NFL	15	15	327	1204	3.7	12	47	249	5.3	3	15	0	90	5
1997—Dallas NFL	16	16	261	1074	4.1	4	40	234	5.9	0	4	1	26	1
1998—Dallas NFL	16	16	319	1332	4.2	13	27	175	6.5	2	15	0	90	3
1999—Dallas NFL	15	15	‡329	1397	4.2	11	27	119	4.4	2	13	0	78	5
2000—Dallas NFL	16	16	294	1203	4.1	9	11	79	7.2	0	9	0	54	6
2001—Dallas NFL	14	14	261	1021	3.9	3	17	116	6.8	0	3	0	18	1
2002—Dallas NFL	16	16	254	975	3.8	5	16	89	5.6	0	5	0	30	3
2003—Arizona NFL	10	5	90	256	2.8	2	14	107	7.6	0	2	0	12	2
2004—Arizona NFL	15	15	267	937	3.5	9	15	105	7.0	0	9	0	54	4
Pro totals (15 years)	226	219	4409	18355	4.2	164	515	3224	6.3	11	175	1	1052	61

SMITH, HUNTER   P   COLTS

PERSONAL: Born August 9, 1977, in Sherman, Texas. ... 6-2/209. ... Full name: Hunter Dwight Smith.
HIGH SCHOOL: Sherman (Texas).
COLLEGE: Notre Dame.
TRANSACTIONS/CAREER NOTES: Selected by Indianapolis Colts in seventh round (210th pick overall) of 1999 NFL draft. ... Signed by Colts (July 22, 1999). ... Granted free agency (March 1, 2002). ... Re-signed by Colts (May 21, 2002). ... Granted unconditional free agency (February 28, 2003). ... Re-signed by Colts (March 16, 2003).
CHAMPIONSHIP GAME EXPERIENCE: Played in AFC championship game (2003 season).

				PUNTING			
Year Team	G	No.	Yds.	Avg.	Net avg.	In. 20	Blk.
1999—Indianapolis NFL	16	58	2467	42.5	30.6	16	†2
2000—Indianapolis NFL	16	65	2906	44.7	36.4	20	0
2001—Indianapolis NFL	16	68	3023	44.5	33.8	12	0
2002—Indianapolis NFL	16	66	2672	40.5	34.9	26	1
2003—Indianapolis NFL	16	62	2617	42.2	35.5	20	1
2004—Indianapolis NFL	16	54	2443	45.2	36.8	21	0
Pro totals (6 years)	96	373	16128	43.2	34.7	115	4

SMITH, JIMMY WR JAGUARS

PERSONAL: Born February 9, 1969, in Detroit, Mich. ... 6-1/208. ... Full name: Jimmy Lee Smith Jr.
HIGH SCHOOL: Callaway (Jackson, Miss.).
COLLEGE: Jackson State.
TRANSACTIONS/CAREER NOTES: Selected by Dallas Cowboys in second round (36th pick overall) of 1992 NFL draft. ... Signed by Cowboys (April 26, 1992). ... On injured reserve with fibula injury (September 2-October 7, 1992); on practice squad (September 28-October 7, 1992). ... On non-football injury list with appendicitis (September 2, 1993-entire season). ... Released by Cowboys (July 11, 1994). ... Signed by Philadelphia Eagles (July 19, 1994). ... Released by Eagles (August 29, 1994). ... Signed by Jacksonville Jaguars (February 28, 1995). ... Granted free agency (February 16, 1996). ... Re-signed by Jaguars (May 28, 1996). ... On reserve/did not report list (July 25-September 1, 2002). ... On suspended list for violating league substance abuse policy (August 31-September 29, 2003).
CHAMPIONSHIP GAME EXPERIENCE: Played in NFC championship game (1992 season). ... Member of Super Bowl championship team (1992 season). ... Played in AFC championship game (1996 and 1999 seasons).
HONORS: Played in Pro Bowl (1997-2000 seasons). ... Named to play in Pro Bowl (2001 season); replaced by Hines Ward due to injury.
SINGLE GAME HIGHS (regular season): Receptions—15 (September 10, 2000, vs. Baltimore); yards—291 (September 10, 2000, vs. Baltimore); and touchdown receptions—3 (September 10, 2000, vs. Baltimore).
STATISTICAL PLATEAUS: 100-yard receiving games: 1996 (4), 1997 (6), 1998 (5), 1999 (9), 2000 (5), 2001 (6), 2002 (2), 2003 (2), 2004 (4). Total: 43.
MISCELLANEOUS: Holds Jacksonville Jaguars all-time record for most receptions (792), most yards receiving (11,264), most touchdowns (63) and most touchdown receptions (61).

			RECEIVING				KICKOFF RETURNS				TOTALS			
Year Team	G	GS	No.	Yds.	Avg.	TD	No.	Yds.	Avg.	TD	TD	2pt.	Pts.	Fum.
1992—Dallas NFL	7	0	0	0	0.0	0	0	0	0.0	0	0	0	0	0
1993—Dallas NFL		Did not play.												
1994—		Did not play.												
1995—Jacksonville NFL	16	4	22	288	13.1	3	24	540	22.5	1	5	0	30	2
1996—Jacksonville NFL	16	9	83	§1244	15.0	7	2	49	24.5	0	7	0	42	1
1997—Jacksonville NFL	16	16	82	1324	16.1	4	0	0	0.0	0	4	0	24	1
1998—Jacksonville NFL	16	15	78	1182	15.2	8	0	0	0.0	0	8	0	48	2
1999—Jacksonville NFL	16	16	*116	1636	14.1	6	0	0	0.0	0	6	1	38	1
2000—Jacksonville NFL	15	14	91	1213	13.3	8	0	0	0.0	0	8	0	48	1
2001—Jacksonville NFL	16	16	112	1373	12.3	8	0	0	0.0	0	8	0	48	1
2002—Jacksonville NFL	16	16	80	1027	12.8	7	0	0	0.0	0	7	1	44	0
2003—Jacksonville NFL	12	12	54	805	14.9	4	0	0	0.0	0	4	0	24	1
2004—Jacksonville NFL	16	16	74	1172	15.8	6	0	0	0.0	0	6	0	36	2
Pro totals (11 years)	162	134	792	11264	14.2	61	26	589	22.7	1	63	2	382	12

SMITH, JONATHAN WR BILLS

PERSONAL: Born November 28, 1981, in Argyle, Ga. ... 5-10/194. ... Full name: Jonathan Dewayne Smith.
HIGH SCHOOL: Cinch County (Homerville, Ala.).
COLLEGE: Georgia Tech.
TRANSACTIONS/CAREER NOTES: Selected by Buffalo Bills in seventh round (214th pick overall) of 2004 NFL draft. ... Signed by Bills (June 8, 2004). ... Released by Bills (September 5, 2004). ... Re-signed by Bills to practice squad (September 6, 2004). ... Activated (November 5, 2004).
SINGLE GAME HIGHS (regular season): Receptions—2 (November 28, 2004, vs. Seattle); yards—11 (December 26, 2004, vs. San Francisco); and touchdown receptions—0.

			RECEIVING				PUNT RETURNS				TOTALS			
Year Team	G	GS	No.	Yds.	Avg.	TD	No.	Yds.	Avg.	TD	TD	2pt.	Pts.	Fum.
2004—Buffalo NFL	9	0	3	21	7.0	0	9	157	17.4	1	1	0	6	0

SMITH, JUSTIN DE BENGALS

PERSONAL: Born September 30, 1979, in Jefferson City, Mo. ... 6-4/270.
HIGH SCHOOL: Jefferson City (Mo.).
COLLEGE: Missouri.
TRANSACTIONS/CAREER NOTES: Selected after junior season by Cincinnati Bengals in first round (fourth pick overall) of 2001 NFL draft. ... Signed by Bengals (September 8, 2001).
HONORS: Named defensive end on THE SPORTING NEWS college All-America third team (2000).

			TOTALS			INTERCEPTIONS			
Year Team	G	GS	Tk.	Ast.	Sks.	No.	Yds.	Avg.	TD
2001—Cincinnati NFL	15	11	41	13	8.5	2	28	14.0	0
2002—Cincinnati NFL	16	16	48	13	6.5	0	0	0.0	0
2003—Cincinnati NFL	16	16	41	19	5.0	0	0	0.0	0
2004—Cincinnati NFL	16	16	42	29	8.0	0	0	0.0	0
Pro totals (4 years)	63	59	172	74	28.0	2	28	14.0	0

S

SMITH, KEITH   CB   LIONS

PERSONAL: Born March 20, 1980, in Leesville, La. ... 5-11/192.
HIGH SCHOOL: Leesville (La.).
COLLEGE: McNeese State.
TRANSACTIONS/CAREER NOTES: Selected by Detroit Lions in third round (73rd pick overall) of 2004 NFL draft. ... Signed by Lions (July 29, 2004).

				TOTALS			INTERCEPTIONS			
Year Team	G	GS	Tk.	Ast.	Sks.	No.	Yds.	Avg.	TD	
2004—Detroit NFL	15	2	22	7	0.0	1	2	2.0	0	

SMITH, LARRY   DT

PERSONAL: Born December 4, 1974, in Kingsland, Ga. ... 6-5/292. ... Full name: Larry Smith Jr.
HIGH SCHOOL: Charlton County (Folkston, Ga.), then Valley Forge (Pa.).
COLLEGE: Florida State.
TRANSACTIONS/CAREER NOTES: Selected after junior season by Jacksonville Jaguars in second round (56th pick overall) of 1999 NFL draft. ... Signed by Jaguars (April 26, 1999). ... Granted unconditional free agency (February 28, 2003). ... Re-signed by Jaguars (May 2, 2003). ... Released by Jaguars (August 13, 2003). ... Signed by Green Bay Packers (August 18, 2003). ... Released by Packers (September 1, 2003). ... Re-signed by Packers (October 9, 2003). ... Granted unconditional free agency (March 3, 2004). ... Re-signed by Packers (March 29, 2004). ... Released by Packers (September 5, 2004). ... Re-signed by Packers (October 7, 2004). ... Released by Packers (October 26, 2004).
CHAMPIONSHIP GAME EXPERIENCE: Played in AFC championship game (1999 season).

			TOTALS		
Year Team	G	GS	Tk.	Ast.	Sks.
1999—Jacksonville NFL	15	0	11	1	3.0
2000—Jacksonville NFL	14	4	15	5	0.0
2001—Jacksonville NFL	7	0	3	0	0.0
2002—Jacksonville NFL	15	3	15	3	1.0
2003—Green Bay NFL	10	0	9	6	1.5
2004—Green Bay NFL	3	0	3	1	0.0
Pro totals (6 years)	64	7	56	16	5.5

SMITH, LAWRENCE   T   BILLS

PERSONAL: Born August 16, 1979, in Atlanta, Ga. ... 6-3/295. ... Full name: Lawrence Anthony Smith.
HIGH SCHOOL: Booker T. Washington (Atlanta, Ga.).
COLLEGE: Tennessee State.
TRANSACTIONS/CAREER NOTES: Signed as non-drafted free agent by Buffalo Bills (January 28, 2004).
PLAYING EXPERIENCE: Buffalo NFL, 2004. ... Games/Games started: 2004 (16/8). Total: 16/8.

SMITH, L.J.   TE   EAGLES

PERSONAL: Born May 13, 1980, in Highland Park, N.J. ... 6-3/258. ... Full name: John Smith.
HIGH SCHOOL: Highland Park (N.J.).
COLLEGE: Rutgers.
TRANSACTIONS/CAREER NOTES: Selected by Philadelphia Eagles in second round (61st pick overall) of 2003 NFL draft. ... Signed by Eagles (July 24, 2003).
CHAMPIONSHIP GAME EXPERIENCE: Played in NFC championship game (2003 and 2004 seasons). ... Played in Super Bowl 39 (2004 season).
SINGLE GAME HIGHS (regular season): Receptions—6 (November 2, 2003, vs. Atlanta); yards—97 (November 2, 2003, vs. Atlanta); and touchdown receptions—1 (December 12, 2004, vs. Washington).

			RECEIVING				TOTALS			
Year Team	G	GS	No.	Yds.	Avg.	TD	TD	2pt.	Pts.	Fum.
2003—Philadelphia NFL	15	5	27	321	11.9	1	1	0	6	1
2004—Philadelphia NFL	16	8	34	377	11.1	5	5	0	30	0
Pro totals (2 years)	31	13	61	698	11.4	6	6	0	36	1

SMITH, MARVEL   T   STEELERS

PERSONAL: Born August 6, 1978, in Oakland, Calif. ... 6-5/321. ... Full name: Marvel Amos Smith.
HIGH SCHOOL: Skyline (Oakland).
COLLEGE: Arizona State.
TRANSACTIONS/CAREER NOTES: Selected after junior season by Pittsburgh Steelers in second round (38th pick overall) of 2000 NFL draft. ... Signed by Steelers (July 16, 2000). ... On injured reserve with neck injury (December 23, 2003-remainder of season).
PLAYING EXPERIENCE: Pittsburgh NFL, 2000-2004. ... Games/Games started: 2000 (12/9), 2001 (16/16), 2002 (16/16), 2003 (6/6), 2004 (16/16). Total: 66/63.
CHAMPIONSHIP GAME EXPERIENCE: Played in AFC championship game (2001 and 2004 seasons).
HONORS: Named offensive tackle on THE SPORTING NEWS college All-America third team (1999). ... Played in Pro Bowl (2004 season).

S

SMITH, MUSA — RB — RAVENS

PERSONAL: Born May 31, 1982, in Elliottsburg, Pa. ... 6-0/232.
HIGH SCHOOL: West Perry (Pa.).
COLLEGE: Georgia.
TRANSACTIONS/CAREER NOTES: Selected after junior season by Baltimore Ravens in third round (77th pick overall) of 2003 NFL draft. ... Signed by Ravens (July 27, 2003). ... On injured reserve with leg injury (November 24, 2004-remainder of season).
SINGLE GAME HIGHS (regular season): Attempts—6 (October 24, 2004, vs. Buffalo); yards—25 (October 31, 2004, vs. Philadelphia); and rushing touchdowns—1 (December 21, 2003, vs. Cleveland).

Year Team	G	GS	RUSHING				RECEIVING				KICKOFF RETURNS				TOTALS			
			Att.	Yds.	Avg.	TD	No.	Yds.	Avg.	TD	No.	Yds.	Avg.	TD	TD	2pt.	Pts.	Fum.
2003—Baltimore NFL	11	0	9	31	3.4	2	0	0	0.0	0	2	17	8.5	0	2	0	12	1
2004—Baltimore NFL	9	0	12	48	4.0	0	2	31	15.5	0	0	0	0.0	0	0	0	0	0
Pro totals (2 years)	20	0	21	79	3.8	2	2	31	15.5	0	2	17	8.5	0	2	0	12	1

SMITH, ONTERRIO — RB — VIKINGS

PERSONAL: Born December 8, 1980, in Sacramento, Calif. ... 5-10/214. ... Full name: Onterrio Raymond Smith.
HIGH SCHOOL: Grant (Sacramento).
COLLEGE: Oregon.
TRANSACTIONS/CAREER NOTES: Selected after junior season by Minnesota Vikings in fourth round (105th pick overall) of 2003 NFL draft. ... Signed by Vikings (July 27, 2003). ... On suspended list for violating league substance abuse policy (October 5-November 2, 2004).
SINGLE GAME HIGHS (regular season): Attempts—27 (December 14, 2003, vs. Chicago); yards—148 (December 14, 2003, vs. Chicago); and rushing touchdowns—3 (December 20, 2003, vs. Kansas City).
STATISTICAL PLATEAUS: 100-yard rushing games: 2003 (2). Total: 2. 100-yard receiving games: 2004 (1). Total: 1.

Year Team	G	GS	RUSHING				RECEIVING				KICKOFF RETURNS				TOTALS			
			Att.	Yds.	Avg.	TD	No.	Yds.	Avg.	TD	No.	Yds.	Avg.	TD	TD	2pt.	Pts.	Fum.
2003—Minnesota NFL	15	3	107	579	‡5.4	5	15	129	8.6	0	27	588	21.8	0	5	1	32	1
2004—Minnesota NFL	11	6	124	544	4.4	2	36	394	10.9	2	9	155	17.2	0	4	1	26	2
Pro totals (2 years)	26	9	231	1123	4.9	7	51	523	10.3	2	36	743	20.6	0	9	2	58	3

SMITH, RAONALL — LB — VIKINGS

PERSONAL: Born October 22, 1978, in Mesa, Ariz. ... 6-2/241. ... Full name: Raonall Aarrig Smith.
HIGH SCHOOL: Peninsula (Gig Harbor, Wash.).
COLLEGE: Washington State.
TRANSACTIONS/CAREER NOTES: Selected by Minnesota Vikings in second round (38th pick overall) of 2002 NFL draft. ... Signed by Vikings (July 26, 2002). ... On injured reserve with shoulder injury (September 11, 2002-remainder of season). ... On injured reserve with concussion (December 15, 2004-remainder of season).

Year Team	G	GS	TOTALS			INTERCEPTIONS			
			Tk.	Ast.	Sks.	No.	Yds.	Avg.	TD
2003—Minnesota NFL	7	0	0	0	0.0	0	0	0.0	0
2004—Minnesota NFL	7	3	12	5	0.0	1	19	19.0	0
Pro totals (2 years)	14	3	12	5	0.0	1	19	19.0	0

SMITH, RICHARD — WR — CHIEFS

PERSONAL: Born July 16, 1980, in Shreveport, La. ... 5-10/191.
HIGH SCHOOL: Evangel Christian (Shreveport, La.).
COLLEGE: Arkansas.
TRANSACTIONS/CAREER NOTES: Signed as non-drafted free agent by Kansas City Chiefs (April 27, 2004). ... Released by Chiefs (September 27, 2004). ... Re-signed by Chiefs to practice squad (September 30, 2004). ... Activated (December 24, 2004).

Year Team	G	GS	RECEIVING				TOTALS			
			No.	Yds.	Avg.	TD	TD	2pt.	Pts.	Fum.
2004—Kansas City NFL	4	0	0	0	0.0	0	0	0	0	0

SMITH, ROBAIRE — DT/DE — TEXANS

PERSONAL: Born November 15, 1977, in Flint, Mich. ... 6-4/328. ... Full name: Robaire Freddick Smith. ... Brother of Fernando Smith, defensive end with four NFL teams (1994-2000).
HIGH SCHOOL: Flint (Mich.).
COLLEGE: Michigan State.
TRANSACTIONS/CAREER NOTES: Selected by Tennessee Titans in sixth round (197th pick overall) of 2000 NFL draft. ... Signed by Titans (July 5, 2000). ... Granted free agency (February 28, 2003). ... Re-signed by Titans (May 8, 2003). ... Granted unconditional free agency (March 3, 2004). ... Signed by Houston Texans (March 4, 2004).
CHAMPIONSHIP GAME EXPERIENCE: Played in AFC championship game (2002 season).
HONORS: Named defensive end on THE SPORTING NEWS college All-America second team (1999).

Year Team	G	GS	TOTALS		
			Tk.	Ast.	Sks.
2000—Tennessee NFL	7	0	5	1	2.5
2001—Tennessee NFL	10	0	5	2	2.0
2002—Tennessee NFL	16	2	25	9	2.5
2003—Tennessee NFL	16	15	20	15	4.5
2004—Houston NFL	16	16	33	19	2.0
Pro totals (5 years)	65	33	88	46	13.5

S

SMITH, ROD — WR — BRONCOS

PERSONAL: Born May 15, 1970, in Texarkana, Ark. ... 6-0/200.
HIGH SCHOOL: Texarkana (Ark.).
COLLEGE: Missouri Southern State.
TRANSACTIONS/CAREER NOTES: Signed as non-drafted free agent by Denver Broncos (March 23, 1995).
CHAMPIONSHIP GAME EXPERIENCE: Played in AFC championship game (1997 and 1998 seasons). ... Member of Super Bowl championship team (1997 and 1998 seasons).
HONORS: Played in Pro Bowl (2000 season). ... Named to play in Pro Bowl (2001 season); replaced by Troy Brown due to injury.
SINGLE GAME HIGHS (regular season): Receptions—14 (September 23, 2001, vs. Arizona); yards—208 (October 31, 2004, vs. Atlanta); and touchdown receptions—3 (October 15, 2000, vs. Cleveland).
STATISTICAL PLATEAUS: 100-yard receiving games: 1997 (6), 1998 (4), 1999 (3), 2000 (8), 2001 (5), 2003 (1), 2004 (1). Total: 28.
MISCELLANEOUS: Holds Denver Broncos all-time record for most receptions (712), most yards receiving (9,772) and most touchdown receptions (59).

			RUSHING				RECEIVING				PUNT RETURNS				KICKOFF RETURNS				TOTALS		
Year Team	G	GS	Att.	Yds.	Avg.	TD	No.	Yds.	Avg.	TD	No.	Yds.	Avg.	TD	No.	Yds.	Avg.	TD	TD	2pt.	Pts.
1995—Den. NFL	16	1	0	0	0.0	0	6	152	25.3	1	0	0	0.0	0	4	54	13.5	0	1	0	6
1996—Den. NFL	10	1	1	1	1.0	0	16	237	14.8	2	23	283	12.3	0	1	29	29.0	0	2	0	12
1997—Den. NFL	16	16	5	16	3.2	0	70	1180	16.9▲	12	1	12	12.0	0	0	0	0.0	0	12	0	72
1998—Den. NFL	16	16	6	63	10.5	0	86	1222	14.2	6	0	0	0.0	0	0	0	0.0	0	7	0	42
1999—Den. NFL	15	15	0	0	0.0	0	79	1020	12.9	4	0	0	0.0	0	1	10	10.0	0	4	0	24
2000—Den. NFL	16	16	6	99	16.5	1	100§	1602	16.0	8	0	0	0.0	0	0	0	0.0	0	9	0	54
2001—Den. NFL	15	14	3	27	9.0	0	*113	1343	11.9	11	0	0	0.0	0	0	0	0.0	0	11	1	68
2002—Den. NFL	16	16	6	9	1.5	0	89	1027	11.5	5	0	0	0.0	0	0	0	0.0	0	5	0	30
2003—Den. NFL	15	15	10	98	9.8	0	74	845	11.4	3	6	127	21.2	1	0	0	0.0	0	4	0	24
2004—Den. NFL	16	16	5	33	6.6	0	79	1144	14.5	7	22	223	10.1	0	0	0	0.0	0	7	0	42
Pro totals (10 years)	151	126	42	346	8.2	1	712	9772	13.7	59	52	645	12.4	1	6	93	15.5	0	62	1	374

SMITH, SHAUN — DT — BENGALS

PERSONAL: Born August 19, 1981, in Brooklyn, N.Y. ... 6-2/320.
HIGH SCHOOL: Wichita Heights (Wichita, Kan.).
COLLEGE: South Carolina.
TRANSACTIONS/CAREER NOTES: Signed as non-drafted free agent by Dallas Cowboys (May 1, 2003). ... Released by Cowboys (August 31, 2003). ... Re-signed by Cowboys to practice squad (September 1, 2003). ... Activated (January 5, 2004). ... Claimed on waivers by Arizona Cardinals (September 1, 2004). ... Released by Cardinals (September 5, 2004). ... Signed by New Orleans Saints to practice squad (September 8, 2004). ... Activated (September 18, 2004). ... Claimed on waivers by Cincinnati Bengals (December 2, 2004).

			TOTALS		
Year Team	G	GS	Tk.	Ast.	Sks.
2003—Dallas NFL	1	0	0	0	0.0
2004—New Orleans NFL	5	1	6	3	0.0
—Cincinnati NFL	3	1	2	0	0.0
Pro totals (2 years)	9	2	8	3	0.0

SMITH, STEVE — WR/PR — PANTHERS

PERSONAL: Born May 12, 1979, in Los Angeles, Calif. ... 5-9/185. ... Full name: Stevonne Smith.
HIGH SCHOOL: University (Los Angeles).
JUNIOR COLLEGE: Santa Monica Junior College.
COLLEGE: Utah.
TRANSACTIONS/CAREER NOTES: Selected by Carolina Panthers in third round (74th pick overall) of 2001 NFL draft. ... Signed by Panthers (June 19, 2001). ... On injured reserve with leg injury (October 27, 2004-remainder of season).
CHAMPIONSHIP GAME EXPERIENCE: Played in NFC championship game (2003 season). ... Played in Super Bowl 38 (2003 season).
HONORS: Named kick returner on THE SPORTING NEWS NFL All-Pro team (2001). ... Played in Pro Bowl (2001 season).
RECORDS: Shares NFL single-game records for most touchdowns by punt returns—2; and most touchdowns by combined kick return—2 (December 8, 2002, vs. Detroit).
SINGLE GAME HIGHS (regular season): Receptions—10 (October 19, 2003, vs. Tennessee); yards—151 (October 19, 2003, vs. Tennessee); and touchdown receptions—1 (December 21, 2003, vs. Detroit).
STATISTICAL PLATEAUS: 100-yard receiving games: 2002 (2), 2003 (3). Total: 5.

			RECEIVING				PUNT RETURNS				KICKOFF RETURNS				TOTALS			
Year Team	G	GS	No.	Yds.	Avg.	TD	No.	Yds.	Avg.	TD	No.	Yds.	Avg.	TD	TD	2pt.	Pts.	Fum.
2001—Carolina NFL	15	1	10	154	15.4	0	34	364	10.7	†1	56	1431	s25.6	†2	3	0	18	8
2002—Carolina NFL	15	13	54	872	16.1	3	*55	470	8.5	†2	26	571	22.0	0	5	0	30	5
2003—Carolina NFL	16	11	88	1110	12.6	7	‡44	439	10.0	1	11	309	28.1	0	8	0	48	5
2004—Carolina NFL	1	1	6	60	10.0	0	0	0	0.0	0	0	0	0.0	0	0	0	0	0
Pro totals (4 years)	47	26	158	2196	13.9	10	133	1273	9.6	4	93	2311	24.8	2	16	0	96	18

SMITH, TERRELLE — FB — BROWNS

PERSONAL: Born March 12, 1978, in West Covina, Calif. ... 6-0/255. ... Full name: Terrelle Vernon Smith.
HIGH SCHOOL: Canyon Springs (Moreno Valley, Calif.).
COLLEGE: Arizona State.

TRANSACTIONS/CAREER NOTES: Selected by New Orleans Saints in fourth round (96th pick overall) of 2000 NFL draft. ... Signed by Saints (July 11, 2000). ... Granted free agency (February 28, 2003). ... Re-signed by Saints (April 22, 2003). ... Granted unconditional free agency (March 3, 2004). ... Signed by Cleveland Browns (March 11, 2004).
SINGLE GAME HIGHS (regular season): Attempts—6 (December 10, 2000, vs. San Francisco); yards—42 (November 19, 2000, vs. Oakland); and rushing touchdowns—0.

				RUSHING				RECEIVING				TOTALS		
Year Team	G	GS	Att.	Yds.	Avg.	TD	No.	Yds.	Avg.	TD	TD	2pt.	Pts.	Fum.
2000—New Orleans NFL	14	9	29	131	4.5	0	12	65	5.4	0	0	0	0	1
2001—New Orleans NFL	14	9	5	8	1.6	0	4	30	7.5	2	2	0	12	1
2002—New Orleans NFL	16	8	5	11	2.2	0	9	30	3.3	0	0	0	0	1
2003—New Orleans NFL	15	10	0	0	0.0	0	6	28	4.7	0	0	0	0	0
2004—Cleveland NFL	16	9	4	9	2.3	0	7	39	5.6	0	0	0	0	0
Pro totals (5 years)	75	45	43	159	3.7	0	38	192	5.1	2	2	0	12	3

SMITH, TRAVIAN   LB   RAIDERS

PERSONAL: Born August 26, 1975, in Shepherd, Texas. ... 6-4/240.
HIGH SCHOOL: Tatum (Texas).
COLLEGE: Oklahoma.
TRANSACTIONS/CAREER NOTES: Selected by Oakland Raiders in fifth round (152nd pick overall) of 1998 NFL draft. ... Signed by Raiders (July 6, 1998). ... Released by Raiders (August 26, 1998). ... Re-signed by Raiders to practice squad (August 31, 1998). ... Activated (December 15, 1998). ... On injured reserve with knee injury (November 19, 2003-remainder of season).
CHAMPIONSHIP GAME EXPERIENCE: Played in AFC championship game (2000 and 2002 seasons). ... Played in Super Bowl 37 (2002 season).

			TOTALS			INTERCEPTIONS			
Year Team	G	GS	Tk.	Ast.	Sks.	No.	Yds.	Avg.	TD
1998—Oakland NFL	2	0	0	0	0.0	0	0	0.0	0
1999—Oakland NFL	16	1	6	1	0.0	0	0	0.0	0
2000—Oakland NFL	16	0	2	0	0.0	0	0	0.0	0
2001—Oakland NFL	16	2	14	11	2.5	1	9	9.0	0
2002—Oakland NFL	16	2	23	7	5.0	0	0	0.0	0
2003—Oakland NFL	10	7	50	10	1.0	0	0	0.0	0
2004—Oakland NFL	8	4	29	11	0.0	0	0	0.0	0
Pro totals (7 years)	84	16	124	40	8.5	1	9	9.0	0

SMITH, TRENT   TE   RAVENS

PERSONAL: Born September 15, 1979, in Norman, Okla. ... 6-5/243.
HIGH SCHOOL: Clinton (Okla.).
COLLEGE: Oklahoma.
TRANSACTIONS/CAREER NOTES: Selected by Baltimore Ravens in seventh round (223rd pick overall) of 2003 NFL draft. ... Signed by Ravens (July 25, 2003). ... On injured reserve with leg injury (August 25, 2003-entire season). ... On injured reserve with leg injury (August 30, 2004-entire season).

SMITH, WADE   T   DOLPHINS

PERSONAL: Born April 26, 1981, in Dallas, Texas. ... 6-4/315.
HIGH SCHOOL: Lake Highlands (Dallas).
COLLEGE: Memphis.
TRANSACTIONS/CAREER NOTES: Selected by Miami Dolphins in third round (78th pick overall) of 2003 NFL draft. ... Signed by Dolphins (July 28, 2003).
PLAYING EXPERIENCE: Miami NFL, 2003-2004. ... Games/Games started: 2003 (16/16), 2004 (6/2). Total: 22/18.

SMITH, WILL   DE   SAINTS

PERSONAL: Born August 4, 1981, in Queens, N.Y. ... 6-3/282.
HIGH SCHOOL: Proctor (Utica, N.Y.).
COLLEGE: Ohio State.
TRANSACTIONS/CAREER NOTES: Selected by New Orleans Saints in first round (18th pick overall) of 2004 NFL draft. ... Signed by Saints (July 31, 2004).
HONORS: Named defensive end on THE SPORTING NEWS college All-America second team (2003).

			TOTALS			INTERCEPTIONS			
Year Team	G	GS	Tk.	Ast.	Sks.	No.	Yds.	Avg.	TD
2004—New Orleans NFL	16	4	32	10	7.5	0	0	0.0	0

SMOOT, FRED   CB   VIKINGS

PERSONAL: Born April 17, 1979, in Jackson, Miss. ... 5-11/174. ... Full name: Fredrick D. Smoot.
HIGH SCHOOL: Provine (Jackson, Miss.).
JUNIOR COLLEGE: Hinds Community College (Miss.).
COLLEGE: Mississippi State.
TRANSACTIONS/CAREER NOTES: Selected by Washington Redskins in second round (45th pick overall) of 2001 NFL draft. ... Signed by Redskins (July 31, 2001). ... Granted unconditional free agency (March 2, 2005). ... Signed by Minnesota Vikings (March 8, 2005).

Year Team	G	GS	TOTALS			INTERCEPTIONS			
			Tk.	Ast.	Sks.	No.	Yds.	Avg.	TD
2001—Washington NFL	14	13	30	3	0.0	5	36	7.2	0
2002—Washington NFL	16	16	49	12	0.0	4	12	3.0	0
2003—Washington NFL	15	15	49	8	0.0	4	35	8.8	0
2004—Washington NFL	15	15	55	6	0.0	3	17	5.7	0
Pro totals (4 years)	60	59	183	29	0.0	16	100	6.3	0

SNEE, CHRIS G GIANTS

PERSONAL: Born January 8, 1982, in Edison, N.J. ... 6-2/314. ... Full name: Christopher Snee.
HIGH SCHOOL: Montrose, Pa.
COLLEGE: Boston College.
TRANSACTIONS/CAREER NOTES: Selected by New York Giants in second round (34th pick overall) of 2004 NFL draft. ... Signed by Giants (July 30, 2004).
PLAYING EXPERIENCE: New York Giants NFL, 2004. ... Games/Games started: 2004 (11/11). Total: 11/11.
HONORS: Named guard on THE SPORTING NEWS Freshman All-America fourth team (2001).

SNOW, JUSTIN TE COLTS

PERSONAL: Born December 21, 1976, in Fort Worth, Texas. ... 6-3/240.
HIGH SCHOOL: Cooper (Abilene, Texas).
COLLEGE: Baylor.
TRANSACTIONS/CAREER NOTES: Signed as non-drafted free agent by Indianapolis Colts (April 20, 2000).
CHAMPIONSHIP GAME EXPERIENCE: Played in AFC championship game (2003 season).

Year Team	G	GS	RECEIVING				TOTALS			
			No.	Yds.	Avg.	TD	TD	2pt.	Pts.	Fum.
2000—Indianapolis NFL	16	0	0	0	0.0	0	0	0	0	0
2001—Indianapolis NFL	16	0	0	0	0.0	0	0	0	0	0
2002—Indianapolis NFL	16	0	0	0	0.0	0	0	0	0	0
2003—Indianapolis NFL	16	0	0	0	0.0	0	0	0	0	0
2004—Indianapolis NFL	16	0	0	0	0.0	0	0	0	0	0
Pro totals (5 years)	80	0	0	0	0.0	0	0	0	0	0

SOLWOLD, MIKE C

PERSONAL: Born September 30, 1977, in Menomonee Falls, Wis. ... 6-6/244.
HIGH SCHOOL: Arrowhead (Wis.).
COLLEGE: Wisconsin.
TRANSACTIONS/CAREER NOTES: Signed as non-drafted free agent by Minnesota Vikings (April 22, 2001). ... Claimed on waivers by Dallas Cowboys (August 28, 2001). ... Released by Cowboys (September 3, 2001). ... Re-signed by Cowboys (November 14, 2001). ... Released by Cowboys (April 18, 2002). ... Signed by Tampa Bay Buccaneers (May 1, 2002). ... On injured reserve with foot injury (October 1, 2002-remainder of season). ... Granted free agency (February 28, 2003). ... Released by Ravens (July 30, 2004). ... Signed by Ravens (December 11, 2004). ... Released by Ravens (December 13, 2004). ... Signed by New England Patriots to practice squad (January 13, 2005). ... Released by Patriots (January 17, 2005).
PLAYING EXPERIENCE: Dallas NFL, 2001; Tampa Bay NFL, 2002; Baltimore NFL, 2004. ... Games/Games started: 2001 (8/0), 2002 (4/0), 2004 (1/0). Total: 13/0.

SORENSEN, NICK S JAGUARS

PERSONAL: Born July 31, 1978, in Winter Haven, Fla. ... 6-3/210. ... Full name: Nicholas Carl Sorensen.
HIGH SCHOOL: George C. Marshall (Vienna, Va.).
COLLEGE: Virginia Tech.
TRANSACTIONS/CAREER NOTES: Signed as non-drafted free agent by Miami Dolphins (April 26, 2001). ... Released by Dolphins (August 26, 2001). ... Signed by St. Louis Rams to practice squad (October 16, 2001). ... Activated (November 16, 2001). ... Released by Rams (November 24, 2001). ... Re-signed by Rams (November 27, 2001). ... Released by Rams (August 31, 2003). ... Signed by Jacksonville Jaguars (September 16, 2003).
CHAMPIONSHIP GAME EXPERIENCE: Played in NFC championship game (2001 season). ... Played in Super Bowl 36 (2001 season).

Year Team	G	GS	TOTALS			INTERCEPTIONS			
			Tk.	Ast.	Sks.	No.	Yds.	Avg.	TD
2001—St. Louis NFL	7	0	1	0	0.0	0	0	0.0	0
2002—St. Louis NFL	16	0	1	0	0.0	0	0	0.0	0
2003—Jacksonville NFL	14	0	0	0	0.0	0	0	0.0	0
2004—Jacksonville NFL	16	0	0	0	0.0	0	0	0.0	0
Pro totals (4 years)	53	0	2	0	0.0	0	0	0.0	0

SORGI, JIM QB COLTS

PERSONAL: Born December 3, 1980, in Fraser, Mich. ... 6-5/196.
HIGH SCHOOL: Fraser (Mich.).
COLLEGE: Wisconsin.

Year Team	G	GS	PASSING									RUSHING				TOTALS		
			Att.	Cmp.	Pct.	Yds.	TD	Int.	Avg.	Skd.	Rat.	Att.	Yds.	Avg.	TD	TD	2pt.	Pts.
2004—Indianapolis NFL............	4	0	29	17	58.6	175	2	0	6.03	1	99.1	8	-5	-0.6	0	0	0	0

SOWELL, JERALD — FB — JETS

PERSONAL: Born January 21, 1974, in Elyria, Ohio. ... 6-0/237. ... Full name: Jerald Monye Sowell.
HIGH SCHOOL: Baker (La.).
COLLEGE: Tulane.
TRANSACTIONS/CAREER NOTES: Selected by Green Bay Packers in seventh round (231st pick overall) of 1997 NFL draft. ... Signed by Packers (July 10, 1997). ... Claimed on waivers by New York Jets (August 25, 1997). ... Granted free agency (February 11, 2000). ... Re-signed by Jets (April 25, 2000). ... Granted unconditional free agency (February 28, 2003). ... Re-signed by Jets (March 3, 2003).
CHAMPIONSHIP GAME EXPERIENCE: Member of Jets for AFC championship game (1998 season); inactive.
SINGLE GAME HIGHS (regular season): Attempts—14 (November 8, 1998, vs. Buffalo); yards—82 (September 20, 1998, vs. Indianapolis); and rushing touchdowns—0.

Year Team	G	GS	RUSHING				RECEIVING				TOTALS			
			Att.	Yds.	Avg.	TD	No.	Yds.	Avg.	TD	TD	2pt.	Pts.	Fum.
1997—New York Jets NFL	9	0	7	35	5.0	0	1	8	8.0	0	0	0	0	0
1998—New York Jets NFL	16	2	40	164	4.1	0	10	59	5.9	0	0	0	0	2
1999—New York Jets NFL	16	0	3	5	1.7	0	0	0	0.0	0	0	0	0	0
2000—New York Jets NFL	16	0	2	0	0.0	0	6	84	14.0	0	0	0	0	0
2001—New York Jets NFL	16	0	4	9	2.3	0	1	19	19.0	0	0	0	0	0
2002—New York Jets NFL	16	0	1	0	0.0	0	9	85	9.4	1	1	0	6	0
2003—New York Jets NFL	16	16	1	2	2.0	0	47	436	9.3	1	1	0	6	0
2004—New York Jets NFL	16	16	2	28	14.0	0	45	342	7.6	1	1	0	6	1
Pro totals (8 years)...........................	121	34	60	243	4.1	0	119	1033	8.7	3	3	0	18	3

SPEARS, MARCUS — T

PERSONAL: Born September 28, 1971, in Baton Rouge, La. ... 6-4/320. ... Full name: Marcus DeWayne Spears.
HIGH SCHOOL: Belaire (Baton Rouge, La.).
COLLEGE: Northwestern State.
TRANSACTIONS/CAREER NOTES: Selected by Chicago Bears in second round (39th pick overall) of 1994 NFL draft. ... Signed by Bears (July 16, 1994). ... Inactive for all 16 games (1994). ... Active for five games (1995); did not play. ... Assigned by Bears to Amsterdam Admirals in 1996 World League enhancement allocation program (February 19, 1996). ... Granted unconditional free agency (February 14, 1997). ... Signed by Green Bay Packers (March 12, 1997). ... Released by Packers (August 19, 1997). ... Signed by Kansas City Chiefs (September 16, 1997). ... On injured reserve with hand injury (December 9, 1998-remainder of season). ... Granted unconditional free agency (February 12, 1999). ... Re-signed by Chiefs (February 16, 1999). ... On injured reserve with arm injury (December 15, 2000-remainder of season). ... Granted unconditional free agency (March 1, 2002). ... Re-signed by Chiefs (May 6, 2002). ... Released by Chiefs (June 16, 2004). ... Signed by Houston Texans (July 1, 2004). ... Granted unconditional free agency (March 2, 2005).
PLAYING EXPERIENCE: Chicago NFL, 1996; Houston NFL, 2004. ... Games/Games started: 1996 (9/0), 1997 (3/0), 1998 (12/0), 1999 (10/2), 2000 (13/0), 2001 (16/16), 2002 (9/0), 2003 (15/0), 2004 (16/3). Total: 103/21.
HONORS: Named offensive lineman on THE SPORTING NEWS college All-America second team (1993).

SPENCER, CODY — LB — TITANS

PERSONAL: Born June 1, 1981, in Port Lavaca, Texas. ... 6-2/242.
HIGH SCHOOL: Grapevine (Texas).
COLLEGE: North Texas.
TRANSACTIONS/CAREER NOTES: Selected by Oakland Raiders in sixth round (182nd pick overall) of 2004 NFL draft. ... Signed by Raiders (July 30, 2004). ... Released by Raiders (September 5, 2004). ... Signed by Tennessee Titans (September 7, 2004). ... Activated (October 7, 2004).

Year Team	G	GS	TOTALS			INTERCEPTIONS			
			Tk.	Ast.	Sks.	No.	Yds.	Avg.	TD
2004—Tennessee NFL..	7	0	1	0	0.0	0	0	0.0	0

SPENCER, SHAWNTAE — CB — 49ERS

PERSONAL: Born February 22, 1982, in Rankin, Pa. ... 6-1/181.
HIGH SCHOOL: Woodland Hills (Pa.).
COLLEGE: Pittsburgh.
TRANSACTIONS/CAREER NOTES: Selected by San Francisco 49ers in second round (58th pick overall) of 2004 NFL draft. ... Signed by 49ers (July 30, 2004).

Year Team	G	GS	TOTALS			INTERCEPTIONS			
			Tk.	Ast.	Sks.	No.	Yds.	Avg.	TD
2004—San Francisco NFL..	16	12	59	8	0.0	0	0	0.0	0

SPICER, PAUL — DE — JAGUARS

PERSONAL: Born August 18, 1975, in Indianapolis, Ind. ... 6-4/287.
HIGH SCHOOL: Northwestern (Indianapolis).
COLLEGE: Saginaw Valley.
TRANSACTIONS/CAREER NOTES: Signed as non-drafted free agent by Seattle Seahawks (April 20, 1998). ... Released by Seahawks (August 24, 1998). ... Signed by Sasketchewan Roughriders of CFL (September 26, 1998). ... Signed by Detroit Lions (February 24, 1999). ... Released by Lions (September 5, 1999). ... Re-signed by Lions to practice squad (September 7, 1999). ... Activated (October 8, 1999). ... Released by Lions (November 6, 1999). ... Re-signed by Lions to practice squad (November 10, 1999). ... Released by Lions (August 22, 2000). ... Signed by Jacksonville Jaguars to practice squad (August 30, 2000). ... Activated (October 4, 2000). ... Assigned by Jaguars to Frankfurt Galaxy in 2001 NFL Europe enhancement allocation program (February 19, 2001). ... Granted free agency (February 28, 2003). ... Re-signed by Jaguars (April 23, 2003). ... On injured reserve with leg injury (September 23, 2004-remainder of season).

Year Team	G	GS	TOTALS			INTERCEPTIONS			
			Tk.	Ast.	Sks.	No.	Yds.	Avg.	TD
1998—Saskatchewan CFL	7	...	...	...	4.0	0	0	0.0	0
1999—Detroit NFL	2	0	0	0	0.0	0	0	0.0	0
2000—Jacksonville NFL	3	0	4	1	1.0	0	0	0.0	0
2001—Jacksonville NFL	16	4	23	5	2.0	0	0	0.0	0
2002—Jacksonville NFL	16	4	35	2	4.0	0	0	0.0	0
2003—Jacksonville NFL	16	1	24	8	0.0	1	2	2.0	0
2004—Jacksonville NFL	2	2	4	1	0.0	0	0	0.0	0
CFL totals (1 year)	7	...	...	...	4.0	0	0	0.0	0
NFL totals (6 years)	55	11	90	17	7.0	1	2	2.0	0
Pro totals (7 years)	62	...	...	...	11.0	1	2	2.0	0

SPIKES, CAMERON — G

PERSONAL: Born November 6, 1976, in Madisonville, Texas. ... 6-4/313. ... Full name: Cameron Wade Spikes.
HIGH SCHOOL: Bryan (Texas).
COLLEGE: Texas A&M.
TRANSACTIONS/CAREER NOTES: Selected by St. Louis Rams in fifth round (145th pick overall) of 1999 NFL draft. ... Signed by Rams (July 19, 1999). ... Granted free agency (March 1, 2002). ... Re-signed by Rams (April 17, 2002). ... Claimed on waivers by Houston Texans (August 26, 2002). ... Granted unconditional free agency (February 28, 2003). ... Signed by Arizona Cardinals (March 28, 2003). ... Granted unconditional free agency (March 2, 2005).
PLAYING EXPERIENCE: St. Louis NFL, 1999-2001; Houston NFL, 2002; Arizona NFL, 2004. ... Games/Games started: 1999 (5/0), 2000 (9/0), 2001 (5/0), 2002 (12/5), 2003 (16/16), 2004 (16/9).
CHAMPIONSHIP GAME EXPERIENCE: Member of Rams for NFC championship game (1999 and 2001 seasons); inactive. ... Member of Super Bowl championship team (1999 season); inactive. ... Played in Super Bowl 36 (2001 season).

SPIKES, TAKEO — LB — BILLS

PERSONAL: Born December 17, 1976, in Sandersville, Ga. ... 6-2/242. ... Full name: Takeo Gerard Spikes. ... Name pronounced: tuh-KEE-oh.
HIGH SCHOOL: Washington County (Sandersville, Ga.).
COLLEGE: Auburn.
TRANSACTIONS/CAREER NOTES: Selected after junior season by Cincinnati Bengals in first round (13th pick overall) of 1998 NFL draft. ... Signed by Bengals (July 25, 1998). ... Designated by Bengals as transition player (February 20, 2003). ... Tendered offer sheet by Buffalo Bills (March 10, 2003). ... Bengals declined to match offer (March 11, 2003).
HONORS: Named inside linebacker on THE SPORTING NEWS college All-America first team (1997). ... Named linebacker on THE SPORTING NEWS NFL All-Pro team (2004). ... Played in Pro Bowl (2003 and 2004 seasons).

Year Team	G	GS	TOTALS			INTERCEPTIONS			
			Tk.	Ast.	Sks.	No.	Yds.	Avg.	TD
1998—Cincinnati NFL	16	16	95	17	2.0	0	0	0.0	0
1999—Cincinnati NFL	16	16	82	23	3.0	2	7	3.5	0
2000—Cincinnati NFL	16	16	109	19	2.0	2	12	6.0	0
2001—Cincinnati NFL	15	15	80	29	6.0	1	66	66.0	1
2002—Cincinnati NFL	16	16	81	32	1.5	0	0	0.0	0
2003—Buffalo NFL	16	16	70	56	2.0	2	1	0.5	0
2004—Buffalo NFL	16	16	64	35	3.0	5	122	24.4	†2
Pro totals (7 years)	111	111	581	211	19.5	12	208	17.3	3

SPIRES, GREG — DE — BUCCANEERS

PERSONAL: Born August 12, 1974, in Marianna, Fla. ... 6-1/265. ... Full name: Greg Tyrone Spires.
HIGH SCHOOL: Mariner (Cape Coral, Fla.).
COLLEGE: Florida State.
TRANSACTIONS/CAREER NOTES: Selected by New England Patriots in third round (83rd pick overall) of 1998 NFL draft. ... Signed by Patriots (July 16, 1998). ... On injured reserve with knee injury (December 15, 1999-remainder of season). ... Granted free agency (March 2, 2001). ... Re-signed by Patriots (April 30, 2001). ... Claimed on waivers by Cleveland Browns (September 4, 2001). ... Granted unconditional free agency (March 1, 2002). ... Signed by Tampa Bay Buccaneers (March 22, 2002). ... On injured reserve with shoulder injury (December 22, 2003-remainder of season).
CHAMPIONSHIP GAME EXPERIENCE: Played in NFC championship game (2002 season). ... Member of Super Bowl championship team (2002 season).

Year Team	G	GS	TOTALS		
			Tk.	Ast.	Sks.
1998—New England NFL	15	1	18	6	3.0
1999—New England NFL	11	1	6	1	0.5
2000—New England NFL	16	2	12	5	6.0

Year Team	G	GS	TOTALS Tk.	Ast.	Sks.
2001—Cleveland NFL	16	4	23	8	4.0
2002—Tampa Bay NFL	16	16	27	10	3.5
2003—Tampa Bay NFL	15	15	24	12	3.5
2004—Tampa Bay NFL	16	16	47	14	8.0
Pro totals (7 years)	105	55	157	56	28.5

SPRAGAN, DONNIE   LB   DOLPHINS

PERSONAL: Born July 12, 1976, in Oakland, Calif. ... 6-3/239.
HIGH SCHOOL: Logan (Union City, Calif.).
COLLEGE: Stanford.
TRANSACTIONS/CAREER NOTES: Signed as non-drafted free agent by New Orleans Saints (April 23, 1999). ... On injured reserve with knee injury (September 6, 1999-entire season). ... Released by Saints (August 22, 2000). ... Signed by Green Bay Packers (July 19, 2001). ... Released by Packers (September 1, 2001). ... Signed by Cleveland Browns to practice squad (October 2, 2001). ... Released by Browns (October 31, 2001). ... Signed by Denver Broncos to practice squad (December 11, 2001). ... Granted free agency (March 3, 2004). ... Re-signed by Broncos (2004). ... Granted unconditional free agency (March 2, 2005). ... Signed by Miami Dolphins (March 11, 2005).

Year Team	G	GS	TOTALS Tk.	Ast.	Sks.	INTERCEPTIONS No.	Yds.	Avg.	TD
2002—Denver NFL	16	0	0	0	0.0	0	0	0.0	0
2003—Denver NFL	16	8	38	8	0.0	0	0	0.0	0
2004—Denver NFL	16	14	44	22	1.0	0	0	0.0	0
Pro totals (3 years)	48	22	82	30	1.0	0	0	0.0	0

SPRINGS, SHAWN   CB   REDSKINS

PERSONAL: Born March 11, 1975, in Silver Spring, Md. ... 6-0/204. ... Son of Ron Springs, running back with Dallas Cowboys (1979-84) and Tampa Bay Buccaneers (1985 and 1986).
HIGH SCHOOL: Springbrook (Silver Spring, Md.).
COLLEGE: Ohio State.
TRANSACTIONS/CAREER NOTES: Selected by Seattle Seahawks in first round (third pick overall) of 1997 NFL draft. ... Signed by Seahawks (August 4, 1997). ... On suspended list for violating league substance abuse policy (November 27-January 4, 2001). ... Granted unconditional free agency (March 3, 2004). ... Signed by Washington Redskins (March 4, 2004).
HONORS: Named cornerback on THE SPORTING NEWS college All-America second team (1996). ... Played in Pro Bowl (1998 season).

Year Team	G	GS	TOTALS Tk.	Ast.	Sks.	INTERCEPTIONS No.	Yds.	Avg.	TD
1997—Seattle NFL	10	10	34	5	0.0	1	0	0.0	0
1998—Seattle NFL	16	16	61	14	0.0	7	142	20.3	▲2
1999—Seattle NFL	16	16	63	10	0.0	5	77	15.4	0
2000—Seattle NFL	16	16	72	13	0.0	2	8	4.0	0
2001—Seattle NFL	8	7	16	4	0.0	1	0	0.0	0
2002—Seattle NFL	15	15	54	5	0.0	3	0	0.0	0
2003—Seattle NFL	12	8	34	5	1.5	1	8	8.0	0
2004—Washington NFL	15	15	52	12	6.0	5	117	23.4	0
Pro totals (8 years)	108	103	386	68	7.5	25	352	14.1	2

STALEY, DUCE   RB   STEELERS

PERSONAL: Born February 27, 1975, in Tampa, Fla. ... 5-11/242. ... Name pronounced: DEUCE.
HIGH SCHOOL: Airport (Columbia, S.C.).
JUNIOR COLLEGE: Itawamba Community College (Miss.).
COLLEGE: South Carolina.
TRANSACTIONS/CAREER NOTES: Selected by Philadelphia Eagles in third round (71st pick overall) of 1997 NFL draft. ... Signed by Eagles (June 12, 1997). ... On injured reserve with foot injury (October 10, 2000-remainder of season). ... On reserve/did not report list (July 29, 2003). ... Activated (August 24, 2003). ... Granted unconditional free agency (March 3, 2004). ... Signed by Pittsburgh Steelers (March 10, 2004).
CHAMPIONSHIP GAME EXPERIENCE: Played in NFC championship game (2001-2003 seasons). ... Played in AFC championship game (2004 season).
SINGLE GAME HIGHS (regular season): Attempts—31 (November 17, 2002, vs. Arizona); yards—201 (September 3, 2000, vs. Dallas); and rushing touchdowns—2 (December 21, 2003, vs. San Francisco).
STATISTICAL PLATEAUS: 100-yard rushing games: 1998 (1), 1999 (5), 2000 (1), 2001 (2), 2002 (4), 2004 (4). Total: 17. 100-yard receiving games: 2001 (1). Total: 1.

Year Team	G	GS	RUSHING Att.	Yds.	Avg.	TD	RECEIVING No.	Yds.	Avg.	TD	KICKOFF RETURNS No.	Yds.	Avg.	TD	TOTALS TD	2pt.	Pts.	Fum.
1997—Philadelphia NFL	16	0	7	29	4.1	0	2	22	11.0	0	47	1139	24.2	0	0	0	0	0
1998—Philadelphia NFL	16	13	258	1065	4.1	5	57	432	7.6	1	1	19	19.0	0	6	0	36	2
1999—Philadelphia NFL	16	16	325	1273	3.9	4	41	294	7.2	2	0	0	0.0	0	6	0	36	5
2000—Philadelphia NFL	5	5	79	344	4.4	1	25	201	8.0	0	0	0	0.0	0	1	0	6	3
2001—Philadelphia NFL	13	10	166	604	3.6	2	63	626	9.9	2	0	0	0.0	0	4	0	24	3
2002—Philadelphia NFL	16	16	269	1029	3.8	5	51	541	10.6	3	0	0	0.0	0	8	1	50	3
2003—Philadelphia NFL	16	4	96	463	4.8	5	36	382	10.6	2	0	0	0.0	0	7	0	42	2
2004—Pittsburgh NFL	10	10	192	830	4.3	1	6	55	9.2	0	0	0	0.0	0	1	0	6	3
Pro totals (8 years)	108	74	1392	5637	4.0	23	281	2553	9.1	10	48	1158	24.1	0	33	1	200	21

STALLWORTH, DONTE' WR SAINTS

PERSONAL: Born November 10, 1980, in Sacramento, Calif. ... 6-0/196. ... Full name: Donte' Lamar Stallworth.
HIGH SCHOOL: Grant (Sacramento, Calif.).
COLLEGE: Tennessee.
TRANSACTIONS/CAREER NOTES: Selected after junior season by New Orleans Saints in first round (13th pick overall) of 2002 NFL draft. ... Signed by Saints (July 29, 2002).
SINGLE GAME HIGHS (regular season): Receptions—10 (November 21, 2004, vs. Denver); yards—122 (November 21, 2004, vs. Denver); and touchdown receptions—1 (December 26, 2004, vs. Atlanta).
STATISTICAL PLATEAUS: 100-yard receiving games: 2002 (1), 2003 (2), 2004 (3). Total: 6.

			RUSHING				RECEIVING				PUNT RETURNS				KICKOFF RETURNS				TOTALS		
Year Team	G	GS	Att.	Yds.	Avg.	TD	No.	Yds.	Avg.	TD	No.	Yds.	Avg.	TD	No.	Yds.	Avg.	TD	TD	2pt.	Pts.
2002—N.O. NFL	13	7	2	2	1.0	0	42	594	14.1	8	0	0	0.0	0	0	0	0.0	0	8	0	48
2003—N.O. NFL	11	3	1	3	3.0	0	25	485	19.4	3	5	44	8.8	0	0	0	0.0	0	3	0	18
2004—N.O. NFL	16	10	6	37	6.2	0	58	767	13.2	5	6	6	1.0	0	0	0	0.0	0	5	0	30
Pro totals (3 years)	40	20	9	42	4.7	0	125	1846	14.8	16	11	50	4.5	0	8	171	21.4	0	16	0	96

STAMER, JOSH LB BILLS

PERSONAL: Born October 11, 1977, in Sutherland, Iowa. ... 6-2/238.
HIGH SCHOOL: Sutherland (Iowa).
COLLEGE: South Dakota.
TRANSACTIONS/CAREER NOTES: Signed as non-drafted free agent by New York Giants (April 26, 2001). ... Released by Giants (June 28, 2002). ... Signed by Seattle Seahawks (July 23, 2002). ... Released by Seahawks (September 1, 2002). ... Signed by Buffalo Bills (January 21, 2003).

			TOTALS			INTERCEPTIONS			
Year Team	G	GS	Tk.	Ast.	Sks.	No.	Yds.	Avg.	TD
2003—Buffalo NFL	16	0	3	1	0.0	0	0	0.0	0
2004—Buffalo NFL	16	0	5	4	0.0	1	0	0.0	0
Pro totals (2 years)	32	0	8	5	0.0	1	0	0.0	0

STANLEY, CHAD P TEXANS

PERSONAL: Born January 29, 1976, in Ore City, Texas. ... 6-3/216. ... Full name: Benjamin Chadwick Stanley.
HIGH SCHOOL: Ore City (Texas).
COLLEGE: Stephen F. Austin.
TRANSACTIONS/CAREER NOTES: Signed as non-drafted free agent by San Francisco 49ers (April 23, 1999). ... Released by 49ers (September 1, 2001). ... Signed by Arizona Cardinals (November 6, 2001). ... Released by Cardinals (December 5, 2001). ... Signed by Houston Texans (February 6, 2002). ... Granted free agency (February 28, 2003). ... Re-signed by Texans (June 1, 2003).
RECORDS: Shares NFL single-season record for most punts—114 (2002).

		PUNTING					
Year Team	G	No.	Yds.	Avg.	Net avg.	In. 20	Blk.
1999—San Francisco NFL	16	69	2737	39.7	30.7	20	†2
2000—San Francisco NFL	16	69	2727	39.5	32.2	15	1
2001—Arizona NFL	4	19	751	39.5	34.2	4	0
2002—Houston NFL	16	*114	§4720	41.4	36.8	*36	2
2003—Houston NFL	16	*97	4028	41.5	36.7	36	0
2004—Houston NFL	16	73	3009	41.2	35.7	19	0
Pro totals (6 years)	84	441	17972	40.8	34.8	130	5

STANLEY, MATT FB

PERSONAL: Born April 27, 1979, in Pasadena, Calif. ... 6-3/245. ... Full name: Matthew Charles Stanley.
HIGH SCHOOL: Bexley (Ohio).
COLLEGE: UCLA.
TRANSACTIONS/CAREER NOTES: Signed as non-drafted free agent by San Francisco 49ers (April 24, 2002). ... Released by 49ers (August 13, 2002). ... Re-signed by 49ers (January 29, 2003). ... Assigned by 49ers to Rhein Fire in 2003 NFL Europe enhancement allocation program (February 4, 2003). ... Released by 49ers (August 31, 2003). ... Re-signed by 49ers (April 13, 2004). ... Released by 49ers (September 5, 2004). ... Re-signed by 49ers to practice squad (September 6, 2004). ... Activated (September 11, 2004). ... Released by 49ers (September 14, 2004). ... Re-signed by 49ers to practice squad (September 15, 2004). ... Released by 49ers from practice squad (September 21, 2004).

STARKS, DUANE CB PATRIOTS

PERSONAL: Born May 23, 1974, in Miami, Fla. ... 5-10/174. ... Full name: Duane Lonell Starks.
HIGH SCHOOL: Miami Beach Senior.
JUNIOR COLLEGE: Holmes Junior College (Miss.).
COLLEGE: Miami (Fla.).
TRANSACTIONS/CAREER NOTES: Selected by Baltimore Ravens in first round (10th pick overall) of 1998 NFL draft. ... Signed by Ravens (August 5, 1998). ... Granted unconditional free agency (March 1, 2002). ... Signed by Arizona Cardinals (March 18, 2002). ... On injured reserve with knee injury (August 27, 2003-entire season). ... Traded by Cardinals with fifth-round (traded to Detroit) pick in 2005 draft to New England Patriots for third- (LB Darryl Blackstock) and fifth- (LB Lance Mitchell) round picks in 2005 draft (March 3, 2005).
CHAMPIONSHIP GAME EXPERIENCE: Played in AFC championship game (2000 season). ... Member of Super Bowl championship team (2000 season).

Year Team	G	GS	TOTALS			INTERCEPTIONS				PUNT RETURNS				TOTALS			
			Tk.	Ast.	Sks.	No.	Yds.	Avg.	TD	No.	Yds.	Avg.	TD	TD	2pt.	Pts.	Fum.
1998—Baltimore NFL	16	8	49	4	0.0	5	3	0.6	0	0	0	0.0	0	0	0	0	0
1999—Baltimore NFL	16	6	39	3	0.0	5	59	11.8	1	0	0	0.0	0	1	0	6	0
2000—Baltimore NFL	15	15	45	4	0.0	6	125	20.8	0	9	135	15.0	0	0	0	0	1
2001—Baltimore NFL	15	15	54	5	0.0	4	9	2.3	0	0	0	0.0	0	0	0	0	0
2002—Arizona NFL	10	10	47	8	0.0	2	3	1.5	0	0	0	0.0	0	0	0	0	0
2003—Arizona NFL	Did not play.																
2004—Arizona NFL	15	8	53	5	1.0	3	46	15.3	1	7	43	6.1	0	1	0	6	0
Pro totals (6 years)	87	62	287	29	1.0	25	245	9.8	2	16	178	11.1	0	2	0	12	1

STARKS, MAX   T   STEELERS

PERSONAL: Born January 10, 1982, in Orlando, Fla. ... 6-7/337. ... Son of Ross Browner, defensive end with Cincinnati Bengals (1978-86) and Green Bay Packers (1987).
HIGH SCHOOL: Lake Highland Prep (Orlando, Fla.).
COLLEGE: Florida.
TRANSACTIONS/CAREER NOTES: Selected by Pittsburgh Steelers in third round (75th pick overall) of 2004 NFL draft. ... Signed by Steelers (July 27, 2004).
PLAYING EXPERIENCE: Pittsburgh NFL, 2004. ... Games/Games started: 2004 (10/0). Total: 10/0.
CHAMPIONSHIP GAME EXPERIENCE: Played in AFC championship game (2004 season).

STARKS, RANDY   DT   TITANS

PERSONAL: Born December 14, 1983, in Petersburg, Va. ... 6-3/307.
HIGH SCHOOL: Westlake (Waldorf, Md.).
COLLEGE: Maryland.
TRANSACTIONS/CAREER NOTES: Selected after junior season by Tennessee Titans in third round (71st pick overall) of 2004 NFL draft. ... Signed by Titans (July 29, 2004).
HONORS: Named defensive tackle on THE SPORTING NEWS Freshman All-America fourth team (2001). ... Named defensive tackle on THE SPORTING NEWS college All-America second team (2003).

Year Team	G	GS	TOTALS		
			Tk.	Ast.	Sks.
2004—Tennessee NFL	14	8	17	11	4.5

STARLING, KENDRICK   WR   TEXANS

PERSONAL: Born December 27, 1979, in Marshall, Texas. ... 6-0/193.
HIGH SCHOOL: Marshall (Texas).
COLLEGE: Auburn.
TRANSACTIONS/CAREER NOTES: Signed as non-drafted free agent by Houston Texans (April 29, 2004). ... Released by Texans (September 21, 2004). ... Re-signed by Texans to practice squad (September 22, 2004). ... Activated (November 17, 2004).

Year Team	G	GS	RECEIVING				TOTALS			
			No.	Yds.	Avg.	TD	TD	2pt.	Pts.	Fum.
2004—Houston NFL	8	0	0	0	0.0	0	0	0	0	0

ST. CLAIR, JOHN   T   DOLPHINS

PERSONAL: Born July 31, 1977, in Roanoke, Va. ... 6-4/320. ... Full name: John Bradley St. Clair.
HIGH SCHOOL: William Fleming (Roanoke, Va.).
COLLEGE: Virginia.
TRANSACTIONS/CAREER NOTES: Selected by St. Louis Rams in third round (94th pick overall) of 2000 NFL draft. ... Signed by Rams (July 20, 2000). ... Granted free agency (February 28, 2003). ... Re-signed by Rams (April 23, 2003). ... Granted unconditional free agency (March 3, 2004). ... Signed by Miami Dolphins (March 11, 2004).
PLAYING EXPERIENCE: St. Louis NFL, 2000-2003; Miami NFL, 2004. ... Games/Games started: 2002 (16/16), 2003 (16/0), 2004 (14/14). Total: 46/30.
CHAMPIONSHIP GAME EXPERIENCE: Member of Rams for NFC championship game (2001 season); inactive. ... Member of Rams for Super Bowl 36 (2001 season); inactive.

STECKER, AARON   RB   SAINTS

PERSONAL: Born November 13, 1975, in Green Bay, Wis. ... 5-10/213.
HIGH SCHOOL: Ashwaubenon (Green Bay).
COLLEGE: Western Illinois.
TRANSACTIONS/CAREER NOTES: Signed as non-drafted free agent by Chicago Bears (April 18, 1999). ... Released by Bears (August 30, 1999). ... Signed by Tampa Bay Buccaneers to practice squad (October 20, 1999). ... Granted free agency (February 28, 2003). ... Re-signed by Buccaneers (April 10, 2003). ... Granted unconditional free agency (March 3, 2004). ... Signed by New Orleans Saints (March 4, 2004).
CHAMPIONSHIP GAME EXPERIENCE: Played in NFC championship game (2002 season). ... Member of Super Bowl championship team (2002 season).
SINGLE GAME HIGHS (regular season): Attempts—18 (September 26, 2004, vs. St. Louis); yards—106 (September 26, 2004, vs. St. Louis); and rushing touchdowns—1 (January 2, 2005, vs. Carolina).
STATISTICAL PLATEAUS: 100-yard rushing games: 2004 (1). Total: 1.

Year Team	G	GS	RUSHING				RECEIVING				KICKOFF RETURNS				TOTALS			
			Att.	Yds.	Avg.	TD	No.	Yds.	Avg.	TD	No.	Yds.	Avg.	TD	TD	2pt.	Pts.	Fum.
2000—Tampa Bay NFL	10	0	12	31	2.6	0	1	15	15.0	0	29	663	22.9	0	0	0	0	1
2001—Tampa Bay NFL	13	0	24	72	3.0	1	10	101	10.1	1	9	259	28.8	0	2	0	12	0
2002—Tampa Bay NFL	16	1	28	174	6.2	0	13	69	5.3	0	37	934	25.2	0	0	0	0	3
2003—Tampa Bay NFL	16	1	37	125	3.4	0	9	48	5.3	1	25	520	20.8	0	1	0	6	1
2004—New Orleans NFL	16	3	58	244	4.2	2	29	174	6.0	0	18	469	26.1	1	3	0	18	1
Pro totals (5 years)	71	5	159	646	4.1	3	62	407	6.6	2	118	2845	24.1	1	6	0	36	6

STEELE, BEN — TE — PACKERS

PERSONAL: Born May 27, 1978, in Denver, Colo. ... 6-5/250.
HIGH SCHOOL: Palisade (Colo.).
COLLEGE: Mesa State.
TRANSACTIONS/CAREER NOTES: Signed as non-drafted free agent by San Francisco 49ers (April 26, 2001). ... Released by 49ers (September 2, 2001). ... Re-signed by 49ers to practice squad (January 2, 2002). ... Assigned by 49ers to Frankfurt Galaxy in 2002 NFL Europe enhancement allocation program (February 13, 2002). ... Released by 49ers (August 27, 2002). ... Signed by Oakland Raiders to practice squad (November 13, 2002). ... Released by Raiders (November 19, 2002). ... Re-signed by Raiders to practice squad (November 27, 2002). ... Released by Raiders (January 7, 2003). ... Re-signed by Raiders (January 28, 2003). ... Claimed on waivers by Seattle Seahawks (May 5, 2003). ... Released by Seahawks (June 26, 2003). ... Signed by Minnesota Vikings (August 13, 2003). ... Released by Vikings (August 31, 2003). ... Re-signed by Vikings (January 22, 2004). ... Released by Vikings (August 31, 2004). ... Signed by Green Bay Packers to practice squad (September 7, 2004). ... Activated (September 15, 2004).
SINGLE GAME HIGHS (regular season): Receptions—2 (December 19, 2004, vs. Jacksonville); yards—27 (January 2, 2005, vs. Chicago); and touchdown receptions—0.

Year Team	G	GS	RECEIVING				TOTALS			
			No.	Yds.	Avg.	TD	TD	2pt.	Pts.	Fum.
2004—Green Bay NFL	15	0	4	42	10.5	0	0	0	0	0

STEINBACH, ERIC — G — BENGALS

PERSONAL: Born April 4, 1980, in New Lenox, Ill. ... 6-6/297.
HIGH SCHOOL: Providence Catholic (New Lenox, Ill.).
COLLEGE: Iowa.
TRANSACTIONS/CAREER NOTES: Selected by Cincinnati Bengals in second round (33rd pick overall) of 2003 NFL draft. ... Signed by Bengals (July 29, 2003).
PLAYING EXPERIENCE: Cincinnati NFL, 2003-2004. ... Games/Games started: 2003 (15/15), 2004 (16/15). Total: 31/30.

STEMKE, KEVIN — P

PERSONAL: Born November 23, 1978, in Green Bay, Wis. ... 6-2/194.
HIGH SCHOOL: Preble (Green Bay, Wis.).
COLLEGE: Wisconsin.
TRANSACTIONS/CAREER NOTES: Signed as non-drafted free agent by Green Bay Packers (April 27, 2001). ... Released by Packers (August 26, 2001). ... Signed by St. Louis Rams (January 10, 2002). ... Released by Rams (August 12, 2002). ... Signed by Oakland Raiders (August 16, 2002). ... Released by Raiders (September 25, 2002). ... Signed by Miami Dolphins (January 24, 2003). ... Assigned by Dolphins to Scottish Claymores in 2003 NFL Europe enhancement allocation program (February 4, 2003). ... Released by Dolphins (August 29, 2003). ... Signed by Washington Redskins (January 13, 2004). ... Released by Redskins (August 30, 2004). ... Signed by Rams (November 26, 2004). ... Released by Rams (May 9, 2005).

Year Team	G	PUNTING					
		No.	Yds.	Avg.	Net avg.	In. 20	Blk.
2002—Oakland NFL	2	5	212	42.4	31.8	1	1
2004—St. Louis NFL	6	28	1115	39.8	36.1	12	0
Pro totals (2 years)	8	33	1327	40.2	29.7	13	1

STEPANOVICH, ALEX — C — CARDINALS

PERSONAL: Born September 25, 1981, in Berea, Ohio. ... 6-4/301.
HIGH SCHOOL: Berea (Ohio).
COLLEGE: Ohio State.
TRANSACTIONS/CAREER NOTES: Selected by Arizona Cardinals in fourth round (100th pick overall) of 2004 NFL draft. ... Signed by Cardinals (July 27, 2004).
PLAYING EXPERIENCE: Arizona NFL, 2004. ... Games/Games started: 2004 (16/16). Total: 16/16.

STEUSSIE, TODD — T — BUCCANEERS

PERSONAL: Born December 1, 1970, in Canoga Park, Calif. ... 6-6/320. ... Full name: Todd Edward Steussie. ... Name pronounced: STEW-see.
HIGH SCHOOL: Agoura (Calif.).
COLLEGE: California.
TRANSACTIONS/CAREER NOTES: Selected by Minnesota Vikings in first round (19th pick overall) of 1994 NFL draft. ... Signed by Vikings (July 13, 1994). ... Released by Vikings (March 14, 2001). ... Signed by Carolina Panthers (March 29, 2001). ... Released by Panthers (March 11, 2004). ... Signed by Tampa Bay Buccaneers (March 15, 2004).
PLAYING EXPERIENCE: Minnesota NFL, 1994-2000; Carolina NFL, 2001-2003; Tampa Bay NFL, 2004. ... Games/Games started: 1994 (16/16), 1995 (16/16), 1996 (16/16), 1997 (16/16), 1998 (15/15), 1999 (16/16), 2000 (16/16), 2001 (16/16), 2002 (16/16), 2003 (16/16), 2004 (16/5). Total: 175/164.

S

CHAMPIONSHIP GAME EXPERIENCE: Played in NFC championship game (1998, 2000 and 2003 seasons). ... Played in Super Bowl 38 (2003 season).
HONORS: Named offensive lineman on THE SPORTING NEWS college All-America second team (1993). ... Played in Pro Bowl (1997 and 1998 seasons).

STEVENS, JERRAMY   TE   SEAHAWKS

PERSONAL: Born November 13, 1979, in Boise, Idaho. ... 6-7/260.
HIGH SCHOOL: River Ridge (Olympia, Wash.).
COLLEGE: Washington.
TRANSACTIONS/CAREER NOTES: Selected after junior season by Seattle Seahawks in first round (28th pick overall) of 2002 NFL draft. ... Signed by Seahawks (July 30, 2002).
SINGLE GAME HIGHS (regular season): Receptions—4 (November 7, 2004, vs. San Francisco); yards—70 (December 22, 2002, vs. St. Louis); and touchdown receptions—1 (January 2, 2005, vs. Atlanta).

			RECEIVING				TOTALS			
Year Team	G	GS	No.	Yds.	Avg.	TD	TD	2pt.	Pts.	Fum.
2002—Seattle NFL	12	1	26	252	9.7	3	3	0	18	1
2003—Seattle NFL	16	2	6	72	12.0	0	0	0	0	0
2004—Seattle NFL	16	5	31	349	11.3	3	3	1	20	0
Pro totals (3 years)	44	8	63	673	10.7	6	6	1	38	1

STEVENS, LARRY   DE   BENGALS

S

PERSONAL: Born January 22, 1982, in Tacoma, Wash. ... 6-2/241.
HIGH SCHOOL: Woodrow Wilson (Tacoma, Wash.).
COLLEGE: Michigan.
TRANSACTIONS/CAREER NOTES: Signed as non-drafted free agent by Cincinnati Bengals (April 27, 2004). ... Released by Bengals (September 5, 2004). ... Signed by Bengals to practice squad (September 6, 2004). ... Activated (November 5, 2004).

			TOTALS			INTERCEPTIONS			
Year Team	G	GS	Tk.	Ast.	Sks.	No.	Yds.	Avg.	TD
2004—Cincinnati NFL	9	0	2	3	0.0	0	0	0.0	0

STEVENSON, DOMINIQUE   LB

PERSONAL: Born December 28, 1977, in Gaffney, S.C. ... 6-0/235. ... Full name: Antone Dominique Stevenson.
HIGH SCHOOL: Gaffney (S.C.).
COLLEGE: Tennessee.
TRANSACTIONS/CAREER NOTES: Selected by Buffalo Bills in seventh round (260th pick overall) of 2002 NFL draft. ... Signed by Bills (July 3, 2002). ... Released by Bills (September 3, 2002). ... Re-signed by Bills to practice squad (September 4, 2002). ... Activated (October 2, 2002). ... Claimed on waivers by Washington Redskins (September 7, 2004). ... Released by Redskins (September 17, 2004).

			TOTALS			INTERCEPTIONS			
Year Team	G	GS	Tk.	Ast.	Sks.	No.	Yds.	Avg.	TD
2002—Buffalo NFL	4	0	0	0	0.0	0	0	0.0	0
2003—Buffalo NFL	16	0	2	0	0.0	0	0	0.0	0
2004—Washington NFL	1	0	0	0	0.0	0	0	0.0	0
Pro totals (3 years)	21	0	2	0	0.0	0	0	0.0	0

STEWART, DALEROY   DT   TEXANS

PERSONAL: Born November 2, 1978, in Vero Beach, Fla. ... 6-4/298. ... Full name: Daleroy Andrew Stewart.
HIGH SCHOOL: Vero Beach (Fla.).
COLLEGE: Southern Miss.
TRANSACTIONS/CAREER NOTES: Selected by Dallas Cowboys in sixth round (171st pick overall) in 2001 NFL draft. ... Signed by Cowboys (July 21, 2001). ... On non-football injury list with shoulder injury (August 28, 2001-remainder of season). ... Inactive for 16 games (2002). ... Released by Cowboys (September 14, 2004). ... Signed by New York Jets (September 16, 2004). ... Claimed on waivers by San Francisco 49ers (September 28, 2004). ... Did not receive qualifying offer from 49ers (March 2, 2005). ... Signed by Houston Texans (April 20, 2005).

			TOTALS		
Year Team	G	GS	Tk.	Ast.	Sks.
2003—Dallas NFL	15	1	12	5	1.5
2004—Dallas NFL	1	0	0	1	0.0
—New York Jets NFL	1	0	0	0	0.0
—San Francisco NFL	9	0	5	3	0.0
Pro totals (2 years)	26	1	17	9	1.5

STEWART, KORDELL   QB

PERSONAL: Born October 16, 1972, in New Orleans, La. ... 6-1/218.
HIGH SCHOOL: John Ehret (Marrero, La.).
COLLEGE: Colorado.
TRANSACTIONS/CAREER NOTES: Selected by Pittsburgh Steelers in second round (60th pick overall) of 1995 NFL draft. ... Signed by Steelers (July 17, 1995). ... Released by Steelers (February 26, 2003). ... Signed by Chicago Bears (March 13, 2003). ... Released by Bears (March 1, 2004). ... Signed by Baltimore Ravens (June 3, 2004). ... Granted unconditional free agency (March 2, 2005).

CHAMPIONSHIP GAME EXPERIENCE: Played in AFC championship game (1995, 1997 and 2001 seasons). ... Played in Super Bowl 30 (1995 season).
HONORS: Played in Pro Bowl (2001 season).
SINGLE GAME HIGHS (regular season): Attempts—48 (December 13, 1997, vs. New England); completions—26 (December 13, 1997, vs. New England); yards—333 (December 16, 2001, vs. Baltimore); and touchdown passes—3 (December 30, 2001, vs. Cincinnati).
STATISTICAL PLATEAUS: 100-yard rushing games: 1996 (1), 1998 (1). Total: 2. 300-yard passing games: 1997 (2), 2001 (1). Total: 3.
MISCELLANEOUS: Regular-season record as starting NFL quarterback: 48-34 (.585). ... Postseason record as starting NFL quarterback: 2-2 (.500). ... Started two games at wide receiver (1995). ... Started two games at wide receiver (1996). ... Started one game at wide receiver (1999).

Year Team	G	GS	PASSING								RUSHING				RECEIVING				TOTALS		
			Att.	Cmp.	Pct.	Yds.	TD	Int.	Avg.	Rat.	Att.	Yds.	Avg.	TD	No.	Yds.	Avg.	TD	TD	2pt.	Pts.
1995—Pittsburgh NFL	10	2	7	5	71.4	60	1	0	8.57	136.9	15	86	5.7	1	14	235	16.8	1	2	0	12
1996—Pittsburgh NFL	16	2	30	11	36.7	100	0	2	3.33	18.8	39	171	4.4	5	17	293	17.2	3	8	0	48
1997—Pittsburgh NFL	16	16	440	236	53.6	3020	21	§17	6.86	75.2	88	476	5.4	11	0	0	0.0	0	11	0	66
1998—Pittsburgh NFL	16	16	458	252	55.0	2560	11	18	5.59	62.9	81	406	5.0	2	1	17	17.0	0	2	0	12
1999—Pittsburgh NFL	16	12	275	160	58.2	1464	6	10	5.32	64.9	56	258	4.6	2	9	113	12.6	1	3	0	18
2000—Pittsburgh NFL	16	11	289	151	52.2	1860	11	8	6.44	73.6	78	436	5.6	7	0	0	0.0	0	7	0	42
2001—Pittsburgh NFL	16	16	442	266	60.2	3109	14	11	7.03	81.7	96	537	5.6	5	0	0	0.0	0	5	0	30
2002—Pittsburgh NFL	8	5	166	109	65.7	1155	6	6	6.96	82.8	43	191	4.4	2	0	0	0.0	0	2	0	12
2003—Chicago NFL	9	7	251	126	50.2	1418	7	12	5.65	56.8	59	290	4.9	3	0	0	0.0	0	3	1	20
2004—Baltimore NFL	2	0	0	0	0.0	0	0	0	0.00	0.0	1	-1	-1.0	0	0	0	0.0	0	0	0	0
Pro totals (10 years) 125		87	2358	1316	55.8	14746	77	84	6.25	70.7	556	2850	5.1	38	41	658	16.0	5	43	1	260

STEWART, MATT   LB   FALCONS

PERSONAL: Born August 31, 1979, in Columbus, Ohio. ... 6-3/232.
HIGH SCHOOL: DeSales (Columbus, Ohio).
COLLEGE: Vanderbilt.
TRANSACTIONS/CAREER NOTES: Selected by Atlanta Falcons in fourth round (102nd pick overall) of 2001 NFL draft. ... Signed by Falcons (May 30, 2001). ... Granted free agency (March 3, 2004). ... Re-signed by Falcons (May 20, 2004). ... Granted unconditional free agency (March 2, 2005). ... Re-signed by Falcons (March 15, 2005).
CHAMPIONSHIP GAME EXPERIENCE: Played in NFC championship game (2004 season).

Year Team	G	GS	TOTALS			INTERCEPTIONS			
			Tk.	Ast.	Sks.	No.	Yds.	Avg.	TD
2001—Atlanta NFL	15	0	9	3	0.0	0	0	0.0	0
2002—Atlanta NFL	16	13	48	5	3.0	0	0	0.0	0
2003—Atlanta NFL	16	16	59	17	2.5	0	0	0.0	0
2004—Atlanta NFL	16	15	56	11	1.5	0	0	0.0	0
Pro totals (4 years)	63	44	172	36	7.0	0	0	0.0	0

STEWART, TONY   TE   BENGALS

PERSONAL: Born August 9, 1979, in Lohne, Germany. ... 6-5/260. ... Full name: Tony Alexander Stewart.
HIGH SCHOOL: Allentown Central (Pa.).
COLLEGE: Penn State.
TRANSACTIONS/CAREER NOTES: Selected by Philadelphia Eagles in fifth round (147th pick overall) of 2001 NFL draft. ... Signed by Eagles (May 22, 2001). ... Released by Eagles (September 10, 2002). ... Re-signed by Eagles to practice squad (September 12, 2002). ... Signed by Cincinnati Bengals off Eagles practice squad (November 23, 2002). ... Granted free agency (March 3, 2004). ... Re-signed by Bengals (April 16, 2004).
CHAMPIONSHIP GAME EXPERIENCE: Member of Eagles for NFC championship game (2001 season); inactive.
SINGLE GAME HIGHS (regular season): Receptions—5 (October 5, 2003, vs. Buffalo); yards—56 (September 28, 2003, vs. Cleveland); and touchdown receptions—1 (November 14, 2004, vs. Washington).

Year Team	G	GS	RECEIVING				TOTALS			
			No.	Yds.	Avg.	TD	TD	2pt.	Pts.	Fum.
2001—Philadelphia NFL	3	1	5	52	10.4	1	1	0	6	0
2002—Cincinnati NFL	3	1	1	6	6.0	0	0	0	0	0
2003—Cincinnati NFL	16	7	21	212	10.1	0	0	0	0	0
2004—Cincinnati NFL	16	9	10	48	4.8	1	1	0	6	0
Pro totals (4 years)	38	17	37	318	8.6	2	2	0	12	0

STILLS, GARY   DE   CHIEFS

PERSONAL: Born July 11, 1974, in Trenton, N.J. ... 6-2/250.
HIGH SCHOOL: Valley Forge (Pa.) Military Academy.
COLLEGE: West Virginia.
TRANSACTIONS/CAREER NOTES: Selected by Kansas City Chiefs in third round (75th pick overall) of 1999 NFL draft. ... Signed by Chiefs (July 26, 1999). ... Assigned by Chiefs to Frankfurt Galaxy in 2001 NFL Europe enhancement allocation program (February 19, 2001). ... Granted free agency (March 1, 2002). ... Re-signed by Chiefs (April 20, 2002). ... Granted unconditional free agency (February 27, 2003). ... Re-signed by Chiefs (February 27, 2003).
HONORS: Played in Pro Bowl (2003 season).

Year Team	G	GS	TOTALS			INTERCEPTIONS			
			Tk.	Ast.	Sks.	No.	Yds.	Avg.	TD
1999—Kansas City NFL	2	0	0	0	0.0	0	0	0.0	0
2000—Kansas City NFL	11	0	0	0	0.0	0	0	0.0	0
2001—Kansas City NFL	10	0	1	0	0.0	0	0	0.0	0
2002—Kansas City NFL	16	1	18	3	2.0	0	0	0.0	0

Year Team	G	GS	TOTALS Tk.	Ast.	Sks.	INTERCEPTIONS No.	Yds.	Avg.	TD
2003—Kansas City NFL	16	0	16	0	3.0	0	0	0.0	0
2004—Kansas City NFL	16	0	8	1	2.5	0	0	0.0	0
Pro totals (6 years)	71	1	43	4	7.5	0	0	0.0	0

STINCHCOMB, JON   T   SAINTS

PERSONAL: Born August 27, 1979, in Lilburn, Ga. ... 6-5/315. ... Full name: Jonathan Stinchcomb. ... Brother of Matt Stinchcomb, offensive lineman, Tampa Bay Buccaneers.
HIGH SCHOOL: Parkview (Lilburn, Ga.).
COLLEGE: Georgia.
TRANSACTIONS/CAREER NOTES: Selected by New Orleans Saints in second round (37th pick overall) of 2003 NFL draft. ... Signed by Saints (July 25, 2003).
PLAYING EXPERIENCE: New Orleans NFL, 2003-2004. ... Games/Games started: 2003 (6/0), 2004 (4/0). Total: 10/0.

STINCHCOMB, MATT   G/T   BUCCANEERS

PERSONAL: Born June 3, 1977, in Lilburn, Ga. ... 6-6/310. ... Full name: Matthew Douglass Stinchcomb. ... Brother of Jon Stinchcomb, offensive tackle, New Orleans Saints.
HIGH SCHOOL: Parkview (Lilburn, Ga.).
COLLEGE: Georgia.
TRANSACTIONS/CAREER NOTES: Selected by Oakland Raiders in first round (18th pick overall) of 1999 NFL draft. ... Signed by Raiders (July 22, 1999). ... Inactive for three games (1999). ... On injured reserve with shoulder injury (October 1, 1999-remainder of season). ... On injured reserve with shoulder injury (November 12, 2003-remainder of season). ... Granted unconditional free agency (March 3, 2004). ... Signed by Tampa Bay Buccaneers (March 5, 2004).
PLAYING EXPERIENCE: Oakland NFL, 1999-2003; Tampa Bay NFL, 2004. ... Games/Games started: 2000 (13/9), 2001 (14/1), 2002 (16/6), 2003 (6/4), 2004 (16/16), Total: 65/36.
CHAMPIONSHIP GAME EXPERIENCE: Member of Raiders for AFC Championship game (2000 season); did not play. ... Played in AFC championship game (2002 season). ... Played in Super Bowl 37 (2002 season).
HONORS: Named offensive tackle on THE SPORTING NEWS college All-America second team (1997 and 1998).

ST. LOUIS, BRAD   TE/LS   BENGALS

PERSONAL: Born August 19, 1976, in Waverly, Mo. ... 6-3/247. ... Full name: Brad Allen St. Louis.
HIGH SCHOOL: Belton (Mo.).
COLLEGE: Southwest Missouri State.
TRANSACTIONS/CAREER NOTES: Selected by Cincinnati Bengals in seventh round (210th pick overall) of 2000 NFL draft. ... Signed by Bengals (July 20, 2000). ... On injured reserve with leg injury (December 5, 2001-remainder of season). ... Granted free agency (February 28, 2003). ... Re-signed by Bengals (March 17, 2003). ... Re-signed by Bengals (December 20, 2003).
PLAYING EXPERIENCE: Cincinnati NFL, 2000-2004. ... Games/Games started: 2000 (16/0), 2001 (11/0), 2002 (16/0), 2003 (16/0), 2004 (16/0). Total: 75/0.

STOKLEY, BRANDON   WR   COLTS

PERSONAL: Born June 23, 1976, in Blacksburg, Va. ... 5-11/197.
HIGH SCHOOL: Comeaux (Lafayette, La.).
COLLEGE: Louisiana-Lafayette.
TRANSACTIONS/CAREER NOTES: Selected by Baltimore Ravens in fourth round (105th pick overall) of 1999 NFL draft. ... Signed by Ravens (July 28, 1999). ... On injured reserve with shoulder injury (October 25, 1999-remainder of season). ... Granted free agency (March 1, 2002). ... Re-signed by Ravens (April 16, 2002). ... On injured reserve with foot injury (November 26, 2002-remainder of season). ... Granted unconditional free agency (February 28, 2003). ... Signed by Indianapolis Colts (March 13, 2003).
CHAMPIONSHIP GAME EXPERIENCE: Played in AFC championship game (2000 and 2003 seasons). ... Member of Super Bowl championship team (2000 season).
SINGLE GAME HIGHS (regular season): Receptions—9 (December 28, 2003, vs. Houston); yards—153 (December 5, 2004, vs. Tennessee); and touchdown receptions—3 (November 25, 2004, vs. Detroit).
STATISTICAL PLATEAUS: 100-yard receiving games: 2004 (5). Total: 5.

Year Team	G	GS	RUSHING Att.	Yds.	Avg.	TD	RECEIVING No.	Yds.	Avg.	TD	TOTALS TD	2pt.	Pts.	Fum.
1999—Baltimore NFL	2	0	0	0	0.0	0	1	28	28.0	1	1	0	6	0
2000—Baltimore NFL	7	1	1	6	6.0	0	11	184	16.7	2	2	0	12	0
2001—Baltimore NFL	16	5	1	1	1.0	0	24	344	14.3	2	2	0	12	1
2002—Baltimore NFL	8	5	6	31	5.2	0	24	357	14.9	2	2	0	12	1
2003—Indianapolis NFL	6	3	0	0	0.0	0	22	211	9.6	3	3	0	18	0
2004—Indianapolis NFL	16	3	0	0	0.0	0	68	1077	15.8	10	10	0	60	1
Pro totals (6 years)	55	17	8	38	4.8	0	150	2201	14.7	20	20	0	120	3

STONE, JOHN   WR   RAIDERS

PERSONAL: Born July 7, 1979... 5-11/180.
HIGH SCHOOL: Mainland Regional (N.J.).
COLLEGE: Wake Forest.

TRANSACTIONS/CAREER NOTES: Signed as non-drafted free agent by Indianapolis Colts (April 26, 2002). ... Released by Colts (August 26, 2002). ... Signed by Oakland Raiders (January 13, 2003). ... Released by Raiders (August 26, 2003). ... Re-signed by Raiders to practice squad (September 2, 2003). ... Activated (December 10, 2003). ... Released by Raiders (August 31, 2004). ... Re-signed by Raiders to practice squad (September 7, 2004). ... Activated (November 21, 2004).

SINGLE GAME HIGHS (regular season): Receptions—2 (December 12, 2004, vs. Atlanta); yards—62 (December 12, 2004, vs. Atlanta); and touchdown receptions—0.

				RECEIVING				TOTALS		
Year Team	G	GS	No.	Yds.	Avg.	TD	TD	2pt.	Pts.	Fum.
2003—Oakland NFL	1	0	0	0	0.0	0	0	0	0	0
2004—Oakland NFL	4	0	3	80	26.7	0	0	0	0	0
Pro totals (2 years)	5	0	3	80	26.7	0	0	0	0	0

STONE, MICHAEL   CB   RAMS

PERSONAL: Born February 13, 1978, in Southfield, Mich. ... 6-0/201. ... Full name: Michael Ahmed Stone.
HIGH SCHOOL: Southfield-Lathrup (Southfield, Mich.).
COLLEGE: Memphis.
TRANSACTIONS/CAREER NOTES: Selected by Arizona Cardinals in second round (54th pick overall) of 2001 NFL draft. ... Signed by Cardinals (July 16, 2001). ... Granted unconditional free agency (March 2, 2005). ... Signed by St. Louis Rams (March 10, 2005).

			TOTALS			INTERCEPTIONS			
Year Team	G	GS	Tk.	Ast.	Sks.	No.	Yds.	Avg.	TD
2001—Arizona NFL	7	0	0	0	0.0	0	0	0.0	0
2002—Arizona NFL	16	0	0	0	0.0	0	0	0.0	0
2004—Arizona NFL	14	0	1	1	0.0	0	0	0.0	0
Pro totals (3 years)	37	0	1	1	0.0	0	0	0.0	0

S

STONE, RON   G   RAIDERS

PERSONAL: Born July 20, 1971, in Boston, Mass. ... 6-5/325.
HIGH SCHOOL: West Roxbury (Mass.).
COLLEGE: Boston College.
TRANSACTIONS/CAREER NOTES: Selected by Dallas Cowboys in fourth round (96th pick overall) of 1993 NFL draft. ... Signed by Cowboys (July 16, 1993). ... Active for four games with Cowboys (1993); did not play. ... Granted free agency (February 16, 1996). ... Tendered offer sheet by New York Giants (March 1, 1996) ... Cowboys declined to match offer (March 7, 1996). ... Granted unconditional free agency (March 1, 2002). ... Signed by San Francisco 49ers (April 12, 2002). ... Released by 49ers (March 2, 2004). ... Signed by Oakland Raiders (March 8, 2004).
PLAYING EXPERIENCE: Dallas NFL, 1994-1995; New York Giants NFL, 1996-2001; San Francisco NFL, 2002-2003; Oakland NFL, 2004. ... Games/Games started: 1994 (16/0), 1995 (16/1), 1996 (16/16), 1997 (16/16), 1998 (14/14), 1999 (16/16), 2000 (15/15), 2001 (15/15), 2002 (15/15), 2003 (13/13), 2004 (5/5). Total: 157/126.
CHAMPIONSHIP GAME EXPERIENCE: Member of Cowboys for NFC championship game (1993 season); inactive. ... Member of Super Bowl championship team (1993 and 1995 seasons). ... Played in NFC championship game (1994, 1995 and 2000 seasons). ... Played in Super Bowl 35 (2000 season).
HONORS: Played in Pro Bowl (2000-2002 seasons).

STOUTMIRE, OMAR   S

PERSONAL: Born July 9, 1974, in Pensacola, Fla. ... 5-11/205.
HIGH SCHOOL: Polytechnic (Long Beach, Calif.).
COLLEGE: Fresno State.
TRANSACTIONS/CAREER NOTES: Selected by Dallas Cowboys in seventh round (224th pick overall) of 1997 NFL draft. ... Signed by Cowboys (July 14, 1997). ... Claimed on waivers by Cleveland Browns (September 6, 1999). ... Inactive for two games with Browns (1999). ... Released by Browns (September 21, 1999). ... Signed by New York Jets (October 6, 1999). ... Granted free agency (February 11, 2000). ... Re-signed by Jets (April 18, 2000). ... Released by Jets (August 27, 2000). ... Signed by New York Giants (August 30, 2000). ... Granted unconditional free agency (March 2, 2001). ... Re-signed by Giants (May 14, 2001). ... Granted unconditional free agency (February 28, 2003). ... Re-signed by Giants (March 19, 2003). ... On injured reserve with knee injury (September 15, 2004-remainder of season). ... Released by Giants (February 22, 2005).
CHAMPIONSHIP GAME EXPERIENCE: Played in NFC championship game (2000 season). ... Played in Super Bowl 35 (2000 season).

			TOTALS			INTERCEPTIONS			
Year Team	G	GS	Tk.	Ast.	Sks.	No.	Yds.	Avg.	TD
1997—Dallas NFL	16	2	38	8	2.0	2	8	4.0	0
1998—Dallas NFL	16	12	36	16	1.0	0	0	0.0	0
1999—New York Jets NFL	12	5	25	4	1.0	2	97	48.5	1
2000—New York Giants NFL	16	0	1	0	0.0	0	0	0.0	0
2001—New York Giants NFL	16	0	2	0	0.0	0	0	0.0	0
2002—New York Giants NFL	16	16	63	18	0.0	0	0	0.0	0
2003—New York Giants NFL	16	16	74	21	1.0	1	34	34.0	0
2004—New York Giants NFL	1	0	1	1	0.0	0	0	0.0	0
Pro totals (8 years)	109	51	240	68	5.0	5	139	27.8	1

STOVER, MATT   K   RAVENS

PERSONAL: Born January 27, 1968, in Dallas, Texas. ... 5-11/178. ... Full name: John Matthew Stover.
HIGH SCHOOL: Lake Highlands (Dallas).
COLLEGE: Louisiana Tech.

TRANSACTIONS/CAREER NOTES: Selected by New York Giants in 12th round (329th pick overall) of 1990 NFL draft. ... Signed by Giants (July 23, 1990). ... On injured reserve with leg injury (September 4, 1990-entire season). ... Granted unconditional free agency (February 1, 1991). ... Signed by Cleveland Browns (March 15, 1991). ... Granted free agency (March 1, 1993). ... Re-signed by Browns (July 24, 1993). ... Released by Browns (August 30, 1993). ... Re-signed by Browns (August 31, 1993). ... Granted unconditional free agency (February 17, 1994). ... Re-signed by Browns (March 4, 1994). ... Browns franchise moved to Baltimore and renamed Ravens for 1996 season (March 11, 1996). ... Granted unconditional free agency (March 3, 2004). ... Re-signed by Ravens (March 9, 2004).

CHAMPIONSHIP GAME EXPERIENCE: Played in AFC championship game (2000 season). ... Member of Super Bowl championship team (2000 season).

HONORS: Named kicker on THE SPORTING NEWS NFL All-Pro team (2000). ... Played in Pro Bowl (2000 season).

RECORDS: Holds NFL record for most consecutive games with one or more field goals made—38 (October 31, 1999-December 2, 2001).

MISCELLANEOUS: Baltimore Ravens all-time scoring leader (1,001 points).

Year Team	G	FIELD GOALS 1-29	30-39	40-49	50+	Tot.	Pct.	Lg.	TOTALS XPM	XPA	Pts.
1990—New York Giants NFL		Did not play.									
1991—Cleveland NFL	16	3-5	8-9	3-6	2-2	16-22	72.7	§55	33	34	81
1992—Cleveland NFL	16	12-12	6-8	2-6	1-3	21-29	72.4	51	29	30	92
1993—Cleveland NFL	16	4-4	5-6	6-8	1-4	16-22	72.7	53	36	36	84
1994—Cleveland NFL	16	8-8	10-11	8-8	0-1	26-28	*92.9	45	32	32	110
1995—Cleveland NFL	16	13-13	9-10	7-9	0-1	29-33	§87.9	47	26	26	113
1996—Baltimore NFL	16	8-8	5-6	5-10	1-1	19-25	76.0	50	34	35	91
1997—Baltimore NFL	16	8-9	12-12	6-11	0-2	26-34	76.5	49	32	32	110
1998—Baltimore NFL	16	6-6	5-5	10-17	0-0	21-28	75.0	48	24	24	87
1999—Baltimore NFL	16	13-13	6-8	7-7	2-5	28-33	84.8	50	32	32	116
2000—Baltimore NFL	16	11-11	12-13	10-12	2-3	*35-*39	89.7	51	30	30	135
2001—Baltimore NFL	16	16-16	9-10	5-9	0-0	30-35	85.7	49	25	25	115
2002—Baltimore NFL	15	9-9	4-5	7-10	1-1	21-25	84.0	51	33	33	96
2003—Baltimore NFL	16	16-16	6-6	11-14	0-2	33-§38	86.8	49	35	35	134
2004—Baltimore NFL	16	11-11	7-8	9-10	2-3	29-32	90.6	50	30	30	117
Pro totals (14 years)	**223**	**138-141**	**104-117**	**96-137**	**12-28**	**350-423**	**82.7**	**55**	**431**	**434**	**1481**

ST. PIERRE, BRIAN — QB — STEELERS

PERSONAL: Born November 28, 1979, in Salem, Mass. ... 6-3/230.

HIGH SCHOOL: St. John's Prep (Danvers, Mass.).

COLLEGE: Boston College.

TRANSACTIONS/CAREER NOTES: Selected by Pittsburgh Steelers in fifth round (163rd pick overall) of 2003 NFL draft. ... Signed by Steelers (July 25, 2003). ... Inactive for all 16 games (2003). ... Released by Steelers (September 6, 2004). ... Re-signed by Steelers to practice squad (September 7, 2004). ... Activated (September 18, 2004). ... Released by Steelers (November 13, 2004). ... Re-signed by Steelers to practice squad (November 16, 2004). ... Activated (December 31, 2004).

CHAMPIONSHIP GAME EXPERIENCE: Member of Steelers for AFC championship game (2004 season); inactive.

Year Team	G	GS	PASSING Att.	Cmp.	Pct.	Yds.	TD	Int.	Avg.	Skd.	Rat.	RUSHING Att.	Yds.	Avg.	TD	TOTALS TD	2pt.	Pts.
2004—Pittsburgh NFL	1	0	1	0	0.0	0	0	0	0.00	0	39.6	4	-3	-0.7	0	0	0	0

STRAHAN, MICHAEL — DE — GIANTS

PERSONAL: Born November 21, 1971, in Houston, Texas. ... 6-5/275. ... Full name: Michael Anthony Strahan. ... Name pronounced: STRAY-han.

HIGH SCHOOL: Westbury (Houston), then Mannheim (West Germany) American.

COLLEGE: Texas Southern.

TRANSACTIONS/CAREER NOTES: Selected by New York Giants in second round (40th pick overall) of 1993 NFL draft. ... Signed by Giants (July 25, 1993). ... On injured reserve with foot injury (January 13, 1994-remainder of playoffs). ... Granted free agency (February 16, 1996). ... Re-signed by Giants (July 8, 1996). ... On injured reserve with pectoral injury (November 9, 2004-remainder of season).

CHAMPIONSHIP GAME EXPERIENCE: Played in NFC championship game (2000 season). ... Played in Super Bowl 35 (2000 season).

HONORS: Named defensive end on THE SPORTING NEWS NFL All-Pro team (1997, 2001 and 2003). ... Played in Pro Bowl (1997-1999 and 2001-2003 seasons).

RECORDS: Holds NFL single-season record for most sacks—22 1/2 (2001).

MISCELLANEOUS: Active NFL leader in sacks (118).

Year Team	G	GS	TOTALS Tk.	Ast.	Sks.	INTERCEPTIONS No.	Yds.	Avg.	TD
1993—New York Giants NFL	9	0	1	2	1.0	0	0	0.0	0
1994—New York Giants NFL	15	15	27	13	4.5	0	0	0.0	0
1995—New York Giants NFL	15	15	48	10	7.5	2	56	28.0	0
1996—New York Giants NFL	16	16	54	9	5.0	0	0	0.0	0
1997—New York Giants NFL	16	16	49	19	14.0	0	0	0.0	0
1998—New York Giants NFL	16	15	53	14	15.0	1	24	24.0	1
1999—New York Giants NFL	16	16	43	15	5.5	1	44	44.0	1
2000—New York Giants NFL	16	16	51	15	9.5	0	0	0.0	0
2001—New York Giants NFL	16	16	62	11	*22.5	0	0	0.0	0
2002—New York Giants NFL	16	16	57	14	11.0	0	0	0.0	0
2003—New York Giants NFL	16	16	60	15	*18.5	0	0	0.0	0
2004—New York Giants NFL	8	8	25	10	4.0	0	0	0.0	0
Pro totals (12 years)	**175**	**165**	**530**	**147**	**118.0**	**4**	**124**	**31.0**	**2**

STRAIT, DERRICK   CB   JETS

PERSONAL: Born August 27, 1980, in Austin, Texas. ... 5-11/189.
HIGH SCHOOL: Lanier (Austin, Texas).
COLLEGE: Oklahoma.
TRANSACTIONS/CAREER NOTES: Selected by New York Jets in third round (76th pick overall) of 2004 NFL draft. ... Signed by Jets (July 29, 2004).
HONORS: Bronko Nagurski Award winner (2003). ... Jim Thorpe Award winner (2003). ... Named defensive back on THE SPORTING NEWS Freshman All-America second team (2000). ... Named cornerback on THE SPORTING NEWS college All-America first team (2003).

			TOTALS			INTERCEPTIONS			
Year Team	G	GS	Tk.	Ast.	Sks.	No.	Yds.	Avg.	TD
2004—New York Jets NFL	5	1	3	2	0.0	0	0	0.0	0

STREETS, TAI   WR

PERSONAL: Born April 20, 1977, in Matteson, Ill. ... 6-3/207.
HIGH SCHOOL: Thornton Township (Harvey, Ill.).
COLLEGE: Michigan.
TRANSACTIONS/CAREER NOTES: Selected by San Francisco 49ers in sixth round (171st pick overall) of 1999 NFL draft. ... Signed by 49ers (July 30, 1999). ... On non-football injury list with Achilles' tendon injury (July 30-November 30, 1999). ... Granted free agency (February 28, 2003). ... Re-signed by 49ers (May 16, 2003). ... Granted unconditional free agency (March 3, 2004). ... Signed by Detroit Lions (March 10, 2004). ... Granted unconditional free agency (March 2, 2005).
SINGLE GAME HIGHS (regular season): Receptions—8 (December 21, 2002, vs. Arizona); yards—90 (December 21, 2002, vs. Arizona); and touchdown receptions—2 (December 30, 2002, vs. St. Louis).

			RECEIVING				TOTALS			
Year Team	G	GS	No.	Yds.	Avg.	TD	TD	2pt.	Pts.	Fum.
1999—San Francisco NFL	2	0	2	25	12.5	0	0	0	0	0
2000—San Francisco NFL	15	1	19	287	15.1	0	0	0	0	1
2001—San Francisco NFL	16	3	28	345	12.3	1	1	0	6	0
2002—San Francisco NFL	16	14	72	756	10.5	5	5	0	30	1
2003—San Francisco NFL	16	16	47	595	12.7	7	7	0	42	0
2004—Detroit NFL	13	12	28	260	9.3	1	1	1	8	0
Pro totals (6 years)	78	46	196	2268	11.6	14	14	1	86	2

STRICKLAND, DONALD   CB   COLTS

PERSONAL: Born November 24, 1980, in Redwood City, Calif. ... 5-10/187.
HIGH SCHOOL: Archbishop Riordan (San Francisco).
COLLEGE: Colorado.
TRANSACTIONS/CAREER NOTES: Selected by Indianapolis Colts in third round (90th pick overall) of 2003 NFL draft. ... Signed by Colts (July 30, 2003). ... On injured reserve with shoulder injury (October 9, 2004-remainder of season).
CHAMPIONSHIP GAME EXPERIENCE: Played in AFC championship game (2003 season).

			TOTALS			INTERCEPTIONS			
Year Team	G	GS	Tk.	Ast.	Sks.	No.	Yds.	Avg.	TD
2003—Indianapolis NFL	11	8	23	13	0.0	2	43	21.5	0
2004—Indianapolis NFL	4	4	15	5	0.0	0	0	0.0	0
Pro totals (2 years)	15	12	38	18	0.0	2	43	21.5	0

STRONG, MACK   FB   SEAHAWKS

PERSONAL: Born September 11, 1971, in Columbus, Ga. ... 6-0/245.
HIGH SCHOOL: Brookstone (Columbus, Ga.).
COLLEGE: Georgia.
TRANSACTIONS/CAREER NOTES: Signed as non-drafted free agent by Seattle Seahawks (April 28, 1993). ... Released by Seahawks (September 4, 1993). ... Re-signed by Seahawks to practice squad (September 6, 1993). ... Released by Seahawks (February 10, 2000). ... Re-signed by Seahawks (February 14, 2000). ... Granted unconditional free agency (March 1, 2002). ... Re-signed by Seahawks (May 1, 2002). ... Granted unconditional free agency (February 28, 2003). ... Re-signed by Seahawks (April 8, 2003).
SINGLE GAME HIGHS (regular season): Attempts—10 (December 11, 1994, vs. Houston); yards—44 (December 11, 1994, vs. Houston); rushing touchdowns—1 (October 12, 2003, vs. San Francisco).

			RUSHING				RECEIVING				KICKOFF RETURNS				TOTALS			
Year Team	G	GS	Att.	Yds.	Avg.	TD	No.	Yds.	Avg.	TD	No.	Yds.	Avg.	TD	TD	2pt.	Pts.	Fum.
1993—Seattle NFL	Did not play.																	
1994—Seattle NFL	8	1	27	114	4.2	2	3	3	1.0	0	0	0	0.0	0	2	0	12	1
1995—Seattle NFL	16	2	8	23	2.9	1	12	117	9.8	3	4	65	16.3	0	4	0	24	2
1996—Seattle NFL	14	8	5	8	1.6	0	9	78	8.7	0	0	0	0.0	0	0	0	0	0
1997—Seattle NFL	16	9	4	8	2.0	0	13	91	7.0	2	1	16	16.0	0	2	0	12	0
1998—Seattle NFL	16	5	15	47	3.1	0	8	48	6.0	0	0	0	0.0	0	2	0	12	2
1999—Seattle NFL	14	1	1	0	0.0	0	1	5	5.0	0	0	0	0.0	0	0	0	0	0
2000—Seattle NFL	16	12	3	9	3.0	0	23	141	6.1	1	1	26	26.0	0	1	0	6	0
2001—Seattle NFL	16	13	17	55	3.2	0	17	141	8.3	0	1	16	16.0	0	0	0	0	0
2002—Seattle NFL	16	12	23	94	4.1	0	22	120	5.5	2	3	54	18.0	0	2	0	12	0
2003—Seattle NFL	16	10	37	174	4.7	1	29	216	7.4	0	3	60	20.0	0	1	0	6	1
2004—Seattle NFL	16	13	36	131	3.6	0	21	99	4.7	0	0	0	0.0	0	0	0	0	2
Pro totals (11 years)	164	86	176	663	3.8	4	158	1059	6.7	10	13	237	18.2	0	14	0	84	8

S

STROTHER, BILLY — LB — DOLPHINS

PERSONAL: Born January 8, 1982, in Evansville, Ind. ... 6-0/230. ... Full name: William Gregory Strother.
HIGH SCHOOL: Evansville Harrison (Evansville, Ind.).
JUNIOR COLLEGE: West Hills (Coalinga, Calif.).
COLLEGE: New Mexico.
TRANSACTIONS/CAREER NOTES: Signed as non-drafted free agent by Washington Redskins (April 28, 2004). ... Claimed on waivers by New Orleans Saints (August 31, 2004). ... Released by Saints (September 5, 2004). ... Re-signed by Saints to practice squad (September 6, 2004). ... Released by Saints from practice squad (September 23, 2004). ... Signed by Redskins to practice squad (October 6, 2004). ... Released by Redskins from practice squad (October 21, 2004). ... Re-signed by Redskins to practice squad (October 29, 2004). ... Activated (November 17, 2004). ... Released by Redskins (December 4, 2004). ... Re-signed by Redskins to practice squad (December 8, 2004). ... Signed by Miami Dolphins off Redskins practice squad (December 23, 2004).

Year Team	G	GS	TOTALS Tk.	Ast.	Sks.	INTERCEPTIONS No.	Yds.	Avg.	TD
2004—Washington NFL	2	0	0	0	0.0	0	0	0.0	0
—Miami NFL	1	0	0	0	0.0	0	0	0.0	0
Pro totals (1 year)	3	0	0	0	0.0	0	0	0.0	0

STROUD, MARCUS — DT — JAGUARS

PERSONAL: Born June 25, 1978, in Thomasville, Ga. ... 6-6/312.
HIGH SCHOOL: Brooks County (Barney, Ga.).
COLLEGE: Georgia.
TRANSACTIONS/CAREER NOTES: Selected by Jacksonville Jaguars in first round (13th pick overall) of 2001 draft. ... Signed by Jaguars (July 26, 2001).
HONORS: Played in Pro Bowl (2003 and 2004 seasons).

Year Team	G	GS	TOTALS Tk.	Ast.	Sks.
2001—Jacksonville NFL	16	0	21	4	0.0
2002—Jacksonville NFL	16	16	41	7	6.5
2003—Jacksonville NFL	16	16	47	18	4.5
2004—Jacksonville NFL	16	16	38	16	4.5
Pro totals (4 years)	64	48	147	45	15.5

STUVAINTS, RUSSELL — S — STEELERS

PERSONAL: Born August 28, 1980, in Pittsburgh, Pa. ... 6-0/202. ... Full name: Russell Stuvaints Jr.
HIGH SCHOOL: McKeesport (Pa.).
COLLEGE: Youngstown State.
TRANSACTIONS/CAREER NOTES: Signed as non-drafted free agent by Pittsburgh Steelers (May 2, 2003). ... Released by Steelers (August 26, 2003). ... Re-signed by Steelers to practice squad (September 1, 2003). ... Released by Steelers (September 30, 2003). ... Re-signed by Steelers to practice squad (October 7, 2003). ... Released by Steelers (October 21, 2003). ... Re-signed by Steelers to practice squad (October 28, 2003). ... Activated (December 2, 2003). ... Released by Steelers (September 5, 2004). ... Signed by New England Patriots to practice squad (September 7, 2004). ... Signed by Steelers off Patriots practice squad (September 13, 2004).
CHAMPIONSHIP GAME EXPERIENCE: Played in AFC championship game (2004 season).

Year Team	G	GS	TOTALS Tk.	Ast.	Sks.	INTERCEPTIONS No.	Yds.	Avg.	TD
2003—Pittsburgh NFL	4	0	0	0	0.0	0	0	0.0	0
2004—Pittsburgh NFL	15	0	14	3	0.0	0	0	0.0	0
Pro totals (2 years)	19	0	14	3	0.0	0	0	0.0	0

SUGGS, LEE — RB — BROWNS

PERSONAL: Born August 11, 1980, in Roanoke, Va. ... 6-0/210. ... Full name: Lee Ernest Suggs Jr.
HIGH SCHOOL: William Fleming (Roanoke, Va.).
COLLEGE: Virginia Tech.
TRANSACTIONS/CAREER NOTES: Selected by Cleveland Browns in fourth round (115th pick overall) of 2003 NFL draft. ... Signed by Browns (August 13, 2003). ... On non-football injury list with shoulder injury (August 31-November 12, 2003).
SINGLE GAME HIGHS (regular season): Attempts—38 (December 26, 2004, vs. Miami); yards—186 (December 28, 2003, vs. Cincinnati); and rushing touchdowns—2 (December 28, 2003, vs. Cincinnati).
STATISTICAL PLATEAUS: 100-yard rushing games: 2003 (1), 2004 (3). Total: 4. 100-yard receiving games: 2004 (1). Total: 1.

Year Team	G	GS	RUSHING Att.	Yds.	Avg.	TD	RECEIVING No.	Yds.	Avg.	TD	KICKOFF RETURNS No.	Yds.	Avg.	TD	TOTALS TD	2pt.	Pts.	Fum.
2003—Cleveland NFL	7	0	56	289	5.2	2	2	0	0.0	0	14	318	22.7	0	2	0	12	2
2004—Cleveland NFL	10	4	199	744	3.7	2	20	178	8.9	1	0	0	0.0	0	3	0	18	6
Pro totals (2 years)	17	4	255	1033	4.1	4	22	178	8.1	1	14	318	22.7	0	5	0	30	8

SUGGS, TERRELL — LB — RAVENS

PERSONAL: Born October 11, 1982, in Minneapolis, Minn. ... 6-3/260. ... Full name: Terrell Raynonn Suggs.
HIGH SCHOOL: Hamilton (Chandler, Ariz.).
COLLEGE: Arizona State.

			TOTALS			INTERCEPTIONS			
Year Team	G	GS	Tk.	Ast.	Sks.	No.	Yds.	Avg.	TD
2003—Baltimore NFL	16	1	19	8	12.0	1	11	11.0	0
2004—Baltimore NFL	16	16	46	14	10.5	0	0	0.0	0
Pro totals (2 years)	32	17	65	22	22.5	1	11	11.0	0

SULFSTED, ALEX T BENGALS

PERSONAL: Born December 21, 1977, in Loveland, Ohio. ... 6-3/320.
HIGH SCHOOL: Mariemont (Ohio).
COLLEGE: Miami (Ohio).
TRANSACTIONS/CAREER NOTES: Selected by Kansas City Chiefs in sixth round (176th pick overall) of 2001 NFL draft. ... Signed by Chiefs (July 18, 2001). ... Released by Chiefs (September 1, 2001). ... Signed by Cincinnati Bengals to practice squad (September 4, 2001). ... Signed by Washington Redskins off Bengals practice squad (October 26, 2001). ... Re-claimed on waivers by Bengals (July 28, 2003). ... Released by Bengals (August 25, 2003). ... Re-signed by Bengals (December 9, 2003). ... Released by Bengals (June 4, 2004). ... Re-signed by Bengals (June 22, 2004). ... Released by Bengals (September 5, 2004). ... Re-signed by Bengals (September 9, 2004).
PLAYING EXPERIENCE: Cincinnati NFL, 2002-2004. ... Games/Games started: 2002 (14/3), 2004 (3/0). Total: 17/3.

SULLIVAN, JOHNATHAN DT SAINTS

PERSONAL: Born January 21, 1981, in Griffin, Ga. ... 6-3/315.
HIGH SCHOOL: Griffin (Ga.).
COLLEGE: Georgia.
TRANSACTIONS/CAREER NOTES: Selected after junior season by New Orleans Saints in first round (sixth pick overall) of 2003 NFL draft. ... Signed by Saints (July 30, 2003).

			TOTALS		
Year Team	G	GS	Tk.	Ast.	Sks.
2003—New Orleans NFL	14	12	26	8	1.0
2004—New Orleans NFL	7	4	11	4	0.5
Pro totals (2 years)	21	16	37	12	1.5

SURTAIN, PATRICK CB CHIEFS

PERSONAL: Born June 19, 1976, in New Orleans, La. ... 5-11/192. ... Full name: Patrick Frank Surtain. ... Name pronounced: sir-TANE.
HIGH SCHOOL: Edna Karr (New Orleans).
COLLEGE: Southern Miss.
TRANSACTIONS/CAREER NOTES: Selected by Miami Dolphins in second round (44th pick overall) of 1998 NFL draft. ... Signed by Dolphins (July 21, 1998). ... Traded by Dolphins with a second-round pick (LB James Grigsby) in 2005 draft to Kansas City Chiefs for second- (DE Matt Roth) and fifth-round (T Anthony Alabi) picks in 2005 draft (April 22, 2005).
HONORS: Named cornerback on THE SPORTING NEWS college All-America second team (1997). ... Named to play in Pro Bowl (2002 season); replaced by Sam Madison due to injury. ... Named cornerback on the THE SPORTING NEWS NFL All-Pro team (2002 and 2003). ... Played in Pro Bowl (2003 season).

			TOTALS			INTERCEPTIONS			
Year Team	G	GS	Tk.	Ast.	Sks.	No.	Yds.	Avg.	TD
1998—Miami NFL	16	0	23	5	0.0	2	1	0.5	0
1999—Miami NFL	16	6	32	5	2.0	2	28	14.0	0
2000—Miami NFL	16	16	44	9	1.0	5	55	11.0	0
2001—Miami NFL	16	16	43	10	1.0	3	74	24.7	1
2002—Miami NFL	14	14	39	19	1.5	6	79	13.2	1
2003—Miami NFL	15	15	34	19	0.0	▲7	59	8.4	0
2004—Miami NFL	15	15	40	18	1.0	4	2	0.5	0
Pro totals (7 years)	108	82	255	85	6.5	29	298	10.3	2

SWINTON, REGGIE WR TEXANS

PERSONAL: Born July 24, 1975, in Little Rock, Ark. ... 6-0/186.
HIGH SCHOOL: Central (Ark.).
COLLEGE: Murray State.
TRANSACTIONS/CAREER NOTES: Signed as non-drafted free agent by Jacksonville Jaguars (April 18, 1998). ... Released by Jaguars (August 25, 1998). ... Signed by Toronto Argonauts of the CFL (February 19, 1999). ... Traded by Argonauts with QB Kerwin Bell to Winnipeg Blue Bombers for Eric Blount and RB Mitch Running (March 1, 1999). ... Released by Blue Bombers (August 16, 1999). ... Signed by Edmonton Eskimos of CFL (September 13, 1999). ... Released by Eskimos (October 12, 1999). ... Signed by Seattle Seahawks (February 24, 2000). ... Released by Seahawks (August 27, 2000). ... Signed by Dallas Cowboys (August 6, 2001). ... Traded by Cowboys to Green Bay Packers for a sixth-round pick (traded to San Francisco) in 2004 draft (September 29, 2003). ... Claimed on waivers by Detroit Lions (October 10, 2003). ... Granted free agency (March 3, 2004). ... Re-signed by Lions (April 19, 2004). ... Released by Lions (September 5, 2004). ... Re-signed by Lions (September 20, 2004). ... Granted unconditional free agency (March 2, 2005). ... Signed by Houston Texans (April 19, 2005).
SINGLE GAME HIGHS (regular season): Receptions—5 (November 7, 2004, vs. Washington); yards—72 (December 23, 2001, vs. Arizona); and touchdown receptions—1 (October 24, 2004, vs. New York Giants).

			RECEIVING				PUNT RETURNS				KICKOFF RETURNS				TOTALS			
Year Team	G	GS	No.	Yds.	Avg.	TD	No.	Yds.	Avg.	TD	No.	Yds.	Avg.	TD	TD	2pt.	Pts.	Fum.
1999—Winnipeg CFL	4	0	11	162	14.7	1	7	235	33.6	1	5	18	3.6	0	2	0	12	0

Year Team	G	GS	RECEIVING No.	Yds.	Avg.	TD	PUNT RETURNS No.	Yds.	Avg.	TD	KICKOFF RETURNS No.	Yds.	Avg.	TD	TOTALS TD	2pt.	Pts.	Fum.
—Toronto CFL	3	3	3	22	7.3	0	9	178	19.8	0	3	33	11.0	0	0	0	0	0
2000—	Did not play.																	
2001—Dallas NFL	15	1	7	117	16.7	1	31	414	13.4	†1	56	1327	23.7	0	2	0	12	4
2002—Dallas NFL	14	0	7	63	9.0	0	19	141	7.4	0	28	697	24.9	1	1	0	6	1
2003—Dallas NFL	1	0	0	0	0.0	0	1	0	0.0	0	3	65	21.7	0	0	0	0	0
—Detroit NFL	11	1	9	100	11.1	0	23	318	13.8	1	40	964	24.1	1	2	0	12	4
2004—Detroit NFL	13	1	18	213	11.8	1	16	104	6.5	0	18	410	22.8	0	1	0	6	1
CFL totals (1 year)	7	0	14	184	13.1	1	16	413	25.8	1	8	51	6.4	0	2	0	12	0
NFL totals (4 years)	54	3	41	493	12.0	2	90	977	10.9	2	145	3463	23.9	2	6	0	36	10
Pro totals (5 years)	61	3	55	677	12.3	3	106	1390	13.1	3	153	3514	23.0	2	8	0	48	10

SYKES, JASHON   LB   BRONCOS

PERSONAL: Born September 25, 1979, in Los Angeles, Calif. ... 6-2/236.
HIGH SCHOOL: Serra (Los Angeles, Calif.).
COLLEGE: Colorado.
TRANSACTIONS/CAREER NOTES: Signed as non-drafted free agent by Denver Broncos (April 22, 2002). ... Released by Broncos (August 31, 2002). ... Re-signed by Broncos to practice squad (September 3, 2002). ... Activated (December 31, 2002).

Year Team	G	GS	TOTALS Tk.	Ast.	Sks.	INTERCEPTIONS No.	Yds.	Avg.	TD
2003—Denver NFL	16	8	38	14	0.0	0	0	0.0	0
2004—Denver NFL	3	0	0	0	0.0	0	0	0.0	0
Pro totals (2 years)	19	8	38	14	0.0	0	0	0.0	0

TAIT, JOHN   T   BEARS

PERSONAL: Born January 26, 1975, in Phoenix, Ariz. ... 6-6/315.
HIGH SCHOOL: McClintock (Tempe, Ariz.).
COLLEGE: Brigham Young.
TRANSACTIONS/CAREER NOTES: Selected after junior season by Kansas City Chiefs in first round (14th pick overall) of 1999 NFL draft. ... Signed by Chiefs (September 9, 1999). ... Designated by Chiefs as franchise player (February 24, 2004). ... Tendered offer sheet by Chicago Bears (March 6, 2004). ... Chiefs declined to match offer (March 12, 2004).
PLAYING EXPERIENCE: Kansas City NFL, 1999-2003; Chicago NFL, 2004. ... Games/Games started: 1999 (12/3), 2000 (15/15), 2001 (16/16), 2002 (16/16), 2003 (16/16), 2004 (13/13). Total: 88/79.

TAPEH, THOMAS   FB   EAGLES

PERSONAL: Born March 28, 1980, in St. Paul, Minn. ... 6-1/243. ... Full name: Thomas Teah Tapeh. ... Name pronounced: Tuh-PAY.
HIGH SCHOOL: Johnson (St. Paul, Minn.).
COLLEGE: Minnesota.
TRANSACTIONS/CAREER NOTES: Selected by Philadelphia Eagles in fifth round (162nd pick overall) of 2004 NFL draft. ... Signed by Eagles (July 27, 2004). ... On injured reserve with hip injury (December 29, 2004-remainder of season).
SINGLE GAME HIGHS (regular season): Attempts—4 (November 21, 2004, vs. Washington); yards—14 (November 21, 2004, vs. Washington); and rushing touchdowns—0.

Year Team	G	GS	RUSHING Att.	Yds.	Avg.	TD	RECEIVING No.	Yds.	Avg.	TD	TOTALS TD	2pt.	Pts.	Fum.
2004—Philadelphia NFL	7	0	12	42	3.5	0	2	15	7.5	0	0	0	0	0

TATE, ROBERT   CB   CARDINALS

PERSONAL: Born October 19, 1973, in Crowley, La. ... 5-11/193.
HIGH SCHOOL: John Harris (Harrisburg, Pa.), then Milford (Conn.) Academy.
COLLEGE: Cincinnati.
TRANSACTIONS/CAREER NOTES: Selected by Minnesota Vikings in sixth round (183rd pick overall) of 1997 NFL draft. ... Signed by Vikings (June 17, 1997). ... On injured reserve with ankle injury (October 8, 1997-remainder of season). ... Released by Vikings (August 21, 2002). ... Signed by Baltimore Ravens (August 22, 2002). ... Granted unconditional free agency (February 28, 2003). ... Signed by Arizona Cardinals (February 26, 2004). ... Granted unconditional free agency (March 2, 2005). ... Re-signed by Cardinals (April 11, 2005).
CHAMPIONSHIP GAME EXPERIENCE: Member of Vikings for NFC championship game (1998 season); inactive. ... Played in NFC championship game (2000 season).
SINGLE GAME HIGHS (regular season): Receptions—1 (October 3, 1999, vs. Tampa Bay); yards—17 (December 3, 1999, vs. Tampa Bay); and touchdown receptions—0.

Year Team	G	GS	TOTALS Tk.	Ast.	Sks.	INTERCEPTIONS No.	Yds.	Avg.	TD	KICKOFF RETURNS No.	Yds.	Avg.	TD	TOTALS TD	2pt.	Pts.	Fum.
1997—Minnesota NFL	4	0	0	0	0.0	0	0	0.0	0	10	196	19.6	0	0	0	0	0
1998—Minnesota NFL	15	1	0	0	0.0	0	0	0.0	0	2	43	21.5	0	0	0	0	0
1999—Minnesota NFL	16	1	0	0	0.0	1	18	18.0	0	25	627	25.1	1	1	0	6	1
2000—Minnesota NFL	16	16	0	0	0.0	2	12	6.0	0	0	0	0.0	0	0	0	0	0
2001—Minnesota NFL	16	5	0	0	0.0	0	0	0.0	0	0	0	0.0	0	0	0	0	0
2002—Baltimore NFL	13	1	0	0	0.0	0	0	0.0	0	17	356	20.9	0	0	0	0	2
2004—Arizona NFL	14	0	12	0	0.0	0	0	0.0	0	0	0	0.0	0	0	0	0	0
Pro totals (7 years)	94	24	12	0	0.0	3	30	10.0	0	54	1222	22.6	1	1	0	6	3

TAUSCHER, MARK   T/G   PACKERS

PERSONAL: Born June 17, 1977, in Marshfield, Wis. ... 6-4/320. ... Full name: Mark Gerald Tauscher.
HIGH SCHOOL: Auburndale (Wis.).
COLLEGE: Wisconsin.
TRANSACTIONS/CAREER NOTES: Selected by Green Bay Packers in seventh round (224th pick overall) of 2000 NFL draft. ... Signed by Packers (June 21, 2000). ... On injured reserve with knee injury (September 18, 2002-remainder of season).
PLAYING EXPERIENCE: Green Bay NFL, 2000-2004. ... Games/Games started: 2000 (16/14), 2001 (16/16), 2002 (2/2), 2003 (16/16), 2004 (16/16). Total: 66/64.

TAYLOR, BEN   LB   BROWNS

PERSONAL: Born August 31, 1978, in Bellaire, Ohio. ... 6-2/245. ... Full name: Benjamin Frazier Taylor.
HIGH SCHOOL: Bellaire (Ohio).
COLLEGE: Virginia Tech.
TRANSACTIONS/CAREER NOTES: Selected by Cleveland Browns in fourth round (111th pick overall) of 2002 NFL draft. ... Signed by Browns (July 19, 2002). ... On injured reserve with hamstring injury (November 25, 2002-remainder of season). ... On injured reserve with pectoral injury (September 28, 2004-remainder of season). ... Granted free agency (March 2, 2005). ... Re-signed by Browns (March 15, 2005).
HONORS: Named linebacker on THE SPORTING NEWS college All-America third team (2001).

				TOTALS			INTERCEPTIONS			
Year Team	G	GS	Tk.	Ast.	Sks.	No.	Yds.	Avg.	TD
2002—Cleveland NFL	7	0	1	2	0.0	0	0	0.0	0
2003—Cleveland NFL	13	8	63	16	0.0	1	0	0.0	0
2004—Cleveland NFL	3	2	2	6	0.0	0	0	0.0	0
Pro totals (3 years)	23	10	66	24	0.0	1	0	0.0	0

TAYLOR, BOBBY   CB   SEAHAWKS

PERSONAL: Born December 28, 1973, in Houston, Texas. ... 6-3/216. ... Full name: Robert Taylor. ... Son of Robert Taylor, silver medalist in 100-meter dash and member of gold-medal winning 400-meter relay team at 1972 Summer Olympics.
HIGH SCHOOL: Longview (Texas).
COLLEGE: Notre Dame.
TRANSACTIONS/CAREER NOTES: Selected after junior season by Philadelphia Eagles in second round (49th pick overall) of 1995 NFL draft. ... Signed by Eagles (July 19, 1995). ... On injured reserve with knee injury (October 17, 1997-remainder of season). ... Granted free agency (February 13, 1998). ... Re-signed by Eagles (June 11, 1998). ... On injured reserve with fractured jaw (December 28, 1999-remainder of season). ... Granted unconditional free agency (March 3, 2004). ... Signed by Seattle Seahawks (March 25, 2004).
CHAMPIONSHIP GAME EXPERIENCE: Played in NFC championship game (2001-2003 seasons).
HONORS: Named defensive back on THE SPORTING NEWS college All-America first team (1993 and 1994). ... Played in Pro Bowl (2002 season).

				TOTALS			INTERCEPTIONS			
Year Team	G	GS	Tk.	Ast.	Sks.	No.	Yds.	Avg.	TD
1995—Philadelphia NFL	16	12	47	5	0.0	2	52	26.0	0
1996—Philadelphia NFL	16	16	55	7	1.0	3	-1	-0.3	0
1997—Philadelphia NFL	6	5	14	4	2.0	0	0	0.0	0
1998—Philadelphia NFL	11	10	22	9	0.0	0	0	0.0	0
1999—Philadelphia NFL	15	14	39	7	0.0	4	59	14.8	1
2000—Philadelphia NFL	16	15	39	7	0.0	3	64	21.3	0
2001—Philadelphia NFL	16	14	36	3	1.0	1	5	5.0	0
2002—Philadelphia NFL	16	16	47	11	0.0	5	43	8.6	1
2003—Philadelphia NFL	7	7	18	1	0.0	1	2	2.0	0
2004—Seattle NFL	10	0	11	2	0.0	0	0	0.0	0
Pro totals (10 years)	129	109	328	56	4.0	19	224	11.8	2

TAYLOR, CHESTER   RB   RAVENS

PERSONAL: Born September 22, 1979, in River Rouge, Mich. ... 5-11/213. ... Full name: Chester Lamar Taylor.
HIGH SCHOOL: River Rouge (Mich.).
COLLEGE: Toledo.
TRANSACTIONS/CAREER NOTES: Selected by Baltimore Ravens in sixth round (207th pick overall) of 2002 NFL draft. ... Signed by Ravens (July 24, 2002). ... Granted free agency (March 2, 2005). ... Tendered offer sheet by Cleveland Browns (March 13, 2005). ... Ravens matched offer (March 21, 2005).
SINGLE GAME HIGHS (regular season): Attempts—25 (December 12, 2004, vs. New York Giants); yards—139 (December 5, 2004, vs. Cincinnati); and rushing touchdowns—1 (December 5, 2004, vs. Cincinnati).
STATISTICAL PLATEAUS: 100-yard rushing games: 2004 (2). Total: 2.

			RUSHING				RECEIVING				KICKOFF RETURNS				TOTALS			
Year Team	G	GS	Att.	Yds.	Avg.	TD	No.	Yds.	Avg.	TD	No.	Yds.	Avg.	TD	TD	2pt.	Pts.	Fum.
2002—Baltimore NFL	15	2	33	122	3.7	0	14	129	9.2	2	10	236	23.6	0	2	1	14	1
2003—Baltimore NFL	16	1	63	276	4.4	2	20	132	6.6	0	23	448	19.5	0	2	0	12	3
2004—Baltimore NFL	16	4	160	714	4.5	2	30	184	6.1	0	0	0	0.0	0	2	0	12	1
Pro totals (3 years)	47	7	256	1112	4.3	4	64	445	7.0	2	33	684	20.7	0	6	1	38	5

TAYLOR, FRED   RB   JAGUARS

PERSONAL: Born January 27, 1976, in Pahokee, Fla. ... 6-1/234. ... Full name: Frederick Antwon Taylor.
HIGH SCHOOL: Glades Central (Belle Glade, Fla.).
COLLEGE: Florida.

TRANSACTIONS/CAREER NOTES: Selected by Jacksonville Jaguars in first round (ninth pick overall) of 1998 NFL draft. ... Signed by Jaguars (July 6, 1998).
CHAMPIONSHIP GAME EXPERIENCE: Played in AFC championship game (1999 season).
HONORS: Named running back on THE SPORTING NEWS college All-America third team (1997).
SINGLE GAME HIGHS (regular season): Attempts—34 (December 21, 2003, vs. New Orleans); yards—234 (November 19, 2000, vs. Pittsburgh); and rushing touchdowns—3 (December 3, 2000, vs. Cleveland).
STATISTICAL PLATEAUS: 100-yard rushing games: 1998 (6), 1999 (3), 2000 (9), 2002 (5), 2003 (7), 2004 (5). Total: 35.
MISCELLANEOUS: Holds Jacksonville Jaguars all-time records for most yards rushing (7,580) and most rushing touchdowns (48).

			RUSHING				RECEIVING				TOTALS			
Year Team	G	GS	Att.	Yds.	Avg.	TD	No.	Yds.	Avg.	TD	TD	2pt.	Pts.	Fum.
1998—Jacksonville NFL	15	12	264	1223	4.6	14	44	421	9.6	3	17	0	102	3
1999—Jacksonville NFL	10	9	159	732	4.6	6	10	83	8.3	0	6	0	36	0
2000—Jacksonville NFL	13	13	292	1399	4.8	12	36	240	6.7	2	14	0	84	4
2001—Jacksonville NFL	2	2	30	116	3.9	0	2	13	6.5	0	0	0	0	1
2002—Jacksonville NFL	16	16	287	1314	4.6	8	49	408	8.3	0	8	2	52	3
2003—Jacksonville NFL	16	16	345	1572	4.6	6	48	370	7.7	1	7	0	42	6
2004—Jacksonville NFL	14	14	260	1224	4.7	2	36	345	9.6	1	3	0	18	3
Pro totals (7 years)	86	82	1637	7580	4.6	48	225	1880	8.4	7	55	2	334	20

TAYLOR, IKE　　　　　　　CB　　　　　　　STEELERS

PERSONAL: Born May 5, 1980, in New Orleans, La. ... 6-1/191. ... Full name: Ivan Taylor.
HIGH SCHOOL: Abramson (Gretna, La.).
COLLEGE: Louisiana-Lafayette.
TRANSACTIONS/CAREER NOTES: Selected by Pittsburgh Steelers in fourth round (125th pick overall) of 2003 NFL draft. ... Signed by Steelers (May 28, 2003).
CHAMPIONSHIP GAME EXPERIENCE: Played in AFC championship game (2004 season).

			RUSHING				RECEIVING				KICKOFF RETURNS				TOTALS			
Year Team	G	GS	Att.	Yds.	Avg.	TD	No.	Yds.	Avg.	TD	No.	Yds.	Avg.	TD	TD	2pt.	Pts.	Fum.
2003—Pittsburgh NFL	16	1	0	0	0.0	0	0	0	0.0	0	37	831	22.5	0	0	0	0	1
2004—Pittsburgh NFL	13	1	0	0	0.0	0	0	0	0.0	0	11	184	16.7	0	0	0	0	1
Pro totals (2 years)	29	2	0	0	0.0	0	0	0	0.0	0	48	1015	21.1	0	0	0	0	2

T

TAYLOR, JAMAAR　　　　　　　WR　　　　　　　GIANTS

PERSONAL: Born February 25, 1981, in Giessen, Germany. ... 6-0/197. ... Full name: Henry Jamaar Taylor.
HIGH SCHOOL: Mission (Texas).
COLLEGE: Texas A&M.
TRANSACTIONS/CAREER NOTES: Selected by New York Giants in sixth round (168th pick overall) of 2004 NFL draft. ... Signed by Giants (July 30, 2004).
SINGLE GAME HIGHS (regular season): Receptions—2 (November 28, 2004, vs. Philadelphia); yards—102 (November 28, 2004, vs. Philadelphia); and touchdown receptions—0.
STATISTICAL PLATEAUS: 100-yard receiving games: 2004 (1). Total: 1.

			RECEIVING				KICKOFF RETURNS				TOTALS			
Year Team	G	GS	No.	Yds.	Avg.	TD	No.	Yds.	Avg.	TD	TD	2pt.	Pts.	Fum.
2004—New York Giants NFL	8	0	6	146	24.3	0	0	0	0.0	0	0	0	0	0

TAYLOR, JASON　　　　　　　DE　　　　　　　DOLPHINS

PERSONAL: Born September 1, 1974, in Pittsburgh, Pa. ... 6-6/255. ... Full name: Jason Paul Taylor.
HIGH SCHOOL: Woodland Hills (Pittsburgh).
COLLEGE: Akron.
TRANSACTIONS/CAREER NOTES: Selected by Miami Dolphins in third round (73rd pick overall) of 1997 NFL draft. ... Signed by Dolphins (July 9, 1997). ... On injured reserve with broken collarbone (December 29, 1998-remainder of playoffs). ... Granted free agency (February 11, 2000). ... Re-signed by Dolphins (April 13, 2000). ... Designated by Dolphins as franchise player (February 22, 2001). ... Re-signed by Dolphins (July 23, 2001).
HONORS: Named defensive end on THE SPORTING NEWS NFL All-Pro team (2000 and 2002). ... Played in Pro Bowl (2000, 2002 and 2004 seasons).
MISCELLANEOUS: Holds Miami Dolphins all-time record for most sacks (80.5).

			TOTALS			INTERCEPTIONS			
Year Team	G	GS	Tk.	Ast.	Sks.	No.	Yds.	Avg.	TD
1997—Miami NFL	13	11	30	12	5.0	0	0	0.0	0
1998—Miami NFL	16	15	34	18	9.0	0	0	0.0	0
1999—Miami NFL	15	15	24	16	2.5	1	0	0.0	0
2000—Miami NFL	16	16	35	28	14.5	1	2	2.0	0
2001—Miami NFL	16	16	48	23	8.5	1	4	4.0	0
2002—Miami NFL	16	16	46	23	*18.5	0	0	0.0	0
2003—Miami NFL	16	16	37	22	13.0	0	0	0.0	0
2004—Miami NFL	16	16	41	27	9.5	1	-3	-3.0	0
Pro totals (8 years)	124	121	295	169	80.5	4	3	0.8	0

TAYLOR, JAY　　　　　　　K

PERSONAL: Born October 23, 1976, in Hershey, Pa. ... 6-1/191.
HIGH SCHOOL: Hershey (Pa.).
COLLEGE: West Virginia.

			FIELD GOALS							TOTALS		
Year Team	G	1-29	30-39	40-49	50+	Tot.	Pct.	Lg.		XPM	XPA	Pts.
2004—Tampa Bay NFL	5	0-0	2-3	1-1	1-1	4-5	80.0	50		11	11	23

TAYLOR, SEAN   DB   REDSKINS

PERSONAL: Born April 1, 1983, in Miami, Fla. ... 6-2/231. ... Full name: Sean Michael Taylor.
HIGH SCHOOL: Gulliver Prep (Miami, Fla.).
COLLEGE: Miami (Fla.).
TRANSACTIONS/CAREER NOTES: Selected after junior season by Washington Redskins in first round (fifth pick overall) of 2004 NFL draft. ... Signed by Redskins (July 27, 2004).
HONORS: Named safety on THE SPORTING NEWS college All-America first team (2003).

		TOTALS			INTERCEPTIONS				PUNT RETURNS				TOTALS			
Year Team	G	GS	Tk.	Ast.	Sks.	No.	Yds.	Avg.	TD	No.	Yds.	Avg.	TD	TD	2pt.	Pts.	Fum.
2004—Washington NFL	15	13	59	17	1.0	4	85	21.3	0	0	0	0.0	0	0	0	0	0

TAYLOR, TRAVIS   WR   VIKINGS

PERSONAL: Born March 30, 1978, in Fernadina, Fla. ... 6-1/210. ... Full name: Travis Lamont Taylor.
HIGH SCHOOL: Camden County (Ga.), then Jean Ribault (Jacksonville).
COLLEGE: Florida.
TRANSACTIONS/CAREER NOTES: Selected after junior season by Baltimore Ravens in first round (10th pick overall) of 2000 NFL draft. ... Signed by Ravens (August 1, 2000). ... On injured reserve with broken clavicle (November 8, 2000-remainder of season). ... Granted unconditional free agency (March 2, 2005). ... Signed by Minnesota Vikings (March 15, 2005).
SINGLE GAME HIGHS (regular season): Receptions—7 (November 7, 2004, vs. Cleveland); yards—138 (October 19, 2003, vs. Cincinnati); and touchdown receptions—2 (October 19, 2003, vs. Cincinnati).
STATISTICAL PLATEAUS: 100-yard receiving games: 2002 (1), 2003 (1). Total: 2.
MISCELLANEOUS: Holds Baltimore Ravens all-time record for most receptions (204).

			RUSHING				RECEIVING				TOTALS			
Year Team	G	GS	Att.	Yds.	Avg.	TD	No.	Yds.	Avg.	TD	TD	2pt.	Pts.	Fum.
2000—Baltimore NFL	9	8	2	11	5.5	0	28	276	9.9	3	3	0	18	1
2001—Baltimore NFL	16	13	5	46	9.2	0	42	560	13.3	3	3	0	18	0
2002—Baltimore NFL	16	15	11	105	9.5	0	61	869	14.2	6	6	0	36	0
2003—Baltimore NFL	16	16	11	62	5.6	0	39	632	16.2	3	3	0	18	0
2004—Baltimore NFL	10	9	0	0	0.0	0	34	421	12.4	0	0	0	0	1
Pro totals (5 years)	67	61	29	224	7.7	0	204	2758	13.5	15	15	0	90	2

TEAGUE, TREY   C   BILLS

PERSONAL: Born December 27, 1974, in Jackson, Tenn. ... 6-5/300. ... Full name: Fred Everette Teague III. ... Name pronounced: TEEG.
HIGH SCHOOL: University (Jackson, Tenn.).
COLLEGE: Tennessee.
TRANSACTIONS/CAREER NOTES: Selected by Denver Broncos in seventh round (200th pick overall) of 1998 NFL draft. ... Signed by Broncos (July 23, 1998). ... Inactive for all 16 games (1998). ... On injured reserve with knee injury (September 12, 2000-remainder of season). ... Granted free agency (March 2, 2001). ... Re-signed by Broncos (May 3, 2001). ... Granted unconditional free agency (March 1, 2002). ... Signed by Buffalo Bills (March 27, 2002).
PLAYING EXPERIENCE: Denver NFL, 1999-2001; Buffalo NFL, 2002-2004. ... Games/Games started: 1999 (16/4), 2000 (2/0), 2001 (16/16), 2002 (16/16), 2003 (16/16), 2004 (12/12). Total: 78/64.
CHAMPIONSHIP GAME EXPERIENCE: Member of Broncos for AFC championship game (1998 season); inactive. ... Member of Super Bowl championship team (1998 season); inactive.

TERCERO, SCOTT   G   RAMS

PERSONAL: Born October 28, 1981, in Whittier, Calif. ... 6-4/303.
HIGH SCHOOL: Loyola (Pico Rivera, Calif.).
COLLEGE: California.
TRANSACTIONS/CAREER NOTES: Selected by St. Louis Rams in sixth round (184th pick overall) of 2003 NFL draft. ... Inactive for four games (2003). ... On injured reserve with shoulder injury (November 16, 2004-remainder of season).
PLAYING EXPERIENCE: St. Louis NFL, 2004. ... Games/Games started: 2004 (8/4). Total: 8/4.

TERRELL, DAVID   WR   PATRIOTS

PERSONAL: Born March 13, 1979, in Richmond, Va. ... 6-3/212.
HIGH SCHOOL: Huguenot (Richmond, Va.).
COLLEGE: Michigan.

TRANSACTIONS/CAREER NOTES: Selected after junior season by Chicago Bears in first round (eighth pick overall) of 2001 NFL draft. ... Signed by Bears (July 31, 2001). ... On injured reserve with foot injury (November 12, 2002-remainder of season). ... Released by Bears (February 28, 2005). ... Signed by New England Patriots (April 5, 2005).

HONORS: Named wide receiver on THE SPORTING NEWS college All-America second team (2000).

SINGLE GAME HIGHS (regular season): Receptions—9 (October 3, 2004, vs. Philadelphia); yards—126 (September 12, 2004, vs. Detroit); and touchdown receptions—2 (October 28, 2001, vs. San Francisco).

STATISTICAL PLATEAUS: 100-yard receiving games: 2004 (2). Total: 2.

				RECEIVING				TOTALS		
Year Team	G	GS	No.	Yds.	Avg.	TD	TD	2pt.	Pts.	Fum.
2001—Chicago NFL	16	6	34	415	12.2	4	4	0	24	0
2002—Chicago NFL	5	1	9	127	14.1	3	3	0	18	0
2003—Chicago NFL	16	7	43	361	8.4	1	1	0	6	1
2004—Chicago NFL	16	15	42	699	16.6	1	1	0	6	1
Pro totals (4 years)	53	29	128	1602	12.5	9	9	0	54	2

TERRELL, DAVID　　　　　　　　S

PERSONAL: Born July 8, 1975, in Floydada, Texas. ... 6-1/190.
HIGH SCHOOL: Sweetwater (Texas).
COLLEGE: Texas-El Paso.
TRANSACTIONS/CAREER NOTES: Selected by Washington Redskins in seventh round (191st pick overall) of 1998 NFL draft. ... Signed by Redskins (May 13, 1998). ... Released by Redskins (August 25, 1998). ... Selected by Rhein Fire in 1999 NFL Europe draft (February 23, 1999). ... Released by Redskins (September 4, 1999). ... Re-signed by Redskins to practice squad (September 14, 1999). ... Granted free agency (February 28, 2003). ... Re-signed by Redskins (April 22, 2003). ... Granted unconditional free agency (March 3, 2004). ... Signed by Oakland Raiders (May 17, 2004). ... Granted unconditional free agency (March 2, 2005).

			TOTALS			INTERCEPTIONS			
Year Team	G	GS	Tk.	Ast.	Sks.	No.	Yds.	Avg.	TD
2000—Washington NFL	16	0	3	0	0.0	0	0	0.0	0
2001—Washington NFL	16	16	61	10	1.0	2	0	0.0	0
2002—Washington NFL	16	16	48	15	0.0	2	41	20.5	0
2003—Washington NFL	13	1	13	4	0.0	2	21	10.5	0
2004—Oakland NFL	16	0	6	1	0.0	0	0	0.0	0
Pro totals (5 years)	77	33	131	30	1.0	6	62	10.3	0

TERRILL, CRAIG　　　　　DT　　　　　SEAHAWKS

PERSONAL: Born June 27, 1980, in Lebanon, Ind. ... 6-2/290. ... Full name: Craig Adam Terrill.
HIGH SCHOOL: Lebanon (Ind.).
COLLEGE: Purdue.
TRANSACTIONS/CAREER NOTES: Selected by Seattle Seahawks in sixth round (189th pick overall) of 2004 NFL draft. ... Signed by Seahawks (June 24, 2004).

			TOTALS		
Year Team	G	GS	Tk.	Ast.	Sks.
2004—Seattle NFL	4	0	1	3	0.0

TERRY, CHRIS　　　　　　　　T

PERSONAL: Born August 8, 1975, in Jacksonville, Fla. ... 6-5/295. ... Full name: Christopher Alexander Terry.
HIGH SCHOOL: Jean Ribault (Jacksonville).
COLLEGE: Georgia.
TRANSACTIONS/CAREER NOTES: Selected by Carolina Panthers in second round (34th pick overall) of 1999 NFL draft. ... Signed by Panthers (May 24, 1999). ... Waived by Panthers (November 20, 2002). ... Claimed on waivers by Seattle Seahawks (November 21, 2002). ... On injured reserve with shoulder injury (December 10, 2004-remainder of season). ... Released by Seahawks (March 18, 2005).
PLAYING EXPERIENCE: Carolina NFL, 1999-2001; Seattle NFL, 2002; Carolina NFL, 2002; Seattle NFL, 2003-2004. ... Games/Games started: 1999 (16/16), 2000 (16/16), 2001 (15/15), 2002 (10/10), 2003 (12/10), 2004 (8/8). Total: 77/75.

TERRY, JEB　　　　　　G　　　　　BUCCANEERS

PERSONAL: Born April 10, 1981, in Dallas, Texas. ... 6-5/311.
HIGH SCHOOL: Culver Military Academy (Bloomington, Ind.).
COLLEGE: North Carolina.
TRANSACTIONS/CAREER NOTES: Selected by Tampa Bay Buccaneers in fifth round (146th pick overall) of 2004 NFL draft. ... Signed by Buccaneers (July 30, 2004).
PLAYING EXPERIENCE: Tampa Bay NFL, 2004. ... Games/Games started: 2004 (4/0). Total: 4/0.

TESTAVERDE, VINNY　　　　　QB

PERSONAL: Born November 13, 1963, in Brooklyn, N.Y. ... 6-5/233. ... Full name: Vincent Frank Testaverde. ... Name pronounced: TESS-tuh-VER-dee.
HIGH SCHOOL: Sewanhaka (Floral Park, N.Y.), then Fork Union (Va.) Military Academy.
COLLEGE: Miami (Fla.).
TRANSACTIONS/CAREER NOTES: Signed by Tampa Bay Buccaneers (April 3, 1987). ... Selected officially by Buccaneers in first round (first pick overall) of 1987 NFL draft. ... On injured reserve with ankle injury (December 20, 1989-remainder of season). ... Granted unconditional

free agency (March 1, 1993). ... Signed by Cleveland Browns (March 31, 1993). ... Browns franchise moved to Baltimore and renamed Ravens for 1996 season (March 11, 1996). ... Released by Ravens (June 2, 1998). ... Signed by New York Jets (June 24, 1998). ... Granted free agency (February 12, 1999). ... Re-signed by Jets (March 1, 1999). ... On injured reserve with torn Achilles' tendon (September 13, 1999-remainder of season). ... Released by Jets (June 2, 2004). ... Signed by Dallas Cowboys (June 3, 2004). ... Granted unconditional free agency (March 2, 2005).

CHAMPIONSHIP GAME EXPERIENCE: Played in AFC championship game (1998 season).

HONORS: Named quarterback on THE SPORTING NEWS college All-America second team (1985). ... Heisman Trophy winner (1986). ... Named College Football Player of the Year by THE SPORTING NEWS (1986). ... Maxwell Award winner (1986). ... Davey O'Brien Award winner (1986). ... Named quarterback on THE SPORTING NEWS college All-America first team (1986). ... Played in Pro Bowl (1996 and 1998 seasons).

SINGLE GAME HIGHS (regular season): Attempts—69 (December 24, 2000, vs. Baltimore); completions—42 (December 6, 1998, vs. Seattle); yards—481 (December 24, 2000, vs. Baltimore); and touchdown passes—5 (October, 23, 2000, vs. Miami).

STATISTICAL PLATEAUS: 100-yard rushing games: 1990 (1). Total: 1. 300-yard passing games: 1987 (1), 1988 (4), 1989 (4), 1990 (1), 1991 (1), 1992 (1), 1993 (1), 1995 (2), 1996 (5), 1997 (3), 1998 (1), 2000 (2), 2003 (1), 2004 (3). Total: 30.

MISCELLANEOUS: Regular-season record as starting NFL quarterback: 87-116-1 (.429). ... Postseason record as starting NFL quarterback: 2-3 (.400). ... Holds Tampa Bay Buccaneers all-time records for most yards passing (14,820) and most touchdown passes (77). ... Holds Baltimore Ravens all-time records for most yards passing (7,148) and most touchdown passes (51). ... Granted unrestricted free agency (March 2, 2005).

			PASSING									RUSHING				TOTALS		
Year Team	G	GS	Att.	Cmp.	Pct.	Yds.	TD	Int.	Avg.	Skd.	Rat.	Att.	Yds.	Avg.	TD	TD	2pt.	Pts.
1987—Tampa Bay NFL	6	4	165	71	43.0	1081	5	6	6.55	18	60.2	13	50	3.8	1	1	0	6
1988—Tampa Bay NFL	15	15	466	222	47.6	3240	13	*35	6.95	33	48.8	28	138	4.9	1	1	0	6
1989—Tampa Bay NFL	14	14	480	258	53.8	3133	20	†22	6.53	38	68.9	25	139	5.6	0	0	0	0
1990—Tampa Bay NFL	14	13	365	203	55.6	2818	17	∞18	s7.72	38	75.6	38	280	7.4	1	1	0	6
1991—Tampa Bay NFL	13	12	326	166	50.9	1994	8	15	6.12	35	59.0	32	101	3.2	0	0	0	0
1992—Tampa Bay NFL	14	14	358	206	57.5	2554	14	16	7.13	35	74.2	36	197	5.5	2	2	0	12
1993—Cleveland NFL	10	6	230	130	56.5	1797	14	9	s7.81	17	85.7	18	74	4.1	0	0	0	0
1994—Cleveland NFL	14	13	376	207	55.1	2575	16	18	6.85	12	70.7	21	37	1.8	2	2	0	12
1995—Cleveland NFL	13	12	392	241	61.5	2883	17	10	7.35	17	87.8	18	62	3.4	2	2	0	12
1996—Baltimore NFL	16	16	549	325	59.2	4177§33	19	7.01		34	88.7	34	188	5.5	2	2	1	14
1997—Baltimore NFL	13	13	470	271	57.7	2971	18	15	6.32	20	75.9	34	138	4.1	0	0	0	0
1998—New York Jets NFL	14	13	421	259	61.5	3256§29	7	7.73		19§101.6	24	104	4.3	1	1	0	6
1999—New York Jets NFL	1	1	15	10	66.7	96	1	1	6.40	0	78.7	0	0	0.0	0	0	0	0
2000—New York Jets NFL	16	16	*590	328	55.6	3732	21	*25	6.33	13	69.0	25	32	1.3	0	0	0	0
2001—New York Jets NFL	16	16	441	260	59.0	2752	15	14	6.24	18	75.3	31	25	0.8	0	0	0	0
2002—New York Jets NFL	5	4	83	54	65.1	499	3	3	6.01	9	78.3	2	23	11.5	0	0	0	0
2003—New York Jets NFL	7	7	198	123	62.1	1385	7	2	6.99	6	90.6	6	17	2.8	0	0	0	0
2004—Dallas NFL	16	15	495	297	60.0	3632	17	†20	7.14	34	76.4	21	38	1.8	1	1	0	6
Pro totals (18 years)	217	204	6420	3631	56.6	44475	268	255	6.93	396	75.4	406	1643	4.0	13	13	1	80

THOMAS, ADALIUS   DE   RAVENS

PERSONAL: Born August 18, 1977, in Equality, Ala. ... 6-2/270. ... Full name: Adalius Donquail Thomas.

HIGH SCHOOL: Central Coosa (Equality, Ala.).

COLLEGE: Southern Miss.

TRANSACTIONS/CAREER NOTES: Selected by Baltimore Ravens in sixth round (186th pick overall) of 2000 NFL draft. ... Signed by Ravens (July 6, 2000). ... Granted free agency (February 28, 2003). ... Re-signed by Ravens (June 17, 2003). ... On injured reserve with arm injury (December 17, 2003-remainder of season). ... Granted unconditional free agency (March 3, 2004). ... Re-signed by Ravens (March 22, 2004).

CHAMPIONSHIP GAME EXPERIENCE: Played in AFC championship game (2000 season). ... Member of Super Bowl championship team (2000 season); inactive.

HONORS: Named defensive end on THE SPORTING NEWS college All-America second team (1999). ... Named to play in Pro Bowl (2003 season); replaced by Gary Stillis due to injury.

			TOTALS			INTERCEPTIONS			
Year Team	G	GS	Tk.	Ast.	Sks.	No.	Yds.	Avg.	TD
2000—Baltimore NFL	3	0	0	1	0.0	0	0	0.0	0
2001—Baltimore NFL	16	2	22	6	3.5	0	0	0.0	0
2002—Baltimore NFL	16	12	30	11	3.0	2	57	28.5	1
2003—Baltimore NFL	13	11	25	2	4.0	0	0	0.0	0
2004—Baltimore NFL	16	16	49	15	8.0	1	8	8.0	0
Pro totals (5 years)	64	41	126	35	18.5	3	65	21.7	1

THOMAS, ANTHONY   RB   COWBOYS

PERSONAL: Born November 7, 1977, in Winnfield, La. ... 6-2/225. ... Full name: Anthony Jermaine Thomas.

HIGH SCHOOL: Winnfield (La.).

COLLEGE: Michigan.

TRANSACTIONS/CAREER NOTES: Selected by Chicago Bears in second round (38th pick overall) of 2001 NFL draft. ... Signed by Bears (July 20, 2001). ... On injured reserve with finger injury (December 10, 2002-remainder of season). ... Granted unconditional free agency (March 2, 2005). ... Signed by Dallas Cowboys (May 3, 2005).

HONORS: Named running back to THE SPORTING NEWS college All-America third team (2000).

SINGLE GAME HIGHS (regular season): Attempts—33 (January 6, 2002, vs. Jacksonville); yards—188 (October 21, 2001, vs. Cincinnati); and rushing touchdowns—2 (November 7, 2004, vs. New York Giants).

STATISTICAL PLATEAUS: 100-yard rushing games: 2001 (4), 2002 (1), 2003 (4), 2004 (1). Total: 10.

			RUSHING				RECEIVING				TOTALS		
Year Team	G	GS	Att.	Yds.	Avg.	TD	No.	Yds.	Avg.	TD	TD	2pt.	Pts.	Fum.
2001—Chicago NFL	14	10	278	1183	4.3	7	22	178	8.1	0	7	1	44	0
2002—Chicago NFL	12	12	214	721	3.4	6	24	163	6.8	0	6	0	36	5

Year Team				RUSHING				RECEIVING				TOTALS			
	G	GS	Att.	Yds.	Avg.	TD	No.	Yds.	Avg.	TD	TD	2pt.	Pts.	Fum.
2003—Chicago NFL	13	13	244	1024	4.2	6	9	36	4.0	0	6	0	36	1
2004—Chicago NFL	12	2	122	404	3.3	2	17	132	7.8	0	2	0	12	1
Pro totals (4 years)	51	37	858	3332	3.9	21	72	509	7.1	0	21	1	128	7

THOMAS, BRYAN   DE   JETS

PERSONAL: Born June 7, 1979, in Birmingham, Ala. ... 6-4/266.
HIGH SCHOOL: Minor (Birmingham, Ala.).
COLLEGE: Alabama-Birmingham.
TRANSACTIONS/CAREER NOTES: Selected by New York Jets in first round (22nd pick overall) of 2002 NFL draft. ... Signed by Jets (June 19, 2002).

Year Team			TOTALS		
	G	GS	Tk.	Ast.	Sks.
2002—New York Jets NFL	15	0	5	4	0.5
2003—New York Jets NFL	16	10	26	16	1.0
2004—New York Jets NFL	14	6	28	15	1.5
Pro totals (3 years)	45	16	59	35	3.0

THOMAS, DONTARRIOUS   LB   VIKINGS

PERSONAL: Born September 2, 1980, in Perry, Ga. ... 6-2/241. ... Full name: Dontarrious Donta Thomas.
HIGH SCHOOL: Perry (Ala.).
COLLEGE: Auburn.
TRANSACTIONS/CAREER NOTES: Selected by Minnesota Vikings in second round (48th pick overall) of 2004 NFL draft. ... Signed by Vikings (August 1, 2004).

Year Team			TOTALS			INTERCEPTIONS			
	G	GS	Tk.	Ast.	Sks.	No.	Yds.	Avg.	TD
2004—Minnesota NFL	16	5	36	15	0.5	0	0	0.0	0

THOMAS, FRED   CB   SAINTS

PERSONAL: Born September 11, 1973, in Bruce, Miss. ... 5-9/185.
HIGH SCHOOL: Bruce (Miss.).
JUNIOR COLLEGE: Northwest Mississippi Community College.
COLLEGE: Tennessee-Martin.
TRANSACTIONS/CAREER NOTES: Selected by Seattle Seahawks in second round (47th pick overall) of 1996 NFL draft. ... Signed by Seahawks (July 19, 1996). ... Granted free agency (February 12, 1999). ... Re-signed by Seahawks (May 27, 1999). ... On injured reserve with broken leg (September 17, 1999-remainder of season). ... Granted unconditional free agency (February 11, 2000). ... Signed by New Orleans Saints (February 14, 2000). ... Granted unconditional free agency (March 3, 2004). ... Re-signed by Saints (March 4, 2004).

Year Team			TOTALS			INTERCEPTIONS			
	G	GS	Tk.	Ast.	Sks.	No.	Yds.	Avg.	TD
1996—Seattle NFL	15	0	4	1	0.0	0	0	0.0	0
1997—Seattle NFL	16	3	24	4	0.0	0	0	0.0	0
1998—Seattle NFL	15	2	32	7	0.0	0	0	0.0	0
1999—Seattle NFL	1	0	0	0	0.0	0	0	0.0	0
2000—New Orleans NFL	11	0	16	0	0.0	0	0	0.0	0
2001—New Orleans NFL	16	16	51	13	0.0	1	0	0.0	0
2002—New Orleans NFL	15	14	69	11	1.0	5	80	16.0	0
2003—New Orleans NFL	16	14	75	11	1.0	4	47	11.8	0
2004—New Orleans NFL	15	7	43	2	0.0	0	0	0.0	0
Pro totals (9 years)	120	56	314	49	2.0	10	127	12.7	0

THOMAS, HOLLIS   DT   EAGLES

PERSONAL: Born January 10, 1974, in Abilene, Texas. ... 6-0/306.
HIGH SCHOOL: Sumner (St. Louis).
COLLEGE: Northern Illinois.
TRANSACTIONS/CAREER NOTES: Signed as non-drafted free agent by Philadelphia Eagles (April 26, 1996). ... On injured reserve with arm/shoulder injury (December 2, 1998-remainder of season). ... On injured reserve with foot injury (December 31, 2001-remainder of season). ... On injured reserve with foot injury (August 27, 2002-remainder of season). ... On injured reserve with biceps injury (October 28, 2003-remainder of season).
CHAMPIONSHIP GAME EXPERIENCE: Played in NFC championship game (2004 season). ... Played in Super Bowl 39 (2004 season).

Year Team			TOTALS		
	G	GS	Tk.	Ast.	Sks.
1996—Philadelphia NFL	16	5	32	10	1.0
1997—Philadelphia NFL	16	16	39	22	2.5
1998—Philadelphia NFL	12	12	34	8	5.0
1999—Philadelphia NFL	16	16	36	13	1.0
2000—Philadelphia NFL	16	16	46	14	4.0
2001—Philadelphia NFL	14	14	43	9	0.0
2002—Philadelphia NFL	Did not play.				
2003—Philadelphia NFL	7	2	13	6	0.0
2004—Philadelphia NFL	13	2	17	4	0.0
Pro totals (8 years)	110	83	260	86	13.5

THOMAS, JOEY   CB   PACKERS

PERSONAL: Born August 29, 1980, in Seattle, Wash. ... 6-1/195. ... Full name: Joseph Thomas.
HIGH SCHOOL: John F. Kennedy (Burien, Wash.).
COLLEGE: Montana State.
TRANSACTIONS/CAREER NOTES: Selected by Green Bay Packers in third round (70th pick overall) of 2004 NFL draft. ... Signed by Packers (July 30, 2004).

			TOTALS			INTERCEPTIONS			
Year Team	G	GS	Tk.	Ast.	Sks.	No.	Yds.	Avg.	TD
2004—Green Bay NFL	14	0	14	1	0.0	0	0	0.0	0

THOMAS, JOSH   DE   COLTS

PERSONAL: Born June 26, 1981, in Plymouth, Mass. ... 6-5/271. ... Full name: Joshua Lloyd Thomas.
HIGH SCHOOL: Orchard Park (N.Y.).
COLLEGE: Syracuse.
TRANSACTIONS/CAREER NOTES: Signed as non-drafted free agent by Indianapolis Colts (May 3, 2004). ... On injured reserve with knee injury (November 30, 2004-remainder of season).

			TOTALS		
Year Team	G	GS	Tk.	Ast.	Sks.
2004—Indianapolis NFL	11	0	7	1	1.0

THOMAS, JUQUA   DE   TITANS

PERSONAL: Born May 15, 1978, in Houston, Texas. ... 6-2/250. ... Full name: Juqua Demail Thomas.
HIGH SCHOOL: Aldine (Texas).
JUNIOR COLLEGE: Northeastern Oklahoma.
COLLEGE: Oklahoma State.
TRANSACTIONS/CAREER NOTES: Signed as non-drafted free agent by Tennessee Titans (April 27, 2001). ... Re-signed by Titans (April 2, 2003). ... Granted free agency (March 3, 2004). ... Re-signed by Titans (March 26, 2004).
CHAMPIONSHIP GAME EXPERIENCE: Member of Titans for AFC championship game (2002 season); inactive.

			TOTALS		
Year Team	G	GS	Tk.	Ast.	Sks.
2001—Tennessee NFL	7	0	4	1	0.0
2002—Tennessee NFL	9	0	9	0	1.0
2003—Tennessee NFL	15	0	12	4	4.0
2004—Tennessee NFL	10	0	5	1	0.0
Pro totals (4 years)	41	0	30	6	5.0

THOMAS, KEVIN   CB

PERSONAL: Born July 28, 1978, in Phoenix, Ariz. ... 6-0/182. ... Full name: Marvin Kevin Thomas.
HIGH SCHOOL: Foothill (Calif.).
COLLEGE: Nevada-Las Vegas.
TRANSACTIONS/CAREER NOTES: Selected by Buffalo Bills in sixth round (176th pick overall) of 2002 NFL draft. ... Signed by Bills (July 23, 2002). ... Granted free agency (March 2, 2005).

			TOTALS			INTERCEPTIONS			
Year Team	G	GS	Tk.	Ast.	Sks.	No.	Yds.	Avg.	TD
2002—Buffalo NFL	6	1	8	0	0.0	1	31	31.0	0
2003—Buffalo NFL	16	1	11	5	0.5	0	0	0.0	0
2004—Buffalo NFL	16	1	30	10	1.0	0	0	0.0	0
Pro totals (3 years)	38	3	49	15	1.5	1	31	31.0	0

THOMAS, KIWAUKEE   CB   JAGUARS

PERSONAL: Born June 19, 1977, in Warner Robins, Ga. ... 5-11/192. ... Full name: Kiwaukee Sanchez Thomas. ... Name pronounced: kee-WA-kee.
HIGH SCHOOL: Perry (Ga.).
COLLEGE: Georgia Southern.
TRANSACTIONS/CAREER NOTES: Selected by Jacksonville Jaguars in fifth round (159th pick overall) of 2000 NFL draft. ... Signed by Jaguars (May 25, 2000). ... Granted free agency (February 28, 2003). ... Re-signed by Jaguars (April 23, 2003).

			TOTALS			INTERCEPTIONS			
Year Team	G	GS	Tk.	Ast.	Sks.	No.	Yds.	Avg.	TD
2000—Jacksonville NFL	16	3	17	1	0.0	0	0	0.0	0
2001—Jacksonville NFL	16	5	40	2	0.0	0	0	0.0	0
2002—Jacksonville NFL	16	0	23	2	0.0	0	0	0.0	0
2003—Jacksonville NFL	11	1	10	3	1.0	0	0	0.0	0
2004—Jacksonville NFL	16	2	9	3	0.0	0	0	0.0	0
Pro totals (5 years)	75	11	99	11	4.0	0	0	0.0	0

THOMAS, RANDY   G   REDSKINS

PERSONAL: Born January 19, 1976, in East Point, Ga. ... 6-5/306.
HIGH SCHOOL: Tri-Cities (East Point, Ga.).
JUNIOR COLLEGE: Copiah-Lincoln Junior College (Miss.).
COLLEGE: Mississippi State.
TRANSACTIONS/CAREER NOTES: Selected by New York Jets in second round (57th pick overall) of 1999 NFL draft. ... Signed by Jets (July 20, 1999). ... Granted unconditional free agency (February 28, 2003). ... Signed by Washington Redskins (March 1, 2003).
PLAYING EXPERIENCE: New York Jets NFL, 1999-2002; Washington NFL, 2003-2004. ... Games/Games started: 1999 (16/16), 2000 (16/16), 2001 (13/13), 2002 (16/16), 2003 (16/16), 2004 (15/15). Total: 92/92.
HONORS: Named offensive guard on THE SPORTING NEWS college All-America second team (1998).

THOMAS, ROBERT   LB   RAMS

PERSONAL: Born July 17, 1980, in El Centro, Calif. ... 6-1/237. ... Full name: Robert W. Thomas.
HIGH SCHOOL: Imperial (Calif.).
COLLEGE: UCLA.
TRANSACTIONS/CAREER NOTES: Selected by St. Louis Rams in first round (31st pick overall) of 2002 NFL draft. ... Signed by Rams (July 23, 2002).
HONORS: Named linebacker on THE SPORTING NEWS college All-America first team (2001).

| | | | TOTALS | | | INTERCEPTIONS | | | |
Year Team	G	GS	Tk.	Ast.	Sks.	No.	Yds.	Avg.	TD
2002—St. Louis NFL	16	10	34	3	0.0	0	0	0.0	0
2003—St. Louis NFL	12	9	61	9	2.0	0	0	0.0	0
2004—St. Louis NFL	14	11	39	15	0.0	0	0	0.0	0
Pro totals (3 years)	42	30	134	27	2.0	0	0	0.0	0

THOMAS, TRA   T   EAGLES

PERSONAL: Born November 20, 1974, in DeLand, Fla. ... 6-7/349. ... Full name: William Thomas III. ... Name pronounced: TRAY.
HIGH SCHOOL: De Land (Fla.).
COLLEGE: Florida State.
TRANSACTIONS/CAREER NOTES: Selected by Philadelphia Eagles in first round (11th pick overall) of 1998 NFL draft. ... Signed by Eagles (June 19, 1998).
PLAYING EXPERIENCE: Philadelphia NFL, 1998-2004. ... Games/Games started: 1998 (16/16), 1999 (16/15), 2000 (16/16), 2001 (15/15), 2002 (16/16), 2003 (15/15), 2004 (15/15). Total: 109/108.
CHAMPIONSHIP GAME EXPERIENCE: Played in NFC championship game (2001-2004 seasons). ... Played in Super Bowl 39 (2004 season).
HONORS: Named offensive tackle on the THE SPORTING NEWS NFL All-Pro team (2002). ... Played in Pro Bowl (2001 and 2002 seasons). ... Named to play in Pro Bowl (2004 season); replaced by Flozell Adams due to injury.

THOMAS, ZACH   LB   DOLPHINS

PERSONAL: Born September 1, 1973, in Pampa, Texas. ... 5-11/230. ... Full name: Zach Michael Thomas.
HIGH SCHOOL: White Deer (Texas), then Pampa (Texas).
COLLEGE: Texas Tech.
TRANSACTIONS/CAREER NOTES: Selected by Miami Dolphins in fifth round (154th pick overall) of 1996 NFL draft. ... Signed by Dolphins (July 10, 1996). ... Granted free agency (February 12, 1999). ... Re-signed by Dolphins (February 12, 1999). ... Re-signed by Dolphins (March 29, 2003).
HONORS: Named linebacker on THE SPORTING NEWS college All-America second team (1994). ... Named linebacker on THE SPORTING NEWS college All-America first team (1995). ... Played in Pro Bowl (1999, 2000, 2002 and 2003 seasons). ... Named to play in Pro Bowl (2001 season); replaced by Al Wilson due to injury.

| | | | TOTALS | | | INTERCEPTIONS | | | |
Year Team	G	GS	Tk.	Ast.	Sks.	No.	Yds.	Avg.	TD
1996—Miami NFL	16	16	120	34	2.0	3	64	21.3	1
1997—Miami NFL	15	15	78	50	0.5	1	10	10.0	0
1998—Miami NFL	16	16	86	51	2.0	3	21	7.0	▲2
1999—Miami NFL	16	16	80	53	1.0	1	0	0.0	0
2000—Miami NFL	11	11	56	43	1.5	1	0	0.0	0
2001—Miami NFL	15	15	96	59	3.0	2	51	25.5	1
2002—Miami NFL	16	16	100	56	0.5	1	7	7.0	0
2003—Miami NFL	15	15	85	68	1.0	3	21	7.0	0
2004—Miami NFL	13	13	85	60	2.0	0	0	0.0	0
Pro totals (9 years)	133	133	786	474	13.5	15	174	11.6	4

THOMPSON, CHAUN   LB   BROWNS

PERSONAL: Born May 22, 1980, in Mount Pleasant, Texas. ... 6-2/250.
HIGH SCHOOL: Mount Pleasant (Texas).
COLLEGE: West Texas A&M.
TRANSACTIONS/CAREER NOTES: Selected by Cleveland Browns in second round (52nd pick overall) of 2003 NFL draft. ... Signed by Browns (July 30, 2003).

Year Team	G	GS	Tk.	Ast.	Sks.	No.	Yds.	Avg.	TD
2003—Cleveland NFL	16	0	4	0	0.0	0	0	0.0	0
2004—Cleveland NFL	16	13	39	19	2.5	0	0	0.0	0
Pro totals (2 years)	32	13	43	19	2.5	0	0	0.0	0

Above the interception columns: **TOTALS** (Tk. Ast. Sks.), **INTERCEPTIONS** (No. Yds. Avg. TD).

THOMPSON, DERRIUS — WR — DOLPHINS

PERSONAL: Born July 5, 1977, in Dallas, Texas. ... 6-2/220. ... Full name: Derrius Damon Thompson.
COLLEGE: Baylor.
TRANSACTIONS/CAREER NOTES: Signed as non-drafted free agent by Washington Redskins (April 21, 1999). ... Released by Redskins (September 4, 1999). ... Re-signed by Redskins to practice squad (September 6, 1999). ... Activated (November 16, 1999). ... Released by Redskins (August 27, 2000). ... Re-signed by Redskins to practice squad (August 28, 2000). ... Activated (September 8, 2000). ... Released by Redskins (September 18, 2000). ... Re-signed by Redskins to practice squad (November 16, 2000). ... Activated (December 18, 2000). ... Granted free agency (March 1, 2002). ... Re-signed by Redskins (June 14, 2002). ... Granted unconditional free agency (February 28, 2003). ... Signed by Miami Dolphins (March 8, 2003).
SINGLE GAME HIGHS (regular season): Receptions—7 (December 15, 2002, vs. Philadelphia); yards—122 (December 8, 2002, vs. New York Giants); and touchdown receptions—1 (December 26, 2004, vs. Cleveland).
STATISTICAL PLATEAUS: 100-yard receiving games: 2002 (1). Total: 1.

			RUSHING			RECEIVING				KICKOFF RETURNS				TOTALS			
Year Team	G	GS	Att.	Yds.	Avg.	TD	No.	Yds.	Avg.	TD	No.	Yds.	Avg.	TD	TD	2pt.	Pts. Fum.
1999—Washington NFL	1	0	0	0	0.0	0	0	0	0.0	0	0	0	0.0	0	0	0	0	0
2000—Washington NFL	4	0	0	0	0.0	0	0	0	0.0	0	0	0	0.0	0	0	0	0	0
2001—Washington NFL	16	0	0	0	0.0	0	3	52	17.3	1	3	17	5.7	0	1	0	6	0
2002—Washington NFL	16	14	10	77	7.7	0	53	773	14.6	4	6	91	15.2	0	4	0	24	2
2003—Miami NFL	16	12	0	0	0.0	0	26	359	13.8	0	0	0	0.0	0	0	0	0	0
2004—Miami NFL	16	3	0	0	0.0	0	23	359	15.6	4	0	0	0.0	0	4	0	24	0
Pro totals (6 years)	69	29	10	77	7.7	0	105	1543	14.7	9	9	108	12.0	0	9	0	54	2

THOMPSON, LAMONT — S

PERSONAL: Born July 30, 1978, in Richmond, Calif. ... 6-1/220. ... Full name: Lamont Darnell Thompson.
HIGH SCHOOL: El Cerrito (Richmond, Calif.).
COLLEGE: Washington State.
TRANSACTIONS/CAREER NOTES: Selected by Cincinnati Bengals in second round (41st pick overall) of 2002 NFL draft. ... Signed by Bengals (July 25, 2002). ... On injured reserve with knee injury (December 12, 2002-remainder of season). ... Released by Bengals (August 31, 2003). ... Signed by Tennessee Titans (September 3, 2003). ... Granted free agency (March 2, 2005).
HONORS: Named free safety on THE SPORTING NEWS college All-America second team (2001).

			TOTALS			INTERCEPTIONS			
Year Team	G	GS	Tk.	Ast.	Sks.	No.	Yds.	Avg.	TD
2002—Cincinnati NFL	13	0	10	0	0.0	1	4	4.0	0
2003—Tennessee NFL	16	0	4	2	0.0	0	0	0.0	0
2004—Tennessee NFL	16	13	55	10	0.0	4	77	19.3	1
Pro totals (3 years)	45	13	69	12	0.0	5	81	16.2	1

THOMPSON, RAY — LB — PACKERS

PERSONAL: Born November 21, 1977, in Los Angeles, Calif. ... 6-3/224. ... Full name: Raynoch Joseph Thompson.
HIGH SCHOOL: St. Augustine (New Orleans).
COLLEGE: Tennessee.
TRANSACTIONS/CAREER NOTES: Selected by Arizona Cardinals in second round (41st pick overall) of 2000 NFL draft. ... Signed by Cardinals (June 21, 2000). ... On injured reserve with knee injury (December 15, 2000-remainder of season). ... On suspended list for violating league substance abuse policy (December 2-29, 2003). ... Released by Cardinals (April 11, 2005). ... Signed by Green Bay Packers (April 22, 2005).

			TOTALS			INTERCEPTIONS			
Year Team	G	GS	Tk.	Ast.	Sks.	No.	Yds.	Avg.	TD
2000—Arizona NFL	11	9	30	13	0.0	0	0	0.0	0
2001—Arizona NFL	14	14	62	21	0.5	0	0	0.0	0
2002—Arizona NFL	16	16	73	31	3.0	0	0	0.0	0
2003—Arizona NFL	12	12	54	9	3.0	0	0	0.0	0
2004—Arizona NFL	11	3	21	13	1.0	0	0	0.0	0
Pro totals (5 years)	64	54	240	87	7.5	0	0	0.0	0

THORNTON, BRUCE — CB — COWBOYS

PERSONAL: Born January 31, 1980, in LaGrange, Ga. ... 5-10/198.
HIGH SCHOOL: LaGrange (Ga.).
COLLEGE: Georgia.
TRANSACTIONS/CAREER NOTES: Selected by Dallas Cowboys in fourth round (121st pick overall) of 2004 NFL draft. ... Signed by Cowboys (July 30, 2004). ... On injured reserve with knee injury (October 12, 2004-remainder of season).

			TOTALS			INTERCEPTIONS			
Year Team	G	GS	Tk.	Ast.	Sks.	No.	Yds.	Avg.	TD
2004—Dallas NFL	1	0	0	0	0.0	0	0	0.0	0

THORNTON, DAVID   LB

PERSONAL: Born November 1, 1978, in Goldsboro, N.C. ... 6-2/230. ... Full name: David Dontay Thornton.
HIGH SCHOOL: Goldsboro (N.C.).
COLLEGE: North Carolina.
TRANSACTIONS/CAREER NOTES: Selected by Indianapolis Colts in fourth round (106th pick overall) of 2002 NFL draft. ... Signed by Colts (July 10, 2002). ... Granted free agency (March 2, 2005).
CHAMPIONSHIP GAME EXPERIENCE: Played in AFC championship game (2003 season).

				TOTALS			INTERCEPTIONS			
Year	Team	G	GS	Tk.	Ast.	Sks.	No.	Yds.	Avg.	TD
2002—Indianapolis NFL		15	0	27	6	0.0	0	0	0.0	0
2003—Indianapolis NFL		16	16	108	32	1.0	2	3	1.5	0
2004—Indianapolis NFL		16	15	66	19	0.0	1	5	5.0	0
Pro totals (3 years)		47	31	201	57	1.0	3	8	2.7	0

THORNTON, JOHN   DT   BENGALS

PERSONAL: Born October 2, 1976, in Philadelphia, Pa. ... 6-3/297. ... Full name: John Jason Thornton.
HIGH SCHOOL: Scotland (Pa.) School for Veterans' Children.
COLLEGE: West Virginia.
TRANSACTIONS/CAREER NOTES: Selected by Tennessee Titans in second round (52nd pick overall) of 1999 NFL draft. ... Signed by Titans (July 26, 1999). ... On injured reserve with shoulder injury (November 8, 2001-remainder of season). ... Granted free agency (March 1, 2002). ... Re-signed by Titans (March 28, 2002). ... Granted unconditional free agency (February 28, 2003). ... Signed by Cincinnati Bengals (May 5, 2003).
CHAMPIONSHIP GAME EXPERIENCE: Played in AFC championship game (1999 and 2002 seasons). ... Played in Super Bowl 34 (1999 season).

				TOTALS		
Year	Team	G	GS	Tk.	Ast.	Sks.
1999—Tennessee NFL		16	3	16	4	4.5
2000—Tennessee NFL		16	16	19	9	4.0
2001—Tennessee NFL		3	0	0	0	0.0
2002—Tennessee NFL		16	16	15	5	2.0
2003—Cincinnati NFL		16	16	19	12	6.0
2004—Cincinnati NFL		16	16	37	20	3.0
Pro totals (6 years)		83	67	106	50	19.5

THORNTON, KALEN   DE

PERSONAL: Born May 12, 1982, in Dallas, Texas. ... 6-3/240. ... Full name: Kalen Bruce Thornton.
HIGH SCHOOL: St. Mark's (Dallas, Texas).
COLLEGE: Texas.
TRANSACTIONS/CAREER NOTES: Signed as non-drafted free agent by Dallas Cowboys (April 30, 2004).
HONORS: Named defensive lineman on THE SPORTING NEWS Freshman All-America first team (2000).

				TOTALS			INTERCEPTIONS			
Year	Team	G	GS	Tk.	Ast.	Sks.	No.	Yds.	Avg.	TD
2004—Dallas NFL		16	0	6	0	0.0	0	0	0.0	0

THRASH, JAMES   WR   REDSKINS

PERSONAL: Born April 28, 1975, in Denver, Colo. ... 6-0/200.
HIGH SCHOOL: Wewoka (Okla.).
COLLEGE: Missouri Southern State.
TRANSACTIONS/CAREER NOTES: Signed as non-drafted free agent by Philadelphia Eagles (April 22, 1997). ... Released by Eagles (July 8, 1997). ... Signed by Washington Redskins (July 11, 1997). ... On injured reserve with shoulder injury (December 8, 1998-remainder of season). ... Granted free agency (February 11, 2000). ... Re-signed with Redskins (April 21, 2000). ... Granted unconditional free agency (March 2, 2001). ... Signed by Eagles (March 9, 2001). ... Traded by Eagles to Washington Redskins for a fifth-round (LB Trent Cole) pick in 2005 draft (March 30, 2004).
CHAMPIONSHIP GAME EXPERIENCE: Played in NFC championship game (2001-2003 seasons).
SINGLE GAME HIGHS (regular season): Receptions—10 (September 23, 2001, vs. Seattle); yards—165 (September 23, 2001, vs. Seattle); and touchdown receptions—2 (November 11, 2001, vs. Minnesota).
STATISTICAL PLATEAUS: 100-yard receiving games: 2000 (2), 2001 (2), 2002 (1). Total: 5.

				RUSHING				RECEIVING				PUNT RETURNS				KICKOFF RETURNS				TOTALS		
Year	Team	G	GS	Att.	Yds.	Avg.	TD	No.	Yds.	Avg.	TD	No.	Yds.	Avg.	TD	No.	Yds.	Avg.	TD	TD	2pt.	Pts.
1997—Was. NFL		4	0	0	0	0.0	0	2	24	12.0	0	0	0	0.0	0	0	0	0.0	0	0	0	0
1998—Was. NFL		10	1	0	0	0.0	0	10	163	16.3	1	0	0	0.0	0	6	129	21.5	0	1	0	6
1999—Was. NFL		16	0	1	37	37.0	0	3	44	14.7	0	0	0	0.0	0	14	355	25.4	1	1	0	6
2000—Was. NFL		16	8	10	82	8.2	0	50	653	13.1	2	10	106	10.6	0	45	1000	22.2	0	2	0	12
2001—Phi. NFL		15	15	6	57	9.5	0	63	833	13.2	8	0	0	0.0	0	5	101	20.2	0	8	0	48
2002—Phi. NFL		16	16	18	126	7.0	2	52	635	12.2	6	0	0	0.0	0	0	0	0.0	0	8	0	48
2003—Phi. NFL		16	16	5	52	10.4	0	49	558	11.4	1	1	2	2.0	0	34	815	24.0	0	1	0	6
2004—Was. NFL		16	3	0	0	0.0	0	17	203	11.9	0	19	162	8.5	0	9	186	20.7	0	0	0	0
Pro totals (8 years)		109	59	40	354	8.9	2	246	3113	12.7	18	30	270	9.0	0	113	2586	22.9	1	21	0	126

THURMAN, ANDRAE   WR   PACKERS

PERSONAL: Born October 25, 1980, in Houston, Texas. ... 5-11/192. ... Full name: D'Andrae Carnell Thurman.
HIGH SCHOOL: Avondale (Ariz.).
COLLEGE: Southern Oregon.
TRANSACTIONS/CAREER NOTES: Signed as non-drafted free agent by New York Giants (May 7, 2004). ... Claimed on waivers by Houston Texans (July 1, 2004). ... Released by Texans (August 30, 2004). ... Signed by Pittsburgh Steelers to practice squad (September 6, 2004). ... Released by Steelers (September 7, 2004). ... Signed by Green Bay Packers to practice squad (September 9, 2004). ... Activated (December 23, 2004).
SINGLE GAME HIGHS (regular season): Receptions—2 (December 24, 2004, vs. Minnesota); yards—12 (December 24, 2004, vs. Minnesota); and touchdown receptions—0.

			RECEIVING				KICKOFF RETURNS				TOTALS			
Year Team	G	GS	No.	Yds.	Avg.	TD	No.	Yds.	Avg.	TD	TD	2pt.	Pts.	Fum.
2004—Green Bay NFL	2	0	2	12	6.0	0	3	59	19.7	0	0	0	0	0

TILLMAN, CHARLES   CB   BEARS

PERSONAL: Born February 23, 1981, in Chicago, Ill. ... 6-1/196.
HIGH SCHOOL: Copperas Cove (Texas).
COLLEGE: Louisiana-Lafayette.
TRANSACTIONS/CAREER NOTES: Selected by Chicago Bears in second round (35th pick overall) of 2003 NFL draft. ... Signed by Bears (July 26, 2003).

			TOTALS			INTERCEPTIONS				PUNT RETURNS				TOTALS			
Year Team	G	GS	Tk.	Ast.	Sks.	No.	Yds.	Avg.	TD	No.	Yds.	Avg.	TD	TD	2pt.	Pts.	Fum.
2003—Chicago NFL	16	13	74	7	1.0	4	27	6.8	0	0	0	0.0	0	0	0	0	0
2004—Chicago NFL	8	7	32	7	0.0	0	0	0.0	0	0	0	0.0	0	0	0	0	0
Pro totals (2 years)	24	20	106	14	1.0	4	27	6.8	0	0	0	0.0	0	0	0	0	0

TILLMAN, TRAVARES   S   DOLPHINS

PERSONAL: Born October 8, 1977, in Lyons, Ga. ... 6-1/190. ... Full name: Travares Arastius Tillman.
HIGH SCHOOL: Toombs County (Lyons, Ga.).
COLLEGE: Georgia Tech.
TRANSACTIONS/CAREER NOTES: Selected by Buffalo Bills in second round (58th pick overall) of 2000 NFL draft. ... Signed by Bills (July 20, 2000). ... Released by Bills (September 1, 2002). ... Signed by Houston Texans (January 14, 2003). ... Claimed on waivers by Carolina Panthers (September 18, 2003). ... Granted free agency (March 3, 2004). ... On injured reserve with arm injury (November 9, 2004-remainder of season). ... Signed by Miami Dolphins (March 4, 2005).
CHAMPIONSHIP GAME EXPERIENCE: Member of Panthers for NFC championship game (2003 season); inactive. ... Member of Panthers for Super Bowl 38 (2003 season); inactive.

			TOTALS			INTERCEPTIONS			
Year Team	G	GS	Tk.	Ast.	Sks.	No.	Yds.	Avg.	TD
2000—Buffalo NFL	15	4	19	3	0.0	0	0	0.0	0
2001—Buffalo NFL	13	6	22	11	0.0	1	0	0.0	0
2003—Carolina NFL	7	0	0	0	0.0	0	0	0.0	0
2004—Carolina NFL	6	1	3	1	0.0	0	0	0.0	0
Pro totals (4 years)	41	11	44	15	0.0	1	0	0.0	0

TIMMERMAN, ADAM   G   RAMS

PERSONAL: Born August 14, 1971, in Cherokee, Iowa. ... 6-4/310. ... Full name: Adam Larry Timmerman.
HIGH SCHOOL: Washington (Cherokee, Iowa).
COLLEGE: South Dakota State.
TRANSACTIONS/CAREER NOTES: Selected by Green Bay Packers in seventh round (230th pick overall) of 1995 NFL draft. ... Signed by Packers (June 2, 1995). ... Granted free agency (February 13, 1998). ... Re-signed by Packers (April 15, 1998). ... Granted unconditional free agency (February 12, 1999). ... Signed by St. Louis Rams (February 15, 1999).
PLAYING EXPERIENCE: Green Bay NFL, 1995-1998; St. Louis NFL, 1999-2004. ... Games/Games started: 1995 (13/0), 1996 (16/16), 1997 (16/16), 1998 (16/16), 1999 (16/16), 2000 (16/15), 2001 (16/16), 2002 (16/16), 2003 (16/16), 2004 (16/16). Total: 157/143.
CHAMPIONSHIP GAME EXPERIENCE: Played in NFC championship game (1995-97, 1999 and 2001 seasons). ... Member of Super Bowl championship team (1996 and 1999 seasons). ... Played in Super Bowl 32 (1997 season). ... Played in Super Bowl 36 (2001 season).
HONORS: Played in Pro Bowl (1999 and 2001 seasons).

TINOISAMOA, PISA   LB   RAMS

PERSONAL: Born July 15, 1981, in San Diego, Calif. ... 6-1/235.
HIGH SCHOOL: Vista (Calif.).
COLLEGE: Hawaii.
TRANSACTIONS/CAREER NOTES: Selected by St. Louis Rams in second round (43rd pick overall) of 2003 NFL draft. ... Signed by Rams (July 24, 2003).

			TOTALS			INTERCEPTIONS			
Year Team	G	GS	Tk.	Ast.	Sks.	No.	Yds.	Avg.	TD
2003—St. Louis NFL	16	15	65	13	2.0	3	46	15.3	0
2004—St. Louis NFL	16	16	73	19	1.5	0	0	0.0	0
Pro totals (2 years)	32	31	138	32	3.5	3	46	15.3	0

TOBECK, ROBBIE   C/G   SEAHAWKS

PERSONAL: Born March 6, 1970, in Tarpon Springs, Fla. ... 6-4/297. ... Full name: Robert L. Tobeck.
HIGH SCHOOL: New Port Richey (Fla.).
COLLEGE: Washington State.
TRANSACTIONS/CAREER NOTES: Signed as non-drafted free agent by Atlanta Falcons (May 7, 1993). ... Released by Falcons (August 30, 1993). ... Re-signed by Falcons to practice squad (August 31, 1993). ... Activated (January 1, 1994). ... Granted unconditional free agency (February 11, 2000). ... Signed by Seattle Seahawks (March 20, 2000). ... On physically unable to perform list with knee injury (August 20-October 14, 2000). ... Granted unconditional free agency (March 2, 2005). ... Re-signed by Seahawks (March 31, 2005).
PLAYING EXPERIENCE: Atlanta NFL, 1994-1999; Seattle NFL, 2000-2004. ... Games/Games started: 1994 (5/0), 1995 (16/16), 1996 (16/16), 1997 (16/15), 1998 (16/16), 1999 (15/15), 2000 (4/0), 2001 (16/16), 2002 (16/16), 2003 (16/16), 2004 (16/16). Total: 152/142.
CHAMPIONSHIP GAME EXPERIENCE: Played in NFC championship game (1998 season). ... Played in Super Bowl 33 (1998 season).

TOEFIELD, LABRANDON   RB   JAGUARS

PERSONAL: Born September 24, 1980, in Independence, La. ... 5-11/232. ... Full name: LaBrandon Cordell Toefield.
HIGH SCHOOL: Independence (La.).
COLLEGE: Louisiana State.
TRANSACTIONS/CAREER NOTES: Selected after junior season by Jacksonville Jaguars in fourth round (132nd pick overall) of 2003 NFL draft. ... Signed by Jaguars (July 24, 2003).
SINGLE GAME HIGHS (regular season): Attempts—12 (November 14, 2004, vs. Detroit); yards—54 (December 7, 2003, vs. Houston); and rushing touchdowns—1 (December 28, 2003, vs. Atlanta).

			RUSHING				RECEIVING				KICKOFF RETURNS				TOTALS			
Year Team	G	GS	Att.	Yds.	Avg.	TD	No.	Yds.	Avg.	TD	No.	Yds.	Avg.	TD	TD	2pt.	Pts.	Fum.
2003—Jacksonville NFL	16	0	53	212	4.0	2	14	105	7.5	1	14	272	19.4	0	3	0	18	0
2004—Jacksonville NFL	14	0	51	169	3.3	0	28	151	5.4	1	3	43	14.3	0	1	0	6	1
Pro totals (2 years)	30	0	104	381	3.7	2	42	256	6.1	2	17	315	18.5	0	4	0	24	1

TOMLINSON, LADAINIAN   RB   CHARGERS

PERSONAL: Born June 23, 1979, in Rosebud, Texas. ... 5-10/221.
HIGH SCHOOL: Waco University (Texas).
COLLEGE: Texas Christian.
TRANSACTIONS/CAREER NOTES: Selected by San Diego Chargers in first round (fifth pick overall) of 2001 draft. ... Signed by Chargers (August 23, 2001).
HONORS: Named running back on THE SPORTING NEWS college All-America third team (1999). ... Named running back on THE SPORTING NEWS college All-America first team (2000). ... Doak Walker Award winner (2000). ... Played in Pro Bowl (2002 and 2004 seasons).
SINGLE GAME HIGHS (regular season): Attempts—39 (October 20, 2002, vs. Oakland); yards—243 (December 28, 2003, vs. Oakland); and rushing touchdowns—3 (December 1, 2002, vs. Denver).
STATISTICAL PLATEAUS: 100-yard rushing games: 2001 (4), 2002 (7), 2003 (6), 2004 (6). Total: 23. 100-yard receiving games: 2003 (2). Total: 2.
MISCELLANEOUS: Holds San Diego Chargers all-time records for most yards rushing (5,899) and most rushing touchdowns (54).

			RUSHING				RECEIVING				TOTALS			
Year Team	G	GS	Att.	Yds.	Avg.	TD	No.	Yds.	Avg.	TD	TD	2pt.	Pts.	Fum.
2001—San Diego NFL	16	16	339	1236	3.6	10	59	367	6.2	0	10	0	60	8
2002—San Diego NFL	16	16	372	1683	4.5	14	79	489	6.2	1	15	0	90	3
2003—San Diego NFL	16	16	313	1645	5.3	13	§100	725	7.3	4	17	0	102	2
2004—San Diego NFL	15	15	339	1335	3.9	*17	53	441	8.3	1	§18	0	108	6
Pro totals (4 years)	63	63	1363	5899	4.3	54	291	2022	6.9	6	60	0	360	19

TONGUE, REGGIE   S   JETS

PERSONAL: Born April 11, 1973, in Baltimore, Md. ... 6-0/204. ... Full name: Reginald Clinton Tongue.
HIGH SCHOOL: Lathrop (Fairbanks, Alaska).
COLLEGE: Oregon State.
TRANSACTIONS/CAREER NOTES: Selected by Kansas City Chiefs in second round (58th pick overall) of 1996 NFL draft. ... Signed by Chiefs (July 26, 1996). ... Granted unconditional free agency (February 11, 2000). ... Signed by Seattle Seahawks (February 22, 2000). ... Granted unconditional free agency (March 3, 2004). ... Signed by New York Jets (March 22, 2004).

			TOTALS			INTERCEPTIONS			
Year Team	G	GS	Tk.	Ast.	Sks.	No.	Yds.	Avg.	TD
1996—Kansas City NFL	16	0	4	0	0.0	0	0	0.0	0
1997—Kansas City NFL	16	16	67	21	2.5	1	0	0.0	0
1998—Kansas City NFL	15	15	78	20	2.0	0	0	0.0	0
1999—Kansas City NFL	16	16	66	10	2.0	1	80	80.0	1
2000—Seattle NFL	16	6	31	9	0.0	0	0	0.0	0
2001—Seattle NFL	16	16	56	20	1.0	3	67	22.3	1
2002—Seattle NFL	16	16	68	25	0.0	5	118	23.6	1
2003—Seattle NFL	14	14	50	13	2.0	4	11	2.8	0
2004—New York Jets NFL	16	16	55	17	0.0	1	23	23.0	0
Pro totals (9 years)	141	115	475	135	9.5	15	299	19.9	3

TOOMER, AMANI   WR   GIANTS

PERSONAL: Born September 8, 1974, in Berkeley, Calif. ... 6-3/208. ... Name pronounced: uh-MAHN-ee.
HIGH SCHOOL: De La Salle Catholic (Concord, Calif.).
COLLEGE: Michigan.
TRANSACTIONS/CAREER NOTES: Selected by New York Giants in second round (34th pick overall) of 1996 NFL draft. ... Signed by Giants (July 21, 1996). ... On injured reserve with knee injury (October 31, 1996-remainder of season). ... Granted free agency (February 12, 1999). ... Re-signed by Giants (July 31, 1999).
CHAMPIONSHIP GAME EXPERIENCE: Played in NFC championship game (2000 season). ... Played in Super Bowl 35 (2000 season).
SINGLE GAME HIGHS (regular season): Receptions—10 (December 22, 2002, vs. Indianapolis); yards—204 (December 22, 2002, vs. Indianapolis); and touchdown receptions—3 (December 22, 2002, vs. Indianapolis).
STATISTICAL PLATEAUS: 100-yard receiving games: 1999 (4), 2000 (5), 2001 (2), 2002 (5), 2003 (3), 2004 (2). Total: 21.
MISCELLANEOUS: Holds New York Giants all-time record for most yards receiving (7,113).

			RECEIVING				PUNT RETURNS				KICKOFF RETURNS				TOTALS			
Year Team	G	GS	No.	Yds.	Avg.	TD	No.	Yds.	Avg.	TD	No.	Yds.	Avg.	TD	TD	2pt.	Pts.	Fum.
1996—New York Giants NFL..	7	1	1	12	12.0	0	18	298	16.6	2	11	191	17.4	0	2	0	12	1
1997—New York Giants NFL..	16	0	16	263	16.4	1	47	455	9.7	∞1	0	0	0.0	0	2	0	12	0
1998—New York Giants NFL..	16	0	27	360	13.3	5	35	252	7.2	0	4	66	16.5	0	5	0	30	0
1999—New York Giants NFL..	16	16	79	1183	15.0	6	1	14	14.0	0	0	0	0.0	0	6	0	36	0
2000—New York Giants NFL..	16	15	78	1094	14.0	7	0	0	0.0	0	0	0	0.0	0	8	0	48	1
2001—New York Giants NFL..	16	14	72	1054	14.6	5	8	41	5.1	0	0	0	0.0	0	5	0	30	2
2002—New York Giants NFL..	16	16	82	1343	16.4	8	0	0	0.0	0	0	0	0.0	0	8	0	48	0
2003—New York Giants NFL..	16	16	63	1057	16.8	5	0	0	0.0	0	0	0	0.0	0	5	0	30	0
2004—New York Giants NFL..	15	14	51	747	14.6	0	0	0	0.0	0	0	0	0.0	0	0	0	0	1
Pro totals (9 years)...............	134	92	469	7113	15.2	37	109	1060	9.7	3	15	257	17.1	0	41	0	246	5

TORBOR, REGGIE   LB   GIANTS

PERSONAL: Born January 25, 1981, in Baton Rouge, La. ... 6-2/254.
HIGH SCHOOL: Lee (Baton Rouge, La.).
COLLEGE: Auburn.
TRANSACTIONS/CAREER NOTES: Selected by New York Giants in fourth round (97th pick overall) of 2004 NFL draft. ... Signed by Giants (July 30, 2004).

			TOTALS			INTERCEPTIONS			
Year Team	G	GS	Tk.	Ast.	Sks.	No.	Yds.	Avg.	TD
2004—New York Giants NFL	16	1	15	6	3.0	0	0	0.0	0

TOWNSEND, DESHEA   CB   STEELERS

PERSONAL: Born September 8, 1975, in Batesville, Miss. ... 5-10/190. ... Full name: Trevor Deshea Townsend.
HIGH SCHOOL: South Panola (Batesville, Miss.).
COLLEGE: Alabama.
TRANSACTIONS/CAREER NOTES: Selected by Pittsburgh Steelers in fourth round (117th pick overall) of 1998 NFL draft. ... Signed by Steelers (July 6, 1998). ... Granted free agency (March 2, 2001). ... Re-signed by Steelers (March 2, 2001). ... Granted unconditional free agency (March 1, 2002). ... Re-signed by Steelers (April 2, 2002).
CHAMPIONSHIP GAME EXPERIENCE: Played in AFC championship game (2001 and 2004 seasons).

			TOTALS			INTERCEPTIONS			
Year Team	G	GS	Tk.	Ast.	Sks.	No.	Yds.	Avg.	TD
1998—Pittsburgh NFL..	12	0	9	2	0.0	0	0	0.0	0
1999—Pittsburgh NFL..	16	4	27	4	0.0	0	0	0.0	0
2000—Pittsburgh NFL..	16	0	20	5	3.5	0	0	0.0	0
2001—Pittsburgh NFL..	16	1	20	4	2.0	2	7	3.5	0
2002—Pittsburgh NFL..	16	5	28	6	0.0	3	3	1.0	0
2003—Pittsburgh NFL..	16	8	37	6	1.0	3	24	8.0	1
2004—Pittsburgh NFL..	15	15	47	9	4.0	4	54	13.5	1
Pro totals (7 years)................................	107	33	188	36	10.5	12	88	7.3	2

TRAFFORD, RODNEY   TE   BILLS

PERSONAL: Born November 28, 1978, in Morristown, N.J. ... 6-3/250.
HIGH SCHOOL: Delbarton (N.J.).
COLLEGE: South Carolina.
TRANSACTIONS/CAREER NOTES: Signed as non-drafted free agent by New England Patriots (January 17, 2003). ... Assigned by Patriots to Scottish Claymores in 2003 NFL Europe enhancement allocation program (February 14, 2003). ... Released by Patriots (August 28, 2003). ... Signed by Philadelphia Eagles to practice squad (September 22, 2004). ... Signed by Buffalo Bills off Eagles practice squad (December 8, 2004).
SINGLE GAME HIGHS (regular season): Receptions—1 (January 2, 2005, vs. Pittsburgh); yards—10 (January 2, 2005, vs. Pittsburgh); and touchdown receptions—0.

			RECEIVING				TOTALS			
Year Team	G	GS	No.	Yds.	Avg.	TD	TD	2pt.	Pts.	Fum.
2004—Buffalo NFL	4	0	3	25	8.3	0	0	0	0	0

TRAYLOR, KEITH   DT   DOLPHINS

PERSONAL: Born September 3, 1969, in Little Rock, Ark. ... 6-2/340. ... Full name: Byron Keith Traylor.
HIGH SCHOOL: Malvern (Ark.).
JUNIOR COLLEGE: Coffeyville (Kan.) Community College.
COLLEGE: Central Oklahoma.
TRANSACTIONS/CAREER NOTES: Selected by Denver Broncos in third round (61st pick overall) of 1991 NFL draft. ... Signed by Broncos for 1991 season. ... Released by Broncos (June 7, 1993). ... Signed by Los Angeles Raiders (June 1993). ... Released by Raiders (August 30, 1993). ... Signed by Green Bay Packers (September 14, 1993). ... Released by Packers (November 9, 1993). ... Signed by Kansas City Chiefs (January 7, 1994). ... Released by Chiefs (January 14, 1994). ... Re-signed by Chiefs (May 18, 1994). ... Released by Chiefs (August 28, 1994). ... Re-signed by Chiefs (February 28, 1995). ... Granted unconditional free agency (February 14, 1997). ... Signed by Broncos (March 10, 1997). ... Released by Broncos (March 14, 2001). ... Signed by Chicago Bears (March 24, 2001). ... Granted unconditional free agency (March 3, 2004). ... Signed by New England Patriots (March 31, 2004). ... Released by Patriots (May 4, 2005). ... Signed by Miami Dolphins (May 23, 2005).
CHAMPIONSHIP GAME EXPERIENCE: Played in AFC championship game (1991, 1997, 1998 and 2004 seasons). ... Member of Super Bowl championship team (1997, 1998 and 2004 seasons).

			TOTALS			INTERCEPTIONS			
Year Team	G	GS	Tk.	Ast.	Sks.	No.	Yds.	Avg.	TD
1991—Denver NFL	16	2	12	15	0.0	0	0	0.0	0
1992—Denver NFL	16	3	21	18	1.0	0	0	0.0	0
1993—Green Bay NFL	5	0	0	1	0.0	0	0	0.0	0
1994—		Did not play.							
1995—Kansas City NFL	16	0	9	2	1.5	0	0	0.0	0
1996—Kansas City NFL	15	1	21	6	1.0	0	0	0.0	0
1997—Denver NFL	16	16	28	11	2.0	1	62	62.0	1
1998—Denver NFL	15	14	24	8	2.0	0	0	0.0	0
1999—Denver NFL	15	15	25	7	1.5	0	0	0.0	0
2000—Denver NFL	16	16	32	5	1.0	0	0	0.0	0
2001—Chicago NFL	16	15	29	4	2.0	1	67	67.0	0
2002—Chicago NFL	15	15	26	5	1.0	0	0	0.0	0
2003—Chicago NFL	10	10	13	4	0.0	0	0	0.0	0
2004—New England NFL	16	10	23	5	0.0	0	0	0.0	0
Pro totals (13 years)	187	117	263	91	13.0	2	129	64.5	1

TREJO, STEPHEN   FB

PERSONAL: Born November 20, 1977, in Mesa, Ariz. ... 6-2/254. ... Full name: Stephen Nicholas Trejo.
HIGH SCHOOL: Casa Grande (Ariz.).
COLLEGE: Arizona State.
TRANSACTIONS/CAREER NOTES: Signed as non-drafted free agent by Detroit Lions (April 27, 2001). ... Granted free agency (March 3, 2004). ... Re-signed by Lions (April 23, 2004). ... Released by Lions (September 5, 2004). ... Signed by St. Louis Rams (September 9, 2004). ... Released by Rams (September 21, 2004). ... Re-signed by Lions (September 28, 2004). ... Granted unconditional free agency (March 2, 2005).
SINGLE GAME HIGHS (regular season): Attempts—1 (September 15, 2002, vs. Carolina); yards—0; and rushing touchdowns—0.

			RUSHING				RECEIVING				TOTALS			
Year Team	G	GS	Att.	Yds.	Avg.	TD	No.	Yds.	Avg.	TD	TD	2pt.	Pts.	Fum.
2001—Detroit NFL	14	0	0	0	0.0	0	5	61	12.2	0	0	0	0	0
2002—Detroit NFL	16	0	1	0	0.0	0	2	13	6.5	0	0	0	0	0
2003—Detroit NFL	16	0	0	0	0.0	0	1	2	2.0	0	0	0	0	0
2004—St. Louis NFL	2	0	0	0	0.0	0	0	0	0.0	0	0	0	0	0
—Detroit NFL	11	2	0	0	0.0	0	4	37	9.3	0	0	0	0	0
Pro totals (4 years)	59	2	1	0	0.0	0	12	113	9.4	0	0	0	0	0

TREU, ADAM   C/LS   RAIDERS

PERSONAL: Born June 24, 1974, in Lincoln, Neb. ... 6-5/300. ... Name pronounced: TRUE.
HIGH SCHOOL: Pius X (Lincoln, Neb.).
COLLEGE: Nebraska.
TRANSACTIONS/CAREER NOTES: Selected by Oakland Raiders in third round (72nd pick overall) of 1997 NFL draft. ... Signed by Raiders for 1997 season.
PLAYING EXPERIENCE: Oakland NFL, 1997-2004. ... Games/Games started: 1997 (16/0), 1998 (16/0), 1999 (16/0), 2000 (16/0), 2001 (16/14), 2002 (16/0), 2003 (16/4), 2004 (16/16). Total: 128/34.
CHAMPIONSHIP GAME EXPERIENCE: Played in AFC championship game (2000 and 2002 seasons). ... Played in Super Bowl 37 (2002 season).

TRIPPLETT, LARRY   DT   COLTS

PERSONAL: Born January 18, 1979, in Los Angeles, Calif. ... 6-2/295.
HIGH SCHOOL: Westchester (Los Angeles).
COLLEGE: Washington.
TRANSACTIONS/CAREER NOTES: Selected by Indianapolis Colts in second round (42nd pick overall) of 2002 NFL draft. ... Signed by Colts (July 26, 2002).
CHAMPIONSHIP GAME EXPERIENCE: Played in AFC championship game (2003 season).
HONORS: Named defensive tackle on THE SPORTING NEWS college All-America second team (2000). ... Named defensive tackle on THE SPORTING NEWS college All-America third team (2001).

Year Team	G	GS	Tk.	Ast.	Sks.
			TOTALS		
2002—Indianapolis NFL	13	10	18	3	0.0
2003—Indianapolis NFL	16	16	29	18	1.0
2004—Indianapolis NFL	16	0	26	3	0.0
Pro totals (3 years)	45	26	73	24	1.0

TROTTER, JEREMIAH LB EAGLES

PERSONAL: Born January 20, 1977, in Texarkana, Texas. ... 6-1/262.
HIGH SCHOOL: Hooks (Texas).
COLLEGE: Stephen F. Austin.
TRANSACTIONS/CAREER NOTES: Selected after junior season by Philadelphia Eagles in third round (72nd pick overall) of 1998 NFL draft. ... Signed by Eagles (July 14, 1998). ... Granted free agency (March 2, 2001). ... Re-signed by Eagles (April 27, 2001). ... Designated by Eagles as franchise player (February 21, 2002). ... Granted unconditional free agency (April 5, 2002). ... Signed by Washington Redskins (April 22, 2002). ... On injured reserve with knee injury (December 2, 2002-remainder of season). ... Released by Redskins (June 2, 2004). ... Signed by Eagles (July 14, 2004). ... Granted unconditional free agency (March 2, 2005). ... Re-signed by Eagles (March 4, 2005).
CHAMPIONSHIP GAME EXPERIENCE: Played in NFC championship game (2001 and 2004 seasons). ... Played in Super Bowl 39 (2004 season).
HONORS: Played in Pro Bowl (2000, 2001 and 2004 seasons).

Year Team	G	GS	Tk.	Ast.	Sks.	No.	Yds.	Avg.	TD
			TOTALS			**INTERCEPTIONS**			
1998—Philadelphia NFL	8	0	3	0	0.0	0	0	0.0	0
1999—Philadelphia NFL	16	16	91	31	2.5	2	30	15.0	0
2000—Philadelphia NFL	16	16	99	21	3.0	1	27	27.0	1
2001—Philadelphia NFL	16	16	93	22	3.5	2	64	32.0	1
2002—Washington NFL	12	12	58	33	0.0	1	2	2.0	0
2003—Washington NFL	16	16	92	23	1.5	1	21	21.0	0
2004—Philadelphia NFL	16	9	55	6	1.0	0	0	0.0	0
Pro totals (7 years)	100	85	491	136	11.5	7	144	20.6	2

TROUPE, BEN TE TITANS

PERSONAL: Born September 1, 1982, in Swainsboro, Ga. ... 6-4/262. ... Full name: Benjamin LaShaun Troupe.
HIGH SCHOOL: Butler (Augusta, Ga.).
COLLEGE: Florida.
TRANSACTIONS/CAREER NOTES: Selected by Tennessee Titans in second round (40th pick overall) of 2004 NFL draft. ... Signed by Titans (July 31, 2004).
HONORS: Named tight end on THE SPORTING NEWS college All-America second team (2003).
SINGLE GAME HIGHS (regular season): Receptions—6 (December 19, 2004, vs. Oakland); yards—75 (January 2, 2005, vs. Detroit); and touchdown receptions—1 (December 19, 2004, vs. Oakland).

Year Team	G	GS	No.	Yds.	Avg.	TD	TD	2pt.	Pts.	Fum.
			RECEIVING				**TOTALS**			
2004—Tennessee NFL	14	6	33	329	10.0	1	1	0	6	2

TRUFANT, MARCUS CB SEAHAWKS

PERSONAL: Born December 25, 1980, in Tacoma, Wash. ... 5-11/199. ... Full name: Marcus Lavon Trufant.
HIGH SCHOOL: Wilson (Tacoma, Wash.).
COLLEGE: Washington State.
TRANSACTIONS/CAREER NOTES: Selected by Seattle Seahawks in first round (11th pick overall) of 2003 NFL draft. ... Signed by Seahawks (July 24, 2003).

Year Team	G	GS	Tk.	Ast.	Sks.	No.	Yds.	Avg.	TD
			TOTALS			**INTERCEPTIONS**			
2003—Seattle NFL	16	16	69	9	0.0	2	21	10.5	0
2004—Seattle NFL	16	16	83	10	1.0	5	141	28.2	0
Pro totals (2 years)	32	32	152	19	1.0	7	162	23.1	0

TRULUCK, R-KAL DE PACKERS

PERSONAL: Born September 30, 1974, in Brooklyn, N.Y. ... 6-4/260. ... Full name: R-Kal K-Quan Truluck.
HIGH SCHOOL: Spring Valley (Rockland County, N.Y.).
COLLEGE: Cortland State.
TRANSACTIONS/CAREER NOTES: Signed as non-drafted free agent by Washington Redskins (April 27, 1997). ... Released by Redskins (August 20, 1997). ... Signed by Saskatchewan Roughriders of CFL (May 1998). ... Signed by St. Louis Rams (April 16, 2001). ... Released by Rams (April 26, 2001). ... Signed by Redskins to practice squad (August 26, 2001). ... Released by Redskins (September 2, 2001). ... Played with Detroit Fury of Arena League (2001-02). ... Signed by Kansas City Chiefs (August 6, 2002). ... Released by Chiefs (September 1, 2002). ... Re-signed by Chiefs to practice squad (September 3, 2002). ... Activated (November 20, 2002). ... Traded by Chiefs to Green Bay Packers for fifth- (traded to Miami) and sixth-round (DE Khari Long) picks in 2005 draft (September 5, 2004).

Year Team	G	GS	Tk.	Ast.	Sks.
			TOTALS		
1998—Saskatchewan CFL	3	0	...	...	4.0
1999—Saskatchewan CFL	18	0	...	...	7.0
2000—Saskatchewan CFL	17	0	...	...	1.0

Year Team	G	GS	TOTALS		
			Tk.	Ast.	Sks.
2002—Kansas City NFL	6	0	6	2	0.5
2003—Kansas City NFL	14	0	10	2	5.0
2004—Green Bay NFL	14	1	12	1	2.5
CFL totals (3 years)	38	0	...	...	12.0
NFL totals (3 years)	34	1	28	5	8.0
Pro totals (6 years)	72	1	...	...	20.0

TUBBS, MARCUS   DT   SEAHAWKS

PERSONAL: Born May 16, 1981, in Dallas, Texas. ... 6-4/320. ... Full name: Marcus Dwayne Tubbs.
HIGH SCHOOL: DeSoto (Texas).
COLLEGE: Texas.
TRANSACTIONS/CAREER NOTES: Selected by Seattle Seahawks in first round (23rd pick overall) of 2004 NFL draft. ... Signed by Seahawks (August 10, 2004).

Year Team	G	GS	TOTALS		
			Tk.	Ast.	Sks.
2004—Seattle NFL	11	3	6	7	1.0

TUCKER, REX   G   RAMS

PERSONAL: Born December 20, 1976, in Midland, Texas. ... 6-5/315. ... Full name: Rex Truman Tucker. ... Brother of Ryan Tucker, offensive tackle, Cleveland Browns.
HIGH SCHOOL: Robert E. Lee (Midland, Texas).
COLLEGE: Texas A&M.
TRANSACTIONS/CAREER NOTES: Selected in third round by Chicago Bears (66th pick overall) of 1999 NFL draft. ... Signed by Bears (July 21, 1999). ... Granted free agency (March 1, 2002). ... Re-signed by Bears (April 19, 2002). ... On injured reserve with ankle injury (October 9, 2002-remainder of season). ... On injured reserve with ankle injury (August 31, 2003-remainder of season). ... On injured reserve with hamstring injury (December 14, 2004-remainder of season). ... Released by Bears (April 18, 2005). ... Signed by St. Louis Rams (April 20, 2005).
PLAYING EXPERIENCE: Chicago NFL, 1999-2004. ... Games/Games started: 1999 (2/1), 2000 (6/0), 2001 (16/16), 2002 (5/5), 2004 (6/5), Total: 35/27.

TUCKER, ROSS   G   BILLS

PERSONAL: Born March 2, 1979, in Wyomissing, Pa. ... 6-4/316.
HIGH SCHOOL: Wyomissing (Pa.).
COLLEGE: Princeton.
TRANSACTIONS/CAREER NOTES: Singed as non-drafted free agent by Washington Redskins (April 25, 2001). ... Claimed on waivers by Dallas Cowboys (October 23, 2002). ... Claimed on waivers by Buffalo Bills (June 16, 2003).
PLAYING EXPERIENCE: Washington NFL, 2001; Dallas NFL, 2002; Washington NFL, 2002; Buffalo NFL, 2003-2004. ... Games/Games started: 2001 (3/0), 2002 (3/0), 2003 (12/5), 2004 (16/12). Total: 34/17.

TUCKER, RYAN   T   BROWNS

PERSONAL: Born June 12, 1975, in Midland, Texas. ... 6-6/320. ... Full name: Ryan Huey Tucker. ... Brother of Rex Tucker, guard, St. Louis Rams.
HIGH SCHOOL: Robert E. Lee (Midland, Texas).
COLLEGE: Texas Christian.
TRANSACTIONS/CAREER NOTES: Selected by St. Louis Rams in fourth round (112th pick overall) of 1997 NFL draft. ... Signed by Rams (July 3, 1997). ... On physically unable to perform list with knee injury (August 19-October 29, 1997). ... Granted free agency (February 11, 2000). ... Tendered offer sheet by Miami Dolphins (February 17, 2000). ... Offer matched by Rams (February 22, 2000). ... Released by Rams (February 28, 2002). ... Signed by Cleveland Browns (March 7, 2002). ... On injured reserve with knee injury (November 24, 2004-remainder of season).
PLAYING EXPERIENCE: St. Louis NFL, 1997-2001; Cleveland NFL, 2002-2004. ... Games/Games started: 1997 (7/0), 1998 (5/0), 1999 (16/0), 2000 (16/16), 2001 (15/15), 2002 (14/14), 2003 (16/16), 2004 (7/7). Total: 96/68.
CHAMPIONSHIP GAME EXPERIENCE: Played in NFC championship game (1999 and 2001 seasons). ... Member of Super Bowl championship team (1999 season). ... Played in Super Bowl 36 (2001 season).

TUCKER, TORRIN   G   COWBOYS

PERSONAL: Born December 25, 1979, in Meridian, Miss. ... 6-6/315.
HIGH SCHOOL: Southeast Lauderdale (Meridian, Miss.).
COLLEGE: Southern Miss.
TRANSACTIONS/CAREER NOTES: Signed as non-drafted free agent by Dallas Cowboys (May 1, 2003). ... Released by Cowboys (August 31, 2003). ... Re-signed by Cowboys to practice squad (September 1, 2003). ... Activated (October 1, 2003). ... Re-signed by Cowboys (March 3, 2004).
PLAYING EXPERIENCE: Dallas NFL, 2003-2004. ... Games/Games started: 2003 (7/1), 2004 (13/13). Total: 20/14.

TUFTS, SEAN   LB   PANTHERS

PERSONAL: Born March 26, 1982, in Englewood, Colo. ... 6-3/236.
HIGH SCHOOL: Cherry Creek (Englewood, Colo.).
COLLEGE: Colorado.

TRANSACTIONS/CAREER NOTES: Selected by Carolina Panthers in sixth round (196th pick overall) of 2004 NFL draft. ... Signed by Panthers (May 21, 2004). ... Released by Panthers (September 4, 2004). ... Re-signed by Panthers to practice squad (September 7, 2004). ... Activated (November 19, 2004).

Year Team	G	GS	TOTALS			INTERCEPTIONS			
			Tk.	Ast.	Sks.	No.	Yds.	Avg.	TD
2004—Carolina NFL	3	0	0	0	0.0	0	0	0.0	0

TUITELE, MAUGAULA   LB

PERSONAL: Born May 26, 1978, in Torrance, Calif. ... 6-1/250. ... Full name: Maugaula Norman Tuitele.
HIGH SCHOOL: Pacific (Calif.).
COLLEGE: Colorado State.
TRANSACTIONS/CAREER NOTES: Signed as non-drafted free agent by New England Patriots (April 19, 2000). ... Released by Patriots (August 28, 2001). ... Re-signed by Patriots to practice squad (September 25, 2001). ... Released by Patriots (September 26, 2001). ... Re-signed by Patriots to practice squad (November 20, 2001). ... Activated (December 2, 2001). ... Released by Patriots (December 5, 2001). ... Re-signed by Patriots to practice squad (December 6, 2001). ... Released by Patriots (December 27, 2001). ... Signed by Tampa Bay Buccaneers to practice squad (December 27, 2001). ... Granted free agency after 2001 season. ... Signed by Patriots (February 11, 2002). ... Assigned by Patriots to Rhein Fire in NFL Europe enhancement allocation program (February 12, 2002). ... Claimed on waivers by Buffalo Bills (September 3, 2002). ... Released by Bills (November 18, 2002). ... Signed by Patriots (December 11, 2002). ... Released by Patriots (August 31, 2003). ... Signed by Oakland Raiders (August 18, 2004). ... Released by Raiders (September 5, 2004). ... Re-signed by Raiders (October 29, 2004). ... Released by Raiders (December 1, 2004).

Year Team	G	GS	TOTALS			INTERCEPTIONS			
			Tk.	Ast.	Sks.	No.	Yds.	Avg.	TD
2000—New England NFL	1	0	0	0	0.0	0	0	0.0	0
2001—New England NFL	1	0	0	0	0.0	0	0	0.0	0
2002—New England NFL	3	0	0	0	0.0	0	0	0.0	0
—Buffalo NFL	9	0	0	0	0.0	0	0	0.0	0
2004—Oakland NFL	1	0	0	0	0.0	0	0	0.0	0
Pro totals (4 years)	15	0	0	0	0.0	0	0	0.0	0

TUMAN, JERAME   TE   STEELERS

PERSONAL: Born March 21, 1976, in Liberal, Kan. ... 6-4/253. ... Full name: Jerame Dean Tuman. ... Name pronounced: Jeromy TOO-man.
HIGH SCHOOL: Liberal (Kan.).
COLLEGE: Michigan.
TRANSACTIONS/CAREER NOTES: Selected by Pittsburgh Steelers in fifth round (136th pick overall) of 1999 NFL draft. ... Signed by Steelers (July 19, 1999). ... On injured reserve with knee injury (October 27, 1999-remainder of season). ... Granted free agency (March 1, 2002). ... Re-signed by Steelers (April 10, 2002). ... Granted unconditional free agency (February 28, 2003). ... Re-signed by Steelers (February 28, 2003).
CHAMPIONSHIP GAME EXPERIENCE: Played in AFC championship game (2001 and 2004 seasons).
HONORS: Named tight end on THE SPORTING NEWS college All-America third team (1997).
SINGLE GAME HIGHS (regular season): Receptions—4 (October 17, 2004, vs. Dallas); yards—32 (October 21, 2001, vs. Tampa Bay); and touchdown receptions—1 (December 26, 2004, vs. Baltimore).

Year Team	G	GS	RECEIVING				TOTALS			
			No.	Yds.	Avg.	TD	TD	2pt.	Pts.	Fum.
1999—Pittsburgh NFL	7	0	0	0	0.0	0	0	0	0	0
2000—Pittsburgh NFL	16	1	0	0	0.0	0	0	0	0	0
2001—Pittsburgh NFL	16	7	7	96	13.7	1	1	0	6	0
2002—Pittsburgh NFL	13	7	4	63	15.8	1	1	0	6	0
2003—Pittsburgh NFL	16	12	12	113	9.4	0	0	0	0	0
2004—Pittsburgh NFL	16	16	9	89	9.9	3	3	0	18	0
Pro totals (6 years)	84	43	32	361	11.3	5	5	0	30	0

TUPA, TOM   P/QB   REDSKINS

PERSONAL: Born February 6, 1966, in Cleveland, Ohio. ... 6-4/225. ... Full name: Thomas Joseph Tupa Jr.
HIGH SCHOOL: Brecksville (Broadview Heights, Ohio).
COLLEGE: Ohio State.
TRANSACTIONS/CAREER NOTES: Selected by Phoenix Cardinals in third round (68th pick overall) of 1988 NFL draft. ... Signed by Cardinals (July 12, 1988). ... Granted free agency (February 1, 1991). ... Re-signed by Cardinals (July 17, 1991). ... Granted unconditional free agency (February 1, 1992). ... Signed by Indianapolis Colts (March 31, 1992). ... Released by Colts (August 30, 1993). ... Signed by Cleveland Browns (November 9, 1993). ... Released by Browns (November 24, 1993). ... Re-signed by Browns (March 30, 1994). ... Granted unconditional free agency (February 16, 1996). ... Signed by New England Patriots (March 15, 1996). ... Granted unconditional free agency (February 12, 1999). ... Signed by New York Jets (February 15, 1999). ... Released by Jets (February 25, 2002). ... Signed by Tampa Bay Buccaneers (May 10, 2002). ... Granted unconditional free agency (February 28, 2003). ... Re-signed by Buccaneers (June 17, 2003). ... Granted unconditional free agency (March 3, 2004). ... Signed by Washington Redskins (March 9, 2004).
CHAMPIONSHIP GAME EXPERIENCE: Played in AFC championship game (1996 season). ... Played in Super Bowl 31 (1996 season). ... Played in NFC championship game (2002 season). ... Member of Super Bowl championship team (2002 season).
HONORS: Played in Pro Bowl (1999 season).
STATISTICAL PLATEAUS: 300-yard passing games: 1991 (1). Total: 1.
MISCELLANEOUS: Regular-season starting record as starting NFL quarterback: 4-9 (.308).

Year Team	G	No.	PUNTING				
			Yds.	Avg.	Net avg.	In. 20	Blk.
1988—Phoenix NFL	2	0	0	0.0	0.0	0	0
1989—Phoenix NFL	14	6	280	46.7	39.7	2	0

Year Team			PUNTING				
	G	No.	Yds.	Avg.	Net avg.	In. 20	Blk.
1990—Phoenix NFL	15	0	0	0.0	0.0	0	0
1991—Phoenix NFL	11	0	0	0.0	0.0	0	0
1992—Indianapolis NFL	3	0	0	0.0	0.0	0	0
1993—Cleveland NFL		Did not play.					
1994—Cleveland NFL	16	80	3211	40.1	35.3	27	0
1995—Cleveland NFL	16	65	2831	43.6	36.2	18	0
1996—New England NFL	16	63	2739	43.5	36.0	14	0
1997—New England NFL	16	78	3569	§45.8	36.1	24	1
1998—New England NFL	16	74	3294	44.5	35.4	13	0
1999—New York Jets NFL	16	81	3659	45.2	38.2	25	0
2000—New York Jets NFL	16	83	3714	44.7	33.2	18	0
2001—New York Jets NFL	15	67	2575	38.4	32.0	21	0
2002—Tampa Bay NFL	16	90	3856	42.8	35.4	30	0
2003—Tampa Bay NFL	16	83	3590	43.3	35.9	26	0
2004—Washington NFL	16	103	4544	∞44.1	35.2	30	1
Pro totals (16 years)	220	873	37862	43.4	35.4	248	2

TURK, MATT   P   DOLPHINS

PERSONAL: Born June 16, 1968, in Greenfield, Wis. ... 6-5/235. ... Brother of Dan Turk, center with five NFL teams (1985-99).
HIGH SCHOOL: Greenfield (Wis.).
COLLEGE: Wisconsin-Whitewater.
TRANSACTIONS/CAREER NOTES: Signed as non-drafted free agent by Green Bay Packers (July 13, 1993). ... Released by Packers (August 4, 1993). ... Signed by Los Angeles Rams (April 1994). ... Released by Rams (August 22, 1994). ... Signed by Washington Redskins (April 5, 1995). ... Traded by Redskins to Miami Dolphins for sventh-round pick (traded to San Francisco) in 2001 draft (March 9, 2000). ... Granted unconditional free agency (March 1, 2002). ... Signed by New York Jets (April 23, 2002). ... Released by Jets (March 7, 2003). ... Signed by Miami Dolphins (September 29, 2003). ... Granted unconditional free agency (March 3, 2004). ... Re-signed by Dolphins (March 23, 2004).
HONORS: Played in Pro Bowl (1996-1998 seasons). ... Named punter on THE SPORTING NEWS NFL All-Pro team (1997).

Year Team			PUNTING				
	G	No.	Yds.	Avg.	Net avg.	In. 20	Blk.
1995—Washington NFL	16	74	3140	42.4	37.7	†29	0
1996—Washington NFL	16	75	3386	*45.1	*39.2	24	0
1997—Washington NFL	16	84	3788	45.1	*39.2	32	1
1998—Washington NFL	16	93	4103	44.1	‡39.0	∞33	∞1
1999—Washington NFL	14	62	2564	41.4	35.6	16	0
2000—Miami NFL	16	92	3870	42.1	36.2	25	0
2001—Miami NFL	16	81	3321	41.0	37.6	28	0
2002—New York Jets NFL	16	63	2584	41.0	34.9	13	0
2003—Miami NFL	13	68	2631	38.7	34.5	23	0
2004—Miami NFL	16	§98	§4088	41.7	37.2	29	0
Pro totals (10 years)	155	790	33475	42.4	37.2	252	2

TURLEY, KYLE   T   RAMS

PERSONAL: Born September 24, 1975, in Moreno Valley, Calif. ... 6-5/309. ... Full name: Kyle John Turley.
HIGH SCHOOL: Valley View (Moreno Valley, Calif.).
COLLEGE: San Diego State.
TRANSACTIONS/CAREER NOTES: Selected by New Orleans Saints in first round (seventh pick overall) of 1998 NFL draft. ... Signed by Saints (July 23, 1998). ... Traded by Saints to St. Louis Rams for second-round pick (DE Courtney Watson) in 2004 draft (March 21, 2003). ... On injured reserve with back injury (August 28, 2004-entire season).
PLAYING EXPERIENCE: New Orleans NFL, 1998-2002; St. Louis NFL, 2003-2004. ... Games/Games started: 1998 (15/15), 1999 (16/16), 2000 (16/16), 2001 (16/16), 2002 (16/16), 2003 (16/16), Total: 95/95.
HONORS: Named offensive tackle on THE SPORTING NEWS college All-America first team (1997).

TURNER, LARRY   C   RAMS

PERSONAL: Born March 8, 1982, in Huber Heights, Ohio. ... 6-2/290. ... Full name: Larry Edward Turner Jr.
HIGH SCHOOL: Wayne (Huber Heights, Ohio).
COLLEGE: Eastern Kentucky.
TRANSACTIONS/CAREER NOTES: Selected by St. Louis Rams in seventh round (238th pick overall) of 2004 NFL draft. ... Signed by Rams (June 24, 2004).
PLAYING EXPERIENCE: St. Louis NFL, 2004. ... Games/Games started: 2004 (14/1). Total: 14/1.

TURNER, MICHAEL   RB   CHARGERS

PERSONAL: Born February 13, 1982, in North Chicago, Ill. ... 5-10/237.
HIGH SCHOOL: North Chicago (Chicago, Ill.).
COLLEGE: Northern Illinois.
TRANSACTIONS/CAREER NOTES: Selected by San Diego Chargers in fifth round (154th pick overall) of 2004 NFL draft. ... Signed by Chargers (July 28, 2004).
HONORS: Named running back on THE SPORTING NEWS college All-America second team (2003).
SINGLE GAME HIGHS (regular season): Attempts—15 (January 2, 2005, vs. Kansas City); yards—87 (January 2, 2005, vs. Kansas City); and rushing touchdowns—0.

Year Team	G	GS	RUSHING				RECEIVING				KICKOFF RETURNS				TOTALS			
			Att.	Yds.	Avg.	TD	No.	Yds.	Avg.	TD	No.	Yds.	Avg.	TD	TD	2pt.	Pts.	Fum.
2004—San Diego NFL............	14	1	20	104	5.2	0	4	8	2.0	0	1	18	18.0	0	0	0	0	1

TYLSKI RICH   G   PANTHERS

PERSONAL: Born February 27, 1971, in San Diego, Calif. ... 6-4/305. ... Full name: Richard Lee Tylski. ... Name pronounced: TILL-skee.
HIGH SCHOOL: Madison (San Diego).
COLLEGE: Utah State.
TRANSACTIONS/CAREER NOTES: Signed as non-drafted free agent by New England Patriots (April 25, 1994). ... Released by Patriots (August 20, 1994). ... Re-signed by Patriots to practice squad (August 30, 1994). ... Claimed on waivers by Jacksonville Jaguars (July 26, 1995). ... Released by Jaguars (August 27, 1995). ... Re-signed by Jaguars to practice squad (August 28, 1995). ... Granted free agency (February 12, 1999). ... Re-signed by Jaguars (May 5, 1999). ... Granted unconditional free agency (February 11, 2000). ... Signed by Pittsburgh Steelers (February 28, 2000). ... Released by Steelers (April 22, 2002). ... Signed by Patriots (May 31, 2002). ... Announced retirement (July 29, 2002). ... Signed by Carolina Panthers (March 10, 2004).
PLAYING EXPERIENCE: Jacksonville NFL, 1996-1999; Pittsburgh NFL, 2000-2001; Carolina NFL, 2004. ... Games/Games started: 1996 (16/7), 1997 (13/13), 1998 (11/8), 1999 (10/8), 2000 (16/16), 2001 (12/10), 2004 (16/1). Total: 94/63.
CHAMPIONSHIP GAME EXPERIENCE: Played in AFC championship game (1999 and 2001 seasons).

TYNES LAWRENCE   K   CHIEFS

PERSONAL: Born May 3, 1978, in Greenock, Scotland. ... 6-1/202. ... Full name: Lawrence James Tynes.
HIGH SCHOOL: Milton (Fla.).
COLLEGE: Troy.
TRANSACTIONS/CAREER NOTES: Signed as non-drafted free agent by Kansas City Chiefs (February 9, 2004).

Year Team	G	FIELD GOALS								TOTALS		
		1-29	30-39	40-49	50+	Tot.	Pct.	Lg.		XPM	XPA	Pts.
2004—Kansas City NFL................................	16	5-5	7-8	3-6	2-4	17-23	73.9	50		58	†60	109

TYREE DAVID   WR   GIANTS

PERSONAL: Born January 3, 1980, in Livingston, N.J. ... 6-0/205. ... Full name: David Mikel Tyree.
HIGH SCHOOL: Montclair (N.J.).
COLLEGE: Syracuse.
TRANSACTIONS/CAREER NOTES: Selected by New York Giants in sixth round (211th pick overall) of 2003 NFL draft. ... Signed by Giants (June 13, 2003).
SINGLE GAME HIGHS (regular season): Receptions—7 (January 2, 2005, vs. Dallas); yards—106 (November 16, 2003, vs. Philadelphia); and touchdown receptions—1 (January 2, 2005, vs. Dallas).
STATISTICAL PLATEAUS: 100-yard receiving games: 2003 (1). Total: 1.

Year Team	G	GS	RECEIVING				PUNT RETURNS				TOTALS			
			No.	Yds.	Avg.	TD	No.	Yds.	Avg.	TD	TD	2pt.	Pts.	Fum.
2003—New York Giants NFL............................	16	3	16	211	13.2	0	0	0	0.0	0	0	0	0	0
2004—New York Giants NFL............................	16	1	10	155	15.5	1	0	0	0.0	0	1	0	6	0
Pro totals (2 years).................................	32	4	26	366	14.1	1	0	0	0.0	0	1	0	6	0

UDEZE KENECHI   DE   VIKINGS

PERSONAL: Born March 5, 1983, in Los Angeles, Calif. ... 6-3/281.
HIGH SCHOOL: Verbum Dei (Los Angeles, Calif.).
COLLEGE: Southern California.
TRANSACTIONS/CAREER NOTES: Selected after junior season by Minnesota Vikings in first round (20th pick overall) of 2004 NFL draft. ... Signed by Vikings (July 30, 2004).
HONORS: Named defensive end on THE SPORTING NEWS Freshman All-America second team (2001). ... Named defensive end on THE SPORTING NEWS college All-America first team (2003).

Year Team	G	GS	TOTALS			INTERCEPTIONS			
			Tk.	Ast.	Sks.	No.	Yds.	Avg.	TD
2004—Minnesota NFL	16	15	25	11	5.0	0	0	0.0	0

ULBRICH, JEFF   LB   49ERS

PERSONAL: Born February 17, 1977, in San Jose, Calif. ... 6-0/249.
HIGH SCHOOL: Live Oak (Morgan Hill, Calif.).
JUNIOR COLLEGE: Gavilan College (Calif.).
COLLEGE: Hawaii.
TRANSACTIONS/CAREER NOTES: Selected by San Francisco 49ers in third round (86th pick overall) of 2000 NFL draft. ... Signed by 49ers (July 13, 2000). ... On injured reserve with shoulder injury (November 20, 2000-remainder of season).

Year Team	G	GS	TOTALS			INTERCEPTIONS			
			Tk.	Ast.	Sks.	No.	Yds.	Avg.	TD
2000—San Francisco NFL..	4	0	0	1	0.0	0	0	0.0	0
2001—San Francisco NFL..	14	14	62	24	0.5	0	0	0.0	0
2002—San Francisco NFL..	14	13	46	22	1.5	0	0	0.0	0
2003—San Francisco NFL..	15	15	53	21	2.5	1	7	7.0	0
2004—San Francisco NFL..	16	14	71	19	1.0	1	19	19.0	0
Pro totals (5 years)..	63	56	232	87	5.5	2	26	13.0	0

ULMER, ARTIE　　　　　　LB

PERSONAL: Born July 30, 1973, in Rincon, Ga. ... 6-3/247. ... Full name: Charles Artie Ulmer.
HIGH SCHOOL: Effingham County (Springfield, Ga.).
COLLEGE: Valdosta State.
TRANSACTIONS/CAREER NOTES: Selected by Minnesota Vikings in seventh round (220th pick overall) of 1997 NFL draft. ... On suspended list for violating league substance abuse policy (August 19-September 23, 1997). ... Signed by Vikings (June 17, 1997). ... Assigned by Vikings to Frankfurt Galaxy in 1998 NFL Europe enhancement allocation program (February 18, 1998). ... Released by Vikings (August 24, 1998). ... Signed by Denver Broncos (January 14, 1999). ... On injured reserve with knee injury (November 4, 1999-remainder of season). ... Granted free agency (February 11, 2000). ... Signed by San Francisco 49ers to practice squad (September 14, 2000). ... Activated (September 19, 2000). ... Released by 49ers (February 19, 2001). ... Signed by Atlanta Falcons (April 16, 2001). ... Granted unconditional free agency (March 1, 2002). ... Re-signed by Falcons (March 22, 2002). ... Granted unconditional free agency (February 28, 2003). ... Re-signed by Falcons (April 1, 2003). ... Granted unconditional free agency (March 3, 2004). ... Re-signed by Falcons (March 19, 2004). ... Granted unconditional free agency (March 2, 2005).
CHAMPIONSHIP GAME EXPERIENCE: Played in NFC championship game (2004 season).

Year Team	G	GS	TOTALS Tk.	Ast.	Sks.	INTERCEPTIONS No.	Yds.	Avg.	TD
1999—Denver NFL	7	0	0	0	0.0	0	0	0.0	0
2000—San Francisco NFL	12	2	6	6	1.0	0	0	0.0	0
2001—Atlanta NFL	15	0	3	1	0.0	0	0	0.0	0
2002—Atlanta NFL	15	0	2	0	0.0	0	0	0.0	0
2003—Atlanta NFL	16	0	4	2	0.0	0	0	0.0	0
2004—Atlanta NFL	16	0	0	0	0.0	0	0	0.0	0
Pro totals (6 years)	81	2	15	9	1.0	0	0	0.0	0

UMENYIORA, OSI　　　　　　DE　　　　　　GIANTS

PERSONAL: Born November 16, 1980, in London, England. ... 6-3/280.
HIGH SCHOOL: Auburn (Ala.).
COLLEGE: Troy.
TRANSACTIONS/CAREER NOTES: Selected by New York Giants in second round (56th pick overall) of 2003 NFL draft. ... Signed by Giants (July 18, 2003).

Year Team	G	GS	TOTALS Tk.	Ast.	Sks.
2003—New York Giants NFL	13	1	13	7	1.0
2004—New York Giants NFL	16	7	42	16	7.0
Pro totals (2 years)	29	8	55	23	8.0

UNCK, MASON　　　　　　LB　　　　　　BROWNS

PERSONAL: Born September 7, 1980, in Ogden, Utah. ... 6-3/235. ... Full name: Mason Douglas Unck.
HIGH SCHOOL: Bonneville (Ogden, Utah).
COLLEGE: Arizona State.
TRANSACTIONS/CAREER NOTES: Signed by Cleveland Browns as a non-drafted free agent (May 2, 2003). ... Waived by Browns (August 31, 2003). ... Re-signed by Browns to practice squad (September 1, 2003). ... Activated (November 26, 2003). ... Assigned by Browns to Frankfurt Galaxy in 2004 NFL Europe enhancement allocation program (February 9, 2004). ... Released by Browns (September 5, 2004). ... Re-signed by Browns to practice squad (September 6, 2004). ... Activated (October 14, 2004).

Year Team	G	GS	TOTALS Tk.	Ast.	Sks.	INTERCEPTIONS No.	Yds.	Avg.	TD
2003—Cleveland NFL	1	0	0	0	0.0	0	0	0.0	0
2004—Cleveland NFL	11	0	4	1	0.0	0	0	0.0	0
Pro totals (2 years)	12	0	4	1	0.0	0	0	0.0	0

UPSHAW, REGAN　　　　　　DE

PERSONAL: Born August 12, 1975, in Berrien Springs, Mich. ... 6-4/265. ... Full name: Regan Charles Upshaw.
HIGH SCHOOL: Pittsburg (Calif.).
COLLEGE: California.
TRANSACTIONS/CAREER NOTES: Selected after junior season by Tampa Bay Buccaneers in first round (12th pick overall) of 1996 NFL draft. ... Signed by Buccaneers (July 21, 1996). ... Traded by Buccaneers to Jacksonville Jaguars for sixth-round pick (RB Jameel Cook) in 2001 draft (October 19, 1999). ... Granted unconditional free agency (February 11, 2000). ... Signed by Oakland Raiders (March 1, 2000). ... On physically unable to perform list with knee injury (August 26-November 20, 2002). ... Released by Raiders (February 27, 2003). ... Signed by Washington Redskins (March 1, 2003). ... Released by Redskins (September 5, 2004). ... Signed by New York Giants (November 30, 2004). ... On injured reserve with hand injury (December 20, 2004-remainder of season). ... Granted unconditional free agency (March 2, 2005).
CHAMPIONSHIP GAME EXPERIENCE: Played in AFC championship game (1999, 2000 and 2002 seasons). ... Played in Super Bowl 37 (2002 season).

Year Team	G	GS	TOTALS Tk.	Ast.	Sks.	INTERCEPTIONS No.	Yds.	Avg.	TD
1996—Tampa Bay NFL	16	15	20	5	4.0	0	0	0.0	0
1997—Tampa Bay NFL	15	15	23	5	7.5	0	0	0.0	0
1998—Tampa Bay NFL	16	16	23	6	7.0	1	26	26.0	0
1999—Tampa Bay NFL	1	0	0	1	0.0	0	0	0.0	0
—Jacksonville NFL	6	0	6	0	0.0	0	0	0.0	0
2000—Oakland NFL	16	7	17	5	6.0	0	0	0.0	0
2001—Oakland NFL	16	15	24	8	7.0	0	0	0.0	0
2002—Oakland NFL	5	1	2	1	2.0	0	0	0.0	0
2003—Washington NFL	16	8	16	5	1.0	0	0	0.0	0
2004—New York Giants NFL	3	0	0	0	0.0	0	0	0.0	0
Pro totals (9 years)	110	77	131	36	34.5	1	26	26.0	0

URBAN, JERHEME   WR   SEAHAWKS

PERSONAL: Born November 26, 1980, in Victoria, Texas. ... 6-3/212.
HIGH SCHOOL: Stroman (Texas).
COLLEGE: Trinity (Texas).
TRANSACTIONS/CAREER NOTES: Signed as non-drafted free agent by Seattle Seahawks (May 1, 2003). ... Released by Seahawks (September 9, 2004). ... Re-signed by Seahawks to practice squad (September 11, 2004). ... Activated (November 5, 2004).
SINGLE GAME HIGHS (regular season): Receptions—2 (December 6, 2004, vs. Dallas); yards—50 (November 7, 2004, vs. San Francisco); and touchdown receptions—1 (December 6, 2004, vs. Dallas).

			RECEIVING				TOTALS		
Year Team	G	GS	No.	Yds.	Avg.	TD	TD	2pt.	Pts.	Fum.
2004—Seattle NFL	7	1	6	117	19.5	1	1	0	6	1

URLACHER, BRIAN   LB   BEARS

PERSONAL: Born May 25, 1978, in Pasco, Wash. ... 6-4/258. ... Full name: Brian Keith Urlacher.
HIGH SCHOOL: Lovington (N.M.).
COLLEGE: New Mexico.
TRANSACTIONS/CAREER NOTES: Selected by Chicago Bears in first round (ninth pick overall) of 2000 NFL draft. ... Signed by Bears (June 16, 2000). ... On injured reserve with hamstring injury (December 22, 2004-remainder of season).
HONORS: Named strong safety on THE SPORTING NEWS college All-America second team (1999). ... Named NFL Rookie of the Year by THE SPORTING NEWS (2000). ... Played in Pro Bowl (2000-2003 seasons). ... Named linebacker on THE SPORTING NEWS NFL All-Pro team (2001 and 2002).

			TOTALS			INTERCEPTIONS			
Year Team	G	GS	Tk.	Ast.	Sks.	No.	Yds.	Avg.	TD
2000—Chicago NFL	16	14	97	26	8.0	2	19	9.5	0
2001—Chicago NFL	16	16	90	27	6.0	3	60	20.0	0
2002—Chicago NFL	16	16	116	36	4.5	1	0	0.0	0
2003—Chicago NFL	16	16	86	29	2.5	0	0	0.0	0
2004—Chicago NFL	9	9	54	18	5.5	1	42	42.0	0
Pro totals (5 years)	73	71	443	136	26.5	7	121	17.3	0

VAN BUREN, COURTNEY   T   CHARGERS

PERSONAL: Born February 22, 1980, in St. Louis, Mo. ... 6-6/350.
HIGH SCHOOL: Ladue (St. Louis).
COLLEGE: Arkansas-Pine Bluff.
TRANSACTIONS/CAREER NOTES: Selected by San Diego Chargers in third round (80th pick overall) of 2003 NFL draft. ... Signed by Chargers (July 17, 2003). ... On injured reserve with knee injury (December 17, 2003-remainder of season). ... On injured reserve with knee injury (September 20, 2004-remainder of season).
PLAYING EXPERIENCE: San Diego NFL, 2003-2004. ... Games/Games started: 2003 (8/7), 2004 (1/0). Total: 9/7.

VANDEN BOSCH, KYLE   DE   TITANS

PERSONAL: Born November 17, 1978, in Larchwood, Iowa. ... 6-4/278.
HIGH SCHOOL: West Lyon (Larchwood, Iowa).
COLLEGE: Nebraska.
TRANSACTIONS/CAREER NOTES: Selected by Arizona Cardinals in second round (34th pick overall) of 2001 NFL draft. ... Signed by Cardinals (July 12, 2001). ... On injured reserve with knee injury (October 25, 2001-remainder of season). ... On injured reserve with knee injury (August 26, 2003-entire season). ... Granted unconditional free agency (March 2, 2005). ... Signed by Tennessee Titans (April 25, 2005).

			TOTALS		
Year Team	G	GS	Tk.	Ast.	Sks.
2001—Arizona NFL	3	3	12	1	0.5
2002—Arizona NFL	16	16	37	13	3.5
2003—Arizona NFL	Did not play.				
2004—Arizona NFL	16	1	11	2	0.0
Pro totals (3 years)	35	20	60	16	4.0

VANDERJAGT, MIKE   K   COLTS

PERSONAL: Born March 24, 1970, in Oakville, ON. ... 6-5/211. ... Name pronounced: vander-JAT.
HIGH SCHOOL: White Oaks (Ont.).
JUNIOR COLLEGE: Allan Hancock College (Calif.).
COLLEGE: West Virginia.
TRANSACTIONS/CAREER NOTES: Signed by Saskatchewan Roughriders prior to 1993 season. ... Signed by Toronto Argonauts of CFL (February 15, 1994). ... Released by Argonauts (June 13, 1994). ... Signed by Hamilton Tiger-Cats of CFL (June 24, 1994). ... Released by Tiger-Cats (July 11, 1994). ... Signed by Argonauts of CFL (March 16, 1995). ... Released by Argonauts (June 25, 1995). ... Re-signed by Argonauts of CFL (May 10, 1996). ... Signed as non-drafted free agent by Indianapolis Colts (March 4, 1998).
CHAMPIONSHIP GAME EXPERIENCE: Member of CFL Championship team (1996 and 1997). ... Played in AFC championship game (2003 season).
HONORS: Named Most Outstanding Canadian Player in Grey Cup (1996). ... Named to CFL All-Star team (1997). ... Named kicker on THE SPORTING NEWS NFL All-Pro team (2003). ... Played in Pro Bowl (2003 season).

RECORDS: Holds NFL career record for highest field-goal percentage—87.0. ... Shares NFL single-season record for highest field-goal percentage—100.0 (2003). ... Holds NFL career record for most consecutive field goals made—42 (December 22, 2002 through September 9, 2004).
MISCELLANEOUS: Colts franchise all-time scoring leader (874 points).

Year Team	G	FIELD GOALS							TOTALS		
		1-29	30-39	40-49	50+	Tot.	Pct.	Lg.	XPM	XPA	Pts.
1993—Saskatchewan CFL	2	...-...	...-...	...-...	...-...	0-0	...	0	0	0	0
1994—		Did not play.									
1995—		Did not play.									
1996—Toronto CFL	18	...-...	...-...	...-...	...-...	40-56	71.4	51	59	59	179
1997—Toronto CFL	18	...-...	...-...	...-...	...-...	33-43	76.7	51	77	77	176
1998—Indianapolis NFL	14	9-9	4-4	8-9	6-9	27-31	87.1	53	23	23	104
1999—Indianapolis NFL	16	12-12	11-13	10-11	1-2	34-38	§89.5	53	43	43	*145
2000—Indianapolis NFL	16	7-7	13-13	5-6	0-1	25-27	§92.6	48	46	46	121
2001—Indianapolis NFL	16	7-8	6-6	12-16	3-4	28-34	82.4	52	41	▲42	§125
2002—Indianapolis NFL	16	8-9	6-7	6-12	3-3	23-31	74.2	54	34	34	103
2003—Indianapolis NFL	16	17-17	7-7	12-12	1-1	§37-37	*100.0	50	46	46	157
2004—Indianapolis NFL	15	6-6	9-11	5-7	0-1	20-25	80.0	47	*59	†60	119
CFL totals (3 years)	38	...-...	...-...	...-...	...-...	73-99	73.7	51	136	136	355
NFL totals (7 years)	109	66-68	56-61	58-73	14-21	194-223	87.0	54	292	294	874
Pro totals (10 years)	147	...-...	...-...	...-...	...-...	267-322	82.9	54	428	430	1229

VASHER, NATHAN — CB — BEARS

PERSONAL: Born November 17, 1981, in Wichita Falls, Texas. ... 5-10/180. ... Full name: Nathanael DeWayne Vasher.
HIGH SCHOOL: Texas (Texarkana, Texas).
COLLEGE: Texas.
TRANSACTIONS/CAREER NOTES: Selected by Chicago Bears in fourth round (110th pick overall) of 2004 NFL draft. ... Signed by Bears (May 24, 2004).
HONORS: Named kick returner on THE SPORTING NEWS college All-America third team (2001).

Year Team		TOTALS				INTERCEPTIONS				PUNT RETURNS				TOTALS			
	G	GS	Tk.	Ast.	Sks.	No.	Yds.	Avg.	TD	No.	Yds.	Avg.	TD	TD	2pt.	Pts.	Fum.
2004—Chicago NFL	16	7	22	1	0.0	5	‡177	35.4	1	0	0	0.0	0	1	0	6	0

VAUGHN, KHALEED — DE

PERSONAL: Born May 20, 1981, in Atlanta, Ga. ... 6-4/276. ... Name pronounced: kuh-LEED.
HIGH SCHOOL: South Atlanta (Ga.).
COLLEGE: Clemson.
TRANSACTIONS/CAREER NOTES: Signed as non-drafted free agent by New York Giants (May 7, 2004). ... Released by Giants (September 5, 2004). ... Signed by Giants to practice squad (September 7, 2004). ... Signed by Atlanta Falcons off Giants practice squad (October 20, 2004).
CHAMPIONSHIP GAME EXPERIENCE: Played in NFC championship game (2004 season).

Year Team			TOTALS		
	G	GS	Tk.	Ast.	Sks.
2004—Atlanta NFL	3	0	3	0	0.0

VERBA, ROSS — T — BROWNS

V

PERSONAL: Born October 31, 1973, in Des Moines, Iowa. ... 6-4/305. ... Full name: Ross Robert Verba.
HIGH SCHOOL: Dowling (West Des Moines, Iowa).
COLLEGE: Iowa.
TRANSACTIONS/CAREER NOTES: Selected by Green Bay Packers in first round (30th pick overall) of 1997 NFL draft. ... Signed by Packers (July 31, 1997). ... Granted unconditional free agency (March 2, 2001). ... Signed by Cleveland Browns (March 23, 2001). ... On physically unable to perform list with back injury (July 23-August 13, 2001). ... On injured reserve with biceps injury (August 31, 2003-remainder of season). ... Re-signed by Browns (April 16, 2004).
PLAYING EXPERIENCE: Green Bay NFL, 1997-2000; Cleveland NFL, 2001-2004. ... Games/Games started: 1997 (16/11), 1998 (16/16), 1999 (11/10), 2000 (16/16), 2001 (15/15), 2002 (16/16), 2004 (16/16), Total: 106/100.
CHAMPIONSHIP GAME EXPERIENCE: Played in NFC championship game (1997 season). ... Played in Super Bowl 32 (1997 season).

VICK, MICHAEL — QB — FALCONS

PERSONAL: Born June 26, 1980, in Newport News, Va. ... 6-0/215. ... Full name: Michael Dwayne Vick.
HIGH SCHOOL: Warwick (Newport News, Va.).
COLLEGE: Virginia Tech.
TRANSACTIONS/CAREER NOTES: Selected after sophomore season by Atlanta Falcons in first round (first pick overall) of 2001 draft. ... Signed by Falcons (May 9, 2001).
CHAMPIONSHIP GAME EXPERIENCE: Played in NFC championship game (2004 season).
HONORS: Named College Football Freshman of the Year by THE SPORTING NEWS (1999). ... Named quarterback on THE SPORTING NEWS college All-America first team (1999). ... Named to play in Pro Bowl (2002 season); replaced by Brad Johnson due to injury. ... Played in Pro Bowl (2004 season).
SINGLE GAME HIGHS (regular season): Attempts—46 (November 10, 2002, vs. Pittsburgh); completions—24 (November 10, 2002, vs. Pittsburgh); yards—337 (December 22, 2002, vs. Detroit); and touchdown passes—2 (December 18, 2004, vs. Carolina).
STATISTICAL PLATEAUS: 100-yard rushing games: 2002 (1), 2003 (1), 2004 (3). Total: 5. 300-yard passing games: 2002 (1). Total: 1.

				PASSING								RUSHING				TOTALS		
Year Team	G	GS	Att.	Cmp.	Pct.	Yds.	TD	Int.	Avg.	Skd.	Rat.	Att.	Yds.	Avg.	TD	TD	2pt.	Pts.
2001—Atlanta NFL	8	2	113	50	44.2	785	2	3	6.95	21	62.7	31	289	9.3	1	1	0	6
2002—Atlanta NFL	15	15	421	231	54.9	2936	16	8	6.97	33	81.6	113	777	*6.9	8	8	0	48
2003—Atlanta NFL	5	4	100	50	50.0	585	4	3	5.85	9	69.0	40	255	6.4	1	1	0	6
2004—Atlanta NFL	15	15	321	181	56.4	2313	14	12	7.21	∞46	78.1	120	902	*7.5	3	3	0	18
Pro totals (4 years)	43	36	955	512	53.6	6619	36	26	6.93	109	76.9	304	2223	7.3	13	13	0	78

VILLARRIAL, CHRIS — G — BILLS

PERSONAL: Born June 9, 1973, in Hummelstown, Pa. ... 6-3/318. ... Name pronounced: vuh-LAR-ree-uhl.
HIGH SCHOOL: Hershey (Pa.).
COLLEGE: Indiana (Pa.).
TRANSACTIONS/CAREER NOTES: Selected by Chicago Bears in fifth round (152nd pick overall) of 1996 NFL draft. ... Signed by Bears (July 11, 1996). ... Granted free agency (February 12, 1999). ... Re-signed by Bears (April 16, 1999). ... Granted unconditional free agency (March 3, 2004). ... Signed by Buffalo Bills (March 3, 2004).
PLAYING EXPERIENCE: Chicago NFL, 1996-2003; Buffalo NFL, 2004. ... Games/Games started: 1996 (14/8), 1997 (11/11), 1998 (16/16), 1999 (15/15), 2000 (16/15), 2001 (16/16), 2002 (15/15), 2003 (13/13), 2004 (16/16). Total: 132/125.

VILMA, JONATHAN — LB — JETS

PERSONAL: Born April 16, 1982, in Coral Gables, Fla. ... 6-1/230. ... Full name: Jonathan Polynice Vilma.
HIGH SCHOOL: Coral Gables (Fla.).
COLLEGE: Miami (Fla.).
TRANSACTIONS/CAREER NOTES: Selected by New York Jets in first round (12th pick overall) of 2004 NFL draft. ... Signed by Jets (July 27, 2004).

			TOTALS			INTERCEPTIONS			
Year Team	G	GS	Tk.	Ast.	Sks.	No.	Yds.	Avg.	TD
2004—New York Jets NFL	16	14	75	30	2.0	3	58	19.3	1

VINATIERI, ADAM — K — PATRIOTS

PERSONAL: Born December 28, 1972, in Yankton, S.D. ... 6-0/202. ... Full name: Adam Matthew Vinatieri. ... Name pronounced: VIN-a-TERRY.
HIGH SCHOOL: Rapid City (S.D.) Central.
COLLEGE: South Dakota State.
TRANSACTIONS/CAREER NOTES: Signed by Amsterdam Admirals of World League for 1996 season. ... Signed as non-drafted free agent by New England Patriots (June 28, 1996). ... Granted free agency (February 12, 1999). ... Re-signed by Patriots (March 12, 1999). ... Granted free agency (March 1, 2002). ... Re-signed by Patriots (March 15, 2002). ... Designated by Patriots as franchise player (February 22, 2005).
CHAMPIONSHIP GAME EXPERIENCE: Played in AFC championship game (1996, 2001, 2003 and 2004 seasons). ... Played in Super Bowl 31 (1996 season). ... Member of Super Bowl championship team (2001, 2003 and 2004 seasons).
HONORS: Named kicker on THE SPORTING NEWS NFL All-Pro team (2004). ... Played in Pro Bowl (2002 and 2004 seasons).

		FIELD GOALS							TOTALS		
Year Team	G	1-29	30-39	40-49	50+	Tot.	Pct.	Lg.	XPM	XPA	Pts.
1996—New England NFL	16	10-11	8-8	8-14	1-2	27-35	77.1	50	39	42	120
1997—New England NFL	16	11-11	7-9	6-8	1-1	25-29	86.2	52	40	40	115
1998—New England NFL	16	11-11	9-14	9-12	2-2	31-39	79.5	55	32	32	125
1999—New England NFL	16	15-15	5-7	5-9	1-2	26-33	78.8	51	29	30	107
2000—New England NFL	16	11-13	8-9	7-8	1-3	27-33	81.8	53	25	25	106
2001—New England NFL	16	9-9	7-8	7-12	1-1	24-30	80.0	54	41	▲42	113
2002—New England NFL	16	6-6	12-12	8-10	1-2	27-§30	*90.0	*57	36	36	117
2003—New England NFL	16	16-17	4-8	5-8	0-1	25-34	73.5	48	37	38	112
2004—New England NFL	16	13-13	7-7	11-12	0-1	*31-33	*93.9	48	48	48	*141
Pro totals (9 years)	144	102-106	67-82	66-93	8-15	243-296	82.1	57	327	333	1056

VINCENT, KEYDRICK — G — RAVENS

PERSONAL: Born April 13, 1978, in Bartow, Fla. ... 6-5/325. ... Full name: Keydrick Trepell Vincent.
HIGH SCHOOL: Lake Gibson (Fla.).
COLLEGE: Mississippi.
TRANSACTIONS/CAREER NOTES: Signed as non-drafted free agent by Pittsburgh Steelers (April 23, 2001). ... Re-signed by Steelers (February 19, 2003). ... Granted free agency (March 3, 2004). ... Re-signed by Steelers (April 22, 2004). ... Granted unconditional free agency (March 2, 2005). ... Signed by Baltimore Ravens (March 11, 2005).
PLAYING EXPERIENCE: Pittsburgh NFL, 2001-2004. ... Games/Games started: 2001 (5/1), 2002 (7/1), 2003 (10/9), 2004 (16/16). Total: 38/27.
CHAMPIONSHIP GAME EXPERIENCE: Played in AFC championship game (2001 and 2004 seasons).

VINCENT, TROY — CB — BILLS

PERSONAL: Born June 8, 1971, in Trenton, N.J. ... 6-1/200. ... Full name: Troy D. Vincent.
HIGH SCHOOL: Pennsbury (Fairless Hills, Pa.).
COLLEGE: Wisconsin.

TRANSACTIONS/CAREER NOTES: Selected by Miami Dolphins in first round (seventh pick overall) of 1992 NFL draft. ... Signed by Dolphins (August 8, 1992). ... Designated by Dolphins as transition player (February 25, 1993). ... On injured reserve with knee injury (December 15, 1993-remainder of season). ... Tendered offer sheet by Philadelphia Eagles (February 24, 1996). ... Dolphins declined to match offer (March 3, 1996). ... Granted unconditional free agency (March 3, 2004). ... Signed by Buffalo Bills (March 15, 2004).

CHAMPIONSHIP GAME EXPERIENCE: Played in AFC championship game (1992 season). ... Played in NFC championship game (2001-2003 seasons).

HONORS: Named defensive back on THE SPORTING NEWS college All-America first team (1991). ... Played in Pro Bowl (1999, 2000, 2002 and 2003 seasons). ... Named to play in Pro Bowl (2001 season); replaced by Champ Bailey due to injury.

Year Team	G	GS	Tk.	Ast.	Sks.	No.	Yds.	Avg.	TD
			TOTALS			**INTERCEPTIONS**			
1992—Miami NFL	15	14	56	21	0.0	2	47	23.5	0
1993—Miami NFL	13	13	58	10	0.0	2	29	14.5	0
1994—Miami NFL	13	12	41	11	0.0	5	113	22.6	1
1995—Miami NFL	16	16	52	10	0.0	5	95	19.0	▲1
1996—Philadelphia NFL	16	16	45	7	0.0	3	144	*48.0	1
1997—Philadelphia NFL	16	16	50	15	0.0	3	14	4.7	0
1998—Philadelphia NFL	13	13	42	8	1.0	2	29	14.5	0
1999—Philadelphia NFL	14	14	62	20	1.0	†7	91	13.0	0
2000—Philadelphia NFL	16	16	64	13	1.0	5	34	6.8	0
2001—Philadelphia NFL	15	15	58	11	1.5	3	0	0.0	0
2002—Philadelphia NFL	15	15	55	12	0.0	2	1	0.5	0
2003—Philadelphia NFL	13	13	49	8	0.0	3	28	9.3	0
2004—Buffalo NFL	7	7	18	9	1.0	1	8	8.0	0
Pro totals (13 years)	**182**	**180**	**650**	**155**	**5.5**	**43**	**633**	**14.7**	**3**

VINES, SCOTTIE — WR — LIONS

PERSONAL: Born April 17, 1979, in Alexander City, Ala. ... 6-2/220.
HIGH SCHOOL: Benjamin Russell (Alexander City, Ala.).
JUNIOR COLLEGE: Eastern Utah.
COLLEGE: Wyoming.
TRANSACTIONS/CAREER NOTES: Signed as non-drafted free agent by Detroit Lions (May 2, 2003). ... Released by Lions (August 26, 2003). ... Signed by Green Bay Packers to practice squad (September 1, 2003). ... Activated (January 26, 2004). ... Released by Packers (September 5, 2004). ... Signed by Lions to practice squad (September 16, 2004). ... Activated (November 20, 2004).
SINGLE GAME HIGHS (regular season): Receptions—2 (January 2, 2005, vs. Tennessee); yards—40 (January 2, 2005, vs. Tennessee); and touchdown receptions—0.

Year Team	G	GS	No.	Yds.	Avg.	TD	TD	2pt.	Pts.	Fum.
			RECEIVING				**TOTALS**			
2004—Detroit NFL	6	1	3	51	17.0	0	0	0	0	0

VOLEK, BILLY — QB — TITANS

PERSONAL: Born April 28, 1976, in Hemet, Calif. ... 6-2/214. ... Full name: John William Volek.
HIGH SCHOOL: Clovis West (Fresno, Calif.).
COLLEGE: Fresno State.
TRANSACTIONS/CAREER NOTES: Signed as non-drafted free agent by Tennessee Titans (April 18, 2000). ... Active for one game (2000); did not play. ... Granted free agency (February 28, 2003). ... Re-signed by Titans (April 9, 2003). ... On injured reserve with spleen injury (December 18, 2003-remainder of season). ... Granted unconditional free agency (March 3, 2004). ... Re-signed by Titans (March 24, 2004).
CHAMPIONSHIP GAME EXPERIENCE: Member of Titans for AFC championship game (2002 season); inactive.
SINGLE GAME HIGHS (regular season): Attempts—60 (December 19, 2004, vs. Oakland); completions—40 (December 19, 2004, vs. Oakland); yards—492 (December 19, 2004, vs. Oakland); and touchdown passes—4 (December 19, 2004, vs. Oakland).
STATISTICAL PLATEAUS: 300-yard passing games: 2004 (3). Total: 3.
MISCELLANEOUS: Regular-season record as starting NFL quarterback: 3-6 (.333).

Year Team	G	GS	Att.	Cmp.	Pct.	Yds.	TD	Int.	Avg.	Skd.	Rat.	Att.	Yds.	Avg.	TD	TD	2pt.	Pts.
			PASSING									**RUSHING**				**TOTALS**		
2000—Tennessee NFL	1	0	0	0	0.0	0	0	0	0.00	0	0.0	0	0	0.0	0	0	0	0
2001—Tennessee NFL	1	0	3	0	0.0	0	0	0	0.00	0	39.6	0	0	0.0	0	0	0	0
2003—Tennessee NFL	7	1	69	44	63.8	545	4	1	7.90	6	101.4	11	4	0.4	1	1	0	6
2004—Tennessee NFL	10	8	357	218	61.1	2486	18	10	6.96	30	87.1	11	50	4.5	1	1	0	6
Pro totals (4 years)	**19**	**9**	**429**	**262**	**61.1**	**3031**	**22**	**11**	**7.07**	**36**	**88.8**	**22**	**54**	**2.5**	**2**	**2**	**0**	**12**

VOLLERS, KURT — T — COWBOYS

PERSONAL: Born April 4, 1979, in San Gabriel, Calif. ... 6-7/300.
HIGH SCHOOL: Servite (Whittier, Calif.).
COLLEGE: Notre Dame.
TRANSACTIONS/CAREER NOTES: Signed as non-drafted free agent by Indianapolis Colts (April 20, 2002). ... Released by Colts (September 1, 2002). ... Re-signed by Colts to practice squad (September 3, 2002). ... Claimed on waivers by Dallas Cowboys (October 23, 2002). ... Granted free agency (March 2, 2005). ... Re-signed by Cowboys (May 4, 2005).
PLAYING EXPERIENCE: Dallas NFL, 2002-2004. ... Games/Games started: 2002 (1/0), 2003 (13/8), 2004 (13/3). Total: 27/11.

V

VON OELHOFFEN, KIMO　　　　　DT　　　　　STEELERS

PERSONAL: Born January 30, 1971, in Kaunakakai, Hawaii. ... 6-4/299. ... Full name: Kimo K. von Oelhoffen. ... Name pronounced: KEE-moe von OHL-hoffen.
HIGH SCHOOL: Molokai (Hoolehua, Hawaii).
JUNIOR COLLEGE: Walla Walla (Wash.) Community College.
COLLEGE: Boise State.
TRANSACTIONS/CAREER NOTES: Selected by Cincinnati Bengals in sixth round (162nd pick overall) of 1994 NFL draft. ... Signed by Bengals (May 9, 1994). ... Granted unconditional free agency (February 11, 2000). ... Signed by Pittsburgh Steelers (February 14, 2000).
CHAMPIONSHIP GAME EXPERIENCE: Played in AFC championship game (2001 and 2004 seasons).

			TOTALS		
Year　Team	G	GS	Tk.	Ast.	Sks.
1994—Cincinnati NFL	7	0	2	0	0.0
1995—Cincinnati NFL	16	1	7	1	0.0
1996—Cincinnati NFL	11	1	11	4	1.0
1997—Cincinnati NFL	13	13	32	10	0.0
1998—Cincinnati NFL	16	16	36	9	0.0
1999—Cincinnati NFL	16	5	24	2	4.0
2000—Pittsburgh NFL	16	16	29	15	1.0
2001—Pittsburgh NFL	15	15	20	8	4.0
2002—Pittsburgh NFL	16	16	12	10	3.0
2003—Pittsburgh NFL	16	16	27	8	8.0
2004—Pittsburgh NFL	16	15	16	8	1.0
Pro totals (11 years)	158	114	216	75	22.0

VRABEL, MIKE　　　　　LB　　　　　PATRIOTS

PERSONAL: Born August 14, 1975, in Akron, Ohio. ... 6-4/261. ... Full name: Michael George Vrabel.
HIGH SCHOOL: Walsh Jesuit (Cuyahoga Falls, Ohio).
COLLEGE: Ohio State.
TRANSACTIONS/CAREER NOTES: Selected by Pittsburgh Steelers in third round (91st pick overall) of 1997 NFL draft. ... Signed by Steelers (July 15, 1997). ... Granted free agency (February 11, 2000). ... Re-signed by Steelers (April 20, 2000). ... Granted unconditional free agency (March 2, 2001). ... Signed by New England Patriots (March 16, 2001).
CHAMPIONSHIP GAME EXPERIENCE: Played in AFC championship game (1997, 2001, 2003 and 2004 seasons). ... Member of Super Bowl championship team (2001, 2003 and 2004 seasons).

			TOTALS			INTERCEPTIONS			
Year　Team	G	GS	Tk.	Ast.	Sks.	No.	Yds.	Avg.	TD
1997—Pittsburgh NFL	15	0	14	3	1.5	0	0	0.0	0
1998—Pittsburgh NFL	11	0	6	3	2.5	0	0	0.0	0
1999—Pittsburgh NFL	10	0	4	1	2.0	0	0	0.0	0
2000—Pittsburgh NFL	15	0	3	2	1.0	0	0	0.0	0
2001—New England NFL	16	12	37	23	3.0	2	27	13.5	0
2002—New England NFL	16	13	51	24	4.5	1	0	0.0	0
2003—New England NFL	13	9	38	14	9.5	2	18	9.0	0
2004—New England NFL	16	15	52	15	5.5	0	0	0.0	0
Pro totals (8 years)	112	49	205	85	29.5	5	45	9.0	0

WADDELL, MICHAEL　　　　　CB　　　　　TITANS

PERSONAL: Born January 9, 1981, in Ellerbe, N.C. ... 5-10/187.
HIGH SCHOOL: Richmond County (Ellerbe, N.C.).
COLLEGE: North Carolina.
TRANSACTIONS/CAREER NOTES: Selected by Tennessee Titans in fourth round (124th pick overall) of 2004 NFL draft. ... Signed by Titans (July 30, 2004).

			TOTALS			INTERCEPTIONS				PUNT RETURNS				KICKOFF RETURNS				TOTALS			
Year　Team	G	GS	Tk.	Ast.	Sks.	No.	Yds.	Avg.	TD	No.	Yds.	Avg.	TD	No.	Yds.	Avg.	TD	TD	2pt.	Pts.	Fum.
2004—Ten. NFL	16	4	30	2	0.0	1	0	0.0	0	9	54	6.0	0	17	342	20.1	0	0	0	0	3

WADE, BOBBY　　　　　WR　　　　　BEARS

PERSONAL: Born February 25, 1981, in Orange County, Calif. ... 5-10/192. ... Full name: Robert Louis Wade Jr.
HIGH SCHOOL: Desert Vista (Phoenix).
COLLEGE: Arizona.
TRANSACTIONS/CAREER NOTES: Selected by Chicago Bears in fifth round (139th pick overall) of 2003 NFL draft. ... Signed by Bears (July 25, 2003).
SINGLE GAME HIGHS (regular season): Receptions—4 (January 2, 2005, vs. Green Bay); yards—71 (September 26, 2004, vs. Minnesota); and touchdown receptions—0.

			RUSHING				RECEIVING				PUNT RETURNS				KICKOFF RETURNS				TOTALS		
Year　Team	G	GS	Att.	Yds.	Avg.	TD	No.	Yds.	Avg.	TD	No.	Yds.	Avg.	TD	No.	Yds.	Avg.	TD	TD	2pt.	Pts.
2003—Chi. NFL	12	1	5	14	2.8	0	12	137	11.4	0	2	9	4.5	0	0	0	0.0	0	0	0	0
2004—Chi. NFL	16	14	12	76	6.3	0	42	481	11.5	0	0	0	0.0	0	0	0	0.0	0	0	0	0
Pro totals (2 years)	28	15	17	90	5.3	0	54	618	11.4	0	2	9	4.5	0	0	0	0.0	0	0	0	0

W

WADE, JOHN   C   BUCCANEERS

PERSONAL: Born January 25, 1975, in Harrisonburg, Va. ... 6-5/299. ... Full name: John Robert Wade.
HIGH SCHOOL: Harrisonburg (Va.).
COLLEGE: Marshall.
TRANSACTIONS/CAREER NOTES: Selected by Jacksonville Jaguars in fifth round (148th pick overall) of 1998 NFL draft. ... Signed by Jaguars (June 1, 1998). ... On injured reserve with broken foot (September 27, 2000-remainder of season). ... On physically unable to perform list with foot injury (July 27-September 2, 2001). ... Granted unconditional free agency (March 1, 2002). ... Re-signed by Jaguars (March 13, 2002). ... Granted unconditional free agency (February 28, 2003). ... Signed by Tampa Bay Buccaneers (March 10, 2003). ... On injured reserve with knee injury (November 10, 2004-remainder of season). ... Re-signed by Buccaneers (March 1, 2005).
PLAYING EXPERIENCE: Jacksonville NFL, 1998-2002; Tampa Bay NFL, 2003-2004. ... Games/Games started: 1998 (5/0), 1999 (16/16), 2000 (2/2), 2001 (15/0), 2002 (16/16), 2003 (16/16), 2004 (8/8). Total: 78/58.
CHAMPIONSHIP GAME EXPERIENCE: Played in AFC championship game (1999 season).

WADE, TODD   T   TEXANS

PERSONAL: Born October 30, 1976, in Greenwood, Miss. ... 6-8/317. ... Full name: Todd McLaurin Wade.
HIGH SCHOOL: Jackson (Miss.) Prep.
COLLEGE: Mississippi.
TRANSACTIONS/CAREER NOTES: Selected by Miami Dolphins in second round (53rd pick overall) of 2000 NFL draft. ... Signed by Dolphins (July 24, 2000). ... Granted unconditional free agency (March 3, 2004). ... Signed by Houston Texans (March 4, 2004).
PLAYING EXPERIENCE: Miami NFL, 2000-2003; Houston NFL, 2004. ... Games/Games started: 2000 (16/16), 2001 (15/15), 2002 (16/16), 2003 (16/16), 2004 (14/13). Total: 77/76.

WAHLE, MIKE   G   PANTHERS

PERSONAL: Born March 29, 1977, in Portland, Ore. ... 6-6/304. ... Full name: Michael James Wahle. ... Name pronounced: WALL.
HIGH SCHOOL: Rim of the World (Lake Arrowhead, Calif.).
COLLEGE: Navy.
TRANSACTIONS/CAREER NOTES: Selected by Green Bay Packers in second round of 1998 supplemental draft (July 9, 1998). ... Signed by Packers (August 6, 1998). ... Granted free agency (March 2, 2001). ... Re-signed by Packers (May 31, 2001). ... Granted unconditional free agency (March 1, 2002). ... Re-signed by Packers (March 8, 2002). ... Released by Packers (March 1, 2005). ... Signed by Carolina Panthers (March 3, 2005).
PLAYING EXPERIENCE: Green Bay NFL, 1998-2004. ... Games/Games started: 1998 (1/0), 1999 (16/13), 2000 (16/6), 2001 (16/16), 2002 (16/16), 2003 (16/16), 2004 (16/16). Total: 97/83.

WAHLROOS, DREW   LB   RAMS

PERSONAL: Born June 7, 1980, in Poway, Calif. ... 6-3/230.
HIGH SCHOOL: Poway (Calif.).
COLLEGE: Colorado.
TRANSACTIONS/CAREER NOTES: Signed as non-drafted free agent by Philadelphia Eagles (January 28, 2003). ... Released by Eagles (August 23, 2003). ... Signed by Tennessee Titans (June 17, 2004). ... Released by Titans (July 27, 2004). ... Signed by St. Louis Rams to practice squad (November 15, 2004). ... Activated (November 16, 2004).

			TOTALS			INTERCEPTIONS			
Year Team	G	GS	Tk.	Ast.	Sks.	No.	Yds.	Avg.	TD
2004—St. Louis NFL	6	0	0	0	0.0	0	0	0.0	0

WALKER, AARON   TE   49ERS

PERSONAL: Born March 14, 1980, in Titusville, Fla. ... 6-6/252. ... Full name: Aaron Scott Walker.
HIGH SCHOOL: Astronaut (Mims, Fla.).
COLLEGE: Florida.
TRANSACTIONS/CAREER NOTES: Selected by San Francisco 49ers in fifth round (161st pick overall) of 2003 NFL draft.
SINGLE GAME HIGHS (regular season): Receptions—3 (October 10, 2004, vs. Arizona); yards—41 (October 10, 2004, vs. Arizona); and touchdown receptions—1 (October 5, 2003, vs. Detroit).

			RECEIVING				TOTALS			
Year Team	G	GS	No.	Yds.	Avg.	TD	TD	2pt.	Pts.	Fum.
2003—San Francisco NFL	16	2	8	116	14.5	1	1	0	6	0
2004—San Francisco NFL	16	4	10	115	11.5	0	0	0	0	0
Pro totals (2 years)	32	6	18	231	12.8	1	1	0	6	0

WALKER, BRACY   S   LIONS

PERSONAL: Born October 28, 1970, in Portsmouth, Va. ... 6-0/202. ... Full name: Bracy Wordell Walker.
HIGH SCHOOL: Pine Forest (Fayetteville, N.C.).
COLLEGE: North Carolina.
TRANSACTIONS/CAREER NOTES: Selected by Kansas City Chiefs in fourth round (127th pick overall) of 1994 NFL draft. ... Signed by Chiefs (July 20, 1994). ... Claimed on waivers by Cincinnati Bengals (October 12, 1994). ... Granted free agency (February 14, 1997). ... Re-signed by Bengals (April 18, 1997). ... Claimed on waivers by Miami Dolphins (August 20, 1997). ... On injured reserve with leg injury (December 2, 1997-remainder of season). ... Granted unconditional free agency (February 13, 1998). ... Re-signed by Dolphins (April 27, 1998). ... Released by Dolphins (August 19, 1998). ... Signed by Chiefs (November 3, 1998). ... Granted unconditional free agency (February 11, 2000). ... Re-

W

signed by Chiefs (February 24, 2000). ... Granted unconditional free agency (March 2, 2002). ... Signed by Detroit Lions (April 15, 2002). ... On injured reserve with liver injury (December 18, 2002-remainder of season). ... Re-signed by Lions (March 11, 2003). ... Granted unconditional free agency (March 3, 2004). ... Re-signed by Lions (March 5, 2004). ... Granted unconditional free agency (March 2, 2005). ... Re-signed by Lions (March 2, 2005).

HONORS: Named defensive back on THE SPORTING NEWS college All-America second team (1993).

Year Team	G	GS	TOTALS			INTERCEPTIONS			
			Tk.	Ast.	Sks.	No.	Yds.	Avg.	TD
1994—Kansas City NFL	2	0	0	0	0.0	0	0	0.0	0
—Cincinnati NFL	7	0	1	1	0.0	0	0	0.0	0
1995—Cincinnati NFL	14	14	60	25	0.0	4	56	14.0	0
1996—Cincinnati NFL	16	16	57	13	0.0	2	35	17.5	0
1997—Miami NFL	12	0	2	0	0.0	0	0	0.0	0
1998—Kansas City NFL	8	0	1	0	0.0	0	0	0.0	0
1999—Kansas City NFL	16	1	8	0	0.0	0	0	0.0	0
2000—Kansas City NFL	15	0	0	0	0.0	0	0	0.0	0
2001—Kansas City NFL	15	0	1	0	0.0	0	0	0.0	0
2002—Detroit NFL	14	1	24	12	1.0	0	0	0.0	0
2003—Detroit NFL	16	1	27	2	0.0	0	0	0.0	0
2004—Detroit NFL	16	16	52	22	1.0	1	0	0.0	0
Pro totals (11 years)	151	49	233	75	2.0	7	91	13.0	0

WALKER, BRIAN   S

PERSONAL: Born May 31, 1972, in Colorado Springs, Colo. ... 6-1/205.
HIGH SCHOOL: Widefield (Colorado Springs, Colo.).
JUNIOR COLLEGE: Snow College (Utah).
COLLEGE: Washington State.
TRANSACTIONS/CAREER NOTES: Signed as non-drafted free agent by Washington Redskins (May 1, 1996). ... Released by Redskins (October 9, 1997). ... Signed by Miami Dolphins (December 9, 1997). ... Active for two games with Dolphins (1997); did not play. ... Claimed on waivers by Seattle Seahawks (September 6, 1999). ... Released by Seahawks (September 14, 1999). ... Re-signed by Seahawks (September 30, 1999). ... On injured reserve with hamstring injury (January 8, 2000-remainder of playoffs). ... Granted unconditional free agency (February 11, 2000). ... Re-signed by Dolphins (February 16, 2000). ... Granted unconditional free agency (March 1, 2002). ... Signed by Detroit Lions (March 5, 2002). ... On injured reserve with knee injury (September 5, 2004-entire season). ... Released by Lions (February 22, 2005).

Year Team	G	GS	TOTALS			INTERCEPTIONS			
			Tk.	Ast.	Sks.	No.	Yds.	Avg.	TD
1996—Washington NFL	16	4	29	9	1.0	0	0	0.0	0
1997—Washington NFL	5	0	0	0	0.0	0	0	0.0	0
1998—Miami NFL	16	0	12	3	0.0	4	12	3.0	0
1999—Seattle NFL	5	0	8	1	0.0	1	21	21.0	0
2000—Miami NFL	16	16	60	28	2.0	▲7	80	11.4	0
2001—Miami NFL	13	13	52	25	0.0	1	0	0.0	0
2002—Detroit NFL	10	9	32	12	1.0	0	0	0.0	0
2003—Detroit NFL	16	16	60	20	0.0	2	0	0.0	0
2004—Detroit NFL			Did not play.						
Pro totals (8 years)	97	58	253	98	4.0	15	113	7.5	0

WALKER, DARWIN   DT   EAGLES

PERSONAL: Born June 15, 1977, in Walterboro, S.C. ... 6-3/294. ... Full name: Darwin Jamar Walker.
HIGH SCHOOL: Walterboro (S.C.).
COLLEGE: Tennessee.
TRANSACTIONS/CAREER NOTES: Selected by Arizona Cardinals in third round (71st pick overall) of 2000 NFL draft. ... Signed by Cardinals (June 19, 2000). ... Claimed on waivers by Philadelphia Eagles (September 12, 2000).
CHAMPIONSHIP GAME EXPERIENCE: Played in NFC championship game (2001-2004 seasons). ... Played in Super Bowl 39 (2004 season).
HONORS: Named defensive tackle on THE SPORTING NEWS college All-America second team (1999).

Year Team	G	GS	TOTALS		
			Tk.	Ast.	Sks.
2000—Arizona NFL	1	0	0	0	0.0
2001—Philadelphia NFL	10	0	4	1	1.0
2002—Philadelphia NFL	16	16	29	6	7.5
2003—Philadelphia NFL	16	16	35	7	6.0
2004—Philadelphia NFL	16	16	22	7	4.5
Pro totals (5 years)	59	48	90	21	19.0

WALKER, DENARD   CB   RAIDERS

PERSONAL: Born August 9, 1973, in Dallas, Texas. ... 6-1/190. ... Full name: Denard Antuan Walker.
HIGH SCHOOL: South Garland (Texas), than Harlingen (Texas) Military Institute.
COLLEGE: Louisiana State.
TRANSACTIONS/CAREER NOTES: Selected by Houston Oilers in third round (75th pick overall) of 1997 NFL draft. ... Oilers franchise moved to Tennessee for 1997 season. ... Signed by Oilers (July 18, 1997). ... Oilers franchise renamed Tennessee Titans for 1999 season (December 26, 1998). ... Granted free agency (February 11, 2000). ... Re-signed by Titans (June 3, 2000). ... On suspended list (September 3-5, 2000). ... Granted unconditional free agency (March 2, 2001). ... Signed by Denver Broncos (March 19, 2001). ... Waived by Broncos (February 25, 2003). ... Signed by Minnesota Vikings (March 12, 2003). ... Waived by Vikings (March 30, 2004). ... Signed by Oakland Raiders (April 15, 2004).
CHAMPIONSHIP GAME EXPERIENCE: Played in AFC championship game (1999 season). ... Played in Super Bowl 34 (1999 season).

W

Year—Team	G	GS	TOTALS Tk.	Ast.	Sks.	INTERCEPTIONS No.	Yds.	Avg.	TD
1997—Tennessee NFL	15	11	56	12	0.0	2	53	26.5	1
1998—Tennessee NFL	16	16	68	15	0.0	2	6	3.0	0
1999—Tennessee NFL	15	14	39	8	0.0	1	27	27.0	0
2000—Tennessee NFL	15	14	44	1	0.0	2	4	2.0	0
2001—Denver NFL	16	15	51	5	0.0	3	60	20.0	1
2002—Denver NFL	16	16	56	8	0.0	1	8	8.0	0
2003—Minnesota NFL	16	8	48	5	0.0	1	0	0.0	0
2004—Oakland NFL	16	5	42	2	0.0	1	45	45.0	0
Pro totals (8 years)	125	99	404	56	0.0	13	203	15.6	2

WALKER, FRANK — CB — GIANTS

PERSONAL: Born August 6, 1980, in Tuskegee, Ala. ... 5-10/198. ... Full name: Frank Bernard Walker Jr.
HIGH SCHOOL: Booker T. Washington (Tuskegee, Ala.).
COLLEGE: Tuskegee.
TRANSACTIONS/CAREER NOTES: Selected by New York Giants in sixth round (207th pick overall) of 2003 NFL draft. ... Signed by Giants (June 26, 2003).

Year—Team	G	GS	TOTALS Tk.	Ast.	Sks.	INTERCEPTIONS No.	Yds.	Avg.	TD
2003—New York Giants NFL	10	7	30	4	0.0	2	74	37.0	1
2004—New York Giants NFL	13	1	10	2	0.0	2	20	10.0	0
Pro totals (2 years)	23	8	40	6	0.0	4	94	23.5	1

WALKER, GARY — DE

PERSONAL: Born February 28, 1973, in Royston, Ga. ... 6-2/324. ... Full name: Gary Lamar Walker.
HIGH SCHOOL: Franklin County (Carnesville, Ga.).
JUNIOR COLLEGE: Hinds Community College (Miss.).
COLLEGE: Auburn.
TRANSACTIONS/CAREER NOTES: Selected by Houston Oilers in fifth round (159th pick overall) of 1995 NFL draft. ... Signed by Oilers (July 10, 1995). ... Oilers franchise moved to Tennessee for 1997 season. ... Granted free agency (February 13, 1998). ... Re-signed by Oilers (July 15, 1998). ... Granted unconditional free agency (February 12, 1999). ... Signed by Jacksonville Jaguars (February 15, 1999). ... Selected by Houston Texans from Jaguars in NFL expansion draft (February 18, 2002). ... Signed by Texans (March 3, 2004). ... Released by Texans (March 21, 2005).
CHAMPIONSHIP GAME EXPERIENCE: Played in AFC championship game (1999 season).
HONORS: Played in Pro Bowl (2001 and 2002 seasons).

Year—Team	G	GS	TOTALS Tk.	Ast.	Sks.
1995—Houston NFL	15	9	22	10	2.5
1996—Houston NFL	16	16	30	15	5.5
1997—Tennessee NFL	15	15	31	13	7.0
1998—Tennessee NFL	16	16	31	16	1.0
1999—Jacksonville NFL	16	16	46	8	10.0
2000—Jacksonville NFL	15	14	40	3	5.0
2001—Jacksonville NFL	16	16	35	8	7.5
2002—Houston NFL	16	16	37	15	6.5
2003—Houston NFL	4	4	7	6	0.0
2004—Houston NFL	15	15	20	10	0.5
Pro totals (10 years)	144	137	299	104	45.5

WALKER, GREG — T — GIANTS

PERSONAL: Born October 1, 1981, in Wichita, Kan. ... 6-5/341. ... Full name: Gregory Walker.
HIGH SCHOOL: Sumter (S.C.).
COLLEGE: Clemson.
TRANSACTIONS/CAREER NOTES: Signed as non-drafted free agent by Detroit Lions (April 30, 2004). ... Released by Lions (May 6, 2004). ... Signed by New York Giants (June 2, 2004). ... On injured reserve with knee injury (January 2, 2005-remainder of season).
PLAYING EXPERIENCE: New York Giants NFL, 2004. ... Games/Games started: 2004 (7/0). Total: 7/0.

W

WALKER, JAVON — WR — PACKERS

PERSONAL: Born October 14, 1978, in Galveston, Texas. ... 6-3/215.
HIGH SCHOOL: St. Thomas More (Lafayette, La.).
JUNIOR COLLEGE: Jones Junior College (Miss.).
COLLEGE: Florida State.
TRANSACTIONS/CAREER NOTES: Selected by Green Bay Packers in first round (20th pick overall) of 2002 NFL draft. ... Signed by Packers (July 23, 2002).
HONORS: Played in Pro Bowl (2004 season).
SINGLE GAME HIGHS (regular season): Receptions—11 (December 19, 2004, vs. Jacksonville); yards—200 (September 26, 2004, vs. Indianapolis); and touchdown receptions—3 (September 26, 2004, vs. Indianapolis).
STATISTICAL PLATEAUS: 100-yard receiving games: 2003 (1), 2004 (5). Total: 6.

Year Team	G	GS	RUSHING				RECEIVING				KICKOFF RETURNS				TOTALS			
			Att.	Yds.	Avg.	TD	No.	Yds.	Avg.	TD	No.	Yds.	Avg.	TD	TD	2pt	Pts.	Fum.
2002—Green Bay NFL	15	2	1	11	11.0	0	23	319	13.9	1	35	769	22.0	0	1	0	6	1
2003—Green Bay NFL	16	3	2	1	0.5	0	41	716	17.5	9	0	0	0.0	0	9	0	54	1
2004—Green Bay NFL	16	12	0	0	0.0	0	89	1382	15.5	12	0	0	0.0	0	12	0	72	2
Pro totals (3 years)	47	17	3	12	4.0	0	153	2417	15.8	22	35	769	22.0	0	22	0	132	4

WALKER, KENYATTA   T   BUCCANEERS

PERSONAL: Born February 1, 1979, in Meridian, Miss. ... 6-5/302. ... Full name: Idrees Kenyatta Walker.
HIGH SCHOOL: Meridian (Miss.).
COLLEGE: Florida.
TRANSACTIONS/CAREER NOTES: Selected after junior season by Tampa Bay Buccaneers in first round (14th pick overall) of 2001 draft. ... Signed by Buccaneers (July 26, 2001). ... On injured reserved with knee injury (December 26, 2003-remainder of season).
PLAYING EXPERIENCE: Tampa Bay NFL, 2001-2004. ... Games/Games started: 2001 (16/16), 2002 (13/13), 2003 (14/14), 2004 (13/11). Total: 56/54.
CHAMPIONSHIP GAME EXPERIENCE: Played in NFC championship game (2002 season). ... Member of Super Bowl championship team (2002 season).

WALKER, LANGSTON   T   RAIDERS

PERSONAL: Born September 3, 1979, in Oakland, Calif. ... 6-8/345.
HIGH SCHOOL: Bishop O'Dowd (Calif.).
COLLEGE: California.
TRANSACTIONS/CAREER NOTES: Selected by Oakland Raiders in second round (53rd pick overall) of 2002 NFL draft. ... Signed by Raiders (July 19, 2002).
PLAYING EXPERIENCE: Oakland NFL, 2002-2004. ... Games/Games started: 2002 (12/2), 2003 (16/8), 2004 (16/1). Total: 44/11.
CHAMPIONSHIP GAME EXPERIENCE: Played in AFC championship game (2002 season). ... Played in Super Bowl 37 (2002 season).

WALLACE, AL   DE   PANTHERS

PERSONAL: Born March 25, 1974, in Delray Beach, Fla. ... 6-5/275. ... Full name: Alonzo Dwight Wallace.
HIGH SCHOOL: Spanish River (Boca Raton, Fla.).
COLLEGE: Maryland.
TRANSACTIONS/CAREER NOTES: Signed as non-drafted free agent by Jacksonville Jaguars (April 21, 1997). ... Released by Jaguars (August 19, 1997). ... Re-signed by Jaguars to practice squad (August 25, 1997). ... Signed by Philadelphia Eagles off Jaguars practice squad (December 2, 1997). ... On injured reserve with ankle injury (September 5, 1999-entire season). ... Released by Eagles (August 27, 2000). ... Signed by Chicago Bears (December 20, 2000). ... Released by Bears (August 28, 2001). ... Signed by Miami Dolphins (January 15, 2002). ... Traded by Dolphins with fourth-round pick (DB Colin Branch) in 2003 draft to Carolina Panthers for DE Jay Williams (July 19, 2002).
CHAMPIONSHIP GAME EXPERIENCE: Played in NFC championship game (2003 season). ... Played in Super Bowl 38 (2003 season).

Year Team	G	GS	TOTALS			INTERCEPTIONS			
			Tk.	Ast.	Sks.	No.	Yds.	Avg.	TD
1997—Philadelphia NFL	1	0	0	0	0.0	0	0	0.0	0
1998—Philadelphia NFL	15	0	14	4	6.0	0	0	0.0	0
1999—Philadelphia NFL			Did not play.						
2002—Carolina NFL	16	4	22	4	3.0	0	0	0.0	0
2003—Carolina NFL	16	2	28	8	5.0	2	58	29.0	0
2004—Carolina NFL	16	0	20	2	1.0	0	0	0.0	0
Pro totals (5 years)	64	6	84	18	15.0	2	58	29.0	0

WALLACE, TACO   WR   SEAHAWKS

PERSONAL: Born April 14, 1981, in Harbor City, Calif. ... 6-1/190.
HIGH SCHOOL: Taft (Woodlands Hills, Calif.).
JUNIOR COLLEGE: Mount San Antonio College (Calif.).
COLLEGE: Kansas State.
TRANSACTIONS/CAREER NOTES: Selected by Seattle Seahawks in seventh round (224th pick overall) of 2003 NFL draft. ... Signed by Seahawks (July 9, 2003). ... Released by Seahawks (September 5, 2004). ... Re-signed by Seahawks to practice squad (September 6, 2004). ... Activated (November 5, 2004).

Year Team	G	GS	RECEIVING				TOTALS			
			No.	Yds.	Avg.	TD	TD	2pt	Pts.	Fum.
2003—Seattle NFL	1	0	0	0	0.0	0	0	0	0	0
2004—Seattle NFL	2	0	0	0	0.0	0	0	0	0	0
Pro totals (2 years)	3	0	0	0	0.0	0	0	0	0	0

WALLS, LENNY   CB   BRONCOS

PERSONAL: Born September 26, 1979, in San Francisco, Calif. ... 6-4/192.
HIGH SCHOOL: Galileo (San Francisco).
JUNIOR COLLEGE: City College of San Francisco.
COLLEGE: Boston College.
TRANSACTIONS/CAREER NOTES: Signed as non-drafted free agent by Denver Broncos (April 22, 2002). ... On injured reserve with shoulder injury (November 30, 2004-remainder of season). ... Granted free agency (March 2, 2005). ... Re-signed by Broncos (April 15, 2005).

W

Year Team	G	GS	TOTALS Tk.	Ast.	Sks.	INTERCEPTIONS No.	Yds.	Avg.	TD
2002—Denver NFL	13	0	0	0	0.0	0	0	0.0	0
2003—Denver NFL	16	16	53	5	0.0	1	0	0.0	0
2004—Denver NFL	7	1	20	1	0.0	0	0	0.0	0
Pro totals (3 years)	36	17	73	6	0.0	1	0	0.0	0

WALLS, RAYMOND　　　CB　　　CARDINALS

PERSONAL: Born July 24, 1979, in Kentwood, La. ... 5-10/188. ... Full name: Raymond Omoncial Tyshone Walls.
HIGH SCHOOL: Kentwood (La.).
COLLEGE: Southern Miss.
TRANSACTIONS/CAREER NOTES: Selected by Indianapolis Colts in fifth round (152nd pick overall) of 2001 NFL draft. ... Signed by Colts (June 13, 2001). ... Released by Colts (September 1, 2001). ... Re-signed by Colts to practice squad (September 3, 2001). ... Activated (October 8, 2001). ... Released by Colts (August 28, 2002). ... Signed by Cleveland Browns to practice squad (September 25, 2002). ... Activated (October 23, 2002). ... Released by Browns (November 14, 2002). ... Re-signed by Browns to practice squad (November 14, 2002). ... Activated (November 26, 2002). ... Waived by Browns (August 4, 2003). ... Signed by Baltimore Ravens (August 20, 2003). ... Granted free agency (March 3, 2004). ... Re-signed by Ravens (April 14, 2004). ... Granted unconditional free agency (March 2, 2005). ... Signed by Arizona Cardinals (April 25, 2005).

Year Team	G	GS	TOTALS Tk.	Ast.	Sks.	INTERCEPTIONS No.	Yds.	Avg.	TD
2001—Indianapolis NFL	4	0	3	0	0.0	1	0	0.0	0
2002—Cleveland NFL	4	0	0	0	0.0	0	0	0.0	0
2003—Baltimore NFL	10	0	4	0	0.0	0	0	0.0	0
2004—Baltimore NFL	16	1	8	4	0.0	0	0	0.0	0
Pro totals (4 years)	34	1	15	4	0.0	1	0	0.0	0

WALTER, KEN　　　P　　　SEAHAWKS

PERSONAL: Born August 15, 1972, in Cleveland, Ohio. ... 6-1/207. ... Full name: Kenneth Matthew Walter Jr.
HIGH SCHOOL: Euclid (Ohio).
COLLEGE: Kent State.
TRANSACTIONS/CAREER NOTES: Signed as non-drafted free agent by Carolina Panthers (April 14, 1997). ... Released by Panthers (April 24, 2001). ... Signed by New England Patriots (October 16, 2001). ... Waived by Patriots (December 2, 2003). ... Re-signed by Patriots (December 12, 2003). ... Granted unconditional free agency (March 3, 2004). ... Signed by Seattle Seahawks (November 24, 2004).
CHAMPIONSHIP GAME EXPERIENCE: Played in AFC championship game (2001 and 2003 seasons). ... Member of Super Bowl championship team (2001 and 2003 seasons).

Year Team	G	No.	PUNTING Yds.	Avg.	Net avg.	In. 20	Blk.
1997—Carolina NFL	16	85	3604	42.4	36.4	29	0
1998—Carolina NFL	16	77	3131	40.7	38.1	20	0
1999—Carolina NFL	16	65	2562	39.4	36.7	18	0
2000—Carolina NFL	16	64	2459	38.4	33.8	19	†2
2001—New England NFL	11	49	1964	40.1	§38.1	24	0
2002—New England NFL	16	70	2723	38.9	33.3	19	1
2003—New England NFL	15	76	2865	37.7	33.6	25	1
2004—Seattle NFL	6	24	920	38.3	33.0	4	1
Pro totals (8 years)	112	510	20228	39.7	35.5	158	5

WALTER, KEVIN　　　WR　　　BENGALS

PERSONAL: Born August 4, 1981, in Lake Forest, Ill. ... 6-3/218. ... Full name: Kevin Patrick Walter.
HIGH SCHOOL: Libertyville (Ill.).
COLLEGE: Eastern Michigan.
TRANSACTIONS/CAREER NOTES: Selected by New York Giants in seventh round (255th pick overall) of 2003 NFL draft. ... Signed by Giants (June 16, 2003). ... Claimed on waivers by Cincinnati Bengals (August 26, 2003). ... Waived by Bengals (August 31, 2003). ... Re-signed by Bengals to practice squad (September 1, 2003). ... Activated (October 16, 2003).
SINGLE GAME HIGHS (regular season): Receptions—2 (November 28, 2004, vs. Cleveland); yards—23 (November 14, 2004, vs. Washington); and touchdown receptions—0.

Year Team	G	GS	RECEIVING No.	Yds.	Avg.	TD	TOTALS TD	2pt.	Pts.	Fum.
2003—Cincinnati NFL	11	0	3	18	6.0	0	0	0	0	0
2004—Cincinnati NFL	16	0	8	67	8.4	0	0	0	0	0
Pro totals (2 years)	27	0	11	85	7.7	0	0	0	0	0

WALTER, TYSON　　　T

PERSONAL: Born March 17, 1978, in Bainbridge, Ohio. ... 6-4/303.
HIGH SCHOOL: Kenston (Ohio).
COLLEGE: Ohio State.
TRANSACTIONS/CAREER NOTES: Selected by Dallas Cowboys in sixth round (179th pick overall) of 2002 NFL draft. ... Signed by Cowboys (July 24, 2002). ... Granted free agency (March 2, 2005).
PLAYING EXPERIENCE: Dallas NFL, 2004. ... Games/Games started: 2002 (10/8), 2003 (16/0), 2004 (13/1). Total: 39/9.

W

WALTERS, TROY   WR   COLTS

PERSONAL: Born December 15, 1976, in Bloomington, Ind. ... 5-7/172. ... Full name: Troy M. Walters.
HIGH SCHOOL: A&M Consolidated (College Station, Texas).
COLLEGE: Stanford.
TRANSACTIONS/CAREER NOTES: Selected by Minnesota Vikings in fifth round (165th pick overall) of 2000 NFL draft. ... Signed by Vikings (July 12, 2000). ... Claimed on waivers by Indianapolis Colts (February 24, 2002). ... Re-signed by Colts (January 5, 2003). ... Granted unconditional free agency (March 2, 2005). ... Re-signed by Colts (March 14, 2005).
CHAMPIONSHIP GAME EXPERIENCE: Played in NFC championship game (2000 season). ... Played in AFC championship game (2003 season).
HONORS: Named wide receiver on THE SPORTING NEWS college All-America first team (1999). ... Fred Biletnikoff Award winner (1999).
SINGLE GAME HIGHS (regular season): Receptions—7 (November 17, 2002, vs. Dallas); yards—91 (November 17, 2002, vs. Dallas); and touchdown receptions—1 (November 30, 2003, vs. New England).

			RUSHING				RECEIVING				PUNT RETURNS				KICKOFF RETURNS				TOTALS		
Year Team	G	GS	Att.	Yds.	Avg.	TD	No.	Yds.	Avg.	TD	No.	Yds.	Avg.	TD	No.	Yds.	Avg.	TD	TD	2pt.	Pts.
2000—Min. NFL	12	0	1	3	3.0	0	1	5	5.0	0	15	217	14.5	0	30	692	23.1	0	0	0	0
2001—Min. NFL	6	0	0	0	0.0	0	0	0	0.0	0	11	69	6.3	0	18	425	23.6	0	0	0	0
2002—Ind. NFL	16	1	2	33	16.5	0	18	207	11.5	0	35	270	7.7	0	53	1150	21.7	0	0	0	0
2003—Ind. NFL	15	4	1	6	6.0	0	36	456	12.7	3	11	105	9.5	0	6	126	21.0	0	3	0	18
2004—Ind. NFL	5	0	0	0	0.0	0	1	5	5.0	0	7	40	5.7	0	1	16	16.0	0	0	0	0
Pro totals (5 years)	54	5	4	42	10.5	0	56	673	12.0	3	79	701	8.9	0	108	2409	22.3	0	3	0	18

WAND, SETH   T   TEXANS

PERSONAL: Born August 6, 1979, in Springfield, Mo. ... 6-7/330.
HIGH SCHOOL: Springfield Catholic (Springfield, Mo.).
COLLEGE: Northwest Missouri State.
TRANSACTIONS/CAREER NOTES: Selected by Houston Texans in third round (75th pick overall) of 2003 NFL draft. ... Signed by Texans (July 18, 2003).
PLAYING EXPERIENCE: Houston NFL, 2003-2004. ... Games/Games started: 2003 (16/2), 2004 (16/16). Total: 32/18.

WARD, DEDRIC   WR

PERSONAL: Born September 29, 1974, in Cedar Rapids, Iowa. ... 5-9/189. ... Full name: Dedric Lamar Ward. ... Name pronounced: DEE-drick.
HIGH SCHOOL: Washington (Cedar Rapids, Iowa).
COLLEGE: Northern Iowa.
TRANSACTIONS/CAREER NOTES: Selected by New York Jets in third round (88th pick overall) of 1997 NFL draft. ... Signed by Jets (July 17, 1997). ... Granted free agency (February 11, 2000). ... Re-signed by Jets (May 3, 2000). ... Granted unconditional free agency (March 2, 2001). ... Signed by Miami Dolphins (April 18, 2001). ... Released by Dolphins (February 26, 2003). ... Signed by New England Patriots (May 22, 2003). ... Released by Patriots (August 31, 2003). ... Signed by Baltimore Ravens (October 6, 2003). ... Waived by Ravens (November 18, 2003). ... Signed by Patriots (November 20, 2003). ... Granted unconditional free agency (March 3, 2004). ... Signed by Dallas Cowboys (June 11, 2004). ... Released by Cowboys (December 31, 2004).
CHAMPIONSHIP GAME EXPERIENCE: Played in AFC championship game (1998 and 2003 seasons). ... Member of Super Bowl championship team (2003 season).
SINGLE GAME HIGHS (regular season): Receptions—8 (December 24, 2000, vs. Baltimore); yards—147 (December 24, 2000, vs. Baltimore); and touchdown receptions—1 (November 30, 2003, vs. Indianapolis).
STATISTICAL PLATEAUS: 100-yard receiving games: 1997 (1), 2000 (3). Total: 4.

			RECEIVING				PUNT RETURNS				KICKOFF RETURNS				TOTALS			
Year Team	G	GS	No.	Yds.	Avg.	TD	No.	Yds.	Avg.	TD	No.	Yds.	Avg.	TD	TD	2pt.	Pts.	Fum.
1997—New York Jets NFL	11	0	18	212	11.8	1	8	55	6.9	0	2	10	5.0	0	1	0	6	1
1998—New York Jets NFL	16	2	25	477	19.1	4	8	72	9.0	0	3	60	20.0	0	4	0	24	0
1999—New York Jets NFL	16	10	22	325	14.8	3	38	288	7.6	0	0	0	0.0	0	3	0	18	2
2000—New York Jets NFL	16	16	54	801	14.8	3	27	214	7.9	0	0	0	0.0	0	3	0	18	1
2001—Miami NFL	13	1	21	209	10.0	0	9	88	9.8	0	0	0	0.0	0	0	0	0	1
2002—Miami NFL	16	1	19	172	9.1	0	16	169	10.6	0	0	0	0.0	0	0	0	0	1
2003—Baltimore NFL	3	0	0	0	0.0	0	3	26	8.7	0	1	20	20.0	0	0	0	0	0
—New England NFL	4	0	7	106	15.1	1	0	0	0.0	0	0	0	0.0	0	1	0	6	0
2004—Dallas NFL	8	0	1	5	5.0	0	14	114	8.1	0	0	0	0.0	0	0	0	0	1
Pro totals (8 years)	103	30	167	2307	13.8	12	123	1026	8.3	0	6	90	15.0	0	12	0	72	7

WARD, DERRICK   RB   GIANTS

PERSONAL: Born August 30, 1980, in Los Angeles, Calif. ... 5-11/233.
HIGH SCHOOL: Valley View (Moreno Valley, Calif.).
COLLEGE: Ottawa.
TRANSACTIONS/CAREER NOTES: Selected by New York Jets in seventh round (235th pick overall) of 2004 NFL draft. ... Signed by Jets (July 29, 2004). ... Released by Jets (September 5, 2004). ... Re-signed by Jets to practice squad (September 6, 2004). ... Signed by New York Giants off Jets practice squad (October 13, 2004).

			RUSHING				RECEIVING				KICKOFF RETURNS				TOTALS			
Year Team	G	GS	Att.	Yds.	Avg.	TD	No.	Yds.	Avg.	TD	No.	Yds.	Avg.	TD	TD	2pt.	Pts.	Fum.
2004—New York Giants NFL	5	0	0	0	0.0	0	0	0	0.0	0	16	436	27.3	1	1	0	6	1

WARD, HINES   WR   STEELERS

PERSONAL: Born March 8, 1976, in Seoul, South Korea. ... 6-0/215. ... Full name: Hines Ward Jr.
HIGH SCHOOL: Forest Park (Ga.).
COLLEGE: Georgia.
TRANSACTIONS/CAREER NOTES: Selected by Pittsburgh Steelers in third round (92nd pick overall) of 1998 NFL draft. ... Signed by Steelers (July 20, 1998). ... Granted free agency (March 2, 2001). ... Re-signed by Steelers (July 1, 2001).
CHAMPIONSHIP GAME EXPERIENCE: Played in AFC championship game (2001 and 2004 seasons).
HONORS: Played in Pro Bowl (2001-2004 seasons).
SINGLE GAME HIGHS (regular season): Receptions—13 (November 30, 2003, vs. Cincinnati); yards—168 (November 17, 2002, vs. Tennessee); and touchdown receptions—2 (November 9, 2003, vs. Arizona).
STATISTICAL PLATEAUS: 100-yard receiving games: 2001 (2), 2002 (4), 2003 (2), 2004 (2). Total: 10.

| | | | RUSHING | | | | RECEIVING | | | | TOTALS | | |
Year Team	G	GS	Att.	Yds.	Avg.	TD	No.	Yds.	Avg.	TD	TD	2pt.	Pts.	Fum.
1998—Pittsburgh NFL	16	0	1	13	13.0	0	15	246	16.4	0	0	0	0	0
1999—Pittsburgh NFL	16	14	2	-2	-1.0	0	61	638	10.5	7	7	1	44	1
2000—Pittsburgh NFL	16	15	4	53	13.3	0	48	672	14.0	4	4	0	24	2
2001—Pittsburgh NFL	16	16	10	83	8.3	0	94	1003	10.7	4	4	0	24	1
2002—Pittsburgh NFL	16	16	12	142	11.8	0	112	1329	11.9	§12	12	3	78	1
2003—Pittsburgh NFL	16	16	11	61	5.5	0	95	1163	12.2	10	10	0	60	0
2004—Pittsburgh NFL	16	16	7	25	3.6	1	80	1004	12.6	4	5	0	30	1
Pro totals (7 years)	112	93	47	375	8.0	1	505	6055	12.0	41	42	4	260	6

WARE, KEVIN   TE

PERSONAL: Born September 30, 1980, in San Diego, Calif. ... 6-3/259.
HIGH SCHOOL: Klein Oak (Houston, Texas).
COLLEGE: Washington.
TRANSACTIONS/CAREER NOTES: Signed as non-drafted free agent by Washington Redskins (May 2, 2003). ... Released by Redskins (August 31, 2003). ... Re-signed by Redskins to practice squad (September 1, 2003). ... Activated (September 12, 2003). ... Released by Redskins (September 15, 2003). ... Re-signed by Redskins to practice squad (September 17, 2003). ... Activated (September 19, 2003). ... Released by Redskins (September 22, 2003). ... Re-signed by Redskins to practice squad (September 24, 2003). ... Activated (October 31, 2003). ... Released by Redskins (June 29, 2004). ... Signed by San Francisco 49ers (August 4, 2004). ... Released by 49ers (September 11, 2004). ... Re-signed by 49ers (September 14, 2004). ... Released by 49ers (September 15, 2004). ... Re-signed by 49ers (October 25, 2004). ... Released by 49ers (November 30, 2004).
SINGLE GAME HIGHS (regular season): Receptions—2 (December 27, 2003, vs. Philadelphia); yards—11 (December 27, 2003, vs. Philadelphia); and touchdown receptions—0.

| | | | RECEIVING | | | | TOTALS | | |
Year Team	G	GS	No.	Yds.	Avg.	TD	TD	2pt.	Pts.	Fum.
2003—Washington NFL	11	2	3	17	5.7	0	0	0	0	0
2004—San Francisco NFL	5	0	1	9	9.0	0	0	0	0	0
Pro totals (2 years)	16	2	4	26	6.5	0	0	0	0	0

WARE, MATT   CB   EAGLES

PERSONAL: Born December 2, 1982, in Santa Monica, Calif. ... 6-2/210. ... Full name: Matthew Jesse Ware.
HIGH SCHOOL: Loyola (Malibu, Calif.).
COLLEGE: UCLA.
TRANSACTIONS/CAREER NOTES: Selected after junior season by Philadelphia Eagles in third round (89th pick overall) of 2004 NFL draft. ... Signed by Eagles (July 27, 2004).
CHAMPIONSHIP GAME EXPERIENCE: Played in NFC championship game (2004 season). ... Played in Super Bowl 39 (2004 season).
HONORS: Named cornerback on THE SPORTING NEWS Freshman All-America first team (2001).
MISCELLANEOUS: Selected by Seattle Mariners organization in 21st round of free-agent baseball draft (June 2001).

| | | | TOTALS | | | INTERCEPTIONS | | | |
Year Team	G	GS	Tk.	Ast.	Sks.	No.	Yds.	Avg.	TD
2004—Philadelphia NFL	12	0	8	0	0.0	0	0	0.0	0

WARFIELD, ERIC   CB   CHIEFS

PERSONAL: Born March 3, 1976, in Vicksburg, Miss. ... 6-0/200. ... Full name: Eric Andrew Warfield.
HIGH SCHOOL: Arkansas (Texarkana, Ark.).
COLLEGE: Nebraska.
TRANSACTIONS/CAREER NOTES: Selected by Kansas City Chiefs in seventh round (216th pick overall) of 1998 NFL draft. ... Signed by Chiefs (May 27, 1998). ... Granted unconditional free agency (March 1, 2002). ... Re-signed by Chiefs (March 4, 2002).

| | | | TOTALS | | | INTERCEPTIONS | | | |
Year Team	G	GS	Tk.	Ast.	Sks.	No.	Yds.	Avg.	TD
1998—Kansas City NFL	12	0	0	0	0.0	0	0	0.0	0
1999—Kansas City NFL	16	1	25	4	0.0	3	0	0.0	0
2000—Kansas City NFL	13	3	19	2	0.0	0	0	0.0	0
2001—Kansas City NFL	16	16	64	6	0.0	4	61	15.3	1
2002—Kansas City NFL	16	16	56	8	0.0	4	30	7.5	0
2003—Kansas City NFL	15	15	62	4	1.0	4	39	9.8	0
2004—Kansas City NFL	16	16	50	8	0.0	4	49	12.3	1
Pro totals (7 years)	104	67	276	32	1.0	19	179	9.4	2

W

PERSONAL: Born June 22, 1971, in Burlington, Iowa. ... 6-2/200. ... Full name: Kurtis Eugene Warner.
HIGH SCHOOL: Regis (Cedar Rapids, Iowa).
COLLEGE: Northern Iowa.
TRANSACTIONS/CAREER NOTES: Signed as non-drafted free agent by Green Bay Packers (April 28, 1994). ... Released by Packers prior to 1994 season. ... Played for Iowa Barnstormers of Arena Football League (1995-97). ... Signed by St. Louis Rams (December 26, 1997). ... Assigned by Rams to Amsterdam Admirals in 1998 NFL Europe enhancement allocation program (February 18, 1998). ... On injured reserve with hand injury (December 12, 2002-remaider of season). ... Released by Rams (June 2, 2004). ... Signed by New York Giants (June 3, 2004). ... Granted unconditional free agency (March 2, 2005). ... Signed by Arizona Cardinals (March 6, 2005).
CHAMPIONSHIP GAME EXPERIENCE: Played in NFC championship game (1999 and 2001 seasons). ... Member of Super Bowl championship team (1999 season). ... Played in Super Bowl 36 (2001 season).
HONORS: Named NFL Player of the Year by THE SPORTING NEWS (1999). ... Named quarterback on THE SPORTING NEWS NFL All-Pro team (1999 and 2001). ... Named Most Valuable Player of Super Bowl 34 (1999 season). ... Played in Pro Bowl (1999 and 2001 seasons). ... Named to play in Pro Bowl (2000 season); replaced by Donovan McNabb due to injury.
RECORDS: Shares NFL record for most consecutive games with 300 or more yards passing—6 (September 4-October 15, 2000).
POST SEASON RECORDS: Holds Super Bowl single-game record for most yards passing—414 (January 30, 2000, vs. Tennessee).
SINGLE GAME HIGHS (regular season): Attempts—54 (September 7, 2003, vs. New York Giants); completions—35 (September 10, 2000, vs. Seattle); yards—441 (September 4, 2000, vs. Denver); and touchdown passes—5 (October 10, 1999, vs. San Francisco).
STATISTICAL PLATEAUS: 300-yard passing games: 1999 (9), 2000 (8), 2001 (9), 2002 (3), 2003 (1). Total: 30.
MISCELLANEOUS: Regular-season record as starting NFL quarterback: 40-19 (.678). ... Postseason record as starting NFL quarterback: 5-2 (.714).

			PASSING									RUSHING				TOTALS		
Year Team	G	GS	Att.	Cmp.	Pct.	Yds.	TD	Int.	Avg.	Skd.	Rat.	Att.	Yds.	Avg.	TD	TD	2pt.	Pts.
1998—St. Louis NFL	1	0	11	4	36.4	39	0	0	3.55	0	47.2	0	0	0.0	0	0	0	0
1999—St. Louis NFL	16	16	499	325	*65.1	4353	*41	13	*8.72	29	*109.2	23	92	4.0	1	1	0	6
2000—St. Louis NFL	11	11	347	235	*67.7	3429	21	18	*9.88	20	98.3	18	17	0.9	0	0	0	0
2001—St. Louis NFL	16	16	546	*375	*68.7	*4830	*36	∞22	*8.85	38	*101.4	28	60	2.1	0	0	0	0
2002—St. Louis NFL	7	6	220	144	65.5	1431	3	11	6.50	21	67.4	8	33	4.1	0	0	0	0
2003—St. Louis NFL	2	1	65	38	58.5	365	I	1	5.62	6	72.9	1	0	0.0	0	0	0	0
2004—New York Giants NFL	10	9	277	174	62.8	2054	6	4	7.42	39	86.5	13	30	2.3	1	1	0	6
Pro totals (7 years)	03	59	1965	1295	65.9	16501	108	69	8.40	153	95.7	91	232	2.5	2	2	0	12

PERSONAL: Born September 26, 1975, in Independence, Kan. ... 6-3/270.
HIGH SCHOOL: Independence (Kan.).
JUNIOR COLLEGE: Independence (Kan.) Community College.
COLLEGE: Kansas.
TRANSACTIONS/CAREER NOTES: Selected by New Orleans Saints in seventh round (239th pick overall) of 1998 NFL draft. ... Signed by Saints (July 23, 1998). ... On non-football injury list with knee injury (August 25-November 4, 1998). ... Released by Saints (September 5, 1999). ... Signed by Washington Redskins to practice (September 14, 1999). ... Released by Redskins (November 24, 1999). ... Signed by Chicago Bears to practice squad (December 22, 1999). ... Granted free agency following 1999 season. ... Signed by Buccaneers (March 4, 2001). ... Released by Buccaneers (September 8, 2001). ... Re-signed by Buccaneers to practice squad (September 10, 2001). ... On suspended list (September 1-30, 2002). ... Released by Buccaneers (October 7, 2002). ... Re-signed by Buccaneers (November 28, 2002). ... Released by Buccaneers (October 7, 2003). ... Signed by Redskins (October 21, 2003). ... Waived by Redskins (October 30, 2003). ... Re-signed by Redskins (December 23, 2003).
CHAMPIONSHIP GAME EXPERIENCE: Played in NFC championship game (2002 season). ... Member of Super Bowl championship team (2002 season).
HONORS: Named outside linebacker on THE SPORTING NEWS college All-America second team (1997).

			TOTALS			INTERCEPTIONS			
Year Team	G	GS	Tk.	Ast.	Sks.	No.	Yds.	Avg.	TD
1998—New Orleans NFL	1	0	2	2	0.0	0	0	0.0	0
2002—Tampa Bay NFL	4	0	0	0	0.0	0	0	0.0	0
2003—Tampa Bay NFL	4	0	0	1	0.0	0	0	0.0	0
—Washington NFL	1	0	0	0	0.0	0	0	0.0	0
2004—Washington NFL	14	2	9	3	3.5	1	39	39.0	0
Pro totals (4 years)	24	2	11	6	3.5	1	39	39.0	0

W

PERSONAL: Born July 25, 1978, in Lake City, Fla. ... 6-4/325. ... Full name: Gerard T. Warren.
HIGH SCHOOL: Union City (Raiford, Fla.).
COLLEGE: Florida.
TRANSACTIONS/CAREER NOTES: Selected by Cleveland Browns in first round (third pick overall) of 2001 draft. ... Signed by Browns (August 1, 2001). ... Traded by Browns to Denver Broncos for fourth-round (traded to Seattle) pick in 2005 draft (March 2, 2005).

			TOTALS		
Year Team	G	GS	Tk.	Ast.	Sks.
2001—Cleveland NFL	15	15	48	13	5.0
2002—Cleveland NFL	16	16	30	10	2.0
2003—Cleveland NFL	16	15	24	8	5.5
2004—Cleveland NFL	13	13	14	5	4.0
Pro totals (4 years)	60	59	116	36	16.5

WARREN, TY   DT/DE   PATRIOTS

PERSONAL: Born February 6, 1981, in Bryan, Texas. ... 6-5/300. ... Full name: Ty'ron Markeith Warren.
HIGH SCHOOL: Bryan (Texas).
COLLEGE: Texas A&M.
TRANSACTIONS/CAREER NOTES: Selected by New England Patriots in first round (13th pick overall) of 2003 NFL draft. ... Signed by Patriots (July 21, 2003).
CHAMPIONSHIP GAME EXPERIENCE: Played in AFC championship game (2003 and 2004 seasons). ... Member of Super Bowl championship team (2003 and 2004 seasons).

			TOTALS		
Year Team	G	GS	Tk.	Ast.	Sks.
2003—New England NFL	16	4	19	14	1.0
2004—New England NFL	16	16	40	9	3.5
Pro totals (2 years)	32	20	59	23	4.5

WARRICK, PETER   WR/PR   BENGALS

PERSONAL: Born June 19, 1977, in Bradenton, Fla. ... 5-11/192.
HIGH SCHOOL: Southeast (Bradenton, Fla.).
COLLEGE: Florida State.
TRANSACTIONS/CAREER NOTES: Selected by Cincinnati Bengals in first round (fourth pick overall) of 2000 NFL draft. ... Signed by Bengals (June 4, 2000). ... On injured reserve with shin injury (November 5, 2004-remainder of season).
HONORS: Named wide receiver on THE SPORTING NEWS college All-America first team (1998 and 1999).
SINGLE GAME HIGHS (regular season): Receptions—11 (December 7, 2003, vs. Baltimore); yards—114 (November 16, 2003, vs. Kansas City); and touchdown receptions—2 (December 8, 2002, vs. Carolina).
STATISTICAL PLATEAUS: 100-yard receiving games: 2001 (1), 2003 (2). Total: 3.

			RUSHING				RECEIVING				PUNT RETURNS				TOTALS			
Year Team	G	GS	Att.	Yds.	Avg.	TD	No.	Yds.	Avg.	TD	No.	Yds.	Avg.	TD	TD	2pt.	Pts.	Fum.
2000—Cincinnati NFL	16	16	16	148	9.3	2	51	592	11.6	4	7	123	17.6	1	7	0	42	2
2001—Cincinnati NFL	16	14	8	14	1.8	0	70	667	9.5	1	18	116	6.4	0	1	0	6	3
2002—Cincinnati NFL	15	10	8	22	2.8	0	53	606	11.4	6	4	14	3.5	0	6	0	36	2
2003—Cincinnati NFL	15	14	18	157	8.7	0	79	819	10.4	7	25	273	10.9	1	8	0	48	2
2004—Cincinnati NFL	4	1	2	14	7.0	0	11	127	11.5	0	0	0	0.0	0	0	0	0	0
Pro totals (5 years)	66	55	52	355	6.8	2	264	2811	10.6	18	54	526	9.7	2	22	0	132	9

WASHINGTON, DEWAYNE   CB

PERSONAL: Born December 27, 1972, in Durham, N.C. ... 5-11/193. ... Full name: Dewayne Neron Washington.
HIGH SCHOOL: Northern (Durham, N.C.).
COLLEGE: North Carolina State.
TRANSACTIONS/CAREER NOTES: Selected by Minnesota Vikings in first round (18th pick overall) of 1994 NFL draft. ... Signed by Vikings (July 14, 1994). ... Granted unconditional free agency (February 13, 1998). ... Signed by Pittsburgh Steelers (February 25, 1998). ... Released by Steelers (February 27, 2003). ... Signed by Jacksonville Jaguars (March 9, 2004). ... Released by Jaguars (March 3, 2005).
CHAMPIONSHIP GAME EXPERIENCE: Played in AFC championship game (2001 season).

			TOTALS			INTERCEPTIONS			
Year Team	G	GS	Tk.	Ast.	Sks.	No.	Yds.	Avg.	TD
1994—Minnesota NFL	16	16	68	7	0.0	3	135	45.0	2
1995—Minnesota NFL	15	14	54	8	0.0	1	25	25.0	0
1996—Minnesota NFL	16	16	69	6	0.0	2	27	13.5	1
1997—Minnesota NFL	16	16	74	10	0.0	4	71	17.8	0
1998—Pittsburgh NFL	16	16	79	14	0.0	5	§178	35.6	▲2
1999—Pittsburgh NFL	16	16	50	2	0.0	4	1	0.3	0
2000—Pittsburgh NFL	16	16	69	9	0.0	5	59	11.8	0
2001—Pittsburgh NFL	16	16	66	11	1.0	1	15	15.0	0
2002—Pittsburgh NFL	16	16	45	9	0.0	3	51	17.0	0
2003—Pittsburgh NFL	16	12	50	5	0.0	1	7	7.0	0
2004—Jacksonville NFL	16	16	68	9	0.0	2	0	0.0	0
Pro totals (11 years)	175	170	692	90	1.0	31	569	18.4	5

WASHINGTON, KEITH   DE

PERSONAL: Born December 18, 1972, in Dallas, Texas. ... 6-4/285. ... Full name: Keith L. Washington.
HIGH SCHOOL: Wilmer-Hutchins (Dallas).
COLLEGE: Nevada-Las Vegas.
TRANSACTIONS/CAREER NOTES: Signed as non-drafted free agent by Minnesota Vikings (April 9, 1995). ... Released by Vikings (August 27, 1995). ... Re-signed by Vikings to practice squad (August 28, 1995). ... Activated (October 9, 1995); did not play. ... On injured reserve with ankle injury (November 15, 1995-remainder of season). ... Released by Vikings (August 25, 1996). ... Signed by Detroit Lions (August 26, 1996). ... Released by Lions (August 26, 1997). ... Signed by Baltimore Ravens (October 15, 1997). ... Granted free agency (February 13, 1998). ... Re-signed by Ravens (April 14, 1998). ... Granted unconditional free agency (February 11, 2000). ... Re-signed by Ravens (March 31, 2000). ... Released by Ravens (March 13, 2001). ... Signed by Denver Broncos (April 6, 2001). ... Released by Broncos (February 25, 2003). ... Signed by New York Giants (March 28, 2003). ... Granted unconditional free agency (March 3, 2004). ... Re-signed by Giants (March 3, 2004). ... On injured reserve with knee injury (November 9, 2004-remainder of season). ... Released by Giants (March 15, 2005).
CHAMPIONSHIP GAME EXPERIENCE: Played in AFC championship game (2000 season). ... Member of Super Bowl championship team (2000 season).

W

Year Team	G	GS	TOTALS			INTERCEPTIONS			
			Tk.	Ast.	Sks.	No.	Yds.	Avg.	TD
1996—Detroit NFL	12	0	7	0	0.0	0	0	0.0	0
1997—Baltimore NFL	10	1	14	4	2.0	0	0	0.0	0
1998—Baltimore NFL	16	0	13	2	1.0	0	0	0.0	0
1999—Baltimore NFL	16	0	9	2	1.0	0	0	0.0	0
2000—Baltimore NFL	16	0	11	7	0.0	0	0	0.0	0
2001—Denver NFL	16	16	27	9	4.0	0	0	0.0	0
2002—Denver NFL	10	0	9	0	0.0	1	-2	-2.0	0
2003—New York Giants NFL	14	6	16	8	1.0	0	0	0.0	0
2004—New York Giants NFL	8	8	12	5	1.0	0	0	0.0	0
Pro totals (9 years)	118	31	118	37	10.0	1	-2	-2.0	0

WASHINGTON, KELLEY — WR — BENGALS

PERSONAL: Born August 21, 1979, in Stephens City, Va. ... 6-3/218. ... Full name: James Kelley Washington.
HIGH SCHOOL: Sherando (Stephens City, Va.).
COLLEGE: Tennessee.
TRANSACTIONS/CAREER NOTES: Selected after junior season by Cincinnati Bengals in third round (65th pick overall) of 2003 NFL draft. ... Signed by Bengals (August 3, 2003).
SINGLE GAME HIGHS (regular season): Receptions—5 (September 26, 2004, vs. Baltimore); yards—61 (November 23, 2003, vs. San Diego); and touchdown receptions—1 (December 12, 2004, vs. New England).
MISCELLANEOUS: Selected by Florida Marlins organization in 10th round of free-agent draft (June 2, 1997).

Year Team	G	GS	RECEIVING				TOTALS			
			No.	Yds.	Avg.	TD	TD	2pt.	Pts.	Fum.
2003—Cincinnati NFL	16	3	22	299	13.6	4	4	0	24	0
2004—Cincinnati NFL	16	2	31	378	12.2	3	3	0	18	0
Pro totals (2 years)	32	5	53	677	12.8	7	7	0	42	0

WASHINGTON, MARCUS — LB — REDSKINS

PERSONAL: Born October 17, 1977, in Auburn, Ala. ... 6-3/247. ... Full name: Marcus Cornelius Washington.
HIGH SCHOOL: Auburn (Ala.).
COLLEGE: Auburn.
TRANSACTIONS/CAREER NOTES: Selected by Indianapolis Colts in second round (59th pick overall) of 2000 NFL draft. ... Signed by Colts (July 13, 2000). ... Granted unconditional free agency (March 3, 2004). ... Signed by Washington Redskins (March 5, 2004).
CHAMPIONSHIP GAME EXPERIENCE: Played in AFC championship game (2003 season).
HONORS: Played in Pro Bowl (2004 season).

Year Team	G	GS	TOTALS			INTERCEPTIONS			
			Tk.	Ast.	Sks.	No.	Yds.	Avg.	TD
2000—Indianapolis NFL	16	0	6	5	2.0	1	1	1.0	0
2001—Indianapolis NFL	16	16	74	20	8.0	0	0	0.0	0
2002—Indianapolis NFL	15	15	47	19	2.0	1	40	40.0	1
2003—Indianapolis NFL	16	16	55	25	6.0	0	0	0.0	0
2004—Washington NFL	16	16	83	19	4.5	0	0	0.0	0
Pro totals (5 years)	79	63	265	88	22.5	2	41	20.5	1

WASHINGTON, RASHAD — DB — JETS

PERSONAL: Born March 15, 1980, in Wichita, Kan. ... 6-1/217.
HIGH SCHOOL: Southeast (Wichita, Kan.).
COLLEGE: Kansas State.
TRANSACTIONS/CAREER NOTES: Selected by New York Jets in seventh round (236th pick overall) of 2004 NFL draft. ... Signed by Jets (June 9, 2004).

Year Team	G	GS	TOTALS			INTERCEPTIONS			
			Tk.	Ast.	Sks.	No.	Yds.	Avg.	TD
2004—New York Jets NFL	6	0	0	0	0.0	0	0	0.0	0

WASHINGTON, TED — DT — RAIDERS

PERSONAL: Born April 13, 1968, in Tampa, Fla. ... 6-5/365. ... Full name: Theodore Washington. ... Son of Ted Washington, linebacker with New York Jets (1973) and Houston Oilers (1974-82).
HIGH SCHOOL: Tampa Bay Vocational Tech Senior.
COLLEGE: Louisville.
TRANSACTIONS/CAREER NOTES: Selected by San Francisco 49ers in first round (25th pick overall) of 1991 NFL draft. ... Signed by 49ers (July 10, 1991). ... Traded by 49ers to Denver Broncos for fifth-round pick (traded to Green Bay) in 1994 draft (April 19, 1994). ... Granted unconditional free agency (February 17, 1995). ... Signed by Buffalo Bills (February 25, 1995). ... Designated by Bills as franchise player (February 13, 1998). ... Free agency status changed from franchise to transitional (February 27, 1998). ... Re-signed by Bills (March 2, 1998). ... Released by Bills (February 22, 2001). ... Signed by Chicago Bears (April 10, 2001). ... On injured reserve with leg injury (November 29, 2002-remainder of season). ... Traded by Bears to New England Patriots for a fourth-round pick (traded to Washington) in 2004 NFL draft (August 19, 2003). ... Granted unconditional free agency (March 3, 2004). ... Signed by Oakland Raiders (March 4, 2004).
CHAMPIONSHIP GAME EXPERIENCE: Played in NFC championship game (1992 and 1993 seasons). ... Played in AFC championship game (2003 season). ... Member of Super Bowl championship team (2003 season).
HONORS: Played in Pro Bowl (1997, 1998, 2000 and 2001 seasons). ... Named defensive tackle on THE SPORTING NEWS NFL All-Pro team (2001).

Year Team	G	GS	TOTALS			INTERCEPTIONS			
			Tk.	Ast.	Sks.	No.	Yds.	Avg.	TD
1991—San Francisco NFL	16	0	20	1	1.0	0	0	0.0	0
1992—San Francisco NFL	16	6	27	8	2.0	0	0	0.0	0
1993—San Francisco NFL	12	12	36	5	3.0	0	0	0.0	0
1994—Denver NFL	15	15	44	12	2.5	1	5	5.0	0
1995—Buffalo NFL	16	15	42	11	2.5	0	0	0.0	0
1996—Buffalo NFL	16	16	70	22	3.5	0	0	0.0	0
1997—Buffalo NFL	16	16	63	17	4.0	0	0	0.0	0
1998—Buffalo NFL	16	16	35	15	4.5	1	0	0.0	0
1999—Buffalo NFL	16	16	35	10	2.5	0	0	0.0	0
2000—Buffalo NFL	16	16	37	21	2.5	0	0	0.0	0
2001—Chicago NFL	16	15	26	8	1.5	0	0	0.0	0
2002—Chicago NFL	2	2	4	1	0.0	0	0	0.0	0
2003—New England NFL	10	10	32	8	2.0	0	0	0.0	0
2004—Oakland NFL	16	16	33	8	3.0	0	0	0.0	0
Pro totals (14 years)	199	171	504	147	34.5	2	5	2.5	0

WASHINGTON, TODD   C   TEXANS

PERSONAL: Born September 19, 1976, in Nassawadox, Va. ... 6-3/317. ... Full name: Todd Page Washington.
HIGH SCHOOL: Nandua (Onley, Va.).
COLLEGE: Virginia Tech.
TRANSACTIONS/CAREER NOTES: Selected by Tampa Bay Buccaneers in fourth round (104th pick overall) of 1998 NFL draft. ... Signed by Buccaneers (June 11, 1998). ... Granted free agency (March 2, 2001). ... Re-signed by Buccaneers (March 14, 2001). ... Granted unconditional free agency (March 1, 2002). ... Re-signed by Buccaneers (March 18, 2002). ... Signed by Houston Texans (March 24, 2003). ... Granted unconditional free agency (March 3, 2004). ... Re-signed by Texans (March 4, 2004).
PLAYING EXPERIENCE: Tampa Bay NFL, 1998-2002; Houston NFL, 2003-2004. ... Games/Games started: 1998 (4/0), 1999 (6/0), 2000 (9/0), 2001 (15/1), 2002 (16/2), 2003 (16/14), 2004 (15/0). Total: 81/17.
CHAMPIONSHIP GAME EXPERIENCE: Played in NFC championship game (1999 and 2002 seasons). ... Member of Super Bowl championship team (2002).

WATERS, BRIAN   G   CHIEFS

PERSONAL: Born February 18, 1977, in Waxahachie, Texas. ... 6-3/318. ... Full name: Brian Demond Waters.
HIGH SCHOOL: Waxahachie (Texas).
COLLEGE: North Texas.
TRANSACTIONS/CAREER NOTES: Signed as non-drafted free agent by Dallas Cowboys (April 23, 1999). ... Released by Cowboys (September 5, 1999). ... Signed by Kansas City Chiefs (January 11, 2000).
PLAYING EXPERIENCE: Kansas City NFL, 2000-2004. ... Games/Games started: 2000 (6/0), 2001 (16/8), 2002 (16/16), 2003 (16/16), 2004 (16/16). Total: 70/56.
HONORS: Named guard on THE SPORTING NEWS NFL All-Pro team (2004). ... Played in Pro Bowl (2004 season).

WATSON, BEN   TE   PATRIOTS

PERSONAL: Born December 18, 1980, in Norfolk, Va. ... 6-3/253. ... Full name: Benjamin Watson.
HIGH SCHOOL: Northwestern (Rock Hill, S.C.).
COLLEGE: Georgia.
TRANSACTIONS/CAREER NOTES: Selected by New England Patriots in first round (32nd pick overall) of 2004 NFL draft. ... Signed by Patriots (August 15, 2004). ... On injured reserve with knee injury (September 29, 2004-remainder of season).
SINGLE GAME HIGHS (regular season): Receptions—2 (September 9, 2004, vs. Indianapolis); yards—16 (September 9, 2004, vs. Indianapolis); and touchdown receptions—0.

Year Team	G	GS	RECEIVING				TOTALS			
			No.	Yds.	Avg.	TD	TD	2pt.	Pts.	Fum.
2004—New England NFL	1	1	2	16	8.0	0	0	0	0	0

WATSON, COURTNEY   LB   SAINTS

PERSONAL: Born September 18, 1980, in Sarasota, Fla. ... 6-1/246.
HIGH SCHOOL: Riverview (Sarasota, Fla.).
COLLEGE: Notre Dame.
TRANSACTIONS/CAREER NOTES: Selected by New Orleans Saints in second round (60th pick overall) of 2004 NFL draft. ... Signed by Saints (July 29, 2004).

Year Team	G	GS	TOTALS			INTERCEPTIONS			
			Tk.	Ast.	Sks.	No.	Yds.	Avg.	TD
2004—New Orleans NFL	12	8	38	17	2.0	0	0	0.0	0

WATSON, KENNY   RB   BENGALS

PERSONAL: Born March 13, 1978, in Harrisburg, Pa. ... 5-11/218.
HIGH SCHOOL: Harrisburg (Pa.).
COLLEGE: Penn State.

W

TRANSACTIONS/CAREER NOTES: Signed as non-drafted free agent by Washington Redskins (April 23, 2001). ... Released by Redskins (October 16, 2001). ... Re-signed by Redskins to practice squad (October 18, 2001). ... Waived by Redskins (August 31, 2003). ... Signed by Cincinnati Bengals (September 30, 2003). ... Granted free agency (March 2, 2005). ... Re-signed by Bengals (April 12, 2005).

SINGLE GAME HIGHS (regular season): Attempts—23 (November 3, 2002, vs. Seattle); yards—110 (December 22, 2002, vs. Houston); and rushing touchdowns—1 (December 29, 2002, vs. Dallas).

STATISTICAL PLATEAUS: 100-yard rushing games: 2002 (2). Total: 2.

			RUSHING				RECEIVING				KICKOFF RETURNS				TOTALS			
Year Team	G	GS	Att.	Yds.	Avg.	TD	No.	Yds.	Avg.	TD	No.	Yds.	Avg.	TD	TD	2pt.	Pts.	Fum.
2002—Washington NFL	16	4	116	534	4.6	1	32	253	7.9	1	23	496	21.6	0	2	0	12	0
2003—Cincinnati NFL	8	0	0	0	0.0	0	0	0	0.0	0	7	113	16.1	0	0	0	0	1
2004—Cincinnati NFL	16	0	26	161	6.2	0	25	171	6.8	1	13	240	18.5	0	1	0	6	2
Pro totals (3 years)	40	4	142	695	4.9	1	57	424	7.4	2	43	849	19.7	0	3	0	18	3

WATTS, DARIUS — WR — BRONCOS

PERSONAL: Born December 19, 1981, in Atlanta, Ga. ... 6-2/188. ... Full name: Darius Orlando Watts.
HIGH SCHOOL: Banneker (College Park, Ga.).
COLLEGE: Marshall.
TRANSACTIONS/CAREER NOTES: Selected by Denver Broncos in second round (54th pick overall) of 2004 NFL draft. ... Signed by Broncos (July 27, 2004).
HONORS: Named wide receiver on THE SPORTING NEWS college All-America fourth team (2001).
SINGLE GAME HIGHS (regular season): Receptions—7 (October 31, 2004, vs. Atlanta); yards—86 (October 31, 2004, vs. Atlanta); and touchdown receptions—1 (October 31, 2004, vs. Atlanta).

			RUSHING				RECEIVING				KICKOFF RETURNS				TOTALS			
Year Team	G	GS	Att.	Yds.	Avg.	TD	No.	Yds.	Avg.	TD	No.	Yds.	Avg.	TD	TD	2pt.	Pts.	Fum.
2004—Denver NFL	16	2	5	33	6.6	0	31	385	12.4	1	0	0	0.0	0	1	0	6	1

WAYNE, NATE — LB — JAGUARS

PERSONAL: Born January 12, 1975, in Chicago, Ill. ... 6-0/237.
HIGH SCHOOL: Noxubee County (Macon, Miss.).
COLLEGE: Mississippi.
TRANSACTIONS/CAREER NOTES: Selected by Denver Broncos in seventh round (219th pick overall) of 1998 NFL draft. ... Signed by Broncos (June 9, 1998). ... Assigned by Broncos to Barcelona Dragons in 1999 NFL Europe enhancement allocation program (February 22, 1999). ... Released by Broncos (September 19, 1999). ... Re-signed by Broncos to practice squad (September 21, 1999). ... Activated (September 22, 1999). ... Traded by Broncos to Green Bay Packers for conditional future draft pick (August 15, 2000). ... Released by Packers (March 10, 2003). ... Signed by Philadelphia Eagles (March 14, 2003). ... Released by Eagles (February 24, 2005). ... Signed by Jacksonville Jaguars (May 12, 2005).
CHAMPIONSHIP GAME EXPERIENCE: Member of Broncos for AFC championship game (1998 season); inactive. ... Played in NFC championship game (2003 and 2004 seasons). ... Member of Super Bowl championship team (1998 season); inactive. ... Played in Super Bowl 39 (2004 season).

			TOTALS			INTERCEPTIONS			
Year Team	G	GS	Tk.	Ast.	Sks.	No.	Yds.	Avg.	TD
1998—Denver NFL	1	0	0	0	0.0	0	0	0.0	0
1999—Denver NFL	16	0	8	2	2.0	0	0	0.0	0
2000—Green Bay NFL	16	13	75	26	2.0	0	0	0.0	0
2001—Green Bay NFL	12	12	60	26	5.5	3	55	18.3	0
2002—Green Bay NFL	16	15	70	41	2.5	3	32	10.7	0
2003—Philadelphia NFL	16	16	69	21	3.0	1	33	33.0	0
2004—Philadelphia NFL	9	7	23	7	1.0	0	0	0.0	0
Pro totals (7 years)	86	63	305	123	16.0	7	120	17.1	0

WAYNE, REGGIE — WR — COLTS

PERSONAL: Born November 17, 1978, in New Orleans, La. ... 6-0/198.
HIGH SCHOOL: Ehret (La.).
COLLEGE: Miami (Fla.).
TRANSACTIONS/CAREER NOTES: Selected by Indianapolis Colts in first round (30th pick overall) of 2001 NFL draft. ... Signed by Colts (July 26, 2001).
CHAMPIONSHIP GAME EXPERIENCE: Played in AFC championship game (2003 season).
SINGLE GAME HIGHS (regular season): Receptions—11 (September 26, 2004, vs. Green Bay); yards—184 (September 26, 2004, vs. Green Bay); and touchdown receptions—2 (November 21, 2004, vs. Chicago).
STATISTICAL PLATEAUS: 100-yard receiving games: 2002 (3), 2003 (2), 2004 (4). Total: 9.

			RECEIVING				TOTALS			
Year Team	G	GS	No.	Yds.	Avg.	TD	TD	2pt.	Pts.	Fum.
2001—Indianapolis NFL	13	9	27	345	12.8	0	0	0	0	0
2002—Indianapolis NFL	16	7	49	716	14.6	4	4	0	24	2
2003—Indianapolis NFL	16	16	68	838	12.3	7	7	0	42	0
2004—Indianapolis NFL	16	16	77	1210	15.7	12	12	0	72	0
Pro totals (4 years)	61	48	221	3109	14.1	23	23	0	138	2

WEARY, FRED — G — TEXANS

PERSONAL: Born September 30, 1977, in Montgomery, Ala. ... 6-4/308. ... Full name: Fred Edward Weary Jr.
HIGH SCHOOL: Robert E. Lee (Montgomery, Ala.).
COLLEGE: Tennessee.

W

TRANSACTIONS/CAREER NOTES: Selected by Houston Texans in third round (66th pick overall) of 2002 NFL draft. ... Signed by Texans (July 17, 2002).

PLAYING EXPERIENCE: Houston NFL, 2002-2004. ... Games/Games started: 2002 (16/12), 2003 (14/2), 2004 (2/1). Total: 32/15.

HONORS: Named guard on THE SPORTING NEWS college All-America second team (2001).

WEAVER, ANTHONY　　　　　DE　　　　　RAVENS

PERSONAL: Born July 28, 1980, in Abilene, Texas. ... 6-3/290. ... Full name: Anthony Lee Weaver.
HIGH SCHOOL: Saratoga Springs (N.Y.).
COLLEGE: Notre Dame.
TRANSACTIONS/CAREER NOTES: Selected by Baltimore Ravens in second round (52nd pick overall) of 2002 NFL draft. ... Signed by Ravens (July 27, 2002).

Year　Team	G	GS	Tk.	Ast.	Sks.	No.	Yds.	Avg.	TD
			TOTALS			**INTERCEPTIONS**			
2002—Baltimore NFL	16	16	27	4	3.5	0	0	0.0	0
2003—Baltimore NFL	15	15	27	9	5.0	0	0	0.0	0
2004—Baltimore NFL	16	15	35	4	4.0	1	1	1.0	0
Pro totals (3 years)	47	46	89	17	12.5	1	1	1.0	0

WEAVER, JED　　　　　TE　　　　　PATRIOTS

PERSONAL: Born August 11, 1976, in Bend, Ore. ... 6-4/258. ... Full name: Timothy Jed Weaver.
HIGH SCHOOL: Redmond (Ore.).
COLLEGE: Oregon.
TRANSACTIONS/CAREER NOTES: Selected by Philadelphia Eagles in seventh round (208th pick overall) of 1999 NFL draft. ... Signed by Eagles (July 16, 1999). ... Claimed on waivers by Miami Dolphins (August 23, 2000). ... Granted free agency (March 1, 2002). ... Re-signed by Dolphins (April 1, 2002). ... Granted unconditional free agency (February 28, 2003). ... Signed by San Francisco 49ers (March 11, 2003). ... Granted unconditional free agency (March 3, 2004). ... Signed by Denver Broncos (March 19, 2004). ... Released by Broncos (September 5, 2004). ... Signed by New England Patriots (September 29, 2004).
CHAMPIONSHIP GAME EXPERIENCE: Member of Patriots for AFC championship game (2004 season); inactive. ... Member of Patriots for Super Bowl 39 (2004 season); inactive.
SINGLE GAME HIGHS (regular season): Receptions—5 (December 24, 2000, vs. New England); yards—76 (December 7, 2003, vs. Arizona); and touchdown receptions—1 (December 27, 2003, vs. Seattle).

Year　Team	G	GS	No.	Yds.	Avg.	TD	TD	2pt.	Pts.	Fum.
			RECEIVING				**TOTALS**			
1999—Philadelphia NFL	16	10	11	91	8.3	0	0	1	2	0
2000—Miami NFL	16	0	10	179	17.9	0	0	0	0	1
2001—Miami NFL	16	7	18	215	11.9	2	2	0	12	1
2002—Miami NFL	16	4	6	75	12.5	3	3	0	18	0
2003—San Francisco NFL	16	16	35	437	12.5	1	1	0	6	1
2004—New England NFL	10	1	8	93	11.6	0	0	0	0	0
Pro totals (6 years)	90	38	88	1090	12.4	6	6	1	38	3

WEBSTER, JASON　　　　　CB　　　　　FALCONS

PERSONAL: Born September 8, 1977, in Houston, Texas. ... 5-9/187. ... Full name: Jason Richmond Webster.
HIGH SCHOOL: Willowridge (Houston).
COLLEGE: Texas A&M.
TRANSACTIONS/CAREER NOTES: Selected by San Francisco 49ers in second round (48th pick overall) of 2000 NFL draft. ... Signed by 49ers (July 18, 2000). ... On physically unable to perform list with knee injury (July 25-September 7, 2003). ... Granted unconditional free agency (March 3, 2004). ... Signed by Atlanta Falcons (March 5, 2004).
CHAMPIONSHIP GAME EXPERIENCE: Played in NFC championship game (2004 season).

Year　Team	G	GS	Tk.	Ast.	Sks.	No.	Yds.	Avg.	TD
			TOTALS			**INTERCEPTIONS**			
2000—San Francisco NFL	16	10	41	14	0.0	2	78	39.0	1
2001—San Francisco NFL	16	16	69	7	0.5	3	61	20.3	0
2002—San Francisco NFL	16	16	71	14	0.0	1	37	37.0	1
2003—San Francisco NFL	5	2	7	3	0.0	1	17	17.0	0
2004—Atlanta NFL	10	9	39	2	0.0	1	18	18.0	0
Pro totals (5 years)	63	53	227	40	0.5	8	211	26.4	2

W

WEBSTER, NATE　　　　　LB　　　　　BENGALS

PERSONAL: Born November 29, 1977, in Miami, Fla. ... 6-0/235. ... Full name: Nathaniel Webster Jr.
HIGH SCHOOL: Northwestern (Miami).
COLLEGE: Miami (Fla.).
TRANSACTIONS/CAREER NOTES: Selected after junior season by Tampa Bay Buccaneers in third round (90th pick overall) of 2000 NFL draft. ... Signed by Buccaneers (July 11, 2000). ... Granted free agency (February 28, 2003). ... Re-signed by Buccaneers (April 24, 2003). ... Granted unconditional free agency (March 3, 2004). ... Signed by Cincinnati Bengals (March 4, 2004). ... On injured reserve with knee injury (September 29, 2004-remainder of season).
CHAMPIONSHIP GAME EXPERIENCE: Played in NFC championship game (2002 season). ... Member of Super Bowl championship team (2002 season).
HONORS: Named linebacker on THE SPORTING NEWS college All-America second team (1999).

Year Team	G	GS	TOTALS Tk.	Ast.	Sks.	INTERCEPTIONS No.	Yds.	Avg.	TD
2000—Tampa Bay NFL	16	0	17	3	0.0	0	0	0.0	0
2001—Tampa Bay NFL	16	1	25	11	0.0	0	0	0.0	0
2002—Tampa Bay NFL	16	0	14	9	0.0	0	0	0.0	0
2003—Tampa Bay NFL	15	5	25	26	1.0	0	0	0.0	0
2004—Cincinnati NFL	3	3	16	5	1.0	0	0	0.0	0
Pro totals (5 years)	66	9	97	54	2.0	0	0	0.0	0

WEINER, TODD　　　　　T　　　　　FALCONS

PERSONAL: Born September 16, 1975, in Bristol, Pa. ... 6-4/297.
HIGH SCHOOL: Taravella (Coral Springs, Fla.).
COLLEGE: Kansas State.
TRANSACTIONS/CAREER NOTES: Selected by Seattle Seahawks in second round (47th pick overall) of 1998 NFL draft. ... Signed by Seahawks (July 15, 1998). ... Granted unconditional free agency (March 1, 2002). ... Signed by Atlanta Falcons (March 6, 2002).
PLAYING EXPERIENCE: Seattle NFL, 1998-2001; Atlanta NFL, 2002-2004. ... Games/Games started: 1998 (6/0), 1999 (11/1), 2000 (16/6), 2001 (16/13), 2002 (16/15), 2003 (16/16), 2004 (16/16). Total: 97/67.
CHAMPIONSHIP GAME EXPERIENCE: Played in NFC championship game (2004 season).
HONORS: Named offensive tackle on THE SPORTING NEWS college All-America second team (1997).

WELBOURN, JOHN　　　　　G/T　　　　　CHIEFS

PERSONAL: Born March 30, 1976, in Torrance, Calif. ... 6-5/310. ... Full name: John R. Welbourn.
HIGH SCHOOL: Palos Verdes Peninsula (Rolling Hills Estate, Calif.).
COLLEGE: California.
TRANSACTIONS/CAREER NOTES: Selected by Philadelphia Eagles in fourth round (97th pick overall) of 1999 NFL draft. ... Signed by Eagles (July 25, 1999). ... On injured reserve with knee injury (September 13, 1999-remainder of season). ... Traded by Eagles to Kansas City Chiefs for fifth-round pick (RB Thomas Tapeh) in 2004 draft and third-round pick (RB Ryan Moats) in 2005 draft (April 25, 2004). ... On injured reserve with knee and hip injuries (November 25, 2004-remainder of season).
PLAYING EXPERIENCE: Philadelphia NFL, 1999-2003; Kansas City NFL, 2004. ... Games/Games started: 1999 (1/1), 2000 (16/16), 2001 (15/15), 2002 (11/11), 2003 (13/13), 2004 (10/10). Total: 66/66.
CHAMPIONSHIP GAME EXPERIENCE: Played in NFC championship game (2001-2003 seasons).

WELKER, WESLEY　　　　　WR/KR　　　　　DOLPHINS

PERSONAL: Born May 1, 1981, in Oklahoma City, Okla. ... 5-9/190.
HIGH SCHOOL: Heritage Hall (Oklahoma City, Okla.).
COLLEGE: Texas Tech.
TRANSACTIONS/CAREER NOTES: Signed as non-drafted free agent by San Diego Chargers (April 30, 2004). ... Released by Chargers (September 15, 2004). ... Signed by Miami Dolphins (September 21, 2004).

Year Team	G	GS	PUNT RETURNS No.	Yds.	Avg.	TD	KICKOFF RETURNS No.	Yds.	Avg.	TD	TOTALS TD	2pt.	Pts.	Fum.
2004—San Diego NFL	1	0	0	0	0.0	0	4	102	25.5	0	0	0	0	0
—Miami NFL	14	0	43	464	10.8	0	57	1313	23.0	1	1	0	6	4
Pro totals (1 year)	15	0	43	464	10.8	0	61	1415	23.2	1	1	0	6	4

WELLS, JONATHAN　　　　　RB

PERSONAL: Born July 21, 1979, in River Ridge, La. ... 6-1/252.
HIGH SCHOOL: John Curtis (River Ridge, La.).
COLLEGE: Ohio State.
TRANSACTIONS/CAREER NOTES: Selected by Houston Texans in fourth round (99th pick overall) of 2002 NFL draft. ... Signed by Texans (July 19, 2002). ... Granted free agency (March 2, 2005).
SINGLE GAME HIGHS (regular season): Attempts—26 (October 3, 2004, vs. Oakland); yards—105 (October 3, 2004, vs. Oakland); and rushing touchdowns—1 (November 28, 2004, vs. Tennessee).
STATISTICAL PLATEAUS: 100-yard rushing games: 2004 (1). Total: 1.

Year Team	G	GS	RUSHING Att.	Yds.	Avg.	TD	RECEIVING No.	Yds.	Avg.	TD	KICKOFF RETURNS No.	Yds.	Avg.	TD	TOTALS TD	2pt.	Pts.	Fum.
2002—Houston NFL	16	11	197	529	2.7	3	9	48	5.3	0	0	0	0.0	0	3	0	18	3
2003—Houston NFL	13	0	5	14	2.8	0	2	17	8.5	0	2	24	12.0	0	0	0	0	0
2004—Houston NFL	16	1	82	299	3.6	3	11	79	7.2	2	2	27	13.5	0	5	1	32	1
Pro totals (3 years)	45	12	284	842	3.0	6	22	144	6.5	2	4	51	12.8	0	8	1	50	4

W

WELLS, RAY　　　　　LB　　　　　49ERS

PERSONAL: Born August 20, 1980, in Oakland, Calif. ... 6-1/234.
HIGH SCHOOL: Mount Miguel (Spring Valley, Calif.).
JUNIOR COLLEGE: Mesa Junior College.
COLLEGE: Arizona.
TRANSACTIONS/CAREER NOTES: Signed as non-drafted free agent by San Francisco 49ers (May 2, 2003). ... Claimed on waivers by Tennessee Titans (September 1, 2003). ... Released by Titans (September 6, 2004). ... Signed by San Francisco 49ers (October 13, 2004). ... Released by 49ers (October 19, 2004). ... Re-signed by 49ers (October 26, 2004).

Year	Team	G	GS	TOTALS			INTERCEPTIONS			
				Tk.	Ast.	Sks.	No.	Yds.	Avg.	TD
2003—Tennessee NFL		16	0	1	0	0.0	0	0	0.0	0
2004—San Francisco NFL		6	0	0	0	0.0	0	0	0.0	0
Pro totals (2 years)		22	0	1	0	0.0	0	0	0.0	0

WELLS, REGGIE   T   CARDINALS

PERSONAL: Born November 3, 1980, in Liberty, Pa. ... 6-4/323.
HIGH SCHOOL: South Park (Liberty, Pa.).
COLLEGE: Clarion.
TRANSACTIONS/CAREER NOTES: Selected by Arizona Cardinals in sixth round (177th pick overall) of 2003 NFL draft. ... Signed by Cardinals (June 4, 2003).
PLAYING EXPERIENCE: Arizona NFL, 2003-2004. ... Games/Games started: 2003 (15/1), 2004 (16/16). Total: 31/17.

WELLS, SCOTT   C   PACKERS

PERSONAL: Born January 7, 1981, in Spring Hill, Tenn. ... 6-2/300. ... Full name: Scott Darvin Wells.
HIGH SCHOOL: Brentwood Academy (Spring Hill, Tenn.).
COLLEGE: Tennessee.
TRANSACTIONS/CAREER NOTES: Selected by Green Bay Packers in seventh round (251st pick overall) of 2004 NFL draft. ... Signed by Packers (July 29, 2004). ... Released by Packers (September 5, 2004). ... Re-signed by Packers to practice squad (September 6, 2004). ... Activated (October 2, 2004).
PLAYING EXPERIENCE: Green Bay NFL, 2004. ... Games/Games started: 2004 (5/2). Total: 5/2.
HONORS: Named offensive lineman on THE SPORTING NEWS Freshman All-America third team (2000).

WESLEY, DANTE   CB

PERSONAL: Born April 5, 1979, in St. Louis, Mo. ... 6-0/211.
HIGH SCHOOL: Watson Chapel (Pine Bluff, Ark.).
COLLEGE: Arkansas-Pine Bluff.
TRANSACTIONS/CAREER NOTES: Selected by Carolina Panthers in fourth round (100th pick overall) of 2002 NFL draft. ... Signed by Panthers (July 15, 2002). ... Granted free agency (March 2, 2005).
CHAMPIONSHIP GAME EXPERIENCE: Played in NFC championship game (2003 season). ... Played in Super Bowl 38 (2003 season).

Year	Team	G	GS	TOTALS			INTERCEPTIONS			
				Tk.	Ast.	Sks.	No.	Yds.	Avg.	TD
2002—Carolina NFL		13	1	15	3	0.0	0	0	0.0	0
2003—Carolina NFL		16	1	7	1	1.0	0	0	0.0	0
2004—Carolina NFL		13	0	4	0	0.0	0	0	0.0	0
Pro totals (3 years)		42	2	26	4	1.0	0	0	0.0	0

WESLEY, GREG   S   CHIEFS

PERSONAL: Born March 19, 1978, in Little Rock, Ark. ... 6-2/206. ... Full name: Gregory Lashon Wesley.
HIGH SCHOOL: England (Ark.).
COLLEGE: Arkansas-Pine Bluff.
TRANSACTIONS/CAREER NOTES: Selected by Kansas City Chiefs in third round (85th pick overall) of 2000 NFL draft. ... Signed by Chiefs (June 6, 2000). ... Granted free agency (February 28, 2003). ... Re-signed by Chiefs (May 16, 2003).

Year	Team	G	GS	TOTALS			INTERCEPTIONS			
				Tk.	Ast.	Sks.	No.	Yds.	Avg.	TD
2000—Kansas City NFL		16	16	69	16	1.0	2	28	14.0	0
2001—Kansas City NFL		16	16	72	11	2.0	2	44	22.0	0
2002—Kansas City NFL		13	13	54	10	1.0	6	170	28.3	0
2003—Kansas City NFL		16	16	87	15	2.0	6	63	10.5	0
2004—Kansas City NFL		12	11	60	7	0.0	4	92	23.0	0
Pro totals (5 years)		73	72	342	59	6.0	20	397	19.9	0

W

WESTBROOK, BRIAN   RB/KR

PERSONAL: Born September 2, 1979, in Washington, DC. ... 5-10/205.
HIGH SCHOOL: DeMatha (Ft. Washington, Md.).
COLLEGE: Villanova.
TRANSACTIONS/CAREER NOTES: Selected by Philadelphia Eagles in third round (91st pick overall) of 2002 NFL draft. ... Signed by Eagles (July 11, 2002). ... On injured reserve with triceps injury (January 7, 2004-remainder of 2003 season). ... Granted free agency (March 2, 2005).
CHAMPIONSHIP GAME EXPERIENCE: Played in NFC championship game (2002 and 2004 seasons). ... Played in Super Bowl 39 (2004 season).
HONORS: Walter Payton Award winner (2001). ... Played in Pro Bowl (2004 season).
SINGLE GAME HIGHS (regular season): Attempts—22 (October 3, 2004, vs. Chicago); yards—119 (October 3, 2004, vs. Chicago); and rushing touchdowns—1 (November 28, 2004, vs. New York Giants).
STATISTICAL PLATEAUS: 100-yard rushing games: 2004 (2). Total: 2. 100-yard receiving games: 2004 (1). Total: 1.

Year	Team	G	GS	RUSHING Att.	Yds.	Avg.	TD	RECEIVING No.	Yds.	Avg.	TD	PUNT RETURNS No.	Yds.	Avg.	TD	KICKOFF RETURNS No.	Yds.	Avg.	TD	TOTALS TD	2pt.	Pts.
2002—Phi. NFL		15	3	46	193	4.2	0	9	86	9.6	0	0	0	0.0	0	0	0	0.0	0	0	0	0
2003—Phi. NFL		15	8	117	613	5.2	7	37	332	9.0	4	20	306	‡15.3	†2	23	487	21.2	0	13	0	78
2004—Phi. NFL		13	12	177	812	4.6	3	73	703	9.6	6	2	14	7.0	0	0	0	0.0	0	9	0	54
Pro totals (3 years)		43	23	340	1618	4.8	10	119	1121	9.4	10	22	320	14.5	2	23	487	21.2	0	22	0	132

WESTMORELAND, ERIC   LB

PERSONAL: Born March 11, 1977, in Jasper, Tenn. ... 6-0/233. ... Full name: Eric Lebron Westmoreland.
HIGH SCHOOL: Marion County (Tenn.).
COLLEGE: Tennessee.
TRANSACTIONS/CAREER NOTES: Selected by Jacksonville Jaguars in third round (73rd pick overall) of 2001 NFL draft. ... Signed by Jaguars (June 4, 2001). ... Waived by Jaguars (October 8, 2003). ... Signed by Cleveland Browns (August 5, 2004). ... Granted unconditional free agency (March 2, 2005).

Year	Team	G	GS	TOTALS Tk.	Ast.	Sks.	INTERCEPTIONS No.	Yds.	Avg.	TD
2001—Jacksonville NFL		11	2	15	4	1.0	0	0	0.0	0
2002—Jacksonville NFL		15	2	21	7	1.0	0	0	0.0	0
2003—Jacksonville NFL		2	0	0	0	0.0	0	0	0.0	0
2004—Cleveland NFL		16	0	6	2	0.0	0	0	0.0	0
Pro totals (4 years)		44	4	42	13	2.0	0	0	0.0	0

WHARTON, TRAVELLE   T   PANTHERS

PERSONAL: Born May 19, 1981, in Greenville, S.C. ... 6-4/312.
HIGH SCHOOL: Hillcrest (Fountain Inn, S.C.).
COLLEGE: South Carolina.
TRANSACTIONS/CAREER NOTES: Selected by Carolina Panthers in third round (94th pick overall) of 2004 NFL draft. ... Signed by Panthers (May 26, 2004).
PLAYING EXPERIENCE: Carolina NFL, 2004. ... Games/Games started: 2004 (11/11). Total: 11/11.
HONORS: Named offensive lineman on THE SPORTING NEWS Freshman All-America second team (2000).

WHEATLEY, TYRONE   RB

PERSONAL: Born January 19, 1972, in Inkster, Mich. ... 6-0/235.
HIGH SCHOOL: Robichaud (Dearborn Heights, Mich.).
COLLEGE: Michigan.
TRANSACTIONS/CAREER NOTES: Selected by New York Giants in first round (17th pick overall) of 1995 NFL draft. ... Signed by Giants (August 9, 1995). ... Traded by Giants to Miami Dolphins for seventh-round pick (LB O.J. Childress) in 1999 draft (February 12, 1999). ... Released by Dolphins (August 3, 1999). ... Signed by Oakland Raiders (August 4, 1999). ... Granted unconditional free agency (February 28, 2003). ... Re-signed by Raiders (March 25, 2003). ... On injured reserve with hamstring injury (December 24, 2004-remainder of season). ... Released by Raiders (March 2, 2005).
CHAMPIONSHIP GAME EXPERIENCE: Played in AFC championship game (2000 and 2002 seasons). ... Played in Super Bowl 37 (2002 season).
SINGLE GAME HIGHS (regular season): Attempts—32 (November 16, 2003, vs. Minnesota); yards—156 (October 22, 2000, vs. Seattle); and rushing touchdowns—2 (November 7, 2004, vs. Carolina).
STATISTICAL PLATEAUS: 100-yard rushing games: 1997 (1), 1999 (2), 2000 (3), 2003 (1), 2004 (1). Total: 8.

Year	Team	G	GS	RUSHING Att.	Yds.	Avg.	TD	RECEIVING No.	Yds.	Avg.	TD	KICKOFF RETURNS No.	Yds.	Avg.	TD	TOTALS TD	2pt.	Pts.	Fum.
1995—New York Giants NFL..		13	1	78	245	3.1	3	5	27	5.4	0	10	186	18.6	0	3	0	18	2
1996—New York Giants NFL..		14	0	112	400	3.6	1	12	51	4.3	2	23	503	21.9	0	3	0	18	6
1997—New York Giants NFL..		14	7	152	583	3.8	4	16	140	8.8	0	0	0	0.0	0	4	0	24	3
1998—New York Giants NFL..		5	0	14	52	3.7	0	0	0	0.0	0	1	16	16.0	0	0	0	0	0
1999—Oakland NFL		16	9	242	936	3.9	8	21	196	9.3	3	0	0	0.0	0	11	0	66	3
2000—Oakland NFL		14	14	232	1046	4.5	9	20	156	7.8	1	0	0	0.0	0	10	0	60	4
2001—Oakland NFL		11	2	88	276	3.1	5	12	61	5.1	1	0	0	0.0	0	6	0	36	3
2002—Oakland NFL		14	0	108	419	3.9	2	12	71	5.9	0	0	0	0.0	0	2	0	12	1
2003—Oakland NFL		15	5	159	678	4.3	4	12	120	10.0	0	0	0	0.0	0	4	0	24	2
2004—Oakland NFL		8	7	85	327	3.8	4	15	78	5.2	0	0	0	0.0	0	4	0	24	0
Pro totals (10 years)		124	45	1270	4962	3.9	40	125	900	7.2	7	34	705	20.7	0	47	0	282	24

WHITE, DEWAYNE   DE   BUCCANEERS

PERSONAL: Born October 19, 1979, in Marbury, Ala. ... 6-2/273.
HIGH SCHOOL: Marbury (Ala.).
COLLEGE: Louisville.
TRANSACTIONS/CAREER NOTES: Selected after junior season by Tampa Bay Buccaneers in second round (64th pick overall) of 2003 NFL draft. ... Signed by Buccaneers (July 18, 2003).

Year	Team	G	GS	TOTALS Tk.	Ast.	Sks.	INTERCEPTIONS No.	Yds.	Avg.	TD
2003—Tampa Bay NFL		12	1	3	3	0.0	0	0	0.0	0
2004—Tampa Bay NFL		16	3	23	7	6.0	0	0	0.0	0
Pro totals (2 years)		28	4	26	10	6.0	0	0	0.0	0

W

WHITE, DEZ   WR   FALCONS

PERSONAL: Born August 23, 1979, in Orange Park, Fla. ... 6-1/215. ... Full name: Edward Dezmon White.
HIGH SCHOOL: Bolles (Orange Park, Fla.).
COLLEGE: Georgia Tech.
TRANSACTIONS/CAREER NOTES: Selected after junior season by Chicago Bears in third round (69th pick overall) of 2000 NFL draft. ... Signed by Bears (July 19, 2000). ... Granted free agency (February 28, 2003). ... Re-signed by Bears (April 25, 2003). ... On injured reserve with knee injury (December 24, 2003-remainder of season). ... Granted unconditional free agency (March 3, 2004). ... Signed by Atlanta Falcons (March 23, 2004).
CHAMPIONSHIP GAME EXPERIENCE: Played in NFC championship game (2004 season).
SINGLE GAME HIGHS (regular season): Receptions—8 (November 24, 2002, vs. Detroit); yards—106 (November 24, 2002, vs. Detroit); and touchdown receptions—2 (December 22, 2002, vs. Carolina).
STATISTICAL PLATEAUS: 100-yard receiving games: 2002 (1). Total: 1.

				RUSHING			RECEIVING				KICKOFF RETURNS				TOTALS			
Year Team	G	GS	Att.	Yds.	Avg.	TD	No.	Yds.	Avg.	TD	No.	Yds.	Avg.	TD	TD	2pt.	Pts.	Fum.
2000—Chicago NFL	15	0	0	0	0.0	0	10	87	8.7	1	0	0	0.0	0	1	0	6	1
2001—Chicago NFL	14	6	0	0	0.0	0	45	428	9.5	0	0	0	0.0	0	0	0	0	0
2002—Chicago NFL	16	14	3	11	3.7	0	51	656	12.9	4	2	47	23.5	0	4	0	24	1
2003—Chicago NFL	15	11	2	13	6.5	0	49	583	11.9	3	0	0	0.0	0	3	0	18	0
2004—Atlanta NFL	16	15	3	14	4.7	0	30	370	12.3	2	0	0	0.0	0	2	0	12	0
Pro totals (5 years)	76	46	8	38	4.8	0	185	2124	11.5	10	2	47	23.5	0	10	0	60	2

WHITE, JAMEL   RB   LIONS

PERSONAL: Born February 11, 1978, in Los Angeles, Calif. ... 5-9/222.
HIGH SCHOOL: Palmdale (Calif.).
COLLEGE: South Dakota.
TRANSACTIONS/CAREER NOTES: Signed as non-drafted free agent by Indianapolis Colts (April 20, 2000). ... Released by Colts (August 27, 2000). ... Signed by Cleveland Browns (August 29, 2000). ... Granted free agency (February 28, 2003). ... Re-signed by Browns (April 18, 2003). ... Released by Browns (March 5, 2004). ... Signed by Tampa Bay Buccaneers (March 18, 2004). ... Released by Buccaneers (November 16, 2004). ... Signed by Baltimore Ravens (November 24, 2004). ... Granted unconditional free agency (March 2, 2005). ... Signed by Detroit Lions (April 1, 2005).
SINGLE GAME HIGHS (regular season): Attempts—23 (September 30, 2001, vs. Jacksonville); yards—131 (December 23, 2001, vs. Green Bay); and rushing touchdowns—2 (December 30, 2001, vs. Tennessee).
STATISTICAL PLATEAUS: 100-yard rushing games: 2001 (1), 2002 (1), 2003 (1). Total: 3.

				RUSHING			RECEIVING				KICKOFF RETURNS				TOTALS			
Year Team	G	GS	Att.	Yds.	Avg.	TD	No.	Yds.	Avg.	TD	No.	Yds.	Avg.	TD	TD	2pt.	Pts.	Fum.
2000—Cleveland NFL	13	0	47	145	3.1	0	13	100	7.7	0	43	935	21.7	0	0	0	0	0
2001—Cleveland NFL	16	7	126	443	3.5	4	44	418	9.5	1	9	189	21.0	0	6	1	38	1
2002—Cleveland NFL	14	6	106	470	4.4	3	63	452	7.2	0	2	21	10.5	0	3	0	18	0
2003—Cleveland NFL	16	3	70	266	3.8	1	46	303	6.6	1	2	2	1.0	0	2	0	12	1
2004—Tampa Bay NFL	7	0	13	20	1.5	0	4	17	4.3	0	4	99	24.8	0	0	0	0	0
—Baltimore NFL	6	0	14	62	4.4	0	2	4	2.0	0	0	0	0.0	0	0	0	0	0
Pro totals (5 years)	72	16	376	1406	3.7	9	172	1294	7.5	2	60	1246	20.8	0	11	1	68	2

WHITE, TRACY   LB

PERSONAL: Born April 14, 1981, in Charleston, S.C. ... 6-0/230.
COLLEGE: Howard.
TRANSACTIONS/CAREER NOTES: Signed as non-drafted free agent by Seattle Seahawks (May 1, 2003). ... On injured reserve with hamstring injury (January 4, 2005-remainder of season). ... Released by Seahawks (January 4, 2005).

			TOTALS			INTERCEPTIONS			
Year Team	G	GS	Tk.	Ast.	Sks.	No.	Yds.	Avg.	TD
2003—Seattle NFL	11	0	0	0	0.0	0	0	0.0	0
2004—Seattle NFL	10	2	19	7	1.0	0	0	0.0	0
Pro totals (2 years)	21	2	19	7	1.0	0	0	0.0	0

WHITEHEAD, WILLIE   DE   SAINTS

W

PERSONAL: Born January 26, 1973, in Tuskegee, Ala. ... 6-3/300. ... Full name: William Whitehead.
HIGH SCHOOL: Tuskegee (Ala.) Institute.
COLLEGE: Auburn.
TRANSACTIONS/CAREER NOTES: Signed as non-drafted free agent by San Francisco 49ers (April 26, 1995). ... Released by 49ers (July 16, 1995). ... Signed by Baltimore Stallions of CFL (August 1995). ... Signed by Montreal Alouettes of CFL to practice squad (1996). ... Signed by Hamilton Tiger-Cats of CFL (May 14, 1997). ... Signed by Detroit Lions (February 11, 1998). ... Released by Lions (August 25, 1998). ... Signed by New Orleans Saints (January 27, 1999). ... Assigned by Saints to Frankfurt Galaxy in 1999 NFL Europe enhancement allocation program (February 22, 1999). ... Granted free agency (March 1, 2002). ... Re-signed by Saints (April 4, 2002). ... Granted unconditional free agency (February 28, 2003). ... Re-signed by Saints (April 25, 2003). ... On physically unable to perform list with knee injury (July 30-November 12, 2004). ... Activated (November 12, 2004).

			TOTALS		
Year Team	G	GS	Tk.	Ast.	Sks.
1995—Baltimore CFL	1	...	...	...	0.0
1996—Montreal CFL	Did not play.				
1997—Hamilton CFL	15	...	...	...	13.0
1998—	Did not play.				

Year	Team			TOTALS			
		G	GS	Tk.	Ast.	Sks.
1999—New Orleans NFL		16	3	24	6	7.0
2000—New Orleans NFL		16	2	17	10	5.5
2001—New Orleans NFL		14	0	18	3	2.0
2002—New Orleans NFL		12	10	24	10	3.0
2003—New Orleans NFL		11	10	34	6	5.5
2004—New Orleans NFL		8	0	6	4	0.0
CFL totals (2 years)		16	...	...	...	13.0
NFL totals (6 years)		77	25	123	39	23.0
Pro totals (8 years)		93	...	...	...	36.0

WHITESIDE, KEYON LB COLTS

PERSONAL: Born January 31, 1980, in Forest City, N.C. ... 6-0/229. ... Full name: Keyon Shontel Whiteside.
HIGH SCHOOL: Chase (Forest City, N.C.).
COLLEGE: Tennessee.
TRANSACTIONS/CAREER NOTES: Selected by Indianapolis Colts in fifth round (162nd pick overall) of 2003 NFL draft. ... Signed by Colts (July 24, 2003). ... Claimed on waivers by Cincinnati Bengals (September 1, 2003). ... Waived by Bengals (October 22, 2003). ... Signed by Colts (November 18, 2003). ... On injured reserve with knee injury (November 11, 2004-remainder of season).
CHAMPIONSHIP GAME EXPERIENCE: Played in AFC championship game (2003 season).

Year	Team			TOTALS			INTERCEPTIONS			
		G	GS	Tk.	Ast.	Sks.	No.	Yds.	Avg.	TD
2003—Indianapolis NFL		5	0	0	0	0.0	0	0	0.0	0
2004—Indianapolis NFL		7	0	0	0	0.0	0	0	0.0	0
Pro totals (2 years)		12	0	0	0	0.0	0	0	0.0	0

WHITFIELD, BOB T GIANTS

PERSONAL: Born October 18, 1971, in Carson, Calif. ... 6-5/310. ... Full name: Bob Whitfield Jr.
HIGH SCHOOL: Banning (Los Angeles).
COLLEGE: Stanford.
TRANSACTIONS/CAREER NOTES: Selected after junior season by Atlanta Falcons in first round (eighth pick overall) of 1992 NFL draft. ... Signed by Falcons (September 4, 1992). ... Granted roster exemption for one game (September 1992). ... On injured reserve with leg injury (November 3, 2003-remainder of season). ... Released by Falcons (September 5, 2004). ... Signed by Jacksonville Jaguars (October 5, 2004). ... Granted unconditional free agency (March 2, 2005). ... Signed by New York Giants (May 4, 2005).
PLAYING EXPERIENCE: Atlanta NFL 1992-2003; Jacksonville NFL, 2004. ... Games/Games started: 1992 (11/0), 1993 (16/16), 1994 (16/16), 1995 (16/16), 1996 (16/16), 1997 (16/16), 1998 (16/16), 1999 (16/16), 2000 (15/15), 2001 (16/16), 2002 (16/16), 2003 (8/8), 2004 (10/0). Total: 188/167.
CHAMPIONSHIP GAME EXPERIENCE: Played in NFC championship game (1998 season). ... Played in Super Bowl 33 (1998 season).
HONORS: Named offensive tackle on THE SPORTING NEWS college All-America first team (1991). ... Played in Pro Bowl (1998 season).

WHITING, BRANDON DE/DT

PERSONAL: Born July 30, 1976, in Santa Rosa, Calif. ... 6-3/285. ... Name pronounced: WHITE-ing.
HIGH SCHOOL: Polytechnic (Long Beach, Calif.).
COLLEGE: California.
TRANSACTIONS/CAREER NOTES: Selected by Philadelphia Eagles in fourth round (112th pick overall) of 1998 NFL draft. ... Signed by Eagles (July 14, 1998). ... Granted free agency (March 2, 2001). ... Re-signed by Eagles (March 20, 2001). ... Traded by Eagles to San Francisco 49ers as part of a three-way trade involving the Baltimore Ravens (March 16, 2004). The Ravens received a fifth-round draft choice from the Eagles as well as a 2004 second-round pick they sent to San Francisco in an earlier trade. The Eagles received WR Terrell Owens from Baltimore. ... On injured reserve with knee injury (November 3, 2004-remainder of season). ... Released by 49ers (March 1, 2005).
CHAMPIONSHIP GAME EXPERIENCE: Played in NFC championship game (2001-2003 seasons).

Year	Team			TOTALS			INTERCEPTIONS			
		G	GS	Tk.	Ast.	Sks.	No.	Yds.	Avg.	TD
1998—Philadelphia NFL		16	5	14	4	1.5	0	0	0.0	0
1999—Philadelphia NFL		13	2	9	7	1.0	1	22	22.0	1
2000—Philadelphia NFL		16	11	23	11	3.5	0	0	0.0	0
2001—Philadelphia NFL		13	12	15	11	2.5	0	0	0.0	0
2002—Philadelphia NFL		16	15	23	16	6.0	0	0	0.0	0
2003—Philadelphia NFL		14	14	32	13	2.0	0	0	0.0	0
2004—San Francisco NFL		5	5	8	3	0.0	0	0	0.0	0
Pro totals (7 years)		93	64	124	65	16.5	1	22	22.0	1

WHITLEY, JAMES CB

PERSONAL: Born May 13, 1979, in Decatur, Ill. ... 5-11/185. ... Full name: James LaVell Whitley.
HIGH SCHOOL: Norview (Va.).
COLLEGE: Michigan.
TRANSACTIONS/CAREER NOTES: Signed by Montreal Alouettes of CFL (2001). ... Signed as non-drafted free agent by St. Louis Rams (February 26, 2002). ... On physically unable to perform list with foot injury (August 26-October 17, 2003). ... Released by Rams (December 2, 2003). ... Signed by Green Bay Packers (December 10, 2003). ... Granted unconditional free agency (March 3, 2004). ... Re-signed by Packers (April 15, 2004). ... Released by Packers (October 19, 2004). ... Signed by Carolina Panthers (November 10, 2004). ... Released by Panthers (November 19, 2004).

Year	Team	G	GS	TOTALS			INTERCEPTIONS			
				Tk.	Ast.	Sks.	No.	Yds.	Avg.	TD
2001—Montreal CFL		14	5	...	...	1.0	2	18	9.0	0
2002—St. Louis NFL		13	1	26	1	3.0	0	0	0.0	0
2003—St. Louis NFL		3	0	3	0	0.0	0	0	0.0	0
—Green Bay NFL		3	0	0	0	0.0	0	0	0.0	0
2004—Green Bay NFL		6	0	1	0	0.0	0	0	0.0	0
CFL totals (1 year)		14	5	...	...	1.0	2	18	9.0	0
NFL totals (3 years)		25	1	30	1	3.0	0	0	0.0	0
Pro totals (4 years)		39	6	...	...	4.0	2	18	9.0	0

WHITLEY, TAYLOR — G — DOLPHINS

PERSONAL: Born February 21, 1980, in Baytown, Texas. ... 6-4/315.
HIGH SCHOOL: Sudan (Texas).
COLLEGE: Texas A&M.
TRANSACTIONS/CAREER NOTES: Selected by Miami Dolphins in third round (87th pick overall) of 2003 NFL draft. ... Signed by Dolphins (July 28, 2003). ... Inactive for all 16 games (2003).
PLAYING EXPERIENCE: Miami NFL, 2004. ... Games/Games started: 2004 (16/11). Total: 16/11.

WHITTED, ALVIS — WR — RAIDERS

PERSONAL: Born September 4, 1974, in Durham, N.C. ... 6-0/185. ... Full name: Alvis James Whitted.
HIGH SCHOOL: Orange (Hillsborough, N.C.).
COLLEGE: North Carolina State.
TRANSACTIONS/CAREER NOTES: Selected by Jacksonville Jaguars in seventh round (192nd pick overall) of 1998 NFL draft. ... Signed by Jaguars (May 19, 1998). ... Released by Jaguars (December 4, 2001). ... Signed by Atlanta Falcons (January 10, 2002). ... Released by Falcons (August 31, 2002). ... Signed by Oakland Raiders (September 25, 2002).
CHAMPIONSHIP GAME EXPERIENCE: Played in AFC championship game (1999 and 2002 seasons). ... Played in Super Bowl 37 (2002 season).
SINGLE GAME HIGHS (regular season): Receptions—4 (December 23, 2000, vs. New York Giants); yards—61 (December 19, 2004, vs. Tennessee); and touchdown receptions—2 (October 29, 2000, vs. Dallas).

Year	Team	G	GS	RUSHING				RECEIVING				KICKOFF RETURNS				TOTALS			
				Att.	Yds.	Avg.	TD	No.	Yds.	Avg.	TD	No.	Yds.	Avg.	TD	TD	2pt.	Pts.	Fum.
1998—Jacksonville NFL		16	0	3	13	4.3	0	2	61	30.5	0	0	0	0.0	0	1	0	6	0
1999—Jacksonville NFL		14	1	1	9	9.0	0	0	0	0.0	0	8	187	23.4	▲1	1	0	6	0
2000—Jacksonville NFL		16	3	0	0	0.0	0	13	137	10.5	3	4	67	16.8	0	3	0	18	1
2001—Jacksonville NFL		11	0	1	4	4.0	0	2	17	8.5	0	0	0	0.0	0	0	0	0	0
2002—Oakland NFL		9	0	0	0	0.0	0	0	0	0.0	0	4	50	12.5	0	0	0	0	0
2003—Oakland NFL		16	2	6	37	6.2	0	7	106	15.1	1	4	48	12.0	0	1	0	6	0
2004—Oakland NFL		11	5	0	0	0.0	0	9	227	25.2	2	1	36	36.0	0	2	1	14	0
Pro totals (7 years)		93	11	11	63	5.7	0	33	548	16.6	6	21	388	18.5	1	8	1	50	1

WHITTLE, JASON — G — GIANTS

PERSONAL: Born March 7, 1975, in Springfield, Mo. ... 6-4/305.
HIGH SCHOOL: Camdenton (Mo.).
COLLEGE: SMS.
TRANSACTIONS/CAREER NOTES: Signed as non-drafted free agent by New York Giants (April 24, 1998). ... Released by Giants (August 30, 1998). ... Re-signed by Giants to practice squad (September 1, 1998). ... Activated (December 16, 1998). ... Granted free agency (March 1, 2002). ... Re-signed by Giants (April 24, 2002). ... Granted unconditional free agency (February 28, 2003). ... Signed by Tampa Bay Buccaneers (March 7, 2003). ... Traded by Buccaneers to New York Giants for seventh-round pick (WR Paris Warren) in 2005 draft (August 31, 2004).
PLAYING EXPERIENCE: New York Giants NFL, 1998-2002; Tampa Bay NFL, 2003; New York Giants NFL, 2004. ... Games/Games started: 1998 (1/0), 1999 (16/1), 2000 (16/2), 2001 (16/2), 2002 (14/14), 2003 (16/5), 2004 (16/16). Total: 95/40.
CHAMPIONSHIP GAME EXPERIENCE: Played in NFC championship game (2000 season). ... Played in Super Bowl 35 (2000 season).

W

WIEGERT, ZACH — T — TEXANS

PERSONAL: Born August 16, 1972, in Fremont, Neb. ... 6-5/305. ... Full name: Zach Allen Wiegert. ... Name pronounced: WEE-gert.
HIGH SCHOOL: Fremont (Neb.) Bergan.
COLLEGE: Nebraska.
TRANSACTIONS/CAREER NOTES: Selected by St. Louis Rams in second round (38th pick overall) of 1995 NFL draft. ... Signed by Rams (July 18, 1995). ... Granted free agency (February 13, 1998). ... Re-signed by Rams (June 17, 1998). ... Designated by Rams as transition player (February 12, 1999). ... Re-signed by Rams (March 24, 1999). ... Released by Rams (April 28, 1999). ... Signed by Jacksonville Jaguars (May 5, 1999). ... On injured reserve with knee injury (October 25, 2000-remainder of season). ... On injured reserve with knee injury (November 6, 2002-remainder of season). ... Granted unconditional free agency (February 28, 2003). ... Signed by Houston Texans (March 1, 2003). ... On injured reserve with knee injury (December 22, 2004-remainder of season).
PLAYING EXPERIENCE: St. Louis NFL, 1995-1998; Jacksonville NFL, 1999-2002; Houston NFL, 2003-2004. ... Games/Games started: 1995 (5/2), 1996 (16/16), 1997 (15/15), 1998 (13/13), 1999 (16/12), 2000 (8/8), 2001 (16/16), 2002 (7/7), 2003 (15/14), 2004 (13/13). Total: 124/116.
CHAMPIONSHIP GAME EXPERIENCE: Played in AFC championship game (1999 season).
HONORS: Outland Trophy Award winner (1994). ... Named offensive lineman on THE SPORTING NEWS college All-America first team (1994).

WIEGMANN, CASEY   C   CHIEFS

PERSONAL: Born July 20, 1973, in Parkersburg, Iowa. ... 6-2/285. ... Name pronounced: WEG-man.
HIGH SCHOOL: Parkersburg (Iowa).
COLLEGE: Iowa.
TRANSACTIONS/CAREER NOTES: Signed as non-drafted free agent by Indianapolis Colts (April 26, 1996). ... Released by Colts (August 25, 1996). ... Re-signed by Colts to practice squad (August 27, 1996). ... Activated (September 10, 1996); did not play. ... Released by Colts (September 22, 1996). ... Re-signed by Colts to practice squad (September 23, 1996). ... Activated (October 15, 1996); did not play. ... Claimed on waivers by New York Jets (October 29, 1996). ... Released by Jets (September 21, 1997). ... Signed by Chicago Bears (September 24, 1997). ... Granted free agency (February 12, 1999). ... Tendered offer sheet by Miami Dolphins (April 5, 1999). ... Offer matched by Bears (April 8, 1999). ... Granted unconditional free agency (March 2, 2001). ... Signed by Kansas City Chiefs (March 15, 2001).
PLAYING EXPERIENCE: Indianapolis NFL, 1996; New York Jets NFL, 1997; Chicago NFL, 1997-2000; Kansas City NFL, 2001-2004. ... Games/Games started: 1997 (1/0), 1998 (16/15), 1999 (16/0), 2000 (16/10), 2001 (15/15), 2002 (16/16), 2003 (16/16), 2004 (16/16), Total: 112/88.

WIGGINS, JERMAINE   TE   VIKINGS

PERSONAL: Born January 18, 1975, in East Boston, Mass. ... 6-2/260.
HIGH SCHOOL: East Boston.
COLLEGE: Georgia.
TRANSACTIONS/CAREER NOTES: Signed by New York Jets as non-drafted free agent (April 19, 1999). ... Released by Jets (August 23, 1999). ... Re-signed by Jets to practice squad (August 28, 1999). ... Claimed on waivers by New England Patriots (November 28, 2000). ... Released by Patriots (May 2, 2002). ... Signed by Indianapolis Colts (May 14, 2002). ... Released by Colts (September 24, 2002). ... Signed by Carolina Panthers (October 8, 2002). ... Granted free agency (February 28, 2003). ... Re-signed by Panthers (May 2, 2003). ... Granted unconditional free agency (March 3, 2004). ... Signed by Minnesota Vikings (March 24, 2004). ... Granted unconditional free agency (March 2, 2005). ... Re-signed by Vikings (March 9, 2005).
CHAMPIONSHIP GAME EXPERIENCE: Played in AFC championship game (2001 and 2003 seasons). ... Member of Super Bowl championship team (2001 and 2003 seasons).
SINGLE GAME HIGHS (regular season): Receptions—8 (November 21, 2004, vs. Detroit); yards—94 (November 14, 2004, vs. Green Bay); and touchdown receptions—2 (October 17, 2004, vs. New Orleans).

			RECEIVING				TOTALS			
Year Team	G	GS	No.	Yds.	Avg.	TD	TD	2pt.	Pts.	Fum.
2000—New York Jets NFL	11	0	2	4	2.0	1	1	0	6	0
—New England NFL	4	2	16	203	12.7	1	1	0	6	1
2001 New England NFL	16	6	14	133	9.5	4	4	0	24	0
2002—Indianapolis NFL	3	0	2	17	8.5	0	0	0	0	1
—Carolina NFL	11	1	8	45	5.6	1	1	0	6	0
2003—Carolina NFL	16	11	8	80	10.0	1	1	0	6	0
2004—Minnesota NFL	14	13	71	705	9.9	4	4	0	24	1
Pro totals (5 years)	75	33	121	1187	9.8	12	12	0	72	3

WILCOX, DANIEL   TE   RAVENS

PERSONAL: Born March 23, 1977, in Atlanta, Ga. ... 6-1/245.
HIGH SCHOOL: Decatur (Ga.).
JUNIOR COLLEGE: Georgia Military College.
COLLEGE: Appalachian State.
TRANSACTIONS/CAREER NOTES: Signed as non-drafted free agent by New York Jets (April 26, 2001). ... Released by Jets (August 2, 2001). ... Re-signed by Jets (August 20, 2001). ... Released by Jets (September 2, 2001). ... Re-signed by Jets to practice squad (September 3, 2001). ... Activated (September 19, 2001); did not play. ... Released by Jets (October 10, 2001). ... Re-signed by Jets to practice squad (October 11, 2001). ... Activated (November 15, 2001). ... Released by Jets (August 28, 2002). ... Re-signed by Jets to practice squad (September 2, 2002). ... Signed off Jets practice squad by Tampa Bay Buccaneers (December 18, 2002). ... Released by Buccaneers (August 24, 2003). ... Re-signed by Buccaneers (September 5, 2003). ... Released by Buccaneers (September 16, 2003). ... Signed by Baltimore Ravens (June 21, 2004).
CHAMPIONSHIP GAME EXPERIENCE: Member of Buccaneers for NFC championship game (2002 season); inactive. ... Member of Super Bowl championship team (2002 season); inactive.
SINGLE GAME HIGHS (regular season): Receptions—6 (January 2, 2005, vs. Miami); yards—72 (January 2, 2005, vs. Miami); and touchdown receptions—1 (October 31, 2004, vs. Philadelphia).

			RECEIVING				TOTALS			
Year Team	G	GS	No.	Yds.	Avg.	TD	TD	2pt.	Pts.	Fum.
2001—New York Jets NFL	1	0	0	0	0.0	0	0	0	0	0
2003—Tampa Bay NFL	2	0	0	0	0.0	0	0	0	0	0
2004—Baltimore NFL	16	5	25	219	8.8	1	1	0	6	1
Pro totals (3 years)	19	5	25	219	8.8	1	1	0	6	1

W

WILDS, GARNELL   CB   REDSKINS

PERSONAL: Born June 8, 1981, in Tampa, Fla. ... 5-11/196. ... Full name: Garnell Wayman Wilds.
HIGH SCHOOL: Hillsborough (Tampa, Fla.).
COLLEGE: Virginia Tech.
TRANSACTIONS/CAREER NOTES: Signed as non-drafted free agent by Washington Redskins (April 27, 2004). ... Released by Redskins (September 5, 2004). ... Re-signed by Redskins to practice squad (September 6, 2004). ... Activated (December 4, 2004).

			TOTALS			INTERCEPTIONS			
Year Team	G	GS	Tk.	Ast.	Sks.	No.	Yds.	Avg.	TD
2004—Washington NFL	2	0	5	0	0.0	0	0	0.0	0

WILEY, CHUCK   DE

PERSONAL: Born March 6, 1975, in Baton Rouge, La. ... 6-5/275. ... Full name: Samuel Charles Wiley Jr.
HIGH SCHOOL: Southern University Lab (Baton Rouge, La.).
COLLEGE: Louisiana State.
TRANSACTIONS/CAREER NOTES: Selected by Carolina Panthers in third round (62nd pick overall) of 1998 NFL draft. ... Signed by Panthers (June 10, 1998). ... On injured reserve with heel injury (August 30, 1998-entire season). ... Claimed on waivers Atlanta Falcons (August 28, 2000). ... Granted unconditional free agency (March 1, 2002). ... Signed by Minnesota Vikings (May 2, 2002). ... Released by Vikings (November 2, 2004). ... Signed by New York Giants (November 10, 2004). ... On injured reserve with knee injury (November 30, 2004-remainder of season). ... Granted unconditional free agency (March 2, 2005).

				TOTALS			INTERCEPTIONS		
Year Team	G	GS	Tk.	Ast.	Sks.	No.	Yds.	Avg.	TD
1998—Carolina NFL		Did not play.							
1999—Carolina NFL	16	16	32	4	0.0	0	0	0.0	0
2000—Atlanta NFL	16	0	25	14	4.0	0	0	0.0	0
2001—Atlanta NFL	16	1	12	5	1.0	1	1	1.0	0
2002—Minnesota NFL	16	0	7	3	0.0	0	0	0.0	0
2003—Minnesota NFL	7	4	5	0	1.0	0	0	0.0	0
2004—Minnesota NFL	5	2	2	1	0.0	0	0	0.0	0
—New York Giants NFL	3	0	1	3	0.5	0	0	0.0	0
Pro totals (6 years)	79	23	84	30	6.5	1	1	1.0	0

WILEY, MARCELLUS   DE   JAGUARS

PERSONAL: Born November 30, 1974, in Compton, Calif. ... 6-4/278. ... Full name: Marcellus Vernon Wiley.
HIGH SCHOOL: Santa Monica (Calif.).
COLLEGE: Columbia.
TRANSACTIONS/CAREER NOTES: Selected by Buffalo Bills in second round (52nd pick overall) of 1997 NFL draft. ... Signed by Bills (June 20, 1997). ... Granted unconditional free agency (March 2, 2001). ... Signed by San Diego Chargers (March 6, 2001). ... Released by Chargers (March 2, 2004). ... Signed by Cowboys (March 11, 2004). ... Released by Cowboys (February 22, 2005). ... Signed by Jacksonville Jaguars (March 30, 2005).
HONORS: Played in Pro Bowl (2001 season).

				TOTALS			INTERCEPTIONS		
Year Team	G	GS	Tk.	Ast.	Sks.	No.	Yds.	Avg.	TD
1997—Buffalo NFL	16	0	12	4	0.0	0	0	0.0	0
1998—Buffalo NFL	16	3	17	7	3.5	0	0	0.0	0
1999—Buffalo NFL	16	1	18	8	5.0	1	52	52.0	0
2000—Buffalo NFL	16	15	40	25	10.5	0	0	0.0	0
2001—San Diego NFL	14	14	38	10	13.0	0	0	0.0	0
2002—San Diego NFL	14	14	31	5	6.0	1	40	40.0	0
2003—San Diego NFL	16	16	38	13	3.0	0	0	0.0	0
2004—Dallas NFL	16	15	31	7	3.0	0	0	0.0	0
Pro totals (8 years)	124	78	225	79	44.0	2	92	46.0	0

WILFORD, ERNEST   WR   JAGUARS

PERSONAL: Born January 14, 1979, in Richmond, Va. ... 6-4/223. ... Full name: Ernest Lee Wilford Jr.
HIGH SCHOOL: Armstrong/Franklin Military (Richmond, Va.), then Fork Union Military Academy (Va.).
COLLEGE: Virginia Tech.
TRANSACTIONS/CAREER NOTES: Selected by Jacksonville Jaguars in fourth round (120th pick overall) of 2004 NFL draft. ... Signed by Jaguars (July 30, 2004).
SINGLE GAME HIGHS (regular season): Receptions—6 (October 3, 2004, vs. Indianapolis); yards—56 (January 2, 2005, vs. Oakland); and touchdown receptions—1 (September 19, 2004, vs. Denver).

			RECEIVING				TOTALS			
Year Team	G	GS	No.	Yds.	Avg.	TD	TD	2pt.	Pts.	Fum.
2004—Jacksonville NFL	15	3	19	271	14.3	2	2	1	14	0

WILFORK, VINCE   DT   PATRIOTS

W

PERSONAL: Born November 4, 1981, in Boynton Beach, Fla. ... 6-2/325. ... Full name: Vince Lamar Wilfork.
HIGH SCHOOL: Santaluces (Boynton Beach, Fla.).
COLLEGE: Miami (Fla.).
TRANSACTIONS/CAREER NOTES: Selected after junior season by New England Patriots in first round (21st pick overall) of 2004 NFL draft. ... Signed by Patriots (July 19, 2004).
CHAMPIONSHIP GAME EXPERIENCE: Played in AFC championship game (2004 season). ... Member of Super Bowl championship team (2004 season).

			TOTALS		
Year Team	G	GS	Tk.	Ast.	Sks.
2004—New England NFL	16	6	27	15	2.0

WILHELM, MATT   LB   CHARGERS

PERSONAL: Born February 2, 1981, in Oberlin, Ohio. ... 6-2/254.
HIGH SCHOOL: Elyria Catholic (Lorain, Ohio).
COLLEGE: Ohio State.

TRANSACTIONS/CAREER NOTES: Selected by San Diego Chargers in fourth round (112th pick overall) of 2003 NFL draft. ... Signed by Chargers (July 19, 2003).

				TOTALS			INTERCEPTIONS			
Year Team	G	GS	Tk.	Ast.	Sks.	No.	Yds.	Avg.	TD
2003—San Diego NFL	2	0	0	0	0.0	0	0	0.0	0
2004—San Diego NFL	7	0	5	0	0.0	1	0	0.0	0
Pro totals (2 years)	9	0	5	0	0.0	1	0	0.0	0

WILKERSON, JIMMY — DE — CHIEFS

PERSONAL: Born January 4, 1981, in Omaha, Texas. ... 6-2/280.
HIGH SCHOOL: Paul H. Pewitt (Omaha, Texas).
COLLEGE: Oklahoma.
TRANSACTIONS/CAREER NOTES: Selected after junior season by Kansas City Chiefs in sixth round (189th pick overall) of 2003 NFL draft. ... Signed by Kansas City Chiefs (July 14, 2003).

			TOTALS		
Year Team	G	GS	Tk.	Ast.	Sks.
2003—Kansas City NFL	12	0	6	3	0.0
2004—Kansas City NFL	15	0	8	1	0.5
Pro totals (2 years)	27	0	14	4	0.5

WILKINS, JEFF — K — RAMS

PERSONAL: Born April 19, 1972, in Youngstown, Ohio. ... 6-2/205. ... Full name: Jeff Allen Wilkins.
HIGH SCHOOL: Austintown Fitch (Youngstown, Ohio).
COLLEGE: Youngstown State.
TRANSACTIONS/CAREER NOTES: Signed as non-drafted free agent by Dallas Cowboys (April 28, 1994). ... Released by Cowboys (July 18, 1994). ... Signed by Philadelphia Eagles (November 14, 1994). ... Released by Eagles (August 14, 1995). ... Signed by San Francisco 49ers (November 8, 1995). ... Granted unconditional free agency (February 14, 1997). ... Signed by St. Louis Rams (March 6, 1997). ... Granted unconditional free agency (March 2, 2001). ... Re-signed by Rams (March 2, 2001).
CHAMPIONSHIP GAME EXPERIENCE: Played in NFC championship game (1999 and 2001 seasons). ... Member of Super Bowl championship team (1999 season). ... Played in Super Bowl 36 (2001 season).
HONORS: Played in Pro Bowl (2003 season).
RECORDS: Holds NFL single-season record for most PATs without a miss—64 (1999). ... Shares NFL single-season record for highest field-goal percentage—100.0 (2000). ... Shares NFL single-season record for most field goals made—39 (2003). ... Shares NFL record for most field goals made, one quarter (4), vs. Baltimore (November 9, 2003, fourth quarter).
POST SEASON RECORDS: Shares NFL postseason single-game records for most field goals made—5; and most field goals attempted—6 (January 10, 2004, vs. Carolina).
MISCELLANEOUS: Rams franchise all-time scoring leader (878 points).

		FIELD GOALS							TOTALS		
Year Team	G	1-29	30-39	40-49	50+	Tot.	Pct.	Lg.	XPM	XPA	Pts.
1994—Philadelphia NFL	6	0-0	0-0	0-0	0-0	0-0	0.0	0	0	0	0
1995—San Francisco NFL	7	6-6	5-5	1-2	0-0	12-13	92.3	40	27	29	63
1996—San Francisco NFL	16	16-16	7-8	7-10	0-0	30-34	88.2	49	40	40	130
1997—St. Louis NFL	16	8-9	8-12	7-14	2-2	25-∞37	67.6	52	32	32	107
1998—St. Louis NFL	16	4-5	8-8	5-7	3-6	20-26	76.9	‡57	25	26	§85
1999—St. Louis NFL	16	6-6	6-7	7-11	1-4	20-28	71.4	51	*64	*64	‡124
2000—St. Louis NFL	11	7-7	6-6	3-3	1-1	17-17	*100.0	51	38	38	89
2001—St. Louis NFL	16	11-11	5-5	6-12	1-1	23-29	79.3	54	*58	*58	127
2002—St. Louis NFL	16	5-5	8-10	6-9	0-1	19-25	76.0	47	37	37	94
2003—St. Louis NFL	16	16-16	11-13	8-9	4-4	*39-*42	92.9	53	46	46	*163
2004—St. Louis NFL	16	7-7	5-6	3-6	4-5	19-24	79.2	53	32	32	89
Pro totals (11 years)	152	86-88	69-80	53-83	16-24	224-275	81.5	57	399	402	1071

WILKINS, MARCUS — LB — BENGALS

PERSONAL: Born January 2, 1980, in Austin, Texas. ... 6-2/235. ... Full name: Marcus Wesley Wilkins.
HIGH SCHOOL: Westwood (Austin, Texas).
COLLEGE: Texas.
TRANSACTIONS/CAREER NOTES: Signed as non-drafted free agent by Green Bay Packers (April 25, 2002). ... On injured reserve with calf injury (January 11, 2004-remainder of 2003 season). ... Granted free agency (March 3, 2004). ... Re-signed by Packers (March 11, 2004). ... Claimed on waivers by Arizona Cardinals (August 20, 2004). ... Claimed on waivers by Cincinnati Bengals (September 1, 2004). ... Granted free agency (March 2, 2005). ... Re-signed by Bengals (March 8, 2005).

W

				TOTALS			INTERCEPTIONS			
Year Team	G	GS	Tk.	Ast.	Sks.	No.	Yds.	Avg.	TD
2002—Green Bay NFL	5	0	1	1	0.0	0	0	0.0	0
2003—Green Bay NFL	7	0	0	0	0.0	0	0	0.0	0
2004—Cincinnati NFL	16	0	0	3	0.0	0	0	0.0	0
Pro totals (3 years)	28	0	1	4	0.0	0	0	0.0	0

WILKINSON, DAN — DT — LIONS

PERSONAL: Born March 13, 1973, in Dayton, Ohio. ... 6-4/335.
HIGH SCHOOL: Paul L. Dunbar (Dayton, Ohio).
COLLEGE: Ohio State.

TRANSACTIONS/CAREER NOTES: Selected after sophomore season by Cincinnati Bengals in first round (first pick overall) of 1994 NFL draft. ... Signed by Bengals (May 5, 1994). ... Designated by Bengals as franchise player (February 11, 1998). ... Tendered offer sheet by Washington Redskins (February 25, 1998). ... Bengals declined to match offer (February 26, 1998); Bengals received first-(LB Brian Simmons) and third-round (G Mike Goff) picks as compensation. ... On injured reserve with calf injury (December 5, 2002-remainder of season). ... Released by Redskins (July 29, 2003). ... Signed by Detroit Lions (August 17, 2003).
HONORS: Named defensive lineman on THE SPORTING NEWS college All-America first team (1993).

Year Team	G	GS	TOTALS Tk.	Ast.	Sks.	INTERCEPTIONS No.	Yds.	Avg.	TD
1994—Cincinnati NFL	16	14	37	7	5.5	0	0	0.0	0
1995—Cincinnati NFL	14	14	30	10	8.0	0	0	0.0	0
1996—Cincinnati NFL	16	16	37	7	6.5	1	7	7.0	0
1997—Cincinnati NFL	15	15	24	10	5.0	0	0	0.0	0
1998—Washington NFL	16	16	38	7	7.5	1	4	4.0	0
1999—Washington NFL	16	16	23	9	8.0	1	88	88.0	1
2000—Washington NFL	16	16	15	5	3.5	0	0	0.0	0
2001—Washington NFL	16	16	19	6	4.0	2	0	0.0	0
2002—Washington NFL	12	11	12	4	0.0	0	0	0.0	0
2003—Detroit NFL	16	16	18	7	2.0	0	0	0.0	0
2004—Detroit NFL	16	16	18	5	1.5	0	0	0.0	0
Pro totals (11 years)	169	166	271	77	51.5	5	99	19.8	1

WILLIAMS, AENEAS — S

PERSONAL: Born January 29, 1968, in New Orleans, La. ... 5-11/200. ... Full name: Aeneas Demetrius Williams. ... Name pronounced: uh-NEE-us.
HIGH SCHOOL: Fortier (New Orleans).
COLLEGE: Southern University.
TRANSACTIONS/CAREER NOTES: Selected by Phoenix Cardinals in third round (59th pick overall) of 1991 NFL draft. ... Signed by Cardinals (July 26, 1991). ... Granted free agency (February 17, 1994). ... Cardinals franchise renamed Arizona Cardinals for 1994 season. ... Re-signed by Cardinals (June 1, 1994). ... Granted unconditional free agency (February 16, 1996). ... Re-signed by Cardinals (February 27, 1996). ... Designated by Cardinals as franchise player (February 22, 2001). ... Re-signed by Cardinals (April 21, 2001). ... Traded by Cardinals to St. Louis Rams for second- (DB Michael Stone) and fourth-round (DT Marcus Bell) picks in 2001 draft (April 21, 2001). ... On injured reserve with broken ankle (October 21, 2002-remainder of season). ... Released by Rams (February 27, 2003). ... Re-signed by Rams (March 1, 2003). ... On injured reserve with neck injury (December 28, 2004-remainder of season). ... Granted unconditional free agency (March 2, 2005).
CHAMPIONSHIP GAME EXPERIENCE: Played in NFC championship game (2001 season). ... Played in Super Bowl 36 (2001 season).
HONORS: Named cornerback on THE SPORTING NEWS NFL All-Pro team (1995, 1997 and 2001). ... Played in Pro Bowl (1994-1999, 2001 and 2003 seasons).
RECORDS: Shares NFL record for longest fumble recovery return for touchdown—104 yards (November 5, 2000, vs. Washington).
POST SEASON RECORDS: Shares NFL single-game postseason record for most interceptions returned for touchdown—2 (January 20, 2002, vs. Green Bay). ... Holds NFL postseason record for most consecutive games with an interceptions—4 (1998-2001).
MISCELLANEOUS: Active NFL leader in interceptions (55).

Year Team	G	GS	TOTALS Tk.	Ast.	Sks.	INTERCEPTIONS No.	Yds.	Avg.	TD
1991—Phoenix NFL	16	15	38	10	0.0	∞6	60	10.0	0
1992—Phoenix NFL	16	16	40	8	0.0	3	25	8.3	0
1993—Phoenix NFL	16	16	37	5	0.0	2	87	43.5	1
1994—Arizona NFL	16	16	40	1	0.0	†9	89	9.9	0
1995—Arizona NFL	16	16	52	10	0.0	6	86	14.3	†2
1996—Arizona NFL	16	16	65	12	1.0	6	89	14.8	1
1997—Arizona NFL	16	16	49	14	0.0	6	95	15.8	∞2
1998—Arizona NFL	16	16	57	13	1.0	1	15	15.0	0
1999—Arizona NFL	16	16	49	7	0.0	2	5	2.5	0
2000—Arizona NFL	16	16	48	14	0.0	5	102	20.4	0
2001—St. Louis NFL	16	16	56	17	0.0	4	69	17.3	†2
2002—St. Louis NFL	6	6	23	6	0.0	1	3	3.0	0
2003—St. Louis NFL	16	16	60	15	1.0	4	82	20.5	1
2004—St. Louis NFL	13	10	40	8	0.0	0	0	0.0	0
Pro totals (14 years)	211	207	654	140	3.0	55	807	14.7	9

WILLIAMS, ANDREW — DE — 49ERS

W

PERSONAL: Born April 18, 1979, in Tampa, Fla. ... 6-2/263. ... Full name: Andrew B. Williams.
HIGH SCHOOL: Hillsborough (Tampa, Fla.).
JUNIOR COLLEGE: Hinds Community College (Miss.).
COLLEGE: Miami (Fla.).
TRANSACTIONS/CAREER NOTES: Selected by San Francisco 49ers in third round (89th pick overall) of 2003 NFL draft. ... Signed by 49ers (July 24, 2003).

Year Team	G	GS	TOTALS Tk.	Ast.	Sks.
2003—San Francisco NFL	2	0	1	0	0.0
2004—San Francisco NFL	7	3	9	2	0.0
Pro totals (2 years)	9	3	10	2	0.0

WILLIAMS, BOBBIE — G — BENGALS

PERSONAL: Born September 25, 1976, in Jefferson, Texas. ... 6-4/330.
HIGH SCHOOL: Jefferson (Texas).
COLLEGE: Arkansas.

TRANSACTIONS/CAREER NOTES: Selected by Philadelphia Eagles in second round (61st pick overall) of 2000 NFL draft. ... Signed by Eagles (July 17, 2000). ... Inactive for all 16 games (2000). ... Granted unconditional free agency (March 3, 2004). ... Signed by Cincinnati Bengals (March 26, 2004).
PLAYING EXPERIENCE: Philadelphia NFL, 2000-2003; Cincinnati NFL, 2004. ... Games/Games started: 2001 (1/1), 2002 (16/0), 2003 (16/11), 2004 (16/16), Total: 49/28.
CHAMPIONSHIP GAME EXPERIENCE: Member of Eagles for NFC championship game (2001 season); inactive. ... Played in NFC championship game (2002 and 2003 seasons).

WILLIAMS, BOO — TE — SAINTS

PERSONAL: Born June 22, 1979, in Tallahassee, Fla. ... 6-4/265. ... Full name: Eddie Lee Williams.
HIGH SCHOOL: Lincoln (Tallahassee, Fla.).
JUNIOR COLLEGE: Coffeyville (Kan.) Community College.
COLLEGE: Arkansas.
TRANSACTIONS/CAREER NOTES: Signed as non-drafted free agent by New Orleans Saints (April 26, 2000). ... Released by Saints (September 2, 2001). ... Re-signed by Saints to practice squad (September 3, 2001). ... Activated (October 27, 2001).
SINGLE GAME HIGHS (regular season): Receptions—9 (November 23, 2003, vs. Philadelphia); yards—110 (November 23, 2003, vs. Philadelphia); and touchdown receptions—2 (November 18, 2001, vs. Indianapolis).
STATISTICAL PLATEAUS: 100-yard receiving games: 2003 (1). Total: 1.

			RECEIVING					TOTALS			
Year Team	G	GS	No.	Yds.	Avg.	TD	TD	2pt.	Pts.	Fum.
2001—New Orleans NFL	11	4	20	202	10.1	3	3	0	18	0
2002—New Orleans NFL	16	3	13	143	11.0	2	2	1	14	0
2003—New Orleans NFL	16	6	41	436	10.6	5	5	0	30	0
2004—New Orleans NFL	16	8	33	362	11.0	2	2	0	12	2
Pro totals (4 years)	59	21	107	1143	10.7	12	12	1	74	2

WILLIAMS, BRETT — T — CHIEFS

PERSONAL: Born May 2, 1980, in Kissimmee, Fla. ... 6-5/321.
HIGH SCHOOL: Osceola (Kissimmee, Fla.).
COLLEGE: Florida State.
TRANSACTIONS/CAREER NOTES: Selected by Kansas City Chiefs in fourth round (113th pick overall) of 2003 NFL draft. ... Signed by Chiefs (July 17, 2003).
PLAYING EXPERIENCE: Kansas City NFL, 2004. ... Games/Games started: 2004 (5/0). Total: 5/0.

WILLIAMS, BRIAN — CB

PERSONAL: Born July 2, 1979, in High Point, N.C. ... 5-11/198.
HIGH SCHOOL: Southwest Guilford (N.C.).
COLLEGE: North Carolina State.
TRANSACTIONS/CAREER NOTES: Selected by Minnesota Vikings in fourth round (105th pick overall) of 2002 NFL draft. ... Signed by Vikings (July 24, 2002). ... Granted free agency (March 2, 2005).

			TOTALS			INTERCEPTIONS			
Year Team	G	GS	Tk.	Ast.	Sks.	No.	Yds.	Avg.	TD
2002—Minnesota NFL	16	7	32	5	0.0	1	2	2.0	0
2003—Minnesota NFL	16	16	54	16	3.0	5	†205	41.0	1
2004—Minnesota NFL	16	16	59	12	0.0	2	14	7.0	0
Pro totals (3 years)	48	39	145	33	3.0	8	221	27.6	1

WILLIAMS, BROCK — CB — RAIDERS

PERSONAL: Born August 11, 1979, in Hammond, La. ... 5-10/195.
HIGH SCHOOL: Hammond (La.).
COLLEGE: Notre Dame.
TRANSACTIONS/CAREER NOTES: Selected by New England Patriots in third round (86th pick overall) of 2001 NFL draft. ... Signed by Patriots (September 10, 2001). ... On injured reserve with knee injury (September 10, 2001-remainder of season). ... Released by Patriots (September 1, 2002). ... Re-signed by Patriots to practice squad (September 3, 2002). ... Released by Patriots (October 18, 2002). ... Signed by Oakland Raiders to practice squad (October 23, 2002). ... Claimed on waivers by Chicago Bears (August 27, 2003). ... Released by Bears (August 26, 2004). ... Signed by Raiders (October 20, 2004). ... Released by Raiders (October 27, 2004). ... Re-signed by Raiders (December 21, 2004).

			TOTALS			INTERCEPTIONS			
Year Team	G	GS	Tk.	Ast.	Sks.	No.	Yds.	Avg.	TD
2003—Chicago NFL	10	0	2	0	0.0	0	0	0.0	0
2004—Oakland NFL	2	0	5	1	0.0	0	0	0.0	0
Pro totals (2 years)	12	0	7	1	0.0	0	0	0.0	0

W

WILLIAMS, CHAD — S

PERSONAL: Born January 22, 1979, in Birmingham, Ala. ... 5-9/207.
HIGH SCHOOL: Wenonah (Birmingham, Ala.).
COLLEGE: Southern Miss.
TRANSACTIONS/CAREER NOTES: Selected by Baltimore Ravens in sixth round (209th pick overall) of 2002 NFL draft. ... Signed by Ravens (July 25, 2002). ... Granted free agency (March 2, 2005).

Year Team	G	GS	TOTALS Tk.	Ast.	Sks.	INTERCEPTIONS No.	Yds.	Avg.	TD
2002—Baltimore NFL	16	0	29	3	0.0	3	98	32.7	1
2003—Baltimore NFL	16	1	20	4	1.0	1	52	52.0	1
2004—Baltimore NFL	16	1	24	4	2.0	3	156	52.0	1
Pro totals (3 years)	48	2	73	11	3.0	7	306	43.7	3

WILLIAMS, COREY — DT — PACKERS

PERSONAL: Born August 17, 1980, in Harmony Grove, Ark. ... 6-4/310.
HIGH SCHOOL: Harmony Grove (Ark.).
COLLEGE: Arkansas State.
TRANSACTIONS/CAREER NOTES: Selected by Green Bay Packers in sixth round (179th pick overall) of 2004 NFL draft. ... Signed by Packers (July 31, 2004).

Year Team	G	GS	TOTALS Tk.	Ast.	Sks.
2004—Green Bay NFL	12	0	12	9	1.0

WILLIAMS, DAVERN — DT — GIANTS

PERSONAL: Born February 13, 1980, in Brewton, Ala. ... 6-3/300.
HIGH SCHOOL: Jefferson Davis (Montgomery, Ala.).
COLLEGE: Troy.
TRANSACTIONS/CAREER NOTES: Selected by Miami Dolphins in seventh round (248th pick overall) of 2003 NFL draft. ... Signed by Dolphins (July 24, 2003). ... On injured reserve with shoulder injury (August 7, 2003-remainder of season). ... Assigned by Dolphins to Cologne Centurions in 2004 NFL Europe enhancement allocation program (February 9, 2004). ... Released by Dolphins (April 8, 2004). ... Signed by New York Giants to practice squad (October 27, 2004). ... Activated (November 30, 2004).

Year Team	G	GS	TOTALS Tk.	Ast.	Sks.
2004—New York Giants NFL	3	1	3	4	0.5

WILLIAMS, DEMORRIO — LB — FALCONS

PERSONAL: Born July 6, 1980, in Beckville, Texas. ... 6-0/232.
HIGH SCHOOL: Beckville (Texas).
JUNIOR COLLEGE: Kilgore (Texas).
COLLEGE: Nebraska.
TRANSACTIONS/CAREER NOTES: Selected by Atlanta Falcons in fourth round (101st pick overall) of 2004 NFL draft. ... Signed by Falcons (July 13, 2004).
CHAMPIONSHIP GAME EXPERIENCE: Played in NFC championship game (2004 season).

Year Team	G	GS	TOTALS Tk.	Ast.	Sks.	INTERCEPTIONS No.	Yds.	Avg.	TD
2004—Atlanta NFL	16	1	38	7	2.5	0	0	0.0	0

WILLIAMS, D.J. — LB — BRONCOS

PERSONAL: Born July 20, 1982, in Pittsburg, Calif. ... 6-1/242. ... Full name: Genos Derwin Williams.
HIGH SCHOOL: Concord De La Salle (Pittsburg, Calif.).
COLLEGE: Miami (Fla.).
TRANSACTIONS/CAREER NOTES: Selected by Denver Broncos in first round (17th pick overall) of 2004 NFL draft. ... Signed by Broncos (July 27, 2004).
HONORS: Named linebacker on THE SPORTING NEWS college All-America second team (2003).

Year Team	G	GS	TOTALS Tk.	Ast.	Sks.	INTERCEPTIONS No.	Yds.	Avg.	TD
2004—Denver NFL	16	14	75	31	2.0	1	10	10.0	0

W

WILLIAMS, GRANT — T — RAMS

PERSONAL: Born May 10, 1974, in Hattiesburg, Miss. ... 6-7/320.
HIGH SCHOOL: Clinton (Miss.).
JUNIOR COLLEGE: Hinds Community College (Miss.).
COLLEGE: Louisiana Tech.
TRANSACTIONS/CAREER NOTES: Signed as non-drafted free agent by Seattle Seahawks (April 22, 1996). ... Granted unconditional free agency (February 11, 2000). ... Signed by New England Patriots (March 17, 2000). ... Granted unconditional free agency (March 1, 2002). ... Re-signed by Patriots (April 19, 2002). ... Traded by Patriots to St. Louis Rams for seventh-round pick (traded to Tennessee) in 2003 draft (August 19, 2002). ... On injured reserve with ankle injury (October 15, 2002-remainder of season). ... Granted unconditional free agency (February 28, 2003). ... Re-signed by Rams (April 16, 2003).
PLAYING EXPERIENCE: Seattle NFL, 1996-1999; New England NFL, 2000-2001; St. Louis NFL, 2002-2004. ... Games/Games started: 1996 (8/0), 1997 (16/8), 1998 (16/0), 1999 (16/15), 2000 (15/8), 2001 (14/4), 2002 (5/3), 2003 (16/0), 2004 (16/11). Total: 122/49.
CHAMPIONSHIP GAME EXPERIENCE: Played in AFC championship game (2001 season). ... Member of Super Bowl championship team (2001 season).

WILLIAMS, JAMAL   DT   CHARGERS

PERSONAL: Born April 28, 1976, in Washington, DC. ... 6-3/348.
HIGH SCHOOL: Archbishop Carroll (Washington, D.C.).
COLLEGE: Oklahoma State.
TRANSACTIONS/CAREER NOTES: Selected by San Diego Chargers in second round of 1998 supplemental draft (July 9, 1998). ... Signed by Chargers (August 7, 1998). ... Granted free agency (March 2, 2001). ... Re-signed by Chargers (May 11, 2001). ... On injured reserve with knee injury (October 3, 2001-remainder of season). ... On injured reserve with ankle injury (December 2, 2002-remainder of season).

			TOTALS			INTERCEPTIONS			
Year Team	G	GS	Tk.	Ast.	Sks.	No.	Yds.	Avg.	TD
1998—San Diego NFL	9	0	5	1	0.0	1	14	14.0	1
1999—San Diego NFL	16	2	22	4	1.0	0	0	0.0	0
2000—San Diego NFL	16	16	46	7	1.0	0	0	0.0	0
2001—San Diego NFL	3	3	2	0	0.0	0	0	0.0	0
2002—San Diego NFL	12	10	20	4	2.5	0	0	0.0	0
2003—San Diego NFL	15	15	24	9	1.0	0	0	0.0	0
2004—San Diego NFL	15	15	25	7	4.0	0	0	0.0	0
Pro totals (7 years)	86	61	144	32	9.5	1	14	14.0	1

WILLIAMS, JAY   DE   RAMS

PERSONAL: Born October 13, 1971, in Washington, DC. ... 6-3/270. ... Full name: Jay Omar Williams.
HIGH SCHOOL: St. John's (Washington, D.C.).
COLLEGE: Wake Forest.
TRANSACTIONS/CAREER NOTES: Signed as non-drafted free agent by Miami Dolphins (April 28, 1994). ... Released by Dolphins (August 28, 1994). ... Signed by Los Angeles Rams to practice squad (September 27, 1994). ... Activated (December 7, 1994); did not play. ... Rams franchise moved from Los Angeles to St. Louis (April 12, 1995). ... On physically unable to perform list with forearm injury (July 31-November 18, 1996). ... Released by Rams (November 20, 1996). ... Re-signed by Rams (December 11, 1996). ... Granted free agency (February 12, 1999). ... Re-signed by Rams (May 4, 1999). ... Granted unconditional free agency (February 11, 2000). ... Signed by Carolina Panthers (February 16, 2000). ... Traded by Panthers to Miami Dolphins for DE Al Wallace and fourth-round pick (DB Colin Branch) in 2003 draft (July 19, 2002). ... Released by Dolphins (February 23, 2005). ... Signed by Rams (March 30, 2005).
CHAMPIONSHIP GAME EXPERIENCE: Played in NFC championship game (1999 season). ... Member of Super Bowl championship team (1999 season).

			TOTALS			INTERCEPTIONS			
Year Team	G	GS	Tk.	Ast.	Sks.	No.	Yds.	Avg.	TD
1994—Los Angeles Rams NFL	Did not play.								
1995—St. Louis NFL	7	0	0	0	0.0	0	0	0.0	0
1996—St. Louis NFL	2	0	0	0	0.0	0	0	0.0	0
1997—St. Louis NFL	16	2	4	3	1.0	0	0	0.0	0
1998—St. Louis NFL	16	1	10	4	1.0	0	0	0.0	0
1999—St. Louis NFL	16	0	13	1	4.0	0	0	0.0	0
2000—Carolina NFL	16	14	21	6	6.0	0	0	0.0	0
2001—Carolina NFL	16	13	27	12	1.0	1	0	0.0	0
2002—Miami NFL	16	0	17	5	6.0	0	0	0.0	0
2003—Miami NFL	16	0	8	4	2.5	0	0	0.0	0
2004—Miami NFL	16	1	21	17	2.0	1	0	0.0	0
Pro totals (10 years)	137	31	121	52	23.5	2	0	0.0	0

WILLIAMS, JIMMY   CB   SAINTS

PERSONAL: Born March 10, 1979, in Baton Rouge, La. ... 5-11/190.
HIGH SCHOOL: Episcopal (Baton Rouge, La.).
COLLEGE: Vanderbilt.
TRANSACTIONS/CAREER NOTES: Selected by Buffalo Bills in sixth round (196th pick overall) of 2001 NFL draft. ... Signed by Bills (June 13, 2001). ... Released by Bills (September 2, 2001). ... Signed by San Francisco 49ers to practice squad (September 5, 2001). ... Activated (October 16, 2001). ... On injured reserve with knee injury (December 10, 2002-remainder of season). ... Re-signed by 49ers (May 6, 2003). ... Granted free agency (March 3, 2004). ... Re-signed by 49ers (March 30, 2004). ... Granted unconditional free agency (March 2, 2005). ... Signed by New Orleans Saints (April 18, 2005).

			TOTALS			INTERCEPTIONS				PUNT RETURNS				KICKOFF RETURNS				TOTALS			
Year Team	G	GS	Tk.	Ast.	Sks.	No.	Yds.	Avg.	TD	No.	Yds.	Avg.	TD	No.	Yds.	Avg.	TD	TD	2pt.	Pts.	Fum.
2001—S.F. NFL	10	0	0	0	0.0	0	0	0.0	0	0	0	0.0	0	0	0	0.0	0	0	0	0	0
2002—S.F. NFL	13	0	0	0	0.0	0	0	0.0	0	20	336	*16.8	1	35	765	21.9	0	1	0	6	2
2003—S.F. NFL	15	0	9	1	0.0	1	6	6.0	0	35	240	6.9	0	11	207	18.8	0	0	0	0	3
2004—S.F. NFL	12	6	35	8	1.0	0	0	0.0	0	0	0	0.0	0	3	58	19.3	0	0	0	0	0
Pro totals (4 years)	50	6	44	9	1.0	1	6	6.0	0	55	576	10.5	1	49	1030	21.0	0	1	0	6	5

WILLIAMS, JOSH   DT   COLTS

PERSONAL: Born August 9, 1976, in Denver, Colo. ... 6-3/285. ... Full name: Josh Sinclair Williams.
HIGH SCHOOL: Cypress Creek (Houston).
COLLEGE: Michigan.
TRANSACTIONS/CAREER NOTES: Selected by Indianapolis Colts in fourth round (122nd pick overall) of 2000 NFL draft. ... Signed by Colts (June 27, 2000). ... Granted free agency (February 28, 2003). ... Re-signed by Colts (April 15, 2003).
CHAMPIONSHIP GAME EXPERIENCE: Played in AFC championship game (2003 season).

W

Year Team	G	GS	Tk.	Ast.	Sks.
			TOTALS		
2000—Indianapolis NFL	14	7	26	16	3.0
2001—Indianapolis NFL	16	16	30	19	3.0
2002—Indianapolis NFL	7	3	10	4	1.0
2003—Indianapolis NFL	16	4	13	4	1.0
2004—Indianapolis NFL	16	15	28	7	0.0
Pro totals (5 years)	69	45	107	50	8.0

WILLIAMS, KARL   WR/PR

PERSONAL: Born April 10, 1971, in Albion, Mich. ... 5-11/182.
HIGH SCHOOL: Garland (Texas).
COLLEGE: Texas A&M-Kingsville.
TRANSACTIONS/CAREER NOTES: Signed as non-drafted free agent by Tampa Bay Buccaneers (April 23, 1996). ... Granted unconditional free agency (March 1, 2002). ... Re-signed by Buccaneers (April 17, 2002). ... Released by Buccaneers (March 2, 2004). ... Signed by Arizona Cardinals (March 18, 2004). ... Released by Cardinals (March 9, 2005).
CHAMPIONSHIP GAME EXPERIENCE: Played in NFC championship game (1999 and 2002 seasons). ... Member of Super Bowl championship team (2002 season).
SINGLE GAME HIGHS (regular season): Receptions—6 (September 26, 2004, vs. Atlanta); yards—90 (September 26, 2004, vs. Atlanta); and touchdown receptions—2 (November 2, 1997, vs. Indianapolis).

Year Team	G	GS	RECEIVING No.	Yds.	Avg.	TD	PUNT RETURNS No.	Yds.	Avg.	TD	KICKOFF RETURNS No.	Yds.	Avg.	TD	TOTALS TD	2pt.	Pts.	Fum.
1996—Tampa Bay NFL	16	0	22	246	11.2	0	13	274	21.1	1	14	383	27.4	0	1	0	6	2
1997—Tampa Bay NFL	16	7	33	486	14.7	4	46	‡597	13.0	∞1	15	277	18.5	0	5	0	30	5
1998—Tampa Bay NFL	13	6	21	252	12.0	1	10	83	8.3	0	0	0	0.0	0	1	0	6	0
1999—Tampa Bay NFL	13	4	21	176	8.4	0	20	153	7.7	0	1	15	15.0	0	0	0	0	2
2000—Tampa Bay NFL	13	0	2	35	17.5	0	31	286	9.2	1	19	453	23.8	0	1	0	6	2
2001—Tampa Bay NFL	15	3	24	314	13.1	1	35	366	10.5	†1	2	35	17.5	0	2	0	12	3
2002—Tampa Bay NFL	16	2	7	77	11.0	0	43	410	9.5	1	3	49	16.3	0	2	0	12	0
2003—Tampa Bay NFL	13	0	7	114	16.3	0	15	110	7.3	0	1	15	15.0	0	0	1	2	0
2004—Arizona NFL	15	2	18	197	10.9	0	42	286	6.8	0	1	18	18.0	0	0	0	0	4
Pro totals (9 years)	130	24	155	1897	12.2	7	255	2565	10.1	5	56	1245	22.2	0	12	1	74	18

WILLIAMS, KEVIN   DE   VIKINGS

PERSONAL: Born August 16, 1980, in Arkadelphia, Ark. ... 6-5/311.
HIGH SCHOOL: Fordyce (Ark.).
COLLEGE: Oklahoma State.
TRANSACTIONS/CAREER NOTES: Selected by Minnesota Vikings in first round (ninth pick overall) of 2003 NFL draft. ... Signed by Vikings (July 25, 2003).
HONORS: Named defensive tackle on THE SPORTING NEWS NFL All-Pro team (2004). ... Played in Pro Bowl (2004 season).

Year Team	G	GS	TOTALS Tk.	Ast.	Sks.	INTERCEPTIONS No.	Yds.	Avg.	TD
2003—Minnesota NFL	16	16	37	15	10.5	1	3	3.0	0
2004—Minnesota NFL	16	16	53	17	11.5	1	7	7.0	0
Pro totals (2 years)	32	32	90	32	22.0	2	10	5.0	0

WILLIAMS, MADIEU   DB   BENGALS

PERSONAL: Born October 18, 1981, in Sierra Leone, West Africa. ... 6-1/193.
HIGH SCHOOL: DuVal (Lanham, Md.).
COLLEGE: Maryland.
TRANSACTIONS/CAREER NOTES: Selected by Cincinnati Bengals in second round (56th pick overall) of 2004 NFL draft. ... Signed by Bengals (July 30, 2004).

Year Team	G	GS	TOTALS Tk.	Ast.	Sks.	INTERCEPTIONS No.	Yds.	Avg.	TD
2004—Cincinnati NFL	16	13	76	15	2.0	3	51	17.0	1

W

WILLIAMS, MAURICE   T   JAGUARS

PERSONAL: Born January 26, 1979, in Detroit, Mich. ... 6-5/310. ... Full name: Maurice Carlos Williams.
HIGH SCHOOL: Pershing (Detroit).
COLLEGE: Michigan.
TRANSACTIONS/CAREER NOTES: Selected by Jacksonville Jaguars in second round (43rd pick overall) of 2001 NFL draft. ... Signed by Jaguars (July 25, 2001). ... On injured reserve with leg injury (October 14, 2002-remainder of season).
PLAYING EXPERIENCE: Jacksonville NFL, 2001-2004. ... Games/Games started: 2001 (16/16), 2002 (5/5), 2003 (16/16), 2004 (16/16). Total: 53/53.

WILLIAMS, MELVIN   DE

PERSONAL: Born February 2, 1979, in St. Louis, Mo. ... 6-2/278.
HIGH SCHOOL: Mehlville (St. Louis, Mo.).
COLLEGE: Kansas State.

TRANSACTIONS/CAREER NOTES: Selected by New Orleans Saints in fifth round (155th pick overall) of 2003 NFL draft. ... Signed by Saints (June 2, 2003). ... Claimed on waivers by San Francisco 49ers (October 5, 2004). ... Released by 49ers (October 19, 2004). ... Re-signed by 49ers (November 3, 2004). ... Claimed on waivers by Miami Dolphins (November 15, 2004). ... Released by Dolphins (November 23, 2004). ... Signed by Washington Redskins (December 29, 2004). ... Released by Redskins (December 31, 2004).

| | | | | TOTALS | | |
Year Team		G	GS	Tk.	Ast.	Sks.
2003—New Orleans NFL		14	2	6	6	0.0
2004—San Francisco NFL		3	0	3	1	0.0
Pro totals (2 years)		17	2	9	7	0.0

WILLIAMS, MIKE   T   BILLS

PERSONAL: Born January 11, 1980, in Dallas, Texas. ... 6-6/360. ... Full name: Michael D. Williams.
HIGH SCHOOL: The Colony (Texas).
COLLEGE: Texas.
TRANSACTIONS/CAREER NOTES: Selected by Buffalo Bills in first round (fourth pick overall) of 2002 NFL draft. ... Signed by Bills (July 28, 2002).
PLAYING EXPERIENCE: Buffalo NFL, 2002-2004. ... Games/Games started: 2002 (14/14), 2003 (13/13), 2004 (15/15). Total: 42/42.
HONORS: Named offensive tackle on THE SPORTING NEWS college All-America second team (2001).

WILLIAMS, MOE   RB   VIKINGS

PERSONAL: Born July 26, 1974, in Columbus, Ga. ... 6-1/205. ... Full name: Maurice Jabari Williams.
HIGH SCHOOL: Spencer (Columbus, Ga.).
COLLEGE: Kentucky.
TRANSACTIONS/CAREER NOTES: Selected after junior season by Minnesota Vikings in third round (75th pick overall) of 1996 NFL draft. ... Signed by Vikings (July 22, 1996). ... On injured reserve with foot injury (December 8, 1998-remainder of season). ... Granted free agency (February 12, 1999). ... Re-signed by Vikings (April 30, 1999). ... Granted unconditional free agency (February 11, 2000). ... Re-signed by Vikings (March 20, 2000). ... Released by Vikings (September 2, 2001). ... Signed by Baltimore Ravens (September 4, 2001). ... Granted unconditional free agency (March 1, 2002). ... Signed by Vikings (May 21, 2002). ... Granted unconditional free agency (February 28, 2003). ... Re-signed by Vikings (March 13, 2003).
CHAMPIONSHIP GAME EXPERIENCE: Played in NFC championship game (2000 season).
SINGLE GAME HIGHS (regular season): Attempts—24 (December 2, 2001, vs. Indianapolis); yards—111 (December 2, 2001, vs. Indianapolis); and rushing touchdowns—2 (October 5, 2003, vs. Atlanta).
STATISTICAL PLATEAUS: 100-yard rushing games: 2001 (1), 2002 (1), 2003 (1). Total: 3. 100-yard receiving games: 2003 (1). Total: 1.

| | | | RUSHING | | | | RECEIVING | | | | KICKOFF RETURNS | | | | TOTALS | | | |
Year Team	G	GS	Att.	Yds.	Avg.	TD	No.	Yds.	Avg.	TD	No.	Yds.	Avg.	TD	TD	2pt.	Pts.	Fum.
1996—Minnesota NFL	9	0	0	0	0.0	0	0	0	0.0	0	0	0	0.0	0	0	0	0	0
1997—Minnesota NFL	14	0	22	59	2.7	1	4	14	3.5	0	16	388	24.3	0	1	0	6	0
1998—Minnesota NFL	12	1	0	0	0.0	0	1	64	64.0	0	2	19	9.5	0	0	0	0	1
1999—Minnesota NFL	14	0	24	69	2.9	1	1	12	12.0	0	10	240	24.0	1	2	0	12	0
2000—Minnesota NFL	16	0	23	67	2.9	0	4	31	7.8	0	10	214	21.4	0	0	1	2	0
2001—Baltimore NFL	15	2	65	291	4.5	0	23	210	9.1	0	0	0	0.0	0	0	0	0	1
2002—Minnesota NFL	16	0	84	414	4.9	11	27	251	9.3	0	24	516	21.5	0	11	0	66	1
2003—Minnesota NFL	16	7	174	745	4.3	5	65	644	9.9	3	0	0	0.0	0	8	0	48	2
2004—Minnesota NFL	14	1	30	161	5.4	3	21	233	11.1	1	0	0	0.0	0	4	0	24	0
Pro totals (9 years)	126	11	422	1806	4.3	21	146	1459	10.0	4	62	1377	22.2	1	26	1	158	5

WILLIAMS, PAT   DT   VIKINGS

PERSONAL: Born October 24, 1972, in Monroe, La. ... 6-3/317. ... Full name: Patrick Williams.
HIGH SCHOOL: Wossman (Monroe, La.).
JUNIOR COLLEGE: Navarro College (Texas).
COLLEGE: Texas A&M.
TRANSACTIONS/CAREER NOTES: Signed as non-drafted free agent by Buffalo Bills (April 25, 1997). ... Granted free agency (February 11, 2000). ... Re-signed by Bills (March 23, 2000). ... Granted unconditional free agency (March 2, 2005). ... Signed by Minnesota Vikings (March 2, 2005).

| | | | TOTALS | | | INTERCEPTIONS | | | |
Year Team	G	GS	Tk.	Ast.	Sks.	No.	Yds.	Avg.	TD
1997—Buffalo NFL	1	0	0	0	0.0	0	0	0.0	0
1998—Buffalo NFL	13	0	11	1	3.5	0	0	0.0	0
1999—Buffalo NFL	16	0	25	7	2.5	0	0	0.0	0
2000—Buffalo NFL	16	4	37	18	2.5	0	0	0.0	0
2001—Buffalo NFL	13	13	41	18	1.5	0	0	0.0	0
2002—Buffalo NFL	16	16	53	31	0.5	0	0	0.0	0
2003—Buffalo NFL	16	16	54	28	0.0	0	0	0.0	0
2004—Buffalo NFL	16	15	37	16	2.5	1	20	20.0	1
Pro totals (8 years)	107	64	258	119	13.0	1	20	20.0	1

WILLIAMS, QUINTIN   DB   DOLPHINS

PERSONAL: Born September 24, 1982, in Goldsboro, N.C. ... 5-11/204.
HIGH SCHOOL: Rosewood (Goldsboro, N.C.).
COLLEGE: Wake Forest.

W

TRANSACTIONS/CAREER NOTES: Signed as non-drafted free agent by Miami Dolphins (April 30, 2004). ... Released by Dolphins (September 5, 2004). ... Re-signed by Dolphins to practice squad (September 6, 2004). ... Activated (November 15, 2004).

Year Team	G	GS	TOTALS			INTERCEPTIONS			
			Tk.	Ast.	Sks.	No.	Yds.	Avg.	TD
2004—Miami NFL	6	0	0	0	0.0	0	0	0.0	0

WILLIAMS, RANDAL — WR

PERSONAL: Born May 21, 1978, in Bronx, N.Y. ... 6-3/211. ... Full name: Randal Ellison Williams.
HIGH SCHOOL: Deerfield Academy (Maine).
COLLEGE: New Hampshire.
TRANSACTIONS/CAREER NOTES: Signed as non-drafted free agent by Jacksonville Jaguars (April 27, 2001). ... Claimed on waivers by Dallas Cowboys (October 29, 2001). ... Granted free agency (March 3, 2004). ... Re-signed by Cowboys (April 19, 2004). ... Released by Cowboys (April 28, 2005).
SINGLE GAME HIGHS (regular season): Receptions—1 (November 7, 2004, vs. Cincinnati); yards—14 (November 7, 2004, vs. Cincinnati); and touchdown receptions—0.

Year Team	G	GS	RECEIVING				KICKOFF RETURNS				TOTALS			
			No.	Yds.	Avg.	TD	No.	Yds.	Avg.	TD	TD	2pt.	Pts.	Fum.
2001—Dallas NFL	7	0	0	0	0.0	0	0	0	0.0	0	0	0	0	0
2002—Dallas NFL	11	0	0	0	0.0	0	0	0	0.0	0	0	0	0	0
2003—Dallas NFL	15	0	0	0	0.0	0	2	60	30.0	1	1	0	6	0
2004—Dallas NFL	2	2	1	14	14.0	0	0	0	0.0	0	0	0	0	0
Pro totals (4 years)	35	2	1	14	14.0	0	2	60	30.0	1	1	0	6	0

WILLIAMS, REGGIE — WR — JAGUARS

PERSONAL: Born May 17, 1983, in Landstuhl, Germany. ... 6-4/223.
HIGH SCHOOL: Lakes (Lakewood, Wash.).
COLLEGE: Washington.
TRANSACTIONS/CAREER NOTES: Selected after junior season by Jacksonville Jaguars in first round (ninth pick overall) of 2004 NFL draft. ... Signed by Jaguars (July 31, 2004).
HONORS: Named wide receiver on THE SPORTING NEWS Freshman All-America first team (2001).
SINGLE GAME HIGHS (regular season): Receptions—5 (October 31, 2004, vs. Houston); yards—62 (December 12, 2004, vs. Chicago); and touchdown receptions—1 (December 12, 2004, vs. Chicago).

Year Team	G	GS	RECEIVING				TOTALS			
			No.	Yds.	Avg.	TD	TD	2pt.	Pts.	Fum.
2004—Jacksonville NFL	16	15	27	268	9.9	1	1	†2	10	1

WILLIAMS, RENAULD — LB — BROWNS

PERSONAL: Born February 23, 1981, in Westbury, N.Y. ... 6-0/211.
HIGH SCHOOL: Friends Academy (Locust Valley, N.Y.).
COLLEGE: Hofstra.
TRANSACTIONS/CAREER NOTES: Signed as non-drafted free agent by San Francisco 49ers (May 2, 2004). ... Released by 49ers (September 5, 2004). ... Signed by Miami Dolphins to practice squad (September 29, 2004). ... Activated (November 23, 2004). ... On injured reserve with wrist injury (December 23, 2004-remainder of season). ... Claimed on waivers by Cleveland Browns (May 5, 2005).

Year Team	G	GS	TOTALS			INTERCEPTIONS			
			Tk.	Ast.	Sks.	No.	Yds.	Avg.	TD
2004—Miami NFL	2	0	0	0	0.0	0	0	0.0	0

WILLIAMS, ROLAND — TE — RAMS

PERSONAL: Born April 27, 1975, in Rochester, N.Y. ... 6-5/265. ... Full name: Roland Lamar Williams.
HIGH SCHOOL: East (Rochester, N.Y.).
COLLEGE: Syracuse.
TRANSACTIONS/CAREER NOTES: Selected by St. Louis Rams in fourth round (98th pick overall) of 1998 NFL draft. ... Signed by Rams (July 13, 1998). ... Granted free agency (March 2, 2001). ... Re-signed by Rams (April 20, 2001). ... Traded by Rams to Oakland Raiders for fourth-round pick (traded to Arizona) in 2001 draft (April 21, 2001). ... On injured reserve with knee and toe injuries (January 18, 2003-remainder of 2002 season). ... Released by Raiders (August 26, 2003). ... Signed by Tampa Bay Buccaneers (November 12, 2003). ... Waived by Buccaneers (March 2, 2004). ... Signed by Oakland Raiders (April 10, 2004). ... Released by Raiders (March 1, 2005). ... Signed by St. Louis Rams (March 9, 2005).
CHAMPIONSHIP GAME EXPERIENCE: Played in NFC championship game (1999 season). ... Member of Super Bowl championship team (1999 season).
SINGLE GAME HIGHS (regular season): Receptions—7 (September 15, 2002, vs. Pittsburgh); yards—55 (September 15, 2002, vs. Pittsburgh); and touchdown receptions—2 (October 24, 1999, vs. Cleveland).

Year Team	G	GS	RECEIVING				TOTALS			
			No.	Yds.	Avg.	TD	TD	2pt.	Pts.	Fum.
1998—St. Louis NFL	13	9	15	144	9.6	1	1	0	6	0
1999—St. Louis NFL	16	15	25	226	9.0	6	6	0	36	0
2000—St. Louis NFL	16	11	11	102	9.3	3	3	1	20	0
2001—Oakland NFL	16	15	33	298	9.0	3	3	0	18	0
2002—Oakland NFL	16	12	27	213	7.9	0	0	0	0	1
2003—Tampa Bay NFL	1	0	0	0	0.0	0	0	0	0	0
2004—Oakland NFL	12	3	0	0	0.0	0	0	0	0	0
Pro totals (7 years)	90	65	111	983	8.9	13	13	1	80	1

W

WILLIAMS, ROY   S   COWBOYS

PERSONAL: Born August 14, 1980, in Redwood City, Calif. ... 6-0/226.
HIGH SCHOOL: James Logan (Union City, Calif.).
COLLEGE: Oklahoma.
TRANSACTIONS/CAREER NOTES: Selected after junior season by Dallas Cowboys in first round (ninth pick overall) of 2002 NFL draft. ... Signed by Cowboys (July 26, 2002).
HONORS: Named strong safety on THE SPORTING NEWS college All-America first team (2001). ... Jim Thorpe Award winner (2001). ... Bronko Nagurski Award winner (2001). ... Named safety on THE SPORTING NEWS NFL All-Pro team (2003). ... Played in Pro Bowl (2003 and 2004 seasons).

				TOTALS			INTERCEPTIONS			
Year Team	G	GS	Tk.	Ast.	Sks.	No.	Yds.	Avg.	TD
2002—Dallas NFL	16	16	81	11	2.0	5	90	18.0	2
2003—Dallas NFL	16	16	53	16	2.0	2	69	34.5	0
2004—Dallas NFL	16	16	70	18	0.0	2	53	26.5	0
Pro totals (3 years)	48	48	204	45	4.0	9	212	23.6	2

WILLIAMS, ROY   WR   LIONS

PERSONAL: Born December 20, 1981, in Odessa, Texas. ... 6-2/212. ... Full name: Roy Eugene Williams.
HIGH SCHOOL: Permian (Odessa, Texas).
COLLEGE: Texas.
TRANSACTIONS/CAREER NOTES: Selected by Detroit Lions in first round (seventh pick overall) of 2004 NFL draft. ... Signed by Lions (July 31, 2004).
HONORS: Named wide receiver on THE SPORTING NEWS Freshman All-America second team (2000).
SINGLE GAME HIGHS (regular season): Receptions—9 (September 26, 2004, vs. Philadelphia); yards—135 (September 26, 2004, vs. Philadelphia); and touchdown receptions—2 (December 19, 2004, vs. Minnesota).
STATISTICAL PLATFAUS: 100-yard receiving games: 2004 (2). Total: 2.

			RUSHING				RECEIVING				TOTALS			
Year Team	G	GS	Att.	Yds.	Avg.	TD	No.	Yds.	Avg.	TD	TD	2pt.	Pts.	Fum.
2004—Detroit NFL	14	12	1	1	1.0	0	54	817	15.1	8	8	0	48	1

WILLIAMS, SAM   DE   RAIDERS

PERSONAL: Born July 28, 1980, in Clayton, Calif. ... 6-5/265.
HIGH SCHOOL: Clayton Valley (Clayton, Calif.).
COLLEGE: Fresno State.
TRANSACTIONS/CAREER NOTES: Selected by Oakland Raiders in third round (83rd pick overall) of 2003 NFL draft. ... Signed by Raiders (July 24, 2003). ... On injured reserve with knee injury (November 19, 2003-remainder of season).

			TOTALS		
Year Team	G	GS	Tk.	Ast.	Sks.
2003—Oakland NFL	1	0	0	0	0.0
2004—Oakland NFL	9	4	21	5	0.0
Pro totals (2 years)	10	4	21	5	0.0

WILLIAMS, SHAUD   RB

PERSONAL: Born October 2, 1980, in Andrews, Texas. ... 5-7/193.
HIGH SCHOOL: Andrews (Texas).
COLLEGE: Alabama.
TRANSACTIONS/CAREER NOTES: Signed as non-drafted free agent by Buffalo Bills (April 26, 2004).
SINGLE GAME HIGHS (regular season): Attempts—17 (December 26, 2004, vs. San Francisco); yards—93 (December 26, 2004, vs. San Francisco); and rushing touchdowns—1 (December 26, 2004, vs. San Francisco).

			RUSHING				RECEIVING				TOTALS			
Year Team	G	GS	Att.	Yds.	Avg.	TD	No.	Yds.	Avg.	TD	TD	2pt.	Pts.	Fum.
2004—Buffalo NFL	4	0	42	167	4.0	2	3	19	6.3	0	2	0	12	1

WILLIAMS, SHAUN   S   GIANTS

PERSONAL: Born October 10, 1976, in Los Angeles, Calif. ... 6-2/218. ... Full name: Shaun LeJon Williams.
HIGH SCHOOL: Crespi (Encino, Calif.).
COLLEGE: UCLA.
TRANSACTIONS/CAREER NOTES: Selected by New York Giants in first round (24th pick overall) of 1998 NFL draft. ... Signed by Giants (July 24, 1998). ... Granted unconditional free agency (March 1, 2002). ... Re-signed by Giants (March 29, 2002). ... On injured reserve with knee injury (November 19, 2003-remainder of season). ... On injured reserve with knee injury (October 6, 2004-remainder of season).
CHAMPIONSHIP GAME EXPERIENCE: Played in NFC championship game (2000 season). ... Played in Super Bowl 35 (2000 season).
HONORS: Named free safety on THE SPORTING NEWS college All-America second team (1997).

			TOTALS			INTERCEPTIONS			
Year Team	G	GS	Tk.	Ast.	Sks.	No.	Yds.	Avg.	TD
1998—New York Giants NFL	13	0	19	5	0.0	2	6	3.0	0
1999—New York Giants NFL	11	0	13	3	0.0	0	0	0.0	0
2000—New York Giants NFL	16	16	68	17	0.0	3	52	17.3	0

W

Year	Team	G	GS	TOTALS			INTERCEPTIONS			
				Tk.	Ast.	Sks.	No.	Yds.	Avg.	TD
2001—New York Giants NFL		16	16	77	19	1.0	3	25	8.3	0
2002—New York Giants NFL		16	16	64	26	2.0	2	-2	-1.0	0
2003—New York Giants NFL		10	10	44	14	1.5	1	14	14.0	0
2004—New York Giants NFL		2	2	11	0	0.0	0	0	0.0	0
Pro totals (7 years)		84	60	296	84	4.5	11	95	8.6	0

WILLIAMS, TANK — S — TITANS

PERSONAL: Born June 30, 1980, in Gulfport, Miss. ... 6-3/223. ... Full name: Clevan Williams.
HIGH SCHOOL: Bay (Bay St. Louis, Miss.).
COLLEGE: Stanford.
TRANSACTIONS/CAREER NOTES: Selected by Tennesse Titans in second round (45th pick overall) of 2002 NFL draft. ... Signed by Titans (July 22, 2002). ... On injured reserve with knee injury (November 29, 2004-remainder of season).
CHAMPIONSHIP GAME EXPERIENCE: Played in AFC championship game (2002 season).

Year	Team	G	GS	TOTALS			INTERCEPTIONS			
				Tk.	Ast.	Sks.	No.	Yds.	Avg.	TD
2002—Tennessee NFL		16	16	46	15	2.0	1	0	0.0	0
2003—Tennessee NFL		16	16	52	22	0.5	2	0	0.0	0
2004—Tennessee NFL		9	9	41	11	1.0	1	13	13.0	0
Pro totals (3 years)		41	41	139	48	3.5	4	13	3.3	0

WILLIAMS, TODD — G/T — TITANS

PERSONAL: Born September 4, 1978, in Bradenton, Fla. ... 6-5/330.
HIGH SCHOOL: Southeast (Bradenton, Fla.).
COLLEGE: Florida State.
TRANSACTIONS/CAREER NOTES: Selected by Tennessee Titans in seventh round (225th pick overall) of 2003 NFL draft. ... Signed by Titans (June 27, 2003).
PLAYING EXPERIENCE: Tennessee NFL, 2004. ... Games/Games started: 2004 (6/0). Total: 6/0.

WILLIAMS, TONY — DT — JAGUARS

PERSONAL: Born July 9, 1975, in Germantown, Tenn. ... 6-2/296. ... Full name: Anthony Demetric Williams.
HIGH SCHOOL: Oakhaven (Memphis, Tenn.), then Germantown (Tenn.).
COLLEGE: Memphis.
TRANSACTIONS/CAREER NOTES: Selected by Minnesota Vikings in fifth round (151st pick overall) of 1997 NFL draft. ... Signed by Vikings (June 17, 1997). ... Granted unconditional free agency (February 11, 2000). ... Re-signed by Vikings (May 18, 2000). ... Granted unconditional free agency (March 2, 2001). ... Signed by Cincinnati Bengals (March 6, 2001). ... On injured reserve with ankle injury (October 29, 2004-remainder of season). ... Granted unconditional free agency (March 2, 2005). ... Signed by Jacksonville Jaguars (April 6, 2005).
CHAMPIONSHIP GAME EXPERIENCE: Played in NFC championship game (1998 and 2000 season).

Year	Team	G	GS	TOTALS		
				Tk.	Ast.	Sks.
1997—Minnesota NFL		6	2	9	3	0.0
1998—Minnesota NFL		14	9	26	10	1.0
1999—Minnesota NFL		16	12	30	15	5.0
2000—Minnesota NFL		14	14	27	6	4.0
2001—Cincinnati NFL		13	13	15	23	5.0
2002—Cincinnati NFL		16	16	30	12	5.0
2003—Cincinnati NFL		16	16	28	10	2.0
2004—Cincinnati NFL		6	6	10	6	0.0
Pro totals (8 years)		101	88	175	85	22.0

WILLIAMS, TYRONE — CB

PERSONAL: Born May 31, 1973, in Bradenton, Fla. ... 5-11/193. ... Full name: Upton Tyrone Williams.
HIGH SCHOOL: Manatee (Bradenton, Fla.).
COLLEGE: Nebraska.
TRANSACTIONS/CAREER NOTES: Selected by Green Bay Packers in third round (93rd pick overall) of 1996 NFL draft. ... Signed by Packers (May 15, 1996). ... Granted free agency (February 12, 1999). ... Re-signed by Packers (May 17, 1999). ... Granted unconditional free agency (February 28, 2003). ... Signed by Atlanta Falcons (March 16, 2003). ... On suspended list for conduct detrimental to team (October 1- 6, 2003). ... Released by Falcons (June 2, 2004). ... Signed by Dallas Cowboys (September 30, 2004). ... On injured reserve with hamstring injury (November 13-December 14, 2004). ... Released by Cowboys (December 14, 2004).
CHAMPIONSHIP GAME EXPERIENCE: Played in NFC championship game (1996 and 1997 seasons). ... Member of Super Bowl championship team (1996 season). ... Played in Super Bowl 32 (1997 season).

Year	Team	G	GS	TOTALS			INTERCEPTIONS			
				Tk.	Ast.	Sks.	No.	Yds.	Avg.	TD
1996—Green Bay NFL		16	0	22	3	0.0	0	0	0.0	0
1997—Green Bay NFL		16	15	49	17	0.0	1	0	0.0	0
1998—Green Bay NFL		16	16	61	8	0.0	5	40	8.0	0
1999—Green Bay NFL		16	16	53	12	0.0	4	12	3.0	0
2000—Green Bay NFL		16	16	50	8	0.0	4	105	26.2	1
2001—Green Bay NFL		16	16	77	12	0.0	4	117	29.2	1

Year Team	G	GS	TOTALS			INTERCEPTIONS			
			Tk.	Ast.	Sks.	No.	Yds.	Avg.	TD
2002—Green Bay NFL	15	15	60	9	1.0	1	0	0.0	0
2003—Atlanta NFL	6	6	18	2	0.0	0	0	0.0	0
2004—Dallas NFL	3	2	7	0	1.0	0	0	0.0	0
Pro totals (9 years)	120	102	397	71	2.0	19	274	14.4	2

WILLIAMS, WALTER   RB

PERSONAL: Born September 8, 1977, in Baton Rouge, La. ... 6-1/206.
HIGH SCHOOL: Brusly (La.).
COLLEGE: Grambling State.
TRANSACTIONS/CAREER NOTES: Signed as non-drafted free agent by New England Patriots (April 27, 2001). ... On injured reserve with knee injury (September 2, 2001-remainder of season). ... Released by Patriots (August 13, 2002). ... Signed by New Orleans Saints (January 7, 2003). ... Released by Saints (August 26, 2003). ... Signed by Green Bay Packers (January 5, 2004). ... Assigned by Packers to Rhein Fire in 2004 NFL Europe enhancement allocation program (February 13, 2004). ... Released by Packers (September 4, 2004). ... Re-signed by Packers to practice squad (September 15, 2004). ... Activated (November 20, 2004). ... On injured reserve with ankle injury (November 29, 2004-remainder of season).
SINGLE GAME HIGHS (regular season): Attempts—6 (November 21, 2004, vs. Houston); yards—42 (November 21, 2004, vs. Houston); and rushing touchdowns—0.

Year Team	G	GS	RUSHING				TOTALS			
			Att.	Yds.	Avg.	TD	TD	2pt.	Pts.	Fum.
2004—Green Bay NFL	1	0	6	42	7.0	0	0	0	0	0

WILLIAMS, WILLIE   CB   STEELERS

PERSONAL: Born December 26, 1970, in Columbia, S.C. ... 5-9/194. ... Full name: Willie James Williams Jr.
HIGH SCHOOL: Spring Valley (Columbia, S.C.).
COLLEGE: Western Carolina.
TRANSACTIONS/CAREER NOTES: Selected by Pittsburgh Steelers in sixth round (162nd pick overall) of 1993 NFL draft. ... Signed by Steelers (July 9, 1993). ... Granted free agency (February 16, 1996). ... Re-signed by Steelers (June 12, 1996). ... Granted unconditional free agency (February 14, 1997). ... Signed by Seattle Seahawks (February 18, 1997). ... Granted unconditional free agency (March 2, 2001). ... Re-signed by Seahawks (May 3, 2001). ... Granted unconditional free agency (February 28, 2003). ... Re-signed by Seahawks (May 2, 2003). ... Granted unconditional free agency (March 3, 2004). ... Signed by Pittsburgh Steelers (May 26, 2004). ... Granted unconditional free agency (March 2, 2005). ... Re-signed by Steelers (March 7, 2005).
CHAMPIONSHIP GAME EXPERIENCE: Played in AFC championship game (1994, 1995 and 2004 seasons). ... Played in Super Bowl 30 (1995 season).

Year Team	G	GS	TOTALS			INTERCEPTIONS			
			Tk.	Ast.	Sks.	No.	Yds.	Avg.	TD
1993—Pittsburgh NFL	16	0	7	2	0.0	0	0	0.0	0
1994—Pittsburgh NFL	16	1	3	0	0.0	0	0	0.0	0
1995—Pittsburgh NFL	16	15	69	8	0.0	§7	122	17.4	▲1
1996—Pittsburgh NFL	15	14	66	10	1.0	1	1	1.0	0
1997—Seattle NFL	16	16	58	9	0.0	1	0	0.0	0
1998—Seattle NFL	14	14	53	13	0.0	2	36	18.0	1
1999—Seattle NFL	15	14	66	6	0.0	5	43	8.6	1
2000—Seattle NFL	16	15	51	9	1.0	4	74	18.5	1
2001—Seattle NFL	14	14	60	12	0.0	4	24	6.0	0
2002—Seattle NFL	15	1	21	4	1.0	1	2	2.0	0
2003—Seattle NFL	15	0	11	3	0.0	0	0	0.0	0
2004—Pittsburgh NFL	16	10	40	14	1.0	1	0	0.0	0
Pro totals (12 years)	184	114	505	90	4.0	26	302	11.6	4

WILLIG, MATT   T   PANTHERS

PERSONAL: Born January 21, 1969, in Santa Fe Springs, Calif. ... 6-8/315. ... Full name: Matthew Joseph Willig.
HIGH SCHOOL: St. Paul (Santa Fe Springs, Calif.).
COLLEGE: Southern California.
TRANSACTIONS/CAREER NOTES: Signed as non-drafted free agent by New York Jets (May 5, 1992). ... Released by Jets (August 24, 1992). ... Re-signed by Jets to practice squad (September 2, 1992). ... Activated (December 24, 1992). ... Active for one game (1992); did not play. ... Signed by Jets (February 14, 1995). ... Released by Jets (April 23, 1996). ... Signed by Atlanta Falcons (May 2, 1996). ... Granted unconditional free agency (February 13, 1998). ... Signed by Green Bay Packers (May 5, 1998). ... Released by Packers (February 23, 1999). ... Signed by Cleveland Browns (August 17, 1999). ... Released by Browns (September 5, 1999). ... Signed by St. Louis Rams (November 30, 1999). ... Granted unconditional free agency (February 11, 2000). ... Signed by San Francisco 49ers (June 7, 2000). ... Granted unconditional free agency (March 1, 2002). ... Re-signed by 49ers (March 7, 2002). ... Granted unconditional free agency (February 28, 2003). ... Signed by Carolina Panthers (August 1, 2003). ... Granted unconditional free agency (March 3, 2004). ... Re-signed by Panthers (May 1, 2004).
PLAYING EXPERIENCE: New York Jets NFL, 1993-1995; Atlanta NFL, 1996-1997; Green Bay NFL, 1998; San Francisco NFL, 2000-2002; Carolina NFL, 2003-2004. ... Games/Games started: 1993 (3/0), 1994 (16/3), 1995 (15/12), 1996 (12/0), 1997 (16/13), 1998 (16/0), 2000 (16/3), 2001 (15/0), 2002 (11/3), 2003 (13/0), 2004 (16/9). Total: 149/43.
CHAMPIONSHIP GAME EXPERIENCE: Member of Rams for NFC championship game (1999 season); inactive. ... Member of Super Bowl championship team (1999 season); inactive. ... Played in NFC championship game (2003 season). ... Played in Super Bowl 38 (2003 season).

W

WILLIS, JASON   WR   SEAHAWKS

PERSONAL: Born July 26, 1980, in Los Angeles, Calif. ... 6-1/196. ... Full name: Jason Patrick Willis.
HIGH SCHOOL: St. Bernard (Eureka, Calif.).
COLLEGE: Oregon.

Year Team			G	GS	RECEIVING No.	Yds.	Avg.	TD	TOTALS TD	2pt.	Pts.	Fum.
2004—Seattle NFL			1	0	0	0	0.0	0	0	0	0	0

WILSON, ADRIAN — S — CARDINALS

PERSONAL: Born October 12, 1979, in High Point, N.C. ... 6-3/222.
HIGH SCHOOL: T.W. Andrews (High Point, N.C.).
COLLEGE: North Carolina State.
TRANSACTIONS/CAREER NOTES: Selected after junior season by Arizona Cardinals in third round (64th pick overall) of 2001 NFL draft. ... Signed by Cardinals (July 24, 2001). ... Granted free agency (March 3, 2004). ... Re-signed by Cardinals (2004).

Year Team	G	GS	TOTALS Tk.	Ast.	Sks.	INTERCEPTIONS No.	Yds.	Avg.	TD
2001—Arizona NFL	16	0	15	7	0.5	2	97	48.5	1
2002—Arizona NFL	14	14	66	27	1.5	4	35	8.8	0
2003—Arizona NFL	16	15	70	9	0.0	0	0	0.0	0
2004—Arizona NFL	16	16	78	22	1.0	3	62	20.7	0
Pro totals (4 years)	62	45	229	65	3.0	9	194	21.6	1

WILSON, AL — LB — BRONCOS

PERSONAL: Born June 21, 1977, in Jackson, Tenn. ... 6-0/240. ... Full name: Aldra Kauwa Wilson.
HIGH SCHOOL: Central Merry (Jackson, Tenn.).
COLLEGE: Tennessee.
TRANSACTIONS/CAREER NOTES: Selected by Denver Broncos in first round (31st pick overall) of NFL draft. ... Signed by Broncos (July 21, 1999).
HONORS: Named inside linebacker on THE SPORTING NEWS college All-America second team (1998). ... Played in Pro Bowl (2001 and 2003 seasons). ... Named to play in Pro Bowl (2002 season); replaced by Kendrell Bell due to injury.

Year Team	G	GS	TOTALS Tk.	Ast.	Sks.	INTERCEPTIONS No.	Yds.	Avg.	TD
1999—Denver NFL	16	12	58	16	1.0	0	0	0.0	0
2000—Denver NFL	15	14	47	13	5.0	3	21	7.0	0
2001—Denver NFL	16	16	72	13	3.0	0	0	0.0	0
2002—Denver NFL	16	15	100	32	5.0	0	0	0.0	0
2003—Denver NFL	16	16	70	18	1.0	0	0	0.0	0
2004—Denver NFL	16	16	72	33	2.5	2	17	8.5	1
Pro totals (6 years)	95	89	419	125	17.5	5	38	7.6	1

WILSON, CEDRICK — WR — STEELERS

PERSONAL: Born December 17, 1978, in Memphis, Tenn. ... 5-10/183.
HIGH SCHOOL: Melrose (Memphis, Tenn.).
COLLEGE: Tennessee.
TRANSACTIONS/CAREER NOTES: Selected by San Francisco 49ers in sixth round (169th pick overall) of 2001 NFL draft. ... Signed by 49ers (July 24, 2001). ... Granted free agency (March 3, 2004). ... Re-signed by 49ers (April 14, 2004). ... Granted unconditional free agency (March 2, 2005). ... Signed by Pittsburgh Steelers (March 8, 2005).
SINGLE GAME HIGHS (regular season): Receptions—7 (September 12, 2004, vs. Atlanta); yards—101 (November 14, 2004, vs. Carolina); and touchdown receptions—2 (December 12, 2004, vs. Arizona).
STATISTICAL PLATEAUS: 100-yard receiving games: 2004 (1). Total: 1.

Year Team	G	GS	RECEIVING No.	Yds.	Avg.	TD	PUNT RETURNS No.	Yds.	Avg.	TD	KICKOFF RETURNS No.	Yds.	Avg.	TD	TOTALS TD	2pt.	Pts.	Fum.
2001—San Francisco NFL	6	0	0	0	0.0	0	2	4	2.0	0	6	127	21.2	0	0	0	0	0
2002—San Francisco NFL	16	0	15	166	11.1	1	8	59	7.4	0	10	195	19.5	0	1	0	6	0
2003—San Francisco NFL	16	3	35	396	11.3	2	1	12	12.0	0	37	836	22.6	1	3	0	18	1
2004—San Francisco NFL	15	15	47	641	13.6	3	2	21	10.5	0	10	196	19.6	0	3	0	18	0
Pro totals (4 years)	53	18	97	1203	12.4	6	13	96	7.4	0	63	1354	21.5	1	7	0	42	1

WILSON, EUGENE — CB — PATRIOTS

PERSONAL: Born August 17, 1980, in Merrillville, Ind. ... 5-10/195. ... Full name: Eugene W. Wilson II.
HIGH SCHOOL: Merrillville (Ind.).
COLLEGE: Illinois.
TRANSACTIONS/CAREER NOTES: Selected by New England Patriots in second round (36th pick overall) of 2003 NFL draft. ... Signed by Patriots (July 21, 2003).
CHAMPIONSHIP GAME EXPERIENCE: Played in AFC championship game (2003 and 2004 seasons). ... Member of Super Bowl championship team (2003 and 2004 seasons).

Year Team	G	GS	TOTALS Tk.	Ast.	Sks.	INTERCEPTIONS No.	Yds.	Avg.	TD
2003—New England NFL	16	15	47	14	0.0	4	18	4.5	0
2004—New England NFL	15	14	56	9	0.0	4	51	12.8	0
Pro totals (2 years)	31	29	103	23	0.0	8	69	8.6	0

WILSON, GIBRIL — DB — GIANTS

PERSONAL: Born November 12, 1981, in San Jose, Calif. ... 6-0/197.
HIGH SCHOOL: Northwest Whitfield (San Jose, Calif.).
JUNIOR COLLEGE: City College of San Francisco (Calif.).
COLLEGE: Tennessee.
TRANSACTIONS/CAREER NOTES: Selected by New York Giants in fifth round (136th pick overall) of 2004 NFL draft. ... Signed by Giants (July 30, 2004).

Year Team	G	GS	TOTALS Tk.	Ast.	Sks.	INTERCEPTIONS No.	Yds.	Avg.	TD
2004—New York Giants NFL	8	7	49	6	3.0	3	39	13.0	0

WILSON, JERRY — S — CHARGERS

PERSONAL: Born July 17, 1973, in Alexandria, La. ... 5-11/190. ... Full name: Jerry Lee Wilson Jr.
HIGH SCHOOL: La Grange (Lake Charles, La.).
COLLEGE: Southern University.
TRANSACTIONS/CAREER NOTES: Selected by Tampa Bay Buccaneers in fourth round (105th pick overall) of 1995 NFL draft. ... Signed by Buccaneers (May 9, 1995). ... On injured reserve with knee injury (August 31, 1995-entire season). ... Released by Buccaneers (August 20, 1996). ... Signed by Miami Dolphins to practice squad (October 29, 1996). ... Activated (November 5, 1996). ... Granted unconditional free agency (March 2, 2001). ... Signed by New Orleans Saints (January 2, 2002). ... Granted unconditional free agency (March 1, 2002). ... Re-signed by Saints (May 2, 2002). ... Released by Saints (September 1, 2002). ... Re-signed by Saints (September 10, 2002). ... Released by Saints (November 12, 2002). ... Signed by San Diego Chargers (November 19, 2002). ... Granted unconditional free agency (February 28, 2003). ... Re-signed by Chargers (March 17, 2003). ... Granted unconditional free agency (March 3, 2004). ... Re-signed by Chargers (March 17, 2004).

Year Team	G	GS	TOTALS Tk.	Ast.	Sks.	INTERCEPTIONS No.	Yds.	Avg.	TD
1996—Miami NFL	2	0	0	0	0.0	0	0	0.0	0
1997—Miami NFL	16	0	9	1	2.0	0	0	0.0	0
1998—Miami NFL	16	0	13	2	0.0	1	0	0.0	0
1999—Miami NFL	16	1	14	1	3.0	1	13	13.0	0
2000—Miami NFL	16	1	30	9	0.5	1	19	19.0	0
2001—New Orleans NFL	1	0	0	0	0.0	0	0	0.0	0
2002—New Orleans NFL	7	0	4	0	0.0	0	0	0.0	0
—San Diego NFL	5	0	3	0	0.0	0	0	0.0	0
2003—San Diego NFL	16	16	63	19	1.0	1	-2	-2.0	0
2004—San Diego NFL	16	16	52	23	0.0	3	12	4.0	0
Pro totals (9 years)	111	34	188	55	6.5	7	42	6.0	0

WILSON, KRIS — TE — CHIEFS

PERSONAL: Born August 22, 1981, in Lancaster, Pa. ... 6-2/251. ... Full name: Kristopher Wilson.
HIGH SCHOOL: J.P. McCaskey (Lancaster, Pa.).
COLLEGE: Pittsburgh.
TRANSACTIONS/CAREER NOTES: Selected by Kansas City Chiefs in second round (61st pick overall) of 2004 NFL draft. ... Signed by Chiefs (July 19, 2004).

Year Team	G	GS	RECEIVING No.	Yds.	Avg.	TD	TOTALS TD	2pt.	Pts.	Fum.
2004—Kansas City NFL	3	0	0	0	0.0	0	0	0	0	0

WILSON, MARK — T — REDSKINS

PERSONAL: Born November 11, 1980, in San Jose, Calif. ... 6-6/295.
HIGH SCHOOL: Fall River (McArthur, Calif.).
COLLEGE: California.
TRANSACTIONS/CAREER NOTES: Selected by Washington Redskins in fifth round (151st pick overall) of 2004 NFL draft. ... Signed by Redskins (July 21, 2004).
PLAYING EXPERIENCE: Washington NFL, 2004. ... Games/Games started: 2004 (2/1). Total: 2/1.
HONORS: Named offensive lineman on THE SPORTING NEWS Freshman All-America third team (2000).

WINBORN, JAMIE — LB — 49ERS

PERSONAL: Born May 14, 1979, in Wetumpka, Ala. ... 5-11/242.
HIGH SCHOOL: Wetumpka (Ala.).
COLLEGE: Vanderbilt.
TRANSACTIONS/CAREER NOTES: Selected after junior season by San Francisco 49ers in second round (47th pick overall) of 2001 NFL draft. ... Signed by 49ers (July 25, 2001). ... On injured reserve with knee injury (January 2, 2003-remainder of 2002 season). ... On injured reserve with neck injury (November 15, 2003-remainder of season).

Year Team	G	GS	TOTALS Tk.	Ast.	Sks.	INTERCEPTIONS No.	Yds.	Avg.	TD
2001—San Francisco NFL	14	4	34	11	0.5	2	40	20.0	0
2002—San Francisco NFL	3	3	18	6	1.0	0	0	0.0	0
2003—San Francisco NFL	9	0	34	3	3.0	0	0	0.0	0
2004—San Francisco NFL	14	10	55	8	4.5	1	1	1.0	0
Pro totals (4 years)	40	17	141	28	9.0	3	41	13.7	0

W

WINEY, BRANDON   T   GIANTS

PERSONAL: Born January 27, 1978, in Lake Charles, La. ... 6-6/311.
HIGH SCHOOL: Washington-Marion (Lake Charles, La.).
COLLEGE: Louisiana State.
TRANSACTIONS/CAREER NOTES: Selected by Miami Dolphins in sixth round (164th pick overall) of 2001 NFL draft. ... Signed by Dolphins (June 15, 2001). ... Released by Dolphins (September 2, 2001). ... Re-signed by Dolphins to practice squad (September 3, 2001). ... Signed by Denver Broncos off Dolphins practice squad (December 11, 2001). ... Released by Broncos (August 26, 2002). ... Signed by Seattle Seahawks to practice squad (September 2, 2002). ... Released by Seahawks (January 6, 2003). ... Signed by Washington Redskins (August 2, 2003). ... Released by Redskins (August 17, 2004). ... Signed by New York Giants (August 23, 2004).
PLAYING EXPERIENCE: Washington NFL, 2003; New York Giants NFL, 2004. ... Games/Games started: 2003 (11/3), 2004 (13/0). Total: 24/3.
HONORS: Named offensive tackle on THE SPORTING NEWS college All-America third team (2000).

WINFIELD, ANTOINE   CB   VIKINGS

PERSONAL: Born June 24, 1977, in Akron, Ohio. ... 5-9/180. ... Full name: Antoine D. Winfield.
HIGH SCHOOL: Garfield (Ohio).
COLLEGE: Ohio State.
TRANSACTIONS/CAREER NOTES: Selected by Buffalo Bills in first round (23rd pick overall) of 1999 NFL draft. ... Signed by Bills (July 30, 1999). ... On injured reserve list with shoulder injury (November 22, 2000-remainder of season). ... Granted unconditional free agency (March 3, 2004). ... Signed by Minnesota Vikings (March 5, 2004).
HONORS: Named cornerback on THE SPORTING NEWS college All-America second team (1997). ... Jim Thorpe Award winner (1998). ... Named cornerback on THE SPORTING NEWS college All-America first team (1998).

			TOTALS			INTERCEPTIONS			
Year Team	G	GS	Tk.	Ast.	Sks.	No.	Yds.	Avg.	TD
1999—Buffalo NFL	16	2	38	1	0.0	2	13	6.5	0
2000—Buffalo NFL	11	11	34	8	0.0	1	8	8.0	0
2001—Buffalo NFL	16	16	69	12	0.0	2	0	0.0	0
2002—Buffalo NFL	13	13	51	5	0.0	0	0	0.0	0
2003—Buffalo NFL	16	16	94	15	1.0	1	11	11.0	0
2004—Minnesota NFL	14	12	64	14	0.0	3	89	29.7	0
Pro totals (6 years)	86	70	350	55	1.0	9	121	13.4	0

WINSLOW, KELLEN   TE   BROWNS

PERSONAL: Born July 21, 1983, in San Diego, Calif. ... 6-4/250. ... Full name: Kellen Boswell Winslow II. ... Son of Kellen Winslow Sr., Hall of Fame tight end, San Diego Chargers (1979-87).
HIGH SCHOOL: Scripps Ranch (San Diego, Calif.).
COLLEGE: Miami (Fla.).
TRANSACTIONS/CAREER NOTES: Selected after junior season by Cleveland Browns in first round (sixth pick overall) of 2004 NFL draft. ... Signed by Browns (August 11, 2004). ... On injured reserve with leg injury (September 28, 2004-remainder of season).
HONORS: John Mackey Award winner (2003). ... Named tight end on THE SPORTING NEWS college All-America second team (2002) and first team (2003).
SINGLE GAME HIGHS (regular season): Receptions—4 (September 12, 2004, vs. Baltimore); yards—39 (September 12, 2004, vs. Baltimore); and touchdown receptions—0.

			RECEIVING				TOTALS			
Year Team	G	GS	No.	Yds.	Avg.	TD	TD	2pt.	Pts.	Fum.
2004—Cleveland NFL	2	2	5	50	10.0	0	0	0	0	0

WIRE, COY   S   BILLS

PERSONAL: Born November 7, 1978, in Camp Hill, Pa. ... 6-0/205.
COLLEGE: Stanford.
TRANSACTIONS/CAREER NOTES: Selected by Buffalo Bills in third round (97th pick overall) of 2002 NFL draft. ... Signed by Bills (July 3, 2002).

			TOTALS			INTERCEPTIONS			
Year Team	G	GS	Tk.	Ast.	Sks.	No.	Yds.	Avg.	TD
2002—Buffalo NFL	16	15	67	25	3.0	0	0	0.0	0
2003—Buffalo NFL	16	1	10	3	1.0	0	0	0.0	0
2004—Buffalo NFL	12	3	10	8	1.0	0	0	0.0	0
Pro totals (3 years)	44	19	87	36	5.0	0	0	0.0	0

WISTROM, GRANT   DE   SEAHAWKS

PERSONAL: Born July 3, 1976, in Webb City, Mo. ... 6-4/272. ... Full name: Grant Alden Wistrom.
HIGH SCHOOL: Webb City (Mo.).
COLLEGE: Nebraska.
TRANSACTIONS/CAREER NOTES: Selected by St. Louis Rams in first round (sixth pick overall) of 1998 NFL draft. ... Signed by Rams (July 18, 1998). ... Granted unconditional free agency (March 3, 2004). ... Signed by Seattle Seahawks (March 4, 2004).
CHAMPIONSHIP GAME EXPERIENCE: Played in NFC championship game (1999 and 2001 seasons). ... Member of Super Bowl championship team (1999 season). ... Played in Super Bowl 36 (2001 season).
HONORS: Named defensive end on THE SPORTING NEWS college All-America first team (1996 and 1997).

W

Year Team	G	GS	TOTALS			INTERCEPTIONS			
			Tk.	Ast.	Sks.	No.	Yds.	Avg.	TD
1998—St. Louis NFL	13	0	14	6	3.0	0	0	0.0	0
1999—St. Louis NFL	16	16	33	6	6.5	2	131	65.5	†2
2000—St. Louis NFL	16	16	51	12	11.0	0	0	0.0	0
2001—St. Louis NFL	15	15	47	9	9.0	2	-4	-2.0	0
2002—St. Louis NFL	15	14	45	2	4.5	1	2	2.0	0
2003—St. Louis NFL	16	16	50	11	7.5	0	0	0.0	0
2004—Seattle NFL	9	9	27	11	3.5	0	0	0.0	0
Pro totals (7 years)	100	86	267	57	45.0	5	129	25.8	2

WITHERSPOON, WILL   LB

PERSONAL: Born August 19, 1980, in San Antonio, Texas. ... 6-1/231. ... Full name: William Cordell Witherspoon.
HIGH SCHOOL: Rutherford (Panama City, Fla.).
COLLEGE: Georgia.
TRANSACTIONS/CAREER NOTES: Selected by Carolina Panthers in third round (73rd pick overall) of 2002 NFL draft. ... Signed by Panthers (June 20, 2002). ... Granted free agency (March 2, 2005).
CHAMPIONSHIP GAME EXPERIENCE: Played in NFC championship game (2003 season). ... Played in Super Bowl 38 (2003 season).

Year Team	G	GS	TOTALS			INTERCEPTIONS			
			Tk.	Ast.	Sks.	No.	Yds.	Avg.	TD
2002—Carolina NFL	15	8	49	14	1.5	0	0	0.0	0
2003—Carolina NFL	16	16	73	24	1.0	1	10	10.0	0
2004—Carolina NFL	16	16	84	18	3.0	4	48	12.0	0
Pro totals (3 years)	47	40	206	56	5.5	5	58	11.6	0

WITHROW, CORY   C   VIKINGS

PERSONAL: Born April 5, 1975, in Spokane, Wash. ... 6-2/287.
HIGH SCHOOL: Mead (Spokane, Wash.).
COLLEGE: Washington State.
TRANSACTIONS/CAREER NOTES: Signed as non-drafted free agent by Minnesota Vikings (April 23, 1998). ... Released by Vikings (August 30, 1998). ... Signed by Cincinnati Bengals to practice squad (December 18, 1998). ... Released by Bengals (April 15, 1999). ... Signed by Vikings (April 30, 1999). ... Released by Vikings (September 5, 1999). ... Re-signed by Vikings to practice squad (September 6, 1999). Activated (October 26, 1999); did not play. ... Released by Vikings (November 30, 1999). ... Re-signed by Vikings to practice squad (December 1, 1999). ... Granted free agency (February 28, 2003). ... Re-signed by Vikings (April 9, 2003). ... Granted unconditional free agency (March 3, 2004). ... Re-signed by Vikings (April 25, 2004). ... Released by Vikings (February 22, 2005). ... Re-signed by Vikings (March 29, 2005).
PLAYING EXPERIENCE: Minnesota NFL, 2000-2004. ... Games/Games started: 2000 (12/0), 2001 (16/1), 2002 (16/0), 2003 (8/0), 2004 (12/5). Total: 64/6.
CHAMPIONSHIP GAME EXPERIENCE: Played in NFC championship game (2000 season).

WITTEN, JASON   TE   COWBOYS

PERSONAL: Born May 6, 1982, in Elizabethton, Tenn. ... 6-5/261. ... Full name: Christopher Jason Witten.
HIGH SCHOOL: Elizabethon (Tenn.).
COLLEGE: Tennessee.
TRANSACTIONS/CAREER NOTES: Selected after junior season by Dallas Cowboys in third round (69th pick overall) of 2003 NFL draft. ... Signed by Cowboys (July 26, 2003).
HONORS: Played in Pro Bowl (2004 season).
SINGLE GAME HIGHS (regular season): Receptions—9 (November 15, 2004, vs. Philadelphia); yards—133 (November 15, 2004, vs. Philadelphia); and touchdown receptions—2 (November 15, 2004, vs. Philadelphia).
STATISTICAL PLATEAUS: 100-yard receiving games: 2004 (2). Total: 2.

Year Team	G	GS	RECEIVING				TOTALS			
			No.	Yds.	Avg.	TD	TD	2pt.	Pts.	Fum.
2003—Dallas NFL	15	7	35	347	9.9	1	1	0	6	0
2004—Dallas NFL	16	15	87	980	11.3	6	6	1	38	2
Pro totals (2 years)	31	22	122	1327	10.9	7	7	1	44	2

WOMACK, FLOYD   T   SEAHAWKS

PERSONAL: Born November 15, 1978, in Cleveland, Miss. ... 6-4/333. ... Full name: Floyd Seneca Womack.
HIGH SCHOOL: East Side (Cleveland, Miss.).
COLLEGE: Mississippi State.
TRANSACTIONS/CAREER NOTES: Selected by Seattle Seahawks in fourth round (128th pick overall) of 2001 NFL draft. ... Signed by Seahawks (June 22, 2001). ... Granted free agency (March 3, 2004). ... Re-signed by Seahawks (April 4, 2004). ... Granted unconditional free agency (March 2, 2005). ... Re-signed by Seahawks (March 16, 2005).
PLAYING EXPERIENCE: Seattle NFL, 2001-2004. ... Games/Games started: 2001 (6/0), 2002 (11/10), 2003 (11/4), 2004 (15/8). Total: 43/22.

WONG, KAILEE   LB   TEXANS

PERSONAL: Born May 23, 1976, in Eugene, Ore. ... 6-2/246.
HIGH SCHOOL: North Eugene (Ore.).
COLLEGE: Stanford.

W

TRANSACTIONS/CAREER NOTES: Selected by Minnesota Vikings in second round (51st pick overall) of 1998 NFL draft. ... Signed by Vikings (July 25, 1998). ... On injured reserve with leg injury (December 31, 1998-remainder of season). ... Granted free agency (March 2, 2001). ... Re-signed by Vikings (April 16, 2001). ... Granted unconditional free agency (March 1, 2002). ... Signed by Houston Texans (March 7, 2002).
CHAMPIONSHIP GAME EXPERIENCE: Played in NFC championship game (2000 season).
MISCELLANEOUS: Holds Houston Texans all-time record for most sacks (14).

Year Team	G	GS	TOTALS			INTERCEPTIONS			
			Tk.	Ast.	Sks.	No.	Yds.	Avg.	TD
1998—Minnesota NFL	15	0	12	2	1.5	0	0	0.0	0
1999—Minnesota NFL	13	8	34	12	0.0	0	0	0.0	0
2000—Minnesota NFL	16	16	83	28	2.0	2	28	14.0	0
2001—Minnesota NFL	16	16	83	16	3.0	1	27	27.0	1
2002—Houston NFL	16	16	34	10	5.5	0	0	0.0	0
2003—Houston NFL	16	16	49	13	3.0	0	0	0.0	0
2004—Houston NFL	16	16	51	20	5.5	3	0	0.0	0
Pro totals (7 years)	108	88	346	101	20.5	6	55	9.2	1

WOODARD, CEDRIC   DT   SEAHAWKS

PERSONAL: Born September 5, 1977, in Bay City, Texas. ... 6-2/310. ... Full name: Cedric Darnell Woodard.
HIGH SCHOOL: Sweeny (Texas).
COLLEGE: Texas.
TRANSACTIONS/CAREER NOTES: Selected by Baltimore Ravens in sixth round (191st pick overall) of 2000 NFL draft. ... Signed by Ravens (June 15, 2000). ... Claimed on waivers by Seattle Seahawks (September 6, 2000). ... Granted free agency (February 28, 2003). ... Re-signed by Seahawks (April 9, 2003). ... Granted unconditional free agency (March 3, 2004). ... Re-signed by Seahawks (March 9, 2004).

Year Team	G	GS	TOTALS		
			Tk.	Ast.	Sks.
2001—Seattle NFL	16	0	3	1	0.0
2002—Seattle NFL	12	0	0	1	0.0
2003—Seattle NFL	16	13	41	16	0.0
2004—Seattle NFL	16	16	28	21	1.0
Pro totals (4 years)	60	29	72	39	1.0

WOODEN, SHAWN   S   DOLPHINS

PERSONAL: Born October 23, 1973, in Philadelphia, Pa. ... 5-11/205. ... Full name: Shawn Anthony Wooden.
HIGH SCHOOL: Abington (Pa.).
COLLEGE: Notre Dame.
TRANSACTIONS/CAREER NOTES: Selected by Miami Dolphins in sixth round (189th pick overall) of 1996 NFL draft. ... Signed by Dolphins (July 10, 1996). ... On injured reserve with knee injury (September 15, 1998-remainder of season). ... Granted free agency (February 12, 1999). ... Re-signed by Dolphins (April 23, 1999). ... Granted unconditional free agency (February 11, 2000). ... Signed by Chicago Bears (March 6, 2000). ... Released by Bears (June 26, 2001). ... Signed by Dolphins (June 29, 2001). ... Released by Dolphins (March 11, 2003). ... Re-signed by Dolphins (April 24, 2003). ... Granted unconditional free agency (March 3, 2004). ... Re-signed by Dolphins (March 6, 2004). ... On injured reserve with back injury (August 31, 2004-entire season).

Year Team	G	GS	TOTALS			INTERCEPTIONS			
			Tk.	Ast.	Sks.	No.	Yds.	Avg.	TD
1996—Miami NFL	16	11	54	13	0.0	2	15	7.5	0
1997—Miami NFL	16	15	56	27	0.0	2	10	5.0	0
1998—Miami NFL	2	1	10	0	0.0	0	0	0.0	0
1999—Miami NFL	15	6	36	15	0.0	0	0	0.0	0
2000—Chicago NFL	11	0	8	3	0.0	0	0	0.0	0
2001—Miami NFL	13	0	2	0	0.0	0	0	0.0	0
2002—Miami NFL	16	2	12	6	0.0	1	0	0.0	0
2003—Miami NFL	15	0	1	0	0.0	0	0	0.0	0
2004—Miami NFL	Did not play.								
Pro totals (8 years)	104	35	179	64	0.0	5	25	5.0	0

WOODS, JEROME   S   CHIEFS

PERSONAL: Born March 17, 1973, in Memphis, Tenn. ... 6-3/205.
HIGH SCHOOL: Melrose (Memphis, Tenn.).
JUNIOR COLLEGE: Northeast Mississippi Community College.
COLLEGE: Memphis.
TRANSACTIONS/CAREER NOTES: Selected by Kansas City Chiefs in first round (28th pick overall) of 1996 NFL draft. ... Signed by Chiefs (August 12, 1996). ... Granted unconditional free agency (February 11, 2000). ... Re-signed by Chiefs (February 11, 2000). ... On injured reserve with broken leg (August 26, 2002-entire season). ... Granted unconditional free agency (March 3, 2004). ... Re-signed by Chiefs (March 3, 2004).
HONORS: Played in Pro Bowl (2003 season).

Year Team	G	GS	TOTALS			INTERCEPTIONS			
			Tk.	Ast.	Sks.	No.	Yds.	Avg.	TD
1996—Kansas City NFL	16	0	5	1	0.0	0	0	0.0	0
1997—Kansas City NFL	16	16	67	19	1.0	4	57	14.3	0
1998—Kansas City NFL	16	16	56	25	0.0	2	47	23.5	0
1999—Kansas City NFL	15	15	70	9	0.0	1	5	5.0	0
2000—Kansas City NFL	16	16	74	8	2.0	2	0	0.0	0
2001—Kansas City NFL	16	16	74	13	1.0	3	48	16.0	0
2002—Kansas City NFL	Did not play.								

W

Year Team	G	GS	TOTALS			INTERCEPTIONS			
			Tk.	Ast.	Sks.	No.	Yds.	Avg.	TD
2003—Kansas City NFL	16	16	61	18	0.0	3	125	41.7	†2
2004—Kansas City NFL	10	10	36	6	1.0	0	0	0.0	0
Pro totals (8 years)	121	105	443	99	5.0	15	282	18.8	2

WOODS, LEVAR   LB   BEARS

PERSONAL: Born March 15, 1978, in Cleveland, Ohio. ... 6-3/244.
HIGH SCHOOL: West Lyon (Inwood, Iowa).
COLLEGE: Iowa.
TRANSACTIONS/CAREER NOTES: Signed as non-drafted free agent by Arizona Cardinals (April 23, 2001). ... Granted free agency (February 27, 2003). ... Re-signed by Cardinals (March 16, 2003). ... Released by Cardinals (April 11, 2005). ... Signed by Chicago Bears (April 15, 2005).

Year Team	G	GS	TOTALS			INTERCEPTIONS			
			Tk.	Ast.	Sks.	No.	Yds.	Avg.	TD
2001—Arizona NFL	15	0	8	0	0.0	0	0	0.0	0
2002—Arizona NFL	15	2	22	7	0.5	0	0	0.0	0
2003—Arizona NFL	16	3	17	4	1.0	0	0	0.0	0
2004—Arizona NFL	14	3	13	5	0.0	0	0	0.0	0
Pro totals (4 years)	60	8	60	16	1.5	0	0	0.0	0

WOODS, RASHAUN   WR   49ERS

PERSONAL: Born October 17, 1980, in Oklahoma City, Okla. ... 6-2/202. ... Full name: Rashaun Dorrell Woods.
HIGH SCHOOL: Millwood (Oklahoma City, Okla.).
COLLEGE: Oklahoma State.
TRANSACTIONS/CAREER NOTES: Selected by San Francisco 49ers in first round (31st pick overall) of 2004 NFL draft. ... Signed by 49ers (July 30, 2004).
HONORS: Named wide receiver on THE SPORTING NEWS college All-America first team (2002).
SINGLE GAME HIGHS (regular season): Receptions—3 (January 2, 2005, vs. New England); yards—76 (January 2, 2005, vs. New England); and touchdown receptions—1 (October 3, 2004, vs. St. Louis).

Year Team	G	GS	RECEIVING				TOTALS			
			No.	Yds.	Avg.	TD	TD	2pt.	Pts.	Fum.
2004—San Francisco NFL	14	0	7	160	22.9	1	1	0	6	0

WOODSON, CHARLES   CB   RAIDERS

PERSONAL: Born October 7, 1976, in Fremont, Ohio. ... 6-1/200.
HIGH SCHOOL: Ross (Fremont, Ohio).
COLLEGE: Michigan.
TRANSACTIONS/CAREER NOTES: Selected after junior season by Oakland Raiders in first round (fourth pick overall) of 1998 NFL draft. ... Signed by Raiders (July 20, 1998). ... Designated by Raiders as franchise player (February 24, 2004). ... Re-signed by Raiders (2004). ... Designated by Raiders as franchise player (February 22, 2005). ... Re-signed by Raiders (March 7, 2005).
CHAMPIONSHIP GAME EXPERIENCE: Played in AFC championship game (2000 and 2002 seasons). ... Played in Super Bowl 37 (2002 season).
HONORS: Named cornerback on THE SPORTING NEWS college All-America second team (1996). ... Heisman Trophy winner (1997). ... Jim Thorpe Award winner (1997). ... Maxwell Award winner (1997). ... Bronko Nagurski Award winner (1997). ... Named College Football Player of the Year by The Sporting News (1997). ... Named cornerback on THE SPORTING NEWS college All-America first team (1997). ... Played in Pro Bowl (1998-2000 seasons). ... Named cornerback on THE SPORTING NEWS NFL All-Pro team (2001). ... Named to played in Pro Bowl (2001 season); replaced by Ty Law due to injury.

Year Team	G	GS	TOTALS			INTERCEPTIONS				PUNT RETURNS				TOTALS			
			Tk.	Ast.	Sks.	No.	Yds.	Avg.	TD	No.	Yds.	Avg.	TD	TD	2pt.	Pts.	Fum.
1998—Oakland NFL	16	16	61	3	0.0	5	118	23.6	1	0	0	0.0	0	1	0	6	0
1999—Oakland NFL	16	16	52	9	0.0	1	15	15.0	1	0	0	0.0	0	1	0	6	0
2000—Oakland NFL	16	16	66	13	0.0	4	36	9.0	0	0	0	0.0	0	0	0	0	0
2001—Oakland NFL	16	15	40	13	2.0	1	64	64.0	0	4	47	11.8	0	0	0	0	0
2002—Oakland NFL	8	7	35	2	0.0	1	3	3.0	0	4	6	1.5	0	0	0	0	0
2003—Oakland NFL	15	15	56	14	1.0	3	67	22.3	0	0	0	0.0	0	0	0	0	0
2004—Oakland NFL	13	12	59	15	2.5	1	25	25.0	0	1	4	4.0	0	0	0	0	0
Pro totals (7 years)	100	97	369	69	5.5	16	328	20.5	2	9	57	6.3	0	2	0	12	0

W

WOODY, DAMIEN   C   LIONS

PERSONAL: Born November 3, 1977, in Beaverdam, Va. ... 6-3/325. ... Full name: Damien Michael Woody.
HIGH SCHOOL: Patrick Henry (Beaverdam, Va.).
COLLEGE: Boston College.
TRANSACTIONS/CAREER NOTES: Selected after junior season by New England Patriots in first round (17th pick overall) of 1999 NFL draft. ... Signed by Patriots (July 30, 1999). ... On injured reserve with knee injury (January 9, 2003-remainder of 2002 season). ... On injured reserve (January 17, 2004-remainder of 2003 season playoffs). ... Granted unconditional free agency (March 3, 2004). ... Signed by Detroit Lions (March 5, 2004).
PLAYING EXPERIENCE: New England NFL, 1999-2003; Detroit NFL, 2004. ... Games/Games started: 1999 (16/16), 2000 (16/16), 2001 (16/15), 2002 (16/15), 2003 (14/14), 2004 (16/16). Total: 94/92.
CHAMPIONSHIP GAME EXPERIENCE: Played in AFC championship game (2001 season). ... Member of Super Bowl championship team (2001 season).
HONORS: Played in Pro Bowl (2002 season).

WOOLFOLK, ANDRE   CB   TITANS

PERSONAL: Born January 26, 1980, in Denver, Colo. ... 6-2/197.
HIGH SCHOOL: Thomas Jefferson (Denver).
COLLEGE: Oklahoma.
TRANSACTIONS/CAREER NOTES: Selected by Tennessee Titans in first round (28th pick overall) of 2003 NFL draft. ... Signed by Titans (July 24, 2003). ... On injured reserve with ankle injury (December 23, 2003-remainder of season). ... On injured reserve with wrist injury (December 31, 2004-remainder of season).

			TOTALS			INTERCEPTIONS			
Year Team	G	GS	Tk.	Ast.	Sks.	No.	Yds.	Avg.	TD
2003—Tennessee NFL	6	1	14	4	0.0	1	4	4.0	0
2004—Tennessee NFL	10	2	36	5	0.0	1	25	25.0	0
Pro totals (2 years)	16	3	50	9	0.0	2	29	14.5	0

WORRELL, CAMERON   S   BEARS

PERSONAL: Born December 14, 1979, in Merced County, Calif. ... 5-11/199.
HIGH SCHOOL: Chowchilla (Calif.).
JUNIOR COLLEGE: Fresno City College (Calif.).
COLLEGE: Fresno State.
TRANSACTIONS/CAREER NOTES: Signed as non-drafted free agent by Chicago Bears (May 4, 2003). ... On injured reserve with ankle injury (December 21, 2004-remainder of season).

			TOTALS			INTERCEPTIONS			
Year Team	G	GS	Tk.	Ast.	Sks.	No.	Yds.	Avg.	TD
2003—Chicago NFL	14	0	1	0	0.0	0	0	0.0	0
2004—Chicago NFL	13	0	7	0	1.0	0	0	0.0	0
Pro totals (2 years)	27	0	8	0	1.0	0	0	0.0	0

WRIGHSTER, GEORGE   TE   JAGUARS

PERSONAL: Born April 1, 1981, in Memphis, Tenn. ... 6-2/260. ... Full name: George Fredrick Wrighster III.
HIGH SCHOOL: Sylmar (Calif.).
COLLEGE: Oregon.
TRANSACTIONS/CAREER NOTES: Selected after junior season by Jacksonville Jaguars in fourth round (104th pick overall) of 2003 NFL draft. ... Signed by Jaguars (July 18, 2003). ... On injured reserve with back injury (December 21, 2004-remainder of season).
SINGLE GAME HIGHS (regular season): Receptions—5 (September 26, 2004, vs. Tennessee); yards—30 (September 26, 2004, vs. Tennessee); and touchdown receptions—1 (September 26, 2004, vs. Tennessee).

			RECEIVING				TOTALS			
Year Team	G	GS	No.	Yds.	Avg.	TD	TD	2pt.	Pts.	Fum.
2003—Jacksonville NFL	15	2	13	150	11.5	2	2	0	12	0
2004—Jacksonville NFL	4	3	10	69	6.9	1	1	0	6	1
Pro totals (2 years)	19	5	23	219	9.5	3	3	0	18	1

WRIGHT, JASON   RB

PERSONAL: Born July 12, 1982, in Upland, Calif. ... 5-10/210. ... Full name: Jason Gormillion Wright.
HIGH SCHOOL: Diamond Bar (Calif.).
COLLEGE: Northwestern.
TRANSACTIONS/CAREER NOTES: Signed as non-drafted free agent by San Francisco 49ers (May 2, 2004). ... Released by 49ers (August 29, 2004). ... Signed by Atlanta Falcons to practice squad (September 7, 2004). ... Activated (October 25, 2004).
CHAMPIONSHIP GAME EXPERIENCE: Member of Falcons for NFC championship game (2004 season); inactive.
SINGLE GAME HIGHS (regular season): Attempts—2 (December 18, 2004, vs. Carolina); yards—8 (December 26, 2004, vs. New Orleans); and rushing touchdowns—0.

			RUSHING				TOTALS			
Year Team	G	GS	Att.	Yds.	Avg.	TD	TD	2pt.	Pts.	Fum.
2004—Atlanta NFL	2	0	3	10	3.3	0	0	0	0	0

WRIGHT, KENNY   CB   JAGUARS

PERSONAL: Born September 14, 1977, in Ruston, La. ... 6-1/207. ... Full name: Kenneth D. Wright.
HIGH SCHOOL: Ruston (La.).
COLLEGE: Northwestern State.
TRANSACTIONS/CAREER NOTES: Selected after junior season by Minnesota Vikings in fourth round (120th pick overall) of 1999 NFL draft. ... Signed by Vikings (July 21, 1999). ... Granted free agency (March 1, 2002). ... Re-signed by Vikings (April 16, 2002). ... Claimed on waivers by Houston Texans (August 1, 2002). ... Re-signed by Texans (April 2, 2003). ... On injured reserve with knee injury (December 22, 2003-remainder of season). ... Granted unconditional free agency (March 2, 2005). ... Signed by Jacksonville Jaguars (March 31, 2005).
CHAMPIONSHIP GAME EXPERIENCE: Member of Vikings for NFC championship game (2000 season); inactive.

			TOTALS			INTERCEPTIONS			
Year Team	G	GS	Tk.	Ast.	Sks.	No.	Yds.	Avg.	TD
1999—Minnesota NFL	16	12	64	10	0.0	1	11	11.0	0
2000—Minnesota NFL	16	6	34	6	0.0	0	0	0.0	0
2001—Minnesota NFL	15	8	34	5	0.0	0	0	0.0	0
2002—Houston NFL	16	0	24	5	1.0	0	0	0.0	0

W

Year Team	G	GS	TOTALS Tk.	Ast.	Sks.	INTERCEPTIONS No.	Yds.	Avg.	TD
2003—Houston NFL	15	5	39	7	1.0	3	-2	-0.7	0
2004—Houston NFL	16	0	5	2	1.0	0	0	0.0	0
Pro totals (6 years)	94	31	200	35	3.0	4	9	2.3	0

WRIGHT, KENYATTA LB JETS

PERSONAL: Born February 19, 1978, in Vian, Okla. ... 6-0/240.
HIGH SCHOOL: Vian (Okla.).
COLLEGE: Oklahoma State.
TRANSACTIONS/CAREER NOTES: Signed as non-drafted free agent by Buffalo Bills (April 23, 2000). ... Granted free agency (March 1, 2002). ... Signed by New York Jets (April 17, 2003). ... Granted free agency (March 3, 2004). ... Re-signed by Jets (March 25, 2004). ... Granted unconditional free agency (March 2, 2005). ... Re-signed by Jets (April 5, 2005).

Year Team	G	GS	TOTALS Tk.	Ast.	Sks.	INTERCEPTIONS No.	Yds.	Avg.	TD
2000—Buffalo NFL	16	1	13	3	0.0	0	0	0.0	0
2001—Buffalo NFL	11	1	26	8	1.5	0	0	0.0	0
2002—			Did not play.						
2003—New York Jets NFL	16	0	2	1	0.0	0	0	0.0	0
2004—New York Jets NFL	16	0	2	0	0.0	0	0	0.0	0
Pro totals (4 years)	59	2	43	12	1.5	0	0	0.0	0

WUNSCH, JERRY T/G SEAHAWKS

PERSONAL: Born January 21, 1974, in Eau Claire, Wis. ... 6-6/339. ... Full name: Gerald Wunsch. ... Name pronounced: WUNCH.
HIGH SCHOOL: West (Wausau, Wis.).
COLLEGE: Wisconsin.
TRANSACTIONS/CAREER NOTES: Selected by Tampa Bay Buccaneers in second round (37th pick overall) of 1997 NFL draft. ... Signed by Buccaneers (July 18, 1997). ... Granted unconditional free agency (March 2, 2001). ... Re-signed by Buccaneers (April 10, 2001). ... Released by Buccaneers (August 25, 2002). ... Signed by Seattle Seahawks (August 27, 2002). ... Granted unconditional free agency (February 28, 2003). ... Re-signed by Seahawks (March 18, 2003). ... On injured reserve with ankle injury (December 26, 2003-remainder of season). ... Released by Seahawks (September 11, 2004). ... Re-signed by Seahawks (October 13, 2004). ... Released by Seahawks (October 23, 2004). ... Re-signed by Seahawks (October 25, 2004).
PLAYING EXPERIENCE: Tampa Bay NFL, 1997-2001; Seattle NFL, 2002-2004. ... Games/Games started: 1997 (16/0), 1998 (16/1), 1999 (16/13), 2000 (16/16), 2001 (16/16), 2002 (15/5), 2003 (12/0), 2004 (5/0). Total: 112/51.
CHAMPIONSHIP GAME EXPERIENCE: Played in NFC championship game (1999 season).

WYMS, ELLIS DE BUCCANEERS

PERSONAL: Born April 12, 1979, in Indianola, Miss. ... 6-3/279. ... Full name: Ellis Rashad Wyms.
HIGH SCHOOL: Gentry (Indianola, Miss.).
COLLEGE: Mississippi State.
TRANSACTIONS/CAREER NOTES: Selected by Tampa Bay Buccaneers in sixth round (183rd pick overall) of 2001 NFL draft. ... Signed by Buccaneers (July 16, 2001). ... On injured reserve with knee injury (December 16, 2003-remainder of season). ... On injured reserve with shoulder injury (October 23, 2004-remainder of season).
CHAMPIONSHIP GAME EXPERIENCE: Played in NFC championship game (2002 season). ... Member of Super Bowl championship team (2002 season).

Year Team	G	GS	TOTALS Tk.	Ast.	Sks.
2001—Tampa Bay NFL	4	0	3	0	0.0
2002—Tampa Bay NFL	14	0	27	8	5.5
2003—Tampa Bay NFL	13	0	20	4	2.0
2004—Tampa Bay NFL	6	0	7	4	0.0
Pro totals (4 years)	37	0	57	16	7.5

WYNN, DEXTER CB EAGLES

PERSONAL: Born February 25, 1981, in Sumter, S.C. ... 5-9/177.
HIGH SCHOOL: Rampart (Colorado Springs, Colo.).
COLLEGE: Colorado State.
TRANSACTIONS/CAREER NOTES: Selected by Philadelphia Eagles in sixth round (192nd pick overall) of 2004 NFL draft. ... Signed by Eagles (July 26, 2004).
CHAMPIONSHIP GAME EXPERIENCE: Played in NFC championship game (2004 season). ... Member of Eagles for Super Bowl 39 (2004 season); inactive.

Year Team	G	GS	TOTALS Tk.	Ast.	Sks.	INTERCEPTIONS No.	Yds.	Avg.	TD	PUNT RETURNS No.	Yds.	Avg.	TD	KICKOFF RETURNS No.	Yds.	Avg.	TD	TOTALS TD	2pt.	Pts.	Fum.
2004—Phi. NFL	12	0	11	0	1.0	0	0	0.0	0	18	194	10.8	0	1	21	21.0	0	0	0	0	1

WYNN, RENALDO DE REDSKINS

PERSONAL: Born September 3, 1974, in Chicago, Ill. ... 6-3/292. ... Full name: Renaldo Levalle Wynn.
HIGH SCHOOL: De La Salle Institute (Chicago).
COLLEGE: Notre Dame.

W

TRANSACTIONS/CAREER NOTES: Selected by Jacksonville Jaguars in first round (21st pick overall) of 1997 NFL draft. ... Signed by Jaguars (July 21, 1997). ... On injured reserve with groin injury (December 25, 1998-remainder of season). ... Granted unconditional free agency (March 1, 2002). ... Signed by Washington Redskins (March 28, 2002).

CHAMPIONSHIP GAME EXPERIENCE: Played in AFC championship game (1999 season).

			TOTALS		
Year Team	G	GS	Tk.	Ast.	Sks.
1997—Jacksonville NFL	16	8	23	5	2.5
1998—Jacksonville NFL	15	15	23	11	1.0
1999—Jacksonville NFL	12	10	10	7	1.5
2000—Jacksonville NFL	14	14	31	5	3.5
2001—Jacksonville NFL	16	16	29	11	5.0
2002—Washington NFL	16	16	30	11	2.5
2003—Washington NFL	16	16	22	7	2.0
2004—Washington NFL	16	16	31	7	3.0
Pro totals (8 years)	121	111	199	64	21.0

WYRICK, JIMMY — CB

PERSONAL: Born December 31, 1976, in DeSoto, Texas. ... 5-9/176.
HIGH SCHOOL: DeSoto (Texas).
COLLEGE: Minnesota.
TRANSACTIONS/CAREER NOTES: Signed as non-drafted free agent by Detroit Lions (April 28, 2000). ... On injured reserve with ankle injury (October 16, 2000-remainder of season). ... Granted free agency (February 28, 2003). ... Re-signed by Lions (February 28, 2003). ... Released by Lions (November 15, 2003). ... Signed by Miami Dolphins (December 1, 2003). ... Granted unconditional free agency (March 3, 2004). ... Re-signed by Dolphins (August 17, 2004). ... Released by Dolphins (September 6, 2004). ... Re-signed by Dolphins (September 14, 2004). ... Granted unconditional free agency (March 2, 2005).

			TOTALS			INTERCEPTIONS			
Year Team	G	GS	Tk.	Ast.	Sks.	No.	Yds.	Avg.	TD
2000—Detroit NFL	6	0	1	3	0.0	0	0	0.0	0
2001—Detroit NFL	16	0	13	2	0.0	0	0	0.0	0
2002—Detroit NFL	15	0	8	0	0.0	0	0	0.0	0
2003—Detroit NFL	7	1	7	0	0.0	0	0	0.0	0
—Miami NFL	4	0	0	0	0.0	0	0	0.0	0
2004—Miami NFL	14	0	5	0	0.0	0	0	0.0	0
Pro totals (5 years)	62	1	34	5	0.0	0	0	0.0	0

YATES, MAX — LB — 49ERS

PERSONAL: Born October 30, 1979, in Newport News, Va. ...6-2/228.
HIGH SCHOOL: Denbigh (Newport News. Va.).
COLLEGE: Marshall.
TRANSACTIONS/CAREER NOTES: Signed as non-drafted free agent by Minnesota Vikings (April 22, 2002). ... Released by Vikings (September 1, 2002). ... Re-signed by Vikings (January 14, 2003). ... Released by Vikings (August 31, 2003).... Re-signed by Vikings (January 9, 2004). ... Released by Vikings (August 31, 2004). ... Re-signed by Vikings to practice squad (September 28, 2004). ...Released by Vikings from practice squad (October 5, 2004). ... Re-signed by Vikings (October 6, 2004). ... Released by Vikings (October 12, 2004). ... Re-signed by Vikings to practice squad (October 13, 2004). ... Released by Vikings from practice squad (November 30, 2004). ... Signed by San Francisco 49ers to practice squad (December 22, 2004). ... Activated (January 5, 2005).
PLAYING EXPERIENCE: Minnesota NFL, 2004. ... Games/Games started: 2004 (1/0). Total: 1/0.

YODER, TODD — TE — JAGUARS

PERSONAL: Born March 18, 1978, in New Palestine, Ind. ... 6-4/250.
HIGH SCHOOL: New Palestine (Ind.).
COLLEGE: Vanderbilt.
TRANSACTIONS/CAREER NOTES: Signed as non-drafted free agent by Tampa Bay Buccaneers (April 17, 2000). ... Granted free agency (February 28, 2003). ... Re-signed by Buccaneers (April 4, 2003). ... Granted unconditional free agency (March 3, 2004). ... Signed by Jacksonville Jaguars (March 5, 2004).
CHAMPIONSHIP GAME EXPERIENCE: Played in NFC championship game (2002 season). ... Member of Super Bowl championship team (2002 season).
SINGLE GAME HIGHS (regular season): Receptions—4 (October 12, 2003, vs. Washington); yards—56 (December 5, 2004, vs. Pittsburgh); and touchdown receptions—2 (October 12, 2003, vs. Washington).

			RECEIVING				TOTALS			
Year Team	G	GS	No.	Yds.	Avg.	TD	TD	2pt.	Pts.	Fum.
2000—Tampa Bay NFL	9	0	1	1	1.0	0	0	0	0	1
2001—Tampa Bay NFL	16	1	4	48	12.0	0	1	0	6	0
2002—Tampa Bay NFL	16	0	2	26	13.0	0	0	0	0	0
2003—Tampa Bay NFL	16	1	7	68	9.7	2	2	0	12	0
2004—Jacksonville NFL	16	8	14	157	11.2	0	0	0	0	0
Pro totals (5 years)	73	10	28	300	10.7	2	3	0	18	1

Y

YOUNG, BRIAN — DT — SAINTS

PERSONAL: Born July 8, 1977, in Lawton, Okla. ... 6-2/298. ... Full name: James Brian Young.
HIGH SCHOOL: Andress (El Paso, Texas).
COLLEGE: Texas-El Paso.

TRANSACTIONS/CAREER NOTES: Selected by St. Louis Rams in fifth round (139th pick overall) of 2000 NFL draft. ... Signed by Rams (July 7, 2000). ... Granted free agency (February 28, 2003). ... Re-signed by Rams (April 25, 2003). ... Granted unconditional free agency (March 3, 2004). ... Signed by New Orleans Saints (March 7, 2004).
CHAMPIONSHIP GAME EXPERIENCE: Played in NFC championship game (2001 season). ... Played in Super Bowl 36 (2001 season).

Year Team	G	GS	TOTALS Tk.	Ast.	Sks.	INTERCEPTIONS No.	Yds.	Avg.	TD
2000—St. Louis NFL	11	0	4	2	0.0	0	0	0.0	0
2001—St. Louis NFL	16	16	33	7	6.5	1	25	25.0	0
2002—St. Louis NFL	16	3	25	9	2.0	0	0	0.0	0
2003—St. Louis NFL	16	12	27	9	2.0	0	0	0.0	0
2004—New Orleans NFL	15	15	40	19	2.5	0	0	0.0	0
Pro totals (5 years)	74	46	129	46	13.0	1	25	25.0	0

YOUNG, BRYANT　　　　DT　　　　49ERS

PERSONAL: Born January 27, 1972, in Chicago Heights, Ill. ... 6-3/291. ... Full name: Bryant Colby Young.
HIGH SCHOOL: Bloom (Chicago Heights, Ill.).
COLLEGE: Notre Dame.
TRANSACTIONS/CAREER NOTES: Selected by San Francisco 49ers in first round (seventh pick overall) of 1994 NFL draft. ... Signed by 49ers (July 26, 1994). ... On injured reserve with broken leg (December 2, 1998-remainder of season). ... On physically unable to perform list with leg injury (July 30-August 10, 1999).
CHAMPIONSHIP GAME EXPERIENCE: Played in NFC championship game (1994 and 1997 seasons). ... Member of Super Bowl championship team (1994 season).
HONORS: Named defensive tackle on THE SPORTING NEWS NFL All-Pro team (1996 and 1998). ... Played in Pro Bowl (1996, 1999, 2001 and 2002 seasons).

Year Team	G	GS	TOTALS Tk.	Ast.	Sks.
1994—San Francisco NFL	16	16	45	4	6.0
1995—San Francisco NFL	12	12	25	3	6.0
1996—San Francisco NFL	16	16	61	15	11.5
1997—San Francisco NFL	12	12	39	6	4.0
1998—San Francisco NFL	12	12	43	11	9.5
1999—San Francisco NFL	16	16	36	5	11.0
2000—San Francisco NFL	15	15	33	12	9.5
2001—San Francisco NFL	16	16	33	6	3.5
2002—San Francisco NFL	16	16	20	8	2.0
2003—San Francisco NFL	16	16	29	6	3.5
2004—San Francisco NFL	16	16	37	11	3.0
Pro totals (11 years)	163	163	409	87	69.5

YOUNG, CHRIS　　　　S　　　　BRONCOS

PERSONAL: Born January 23, 1980, in Senoia, Ga. ... 6-0/210. ... Full name: Christopher Lamont Young.
HIGH SCHOOL: East Cowetta (Ga.).
COLLEGE: Georgia Tech.
TRANSACTIONS/CAREER NOTES: Selected by Denver Broncos in seventh round (228th pick overall) of 2002 NFL draft. ... Signed by Broncos (June 11, 2002). ... Released by Broncos (September 1, 2002). ... Re-signed by Broncos to practice squad (September 3, 2002). ... Activated (December 31, 2002). ... Assigned by Broncos to Frankfurt Galaxy in 2003 NFL Europe enhancement allocation program (February 4, 2003).

Year Team	G	GS	TOTALS Tk.	Ast.	Sks.	INTERCEPTIONS No.	Yds.	Avg.	TD
2003—Denver NFL	11	0	0	1	0.0	0	0	0.0	0
2004—Denver NFL	10	0	0	0	0.0	0	0	0.0	0
Pro totals (2 years)	21	0	0	1	0.0	0	0	0.0	0

YOVANOVITS, DAVE　　　　T　　　　JETS

PERSONAL: Born March 6, 1981, in Stanhope, N.J. ... 6-3/294.
HIGH SCHOOL: Hopatcong (N.J.).
COLLEGE: Temple.
TRANSACTIONS/CAREER NOTES: Selected by New York Jets in seventh round (237th pick overall) of 2003 NFL draft. ... Released by Jets (September 5, 2004). ... Re-signed by Jets to practice squad (September 6, 2004). ... Activated (October 13, 2004).
PLAYING EXPERIENCE: New York Jets NFL, 2004. ... Games/Games started: 2004 (4/0). Total: 4/0.

ZASTUDIL, DAVE　　　　P　　　　RAVENS

PERSONAL: Born October 26, 1978, in Bay Village, Ohio. ... 6-3/215.
HIGH SCHOOL: Bay Village (Ohio).
COLLEGE: Ohio.
TRANSACTIONS/CAREER NOTES: Selected by Baltimore Ravens in fourth round (112th pick overall) of 2002 NFL draft. ... Signed by Ravens (July 26, 2002). ... Granted free agency (March 2, 2005). ... Re-signed by Ravens (March 18, 2005).
HONORS: Named punter on THE SPORTING NEWS college All-America third team (2001).

Year Team	G	No.	PUNTING Yds.	Avg.	Net avg.	In. 20	Blk.
2002—Baltimore NFL	16	81	3368	41.6	33.7	31	2
2003—Baltimore NFL	16	89	3649	41.0	35.2	21	0
2004—Baltimore NFL	13	73	2948	40.4	34.6	26	0
Pro totals (3 years)	45	243	9965	41.0	34.5	78	2

ZELENKA, JOE — TE/LS — JAGUARS

PERSONAL: Born March 9, 1976, in Cleveland, Ohio. ... 6-3/270. ... Full name: Joseph John Zelenka.
HIGH SCHOOL: Benedictine (Cleveland).
COLLEGE: Wake Forest.
TRANSACTIONS/CAREER NOTES: Signed as non-drafted free agent by San Francisco 49ers (April 23, 1999). ... Traded by 49ers to Washington Redskins for seventh-round pick (TE Eric Johnson) in 2001 draft (April 17, 2000). ... Released by Redskins (March 9, 2001). ... Signed by Jacksonville Jaguars (August 13, 2001). ... Granted unconditional free agency (February 28, 2003). ... Re-signed by Jaguars (February 28, 2003). ... Granted unconditional free agency (March 3, 2004). ... Re-signed by Jaguars (March 3, 2004). ... Granted unconditional free agency (March 2, 2005). ... Re-signed by Jaguars (March 2, 2005).
PLAYING EXPERIENCE: San Francisco NFL, 1999; Washington NFL, 2000; Jacksonville NFL, 2001-2004. ... Games/Games started: 1999 (13/0), 2000 (16/0), 2001 (16/0), 2002 (16/0), 2003 (16/0), 2004 (16/0). Total: 93/0.

ZELLNER, PEPPI — DE — CARDINALS

PERSONAL: Born March 14, 1975, in Forsyth, Ga. ... 6-5/262. ... Full name: Hunndens Guiseppi Zellner.
HIGH SCHOOL: Mary Persons (Forsythe, Ga.).
JUNIOR COLLEGE: Georgia Military College.
COLLEGE: Fort Valley State.
TRANSACTIONS/CAREER NOTES: Selected by Dallas Cowboys in fourth round (132nd pick overall) of 1999 NFL draft. ... Signed by Cowboys (July 27, 1999). ... On injured reserve with knee injury (December 12, 2000-remainder of season). ... On physically unable to perform list with knee injury (July 22-August 14, 2001). ... Granted unconditional free agency (February 28, 2003). ... Signed by Washington Redskins (May 13, 2003). ... Granted unconditional free agency (March 3, 2004). ... Signed by Oakland Raiders (August 17, 2004). ... Traded by Raiders with RB Troy Hambrick to Arizona Cardinals for an undisclosed 2005 draft choice (August 31, 2004). ... Granted unconditional free agency (March 2, 2005). ... Re-signed by Cardinals (March 9, 2005).

| | | | TOTALS | | |
Year Team	G	GS	Tk.	Ast.	Sks.
1999—Dallas NFL	13	0	9	0	1.0
2000—Dallas NFL	12	0	7	3	2.0
2001—Dallas NFL	16	15	36	10	3.0
2002—Dallas NFL	16	2	22	7	0.0
2003—Washington NFL	16	0	12	2	1.0
2004—Arizona NFL	16	14	16	6	2.0
Pro totals (6 years)	89	31	102	28	9.0

ZEREOUE, AMOS — RB

PERSONAL: Born October 8, 1976, in Hempstead, N.Y. ... 5-8/205. ... Name pronounced: zer-O-way.
HIGH SCHOOL: W.C. Mepham (Hempstead, N.Y.).
COLLEGE: West Virginia.
TRANSACTIONS/CAREER NOTES: Selected after junior season by Pittsburgh Steelers in third round (95th pick overall) of 1999 NFL draft. ... Signed by Steelers (July 30, 1999). ... Granted free agency (March 1, 2002). ... Re-signed by Steelers (June 13, 2002). ... Released by Steelers (March 11, 2004). ... Signed by Oakland Raiders (April 29, 2004). ... Granted unconditional free agency (March 2, 2005).
CHAMPIONSHIP GAME EXPERIENCE: Played in AFC championship game (2001 season).
HONORS: Named running back on THE SPORTING NEWS college All-America third team (1997).
SINGLE GAME HIGHS (regular season): Attempts—37 (November 10, 2002, vs. Atlanta); yards—123 (November 10, 2002, vs. Atlanta); and rushing touchdowns—2 (October 3, 2004, vs. Houston).
STATISTICAL PLATEAUS: 100-yard rushing games: 2002 (3), 2004 (1). Total: 4.

| | | | RUSHING | | | | RECEIVING | | | | KICKOFF RETURNS | | | | TOTALS | | | |
Year Team	G	GS	Att.	Yds.	Avg.	TD	No.	Yds.	Avg.	TD	No.	Yds.	Avg.	TD	TD	2pt.	Pts.	Fum.
1999—Pittsburgh NFL	8	0	18	48	2.7	0	2	17	8.5	0	7	169	24.1	0	0	0	0	0
2000—Pittsburgh NFL	12	0	6	14	2.3	0	0	0	0.0	0	0	0	0.0	0	0	0	0	0
2001—Pittsburgh NFL	14	0	85	441	5.2	1	13	154	11.8	1	0	0	0.0	0	2	0	12	3
2002—Pittsburgh NFL	16	5	193	762	3.9	4	42	341	8.1	0	0	0	0.0	0	4	0	24	2
2003—Pittsburgh NFL	16	6	132	433	3.3	2	40	310	7.8	0	0	0	0.0	0	2	0	12	0
2004—Oakland NFL	15	6	112	425	3.8	3	39	284	7.3	0	0	0	0.0	0	3	0	18	1
Pro totals (6 years)	81	17	546	2123	3.9	10	136	1106	8.1	1	7	169	24.1	0	11	0	66	6

ZGONINA, JEFF — DT — DOLPHINS

PERSONAL: Born May 24, 1970, in Chicago, Ill. ... 6-2/285. ... Full name: Jeffrey Marc Zgonina. ... Name pronounced: ska-KNEE-na.
HIGH SCHOOL: Mount Carmel (Chicago).
COLLEGE: Purdue.
TRANSACTIONS/CAREER NOTES: Selected by Pittsburgh Steelers in seventh round (185th pick overall) of 1993 NFL draft. ... Signed by Steelers (July 16, 1993). ... Claimed on waivers by Carolina Panthers (August 28, 1995). ... Granted free agency (February 16, 1996). ... Re-signed by Panthers (April 11, 1996). ... Released by Panthers (August 19, 1996). ... Signed by Atlanta Falcons (October 8, 1996). ... Granted unconditional free agency (February 14, 1997). ... Signed by St. Louis Rams (March 17, 1997). ... Released by Rams (August 30, 1998). ... Signed by Oakland Raiders (October 13, 1998). ... Released by Raiders (October 18, 1998). ... Signed by Indianapolis Colts (November 25, 1998). ... Granted unconditional free agency (February 12, 1999). ... Signed by Rams (April 5, 1999). ... Released by Rams (April 1, 2002). ... Re-signed by Rams (April 2, 2002). ... Granted unconditional free agency (February 28, 2003). ... Signed by Miami Dolphins (March 31, 2003).
CHAMPIONSHIP GAME EXPERIENCE: Played in AFC championship game (1994 season). ... Played in NFC championship game (1999 and 2001 seasons). ... Member of Super Bowl championship team (1999 season). ... Played in Super Bowl 36 (2001 season).

Year Team	G	GS	TOTALS			INTERCEPTIONS			
			Tk.	Ast.	Sks.	No.	Yds.	Avg.	TD
1993—Pittsburgh NFL	5	0	11	5	0.0	0	0	0.0	0
1994—Pittsburgh NFL	16	0	6	5	0.0	0	0	0.0	0
1995—Carolina NFL	2	0	2	0	0.0	0	0	0.0	0
1996—Atlanta NFL	8	0	7	5	1.0	0	0	0.0	0
1997—St. Louis NFL	15	0	19	2	2.0	0	0	0.0	0
1998—Indianapolis NFL	2	0	0	0	0.0	0	0	0.0	0
1999—St. Louis NFL	16	0	26	5	4.5	0	0	0.0	0
2000—St. Louis NFL	16	10	30	7	2.0	0	0	0.0	0
2001—St. Louis NFL	13	13	32	6	0.0	0	0	0.0	0
2002—St. Louis NFL	16	16	29	9	4.0	0	0	0.0	0
2003—Miami NFL	16	3	22	17	3.0	1	0	0.0	0
2004—Miami NFL	16	14	32	31	5.0	0	0	0.0	0
Pro totals (12 years)	141	56	216	92	21.5	1	0	0.0	0

ZUKAUSKAS, PAUL   T

PERSONAL: Born July 12, 1979, in Weymouth, Mass. ... 6-5/320. ... Full name: Paul Malcolm Zukauskas.
HIGH SCHOOL: Boston College (Ma.).
COLLEGE: Boston College.
TRANSACTIONS/CAREER NOTES: Selected by Cleveland Browns in seventh round (203rd pick overall) of 2001 NFL draft. ... Signed by Browns (July 20, 2001). ... Released by Browns (September 1, 2001). ... Re-signed by Browns to practice squad (September 3, 2001). ... Activated (November 21, 2001). ... Granted free agency (March 3, 2004). ... Re-signed by Browns (April 8, 2004). ... Granted unconditional free agency (March 2, 2005).
PLAYING EXPERIENCE: Cleveland NFL, 2001-2004. ... Games/Games started: 2001 (1/0), 2002 (16/3), 2003 (12/10), 2004 (14/5). Total: 43/18.
HONORS: Named guard on THE SPORTING NEWS college All-America second team (2000).

ABDULLAH, HAMZA   S   BUCCANEERS

PERSONAL: Born August 20, 1983. ... 6-3/214.
HIGH SCHOOL: Pomona (Calif.).
COLLEGE: Washington State.
TRANSACTIONS/CAREER NOTES: Selected by Tampa Bay Buccaneers in seventh round (231st pick overall) of 2005 NFL draft.

			INTERCEPTIONS			
Year Team	G	Sks.	No.	Yds.	Avg.	TD
2001—Washington State	7	0.0	0	0	0.0	0
2002—Washington State	9	0.0	0	0	0.0	0
2003—Washington State	12	0.0	0	0	0.0	0
2004—Washington State	11	1.0	1	3	3.0	0
College totals (4 years)	39	1.0	1	3	3.0	0

ALABI, ANTHONY   T   DOLPHINS

PERSONAL: Born February 16, 1981, in San Antonio, Texas. ... 6-5/313. ... Full name: Anthony Abayomi Alabi.
HIGH SCHOOL: Antonian College Prep (San Antonio, Texas).
COLLEGE: United States Naval Academy, then Texas Christian.
TRANSACTIONS/CAREER NOTES: Selected by Miami Dolphins in fifth round (162nd pick overall) of 2005 NFL draft.
PLAYING EXPERIENCE: Texas Christian, 2001-2004. ... Games played: 2001 (10), 2002 (12), 2003 (12), 2004 (11). Total: 45.

ANDERSON, DEREK   QB   RAVENS

PERSONAL: Born June 15, 1983, in Portland, Ore. ... 6-6/242.
HIGH SCHOOL: Scappoose (Ore.).
COLLEGE: Oregon State.
TRANSACTIONS/CAREER NOTES: Selected by Baltimore Ravens in sixth round (213th pick overall) of 2005 NFL draft.

		PASSING								RUSHING				TOTALS	
Year Team	G	Att.	Cmp.	Pct.	Yds.	TD	Int.	Avg.	Rat.	Att.	Yds.	Avg.	TD	TD	Pts.
2001—Oregon State	5	41	17	41.5	263	1	3	6.41	88.8	5	-25	-5.0	0	0	0
2002—Oregon State	13	449	211	47.0	3313	25	13	7.38	121.6	45	-231	-5.1	2	2	12
2003—Oregon State	13	509	261	51.3	4058	24	24	7.97	124.4	57	-125	-2.2	4	4	24
2004—Oregon State	12	515	279	54.2	3615	29	17	7.02	125.1	75	-152	-2.0	2	2	12
College totals (4 years)	43	1514	768	50.7	11249	79	57	7.43	122.8	182	-533	-2.9	8	8	48

ARMSTRONG, CALVIN   T   EAGLES

PERSONAL: Born March 31, 1982, in Seattle, Wash. ... 6-7/325.
HIGH SCHOOL: Centralia (Wash.).
COLLEGE: Washington State.
TRANSACTIONS/CAREER NOTES: Selected by Philadelphia Eagles in sixth round (211th pick overall) of 2005 NFL draft.
PLAYING EXPERIENCE: Washington State, 2001-2004. ... Games played: 2001 (12), 2002 (12), 2003 (13), 2004 (11). Total: 48.
HONORS: Named offensive tackle on THE SPORTING NEWS Freshman All-America third team (2001).

ARRINGTON, J.J.   RB   CARDINALS

PERSONAL: Born January 23, 1983, in Rocky Mount, N.C. ... 5-9/214.
HIGH SCHOOL: Northern Nash (Rocky Mount, N.C.).
JUNIOR COLLEGE: College of the Canyons (Santa Clarita, Calif.).
COLLEGE: California.
TRANSACTIONS/CAREER NOTES: Selected by Arizona Cardinals in second round (44th pick overall) of 2005 NFL draft.
MISCELLANEOUS: Named running back on THE SPORTING NEWS college All-America first team (2004).

		RUSHING				RECEIVING				TOTALS	
Year Team	G	Att.	Yds.	Avg.	TD	No.	Yds.	Avg.	TD	TD	Pts.
2003—California	13	107	607	5.7	5	21	178	8.5	3	8	48
2004—California	12	289	2018	7.0	15	21	121	5.8	0	15	90
College totals (2 years)	25	396	2625	6.6	20	42	299	7.1	3	23	138

ATOGWE, OSHIOMOGHO   S   RAMS

PERSONAL: Born June 23, 1981, in Windsor, Ontario. ... 5-11/219.
HIGH SCHOOL: W.F. Herman (Ontario, Canada).
COLLEGE: Stanford.
TRANSACTIONS/CAREER NOTES: Selected by St. Louis Rams in third round (66th pick overall) of 2005 NFL draft.

			INTERCEPTIONS			
Year Team	G	Sks.	No.	Yds.	Avg.	TD
2001—Stanford	11	0.0	0	0	0.0	0
2002—Stanford	11	1.0	3	43	14.3	0
2003—Stanford	11	0.0	2	5	2.5	0
2004—Stanford	11	0.0	4	33	8.3	0
College totals (4 years)	44	1.0	9	81	9.0	0

BAAS, DAVID   G   49ERS

PERSONAL: Born September 28, 1981, in Sarasota, Fla. ... 6-4/319. ... Full name: David Andrew Baas.
HIGH SCHOOL: Riverview (Sarasota, Fla.).
COLLEGE: Michigan.
TRANSACTIONS/CAREER NOTES: Selected by San Francisco 49ers in second round (33rd pick overall) of 2005 NFL draft.
PLAYING EXPERIENCE: Michigan, 2001-2004. ... Games played: 2001 (6), 2002 (13), 2003 (13), 2004 (12). Total: 44.
HONORS: Co-recipient (with LSU's Ben Wilkerson) of Dave Rimington Trophy (2004). ... Named guard on THE SPORTING NEWS college All-America second team (2003 and 2004).

BABINEAUX, JONATHAN   DT   FALCONS

PERSONAL: Born October 12, 1981, in Port Arthur, Texas. ... 6-2/286.
HIGH SCHOOL: Lincoln (Texas).
COLLEGE: Iowa.
TRANSACTIONS/CAREER NOTES: Selected by Atlanta Falcons in second round (59th pick overall) of 2005 NFL draft.

Year Team	G	SACKS
2000—Iowa	11	0.0
2002—Iowa	12	7.0
2003—Iowa	7	1.0
2004—Iowa	12	11.0
College totals (4 years)	42	19.0

BAJEMA, BILLY   TE   49ERS

PERSONAL: Born October 31, 1982, in Oklahoma City, Okla. ... 6-5/259. ... Full name: William Bajema.
HIGH SCHOOL: Westmoore (Oklahoma City, Okla.).
COLLEGE: Oklahoma State.
TRANSACTIONS/CAREER NOTES: Selected by San Francisco 49ers in seventh round (249th pick overall) in the 2005 NFL draft.

		RECEIVING			
Year Team	G	No.	Yds.	Avg.	TD
2001—Oklahoma State	8	4	16	4.0	0
2002—Oklahoma State	13	16	271	16.9	1
2003—Oklahoma State	13	12	129	10.8	2
2004—Oklahoma State	12	20	293	14.7	1
College totals (4 years)	46	52	709	13.6	4

BARBER, MARION   RB   COWBOYS

PERSONAL: Born June 10, 1983, in Plymouth, Minn. ... 5-11/221. ... Full name: Marion Barber III. ... Son of Marion Barber, running back with New York Jets (1982-88).
HIGH SCHOOL: Wayzata (Plymouth, Minn.).
COLLEGE: Minnesota.
TRANSACTIONS/CAREER NOTES: Selected after junior season by Dallas Cowboys in fourth round (109th pick overall) of 2005 NFL draft.
HONORS: Named running back on THE SPORTING NEWS Freshman All-America third team (2001).

		RUSHING				RECEIVING				PUNT RETURNS				KICKOFF RETURNS				TOTALS	
Year Team	G	Att.	Yds.	Avg.	TD	No.	Yds.	Avg.	TD	No.	Yds.	Avg.	TD	No.	Yds.	Avg.	TD	TD	Pts.
2001—Minnesota	11	118	742	6.3	7	2	19	9.5	0	0	0	0.0	0	5	136	27.2	0	7	42
2002—Minnesota	2	19	69	3.6	0	3	25	8.3	0	0	0	0.0	0	0	0	0.0	0	0	0
2003—Minnesota	13	207	1196	5.8	17	13	119	9.2	0	28	405	14.5	0	8	172	21.5	0	17	102
2004—Minnesota	12	231	1269	5.5	11	3	27	9.0	0	19	110	5.8	0	10	206	20.6	0	11	66
College totals (4 years)	38	575	3276	5.7	35	21	190	9.0	0	47	515	11.0	0	23	514	22.3	0	35	210

BARNES, KHALIF   T   JAGUARS

PERSONAL: Born April 21, 1982, in San Diego, Calif. ... 6-6/305.
HIGH SCHOOL: Mount Miguel (Spring Valley, Calif.).
COLLEGE: Washington.
TRANSACTIONS/CAREER NOTES: Selected by Jacksonville Jaguars in second round (52nd pick overall) of 2005 NFL draft.
PLAYING EXPERIENCE: Washington, 2001-2004. ... Games played: 2001 (10), 2002 (13), 2003 (12), 2004 (5). Total: 40.

BARRON, ALEX   T   RAMS

PERSONAL: Born September 28, 1982, in Orangeburg, S.C. ... 6-8/320.
HIGH SCHOOL: Wilkinson (Orangeburg, S.C.).
COLLEGE: Florida State.
TRANSACTIONS/CAREER NOTES: Selected by St. Louis Rams in first round (19th pick overall) of 2005 NFL draft.
PLAYING EXPERIENCE: Florida State, 2001-2004. ... Games played: 2001 (4), 2002 (14), 2003 (13), 2004 (12). Total: 43.
HONORS: Named offensive tackle on THE SPORTING NEWS college All-America first team (2004).

BARTELL, RONALD   CB   RAMS

PERSONAL: Born February 22, 1982, in Detroit, Mich. ... 6-1/211. ... Full name: Ronald Bartell Jr.
HIGH SCHOOL: Renaissance (Detroit, Mich.).
COLLEGE: Central Michigan, then Howard.
TRANSACTIONS/CAREER NOTES: Selected by St. Louis Rams in second round (50th pick overall) of 2005 NFL draft.

Year Team	G	Sks.	INTERCEPTIONS No.	Yds.	Avg.	TD
2001—Central Michigan	11	1.0	0	0	0.0	0
2002—Central Michigan	12	1.0	0	0	0.0	0
2003—Howard	11	0.0	1	33	33.0	0
2004—Howard	11	0.0	1	6	6.0	0
College totals (4 years)	45	2.0	2	39	19.5	0

BECK, JORDAN   LB   FALCONS

PERSONAL: Born April 18, 1983, in Santa Cruz, Calif. ... 6-2/233.
HIGH SCHOOL: San Lorenzo Valley (Mount Hermon, Calif.).
COLLEGE: Cal State Poly.
TRANSACTIONS/CAREER NOTES: Selected by Atlanta Falcons in third round (90th pick overall) of 2005 NFL draft.
MISCELLANEOUS: Buck Buchanan Award winner (2004).

Year Team	G	Sks.	INTERCEPTIONS No.	Yds.	Avg.	TD
2001—Cal Poly	10	2.5	0	0	0.0	0
2002—Cal Poly	11	4.5	0	0	0.0	0
2003—Cal Poly	11	4.0	0	0	0.0	0
2004—Cal Poly	11	5.5	4	108	27.0	2
College totals (4 years)	43	16.5	4	108	27.0	2

BENSON, CEDRIC   RB   BEARS

PERSONAL: Born December 28, 1982, in Midland, Texas. ... 5-11/222. ... Full name: Cedric Myron Benson.
HIGH SCHOOL: Lee (Midland, Texas).
COLLEGE: Texas.
TRANSACTIONS/CAREER NOTES: Selected by Chicago Bears in first round (fourth pick overall) of 2005 NFL draft.
HONORS: Doak Walker Award winner (2004). ... Named running back on THE SPORTING NEWS Freshman All-America first team (2001). ... Named running back on THE SPORTING NEWS college All-America second team (2004).

Year Team	G	RUSHING Att.	Yds.	Avg.	TD	RECEIVING No.	Yds.	Avg.	TD	TOTALS TD	Pts.
2001—Texas	12	223	1053	4.7	12	17	203	11.9	1	13	78
2002—Texas	13	305	1293	4.2	12	21	119	5.7	0	12	72
2003—Texas	12	258	1360	5.3	21	9	120	13.3	1	22	134
2004—Texas	12	326	1834	5.6	19	22	179	8.1	1	20	120
College totals (4 years)	49	1112	5540	5.0	64	69	621	9.0	3	67	404

BERGER, JOE   G/C   PANTHERS

PERSONAL: Born May 25, 1982, in Fremont, Mich. ... 6-5/303.
COLLEGE: Michigan Tech.
TRANSACTIONS/CAREER NOTES: Selected by Carolina Panthers in sixth round (207th pick overall) of 2005 NFL draft.
PLAYING EXPERIENCE: Michigan Tech, 2001-2004. ... Games played: 2001 (7), 2002 (8), 2003 (10), 2004 (10). Total: 35.

BERGERON, DAVID   LB   EAGLES

PERSONAL: Born December 4, 1981, in Lake Oswego, Utah. ... 6-3/241.
HIGH SCHOOL: Lakeridge (Ore.).
COLLEGE: Stanford.
TRANSACTIONS/CAREER NOTES: Selected by Philadelphia Eagles in seventh round (252nd pick overall) of 2005 NFL draft.

Year Team	G	Sks.	INTERCEPTIONS No.	Yds.	Avg.	TD
2001—Stanford	9	0.0	0	0	0.0	0
2002—Stanford	11	1.5	0	0	0.0	0
2003—Stanford	11	0.0	1	10	10.0	0
2004—Stanford	10	0.5	0	0	0.0	0
College totals (4 years)	41	2.0	1	10	10.0	0

BERIAULT, JUSTIN   S   COWBOYS

PERSONAL: Born August 23, 1981, in Indianapolis, Ind. ... 6-3/204. ... Full name: Arthur Justin Beriault.
HIGH SCHOOL: Warren Central (Indianapolis, Ind.).
COLLEGE: Ball State.
TRANSACTIONS/CAREER NOTES: Selected by Dallas Cowboys in sixth round (208th pick overall) of 2005 NFL draft.

Year Team	G	Sks.	INTERCEPTIONS No.	Yds.	Avg.	TD
2001—Ball State	11	0.0	1	0	0.0	0
2002—Ball State	12	0.0	1	0	0.0	0
2003—Ball State	12	0.0	1	6	6.0	0
2004—Ball State	11	0.0	1	18	18.0	0
College totals (4 years)	46	0.0	4	24	6.0	0

BLACKSTOCK, DARRYL   LB   CARDINALS

PERSONAL: Born May 30, 1983, in Newport News, Va. ... 6-3/238. ... Full name: Darryl Tyger Blackstock.
HIGH SCHOOL: Heritage (Newport News, Va.).

COLLEGE: Virginia.
TRANSACTIONS/CAREER NOTES: Selected after junior season by Arizona Cardinals in third round (95th pick overall) of 2005 NFL draft.
HONORS: Named linebacker on THE SPORTING NEWS Freshman All-America first team (2002).

				INTERCEPTIONS		
Year Team	G	Sks.	No.	Yds.	Avg.	TD
2002—Virginia	14	10.0	1	9	9.0	0
2003—Virginia	13	6.0	0	0	0.0	0
2004—Virginia	12	11.0	0	0	0.0	0
College totals (3 years)	39	27.0	1	9	9.0	0

BOLEY, MICHAEL — LB — FALCONS

PERSONAL: Born August 24, 1982, in Athens, Ala. ... 6-3/236.
HIGH SCHOOL: Elkmont (Athens, Ala.).
COLLEGE: Southern Mississippi.
TRANSACTIONS/CAREER NOTES: Selected by Atlanta Falcons in fifth round (160th pick overall) of 2005 NFL draft.
HONORS: Named linebacker on THE SPORTING NEWS college All-America second team (2004).

				INTERCEPTIONS		
Year Team	G	Sks.	No.	Yds.	Avg.	TD
2001—Southern Mississippi	9	0.5	0	0	0.0	0
2002—Southern Mississippi	13	8.0	1	54	54.0	1
2003—Southern Mississippi	13	11.0	0	0	0.0	0
2004—Southern Mississippi	12	9.0	2	75	37.5	1
College totals (4 years)	47	28.5	3	129	43.0	2

BRACKINS, LARRY — WR — BUCCANEERS

PERSONAL: Born November 5, 1982. ... 6-4/205.
HIGH SCHOOL: Dothan (Ala.).
COLLEGE: Feather River Community College, then Pearl River Community College.
TRANSACTIONS/CAREER NOTES: Selected after junior season by Tampa Bay Buccaneers in fifth round (155th pick overall) of 2005 NFL draft.

BRADLEY, MARK — WR — BEARS

PERSONAL: Born January 29, 1982... 6-1/201.
HIGH SCHOOL: Pine Bluff (Ark.).
COLLEGE: Arkansas-Pine Bluff, then Oklahoma.
TRANSACTIONS/CAREER NOTES: Selected by Chicago Bears in second round (39th pick overall) of 2005 NFL draft.

		RUSHING			RECEIVING				PUNT RETURNS				KICKOFF RETURNS				TOTALS	
Year Team	G	Att.	Yds.	Avg.	TD	No.	Yds.	Avg.	TD	No.	Yds.	Avg.	TD	No.	Yds.	Avg.	TD	TD Pts.
2000—Arkansas-Pine Bluff	7	0	0	0.0	0	11	256	23.3	4	0	0	0.0	0	0	0	0.0	0	4 24
2001—Arkansas-Pine Bluff	5	0	0	0.0	0	13	203	15.6	2	7	196	28.0	2	3	40	13.3	0	4 24
2003—Oklahoma	12	0	0	0.0	0	11	194	17.6	2	0	0	0.0	0	7	247	35.3	1	3 18
2004—Oklahoma	13	4	73	18.3	1	23	491	21.3	7	1	3	3.0	0	12	236	19.7	0	8 48
College totals (4 years)	37	4	73	18.3	1	58	1144	19.7	15	8	199	24.9	2	22	523	23.8	1	19 114

BRAGG, CRAIG — WR — PACKERS

PERSONAL: Born March 15, 1982, in San Jose, Calif. ... 6-1/196. ... Full name: Craig Milton Bragg.
HIGH SCHOOL: Bellarmine College Prep (San Jose, Calif.).
COLLEGE: UCLA.
TRANSACTIONS/CAREER NOTES: Selected by Green Bay Packers in sixth round (195th pick overall) of 2005 NFL draft.

		RECEIVING				PUNT RETURNS				TOTALS	
Year Team	G	No.	Yds.	Avg.	TD	No.	Yds.	Avg.	TD	TD	Pts.
2001—UCLA	11	29	408	14.1	2	14	118	8.4	0	4	24
2002—UCLA	13	55	889	16.2	8	16	256	16.0	1	9	54
2003—UCLA	13	73	1065	14.6	5	38	302	7.9	0	5	30
2004—UCLA	9	36	483	13.4	4	19	285	15.0	1	5	30
College totals (4 years)	46	193	2845	14.7	19	87	961	11.0	2	23	138

BRITT, WESLEY — T — CHARGERS

PERSONAL: Born November 21, 1981, in Cullman, Ala. ... 6-7/314.
HIGH SCHOOL: Cullman (Ala.).
COLLEGE: Alabama.
TRANSACTIONS/CAREER NOTES: Selected by San Diego Chargers in fifth round (164th pick overall) of 2005 NFL draft.
PLAYING EXPERIENCE: Alabama, 2001-2003. ... Games played: 2001 (11), 2002 (13), 2003 (9). Total: 33.
HONORS: Named offensive tackle on THE SPORTING NEWS Freshman All-America fourth team (2001).

BROUGHTON, NEHEMIAH — RB — REDSKINS

PERSONAL: Born November 4, 1982... 5-11/245.
HIGH SCHOOL: North Charleston (S.C.).
COLLEGE: The Citadel.
TRANSACTIONS/CAREER NOTES: Selected by Washington Redskins in seventh round (222nd pick overall) of 2005 NFL draft.

		RUSHING				RECEIVING				TOTALS	
Year Team	G	Att.	Yds.	Avg.	TD	No.	Yds.	Avg.	TD	TD	Pts.
2001—The Citadel	8	13	34	2.6	1	0	0	0.0	0	1	6

Year Team	G	RUSHING				RECEIVING				TOTALS	
		Att.	Yds.	Avg.	TD	No.	Yds.	Avg.	TD	TD	Pts.
2002—The Citadel	12	224	1038	4.6	11	18	181	10.1	1	12	72
2003—The Citadel	10	165	778	4.7	8	21	239	11.4	2	10	60
2004—The Citadel	10	179	788	4.4	5	8	35	4.4	0	5	30
College totals (4 years)	40	581	2638	4.5	25	47	455	9.7	3	28	168

BROWN, C.C.   S   TEXANS

PERSONAL: Born January 27, 1983, in Greenwood, Miss. ... 6-0/208. ... Full name: Ceandris Nehemiah Brown.
HIGH SCHOOL: Greenwood (Miss.).
JUNIOR COLLEGE: Mississippi Delta Community College (Moorhead, Miss.).
COLLEGE: Louisiana-Lafayette.
TRANSACTIONS/CAREER NOTES: Selected by Houston Texans in sixth round (188th pick overall) in 2005 NFL draft.

Year Team	G	Sks.	INTERCEPTIONS			
			No.	Yds.	Avg.	TD
2003—Louisiana-Lafayette	11	1.0	2	7	3.5	0
2004—Louisiana-Lafayette	11	0.0	0	0	0.0	0
College totals (2 years)	22	1.0	2	7	3.5	0

BROWN, ELTON   G   CARDINALS

PERSONAL: Born May 22, 1982, in Hampton, Va. ... 6-5/329. ... Full name: Elton Gillett Brown.
HIGH SCHOOL: Hampton (Va.).
COLLEGE: Virginia.
TRANSACTIONS/CAREER NOTES: Selected by Arizona Cardinals in fourth round (111th pick overall) of 2005 NFL draft.
PLAYING EXPERIENCE: Virginia, 2001-2004. ... Games played: 2001 (10), 2002 (12), 2003 (11), 2004 (11). Total: 44.
HONORS: Named guard on THE SPORTING NEWS college All-America first team (2004).

BROWN, JAMMAL   T   SAINTS

PERSONAL: Born March 30, 1981, in El Paso, Texas. ... 6-6/316. ... Full name: Jammal F. Brown.
HIGH SCHOOL: MacArthur (Lawton, Okla.).
COLLEGE: Oklahoma.
TRANSACTIONS/CAREER NOTES: Selected by New Orleans Saints in first round (13th pick overall) of 2005 NFL draft.
PLAYING EXPERIENCE: Oklahoma, 2001-2004. ... Games played: 2001 (3), 2002 (14), 2003 (14), 2004 (13). Total: 44.
HONORS: Outland Trophy winner (2004). ... Named offensive tackle on THE SPORTING NEWS college All-America second team (2003). ... Named offensive tackle on THE SPORTING NEWS college All-America first team (2004).

BROWN, JASON   C   RAVENS

PERSONAL: Born May 5, 1983, in Henderson, N.C. ... 6-3/309. ... Full name: J.W. Jason Brown.
HIGH SCHOOL: Northern Vance (Henderson, N.C.).
COLLEGE: North Carolina.
TRANSACTIONS/CAREER NOTES: Selected by Baltimore Ravens in fourth round (124th pick overall) of 2005 NFL draft.
PLAYING EXPERIENCE: North Carolina, 2001-2004. ... Games played: 2001 (8), 2002 (12), 2003 (12), 2004 (12). Total: 44.

BROWN, REGGIE   WR   EAGLES

PERSONAL: Born January 13, 1981, in Carrollton, Ga. ... 6-2/195.
HIGH SCHOOL: Carrollton (Ga.).
COLLEGE: Georgia.
TRANSACTIONS/CAREER NOTES: Selected by Philadelphia Eagles in second round (35th pick overall) of 2005 NFL draft.

Year Team	G	RUSHING				RECEIVING				TOTALS	
		Att.	Yds.	Avg.	TD	No.	Yds.	Avg.	TD	TD	Pts.
2000—Georgia	10	2	-20	-10.0	0	13	143	11.0	1	1	6
2001—Georgia	3	0	0	0.0	0	6	47	7.8	0	0	0
2002—Georgia	14	1	3	3.0	0	23	296	12.9	2	2	12
2003—Georgia	13	4	69	17.3	0	49	662	13.5	3	3	18
2004—Georgia	12	4	35	8.8	0	53	860	16.2	6	6	36
College totals (5 years)	52	11	87	7.9	0	144	2008	13.9	12	12	72

BROWN, RONNIE   RB   DOLPHINS

PERSONAL: Born December 12, 1981, in Rome, Ga. ... 6-0/233.
HIGH SCHOOL: Cartersville (Ga.).
COLLEGE: Auburn.
TRANSACTIONS/CAREER NOTES: Selected by Miami Dolphins in first round (second pick overall) of 2005 NFL draft.
MISCELLANEOUS: Selected by Seattle Mariners organization in 50th round of free-agent draft (June 1, 2000); did not sign.

Year Team	G	RUSHING				RECEIVING				TOTALS	
		Att.	Yds.	Avg.	TD	No.	Yds.	Avg.	TD	TD	Pts.
2001—Auburn	11	84	330	3.9	2	7	109	15.6	0	2	12
2002—Auburn	12	175	1008	5.8	13	9	166	18.4	1	14	84
2003—Auburn	11	95	446	4.7	5	8	80	10.0	0	5	30
2004—Auburn	12	153	913	6.0	8	34	313	9.2	1	9	54
College totals (4 years)	46	507	2697	5.3	28	58	668	11.5	2	30	180

BRYANT, ANTHONY   DT   BUCCANEERS

PERSONAL: Born November 6, 1981, in Newbern, Ala. ... 6-3/332.
HIGH SCHOOL: Sunshine (Newbern, Ala.).
COLLEGE: Alabama.
TRANSACTIONS/CAREER NOTES: Selected by Tampa Bay Buccaneers in sixth round (178th pick overall) of 2005 NFL draft.

Year Team	G	SACKS
2001—Alabama	11	0.5
2002—Alabama	13	0.0
2003—Alabama	13	0.0
2004—Alabama	12	1.5
College totals (4 years)	49	2.0

BUENNING, DAN   G   BUCCANEERS

PERSONAL: Born October 26, 1981... 6-4/320.
HIGH SCHOOL: Bay Port (Green Bay, Wisc.).
COLLEGE: Wisconsin.
TRANSACTIONS/CAREER NOTES: Selected by Tampa Bay Buccaneers in fourth round (107th pick overall) of 2005 NFL draft.
PLAYING EXPERIENCE: Wisconsin, 2001-2004. ... Games played: 2001 (12), 2002 (13), 2003 (13), 2004 (12). Total: 50.
HONORS: Named guard on THE SPORTING NEWS Freshman All-America fourth team (2001). ... Named guard on THE SPORTING NEWS college All-America second team (2004).

BULLOCKS, JOSH   S   SAINTS

PERSONAL: Born February 28, 1983, in Chattanooga, Tenn. ... 6-0/209. ... Full name: Joshua Bullocks.
HIGH SCHOOL: Hixson (Chattanooga, Tenn.).
COLLEGE: Nebraska.
TRANSACTIONS/CAREER NOTES: Selected after junior season by New Orleans Saints in second round (40th pick overall) of 2005 NFL draft.
HONORS: Named safety on THE SPORTING NEWS college All-America first team (2003).

Year Team	G	Sks.	INTERCEPTIONS No.	Yds.	Avg.	TD
2002—Nebraska	13	0.0	1	19	19.0	0
2003—Nebraska	13	0.0	10	154	15.4	0
2004—Nebraska	11	0.0	2	38	19.0	0
College totals (3 years)	37	0.0	13	211	16.2	0

BURNETT, KEVIN   LB   COWBOYS

PERSONAL: Born December 24, 1982, in Englewood, Calif. ... 6-3/230. ... Full name: Kevin Bradley Burnett.
HIGH SCHOOL: Dominguez (Carson, Calif.).
COLLEGE: Tennessee.
TRANSACTIONS/CAREER NOTES: Selected by Dallas Cowboys in second round (42nd pick overall) of 2005 NFL draft.

Year Team	G	Sks.	INTERCEPTIONS No.	Yds.	Avg.	TD
2000—Tennessee	11	2.0	0	0	0.0	0
2001—Tennessee	11	3.5	0	0	0.0	0
2002—Tennessee	1	0.0	0	0	0.0	0
2003—Tennessee	13	1.5	0	0	0.0	0
2004—Tennessee	13	1.0	1	0	0.0	0
College totals (5 years)	49	8.0	1	0	0.0	0

BURNS, VINCENT   DE   COLTS

PERSONAL: Born June 21, 1981, in Valdosta, Ga. ... 6-2/268. ... Full name: Vincent Eric Burns Jr.
HIGH SCHOOL: Lowndes (Valdosta, Ga.).
COLLEGE: Northern Arizona, then Kentucky.
TRANSACTIONS/CAREER NOTES: Selected by Indianapolis Colts in third round (92nd pick overall) of 2005 NFL draft.

Year Team	G	Sks.	INTERCEPTIONS No.	Yds.	Avg.	TD
2000—Northern Arizona	9	2.0	1	16	16.0	0
2002—Kentucky	12	3.0	0	0	0.0	0
2003—Kentucky	12	2.0	0	0	0.0	0
2004—Kentucky	9	0.0	1	3	3.0	0
College totals (4 years)	42	7.0	2	19	9.5	0

CAMPBELL, JASON   QB   REDSKINS

PERSONAL: Born December 31, 1981, in Laurel, Miss. ... 6-5/227.
HIGH SCHOOL: Taylorsville (Miss.).
COLLEGE: Auburn.
TRANSACTIONS/CAREER NOTES: Selected by Washington Redskins in first round (25th pick overall) of 2005 NFL draft.

Year Team	G	PASSING Att.	Cmp.	Pct.	Yds.	TD	Int.	Avg.	Rat.	RUSHING Att.	Yds.	Avg.	TD	TOTALS TD	Pts.
2002—Auburn	10	142	89	62.7	1117	4	4	7.87	132.4	46	72	1.6	2	2	12
2002—Auburn	13	149	94	63.1	1215	11	5	8.15	149.2	72	206	2.9	3	3	22
2003—Auburn	13	293	181	61.8	2267	10	8	7.74	132.6	73	-1	0.0	1	1	8
2004—Auburn	13	270	188	69.6	2700	20	7	10.00	172.9	58	30	0.5	3	3	18
College totals (4 years)	49	854	552	64.6	7299	45	24	8.55	148.2	249	307	1.2	9	9	60

CAMPBELL, KURT — LB — PACKERS

PERSONAL: Born July 30, 1982, in Kingston, Jamaica. ... 6-1/225.
HIGH SCHOOL: Palm Beach Gardens (Fla.).
COLLEGE: Albany (N.Y.).
TRANSACTIONS/CAREER NOTES: Selected by Green Bay Packers in seventh round (245th pick overall) of 2005 NFL draft.

			INTERCEPTIONS			
Year Team	G	Sks.	No.	Yds.	Avg.	TD
2001—Albany	10	0.0	1	0	0.0	0
2002—Albany	9	0.0	0	0	0.0	0
2003—Albany	5	0.0	0	0	0.0	0
2004—Albany	10	0.0	0	0	0.0	0
College totals (4 years)	34	0.0	1	0	0.0	0

CANTY, CHRISTOPHER — DE — COWBOYS

PERSONAL: Born November 10, 1982, in Bronx, New York. ... 6-7/279. ... Full name: Christopher Lee Canty.
HIGH SCHOOL: Charlotte Latin (Charlotte, N.C.).
COLLEGE: Virginia.
TRANSACTIONS/CAREER NOTES: Selected by Dallas Cowboys in fourth round (132nd pick overall) of 2005 NFL draft.

Year Team	G	SACKS
2001—Virginia	12	0.0
2002—Virginia	11	2.0
2003—Virginia	13	4.0
2004—Virginia	4	1.0
College totals (4 years)	40	7.0

CARTER, JEROME — S — RAMS

PERSONAL: Born October 25, 1982, in Lake City, Fla. ... 6-0/217.
HIGH SCHOOL: Columbia (Lake City, Fla.).
COLLEGE: Florida State.
TRANSACTIONS/CAREER NOTES: Selected by St. Louis Rams in fourth round (117th pick overall) of 2005 NFL draft.

			INTERCEPTIONS			
Year Team	G	Sks.	No.	Yds.	Avg.	TD
2001—Florida State	6	0.0	0	0	0.0	0
2002—Florida State	14	1.0	0	0	0.0	0
2003—Florida State	13	0.5	2	38	19.0	0
2004—Florida State	12	1.0	1	3	3.0	0
College totals (4 years)	45	2.5	3	41	13.7	0

CASSEL, MATT — QB — PATRIOTS

PERSONAL: Born May 17, 1982, in Northridge, Calif. ... 6-5/230.
HIGH SCHOOL: Chatsworth (Calif.).
COLLEGE: Southern California.
TRANSACTIONS/CAREER NOTES: Selected by New England Patriots in seventh round (230th pick overall) of 2005 NFL draft.

		PASSING							RUSHING				TOTALS	
Year Team	G	Att.	Cmp.	Pct.	Yds.	TD	Int.	Avg.	Rat.	Att.	Yds.	Avg.	TD	TD	Pts.
2001—Southern California	7	2	1	50.0	5	0	0	2.50	71.0	3	22	7.3	0	0	0
2002—Southern California	10	4	3	75.0	27	0	0	6.75	131.7	1	1	1.0	0	0	0
2003—Southern California	8	13	6	46.2	63	0	0	4.85	86.9	1	-2	-2.0	0	0	0
2004—Southern California	5	14	10	71.4	97	0	1	6.93	115.3	6	11	1.8	0	0	0
College totals (4 years)	30	33	20	60.6	192	0	1	5.82	103.4	11	32	2.9	0	0	0

CASTILLO, LUIS — DT — CHARGERS

PERSONAL: Born August 4, 1983... 6-3/305. ... Full name: Luis Alberto Castillo.
HIGH SCHOOL: Garfield (N.J.).
COLLEGE: Northwestern.
TRANSACTIONS/CAREER NOTES: Selected by San Diego Chargers in first round (28th pick overall) of 2005 NFL draft.

Year Team	G	SACKS
2001—Northwestern	5	0.0
2002—Northwestern	12	0.0
2003—Northwestern	13	2.5
2004—Northwestern	12	2.0
College totals (4 years)	42	4.5

CLARETT, MAURICE — RB — BRONCOS

PERSONAL: Born October 29, 1983, in Youngstown, Ohio. ... 5-11/236.
HIGH SCHOOL: Warren Harding (Youngstown, Ohio).
COLLEGE: Ohio State.
TRANSACTIONS/CAREER NOTES: Selected by Denver Broncos in third round (101st pick overall) of 2005 NFL draft.
HONORS: Named College Football Freshman of the Year by THE SPORTING NEWS (2002). ... Named running back on THE SPORTING NEWS Freshman All-America first team (2002).

		RUSHING				RECEIVING				TOTALS	
Year Team	G	Att.	Yds.	Avg.	TD	No.	Yds.	Avg.	TD	TD	Pts.
2002—Ohio State	11	222	1237	5.6	16	12	104	8.7	2	18	108

CLARIDGE, RYAN   LB   PATRIOTS

PERSONAL: Born April 12, 1981, in Rochester, Mich. ... 6-2/254. ... Full name: Ryan Quinlan Claridge. ... Brother of Travis Claridge, guard with Atlanta Falcons (2000-03).
HIGH SCHOOL: Almont (Almont, Mich.).
COLLEGE: Nevada-Las Vegas.
TRANSACTIONS/CAREER NOTES: Selected by New England Patriots in fifth round (170th pick overall) of 2005 NFL draft.

				INTERCEPTIONS		
Year Team	G	Sks.	No.	Yds.	Avg.	TD
2000—UNLV	12	2.0	0	0	0.0	0
2001—UNLV	11	2.0	0	0	0.0	0
2003—UNLV	12	5.5	2	16	8.0	0
2004—UNLV	10	9.0	0	0	0.0	0
College totals (4 years)	45	18.5	2	16	8.0	0

CLAYTON, MARK   WR   RAVENS

PERSONAL: Born July 2, 1982, in Oklahoma City, Okla. ... 5-10/193.
HIGH SCHOOL: Sam Houston (Arlington, Texas).
COLLEGE: Oklahoma.
TRANSACTIONS/CAREER NOTES: Selected by Baltimore Ravens in first round (22nd pick overall) of 2005 NFL draft.
HONORS: Named wide receiver on THE SPORTING NEWS college All-America first team (2003). ... Named wide receiver on THE SPORTING NEWS college All-America second team (2004).

		RUSHING				RECEIVING				PUNT RETURNS				KICKOFF RETURNS				TOTALS	
Year Team	G	Att.	Yds.	Avg.	TD	No.	Yds.	Avg.	TD	No.	Yds.	Avg.	TD	No.	Yds.	Avg.	TD	TD	Pts.
2001—Oklahoma	12	0	0	0.0	0	45	519	11.5	3	0	0	0.0	0	0	0	0.0	0	3	18
2002—Oklahoma	12	1	9	9.0	0	26	416	16.0	5	0	0	0.0	0	0	0	0.0	0	5	30
2003—Oklahoma	14	9	62	6.9	0	83	1425	17.2	15	0	0	0.0	0	3	53	17.7	0	15	90
2004—Oklahoma	13	4	11	2.8	0	66	876	13.3	8	7	101	14.4	1	3	67	22.3	0	9	54
College totals (4 years)	51	14	82	5.9	0	220	3236	14.7	31	7	101	14.4	1	6	120	20.0	0	32	192

COBB, DEANDRA   RB   FALCONS

PERSONAL: Born May 18, 1981, in Las Vegas, Nev. ... 5-10/196.
HIGH SCHOOL: Clark (Las Vegas, Nev.).
JUNIOR COLLEGE: Antelope Valley (Lancaster, Calif.).
COLLEGE: Michigan State.
TRANSACTIONS/CAREER NOTES: Selected by Atlanta Falcons in sixth round (201st pick overall) of 2005 NFL draft.

		RUSHING				RECEIVING				KICKOFF RETURNS				TOTALS	
Year Team	G	Att.	Yds.	Avg.	TD	No.	Yds.	Avg.	TD	No.	Yds.	Avg.	TD	TD	Pts.
2003—Michigan State	12	38	172	4.5	0	8	79	9.9	0	28	763	27.3	3	3	18
2004—Michigan State	12	96	728	7.6	4	7	10	1.4	0	36	869	24.1	1	5	30
College totals (2 years)	24	134	900	6.7	4	15	89	5.9	0	64	1632	25.5	4	8	48

CODY, DAN   OLB   RAVENS

PERSONAL: Born December 1, 1981, in Ada, Okla. ... 6-5/257. ... Full name: Daniel Price Cody.
HIGH SCHOOL: Ada (Okla.).
COLLEGE: Oklahoma.
TRANSACTIONS/CAREER NOTES: Selected by Baltimore Ravens in second round (53rd pick overall) of 2005 NFL draft.

Year Team	G	SACKS
2000—Oklahoma	10	2.0
2001—Oklahoma	1	0.0
2002—Oklahoma	12	3.0
2003—Oklahoma	13	10.0
2004—Oklahoma	13	10.0
College totals (5 years)	49	25.0

CODY, SHAUN   DT   LIONS

PERSONAL: Born January 22, 1983, in Whittier, Calif. ... 6-4/292.
HIGH SCHOOL: Los Altos (Hacienda Heights, Calif.).
COLLEGE: Southern California.
TRANSACTIONS/CAREER NOTES: Selected by Detroit Lions in second round (37th pick overall) of 2005 NFL draft.
HONORS: Named defensive tackle on THE SPORTING NEWS Freshman All-America first team (2001). ... Named defensive tackle on THE SPORTING NEWS college All-America second team (2004).

Year Team	G	SACKS
2001—Southern California	12	5.0
2002—Southern California	6	0.0
2003—Southern California	13	6.0
2004—Southern California	13	10.0
College totals (4 years)	44	21.0

COLE, TRENT   DE   EAGLES

PERSONAL: Born October 5, 1982, in Xenia, Ohio. ... 6-2/236. ... Full name: Trent Cole Jr.
HIGH SCHOOL: Xenia (Ohio).
COLLEGE: Cincinnati.
TRANSACTIONS/CAREER NOTES: Selected by Philadelphia Eagles in fifth round (146th pick overall) of 2005 NFL draft.

Year Team	G	SACKS
2002—Cincinnati	14	5.0
2003—Cincinnati	12	5.5
2004—Cincinnati	12	8.5
College totals (3 years)	38	19.0

COLLINS, JEROME TE RAMS

PERSONAL: Born August 18, 1982, in Warrenville, Ill. ... 6-4/267. ... Full name: Jerome Vincent Collins.
HIGH SCHOOL: Wheaton-Warrenville South (Warrenville, Ill.).
COLLEGE: Notre Dame.
TRANSACTIONS/CAREER NOTES: Selected by St. Louis Rams in fifth round (144th pick overall) of 2005 NFL draft.

		RECEIVING			
Year Team	G	No.	Yds.	Avg.	TD
2001—Notre Dame	3	0	0	0.0	0
2002—Notre Dame	11	0	0	0.0	0
2003—Notre Dame	10	0	0	0.0	0
2004—Notre Dame	12	6	67	11.2	0
College totals (4 years)	36	6	67	11.2	0

COLLINS, NICK S PACKERS

PERSONAL: Born August 16, 1983, in Gainesville, Fla. ... 5-11/201.
HIGH SCHOOL: Dixie County (Cross City, Fla.).
COLLEGE: Bethune-Cookman.
TRANSACTIONS/CAREER NOTES: Selected by Green Bay Packers in second round (51st pick overall) of 2005 NFL draft.

			INTERCEPTIONS				KICKOFF RETURNS				TOTALS	
Year Team	G	Sks.	No.	Yds.	Avg.	TD	No.	Yds.	Avg.	TD	TD	Pts.
2002—Bethune-Cookman	13	0.5	1	0	0.0	0	8	181	22.6	0	0	0
2003—Bethune-Cookman	11	0.0	6	84	14.0	1	0	0	0.0	0	1	6
2004—Bethune-Cookman	10	0.0	6	108	18.0	1	2	34	17.0	0	1	6
College totals (3 years)	34	0.5	13	192	14.8	2	10	215	21.5	0	2	12

COLMER, CHRIS T BUCCANEERS

PERSONAL: Born November 21, 1980... 6-5/306. ... Full name: Christopher Colmer.
HIGH SCHOOL: Port Jefferson (N.Y.).
COLLEGE: North Carolina State.
TRANSACTIONS/CAREER NOTES: Selected by Tampa Bay Buccaneers in third round (91st pick overall) of 2005 NFL draft.
PLAYING EXPERIENCE: North Carolina State, 2000-2004. ... Games played: 2000 (11), 2001 (11), 2002 (14), 2004 (11). Total: 47.

COLQUITT, DUSTIN P CHIEFS

PERSONAL: Born May 6, 1982, in Knoxville, Tenn. ... 6-2/207. ... Full name: Dustin Farr Colquitt.
HIGH SCHOOL: Bearden (Knoxville, Tenn.).
COLLEGE: Tennessee.
TRANSACTIONS/CAREER NOTES: Selected by Kansas City Chiefs in third round (99th pick overall) of 2005 NFL draft.
HONORS: Named punter on THE SPORTING NEWS college All-America first team (2003).

				PUNTING			
Year Team	G	No.	Yds.	Avg.	Net avg.	In. 20	Blk.
2001—Tennessee	12	51	2020	39.6	39.6	13	0
2002—Tennessee	13	65	2833	43.6	42.3	22	2
2003—Tennessee	13	68	3081	45.3	44.7	20	1
2004—Tennessee	13	56	2282	40.8	40.0	17	1
College totals (4 years)	51	240	10216	42.6	0.0	72	4

CONSIDINE, SEAN S EAGLES

PERSONAL: Born October 28, 1981... 6-0/212.
HIGH SCHOOL: Byron (Ill.).
COLLEGE: Iowa.
TRANSACTIONS/CAREER NOTES: Selected by Philadelphia Eagles in fourth round (102nd pick overall) of 2005 NFL draft.

			INTERCEPTIONS			
Year Team	G	Sks.	No.	Yds.	Avg.	TD
2001—Iowa	11	0.0	0	0	0.0	0
2002—Iowa	13	0.0	0	0	0.0	0
2003—Iowa	13	0.0	3	44	14.7	0
2004—Iowa	10	0.0	3	62	20.7	0
College totals (4 years)	47	0.0	6	106	17.7	0

COSTON, JUNIUS C PACKERS

PERSONAL: Born November 5, 1983, in Framingham, Mass. ... 6-3/310.
HIGH SCHOOL: Broughton (Raleigh, N.C.).
COLLEGE: North Carolina A&T.
TRANSACTIONS/CAREER NOTES: Selected by Green Bay Packers in fifth round (143rd pick overall) of 2005 NFL draft. ... Signed by Packers (May 16, 2005).
PLAYING EXPERIENCE: North Carolina A&T, 2001-2004. ... Games played: 2001 (7), 2002 (12), 2003 (13), 2004 (9). Total: 41.

CROWDER, CHANNING LB DOLPHINS

PERSONAL: Born December 2, 1983, in State College, Pa. ... 6-2/242. ... Full name: Randolph Channing Crowder.
HIGH SCHOOL: North Springs (Atlanta, Ga.).
COLLEGE: Florida.
TRANSACTIONS/CAREER NOTES: Selected after sophomore season by Miami Dolphins in third round (70th pick overall) of 2005 NFL draft.
HONORS: Named College Football Freshman of the Year by THE SPORTING NEWS (2003).

Year Team	G	Sks.	INTERCEPTIONS			
			No.	Yds.	Avg.	TD
2003—Florida	11	2.0	0	0	0.0	0
2004—Florida	9	2.0	1	22	22.0	0
College totals (2 years)	20	4.0	1	22	22.0	0

CURRIE, AIRESE   WR   BEARS

PERSONAL: Born November 16, 1982... 5-11/186.
HIGH SCHOOL: Richland Northeast (Columbia, S.C.).
COLLEGE: Clemson.
TRANSACTIONS/CAREER NOTES: Selected by Chicago Bears in fifth round (140th pick overall) of 2005 NFL draft.

Year Team	G	RUSHING				RECEIVING				KICKOFF RETURNS				TOTALS	
		Att.	Yds.	Avg.	TD	No.	Yds.	Avg.	TD	No.	Yds.	Avg.	TD	TD	Pts.
2001—Clemson	11	4	-4	-1.0	0	17	315	18.5	1	0	0	0.0	0	1	6
2002—Clemson	13	3	20	6.7	0	16	282	17.6	3	0	0	0.0	0	3	18
2003—Clemson	10	1	2	2.0	0	43	560	13.0	4	0	0	0.0	0	4	24
2004—Clemson	11	6	8	1.3	0	61	868	14.2	2	8	212	26.5	0	2	12
College totals (4 years)	45	14	26	1.9	0	137	2025	14.8	10	8	212	26.5	0	10	60

DANIELS, TRAVIS   CB   DOLPHINS

PERSONAL: Born September 8, 1982, in Hollywood, Fla. ... 6-1/192. ... Full name: Travis Antwon Daniels.
HIGH SCHOOL: South Broward (Hollywood, Fla.).
COLLEGE: Louisiana State.
TRANSACTIONS/CAREER NOTES: Selected by Miami Dolphins in fourth round (104th pick overall) of 2005 NFL draft.

Year Team	G	Sks.	INTERCEPTIONS			
			No.	Yds.	Avg.	TD
2001—Louisiana State	1	0.0	0	0	0.0	0
2002—Louisiana State	5	0.0	0	0	0.0	0
2003—Louisiana State	14	2.0	2	48	24.0	1
2004—Louisiana State	12	0.0	0	1	0.0	1
College totals (4 years)	32	2.0	2	49	24.5	2

DAVIS, ANTHONY   RB   COLTS

PERSONAL: Born May 21, 1982, in Plainfield, N.J. ... 5-7/200.
HIGH SCHOOL: Plainfield (N.J.).
COLLEGE: Wisconsin.
TRANSACTIONS/CAREER NOTES: Selected by Indianapolis Colts in seventh round (243rd pick overall) of 2005 NFL draft.
HONORS: Named running back on THE SPORTING NEWS Freshman All-America first team (2001).

Year Team	G	RUSHING				RECEIVING				TOTALS	
		Att.	Yds.	Avg.	TD	No.	Yds.	Avg.	TD	TD	Pts.
2001—Wisconsin	11	291	1466	5.0	11	0	0	0.0	0	11	66
2002—Wisconsin	13	300	1555	5.2	13	6	48	8.0	0	13	78
2003—Wisconsin	8	116	682	5.9	7	3	54	18.0	0	7	42
2004—Wisconsin	8	201	973	4.8	11	13	96	7.4	0	11	66
College totals (4 years)	40	908	4676	5.1	42	22	198	9.0	0	42	252

DAVIS, CHAUNCEY   DE   FALCONS

PERSONAL: Born January 27, 1983, in Auburndale, Fla. ... 6-2/274.
HIGH SCHOOL: Auburndale (Fla.).
JUNIOR COLLEGE: Jones County (Ellisville, Miss.).
COLLEGE: Florida State.
TRANSACTIONS/CAREER NOTES: Selected by Atlanta Falcons in fourth round (128th pick overall) of 2005 NFL draft.

Year Team	G	SACKS
2003—Florida State	13	2.0
2004—Florida State	11	5.0
College totals (2 years)	24	7.0

DAVIS, THOMAS   OLB   PANTHERS

PERSONAL: Born March 22, 1983, in Shellman, Ga. ... 6-1/227. ... Full name: Thomas Antonio Davis.
HIGH SCHOOL: Randolph-Clay (Shellman, Ga.).
COLLEGE: Georgia.
TRANSACTIONS/CAREER NOTES: Selected after junior season by Carolina Panthers in first round (14th pick overall) of 2005 NFL draft.
HONORS: Named safety on THE SPORTING NEWS college All-America second team (2003). ... Named strong safety on THE SPORTING NEWS college All-America first team (2004).

Year Team	G	Sks.	INTERCEPTIONS			
			No.	Yds.	Avg.	TD
2002—Georgia	14	3.0	1	11	11.0	0
2003—Georgia	13	4.5	1	34	34.0	0
2004—Georgia	11	3.0	1	0	0.0	0
College totals (3 years)	38	10.5	3	45	15.0	0

DREESSEN, JOEL   TE   JETS

PERSONAL: Born July 26, 1982, in Ida Grove, Iowa. ... 6-4/260. ... Full name: Joel Clifford Dreessen.
HIGH SCHOOL: Fort Morgan (Colo.).
COLLEGE: Colorado State.
TRANSACTIONS/CAREER NOTES: Selected by New York Jets in sixth round (198th pick overall) of 2005 NFL draft.

Year Team	G	No.	RECEIVING Yds.	Avg.	TD
2001—Colorado State	11	22	205	9.3	2
2002—Colorado State	14	29	340	11.7	2
2003—Colorado State	9	29	323	11.1	3
2004—Colorado State	11	43	427	9.9	3
College totals (4 years)	45	123	1295	10.5	10

DUNN, JON — T — BROWNS

PERSONAL: Born December 12, 1981, in Norfolk, Va. ... 6-7/331. ... Full name: Jonathan Paul Dunn.
HIGH SCHOOL: Tallwood (Virginia Beach, Va.).
COLLEGE: Virginia Tech.
TRANSACTIONS/CAREER NOTES: Selected by Cleveland Browns in seventh round (217th pick overall) of 2005 NFL draft.
PLAYING EXPERIENCE: Virginia Tech, 2001-2004. ... Games played: 2001 (10), 2002 (14), 2003 (12), 2004 (13). Total: 49.

EDWARDS, BRAYLON — WR — BROWNS

PERSONAL: Born February 21, 1983, in Detroit, Mich. ... 6-3/210. ... Full name: Braylon Jamel Edwards. ... Son of Stanley Edwards, running back with Houston Oilers (1982-86) and Detroit Lions (1987).
HIGH SCHOOL: Bishop Gallagher (Detroit, Mich.).
COLLEGE: Michigan.
TRANSACTIONS/CAREER NOTES: Selected by Cleveland Browns in first round (third pick overall) of 2005 NFL draft.
HONORS: Fred Biletnikoff Award winner (2004). ... Named wide receiver on THE SPORTING NEWS college All-America first team (2004).

Year Team	G	RUSHING Att.	Yds.	Avg.	TD	RECEIVING No.	Yds.	Avg.	TD	TOTALS TD	Pts.
2001—Michigan	6	0	0	0.0	0	3	38	12.7	0	0	0
2002—Michigan	13	1	-10	-10.0	0	67	1035	15.4	10	10	60
2003—Michigan	13	3	21	7.0	0	85	1138	13.4	14	14	86
2004—Michigan	12	6	61	10.2	0	97	1330	13.7	15	15	90
College totals (4 years)	44	10	72	7.2	0	252	3541	14.1	39	39	236

ELLISON, ATIYYAH — DT — PANTHERS

PERSONAL: Born September 29, 1981, in St. Louis, Mo. ... 6-4/305.
HIGH SCHOOL: Parkway South (St. Louis, Mo.).
JUNIOR COLLEGE: Coffeyville (Kan.).
COLLEGE: Missouri.
TRANSACTIONS/CAREER NOTES: Selected by Carolina Panthers in third round (89th pick overall) of 2005 NFL draft.

Year Team	G	SACKS
2002—Missouri	12	0.0
2003—Missouri	13	4.0
2004—Missouri	11	2.5
College totals (3 years)	36	6.5

EMANUEL, BEN — S — PANTHERS

PERSONAL: Born June 18, 1982, in Friendswood, Texas. ... 6-3/209.
COLLEGE: UCLA.
TRANSACTIONS/CAREER NOTES: Selected by Carolina Panthers in fifth round (171st pick overall) of 2005 NFL draft.

Year Team	G	Sks.	INTERCEPTIONS No.	Yds.	Avg.	TD
2001—UCLA	11	0.0	2	29	14.5	1
2002—UCLA	12	0.0	4	77	19.3	1
2003—UCLA	12	0.0	1	2	2.0	0
2004—UCLA	12	0.0	1	0	0.0	0
College totals (4 years)	47	0.0	8	108	13.5	2

ERNSTER, PAUL — P — BRONCOS

PERSONAL: Born January 26, 1982, in Phoenix, Ariz. ... 6-0/217. ... Full name: Paul T. Ernster.
HIGH SCHOOL: Ironwood (Glendale, Ariz.).
COLLEGE: Northern Arizona.
TRANSACTIONS/CAREER NOTES: Selected by Denver Broncos in seventh round (239th pick overall) of 2005 NFL draft.

Year Team	G	PUNTING No.	Yds.	Avg.	Net avg.	In. 20	Blk.	KICKING XPM	XPA	Pts.	TOTALS XPM	XPA	Pts.
2001—Northern Arizona	10	4	179	44.8	44.8	0	0	0	0	0	0	0	0
2002—Northern Arizona	11	1	40	40.0	40.0	0	0	27	29	66	27	29	66
2003—Northern Arizona	13	0	0	0.0	0.0	0	0	47	49	101	47	49	101
2004—Northern Arizona	11	55	2631	47.8	47.0	19	1	27	27	54	27	27	54
College totals (4 years)	45	60	2850	47.5	0.0	19	1	202	210	442	202	210	442

ESSEX, TRAI — T — STEELERS

PERSONAL: Born December 5, 1982, in Fort Wayne, Ind. ... 6-4/316. ... Full name: Trai J. Essex.
HIGH SCHOOL: Paul Harding (Fort Wayne, Ind.).
COLLEGE: Northwestern.

ESTES, PATRICK   TE   49ERS

PERSONAL: Born February 4, 1983, in Richmond, Va. ... 6-6/268. ... Full name: Patrick Brion Estes.
HIGH SCHOOL: Benedictine (Richmond, Va.).
COLLEGE: Virginia.
TRANSACTIONS/CAREER NOTES: Selected by San Francisco 49ers in seventh round (248th pick overall) of 2005 NFL draft.

		RECEIVING			
Year Team	G	No.	Yds.	Avg.	TD
2001—Virginia	11	3	33	11.0	0
2002—Virginia	13	13	97	7.5	4
2003—Virginia	11	6	48	8.0	1
2004—Virginia	12	6	74	12.3	0
College totals (4 years)	47	28	252	9.0	5

EVERETT, KEVIN   TE   BILLS

PERSONAL: Born February 5, 1982, in Kilgore, Texas. ... 6-5/241.
HIGH SCHOOL: Thomas Jefferson (Port Arthur, Texas).
JUNIOR COLLEGE: Kilgore (Texas).
COLLEGE: Miami (Fla.).
TRANSACTIONS/CAREER NOTES: Selected by Buffalo Bills in third round (86th pick overall) of 2005 NFL draft.

		RECEIVING			
Year Team	G	No.	Yds.	Avg.	TD
2003—Miami (Fla.)	13	9	90	10.0	3
2004—Miami (Fla.)	11	23	310	13.5	0
College totals (2 years)	24	32	400	12.5	3

FANENE, JONATHAN   DE   BENGALS

PERSONAL: Born March 19, 1982... 6-3/290. ... Full name: Jonathan David Fanene. ... Name pronounced: fa-nay-nay.
HIGH SCHOOL: Tafuna (American Samoa).
JUNIOR COLLEGE: College of the Canyons (Pago Pago, American Samoa).
COLLEGE: Utah.
TRANSACTIONS/CAREER NOTES: Selected by Cincinnati Bengals in seventh round (233rd pick overall) of 2005 NFL draft.

			INTERCEPTIONS		
Year Team	G	Sks.	No.	Yds.	Avg.	TD
2003—Utah	9	2.0	0	0	0.0	0
2004—Utah	11	3.0	1	76	76.0	1
College totals (2 years)	20	5.0	1	76	76.0	1

FASON, CIATRICK   RB   VIKINGS

PERSONAL: Born October 29, 1982, in Atlanta, Ga. ... 6-1/209. ... Full name: Ciatrick Antione Fason.
HIGH SCHOOL: Fletcher (Neptune Beach, Fla.).
COLLEGE: Florida.
TRANSACTIONS/CAREER NOTES: Selected after junior season by Minnesota Vikings in fourth round (112th pick overall) of 2005 NFL draft.

		RUSHING				RECEIVING				TOTALS	
Year Team	G	Att.	Yds.	Avg.	TD	No.	Yds.	Avg.	TD	TD	Pts.
2002—Florida	13	9	27	3.0	1	0	0	0.0	0	1	6
2003—Florida	13	84	583	6.9	3	11	142	12.9	3	6	36
2004—Florida	12	222	1267	5.7	10	35	266	7.6	2	12	72
College totals (3 years)	38	315	1877	6.0	14	46	408	8.9	5	19	114

FIELDS, RONALD   DT   49ERS

PERSONAL: Born September 13, 1981, in Bogalusa, La. ... 6-2/298. ... Full name: Ronald J. Fields.
HIGH SCHOOL: Bogalusa (La.), then Hargrave Military Academy (Hargrave, Va.).
COLLEGE: Mississippi State.
TRANSACTIONS/CAREER NOTES: Selected by San Francisco 49ers in fifth round (137th pick overall) of 2005 NFL draft.

Year Team	G	SACKS
2001—Mississippi State	11	0.0
2002—Mississippi State	12	0.0
2003—Mississippi State	12	1.0
2004—Mississippi State	11	0.0
College totals (4 years)	46	1.0

FINCHER, ALFRED   LB   SAINTS

PERSONAL: Born August 15, 1983, in Key West, Fla. ... 6-1/240. ... Full name: Alfred William Fincher.
HIGH SCHOOL: Norwood (Norwood, Mass.).
COLLEGE: Connecticut.
TRANSACTIONS/CAREER NOTES: Selected by New Orleans Saints in third round (82nd pick overall) of 2005 NFL draft.

			INTERCEPTIONS		
Year Team	G	Sks.	No.	Yds.	Avg.	TD
2001—Connecticut	11	0.0	0	0	0.0	0
2002—Connecticut	12	1.5	1	19	19.0	0
2003—Connecticut	12	1.5	1	26	26.0	0
2004—Connecticut	12	2.0	2	16	8.0	1
College totals (4 years)	47	5.0	4	61	15.3	1

FITZPATRICK, RYAN   QB   RAMS

PERSONAL: Born November 24, 1982, in Gilbert, Ariz. ... 6-2/221. ... Full name: Ryan Joseph Fitzpatrick.
HIGH SCHOOL: Highland (Gilbert, Ariz.).
COLLEGE: Harvard.
TRANSACTIONS/CAREER NOTES: Selected by St. Louis Rams in seventh round (250th pick overall) of 2005 NFL draft.

				PASSING							RUSHING				TOTALS	
Year Team	G	Att.	Cmp.	Pct.	Yds.	TD	Int.	Avg.	Rat.	Att.	Yds.	Avg.	TD	TD	Pts.
2001—Harvard	4	37	25	67.6	323	2	1	8.73	153.3	23	86	3.7	0	0	0
2002—Harvard	10	150	94	62.7	1155	8	0	7.70	144.9	115	523	4.5	5	5	30
2003—Harvard	7	178	107	60.1	1770	16	8	9.94	164.3	109	430	3.9	6	6	38
2004—Harvard	10	276	158	57.2	1986	13	6	7.20	128.9	118	448	3.8	5	5	34
College totals (4 years)	31	641	384	59.9	5234	39	15	8.17	143.9	365	1487	4.1	16	16	102

FOX, DUSTIN   S   VIKINGS

PERSONAL: Born October 8, 1982, in Canton, Ohio. ... 5-11/191.
HIGH SCHOOL: GlenOak (Canton, Ohio).
COLLEGE: Ohio State.
TRANSACTIONS/CAREER NOTES: Selected by Minnesota Vikings in third round (80th pick overall) of 2005 NFL draft.
HONORS: Named safety on THE SPORTING NEWS Freshman All-America fourth team (2001).

			INTERCEPTIONS			
Year Team	G	Sks.	No.	Yds.	Avg.	TD
2001—Ohio State	12	0.0	1	0	0.0	0
2002—Ohio State	14	0.0	3	12	4.0	0
2003—Ohio State	13	0.0	3	6	2.0	0
2004—Ohio State	9	0.0	0	0	0.0	0
College totals (4 years)	48	0.0	7	18	2.6	0

FOXWORTH, DOMONIQUE   CB   BRONCOS

PERSONAL: Born March 27, 1983, in Oxford, England... 6-0/183.
HIGH SCHOOL: Western Tech (Randallstown, Md.).
COLLEGE: Maryland.
TRANSACTIONS/CAREER NOTES: Selected by Denver Broncos in third round (97th pick overall) of 2005 NFL draft.
HONORS: Named cornerback on THE SPORTING NEWS college All-America second team (2004).

			INTERCEPTIONS			
Year Team	G	Sks.	No.	Yds.	Avg.	TD
2001—Maryland	2	0.0	0	0	0.0	0
2002—Maryland	14	0.0	5	64	12.8	0
2003—Maryland	13	0.0	3	64	21.3	1
2004—Maryland	11	0.0	0	0	0.0	0
College totals (4 years)	40	0.0	8	128	16.0	1

FRYE, CHARLIE   QB   BROWNS

PERSONAL: Born August 28, 1981, in Willard, Ohio. ... 6-4/225.
HIGH SCHOOL: Willard (Ohio).
COLLEGE: Akron.
TRANSACTIONS/CAREER NOTES: Selected by Cleveland Browns in third round (67th pick overall) of 2005 NFL draft.

				PASSING							RUSHING				TOTALS	
Year Team	G	Att.	Cmp.	Pct.	Yds.	TD	Int.	Avg.	Rat.	Att.	Yds.	Avg.	TD	TD	Pts.
2001—Akron	11	289	170	58.8	2053	9	6	7.10	124.6	62	22	0.4	3	3	18
2002—Akron	12	380	250	65.8	2824	15	9	7.43	136.5	102	125	1.2	7	7	42
2003—Akron	12	421	273	64.8	3549	22	9	8.43	148.6	111	288	2.6	7	7	42
2004—Akron	11	346	220	63.6	2623	18	8	7.58	139.8	100	-6	-0.1	2	2	12
College totals (4 years)	46	1436	913	63.6	11049	64	32	7.69	138.5	375	429	1.1	19	19	114

FULLER, VINCENT   S   TITANS

PERSONAL: Born August 3, 1982, in Baltimore, Md. ... 6-1/187. ... Full name: Vincent Fuller II.
HIGH SCHOOL: Woodlawn (Baltimore, Md.).
COLLEGE: Virginia Tech.
TRANSACTIONS/CAREER NOTES: Selected by Tennessee Titans in fourth round (108th pick overall) of 2005 NFL draft.

			INTERCEPTIONS			
Year Team	G	Sks.	No.	Yds.	Avg.	TD
2001—Virginia Tech	10	0.0	0	0	0.0	0
2002—Virginia Tech	14	0.5	4	0	0.0	0
2003—Virginia Tech	13	0.0	1	33	33.0	0
2004—Virginia Tech	13	0.0	3	12	4.0	0
College totals (4 years)	50	0.5	8	45	5.6	0

GANDY, DYLAN   G/C   COLTS

PERSONAL: Born March 8, 1982, in Harlingen, Texas. ... 6-3/304.
HIGH SCHOOL: Pflugerville (Texas).
COLLEGE: Texas Tech.
TRANSACTIONS/CAREER NOTES: Selected by Indianapolis Colts in fourth round (129th pick overall) of 2005 NFL draft.
PLAYING EXPERIENCE: Texas Tech, 2001-2004. ... Games played: 2001 (11), 2002 (14), 2003 (13), 2004 (12). Total: 50.

GATES, LIONEL   RB   BILLS

PERSONAL: Born March 13, 1982, in Jacksonville, Fla. ... 6-0/223. ... Full name: Lionel Theron Gates.
HIGH SCHOOL: Parker (Jacksonville, Fla.).
COLLEGE: Louisville.
TRANSACTIONS/CAREER NOTES: Selected by Buffalo Bills in seventh round (236th pick overall) of 2005 NFL draft.

| | | RUSHING | | | | RECEIVING | | | | TOTALS | |
Year Team	G	Att.	Yds.	Avg.	TD	No.	Yds.	Avg.	TD	TD	Pts.
2001—Louisville	3	30	87	2.9	1	1	1	1.0	0	1	6
2002—Louisville	12	72	209	2.9	1	4	29	7.3	0	1	6
2003—Louisville	13	141	817	5.8	11	25	368	14.7	0	11	66
2004—Louisville	9	76	373	4.9	7	10	71	7.1	2	9	54
College totals (4 years)	37	319	1486	4.7	20	40	469	11.7	2	22	132

GEISINGER, JUSTIN   G   BILLS

PERSONAL: Born May 24, 1982, in Pittsburgh, Pa. ... 6-4/320.
HIGH SCHOOL: Mount Lebanon (Pittsburgh, Pa.).
COLLEGE: Vanderbilt.
TRANSACTIONS/CAREER NOTES: Selected by Buffalo Bills in sixth round (197th pick overall) of 2005 NFL draft.
PLAYING EXPERIENCE: Vanderbilt, 2001-2004. ... Games played: 2001 (9), 2002 (12), 2003 (12), 2004 (9). Total: 42.

GHIACIUC, ERIC   C   BENGALS

PERSONAL: Born May 28, 1981, in Oxford, Mich. ... 6-4/300.
HIGH SCHOOL: Oxford (Detroit, Mich.).
COLLEGE: Central Michigan.
TRANSACTIONS/CAREER NOTES: Selected by Cincinnati Bengals in fourth round (119th pick overall) of 2005 NFL draft.
PLAYING EXPERIENCE: Central Michigan, 2002-2004. ... Games played: 2002 (12), 2003 (12), 2004 (10). Total: 34.

GIBSON, FRED   WR   STEELERS

PERSONAL: Born October 26, 1981, in Waycross, Ga. ... 6-4/196.
HIGH SCHOOL: Ware County (Waycross, Ga.).
COLLEGE: Georgia.
TRANSACTIONS/CAREER NOTES: Selected by Pittsburgh Steelers in fourth round (131st pick overall) of 2005 NFL draft.

| | | RECEIVING | | | |
Year Team	G	No.	Yds.	Avg.	TD
2001—Georgia	10	33	772	23.4	6
2002—Georgia	12	43	758	17.6	4
2003—Georgia	11	36	553	15.4	3
2004—Georgia	12	49	801	16.3	7
College totals (4 years)	45	161	2884	17.9	20

GIORDANO, MATT   S   COLTS

PERSONAL: Born October 16, 1982, in Fresno, Calif. ... 5-10/196. ... Full name: Matthew Giordano.
HIGH SCHOOL: Buchanan (Fresno, Calif.).
JUNIOR COLLEGE: Fresno City College.
COLLEGE: California.
TRANSACTIONS/CAREER NOTES: Selected by Indianapolis Colts in fourth round (135th pick overall) of 2005 NFL draft.

| | | | INTERCEPTIONS | | | |
Year Team	G	Sks.	No.	Yds.	Avg.	TD
2003—California	13	0.0	1	15	15.0	0
2004—California	12	1.0	1	0	0.0	0
College totals (2 years)	25	1.0	2	15	7.5	0

GODDARD, JONATHAN   OLB   LIONS

PERSONAL: Born May 11, 1981, in San Diego, Calif. ... 6-0/238. ... Full name: Jonathan Bruce Goddard.
HIGH SCHOOL: Ed White (Jacksonville, Fla.).
COLLEGE: Marshall.
TRANSACTIONS/CAREER NOTES: Selected by Detroit Lions in sixth round (206th pick overall) of 2005 NFL draft.

| | | | INTERCEPTIONS | | | |
Year Team	G	Sks.	No.	Yds.	Avg.	TD
2001—Marshall	11	2.0	0	0	0.0	0
2002—Marshall	13	3.0	0	0	0.0	0
2003—Marshall	12	6.5	0	0	0.0	0
2004—Marshall	12	16.0	1	23	23.0	1
College totals (4 years)	48	27.5	1	23	23.0	1

GORE, FRANK   RB   49ERS

PERSONAL: Born May 14, 1983, in Coral Gables, Fla. ... 5-10/208. ... Full name: Franklin Gore.
HIGH SCHOOL: Coral Gables (Fla.).
COLLEGE: Miami (Fla.).
TRANSACTIONS/CAREER NOTES: Selected after junior season by San Francisco 49ers in third round (65th pick overall) of 2005 NFL draft.
HONORS: Named running back on THE SPORTING NEWS Freshman All-America fourth team (2001).

Year Team		RUSHING				RECEIVING				TOTALS	
	G	Att.	Yds.	Avg.	TD	No.	Yds.	Avg.	TD	TD	Pts.
2001—Miami (Fla.)	11	62	562	9.1	5	1	14	14.0	0	5	30
2003—Miami (Fla.)	5	89	468	5.3	4	12	105	8.8	0	4	24
2004—Miami (Fla.)	12	197	945	4.8	8	10	106	10.6	0	8	48
College totals (3 years)	28	348	1975	5.7	17	23	225	9.8	0	17	102

GREEN, ERIC — CB — CARDINALS

PERSONAL: Born March 16, 1982, in Pahokee, Fla. ... 5-11/198. ... Full name: Eric Denaud Green.
HIGH SCHOOL: Clewiston (Fla.).
COLLEGE: Virginia Tech.
TRANSACTIONS/CAREER NOTES: Selected by Arizona Cardinals in third round (75th pick overall) of 2005 NFL draft.

Year Team			INTERCEPTIONS			
	G	Sks.	No.	Yds.	Avg.	TD
2000—Virginia Tech	11	0.0	4	51	12.8	0
2001—Virginia Tech	10	0.0	0	0	0.0	0
2003—Virginia Tech	13	0.0	3	166	55.3	2
2004—Virginia Tech	13	0.0	1	47	47.0	0
College totals (4 years)	47	0.0	8	264	33.0	2

GREEN, JUSTIN — FB — RAVENS

PERSONAL: Born April 30, 1982, in San Diego, Calif. ... 5-11/242.
HIGH SCHOOL: University of San Diego (Calif.).
COLLEGE: San Diego State, then Montana.
TRANSACTIONS/CAREER NOTES: Selected by Baltimore Ravens in fifth round (158th pick overall) of 2005 NFL draft.

Year Team		RUSHING				RECEIVING				TOTALS	
	G	Att.	Yds.	Avg.	TD	No.	Yds.	Avg.	TD	TD	Pts.
2001—San Diego State	11	24	133	5.5	1	0	0	0.0	0	1	6
2003—Montana	13	252	1146	4.5	14	6	25	4.2	0	14	84
2004—Montana	14	160	638	4.0	8	9	68	7.6	0	8	48
College totals (3 years)	38	436	1917	4.4	23	15	93	6.2	0	23	138

GREENE, DAVID — QB — SEAHAWKS

PERSONAL: Born June 22, 1982... 6-3/226.
HIGH SCHOOL: South Gwinnett (Snellville, Ga.).
COLLEGE: Georgia.
TRANSACTIONS/CAREER NOTES: Selected by Seattle Seahawks in third round (85th pick overall) of 2005 NFL draft.
HONORS: Named quarterback on THE SPORTING NEWS Freshman All-America second team (2001).

Year Team		PASSING								RUSHING				TOTALS	
	G	Att.	Cmp.	Pct.	Yds.	TD	Int.	Avg.	Rat.	Att.	Yds.	Avg.	TD	TD	Pts.
2001—Georgia	11	324	192	59.3	2789	17	9	8.61	143.3	47	41	0.9	1	1	6
2002—Georgia	14	379	218	57.5	2924	22	8	7.72	137.3	65	-52	-0.8	2	2	12
2003—Georgia	14	438	264	60.3	3307	13	11	7.55	128.5	69	-180	-2.6	1	1	6
2004—Georgia	12	299	175	58.5	2508	20	4	8.39	148.4	23	-67	-2.9	1	1	6
College totals (4 years)	51	1440	849	59.0	11528	72	32	8.01	138.3	204	-258	-1.3	5	5	30

GRIGSBY, BOOMER — LB — CHIEFS

PERSONAL: Born November 15, 1981, in Canton, Ill. ... 6-0/249. ... Full name: James Grigsby.
HIGH SCHOOL: Canton (Ill.).
COLLEGE: Illinois State.
TRANSACTIONS/CAREER NOTES: Selected by Kansas City Chiefs in fifth round (138th pick overall) of 2005 NFL draft.

Year Team			INTERCEPTIONS			
	G	Sks.	No.	Yds.	Avg.	TD
2001—Illinois State	11	3.0	0	0	0.0	0
2002—Illinois State	11	4.0	0	0	0.0	0
2003—Illinois State	12	3.0	0	0	0.0	0
2004—Illinois State	10	3.0	0	0	0.0	0
College totals (4 years)	44	13.0	0	0	0.0	0

HAGLER, TYJUAN — LB — COLTS

PERSONAL: Born December 3, 1981, in Kankakee, Ill. ... 6-0/238.
HIGH SCHOOL: Bishop McNamara (Kankakee, Ill.).
COLLEGE: Cincinnati.
TRANSACTIONS/CAREER NOTES: Selected by Indianapolis Colts in fifth round (173rd pick overall) of 2005 NFL draft.

Year Team			INTERCEPTIONS			
	G	Sks.	No.	Yds.	Avg.	TD
2001—Cincinnati	3	0.0	0	0	0.0	0
2002—Cincinnati	14	3.0	1	15	15.0	1
2003—Cincinnati	12	3.0	0	0	0.0	0
2004—Cincinnati	12	1.0	0	0	0.0	0
College totals (4 years)	41	7.0	1	15	15.0	1

HANGARTNER, GEOFF — T — PANTHERS

PERSONAL: Born April 22, 1982, in New Braunfels, Texas. ... 6-5/301. ... Full name: Geoffrey Thomas Hangartner.
HIGH SCHOOL: New Braunfels (New Braunfels, Texas).

COLLEGE: Texas A&M.
TRANSACTIONS/CAREER NOTES: Selected by Carolina Panthers in fifth round (169th pick overall) of 2005 NFL draft.
PLAYING EXPERIENCE: Texas A&M, 2001-2004. ... Games played: 2001 (2), 2002 (12), 2003 (12), 2004 (12). Total: 38.

HARRIS, CHRIS   S   BEARS

PERSONAL: Born August 6, 1982, in Little Rock, Ark. ... 6-1/206.
HIGH SCHOOL: J.A. Fair (Little Rock, Ark.).
COLLEGE: Louisiana-Monroe.
TRANSACTIONS/CAREER NOTES: Selected by Chicago Bears in sixth round (181st pick overall) of 2005 NFL draft.

			INTERCEPTIONS			
Year Team	G	Sks.	No.	Yds.	Avg.	TD
2001—Louisiana-Monroe	11	0.0	2	0	0.0	0
2002—Louisiana-Monroe	12	0.0	1	0	0.0	0
2003—Louisiana-Monroe	11	1.0	4	0	0.0	0
2004—Louisiana-Monroe	11	0.0	7	11	1.6	0
College totals (4 years)	45	1.0	14	11	0.8	0

HAWKINS, MIKE   CB   PACKERS

PERSONAL: Born July 15, 1983, in Dallas, Texas. ... 6-2/178. ... Full name: Micheal Hawkins.
HIGH SCHOOL: R.L. Daniels (Carrollton, Texas).
COLLEGE: Oklahoma.
TRANSACTIONS/CAREER NOTES: Selected by Green Bay Packers in fifth round (167th pick overall) of 2005 NFL draft.

			INTERCEPTIONS			
Year Team	G	Sks.	No.	Yds.	Avg.	TD
2002—Oklahoma	8	0.0	1	45	45.0	1

HAWTHORNE, ANTTAJ   DT   RAIDERS

PERSONAL: Born November 15, 1981, in New Haven, Conn. ... 6-3/321.
HIGH SCHOOL: Hamden (Conn.).
COLLEGE: Wisconsin.
TRANSACTIONS/CAREER NOTES: Selected by Oakland Raiders in the sixth round (175th overall) of 2005 NFL draft.

			INTERCEPTIONS			
Year Team	G	Sks.	No.	Yds.	Avg.	TD
2001—Wisconsin	11	0.0	0	0	0.0	0
2002—Wisconsin	14	2.0	0	0	0.0	0
2003—Wisconsin	13	4.0	0	0	0.0	0
2004—Wisconsin	12	6.0	1	15	15.0	0
College totals (4 years)	50	12.0	1	15	15.0	0

HAYDEN, KELVIN   CB   COLTS

PERSONAL: Born July 23, 1983, in Chicago, Ill. ... 5-10/198. ... Full name: Kelvin Darnell Hayden Jr.
HIGH SCHOOL: Hubbard (Chicago, Ill.).
JUNIOR COLLEGE: Joliet (Ill.).
COLLEGE: Illinois.
TRANSACTIONS/CAREER NOTES: Selected by Indianapolis Colts in second round (60th pick overall) of 2005 NFL draft.

			INTERCEPTIONS			
Year Team	G	Sks.	No.	Yds.	Avg.	TD
2003—Illinois	10	0.0	0	0	0.0	0
2004—Illinois	11	0.0	4	84	21.0	1
College totals (2 years)	21	0.0	4	84	21.0	1

HAYE, JOVAN   DE   PANTHERS

PERSONAL: Born June 21, 1982, in Jamaica. ... 6-2/287.
HIGH SCHOOL: Dillard (Fort Lauderdale, Fla.).
COLLEGE: Vanderbilt.
TRANSACTIONS/CAREER NOTES: Selected after junior season by Carolina Panthers in sixth round (189th pick overall) of 2005 NFL draft.

Year Team	G	SACKS
2002—Vanderbilt	12	1.0
2003—Vanderbilt	12	8.5
2004—Vanderbilt	11	1.0
College totals (3 years)	35	10.5

HEDGECOCK, MADISON   FB   RAMS

PERSONAL: Born August 27, 1981, in Winston-Salem, N.C. ... 6-3/259. ... Full name: Madison Smith Hedgecock.
HIGH SCHOOL: Ledford (Thomasville, N.C.).
COLLEGE: North Carolina.
TRANSACTIONS/CAREER NOTES: Selected by St. Louis Rams in seventh round (251st pick overall) of 2005 NFL draft.

		RUSHING				RECEIVING				TOTALS	
Year Team	G	Att.	Yds.	Avg.	TD	No.	Yds.	Avg.	TD	TD	Pts.
2001—North Carolina	12	1	1	1.0	0	0	0	0.0	0	0	0
2002—North Carolina	12	3	11	3.7	0	2	7	3.5	0	0	0
2003—North Carolina	12	0	0	0.0	0	0	0	0.0	0	0	0
2004—North Carolina	12	30	118	3.9	2	4	35	8.8	0	2	12
College totals (4 years)	48	34	130	3.8	2	6	42	7.0	0	2	12

HENRY, CHRIS — WR — BENGALS

PERSONAL: Born May 17, 1983, in Belle Chasse, La. ... 6-4/197. ... Full name: Christopher Henry.
HIGH SCHOOL: Belle Chasse (La.).
COLLEGE: West Virginia.
TRANSACTIONS/CAREER NOTES: Selected after junior season by Cincinnati Bengals in third round (83rd pick overall) of 2005 NFL draft.

			RECEIVING		
Year Team	G	No.	Yds.	Avg.	TD
2003—West Virginia	12	41	1006	24.5	10
2004—West Virginia	11	52	872	16.8	12
College totals (2 years)	23	93	1878	20.2	22

HERREMANS, TODD — T — EAGLES

PERSONAL: Born October 13, 1982... 6-6/321.
HIGH SCHOOL: Ravenna (Mich.).
COLLEGE: Saginaw Valley State.
TRANSACTIONS/CAREER NOTES: Selected by Philadelphia Eagles in fourth round (126th pick overall) of 2005 NFL draft.
PLAYING EXPERIENCE: Saginaw Valley, 2001-2004. ... Games played: 2001 (13), 2002 (11), 2003 (12), 2004 (10). Total: 46.

HERRON, NOAH — RB — STEELERS

PERSONAL: Born April 3, 1982, in Mattawan, Mich. ... 5-10/224. ... Full name: Noah Scott Herron.
HIGH SCHOOL: Mattawan (Mich.).
COLLEGE: Northwestern.
TRANSACTIONS/CAREER NOTES: Selected by Pittsburgh Steelers in seventh round (244th pick overall) of 2005 NFL draft.

		RUSHING				RECEIVING				TOTALS	
Year Team	G	Att.	Yds.	Avg.	TD	No.	Yds.	Avg.	TD	TD	Pts.
2001—Northwestern	8	3	39	13.0	0	2	18	9.0	0	0	0
2002—Northwestern	12	66	365	5.5	7	15	184	12.3	0	7	42
2003—Northwestern	13	119	739	6.2	5	19	228	12.0	1	6	36
2004—Northwestern	12	274	1381	5.0	14	36	351	9.8	1	15	90
College totals (4 years)	45	462	2524	5.5	26	72	781	10.8	2	28	168

HILL, LEROY — LB — SEAHAWKS

PERSONAL: Born September 14, 1982... 6-1/229. ... Full name: LeRoy Hill Jr.
HIGH SCHOOL: Baldwin (Haddock, Ga.).
COLLEGE: Clemson.
TRANSACTIONS/CAREER NOTES: Selected by Seattle Seahawks in third round (98th pick overall) of 2005 NFL draft.

Year Team	G	SACKS
2001—Clemson	9	0.0
2002—Clemson	13	0.0
2003—Clemson	13	8.0
2004—Clemson	11	8.0
College totals (4 years)	46	16.0

HILL, REYNALDO — CB — TITANS

PERSONAL: Born August 28, 1982, in Pahokee, Fla. ... 5-11/187.
HIGH SCHOOL: Stranahan (Fort Lauderdale, Fla.).
JUNIOR COLLEGE: Dodge City Community College (Kan.).
COLLEGE: Florida.
TRANSACTIONS/CAREER NOTES: Selected by Tennessee Titans in seventh round (218th pick overall) of 2005 NFL draft.

			INTERCEPTIONS			
Year Team	G	Sks.	No.	Yds.	Avg.	TD
2003—Florida	13	0.0	0	0	0.0	0
2004—Florida	12	0.0	1	0	0.0	0
College totals (2 years)	25	0.0	1	0	0.0	0

HOBBS, ELLIS — CB — PATRIOTS

PERSONAL: Born May 16, 1983, in Niagara Falls, N.Y. ... 5-8/188. ... Full name: Ellis Hobbs III.
HIGH SCHOOL: DeSoto (Texas).
COLLEGE: Iowa State.
TRANSACTIONS/CAREER NOTES: Selected by New England Patriots in third round (84th pick overall) of 2005 NFL draft.

			INTERCEPTIONS				KICKOFF RETURNS				TOTALS	
Year Team	G	Sks.	No.	Yds.	Avg.	TD	No.	Yds.	Avg.	TD	TD	Pts.
2001—Iowa State	11	0.0	1	4	4.0	0	6	91	15.2	0	0	0
2002—Iowa State	14	0.0	2	0	0.0	0	0	0	0.0	0	0	0
2003—Iowa State	12	1.0	1	0	0.0	0	6	111	18.5	0	0	0
2004—Iowa State	12	1.0	5	117	23.4	1	12	288	24.0	0	1	6
College totals (4 years)	49	2.0	9	121	13.4	1	24	490	20.4	0	1	6

HODGDON, DREW — C/G — TEXANS

PERSONAL: Born November 15, 1981, in Palo Alto, California. ... 6-3/309. ... Full name: Lincoln Andrew Hodgdon.
HIGH SCHOOL: Palo Alto (Calif.).
COLLEGE: Arizona State.
TRANSACTIONS/CAREER NOTES: Selected by Houston Texans in fifth round (151st pick overall) of 2005 NFL draft.
PLAYING EXPERIENCE: Arizona State, 2001-2004. ... Games played: 2001 (10), 2002 (14), 2003 (12), 2004 (9). Total: 45.

HODGE, ALPHONSO   CB   CHIEFS

PERSONAL: Born May 30, 1982, in Cleveland, Ohio. ... 5-11/203.
HIGH SCHOOL: St. Edward (Cleveland, Ohio).
COLLEGE: Miami (Ohio).
TRANSACTIONS/CAREER NOTES: Selected by Kansas City Chiefs in fifth round (147th pick overall) of 2005 NFL draft.

Year Team	G	SACKS
2001—Miami of Ohio	7	0.0
2002—Miami of Ohio	12	2.0
2003—Miami of Ohio	14	1.0
2004—Miami of Ohio	13	5.0
College totals (4 years)	46	8.0

HODGES, REGGIE   P   RAMS

PERSONAL: Born January 26, 1987, in Champaign, Ill. ... 6-0/226. ... Full name: Reggie A. Hodges.
HIGH SCHOOL: Centennial (Champaign, Ill.).
COLLEGE: Ball State.
TRANSACTIONS/CAREER NOTES: Selected by St. Louis Rams in sixth round (210th pick overall) of 2005 NFL draft.

Year Team	G	No.	Yds.	Avg.	Net avg.	In. 20	Blk.
2000—Ball State	11	64	2321	36.3	35.7	18	1
2001—Ball State	11	60	2481	41.4	40.0	12	2
2002—Ball State	11	57	2299	40.3	40.3	23	0
2004—Ball State	11	73	3109	42.6	40.4	25	4
College totals (4 years)	44	254	10210	40.2	0.0	78	7

HOFFMAN, ANDREW   DT   BROWNS

PERSONAL: Born February 15, 1982, in Fairfax, Va. ... 6-4/296. ... Full name: Andrew Judson Hoffman.
HIGH SCHOOL: Park View-Sterling (South Riding, Va.).
COLLEGE: Virginia.
TRANSACTIONS/CAREER NOTES: Selected by Cleveland Browns in sixth round (203rd pick overall) of 2005 NFL draft.

Year Team	G	SACKS
2000—Virginia	7	0.0
2002—Virginia	14	0.0
2003—Virginia	13	0.0
2004—Virginia	12	3.0
College totals (4 years)	46	3.0

HOLLY, DAVEN   CB   49ERS

PERSONAL: Born August 8, 1982, in McKeesport, Pa. ... 5-10/192.
HIGH SCHOOL: Clairton (Pa.).
COLLEGE: Cincinnati.
TRANSACTIONS/CAREER NOTES: Selected by San Francisco 49ers in seventh round (215th pick overall) of 2005 NFL draft.

			INTERCEPTIONS			
Year Team	G	Sks.	No.	Yds.	Avg.	TD
2001—Cincinnati	11	0.0	0	0	0.0	0
2002—Cincinnati	14	0.0	1	0	0.0	0
2003—Cincinnati	12	0.0	6	58	9.7	1
2004—Cincinnati	12	0.0	2	0	0.0	0
College totals (4 years)	49	0.0	9	58	6.4	1

HOUSTON, CEDRIC   RB   JETS

PERSONAL: Born June 28, 1982, in Little Rock, Ark. ... 5-11/223. ... Full name: Cedric Leonard Houston.
HIGH SCHOOL: Clarendon (Ark.).
COLLEGE: Tennessee.
TRANSACTIONS/CAREER NOTES: Selected by New York Jets in sixth round (182nd pick overall) of 2005 NFL draft.

		RUSHING				RECEIVING				TOTALS	
Year Team	G	Att.	Yds.	Avg.	TD	No.	Yds.	Avg.	TD	TD	Pts.
2001—Tennessee	12	18	106	5.9	1	0	0	0.0	0	1	6
2002—Tennessee	12	153	779	5.1	6	9	55	6.1	0	6	36
2003—Tennessee	12	149	744	5.0	2	14	134	9.6	0	2	12
2004—Tennessee	13	181	1005	5.6	8	16	180	11.3	1	9	56
College totals (4 years)	49	501	2634	5.3	17	39	369	9.5	1	18	110

HUCKEBA, JEB   DE   SEAHAWKS

PERSONAL: Born May 20, 1982... 6-5/252. ... Name pronounced: Huck-a-bee.
HIGH SCHOOL: Harding Academy (Searcy, Ark.).
COLLEGE: Arkansas.
TRANSACTIONS/CAREER NOTES: Selected by Seattle Seahawks in fifth round (159th pick overall) of 2005 NFL draft.

Year Team	G	SACKS
2001—Arkansas	11	0.0
2002—Arkansas	13	0.0
2003—Arkansas	13	0.0
2004—Arkansas	11	6.5
College totals (4 years)	48	6.5

HUNT, ROB C COLTS

PERSONAL: Born March 3, 1981, in Cavalier, N.D. ... 6-4/301. ... Full name: Robert Hunt.
HIGH SCHOOL: Cavalier (N.D.).
COLLEGE: North Dakota State.
TRANSACTIONS/CAREER NOTES: Selected by Indianapolis Colts in fifth round (165th pick overall) of 2005 NFL draft.
PLAYING EXPERIENCE: North Dakota State, 2001-2004. ... Games played: 2001 (10), 2002 (10), 2003 (11), 2004 (11). Total: 42.

INCOGNITO, RICHIE C RAMS

PERSONAL: Born July 5, 1983, in Englewood, N.J. ... 6-3/305. ... Full name: Richard Incognito.
HIGH SCHOOL: Mountain Ridge (Glendale, Ariz.).
COLLEGE: Nebraska.
TRANSACTIONS/CAREER NOTES: Selected after junior season by St. Louis Rams in third round (81st pick overall) of 2005 NFL draft.
PLAYING EXPERIENCE: Nebraska, 2002-2003. ... Games played: 2002 (14), 2003 (13). Total: 27.

JACKSON, MARLIN CB COLTS

PERSONAL: Born June 30, 1983, in Sharon, Pa. ... 6-1/198. ... Full name: Marlin Tyrell Jackson.
HIGH SCHOOL: Sharon (Pa.).
COLLEGE: Michigan.
TRANSACTIONS/CAREER NOTES: Selected by Indianapolis Colts in first round (29th pick overall) of 2005 NFL draft.
HONORS: Named cornerback on THE SPORTING NEWS Freshman All-America first team (2001). ... Named cornerback on THE SPORTING NEWS college All-America first team (2004).

| | | | | INTERCEPTIONS | | |
Year Team	G	Sks.	No.	Yds.	Avg.	TD
2001—Michigan	10	0.0	3	0	0.0	0
2002—Michigan	13	1.0	3	40	13.3	1
2003—Michigan	9	0.0	2	3	1.5	0
2004—Michigan	12	1.0	1	34	34.0	0
College totals (4 years)	44	2.0	9	77	8.6	1

JACKSON, TONY FB SEAHAWKS

PERSONAL: Born July 5, 1982... 6-2/268.
HIGH SCHOOL: Willow Run (Ypsilanti, Mich.).
COLLEGE: Iowa.
TRANSACTIONS/CAREER NOTES: Selected by Seattle Seahawks in sixth round (196th pick overall) of 2005 NFL draft.

| | | RECEIVING | | | |
Year Team	G	No.	Yds.	Avg.	TD
2001—Iowa	9	0	0	0.0	0
2002—Iowa	13	2	10	5.0	0
2003—Iowa	13	5	42	8.4	1
2004—Iowa	12	7	82	11.7	1
College totals (4 years)	47	14	134	9.6	2

JACKSON, VINCENT WR CHARGERS

PERSONAL: Born January 14, 1983... 6-5/238.
HIGH SCHOOL: Widefield (Colorado Springs, Colo.).
COLLEGE: Northern Colorado.
TRANSACTIONS/CAREER NOTES: Selected by San Diego Chargers in second round (61st pick overall) of 2005 NFL draft.

| | | RECEIVING | | | | PUNT RETURNS | | | | KICKOFF RETURNS | | | | TOTALS | |
Year Team	G	No.	Yds.	Avg.	TD	No.	Yds.	Avg.	TD	No.	Yds.	Avg.	TD	TD	Pts.
2001—Northern Colorado	10	9	259	28.8	2	17	306	18.0	2	11	264	24.0	0	0	0
2002—Northern Colorado	14	22	445	20.2	3	27	256	9.5	0	15	379	25.3	0	0	0
2003—Northern Colorado	11	66	1462	22.2	21	19	166	8.7	0	13	321	24.7	0	21	126
2004—Northern Colorado	11	80	1382	17.3	11	25	296	11.8	0	13	274	21.1	0	11	66
College totals (4 years)	46	177	3548	20.0	37	88	1024	11.6	2	52	1238	23.8	0	32	192

JACOBS, BRANDON RB GIANTS

PERSONAL: Born July 6, 1982, in Houma, La. ... 6-4/264.
HIGH SCHOOL: Assumption (Napoleanville, La.).
COLLEGE: Auburn, then Southern Illinois.
TRANSACTIONS/CAREER NOTES: Selected by New York Giants in fourth round (110th pick overall) of 2005 NFL draft.

| | | RUSHING | | | | RECEIVING | | | | KICKOFF RETURNS | | | | TOTALS | |
Year Team	G	Att.	Yds.	Avg.	TD	No.	Yds.	Avg.	TD	No.	Yds.	Avg.	TD	TD	Pts.
2003—Auburn	13	72	446	6.2	3	1	34	34.0	0	0	0	0.0	0	3	18
2004—Southern Illinois	12	150	992	6.6	19	8	83	10.4	0	6	140	23.3	0	19	114
College totals (2 years)	25	222	1438	6.5	22	9	117	13.0	0	6	140	23.3	0	22	132

JAMES, ERASMUS DE VIKINGS

PERSONAL: Born November 4, 1982, in St. Kitts, Caribbean. ... 6-4/266.
HIGH SCHOOL: McArthur (Pembroke Pines, Fla.).
COLLEGE: Wisconsin.
TRANSACTIONS/CAREER NOTES: Selected by Minnesota Vikings in first round (18th pick overall) of 2005 NFL draft.

Year	Team	G	SACKS
2001—Wisconsin		12	6.0
2002—Wisconsin		14	4.0
2004—Wisconsin		11	8.0
College totals (3 years)		37	18.0

JEFFERSON, JASON — DT — SAINTS

PERSONAL: Born December 20, 1981, in Chicago, Ill. ... 6-2/310.
HIGH SCHOOL: Leo (Chicago, Ill.).
COLLEGE: Wisconsin.
TRANSACTIONS/CAREER NOTES: Selected by New Orleans Saints in sixth round (193rd pick overall) of 2005 NFL draft.

Year	Team	G	SACKS
2001—Wisconsin		3	0.0
2002—Wisconsin		14	1.0
2003—Wisconsin		13	1.0
2004—Wisconsin		12	3.0
College totals (4 years)		42	5.0

JOHNSON, DERRICK — LB — CHIEFS

PERSONAL: Born November 22, 1982, in Waco, Texas. ... 6-3/242. ... Full name: Derrick O'Hara Johnson. ... Brother of Dwight Johnson, defensive lineman with Philadelphia Eagles (2000) and New York Giants (2002).
HIGH SCHOOL: Waco (Texas).
COLLEGE: Texas.
TRANSACTIONS/CAREER NOTES: Selected by Kansas City Chiefs in first round (15th pick overall) of 2005 NFL draft.
HONORS: Dick Butkus Award winner (2004). ... Bronko Nagurski Award winner (2004). ... Named College Football Defensive Player of the Year by THE SPORTING NEWS (2004). ... Named linebacker on THE SPORTING NEWS Freshman All-America first team (2001). ... Named linebacker on THE SPORTING NEWS college All-America second team (2003). ... Named linebacker on THE SPORTING NEWS college All-America first team (2004).

Year	Team	G	Sks.	INTERCEPTIONS No.	Yds.	Avg.	TD
2001—Texas		12	4.5	0	0	0.0	0
2002—Texas		13	2.0	4	85	21.3	0
2003—Texas		13	2.0	4	92	23.0	1
2004—Texas		12	2.0	1	18	18.0	0
College totals (4 years)		50	10.5	9	195	21.7	1

JOHNSON, DERRICK — CB — 49ERS

PERSONAL: Born February 9, 1982, in Riverside, Calif. ... 5-11/188.
HIGH SCHOOL: Notre Dame (Riverside, Calif.).
COLLEGE: Washington.
TRANSACTIONS/CAREER NOTES: Selected by San Francisco 49ers in sixth round (205th pick overall) of 2005 NFL draft.

Year	Team	G	Sks.	INTERCEPTIONS No.	Yds.	Avg.	TD
2000—Washington		11	0.0	0	0	0.0	0
2002—Washington		13	0.0	5	56	11.2	1
2003—Washington		12	0.0	6	62	10.3	1
2004—Washington		10	1.0	0	0	0.0	0
College totals (4 years)		46	1.0	11	118	10.7	2

JOHNSON, MARCUS — OL — VIKINGS

PERSONAL: Born December 1, 1981, in Greenville, Miss. ... 6-6/310. ... Full name: Marcus Allen Johnson. ... Brother of Belton Johnson, offensive lineman with Cincinnati Bengals.
HIGH SCHOOL: Coffeeville (Miss.).
COLLEGE: Mississippi.
TRANSACTIONS/CAREER NOTES: Selected by Minnesota Vikings in second round (49th pick overall) of 2005 NFL draft.
PLAYING EXPERIENCE: Mississippi, 2001-2004. ... Games played: 2001 (11), 2002 (13), 2003 (13), 2004 (11). Total: 48.
HONORS: Named guard on THE SPORTING NEWS Freshman All-America fourth team (2001).

JOHNSON, TRAVIS — DT — TEXANS

PERSONAL: Born April 26, 1982, in Sherman Oaks, Calif. ... 6-4/296.
HIGH SCHOOL: Notre Dame (Sherman Oaks, Calif.).
COLLEGE: Florida State.
TRANSACTIONS/CAREER NOTES: Selected by Houston Texans in first round (16th pick overall) of 2005 NFL draft.
HONORS: Named defensive end on THE SPORTING NEWS Freshman All-America first team (2001).

Year	Team	G	SACKS
2000—Florida State		2	1.0
2001—Florida State		10	2.0
2002—Florida State		14	4.0
2003—Florida State		13	0.5
2004—Florida State		12	2.5
College totals (5 years)		51	10.0

JONES, ADAM — CB — TITANS

PERSONAL: Born September 30, 1983, in Atlanta, Ga. ... 5-10/183.
HIGH SCHOOL: Westlake (Atlanta, Ga.).
COLLEGE: West Virginia.

TRANSACTIONS/CAREER NOTES: Selected after junior season by Tennessee Titans in first round (sixth pick overall) of 2005 NFL draft.

			INTERCEPTIONS			
Year Team	G	Sks.	No.	Yds.	Avg.	TD
2002—West Virginia	11	0.0	1	14	14.0	0
2003—West Virginia	13	0.0	4	91	22.8	1
2004—West Virginia	12	2.0	3	51	17.0	0
College totals (3 years)	36	2.0	8	156	19.5	1

JONES, BRANDON　　　WR　　　TITANS

PERSONAL: Born October 6, 1982, in Texarkana, Texas. ... 6-2/208. ... Full name: Brandon Virgil Jones.
HIGH SCHOOL: Liberty Eylau (Texarkana, Texas).
COLLEGE: Oklahoma.
TRANSACTIONS/CAREER NOTES: Selected by Tennessee Titans in third round (96th pick overall) of 2005 NFL draft.

		RECEIVING			
Year Team	G	No.	Yds.	Avg.	TD
2001—Oklahoma	12	2	16	8.0	0
2002—Oklahoma	12	7	117	16.7	3
2003—Oklahoma	14	46	709	15.4	8
2004—Oklahoma	13	27	345	12.8	3
College totals (4 years)	51	82	1187	14.5	14

JONES, MATT　　　WR　　　JAGUARS

PERSONAL: Born April 22, 1983, in Fort Smith, Ark. ... 6-6/242. ... Full name: Matthew Jones.
HIGH SCHOOL: Van Buren (Ark.), then Northside (Fort Smith, Ark.).
COLLEGE: Arkansas.
TRANSACTIONS/CAREER NOTES: Selected by Jacksonville Jaguars in first round (21st pick overall) of 2005 NFL draft.

		PASSING								RUSHING				TOTALS	
Year Team	G	Att.	Cmp.	Pct.	Yds.	TD	Int.	Avg.	Rat.	Att.	Yds.	Avg.	TD	TD	Pts.
2001—Arkansas	8	27	12	44.4	275	4	3	10.19	156.7	74	592	8.0	5	5	30
2002—Arkansas	14	234	122	52.1	1592	16	8	6.80	125.0	129	614	4.8	5	5	30
2003—Arkansas	13	230	132	57.4	1917	18	7	8.33	147.1	96	707	7.4	8	8	48
2004—Arkansas	11	264	151	57.2	2073	15	12	7.85	132.8	83	622	7.5	6	6	36
College totals (4 years)	46	755	417	55.2	5857	53	30	7.76	135.6	382	2535	6.6	24	24	144

KACZUR, NICK　　　G　　　PATRIOTS

PERSONAL: Born July 28, 1979, in Brantford, Ontario. ... 6-4/319. ... Full name: Nicholas Jesse Kaczur.
HIGH SCHOOL: Collegiate (Brantford, Ontario).
COLLEGE: Toledo.
TRANSACTIONS/CAREER NOTES: Selected by New England Patriots in third round (100th pick overall) of 2005 NFL draft.
PLAYING EXPERIENCE: Toledo, 2001-2004. ... Games played: 2001 (10), 2002 (14), 2003 (12), 2004 (13). Total: 49.
HONORS: Named offensive tackle on THE SPORTING NEWS Freshman All-America third team (2001).

KEMOEATU, CHRIS　　　G　　　STEELERS

PERSONAL: Born January 4, 1983, in Kahuku, Hawaii. ... 6-3/344. ... Full name: Uikelotu Christopher Kemoeatu. ... Name pronounced: kay-moy-ah-too. ... Brother of Maake Kemoeatu, defensive tackle with Baltimore Ravens.
HIGH SCHOOL: Kahuku (Hawaii).
COLLEGE: Utah.
TRANSACTIONS/CAREER NOTES: Selected by Pittsburgh Steelers in sixth round (204th pick overall) of 2005 NFL draft. ... Signed by Steelers (May 19, 2005).
PLAYING EXPERIENCE: Utah, 2001-2004. ... Games played: 2001 (3), 2002 (11), 2003 (8), 2004 (11). Total: 33.

KIEFT, ADAM　　　T　　　BENGALS

PERSONAL: Born August 21, 1982, in Rockford, Mich. ... 6-7/335.
HIGH SCHOOL: Rockford (Mich.).
COLLEGE: Central Michigan.
TRANSACTIONS/CAREER NOTES: Selected by Cincinnati Bengals in fifth round (153rd pick overall) of 2005 NFL draft.
PLAYING EXPERIENCE: Central Michigan, 2001-2004. ... Games played: 2001 (8), 2002 (12), 2003 (12), 2004 (10). Total: 42.

KILIAN, JAMES　　　QB　　　CHIEFS

PERSONAL: Born October 24, 1980, in Caldwell, Kan. ... 6-3/218.
HIGH SCHOOL: Medford (Okla.).
COLLEGE: Tulsa.
TRANSACTIONS/CAREER NOTES: Selected by Kansas City Chiefs in seventh round (229th pick overall) of 2005 NFL draft.

		PASSING								RUSHING				TOTALS	
Year Team	G	Att.	Cmp.	Pct.	Yds.	TD	Int.	Avg.	Rat.	Att.	Yds.	Avg.	TD	TD	Pts.
2001—Tulsa	7	38	16	42.1	193	0	1	5.08	79.5	23	110	4.8	2	2	12
2002—Tulsa	6	52	22	42.3	208	1	2	4.00	74.6	23	86	3.7	2	2	12
2003—Tulsa	13	331	188	56.8	2217	22	11	6.70	128.3	133	605	4.5	7	7	42
2004—Tulsa	12	337	184	54.6	2247	13	16	6.67	113.8	150	282	1.9	8	8	48
College totals (4 years)	38	758	410	54.1	4865	36	30	6.42	115.8	329	1083	3.3	19	19	114

KING, ERIC　　　CB　　　BILLS

PERSONAL: Born May 10, 1982, in Baltimore, Md. ... 5-8/184.
HIGH SCHOOL: McDonogh (Woodstock, Md.).
COLLEGE: Wake Forest.

TRANSACTIONS/CAREER NOTES: Selected by Buffalo Bills in fifth round (156th pick overall) of 2005 NFL draft.

Year Team	G	Sks.	No.	INTERCEPTIONS Yds.	Avg.	TD
2001—Wake Forest	11	0.0	0	0	0.0	0
2002—Wake Forest	13	0.0	3	16	5.3	0
2003—Wake Forest	12	0.0	3	127	42.3	1
2004—Wake Forest	10	2.0	1	0	0.0	0
College totals (4 years)	46	2.0	7	143	20.4	1

LEFORS, STEFAN — QB — PANTHERS

PERSONAL: Born June 7, 1981, in Baton Rouge, La. ... 6-0/208.
HIGH SCHOOL: Christian Life Academy (Baton Rouge, La.).
COLLEGE: Louisville.
TRANSACTIONS/CAREER NOTES: Selected by Carolina Panthers in fourth round (121st pick overall) of 2005 NFL draft.

Year Team	G	PASSING Att.	Cmp.	Pct.	Yds.	TD	Int.	Avg.	Rat.	RUSHING Att.	Yds.	Avg.	TD	TOTALS TD	Pts.
2001—Louisville	5	9	3	33.3	63	0	0	7.00	92.1	4	18	4.5	0	0	0
2002—Louisville	3	7	5	71.4	49	1	0	7.00	177.4	0	0	0.0	0	0	0
2003—Louisville	13	357	219	61.3	3145	17	10	8.81	145.5	71	405	5.7	3	4	28
2004—Louisville	12	257	189	73.5	2596	20	3	10.10	181.7	71	333	4.7	3	3	20
College totals (4 years)	33	630	416	66.0	5853	38	13	9.29	159.8	146	756	5.2	6	7	48

LONG, KHARI — DE — CHIEFS

PERSONAL: Born May 23, 1982, in Wichita Falls, Texas. ... 6-4/257. ... Full name: Khari Ahmad Long.
HIGH SCHOOL: Rider (Wichita Falls, Texas).
COLLEGE: Baylor.
TRANSACTIONS/CAREER NOTES: Selected by Kansas City Chiefs in sixth round (199th pick overall) of 2005 NFL draft.

Year Team	G	SACKS
2001—Baylor	7	1.0
2002—Baylor	11	4.5
2003—Baylor	10	1.5
2004—Baylor	11	2.0
College totals (4 years)	39	9.0

LOPER, DANIEL — T — TITANS

PERSONAL: Born January 15, 1982, in Houston, Texas. ... 6-6/306.
HIGH SCHOOL: Episcopal (Houston, Texas).
COLLEGE: Texas Tech.
TRANSACTIONS/CAREER NOTES: Selected by Tennessee Titans in fifth round (150th pick overall) of 2005 NFL draft.
PLAYING EXPERIENCE: Texas Tech, 2001-2004. ... Games played: 2001 (11), 2002 (14), 2003 (13), 2004 (12). Total: 50.

LYMAN, CHASE — WR — SAINTS

PERSONAL: Born September 4, 1982, in Mountain View, Ca. ... 6-3/217.
HIGH SCHOOL: St. Francis (Los Altos Hills, Ca.).
COLLEGE: California.
TRANSACTIONS/CAREER NOTES: Selected by New Orleans Saints in fourth round (118th pick overall) of 2005 NFL draft.

Year Team	G	RECEIVING No.	Yds.	Avg.	TD
2000—California	11	19	313	16.5	2
2001—California	5	9	106	11.8	1
2003—California	10	12	256	21.3	1
2004—California	4	14	414	29.6	5
College totals (4 years)	30	54	1089	20.2	9

MADDOX, ANDRE — S — JETS

PERSONAL: Born October 8, 1982, in Miami, Fla. ... 6-0/208.
HIGH SCHOOL: Killian (Miami, Fla.).
COLLEGE: North Carolina State.
TRANSACTIONS/CAREER NOTES: Selected by New York Jets in fifth round (161st pick overall) of 2005 NFL draft.

Year Team	G	SACKS
2001—North Carolina State	10	0.0
2002—North Carolina State	14	4.0
2003—North Carolina State	13	2.0
2004—North Carolina State	10	2.0
College totals (4 years)	47	8.0

MANKINS, LOGAN — OL — PATRIOTS

PERSONAL: Born March 10, 1982, in Catheys Valley, Calif. ... 6-4/307.
HIGH SCHOOL: Mariposa (Catheys Valley, Calif.).
COLLEGE: Fresno State.
TRANSACTIONS/CAREER NOTES: Selected by New England Patriots in first round (32nd pick overall) of 2005 NFL draft.

MARSHALL, KEYONTA — DT — EAGLES

PERSONAL: Born August 13, 1981, in Saginaw, Mich. ... 6-1/330.
HIGH SCHOOL: Saginaw (Mich.).
COLLEGE: Hawaii, then Saginaw Valley State, then Grand Valley State.
TRANSACTIONS/CAREER NOTES: Selected by Philadelphia Eagles in seventh round (247th pick overall) of 2005 NFL draft.

Year Team	G	SACKS
2001—Grand Valley State	13	4.0
2002—Grand Valley State	14	12.0
2003—Grand Valley State	15	4.0
2004—Grand Valley State	13	6.0
College totals (4 years)	55	26.0

MARSHALL, RASHEED — WR — 49ERS

PERSONAL: Born July 11, 1981, in Pittsburgh, Pa. ... 5-11/185.
HIGH SCHOOL: Brashear (Pittsburgh, Pa.).
COLLEGE: West Virginia.
TRANSACTIONS/CAREER NOTES: Selected by San Francisco 49ers in fifth round (174th pick overall) of 2005 NFL draft.

Year Team	G	PASSING								RUSHING				TOTALS	
		Att.	Cmp.	Pct.	Yds.	TD	Int.	Avg.	Rat.	Att.	Yds.	Avg.	TD	TD	Pts.
2001—West Virginia	5	79	41	51.9	327	2	4	4.14	84.9	48	210	4.4	3	3	18
2002—West Virginia	13	259	139	53.7	1616	9	5	6.24	113.7	173	666	3.8	12	13	78
2003—West Virginia	12	215	109	50.7	1729	15	8	8.04	133.8	101	303	3.0	4	4	24
2004—West Virginia	12	242	144	59.5	1886	19	9	7.79	143.4	169	861	5.1	4	4	24
College totals (4 years)	42	795	433	54.5	5558	45	26	6.99	125.3	491	2040	4.2	23	24	144

MATHIS, EVAN — G — PANTHERS

PERSONAL: Born November 1, 1981, in Homewood, Ala. ... 6-5/312.
HIGH SCHOOL: Homewood (Ala.).
COLLEGE: Alabama.
TRANSACTIONS/CAREER NOTES: Selected by Carolina Panthers in third round (79th pick overall) of 2005 NFL draft.
PLAYING EXPERIENCE: Alabama, 2001-2004. ... Games played: 2001 (11), 2002 (13), 2003 (13), 2004 (12). Total: 49.

MATHIS, JEROME — WR — TEXANS

PERSONAL: Born July 26, 1983, in Petersburg, Va. ... 5-11/181.
HIGH SCHOOL: Petersburg (Va.).
COLLEGE: Hampton.
TRANSACTIONS/CAREER NOTES: Selected by Houston Texans in fourth round (114th pick overall) of 2005 NFL draft.

Year Team	G	RUSHING				RECEIVING				KICKOFF RETURNS				TOTALS	
		Att.	Yds.	Avg.	TD	No.	Yds.	Avg.	TD	No.	Yds.	Avg.	TD	TD	Pts.
2002—Hampton	12	20	188	9.4	1	24	615	25.6	3	20	417	20.9	1	5	30
2003—Hampton	11	9	29	3.2	0	40	977	24.4	9	17	343	20.2	0	9	54
2004—Hampton	12	14	173	12.4	2	29	864	29.8	9	25	888	35.5	5	16	96
College totals (3 years)	35	43	390	9.1	3	93	2456	26.4	21	62	1648	26.6	6	30	180

MAXWELL, MARCUS — WR — 49ERS

PERSONAL: Born July 8, 1983, in Berkley, Calif. ... 6-5/205. ... Full name: Marcus James Maxwell.
HIGH SCHOOL: Pinole Valley (Pinole, Calif.).
JUNIOR COLLEGE: Diablo Valley (Pleasant Hill, Calif.).
COLLEGE: Oregon.
TRANSACTIONS/CAREER NOTES: Selected by San Francisco 49ers in seventh round (223rd pick overall) of 2005 NFL draft.

Year Team	G	RECEIVING			
		No.	Yds.	Avg.	TD
2003—Oregon	7	11	114	10.4	0
2004—Oregon	11	25	287	11.5	2
College totals (2 years)	18	36	401	11.1	2

McCOY, LERON — WR — CARDINALS

PERSONAL: Born January 24, 1982, in Harrisburg, Pa. ... 6-2/205.
HIGH SCHOOL: Bishop McDevitt (Harrisburg, Pa.).
COLLEGE: Indiana (Pa.).
TRANSACTIONS/CAREER NOTES: Selected by Arizona Cardinals in seventh round (226th pick overall) of 2005 NFL draft.

Year Team	G	RUSHING				RECEIVING				TOTALS	
		Att.	Yds.	Avg.	TD	No.	Yds.	Avg.	TD	TD	Pts.
2001—Indiana (Pa.)	10	2	8	4.0	0	8	234	29.3	1	0	0
2002—Indiana (Pa.)	13	4	27	6.8	0	30	640	21.3	8	0	0
2003—Indiana (Pa.)	10	5	97	19.4	2	36	521	14.5	6	0	2
2004—Indiana (Pa.)	10	7	44	6.3	1	36	701	19.5	10	0	0
College totals (4 years)	43	18	176	9.8	3	110	2096	19.1	25	0	2

MCCOY, MATT   LB   EAGLES

PERSONAL: Born October 14, 1982, in Orange County, Calif. ... 6-0/234.
HIGH SCHOOL: Tustin (Orange County, Calif.).
COLLEGE: San Diego State.
TRANSACTIONS/CAREER NOTES: Selected after junior season by Philadelphia Eagles in second round (63rd pick overall) of 2005 NFL draft.

				INTERCEPTIONS			
Year Team	G	Sks.	No.	Yds.	Avg.	TD	
2002—San Diego State	13	1.0	0	0	0.0	0	
2003—San Diego State	12	4.0	0	0	0.0	0	
2004—San Diego State	11	3.0	0	0	0.0	0	
College totals (3 years)	36	8.0	0	0	0.0	0	

MCCUNE, ROBERT   LB   REDSKINS

PERSONAL: Born March 9, 1979... 6-0/244.
HIGH SCHOOL: LeFlore (Mobile, Ala.).
COLLEGE: Louisville.
TRANSACTIONS/CAREER NOTES: Selected by Washington Redskins in fifth round (154th pick overall) of 2005 NFL draft.

				INTERCEPTIONS			
Year Team	G	Sks.	No.	Yds.	Avg.	TD	
2001—Louisville	13	0.0	0	0	0.0	0	
2002—Louisville	13	0.0	0	0	0.0	0	
2003—Louisville	13	4.0	1	0	0.0	0	
2004—Louisville	12	2.0	1	7	7.0	0	
College totals (4 years)	51	6.0	2	7	3.5	0	

MCFADDEN, BRYANT   CB   STEELERS

PERSONAL: Born November 21, 1981, in Hollywood, Fla. ... 5-11/188.
HIGH SCHOOL: McArthur (Hollywood, Fla.).
COLLEGE: Florida State.
TRANSACTIONS/CAREER NOTES: Selected by Pittsburgh Steelers in second round (62nd pick overall) of 2005 NFL draft.

				INTERCEPTIONS			
Year Team	G	Sks.	No.	Yds.	Avg.	TD	
2001—Florida State	11	0.0	0	0	0.0	0	
2002—Florida State	14	0.0	3	8	2.7	0	
2003—Florida State	12	0.0	0	0	0.0	0	
2004—Florida State	12	0.0	1	0	0.0	0	
College totals (4 years)	49	0.0	4	8	2.0	0	

MCMAHON, PETE   T   RAIDERS

PERSONAL: Born October 15, 1981, in Dubuque, Iowa... 6-8/329. ... Full name: Peter McMahon.
HIGH SCHOOL: Wahlert (Dubuque, Iowa).
COLLEGE: Iowa.
TRANSACTIONS/CAREER NOTES: Selected by Oakland Raiders in sixth round (214th pick overall) of 2005 NFL draft.
PLAYING EXPERIENCE: Iowa, 2001-2004. ... Games played: 2001 (9), 2002 (13), 2003 (13), 2004 (12). Total: 47.

MCMILLAN, DAVID   DE   BROWNS

PERSONAL: Born September 20, 1981, in Hinesville, Ga. ... 6-3/260.
HIGH SCHOOL: Killeen (Texas).
COLLEGE: Kansas.
TRANSACTIONS/CAREER NOTES: Selected by Cleveland Browns in fifth round (139th pick overall) of 2005 NFL draft.

Year Team	G	SACKS
2001—Kansas	10	2.0
2002—Kansas	12	3.0
2003—Kansas	13	3.0
2004—Kansas	11	7.0
College totals (4 years)	46	15.0

MCPHERSON, ADRIAN   QB   SAINTS

PERSONAL: Born May 8, 1983, in Bradenton, Fla. ... 6-3/218. ... Full name: Adrian Jamal McPherson.
HIGH SCHOOL: Southeast (Bradenton, Fla.).
COLLEGE: Florida State.
TRANSACTIONS/CAREER NOTES: Selected by New Orleans Saints in fifth round (152nd pick overall) of 2005 NFL draft.

		PASSING							RUSHING				TOTALS	
Year Team	G	Att.	Cmp.	Pct.	Yds.	TD	Int.	Avg.	Rat.	Att.	Yds.	Avg.	TD	TD	Pts.
2001—Florida State	7	37	18	48.6	198	2	0	5.35	111.4	23	16	0.7	0	0	0
2002—Florida State	9	155	80	51.6	1017	12	1	6.56	131.0	48	180	3.8	0	0	0
College totals (2 years)	16	192	98	51.0	1215	14	1	6.33	127.2	71	196	2.8	0	0	0

MERRIMAN, SHAWNE   DE   CHARGERS

PERSONAL: Born May 25, 1984... 6-4/245. ... Full name: Shawne DeAndre Merriman.
HIGH SCHOOL: Frederick Douglass (Upper Marlboro, Md.).
COLLEGE: Maryland.
TRANSACTIONS/CAREER NOTES: Selected after junior season by San Diego Chargers in first round (12th pick overall) of 2005 NFL draft.

Year Team	G	SACKS
2002—Maryland	14	5.0
2003—Maryland	13	8.5
2004—Maryland	11	8.5
College totals (3 years)	38	22.0

MILLER, HEATH — TE — STEELERS

PERSONAL: Born October 22, 1982, in Richlands, Va. ... 6-5/255. ... Full name: Earl Heath Miller.
HIGH SCHOOL: Honaker (Swords Creek, Va.).
COLLEGE: Virginia.
TRANSACTIONS/CAREER NOTES: Selected after junior season by Pittsburgh Steelers in first round (30th pick overall) of 2005 NFL draft.

Year Team	G	RECEIVING No.	Yds.	Avg.	TD
2002—Virginia	14	33	327	9.9	9
2003—Virginia	13	70	835	11.9	6
2004—Virginia	12	41	541	13.2	5
College totals (3 years)	39	144	1703	11.8	20

MILLER, JUSTIN — CB — JETS

PERSONAL: Born February 14, 1984, in Owensboro, Ky. ... 5-10/201.
HIGH SCHOOL: Owensboro (Ky.).
COLLEGE: Clemson.
TRANSACTIONS/CAREER NOTES: Selected after junior season by New York Jets in second round (57th pick overall) of 2005 NFL draft.
HONORS: Named cornerback on THE SPORTING NEWS Freshman All-America first team (2002).

Year Team	G	Sks.	INTERCEPTIONS No.	Yds.	Avg.	TD	PUNT RETURNS No.	Yds.	Avg.	TD	KICKOFF RETURNS No.	Yds.	Avg.	TD	TOTALS TD	Pts.
2002—Clemson	13	0.0	8	50	6.3	0	0	0	0.0	0	13	456	35.1	1	1	6
2003—Clemson	13	1.0	2	30	15.0	0	8	73	9.1	0	17	417	24.5	0	1	6
2004—Clemson	11	0.0	3	14	4.7	0	26	339	13.0	1	20	661	33.1	2	3	18
College totals (3 years)	37	1.0	13	94	7.2	0	34	412	12.1	2	50	1534	30.7	3	5	30

MITCHELL, LANCE — LB — CARDINALS

PERSONAL: Born October 9, 1981, in Los Banos, Calif. ... 6-2/245.
HIGH SCHOOL: Los Banos (Calif.).
JUNIOR COLLEGE: Community College of San Francisco (Calif.).
COLLEGE: Oklahoma.
TRANSACTIONS/CAREER NOTES: Selected by Arizona Cardinals in fifth round (168th pick overall) of 2005 NFL draft.

Year Team	G	Sks.	INTERCEPTIONS No.	Yds.	Avg.	TD
2002—Oklahoma	14	3.0	0	0	0.0	0
2003—Oklahoma	3	0.0	0	0	0.0	0
2004—Oklahoma	13	2.0	0	0	0.0	0
College totals (3 years)	30	5.0	0	0	0.0	0

MOATS, RYAN — RB — EAGLES

PERSONAL: Born December 17, 1982, in Dallas, Texas. ... 5-8/210.
HIGH SCHOOL: Bishop Lynch (Dallas, Texas).
COLLEGE: Louisiana Tech.
TRANSACTIONS/CAREER NOTES: Selected after junior season by Philadelphia Eagles in third round (77th pick overall) of 2005 NFL draft.

Year Team	G	RUSHING Att.	Yds.	Avg.	TD	RECEIVING No.	Yds.	Avg.	TD	TOTALS TD	Pts.
2002—Louisiana Tech	10	12	38	3.2	0	6	74	12.3	0	0	0
2003—Louisiana Tech	12	199	1300	6.5	10	27	251	9.3	1	11	68
2004—Louisiana Tech	12	288	1774	6.2	18	15	116	7.7	1	19	114
College totals (3 years)	34	499	3112	6.2	28	48	441	9.2	2	30	182

MONTGOMERY, MIKE — DE — PACKERS

PERSONAL: Born August 18, 1983, in Carthage, Texas. ... 6-5/276. ... Full name: Michael Lewis Montgomery.
HIGH SCHOOL: Center (Tenaha, Texas).
JUNIOR COLLEGE: Navarro (Texas).
COLLEGE: Texas A&M.
TRANSACTIONS/CAREER NOTES: Selected by Green Bay Packers in sixth round (180th pick overall) of 2005 NFL draft.

Year Team	G	Sks.	INTERCEPTIONS No.	Yds.	Avg.	TD
2003—Texas A&M	10	4.0	0	0	0.0	0
2004—Texas A&M	12	6.0	1	14	14.0	0
College totals (2 years)	22	10.0	1	14	14.0	0

MOORE, ERIC — DE — GIANTS

PERSONAL: Born February 28, 1981, in Pahokee, Fla. ... 6-4/261.
HIGH SCHOOL: Pahokee (Fla.).
COLLEGE: Florida State.
TRANSACTIONS/CAREER NOTES: Selected by New York Giants in sixth round (186th pick overall) of 2005 NFL draft.

Year Team	G	SACKS
2001—Florida State	9	1.0
2002—Florida State	10	3.0

Year Team	G	SACKS
2003— Florida State	12	7.5
2004— Florida State	10	2.5
College totals (4 years)	41	14.0

MORENCY, VERNAND   RB   TEXANS

PERSONAL: Born February 4, 1980, in Miami, Fla. ... 5-10/212.
HIGH SCHOOL: Northwestern (Miami, Fla.).
COLLEGE: Oklahoma State.
TRANSACTIONS/CAREER NOTES: Selected after junior season by Houston Texans in third round (73rd pick overall) of 2005 NFL draft.

		RUSHING				RECEIVING				TOTALS	
Year Team	G	Att.	Yds.	Avg.	TD	No.	Yds.	Avg.	TD	TD	Pts.
2002—Oklahoma State	6	58	269	4.6	3	2	-2	-1.0	0	3	18
2003—Oklahoma State	13	135	918	6.8	8	4	20	5.0	0	8	48
2004—Oklahoma State	11	258	1474	5.7	12	5	101	20.2	1	13	78
College totals (3 years)	30	451	2661	5.9	23	11	119	10.8	1	24	144

MORRISON, KIRK   LB   RAIDERS

PERSONAL: Born February 19, 1982, in Oakland, Calif. ... 6-1/234.
HIGH SCHOOL: Bishop O'Dowd (Oakland, Calif.).
COLLEGE: San Diego State.
TRANSACTIONS/CAREER NOTES: Selected by Oakland Raiders in third round (78th pick overall) of 2005 NFL draft.
HONORS: Named linebacker on THE SPORTING NEWS Freshman All-America fourth team (2001). ... Named linebacker on THE SPORTING NEWS college All-America second team (2004).

			INTERCEPTIONS			
Year Team	G	Sks.	No.	Yds.	Avg.	TD
2001—San Diego State	11	3.0	1	0	0.0	0
2002—San Diego State	13	3.0	3	91	30.3	1
2003—San Diego State	12	3.5	1	0	0.0	0
2004—San Diego State	11	0.0	1	14	14.0	0
College totals (4 years)	47	9.5	6	105	17.5	1

MOSLEY, C.J.   DT   VIKINGS

PERSONAL: Born August 6, 1983, in Fort Knox, Ky. ... 6-2/312. ... Full name: Calvin Michael Mosley Jr.
HIGH SCHOOL: Waynesville (Mo.).
COLLEGE: Missouri.
TRANSACTIONS/CAREER NOTES: Selected after junior season by Minnesota Vikings in sixth round (191st pick overall) of 2005 NFL draft.

Year Team	G	SACKS
2002—Missouri	12	3.0
2003—Missouri	13	6.0
2004—Missouri	11	6.5
College totals (3 years)	36	15.5

MRUCZKOWSKI, SCOTT   C   CHARGERS

PERSONAL: Born April 5, 1982... 6-4/321. ... Full name: Scott Allen Mruczkowski. ... Brother of Gene Mruczkowski, center with New England Patriots.
HIGH SCHOOL: Benedictine (Cleveland, Ohio).
COLLEGE: Bowling Green.
TRANSACTIONS/CAREER NOTES: Selected by San Diego Chargers in seventh round (242nd pick overall) of 2005 NFL draft.
PLAYING EXPERIENCE: Bowling Green, 2001-2004. ... Games played: 2001 (11), 2002 (12), 2003 (14), 2004 (12). Total: 49.

MURPHY, TERRENCE   WR   PACKERS

PERSONAL: Born December 15, 1982, in Tyler, Texas. ... 6-1/202. ... Full name: Terrence Cardene Murphy.
HIGH SCHOOL: Chapel Hill (Tyler, Texas).
COLLEGE: Texas A&M.
TRANSACTIONS/CAREER NOTES: Selected by Green Bay Packers in second round (58th pick overall) of 2005 NFL draft.
HONORS: Named wide receiver on THE SPORTING NEWS Freshman All-America fourth team (2001).

		RUSHING				RECEIVING				KICKOFF RETURNS				TOTALS	
Year Team	G	Att.	Yds.	Avg.	TD	No.	Yds.	Avg.	TD	No.	Yds.	Avg.	TD	TD	Pts.
2001—Texas A&M	11	3	28	9.3	0	36	518	14.4	3	1	19	19.0	0	3	18
2002—Texas A&M	11	0	0	0.0	0	36	599	16.6	4	0	0	0.0	0	4	24
2003—Texas A&M	12	10	150	15.0	1	44	762	17.3	0	23	626	27.2	0	1	6
2004—Texas A&M	11	4	31	7.8	0	56	721	12.9	3	7	116	16.6	0	3	18
College totals (4 years)	45	17	209	12.3	1	172	2600	15.1	10	31	761	24.5	0	11	66

MYERS, CHRIS   G   BRONCOS

PERSONAL: Born September 15, 1981... 6-5/301.
HIGH SCHOOL: Palmetto (Miami, Fla.).
COLLEGE: Miami (Fla.).
TRANSACTIONS/CAREER NOTES: Selected by Denver Broncos in sixth round (200th pick overall) of 2005 NFL draft.
PLAYING EXPERIENCE: Miami (Fla.), 2001-2004. ... Games played: 2001 (7), 2002 (13), 2003 (13), 2004 (12). Total: 45.

NASH, DAMIEN   RB   TITANS

PERSONAL: Born April 14, 1982, in St. Louis, Mo. ... 5-10/210. ... Full name: Damien Darnell Nash.
HIGH SCHOOL: Riverview Gardens (St. Louis, Mo.), then East St. Louis (Ill.).
JUNIOR COLLEGE: Coffeyville (Kan.).
COLLEGE: Missouri.
TRANSACTIONS/CAREER NOTES: Selected by Tennessee Titans in fifth round (142nd pick overall) of 2005 NFL draft.

Year Team	G	RUSHING				RECEIVING				TOTALS	
		Att.	Yds.	Avg.	TD	No.	Yds.	Avg.	TD	TD	Pts.
2003—Missouri	13	89	462	5.2	5	11	105	9.5	1	6	36
2004—Missouri	10	164	792	4.8	7	25	176	7.0	1	8	50
College totals (2 years)	23	253	1254	5.0	12	36	281	7.8	2	14	86

NEWBERRY, JARED   LB   REDSKINS

PERSONAL: Born November 11, 1981... 6-1/234.
HIGH SCHOOL: DeLaSalle (Minneapolis, Minn.).
COLLEGE: Stanford.
TRANSACTIONS/CAREER NOTES: Selected by Washington Redskins in sixth round (183rd pick overall) of 2005 NFL draft.

Year Team	G	Sks.	INTERCEPTIONS			
			No.	Yds.	Avg.	TD
2001—Stanford	10	0.0	0	0	0.0	0
2002—Stanford	11	3.0	1	5	5.0	0
2003—Stanford	11	3.0	1	14	14.0	0
2004—Stanford	11	0.5	1	9	9.0	0
College totals (4 years)	43	6.5	3	28	9.3	0

NICHOLSON, DONTE   S   BUCCANEERS

PERSONAL: Born December 18, 1981, in Los Angeles, Calif. ... 6-1/209. ... Full name: Donte Lamar Nicholson.
HIGH SCHOOL: Diamond Bar (Calif.).
JUNIOR COLLEGE: Mt. San Antonio (Walnut, Calif.).
COLLEGE: Oklahoma.
TRANSACTIONS/CAREER NOTES: Selected by Tampa Bay Buccaneers in fifth round (141st pick overall) of 2005 NFL draft.

Year Team	G	Sks.	INTERCEPTIONS			
			No.	Yds.	Avg.	TD
2003—Oklahoma	14	6.0	2	0	0.0	0
2004—Oklahoma	13	2.0	1	32	32.0	0
College totals (2 years)	27	8.0	3	32	10.7	0

NIENHUIS, DOUG   T   SEAHAWKS

PERSONAL: Born February 16, 1982, in Long Beach, Calif. ... 6-6/307.
HIGH SCHOOL: Woodbridge (Irvine, Calif.).
COLLEGE: Oregon State.
TRANSACTIONS/CAREER NOTES: Selected by Seattle Seahawks in seventh round (254th pick overall) of 2005 NFL draft.
PLAYING EXPERIENCE: Oregon State, 2001-2004. ... Games played: 2001 (9), 2002 (13), 2003 (13), 2004 (12). Total: 47.

NUA, SHAUN   DE   STEELERS

PERSONAL: Born May 22, 1981, in Pago Pago, American Samoa. ... 6-5/270.
HIGH SCHOOL: Tafuna (Pago Pago, American Samoa).
JUNIOR COLLEGE: E. Arizona (Thatcher, Ariz.).
COLLEGE: Brigham Young.
TRANSACTIONS/CAREER NOTES: Selected by Pittsburgh Steelers in seventh round (228th pick overall) of 2005 NFL draft.

Year Team	G	SACKS
2002—Brigham Young	12	4.0
2004—Brigham Young	11	6.0
College totals (2 years)	23	10.0

NUGENT, MIKE   K   JETS

PERSONAL: Born March 2, 1982, in Centerville, Ohio. ... 6-0/182. ... Full name: Michael Nugent.
HIGH SCHOOL: Centerville (Ohio).
COLLEGE: Ohio State.
TRANSACTIONS/CAREER NOTES: Selected by New York Jets in second round (47th pick overall) of 2005 NFL draft.
HONORS: Lou Groza Award winner (2004). ... Named kicker on THE SPORTING NEWS college All-America first team (2004).

Year Team	G	KICKING						
		50+	Tot.	Pct.	Lg.	XPM	XPA	Pts.
2001—Ohio State	9	0-0	7-14	50.0	44	23	25	44
2002—Ohio State	14	1-1	25-28	89.3	51	45	46	120
2003—Ohio State	13	2-2	16-19	84.2	53	38	38	86
2004—Ohio State	12	5-6	24-27	88.9	55	30	30	102
College totals (4 years)	48	8-9	72-88	81.8	55	136	139	352

OMIYALE, FRANK   T   FALCONS

PERSONAL: Born November 23, 1982, in Nashville, Tenn. ... 6-4/310. ... Full name: Frank Tayo Omiyale.
HIGH SCHOOL: Whites Creek (Tenn.).
COLLEGE: Tennessee Tech.

TRANSACTIONS/CAREER NOTES: Selected by Atlanta Falcons in fifth round (163rd pick overall) of 2005 NFL draft.
PLAYING EXPERIENCE: Tennessee Tech, 2001-2004. ... Games played: 2001 (3), 2002 (12), 2003 (10), 2004 (10). Total: 35.

ORLOVSKY, DAN — QB — LIONS

PERSONAL: Born August 18, 1983, in Bridgeport, Conn. ... 6-5/230. ... Full name: Daniel John Orlovsky.
HIGH SCHOOL: Shelton (Shelton, Conn.).
COLLEGE: Connecticut.
TRANSACTIONS/CAREER NOTES: Selected by Detroit Lions in fifth round (145th pick overall) of 2005 NFL draft.

		PASSING								RUSHING				TOTALS	
Year Team	G	Att.	Cmp.	Pct.	Yds.	TD	Int.	Avg.	Rat.	Att.	Yds.	Avg.	TD	TD	Pts.
2001—Connecticut	10	269	128	47.6	1379	9	11	5.13	93.5	31	-117	-3.8	2	2	12
2002—Connecticut	12	366	221	60.4	2488	19	11	6.80	128.6	50	-86	-1.7	4	4	24
2003—Connecticut	12	475	279	58.7	3485	33	14	7.34	137.4	30	-41	-1.4	0	0	0
2004—Connecticut	12	457	288	63.0	3354	23	15	7.34	134.7	32	-41	-1.3	0	0	0
College totals (4 years)	46	1567	916	58.5	10706	84	51	6.83	127.0	143	-285	-2.0	6	6	36

ORTON, KYLE — QB — BEARS

PERSONAL: Born November 14, 1982... 6-4/233. ... Full name: Kyle Raymond Orton.
HIGH SCHOOL: Southeast Polk (Altoona, Iowa).
COLLEGE: Purdue.
TRANSACTIONS/CAREER NOTES: Selected by Chicago Bears in fourth round (106th pick overall) of 2005 NFL draft.

		PASSING								RUSHING				TOTALS	
Year Team	G	Att.	Cmp.	Pct.	Yds.	TD	Int.	Avg.	Rat.	Att.	Yds.	Avg.	TD	TD	Pts.
2001—Purdue	6	142	69	48.6	686	2	3	4.83	89.6	27	-63	-2.3	0	0	0
2002—Purdue	13	317	192	60.6	2257	13	9	7.12	128.2	43	47	1.1	0	0	0
2003—Purdue	13	414	251	60.6	2885	15	7	6.97	127.7	112	237	2.1	3	3	18
2004—Purdue	11	389	236	60.7	3090	31	5	7.94	151.1	80	112	1.4	3	3	18
College totals (4 years)	43	1262	748	59.3	8918	61	24	7.07	130.8	262	333	1.3	6	6	36

OWENS, CHAD — WR — JAGUARS

PERSONAL: Born April 3, 1982, in Honolulu, Hawaii. ... 5-7/181.
HIGH SCHOOL: Roosevelt (Honolulu, Hawaii).
COLLEGE: Hawaii.
TRANSACTIONS/CAREER NOTES: Selected by Jacksonville Jaguars in sixth round (185th pick overall) of 2005 NFL draft.

		RECEIVING				PUNT RETURNS				TOTALS	
Year Team	G	No.	Yds.	Avg.	TD	No.	Yds.	Avg.	TD	TD	Pts.
2001—Hawaii	10	5	57	11.4	1	18	216	12.0	1	5	30
2002—Hawaii	10	47	550	11.7	2	17	131	7.7	0	2	12
2003—Hawaii	11	85	1134	13.3	9	14	136	9.7	0	9	54
2004—Hawaii	13	102	1290	12.6	17	36	531	14.8	5	22	132
College totals (4 years)	44	239	3031	12.7	29	85	1014	11.9	6	38	228

PARQUET, JEREMY — T — CHIEFS

PERSONAL: Born April 11, 1982, in Norco, La. ... 6-7/323.
HIGH SCHOOL: Destrehan (Norco, La.).
COLLEGE: Southern Mississippi.
TRANSACTIONS/CAREER NOTES: Selected by Kansas City Chiefs in seventh round (238th pick overall) of 2005 NFL draft.
PLAYING EXPERIENCE: Southern Mississippi, 2001-2004. ... Games played: 2001 (6), 2002 (13), 2003 (13), 2004 (12). Total: 44.

PARRISH, ROSCOE — WR — BILLS

PERSONAL: Born July 16, 1982, in Miami, Fla. ... 5-10/170.
HIGH SCHOOL: Miami Senior (Miami, Fla.).
COLLEGE: Miami (Fla.).
TRANSACTIONS/CAREER NOTES: Selected after junior season by Buffalo Bills in second round (55th pick overall) of 2005 NFL draft.

		RUSHING				RECEIVING				PUNT RETURNS				TOTALS	
Year Team	G	Att.	Yds.	Avg.	TD	No.	Yds.	Avg.	TD	No.	Yds.	Avg.	TD	TD	Pts.
2002—Miami (Fla.)	13	4	69	17.3	0	19	340	17.9	2	27	392	14.5	0	3	18
2003—Miami (Fla.)	11	6	57	9.5	0	24	322	13.4	2	23	240	10.4	1	3	18
2004—Miami (Fla.)	12	9	60	6.7	0	43	693	16.1	8	20	324	16.2	2	10	60
College totals (3 years)	36	19	186	9.8	1	86	1355	15.8	12	70	956	13.7	3	16	96

PATTERSON, MIKE — DT — EAGLES

PERSONAL: Born September 1, 1983, in Sacramento, Calif. ... 5-11/291. ... Full name: Michael Patterson.
HIGH SCHOOL: Los Alamitos (Calif.).
COLLEGE: Southern California.
TRANSACTIONS/CAREER NOTES: Selected by Philadelphia Eagles in first round (31st pick overall) of 2005 NFL draft.
HONORS: Named defensive tackle on THE SPORTING NEWS college All-America first team (2004).

Year Team	G	SACKS
2001—Southern California	11	3.0
2002—Southern California	13	5.5
2003—Southern California	13	7.0
2004—Southern California	13	5.5
College totals (4 years)	50	21.0

PAYMAH, KARL — CB — BRONCOS

PERSONAL: Born November 29, 1982, in Culver City, Calif. ... 6-0/204.
HIGH SCHOOL: Culver City (Calif.).
COLLEGE: Washington State.
TRANSACTIONS/CAREER NOTES: Selected by Denver Broncos in third round (76th pick overall) of 2005 NFL draft.

				INTERCEPTIONS			
Year Team	G	Sks.	No.	Yds.	Avg.	TD	
2001—Washington State	12	0.0	0	0	0.0	0	
2002—Washington State	12	0.0	0	0	0.0	0	
2003—Washington State	13	0.0	1	0	0.0	0	
2004—Washington State	11	0.0	2	5	2.5	0	
College totals (4 years)	48	0.0	3	5	1.7	0	

PEARMAN, ALVIN — RB — JAGUARS

PERSONAL: Born August 10, 1982, in Princeton, N.J. ... 5-9/205. ... Full name: Francis Alvin Pearman II.
HIGH SCHOOL: Country Day (Charlotte, N.C.).
COLLEGE: Virginia.
TRANSACTIONS/CAREER NOTES: Selected by Jacksonville Jaguars in fourth round (127th pick overall) of 2005 NFL draft.

		RUSHING				RECEIVING				PUNT RETURNS				KICKOFF RETURNS				TOTALS	
Year Team	G	Att.	Yds.	Avg.	TD	No.	Yds.	Avg.	TD	No.	Yds.	Avg.	TD	No.	Yds.	Avg.	TD	TD	Pts.
2001—Virginia	12	88	371	4.2	1	25	283	11.3	3	27	247	9.1	0	13	266	20.5	0	4	24
2002—Virginia	9	83	343	4.1	4	21	193	9.2	0	1	1	1.0	0	0	0	0.0	0	4	24
2003—Virginia	13	134	643	4.8	4	63	518	8.2	4	5	38	7.6	0	6	128	21.3	0	8	48
2004—Virginia	12	195	1037	5.3	10	29	402	13.9	1	28	314	11.2	1	5	185	37.0	0	12	72
College totals (4 years)	46	500	2394	4.8	19	138	1396	10.1	8	61	600	9.8	1	24	579	24.1	0	28	168

PERKINS, ANTONIO — CB — BROWNS

PERSONAL: Born January 9, 1982, in Lawton, Okla. ... 5-11/190. ... Full name: Antonio D. Perkins.
HIGH SCHOOL: Lawton (Okla.).
COLLEGE: Oklahoma.
TRANSACTIONS/CAREER NOTES: Selected by Cleveland Browns in fourth round (103rd pick overall) of 2005 NFL draft.
HONORS: Named cornerback on THE SPORTING NEWS Freshman All-America second team (2001). ... Named kick returner on THE SPORTING NEWS college All-America first team (2003).

			INTERCEPTIONS				KICKOFF RETURNS				TOTALS	
Year Team	G	Sks.	No.	Yds.	Avg.	TD	No.	Yds.	Avg.	TD	TD	Pts.
2001—Oklahoma	9	0.0	3	26	8.7	0	0	0	0.0	0	0	0
2002—Oklahoma	14	0.0	4	111	27.8	1	43	643	15.0	3	4	24
2003—Oklahoma	14	0.0	3	13	4.3	0	53	642	12.1	4	4	24
2004—Oklahoma	11	1.0	1	0	0.0	0	17	156	9.2	1	1	6
College totals (4 years)	48	1.0	11	150	13.6	1	113	1441	12.8	8	9	54

PERRY, TAB — WR — BENGALS

PERSONAL: Born January 20, 1982, in Milpitas, Calif. ... 6-3/229. ... Full name: Tab Wilson Perry.
HIGH SCHOOL: Milpitas (Calif.).
COLLEGE: UCLA.
TRANSACTIONS/CAREER NOTES: Selected by Cincinnati Bengals in sixth round (190th pick overall) of 2005 NFL draft.

		RECEIVING				KICKOFF RETURNS				TOTALS	
Year Team	G	No.	Yds.	Avg.	TD	No.	Yds.	Avg.	TD	TD	Pts.
2000—UCLA	10	6	58	9.7	0	27	556	20.6	0	0	0
2001—UCLA	9	21	416	19.8	2	2	38	19.0	0	2	12
2002—UCLA	12	35	698	19.9	1	25	626	25.0	0	1	6
2004—UCLA	11	22	375	17.0	3	11	214	19.5	0	4	24
College totals (4 years)	42	84	1547	18.4	6	65	1434	22.1	0	7	42

PETITTI, ROB — T — COWBOYS

PERSONAL: Born May 21, 1982, in Clark, N.J. ... 6-6/347. ... Full name: Rob Christopher Petitti.
HIGH SCHOOL: Rumson-Fair Haven Regional (Rumson, NJ).
COLLEGE: Pittsburgh.
TRANSACTIONS/CAREER NOTES: Selected by Dallas Cowboys in sixth round (209th pick overall) of 2005 NFL draft.
PLAYING EXPERIENCE: Pittsburgh, 2001-2004. ... Games played: 2001 (11), 2002 (13), 2003 (13), 2004 (11). Total: 48.
HONORS: Named offensive lineman on THE SPORTING NEWS Freshman All-America second team (2001). ... Named offensive tackle on THE SPORTING NEWS college All-America second team (2004).

PETTWAY, KENNETH — DE — TEXANS

PERSONAL: Born November 13, 1982, in Gilmer, Texas. ... 6-3/236. ... Full name: Kenneth Aaron Pettway.
HIGH SCHOOL: Gilmer (Texas).
COLLEGE: Southern Arkansas, then Grambling State.
TRANSACTIONS/CAREER NOTES: Selected by Houston Texans in seventh round (227th pick overall) of 2005 NFL draft.

Year Team	G	SACKS
2000—Southern Arkansas	8	6.0
2001—Southern Arkansas	8	4.0
2003—Grambling State	12	5.0
2004—Grambling State	11	8.5
College totals (4 years)	39	23.5

POLLACK, DAVID　　　　　OLB　　　　　BENGALS

PERSONAL: Born June 19, 1982, in Snellville, Ga. ... 6-2/265. ... Full name: David M. Pollack.
HIGH SCHOOL: Shiloh (Snellville, Ga.).
COLLEGE: Georgia.
TRANSACTIONS/CAREER NOTES: Selected by Cincinnati Bengals in first round (17th pick overall) of 2005 NFL draft.
HONORS: Ted Hendricks Award winner (2003). ... Chuck Bednarik Award winner (2004). ... Vince Lombardi Award winner (2004). ... Named defensive tackle on THE SPORTING NEWS Freshman All-America fourth team (2001). ... Named defensive end on THE SPORTING NEWS college All-America first team (2002). ... Named defensive end on THE SPORTING NEWS college All-America second team (2004).

Year　Team	G	SACKS
2001—Georgia	10	2.0
2002—Georgia	14	14.0
2003—Georgia	14	7.5
2004—Georgia	12	12.5
College totals (4 years)	**50**	**36.0**

POOL, BRODNEY　　　　　S　　　　　BROWNS

PERSONAL: Born May 24, 1984, in Houston, Texas. ... 6-1/201.
HIGH SCHOOL: Westbury (Houston, Texas).
COLLEGE: Oklahoma.
TRANSACTIONS/CAREER NOTES: Selected after junior season by Cleveland Browns in second round (34th pick overall) of 2005 NFL draft.

Year　Team	G	Sks.	INTERCEPTIONS No.	Yds.	Avg.	TD
2002—Oklahoma	10	0.0	0	0	0.0	0
2003—Oklahoma	14	2.0	7	79	11.3	0
2004—Oklahoma	13	0.0	2	42	21.0	0
College totals (3 years)	**37**	**2.0**	**9**	**121**	**13.4**	**0**

POPPINGA, BRADY　　　　　LB　　　　　PACKERS

PERSONAL: Born September 21, 1979, in Evanston, Wyo. ... 6-3/259.
HIGH SCHOOL: Evanston (Wyo.).
COLLEGE: Brigham Young.
TRANSACTIONS/CAREER NOTES: Selected by Green Bay Packers in fourth round (125th pick overall) of 2005 NFL draft.

Year　Team	G	SACKS
2001—Brigham Young	12	0.0
2002—Brigham Young	12	8.0
2003—Brigham Young	12	5.0
2004—Brigham Young	11	6.0
College totals (4 years)	**47**	**19.0**

POUHA, SIONE　　　　　DT　　　　　JETS

PERSONAL: Born February 3, 1979, in Salt Lake City, Utah. ... 6-4/318. ... Full name: Sione Sonasi Pouha.
HIGH SCHOOL: East (Salt Lake City, Utah).
COLLEGE: Utah.
TRANSACTIONS/CAREER NOTES: Selected by New York Jets in third round (88th pick overall) of 2005 NFL draft.

Year　Team	G	Sks.	INTERCEPTIONS No.	Yds.	Avg.	TD
2001—Utah	7	1.0	0	0	0.0	0
2002—Utah	11	2.0	0	0	0.0	0
2003—Utah	12	2.0	0	0	0.0	0
2004—Utah	10	2.0	1	0	0.0	0
College totals (4 years)	**40**	**7.0**	**1**	**0**	**0.0**	**0**

PRESTON, DUKE　　　　　C　　　　　BILLS

PERSONAL: Born June 12, 1982, in San Diego, Calif. ... 6-5/311. ... Full name: Raymond Newton Preston III.
HIGH SCHOOL: Mt. Carmel (San Diego, Calif.).
COLLEGE: Illinois.
TRANSACTIONS/CAREER NOTES: Selected by Buffalo Bills in fourth round (122nd pick overall) of 2005 NFL draft.
PLAYING EXPERIENCE: Illinois, 2001-2004. ... Games played: 2001 (2), 2002 (12), 2003 (12), 2004 (11). Total: 37.

RATLIFF, JAY　　　　　DE　　　　　COWBOYS

PERSONAL: Born August 29, 1981, in St. Petersburg, Fla. ... 6-3/275. ... Full name: Jeremiah J. Ratliff.
HIGH SCHOOL: Lowndes County (Valdosta, Ga.).
COLLEGE: Auburn.
TRANSACTIONS/CAREER NOTES: Selected by Dallas Cowboys in seventh round (224th pick overall) of 2005 NFL draft.

Year　Team	G	SACKS
2001—Auburn	12	0.0
2002—Auburn	12	1.0
2003—Auburn	9	0.0
2004—Auburn	13	1.0
College totals (4 years)	**46**	**2.0**

RAYNER, DAVE　　　　　K　　　　　COLTS

PERSONAL: Born October 26, 1982, in Oxford, Mich. ... 6-2/209.
HIGH SCHOOL: Oxford (Mich.).

COLLEGE: Michigan State.
TRANSACTIONS/CAREER NOTES: Selected by Indianapolis Colts in sixth round (202nd pick overall) of 2005 NFL draft.

Year Team	G			PUNTING					KICKING			TOTALS		
		No.	Yds.	Avg.	Net avg.	In. 20	Blk.	XPM	XPA	Pts.	XPM	XPA	Pts.
2001—Michigan State	9	0	0	0.0	0.0	0	0	31	31	52	31	31	52
2002—Michigan State	12	0	0	0.0	0.0	0	0	34	35	64	34	35	64
2003—Michigan State	13	14	565	40.4	40.4	8	0	39	40	105	39	40	105
2004—Michigan State	12	5	172	34.4	34.4	1	0	39	39	105	39	39	105
College totals (4 years)	46	19	737	38.8	0.0	9	0	286	290	652	286	290	652

RAZZANO, RICK — FB — BUCCANEERS

PERSONAL: Born January 28, 1981... 5-11/241. ... Full name: Richard Anthony Razzano. ... Son of Rick Razzano, linebacker for Cincinnati Bengals (1980-84).
HIGH SCHOOL: Milford (Ohio).
COLLEGE: Mississippi.
TRANSACTIONS/CAREER NOTES: Selected by Tampa Bay Buccaneers in seventh round (221st pick overall) of 2005 NFL draft.

Year Team	G	RUSHING				RECEIVING				TOTALS	
		Att.	Yds.	Avg.	TD	No.	Yds.	Avg.	TD	TD	Pts.
2001—Mississippi	11	4	13	3.3	0	1	8	8.0	0	0	0
2002—Mississippi	13	26	60	2.3	1	23	180	7.8	0	1	6
2003—Mississippi	9	5	12	2.4	0	9	55	6.1	1	1	6
2004—Mississippi	8	15	58	3.9	0	8	69	8.6	0	0	0
College totals (4 years)	41	50	143	2.9	1	41	312	7.6	1	2	12

RHODES, KERRY — S — JETS

PERSONAL: Born August 2, 1982, in Birmingham, Ala. ... 6-3/208.
HIGH SCHOOL: Lanier (Bessemer, Ala.).
COLLEGE: Louisville.
TRANSACTIONS/CAREER NOTES: Selected by New York Jets in fourth round (123rd pick overall) of 2005 NFL draft.

Year Team	G	Sks.	INTERCEPTIONS			
			No.	Yds.	Avg.	TD
2001—Louisville	6	0.0	1	0	0.0	0
2002—Louisville	13	0.0	1	17	17.0	0
2003—Louisville	13	1.0	3	33	11.0	1
2004—Louisville	12	0.0	6	56	9.3	1
College totals (4 years)	44	1.0	11	106	9.6	2

RIDDLE, RYAN — DE — RAIDERS

PERSONAL: Born July 5, 1981, in Los Angeles, Calif. ... 6-2/253.
HIGH SCHOOL: Culver City (Calif.).
JUNIOR COLLEGE: El Camino (Torrance, Calif.).
COLLEGE: California.
TRANSACTIONS/CAREER NOTES: Selected by Oakland Raiders in sixth round (212th pick overall) of 2005 NFL draft.
HONORS: Named defensive end on THE SPORTING NEWS college All-America first team (2004).

Year Team	G	SACKS
2003—California	13	6.5
2004—California	12	14.5
College totals (2 years)	25	21.0

RIDGEWAY, DANTE — WR — RAMS

PERSONAL: Born April 18, 1984, in Chicago, Ill. ... 5-11/206. ... Full name: Dante DeAndre Ridgeway.
HIGH SCHOOL: Douglas MacArthur (Decatur, Ill.).
COLLEGE: Ball State.
TRANSACTIONS/CAREER NOTES: Selected after junior season by St. Louis Rams in sixth round (192nd pick overall) of 2005 NFL draft.

Year Team	G	RECEIVING				PUNT RETURNS				TOTALS	
		No.	Yds.	Avg.	TD	No.	Yds.	Avg.	TD	TD	Pts.
2002—Ball State	12	44	556	12.6	4	0	0	0.0	0	4	24
2003—Ball State	12	89	1075	12.1	10	3	16	5.3	0	11	66
2004—Ball State	11	105	1399	13.3	8	3	15	5.0	0	8	50
College totals (3 years)	35	238	3030	12.7	22	6	31	5.2	0	23	140

ROBERSON, CHRIS — CB — JAGUARS

PERSONAL: Born June 3, 1983, in Farmington Hills, Mich. ... 5-11/185. ... Full name: Christopher Robert Roberson.
HIGH SCHOOL: Harrison (Farmington Hills, Mich.).
COLLEGE: Eastern Michigan.
TRANSACTIONS/CAREER NOTES: Selected by Jacksonville Jaguars in seventh round (237th pick overall) of 2005 NFL draft.

Year Team	G	RUSHING				RECEIVING				PUNT RETURNS				KICKOFF RETURNS				TOTALS	
		Att.	Yds.	Avg.	TD	No.	Yds.	Avg.	TD	No.	Yds.	Avg.	TD	No.	Yds.	Avg.	TD	TD	Pts.
2001—Eastern Michigan	11	167	755	4.5	3	23	91	4.0	1	6	42	7.0	0	12	277	23.1	0	4	24
2002—Eastern Michigan	12	6	22	3.7	0	40	379	9.5	7	21	232	11.0	1	16	328	20.5	0	8	48
2003—Eastern Michigan	12	3	13	4.3	0	34	338	9.0	2	11	48	4.4	0	7	118	16.9	0	2	12
2004—Eastern Michigan	11	0	0	...	0	0	0	...	0	0	0	...	0	1	12	12.0	0	0	0
College totals (4 years)	46	176	790	4.5	3	97	808	8.3	10	38	322	8.5	1	36	735	20.4	0	14	84

ROBY, COURTNEY — WR — TITANS

PERSONAL: Born January 10, 1983... 6-0/189.
HIGH SCHOOL: North Central (Indianapolis, Ind.).
COLLEGE: Indiana.
TRANSACTIONS/CAREER NOTES: Selected by Tennessee Titans in third round (68th pick overall) of 2005 NFL draft.

		RUSHING				RECEIVING				KICKOFF RETURNS				TOTALS	
Year Team	G	Att.	Yds.	Avg.	TD	No.	Yds.	Avg.	TD	No.	Yds.	Avg.	TD	TD	Pts.
2001—Indiana	11	1	-8	-8.0	0	11	171	15.5	1	4	80	20.0	0	1	6
2002—Indiana	12	2	37	18.5	0	59	1039	17.6	4	11	227	20.6	0	4	24
2003—Indiana	11	7	43	6.1	0	45	504	11.2	0	10	193	19.3	0	0	0
2004—Indiana	11	21	135	6.4	2	55	810	14.7	7	3	67	22.3	0	9	54
College totals (4 years)	45	31	207	6.7	2	170	2524	14.8	12	28	567	20.3	0	14	84

RODGERS, AARON — QB — PACKERS

PERSONAL: Born December 2, 1983, in Chico, Calif. ... 6-2/223.
HIGH SCHOOL: Pleasant Valley (Chico, Calif.).
JUNIOR COLLEGE: Butte College (Oroville, Calif.).
COLLEGE: California.
TRANSACTIONS/CAREER NOTES: Selected after junior season by Green Bay Packers in first round (24th pick overall) of 2005 NFL draft.

		PASSING								RUSHING				TOTALS	
Year Team	G	Att.	Cmp.	Pct.	Yds.	TD	Int.	Avg.	Rat.	Att.	Yds.	Avg.	TD	TD	Pts.
2003—California	13	349	215	61.6	2903	19	5	8.32	146.6	86	210	2.4	5	5	30
2004—California	12	316	209	66.1	2566	24	8	8.12	154.3	74	126	1.7	3	3	18
College totals (2 years)	25	665	424	63.8	5469	43	13	8.22	150.3	160	336	2.1	8	8	48

ROGERS, CARLOS — CB — REDSKINS

PERSONAL: Born July 2, 1981... 6-0/196.
HIGH SCHOOL: Butler (Augusta, Ga.), then Hargrave Academy.
COLLEGE: Auburn.
TRANSACTIONS/CAREER NOTES: Selected by Washington Redskins in first round (ninth pick overall) of 2005 NFL draft.
HONORS: Jim Thorpe Award winner (2004). ... Named cornerback on THE SPORTING NEWS Freshman All-America second team (2001).

			INTERCEPTIONS			
Year Team	G	Sks.	No.	Yds.	Avg.	TD
2001—Auburn	12	0.0	0	0	0.0	0
2002—Auburn	13	0.0	4	48	12.0	0
2003—Auburn	12	0.0	1	0	0.0	0
2004—Auburn	13	1.0	2	53	26.5	1
College totals (4 years)	50	1.0	7	101	14.4	1

ROLLE, ANTREL — CB — CARDINALS

PERSONAL: Born December 16, 1982, in Homestead, Fla. ... 6-1/197.
HIGH SCHOOL: South Dade (Homestead, Fla.).
COLLEGE: Miami (Fla.).
TRANSACTIONS/CAREER NOTES: Selected by Arizona Cardinals in first round (eighth pick overall) of 2005 NFL draft.
HONORS: Named free safety on THE SPORTING NEWS college All-America first team (2004).

			INTERCEPTIONS			
Year Team	G	Sks.	No.	Yds.	Avg.	TD
2001—Miami (Fla.)	8	0.0	1	0	0.0	0
2002—Miami (Fla.)	13	2.0	1	22	22.0	0
2003—Miami (Fla.)	12	1.0	2	45	22.5	1
2004—Miami (Fla.)	12	1.5	1	6	6.0	0
College totals (4 years)	45	4.5	5	73	14.6	1

ROOS, MICHAEL — T — TITANS

PERSONAL: Born October 5, 1982, in Tallin, Estonia. ... 6-7/320.
HIGH SCHOOL: Mountain View (Vancouver, Wash.).
COLLEGE: Eastern Washington.
TRANSACTIONS/CAREER NOTES: Selected by Tennessee Titans in the second round (41st overall) of 2005 NFL draft.
PLAYING EXPERIENCE: Eastern Washington, 2001-2004. ... Games played: 2001 (8), 2002 (11), 2003 (11), 2004 (13). Total: 43.

ROTH, MATT — DE — DOLPHINS

PERSONAL: Born October 14, 1982, in Villa Park, Ill. ... 6-4/278. ... Full name: Matthew Roth.
HIGH SCHOOL: Willowbrook (Villa Park, Ill.).
COLLEGE: Iowa.
TRANSACTIONS/CAREER NOTES: Selected by Miami Dolphins in second round (46th pick overall) of 2005 NFL draft.
HONORS: Named defensive end on THE SPORTING NEWS college All-America second team (2004).

Year Team	G	SACKS
2001—Iowa	11	0.0
2002—Iowa	13	10.0
2003—Iowa	13	12.0
2004—Iowa	12	8.0
College totals (4 years)	49	30.0

ROUTT, STANFORD   CB   RAIDERS

PERSONAL: Born July 23, 1983, in Austin, Texas. ... 6-1/190.
HIGH SCHOOL: Connally (Austin, Texas).
COLLEGE: Houston.
TRANSACTIONS/CAREER NOTES: Selected by Oakland Raiders in second round (38th pick overall) of 2005 NFL draft.

			INTERCEPTIONS			
Year Team	G	Sks.	No.	Yds.	Avg.	TD
2001—Houston	11	0.0	1	15	15.0	0
2002—Houston	11	0.0	0	0	0.0	0
2003—Houston	13	0.0	4	44	11.0	0
2004—Houston	11	0.0	2	37	18.5	0
College totals (4 years)	46	0.0	7	96	13.7	0

RUSSELL, J.R.   WR   BUCCANEERS

PERSONAL: Born December 5, 1981... 6-3/206. ... Full name: Jeremiah Russell.
HIGH SCHOOL: Gaither (Tampa, Fla.).
COLLEGE: Louisville.
TRANSACTIONS/CAREER NOTES: Selected by Tampa Bay Buccaneers in seventh round (253rd pick overall) of 2005 NFL draft.

		RECEIVING			
Year Team	G	No.	Yds.	Avg.	TD
2001—Louisville	12	14	151	10.8	2
2002—Louisville	13	24	287	12.0	2
2003—Louisville	13	75	1213	16.2	8
2004—Louisville	12	73	968	13.3	7
College totals (4 years)	50	186	2619	14.1	19

RUUD, BARRETT   LB   BUCCANEERS

PERSONAL: Born May 20, 1983, in Lincoln, Neb. ... 6-3/241. ... Full name: Barrett James Ruud.
HIGH SCHOOL: Southeast (Lincoln, Neb.).
COLLEGE: Nebraska.
TRANSACTIONS/CAREER NOTES: Selected by Tampa Bay Buccaneers in second round (38th overall) of 2005 NFL draft.
HONORS: Named linebacker on THE SPORTING NEWS Freshman All-America second team (2001).

			INTERCEPTIONS			
Year Team	G	Sks.	No.	Yds.	Avg.	TD
2001—Nebraska	12	0.5	0	0	0.0	0
2002—Nebraska	14	2.0	0	0	0.0	0
2003—Nebraska	13	2.5	1	27	27.0	1
2004—Nebraska	11	3.0	0	0	0.0	0
College totals (4 years)	50	8.0	1	27	27.0	1

SANDERS, JAMES   SS   PATRIOTS

PERSONAL: Born November 11, 1983... 5-11/214.
HIGH SCHOOL: Monache (Porterville, Calif.).
COLLEGE: Fresno State.
TRANSACTIONS/CAREER NOTES: Selected after junior season by New England Patriots in fourth round (133rd pick overall) of 2005 NFL draft.

			INTERCEPTIONS			
Year Team	G	Sks.	No.	Yds.	Avg.	TD
2002—Fresno State	14	3.0	2	23	11.5	0
2003—Fresno State	13	2.0	2	2	1.0	0
2004—Fresno State	12	2.0	3	60	20.0	1
College totals (3 years)	39	7.0	7	85	12.1	1

SCAIFE, BO   TE   TITANS

PERSONAL: Born January 6, 1981, in Denver, Colo. ... 6-3/249. ... Full name: Oliver Edward Scaife III.
HIGH SCHOOL: Mullen Prep (Denver, Colo.).
COLLEGE: Texas.
TRANSACTIONS/CAREER NOTES: Selected by Tennessee Titans in sixth round (179th pick overall) of 2005 NFL draft.

		RECEIVING			
Year Team	G	No.	Yds.	Avg.	TD
1999—Texas	7	3	48	16.0	0
2001—Texas	12	30	396	13.2	1
2003—Texas	13	16	205	12.8	2
2004—Texas	12	26	348	13.4	2
College totals (4 years)	44	75	997	13.3	5

SENSABAUGH, GERALD   S   JAGUARS

PERSONAL: Born June 13, 1983, in Kingsport, Tenn. ... 6-1/211.
HIGH SCHOOL: Dobyns-Bennett (Kingsport, Tenn.).
COLLEGE: East Tennessee State, then North Carolina.
TRANSACTIONS/CAREER NOTES: Selected by Jacksonville Jaguars in fifth round (157th pick overall) of 2005 NFL draft.

			INTERCEPTIONS			
Year Team	G	Sks.	No.	Yds.	Avg.	TD
2001—East Tennessee State	11	3.0	2	1	0.5	0
2002—East Tennessee State	11	0.0	1	32	32.0	1

Year	Team	G	Sks.	No.	Yds.	Avg.	TD
				INTERCEPTIONS			
2003—East Tennessee State		12	2.0	0	0	0.0	0
2004—North Carolina		12	3.0	1	0	0.0	0
College totals (4 years)		46	8.0	4	33	8.3	1

SEWARD, ADAM — LB — PANTHERS

PERSONAL: Born June 15, 1982, in Champaign, Ill. ... 6-2/248. ... Full name: Adam Hartford Seward.
HIGH SCHOOL: Bonanza (Las Vegas, Nevada).
COLLEGE: Nevada-Las Vegas.
TRANSACTIONS/CAREER NOTES: Selected by Carolina Panthers in fifth round (149th pick overall) of 2005 NFL draft.

Year	Team	G	Sks.	No.	Yds.	Avg.	TD
				INTERCEPTIONS			
2001—UNLV		11	3.0	0	0	0.0	0
2002—UNLV		12	1.5	0	0	0.0	0
2003—UNLV		12	0.5	2	22	11.0	0
2004—UNLV		11	1.0	0	0	0.0	0
College totals (4 years)		46	6.0	2	22	11.0	0

SHELTON, ERIC — RB — PANTHERS

PERSONAL: Born June 23, 1983... 6-2/245.
HIGH SCHOOL: Bryan Station (Lexington, Ky.).
COLLEGE: Florida State, then Louisville.
TRANSACTIONS/CAREER NOTES: Selected after junior season by Carolina Panthers in second round (54th pick overall) of 2005 NFL draft.

Year	Team	G	Att.	Yds.	Avg.	TD	No.	Yds.	Avg.	TD	TD	Pts.
			RUSHING				RECEIVING				TOTALS	
2001—Florida State		11	29	130	4.5	0	0	0	0.0	0	0	0
2003—Louisville		10	166	790	4.8	10	1	19	19.0	0	10	60
2004—Louisville		12	146	938	6.4	20	6	35	5.8	0	20	120
College totals (3 years)		33	341	1858	5.4	30	7	54	7.7	0	30	180

SHROPSHIRE, DARRELL — DT — FALCONS

PERSONAL: Born March 18, 1983, in Kershaw, S.C. ... 6-2/301.
HIGH SCHOOL: Andrew Jackson (Kershaw, S.C.).
JUNIOR COLLEGE: Coffeyville (Kan.).
COLLEGE: South Carolina.
TRANSACTIONS/CAREER NOTES: Selected by Atlanta Falcons in seventh round (241st pick overall) of 2005 NFL draft.

Year	Team	G	SACKS
2003—South Carolina		12	0.0
2004—South Carolina		11	2.0
College totals (2 years)		23	2.0

SIMS, WES — G — CHARGERS

PERSONAL: Born April 8, 1981... 6-3/317. ... Full name: Wesley O. Sims.
HIGH SCHOOL: Weatherford (Okla.).
COLLEGE: Oklahoma.
TRANSACTIONS/CAREER NOTES: Selected by San Diego Chargers in sixth round (177th pick overall) of 2005 NFL draft.
PLAYING EXPERIENCE: Oklahoma, 2001-2004. ... Games played: 2001 (7), 2002 (14), 2003 (14), 2004 (13). Total: 48.
HONORS: Named offensive lineman on THE SPORTING NEWS Freshman All-America first team (2001).

SMITH, ALEX — TE — BUCCANEERS

PERSONAL: Born May 22, 1982... 6-4/258. ... Son of Ed Smith, defensive end with Denver Broncos (1973-74).
HIGH SCHOOL: Mullen (Denver, Colo.).
COLLEGE: Stanford.
TRANSACTIONS/CAREER NOTES: Selected by Tampa Bay Buccaneers in third round (71st pick overall) of 2005 NFL draft.

Year	Team	G	No.	Yds.	Avg.	TD
			RECEIVING			
2001—Stanford		11	1	20	20.0	0
2002—Stanford		11	30	380	12.7	2
2003—Stanford		11	24	185	7.7	3
2004—Stanford		11	52	706	13.6	3
College totals (4 years)		44	107	1291	12.1	8

SMITH, ALEX — QB — 49ERS

PERSONAL: Born May 7, 1984, in Seattle, Wash. ... 6-4/217. ... Full name: Alexander D. Smith.
HIGH SCHOOL: Helix (Calif.).
COLLEGE: Utah.
TRANSACTIONS/CAREER NOTES: Selected after junior season by San Francisco 49ers in first round (first pick overall) of 2005 NFL draft.

Year	Team	G	Att.	Cmp.	Pct.	Yds.	TD	Int.	Avg.	Rat.	Att.	Yds.	Avg.	TD	TD	Pts.
			PASSING								RUSHING				TOTALS	
2002—Utah		2	4	2	50.0	4	0	1	1.00	8.4	2	-11	-5.5	0	0	0
2003—Utah		11	266	173	65.0	2247	15	3	8.45	152.3	149	452	3.0	5	5	30
2004—Utah		12	317	214	67.5	2952	32	4	9.31	176.5	135	631	4.7	10	10	60
College totals (3 years)		25	587	389	66.3	5203	47	8	8.86	164.4	286	1072	3.7	15	15	90

SMITH, MIKE — LB — RAVENS

PERSONAL: Born September 2, 1981, in Lubbock, Texas. ... 6-1/240.
HIGH SCHOOL: Coronado (Calif.).
COLLEGE: Texas Tech.
TRANSACTIONS/CAREER NOTES: Selected by Baltimore Ravens in seventh round (234th pick overall) of 2005 NFL draft.

			INTERCEPTIONS			
Year Team	G	Sks.	No.	Yds.	Avg.	TD
2001—Texas Tech	11	2.0	0	0	0.0	0
2002—Texas Tech	14	1.0	2	9	4.5	0
2003—Texas Tech	12	3.0	0	0	0.0	0
2004—Texas Tech	12	1.0	0	0	0.0	0
College totals (4 years)	49	7.0	2	9	4.5	0

SNYDER, ADAM — G — 49ERS

PERSONAL: Born January 30, 1982, in Fullerton, Calif. ... 6-5/316. ... Full name: Adam Richard Snyder.
HIGH SCHOOL: La Serna (Whittier, Calif.).
COLLEGE: Oregon.
TRANSACTIONS/CAREER NOTES: Selected by San Francisco 49ers in third round (94th pick overall) of 2005 NFL draft.
PLAYING EXPERIENCE: Oregon, 2001-2004. ... Games played: 2001 (10), 2002 (13), 2003 (13), 2004 (11). Total: 47.

SPEARS, MARCUS — DE — COWBOYS

PERSONAL: Born March 8, 1983, in Baton Rouge, La. ... 6-4/307. ... Full name: Marcus Raishon Spears.
HIGH SCHOOL: Southern Lab (Baton Rouge, La.).
COLLEGE: Louisiana State.
TRANSACTIONS/CAREER NOTES: Selected by Dallas Cowboys in first round (20th pick overall) of 2005 NFL draft.

			INTERCEPTIONS			
Year Team	G	Sks.	No.	Yds.	Avg.	TD
2001—Louisiana State	11	1.0	0	0	0.0	0
2002—Louisiana State	12	3.0	2	29	14.5	0
2003—Louisiana State	14	6.0	1	20	20.0	1
2004—Louisiana State	12	9.0	1	35	35.0	1
College totals (4 years)	49	19.0	4	84	21.0	2

SPEEGLE, NICK — OLB — BROWNS

PERSONAL: Born November 29, 1981, in Albuquerque, N.M. ... 6-6/241. ... Full name: Nicholas David Speegle.
HIGH SCHOOL: La Cueva (Albuquerque, N.M.).
COLLEGE: New Mexico.
TRANSACTIONS/CAREER NOTES: Selected by Cleveland Browns in sixth round (176th pick overall) of 2005 NFL draft.

			INTERCEPTIONS			
Year Team	G	Sks.	No.	Yds.	Avg.	TD
2001—New Mexico	11	2.0	0	0	0.0	0
2002—New Mexico	14	5.0	1	2	2.0	0
2003—New Mexico	13	2.5	1	23	23.0	0
2004—New Mexico	12	1.5	0	0	0.0	0
College totals (4 years)	50	11.0	2	25	12.5	0

SPENCER, CHRIS — C — SEAHAWKS

PERSONAL: Born March 28, 1982... 6-3/308. ... Full name: Christopher Clarks Spencer.
HIGH SCHOOL: Madison Central (Miss.).
COLLEGE: Mississippi.
TRANSACTIONS/CAREER NOTES: Selected after junior season by Seattle Seahawks in first round (26th pick overall) of 2005 NFL draft.
PLAYING EXPERIENCE: Mississippi, 2002-2004. ... Games played: 2002 (13), 2003 (13), 2004 (11). Total: 37.

SPROLES, DARREN — RB — CHARGERS

PERSONAL: Born June 20, 1983, in Waterloo, Iowa. ... 5-6/187. ... Full name: Darren Lee Sproles.
HIGH SCHOOL: Olathe North (Kan.).
COLLEGE: Kansas State.
TRANSACTIONS/CAREER NOTES: Selected by San Diego Chargers in fourth round (130th pick overall) of 2005 NFL draft.
HONORS: Named running back on THE SPORTING NEWS college All-America second team (2003).

		RUSHING				RECEIVING				PUNT RETURNS				KICKOFF RETURNS				TOTALS	
Year Team	G	Att.	Yds.	Avg.	TD	No.	Yds.	Avg.	TD	No.	Yds.	Avg.	TD	No.	Yds.	Avg.	TD	TD	Pts.
2001—Kansas State	6	28	210	7.5	1	0	0	0.0	0	0	0	0.0	0	0	0	0.0	0	1	6
2002—Kansas State	13	237	1465	6.2	17	9	99	11.0	0	15	154	10.3	0	4	82	20.5	0	17	104
2003—Kansas State	15	306	1986	6.5	16	25	287	11.5	2	19	190	10.0	1	10	272	27.2	0	19	114
2004—Kansas State	11	244	1318	5.4	11	32	223	7.0	0	6	34	5.7	0	21	492	23.4	0	11	68
College totals (4 years)	45	815	4979	6.1	45	66	609	9.2	2	40	378	9.5	1	35	846	24.2	0	48	292

STARKS, SCOTT — CB — JAGUARS

PERSONAL: Born June 27, 1983, in St. Louis (Mo.). ... 5-9/172.
HIGH SCHOOL: Hazelwood East (St. Louis, Mo.).
COLLEGE: Wisconsin.
TRANSACTIONS/CAREER NOTES: Selected by Jacksonville Jaguars in third round (87th pick overall) of 2005 NFL draft.

Year Team	G	Sks.	INTERCEPTIONS No.	Yds.	Avg.	TD	KICKOFF RETURNS No.	Yds.	Avg.	TD	TOTALS TD	Pts.
2001—Wisconsin	12	0.0	3	17	5.7	0	0	0	0.0	0	0	0
2002—Wisconsin	14	0.0	2	46	23.0	0	0	0	0.0	0	0	0
2003—Wisconsin	13	0.0	1	26	26.0	0	0	0	0.0	0	0	0
2004—Wisconsin	12	1.0	1	16	16.0	0	6	119	19.8	0	1	6
College totals (4 years)	51	1.0	7	105	15.0	0	6	119	19.8	0	1	6

STEWART, DAVID — T — TITANS

PERSONAL: Born August 28, 1982, in Moulton, Ala. ... 6-7/318. ... Full name: James David Stewart.
HIGH SCHOOL: Lawrence County (Moulton, Ala.).
COLLEGE: Mississippi State.
TRANSACTIONS/CAREER NOTES: Selected by Tennessee Titans in fourth round (113th pick overall) of 2005 NFL draft.
PLAYING EXPERIENCE: Mississippi State, 2001-2004. ... Games played: 2001 (6), 2002 (12), 2003 (12), 2004 (11). Total: 41.

STOKES, ANDY — TE — PATRIOTS

PERSONAL: Born June 2, 1981, in St. George, Utah. ... 6-5/245. ... Full name: Thomas Andrew Stokes.
HIGH SCHOOL: Moapa Valley (Utah).
JUNIOR COLLEGE: Snow (Ephraim, Utah).
COLLEGE: William Penn.
TRANSACTIONS/CAREER NOTES: Selected by New England Patriots in seventh round (255th pick overall) of 2005 NFL draft.

Year Team	G	RECEIVING No.	Yds.	Avg.	TD
2002—William Penn	10	32	417	13.0	2
2003—William Penn	10	30	408	13.6	3
2004—William Penn	11	42	753	17.9	5
College totals (3 years)	31	104	1578	15.2	10

SVITEK, WILL — T — CHIEFS

PERSONAL: Born January 8, 1982, in Prague, Czech Republic. ... 6-6/300.
HIGH SCHOOL: Newbury Park (Calif.).
COLLEGE: Stanford.
TRANSACTIONS/CAREER NOTES: Selected by Kansas City Chiefs in sixth round (187th pick overall) of 2005 NFL draft.
PLAYING EXPERIENCE: Stanford, 2001-2004. ... Games played: 2001 (8), 2002 (10), 2003 (11), 2004 (9). Total: 38.

SWANCUTT, BILL — DE — LIONS

PERSONAL: Born September 4, 1982, in Salem, Ore. ... 6-4/270.
HIGH SCHOOL: Sprague (Salem, Ore.).
COLLEGE: Oregon State.
TRANSACTIONS/CAREER NOTES: Selected by Detroit Lions in sixth round (184th pick overall) of 2005 NFL draft.

Year Team	G	Sks.	INTERCEPTIONS No.	Yds.	Avg.	TD
2001—Oregon State	11	3.0	0	0	0.0	0
2002—Oregon State	13	11.5	0	0	0.0	0
2003—Oregon State	13	11.0	0	0	0.0	0
2004—Oregon State	12	11.5	1	0	0.0	0
College totals (4 years)	49	37.0	1	0	0.0	0

TATUPU, LOFA — LB — SEAHAWKS

PERSONAL: Born November 15, 1982, in Wrentham, Mass. ... 6-0/240. ... Son of Mosi Tatupu, running back with New England Patriots and Los Angeles Rams (1978-91).
HIGH SCHOOL: King Philip Regional (Wrentham, Mass.).
COLLEGE: Maine, then Southern California.
TRANSACTIONS/CAREER NOTES: Selected after junior season by Seattle Seahawks in second round (45th pick overall) of 2005 NFL draft.

Year Team	G	Sks.	INTERCEPTIONS No.	Yds.	Avg.	TD
2001—Maine	12	3.5	3	50	16.7	0
2003—Southern California	12	3.0	4	126	31.5	1
2004—Southern California	13	6.0	3	38	12.7	0
College totals (3 years)	37	12.5	10	214	21.4	1

TERRELL, CLAUDE — G — RAMS

PERSONAL: Born April 20, 1982, in Texas City, Texas. ... 6-2/343. ... Full name: Claude Edward Terrell.
HIGH SCHOOL: La Marque (Texas).
COLLEGE: New Mexico.
TRANSACTIONS/CAREER NOTES: Selected by St. Louis Rams in fourth round (134th pick overall) of 2005 NFL draft.
PLAYING EXPERIENCE: New Mexico, 2001-2004. ... Games played: 2001 (11), 2002 (14), 2003 (13), 2004 (12). Total: 50.

TERRY, ADAM — T — RAVENS

PERSONAL: Born September 1, 1982, in Glen Falls, N.Y. ... 6-8/330.
HIGH SCHOOL: Queensbury (N.Y.).
COLLEGE: Syracuse.
TRANSACTIONS/CAREER NOTES: Selected by Baltimore Ravens in second round (64th pick overall) of 2005 NFL draft.

2005 DRAFT PICKS

PLAYING EXPERIENCE: Syracuse, 2001-2004. ... Games played: 2001 (4), 2002 (11), 2003 (12), 2004 (12). Total: 39.

THOMAS, PAT   LB   JAGUARS

PERSONAL: Born January 26, 1983, in Miami, Fla. ... 6-1/237.
HIGH SCHOOL: Killian (Miami, Fla.).
COLLEGE: North Carolina State.
TRANSACTIONS/CAREER NOTES: Selected by Jacksonville Jaguars in sixth round (194th pick overall) of 2005 NFL draft.

Year Team	G	Sks.	INTERCEPTIONS No.	Yds.	Avg.	TD
2001—North Carolina State	11	0.0	0	0	0.0	0
2002—North Carolina State	14	3.0	0	0	0.0	0
2003—North Carolina State	13	8.0	0	0	0.0	0
2004—North Carolina State	11	4.5	0	0	0.0	0
College totals (4 years)	49	15.5	0	0	0.0	0

THORPE, CRAPHONSO   WR   CHIEFS

PERSONAL: Born June 27, 1983, in Tallahassee, Fla. ... 6-1/187.
HIGH SCHOOL: Lincoln (Tallahassee, Fla.).
COLLEGE: Florida State.
TRANSACTIONS/CAREER NOTES: Selected by Kansas City Chiefs in fourth round (116th pick overall) of 2005 NFL draft.

Year Team	G	RECEIVING No.	Yds.	Avg.	TD
2001—Florida State	11	15	286	19.1	1
2002—Florida State	14	17	377	22.2	4
2003—Florida State	11	51	994	19.5	11
2004—Florida State	11	40	496	12.4	2
College totals (4 years)	47	123	2153	17.5	18

THURMAN, ODELL   LB   BENGALS

PERSONAL: Born July 9, 1983, in Monticello, Ga. ... 6-0/233. ... Full name: Odell Lamar Thurman.
HIGH SCHOOL: Monticello (Ga.).
COLLEGE: Georgia.
TRANSACTIONS/CAREER NOTES: Selected after junior season by Cincinnati Bengals in second round (48th pick overall) of 2005 NFL draft.

Year Team	G	Sks.	INTERCEPTIONS No.	Yds.	Avg.	TD
2003—Georgia	13	6.5	2	125	62.5	1
2004—Georgia	9	3.0	0	0	0.0	0
College totals (2 years)	22	9.5	2	125	62.5	1

TUCK, JUSTIN   DE   GIANTS

PERSONAL: Born March 29, 1983, in Kellyton, Ala. ... 6-5/275. ... Full name: Justin Lee Tuck.
HIGH SCHOOL: Central Coosa County (Kellyton, Ala.).
COLLEGE: Notre Dame.
TRANSACTIONS/CAREER NOTES: Selected after junior season by New York Giants in third round (74th pick overall) of 2005 NFL draft.

Year Team	G	SACKS
2002—Notre Dame	13	5.0
2003—Notre Dame	12	13.5
2004—Notre Dame	11	6.0
College totals (3 years)	36	24.5

UNDERWOOD, MARVIEL   S   PACKERS

PERSONAL: Born February 17, 1982, in Oakland, Calif. ... 5-10/197.
HIGH SCHOOL: San Leandro (Calif.).
COLLEGE: San Diego State.
TRANSACTIONS/CAREER NOTES: Selected by Green Bay Packers in fourth round (115th pick overall) of 2005 NFL draft.

Year Team	G	Sks.	INTERCEPTIONS No.	Yds.	Avg.	TD
2001—San Diego State	11	0.0	0	0	0.0	0
2002—San Diego State	12	0.0	3	10	3.3	0
2003—San Diego State	12	1.0	2	106	53.0	1
2004—San Diego State	11	0.0	2	21	10.5	0
College totals (4 years)	46	1.0	7	137	19.6	1

VERDON, JIMMY   DE   SAINTS

PERSONAL: Born November 4, 1981, in Pomona, Calif. ... 6-3/280. ... Full name: Jimmy Lee Verdon.
HIGH SCHOOL: Pomona (Calif.).
COLLEGE: Arizona State.
TRANSACTIONS/CAREER NOTES: Selected by New Orleans Saints in seventh round (232nd pick overall) of 2005 NFL draft.

Year Team	G	SACKS
2001—Arizona State	11	1.0
2002—Arizona State	14	4.0
2003—Arizona State	12	3.0
2004—Arizona State	12	2.0
College totals (4 years)	49	10.0

VICKERSON, KEVIN　　　　　DT　　　　　DOLPHINS

PERSONAL: Born January 8, 1983, in Detroit, Mich. ... 6-5/308.
HIGH SCHOOL: Martin Luther King (Detroit, Mich.).
COLLEGE: Michigan State.
TRANSACTIONS/CAREER NOTES: Selected by Miami Dolphins in seventh round (216th pick overall) of 2005 NFL draft.

			INTERCEPTIONS			
Year　Team	G	Sks.	No.	Yds.	Avg.	TD
2001—Michigan State	8	1.0	0	0	0.0	0
2002—Michigan State	12	1.0	0	0	0.0	0
2003—Michigan State	13	2.0	0	0	0.0	0
2004—Michigan State	12	4.5	0	0	0.0	0
College totals (4 years)	45	8.5	0	0	0.0	0

WALLACE, RIAN　　　　　LB　　　　　STEELERS

PERSONAL: Born May 24, 1982, in Pottstown, Penn. ... 6-2/241.
HIGH SCHOOL: Pottstown (Penn.).
COLLEGE: Temple.
TRANSACTIONS/CAREER NOTES: Selected after junior season by Pittsburgh Steelers in fifth round (166th pick overall) of 2005 NFL draft. ... Signed by Steelers (May 26, 2005).

			INTERCEPTIONS			
Year　Team	G	Sks.	No.	Yds.	Avg.	TD
2002—Temple	12	1.0	1	-4	-4.0	0
2003—Temple	12	1.0	0	0	0.0	0
2004—Temple	10	0.0	1	0	0.0	0
College totals (3 years)	34	2.0	2	-4	-2.0	0

WALTER, ANDREW　　　　　QB　　　　　RAIDERS

PERSONAL: Born May 11, 1982, in Phoenix, Ariz. ... 6-6/233. ... Full name: Andrew Scott Walter.
HIGH SCHOOL: Grand Junction (Colo.).
COLLEGE: Arizona State.
TRANSACTIONS/CAREER NOTES: Selected by Oakland Raiders in third round (69th pick overall) of 2005 NFL draft.

		PASSING								RUSHING				TOTALS	
Year　Team	G	Att.	Cmp.	Pct.	Yds.	TD	Int.	Avg.	Rat.	Att.	Yds.	Avg.	TD	TD	Pts.
2001—Arizona State	11	86	38	44.2	546	3	2	6.35	104.4	28	-22	-0.8	0	0	0
2002—Arizona State	14	483	274	56.7	3877	28	15	8.03	137.1	56	-216	-3.9	0	0	0
2003—Arizona State	12	421	221	52.5	3044	24	10	7.23	127.3	33	-125	-3.8	0	0	0
2004—Arizona State	11	426	244	57.3	3150	30	9	7.39	138.4	58	-112	-1.9	0	0	0
College totals (4 years)	48	1416	777	54.9	10617	85	36	7.50	132.6	175	-475	-2.7	0	0	0

WARD, ADRIAN　　　　　CB　　　　　VIKINGS

PERSONAL: Born July 1, 1982, in Berkeley, Calif. ... 5-11/175. ... Full name: Adrian Michael Ward.
HIGH SCHOOL: Hayward (Oakland, Calif.).
JUNIOR COLLEGE: Chabot (Hayward, Calif.).
COLLEGE: Texas-El Paso.
TRANSACTIONS/CAREER NOTES: Selected by Minnesota Vikings in seventh round (219th pick overall) of 2005 NFL draft.

Year　Team	G	SACKS
2003—Texas-El Paso	13	0.0
2004—Texas-El Paso	12	0.0
College totals (2 years)	25	0.0

WARE, DEMARCUS　　　　　DE/OLB　　　　　COWBOYS

PERSONAL: Born July 31, 1982, in Auburn, Ala. ... 6-4/251.
HIGH SCHOOL: Auburn (Ala.).
COLLEGE: Troy.
TRANSACTIONS/CAREER NOTES: Selected by Dallas Cowboys in first round (11th pick overall) of 2005 NFL draft.

Year　Team	G	SACKS
2001—Troy	8	2.0
2002—Troy	12	9.0
2003—Troy	12	6.0
2004—Troy	12	10.5
College totals (4 years)	44	27.5

WARREN, PARIS　　　　　WR　　　　　BUCCANEERS

PERSONAL: Born September 6, 1982... 6-3/213. ... Full name: Paris Jazz Warren.
HIGH SCHOOL: Grant (Sacramento, Calif.).
COLLEGE: Oregon, then Utah.
TRANSACTIONS/CAREER NOTES: Selected by Tampa Bay Buccaneers in seventh round (225th pick overall) of 2005 NFL draft.

		RUSHING				RECEIVING				PUNT RETURNS				TOTALS	
Year　Team	G	Att.	Yds.	Avg.	TD	No.	Yds.	Avg.	TD	No.	Yds.	Avg.	TD	TD	Pts.
2001—Oregon	10	0	0	0.0	0	0	0	0.0	0	0	0	0.0	0	0	0
2003—Utah	11	20	124	6.2	1	76	809	10.6	4	23	177	7.7	0	5	30
2004—Utah	12	28	157	5.6	2	80	1076	13.5	12	5	12	2.4	0	14	84
College totals (3 years)	33	48	281	5.9	3	156	1885	12.1	16	28	189	6.8	0	19	114

WASHINGTON, FABIAN — CB — RAIDERS

PERSONAL: Born June 9, 1983, in Bradenton, Fla. ... 5-11/188.
HIGH SCHOOL: Bayshore (Bradenton, Fla.).
COLLEGE: Nebraska.
TRANSACTIONS/CAREER NOTES: Selected after junior season by Oakland Raiders in first round (23rd pick overall) of 2005 NFL draft.

Year Team	G	Sks.	INTERCEPTIONS No.	Yds.	Avg.	TD
2002—Nebraska	13	0.0	4	35	8.8	1
2003—Nebraska	13	0.0	4	14	3.5	0
2004—Nebraska	11	0.0	3	23	7.7	0
College totals (3 years)	37	0.0	11	72	6.5	1

WEBSTER, COREY — CB — GIANTS

PERSONAL: Born March 2, 1982, in Vacherie, La. ... 6-0/199. ... Full name: Corey Jonas Webster.
HIGH SCHOOL: St. James (Vacherie, La.).
COLLEGE: Louisiana State.
TRANSACTIONS/CAREER NOTES: Selected by New York Giants in second round (43rd pick overall) of 2005 NFL draft.
HONORS: Named cornerback on THE SPORTING NEWS college All-America first team (2004).

Year Team	G	Sks.	INTERCEPTIONS No.	Yds.	Avg.	TD
2001—Louisiana State	12	0.0	0	0	0.0	0
2002—Louisiana State	13	0.0	7	75	10.7	1
2003—Louisiana State	14	1.0	7	60	8.6	0
2004—Louisiana State	11	0.0	2	46	23.0	0
College totals (4 years)	50	1.0	16	181	11.3	1

WELSH, JONATHAN — DE — COLTS

PERSONAL: Born June 9, 1982, in Houston, Texas. ... 6-3/244.
HIGH SCHOOL: B.T. Washington (Houston, Texas).
COLLEGE: Wisconsin.
TRANSACTIONS/CAREER NOTES: Selected by Indianapolis Colts in fifth round (148th pick overall) of 2005 NFL draft.

Year Team	G	SACKS
2001—Wisconsin	9	2.0
2002—Wisconsin	14	1.0
2003—Wisconsin	13	8.0
2004—Wisconsin	12	2.0
College totals (4 years)	48	13.0

WHITE, MANUEL — RB — REDSKINS

PERSONAL: Born July 2, 1982, in Panorama City, Calif. ... 6-2/244. ... Full name: Manuel White Jr.
HIGH SCHOOL: Valencia (Placentia, Calif.).
COLLEGE: UCLA.
TRANSACTIONS/CAREER NOTES: Selected by Washington Redskins in fourth round (120th pick overall) of 2005 NFL draft.

Year Team	G	RUSHING Att.	Yds.	Avg.	TD	RECEIVING No.	Yds.	Avg.	TD	TOTALS TD	Pts.
2001—UCLA	11	63	290	4.6	3	5	64	12.8	0	3	18
2002—UCLA	9	85	381	4.5	5	17	238	14.0	2	7	42
2003—UCLA	8	96	379	3.9	3	10	101	10.1	0	3	20
2004—UCLA	12	164	764	4.7	8	20	115	5.8	1	9	56
College totals (4 years)	40	408	1814	4.4	19	52	518	10.0	3	22	136

WHITE, RODDY — WR — FALCONS

PERSONAL: Born November 2, 1981, in James Island, S.C. ... 6-1/204. ... Full name: Sharod L. White.
HIGH SCHOOL: James Island (Charleston, S.C.).
COLLEGE: Alabama-Birmingham.
TRANSACTIONS/CAREER NOTES: Selected by Atlanta Falcons in first round (27th pick overall) of 2005 NFL draft.

Year Team	G	RECEIVING No.	Yds.	Avg.	TD
2001—UAB	9	14	236	16.9	2
2002—UAB	12	39	580	14.9	3
2003—UAB	12	39	844	21.6	7
2004—UAB	12	71	1452	20.5	14
College totals (4 years)	45	163	3112	19.1	26

WHITTICKER, WILLIAM — G — PACKERS

PERSONAL: Born August 2, 1982, in Evansville, Ind. ... 6-5/336.
HIGH SCHOOL: Marion (Ind.).
COLLEGE: Michigan State.
TRANSACTIONS/CAREER NOTES: Selected by Green Bay Packers in seventh round (246th pick overall) of 2005 NFL draft.
PLAYING EXPERIENCE: Michigan State, 2001-2004. ... Games played: 2001 (11), 2002 (12), 2003 (13), 2004 (12). Total: 48.

WILLIAMS, CARNELL   RB   BUCCANEERS

PERSONAL: Born April 21, 1982... 5-11/217.
HIGH SCHOOL: Etowah (Attala, Ala.).
COLLEGE: Auburn.
TRANSACTIONS/CAREER NOTES: Selected by Tampa Bay Buccaneers in first round (fifth pick overall) of 2005 NFL draft.
HONORS: Named running back on THE SPORTING NEWS Freshman All-America second team (2001). ... Named running back on THE SPORTING NEWS college All-America second team (2004).

		RUSHING				RECEIVING				PUNT RETURNS				KICKOFF RETURNS				TOTALS	
Year Team	G	Att.	Yds.	Avg.	TD	No.	Yds.	Avg.	TD	No.	Yds.	Avg.	TD	No.	Yds.	Avg.	TD	TD	Pts.
2001—Auburn	9	120	614	5.1	6	13	140	10.8	0	0	0	0.0	0	8	190	23.8	0	6	36
2002—Auburn	7	141	745	5.3	10	6	30	5.0	0	0	0	0.0	0	0	0	0.0	0	10	60
2003—Auburn	13	241	1307	5.4	17	5	20	4.0	0	6	51	8.5	0	13	269	20.7	0	17	102
2004—Auburn	13	239	1165	4.9	12	21	152	7.2	1	22	251	11.4	0	8	150	18.8	0	13	78
College totals (4 years)	42	741	3831	5.2	45	45	342	7.6	1	28	302	10.8	0	29	609	21.0	0	46	276

WILLIAMS, DARRENT   CB   BRONCOS

PERSONAL: Born September 27, 1982, in Fort Worth, Texas. ... 5-9/176.
HIGH SCHOOL: O.D. Wyatt (Ft. Worth, Texas).
COLLEGE: Oklahoma State.
TRANSACTIONS/CAREER NOTES: Selected by Denver Broncos in second round (56th pick overall) of 2005 NFL draft.

			INTERCEPTIONS				PUNT RETURNS				TOTALS	
Year Team	G	Sks.	No.	Yds.	Avg.	TD	No.	Yds.	Avg.	TD	TD	Pts.
2001—Oklahoma State	10	0.0	2	105	52.5	2	0	0	0.0	0	2	12
2002—Oklahoma State	13	0.0	3	47	15.7	1	0	0	0.0	0	1	6
2003—Oklahoma State	11	0.0	6	130	21.7	2	13	233	17.9	2	4	24
2004—Oklahoma State	7	0.0	0	0	0.0	0	9	249	27.7	1	1	6
College totals (4 years)	41	0.0	11	282	25.6	5	22	482	21.9	3	8	48

WILLIAMS, HARRY   WR   JETS

PERSONAL: Born August 10, 1982, in Augusta, Ga. ... 6-2/175.
HIGH SCHOOL: Jackson-Olin (Birmingham, Ala.).
COLLEGE: Tuskegee.
TRANSACTIONS/CAREER NOTES: Selected by New York Jets in seventh round (240th pick overall) of 2005 NFL draft.

WILLIAMS, MIKE   WR   LIONS

PERSONAL: Born January 4, 1984, in Tampa, Fla. ... 6-5/229. ... Full name: Michael Williams.
HIGH SCHOOL: Plant (Tampa, Fla.).
COLLEGE: Southern California.
TRANSACTIONS/CAREER NOTES: Selected by Detroit Lions in first round (10th pick overall) of 2005 NFL draft.
HONORS: Named wide receiver on THE SPORTING NEWS Freshman All-America first team (2002). ... Named wide receiver on THE SPORTING NEWS college All-America second team (2003).

		RECEIVING			
Year Team	G	No.	Yds.	Avg.	TD
2002—Southern California	13	81	1265	15.6	14
2003—Southern California	13	95	1314	13.8	16
College totals (2 years)	26	176	2579	14.7	30

WILLIAMS, ROYDELL   WR   TITANS

PERSONAL: Born March 14, 1981, in New Orleans, La. ... 6-1/187.
HIGH SCHOOL: East St. John (Reserve, La.).
COLLEGE: Tulane.
TRANSACTIONS/CAREER NOTES: Selected by Tennessee Titans in fourth round (136th pick overall) of 2005 NFL draft.

		RECEIVING			
Year Team	G	No.	Yds.	Avg.	TD
2000—Tulane	11	26	338	13.0	2
2001—Tulane	12	56	886	15.8	11
2002—Tulane	3	15	151	10.1	1
2003—Tulane	12	66	1006	15.2	9
2004—Tulane	10	52	826	15.9	12
College totals (5 years)	48	215	3207	14.9	35

WILLIAMSON, TROY   WR   VIKINGS

PERSONAL: Born April 30, 1983, in Jersey City, N.J. ... 6-1/203.
HIGH SCHOOL: Silver Bluff (Jackson, S.C.).
COLLEGE: South Carolina.
TRANSACTIONS/CAREER NOTES: Selected after junior season by Minnesota Vikings in first round (seventh pick overall) of 2005 NFL draft.

		RUSHING				RECEIVING				KICKOFF RETURNS				TOTALS	
Year Team	G	Att.	Yds.	Avg.	TD	No.	Yds.	Avg.	TD	No.	Yds.	Avg.	TD	TD	Pts.
2002—South Carolina	11	3	47	15.7	0	17	491	28.9	4	3	74	24.7	0	4	24
2003—South Carolina	12	5	24	4.8	0	31	428	13.8	2	14	268	19.1	0	2	12
2004—South Carolina	11	4	30	7.5	0	43	835	19.4	7	7	150	21.4	0	7	42
College totals (3 years)	34	12	101	8.4	0	91	1754	19.3	13	24	492	20.5	0	13	78

WILLIS, RAY   T   SEAHAWKS

PERSONAL: Born August 13, 1982... 6-5/325.
HIGH SCHOOL: Angleton (Texas).
COLLEGE: Florida State.
TRANSACTIONS/CAREER NOTES: Selected by Seattle Seahawks in fourth round (105th pick overall) of 2005 NFL draft.
PLAYING EXPERIENCE: Florida State, 2001-2004. ... Games played: 2001 (11), 2002 (14), 2003 (13), 2004 (13). Total: 51.

WILSON, RODRIQUES   LB   BEARS

PERSONAL: Born November 12, 1981... 6-2/217.
HIGH SCHOOL: Cross (S.C.).
COLLEGE: South Carolina.
TRANSACTIONS/CAREER NOTES: Selected by Chicago Bears in seventh round (220th pick overall) of 2005 NFL draft.

Year Team	G	SACKS
2000—South Carolina	1	0.0
2001—South Carolina	9	0.0
2002—South Carolina	12	0.0
2003—South Carolina	8	0.0
2004—South Carolina	11	3.0
College totals (5 years)	41	3.0

WILSON, STANLEY   CB   LIONS

PERSONAL: Born November 5, 1982, in Carson, Calif. ... 6-0/185. ... Son of Stanley Wilson, running back with Cincinnati Bengals (1983-88).
HIGH SCHOOL: Bishop Montgomery (Carson, Calif.).
COLLEGE: Stanford.
TRANSACTIONS/CAREER NOTES: Selected by Detroit Lions in third round (72nd pick overall) of 2005 NFL draft.

Year Team	G	Sks.	INTERCEPTIONS No.	Yds.	Avg.	TD
2001—Stanford	6	0.0	1	17	17.0	0
2002—Stanford	11	0.0	2	35	17.5	0
2003—Stanford	11	0.0	1	0	0.0	0
2004—Stanford	11	0.0	1	51	51.0	0
College totals (4 years)	39	0.0	5	103	20.6	0

WORTHAM, CORNELIUS   LB   SEAHAWKS

PERSONAL: Born January 25, 1982, in Calhoun City, Miss. ... 6-1/231. ... Full name: James Wortham.
HIGH SCHOOL: Calhoun City (Miss.).
COLLEGE: Alabama.
TRANSACTIONS/CAREER NOTES: Selected by Seattle Seahawks in seventh round (235th pick overall) of 2005 NFL draft.

Year Team	G	Sks.	INTERCEPTIONS No.	Yds.	Avg.	TD
2000—Alabama	11	0.0	0	0	0.0	0
2001—Alabama	11	1.0	0	0	0.0	0
2002—Alabama	13	1.0	0	0	0.0	0
2004—Alabama	12	1.0	1	0	0.0	0
College totals (4 years)	47	3.0	1	0	0.0	0

YOUNG, SCOTT   G   EAGLES

PERSONAL: Born July 15, 1981... 6-4/312.
HIGH SCHOOL: Hillcrest (Salt Lake City, Utah).
JUNIOR COLLEGE: Dixie State (St. George, Utah).
COLLEGE: Brigham Young.
TRANSACTIONS/CAREER NOTES: Selected by Philadelphia Eagles in the fifth round (172nd overall) of 2005 NFL draft.
PLAYING EXPERIENCE: Brigham Young, 2002-2004. ... Games played: 2002 (10), 2004 (11). Total: 21.

HEAD COACHES

BELICHICK, BILL — PATRIOTS

PERSONAL: Born April 16, 1952, in Nashville, Tenn. ... Full name: William Stephen Belichick. ... Son of Steve Belichick, fullback with Detroit Lions (1941); head coach at Hiram (Ohio) College (1946-49); assistant coach, Vanderbilt (1949-53); assistant coach, North Carolina (1953-56); assistant coach, Navy (1956-83); and administrative assistant, Navy (1983-89).
HIGH SCHOOL: Annapolis (Md.), then Phillips Academy (Andover, Mass.).
COLLEGE: Wesleyan.

HEAD COACHING RECORD

BACKROUND: Assistant special teams coach, Baltimore Colts NFL (1975). ... Assistant special teams coach, Detroit Lions NFL (1976 and 1977). ... Assistant special teams coach/assistant to defensive coordinator, Denver Broncos NFL (1978). ... Special teams coach, New York Giants NFL (1979 and 1980). ... Special teams/linebackers coach, Giants (1981 and 1982). ... Linebackers coach, Giants (1983 and 1984). ... Defensive coordinator/linebackers coach, Giants (1985-1988). ... Defensive coordinator/secondary coach, Giants (1989 and 1990). ... Assistant head coach/secondary coach, New England Patriots NFL (1996). ... Assistant head coach/secondary coach, New York Jets NFL (1997-1999).
HONORS: Named NFL Coach of the Year by THE SPORTING NEWS (2003).

	\nW\n REGULAR SEASON					POST-SEASON	
	W	L	T	Pct.	Finish	W	L
1991—Cleveland NFL	6	10	0	.375	3rd/AFC Central Division	0	0
1992—Cleveland NFL	7	9	0	.438	3rd/AFC Central Division	0	0
1993—Cleveland NFL	7	9	0	.438	3rd/AFC Central Division	0	0
1994—Cleveland NFL	11	5	0	.688	2nd/AFC Central Division	1	1
1995—Cleveland NFL	5	11	0	.313	4th/AFC Central Division	0	0
2000—New England NFL	5	11	0	.313	5th/AFC Eastern Division	0	0
2001—New England NFL	11	5	0	.688	1st/AFC Eastern Division	3	0
2002—New England NFL	9	7	0	.563	2nd/AFC East Division	0	0
2003—New England NFL	14	2	0	.875	1st/AFC East Division	3	0
2004—New England NFL	14	2	0	.875	1st/AFC East Division	3	0
Pro totals (10 years)	89	71	0	.556	Pro totals (4 years)	10	1

NOTES:
1994—Defeated New England, 20-13, in first-round playoff game; lost to Pittsburgh, 29-9, in conference playoff game.
2001—Defeated Oakland, 16-13 (OT), in conference playoff game; defeated Pittsburgh, 24-17, in AFC championship game; defeated St. Louis, 20-17, in Super Bowl 36.
2003—Defeated Tennessee, 17-14, in first-round playoff game; defeated Indianapolis, 24-14, in AFC championship game; defeated Carolina, 32-29, in Super Bowl 38.
2004—Defeated Indianapolis, 20-3, in conference playoff game; defeated Pittsburgh, 41-27, in AFC championship game; defeated Philadelphia, 24-21 in Super Bowl 39.

BILLICK, BRIAN — RAVENS

PERSONAL: Born February 28, 1954, in Fairborn, Ohio. ... Full name: Brian Harold Billick. ... Played tight end.
HIGH SCHOOL: Redlands (Calif.).
COLLEGE: Air Force, then Brigham Young.
TRANSACTIONS/CAREER NOTES: Selected by San Francisco 49ers in 11th round of 1977 NFL draft. ... Signed by 49ers for 1977 season. ... Released by 49ers (August 30, 1977). ... Signed by Dallas Cowboys (May 1978). ... Released by Cowboys before 1978 season.

HEAD COACHING RECORD

BACKROUND: Assistant coach, University of Redlands (1977). ... Graduate assistant, Brigham Young (1978). ... Assistant public relations director, San Francisco 49ers NFL (1979 and 1980). ... Assistant coach and recruiting coordinator, San Diego State (1981-1985). ... Offensive coordinator, Utah State (1986-1988). ... Assistant coach, Stanford (1989-1991). ... Tight ends coach, Minnesota Vikings (1992). ... Offensive coordinator, Minnesota Vikings (1993-1998).

	REGULAR SEASON					POST-SEASON	
	W	L	T	Pct.	Finish	W	L
1999—Baltimore NFL	8	8	0	.500	3rd/AFC Central Division	0	0
2000—Baltimore NFL	12	4	0	.750	2nd/AFC Central Division	4	0
2001—Baltimore NFL	10	6	0	.625	2nd/AFC Central Division	1	1
2002—Baltimore NFL	7	9	0	.438	3rd/AFC North Division	0	0
2003—Baltimore NFL	10	6	0	.625	1st/AFC North Division	0	1
2004—Baltimore NFL	9	7	0	.563	2nd/AFC North Division	0	0
Pro totals (6 years)	56	40	0	.583	Pro totals (3 years)	5	2

NOTES:
2000—Defeated Denver, 21-3, in first-round playoff game; defeated Tennessee, 24-10, in conference playoff game; defeated Oakland, 16-3, in AFC championship game; defeated New York Giants, 34-7, in Super Bowl 35.
2001—Defeated Miami, 20-3, in first-round playoff game; lost to Pittsburgh, 27-10, in conference playoff game.
2003—Lost to Tennessee, 20-17, in first-round playoff game.

CAPERS, DOM — TEXANS

PERSONAL: Born August 7, 1950, in Cambridge, Ohio. ... Full name: Dominic Capers.
HIGH SCHOOL: Meadowbrook (Byesville, Ohio).
COLLEGE: Mount Union, Ohio (bachelor's degree in psychology and physical education), then Kent State (master's degree in administration).

HEAD COACHING RECORD

BACKROUND: Graduate assistant, Kent State (1972-1974). ... Graduate assistant, Washington (1975). ... Defensive backs coach, Hawaii (1976). ... Defensive backs coach, San Jose State (1977). ... Defensive backs coach, California (1978 and 1979). ... Defensive backs coach, Tennessee (1980 and 1981). ... Defensive backs coach, Ohio State (1982 and 1983). ... Defensive backs coach, Philadelphia Stars USFL (1984). ... Defensive backs coach, Baltimore Stars USFL (1985). ... Defensive backs coach, New Orleans Saints NFL (1986-1991). ... Defensive coordinator, Pittsburgh Steelers NFL (1992-1994). ... Defensive coordinator, Jacksonville Jaguars NFL (1999 and 2000). ...

HONORS: Named NFL Coach of the Year by THE SPORTING NEWS (1996).

	W	L	T	Pct.	REGULAR SEASON Finish	POST-SEASON W	L
1995—Carolina NFL	7	9	0	.438	4th/NFC Western Division	0	0
1996—Carolina NFL	12	4	0	.750	1st/NFC Western Division	1	1
1997—Carolina NFL	7	9	0	.438	2nd/NFC Western Division	0	0
1998—Carolina NFL	4	12	0	.250	4th/NFC Western Division	0	0
2002—Houston NFL	4	12	0	.250	4th/AFC South Division	0	0
2003—Houston NFL	5	11	0	.313	4th/AFC South Division	0	0
2004—Houston NFL	7	9	0	.438	3rd/AFC South Division	0	0
Pro totals (7 years)	46	66	0	.411	**Pro totals (1 year)**	1	1

NOTES:
1996—Defeated Dallas, 26-17, in conference playoff game; lost to Green Bay, 30-13, in NFC championship game.

COUGHLIN, TOM   GIANTS

PERSONAL: Born August 31, 1946, in Waterloo, N.Y. ... Full name: Thomas Richard Coughlin.
HIGH SCHOOL: Waterloo (N.Y.) Central.
COLLEGE: Syracuse.

HEAD COACHING RECORD
BACKROUND: Graduate assistant, Syracuse (1969). ... Quarterbacks/offensive backfield coach, Syracuse (1974-1976). ... Offensive coordinator, Syracuse (1977-1980). ... Quarterbacks coach, Boston College (1980-1983). ... Receivers coach, Philadelphia Eagles NFL (1984 and 1985). ... Receivers coach, Green Bay Packers NFL (1986 and 1987). ... Receivers coach, New York Giants NFL (1988-1990).

	W	L	T	Pct.	REGULAR SEASON Finish	POST-SEASON W	L
1970—Rochester Tech	4	3	0	.571	Eastern College Athletic Conference	0	0
1971—Rochester Tech	5	2	1	.714	Eastern College Athletic Conference	0	0
1972—Rochester Tech	4	5	0	.444	Eastern College Athletic Conference	0	0
1973—Rochester Tech	3	5	1	.375	Eastern College Athletic Conference	0	0
1991—Boston College	4	7	0	.364	7th/Big East Conference	0	0
1992—Boston College	8	2	1	.800	3rd/Big East Conference	0	1
1993—Boston College	9	3	0	.727	3rd/Big East Conference	1	0
1995—Jacksonville NFL	4	12	0	.250	5th/AFC Central Division	0	0
1996—Jacksonville NFL	9	7	0	.563	2nd/AFC Central Division	2	1
1997—Jacksonville NFL	11	5	0	.688	2nd/AFC Central Division	0	1
1998—Jacksonville NFL	11	5	0	.688	1st/AFC Central Division	1	1
1999—Jacksonville NFL	14	2	0	.875	1st/AFC Central Division	1	1
2000—Jacksonville NFL	7	9	0	.438	4th/AFC Central Division	0	0
2001—Jacksonville NFL	6	10	0	.375	5th/AFC Central Division	0	0
2002—Jacksonville NFL	6	10	0	.375	3rd/AFC South Division	0	0
2004—New York Giants NFL	6	10	0	.375	2nd/NFC East Division	0	0
College totals (7 years)	37	27	3	.578	**College totals (2 years)**	1	1
Pro totals (9 years)	74	70	0	.514	**Pro totals (4 years)**	4	4

NOTES:
1992—Lost to Tennessee, 38-23, in Hall of Fame Bowl.
1993—Defeated Virginia, 31-13, in Carquest Bowl.
1996—Defeated Buffalo, 30-27, in first-round playoff game; defeated Denver, 30-27, in conference playoff game; lost to New England, 20-6, in AFC championship game.
1997—Lost to Denver, 42-17, in first-round playoff game.
1998—Defeated New England, 25-10, in first-round playoff game; lost to New York Jets, 34-24, in conference playoff game.
1999—Defeated Miami, 62-7, in conference playoff game; lost to Tennessee, 33-14, in AFC championship game.

COWHER, BILL   STEELERS

PERSONAL: Born May 8, 1957, in Pittsburgh. ... Full name: William Laird Cowher. ... Played linebacker.
HIGH SCHOOL: Carlynton (Carnegie, Pa.).
COLLEGE: North Carolina State.
TRANSACTIONS/CAREER NOTES: Signed as non-drafted free agent by Philadelphia Eagles (May 8, 1979). ... Released by Eagles (August 14, 1979). ... Signed by Cleveland Browns (February 27, 1980). ... On injured reserve with knee injury (August 20, 1981-entire season). ... Traded by Browns to Eagles for ninth-round pick (WR Don Jones) in 1984 draft (August 21, 1983). ... On injured reserve with knee injury (September 25, 1984-remainder of season).

HEAD COACHING RECORD
BACKROUND: Special teams coach, Cleveland Browns NFL (1985 and 1986). ... Defensive backs coach, Browns (1987 and 1988). ... Defensive coordinator, Kansas City Chiefs NFL (1989-1991).
HONORS: Named NFL Coach of the Year by The Sporting News (1992 and 2004).

	W	L	T	Pct.	REGULAR SEASON Finish	POST-SEASON W	L
1992—Pittsburgh NFL	11	5	0	.688	1st/AFC Central Division	0	1
1993—Pittsburgh NFL	9	7	0	.563	2nd/AFC Central Division	0	1
1994—Pittsburgh NFL	12	4	0	.750	1st/AFC Central Division	1	1
1995—Pittsburgh NFL	11	5	0	.688	1st/AFC Central Division	2	1
1996—Pittsburgh NFL	10	6	0	.625	1st/AFC Central Division	1	1
1997—Pittsburgh NFL	11	5	0	.688	1st/AFC Central Division	1	1
1998—Pittsburgh NFL	7	9	0	.438	3rd/AFC Central Division	0	0
1999—Pittsburgh NFL	6	10	0	.375	4th/AFC Central Division	0	0
2000—Pittsburgh NFL	9	7	0	.563	3rd/AFC Central Division	0	0

	W	L	T	Pct.	Finish	POST-SEASON W	L
2001—Pittsburgh NFL	13	3	0	.813	1st/AFC Central Division	1	1
2002—Pittsburgh NFL	10	5	1	.667	1st/AFC North Division	1	1
2003—Pittsburgh NFL	6	10	0	.375	3rd/AFC North Division	0	0
2004—Pittsburgh NFL	15	1	0	.938	1st/AFC North Division	1	1
Pro totals (13 years)	130	77	1	.628	Pro totals (9 years)	8	9

NOTES:
1992—Lost to Buffalo, 24-3, in conference playoff game.
1993—Lost to Kansas City, 27-24 (OT), in first-round playoff game.
1994—Defeated Cleveland, 29-9, in conference playoff game; lost to San Diego, 17-13, in AFC championship game.
1995—Defeated Buffalo, 40-21, in conference playoff game; defeated Indianapolis, 20-16, in AFC championship game; lost to Dallas, 27-17, in Super Bowl 30.
1996—Defeated Indianapolis, 42-14, in first-round playoff game; lost to New England, 28-3, in conference playoff game.
1997—Defeated New England, 7-6, in conference playoff game; lost to Denver, 24-21, in AFC championship game.
2001—Defeated Baltimore, 27-10, in conference playoff game; lost to New England, 24-17, in AFC championship game.
2002—Defeated Cleveland, 36-33, in first-round playoff game; lost to Tennessee, 34-31 (OT), in conference playoff game.
2004—Defeated N.Y. Jets, 20-17 (OT), in conference playoff game; lost to New England, 41-27, in AFC championship game.

CRENNEL, ROMEO   BROWNS

PERSONAL: Born June 18, 1947, in Lynchburg, Va.
HIGH SCHOOL: Fort Knox (Ky.), then Central (Amherst, Va.).
COLLEGE: Western Kentucky.

COACHING RECORD
BACKROUND: Graduate assistant, Western Kentucky (1970). ... Defensive line coach, Western Kentucky (1971-74). ... Defensive assistant, Texas Tech (1975-77). ... Defensive ends coach, Mississippi (1978-79). ... Defensive line coach, Georgia Tech (1980). ... Special teams coach/defensive assistant, New York Giants NFL (1981-82). ... Special teams coach, Giants (1983-89). ... Defensive line coach, Giants (1990-92). ... Defensive line coach, New England Patriots NFL (1993-96). ... Defensive line coach, New York Jets NFL (1997-99). ... Defensive coordinator/defensive line coach, Cleveland Browns NFL (2000). ... Defensive coordinator, Patriots (2001 and 2004). ... Defensive coordinator/defensive line coach, Patriots (2002-03).

DEL RIO, JACK   JAGUARS

PERSONAL: Born April 4, 1963, in Castro Valley, Calif. ... Full name: Jack Del Rio Jr.
HIGH SCHOOL: Hayward (Calif.).
COLLEGE: Southern California.
TRANSACTIONS/CAREER NOTES: Selected by Los Angeles Express in 1985 USFL territorial draft. ... Selected by New Orleans Saints in third round (68th pick overall) of 1985 NFL draft. ... Signed by Saints (July 31, 1985). ... Traded by Saints to Kansas City Chiefs for fifth-round pick (TE Greg Scales) in 1988 draft (August 17, 1987). ... On injured reserve with knee injury (December 13, 1988-remainder of season). ... Claimed on waivers by Dallas Cowboys (August 31, 1989). ... Granted free agency (February 1, 1991). ... Re-signed by Cowboys (July 25, 1991). ... Granted unconditional free agency (February 1, 1992). ... Signed by Minnesota Vikings (March 3, 1992). ... Released by Vikings (February 13, 1996). ... Signed by Miami Dolphins (June 2, 1996). ... Released by Dolphins (August 5, 1996).
HONORS: Played in Pro Bowl (1994 season).
MISCELLANEOUS: Selected by Toronto Blue Jays organization in 22nd round of free-agent baseball draft (June 8, 1981); did not sign.

			TOTALS			INTERCEPTIONS			
Year Team	G	GS	Tk.	Ast.	Sks.	No.	Yds.	Avg.	TD
1985—New Orleans NFL	16	9	0	0	0.0	2	13	6.5	0
1986—New Orleans NFL	16	1	0	0	0.0	0	0	0.0	0
1987—Kansas City NFL	10	7	0	0	3.0	0	0	0.0	0
1988—Kansas City NFL	15	10	0	0	1.0	1	0	0.0	0
1989—Dallas NFL	14	12	0	0	0.0	0	0	0.0	0
1990—Dallas NFL	16	16	0	0	1.5	0	0	0.0	0
1991—Dallas NFL	16	16	0	0	0.0	0	0	0.0	0
1992—Minnesota NFL	16	16	0	0	2.0	2	92	46.0	1
1993—Minnesota NFL	16	16	0	0	0.5	4	3	0.8	0
1994—Minnesota NFL	16	16	0	0	2.0	3	5	1.7	0
1995—Minnesota NFL	9	9	0	0	3.0	1	15	15.0	0
Pro totals (11 years)	160	128	0	0	13.0	13	128	9.8	1

HEAD COACHING RECORD
BACKROUND: Linebackers coach/assistant strength coach, New Orleans Saints NFL (1997 and 1998). ... Linebackers coach, Baltimore Ravens NFL (1999-2001). ... Defensive coordinator, Carolina Panthers NFL (2002).

						POST-SEASON	
	W	L	T	Pct.	REGULAR SEASON Finish	W	L
2003—Jacksonville NFL	5	11	0	.313	3rd/AFC South Division	0	0
2004—Jacksonville NFL	9	7	0	.563	2nd/AFC South Division	0	0
Pro totals (2 years)	14	18	0	.438			

DUNGY, TONY   COLTS

PERSONAL: Born October 6, 1955, in Jackson, Mich. ... Full name: Anthony Kevin Dungy. ... Name pronounced: DUN-gee. ... Played defensive back and quarterback.
HIGH SCHOOL: Parkside (Jackson, Mich.).
COLLEGE: Minnesota.
TRANSACTIONS/CAREER NOTES: Signed as non-drafted free agent by Pittsburgh Steelers (May 1977). ... Traded by Steelers to San Francisco 49ers for 10th-round pick in 1980 draft (August 21, 1979). ... Traded by 49ers with RB Mike Hogan to New York Giants for WR Jimmy Robinson and CB Ray Rhodes (March 27, 1980).

CHAMPIONSHIP GAME EXPERIENCE: Played in AFC championship game (1978 season). ... Played in Super Bowl XIII (1978 season).

			INTERCEPTIONS			
Year Team		G	No.	Yds.	Avg.	TD
1977—Pittsburgh NFL		14	3	37	12.3	0
1978—Pittsburgh NFL		16	6	95	15.8	0
1979—San Francisco NFL		15	0	0	0.0	0
Pro totals (3 years)		45	9	132	14.7	0

HEAD COACHING RECORD

BACKROUND: Defensive backs coach, University of Minnesota (1980). ... Defensive assistant, Pittsburgh Steelers NFL (1981). ... Defensive backs coach, Steelers (1982 and 1983). ... Defensive coordinator, Steelers (1984-1988). ... Defensive backs coach, Kansas City Chiefs NFL (1989-1991). ... Defensive coordinator, Minnesota Vikings NFL (1992-1995).

				REGULAR SEASON		POST-SEASON	
	W	L	T	Pct.	Finish	W	L
1996—Tampa Bay NFL	6	10	0	.375	4th/NFC Central Division	0	0
1997—Tampa Bay NFL	10	6	0	.625	2nd/NFC Central Division	1	1
1998—Tampa Bay NFL	8	8	0	.500	3rd/NFC Central Division	0	0
1999—Tampa Bay NFL	11	5	0	.688	1st/NFC Central Division	1	1
2000—Tampa Bay NFL	10	6	0	.625	2nd/NFC Central Division	0	1
2001—Tampa Bay NFL	9	7	0	.563	3rd/NFC Central Division	0	1
2002—Indianapolis NFL	10	6	0	.625	2nd/AFC South Division	0	1
2003—Indianapolis NFL	12	4	0	.750	1st/AFC South Division	2	1
2004—Indianapolis NFL	12	4	0	.750	1st/AFC South Division	1	1
Pro totals (9 years)	88	56	0	.611	**Pro totals (7 years)**	5	7

NOTES:
1997—Defeated Detroit, 20-10, in first-round playoff game; lost to Green Bay, 21-7, in conference playoff game.
1999—Defeated Washington, 14-13, in conference playoff game; lost to St. Louis, 11-6, in NFC championship game.
2000—Lost to Philadelphia, 21-3, in first-round playoff game.
2001—Lost to Philadelphia, 31-9, in first-round playoff game.
2002—Lost to New York Jets, 41-0, in first-round playoff game.
2003—Defeated Denver, 41-10, in first-round playoff game; defeated Kansas City, 38-31, in conference playoff game; lost to New England, 24-14, in AFC championship game.
2004—Defeated Denver, 49-24, in first-round playoff game; lost to New England, 20-3, in conference playoff game.

EDWARDS, HERMAN — JETS

PERSONAL: Born April 27, 1954, in Fort Monmouth, N.J. ... Full name: Herman Lee Edwards. ... Played cornerback.
HIGH SCHOOL: Monterey (Calif.).
JUNIOR COLLEGE: Monterey (Calif.) Peninsula College.
COLLEGE: California, then San Diego State.
TRANSACTIONS/CAREER NOTES: Signed as non-drafted free agent by Philadelphia Eagles (May 1977). ... Released by Eagles (September 8, 1986). ... Signed by Los Angeles Rams (September 15, 1986). ... Released by Rams (October 20, 1986). ... Signed by Atlanta Falcons (November 3, 1986). ... Announced retirement (November 11, 1986).
CHAMPIONSHIP GAME EXPERIENCE: Played in NFC championship game (1980 season). ... Played in Super Bowl 15 (1980 season).

			INTERCEPTIONS			
Year Team		G	No.	Yds.	Avg.	TD
1977—Philadelphia NFL		14	6	9	1.5	0
1978—Philadelphia NFL		16	7	59	8.4	0
1979—Philadelphia NFL		16	3	6	2.0	0
1980—Philadelphia NFL		16	3	12	4.0	0
1981—Philadelphia NFL		16	3	1	0.3	0
1982—Philadelphia NFL		9	5	3	0.6	0
1983—Philadelphia NFL		16	1	0	0.0	0
1984—Philadelphia NFL		16	2	0	0.0	0
1985—Philadelphia NFL		16	3	8	2.7	1
1986—Los Angeles Rams NFL		4	0	0	0.0	0
—Atlanta NFL		3	0	0	0.0	0
Pro totals (10 years)		142	33	98	3.0	1

HEAD COACHING RECORD

BACKROUND: Defensive backs coach, San Jose State (1987-1989). ... Scout, Kansas City Chiefs NFL (1990, 1991 and 1995). ... Defensive backs coach, Chiefs (1992-1994). ... Assistant head coach/defensive backs coach, Tampa Bay Buccaneers NFL (1996-2000).

				REGULAR SEASON		POST-SEASON	
	W	L	T	Pct.	Finish	W	L
2001—New York Jets NFL	10	6	0	.625	3rd/AFC Eastern Division	0	1
2002—New York Jets NFL	9	7	0	.563	1st/AFC East Division	1	1
2003—New York Jets NFL	6	10	0	.375	4th/AFC East Division	0	0
2004—New York Jets NFL	10	6	0	.625	2nd/AFC East Division	1	1
Pro totals (4 years)	35	29	0	.547	**Pro totals (3 years)**	2	3

NOTES:
2001—Lost to Oakland, 38-24, in first-round playoff game.
2002—Defeated Indianapolis, 41-0, in first-round playoff game; lost to Oakland, 30-10, in conference playoff game.
2004—Defeated San Diego, 20-17 (OT), in first-round playoff game; lost to Pittsburgh, 20-17 (OT), in conference playoff game.

HEAD COACHES

FISHER, JEFF — TITANS

PERSONAL: Born February 25, 1958, in Culver City, Calif. ... Full name: Jeffrey Michael Fisher. ... Played safety.
HIGH SCHOOL: Taft (Woodland Hills, Calif.).
COLLEGE: Southern California.
TRANSACTIONS/CAREER NOTES: Selected by Chicago Bears in seventh round (177th pick overall) of 1981 NFL draft. ... On injured reserve with broken leg (October 24, 1983-remainder of season). ... On injured reserve with ankle injury entire 1985 season.
CHAMPIONSHIP GAME EXPERIENCE: Played in NFC championship game (1984 season).

			INTERCEPTIONS				PUNT RETURNS				KICKOFF RETURNS				TOTALS		
Year Team	G	No.	Yds.	Avg.	TD	No.	Yds.	Avg.	TD	No.	Yds.	Avg.	TD	TD	2pt.	Pts.	Fum.
1981—Chicago NFL	16	2	3	1.5	0	43	509	11.8	1	7	102	14.6	0	1	0	6	3
1982—Chicago NFL	9	3	19	6.3	0	7	53	7.6	0	7	102	14.6	0	0	0	0	2
1983—Chicago NFL	8	0	0	0.0	0	13	71	5.5	0	0	0	0.0	0	0	0	0	0
1984—Chicago NFL	16	0	0	0.0	0	57	492	8.6	0	0	0	0.0	0	0	0	0	4
1985—Chicago NFL	Did not play.																
Pro totals (4 years)	49	5	22	4.4	0	120	1125	9.4	1	14	204	14.6	0	1	0	6	9

HEAD COACHING RECORD

BACKROUND: Defensive backs coach, Philadelphia Eagles NFL (1986-1988). ... Defensive coordinator, Eagles (1989 and 1990). ... Defensive coordinator, Los Angeles Rams NFL (1991). ... Defensive backs coach, San Francisco 49ers NFL (1992 and 1993). ... Defensive coordinator, Houston Oilers NFL (February 9-November 14, 1994). ... Oilers franchise moved to Tennessee for 1997 season.

	REGULAR SEASON					POST-SEASON	
	W	L	T	Pct.	Finish	W	L
1994—Houston NFL	1	5	0	.167	4th/AFC Central Division	0	0
1995—Houston NFL	7	9	0	.438	3rd/AFC Central Division	0	0
1996—Houston NFL	8	8	0	.500	4th/AFC Central Division	0	0
1997—Tennessee NFL	8	8	0	.500	3rd/AFC Central Division	0	0
1998—Tennessee NFL	8	8	0	.500	2nd/AFC Central Division	0	0
1999—Tennessee NFL	13	3	0	.813	2nd/AFC Central Division	3	1
2000—Tennessee NFL	13	3	0	.813	1st/AFC Central Division	0	1
2001—Tennessee NFL	7	9	0	.438	4th/AFC Central Division	0	0
2002—Tennessee NFL	11	5	0	.688	1st/AFC South Division	1	1
2003—Tennessee NFL	12	4	0	.750	2nd/AFC South Division	1	1
2004—Tennessee NFL	5	11	0	.313	4th/AFC South Division	0	0
Pro totals (11 years)	93	73	0	.560	Pro totals (4 years)	5	4

NOTES:
1994—Replaced Jack Pardee as head coach (November 14) with 1-9 record and club in fourth place.
1999—Defeated Buffalo, 22-16, in first-round playoff game; defeated Indianapolis, 19-16, in conference playoff game; defeated Jacksonville, 33-14, in AFC championship game; lost to St. Louis, 23-16, in Super Bowl 34.
2000—Lost to Baltimore, 24-10, in conference playoff game.
2002—Defeated Pittsburgh, 34-31 (OT), in conference playoff game; lost to Oakland, 41-24, in AFC championship game.
2003—Defeated Baltimore, 20-17, in first-round playoff game; lost to New England, 17-14, in AFC conference playoff game.

FOX, JOHN — PANTHERS

PERSONAL: Born February 8, 1955, in Virginia Beach, Va.
HIGH SCHOOL: Castle Park (Chula Vista, Calif.).
JUNIOR COLLEGE: Southwestern (Calif.).
COLLEGE: San Diego State.

HEAD COACHING RECORD

BACKROUND: Graduate assistant, San Diego State (1978). ... Assistant coach, U.S. International University, Calif. (1979). ... Secondary coach, Boise State (1980). ... Secondary coach, Long Beach State (1981). ... Secondary coach, University of Utah (1982). ... Secondary coach, University of Kansas (1983). ... Secondary coach, Iowa State (1984). ... Secondary coach, Los Angeles Express USFL (1985). ... Defensive coordinator/secondary coach, University of Pittsburgh (1986-1988). ... Secondary coach, Pittsburgh Steelers NFL (1989-1991). ... Secondary coach, San Diego Chargers NFL (1992-1993). ... Defensive coordinator, Los Angeles Raiders NFL (1994). ... Defensive coordinator, Oakland Raiders NFL (1995). ... Consultant, St. Louis Rams NFL (1996). ... Defensive coordinator, New York Giants NFL (1997-2001).

	REGULAR SEASON					POST-SEASON	
	W	L	T	Pct.	Finish	W	L
2002—Carolina NFL	7	9	0	.438	4th/NFC South Division	0	0
2003—Carolina NFL	11	5	0	.688	1st/NFC South Division	3	1
2004—Carolina NFL	7	9	0	.438	3rd/NFC South Division	0	0
Pro totals (3 years)	25	23	0	.521	Pro totals (1 year)	3	1

NOTES:
2003—Defeated Dallas, 29-10, in first-round playoff game; defeated St. Louis, 29-23 (2OT), in conference playoff game; defeated Philadelphia, 14-3, in NFC championship game; lost to New England, 32-29, in Super Bowl 38.

GIBBS, JOE — REDSKINS

PERSONAL: Born November 25, 1940, in Mocksville, N.C. ... Full name: Joe Jackson Gibbs.
HIGH SCHOOL: Spring (Santa Fe, Calif.).
JUNIOR COLLEGE: Cerritos (Calif.).
COLLEGE: San Diego State.

HEAD COACHING RECORD

BACKROUND: Graduate assistant, San Diego State (1964-65). ... Assistant coach, San Diego State (1966). ... Assistant coach, Florida State (1967-68). ... Assistant coach, Southern California (1969-70). ... Assistant coach, Arkansas (1971-72). ... Assistant coach, St. Louis Cardinals NFL (1973-77). ... Assistant coach, Tampa Bay Buccaneers NFL (1978). ... Assistant coach, San Diego Chargers NFL (1979-80).
HONORS: Named NFL Coach of the Year by The Sporting News (1982, 1983 and 1991).

						POST-SEASON	
	W	L	T	Pct.	Finish	W	L
1981—Washington NFL	8	8	0	.500	4th/NFC Eastern Division	0	0
1982—Washington NFL	8	1	0	.889	1st/NFC	4	0
1983—Washington NFL	14	2	0	.875	1st/NFC Eastern Division	2	1
1984—Washington NFL	11	5	0	.688	1st/NFC Eastern Division	0	1
1985—Washington NFL	10	6	0	.625	3rd/NFC Eastern Division	0	0
1986—Washington NFL	12	4	0	.750	2nd/NFC Eastern Division	2	1
1987—Washington NFL	11	4	0	.733	1st/NFC Eastern Division	3	0
1988—Washington NFL	7	9	0	.438	3rd/NFC Eastern Division	0	0
1989—Washington NFL	10	6	0	.625	3rd/NFC Eastern Division	0	0
1990—Washington NFL	10	6	0	.625	3rd/NFC Eastern Division	1	1
1991—Washington NFL	14	2	0	.875	1st/NFC Eastern Division	3	0
1992—Washington NFL	9	7	0	.563	3rd/NFC Eastern Division	1	1
2004—Washington NFL	6	10	0	.375	4th/NFC East Division	0	0
Pro totals (13 years)	**130**	**70**	**0**	**.650**	**Pro totals (8 years)**	**16**	**5**

NOTES:
1982—Defeated Detroit, 31-7, in first-round playoff game; defeated Minnesota, 21-7, in conference playoff game; defeated Dallas, 31-17, in NFC championship game; defeated Miami, 27-17, in Super Bowl 17.
1983—Defeated Los Angeles Rams, 51-7, in conference playoff game; defeated San Francisco, 24-21, in NFC championship game; lost to Los Angeles Raiders, 38-9, in Super Bowl 18.
1984—Lost to Chicago, 23-19, in conference playoff game.
1986—Defeated Los Angeles Rams, 19-7, in first-round playoff game; defeated Chicago, 27-13, in conference playoff game; lost to New York Giants, 17-0, in NFC championship game.
1987—Defeated Chicago, 21-17, in conference playoff game; defeated Minnesota, 17-10, in NFC championship game; defeated Denver, 42-10, in Super Bowl 22.
1990—Defeated Philadelphia, 20-6, in first-round playoff game; lost to San Francisco, 28-10, in conference playoff game.
1991—Defeated Atlanta, 24-7, in conference playoff game; defeated Detroit, 41-10, in NFC championship game; defeated Buffalo, 37-24, in Super Bowl 26.
1992—Defeated Minnesota, 24-7, in first-round playoff game; lost to San Francisco, 20-13, in conference playoff game.

GREEN, DENNIS — CARDINALS

PERSONAL: Born February 17, 1949, in Harrisburg, Pa.
HIGH SCHOOL: John Harris (Harrisburg, Pa.).
COLLEGE: Iowa.

HEAD COACHING RECORD

BACKROUND: Graduate assistant, University of Iowa (1972). ... Running backs/receivers coach, Dayton (1973). ... Running backs/receivers coach, Iowa (1974-1976). ... Running backs coach, Stanford (1977 and 1978). ... Special teams coach, San Francisco 49ers NFL (1979). ... Offensive coordinator, Stanford (1980). ... Receivers coach, 49ers (1986-1988).

						POST-SEASON	
	W	L	T	Pct.	Finish	W	L
1981—Northwestern	0	11	0	.000	10th/Big Ten Conference	0	0
1982—Northwestern	3	8	0	.273	T8th/Big Ten Conference	0	0
1983—Northwestern	2	9	0	.182	T8th/Big Ten Conference	0	0
1984—Northwestern	2	9	0	.182	9th/Big Ten Conference	0	0
1985—Northwestern	3	8	0	.273	T9th/Big Ten Conference	0	0
1989—Stanford	3	8	0	.273	T7th/Pacific-10 Conference	0	0
1990—Stanford	5	6	0	.455	T6th/Pacific-10 Conference	0	0
1991—Stanford	8	3	0	.727	T2nd/Pacific-10 Conference	0	1
1992—Minnesota NFL	11	5	0	.688	1st/NFC Central Division	0	1
1993—Minnesota NFL	9	7	0	.563	2nd/NFC Central Division	0	1
1994—Minnesota NFL	10	6	0	.625	1st/NFC Central Division	0	1
1995—Minnesota NFL	8	8	0	.500	4th/NFC Central Division	0	0
1996—Minnesota NFL	9	7	0	.563	2nd/NFC Central Division	0	1
1997—Minnesota NFL	9	7	0	.563	4th/NFC Central Division	1	1
1998—Minnesota NFL	15	1	0	.938	1st/NFC Central Division	1	1
1999—Minnesota NFL	10	6	0	.625	2nd/NFC Central Division	1	1
2000—Minnesota NFL	11	5	0	.688	1st/NFC Central Division	1	1
2001—Minnesota NFL	5	10	0	.333	4th/NFC Central Division	0	0
2004—Arizona NFL	6	10	0	.375	3rd/NFC West Division	0	0
College totals (8 years)	**26**	**62**	**0**	**.295**	**College totals (1 year)**	**0**	**1**
Pro totals (11 years)	**103**	**72**	**0**	**.589**	**Pro totals (8 years)**	**4**	**8**

NOTES:
1991—Lost to Georgia Tech, 18-17, in Aloha Bowl.
1992—Lost to Washington, 24-7, in first-round playoff game.
1993—Lost to New York Giants, 17-10, in first-round playoff game.
1994—Lost to Chicago, 35-18, in first-round playoff game.
1996—Lost to Dallas, 40-15, in first-round playoff game.
1997—Defeated New York Giants, 23-22, in first-round playoff game; lost to San Francisco, 38-22, in conference playoff game.
1998—Defeated Arizona, 41-21, in conference playoff game; lost to Atlanta, 30-27, in NFC championship game.
1999—Defeated Dallas, 27-10, in first-round playoff game; lost to St. Louis, 49-37, in conference playoff game.
2000—Defeated New Orleans, 34-16, in conference playoff game; lost to New York Giants, 41-0, in NFC championship game.
2001—Replaced as head coach by Mike Tice (January 4, 2002) and club in fourth place.

PERSONAL: Born August 17, 1963, in Sandusky, Ohio. ... Son of Jim Gruden, scout, San Francisco 49ers; and brother of Jay Gruden, quarterback with Tampa Bay Storm of Arena League (1991-96) and current head coach, Orlando Predators of Arena League.
HIGH SCHOOL: Clay (South Bend, Ind.).
COLLEGE: Dayton, then Tennessee.

HEAD COACHING RECORD
BACKROUND: Graduate assistant, Tennessee (1986 and 1987). ... Passing game coordinator, Southeast Missouri State (1988). ... Wide receivers coach, Pacific (1989). ... Assistant coach, San Francisco 49ers NFL (1990) ... Wide receivers coach, University of Pittsburgh (1991). ... Offensive/quality control coach, Green Bay Packers NFL (1992). ... Wide receivers coach, Packers (1993 and 1994). ... Offensive coordinator, Philadelphia Eagles NFL (1995-1997).

			REGULAR SEASON			POST-SEASON	
	W	L	T	Pct.	Finish	W	L
1998—Oakland NFL	8	8	0	.500	2nd/AFC Western Division	0	0
1999—Oakland NFL	8	8	0	.500	4th/AFC Western Division	0	0
2000—Oakland NFL	12	4	0	.750	1st/AFC Western Division	1	1
2001—Oakland NFL	10	6	0	.625	1st/AFC Western Division	1	1
2002—Tampa Bay NFL	12	4	0	.750	1st/NFC South Division	3	0
2003—Tampa Bay NFL	7	9	0	.438	3rd/NFC South Division	0	0
2004—Tampa Bay NFL	5	11	0	.313	4th/NFC South Division	0	0
Pro totals (7 years)	62	50	0	.554	Pro totals (3 years)	5	2

NOTES:
2000—Defeated Miami, 27-0, in conference playoff game; lost to Baltimore, 16-3, in AFC championship game.
2001—Defeated New York Jets, 38-24, in first-round playoff game; lost to New England, 16-13 (OT), in conference playoff game.
2002—Defeated San Francisco, 31-6, in conference playoff game; defeated Philadelphia, 27-10, in NFC championship game; defeated Oakland, 48-21, in Super Bowl 37.

PERSONAL: Born December 9, 1957, in Pittsburgh. ... Full name: James Donald Haslett. ... Played linebacker.
HIGH SCHOOL: Avalon (Pittsburgh).
COLLEGE: Indiana (Pa.).
TRANSACTIONS/CAREER NOTES: Selected by Buffalo Bills in second round (51st pick overall) of 1979 NFL draft. ... On injured reserve with back injury (September 13-November 17, 1983). ... On injured reserve with broken leg (September 1, 1986-entire season). ... Released by Bills (September 7, 1987). ... Signed by New York Jets as replacement player (September 30, 1987). ... On injured reserve with back injury (October 20, 1987-remainder of season).
HONORS: Played in Pro Bowl (1980 and 1981 seasons).

		INTERCEPTIONS			
Year Team	G	No.	Yds.	Avg.	TD
1979—Buffalo NFL	16	2	15	7.5	0
1980—Buffalo NFL	16	2	30	15.0	0
1981—Buffalo NFL	16	0	0	0.0	0
1982—Buffalo NFL	6	0	0	0.0	0
1983—Buffalo NFL	5	0	0	0.0	0
1984—Buffalo NFL	15	0	0	0.0	0
1985—Buffalo NFL	16	1	40	40.0	0
1986—Buffalo NFL	Did not play.				
1987—New York Jets NFL	3	1	9	9.0	0
Pro totals (8 years)	93	6	94	15.7	0

HEAD COACHING RECORD
BACKROUND: Linebackers coach, University of Buffalo (1988). ... Defensive coordinator, University of Buffalo (1989 and 1990). ... Defensive coordinator, Sacramento Surge W.L. (1991 and 1992). ... Linebackers coach, Los Angeles Raiders NFL (1993 and 1994). ... Linebackers coach, New Orleans Saints NFL (1995). ... Defensive coordinator, Saints (1996). ... Defensive coordinator, Pittsburgh Steelers NFL (1997-1999).

			REGULAR SEASON			POST-SEASON	
	W	L	T	Pct.	Finish	W	L
2000—New Orleans NFL	10	6	0	.625	1st/NFC Western Division	1	1
2001—New Orleans NFL	7	9	0	.438	3rd/NFC Western Division	0	0
2002—New Orleans NFL	9	7	0	.563	3rd/NFC South Division	0	0
2003—New Orleans NFL	8	8	0	.500	2nd/NFC South Division	0	0
2004—New Orleans NFL	8	8	0	.500	2nd/NFC South Division	0	0
Pro totals (5 years)	42	38	0	.525	Pro totals (1 year)	1	1

NOTES:
2000—Defeated St. Louis, 31-28, in first-round playoff game; lost to Minnesota, 34-16, in conference playoff game.

PERSONAL: Born June 15, 1948, in San Francisco. ... Full name: Michael George Holmgren. ... Played quarterback.
HIGH SCHOOL: Lincoln (San Francisco).
COLLEGE: Southern California.
TRANSACTIONS/CAREER NOTES: Selected by St. Louis Cardinals in eighth round of 1970 NFL draft. ... Released by Cardinals (1970).

HEAD COACHING RECORD
BACKROUND: Coach, Lincoln High, San Francisco (1971). ... Assistant coach, Sacred Heart Cathedral Prep School, San Francisco (1972 and 1973). ... Assistant coach, Oak Grove High School, San Jose, Calif. (1975-1980). ... Offensive coordinator/quarterbacks coach, San Francisco State (1981). ... Quarterbacks coach, Brigham Young (1982-1985). ... Quarterbacks coach, San Francisco 49ers NFL (1986-1988). ... Offensive coordinator, 49ers (1989-1991).

	W	L	T	Pct.	Finish	W	L
1992—Green Bay NFL	9	7	0	.563	2nd/NFC Central Division	0	0
1993—Green Bay NFL	9	7	0	.563	3rd/NFC Central Division	1	1
1994—Green Bay NFL	9	7	0	.563	2nd/NFC Central Division	1	1
1995—Green Bay NFL	11	5	0	.688	1st/NFC Central Division	2	1
1996—Green Bay NFL	13	3	0	.813	1st/NFC Central Division	3	0
1997—Green Bay NFL	13	3	0	.813	1st/NFC Central Division	2	1
1998—Green Bay NFL	11	5	0	.688	2nd/NFC Central Division	0	1
1999—Seattle NFL	9	7	0	.563	1st/AFC Western Division	0	1
2000—Seattle NFL	6	10	0	.375	4th/AFC Western Division	0	0
2001—Seattle NFL	9	7	0	.563	2nd/AFC Western Division	0	0
2002—Seattle NFL	7	9	0	.438	3rd/NFC West Division	0	0
2003—Seattle NFL	10	6	0	.625	2nd/NFC West Division	0	1
2004—Seattle NFL	9	7	0	.563	1st/NFC West Division	0	1
Pro totals (13 years)	125	83	0	.601	Pro totals (9 years)	9	8

NOTES:

1993—Defeated Detroit, 28-24, in first-round playoff game; lost to Dallas 27-17, in conference playoff game.
1994—Defeated Detroit, 16-12, in first-round playoff game; lost to Dallas, 35-9, in conference playoff game.
1995—Defeated Atlanta, 37-20, in first-round playoff game; defeated San Francisco, 27-17, in conference playoff game; lost to Dallas, 38-27, in NFC championship game.
1996—Defeated San Francisco, 35-14, in conference playoff game; defeated Carolina, 30-13, in NFC championship game; defeated New England, 35-21, in Super Bowl 31.
1997—Defeated Tampa Bay, 21-7, in conference playoff game; defeated San Francisco, 23-10, in NFC championship game; lost to Denver, 31-24, in Super Bowl 32.
1998—Lost to San Francisco, 30-27, in first-round playoff game.
1999—Lost to Miami, 20-17, in first-round playoff game.
2003—Lost to Green Bay, 33-27 (OT), in first-round playoff game.
2004—Lost to St. Louis, 27-20, in first-round playoff game.

LEWIS, MARVIN — BENGALS

PERSONAL: Born September 23, 1958, in McDonald, Pa.
HIGH SCHOOL: Fort Cherry (McDonald, Pa.).
COLLEGE: Idaho State.

HEAD COACHING RECORD

BACKROUND: Linebackers coach, Idaho State (1981-1984). ... Linebackers coach, Long Beach State (1985 and 1986). ... Linebackers coach, University of New Mexico (1987-1989). ... Outside linebackers coach, University of Pittsburgh (1990 and 1991). ... Linebackers coach, Pittsburgh Steelers NFL (1992-1995). ... Defensive coordinator, Baltimore Ravens NFL (1996-2001). ... Defensive coordinator/assistant head coach, Washington Redskins NFL (2002).

	W	L	T	Pct.	Finish	W	L
2003—Cincinnati NFL	8	8	0	.500	2nd/AFC North Division	0	0
2004—Cincinnati NFL	8	8	0	.500	3rd/AFC North Division	0	0
Pro totals (2 years)	16	16	0	.500			

MARIUCCI, STEVE — LIONS

PERSONAL: Born November 4, 1955, in Iron Mountain, Mich. ... Full name: Steven Mariucci. ... Played quarterback.
HIGH SCHOOL: Iron Mountain (Mich.).
COLLEGE: Northern Michigan.

HEAD COACHING RECORD

BACKROUND: Quarterbacks/running backs coach, Northern Michigan (1978 and 1979). ... Quarterbacks/special teams coordinator, Cal State Fullerton (1980-1982). ... Assistant head coach, Louisville (1983 and 1984). ... Receivers coach, Orlando Renegades USFL (1985). ... Quality control coach, Los Angeles Rams NFL (fall 1985). ... Wide receivers/special teams coach, University of California (1987-1989). ... Offensive coordinator/quarterbacks coach, University of California (1990 and 1991). ... Quarterbacks coach, Green Bay Packers NFL (1992-1995).

	W	L	T	Pct.	Finish	W	L
1996—California	6	6	0	.500	T5th/Pacific-10 Conference	0	1
1997—San Francisco NFL	13	3	0	.813	1st/NFC Western Division	1	1
1998—San Francisco NFL	12	4	0	.750	2nd/NFC Western Division	1	1
1999—San Francisco NFL	4	12	0	.250	4th/NFC Western Division	0	0
2000—San Francisco NFL	6	10	0	.375	4th/NFC Western Division	0	0
2001—San Francisco NFL	12	4	0	.750	2nd/NFC Western Division	0	1
2002—San Francisco NFL	10	6	0	.625	1st/NFC West Division	1	1
2003—Detroit NFL	5	11	0	.313	4th/NFC North Division	0	0
2004—Detroit NFL	6	10	0	.625	3rd/NFC North Division	0	0
College totals (1 year)	6	6	0	.500	College totals (1 year)	0	1
Pro totals (8 years)	68	60	0	.563	Pro totals (4 years)	3	4

NOTES:

1996—Lost to Navy, 42-38, in Aloha Bowl.
1997—Defeated Minnesota, 38-22, in conference playoff game; lost to Green Bay, 23-10, in NFC championship game.
1998—Defeated Green Bay, 30-27, in first-round playoff game; lost to Atlanta, 20-18, in conference playoff game.
2001—Lost to Green Bay, 25-15, in first-round playoff game.
2002—Defeated New York Giants, 39-38, in first-round playoff game; lost to Tampa Bay, 31-6, in conference playoff game.

...orn May 13, 1951, in Sioux Falls, S.D.
...OOL: Madison (San Diego).
...COLLEGE: San Diego Mesa Community College.
...LLEGE: UC Santa Barbara, then Fresno State.

HEAD COACHING RECORD

BACKROUND: Assistant coach, Bullard High School, Fresno, Calif. (1973). ... Assistant coach, San Diego Mesa Community College (1974, 1976 and 1977). ... Assistant coach, San Jose State (1975). ... Assistant coach, Santa Ana College (1978). ... Assistant coach, Fresno State (1979). ... Assistant coach, Pacific University (1980 and 1981). ... Running backs coach, University of Minnesota (1982). ... Quarterbacks/receivers coach, Arizona State (1983, 1986 and 1987). ... Offensive coordinator, Arizona State (1984 and 1988-1991). ... Offensive assistant, Los Angeles Rams NFL (1992 and 1993). ... Quarterbacks coach, Rams (1994). ... Wide receivers coach, St. Louis Rams NFL (1995 and 1996). ... Quarterbacks coach, Washington Redskins NFL (1997 and 1998). ... Offensive coordinator, Rams (1999).

				REGULAR SEASON		POST-SEASON	
	W	L	T	Pct.	Finish	W	L
2000—St. Louis NFL	10	6	0	.625	2nd/NFC Western Division	0	1
2001—St. Louis NFL	14	2	0	.875	1st/NFC Western Division	2	1
2002—St. Louis NFL	7	9	0	.438	2nd/NFC West Division	0	0
2003—St. Louis NFL	12	4	0	.750	1st/NFC West Division	0	1
2004—St. Louis NFL	8	8	0	.500	2nd/NFC West Division	1	1
Pro totals (5 years)	**51**	**29**	**0**	**.638**	**Pro totals (4 years)**	**3**	**4**

NOTES:
2000—Lost to New Orleans, 31-28, in first-round playoff game.
2001—Defeated Green Bay, 45-17, in conference playoff game; defeated Philadelphia, 29-24, in NFC championship game; lost to New England, 20-17, in Super Bowl 36.
2003—Lost to Carolina, 29-23 (OT), in conference playoff game.
2004—Defeated Seattle, 27-20, in first-round playoff game; lost to Atlanta, 47-17, in conference playoff game.

MORA, JIM   FALCONS

PERSONAL: Born November 19, 1961, in Los Angeles. ... Full name: Jim Mora Jr. ... Son of Jim Mora, coach, New Orleans Saints (1986-96) and Indianapolis Colts (1998-2001).
HIGH SCHOOL: Interlake (Bellevue, Wash.).
COLLEGE: Washington.

HEAD COACHING RECORD

BACKROUND: Assistant coach, University of Washington (1984). ... Assistant secondary coach, San Diego Chargers NFL (1986-88). ... Secondary coach, Chargers (1989-91). ... Secondary coach, New Orleans Saints NFL (1992-96). ... Defensive backs coach, San Francisco 49ers NFL (1997-98). ... Defensive coordinator, 49ers (1999-2003).

				REGULAR SEASON		POST-SEASON	
	W	L	T	Pct.	Finish	W	L
2004—Atlanta NFL	11	5	0	.688	1st/NFC South Division	1	1

NOTES:
2004—Defeated St. Louis, 47-17, in conference playoff game; lost to Philadelphia, 27-10, in NFC championship game.

MULARKEY, MIKE   BILLS

PERSONAL: Born November 19, 1961, in Fort Lauderdale, Fla. ... Full name: Michael Rene Mularkey.
HIGH SCHOOL: Northeast (Fort Lauderdale).
COLLEGE: Florida.
TRANSACTIONS/CAREER NOTES: Selected by Tampa Bay Bandits in 1983 USFL territorial draft. ... Selected by San Francisco 49ers in ninth round (229th pick overall) of 1983 NFL draft. ... Signed by 49ers (June 1, 1983). ... Released by 49ers (August 29, 1983). ... Claimed on waivers by Minnesota Vikings (August 30, 1983). ... On injured reserve with ankle injury (September 30, 1983-remainder of season). ... On injured reserve with knee injury (September 8-October 31, 1987). ... Crossed picket line during players strike (October 7, 1987). ... Returned to picket line (October 12, 1987). ... Granted unconditional free agency (February 1, 1989). ... Signed by Pittsburgh Steelers (March 31, 1989). ... Granted unconditional free agency (February 1-April 1, 1991). ... Re-signed by Steelers for 1991 season. ... On injured reserve with back injury (December 6, 1991-remainder of season). ... Granted unconditional free agency (February 1-April 1, 1992). ... Re-signed by Steelers for 1992 season. ... Released by Steelers (June 29, 1992).

			RECEIVING				TOTALS			
Year Team	G	GS	No.	Yds.	Avg.	TD	TD	2pt.	Pts.	Fum.
1983—Minnesota NFL	3	0	0	0	0.0	0	0	0	0	0
1984—Minnesota NFL	16	0	14	134	9.6	2	0	0	0	0
1985—Minnesota NFL	15	0	13	196	15.1	1	0	0	0	0
1986—Minnesota NFL	16	0	11	89	8.1	2	0	0	0	0
1987—Minnesota NFL	9	0	1	6	6.0	0	0	0	0	0
1988—Minnesota NFL	16	0	3	39	13.0	0	0	0	0	0
1989—Pittsburgh NFL	14	0	22	326	14.8	1	0	0	0	0
1990—Pittsburgh NFL	16	0	32	365	11.4	3	0	0	0	0
1991—Pittsburgh NFL	9	0	6	67	11.2	0	0	0	0	0
Pro totals (9 years)	**114**	**0**	**102**	**1222**	**12.0**	**9**	**0**	**0**	**0**	**0**

HEAD COACHING RECORD
BACKROUND: Offensive line coach, Concordia (Minn.) College (1993). ... Quality control coach, Tampa Bay Buccaneers NFL (1994). ... Tight ends coach, Buccaneers (1995). ... Tight ends coach, Pittsburgh Steelers NFL (1996-2000). ... Offensive coordinator, Steelers (2001-03).

	REGULAR SEASON				
	W	L	T	Pct.	Finish
2004—Buffalo NFL	9	7	0	.563	3rd/AFC East Division

NOLAN, MIKE

PERSONAL: Born March 7, 1959, in Baltimore, Md. ... Son of Dick Nolan, coach, San Francisco 49ers (1968-75) and New O... (1978-80).
HIGH SCHOOL: Woodside (Calif.).
COLLEGE: Oregon.

COACHING RECORD

BACKROUND: Graduate assistant, Oregon (1981). ... Defensive backs coach, Stanford (1982). ... Linebackers coach, Stanford (1983). ... Defensive backs coach, Rice (1984-85). ... Linebackers coach, Louisiana State (1986). ... Special teams coach/defensive assistant, Denver Broncos NFL (1987-88). ... Linebackers coach, Broncos (1989-92). ... Defensive coordinator, New York Giants (1993-96). ... Defensive coordinator, Washington Redskins NFL (1997-99). ... Defensive coordinator, New York Jets NFL (2000). ... Defensive coordinator, Baltimore Ravens NFL (2001-04).

PARCELLS, BILL   COWBOYS

PERSONAL: Born August 22, 1941, in Englewood, N.J. ... Full name: Duane Charles Parcells.
HIGH SCHOOL: River Dell (Oradell, N.J.).
COLLEGE: Colgate, then Wichita State.

HEAD COACHING RECORD

BACKROUND: Defensive assistant coach, Hastings (Neb.) College (1964). ... Defensive line coach, Wichita State (1965). ... Linebackers coach, Army (1966-1969). ... Linebackers coach, Florida State (1970-1972). ... Defensive coordinator, Vanderbilt (1973 and 1974). ... Defensive coordinator, Texas Tech (1975-1977). ... Assistant coach, New York Giants NFL (1979). ... Linebackers coach, New England NFL (1980). ... Defensive coordinator/linebackers coach, New York Giants NFL (1981 and 1982). ... NFL Analyst, NBC Sports (1991 and 1992).
HONORS: Named NFL Coach of the Year by THE SPORTING NEWS (1986).

	REGULAR SEASON					POST-SEASON	
	W	L	T	Pct.	Finish	W	L
1978—Air Force	3	8	0	.273	Independent	0	0
1983—New York Giants NFL	3	12	1	.200	5th/NFC Eastern Division	0	0
1984—New York Giants NFL	9	7	0	.563	2nd/NFC Eastern Division	1	1
1985—New York Giants NFL	10	6	0	.625	2nd/NFC Eastern Division	1	1
1986—New York Giants NFL	14	2	0	.875	1st/NFC Eastern Division	3	0
1987—New York Giants NFL	6	9	0	.400	5th/NFC Eastern Division	0	0
1988—New York Giants NFL	10	6	0	.625	2nd/NFC Eastern Division	0	0
1989—New York Giants NFL	12	4	0	.750	1st/NFC Eastern Division	0	1
1990—New York Giants NFL	13	3	0	.813	1st/NFC Eastern Division	3	0
1993—New England NFL	5	11	0	.313	4th/AFC Eastern Division	0	0
1994—New England NFL	10	6	0	.625	2nd/AFC Eastern Division	0	1
1995—New England NFL	6	10	0	.375	4th/AFC Eastern Division	0	0
1996—New England NFL	11	5	0	.688	1st/AFC Eastern Division	2	1

	REGULAR SEASON					POST-SEASON	
	W	L	T	Pct.	Finish	W	L
1997—New York Jets NFL	9	7	0	.563	3rd/AFC Eastern Division	0	0
1998—New York Jets NFL	12	4	0	.750	1st/AFC Eastern Division	1	1
1999—New York Jets NFL	8	8	0	.500	4th/AFC Eastern Division	0	0
2003—Dallas NFL	10	6	0	.625	2nd/NFC East Division	0	1
2004—Dallas NFL	6	10	0	.375	3rd/NFC East Division	0	0
College totals (1 year)	3	8	0	.273			
Pro totals (17 years)	154	116	1	.570	Pro totals (9 years)	11	7

NOTES:
1984—Defeated Los Angeles Rams, 16-13, in first-round playoff game; lost to San Francisco, 21-10, in conference playoff game.
1985—Defeated San Francisco, 17-3, in first-round playoff game; lost to Chicago, 21-0, in conference playoff game.
1986—Defeated San Francisco, 49-3, in conference playoff game; defeated Washington, 17-0, in NFC championship game; defeated Denver, 39-20, in Super Bowl 21.
1989—Lost to Los Angeles Rams, 19-13 (OT), in conference playoff game.
1990—Defeated Chicago, 31-3, in conference playoff game; defeated San Francisco, 15-13, in NFC championship game; defeated Buffalo, 20-19, in Super Bowl 25.
1994—Lost to Cleveland, 20-13, in first-round playoff game.
1996—Defeated Pittsburgh, 28-3, in conference playoff game; defeated Jacksonville, 20-6, in AFC championship game; lost to Green Bay, 35-21, in Super Bowl 31.
1998—Defeated Jacksonville, 34-24, in conference playoff game; lost to Denver, 23-10, in AFC championship game.
2003—Lost to Carolina, 29-10, in first-round playoff game.

REID, ANDY   EAGLES

PERSONAL: Born March 19, 1958, in Los Angeles. ... Full name: Andrew Walter Reid.
HIGH SCHOOL: John Marshall (Los Angeles).
JUNIOR COLLEGE: Glendale (Calif.).
COLLEGE: Brigham Young.

HEAD COACHING RECORD

BACKROUND: Graduate assistant, Brigham Young University (1982). ... Offensive coordinator, San Francisco State (1983-1985). ... Offensive line coach, Northern Arizona University (1986). ... Offensive line coach, University of Texas-El Paso (1987 and 1988). ... Offensive line coach,

University of Missouri (1989-1991). ... Tight ends coach, Green Bay Packers NFL (1992-1996). ... Quarterbacks coach, Packers (1997 and 1998).

HONORS: Named NFL Coach of the Year by THE SPORTING NEWS (2000 and 2002).

		REGULAR SEASON				POST-SEASON	
	W	L	T	Pct.	Finish	W	L
1999—Philadelphia NFL	5	11	0	.313	5th/NFC Eastern Division	0	0
2000—Philadelphia NFL	11	5	0	.688	2nd/NFC Eastern Division	1	1
2001—Philadelphia NFL	11	5	0	.688	1st/NFC Eastern Division	2	1
2002—Philadelphia NFL	12	4	0	.750	1st/NFC East Division	1	1
2003—Philadelphia NFL	12	4	0	.750	1st/NFC East Division	1	1
2004—Philadelphia NFL	13	3	0	.813	1st/NFC East Division	2	1
Pro totals (6 years)	**64**	**32**	**0**	**.667**	**Pro totals (5 years)**	**7**	**5**

NOTES:
2000—Defeated Tampa Bay, 21-3, in first-round playoff game; lost to New York Giants, 20-10, in conference playoff game.
2001—Defeated Tampa Bay, 31-9, in first-round playoff game; defeated Chicago, 33-19, in conference playoff game; lost to St. Louis, 29-24, in NFC championship game.
2002—Defeated Atlanta, 20-6, in conference playoff game; lost to Tampa Bay, 27-10, in NFC championship game.
2003—Defeated Green Bay, 20-17 (OT), in conference playoff game; lost to Carolina, 14-3, in NFC championship game.
2004—Defeated Minnesota, 27-14, in conference playoff game; defeated Atlanta, 27-10, in NFC championship game; lost to New England, 24-21, in Super Bowl 39.

SABAN, NICK — DOLPHINS

PERSONAL: Born October 31, 1951, in Fairmont, W.Va. ... Full name: Nick Lou Saban.
HIGH SCHOOL: Monongah (W.Va.).
COLLEGE: Kent State.

HEAD COACHING RECORD

BACKROUND: Graduate assistant, Kent State (1973-74). ... Linebackers coach, Kent State (1975-76). ... Outside linebackers coach, Syracuse (1977). ... Defensive backs coach, West Virginia (1978-79). ... Defensive backs coach, Ohio State (1980-81). ... Defensive backs coach, Navy (1982). ... Defensive coordinator/secondary coach, Michigan State (1983-87). ... Defensive backs coach, Houston Oilers NFL (1988-89).

		REGULAR SEASON				POST-SEASON	
	W	L	T	Pct.	Finish	W	L
1990—Toledo	9	2	0	.818	T1st/Mid-American Conference	0	0
1995—Michigan State	6	4	1	.600	5th/Big Ten Conference	0	1
1996—Michigan State	6	5	0	.545	T5th/Big Ten Conference	0	1
1997—Michigan State	7	4	0	.636	T6th/Big Ten Conference	0	1
1998—Michigan State	6	6	0	.500	6th/Big Ten Conference	0	0
1999—Michigan State	9	2	0	.818	T2nd/Big Ten Conference	1	0
2000—Louisiana State	7	4	0	.636	2nd/Southeastern Conference (West Division)	1	0
2001—Louisiana State	9	3	0	.750	1st/Southeastern Conference (West Division)	1	0
2002—Louisiana State	8	4	0	.667	1st/Southeastern Conference (West Division)	0	1
2003—Louisiana State	12	1	0	.923	1st/Southeastern Conference (West Division)	1	0
2004—Louisiana State	9	2	0	.818	2nd/Southeastern Conference (West Division)	0	1
College totals (11 years)	**88**	**37**	**1**	**.704**	**College totals (9 years)**	**4**	**5**

NOTES:
1995—Lost to LSU, 45-26, in Independence Bowl.
1996—Lost to Stanford, 38-0, in Sun Bowl.
1997—Lost to Washington, 51-23, in Aloha Bowl.
1999—Defeated Florida, 37-34, in Citrus Bowl.
2000—Defeated Georgia Tech, 28-14, in Peach Bowl.
2001—Defeated Illinois, 47-34, in Sugar Bowl.
2002—Lost to Texas, 35-20, in Cotton Bowl.
2003—Defeated Oklahoma, 21-14, in Sugar Bowl.
2004—Lost to Iowa, 30-25, in Capital One Bowl.

SCHOTTENHEIMER, MARTY — CHARGERS

PERSONAL: Born September 23, 1943, in Canonsburg, Pa. ... Full name: Martin Edward Schottenheimer. ... Played linebacker. ... Brother of Kurt Schottenheimer, secondary coach, St. Louis Rams; father of Brian Schottenheimer, quarterbacks coach, San Diego Chargers.
HIGH SCHOOL: Fort Cherry (McDonald, Pa.).
COLLEGE: Pittsburgh.
TRANSACTIONS/CAREER NOTES: Selected by Buffalo Bills in seventh round of 1965 AFL draft. ... Released by Bills (1969). ... Signed by Boston Patriots (1969). ... Patriots franchise renamed New England Patriots for 1971 season. ... Traded by New England Patriots to Pittsburgh Steelers for OT Mike Haggerty and a draft choice (July 10, 1971). ... Released by Steelers (1971).
CHAMPIONSHIP GAME EXPERIENCE: Member of AFL championship team (1965 season). ... Played in AFL championship game (1966 season).
HONORS: Played in AFL All-Star Game (1965 season).

		INTERCEPTIONS			
Year Team	G	No.	Yds.	Avg.	TD
1965—Buffalo AFL	14	0	0	0.0	0
1966—Buffalo AFL	14	1	20	20.0	0
1967—Buffalo AFL	14	3	88	29.3	1
1968—Buffalo AFL	14	1	22	22.0	0
1969—Boston AFL	11	1	3	3.0	0
1970—Boston NFL	12	0	0	0.0	0
AFL totals (5 years)	**67**	**6**	**133**	**22.2**	**1**
NFL totals (1 year)	**12**	**0**	**0**	**0.0**	**0**
Pro totals (6 years)	**79**	**6**	**133**	**22.2**	**1**

HEAD COACHING RECORD

BACKROUND: Linebackers coach, Portland Storm WFL (1974). ... Linebackers coach, New York Giants NFL (1975 and 1976). ... Defensive coordinator, Giants (1977). ... Linebackers coach, Detroit Lions NFL (1978 and 1979). ... Defensive coordinator, Cleveland Browns NFL (1980-October 22, 1984).

	W	L	T	Pct.	REGULAR SEASON Finish	POST-SEASON W	L
1984—Cleveland NFL	4	4	0	.500	3rd/AFC Central Division	0	0
1985—Cleveland NFL	8	8	0	.500	1st/AFC Central Division	0	1
1986—Cleveland NFL	12	4	0	.750	1st/AFC Central Division	1	1
1987—Cleveland NFL	10	5	0	.667	1st/AFC Central Division	1	1
1988—Cleveland NFL	10	6	0	.625	2nd/AFC Central Division	0	1
1989—Kansas City NFL	8	7	1	.533	2nd/AFC Western Division	0	0
1990—Kansas City NFL	11	5	0	.688	2nd/AFC Western Division	0	1
1991—Kansas City NFL	10	6	0	.625	2nd/AFC Western Division	1	1
1992—Kansas City NFL	10	6	0	.625	2nd/AFC Western Division	0	1

	W	L	T	Pct.	REGULAR SEASON Finish	POST-SEASON W	L
1993—Kansas City NFL	11	5	0	.688	1st/AFC Western Division	2	1
1994—Kansas City NFL	9	7	0	.563	2nd/AFC Western Division	0	1
1995—Kansas City NFL	13	3	0	.813	1st/AFC Western Division	0	1
1996—Kansas City NFL	9	7	0	.563	2nd/AFC Western Division	0	0
1997—Kansas City NFL	13	3	0	.813	1st/AFC Western Division	0	1
1998—Kansas City NFL	7	9	0	.438	4th/AFC Western Division	0	0
2001—Washington NFL	8	8	0	.500	2nd/NFC Eastern Division	0	0
2002—San Diego NFL	8	8	0	.500	3rd/AFC West Division	0	0
2003—San Diego NFL	4	12	0	.250	4th/AFC West Division	0	0
2004—San Diego NFL	12	4	0	.750	1st/AFC West Division	0	1
Pro totals (19 years)	**177**	**117**	**1**	**.602**	**Pro totals (12 years)**	**5**	**12**

NOTES:
1984—Replaced Sam Rutigliano as head coach (October 22) with 1-7 record and club in third place.
1985—Lost to Miami, 24-21, in conference playoff game.
1986—Defeated New York Jets, 23-20 (2 OT), in conference playoff game; lost to Denver, 23-20 (OT), in AFC championship game.
1987—Defeated Indianapolis, 38-21, in conference playoff game; lost to Denver, 38-33, in AFC championship game.
1988—Lost to Houston, 24-23, in first-round playoff game.
1990—Lost to Miami, 17-16, in first-round playoff game.
1991—Defeated Los Angeles Raiders, 10-6, in first-round playoff game; lost to Buffalo, 37-14, in conference playoff game.
1992—Lost to San Diego, 17-0, in first-round playoff game.
1993—Defeated Pittsburgh, 27-24 (OT), in first-round playoff game; defeated Houston, 28-20, in conference playoff game; lost to Buffalo, 30-13, in AFC championship game.
1994—Lost to Miami, 27-17, in first-round playoff game.
1995—Lost to Indianapolis, 10-7, in conference playoff game.
1997—Lost to Denver, 14-10, in conference playoff game.
2004—Lost to N.Y. Jets, 20-17 (OT), in first-round playoff game.

SHANAHAN, MIKE   BRONCOS

PERSONAL: Born August 24, 1952, in Oak Park, Ill. ... Full name: Michael Edward Shanahan.
HIGH SCHOOL: East Leyden (Franklin Park, Ill.).
COLLEGE: Eastern Illinois.

HEAD COACHING RECORD

BACKROUND: Graduate assistant, Eastern Illinois (1973 and 1974). ... Running backs/wide receivers coach, Oklahoma (1975 and 1976). ... Backfield coach, Northern Arizona (1977). ... Offensive coordinator, Eastern Illinois (1978). ... Offensive coordinator, University of Minnesota (1979). ... Offensive coordinator, University of Florida (1980-1983). ... Receivers coach, Denver Broncos NFL (1984). ... Offensive coordinator, Broncos (1985-1987 and 1991). ... Quarterbacks coach, Broncos (1989 and 1990). ... Offensive coordinator, San Francisco 49ers NFL (1992-1994).

	W	L	T	Pct.	REGULAR SEASON Finish	POST-SEASON W	L
1988—Los Angeles Raiders NFL	7	9	0	.438	3rd/AFC Western Division	0	0
1989—Los Angeles Raiders NFL	1	3	0	.250	3rd/AFC Western Division	0	0
1995—Denver NFL	8	8	0	.500	4th/AFC Western Division	0	0
1996—Denver NFL	13	3	0	.813	1st/AFC Western Division	0	1
1997—Denver NFL	12	4	0	.750	2nd/AFC Western Division	4	0
1998—Denver NFL	14	2	0	.875	1st/AFC Western Division	3	0
1999—Denver NFL	6	10	0	.375	5th/AFC Western Division	0	0
2000—Denver NFL	11	5	0	.688	2nd/AFC Western Division	0	1
2001—Denver NFL	8	8	0	.500	3rd/AFC Western Division	0	0
2002—Denver NFL	9	7	0	.563	2nd/AFC West Division	0	0
2003—Denver NFL	10	6	0	.625	2nd/AFC West Division	0	1
2004—Denver NFL	10	6	0	.625	2nd/AFC West Division	0	1
Pro totals (12 years)	**109**	**71**	**0**	**.606**	**Pro totals (6 years)**	**7**	**4**

NOTES:
1989—Replaced as Raiders coach by Art Shell (October 3) with club tied for fourth place.
1996—Lost to Jacksonville, 30-27, in conference playoff game.
1997—Defeated Jacksonville, 42-17, in first-round playoff game; defeated Kansas City, 14-10, in conference playoff game; defeated Pittsburgh, 24-21, in AFC championship game; defeated Green Bay, 31-24, in Super Bowl 32.
1998—Defeated Miami, 38-3, in conference playoff game; defeated New York Jets, 23-10, in AFC championship game; defeated Atlanta, 34-19, in Super Bowl 33.
2000—Lost to Baltimore, 21-3, in first-round playoff game.
2003—Lost to Indianapolis, 41-10, in first-round playoff game.
2004—Lost to Indianapolis, 49-24, in first-round playoff game.

PACKERS

Sherman.

ach, Worcester (Mass.) Academy (1979 and 1980). ...
Tulane (1983 and 1984). ... Offensive line coach, Holy
ach, Texas A&M (1989-1993). ... Offensive line coach,
Green Bay Packers NFL (1997-1998). ... Offensive coor-

	POST-SEASON	
	W	L
Division	0	0
Division	1	1
ivision	0	1
ivision	1	1
Division	0	1
ears)	2	4

7, in conference playoff game.

-17 (OT), in conference playoff game.

BEARS

RECORD
Assistant coach, Cascia Hall (Okla.) Prep (1981). ... Linebackers
ebackers coach, Arizona State (1988-91). ... Outside linebackers
... Defensive backs coach, Ohio State (1995). ... Linebackers coach,
uis Rams NFL (2001-02). ... Assistant head coach/defensive coor-

LAR SEASON	POST-SEASON	
h	W	L
/NFC North Division	0	0

VIKINGS

lichael Peter Tice. ... Played tight end. ... Brother of John Tice, tight end,

by Seattle Seahawks (April 30, 1981). ... On injured reserve with fractured
e agency (February 1, 1989). ... Signed by Washington Redskins (February
d by Seahawks (November 28, 1990). ... Granted unconditional free agency
91). ... Granted unconditional free agency (February 1, 1992). ... Signed by
ack injury (September 25-October 21, 1992). ... Granted unconditional free
... Released by Vikings (August 30, 1993). ... Re-signed by Vikings (August
94). ... Re-signed by Vikings (December 7, 1995). ... Granted unconditional

hip game (1983 season).

	RECEIVING			KICKOFF RETURNS				TOTALS			
No.	Yds.	Avg.	TD	No.	Yds.	Avg.	TD	TD	2pt.	Pts.	Fum.
5	47	9.4	0	0	0	0.0	0	0	0	0	0
9	46	5.1	0	0	0	0.0	0	0	0	0	0
0	0	0.0	0	2	28	14.0	0	0	0	0	0
8	90	11.3	3	0	0	0.0	0	3	0	18	0
2	13	6.5	0	1	17	17.0	0	0	0	0	0
15	150	10.0	0	1	17	17.0	0	0	0	0	0
14	106	7.6	2	0	0	0.0	0	2	0	12	0
29	244	8.4	0	1	17	17.0	0	0	0	0	1
1	2	2.0	0	0	0	0.0	0	0	0	0	0
0	0	0.0	0	0	0	0.0	0	0	0	0	0
10	70	7.0	4	3	46	15.3	0	4	0	24	0
5	65	13.0	1	0	0	0.0	0	1	0	6	0
6	39	6.5	1	0	0	0.0	0	1	0	6	1
3	22	7.3	0	0	0	0.0	0	0	0	0	0
107	894	8.4	11	8	125	15.6	0	11	0	66	2

HEAD COACHING RECORD
. (1996). ... Offensive line coach, Vikings (1997-2000). ... Assistant head coach/offen-

		REGULAR SEASON	POST-SEASON	
T	Pct.	Finish	W	L
0	.000	4th/NFC Central Division	0	0
0	.375	2nd/NFC North Division	0	0

RAIDERS

Turner, offensive coordinator, Chicago

79). ... Defensive backs coach, USC
oach, Los Angeles Rams NFL (1985-

	POST-SEASON	
	W	L
	0	0
	0	0
	0	0
	0	0
	1	1
	0	0
	1	1

CHIEFS

Vermeil, conditioning coach with
es (1978-82).

chool, San Mateo, Calif. (1960-
1968). ... Assistant coach, Los

	POST-SEASON	
	W	L
	0	0
	0	0
	1	0
	0	0
	0	1
	1	1
	2	1
	0	0
	0	0
	3	0
	0	0
	0	1
	0	0
	1	0
	6	5

d, 27-10, in Super Bowl 15.

Tennessee, 23-16, in Super

game.

	REGULAR SEASON				
	W	L	T	Pct.	Finish
2003—Minnesota NFL	9	7	0	.563	2nd/NFC North Division
2004—Minnesota NFL	8	8	0	.500	2nd/NFC North Division
Pro totals (4 years)	23	26	0	.469	**Pro totals (1 year)**

NOTES:
2001—Replaced Dennis Green as head coach (January 4) with 5-10 record and club in fourth place.
2004—Defeated Green Bay, 31-17, in first-round playoff game; lost to Philadelphia, 27-14, in conference playoff

TURNER, NORV

PERSONAL: Born May 17, 1952, in LeJeune, N.C. ... Full name: Norval Eugene Turner. ... Brother of Ror
Bears.
HIGH SCHOOL: Alhambra (Calif.).
COLLEGE: Oregon.

HEAD COACHING RECORD
BACKROUND: Graduate assistant, Oregon (1975). ... Receivers coach, Southern California (1976-19
(1980). ... Quarterbacks coach, USC (1981-1983). ... Offensive coordinator, USC (1984). ... Receivers c
1990). ... Offensive coordinator, Dallas Cowboys NFL (1991-1993).

	REGULAR SEASON				
	W	L	T	Pct.	Finish
1994—Washington NFL	3	13	0	.188	5th/NFC Eastern Division
1995—Washington NFL	6	10	0	.375	3rd/NFC Eastern Division
1996—Washington NFL	9	7	0	.563	3rd/NFC Eastern Division
1997—Washington NFL	8	7	1	.533	2nd/NFC Eastern Division
1998—Washington NFL	6	10	0	.375	4th/NFC Eastern Division
1999—Washington NFL	10	6	0	.625	1st/NFC Eastern Division
2000—Washington NFL	7	6	0	.538	3rd/NFC Eastern Division
2004—Oakland NFL	5	11	0	.313	4th/AFC West Division
Pro totals (8 years)	54	70	1	.435	**Pro totals (1 year)**

NOTES:
1999—Defeated Detroit, 27-13, in first-round playoff game; lost to Tampa Bay, 14-13, in conference playoff game.

VERMEIL, DICK

PERSONAL: Born October 30, 1936, in Calistoga, Calif. ... Full name: Richard Albert Vermeil. ... Brother of Al
San Francisco 49ers (1979-82) and brother-in-law of Louie Giammona, running back with Philadelphia Eagl
HIGH SCHOOL: Calistoga (Calif.).
JUNIOR COLLEGE: Napa College.
COLLEGE: San Jose State (master's degree in physical education, 1959).

HEAD COACHING RECORD
BACKROUND: Assistant coach, Del Mar High School, San Jose, Calif. (1959). ... Head coach, Hillsdale High S
1962; record: 17-9-1). ... Assistant coach, College of San Mateo (1963). ... Assistant coach, Stanford (1965
Angeles Rams NFL (1969 and 1971-1973). ... Offensive coordinator, UCLA (1970).
HONORS: Named NFL Coach of the Year by THE SPORTING NEWS (1979 and 1999).

	REGULAR SEASON				
	W	L	T	Pct.	Finish
1964—Napa College	8	1	0	.889	2nd/Golden Valley Conference
1974—UCLA	6	3	2	.667	T3rd/Pacific-8 Conference
1975—UCLA	8	2	1	.800	T1st/Pacific-8 Conference
1976—Philadelphia NFL	4	10	0	.286	4th/NFC Eastern Division
1977—Philadelphia NFL	5	9	0	.357	4th/NFC Eastern Division
1978—Philadelphia NFL	9	7	0	.563	2nd/NFC Eastern Division
1979—Philadelphia NFL	11	5	0	.688	2nd/NFC Eastern Division
1980—Philadelphia NFL	12	4	0	.750	1st/NFC Eastern Division
1981—Philadelphia NFL	10	6	0	.625	2nd/NFC Eastern Division
1982—Philadelphia NFL	3	6	0	.333	5th/NFC Eastern Division
1997—St. Louis NFL	5	11	0	.313	5th/NFC Western Division
1998—St. Louis NFL	4	12	0	.250	5th/NFC Western Division
1999—St. Louis NFL	13	3	0	.813	1st/NFC Western Division
2001—Kansas City NFL	6	10	0	.375	4th/AFC Western Division
2002—Kansas City NFL	8	8	0	.500	4th/AFC West Division
2003—Kansas City NFL	13	3	0	.813	1st/AFC West Division
2004—Kansas City NFL	7	9	0	.438	3rd/AFC West Division
College totals (2 years)	14	5	3	.737	**College totals (1 year)**
Pro totals (14 years)	110	103	0	.516	**Pro totals (6 years)**

NOTES:
1975—Defeated Ohio State, 23-10, in Rose Bowl.
1978—Lost to Atlanta, 14-13, in conference playoff game.
1979—Defeated Chicago, 27-17, in first-round playoff game; lost to Tampa Bay, 24-17, in conference playoff game.
1980—Defeated Minnesota, 31-16, in conference playoff game; defeated Dallas, 20-7, in NFC championship game; lost to Oakla
1981—Lost to New York Giants, 27-21, in conference playoff game.
1982—Only nine of 16 games were played due to the cancellation of games because of a players strike.
1999—Defeated Minnesota, 49-37, in conference playoff game; defeated Tampa Bay, 11-6, in NFC championship game; defeated
   Bowl 34.
2003—Lost to Indianapolis, 38-31, in conference playoff game.

PERSONAL: Born December 19, 1954, in Norwood, Mass. ... Full name: Michael Francis Sherman.
COLLEGE: Central Connecticut State.

HEAD COACHING RECORD

BACKROUND: Head coach, Stamford High School, Stamford, Conn. (1978). ... Head coach, Worcester (Mass.) Academy (1979 and 1980). ... Graduate assistant, University of Pittsburgh (1981 and 1982). ... Offensive line coach, Tulane (1983 and 1984). ... Offensive line coach, Holy Cross (1985-1987). ... Offensive coordinator, Holy Cross (1988). ... Offensive line coach, Texas A&M (1989-1993). ... Offensive line coach, UCLA (1994). ... Offensive line coach, Texas A&M (1995-1996). ... Tight ends coach, Green Bay Packers NFL (1997-1998). ... Offensive coordinator/tight ends coach, Seattle Seahawks NFL (1999).

							POST-SEASON	
		REGULAR SEASON						
	W	L	T	Pct.	Finish		W	L
2000—Green Bay NFL	9	7	0	.563	3rd/NFC Central Division		0	0
2001—Green Bay NFL	12	4	0	.750	2nd/NFC Central Division		1	1
2002—Green Bay NFL	12	4	0	.750	1st/NFC North Division		0	1
2003—Green Bay NFL	10	6	0	.625	1st/NFC North Division		1	1
2004—Green Bay NFL	10	6	0	.625	1st/NFC North Division		0	1
Pro totals (5 years)	**53**	**27**	**0**	**.663**	**Pro totals (4 years)**		**2**	**4**

NOTES:
2001—Defeated San Francisco, 25-15, in first-round playoff game; lost to St. Louis, 45-17, in conference playoff game.
2002—Lost to Atlanta, 27-7, in first-round playoff game.
2003—Defeated Seattle, 33-27 (OT), in first-round playoff game; lost to Philadelphia, 20-17 (OT), in conference playoff game.
2004—Lost to Minnesota, 31-17, in first-round playoff game.

PERSONAL: Born May 8, 1958, in Big Sandy, Texas.
HIGH SCHOOL: Big Sandy (Texas).
COLLEGE: Tulsa.

HEAD COACHING RECORD

BACKROUND: Assistant coach, Big Sandy (Tex.) High School (1980). ... Assistant coach, Cascia Hall (Okla.) Prep (1981). ... Linebackers coach, Tulsa (1983-86). ... Linebackers coach, Wisconsin (1987). ... Linebackers coach, Arizona State (1988-91). ... Outside linebackers coach, Kentucky (1992). ... Defensive backs coach, Tennessee (1993-94). ... Defensive backs coach, Ohio State (1995). ... Linebackers coach, Tampa Bay Buccaneers NFL (1996-2000). ... Defensive coordinator, St. Louis Rams NFL (2001-02). ... Assistant head coach/defensive coordinator, Rams (2003).

							POST-SEASON	
		REGULAR SEASON						
	W	L	T	Pct.	Finish		W	L
2004—Chicago NFL	5	11	0	.313	4th/NFC North Division		0	0

PERSONAL: Born February 2, 1959, in Bayshore, N.Y. ... Full name: Michael Peter Tice. ... Played tight end. ... Brother of John Tice, tight end, New Orleans Saints (1983-1992).
HIGH SCHOOL: Central Islip (N.Y.).
COLLEGE: Maryland.
TRANSACTIONS/CAREER NOTES: Signed as non-drafted free agent by Seattle Seahawks (April 30, 1981). ... On injured reserve with fractured ankle (October 15-December 7, 1985). ... Granted unconditional free agency (February 1, 1989). ... Signed by Washington Redskins (February 20, 1989). ... Released by Redskins (September 4, 1990). ... Signed by Seahawks (November 28, 1990). ... Granted unconditional free agency (February 1-April 1, 1991). ... Re-signed by Seahawks (July 19, 1991). ... Granted unconditional free agency (February 1, 1992). ... Signed by Minnesota Vikings (March 18, 1992). ... On injured reserve with back injury (September 25-October 21, 1992). ... Granted unconditional free agency (March 1, 1993). ... Re-signed by Vikings (May 4, 1993). ... Released by Vikings (August 30, 1993). ... Re-signed by Vikings (August 31, 1993). ... Granted unconditional free agency (February 17, 1994). ... Re-signed by Vikings (December 7, 1995). ... Granted unconditional free agency (February 16, 1996).
CHAMPIONSHIP GAME EXPERIENCE: Played in AFC championship game (1983 season).

			RECEIVING				KICKOFF RETURNS				TOTALS			
Year Team	G	GS	No.	Yds.	Avg.	TD	No.	Yds.	Avg.	TD	TD	2pt.	Pts.	Fum.
1981—Seattle NFL	16	3	5	47	9.4	0	0	0	0.0	0	0	0	0	0
1982—Seattle NFL	9	9	9	46	5.1	0	0	0	0.0	0	0	0	0	0
1983—Seattle NFL	15	1	0	0	0.0	0	2	28	14.0	0	0	0	0	0
1984—Seattle NFL	16	8	8	90	11.3	3	0	0	0.0	0	3	0	18	0
1985—Seattle NFL	9	2	2	13	6.5	0	1	17	17.0	0	0	0	0	0
1986—Seattle NFL	16	15	15	150	10.0	0	1	17	17.0	0	0	0	0	0
1987—Seattle NFL	12	12	14	106	7.6	2	0	0	0.0	0	2	0	12	0
1988—Seattle NFL	16	16	29	244	8.4	0	1	17	17.0	0	0	0	0	1
1989—Washington NFL	16	5	1	2	2.0	0	0	0	0.0	0	0	0	0	0
1990—Seattle NFL	5	2	0	0	0.0	0	0	0	0.0	0	0	0	0	0
1991—Seattle NFL	16	15	10	70	7.0	4	3	46	15.3	0	4	0	24	0
1992—Minnesota NFL	12	9	5	65	13.0	1	0	0	0.0	0	1	0	6	0
1993—Minnesota NFL	16	12	6	39	6.5	1	0	0	0.0	0	1	0	6	1
1995—Minnesota NFL	3	1	3	22	7.3	0	0	0	0.0	0	0	0	0	0
Pro totals (14 years)	**177**	**110**	**107**	**894**	**8.4**	**11**	**8**	**125**	**15.6**	**0**	**11**	**0**	**66**	**2**

HEAD COACHING RECORD

BACKROUND: Tight ends coach, Minnesota Vikings NFL (1996). ... Offensive line coach, Vikings (1997-2000). ... Assistant head coach/offensive line coach, Vikings (2001).

							POST-SEASON	
		REGULAR SEASON						
	W	L	T	Pct.	Finish		W	L
2001—Minnesota NFL	0	1	0	.000	4th/NFC Central Division		0	0
2002—Minnesota NFL	6	10	0	.375	2nd/NFC North Division		0	0

	W	L	T	Pct.	Finish		W	L
2003—Minnesota NFL	9	7	0	.563	2nd/NFC North Division		0	0
2004—Minnesota NFL	8	8	0	.500	2nd/NFC North Division		1	1
Pro totals (4 years)	23	26	0	.469	**Pro totals (1 year)**		1	1

NOTES:
2001—Replaced Dennis Green as head coach (January 4) with 5-10 record and club in fourth place.
2004—Defeated Green Bay, 31-17, in first-round playoff game; lost to Philadelphia, 27-14, in conference playoff game.

TURNER, NORV   RAIDERS

PERSONAL: Born May 17, 1952, in LeJeune, N.C. ... Full name: Norval Eugene Turner. ... Brother of Ron Turner, offensive coordinator, Chicago Bears.
HIGH SCHOOL: Alhambra (Calif.).
COLLEGE: Oregon.

HEAD COACHING RECORD
BACKROUND: Graduate assistant, Oregon (1975). ... Receivers coach, Southern California (1976-1979). ... Defensive backs coach, USC (1980). ... Quarterbacks coach, USC (1981-1983). ... Offensive coordinator, USC (1984). ... Receivers coach, Los Angeles Rams NFL (1985-1990). ... Offensive coordinator, Dallas Cowboys NFL (1991-1993).

	W	L	T	Pct.	Finish		W	L
1994—Washington NFL	3	13	0	.188	5th/NFC Eastern Division		0	0
1995—Washington NFL	6	10	0	.375	3rd/NFC Eastern Division		0	0
1996—Washington NFL	9	7	0	.563	3rd/NFC Eastern Division		0	0
1997—Washington NFL	8	7	1	.533	2nd/NFC Eastern Division		0	0
1998—Washington NFL	6	10	0	.375	4th/NFC Eastern Division		0	0
1999—Washington NFL	10	6	0	.625	1st/NFC Eastern Division		1	1
2000—Washington NFL	7	6	0	.538	3rd/NFC Eastern Division		0	0
2004—Oakland NFL	5	11	0	.313	4th/AFC West Division		0	0
Pro totals (8 years)	54	70	1	.435	**Pro totals (1 year)**		1	1

NOTES:
1999—Defeated Detroit, 27-13, in first-round playoff game; lost to Tampa Bay, 14-13, in conference playoff game.

VERMEIL, DICK   CHIEFS

PERSONAL: Born October 30, 1936, in Calistoga, Calif. ... Full name: Richard Albert Vermeil. ... Brother of Al Vermeil, conditioning coach with San Francisco 49ers (1979-82) and brother-in-law of Louie Giammona, running back with Philadelphia Eagles (1978-82).
HIGH SCHOOL: Calistoga (Calif.).
JUNIOR COLLEGE: Napa College.
COLLEGE: San Jose State (master's degree in physical education, 1959).

HEAD COACHING RECORD
BACKROUND: Assistant coach, Del Mar High School, San Jose, Calif. (1959). ... Head coach, Hillsdale High School, San Mateo, Calif. (1960-1962; record: 17-9-1). ... Assistant coach, College of San Mateo (1963). ... Assistant coach, Stanford (1965-1968). ... Assistant coach, Los Angeles Rams NFL (1969 and 1971-1973). ... Offensive coordinator, UCLA (1970).
HONORS: Named NFL Coach of the Year by THE SPORTING NEWS (1979 and 1999).

	W	L	T	Pct.	Finish		W	L
1964—Napa College	8	1	0	.889	2nd/Golden Valley Conference		0	0
1974—UCLA	6	3	2	.667	T3rd/Pacific-8 Conference		0	0
1975—UCLA	8	2	1	.800	T1st/Pacific-8 Conference		1	0
1976—Philadelphia NFL	4	10	0	.286	4th/NFC Eastern Division		0	0
1977—Philadelphia NFL	5	9	0	.357	4th/NFC Eastern Division		0	0
1978—Philadelphia NFL	9	7	0	.563	2nd/NFC Eastern Division		0	1
1979—Philadelphia NFL	11	5	0	.688	2nd/NFC Eastern Division		1	1
1980—Philadelphia NFL	12	4	0	.750	1st/NFC Eastern Division		2	1
1981—Philadelphia NFL	10	6	0	.625	2nd/NFC Eastern Division		0	1
1982—Philadelphia NFL	3	6	0	.333	5th/NFC Eastern Division		0	0
1997—St. Louis NFL	5	11	0	.313	5th/NFC Western Division		0	0
1998—St. Louis NFL	4	12	0	.250	5th/NFC Western Division		0	0
1999—St. Louis NFL	13	3	0	.813	1st/NFC Western Division		3	0
2001—Kansas City NFL	6	10	0	.375	4th/AFC Western Division		0	0
2002—Kansas City NFL	8	8	0	.500	4th/AFC West Division		0	0
2003—Kansas City NFL	13	3	0	.813	1st/AFC West Division		0	1
2004—Kansas City NFL	7	9	0	.438	3rd/AFC West Division		0	0
College totals (2 years)	14	5	3	.737	**College totals (1 year)**		1	0
Pro totals (14 years)	110	103	0	.516	**Pro totals (6 years)**		6	5

NOTES:
1975—Defeated Ohio State, 23-10, in Rose Bowl.
1978—Lost to Atlanta, 14-13, in conference playoff game.
1979—Defeated Chicago, 27-17, in first-round playoff game; lost to Tampa Bay, 24-17, in conference playoff game.
1980—Defeated Minnesota, 31-16, in conference playoff game; defeated Dallas, 20-7, in NFC championship game; lost to Oakland, 27-10, in Super Bowl 15.
1981—Lost to New York Giants, 27-21, in conference playoff game.
1982—Only nine of 16 games were played due to the cancellation of games because of a players strike.
1999—Defeated Minnesota, 49-37, in conference playoff game; defeated Tampa Bay, 11-6, in NFC championship game; defeated Tennessee, 23-16, in Super Bowl 34.
2003—Lost to Indianapolis, 38-31, in conference playoff game.